Figuring Style

Studies in Rhetoric/Communication
Thomas W. Benson, Series Editor

Figuring Style

The Legacy of Renaissance Rhetoric

NANCY L. CHRISTIANSEN

The University of South Carolina Press

Published by the University of South Carolina Press
Columbia, South Carolina 29208

www.sc.edu/uscpress

Manufactured in the United States of America

22 21 20 19 18 17 16 15 14 13 10 9 8 7 6 5 4 3 2 1

Library of Congress Cataloging-in-Publication Data

Christiansen, Nancy.
Figuring style : the legacy of Renaissance rhetoric / Nancy L. Christiansen.
pages cm — (Studies in rhetoric/communication)
ISBN 978-1-61117-240-9 (hardbound : alk. paper) 1. Rhetoric,
Renaissance—History and criticism. I. Title.
II. Series: Studies in rhetoric/communication.
PN721.C47 2013
809'.031—dc23
2013018792

To Richard A. Lanham

Contents

Series Editor's Preface

Nancy L. Christiansen's *Figuring Style: The Legacy of Renaissance Rhetoric* is both a handbook of stylistic figures in Renaissance rhetoric and a vigorous interpretation of the role of figures in Renaissance composition, reading, and education. In a comprehensive investigation of figures, Christiansen argues that Renaissance educators understood all language as structured in a web of figures. Figures were not simply an occasional decoration or an alternative to nonfigurative language, but the core of language itself. She traces this claim from the rhetorics of Isocrates and Cicero to Roger Ascham, Bernard Lamy, George Puttenham, and other Renaissance scholars, who understood language as persuasion and performance, structuring at once speech, thought, and action. These understandings Christiansen illustrates in readings of passages in Milton and Shakespeare.

Christiansen provides a comprehensive handlist of figures with extensive historical references from the rhetorical tradition. This is a major work of scholarship sure to be essential as a reference and illuminating as an interpretation.

Thomas W. Benson

Preface

The purposes of the book are threefold: first to make available a fairly comprehensive handlist of the rhetorical figures of speech and of thought that were known in the Renaissance, the historical period when figures most proliferated and style received most attention; second to provide a practical method for stylistic analysis using the figures; and third to explicate the predominant philosophies of style found in the classical and Renaissance rhetorical traditions, contextualizing the figures in the stylistic instruction surrounding them. This study contributes to a history of the figures, a history that James J. Murphy exhorts to be written ("Topos and Figura" 24). It also contributes to the histories of stylistic instruction and of classical and Renaissance rhetoric. The book serves as a general handbook explicating Renaissance style and rhetorical theory.

Because of these purposes, this book will be useful to students of Renaissance studies, whether literary, cultural, or rhetorical; to those interested in the history and philosophy of rhetoric or of style; to those interested in philosophy of language or history of education; and to those who wish to improve their own skills in both stylistic analysis and craftsmanship.

Four appendixes are included as well. Appendix 1 is a collection of Renaissance figures of speech and of thought, a list that both provides evidence for the claims of the preliminary discussion and serves as a reference and heuristic for current use. Appendix 2 lists chronologically each of the manuals cited in the glossary and gives its abbreviation as it appears in the following alphabetical appendix. Appendix 3 is an alphabetical listing of the names that have been given of the figures. This chart indicates under which category (that is, discourse level) in the glossary each figure can be found, provides the head word for the entry, and cites the classical and Renaissance sources that provide this name for this figure. Since most complete rhetoric manuals treat of most of these forms, I only cite here those sources that call these forms figures. I only make an exception when I must cite from someone who serves as a source for a name, definition, or derivation. In these cases, however, I place the reference within brackets. This resource will be helpful when one knows the name of a figure and needs to find the corresponding entry in the preceding glossary. When used in conjunction with the glossary entry, where all the names for the given figure are listed, this appendix will also be helpful in identifying which authors attribute which names to the figure, in tracing the figure's origins, determining its frequency of citation, and showing lines of influence among authors. Appendix 4 details correspondences between the contents of the language arts curriculum and the stylistic figures. It both outlines the typical syllabi of the trivium and demonstrates that nearly all the forms taught in grammar, logic, and rhetoric appear as figures in handbooks of style. For those readers unfamiliar with this curriculum, this chart provides an overview.

NO PROJECT OF THIS SIZE CAN BE completed without contributions from others. My deepest gratitude I extend to my colleagues Grant Boswell, Gideon Burton, and John Talbot for their help with translations from the Latin texts (I acknowledge Boswell's translations throughout the text); to another colleague, David Paxman, for valuable feedback on several early drafts of the manuscript; to my research assistants, Sheridan Green, Sean Northrup, Leda Wilkins, and Eric Meyer; to Hannah Terrill, a student secretary, and Wendy Cloutier, from our faculty support staff, for formatting and typing appendix 3; to my department chair, Ed Cutler, and the dean of the College of Humanities, John Rosenberg, for their support; to the readers of the submitted copy for helpful suggestions to guide the final revision; and finally to my family for their patience, faith, and encouragement.

ntroduction

The Philosophy of Style in the Renaissance Rhetorical Curriculum

Competing Views of Style

Current Views

Style in language has been during the last century a subject of only peripheral concern. This neglect stems from the four most prevalent views of style during this time. In the first view, style is generally understood as the manner of linguistic expression. Less important than the information conveyed, style is fluff.[1] What matters in today's nonfiction prose is content, not style, *res* not *verba.* This belief in the marked differentiation between idea and expression, with the corollary belief that styles can change without changing content, is known as stylistic dualism. Style is linguistic choice. When applied to literature or oratory, this view focuses on figures of speech, those deviations from ordinary language that make style literary and emotional. Style now becomes the study of ornate form.[2] A second view of style is seen among some critics who interpret literary language. Fiction, of course, has no real content and is only style, only fluff. These nonserious belletristic genres use figurative language to create an imaginary reality. Since in these genres changes to the verbal form change the imaginary world evoked, these critics consider style to be the content. This view of style is known as aesthetic monism. The consequence of this organic theory is that style disappears into content. Style is the meaning, the literary work itself.[3] A third view of style is that artistic success in literary or personal expression results from a mysterious natural talent. Each one's style is one's own. Style cannot be reduced to rules, cannot be an art or technique, and cannot be changed. Those who adopt this position of psychological monism[4] usually quote the aphorism "Style is the man himself," coined by Comte de Buffon in his 1753 *Discours sur le style.*[5] These critics read style as a manifestation of an author's peculiar linguistic mannerisms or as an indicator of his or her unique cognitive orientation. They collapse style into the author, considering style as symptom.[6] Sometimes this third view collapses with the second, turning the literary work into the author, the work's aesthetic qualities projecting the author's personal qualities. In this hybrid view, the work is seen, in M. H. Abrams's words, as a transparency opening directly into the soul of its author (227).[7]

More recently, some postmodernists have provided a fourth view of style, one we might call cultural monism. Assuming that there are not two kinds of language but only one—the metaphorical, poetic—that governs thought as well as speech and further assuming the same mind/body split as do the stylistic dualists, these critics follow Friedrich Nietzsche in concluding that words cannot impart factual information, only fictional perspectives.[8] Since these perspectives are determined by the linguistic and cultural systems that shape an individual's upbringing—a combination of the Whorfian hypothesis and social constructionist pragmatism—language and culture construct the individual's mind and self.[9] Nurture creates nature, mind (culture, language, *verba*) creates reality (*res*), and the meanings and values of expressive forms are arbitrarily and provisionally grounded in general usage and conventional agreement within a community. Further, forms have no meanings outside of the social and cultural contexts in which they are inextricably embedded and which are innately political and ideological. These forms belong not to individuals, but to the systems of interpretation within which individuals operate. Style is again symptom, but this time of the culture's preferred modes of expression—the modes of power—and these preferred forms reveal the ideology of a culture at large.[10] But, although society is composed of multiple systems of interpretation, ideologies, and perspectives, ultimately there are only forms and no content, because metaphors cannot refer in any stable way to an absolute exterior transcendental truth. The later Roland Barthes, for example, declares, "We can no longer see a text as a binary structure of Content and Form; the text is not double but multiple; within it there are only forms, or more exactly, the text in its entirety is only a multiplicity of forms without a content" (6).

These four views all discourage attention to style in the composition classroom. The "expressivists," who emphasize primarily creative or personal writing and consider style an individual's natural, unique, and inalterable manner of self-expression, encourage writers simply to be themselves, for style cannot be taught.[11] On the other extreme, teachers of scientific and professional expository writing espouse a more utilitarian approach, wherein style must be invisible, without figurative flourish or grammatical error, and clearly denotive of subject matter, with proper usage and observance of syntactical and formal conventions.[12] When style draws attention to itself, it is suspect, indicative of either a lack of seriousness or covert designs against the audience. Fearful of these designs and the subtle manipulative power latent in poetic diction and syntax, a power commonly supposed to rest in emotion and fantasy, not in logic and facts, teachers of persuasive writing focus on good reasoning rather than style.[13] Strong cultural monists tend to deny even the possibility for stylistic study in the composition classroom, since rules, abstractions, or forms cannot be disembedded from practices, interpretations, or ideologies. Criticism can only describe forms within their particular contexts and not prescribe transcendental or transferable principles. Stanley Fish, for example, remarks:

> Here my thesis is that formal patterns are themselves the products of interpretation and that therefore there is no such thing as a formal pattern, at least in the sense necessary for the practice of stylistics: that is, no pattern that one can observe before interpretation is hazarded and which therefore can be used to prefer one interpretation to another. The conclusion, however, is not that there are no formal patterns but that there are always formal patterns; it is just that the formal patterns there always are will always be the product of a prior interpretive act, and therefore will be available for discerning only so long as that act is in force. (*Is There a Text in This Class* 267)

If the sincere and poetic styles flow from nature; if the clear style results from a focus on content and linguistic correctness; if honest persuasive composition results from reason; or if formal patterns cannot be isolated and taught, then why, when teaching writing, pay much attention to style? Indeed the only aspects of style that some students may be taught today are proper grammar, usage, conventions, and perhaps syntactical variety; yet even grammar and syntax are out of fashion, associated with remediation and dreary rule-bound pedagogy.[14]

When reading texts, students find themselves with equally little guidance. In nonliterary prose they are expected to ignore style altogether and read through the text for the ideas, since discourses of this kind supposedly lack style. In literature, or texts that have style, where looking at the expression counts, students will be given conflicting directions.[15] Depending on which critic a student may consult, style will either be the decoration, representation, or incarnation of subject matter. Likewise students will see little consensus regarding the relationship between style and author. Early twentieth-century literary critics and many linguists who began the science of stylistics in mid-century read fiction as the unconscious revelation of the author, a method rejected for its biographical fallacy by the next generation of formalist critics, who denied in the literary work such access to an author's intentions, emotion, or presence. Since then students have been taught that style in literature produces tone; however, this is a nebulous concept to both formalists and poststructuralists, who divorce texts from authors and so from an individual's voice.[16] Today's approaches vary depending on the interests of the critic: a rhetorical critic will connect style to pathos (emotional persuasion) or ethos (the persuasive persona a writer projects), although there is still question as to whether fiction can be subject to rhetorical analysis;[17] a philologist will talk about an author's particular linguistic traits or personal idiolect; a literary historian will gather together a set of formal characteristics that predominate during certain time periods and that identify given genres; a psychologist will discover the unconscious life and personality of the author in his work; a new historicist will find cultural ideologies; and pluralists will combine various of the above approaches, but usually without a unifying rationale.

Without a very comprehensive art of style to guide analysis or explain literariness, students also experience confusion as to what features of text constitute style. The majority of analysts usually restrict their attention to lexical and syntactical choices beyond grammatical constraints. To literary and rhetorical critics, the relevant forms are figures of speech. Usually, though, these critics only examine tropes and a few additional figures. Linguists likewise narrow their analyses to the few unique and distinguishing lexical and syntactical features that either recur most often in a text or vary from an identified norm. Some critics even restrict their data to evidence of the unconscious and habitual options an author uses, since it is only these that truly identify the author's personal and fixed style.[18] Those who see stylistic choices as cultural choices identify cultural norms in texts.[19] Although new theorists are arguing in favor of expanding the definition of style to include grammar, sound, and larger discourse forms, the domain of style remains a disputed territory.[20] Equally disputed are varying methods of analysis. Do statistical and quantitative studies alone produce significant descriptions, or do stylistic features require qualitative interpretation according to their contexts because they contribute meanings that vary as contexts change?

The result of this confusion for both teachers and students is that style—what it is, how to describe it, and how it functions—remains pretty much a mystery, without a clear anatomy or nomenclature. Roderick P. Hart, in his and Suzanne Daughton's 2005 edition of *Modern Rhetorical Criticism,* even writes, "Perhaps stylistic criticism seems somewhat mystical. It is. Somewhat" (149). Descriptions of style, when they are made at all, tend to be either abstract and impressionistic or overly behavioristic and deterministic.[21] Despite recent efforts by a small group of linguists and a handful of rhetoricians attempting to revitalize the study of style, there still remains a general neglect of the field, a meager body of stylistic analyses, and a lack of coherent theory to fill adequately the gap left by this neglect.[22] As Elizabeth Rankin has commented not too long ago, "Style is out of style" (8), and as Richard Lanham has observed, "We are in fact, English teachers included, wonderfully inept at describing the 'good writing' we all say we cherish. We don't know what to look for, nor what to call it when it trips us up. And so, mostly, we don't look at all" (*Analyzing Prose* xv).

The Renaissance View

This modern disinterest in and plurality of approaches toward style contrast sharply with the attitude and fairly unified pedagogy we find in British Renaissance rhetorical instruction.[23] Embedded in the curriculum at the center of Renaissance grammar school and university education, style joined invention, arrangement, memory, and delivery to form the five offices of rhetoric. Rhetoric—the umbrella of the language arts and so inclusive of grammar and logic—was the art of persuasion become the art of communication, designed to produce the person who with practical and moral judgment could speak extemporaneously yet appropriately on any subject, before any audience, and on any occasion. So important and yet so demanding was the mastery of style to this speaker that often style was touted as the canon deserving the most attention. This stylistic avidity in the Renaissance promoted a flurry of books devoted exclusively to the subject, a meticulous attention to the details and functions of form, and a proliferation of figures of speech and thought that went well beyond the already numerous collection inherited from classical sources. In fact so prominent were these figures that in some texts they became the central features of not only stylistic but also rhetorical instruction.

Indeed given the biases of early and mid-twentieth-century scholars, it is no wonder that when they turned their attention to Renaissance stylistic instruction, they responded with both dismay and dismissal. This apparent preference for fluff led many influential Renaissance scholars such as Donald Lemen Clark, C. S. Lewis, R. R. Bolgar, Paul Oskar Kristeller, T. W. Baldwin, and Morris W. Croll to conclude that the Renaissance language arts curriculum primarily reduced rhetoric to style.[24] This belief has persisted, underlying the work of even contemporary scholars,[25] despite a few recent attempts to point out that the Renaissance curriculum is distinguished from the medieval precisely because of the reintegration of rhetoric's five parts and the subordination of logic to rhetoric, restoring to the art a focus on content and returning the art to a wholeness it had in Greco-Roman times but lost in the aftermath of Rome's collapse.[26] Following Wilbur Samuel Howell in his seminal history *Logic and Rhetoric in England, 1500–1700,* a third group of scholars classify Renaissance rhetoric according to a manual's form: traditional (with all five of rhetoric's canons), stylistic (with only style), or Ramistic (with style and delivery).[27] Yet all three sets of researchers have generally concluded, as George Kennedy so aptly puts it, that style involves verbal expression "'laid on' to the thoughts which invention [provides] and disposition set[s] out, rather than as something integral to the whole speech" (*Classical Rhetoric* 125).[28] Louis T. Milic, a linguist, sums up the scholarly consensus by calling this view "rhetorical dualism" and its use of words and forms to decorate the content the theory of "ornate form" ("Theories" 67).[29]

Additionally scholars have tended to discount the significance of such enthusiasm for figuration. This interest in what seems frivolous minutiae and excessive attention to decorative formulas has prompted critics to characterize this rhetorical curriculum as mechanistic and literary and to see this stylistic exuberance as further evidence that Renaissance rhetoricians, like their classical forebears, viewed style's sole purpose as technique for persuasion or manipulation. Howell observes that Renaissance rhetoricians equated "true elegance and hence true effectiveness with a system of studied departures from the established pattern of everyday speech" and from variations that prevent speech's "accurate correspondence to states of reality" (*Logic* 17, 128). He complains about what appears to him a "mechanical routine": "It may seem strange that human energy should be applied so diligently to this interminable enumeration of stylistic devices, when the subject of communication offers more philosophic and more humane approaches, . . . [Henry] Peacham and his school appear more concerned with the husks than with the kernels of style" (133–34).

Recognizing that sixteenth-century rhetorical style was largely, sometimes exclusively, taught in terms of tropes and schemes, Howell complains that the "list of schemes and tropes was long in sixteenth-century textbooks, as English schoolboys knew to their dismay" (*Poetics, Rhetoric, and Logic* 158). Herbert W. Hildebrandt, the modern editor of Richard Sherry's *A Treatise of Schemes and Tropes,* sees Renaissance style as decoration (introduction viii).[30] In a previous collection of figures from Renaissance handlists, *A Handbook to Sixteenth-Century Rhetoric,* Lee A. Sonnino describes this instruction as the "study of rhetorical ornament" and finds the lengthy lists "dreary and unimaginative" and "only material for that consistently disintegrating attention to ornament alone which was the chief renaissance abuse of the classical tradition" (5, 7). Marion Trousdale reiterates these characterizations in *Shakespeare and the Rhetoricians:*

> By definition such figures were syntactic and semantic turnings of language away from the literal and the commonplace toward patterns and forms that were consciously artful, causing the listener both to admire the art or skill of the conveyance and to be moved by delight in the artifice. . . . A metaphor, a metonymy, an anaphora are essentially transformations, which the Elizabethans called translations (*translatio*). They do not provide the means by which meaning is discovered or altered. Rather, they provide the means by which the "bare and naked body" is "attired in rich and gorgious apparell" so that it "seemeth to the common usage of th' eye much more comely & bewtifull then the naturall."[31] What can be said by figures, then, theoretically can be said without figures. They provide in the strictest sense, albeit in small compass, the poetic means of variation. (82–83)

Assuming, as is customary today, that figures are linguistic deviations, poetic devices that "depart from customary construction, order, or significance," to quote from Harmon and Holman's current edition of the *Handbook to Literature* (217), Quentin Skinner interprets these figures of speech as "linguistic corruptions" that amplify, stretch, and exaggerate facts "to make them appear more favorable to our cause than they are in strict truth" and that this method of speaking was understood in the Renaissance as the "only one possible way" for moving the mind of the audience "to a willing consent" ("Moral Ambiguity" 272–75). Similarly Russ McDonald in *Shakespeare and the Arts of Language* links the orator's application of these formulas and verbal patternings to the creation of the linguistic artificiality necessary for wielding power over others' minds (24, 29).[32]

Today's scholars' belief in two types of language, the figured and the unfigured, has also produced studies that identify in the Renaissance either a self-conscious, ornate rhetorical style or a plain nonrhetorical style, the first associated primarily with the so-called Ciceronianism of the Elizabethan period and the second with the countermovements of Anti-Ciceronianism, Senecanism, or Atticism, as well as the rise of science and the Puritan emphasis on plain preaching in the seventeenth century. From Richard

Foster Jones's essays in the 1920s and 1930s to the twenty-first century, the popular belief in these two types of language has imposed overly rigid classifications on Renaissance styles and continues to influence commentary on Renaissance rhetorical practice.[33] The most recent edition of *The Norton Anthology of English Literature* provides the following introduction to Renaissance stylistics:

> In Renaissance England, certain syntactic forms of patterns of words known as "figures" (also called "schemes") were shaped and repeated in order to confer beauty or heighten expressive power. . . .
>
> As certain grotesquely inflated Renaissance texts attest, lessons from *De copia* and similar rhetorical guides could encourage prolixity and verbal self-display. Elizabethans had a taste for elaborate ornament in language as in clothing, jewelry, and furniture, and, if we are to appreciate their accomplishments, it helps to set aside the modern preference, particularly in prose, for unadorned simplicity and directness. . . .
>
> Elizabethans were certainly capable of admiring plainness of speech—in *King Lear* Shakespeare contrasts the severe directness of the virtuous Cordelia to the "glib and oily art" of her wicked sisters—and such poets as George Gascoigne, Thomas Nashe, and, in the early seventeenth century, Ben Jonson wrote restrained, aphoristic, moralizing lyrics in a plain style whose power depends precisely on the avoidance of richly figurative verbal pyrotechnics. (Greenblatt 501–2)

Since critics have generally assumed that dualism and monism, positions that are contradictory by nature, are the only theoretical positions possible, those few scholars who notice the Renaissance humanists' connection of style to the speaker, a connection that questions a simple dualism, have generally concluded that Renaissance stylistic theory is a theory of contradictions. Bennison Gray, a formalist, makes the point quite directly: "George Puttenham was well within the Renaissance critical tradition when he defined style in his *Arte of English Poesie* (1589) as the ornament and dress of poetry. According to the principle of decorum, style, as ornament, must be suited to the 'matter' and subject of the work and can be judged, by itself, as appropriate or inappropriate. Yet Puttenham was contradicting his notion of style as ornament when he also held that there is an individuality of language which expresses character" (34–35).[34] Terence Cave, a poststructualist, makes the same point, although from opposite assumptions. He notes Erasmus's insistence in *Ciceronianus* (1528) that because nature "intended speech to be a mirror of the mind," the "very thing that delights the reader" is to "discover from the language the feelings, the characteristics, the judgment, and the ability of the writer as well as if one had known him for years" (121). Yet Cave points out that, contrary to Erasmus's belief, this essentiality of identity is always compromised, for Erasmus always creates changing personae for himself in his writings, teaches the duality of words and ideas, and must "become an alien surface in order to constitute himself as an identity, an *apparent* nature, grafted (perhaps) only on the culture of discourse. The Erasmian *sensus* [intention] or *sententia* [idea], issuing supposedly from a unique identity, translates itself into words, and thus inevitably betrays itself" (48).

More recently Richard Waswo has also taken as contradictions these two views in Renaissance thought: "When language is talked about, it is consciously regarded as clothing of preexistent meanings; but when language is employed to reflect on its various functions—to recommend a style, to praise a vernacular, to teach the figures of speech, to urge a method of interpreting Scripture, or to compose literature—it is often implicitly regarded as constitutive of meaning" (80).

The argument of this book, however, is that these characterizations of Renaissance stylistic theory are reductions that have obscured the comprehensive composing and reading method taught by Renaissance rhetoricians. This method points the way to a coherent reconciliation between the dualistic and monistic extremes offered in contemporary theory and offers a useful heuristic and analytic paradigm to supply the guidance missing in today's classrooms.

Specifically the Renaissance language arts program, as ideally conceived, treats the fundamental pairs of content and expression, idea and form, mind and speech, and nature and art not as contradictory things, as do dualists who split them into oppositions, nor as the same thing, as do monists who collapse them, but rather as different but coextensive and complementary dimensions of the same thing—human behavior, the true center of style. While apparent in both the stylistic and rhetorical advice these pedagogues give, this reconciliation occurs most significantly in their treatment of figures. Dissecting style and rhetoric into extensive lists of the figures of speech and of thought, Renaissance manuals de facto treat figures as forms in general that become "ornaments" when appropriate to all the requisites of the speech act, rather than as specialized alterations that by themselves make a style literary. When taken in total, these so-called figures come to include nearly the entirety of forms commonly taught in the trivium, expanding style's domain to encompass the whole of the language arts curriculum. This curriculum itself unites grammar, logic and rhetoric into one art of human communication, whose reach extends beyond verbal to all genres of human creation. Figures, then, are shown to structure all three dimensions of language—speech, thought, and action—and, in being forms, to be essentially behaviors. As a consequence in this paradigm there are not two types of language, the figured and the unfigured, but a single language composed of a web of figures/behaviors with both fictional and nonfictional properties. False oppositions between philosophy and rhetoric, the low and high styles, scientific and literary genres, and reason and emotion disappear without undermining either member in the pair.

As behaviors with both particular and universal aspects, figures/forms in use are inherently meaningful, pointing to both conscious craftsmanship and natural expressivity. Seeing figures as behaviors prompts us to read them not only as signs for some referent in the outside world, but also as a person's chosen formulations, with varying degrees of purposefulness and effectiveness within the context of the persuasive drama that is human life itself. Forms/behaviors are, on the one hand, assertions of relations or lines of argument and, on the other, reflections of the speaker's lines of thinking and so indicative of choices, intentions, emotions, assumptions, and judgments. The arguments figures make, then, have logical, emotional, and ethical significance at once.

A figural/stylistic/rhetorical analysis is ultimately behavioral analysis, applicable to all human arts and revelatory of all that behavior reveals: a speaker's conceptions about reality (both explicit and implicit), a speaker's purposes and achievement (both intentional and unintentional), a speaker's indebtedness to and departure from cultural influences (both self-conscious and not), and aspects of a speaker's personality and character (both crafted and actual).

The Renaissance method of using figures to guide both the creation and interpretation of text highlights the figure/behavior, not the word or single sign, as the fundamental unit of discourse. Being both argument and performance, the figure itself becomes a representation of human utterance, showing that language is at once both dualistic and monistic: that expression both is not and is content, that form both is not and is idea, that outward speech and action both are not and are manifestations of the originating mind, and that a man both is not and is his style. This broad notion of figure and text provides a heuristic that pulls multiplicity into unity and becomes abundantly explanatory of human meaning making.

Additional Contexts: Philosophical, Historical, Methodological

Before examining the centrality of figures and their functions to style and to rhetoric, we need to set the context by first examining how both dualisms and monisms are reconciled in the philosophy of style implicit in Renaissance teachings generally. A brief explanation of these tenets at the outset will clarify this view's breadth and its differences from narrower views. Second we must contextualize this philosophy by identifying its place in the history of rhetoric and in the age-old debate between the philosophers and rhetoricians. Doing so clarifies the issues Renaissance rhetoricians engage with and reveals both the lineage of their ideas and their unique contributions to theory. Third we need to characterize the status of Renaissance instruction as theory to justify the methodology of the following inquiry.

Reconciliations in Renaissance Rhetoric's Philosophy of Style

A few contemporary style theorists have argued that a useful stylistic paradigm requires a reconciliation between dualisms and monisms. Believing that this reconciliation is impossible, Milic recommends that dualism is best for composition teaching, but that psychological monism is best for literary analysis, wherein the reader notes the stylistic options a writer chooses unconsciously and habitually ("Theories" 126). Richard Young asserts that the "durability of these two fundamental conceptions of rhetorical art and the effectiveness of the pedagogical methods based on them suggest that in some sense both are true—in spite of the fact that they seem incompatible" ("Arts" 60). John T. Gage argues that we do actually have it both ways: "In the first place, by stressing revision, we are advocating a separation between the way a thing is said, in its unrevised form, and the ideas themselves, unclothed, that is, in words. In the second place, however, by stressing clarity and the 'plain style'—the precise and straightforward way of saying a thing—we seem to call upon precisely the opposite assumption, namely that there is one ideally suited linguistic formula for each idea" (619–20). He goes on, "It seems to me that this requires acknowledging both sets of assumptions at once, by acknowledging that a change in style is a change in thought—if we consider monistically that ideas and their expression are inseparable—and at the same time that a change in style is not a change in thought—if we consider dualistically that intention and its expression must be separable or we could never know what we wanted to say until we had already said it" (620). Lanham offers another way to incorporate the two approaches with his suggestion that readers must look both "through" the text for the subject matter and "at" the text for the information imparted by the style (*Analyzing Prose* 1). A postmodernist, Rankin attempts to resolve the seeming contradictions by pointing out that if the self and the meaning of utterance are created by language, then the dualist position holds, but if "these constructs are seen as existing within a rhetorical (or interpretative) community, they can be provisionally regarded as determinant," a monistic position, "even while their relativistic nature is acknowledged" (12).

These few efforts to reunite the two views, however, still create a less complex picture of reality than does mainstream Renaissance stylistic instruction, wherein *res* and *verba* are shown to be at once both separable and inseparable because of the multidimensionality of language; that is, *res* and *verba* are always separable on one level but simultaneously inseparable on another. Content and expression, idea and form, mind and speech, and nature and art are each two irreducible faces of one communicative phenomenon.

Content and Expression

First, in Renaissance manuals content and expression are both separable and inseparable. Expression is often described as "clothing for the thought"; the means for communicating ideas are separate from the ideas themselves. "Outer" is separate from "inner," making possible various ways of expressing one's ideas. To develop eloquence, Desiderius Erasmus (1465–1536) in *De copia* (1512) models how to turn an idea or sentence "into more shapes than Proteus himself is supposed to have turned into" (302) by rewriting one sentence, "Always, as long as I live, I shall remember you," in two hundred different ways (354–64). But this metaphor of clothing does not suggest fluff, for clothing is necessary and is itself a set of signs that have meaning. Thomas Wilson (c. 1524–81) in *The Art of Rhetoric* (1553) rebuffs the dualists of his day by claiming that an idea is not complete—it is "both bare and naked" (187)—until it is properly dressed for the speech occasion and ready for public appearance.[35] The outward expression can make the idea dignified, "clad in purple," or slovenly:

> Wherefore I much marvel that so many seek the only knowledge of things without any mind to commend or set forth their intendment, seeing none can know either what they are or what they have without the gift of utterance. Yea, bring them to speak their mind and enter in talk with such as are said to be learned, and you shall find in them such lack of utterance that if you judge them by their tongue and expressing their mind, you must needs say they have no learning. Wherein methinks they do like some rich snudges that having great wealth go with their hose out at

> heels, their shoes out at toes, and their coats out at both elbows. For who can tell if such men are worth a groat, when their apparel is so homely and all their behavior so base? I can call them by none other name but slovens that may have good gear and neither can nor yet will once wear it cleanly. (187–88)

If the manner of expression has meaning, it becomes part of the content, and the trick, as every writer knows, is to get the meaning of one's expression to capture and complement one's ideas, or, as Erasmus advises, to get the clothing to "fit":

> Just as dress and outward appearance can enhance or disfigure the beauty and dignity of the body, so words can enhance or disfigure thought. Accordingly a great mistake is made by those who consider that it makes no difference how anything is expressed, provided it can be understood somehow or other. . . . Our first concern should be to see that the garment is clean, that it fits, and that it is not wrongly made up. It would be a pity to have people put off by a spotty, dirty garment, when the underlying form is itself good. It would be ludicrous to have a man go out in public dressed like a woman, and objectionable to see a person wearing his clothes back to front or upside down. (306)

Erasmus further warns, "In introducing variations one must take care not to confuse the different implications of words, as most professors of dialectic do" (403). Sensitivity to these meanings, to the nuances of forms, contributes to these humanists' reputation for being good translators and textual critics. Indeed the classroom practice of translation and transformation of model texts enables both language acquisition and fluency and demonstrates this very oscillation between dualism and monism.[36] Philip Melanchthon (1497–1560) states this oscillation clearly in his "Reply to Pico" (1558): "Though there is more than one way of saying a thing, yet when we wish to communicate our mind's cogitations to others, it requires the use of a very definite kind of speech to set forth what we are talking about correctly and in order, with words that are known and are rightly put together" (trans. Breen 58).

To Renaissance rhetoricians an utterance provides not merely information about the world, but also information about a speaker's perspectives, attitudes, emotions, intentions, and characteristics. As Erasmus points out, "the reader . . . discover[s] from the language the feelings, the characteristics, the judgment, and the ability of the writer as well as if one had known him for years" (*Ciceronianus* 121). Every utterance conveys these meanings because it is a motivated act of a speaker to induce a response from an audience on a particular occasion that is itself part of an ongoing drama. To the Renaissance mind, life is a stage, evidenced when Juan Luis Vives (1492–1540), for example, calls life "this theatre, in which man was placed by God" (*De tradendis disciplinis* [1531]; trans. Watson 16).[37]

Renaissance rhetoric presents the declamation, which is an argument delivered on the stage of life, as the fundamental genre of human communication. Other scholars have noted the tyranny of the declamation at this time. Don Paul Abbott remarks that "the oration remained fixed as the supreme form of discourse" (155), and Walter J. Ong notices that the oration "tyrannized over ideas of what expression as such—literary or other—was" (*Rhetoric, Romance and Technology* 53). As a declamation an utterance is always both a situated argument and performance. In *The Art of English Poesie* (1589), George Puttenham (c. 1529–90) indicates that the function of language is persuasion: "Utterance also and language is given by nature to man for persuasion of others, and aid of them selves" (24). Rudolph Agricola (1444–85) in his logic manual *De inventione dialectica* (1515) makes explicit the ground-floor assumption of these Renaissance humanists that all expression is argument: "Every discourse on whatever subject, and indeed all language by which we reveal our thoughts, is undertaken for the purpose of teaching something to the person listening, and it seems to have this as its first and proper function" (1.1.1; trans. Mack, *Renaissance Argument* 124). "To teach," he explains "is to speak convincingly," which "is the proper function of him who speaks" (2.4; trans. McNally 413).[38] Julius Caesar Scaliger (1484–1558) introduces his *Poetices libri septem* (1561) by asserting, "Is there not one end, and one only, in philosophical exposition, in oratory, and in the drama? Assuredly such is the case. All have one and the same end—persuasion . . . . Its end is to convince, or secure the doing of something" (1.1.3; trans. Vickers, *In Defence* 285).[39] William Fulwood (d. 1593), in the first epistolary manual in English, *The Enimie of Idleness* (1568), explicitly declares that "the true definition of an Epistle or letter [is] nothing else but an Oration written" and recommends to those who would like a fuller treatment of writing instruction "the Rhetorike of Master Doctor Wilson, or Master Richard Rainolde" (A7r; qtd. in Crane 108). Besides oratory, poetry, and epistles, rhetoric also is commonly attributed to sermons, meditation, prayer, conversation, manners, military arts, music, dance, and painting. In no other time period, until today perhaps, has the domain of rhetoric been as broadly conceived.

All utterance is also performance. With delivery the final elaboration of any text, rhetoric presents text not as words primarily but as actions. Texts of all kinds are read as if dramas. Matthias Flacius Illyricus (1520–75), in *Clavis Scripturae Sacrae* (1562), a rhetoric on the art of preaching, describes the Bible as "a comedy . . . staged in the theater of the whole world" (2:488; trans. Shuger 74). The same metaphor appears in a preaching manual a century later, John Prideaux's *Sacred Eloquence: Or, the Art of Rhetorick, As it is layd down in Scripture* (1659). Prideaux (1578–1650) says that the Bible brings a character "in upon the stage speaking as if he were present" (68; qtd. in Shuger 98). Sir Philip Sidney calls the characters in his fictional narrative *Arcadia* "actors," and Thomas Nashe refers to Sidney's sonnet cycle, *Astrophel and Stella,* as a "tragicomedy of love" to be performed in "this Theater of pleasure" ("The Preface to Sidney's *Astrophel and Stella,*" in Smith 2:223). Erasmus describes the ever-changing situations of the speech act as changing scenes: "Wherever I turn I see things changed, I stand on another stage, I see another theater, yes, another world" (*Ciceronianus* 62).[40]

Consequently the means of expression include signs not merely linguistic but also visual, aural, tactile, behavioral. Delivery, the use of voice, gesture, and physical presentation, accompanies verbal expression and clothes the words. John Bulwer (c. 1606–56) in his *Chironomia* (1644) remarks, "[Words] would prove naked unless the clothing hands do neatly move to adorn and hide their nakedness with their comely and ministerial parts of speech" (165). Gesture, word, and idea are envisioned as layers, dimensions of discourse, each with meaning. A distinction is not made between spoken and written text; rather the written text is merely a record of oral performance and, when read, should be brought back to life, to embodied performance. Puttenham repeats the idea expressed by Quintilian, the renowned Roman schoolmaster: "Writing is no more than the image or character of speech" (271).[41] Furthermore both Donatus (c. 350) and Priscian (c. 500), the late Latin authors of grammar textbooks commonly used in Renaissance schools, call speech *vox,* "voiced sound," and *oratio,* "the arrangement of words into an agreeing (i.e. grammatical) and complete thought or meaning" (Priscian, *Institutio* 44–45; trans. Donawerth 19). *Verba,* then, connotes oral performance, not the silent notation we moderns assume. The close relations between style and delivery often lead Renaissance rhetoricians to subsume delivery under style or to conflate style and delivery, as we will see. The notion that the "clothing" must "fit," then, involves more than merely attaching written words to ideas and ties meaning to the criterion of decorum, "fitness."[42]

The problems with the dualist supposition that style is "fluff," as Renaissance rhetoricians point out, then, are the following: first, it leads to antisocial behavior, for by assuming that any form of expression will do, dualists ignore communication as a social act; second, it leads to loss of choice, for if style is ignored, awareness of options is lost; and third, it leads to blindness to the argumentative function of style and hence to how style can add to or detract from the merit of one's ideas. Ironically this preference for one side of the dualism reveals a monistic underside to the dualists' position. The monist belief that any idea automatically comes with its own form of expression, making *paraphrasis* impossible, also leads to loss of choice, lack of concern for stylistic "fitness," and undue rigidity when assigning meaning to the form. The opposite monist belief that forms ultimately have no content or only conventional signification produces the same blindness to aspects of style's meaning and of the complex judgment necessary to use style well.

Idea and Form

Like content and style, so the second pair of coordinates, idea and form, are also both separable and inseparable, according to Renaissance rhetorical precepts. There is both idea (meaning) and form (that which imparts/creates meaning). Form is not external to idea; rather ideas are ideas because they have forms, and forms have identities because of the ideas they assert. Because form is the bodying forth of idea, the notion of "style as garment," then, as Rosemund Tuve argues, is connected in common Renaissance understanding to the sense that "flesh is the soul's garment" (61). Erasmus, for example, uses this metaphor in *Ecclesiastes* (1535), wherein he applies the principles of rhetoric and dialectic to preaching: "Elocution is the flesh and skin of the living body; the decent clothing for bones and nerves" (2.279.713). We see this relationship on the macro-scale in that signs (sounds, words, gestures, images) by themselves have only potential, conventional meanings until put into use or, in other words, placed into forms, figures, contexts. Priscian makes this point in his grammatical instruction, saying sounds become words because of the context (43–44; Donawerth 19). Erasmus makes the same point when he advises that proper interpretation of a passage requires giving heed to the whole context. In his *Methodus* (1516) he stipulates, "Let him not consider it adequate to pull out four or five little words; let him consider the origin of what is said, by whom it is said, to whom it is said, when, on what occasion, in what words, what precedes it, what follows. For it is from a comprehensive examination of these things that one learns the meaning of a given utterance" (64; trans. Grafton and Jardine 147).

We also see this relationship on the micro-scale, for the same insight applies to thought and becomes evident in Renaissance dialectic manuals, wherein the invention of propositions/arguments is shown to result from the combination of forms, and the supposed universal forms or frames of thinking, being fundamental pairs of relations like similarity/difference, cause/effect, substance/adjunct, part/whole, genus/species, and so forth, are the fundamental ideas that compose all propositions. These fundamental relations are the *loci* or *topoi* or "places" of logic that in conjunction with syllogistic form produce predicates and thereby generate statements when a subject is taken from place to place and seen from different perspectives. Whether the list of *topoi* is complete or accurate matters less for our purposes than the fact that words and sentences are shown to become meaningful, to become arguments, when placed into forms or, in other words, when seen from various places. These frames do double duty: they make possible both the finding (or constructing) of arguments and the judging of arguments, showing that ideas are already placed when they are found—that arranging ideas is to give them another place, another meaning, another context and form—and that quality depends upon "fitness" within and among forms. In Abraham Fraunce's words, a proposition or axiom is "a disposition of one argument with another" (*The Lawiers Logike* [1588] 86v) and an argument is "any several conceit apt to argue that whereunto in reason it is referred" (4v). Because any argument by nature is composed of multiple schema, which are themselves capable of multiple and varied combinations, ideas and forms can be taken apart and put back together in new arrangements.

Recognizing ideas as constructions, Renaissance humanists see that expression does not refer directly to objects in the outside world but rather to conceptions, constructions in the speaker's mind. As John Hoskins (1566–1638) says in *Directions for Speech and Style* (1599), "The conceits of the mind are Pictures of things, and the tongue is the Interpreter of those Pictures" (2). A similar statement appears in *L'académie française* (1577–1594) by Pierre de la Primaudaye (c. 1545–c. 1610): "In the writings of the learned we find mention made of a double speech or reason: the one internal or of the mind, called the divine guide: the other uttered in speech, which is the messenger of the conceits and thoughts of man" (126–27; trans. T. Bowes in *The French Academie* [1586]).[43] When Renaissance rhetoricians say that words refer to "things," they include in this category not only objects such as man, but also concepts such as truth, ambition, friendship, philosophy, and "praiseworthy" (Wilson, *Rule of Reason* [1551] B.iiii.r) or desire, hunger, and "feigned" (Hoskins 8).

The meaning of *res* (content, idea) to Renaissance rhetoricians, then, differs from the meaning the term has among many language philosophers today, a meaning the term acquired in late seventeenth-century usage due to the growing influence of Cartesian philosophy and the rise of science. Despite their failure to recognize the significance of this difference, several of the early Renaissance scholars note it. Wesley Trimpi interprets the Renaissance notion of *res* most acutely: "A writer's subject matter is not objective reality, that which he assumes to be both antecedent to and independent of his perception of it, but his and other men's relation to that reality, their experience of it" (31). Richard Foster Jones is an early observer of the change to a more referential semantics, commenting that "with the [seventeenth-century] scientists the term [reality or *res*] generally means a material reality," while the rhetoricians "used it to refer much more widely to rationalistic explanations of human experience. Though in both 'things' are preferred to 'words,' the experimental philosophers had concrete objects in mind, while the others were thinking of intellectual or moral conceptions" (106). A. C. Howell concurs: "As will appear, the term *res,* meaning *subject-matter,* seems to become confused with *res* meaning *things,* and the tendency to assume that *things* should be expressible in *words,* or conversely, *words* should represent *things,* not metaphysical and abstract concepts, may be discerned" (131).[44]

This change is especially seen in John Wilkins (1614–72), who replaces words with marks for objects so as to dispense with metaphor and connotation in his *Essay towards a Real Character and a Philosophical Language* (1668). It is this attempt to create a perfectly denotative sign system that Jonathan Swift satirizes in book 3 of *Gulliver's Travels* when Gulliver describes the Grand Academy of Lagado's attempt to frame a universal language:

> The other project was a scheme for entirely abolishing all words whatsoever; and this was urged as a great advantage in point of health as well as brevity. . . . An expedient was therefore offered, that since words are only names for things, it would be more convenient for all men to carry about them such things as were necessary to express the particular business they are to discourse on. And this invention would certainly have taken place, to the great ease as well as health of the subject, if the women in conjunction with the vulgar and illiterate had not threatened to raise a rebellion, unless they might be allowed the liberty to speak with their tongues, after the manner of their forefathers; such constant irreconcilable enemies to science are the common people. However, many of the most learned and wise adhere to the new scheme of expressing themselves by *things,* which hath only this inconvenience attending it, that if a man's business be very great, and of various kinds, he must be obliged in proportion to carry a greater bundle of *things* upon his back, unless he can afford one or two strong servants to attend him. (150–51)[45]

Yet Brian Vickers has argued that Wilkins is alone among Englishmen in wanting "to abolish written or spoken language" and that evidence is scarce that the English in the seventeenth century reflect this change toward referential semantics ("Royal Society" 25).

The change is much more evident in French philosopher René Descartes (1596–1650), who argues in *Discourse on Method* (1637) that thought is primary and language or expression secondary. Thinking is not a language art but the means for intuiting and reasoning about pure and clear "Ideas" that lead to certain knowledge, the basis of science and philosophy (3.27). Thinking does not require the *topoi* nor the syllogistic forms of argument (2.15; 3.20), and expression no longer automatically implies a constructing consciousness but instead includes a kind of style capable of presenting physical reality and absolute truths as they are, unmediated by human formulation. Samuel Ijsseling explains that in Descartes "thought is no longer tied to language" and "language has become a completely neutral medium" (65). Descartes remarks that rhetoric and poetics, two arts distinct from science and philosophy, are nice but are unnecessary "gifts of nature," not study (1.7), concerned respectively only with "force and beauty" or "ravishing graces and delights" (1.6). Persuasion is only necessary "whenever there is ground for further doubt" ("Letter to Regius," May 24, 1640; qtd. in Ijsseling 62). The implication of these divisions is that content and expression, idea and form, mind and speech, and nature and art have been turned into dualisms, much as body and mind, reason and emotion, exposition and persuasion, and philosophy and rhetoric have also been.[46]

With ideas shown to be constructions in Renaissance rhetoric, human knowledge is shown to be opinion. This fact does not push these Christian humanists into extreme relativism as it does cultural monists, however. The fundamental principles and forms of reason and rhetoric are to humanists not varying cultural contingencies, but universal constants, which have been, in Thomas Blundeville's words, "grafted in man's mind of God, to the intent that by the help thereof he might invent such arts as are necessary in this life for man's behoof" (*The Art of Logike* [1599] 141). Calling these principles "natural," Wilson writes, "Nature is a right that fantasy hath not framed, but God hath grafted and given man power there unto" (*Art of Rhetoric* 74). These universal forms and laws of reason operate in conjunction with empiricism, and together these two foundations—both mind and body—lead to a knowledge of truth, made increasingly reliable the more commonly shared the experience/perspective is. Man's knowledge grows, Blundeville (fl. 1558–61) tells us, through "tried and approved experience" (25) reinforced by reasoned agreement among "men as well learned as unlearned being in their right wits," or "to the most part of men, or to all wise men, or to the most part of wise men, or else to the most approved wise men" (146). In other words, to humanists knowledge is socially constructed, but in being so not therefore hopelessly uncertain and merely relative to cultural preferences. Being a construction, knowledge remains interpretation without guarantee of absolute certainty, but because it can and must be grounded by universal paradigms and universal experience, it achieves varying degrees of probability. Hence, dialectic, like rhetoric, these humanists all agree, provides the means of disputing "probably on both sides of any matter that is propounded" (Blundeville 1).[47] Without assumed universal foundations, probability becomes a meaningless term. Arguments, then, become important, and it is the most probable argument that deserves credence. Renaissance humanists do not accept the Cartesian mind/body split, the postmodernist reduction of body into mind, nor the behaviorist reduction of mind into body. While quite aware of the imperfections human reason and speech can fall prey to when influenced by an "infected will" or disabled body—fallibilities that keep them skeptical critics,[48] these humanists at the same time retain an optimism about both the human capacity to discover these laws of both physical and mental nature and to learn to behave in accordance with both. Wilson explains that "God, still tendering his own workmanship, stirred up his faithful and elect," who, "seeing by much observation and diligent practice the compass of divers causes, compiled thereupon precepts and lessons," so that "eloquence came not up first by the art, but the art rather was gathered upon eloquence" (*Art of Rhetoric* 41, 48). Wilson goes on, "Rules were therefore given, and by much observation gathered together, that those which could not see art hid in another man's doings should yet see the rules open, all in an order set together, and thereby judge of their doings and by earnest imitation seek to resemble such their invention" (185).

Although the principles of the arts are universals, man's understanding of these universals necessarily remains incomplete. The principles of the arts, then, like all other human inquiries, are up for question, and each manual writer may contribute to the arts by improving upon the work of predecessors: "Man's authority hath no such great force, although noble men, learned Philosophers, and stout captains have pronounced many things most wisely. . . . For except I be persuaded by reason, it is in my choice, either to admit, or to refute such authorities" (Wilson, *Rule of Reason* M.vi.r–v). This learned dialogue between "authorities" and individual challengers again enacts the dynamic between dual complementary forces at work in knowledge-building and prevents the culture from swallowing up the individual or the individual from assuming full independence from the culture.

Although espousing a foundationalist epistemology, the humanists do not embrace positivism, as dualists do, but, like cultural monists, frankly acknowledge their beliefs as an ideology, one compatible with their Christian faith. They also recognize the existence of other ideologies and the framing-function and historicity of such world views. In doing so, they avoid the strict absolutism postmodern relativists levy against foundationalisms. The humanists also, however, offer a philosophy that makes room for both absolutes and relatives, so that the other error relativists accuse foundationalists of—the attempt to identify metaphysical, universal transcendentals—is not an error to these humanists. Rather, since all thinking follows from an ideology, all ideologies perforce postulate some transcendental truths,[49] and cognitive activity naturally requires movement between universals and particulars, the question is not whether to posit universals, but which universals are the most useful in providing heuristic and hermeneutic guidance—which ones provide what Kenneth Burke has more recently called "a representative anecdote" of reality: "A terminology of conceptual analysis, if it is not to lead to misrepresentation, must be constructed in conformity with a representative anecdote" (*Grammar of Motives* 510).

Despite the figurative nature of reasoning and the contingency of human knowledge, there is still always meaning to these humanists, for such a form/thought is an assertion of relations and both guides and reflects all of the mental processes/behaviors that have gone on to construct it. While a reading of this meaning is always interpretation, it nevertheless is not open to an infinity of possibilities, given the text has a definite structure and placement within some, but not all, contexts. Yet its interpretation is also not easily construed, given the complexity of the text's structure and framing, whose meaning accrues through an interaction among the various relevant frames ("places"), not through an accretion of discrete conventional signs. Both monists and dualists in contrast over-simplify this interpretive process by assigning fixed meanings to specific forms/conventions rather than by recognizing that the figures/forms themselves in combination with principles of framing act as not mere referrals or deferrals, but transcendental guides to meaning creation. The humanist assumption of ever-present meaning follows if idea and form are two faces of a figure always contextualized within an act of utterance.

Another implication follows. If ideas have styles, so do one's thoughts. It follows, then, that ideas help to create a style: grand ideas help make a style grand, and trivial ideas help make a style jejune, advice commonly given in these manuals. Hence also comes the frequent warning against devoting attention solely to words and expression. A focus on words and expression alone leads to "mere glibness," Erasmus warns in *De copia* (5)—"only a kind of outer skin," he declares in *Ciceronianus* (84). If one imitates only Cicero's "words, figures, rhythms," one can rightly ask, "Where is the brain, the flesh, the veins, the muscles and bones, the intestines, the blood, the breath and the phlegm, life, movement, sense, voice and speech, and what belong to man peculiarly—mind, talent, memory, judgment?" (52–53). This reciprocity between idea and form also precipitates the advice commonly given to find clear ideas so that words will follow. Erasmus, for example, teaches, "But let your first and chief care be to know the subject which you undertake to present. This will furnish you wealth of speech and true, natural emotions. Your language will live, breathe, persuade, convince, and fully express your self" (123). Reciprocally one can generate ideas from forms and figures, and hence the humanists provide heuristics for both invention and style.

"Fitness" of speech to idea, of "clothing" to thought, then, is not simply the appropriateness of words to objects in the outside world or in the mind—the correspondence theory of meaning that underlies most current stylistic instruction. Instead the stylistic virtue of clarity results from the coherence of all the forms in all the dimensions of the performance, and the stylistic virtue known as discretion or appropriateness results from the relevance of the formal combinations to each other and to all the dimensions of the performance: that is, the forms in the world, the forms of the ideas, the forms of speech and of action, the speaker's intentions (which are also forms), and the speech situation (another form). Fitness derives from congruency both inter- and intratextual. Of Erasmus's two hundred ways to say "Always, as long as I live, I shall remember you," each variation has nuances that make it slightly different in meaning from its fellows and hence appropriate to slightly different situations and contexts. The speaker must exercise judgment in choosing among options, as Erasmus cautions: "But here we must take special care not to do what some do and use the first thing that presents itself out of the heap in any context without exercising any choice at all. For in the first place you will hardly find two words anywhere so isodynamic that they are not kept apart by some distinction. . . . Some words are more respectable than others, or more exalted, or more polished or delightful or powerful or sonorous, or more conducive to harmonious arrangement. Accordingly the man who is about to speak should exercise choice and take what is best" (*De copia* 307–8).

Consequently if a figure is only used to provide some decorative value added to a supposedly complete expression of an idea without awareness of how the figure actually contributes to the expression of the idea, Renaissance rhetoricians point out how the figure is misused and condemn the speaker's lack of judgment. Vives, for example, distinguishes "natural color" from the "artificially painted": "There is also a certain natural color, as Cicero says, which is evenly and healthfully flesh-colored but not splotched with red. Such a color is the result of apt words, clearly set forth, and of figures that are modest, decent, clean, not far-fetched but with the appearance of being fresh and newborn. . . . Opposite to natural is the artificial, the painted, in which decoration appears as something applied from without" (*De ratione dicendi* [1533] 98–99). Renaissance rhetoricians do not believe, as many twentieth-century dualists do, that something said in a poetic style can be said just as well without the poetic style. Rather some ideas are properly expressed in a poetic style, and others are properly expressed in other styles. Renaissance doctrines suggest that a correspondence theory of meaning cannot fully teach the stylistic virtues of clarity and appropriateness.

Mind and Speech

The third set of pairs, mind and speech, exhibits the same reciprocity and is also both inseparable and separable. Renaissance educators agree with cultural monists that individuals inherit a set of particular forms and customary ways to combine those forms from the linguistic and cultural systems they learn. Puttenham, for example, remarks that "the ability to speak" is "given by nature to man" (24, 156), but that "speech it self is artificial and made by man" (24). Once a language "is fully fashioned to the common understanding, and accepted by consent of a whole country and nation, it is called a language, and receiveth no allowed alteration, but by extraordinary occasions by little and little, as it were insensibly bringing in of many corruptions that creep along with the time" (156). Any language is governed by a preferred mode of expression, based in usage: Puttenham declares that use and custom are "the only umpires of speech" (160), the standard reflected in those "civil and graciously behaviored and bred" (157). Similar measures of appropriate behavior have been ordained by "custom and civility" (149, 303). One learns language and behavior through imitation of precept and example. For example Roger Ascham (1515–68), one of the childhood tutors of Queen Elizabeth, explains that "all languages, both learned and mother tongues, be gotten, and gotten only by Imitation" (*Scholemaster* [1570] 264). Consequently "if you be born or brought up in a rude country, ye shall not choose but speak rudely" (265). Because the term *logos,* meaning both reason and word, unites in itself thought and speech and because logic in the Renaissance is a language art whose place, like grammar's, is a part of rhetoric,[50] this acknowledgment of a tongue's cultural relativity and of the role of imitation in learning allows Renaissance readers to recognize the particular constructedness of an individual's mind and speech. Bernard Lamy (1640–1715), for example, perceives cultural traits from an individual's speech: "We know not only the Humor of a man by his Style, but also his Country: Every Climate hath its style" (*Art of Speaking* [1675] 4.19). This style varies from historical period to period: "Every age has its preferred mode" (4.21). Since expression and thought share the same forms, as the lore of the figures will demonstrate, sometimes these forms do govern, even determine, the way humans think. Samuel Shaw (1635–96), the headmaster of Ashby-de-la-Zouch grammar school from 1668 to 1696, observes that these forms in speech (tropes and figures) can shape the mind. In his play *Words Made Visible* (1679), wherein aspects of rhetoric are personified characters, he puts into the mouth of the character Trope: "It is no great thing for us now to be masters of men's tongues . . . [for] we have set up the Dominions of [Style] in the very constitutions of men's minds, and made their conversations voluntary tributaries thereunto" (107–8). Thought, inasmuch as it is prompted by forms in speech and action, is shaped by expression, and speech and action, inasmuch as they flow from thought, mirror forms in the thought. In *Ecclesiastes* Erasmus states, "The internal form of the mind migrates into the external human being and transforms him altogether into its image" (2.247.8–11).

But mind need not be determined by speech or action and preestablished forms need not dictate one's ideas and roles, because mind, speech, and action are separate, equally primary, and mutually causal dimensions of language. Because these three dimensions are separable, thinking can go on without verbalizing, and verbal behaviors need not imitate all mental behaviors. Lorenzo Valla (1407–57) points out this separability when he enumerates kinds of deception in his *Dialecticae disputationes* (1439): "Sometimes they [concepts of truth and falsehood] are not manifested in the mind but in the mouth. Therefore an utterance can be false while the mind is not mistaken—when someone speaks otherwise than he feels—and can likewise be true while the mind is mistaken—when someone deceives not another, as before, but rather himself" (I.ii.649; trans. Waswo 96). Outward behavior, too, may not correspond to one's speech or all of one's thoughts. This separability makes possible not only dissembling, however, but also learning and change. It makes possible the arts. It also makes possible persuasion, in fact puts persuasion at the center of human activity, where Renaissance rhetoricians put it. If there is persuasion, there is choice. Because there are always options, styles result from an individual's choices, choices that can either uphold or violate rules, customs, and conventions. Any language is by nature creative: its natural function requires individuals to take forms apart and put them together in new ways according to the ever-changing circumstances of speech acts. This function ensures that individual utterances are always new constructions, so that choice supersedes particular convention, and individual judgment is as much a part of language use as the inherited forms and means for combining them. Consequently any text primarily reflects the individual mind doing the constructing and the transcendent principles and paradigms of metalanguague or Culture enabling the construction. Only secondarily does the text reflect the particular culture's influences on that mind. Like Erasmus, Lamy takes for granted the inevitable individuality of style: "Discourse is the image of the Mind; we shew our Humours and Inclinations in our Words before we think of it. The Minds then being different, what wonder if the Style of every Author has a character that distinguishes it from all others, though all use the same Terms and Expressions in the same Language" (4.6–7).

The reciprocity between mind and expression also ensures that styles have effects. Styles have cognitive and emotional effects on audiences because speakers through their styles express thoughts and feelings. Much as Cicero teaches that the orator in order to move the audience must first stir up the same passions within himself (*De Oratore* 2.45.189), so Wilson advises that we will not persuade "except we bring the same affections in our own heart, the which we would the judges should bear towards our own matter" (*Art of Rhetoric* 163). But the separability between mind and expression means audiences still have choice whether to be moved.

Additionally Renaissance doctrines also differ from those of cultural monists in the breadth allotted to language. Whereas cultural monists generally reduce language to linguistics, Renaissance humanists conceive of language as behavior. Being placings into relations, forms are always mental processes, so that mind is not reduced to speech, but both speech and mind are separate manifestations of the broadest category—behavior. Not only are the forms of discourse not restricted to linguistic patterns, being inclusive of logical, situational, and behavioral ones as well, but also all forms are either mental, verbal, or physical behaviors. Although he does not pursue the stylistic implications of such an insight, Thomas O. Sloane has noticed this perspective in Erasmus and rhetoricians like him: "It is a view that sees discourse as someone's behavior" (*Donne, Milton* 79).[51] This awareness is manifest in both the Renaissance approach to text as drama and the recognition of figures as behaviors, as we will see.

Because there is always choice, judgment is at the center of stylistic instruction. This focus on judgment is repeated again and again by these humanists. It is this good judgment that Melanchthon declares is lost when style is neglected:

> For this reason, at the very beginning of this work, we must censure the mistake of those who despise the precepts of style and falsely believe that the rules of proper speech have been contrived, not out of necessity, but for empty ostentation. This is the mistaken reason on account of which the study of public speaking was once interrupted and is now neglected, and as a consequence, countless works have come into existence at a disadvantage. For after the rules of proper speech were neglected, all arts and subjects began to be handed down [taught] in a confused and obscure way, because things cannot be understood if they are not explained in words which are meaningful and well known. One thing is connected by nature to another, so that those who are negligent in their speech are much more so in their arrangement of facts. And because they do not follow the rules of proper speaking, they are often muddled in their judgment of facts, which cannot be understood without knowing the type of speech [in which they are used]. (*Elementorum Rhetorices Libri Duo* [1529] 32r; trans. La Fontaine 218–19)

Ascham connects this judgment to moral judgment when he decries against those who favor philosophy (unsocialized utterance) over rhetoric (socialized utterance):

> Ye know not, what hurt ye do to learning, that care not for words, but for matter, and so make a divorce betwixt the tongue and the heart. For mark all ages: look upon the whole course of both the Greek and Latin tongue, and ye shall surely find that when apt and good words began to be neglected and properties of those two tongues to be confounded, then also began ill deeds to spring: strange manners to oppress good orders, new and fond opinions to strive with old and true doctrine, first in Philosophy and after in Religion: right judgment of all things to be perverted, and so virtue with learning is condemned and study left off: of ill thoughts cometh perverse judgment: of ill deeds springeth lewd talk. Which sour misorders [*sic*], as they mar man's life, so destroy they good learning withal. (*Scholemaster* 265–66)[52]

Thomas M. Greene states the proper relationship expressed here: "There is no question of competition between words and matter; what is at stake is a *continuum* . . . properly aligning style, thought, judgment, and action." He continues, "For Ascham thought . . . that the activity of choosing words sharpened the judgment to enable it better to choose actions. The series of manifold tiny decisions required to write a paragraph resembles, he thought, the larger decisions required to act judiciously in society. . . . Barbarous writing involved something like a moral failure, just as barbarous conduct offended the sense of decorum" ("Roger Ascham" 614–15).

If language is fundamentally behavior meant to communicate messages directed to audiences from whom a speaker desires a response, moral judgment is not only one aspect of, but also one with, stylistic judgment. This judgment, as we have seen, is guided by decorum or *aptum:* appropriateness among expression, subject matter, audience, speaker, occasion, purposes, and world. This appropriateness depends in part on grammatical correctness and conventional usage, in part on particular societal rules, manners, and customs, and in part on a universal standard—"a convenient proportion" or "conformity" that pulls the multiplex forms in any utterance into a "uniformity," "congruency," or "decency" (Puttenham 269–70). The writer must make his "multiformitie uniforme," as Puttenham explains (34). In other words decorum rests on both particular and universal criteria. This universal criterion of "decency" is natural, built into the processes of human intellectual activity: "This lovely conformity, or proportion, or convenience between the sense and the sensible hath nature herself first most carefully observed in all her own works, then also by kind graft it in the appetites of every creature working by intelligence to covet and desire: and in their actions to imitate and perform: and of man chiefly before any other creature as well in his speeches as in every other part of his behavior. And this in generality and by an usual term is that which the Latins call [*decorum*]" (Puttenham 269). This universal sense of appropriateness is hard to define more specifically and teach because, due to its general nature, the ever-changing circumstances to which it applies, and the number of choices and dimensions involved simultaneously in every speech act, it cannot be reduced to more specific rules. As Puttenham explains, "But herein resteth the difficulty, to know what this good grace is, and wherein it consisteth, for peradventure it be easier to conceive than to express" (268). It is always a mean between extremes, and hence rhetoricians attempt to impart it by warning against the extremes. Wilson, for example, describes good composition, "the apt joining together of words in such order that neither the ear shall espy any jar, nor yet any man shall be dulled with overlong drawing out of a sentence, nor yet much confounded with mingling of clauses" (192). He warns against too much brevity and too much verbosity, too much repetition and too little, too much poetical fineness and too little, and so forth (192–93). He repeats the commonplace advice that errors occur "when no mean is regarded" (193). Decorum also requires an adaptability to circumstances held in check by the necessity of maintaining congruency among parts and whole. Finally decorum requires creating coherence within the most comprehensive frame relevant to the circumstances. This discretion comes only through lengthy experience and much observation and, as Puttenham explains, shows itself in one who "can make the best and most differences of things by reasonable and witty distinction" (270). While the universal principle is constant, its particular applications are relative to situation, and these individual judgments are always up for debate (282). Manfred Hoffmann summarizes Erasmus's notions of appropriateness similarly:

> Speech is rendered apt in a number of ways. First of all, thought must be fitted to words, and language must be accommodated to the subject matter, to the audience, and to the circumstances. Moreover, the parts of speech must be matched one with another to form a proportionate whole. Last but not least, speech must be adapted to a moral goal. In other words, *aptum* includes: the linguistic adaptation of *res* to *verba;* the pedagogical adjustment of the speaker to the hearers and their circumstances; the rhetorical fitting of discourse into its proper order, relating harmoniously the parts to the whole and the whole to the parts, embellishing oratory so as to make it attractive and persuasive, and synchronizing it with the moral goal so that it brings about transformation, which happens most conveniently when the propriety of the speech fits the probity of the speaker, when the speaker's life agrees with the content and style of speech. (178)

Hoffmann also notes that the aesthetic and the moral are indeed one in Erasmus (176, 182). This conflating of aesthetic and moral judgment in humanist writings the historian Hanna H. Gray has also noticed:

> The terms "*decorum*" and "*imitatio,*" for example, are central in both rhetoric and moral philosophy, and the humanists often appear to fuse their meanings whatever the context. Thus, the imitation of stylistic and of ethical models are spoken of in identical terms; or the idea of always speaking appropriately, of suiting style and manner to subject, aim, and audience is treated as the exact analogue of behaving with decorum, of choosing the actions and responses which are best in harmony with and most appropriate to individual character and principles on the one hand, the nature of circumstances on the other. (506)

It is this universal principle of unity in multiplicity carried out to the social sphere that ultimately prevents style, whether of idea, expression, or action, from being merely outward fashioning or fluff, as dualists would have style be. It also places moral philosophy, which is one of the meanings of wisdom or prudence in the Renaissance, at the center of rhetoric, without prescribing any specific creed.[53] Operating within all levels of discourse—the linguistic, cognitive, and social, this principle of good judgment, although inextricably embedded in practice, as cultural monists claim, is at the same time a transferable signifier that functions heuristically, not algorithmically, because suitably general. To conclude that external forms construct the individual consciousness and then determine one's perspective and practice, as cultural monists do, is to deny this fact of individual judgment at the ultimate level and to suggest, albeit inadvertently perhaps, that learning and language use result more from rote, mindless imitation than critical engagement and inventive play.

Ironically this rote, mindless imitation is the kind of learning many modern scholars have accused Renaissance schoolroom practice of fostering,[54] but this accusation is unjustified as far as Renaissance pedagogical theory is concerned. Renaissance humanists, who acknowledge that learning requires imitation, go out of their way to warn schoolmasters and students alike against rote and formulaic copying.[55] For example Angel Day (fl. 1575–95), an author of a popular letter-writing manual called *The English Secretary* (1586), emphasizes that the writer must always consider the new and unique circumstances within which he composes and that always require adaptation, or else he will appear a fool:

> Nothing is more disordered, fond, or vain, than for anyone, of a thing well done, to take forth a precedent, and think to make unto himself thereof a common platform for every other accident, who without consideration of the gravity or lightness of the cause he taketh in hand (much like unto a foolish Shoemaker, that making his shoes after one fashion, quantity and proportion: supposeth the same forthwith of ability fit to serve every man's foot) includeth in like sort a common method unto every matter. Such imitators who rather by rote than reason make havoc of wit with purchase of small discretion, . . . are better prepared to deliver unto view the ridiculous Pike of Horace with an Ass's head monstrously shaped whereat Readers may laugh, and every one may sport, than certainly to manifest their argument with such correspondent speeches as thereunto may be deemed incident. (4–5)

Erasmus objects to the Ciceronians who believe that following Cicero means taking only Cicero as a model and refusing to use any Latin words or expressions Cicero did not use. In doing so they arbitrarily limit themselves and ignore both the exigencies of their present discourse situation and the flexible and discerning judgment Cicero used to guide his own composing (*Ciceronianus* 61, 80). As Melanchthon says, the true imitator of Cicero must capture the *hexis,* or the mind-set, of Cicero, which requires deviating from the model's particular forms when decorum requires it (*Elem.* 58r).[56] Proper imitation is the seeing of principles in practice, the seeing of how other writers adapted their language, subject matter, and behavior to the exigencies of their own speech occasions. It is not focused on only the actual words, expressions, quotable material, roles, strategies, or content of the original, although noting these transportable features can enlarge the pupil's repertoire. Instead it is focused primarily on evaluating the original author's intentions and quality of judgment in achieving those intentions. Ultimately it compares the original author's accomplishment with the universal principles of decorum. Vives advises, "The zealous imitator will study, with the greatest attention, the model he has set up for himself, and will consider by what art, by what method, such and such was achieved by the author, in order that he himself with a similar artifice may accomplish his own intention in his own work" (*De tradendis disciplinis* 195). Because imparting good judgment is the focus of this training, educators are advised to show pupils the differences between good and bad examples. Pilfering and plagiarism occur if the fragments taken from elsewhere have not been properly "digested" and reframed in order to reflect a "well-stored mind" (Erasmus, *Cic.* 81) and if the imitator regards "not so much the mind of the orator in his expression, as the outward appearance of his words and the external form of his style" (Vives, *De tradendis disciplinis* 191). This focus on judgment is the reason imitation exercises always involve transformations of and competitions with models in order to surpass their artistry. Johann Sturm (1507–89), for example, reminds the schoolmaster of the typical means by which imitations should proceed: schoolboys practice by adding to, subtracting from, substituting for, altering, and transposing the details of a model's subject or style (*Nobilitas Literata* [1549]; trans. T.B. as *A Ritch Storehouse* [1570] 37v–38v). Erasmus gives to would-be imitators of Cicero the warning that will be repeated throughout the period: "Furthermore imitation must fail which desires to follow only, not to surpass" (*Cic.* 55).[57]

Nature and Art

Lastly the fourth pair of coordinates, nature and art, relate to each other as do the previous pairs. Because mind and speech are both separable and inseparable, so nature and art are both separable and inseparable.[58] Style does naturally flow from the mind of the speaker, but the speaker must and can learn to craft thought and expression consciously, developing stylistic versatility and self-conscious artistry. Art, which makes conscious the workings of universal nature—the process of meaning making—enables the perfection of an individual's second nature, one's learned ability to master consciously the process of meaning making. Vives points out what all other humanists also believe—that the language arts merely mirror or make evident the underlying natural principles of human communication: "Now whatever is in the arts was in nature first, just as pearls are in shells, or gems in the sand, but because the dull eyes of many men passed them by without notice, they were pointed out by men, more alert, and the latter were called discoverers, not as if they themselves had made something which previously had no existence, but because they revealed what had been hid" (*De tradendis disciplinis* 20). Fraunce (c. 1561–1633) emphasizes the power of art to change individual nature: "So that, Art, which first was but the scholar of nature, is now become the mistress of nature, and as it were a Glass wherein she seeing and viewing herself, may wash out those spots and blemishes of natural imperfection" (*Lawiers Logike* 2r). When art has brought about this perfected second nature, art has become natural, or in other words art has hidden art. This "hiding of art" is only the naturalizing of it, not the dissembling of sincerity to cover up deception. It is this notion that we must understand when

Puttenham, for example, advises the poet "to be a dissembler only in the subtleties of his art: that is, when he is most artificial, so to disguise and cloak it as it may not appear, nor seem to proceed from him by any study or trade of rules, but to be his natural" (308). When the figure draws attention to itself, to the fact that the speaker is using art, the speaker has not fully integrated the figure into the whole design and shows he has not yet mastered the art. It is handled "indecently," and "all is amisse" (262–63).

These humanists, though optimistic about man's power to fashion himself, remain realistic, however. Despite the tremendous power of art (the mirror of universal nature) to improve one's natural abilities, one's own individual nature remains a limiting force. Erasmus acknowledges that "Ciceronian style does not always accord with one's bent of mind, in which case the effort will turn out badly" (*Cic.* 120). As a consequence he favors "imitation of a model agreeing with [one's] genius" that "aids rather than hinders nature; that corrects rather than destroys nature's gifts" (123). Sturm reminds the teacher that some things, such as ideas and means of expression, can be imitated, and other things, such as quickness of wit and facility, cannot (*Ritch Storehouse* 33v). Hence while kinds of style can be identified, described, and taught, not everyone can master all styles. Furthermore there are as many styles as there are orators (Cicero, *De Oratore* 3.9.34; Quintilian 12.10.10; Puttenham 161). Reciprocally one's own individual genius may also promote one's ability to excel even without formal training. But the humanists' consensus is that a pupil progresses most rapidly when art is a helpmate to individual nature. Wilson makes this point:

> I cannot deny but that a right wise man unlearned shall do more good by his natural wit than twenty of these common wits that want nature to help art. And I know that rules were made first by wise men and not wise men made by rules. For these precepts serve only to help our need such as by nature have not such plentiful gifts. . . . [Yet] none is so wise but counsel may do him good. Yea, he shall do much better that knoweth what art other men have used, what invention they have followed, what order they have kept, and how they have best done in every part. If he like not theirs, he may use his own, and yet none doth so evil, I think, but some good may be got by him. The wise, therefore, will not refuse to hear, and the ignorant for want had need to seek a will. (*Art of Rhetoric* 185–86)

This artistry, this self-consciousness that creates within the individual at least two identities—that of performer and that of critic—enables self-reflection as well as critical thinking and hence the power to escape from blind submission to one's own and others' forms of thought and expression. Since ideas are constructions and can therefore be taken apart and reconstructed, just as forms in expression can be taken apart and changed, one's perspective can change as one's style can change. Furthermore the changing circumstances of life and speech acts require adaptability in one's style, and through practice one can become master of many styles. While a speaker's style will be constrained somewhat by the forms and roles available, a knowledge of the language arts will give every speaker the ability both to conceive of new formal combinations and to collect additional forms as he or she acquires the knowledge of additional languages and cultures. In fact these arts, identifying a metalanguage all humans share, make possible this adaptability both within and between languages, this ability to translate or transfer from one particular expression to another, one culture to another, one role to another. Lamy explains, "Though [this Treatise] was composed in French, it may serve for all Languages, because it inquires into the Fundamentals of Speech, and the Rules prescribed in it, are not peculiar to any one Language" (Preface A7v). The precepts of this metalanguage are not formulaic or algorithmic but heuristic, spurring creativity while constraining incongruency. Renaissance rhetorical training highlights the principles of this metalanguage not only by providing heuristics to guide the learner's use of his own medium but also by exposing learners to multiple tongues and cultures. Schoolboys begin studying both Latin and their own mother tongue and then add a bit of Greek, perhaps Hebrew, and a smattering of other European languages.[59] Such broad language experience enhances capacity and imparts an awareness that both particulars and universals operate within each peculiar linguistic system. Cultural monists, in denying universals, fail to explain fully what makes the processes of critical analysis, translation, adaptability, and transformation possible.

Art liberates. By imparting self-consciousness art increases choice, adaptability, judgment, freedom, and power. Wilson explains that the goal of an education in the arts is independence of judgment: "Now a wise man that hath good experience in these affairs, and is able to make himself a rhetoric for every matter, will not be bound to any precise rules nor keep any one order, but such only as by reason he shall think best to use, being master over art rather than art should be master over him, rather making art by wit than confounding wit by art" (*Art of Rhetoric* 185). Shaw's primary purpose as both schoolmaster and playwright is to correct errors in thought, speech, and action in order to improve judgment and morals: "The design is an innocent *Satire* to promote *Morality,* and by a surprising kind of raillery Tax the grave *fopperies* and beloved vices of the doting world; when men have made the most serious *things* dwindle into *mere words;* and *Virtue* and *honesty,* (not to say, *Religion* and *Conscience* it self) are esteem'd or made use of, but as *Terms of Art* to deceive the ignorant, and serve the *turns* of *interest, faction,* or *ambition,* 'tis time for some Philosophical *Priscian* to Lash such real *Solecisms*" (Preface). The problem with monisms is precisely the denial of such arts and, as a consequence, of the powers self-consciousness provides to individuals.

Such artistry can enable a speaker to create carefully a public persona, a role enactment appropriate to the circumstances, but the very act of creating the persona still points back to the speaker's actual judgment. A speech act is then, regardless of genre, both a literary/fictional and an expository/nonfictional production. While a skilled artist can use the persona as a mask behind which to hide less-than-honorable intentions, such hiding requires that the performer keep parts of the text inaccessible to the audience. The total performance still points to those motives he is attempting to conceal, and while he may succeed in keeping portions of the speech act hidden temporarily, he cannot keep the mask up indefinitely, for to portray always a character is to be that character. Furthermore speakers can play many roles and exhibit multiple qualities that are nevertheless aspects, sometimes mutually congruent and sometimes contradictory, of one consciousness. Speakers can also purposefully choose some behaviors while simultaneously performing others that result from subconscious habit or inattention. Consequently no one utterance absolutely characterizes the speaker, but a good number of varied utterances on varied occasions do, and multiple motives are always at work. This awareness makes these humanists again skeptical and careful readers, always on the lookout for congruencies and incongruencies between persona and person, performance and performer, and always reluctant to consider a character assessment as more than provisional until a sufficient number of performances have been analyzed. This approach Erasmus demonstrates in *Ciceronianus* when he remarks that Cicero has many styles, varied according to genre and circumstances (86), sometimes reflective of prudent judgment and sometimes less so when he falls into boasting, intemperance, and absentminded solecisms (43, 45, 47).

Identities are composed of both general and particular traits: those involving morals and those involving idiosyncratic mannerisms and habits. Wilson notes both kinds. He observes the ostentatiousness of "far-journeyed gentlemen" who "like as they love to go in foreign apparel so they will powder their talk with overseas language" (*Art of Rhetoric* 188), and he points out that while speaking one "blows at their nostrils" and another "sighs out their words" (242). Of these two kinds of traits, however, Renaissance commentators focus primarily on moral qualities. Nevertheless they do not characterize speakers only as types. Melanchthon asserts that Cicero "spoke in a style of his own" and that "the arrangement and the entire body of the speech represent Cicero" (*Elem.* 58v; La Fontaine 320). This awareness of actual character underlying utterance keeps fundamental to Renaissance critics the analysis of complex individual motives, an analysis curtailed in dualists who either read only for a text's explicit subject matter or for the persona created by a speech, in psychological monists who read only for the revelation of unconscious or habitual idiosyncrasies, and in cultural monists who only look beyond individual speakers to typologies or power relations in the culture at large.

According to this philosophy, then, style is an artistic tool by which a speaker may teach, delight, and move an audience, but it is also a natural mirror of the mind of a speaker. Style can be taught and changed; at the same time it always reflects the speaker's mannerisms, attitudes, judgment, and qualities of character. And instruction in style, which imparts good judgment regarding choice of thought, speech, and action, inevitably teaches ethics and character-fashioning, as the Roman schoolmaster Quintilian and many in the Renaissance declare. Quintilian, whose influence on Renaissance humanists is widely evident, insists that an education in rhetoric produces the good man and defines rhetoric as "the science of speaking well," because "this definition includes all the virtues of oratory and the character of the orator as well, since no man can speak well who is not good himself" (*Institutio Oratoria* 2.15.34). This connection to character was denied, Quintilian avers, "as soon as speaking became a means of livelihood and the practice of making an evil use of the blessings of eloquence came into vogue" (1.Pr.13). Following suit, Erasmus in the dramatized dialogue in *Ciceronianus* has Bulephorus reply to Nosoponus's request to "leave off talking of personal characteristics and revert to the discussion of strength and beauty of speech" by responding, "I should gladly do so if the rhetoricians did not declare that one cannot be a good orator who is not also a good man" (45). Wilson also repeats: "The good will not speak evil and the wicked cannot speak well" (*Art of Rhetoric* 244). Such an insight explains the Renaissance attention to style in its very broad demesne.

Historical Context and Significance

Besides contemporary style theory, a second necessary context within which to regard Renaissance teachings is ancient style theory, particularly the differing philosophies of Aristotle and those rhetoricians who advocate the precepts and practices of the Greco-Roman language arts curriculum. Comparing and contrasting the relevant ancient philosophies with those in the Renaissance introduces to the discussion questions that have historically shaped the debate between the philosophers and the rhetoricians: the relationships between rhetoric and poetics, rhetoric and philosophy (epistemology and science), and rhetoric and ethics. The contrast also enables us to make three corrections to the way the history of style (and rhetoric) has hitherto been told: (1) Aristotle's views do not correspond with Renaissance rhetoric but rather with Renaissance philosophy; (2) the Greek and Roman rhetoricians who advocate the classical language arts curriculum originated the philosophy of style undergirding Renaissance rhetoric; and (3) Renaissance rhetoricians go beyond their classical sources in reconciling dualisms and monisms and in making evident that poetics, philosophy, and ethics are both subdisciplines of and synonyms with rhetoric. The defense of these assertions comes in the following chapters, but a brief introduction here justifies this historical focus.

Perhaps because of Aristotle's fame as a philosopher; because his *Rhetoric* was the first of the classical rhetorical texts to be restudied by revivalist rhetoricians in this century; because they have lacked a knowledge of rhetoric's history, which is characterized by the ongoing debate between the philosophers and the rhetoricians; or because they have not read thoroughly, most scholars, until recently, have taken Aristotle as the spokesman for the entire classical and Renaissance rhetorical tradition.[60] The dualistic philosophy scholars have ascribed to Renaissance rhetoric is indeed found in Aristotle. Confining rhetoric to particular genres of political discourse wherein winning marks the orator's success, Aristotle (384–322 B.C.) believes style is only important in rhetoric and poetry, where it and figures are persuasive verbal fluff. He separates the scientific plain style from the rhetorical high style, and though recognizing somewhat style's contributions to the creation of a speaker's persona, he discounts any essential connection between an individual and his or her speech. Separating philosophy and rhetoric and treating figures as merely poetic devices, Aristotle cannot fully justify rhetoric as an ethical enterprise.

But this dominance of Aristotle in modern rhetorical scholarship has hidden from view not only notions of style that historically have been more dominant than Aristotle's, but also the fact that there is not one view of style and rhetoric in either the classical period or the Renaissance.[61] We can, however, talk of two predominant views in the Renaissance, one held by the majority of philosophers, who are Aristotle's descendants, and the other by the rhetoricians, who reject the Scholastics' educational program in favor of the newly rediscovered Greco-Roman language arts curriculum. This Greco-Roman system derives not from Aristotle but from the Hellenistic curriculum the Romans adopted when they conquered the Greek empire—a curriculum fathered by Isocrates (436–338 B.C.),[62] modified over time with contributions from many teachers of various schools, and then adapted again by the Romans, who themselves tended to be eclectic.[63] Marcus Tullius Cicero (106–43 B.C.), who does much to advocate this Greek learning for Romans, was instrumental in encouraging this synthesis, for his own approach in his mature works combines what he considers valuable from the various Greek philosophical and rhetorical schools he attended with his own contributions. Although Cicero has high praise for Aristotle, he also finds him deficient and purposely combines the best from him with the best from Isocrates.[64] Heavily influenced by Cicero, Marcus Fabius Quintilianus (c. 35–c. 95 A.D.), the lawyer turned schoolmaster, also synthesizes ancient and contemporary thinking in his commentary on the liberal arts curriculum he describes in *Institutio Oratoria* (c. 90 A.D.).

The recovery of the full text of Quintilian's *Institutio Oratoria* in 1416 and of Cicero's mature works *De Oratore* (55 B.C.), *Brutus* (46 B.C.), and *Orator* (46 B.C.) in 1421, along with many of his speeches in the succeeding years, enabled the humanists to reintegrate the language arts from the fragmentation and segregation they underwent in the Middle Ages and inspired the humanists' educational reform movement.[65] The name *humanist* comes from the Latin *humanista,* the teacher of this curriculum, which Cicero had called the *studia humanitatis.*[66] Cicero's later works provide what his earlier *De Inventione* (a book that was available in the Middle Ages) does not: both a more complete description of the art with modifications he proposes and a philosophical rationale for its precepts. Quintilian's *Institutio Oratoria* gives the most detailed and complete description available of Roman education. Donald A. Russell has explained that because of the "conservatism of rhetorical teaching over such a long period of time," Quintilian's account can serve as a fairly accurate description of the Greco-Roman system (25).[67] The anonymous *Rhetorica ad Herennium* (c. 85 B.C.), which was available during the Middle Ages and was sometimes erroneously attributed to Cicero, and the late Latin grammars of Donatus (c. 350 A.D.), Diomedes (c. 370 A.D.), and Priscian (c. 500 A.D.) join these works to form the primary corpus on which Renaissance language arts instruction was based.

Their interest in recuperating as much of classical culture as possible led these humanists to consult as many of the available texts as they could. When George of Trebizond (1395–1483), otherwise known as Trapezuntius, published his *Rhetoricorum libri quinque* (1470), he combined this rhetorical corpus with that from the Greek rhetorician Hermogenes of Tarsus, thereby producing the first new full-scale rhetoric of the Renaissance and introducing Hermogenes to the Latin West.[68] During Byzantine times Hermogenes's *On Types of Style* (180 A.D.) was assembled with four additional teaching texts to form a comprehensive "Art of Rhetoric," and this "Hermogenic Corpus" provided the standard textbooks used in Greek schools thereafter.[69] Three additional Greek texts of particular importance to Renaissance rhetoricians are *On Style* by Demetrius (second to early first century B.C.), *On the Sublime* by Longinus (c. first century A.D.), and *On the Figures of Thought and Speech* by Alexander Numenios (c. early second century A.D.).[70] The archival interest also led to the discovery of other *rhetores Latini minores,* of whom Rutilius Lupus (c. 15 A.D.), Aquila Romanus (c. 200 A.D.), and Julius Rufinianus (c. 300 A.D.) are the most frequently cited in humanist discussions of style.[71]

Significantly these sources all share a common stylistic philosophy with precepts, unlike Aristotle's but like those in the Renaissance, that unite without collapsing philosophy, poetics, and rhetoric, reconcile the dualistic and monistic aspects of expression, and thereby give to rhetoric a moral center. Inasmuch as these sources share these common assumptions, we can reasonably suppose this stylistic philosophy to have been passed along in the Hellenistic curriculum.[72] These common assumptions provide evidence that we must also distinguish the philosophy undergirding the Greco-Roman curriculum from that often attributed to the ancient sophists whose relativism and sociopolitical pragmatism contemporary cultural monists such as Fish associate with the entire rhetorical tradition and take as intellecutal precedent (*Doing What Comes Naturally* 478–82).[73]

Although a complete Aristotle's *Rhetoric* also became more widely available in the late fifteenth century and grew in availability during the Renaissance, having received relatively little attention in western Europe's Middle Ages,[74] the majority of humanists either assimilated his briefer and more piecemeal discussion of style within Cicero's more extensive treatment or rejected Aristotle's in favor of Cicero's and Hermogenes's. The observation Lawrence D. Green makes about early Italian humanists serves equally well for the later northern European humanists consulted in this study. Green notices that "pedagogues had little need for Aristotle when they taught practical rhetoric. Renaissance writers had already embraced the more elaborate and preceptive stylistic discussions of Cicero and, more recently, of Hermogenes, and when they came to Book 3 of Aristotle's *Rhetoric,* some felt he added little of immediate use" ("Aristotelian *Lexis*" 163). Speaking of Renaissance commentators of Aristotle, Green explains, "Many commentators seemed to approach Book 3 with the conviction that they already knew what Aristotle meant to say, even if Aristotle himself was clumsy in saying it. For these commentators, Aristotle meant to say what Cicero and Quintilian later said, and the task of commentary was to clarify the muddy correspondences" (150). To read Cicero as if Aristotelian, as moderns have done, or Aristotle as if Ciceronian, as many Renaissance rhetoricians do, is precisely the reason neither group has been able to explicate successfully the humanists' philosophy of style.[75]

The final distinction scholars have failed to notice is that Renaissance pedagogues make both curricular and theoretical innovations that advance this stylistic theory beyond its classical precedents. Because they point to the figure as the fundamental stylistic unit that structures not only all genres of speech but also of thought and action and because they make more obvious the figure itself as both form and content, both tool and mirror, thereby uniting *res* and *verba* without collapsing them, Renaissance teachings provide an even more complete reconciliation between stylistic dualisms and monisms than do Cicero and Hermogenes. In doing so Renaissance teachings presage contemporary explorations into questions regarding the fundamentally figured nature of language and of mind, the identity of speech as action, the epistemic function of figures, the significance of frames for semantics, and the primacy of "utterance," as M. M. Bakhtin coins the term, not word or sentence, as the basic unit of human communication.[76] But unlike contemporary forays into these issues thus far, Renaissance insights come already united within a coherent and ubiquitously applicable stylistic paradigm that appears to be a fairly comprehensive heuristic for both composition and hermeneutics. These contributions, then, require us to acknowledge the Renaissance as the moment in history not only when the repertoire of figurative devices reaches its longest enumeration, but also when style is depicted in its broadest contours.

Status of Theory in the Renaissance

To recognize the breadth and coherence of the humanists' stylistic doctrines is not to assert that Renaissance rhetoricians have fully explicated the theory and its implications, nor is it to attribute to Renaissance rhetoricians "theoretical positions that they had not in fact attained," something Waswo cautions us against doing (80). Rather it is to acknowledge theoretical positions that underlie their principles and practices, even when they themselves do not fully do so. For the most part, this theory and its implications remain implicit in the precepts of the instruction, which is standard enough throughout both the sixteenth and seventeenth centuries to allow us to talk about a mainstream rhetorical curriculum.[77] The fact that all the pedagogues consulted for this study share this traditional curriculum suggests that differences among them are less significant than their similarities. Besides, the authors of these textbooks typically draw from among the same classical precedents and leading contemporaries. Consequently it matters little which ones are consulted. These similarities allow us to mine evidence from even the least influential of manuals without distorting our generalizations about their common perspective.

Being teachers primarily, Renaissance rhetoricians are more interested in practice than theory and turn to practice, rather than theory, to see how discourse works. It is for this reason, as Kees Meerhoff points out, that humanist textbooks so often repeat "*reliqua usus docebit,*" or "practice will teach you the rest" ("Significance" 50).[78] As Hanna H. Gray explains, "[Humanists] were more interested in showing essential similarities and compatibilities among ideas than in making close discriminations among different schools of thought. . . . Over-attention to precise contrasts could be criticized as word-splitting and concentration on points of little import, [since what was important to the humanists was directing learning to] the problem of how to find and lead the best life, not pursuing studies for their own sake" (507). While this interest in practice leads to occasional refinements of precepts, it also prevents many pedagogues from adequately theorizing the art or correcting theoretical errors being passed along in the tradition. There are occasional contradictions that lead John M. Steadman to observe, "We should rather remain aware that in virtually all the literary and artistic debates of the Renaissance there was 'a notable discrepancy between theory and practice'" (viii).[79] Generally speaking, doctrines of style are found primarily in textbooks designed to teach the interdependent activities of textual analysis and composition, where we rarely find explicated at any great length the philosophical or theoretical rationale for the principles and practices taught and where sometimes the rationale given does not match the practice. Consequently in order to understand the theory of style imparted by this curriculum, we must find the coherence in the body of precepts rather than rely solely on the little rhetoricians say by way of explanation.

Unfortunately it is their failure to explicate this more complete and consistent theoretical justification of their curriculum that contributed to the arts' eventual dismantling and splintering in the eighteenth and nineteenth centuries. Dualistic thinking eventually overtook the more unified, comprehensive Renaissance approach. This simplification is due in part to the growing popularity of the curricular reforms of the Frenchman Pierre de la Ramée, or Peter Ramus (1515–72), who in the mid–sixteenth century attempted to simplify and shorten education. In doing so he narrowed the view toward style by reorganizing the materials of instruction in such a way as to increase the sense of separability between idea and expression and to limit style to ornate verbal forms. While his reforms do not constitute much of a shift in overall pedagogical design at first, they do eventually, by decreasing content and coherence, lean the instruction toward the narrower dualistic tendencies evident in the Scholastic philosophical tradition and even further back in Aristotle.[80] This simplification gained impetus in the seventeenth century under combined pressures from the growing influence of Aristotle's *Rhetoric,* Cartesian philosophy, the rise of science, and the newly dominant mercantile class's impatience with the lengthy liberal arts degree.[81] This dualistic perspective then, in turn, evoked the monistic countermovement of the emerging eighteenth-century Romantics, setting in motion the seemingly irreconcilable tensions between dualisms and monisms that characterize stylistic approaches today.

NOW WE WILL TURN TO a four-way comparison between the precepts of Aristotle, those ancients in the Isocratean/Ciceronian/Hermogenean tradition, the Renaissance humanists, and contemporary theorists in regard to the definitions, applications, and functions of figures in order to demonstrate that Renaissance insights show the figure to unite dualisms and monisms and to stand as the paradigm of meaning making. I argue that the figure's primacy emerges because, following the Ciceronian/Hermogenean tradition of conceiving of style broadly and figures loosely, Renaissance rhetoricians then tend to conflate form with figure, depict not only all speech but also thought and action as fundamentally figure, and demonstrate that figures, being both arguments and behaviors, function as both persuasive tools and reflective mirrors simultaneously. Despite the inadequacy of the theory that accompanies them, Renaissance doctrines provide coherence beyond either classical or contemporary alternatives. These doctrines point the way to a new conception of figure, of text, and of language. They also provide the rationale for seeing the equivalence of aesthetic, rational, and ethical judgment. Following this analysis comes an application of the figures to textual analysis, serving to illustrate both the philosophy implicit in the precepts and the usefulness of the theory in practice.

Chapter 1

he Comprehensiveness of Figures

A quick look at the glossary in appendix 1 reveals how expansive the domain of figures becomes in the Renaissance. Compiled from the Latin textbooks most well-known and used in both grammar schools and universities, along with the English manuals attempting either to compete with these texts or to popularize the art more generally, the figures from the rhetorical handbooks consulted for this study total approximately 600. This number increases by about 125 those figures named in the classical sources these Renaissance manuals most frequently cite. The variety calls attention to how comprehensively the figures cover aspects of discourse. The features included as figures belong to every conceivable level of discourse, from sound and rhythm to grammar, diction, syntax, speech acts, gestures, logical proofs and forms, organizational strategies, genres, and qualities of style. Such comprehensiveness shows the error of assuming, as Edward P. J. Corbett does, that classical and Renaissance "stylistic study rarely extended beyond the limits of the sentence" or the "lexical and syntactical resources of the language" ("Teaching Style" 216, 210). Jeanne Fahnestock's assessment that figures included "verbal forms and discourse functions or speech acts" (*Rhetorical Figures* 14) comes somewhat closer to the truth. But figures and style include a domain much more expansive than scholars have yet noticed.

Another look at the glossary also reveals that figures are not restricted to "alterations from normal idiom" or "poetic features" that elevate one's style but encompass nearly every identifiable option at a speaker's disposal, whether of grammar, logic, or rhetoric, as outlined in the Renaissance language arts curriculum. None of these classical or Renaissance authors treats figures with the discriminating precision Heinrich Lausberg does, when in his seminal *Handbook of Literary Rhetoric* he summarizes "the tradition," which he takes to be unitary and unproblematic. Seeing figures as poetic or literary devices, Lausberg insists that all figures of both speech and thought were considered to be alterations of normal idiom, created by means of addition, subtraction, transmutation, and substitution/change (§471, 499–527, 604–754, 755–910). Even though he recognizes that "many *figurae sententiae* are by origin components of status theory and inventio," he insists that these forms only become figures when used outside of their proper contexts: when "they have been lifted out of status theory and inventio, and become generalized so that they can be used freely in the context (i.e., outside the status in question, and outside the part of inventio in question)" (755). Lausberg is spokesman for the typical notions about figures among scholars today. In contrast William G. Crane, a lone, early twentieth-century scholar, noticed that "style came to be almost synonymous with rhetoric in the Renaissance," since manuals moved "nearly all that was considered of significance in rhetoric to tables of tropes and figures" (57).[1] But it was Sister Miriam Joseph who began to demonstrate the extensiveness of the domain covered by Renaissance figures in her 1947 groundbreaking study, *Shakespeare's Use of the Arts of Language,* wherein she compares about two hundred figures from Renaissance handlists with the content of the language arts trivium. She concludes, "A closer examination of [the figurists' work] shows that their concept of figures is so inclusive as to omit little of what has ever been included in a theory of composition, for the approximately two hundred figures of speech which they distinguish represent an analysis of practically every aspect of grammar, logic, and rhetoric" (17–18). Joseph documents only about one third of the figures that were known in the Renaissance, however. The following list in appendix 1 confirms their near all-inclusiveness. Those forms not yet named and anatomized seem rather left off than excluded for any good reason, and the list becomes suggestive, rather than definitive, even in its extensiveness. Appendix 4 charts a detailed comparison between figures and the contents of the rhetorical curriculum, showing that such a list does not reduce style or even rhetoric to ornamental figures but rather expands figures to encompass all the forms in rhetoric. In practice a figure is not restricted to being a specialized form but has become a plastic notion of form itself.

Two crucial questions arise at this point. First, given that this glossary is a compilation longer than any single Renaissance handlist, can this glossary (and the philosophy of figures/style it implies) be truly representative of mainstream Renaissance notions of figures and style? In other words do Renaissance rhetoricians generally approach figures as if form itself and as if isomorphic with the whole of rhetoric? The answer to this question is both no and yes. On the one hand, we can divide Renaissance rhetoricians into a majority who define figures as a set of specialized stylistic devices that alter "common" usage and a minority who actually do declare all forms as figures.[2] On the other hand, even those who give the narrower definition actually do treat forms in general as if de facto figures, since distinctions are so lax as to be insignificant in either their theory or practice.

Figures move from the periphery to the center of style and rhetoric in the Renaissance because humanists follow Cicero, and at times Hermogenes, in understanding style as form or embellishment generally and then either conflate embellishments with figures as does the *Rhetorica ad Herennium* or, like Cicero and Hermogenes, fail to abide by consistent restrictions on the category, so that forms from other departments of style and rhetoric migrate to figure lists. This conflation in some manuals results from theoretical sloppiness, in others from apparent purposefulness. Combined with the fact that none of the definitions offered for figures satisfactorily delimits the category and that the norm from which figures vary is constantly shifting, this practice suggests that a distinction between form and figure is of only secondary importance to these humanists. This practice also shows that they do not distinguish nonliterary and literary language by the absence and presence of figures, as dualists do, but instead by the lesser to greater degree of appropriateness and hence artistry in the author's use of figures. This perspective, which unites without collapsing natural and artistically shaped language, further undermines any strict dichotomy between form and figure. Consequently despite inadequate justification and often contradictory instruction, the figure does take center stage in both Renaissance style and rhetorical theory.

Second, given that the restricted definitions for figures in both the classical and Renaissance manuals do not fit with all the forms they call figures and that no distinction commonly made to separate figures into a class of their own always holds true, we are led to ask whether retaining such a category is useful. Renaissance instruction suggests no. Instead what is useful is recognizing that all forms are designs that have both representational and indicative functions and that become "ornaments" to the degree that they are used appropriately. Inasmuch as these figures or embellishments serve as heuristics for both invention and style, humanist doctrines also unite content and form on the grounds of figure, bringing invention and style together as the two faces of utterance and making these two departments of rhetoric supreme and mirror images of each other.

Style as Form

The first key belief in mainstream Renaissance stylistic instruction is that style is not concerned with merely verbal but rather all the forms of rhetoric. This focus allots comprehensive breadth to the field, pulling even physical signs and types of subject matter and argument into the stylistic realm. This broad view of style comes from Cicero and later Greeks, not from Aristotle.

Classical Precedents

Aristotle treats style briefly in his *Rhetoric* as an "after-the-fact" and cosmetic consideration. Once one has found one's proofs during invention and arranged them in disposition, style is the question of "how to set [these] facts out in language" (*Rhetoric* 3.1 1403b19). While delivery is a facet of style, style does not include the forms of thought. With his preference for proofs, the "only true constituents of the art" (1.1 1354a14), to Aristotle style is "fluff," the "merely accessory" outward expression, which only matters when audiences cannot tell the difference between substance and appearance.[3] Hence to him style is dispensable except in rhetoric and poetics, the two arts aimed at the populace:

> Still, the whole business of rhetoric being concerned with appearances, we must pay attention to the subject of delivery [and style], unworthy though it is, because we cannot do without it. The right thing in speaking really is that we should be satisfied not to annoy our hearers, without trying to delight them: we ought in fairness to fight our case with no help beyond the bare facts: nothing, therefore, should matter except the proof of those facts. Still, as has been already said, other things affect the result considerably, owing to the defects of our hearers. The arts of language cannot help having a small but real importance, whatever it is we have to expound to others: the way in which a thing is said does affect its intelligibility. Not, however, so much importance as people think. All such arts are fanciful and meant to charm the hearer. Nobody uses fine language when teaching geometry. (3.1 1404a5–6)

Despite a brief mention of the virtues of grammatical correctness, clarity, and appropriateness to subject matter, genre, emotion, and speaker's social class and age, Aristotle's focus is on the virtue of ornateness, which he defines as "fine language," that which departs from the ordinary (3.2 1404b9–10). This ornateness arises from unusual word choice and arrangement of words (composition), including rhythm, connection, and various shapes (3.2–12). So important is this ornateness to oratorical style that he treats the appropriate as the ornate, the "avoiding of meanness" without excess through poetic elevation (3.2). Coming early in the development of style theory, Aristotle's discussion of each of these is haphazard and sparse. Briefly acknowledging that delivery, which is a subject that has hitherto been neglected, involves expressing emotions through volume, modulation of pitch, and rhythm, Aristotle declares that when its "principles have been worked out, they will produce the same effect as on the stage" (3.1 1404a14). To Aristotle, then, rhetorical or poetic style is an extricable, value-added, ornate verbal form.[4] He pays heed to it because "poets seemed to win fame through their fine language when their thoughts were simple enough" and because regrettably "most uneducated people think that poetical language makes the finest discourses" (3.1 1404a24–7).

Cicero, in contrast, does not restrict rhetorical style to poetic expression but rather broadens style to encompass all the elements that contribute to the quality of any expression. In book 3 of *De Oratore,* Cicero has Crassus enumerate the principles of style after Antonius has done the same with invention, arrangement, and memory. Crassus begins by insisting that the division Antonius has imposed upon rhetoric is artificial and then reorganizes all the departments of rhetoric under the "embellishments" (*ornatus*) of style. The following diagram charts these embellishments, which include not only the aspects of grammar, diction, composition, and delivery but also of invention and arrangement.[5]

Here we must note that the Latin terms *ornatus* and *exornatione,* or the Greek equivalent, *kataskeue,* do not mean mere decoration but connote instead "necessary accouterments," "furnishings," "equipment," "preparation," "praise," and "honor,"[6] being associated with all the forms and elements necessary for constructing a speech and with the notion of a good or appropriate design. *Ornatus* is also related to the Greek *kosmos,* or "order," or "an order of parts taken together as a whole."[7]

Cicero, *De Oratore*

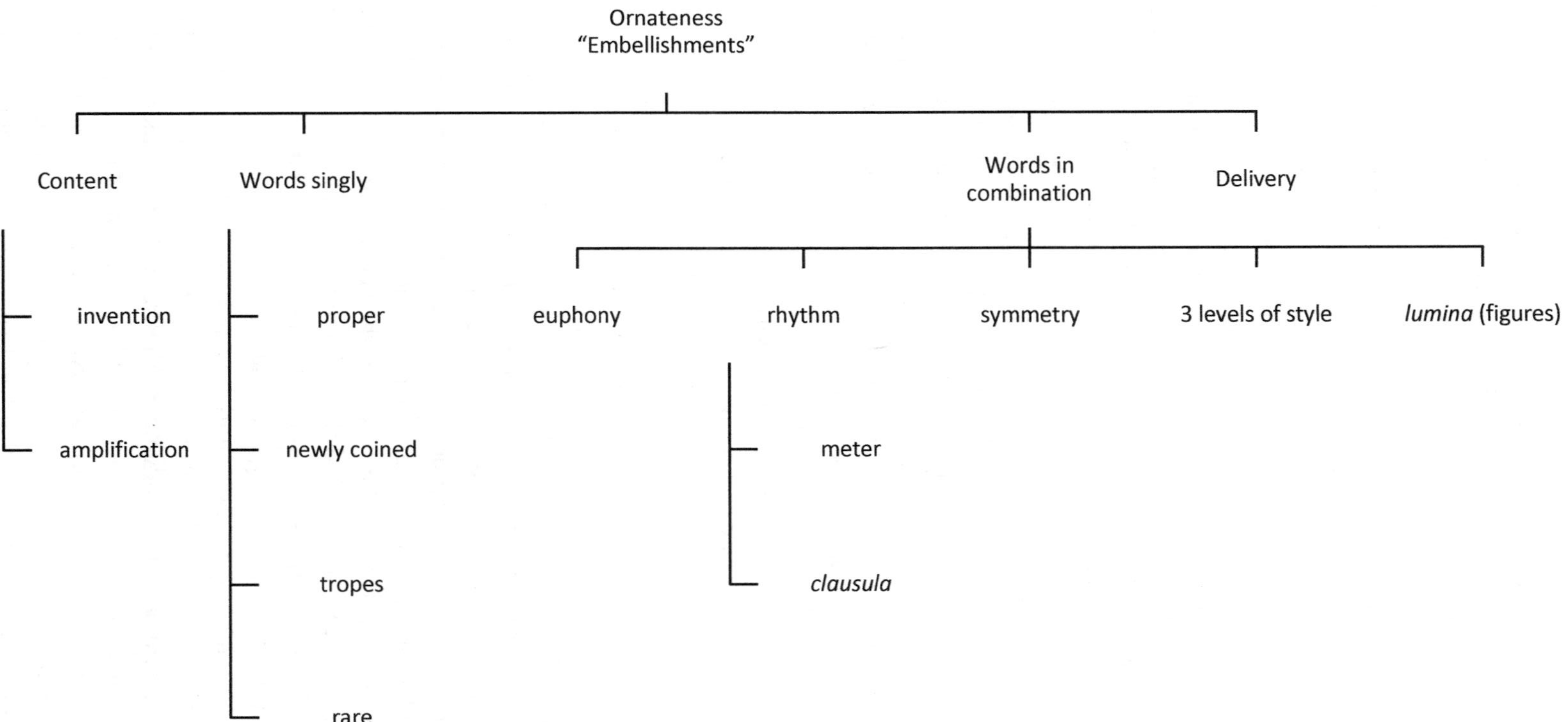

Cicero also uses the term *embellishment,* not only for all these forms but also for what have become by this time the four standard virtues of style: correctness, lucidity, ornateness, and appropriateness.[8] Correctness comes from a knowledge of grammar and clarity from the proper choice and arrangement of diction (3.10.37). Both virtues also arise from correct and careful pronunciation (3.11.40). Ornateness comes from proper embellishment, and appropriateness comes from congruency between forms and subject matter, audience, speaker, situation, and purpose. Rather than keep these virtues completely separate, though, Cicero remarks that correctness, clarity, and appropriateness produce ornateness and that correctness, clarity, and ornateness arise from appropriateness (3.6.24; 3.14.52). In this way Cicero equates appropriateness and ornateness as the overarching virtue. To Cicero it is the appropriate speech that is the truly embellished speech: "Well then, the embellishment of oratory is achieved in the first place by general style and by a sort of inherent colour and flavour; for that it shall be weighty and pleasing and scholarly and gentlemanly and attractive and polished, and shall possess the requisite amount of feeling and pathos, is not a matter of particular divisions of the framework, but these qualities must be visible in the whole of the structure" (3.25.96). In this view style is not "fluff" but the formal essence of speech to be constructed with good judgment. Stylistic instruction is not restricted to ornate form but rather more broadly focused on form used ornately, that is, appropriately or decorously to the whole speech situation.[9]

Cicero makes a point to emphasize subject matter and expression as equal components of style, for he has Crassus assert that neither the speaker without knowledge of the subject nor the speaker without polished and fluent language can be eloquent (1.14.63). Crassus also declares that "excellence in speaking cannot be made manifest unless the speaker fully comprehends the matter he speaks about" (1.11.49), for "this style, if the underlying subject-matter be not comprehended and mastered by the speaker, must inevitably be of no account or even become the sport of universal derision. For what so effectually proclaims the madman as the hollow thundering of words—be they never so choice and resplendent—which have no thought or knowledge behind them?" (1.12.50–51). He again asserts that "it is impossible to achieve an ornate style without first procuring ideas and putting them into shape" (3.6.24). Hence when Crassus remarks that the essential concern of the orator is "a style that is dignified and graceful and in conformity with the general modes of thought and judgement" (1.12.54), Cicero has in mind that this concern involves the whole of the art of rhetoric.[10] Cicero here purposely unites the various connotations of the term *elocutio:* style, copiousness, rhetoric, and good speaking.

This same scope is also found in Demetrius, Hermogenes, and Longinus, who treat as components of style not only verbal elements but also thought, larger features of arrangement, and good judgment. All three writers enumerate the various textual features that create different kinds of styles and emphasize their appropriate use. In *On Style* Demetrius identifies four primary styles—the plain (*ischnos*), the polished (*glaphyros*), the grand (*megaloprepes*), and the forceful (*deinos*)—and their respective opposites: the arid (*tò xeron*), the affected (*cacozelia*), the frigid (*psychrotes*), and the repulsive

Demetrius, *On Style*

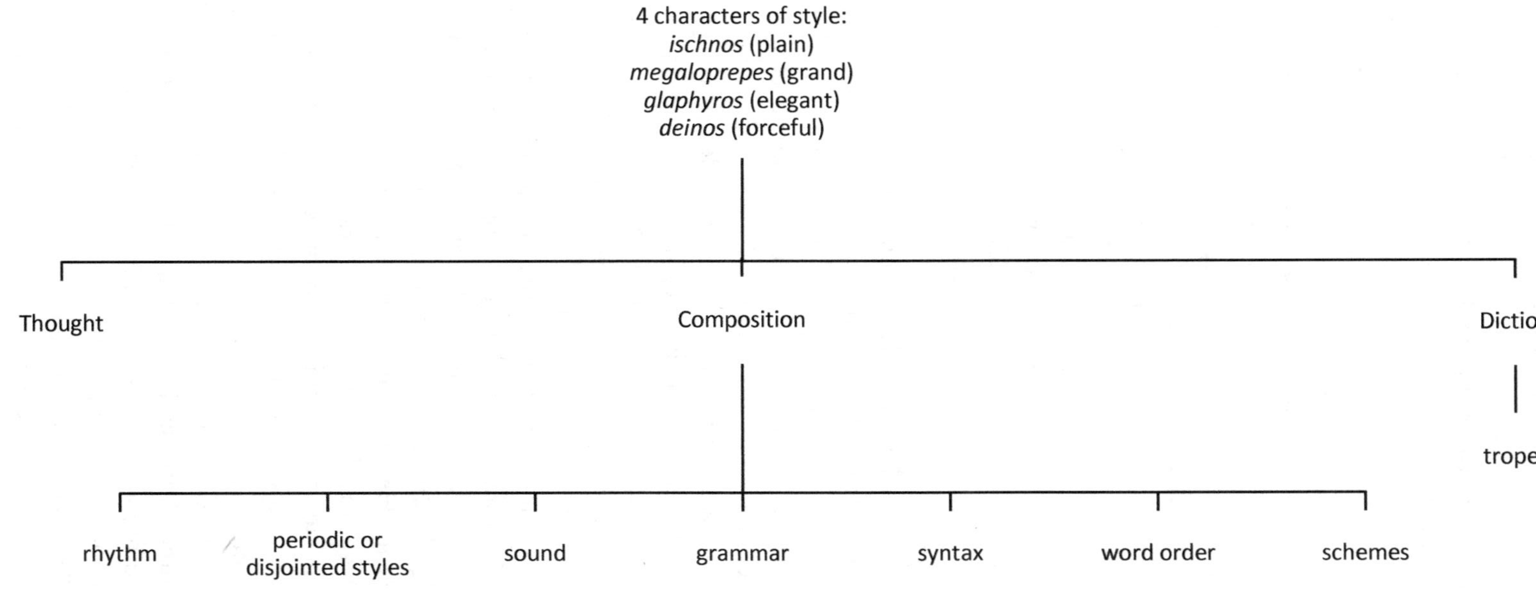

(*acharis*). Demetrius organizes the features of each into three categories: thought (subject, proofs [*apodeixis*]), composition, and diction. Thought is a feature of style because the type of subject matter or proof has an effect and because the degree of appropriateness between subject matter and expression also has an effect. Composition focuses on the arrangement and combination of words, entailing considerations such as rhythm, periodic or disjointed structures, sound, grammar, syntax, word order, and schemes. Diction focuses on word choice.

In *On Types of Style,* Hermogenes greatly increases both the number of stylistic elements and of styles he takes into account. The categories of stylistic elements he expands from three to eight: thought, approach, diction, schemes, clauses, word order, cadences, and rhythm. By "approach" or "method" he means speech acts, genre considerations, and idea arrangements. These elements he analyzes in twenty different kinds of style arranged under seven fundamental styles.

In addition to these twenty, Hermogenes also mentions three faulty styles: *cacozelias* (affected), the opposite of *glykytes* (sweetness); *hyptiotes* (supine), the opposite of *gorgotes* (rapidity); and *psychrotes* (frigidity), the opposite of *drimytes* (subtlety). The Renaissance rhetorician Trebizond explains that Hermogenes is working within a tradition of stylistic forms stretching back to Isocrates,[11] and Joannes Siceliota's commentary for *On Forms* gives the same information (Monfasani, *George* 288).

Longinus in *On the Sublime* similarly examines grand conceptions, vehement emotion, proper construction of figures, elevated diction, dignified word arrangement, and appropriateness as components of one of the panoply of styles—the grand style.

Now the anonymous author of the *Rhetorica Ad Herennium* and Quintilian are less self-consistent because they make a cleaner divide between content and style by reducing style to verbal expression, but they at the same time fail to follow their own restriction. As a consequence from these two sources, some Renaissance rhetoricians inherit precepts that accord with Cicero's broad vision and a content/expression dichotomy reminiscent of Aristotle that does not.

The oldest surviving Latin treatise on rhetoric in its five parts, the *Rhetorica Ad Herennium* identifies style with verbal expression: "Style is the adaptation of suitable words and sentences to the matter devised" (1.2.3). Organizing his discussion of style under a slightly altered list of the virtues, this author appears to focus primarily on verbal elements. He also confines embellishments or *exornationes* to figures of diction and of thought that belong to the stylistic virtue of distinction (*dignitatem*). Yet he freely incorporates argument forms as kinds of "exornations," as we will see, so that his restriction to verbal elements is more apparent than real. Also like Cicero this author regards appropriateness or propriety as the reigning stylistic virtue to which all others contribute, remarking that "an appropriate and finished style," one "suitable to the speaker's purpose" and subject matter, will have "taste (*elegantium*) [which consists of *latinitas* (purity) and *explanatio* (clarity)], artistic composition (*conpositionem*), and distinction (*dignitatem*)" (4.12.17).

Quintilian also restricts style to "individual words" and "groups of words" (8.1.1). This reduced domain focuses his discussion on outward linguistic expression, "the

Hermogenes, *On Types of Style*

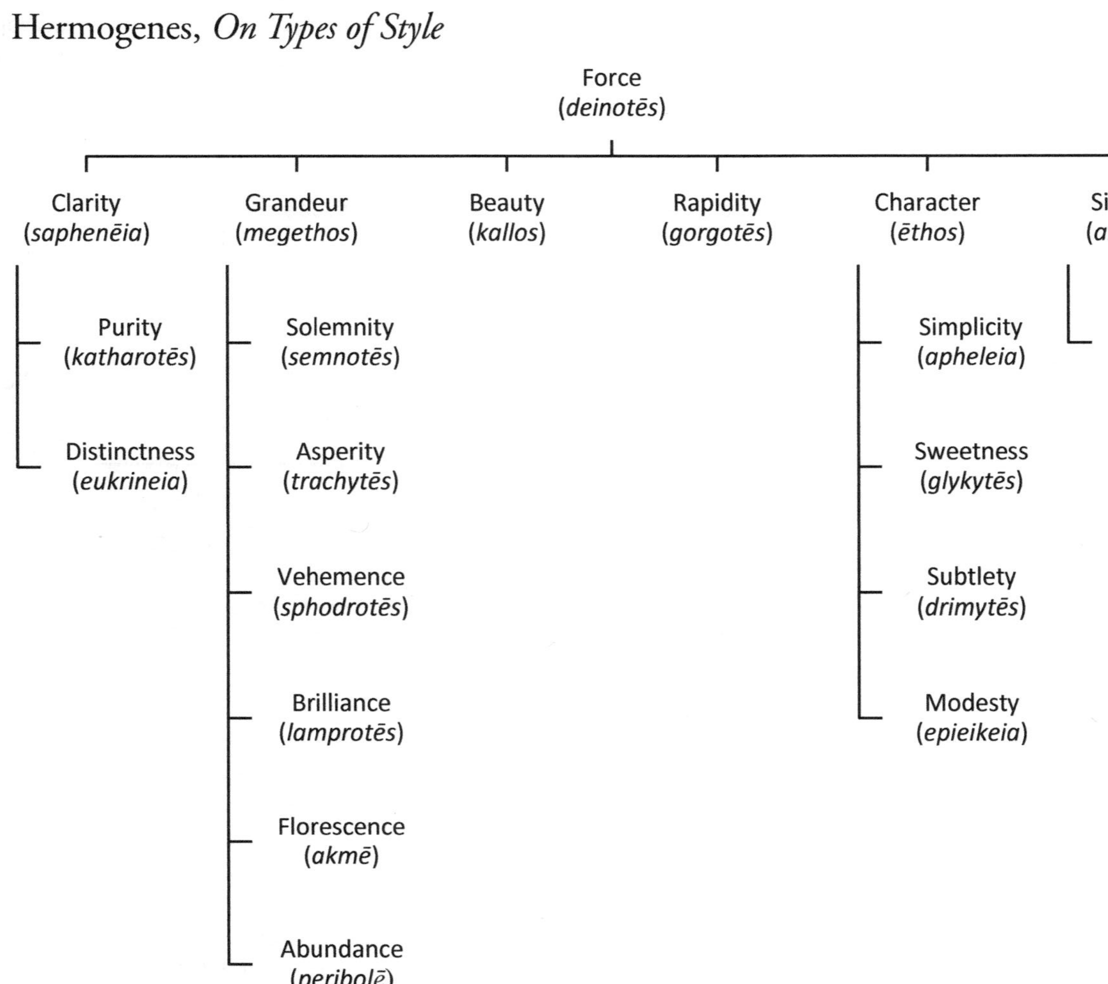

Rhetorica Ad Herennium

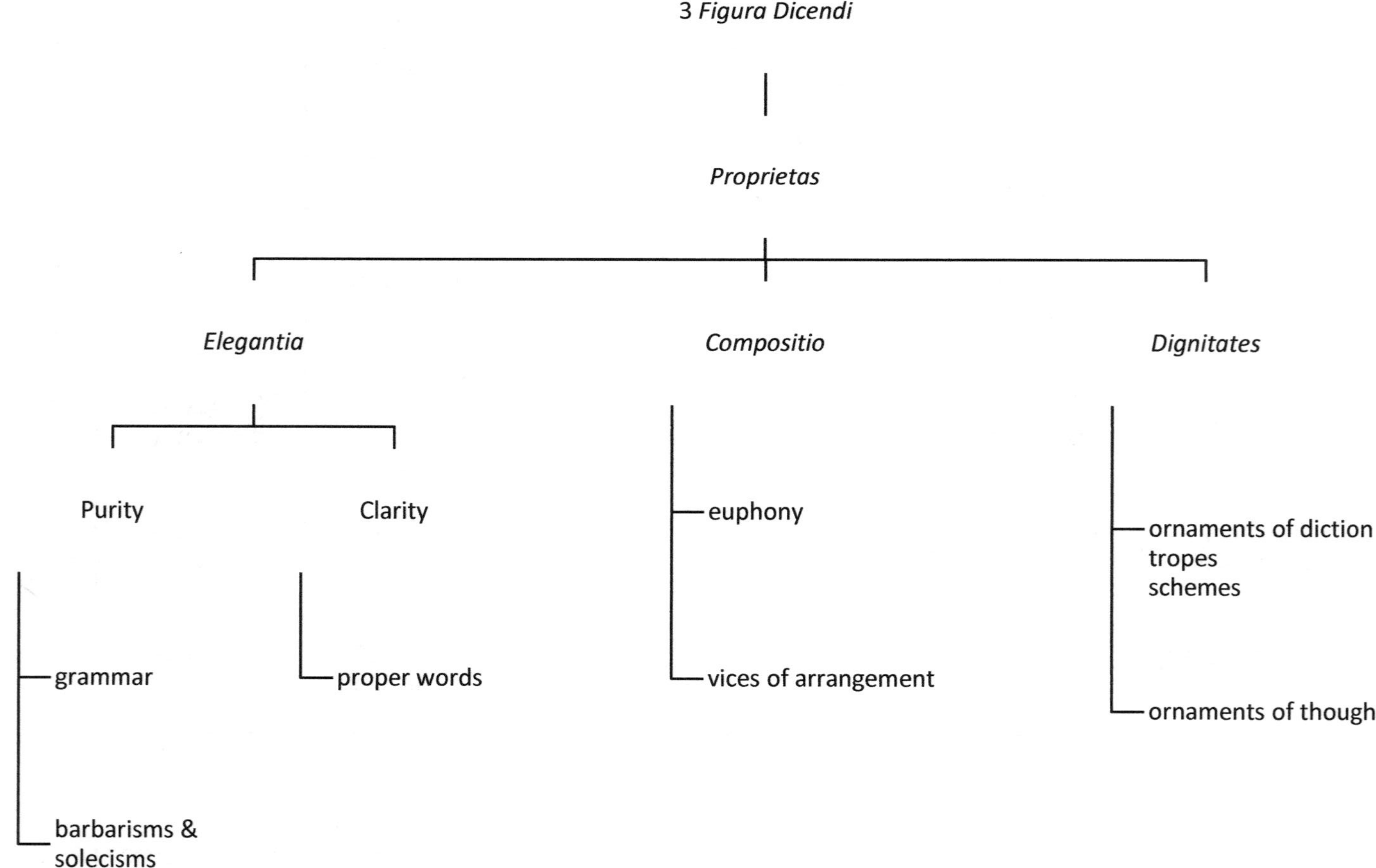

Quintilian, *Institutio Oratoria*

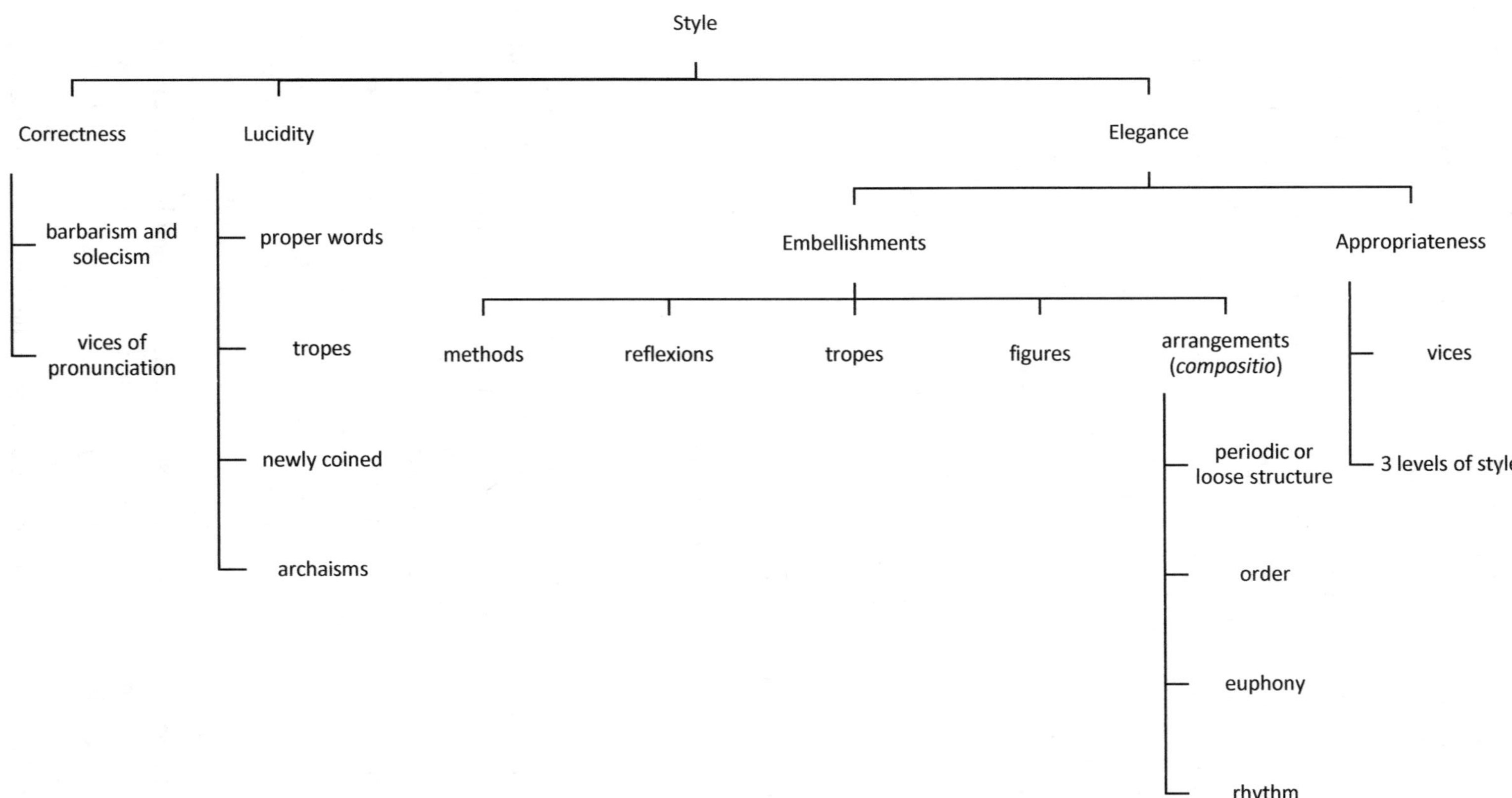

production and communication to the audience of all that the speaker has conceived in his mind, and without this power all the preliminary accomplishments of oratory are as useless as a sword that is kept permanently concealed within its sheath" (8.Pr.15). Like Cicero he merges the virtues of ornateness and appropriateness into the virtue "elegance" (which includes the grammatically correct and lucid), but the elements he treats under elegance emphasize style as the art of "ornate and appropriate language" (8.Pr.13). Much curtailed from Cicero's list, Quintilian's stylistic embellishments include methods, reflexions, tropes, figures, and composition (8.3.41).

Despite excising invention, disposition, and delivery from stylistic concerns, Quintilian has trouble keeping them out, though, for he concedes that the ornate "consists firstly in forming a clear conception of what we wish to say, secondly in giving this adequate expression, and thirdly in lending it additional brilliance" (8.3.61). In his discussion of invention, he declares that giving support to arguments not only strengthens them but also ornaments them, "since we shall have produced something more than a mere fleshless skeleton" (5.12.6), and he admits in his discussion of style that "even the type of simile which I discussed in connexion with arguments is an ornament to oratory, and serves to make it sublime, rich, attractive, or striking" (8.3.74). Although he keeps delivery a separate department, he acknowledges that delivery works upon the same principles as style (11.3.30).

The Renaissance View

In the Renaissance rhetoricians generally follow Cicero and Hermogenes, allotting to style a wide domain, some self-consciously so and others, like the author of the *Ad Herennium* or Quintilian, less self-consciously so. Ramists ostensibly take a narrower view and appear to be the exception, but even some of their precepts point toward the broad view of style.

To Ramus style consists only of rhetorical tropes and figures, which he sees as belonging to verbal language (*Arguments* [1549] 130). He states that grammatical figures should be placed under the purview of grammar (147), although when he writes his own grammar textbook, he does not identify these figures.[12] This reduction gives the appearance of restricting style's domain to ornate verbal form, but in reality this canon includes more. Ramus compromises the firm boundaries he has set when he admits that subject matter helps to determine the style: "For the distinction between high, low and middle style in speech is drawn not only from words but from the subjects themselves, so that this partition is common to invention along with style" (159). Delivery, although a separate department in name, also inevitably becomes part of style in Ramist textbooks. Ramus's collaborator, Audomarus Talaeus (Omer Talon), whose name appears on their joint rhetoric textbook, *Rhetorica* (1545), actually admits that delivery amounts to the same thing as style (83–86). Fraunce, an English Ramist, broadens the domain of style even further by keeping grammar under its purview (*Arcadian Rhetoric* A2r–v). He also, like Talon, regards delivery as another aspect of style, for by giving examples from literature of the various kinds of voices, which end up being various passions, he, like Talon, gives examples of various styles: the sharp, the mild, the angry, the moderate, the pitiful, and so forth. Also, as we will see, the tropes and figures in Ramist handbooks are not merely verbal forms.

Non-Ramist manuals, however, clearly give style an expansive territory. The leading humanist of his day and an advocate of a Ciceronian perspective, Erasmus spearheads a very self-conscious adoption of the broad conception of style. In *De duplici copia rerum et verborum* (1512), which he published at John Colet's request for the new St. Paul's grammar school in London, Erasmus provides instruction and practice in the abundant style. But to do so he must also demonstrate the opposite, the compressed style, so that the true end of his instruction becomes stylistic facility in general. Erasmus admits, "The purpose of these instructions is to enable you so to include the essential in the fewest possible words that nothing is lacking, or so to enlarge and enrich your expression of it that even so nothing is redundant; and to give you the choice, once you understand the principles, of emulating the Laconic style if you so fancy, or of imitating the exuberance of Asianism, or of expressing yourself in the intermediate style of Rhodes" (301). Erasmus teaches that style has two parts: content and expression (295). Consequently book 1 treats expression, and book 2 treats subject matter. Nevertheless he explains that these two aspects, although separated for instructional purposes, are "so interconnected in reality that one cannot easily separate one from the other, and . . . they interact so closely that any distinction between them belongs to theory rather than practice" (301).

When teaching how to find an abundance of subject matter, Erasmus provides instruction in invention and disposition. For example method 10 in the second book reviews how to find as many propositions (*hypotheses* and *theses*) as possible for any given case, so that one can choose those necessary and be prepared to answer those that will possibly be introduced by the opposition. Erasmus's instruction here parallels Quintilian's discussion of proofs in 4.4 and 5.10. Inasmuch as propositions require reasons for support, Erasmus also demonstrates how to find reasons to support them. This discussion includes a recourse to the dialectical topics (595–605). To follow up Erasmus then devotes method 11 to the finding of proofs and arguments, called *pisteis*, which fall into two classes: the artificial (*entechnoi*) and the inartificial (*atechnoi*). This discussion summarizes Quintilian 5.9–10 and also reviews the dialectical topics, along with methods for generating examples, parallels, comparisons, common places (*kriseis*), maxims, elaborations (*expolitio*), fables, dreams, fictional narratives, and scriptural allegories (605–35). Erasmus also treats of logical forms, such as *epagoge* (induction), *apodeixis* (demonstration), *aetiologia* (giving a reason), and *propositio* (a premise in a syllogism), under enrichment of subject matter. Additionally he includes various of the *progymnasmata* (preliminary composition exercises) and ends the book with a discussion of disposition. Paul Butler notices that Erasmus "helps expand the notion of style during the Renaissance, connecting style closely to invention through his emphasis on an abundance of words and ideas" (*Out of Style* 44). But Erasmus's originality is not this broad view but rather the elaboration of the view in his original instructional design. Inasmuch as Erasmus set with this textbook the pattern for stylistic instruction in many Renaissance grammar schools, many rhetoricians after him reflect his breadth.

One of these is Sturm, the rector of the gymnasium at Strasbourg, who is, along with Erasmus, Vives, and Melanchthon, one of the four great preceptors of Renaissance humanism. Sturm provides another comprehensive treatment of style in his eight-hundred-page *De Universa Elocutionis Rhetoricae, libri IIII* (1575). Following Hermogenes, he examines the eight parts of style—thought, method, diction, scheme, clauses, composition (connection of words), cadences (*membra*), and rhythm—in relation to the numerous kinds of styles these elements can create. To this discussion he adds the three genres of oratory, the parts of the oration, the *stases,* the inventive *topoi,* and argument forms, subsuming, like Cicero, all under style.

Less self-aware but still expansive in their views are other influential early humanists. Trebizond in *Rhetoricorum libri quinque* (1470) associates style with words and divides it from invention, which he associates with reason and subject matter, saying, "Thus, if a person claims to know about the revolution of the earth, the causes of things, the nature of the heavens, and whence things come into being and where they will fall into ruin, he will appear destitute of all knowledge unless he also adorns and illuminates what he teaches with a rich abundance of words as if with gold and gems" (trans. Rebhorn, in *Renaissance Debates* 30). Nevertheless like Cicero and Hermogenes, he includes "thought" and "method" as aspects of style. The other two of the four great humanist preceptors also belong in this category. Melanchthon, professor at the University of Wittenberg, reduces style to verbal expression, on the one hand. In his *Elementorum rhetoricae libri duo* (1529), he writes, "Therefore, the choosing of the subject matter [invention] and the arrangement of the material [disposition] revolve around content; style is concerned with words. For those things which we have turned over in our minds and arranged in a certain order must afterwards be presented in meaningful terms" (5v; trans. La Fontaine 81). On the other hand, Melanchthon also acknowledges that stylistic decisions include choice of subject matter, genre, and arrangement. Style, he says, consists of grammar and embellishments (33r). Since embellishments include aspects of amplification, style includes enrichment of subject matter.[13] Melanchthon also declares that style includes choosing "the type of speech in which the information we have found ought to be presented and illustrated" (31v; La Fontaine 218). Additionally he instructs that proper disposition or order (*oeconomia*) is an aspect of style (composition), since "if [a speech] lacks order in the presentation of the matter, [it] is just sounds without meaning" (31v; 217) and coherence of sentences depends upon "the right order of ideas" (59v; 323). In fact clarity depends upon proper invention and arrangement as much as words: "For a speech is made more clear if the ideas are suitably connected, if the parts and argument are not left incomplete, if the parts which it is especially profitable to consider are conspicuous and prominent, if embellishments have been used as clothing, if the lengths of the periods are moderate, if the periods are not scattered by transposition of words" (61r–v; 332–33). Similarly Vives in *De ratione dicendi* (1533), a book on style, presents rhetoric as if the art of expression is separate from content but then concedes that speech is "an outflowing of reason" (27) and that words and sense "are so interrelated that we treat them together when we speak of color and ornament" (88). In this book wherein he presents a new synthesis of rhetorical principles, he also includes argumentation, arrangement, the duties of the orator, choice of genre, and instruction in prudence as aspects of style.

This breadth then becomes characteristic of Renaissance stylistic instruction, even when style is ostensibly listed as only one of rhetoric's five departments. As Puttenham teaches in his *The Arte of English Poesie* (1589), both the "inward conceits" and the "manner of utterance" constitute one's style (161). There seems to be a healthy dual vision commonly evoked in these manuals: style is one aspect of rhetoric, but at the same time the entire art of rhetoric can be viewed from the perspective of style. This inclusive view lasts until the end of the period. The Frenchman Lamy as late as 1675 includes within style aspects of delivery (3.106) and of invention and arrangement, reminding the reader that the "Quality of Style" depends upon "a capacity to discover abundantly all that may be said upon any proposed subject" (4.16), along with "the form, the clearness, the good Order of our Ideas" (4.5).

Form as Figure

Conceiving of style broadly as forms in general, Renaissance rhetoricians then tend to go beyond their classical precedents by equating embellishments and style with figures. This conflation occurs in textbooks that divide style into various elements, with figures ostensibly being only one of those elements, and in manuals that expressly present style as figure. This conflation results from mixing together the influences of the classical authorities, who treat figures with imprecision; from defining figures even more imprecisely than their classical sources do; and from failing to abide by restrictions on the figure category. More concerned with the effects forms produce than distinctions among forms, these pedagogues also do not associate the figures with poetic elevation only, as does Aristotle, but, like Cicero and Hermogenes do, with all kinds of stylistic effects. They also insist, more than do their classical ancestors, that both natural and artful expressions have figures. The handful of Renaissance rhetoricians who purposely broaden the notion of figure to form of any kind, then, simply bring theory into alignment with general practice.

Greek and Roman Imprecision

Classical precedents provide three primary views of figures. The first and oldest is the notion of *schema* (Greek) or *figura* (Latin) as form in general. The second is a much more restricted notion of figure as a special kind of linguistic alteration that poeticizes language, making it more indirect (allegorical) and guileful (ironic). And the third, which is looser than the second but more restricted than the first, is the notion of figure as a particularly effective configuration that gives an utterance artistic polish and elegance. Once the more narrow meanings of the term emerge, talk of figures in a restricted sense becomes a standard feature of the Greco-Roman curriculum. Nonetheless debate continues regarding their proper identity, and there seems to continue a tendency for the general view of *schema* as form to keep encroaching on the narrower view of *schema* as a specialized device. This tendency is evident in all those sources most influential on the Renaissance, and except for Quintilian and Alexander of Numenius, all take little interest in clear differentiation among kinds of stylistic features and so blur the boundaries between the more general and more specialized meanings of the term.

Early in rhetoric's history, the Greeks used the term *schema* to refer to any form or configuration.[14] Sometimes *schema* retained a synonymity with content, for Isocrates treats as synonyms *schema* (construction of word or thought) and *idea* or *eidos* (genre of style, the way a man "carries himself," "real essence," and "thought elements or ideas" that "the orator has ready as a part of his stock in trade"), as H. M. Hubbell points out (6–7). At other times *schema* is restricted to "the purely perceptual or outward shape" and distinguished from *eidos* or the form or idea that informs matter, as in Plato and Aristotle (Auerbach 14).

The narrower meaning of *schema* as a deviation from common speech began after Aristotle, when a theory of figuration gradually developed. We are not certain of much of this development. Aristotle mentions that Gorgias, a sophist, pulled from poetry into public oratory forms that elevate the style and make it more impressive (*Rhetoric* 3.1 1404a24–25). Quintilian indicates that the earliest known definition of a scheme in the narrow sense—"to pretend one thing and say another"—was made by Zoilus in the fourth century B.C. (9.1.14). Theophrastus, Aristotle's student, apparently provided the first direct discussion of kinds of amplification and of schemes.[15] The first separation made between figures of speech and figures of thought occured before Demetrius's *On Style*, for here Demetrius makes brief reference to these categories without definition or explanation. Scholars surmise that it is the Stoic grammarians who probably developed a theory of the tropes in this same late first century B.C., defined tropes as "turnings of signification," made a distinction between the tropes and figures, and likely arranged the figures, which they conceived as kinds of deviations, into those created by addition, omission, substitution, and transposition, categories identical to the four sources of grammatical barbarisms and solecisms.[16] Yet Kennedy also notes that it is Cicero who in *Brutus* (69) first expressly made the distinction between tropes and figures (*Art of Persuasion* 297). Quintilian records that even in his day teachers often did not make this separation (9.1.1). Russell argues that the definitive systematization of the figures into those of speech and of thought "were made in the first century B.C. by two men: Gorgias, who taught Cicero's son at Athens in 44 B.C. and later declaimed at Rome in the hearing of the elder Seneca; and Caecilius of Caleacte, better known as the opponent attacked in [Longinus's] *On Sublimity*" (145–46).

But the general notion of figure as form persisted even when the specialized meaning of the term came into vogue, for both Quintilian and Alexander of Numenius felt the need to argue against the more general notion. Quintilian makes this acknowledgment:

> For the term is used in two senses. In the first it is applied to any form in which thought is expressed, just as it is to bodies which, whatever their composition, must have some shape. In the second and special sense, in which it is called a *schema*, it means a rational change in meaning or language from the ordinary and simple form, that is to say, a change analogous to that involved by sitting, lying down on something or looking back. Consequently when a student tends to continuous

> or at any rate excessive use of the same cases, tenses, rhythms or even feet, we are in the habit of instructing him to vary his figures with a view to the avoidance of monotony. In so doing we speak as if every kind of language possessed a *figure:* . . . Therefore in the first and common sense of the word everything is expressed by *figures.* . . . If, on the other hand, the name is to be applied to certain attitudes, or I might say gestures of language, we must interpret *schema* in the sense of that which is poetically or rhetorically altered from the simple and obvious method of expression. It will then be true to distinguish between the style which is devoid of figures (or *aschematiston*) and that which is adorned with figures (*eschematismen*). (9.1.10–13)

Several years later Alexander, also known as Alexander Rhetor, makes an argument very similar to Quintilian's, showing that controversy over the figures' domain was far from over. In his treatise *On the Figures of Thought and Speech,* he writes:

> Before proceeding first to consider Figures (*schēmata*) of Thought, let us briefly answer those who entirely deny their existence. There are some who say that there is nothing special about a Figure of Thought, for no unfigured discourse (*logos*) can easily be found. This, they say, is inevitable, since discourse depends on the configuration (*diatupōsis*) of the mind (*psuchē*), and indeed was invented to express the mind's forms, experience and movements in general. Now the mind is in constant motion, and takes on many figurations (*schēmatismoi*), e.g. when it defines, reproves, takes counsel, or does or experiences any one of the things which happen to it. Thus discourse, inasmuch as it is a copy (*mimēma*) of the mind, will necessarily have some figure (*schēma*) or other. (trans. Russell 176–77)[17]

The notion of scheme as form in general especially seems paramount in Demetrius, Hermogenes, and Longinus. In all three their focus is on describing how to create various styles, with little concern for distinguishing between *schemata* and other forms. Although all name *schema* as one kind of stylistic element, none defines the term and all fail to treat the so-called category with any kind of consistency or precision. So nebulous is the concept of *schema* in these texts that they pass on a preference for thinking about style and *schema* as form in general[18] and even retain the overlap found in Isocrates between *schema* and idea.

Only fourteen of the one hundred stylistic features Demetrius identifies he expressly calls schemes, and these appear randomly in either discussions of diction or composition. The tropes are undesignated and appear side by side with other undesignated features belonging to both diction and composition. Similarly in Longinus one category of features is the proper construction of schemes. However it is not clear how these features he discusses under schemes differ from those he examines in his other stylistic categories, because features do not belong to only one category. For example *diatyposis* is a scheme but also a feature of thought (§15); *orcos* itself provides ideas, being "a proof that no mistake has been made, an example, a sworn confirmation, an encomium, and an exhortation" (§16). Metaphor Longinus treats under diction (§32), and because he claims that all schemes "serve to lend emotion and excitement to the style" (§29), he blurs the boundaries between schemes and his category of vehement emotion. Since devices he discusses under other categories, such as *parabole,* hyperbole, *auxesis,* and *periodos,* have already been listed as figures by predecessors, he appears to be not much concerned with making careful distinctions, and his treatment works to level the features. This lack of precision makes distinguishing between the figure and nonfigure in both Demetrius and Longinus unhelpful.

Particularly influential is Hermogenes's imprecision. Although he lists schemes as one of the eight kinds of stylistic features, he cares little about rigorous categorization, and he does not conceive of schemes as deviant or exceptional in any way. First of all, the separate category of methods or approaches he admits to be figures of thought (*schemata tes dianoias*) (1.1.223). Second, when he comments on his categorization of devices, he usually admits to the ambiguity of the choice. For example about *diaporesis* (perplexity, doubting), he says, "This is either a figure or an approach, as we said, but we have chosen to discuss it with the figures that convey spontaneity or animation" (2.7.361). Again, he remarks, "Replies [to objections] (*anthypophora, lysis*) are not figures but approaches of sorts, or at any rate thoughts" (2.7.357). Furthermore he variously lists the same device in one spot as a scheme and in another as an approach or as a thought. For example *merismus* (a division) is a scheme in his discussion of clarity (1.4.238) but an approach in his discussion of the simple style (2.3.326). *Epikrisis* (value judgment) he treats as a scheme, even though he acknowledges it also as a thought (1.6.250). Amplification he lists as a scheme in the brilliant style (1.9.268) but a thought in the abundant style (1.11.281). Refutation is a thought in *sphodrotes* or vehemence (1.8.261) but a scheme in *akme,* the florescent style (1.10.271). *Orthotes* is a scheme (1.3.230), but *kommata,* a related syntactical pattern, is a feature of clause (1.3.232). Hermogenes has no category for tropes but treats them as aspects of diction, except for allegory, which is an approach (1.6.246).

Third, besides this carelessness in categorization, Hermogenes does not conceive of schemes as deviant constructions. The direct, simple sentence (*orthotes*), for example, is a figure: "The figure that is most characteristic of Purity is the use of a straightforward construction with the noun in the nominative case" (1.3.229). To create both vehemence and sincerity, one can use the figure *deiktikon* or "pointing expression," created through the use of demonstrative pronouns (1.8.263; 2.7.361). To create brilliance one can use direct denial (*anairesis*), saying, for example, "I did not fortify the city" (1.9.267). Only when Hermogenes discusses "Beauty" does he focus on schemes that "call attention to their ornamental nature and show clearly that the style has been embellished" (1.12.299), suggesting that some schemes, then, do not call attention to themselves. Also significant is his demonstration that purity, clarity, ornamentation, and appropriateness (force)—the four standard virtues of style, which become in his treatment four kinds of style—are all produced by differing schemes.

We find this same looseness in other books passed down in the Hermogenic corpus. In book 4 of *On Invention,* the author gives some suggestions for prose style, treating forty-eight varied devices, calling some schemes and leaving others undesignated. In

On the Method of Forcefulness, we again find treated a miscellaneous and undifferentiated collection of forty-nine stylistic devices, consisting of speech acts, syntactical forms, and kinds of styles. *On Invention* explicitly calls the *comma*, *colon*, and various kinds of *periods* schemes, whereas in *On Types of Style* these features are treated under clauses. Such looseness actually invites all the features Hermogenes discusses to be considered figures. Indeed like those in Demetrius, nearly all the features he examines will appear on figure lists in Renaissance manuals.

The second definition of figures handed down from antiquity refers to self-conscious alterations that make speech more indirect or guileful. This highly restrictive use of the term is found primarily in Quintilian, although the notion of such a set of devices is incipient in Aristotle and is repeated in some later Greek manuals, of which Alexander is an example.[19]

Although Aristotle wrote before the doctrines of the tropes and schemes had officially begun, his emphasis on the need for the public speaker to use linguistic alterations in order to give his speech a poetic flair points to the narrowest view: "Now it was because poets seemed to win fame through their fine language when their thoughts were simple enough, that the language of oratorical prose at first took a poetical colour, e.g. that of Gorgias" (3.1 1413b24–26). This poetical style must be both perspicuous and ornate—that is, it must have an appropriate mix of "proper" words to achieve clarity and "unusual" words (metaphors and coined, foreign, and compound words), along with an appropriate rhythm, to give the speech dignity or stateliness (3.2 1404a1–8). Again in the *Poetics* Aristotle defines "embellished language" as that which is patterned by rhythm, harmony, and song (1449b28–31). The unusual or poetic gives the rhetorical speech "an unfamiliar air," lifting it above ordinary conversation, and is necessary and effective because "men are struck by what is out of the way" (*Rhetoric* 3.2 1404a9–12). He treats of verbal devices such as metaphor, simile, epithet, description, *polysyndeton, asyndeton,* antithesis, *hypotyposis, enigma,* jokes, meter, period, *ploce,* proverbs, hyperbole, *parisosis (isocolon), paromoeosis, homoeoteleuton, polyptoton, anaphora, conduplicatio*, homonyms and synonyms to give the speech this poetic quality.[20] Not regarding these devices common to regular speech, he advises that the writer avoid an excess of them in order to "give the impression of speaking naturally and not artificially" (3.2 1404b17–18).

Having been influenced but not restricted by Aristotle's discussion,[21] Quintilian positions himself with those of his contemporaries who favor restricting *figura* ("shapes"—he is the first to use this term) to "the unusual" and claims that this restricted view of figures meets with common acceptance at his time (9.1.14). Agreeing with Zoilus that a scheme is "to pretend one thing and say another" (9.1.14), Quintilian objects to the latitude many of his precursors and contemporaries have given to the figurative domain and argues that figures of speech (*figurae dictionis*) and thought (*figurae sententiae*) must "involve a certain departure from the straight line and have the merit of variation from ordinary usage" (2.13.11). In fact figures differ from other stylistic features by having all three of these characteristics: they are groups of words "poetically or rhetorically altered from the simple and straightforward method of expression" (9.1.3); they result from pretense and guile, so that "the speaker pretends to say something other than that which he actually does say" (9.1.14); and they give "a new aspect" by purposeful "art" (9.1.14). Tropes ("turnings") are a separate set, defined as "the artistic alteration of a word or phrase from its proper meaning to another" (8.6.35) or, in other words, "the transference of words and phrases from the place which is strictly theirs to another to which they do not properly belong" (9.1.4).

Figures of speech Quintilian divides into the grammatical (form of words and grammar) and the rhetorical (arrangement of words) (9.3.2). The first class (*metaplasmus* and *enallage*) is formed through either addition, omission, transposition, or mutation, being vices of language used to good effect (9.3.2; 1.5.5–54). The second class—pertaining to syntax—is formed through addition, omission, resemblance, or contrast (9.3.28–86). Figures of thought he organizes loosely under those that "increase the force and cogency of proof" (9.2.6), those of simulation (9.2.26), those of dissimulation or irony (9.2.44), those of hidden meaning (9.2.65), and those that "enhance the elegance of our style" (9.2.96). Due to these strictures, Quintilian also insists that arguments and argument forms are not figures (9.3.99), nor are "explanation, proposition, promise of proofs, definition, distinction, exposition of our own opinion, logical conclusion, defence by anticipation, introduction of comparisons or precedents, disposition and distribution, interruption, repression of those who interrupt us, antithesis, exculpation and personal attack . . . amplification and its opposite . . . reproach, [wish, execration,] commendation, conciliation and humour . . . repetition, [digression, diversion of blame, and omission]" (9.2.2–4). These forms, though, "admit of figures" when manifested in disguise (9.2.5). Because he insists upon this narrow classification, he argues that of the 305 features he discusses, most of which had been called figures by predecessors, only 103 should be properly regarded as figures and 20 as tropes. The other stylistic features he categorizes instead as methods, reflections, or aspects of word arrangement (*compositio*) (8.3.41).

Quintilian's view differs from Aristotle's in that figures do not necessarily produce elevation. Rather like forms generally, they can produce multiple effects, functioning "to enhance or attenuate, to express with vigour or calm, in luxuriant or austere language, at length or with conciseness, with gentleness or asperity, magnificence or subtlety, gravity or wit" (8.3.40). This change in focus shifts the stylistic ideal from the strictly poetic to the artistic or appropriate and deemphasizes the differences among the various kinds of forms.

Alexander has a position similar to Quintilian's in that figures are those configurations that are dissimulated—purposefully mimed with an element of pretense and indirection:

> Even if one were to grant that every discourse has its own figure by nature, nevertheless, oratorical and literary discourse (*politikos kai sungraphikos logos*) does not possess this naturally, but by imitation of the other kind. Evidence of this may be seen in the following example. There is a way of speaking which naturally expresses a certain distraction of the mind: "Which way shall I go—this or that?" (Euripides,

> *Hecuba* 163). This expression does not have a figure, we say: and why? Because it is expressed naturally and the speaker is really at a loss. There is another expression, produced in imitation of this, also involving doubt [*aporia*]: "In the other Greeks—should we say their cowardice or their ignorance or both? . . ." (*De corona* 20). Now this does contain a figure. The speaker is not really at a loss, but pretends to be so, and imitates a bewildered speaker by avoiding straightforward expression. We can therefore answer those who deny the existence of Figures of Thought by saying that, even if every discourse has its own figure by nature, there is nothing to prevent discourse from being contrived and feigned in imitation of this. (trans. Russell 177–78)

These devices adorn because they add a certain efficacy: he claims that a scheme is composed of several words making "an alteration for the better in diction or thought" and is distinguished from a trope, which is a single word used in a sense other than its proper one. In his *On the Figures of Thought and Speech,* Alexander lists fifty-nine of these alterations as either schemes of thought or diction, excluding tropes (except irony, which is a separate figure of thought).[22]

Problems in both Quintilian and Alexander, however, compromise their attempts to draw adequate boundaries. First the line between tropes and figures blurs in both. If figures by definition involve pretense and guile, they all contain irony. Furthermore simulation and dissimulation also involve allegory, an observation Quintilian makes as well when he admits that "all such devices which consist in saying one thing, while intending something else to be understood, have a strong resemblance to allegory" (9.2.92). To be consistent Quintilian and Alexander should place figures as species of allegory and irony in combination. Quintilian does acknowledge the unimportance of carefully distinguishing figures from tropes (9.1.7–8) but does not pursue the implications. Second this distinction associates figures with fiction and nonfigures with nonfiction. This dichotomy oversimplifies matters, as Alexander unwittingly demonstrates when he asserts that *aporia* in the fictional speech of Hecuba (above) is not a figure since it is a genuine expression of doubt. Of course Alexander could have pointed out that this same *aporia* is still a simulation, since the poet has certainly contrived and mimed a pattern of thinking for Hecuba in this *prosopopoeia,* and irony is still present in the poet's discourse, even if not in Hecuba's. But the two frames at work here show the problem. The same form can be both authentic and ironic at once in different contexts. To call one use a form and another a figure only distinguishes intent, not forms (except irony). Since all forms can be either feigned (combined with irony) or authentic depending on use, both Quintilian and Alexander err in withholding any form from figure lists. In addition to associate only some forms with fiction and some with nonfiction promotes the false idea that some forms are representational while others are not. Third both Quintilian and Alexander are as responsible as anyone for passing along a broad view of figures. Quintilian includes many of those he rejects in order both to offer coverage and to engage in debate with previous authorities. Similarly Alexander does not maintain the line he establishes between figures and normal forms, for he includes as the most important figures of diction the complete sentence (*periodos*), the clause (*kolon*), and the phrase (*komma*). He restricts none of these three to their specialized senses: the periodic sentence, the compound subject or predicate, and the brief expression, respectively. Instead they have their common grammatical meanings of a sentence with two or more clauses, a clause of any kind, and a phrase of any kind. How then are these features alterations of the normal linguistic idiom or dissimulations?

The third definition of figures—the looser, specialized sense—is that these devices are not indirections necessarily but particularly effective configurations for creating useful effects. This definition comes primarily from the author of the *Rhetorica Ad Herennium* and from Cicero. These two rhetoricians allow much looseness to the category: the definition is hardly exclusive, neither one explains what makes these configurations particularly effective, and both allow a wide variety of discourse forms as figures. The author of the *Ad Herennium* clearly sees "exornations" as a specialized set—those features that belong to the stylistic virtue of *dignitas* (dignity or ornament) and that should be "distributed sparingly" and not "packed in close succession" so as to "set the style in relief, as with colours," and avoid calling attention to the artifice (4.11.16).[23] These are "excellencies" of style—the means by which we polish, add variety, and impart dignity to the language: "It is a figure of diction if the adornment is comprised in the fine polish of the language itself. A figure of thought derives a certain distinction from the idea, not from the words" (4.13.18). But despite setting figures off from other forms, this author compromises boundaries. He includes as figures effective argument forms: *similitudo, comparatio, exemplum, expeditio,* and *contrarium,* features he acknowledges earlier in the book as parts of arguments (2.14.21, 2.29.46). Figures not only adorn but also create clarity and force. Omitting any kind of grouping within the two divisions of figures he lists, except a category for tropes under figures of diction (4.31.42), he rarely explains how a figure differs from a nonfigure. Occasional examples give a figure wide application. For instance *licentia* (frankness of speech) can be used both directly and indirectly, both "with pungency" and "with pretense" (4.37.50). The *expolitio* (development of an argument) becomes synonymous with the schoolroom exercise known as the *chreia* (4.42.54–44.58). His almost exclusive attention to these seventy ornaments that function to create and polish one's style, making it appropriate and effective, works to associate figuration with stylistic craftsmanship generally.

Cicero lists as a separate category from other stylistic features the *formae* (forms) or *lumina* ("lights" and "brilliant touches")—his terms for the figures—that "like those objects which in the embellishment of a stage or of a forum are called 'ornaments,' not because they are the only ornament, but because they stand out from the others" (*Orator* 39.134). These forms "provide grace and neatness of structure in words and impressiveness in expressing thoughts" (*De Oratore* 3.53.202). These are one kind of embellishment—"flowers of language and gems of thought [which] must be so distributed that there may be brilliant jewels placed at various points as a sort of decoration" (3.25.96). Yet while he specifies that these *lumina* do not include "what is pleasant in sound" or "what is regulated by rhythmical law" (*Orator* 44.182), they are quite inclusive of strategies and forms that are not deviations, ironies, poetic expressions, or even alterations at all and that easily encroach upon concerns of invention and arrangement, such as "the exposition of what one is going to say, and its distinction from what has already been said; . . . a return to a point set out already, . . . the use of a formal syllogism; . . . the statement of one's own opinion; . . . comparison and example; division into parts, . . . contrast of opposites," and so forth (*De Oratore* 3.53.203). Because figures are potentially innumerable—he says, "Now there is an almost incalculable supply both of figures of speech and of figures of thought" (3.52.200)—he indicates that those ninety-three he mentions in *De Oratore* are merely representative. It is true that Cicero only lists fifty-nine *lumina* in the *Orator,* a fact that Quintilian interprets as a signal of Cicero's growing desire to limit the domain (9.3.90). But even here Cicero names several he has not mentioned in *De Oratore* and announces that he is still only providing a sampling (40.137). He leaves the boundary around figures quite blurry not only by neglecting to distinguish them further but also by almost admitting all forms to be figures when he associates the figures with giving to the style its particular character (*χαρακτήρ*) (39.134), and when in his *De Optimo Genere Oratorum,* he remarks of his translations of Aeschines and Demosthenes: "And I did not translate them as an interpreter, but as an orator, keeping the same ideas and the forms, or as one might say, the 'figures' of thought, but in language which conforms to our usage" (5.14). Boundaries around tropes he also leaves blurry. Tropes appear under a separate category of embellishment—words considered singly but along with *onomatopoeia* (coined words) and *archaismus* (old and rare words), which Cicero does not call tropes. But, the first of these is a trope in the *Ad Herennium,* and the second is a figure of speech in Quintilian. Finally since Cicero discusses all the embellishments, of which figures are a part, in the context of the various styles and effects they create, he, like the Greeks, cares little about distinguishing carefully among the kinds of forms but greatly about using forms to accomplish one's purposes.

Other sources wherein *figura* are hardly distinguished from forms in general are the Latin handlists of Rutilius, Aquila, and Rufinianus, all of whom allow a broad application of the term. Rutilius bases his Latin handlist *De figuris sententiarum et elocutionis libri II* (c. 15 A.D.) on the work of an older contemporary, the Greek critic Gorgias the Younger, who lived during the time of Augustus. The two short extant books of Rutilius, which contain forty-one figures primarily of diction, are only a portion of the original treatise, which had also included figures of thought. We learn from Quintilian that some of these additional *schemata dianoeas* included *diallage, epakolouthesis, syllogismus, cataplexis, parainetikon, anamnesis, anthypophora, antirrhesis, parauxesis, proecthesis, enantiotes,* and the trope *metalepsis* (9.2.102–6). These inclusions illustrate that both Gorgias and Rutilius held to a broader notion than Quintilian can accept, because they allowed common argument forms to be considered figures (9.3.99). The *De nominibus figurarum et exemplis liber I* (c. 200 A.D.) may be short, listing sixteen figures of thought and thirty of speech, but herein Aquila discusses the careless (loose), continuous (connected), and periodic styles as if types of figures that are themselves created by other figures like *asyndeton, polysyndeton,* and *periodon* (§18), and he declares that figures add not only ornament but also strength and weight (§0).

Finally Rufinianus in *De figuris sententiarum et elocutionis libri 1* (c. 300 A.D.) allots a liberal domain to figures, for although he lists ninety-two, these include such proofs as *paradigma, icon, epagoge,* and *dianoia;* such argument forms as *enthymema, anasceue,* and *anthypophora;* and such features of disposition as *distributio.* Also he enumerates as unnamed figures of speech options in word choice and syntax not traditionally covered under *enallage* or *solecismus,* options made by means of varying cases, rhythms, the placement of prepositions, the tenses and voices of verbs, the properties of adverbs, the qualities of words, and effective word choice (§27–44). Some of these options receive names in the Renaissance handlists, such as *isodynamia* and *plotike.* These conformations are not linguistic violations but legitimate grammatical and lexical options. Their inclusion may suggest that he views all stylistic choices as figures.

Renaissance Imprecision

Because they draw from among all these sources and from their own contemporaries, sometimes indiscriminately, Renaissance rhetoricians tend to be even less precise than their predecessors. While we can separate the humanists with more conservative views of figures from those with more liberal, we cannot attribute to any the narrow views of Aristotle, Quintilian, or Alexander.[24] Only Ramus and his collaborator, Talon, approximate Quintilian's restrictiveness, but they do so only superficially. The majority define figures briefly, as do Cicero or the author of the *Ad Herennium,* as forms that are particularly efficacious in creating desirable stylistic effects. But in reality this majority treat figures more generally as those forms that become "ornaments" or virtues because appropriate to all the requisites of the speech act. Since any form can be effective in a given situation, forms migrate to figure lists. Those rhetoricians who innovate by explicitly equating figures or ornaments with forms well used, then, make explicit the assumption underlying general practice. This definition follows from Cicero's teaching that ornateness or embellishment results from appropriate use (*De Oratore* 3.25.96) and changes the meaning of elevation from elaborate expression to aesthetic excellence. Vickers has also argued that this notion is the predominant one: "Far from being 'violations of our daily speech,' they [figures] are perfections of it: language reaches the highest degree of formalization and expressivity in the tropes and figures of rhetoric" ("Rhetorical and Anti-rhetorical Tropes" 110).[25] Because figures occur naturally, though, and because vices of speech are sometimes precisely the appropriate forms for an utterance, other rhetoricians who simply return to the original meaning of *schema* as form in general provide the most consistent definition of all, allowing for figures/forms to be both ill and well used. According to this perspective, the important differentiation is not between figured and unfigured speech but instead between discourse in which *schemata* are not applied with skill—lots of inconsistency among forms, aims, circumstances, participants, and subject matter—and discourse in which the *schemata* are applied with consistency or good judgment. This perspective is, after all, the one that guides Renaissance instruction in the language arts.

The easiest way to illustrate this imprecision and breadth, while still identifying both conservative and liberal views and lines of influence among texts, is to examine the manuals chronologically within the following categories: first the early influential humanists; second the handlists of figures; third the later traditional rhetoric textbooks; and fourth the Ramist manuals, the arts of poetry, and the grammar books.

The Early Influential Humanists

Influencing nearly every manual thereafter, early Renaissance textbooks all adopt a liberal attitude toward figures and encourage, either implicitly or explicitly, the conflation of style and figure and the view of figure as form in general.

Like the author of the *Ad Herennium,* Trebizond assigns the term *embellishment* to figure. Even though he does not yet reduce style to figures—he divides stylistic forms according to thought, method, and *compositio* (diction, embellishments, clauses, placement, endings, and rhythm)—he, like Hermogenes, does blur categories and demonstrates a propensity to consider most features figures. He remarks that "method" is actually a part of *compositio* (498–99) and that all the features of composition affect "the mind of the listener with embellishing" (469). Like Hermogenes he acknowledges the difficulty of placing features in categories, for he says he will not try to decide whether *resumptio* is a figure or method, since either way it adds elegance and clarity to the speech (527). He leaves unclear whether allegory (which he has already treated under diction as a trope) is also a method or a figure, and he mentions *negatio,* which is a figure in the *Ad Herennium,* as a method (536). Additionally periodic structure (*circumductio*) is a figure but also a feature of "clauses" and the full and abundant style itself. He comments on this issue of categorization, "I don't get involved in this" (527). Additionally like Hermogenes his focus is on describing the forms that create each of the stylistic characters, not on distinguishing carefully among types of forms. His remark, "There are as many schemes for speaking as there are colors for painting" (529), applies to forms generally. This approach encourages the view of style as figure. It also encourages the view of form as figure, for Trebizond lists as a figure, like Hermogenes, the direct, simple sentence (*orthotes* or *rectitudo*) and others that do not deviate from straightforward speech, such as listing in order of sequence (*ordinatio*) or dividing a subject into its parts (*partitio*). He also adds figures his immediate sources do not name, schemes such as attaching the consequences to an event (*consecutio*) and explaining that one is choosing to do something of necessity (*electio*). Finally he defines figures as "particular refinements of words whereby we dress and make appropriate the substance as if with a colored garment" (461, 498), connecting figures with the virtues of both appropriateness and ornateness.

Whereas the extent of Trebizond's influence remains questionable,[26] the four leading preceptors of the Renaissance encourage even more obviously a liberal view. Erasmus in *De copia* simply ignores distinctions. He names and gives examples of many of the classical figures, sometimes calling the device a figure and sometimes neglecting to do so. He never defines either tropes or schemes, uses both terms interchangeably,[27] and mixes together such a myriad of both verbal and discourse forms that apply to both content and expression as to leave the impression that all the textual features he discusses are figures. Freely using the term *figure* for many elements of discourse, Erasmus may indeed have believed that all forms are figures. Melanchthon certainly reads *De copia* as a book of figures: "To this purpose have been written the exceedingly useful books of Erasmus on fullness of expression, the first of which contains figures by which the words are varied. The one following contains figures which provide the greater abundance of circumstances" (*Elem.* 45v; La Fontaine 262). M. Veltkirchius (Joannes Velcurio or John Doelsch), who adds a commentary to *De copia* in 1534 with a revision in 1539, reads Erasmus's intention in this way also: "The nineteenth chapter of the *De copia* has to do with the multiplication of the parts of the oration, and although this chapter is the chief one of invention and not of style, you plainly see that Erasmus does not entirely separate the parts of invention in this commentary from the parts and figures of style, since both pertain equally to the knowledge and copiousness of rhetorical speech" (192v–193r; trans. Boswell). This impression is strengthened by Erasmus's equally lax attention to distinctions in *De conscribendis epistolis* (1521) and *Ecclesiastae sive de ratione concionandi quatuor* (1535). The first of these applies to the writer of letters the same composition method that applies to the orator. Whereas Erasmus does separate out the various elements of style in a comment such as "The most effective means of rousing the emotions seem to be subject-matter, choice of words, amplification, figures, and composition" (*De conscribendis epistolis* 90), he just as easily lumps these elements together indiscriminately when he describes, for example, how to write the letter of consolation (148) or of advice (189). The same avoidance of strict classifications we find in the *Ecclesiastes,* wherein he applies the rhetoric of Cicero and of Hermogenes to Christian preaching and scriptural hermeneutics. Figures appear throughout this treatise, sometimes identified and sometimes not, subordinated to the logical and rhetorical topics of invention, to instructions about disposition and pronunciation, and to style. In his discussion of style, he simply lumps qualities and kinds of style together, calls them all virtues, and subordinates them under the heading of *schemata;* he then turns around and describes the *schemata* or figures conducive to creating the various qualities and kinds of style (3.98.903–162.212).[28] He does not attempt to provide a complete list of the figures but refers the reader to other sources for more extensive treatment, and he, like Cicero, admonishes that there are more figures that have not yet been named (3.176.495–96). All three of these texts were published widely, the *De copia* and *De conscribendis epistolis* often used as textbooks in both grammar schools and universities and the *Ecclesiastes* a stipulated textbook on university statutes in England.[29]

In *De ratione dicendi* (1533), with three printings,[30] Vives also adopts a lax approach. In part 1 he divides style into words, order, sounds, emphasis, amplification, periods, and arrangement of words. In part 2 he describes ways to create many styles and the four ends of rhetoric (to teach, to persuade, to move, and to hold attention). He ends with a concluding section on decorum. In part 3 he gives instructions for writing various genres (description, history, probable narration, fable, poetic fiction, paraphrase, epitome, commentary, and translation), now also incorporating concerns of invention and disposition. Tropes and schemes appear throughout the whole treatise, only sometimes named and never clearly distinguished from other forms. It is impossible to discern which forms should be seen as figures and which not. For example under words Vives names various types, such as archaic, technical, poetic, rustic, vile, natural, tropological, and compound. He also describes various schemes created by means of repetition, reversal, substitution, change of meaning, and subtraction of words. Under periods and word arrangements, all options seem to be figures. Under styles he provides descriptions that echo those of Hermogenes. Here is his description of the devices that create the "pugnacious style": "Periods whose members are well connected are effective for fighting and for driving home a point, and certainly, with a kind of beauty, especially if the last member is shorter than the rest, for then it pierces into the minds of the hearers. . . . It is said that short and sharp sentences, powerful and well-aimed arguments, with carefully honed words and well-turned constructions, strike and pierce so deeply in the heart that they leave their darts in the minds of the hearers. . . . Likewise the audience is stirred by apostrophe, interrogation, and deliberation" (112). Likewise he describes the "rustic" style by enumerating its figures/forms: "Farmers differ from city people in so far as they use rustic words not commonly used in the city, because in pronouncing they exchange letters and syllables, and because they use all kinds of metaphors, similitudes, and examples taken from the country" (129).

Vives uses the term *ornament* in place of *figure,* even pointing out the common slippage between "color" in general and a particular kind of "color." He declares that "ornament is nothing else than color" (102). Then he explains that, deriving from "the condition and nature of each of the words, and from the form, composition, and sound of the whole speech," color "is sometimes used to describe the entire class, character, and condition of a speech" (98) and sometimes restricted to name a specific aspect of the speech, "a special kind of color which is also called ornament" (98). Accordingly Vives defines a figure broadly as any embellishment and embellishment as any feature of language that "gives elegance, grace, and distinctive color to speech" (42). As a consequence some figures "depart from the simplicity of current language," and others do not (43). "Some ornaments are chaste and native, others are exotic and foreign" (102). By some "a hearer understands something different from what the speaker says" (74); other figures contribute to straightforward meaning (57, 59). In general a feature becomes a figure when used appropriately. Vives's lack of concern for precise restrictions becomes apparent when he remarks, "Amplification and development of meaning at times are one and the same thing and are derived from the same sources. But this fact is not important to those learning it, not even to those making use of it. For we turn our eyes to the results, not to the means" (60). Vives probably regards this precision unnecessary "pedantry," a "corruption" he complains of in medieval teaching, wherein rhetoricians engaged in endless, pointless disputes regarding the genera and species of the tropes and figures.[31] His statement that the "Greeks left nothing without figures" (43) suggests his understanding that the figure category has a wide domain. This attention to form in general and to figures as forms well used shows Vives's allegiance to those authorities he most often cites: Cicero, Hermogenes, and Erasmus.[32]

Taking as his authorities the *Ad Herennium,* Cicero, and Quintilian, Melanchthon is more conservative at first than his three older colleagues but more liberal than his ancient sources and increasingly liberal as his career advances. He reworked his *De rhetorica libri tres* (1519) twice, the second edition called *Institutiones rhetoricae* (1521) and the third *Elementorum rhetoricae libri duo* (1529). These latter two editions had thirty and eighty printings respectively and appeared on an early grammar school statute and on university booklists in England.[33]

Reorganizing the art's precepts into a unique presentation, he divides style in the *Institutiones* into ornament and amplification (all figures)[34] and in the later *Elementorum* into grammar and embellishments (33r). Under grammar he treats the virtues of purity and clarity. Under embellishment or figure, which is the third stylistic virtue, he treats tropes and schemes. A trope he defines as a "transfer figure," when "a word is shifted from the proper meaning to something similar or closely allied" (*Elem.* 35r; La Fontaine 233). He defines a scheme as "an expression for effect, where it is not necessary that the meaning of the word be changed" (42r; 247) or "a byplay, as it were, of a speech" (35r; 233). Both kinds of figures should be "interspersed" throughout, for they draw a speech away from "plainness" (34v). What he means by "plainness" he does not explain. In the *Institutiones* he divides tropes into those of word and those of thought and schemes into the grammatical and the rhetorical. The rhetorical further subdivide into those of diction, of thought, and of amplification. In the *Elementorum* he further subdivides grammatical schemes into those of pronunciation (phonetic and orthographical), of syntax, and of diction. The first two species he mentions only, since they are usually taught by the grammarian, while he justifies his attention to the third group because it is also taught in rhetoric (42v; 249). The rhetorical schemes he divides into those of thought that give action to the speech and those methods of amplification that enlarge or diminish words and ideas (42v; 248). This last group he now organizes under the topics of invention from which they derive. The total number of different figures treated in both editions is 114.

Although he loosely echoes Quintilian's divisions of figures, he does not retain Quintilian's strictures on the category. Indirection and irony are no longer criteria, and of these devices that Quintilian lists as arguments—*peristasis, epagoge, paradigma, similitudo*, poetic fictions, proverbs, simile, *parabole, icon, kriseis,* and *epagoge*—Melanchthon lists all as figures but *epagoge.* Furthermore he ties all of the methods of amplification to the logical topics from which they derive. While he tries to maintain a distinction between figure (amplification) and argumentation on the basis of function, this distinction breaks down in his own analyses:

> The zealous reader will observe that all the figures, especially those that enhance a speech, have their origin in dialectical expressions, and if one has practical knowledge to associate them, he will be able to evaluate very many in cases subtly and keenly and better perceive the distinct divisions of the work. For the same expressions, when applied for the purpose of confirming or confuting, are bases for argument and the sinews, as they are called. When applied for the purpose of adorning, they are called rhetorical ornaments. And very many not only have been adapted to give a show of battle, but do add weight to the arguments. (45v; 263–64)

In other words any given feature can be either an argument or an embellishment depending on whether it functions to establish or to elaborate a point. Either way, however, the form becomes a proof, must serve "to the illustration of the case" (61r; 331), and belongs to invention, where Melanchthon uses "embellishment" to mean anything added to the statement of a position. For example in order to defend the proposition "Emperor Constantine acted rightly when he made war on Licinius in defense of the Christians" since "it is a natural law to undertake a defense against unjust cruelty," one can "enlarge by elaborating on the impious act of Licinius" and bringing in God's laws, *sententia* from scripture, and parallel examples (16r–17r; 138–41), which options are all figures. Melanchthon also teaches that *theses* or *loci communes,* which he calls figures and which one brings in to add to the *hypotheses* for enrichment purposes, serve as the major premises of the syllogisms in which the *hypotheses* become the minor premises: "For the commonplace contains the major premise in the main syllogism of the case" (46v; 266). Both the major and minor premises derive from the topics, and both serve to amplify (47v). As Peter E. Medine observes, "With their sources connected in this fashion, the argumentation and adornment of eloquent statement become virtually one" (introduction to Wilson's *Art of Rhetoric* 13). Additionally Melanchthon treats *concessio, purgatio* (*dicaelogia*), and *deprecatio* as both arguments appropriate for refuting (17v) and as figures (53r, 50v, 54v); he also unites figures and arguments by declaring that ethos and pathos result from amplifications (figures), which derive ultimately from logical roots: "But from all logical places, we shall provide amplifications in order to arouse people's minds with either the mild (*ethe*) or the violent (*pathe*) emotions" (28v; 202).

It seems, in fact, that two years after he published these comments in the *Elements of Rhetoric,* he has discovered his inconsistency, for in his 1533 commentary on Cicero's *Topica,* he regards arguments as figures of thought: "[This book] belongs to that part of rhetoric which describes the method of finding arguments, and the ways in which discourse can be amplified. As such, it clearly parallels the second book of Erasmus' *De Copia;* in fact, the subject-matter of both books is identical, because there is no real difference between arguments and figures of thought" (*Corpus Reformatorum,* 16:807; trans. Meerhoff, "Significance" 47). This comment suggests that he has abandoned the effort to keep the figure category exclusive and has adopted instead the very broad view of Erasmus. He seems also to have been influenced by Veltkirchius. Another indication of his lack of regard for firm boundaries comes near the end of his *Elementorum,* when he takes up the stylistic virtue of *compositio.* Rather than discuss this virtue as a separate department of style entailing sentence construction, harmony, and rhythm, he instead expands the topic to cover coherence in the speech generally (54v–55r). Possibly he does not regard elements of *compositio,* such as the nonspecialized comma, colon, and period, as figures, since these forms belong to grammar and contribute to clarity (33v, 59v). However, because he shows how amplification, comparison, contrast, antithesis, and *aetiologia* necessarily connect ideas and create coherence in both sentences and passages, as do also the comma, colon, and period (59r–v); and because in this discussion he does not distinguish between the figure and nonfigure, he again deemphasizes the differences among these forms.

Finally both Veltkirchius and Sturm offer the most explicitly liberal views of all. Both self-consciously adopt the original meaning of schema as form in general. A professor of rhetoric at Wittenberg, Veltkirchius (d. 1607) calls every device, feature, form, vice, or virtue of the rhetorical art a figure. The commentary he appends to Erasmus's *De copia* makes the book a complete Ciceronian rhetoric, supplementing the instruction with the principles of the art Erasmus had not included, providing names for the figures and devices Erasmus had only described, and making explicit how Erasmus's instruction fit into the entire language arts curriculum. Because his commentary adds to *De copia* a review of all five parts of rhetoric and two parts of dialectic, making this one manual a nearly complete rendition of the art (it lacks only the basics of Latin grammar), Veltkirchius brings the whole art within the domain of figure. He recognizes that figures such as *partitio* (division into parts), *enumeratio* (enumeration), *similitudo* (likeness), *peristasis* (addition of circumstances), and so forth correspond to the proofs one finds by means of the dialectical topics (112r–v) and explains that while the places of dialectic and the *stases* produce *theses* or *loci communes,* these forms, which are figures, then turn around and function in syllogisms (184v–186r), which are also figures (194v).

It is not until the end of the commentary that Veltkirchius defines figures, adding a discussion Erasmus had omitted. The definition he gives is broad enough to encompass all discourse features: schemes or figures are "qualities, forms, or habits in both matter and speech resulting from either ingenuity or chance" (193r; trans. Boswell). These schemes, he says, include both direct and indirect, both simple and altered, and both proper and improper elements (193r). Besides tropes he divides schemes into three additional kinds: (1) figures of diction (found in *De copia* 1.30 and Quintilian 9.3); (2) figures of speech (*De copia* 1.32 and Quintilian 9.2); and (3) figures of thought (*De copia* book 2 and Quintilian 8.3 and 9.2). He explains that figures of this third kind have been called by various names, such as ornaments, the forms of amplification, the virtues of speech, lights, colors, and even arguments (193v). Even though some of these schemes are "brought to bear not for the sake of proving, but for the sake of ornamenting," others are "parts of cases which cannot be omitted to any advantage" (193v). He cites Quintilian as one who calls these forms arguments and obviously ignores Quintilian's refusal to call these arguments figures. Veltkirchius lists *syllogismus, enthymema, inductio, consequentia* (conclusion), *consummatio* (many reasons), and *apodeixis* (the complete demonstration) as sample figures (194v). He also claims that Erasmus does too: "Others call them [i.e., schemes of thought] the proof of things [*argumenta rerum*] because by them not only is the body of the speech increased, but also the body of the case. Such Erasmus considered in his second book, not separating the parts of causes, that is the arguments and the places of invention, from the schemes, that is the ornaments and the places [*locis*] of style" (193v). Veltkirchius lists the virtues of speech in an original way that places them also under figures. The four specific virtues of style are purity (*latinitas*), clarity (*perspicuity*), musicality (*euphonia*), and good composition (*oeconomia*) (9r–12r). The two general virtues overarch these specific ones, entail each other, and produce figures: appropriateness brings about ornateness (embellishment). He organizes the vices of style under the four opposite categories: *barbarismus, obscuritas, cacophonia,* and *onoiconometon* (9r–12r). He calls these figures too. The total number of figures Veltkirchius names approximates 230. He would readily agree that there are more but warns that we should not number up a multitude of schemes, lest we separate forms that are related, create confusion, and ignore the intent of the ancient authorities (194r). Editions of *De copia* after 1524 frequently included Veltkirchius's commentary.[35] Almost all the textual forms Erasmus and Veltkirchius discuss show up on later figure lists.

In his *De Universa Ratione Elocutionis Rhetoricae, libri IIII,* where he has pulled all of rhetoric into style, Sturm declares that all speech is "skemmatike" (3.1.441) and calls all discursive features figures. He follows Hermogenes in dividing style into the eight types of elements but then explicitly treats the forms subordinated under each of these categories as either figures of speech or of thought. He treats thought as kinds of "*sententia,*" which he calls figures (3.1.437); methods as "ornaments" and "*schemata tes dianoias*" (1.15.36); diction as tropes and figures of speech (2.1.265); schemes as both figures of speech and of thought having phonetic, grammatical, syntactic, pragmatic, logical, and discourse conformations (2.27.434); clauses as "ornaments" and "schemes" involving the comma, colon, period, and their various configurations (3.1.441; 3.3.483); and word order, cadences, and rhythm as aspects of the figure *compositio* or *synthesis* (3.4.507). In fact Sturm rearranges all the traditional figures to be species of these eight types of elements. He even pulls into the figure domain additional strategies discussed by Demetrius and Hermogenes and new forms he names. He also includes proofs and argument forms, the parts of the oration, and the stylistic virtues and vices as figures. Like Aquila and Erasmus, he calls the various characters of style figures (1.3.8; 3.6.545).[36] Once Sturm has introduced all these figures, he then describes the various Hermogenean stylistic characters by enumerating all the figures that create each one and illustrating each in Cicero, who is to Latin what Demosthenes is to Greek oratory (1.4.8). Although Hermogenes provides the framework for his discussion, Sturm has also drawn, as he says, from Aristotle, Demetrius, Rutilius, Aquila, Rufinianus, the *Ad Herennium,* Cicero, Quintilian, Longinus, Trapezuntius, and probably Erasmus, Veltkirchius, and Scaliger. In this particular book, which had three printings, Sturm names 314 figures.

Handlists of Figures

Almost every treatment of style in later rhetoric manuals turns style into embellishment or figure and figures into a broad-ranging collection of forms of both speech and thought that encroach upon the other canons of style and of rhetoric. Many handlists of figures that are presented as handbooks of style and even of rhetoric reflect this trend. Some of these handlists became school texts. A teacher of Greek at Freiburg and Leipzig, Petrus Mosellanus, or Peter Schade (1493–1524), in *Tabulae de schematibus et tropis* (1516) divides figures into three groups: figures of speech (those of diction, locution, and construction), the vices (those suitable for poetry but not prose), and the virtues (those of propriety and of ornament). He acknowledges the category of figures of thought but omits it, treating the subject as a grammarian (a.iii.r). Figures of diction are phonetic and orthographical schemes, corresponding to the subtypes of metaplasm. Figures of locution include a hodgepodge collection of phonetic, syntactical, and pragmatic features inclusive of the periodic sentence, the answering of tacit objections (*anthypophora*), and impersonation (*prosopopoeia*). These include some features that others list as figures of thought. Figures of construction are grammatical schemes. The vices he lists under the categories *obscurum, inordinatum,* and *barbarum.*[37] Under propriety he places analogy (*analogia*), proper pronunciation (*tasis*), and conciseness (*syntomia*); under ornament he places tropes, good composition (*synthesis*), and proper or normal usage (*cyriologia*). Mosellanus's looseness toward the figure category is demonstrated by this subsuming of the common topics and virtues of style under figures, influenced perhaps by Erasmus. He names Erasmus, Diomedes, Cicero, and Quintilian as sources throughout. Mack identifies the influence of the *Ad Herennium* as well (*History* 216). This book, with ninety-eight figures, had eighty-six printings up to 1590[38] and is recommended on grammar school statutes in England in the first half of the sixteenth century.[39]

A prescribed handlist of the tropes and schemes for some English grammar schools in the latter half of the sixteenth century is Joannes Susenbrotus's *Epitome Troporum ac Schematum, Grammaticorum et Rhetoricorum* (c. 1535), first published in London in 1562 but printed thirty times between 1540 and 1635 throughout western Europe. Similar to the author of the *Ad Herennium,* Susenbrotus (c. 1485–1543), the schoolmaster at Ravensburg, takes a less expansive view toward the domain of figures than does Veltkirchius, but one broader than Quintilian. He gathers 167 figures (he gives the total as 132) from numerous Latin, medieval, and Renaissance antecedents.[40] Assuming that figures are a set of specialized devices, Susenbrotus provides a definition that mixes Quintilian's notion with Cicero's: a figure is "a certain method, by which the direct and simple kind of speaking is altered with a certain strength in the expression" (5; trans. Mack, *History* 219). He divides figures into tropes and schemes. Adopting Melanchthon's partition, he includes among tropes those of diction and of thought and divides schemes into the grammatical and rhetorical. Grammatical figures are orthographical and syntactical features formed by means of addition, deletion, transposition, and substitution. Here Susenbrotus reiterates Quintilian and the grammarians. Rhetorical figures, whose means of creation are unspecified, include those pertaining to diction, to thought, and to amplification. He includes as rhetorical figures several of the tropes he had discussed earlier (*onomatopoeia, antonomasia, metonymy, catachresis,* and *allegory*), plus such forms from invention and disposition as *sententia, icon, paradigma, parabola, comparatio, similitudo, aetiologia, amplificatio, distributio, antirrhesis,* and *anangeon,* all of which Quintilian had rejected as too straightforward. Like the author of the *Ad Herennium,* Susenbrotus also includes as a figure the periodic sentence, regards the figure *expolitio* as a general term for the development of an argument with seven parts (90), and connects *similitudo* with proof (100). Like Mosellanus he includes as figures some vices and virtues of style, and like Melanchthon he links *comparatio* and *distributio* with the logical topics they derive from (72, 91). But he also, like Quintilian, neglects to include other argument forms, such as *enthymema, conclusio, epiphonema,* and *epagoge,* and he differentiates the figure *definitio* from the argument of the same name (85). An interesting mixture of perspectives, this handlist would not do much to limit the figure domain, especially if used in the schools with *De copia.*[41]

Other handlists, which were written with the hopes of becoming school texts or of simply making the art available for the general public, also push the boundaries of the figure category. Although these manuals lack the influence of the more widely available textbooks, they still reflect the tendencies of the time. These handlists demonstrate either a conservative or liberal attitude toward the figure domain, but even the conservative approach is quite broad and loose.

Richard Sherry's two books, *A Treatise of Schemes and Tropes* (1550), with two printings, and *A Treatise of the Figures of Grammar and Rhetorike* (1555), with only one, show a schoolmaster[42] who at first liberally subsumes all of style under figures but then in his second edition strives for more precision and restriction. Nevertheless even his second edition has more similarities to the *Ad Herennium* than to Quintilian. Influenced by Erasmus, Mosellanus, and Melanchthon, along with the *Ad Herennium,* Cicero, and Quintilian, Sherry (c. 1506–c. 1556) in his first book lists 145 figures, which span the usual departments of both style and rhetoric. Like Mosellanus, Sherry divides schemes into figures, faults, and virtues. Being more expansive than Mosellanus, he includes figures not only of words (*lexeos*) but also of thought (*dianoias*). Like Melanchthon figures of words or the grammatical are again divided into two: diction (the transformation of one word either written or pronounced) and construction (the transformation of word order). Figures of thought, or the rhetorical, are divided into those of diction, of sentence, and of amplification. Like Mosellanus, Sherry divides the faults into the obscure, the inordinate (lacking order or dignity), and the barbarous (foul and rude). These faults are appropriate in poetry but not prose (32). The virtues are propriety and garnishing. Propriety includes proportion (*analogia*) and proper accent (*tasis*). Garnishing includes composition (*synthesis*) and exornation (tropes of word and of thought and rhetorical figures). When Sherry discusses the three levels of style, he also calls them figures (21–24),[43] and he includes under figures of amplification both artificial and inartificial proofs and the various parts of an oration, echoing Erasmus.

Sherry may not intend to imply that all forms are figures. In this first edition, he purposely reduces the term *scheme* from its general meaning as "the form, fashion, and shape of any thing expressed in writing or painting" to "the fashion of a word, saying, or sentence, otherwise written or spoken than after the vulgar and common usage" ([1550] 25). Yet "vulgar usage" seems to mean not only the "usual" but also the "inartistic," given the forms he allows to be figures and his definition of figures as the virtues that bestow "grace and dignity in speaking" and lift up and beautify an utterance "above the common manner of speaking of the people" ([1550] 37). More in keeping with an attempt to restrict the figure category, his second edition appears much more like the *Ad Herennium.* Sherry divides his discussion according to the three virtues of style: plainness, composition, and dignity. He covers the various vices, which are the opposites of these three, in this introduction. Then he provides a list of 157 figures, divided into the grammatical and rhetorical. The grammatical entails those of orthography and construction; the rhetorical entails tropes (of word and of thought) and schemes of word and of thought (sentence and oration). The three kinds of style end the discussion but are still called figures (H.iii.v). Although he has removed his explicit discussion of invention and arrangement and he repeats Melanchthon's observation that figures are "not put in matters, to prove any thing, but to garnish it" (H.i.r), he has still retained as figures kinds of evidence, such as the example, similitude, quotation from authority (*indicatio*), pithy saying (*sententia*), exposition of someone's statement or deed (*chreia*), moral from a fable (*aenos*), quotation from scripture (*oraculum*), and addition of a reason (*aetiologia*), plus various forms of argument and aspects of arrangement. He even acknowledges that Quintilian had called some of these arguments (H.i.r).

Franciscus Robertellus (1516–67) in *De artificio dicendi* (1567) collates and compares the figures found in Rutilius, Aquila, Rufinianus, Cicero's *Orator,* Quintilian, and Cornificius (the supposed author of the *Ad Herennium*), along with several additional devices from Demetrius, Hermogenes, Phalereus, and Celsus that Robertellus argues should also be regarded as figures. He has also consulted Aristotle, Alexander Rhetor, and Longinus, the last of whom he praises as the best at explaining the art (36v). Pointing out the inadequacies of traditional definitions, Robertellus enlarges his definition, arguing that a figure should be seen as "a color, sprung from emotion, which is put on over an argument" (42v; trans. Boswell). All forms that express emotions, then, are figures. Even though separate from arguments, figures nonetheless always overlie arguments and belong to all expression, both natural and artificial. Arguing with both Quintilian and Alexander, he states that there is no unfigured—uncolored—speech (25v), "for all speech is figured as it exits our mouths" (26r). The rhetorician simply makes art imitate nature by choosing the forms "in accordance with a selected rationale of character and disposition of the mind . . . , which makes it so that we speak in this or that way" (27r). The only forms Robertellus excludes from the figure category are arguments, such as *enthymeme* (43r), *comparatio* (45r), and *enantiotes* (46r), although he allows readers to retain them as figures of proof if they choose. He also argues that stylistic vices should not be considered figures, since figures must be virtues (29v). Otherwise he treats style as embellishment, listing 240 figures, with the category inclusive of many forms that Quintilian had rejected, such as *diallage, syllogismus, cataplexis, parainesis, asseveratio, propositio, anthypophora, antirrhesis,* and *proecthesis* (29v). Robertellus divides figures into five categories. Figures of thought have two species: those of *affectio* or passion and those of proof. Figures of speech have two species: those of diction (formed by subtraction or addition, by contraction or expansion, by dissolution or composition, and by substitution/change) and those of structure (subdivided into those of order and those of symmetry). Finally there are figures of number (meter), which he does not discuss. Robertellus recognizes that tropes are either of word or of thought, but he places them under the figures of diction formed by change (*immutatio locutionis*). Additionally he points out that some figures are common to both thought and words (28r). He also claims that making a category for figures of passion is his contribution (13r). Even though his book had only one printing, it wielded influence on later rhetoricians.

Finally Angel Day (fl. 1575–95), a man of letters, appends to the second edition of his letter-writing manual, *The English Secretary* (1592), a handlist of figures. With at least eight printings until 1700, Day makes available to the popular audience a fairly typical and conservative collection of figures, which he draws primarily from Susenbrotus. The 1599 edition treats of ninety-three figures, about a dozen more than the 1592 edition. Less ambiguously than Susenbrotus, however, Day echoes the *Ad Herennium* by defining the figure broadly as "a certain mean whereby from a simple and ordinary kind of speaking, we grow into a more cunning and excellent delivery" ([1599] 77). Day divides figures into tropes and schemes but acknowledges that some rhetoricians do not differentiate between these two classes since "often times they run into one another's meaning" (77). Tropes are of diction or thought. He divides schemes into the grammatical and rhetorical. The grammatical divide into the orthographical (*metaplasmus*) and syntactical (those commonly found in the grammarians). Day does not deal with the orthographical, however, because they apply to poetic, not epistolary, uses (81). The rhetorical schemes he does not divide, but they include a mixture of sentence- and passage-level devices of speech and of thought, some of which the grammarians list as tropes. Although a conservative listing, his collection reflects his unconcern for careful distinctions, an impression also communicated when he randomly names and mixes together without distinction the forms of invention and disposition along with the figures of style in the marginal notations of his sample epistles.

Those who self-consciously adopt the more liberal approach of Erasmus or Veltkirchius do encompass within figures the entire rhetorical art. Giving broad scope to figures is the rector Henry Peacham (1546–1634),[44] whose 203 embellishments in the two editions of *The Garden of Eloquence* (1577 and 1593) clearly span the departments of invention, arrangement, and style. Compiling these handlists to show the rhetorical figures in English, he divides them into tropes and schemes: tropes are either of a word or of a passage, and schemes are either grammatical or rhetorical. The grammatical are either orthographical or syntactical and include many of the vices of style. In the first edition, the rhetorical are divided into those of diction, of sentence, and of amplification. In the second edition, he omits the grammatical schemes but provides an even more detailed division of the rhetorical schemes, wherein he slips in some of the grammatical: those of diction (formed by repetition, omission, conjunction, and separation) and those of sentence (expressing affection or providing amplification/proof). Figures of affection divide again into four species: exclamation, moderation, consultation, and permission. Those of amplification also consist of four species: distribution, description, comparison, and collection. Those in these last categories include forms pertaining unabashedly to logical idea development, evidence, arrangement, and genre. The vices of style are not listed as figures in the second edition but reappear in the new discussions he added on the "use" and "cautions" of each figure. Peacham even shows his understanding that Cicero had united all forms under the name of ornament, which Peacham now calls figure: "Figures of the Grecians are called Tropes and Schemates, and of the Latins Figures, Exornations, Lights, Colors, and Ornaments of Speech. Cicero who supposed them to be named of the Grecians Schemates, as a gesture and countenance of speech, called them Concinnitie [*sic*], that is properness, aptness, featness, also conformations, forms, and fashions, comprising all ornaments of speech under one name" ([1577] B.i.r). Crane was moved to acknowledge, as Peacham's first modern editor, that in Peacham "under the guise of style considerable attention was still given to the other branches of rhetoric" (introduction to *Garden of Eloquence* [1593] 8).

Peacham also clearly associates figures not with alterations of normal idiom but instead with the appropriate, proper configurations for an utterance. His contribution may indeed be this explicit definition of figure as the appropriate form. He clarifies that the norm from which figures vary is improperly formed speech, defining a figure as "a fashion of words, oration, or sentence, made new by Art, differing from the vulgar manner and custom of writing or speaking" ([1593] 1). "Vulgar" could mean "ordinary," but it seems that he has in mind "improper" or "unrefined" here, for "Art" is "properness, aptness, featness" ([1577] B.i.r). Peacham also equates figure with rhetoric or eloquence, meaning not poetized but rather appropriate speech. His handlist anatomizes rhetoric into figures, which are "the principal instruments of man's help in this wonderful effect" ([1593] AB.iii.v). Finally he acknowledges that figures do not simply elevate or make more indirect but create all sorts of effects: "By figures he may make his speech as clear as the noon day: or contrary wise, as it were with clouds and foggy mists, he may cover it with darkness: he may stir up storms, & troublesome tempests, or contrary wise, cause and procure a quiet and silent calmness; he may set forth any matter with goodly perspicuity, and paint out any person, deed, or thing, so cunningly with these colors, that it shall seem rather a lively Image painted in tables, than a report expressed with the tongue" ([1577] A.iii.r). Peacham acknowledges his debt to Cicero, Quintilian, Erasmus, Melanchthon, and Wilson. He also appears to have modeled his work on Susenbrotus and to have drawn from the *Ad Herennium,* Sherry, Robertellus, and others.[45]

A similar liberality of coverage and conception of figure are also evident in later manuals, such as John Hoskins's *Directions for Speech and Style* (1599) with seventy-two figures, Thomas Blount's *The Academie of Eloquence* (1653), which, though plagiarizing Hoskins's book in nearly its entirety, adds several additional figures; and John Smith's *The Mystery of Rhetoric Unveiled* (1657) with 160 figures. All three of these handlists turn style into figure and subsume style, argument forms, and aspects of arrangement under stylistic figures. Hoskins (and Blount) provides an original division of figures into those of varying (inclusive of the tropes), of amplification, and of illustration. Both figures of speech and of thought appear in each of these categories. Hoskins (and Blount) does not distinguish the figure from the argument: in fact he not only declares that the figures *definitio* and *divisio* derive from the logical *topoi* of the same names but also provides arguments as examples of these figures (44, 24). Smith may say, as Ramists do, that rhetoric entails "garnishing of speech" (elocution) and "garnishing of the manner of utterance" (pronunciation) (B1r). He may also divide tropes (*verborum immutatio*) into the primary and secondary species. Figures divide into those of diction and of thought. Those of diction are either of dimension (metaplasm), repetition, or miscellaneous; those of thought are either in "musing" (*logismo*) or in "questioning and answering" (*dialogismo*). But his indebtedness to Ramism ends here, as does the neatness of this division, for his handlist of tropes and figures is a rather random collection of devices that include many common forms of invention and disposition, such as the logical syllogism (*syllogismus*), the rhetorical syllogism (*epicheireme*), *enthymema* (both kinds), demonstration (*apodeixis*), an indefinite proposition (*thesis*), and both the hypothetical and the particular propositions (*hypothesis*).[46] Like Hoskins, whose work he draws from, Smith does not distinguish between the figures of *comparatio, dissimilitudo,* and *horismos* and these same arguments of invention.

All three of these handlists also equate figures with appropriateness. Hoskins teaches style or "fashioning" by means of figures or "the Art of the best English" (title page). Reappropriating the definition in Alexander, Blount avers, "Figures and Tropes (says Alexander the Sophister) are the virtues of Speech and Style, as Barbarisms and Solecisms are the vices" (1). Smith says that by means of tropes and figures "the speech it self is beautified and made fine" (2). Finally all three books point to all forms being figures. When Hoskins (Blount) remarks "But let discretion be the greatest and general figure of figures" (15), he subsumes the stylistic virtues under figures. When Smith makes his handlist of tropes and schemes simultaneous with a glossary of rhetorical terms, he conflates all forms with figures.

These books, although not school texts, still wielded considerable influence. Drawing from Aristotle, Hermogenes, Quintilian, Cicero, Sturm, Talaeus, and probably Erasmus, Susenbrotus, and Wilson, the schoolmaster-turned-lawyer Hoskins[47] wrote his epistolary rhetoric to instruct a young gentleman of the Temple, the son of a friend. He did not publish the manuscript, but it circulated so as to influence both the lawyer Blount (1618–79) and the poet Ben Jonson (1572–1637), who quotes substantially from it in his *Timber, or Discoveries Made upon Men and Matter* (1641).[48] Smith (fl. 1657), in turn, draws heavily from Blount's book, which had seven printings between 1653 and 1683.[49] Smith also draws from Fenner, Farnaby, and Peacham,[50] and his book enjoyed six printings between 1657 and 1688. In *A New Discovery of the Old Art of Teaching School* (1660), Charles Hoole recommends "the late English Rhetorick" as a book for reference, meaning either Blount's *The Academy of Eloquence* or Smith's *Mysterie of Rhetorique Unvail'd* (133).[51]

Later Rhetoric Textbooks

Widely used textbooks on the whole art of rhetoric also give to figures a large domain and either depict style as figure or compromise the boundaries so as to dissolve them. The only exception to this tendency among the comprehensive rhetoric texts is Soarez's *De Arte Rhetorica* (1557), a manual not influential in England[52] and one that still leaves the boundary around figures ambiguous. Since there was no suitable text available in Jesuit schools to take pupils from the study of grammar to the study of rhetoric, Cyprian Soarez, SJ (1524–93), priest and teacher of the Society of Jesus, produced this textbook to fill the void and prepare "young men to read the learned books of Aristotle, Cicero, and Quintilian wherein lie the well-springs of eloquence" (108). According to his own admission, Soarez primarily summarizes the rhetorical precepts found in the

Ad Herennium, Cicero, Quintilian, and Aristotle (in that order), whom Soarez treats as participants in one tradition (104–9). This book covers the five parts of rhetoric but gives expression or style the most attention. His interpretation of the classical tradition's stylistic instruction, unmediated through earlier Renaissance renditions, aligns fairly closely with Quintilian's approach, except that he will define figures as does the *Ad Herennium,* saying a figure is "a shaping of discourse different from the ordinary and the obvious" (303) but "consists in the marked polishing of language itself" (305). The definition makes the inartistic or improper form the norm from which figures vary. In his treatment of *elocutio,* Soarez acknowledges the four traditional virtues of style—correctness, clarity, embellishment (composition), and appropriateness—but then focuses his discussion on embellishment, which he divides into word choice (wherein he includes eleven tropes), figures, order, sound, rhythm, periodic structure, coherence, and the three levels of style. Under figures he treats of seventy-eight features of speech or of thought. Figures of speech are formed by addition, omission, or similarity (307) and must be used sparingly (333). Figures of thought or *schemata,* which concern subject matter (335) and explain our thoughts (336), are not subdivided but exclude most argument forms and the other features usually associated with *compositio.* The relatively low number of figures is not indicative, however, of an attempt to limit the figure domain necessarily. Rather Soarez is merely being a conservative purveyor of a tradition. He prefaces his remarks on the subject with the disclaimer that he has no intention of contributing a theoretical argument: "Because there is little agreement among authors, however, concerning the number and the names of the figures, and because there is also much disagreement, since certain figures which some listed among ornaments of thought are classed by others among those of speech, we, who have taken a middle course, shall explain those upon which the most distinguished writers commonly agree" (306). He, like Cicero, also keeps the figure category open and concludes that since rules "concerning the tropes and figures, are very slight and insignificant, . . . it makes little difference whether you decide this way or that [when it comes to categorizing forms as figures]" (362–63).

Other later continental texts, however, clearly reflect the liberal trend. Influential in northern Europe and in seventeenth-century England,[53] Bartholomaus Keckermann (c. 1571–1609) in his *Systema Rhetoricae* (1606) equates style with embellishment or figure. Style, he says, is composed of "schemes or figures of speech, which embellishment is" (*Systema* 1471). Treating of 208 figures, he organizes them into the following categories: (1) tropes (primary and secondary); (2) *formulae* (methods of treatment, arrangement, and adornment) and *sententia* (propositions that come from logic [1476] and are solitary or combined); (3) schemes of invention (explanation, proofs, amplification); (4) schemes of disposition; (5) schemes of emotion; (6) schemes of diction (grammatical, orthographical, phonetic), created by means of omission, addition, transposition, and repetition; (7) number; (8) intervals (comma, colon, and period with syntactical variations); and (9) *copia.* The first five categories belong to figures of thought, the next four belong to figures of speech, and the last contains both figures of thought and of speech. He does separate out figures from other stylistic concerns near the end when he summarizes, "We have seen thus far by what means oratory may be adorned through tropes, figures, euphony, rhythm, elegance of rhythm, and also intervals. There remains the last mode or rather medium of adornment of oratory, which is from quantity and fullness of oration" (1546). Yet he has filled these latter categories from euphony to *copia* with figures, such as species of *metaplasmus,* varieties of sentence construction, plus *paraphrasis, tmesis, epicherema, parenthesis, dialysis, epembole, remotio, congeries, epanodos,* and *climax,* so that it makes more sense to trust his first statement—that all are categories of schemes. Additionally although Keckermann draws from the *Ad Herennium,* Cicero, Quintilian, Rufinianus, Erasmus, Melanchthon, and Robertellus, besides others,[54] much of his discussion is indebted to Sturm. Like Cicero he admits that the domain of figures is limitless: "There are as many ways by which the mind, will, and emotion of man can be expressed as there are figures: it is infinite" (1481). He does acknowledge a distinction between speech that is "nude" and speech that is "figured" or "painted by color" (1480), but he leaves the precise difference obscure.

Influenced by Keckermann along with Aristotle, Demetrius, Cicero, Cornificius, Rutilius, Hermogenes, Menander Rhetor, Quintilian, Aquila, Rufinianus, Talaeus, Melanchthon, Scaliger, Caussin, and Sturm, the rhetoric professor Gerard Johann Vossius (1577–1649), in *Rhetorices contractae, sive partitionum oratoriarum libri quinque* (1621), mixes the conservative and liberal views. Vossius does not say that style is figure. Like the *Ad Herennium,* he organizes his discussion of style under the virtues of elegance (correctness and perspicuity), ornament (figure), and composition. His sections divide as follows: (1) Perspicuity; (2) Tropes; (3) Schemes; (4) Composition; and (5) Characters of Style. He names only 129 figures in his discussion of tropes and schemes. However under each of style's sections, he mentions relevant figures (as he acknowledges), bringing the total of those he treats here to 153 and essentially turning style into figure. Furthermore figures are not strictly alterations from the grammatical norm but also from the "ill-polished" norm, for embellishments, he says, make a style favorable, good, and successful (4.3.208), with a scheme being "a form of speech whereby speech is changed from common usage into a better one" (4.11.229). Tropes are composed of the four primary, with subspecies. Schemes he divides into those of diction, formed by omission, addition, repetition, and similarity of sound, and those of thought, which he calls "ornaments of invention and disposition" (4.14.243) and which he divides into nine species based on function: (1) to prove; (2) to explicate; (3) to make clearer; (4) to assimilate and to contrast; (5) to oppose; (6) to provide extra content; (7) to exaggerate; (8) to make emotional appeals; and (9) to arrange. Figures under these categories include "normal" features of invention and disposition, such as the proposition of an argument (*protasis*) and conclusion to a syllogism (*conclusio*). Vossius also counts the periodic sentence and its parts, the *protasis* and *apodosis,* along with the simple sentence (*apheles*), as figures.

Additionally Vossius intermixes figures throughout his treatments of invention and disposition earlier in the book, where forms and figures are not strictly distinguished. In the confirmation *syllogismus, enthymeme, inductio, exemplum,* and *amplificatio* create arguments (3.7.179–83). In the confutation *elenktikon, apoplanesis, accusatio,* and *indignatio* apply and appear in the company of *interrogatio* and *subjectio,* the latter two explicitly called *schemata* (3.8.183–85). In the epilogue, as we would expect, we find *anacephalaeosis* or *enumeratio* and *pathopoeia,* created, he says explicitly, by means of various figures (3.9.186–87). Like Melanchthon he divides the three oratorical genres into subspecies based on type of emotion and purpose (book 2). Many of these correspond to what we have learned to see as figures in earlier writers: *indignatione* (*indignatio*), *misericordia* (*commiseratio*), *moribus* (*ethikon* or *ethopoeia*),[55] *gratiarum actio, oratione lamentatoria* (*threnos*), *querimonia, commendatio, conciliatio, adhortatio, dehortatio, consolatio, objurgatio, oratione gratulatoria, concitatione, expostulatione, exprobatione,* and *deprecatio.* He actually does list *objurgatio* again as a scheme in book 4. Certainly many of these help to create *pathopoeia,* which he explains arises because of figures. Should we view all of these subgenres as figures, then? If they are, then the number of figures found in Vossius rises again. In any case his treating these features as genres or forms of argument is evidence of their elasticity—that is, their applicability to both small- and large-scale forms—and of their transportability from one department of rhetoric to another. This ambiguity keeps the boundary line loose in Vossius. Furthermore Vossius lists more figures in his *Commentarium rhetoricorum, sive Oratoriarum Institutionum Libri sex* (1606), which was a reissue of his major work on rhetoric, called *Institutiones oratoriae* (1605). His *Rhetorices contractae* is the abridged textbook version of this major work and the publication with more influence, becoming the state-mandated school text for the Netherlands in 1627 and having thirty-one printings during the seventeenth century. With seven Oxford editions, the book was also widely used in England and Scotland.[56]

Finally Lamy's *The Art of Speaking* (1672) does not so much adopt either a conservative or liberal attitude toward the figure domain as reflect confusion surrounding the subject. Lamy refers to Longinus, Cicero, and Quintilian as his authorities but also draws from Scaliger. With ten French printings and only two English printings before 1700, this tome did not wield the same degree of influence in England as those on school booklists. Lamy divides his discussion on style (speaking) into the topics of grammar, tropes and figures, delivery, and characters. But figures come up in all divisions. Under grammar he covers parts of speech, choice of proper words, the proper combination of words, and faults. Here he identifies one figure but discusses other features that have been called figures in the past. Under tropes and figures, he discusses ten tropes and a miscellaneous collection of forty-seven figures of thought. Twenty-six of these figures come in a straightforward list; the others are named throughout his following commentary. Under delivery he takes up sounds, composition, twelve figures of repetition, and measures (meter and feet). Under characters he discusses the three levels of style, the virtues of style (perspicuity, strength, pleasantness, and succinctness), the styles of the differing genres—oratory, history, poetry, and dogmatic assertion (mathematics, philosophy, theology)—and the overall virtue of appropriateness. One additional figure he names in this discussion. He identifies seventy-one figures in all but admits, like Cicero, that "the number of Figures is infinite" (2.96) and that he lists "only those which the Rhetoricians do place frequently in that number" (2.134). Appended to these four books on style is a book 5, "A Discourse, in Which Is Given an Idea of the Art of Persuasion," wherein Lamy provides instruction in invention and disposition. He leaves memory out because it is a gift of nature, only to be improved by exercise, and he postpones discussing pronunciation in detail because it deserves "to be treated at large" (5.162–63).

Confusion arises because Lamy's divisions melt into each other. Figures, he says, are "Manners of Speaking, different and remote from the ways that are ordinary and natural" (2.94). Figures include tropes (2.123), which make use of an "improper word" transferred out of its customary context into another (2.71). Otherwise the standard from which figures vary is variable and not explicitly acknowledged. Some figures are the transgressions of grammar or usage used to good effect (1.40–41); others are elaborations or variations of linguistic features for good effect (3.157–58), for show (2.146), or for ill effect, when they become "fallacious ornaments" (4.73); and others are the formal epitome of emotions or attitudes one expresses, whether intentionally or not (2.94–95). The first two criteria apply to figures of speech and the last to figures of thought, although Lamy does not make this specification explicit. Tropes can conform to all three of the criteria (1.46; 2.123; 4.71). These different norms compete with one another. Proper grammar and usage express attitude, as Lamy explains (1.46–47). How, then, do we exclude the so-called normal forms from the figure category? Lamy mentions hebraisms, *hellenismus,* and *archaismus* in his discussion of grammar but not as figures (1.59). How are these not variations of a customary idiom? Cannot the faults Lamy mentions, the faults of *barbarismus, solecismus, hyperbaton, pleonasmus, perissologia, tautologia, amphibologia, pleonasmus,* and *parenthesis*, express emotion at times and be used to good effect so as to be included as figures? Lamy does indicate that *hyperbaton* and *pleonasmus* are figures when used to good effect (1.40). The others, then, should be counted among the figures. Additionally if other tropes and figures can be used to ill effect and still remain figures, then why stipulate that the grammatical vices are only figures when used to good effect? Furthermore echoing Scaliger, Lamy counts "kind[s] of Arguments that are used in Logic" among the figures of thought, because these forms are both "extraordinary" and expressive of passion:

> And yet it is manifest they are real Figures, being extraordinary ways of reasoning never used but in passion, or ardent desire to persuade or dissuade those to whom we speak. These Reasonings or Figures are wonderfully effectual in this, That joining a clear and incontestable Proposition, with another that is more doubtful and contestable, the clearness of the one dissipates the obscurity of the other, and the two Propositions being strictly connexed, if the reasoning be good we cannot grant the one to be true, but we must confess the other to be so likewise. . . . A solid Argument suppresses and disarms the most obstinate Adversary. (2.134)

This inclusion implies that another norm characterizing the "common" is the uneducated and unskillful (see also 1.66–67), now suggesting that the figures are the appropriate forms for the utterance. Since "nature" has provided these figures, the educated are those who best understand nature (2.92–99; 4.45). Yet Lamy also asserts the opposite: "it is easier to speak by Figures than to speak Naturally" (4.33).

Problems continue. Lamy refers to cadences as figures (4.73) and calls the means for creating cadences figures (2.145). Meter and verse are such figures of measure, as are periods, their variations, and their various parts (3.135). Because figures of speech "are elaborate and studied," they must be constructed "with a mind that is quiet," Lamy says, and "are only fit for diversion" (3.157). These are the flowers of discourse, and he includes periodic structure here (3.163). Yet he separates periodic and figurative features (3.147), while still attributing to periods the same ends he attributes to figures of speech—artistic discourse (3.146) and pleasure (3.146). Furthermore he includes as a figure of speech the *epizeuxis.* But this figure in "My God, my God, why hast thou forsaken me?" (3.159) can hardly be divorced from emotion. Lamy's generalizations do not reflect careful discrimination. He refers to figures as "the flowers and ornaments of rhetoric" (4.40), but he also calls all appropriate choices ornaments (4.61). This confusion must have contributed to the art's decline in the eighteenth century.

Rhetoric textbooks written by Englishmen demonstrate a more deliberate and consistent looseness. The first complete treatise on rhetoric in English, Thomas Wilson's *The Arte of Rhetorique* (1553), combines influences from the *Ad Herennium,* Cicero, Quintilian, Erasmus, and Melanchthon. A scholar, lawyer, and government official, Wilson writes this book, along with its companion tome, *The Rule of Reason* (1551), to make the arts of logic and rhetoric available to the general English populace. His book was popular, with eight printings, the last in 1585. Wilson divides his discussion of style into what he regards as the four virtues: plainness, appropriateness, composition, and exornation. The last, exornation or embellishment, "beautif[ies] our talk" and consists of two parts: the first is the proper use of high, middle, and low styles and the second invests the speech with "goodly colors" and variety of excellencies, like "stars in the firmament or flowers in a garden" (*Art of Rhetoric* 195). Here Wilson discusses ninety-two figures. Although he does not explicitly collapse style and figure, he does so conceptually, for the figures or "excellencies" are the appropriate forms that create the other virtues of clarity, composition, and polished speech.

His definition of a figure as "a certain kind either of sentence, oration, or word, used after some new or strange wise, much unlike to that which men commonly use to speak" (195) assumes both a usage norm and an inartistic norm from which figures deviate, as is also evident from the broad range of features he includes as figures. He divides the figure category into three species. The first kind is tropes, the second kind alters the sounds of words or sentences "contrary to the vulgar custom of our speech," and the third kind, called "colors of rhetoric," is variety, amplification, and "exornation" of the sentence or passage (195–96, 202). In the third kind, Wilson includes common features of an oration that are necessities for a clear, logical, and coherent presentation: for example the statement of one's main points (*propositio*), the dividing of the main idea into its several parts (*distributio*), the recapitulation in the conclusion (*frequentatio*), and various kinds of evidence and argument forms. Wilson further blurs the boundaries between figures and forms in general because under invention, as part of his instruction regarding the peroration, he reviews thirty devices of amplification, affections, and humor. These devices commonly appear on others' figure lists. Does

Wilson suggest, because he treats these devices in invention, that they are not figures? The supposition seems absurd, considering that the devices he exemplifies here include such well-known figures as *sententia, antithesis, paroemia, auxesis, meiosis, comparatio, incrementum, diminutio, frequentatio, pathopoeia, hypotyposis, commiseratio, scematismus, antanaclasis, sarcasmus, improvisum quiddam,* and so forth (152–82). Additionally when he lists "mirth-making" (*ad hilaritatem impulsio*) under figures, he comments that he has already given examples of this figure in his earlier discussion of humor (213). Adding these to the others he covers in style, Wilson treats of approximately 122 figures. But now that we have found figures outside of the designated spot in stylistic instruction, what is to keep us from finding them elsewhere, since other features he discusses in invention, such as the "places" for the "state assumptive" (that is, *confessio, trajectio in alium, metastasis,* and *deprecatio*) and the common "places" (*comparatio, definitio, paradeigma,* and *kriseis*) are also widely recognized as figures at the time and since Wilson allows into the figure category arguments and argument forms? Besides Wilson acknowledges that there are more figures: "but I had rather offend in speaking too little than deserve rebuke in saying too much" (232).

Similarly the schoolmaster Thomas Farnaby (c. 1575–1647) in his compact *Index Rhetoricus* (1625) is not as concerned with distinctions among forms as with the forms themselves. He divides his stylistic instruction according to the *Ad Herennium*'s three stylistic virtues: elegance, composition, and dignity (tropes, schemes, and stylistic characters). Figures he subdivides into the grammatical and rhetorical. The grammatical schemes are those of orthography, prosody, and syntax. The rhetorical figures include the tropes, the schemes of diction, and the schemes of thought. The schemes of thought are further subdivided into those of explanation, proof, amplification, emotion, and copia. Herein he lists 102 figures. But like Wilson he compromises the neat divisions in several ways. First he indicates that the stylistic virtue of dignity arises from the appropriate use of ornament (20). Second his definition of *figure* aligns with Peacham's. He declares that schemes "shape by a more elegant attire and form" either words or thoughts. Words in schemes "resound pleasingly according to their appropriate placement among themselves," and thoughts are "strengthened by proportion and weight, or affected by an impulse of the mind" (20). Third the figure category is broad, including strategies of argument (*aetiologia, inversio, epitrope*). Fourth Farnaby names thirty-one additional devices that have commonly been called figures in his discussions of invention, arrangement, and stylistic composition but without identifying them as figures. Should we assume that his placing of these schemes under other categories reflects his belief that these devices should not be considered figures? This assumption seems unlikely for four reasons. First several mentioned in these earlier lists, such as *incrementum* and *ironia,* he mentions again under style as figures. Second the majority are traditionally regarded as figures (*congeries, diminutio, fabula, sententia, apophthegmata, allusione, interrogatio, isocolon, homoioteleuton, homoioptoton, parison,* and *antithesis*). Perhaps those associated with proof (*amplificatio, similitudo, contrario, exemplum, epicheireme, syllogismus, enthymema, inductio, comparatio,* and *inter se pugnantia*) we can excuse, since these have been the subject of controversy; perhaps too those commonly associated with the peroration (*enumeratio, indignatio,* and *misericordium*) and those associated with *compositio* (*hiatus, periodus, comma,* and *colon*) do not belong to figures, as Quintilian argues. But these features are listed together in Farnaby's discussion so that if we accept the *isocolon, parison,* or antithesis as figures, we must also accept the comma, colon, and variations of the period. If we accept *incrementum,* so too *comparatio, ratiocinatio,* and *congeries.* If we accept *diminutio* or *sententia,* so too *similitudo, contrario, fabula, amplificatio,* and so forth. Third we cannot conclude with certainty that Farnaby wants to restrict the number of figures, for he intends this work for young schoolboys and so attempts here only to provide a representative sampling as part of his short compendium of rhetoric. Fourth, in his discussion of practice at the end of the manual, he describes style as if inclusive of invention and arrangement:

> Moreover, with high hope he will make progress toward the fullest praises, if he shall have surrendered himself entirely and properly to Style, the best and foremost teacher, author, and producer of good speaking. . . .
>
> Before he takes pen in hand, therefore, let him first take care that he understands the subjects under consideration, and what has to be said about the nature, classification, and status of the case. . . . He will evaluate the circumstances, seek out the hiding places of arguments, and bring out whatever contributes toward winning goodwill, instilling trust, and arousing emotions. He will have at hand an abundance of rhetorical resources. . . .
>
> When he will have listed on one page of a tablet all the resources of arguments, examples, similes, ideas, so that they appear as if in battle order, the next task will be that of making a choice. You must consider not only from what rank they step forth, but also in what equipment, how strong they are and how handsome, so that a speech of words adorned with stars, of phrases shining like the constellations, of ideas decked with ornaments of style, may glitter with elegance, flow smoothly in its composition, and gleam with adornment. (38–39; trans. Nadeau, "Renaissance Schoolmaster" 176–77)

It rather seems that Farnaby is simply discussing the forms as relevant when he covers each of the departments of rhetoric and uses the customary names for the forms. The question of whether these features are figures or not seems unimportant.

Apparently Farnaby's compact summary of rhetoric was widely used, with twenty-two printings in the seventeenth century and several more in the eighteenth. Hoole recommends it in his *New Discovery of the Old Art of Teaching School* (181), and the manuscript must have circulated before the first printing, for the grammarian Alexander Gill in his *Logonomia Anglica* (1619) references Farnaby in the discussions of *circumlocutio* and *polysyndeton* (158). Like his contemporaries Farnaby is a synthesizer, citing as his sources Aristotle, Theon, Hermogenes, Longinus, Aphthonius, Cicero, the *Ad Herennium,* Quintilian, Fortunatianus, Sulpitius Victor, Victorinus, Capella, Alcuin, Erasmus, Caussin, Sturm, Keckermann, Soarez, Vossius, and several other minor rhetoricians.

In his brief manual *Some Instructions Concerning the Art of Oratory* (1659), Obadiah Walker (1616–99), a master at Oxford, reorganizes rhetoric's five parts into two:

invention and style (1). He makes arrangement part of invention and delivery part of style. Three-fourths of the book discusses style, to which he assigns words, periods, figures, styles, pronunciation, and action (24). But this division is misleading in the sense that each of these categories is populated with figures. For example under words Walker treats of archaisms, neologisms, epithets, various forms of repetition, *polyptoton, homoeoptoton, zeugma, asyndeton,* and so forth. Under periods he discusses not only the comma, colon, and period but also *enthymema, parison, isocolon,* interposition, *anaphora, epistrophe, symploce,* and *pleonasmus.* Under styles he includes the devices of *interrogatio, transitio, apostrophe, prosopopoeia, dubitatio, admiratio, exclamatio, praeoccupatio,* and *digressio,* along with others; and under pronunciation he mentions rhythm, euphony, and phonetic figures. All these devices he still calls figures. Consequently Walker treats style as essentially figure, which he defines as an ornament or habit "for setting out the matter more speciously, and making our Inventions more lively and plausible, grave and persuasive" (51). The breadth Walker gives to the figure category is especially evident when under the section of figures, he includes not only metaphor and allegory but also logical syllogisms, enthymemes, inductions, examples, theses, and numerous legitimate ways to provide proof, rebut, argue, amplify, and arrange one's speech (80–82). This overlap of style and invention compromises not only the initial division he makes between them but also the possible implication that figures have only to do with appearance. Despite treating only seventy-eight figures directly, Walker's approach to the subject reflects the liberal trend of the time. Walker quotes from Cicero, Quintilian, Scaliger, and Farnaby but has probably also drawn from Erasmus and other like-minded contemporaries. W. S. Howell's conclusion that Walker's focus on style reveals an indirect influence of Ramus (*Logic* 325) seems hasty, since Cicero provides a model for viewing rhetoric from the perspective of style and since Walker gives the breadth to style that Cicero does and Ramus does not. Reprinted three additional times until 1682, this textbook received some use.

The Ramists, the Arts of Poetry, and the Arts of Grammar

Exceptions to this broad view may appear at first glance to be the Ramists, the *ars poetica* and the *ars grammatica* manuals, but these are only partial exceptions. Only Ramus and Talon (c. 1510–62) come close to adhering to Quintilian's strictures on the figure category. In *Arguments in Rhetoric against Quintilian* (1549), Ramus agrees with Quintilian that figures should be restricted to guileful indirections and unusual alterations of speech and even criticizes Quintilian for not being restrictive enough. Illustration, interrogation, and reply should not be figures, "for all of these can be *aschemata,* that is, straightforward and non-figural" (144).[57] Ramus declares that "ornament of style involves a change in speaking from the proper but common manner to some more elegant and brilliant one" (141). In the 1574 edition of the *Rhetorica,* even though he exhibits style as figure or "garnishing," Talon writes that "a figure varies the 'clothing' of speech (*orationis habitus*) from the straightforward and simple" (24; trans. Ong, *Ramus, Method* 274). Because Ramus argues that Quintilian's list of figures should be reduced, Talon only treats of fifty-seven tropes and figures in the 1548 edition, organized under a simplified rubric. He identifies four primary tropes (metaphor, metonymy, synecdoche, and irony) and five species of these, called secondary tropes. Figures divide into those of diction and of thought. Figures of diction divide into three kinds: those of repetition, change, and rhythm. Figures of thought have four species: asking and answering, counterfeiting (*fictione*), separating (*abruptione*), and amplifying (23). All but two of these figures are clearly indirections and unusual alterations. Later editions simplify the divisions and reduce the number of figures even more. In the 1576 edition, figures of speech divide into those of number and those of repetition, with this latter kind dividing into those that repeat the same sound (*epizeuxis, anadiplosis, climax, anaphora, epistrophe, epanalepsis,* and *epanodos*) and those that repeat similar sounds (*paronomasia* and *polyptoton*). Figures of thought divide into the monologic (*epiphonema, licentia, correctio, reticentia, apostrophe,* and *prosopopoeia*) and dialogic (*addubitatio, communicatio,* and *permissio* or *concessio*) for a total of twenty figures in addition to the tropes.[58]

Yet Ramus and Talon still encourage a kind of looseness to the category. They add meter and rhythm to the figure list. They argue that Quintilian is inconsistent in excluding artistic structure, since "structure and rhythm are a fashioning of style removed from everyday usage" (*Arguments* 149; *Rhetorica* [1548] 72). In attempting to separate clearly tropes and figures by arguing that irony, since it is a trope, should not be a figure of thought (145), Ramus unwittingly loosens Quintilian's distinction between figures and nonfigures. In 1548 Talon also includes *subjectio* (or *anthypophora,* the answering of objections) as a figure, which Quintilian had rejected as too straightforward (9.2.106), and a new figure, *salutatio* (a salutation), as a species of *exclamatio* (exclamation) that also seems rather straightforward. The norm from which figures vary also shifts from proper usage to unskillfulness. Talon says in the 1548 edition that figures change speech from the vulgar and make it "proper, suitable, or advantageous" and "tasteful or graceful" (22). Ramus and Talon, then, remain burdened with the same vagueness prevalent in other discussions of the figures. Ong states the problem succinctly: "The Ramist difficulty here is the difficulty of practically all such rhetoric text books: it may be traced to the attempt to describe and classify the unusual without being able to identify what the usual is" (*Ramus* 274). Finally Ramus himself, in his own commentaries, points out forms and figures not specifically included in his own textbooks (such as *antapodosis, enumeratio, amplificatio, accusatio, reprehensio, laudatio,* and *transitio*), mixes them together without careful distinction, and treats them all as if components of arguments.[59]

Sixteenth-century English Ramists have more in common with either the *Ad Herennium* or with Cicero than with Ramus, for though they retain the Ramistic divisions of style and figures, they emphasize not indirection but appropriateness as the marker for figures, they allow authentic and sincere expressions as figures, and they consider figures an open category. Dudley Fenner (c. 1558–87), a Calvinist clergyman, in *The Arte of Rethorike* (1584) calls tropes "the fine manner of word" and figures "the fine shape or frame of speech" (168) that occur when the speech "is changed from the more simple and plain manner of speaking unto that which is more full of excellency and grace" (171). The lawyer Fraunce in *The Arcadian Rhetoric* (1588) may say that "of speeches, some be simple and natural, some finely fashioned and figured artificially," but he defines a figure as "a certain decking of speech, whereby the usual and simple fashion thereof is altered and changed to that which is more elegant and conceited" (B8r). To illustrate *commiseratio* Fenner quotes Christ's genuine lament from Matthew 23:37: "O Jerusalem, Jerusalem, thou that killest the prophets, and stonest them . . . !" To illustrate *desperatio* he quotes Paul's heartfelt plea in Romans 7:24: "O wretched man that I am! who shall deliver me from this body of sin?" (173). To illustrate *aporia* Fraunce pulls from Sir Philip Sidney's *Old Arcadia* Gynecia's tortured self-deliberation (G7v), much like the example above from Euripides's *Hecuba* that Alexander cites and denies is a figure. Although Fenner lists only forty-three and Fraunce only forty-six embellishments, this number does not represent the total they would allow. Fenner seems only to be providing a quick summation of the art's basic principles. He knows of other figures and mentions seven more while discussing sophistry in his *The Arte of Logike* (1584). Treated as devices that can lead to fallacious arguments are *archaismus, onomatopoeia, bomphiologia, homonymia, amphibolia, tautologia, skotison,* and *heterogenium* (arguing beside the point) (176–80). (The last is the only one of the set that has never also appeared as a figure). Perhaps all of these, when faults, cannot be figures, if figures are only the appropriate forms, but Fenner's reference to them shows his awareness of a larger set of figures. Additionally that these forms appear in a discussion of argument reveals them as substantive, not decorative, in nature. If we do take them as figures, then why not add *heterogenium* to the figure list? Likewise Fraunce gives attention to a good number of additional figures of thought in his logic text, *The Lawiers Logike* (1588), calling them both figures and arguments and showing a much broader notion of both figure and style than does Ramus or Fenner.[60]

Some seventeenth-century Ramists in England may hold more strictly to the notion of figures as alterations but still leave the boundary lines ambiguous. Charles Butler (1560–1647), the schoolmaster and vicar of Wotten, produced an adaptation of Talon's rhetoric in *Rhetorica libri duo* (1598). He retains the conservative definition of figure as "a change from straightforward and simple usage" (39) and the Ramist classification system (38), but he expands the list to 102 tropes and figures, "supplying very many things wanting in Talaeus" (204). His inclusions pull into the figure domain features of expression that can be used in a straightforward way, such as equivalent phrases (*isodynamia*), or features that improve coherence and hence appropriateness, such as transitions (*transitio*). He also references Aristotle, Cicero's *De Oratore,* and Quintilian, besides Talon, showing familiarity with the broader tradition. Nevertheless Butler is the most conservative of these English Ramists. In contrast to the one printing of Fraunce's rhetoric and the three of his logic, the seven printings of Fenner's *Artes* and the fifteen printings of Butler's textbook until 1700 show that Ramist reductions had influence in England and, despite ambiguities, supplied a narrower view to compete with the more liberal trend.

The two arts of poetry manuals significant for their treatments of figures are Julius Caesar Scaliger's *Poetices libri septem* (1561) and Puttenham's *The Arte of English Poesie* (1589), both of which give inadequate attention to the boundaries of the figure domain.

One of the few who does not conflate embellishments and figures, Scaliger (1484–1558) distinguishes the nonfigure and the figure, the simple and more elaborate, or the "bare" and "dressed up" forms (3.93.363), both of which are embellishments or the "fitting out" of one's ideas (4.1.449). This humanist physician, philosopher, and grammarian explains that we "dress the matter by whatever words we please, but we furnish with the modulation, alteration, and color of figures" (4.1.450). A figure he defines as "an acceptable delineation of notions which are in the mind, different from ordinary usage" (3.30.303; trans. Mack, *History* 223). Associating the figures with emotional expression, he calls them "colors" or "the impulses" by which the speaker carries his facts to the crowd (3.31.305). Figures of diction give speech a "beautiful face different from the common face" (4.26.496) and are grammatical and syntactical patterns formed by omission, addition (of the same, the similar, the different, the contrary), transposition, quantity, and quality.[61] Figures of thought are all tropes—Scaliger corrects and expands on Quintilian and Alexander here (3.31.305; 4.26.496)—and divide into seven species: those formed by contraries (irony), similarities or equality (*tractatione*), the more (hyperbole), the less (*detractione*), the different (*allegoria*), one thing in many (*periphrasis*), and the many in one (*collectione*). He seems to regard forms such as *sententia* (aphoristic sentence), *purgatio* (self-justification), *conciliatio* (ingratiation), and *ad hilaritatem impulsio* (humor) nonfigures when nontropological and figures when tropological (3.93.363). He also carefully distinguishes types or characters of style from figures: for example brevity and *expolitio* are not figures but the resulting style or form of speech (3.46.316).

Yet despite insisting that figures are acceptable variations from common use, Scaliger allows the norm of "common use" a wide latitude with shifting grounds. "Common use" spans the meanings of most frequent, most customary, most literal, and least polished or shaped. He also includes as figures features that belong to plain, common speech: the *periodus,* which is, as Alexander defines it, a complete thought in either simple or complex form (4.25.493); *orthotes* (a straightforward declaration), which he has pulled from Hermogenes; and argumentation, because "what is more removed from popular use than the entire species of arguments?" (3.71.339–40). If these forms are figures, then the distinction between the usual and unusual or the "bare" and "dressed up" forms becomes problematic. The distinction blurs again when he grants to figures both dissimulated and genuine expressions (3.31.305). More ambiguity arises when he later announces that there are two types of embellishments of speech: figures and rhythm (4.1.439), as if *schemata lexeos* are now inclusive of all linguistic choices except rhythm. Furthermore he hardly separates rhythm from scheme, for he leaves unanswered whether poetic rhythm differs from common use and he simply segues into his discussion of *numerus* (rhythm) as if it is simply the last kind of verbal scheme (4.44.516–20). Additionally Scaliger considers the figure category elastic, discussing 190 forms that cover a wide range of discourse features from sound patterns to genres and that create a myriad of heightening and diminishing effects. He even introduces several new figures, pulling from Demetrius, Hermogenes, and Celsus or inventing several himself. Drawing upon Aquila, Rufinianus, the *Ad Herennium,* Quintilian,

Trapezuntius, Alexander Rhetor, Demetrius, and Hermogenes and also having read Aristotle and Dionysius of Halicarnassus, Scaliger again reflects the synthesizing trend of the Renaissance.[62] Printed ten times until 1617, his book had influence among scholars.

Puttenham's one edition of *The Art of English Poesie* also confuses the issue of definition. In this first full-scale art of poetry in English, Puttenham, like Scaliger, identifies two types of poetic embellishment: proportion (rhythm, rime, cadences, composition, verse form, visual form, emblem, and anagram) and ornament (figures, vices, virtues, and decorum). There are three kinds of figures: (1) those that set a "goodly outward show" upon the matter and "delight the ear only" (155); (2) those that through the sense of words and speeches stir the mind (155); and (3) those that "serve as well the ear as the conceit" (171). The first, which are formed by defect, surplusage, disorder, or "immutation," he calls auricular (with phonetic, orthographical, grammatical, and syntactical manifestations); the second, which belong to either single words or passages, he calls *sensable* (the tropes); and the third, which result from repetition or amplification, he calls sententious or rhetorical (with syntactical, lexical, pragmatic, logical, and discoursal manifestations). He treats 119 figures in this discussion.

But Puttenham offers conflicting definitions of figures that compromise his neat division. At first like Quintilian Puttenham declares that guile underlies figures: "As figures be the instruments of ornament in every language, so be they also in a sort abuses or rather trespasses in speech, because they pass the ordinary limits of common utterance, and be occupied of purpose to deceive the ear and also the mind, drawing it from plainness and simplicity to a certain doubleness, whereby our talk is the more guileful and abusing" (166). Again like Quintilian he regards dissimulation, or allegory, as he calls it, the "chief ringleader and captain of all other figures, either in the Poetical or oratorical science": "And ye shall know that we may dissemble, I mean speak otherwise than we think, in earnest as well as in sport, under covert and dark terms, and in learned and apparent speeches, in short sentences, and by long ambage [*sic*] and circumstance of words, and finally as well when we lie as when we tell truth. To be short every speech wrested from his own natural signification to another not altogether so natural is a kind of dissimulation, because the words bear contrary countenance to th' intent" (197). Yet Puttenham's examples of the first two above statements involve only tropes, and he does not restrict schemes to ironies or allegories, nor to deliberate artifice. For example unlike Quintilian, Puttenham allows some straightforward forms of arguments as figures, including *aetiologia, paradeigma, sententia, expeditio, similitudo,* and *dilemma.* Furthermore unlike Quintilian, Puttenham does not restrict figures to purposeful shaping but says, like Robertellus, that it "maketh no matter whether the same eloquence be natural to them or artificial" (152), for "good utterance . . . resteth altogether in figurative speeches, being well used whether it come by nature or by art or by exercise" (152). Also figures are natural forms that happen by chance or by intent: "All your figures Poetical or Rhetorical, are but observations of strange speeches, and such as without any art at all we should use, and commonly do, even by very nature without discipline. But more or less aptly and decently, or scarcely, or abundantly, or of this or that kind of figure, and one of us more than another, according to the disposition of our nature, constitution of the heart, and facility of that form: but art aideth the judgment of his use and application" (304).

Additionally like Quintilian, Puttenham defines figures as alterations of a normal idiom through either addition, subtraction, transposition, or mutation:

> Figurative speech is a novelty of language evidently (and yet not absurdly) estranged from the ordinary habit and manner of our daily talk and writing and figure itself is a certain lively or good grace set upon words, speeches and sentences to some purpose and not in vain, giving them ornament or efficacy by many manner of alterations in shape, in sound, and also in sense, sometime by way of surplusage, sometime by defect, sometime by disorder, or mutation, and also by putting into our speeches more pith and substance, subtlety, quickness, efficacy or moderation, in this or that sort tuning and tempering them, by amplification, abridgement, opening, closing, enforcing, meekening or otherwise disposing them to the best purpose. (171)

But unlike Quintilian and like Cicero, Puttenham conceives of alteration as a change not merely from some set custom but also from a less to a more effective configuration. He calls devices figures when, being congruent with an author's purposes and a speech's circumstances, they "enforce the sense" and thereby have "subtlety," which make them "excellencies" (212). These excellencies are the proper and hence beautiful uses of language: "Whereupon it came to pass, that all the commendable parts of speech were set forth by the name of figures, and all the ill-laudable parts under the name of vices" (168), since good utterance "resteth altogether in figurative speech" (152) and "ornament is but the good or rather beautiful habit of language or style" (155). What determines the good and beautiful is decorum, or appropriateness: if any device has "foul indecency or disproportion of sound, situation, or sense," it is a vice of speech and not a figure (167). As a consequence he regards the brief recapitulation of one's points in the peroration, "the recapitulatour," as a figure (244). A common feature of the peroration, this recapitulation (*frequentatio*) is not a figure in Quintilian. Additionally even the vices of style can become figures when used appropriately (257), and the virtues of style become conflated with figures. Since this is the case, the number of figures Puttenham actually treats totals 140.

Finally without awareness of self-contradiction, Puttenham changes his definition of figure again and, like Veltkirchius or Sturm, equates figuration itself with all forms, for "figurative speeches [are] the instrument wherewith we burnish our language, fashioning it to this or that measure and proportion, whence finally resulteth a long and continual phrase or manner of writing or speech, which we call by the name of style" (155). He reinforces this view by calling the visual shapes of poems and the emblem "figures" (104), anticipating concerns of visual rhetoric today. With this liberality the other aspects of rhythm, rhyme, and composition easily meld into the category of figure.

Even grammar texts used in the Renaissance impart a liberal view of figures. Whether deeming grammar's purview to include a limited or expansive treatment of figures, grammarians acknowledge they offer only an introduction to prepare students for the more extensive study under the rhetorician.

The late Latin grammarians frequently consulted for figures, Donatus and Diomedes, both state that figures of grammar pertain to the grammarian but figures of thought pertain to the rhetorician. Donatus divides the grammatical figures into thirty-one vices, seventeen *schemata lexeos,* and twenty-eight tropes, for a total of seventy-six figures. Diomedes divides the figures he covers into forty-seven vices (organized under *obscuritas, inordinatae,* and *barbarae*) and twenty-eight tropes. He categorizes the *schemata lexeos* under the vice *solecismus* (a species of *barbarae*) and lists twenty-one of these figures. His total is seventy-five. The "authorized" grammar in England, William Lily's *A Short Introduction of Grammar* (1540), introduces the pupil to only twenty-three figures, those relevant to poetic scansion and to grammar: the fourteen species of *metaplasmus,* seven of grammar, one virtue of construction (*synthesis*), and *caesura.* But Lily (1468–1522), who was the first high master of St. Paul's grammar school, defines a figure broadly as "a form of speaking (*dicendi forma*) made new by art" (G.i.r), and this little book was originally compiled to be an antecedent to Eramsus's *De copia.* Charles Hoole's *The Latine Grammar* (1651), which was a tidying up of Lily's textbook, provides a slightly expanded treatment of the figures. The schoolmaster Hoole (1609–67) divides grammatical figures into those that "any way changeth the form of the word" (262) and those that "any way changeth the frame of a speech" (264). Under those of word, he includes ten species of *metaplasmus,* plus *enallage, tmesis,* and *archaismus.* Under those of construction, he includes fifteen schemes of grammar and syntax. In an appendix he treats of the *colon* and its various forms (*monocolon, dicolon, tricolon,* and *polycolon*), poetic meter, *caesura,* and four additional species of metaplasm for a total of thirty-nine figures. Hoole indicates, though, that the norm from which figures vary shifts: grammarians handle those figures that involve an "altering of a word or speech from the usual manner of speaking" (262), but rhetoricians treat of figures "which belong rather to the handsoming than the making of a Speech" (268). Hoole's book had six printings until 1670.

Other grammar textbooks in wide use give more coverage to figures. For example Antonio Mancinelli's *Carmen de figuris* (1489) lists 108 figures. Following principally Donatus and Diomedes but drawing also from the *Ad Herennium* and Quintilian, Mancinelli (1452–1505) divides the figures into fourteen vices, sixteen metaplasms, twenty-one *schemata lexeos,* and fifty-seven tropes. *De figuris* (1512) by the Flemish grammarian Johannes Despauterius, or de Spauter (c. 1460–1520), divides figures into sixteen types of *metaplasmus,* eighteen *schemata lexeos,* and twenty-seven tropes but also includes a list of seventeen vices and a miscellaneous category inclusive of other tropes, grammatical figures, and figures of thought, such as *descriptio, anthypophora,* and *erotema,* numbering twenty-five. Despauterius lists 103 figures in all, which he defines broadly as "a form of speech altered by a certain art" (C1v). His primary sources include Quintilian, Donatus, Diomedes, and Mancinelli.[63] Similarly one of the translators of the King James Bible and later high master at St. Paul's School,[64] Gill (1567–1635) makes reference to ninety-two figures of speech in his *Logonomia Anglica,* a grammar of the English language, written in Latin and addressed to foreigners studying the English tongue.[65] Claiming Mancinelli and Despauterius as his sources, Gill argues that instruction in figures of speech belongs to the grammarian and that the teacher of rhetoric addresses figures of thought (150). While declaring that a figure of speech "differs from ordinary speech" and is "embodied either in the choice of words or in their use" (151), Gill acknowledges that figures of thought "vary the style of speech" without altering it "from the fundamental syntactical nature" (150). He divides figures of speech into three types: tropes, figures of words, and figures of sentence. He discusses four primary and eighteen secondary tropes. Figures of words divide into fourteen of sound (repetition of meaning or of sound) and fifteen of syntax (omission, addition, or changing of single words). Figures occur in the sentence when word order is either simple and uninterrupted, complex, or confused, or when meaning is either rapidly advanced, corrected, extended, or restrained (163), and total forty-one. These figures (ornaments) of word and syntax are more common in poetry than prose (172), but those of thought belong more properly to prose (150). Although they can be used artfully, figures occur naturally, for "English is neither written, nor spoken without figures of speech" (151). Gill's grammar was published twice before 1700.

Implications

Finding a way to bracket off suitably a set of specialized forms has always posed difficulties. None of the distinctions historically offered to separate the figure from the nonfigure always holds true, and the question of what is the norm from which figures depart is never clearly settled, receiving very little attention in the Renaissance.[66] This difficulty was recognized by the ancients. Longinus, for example, acknowledges, "Thus a common expression sometimes proves far more vivid than elegant language. Being taken from our common life it is immediately recognized, and what is familiar is thereby the more convincing" (§31). Again he acknowledges that "phrases exceedingly ordinary" can become "sublime by being apt to the situation" (§40). Vives makes a similar observation: "Adornments should be carefully chosen from common language with good taste and with no other desire than that which a person might have who in a meadow or garden would gather a bouquet or weave a crown of flowers. But just as a simple twig or green herb can be a cause of delight to some, so there is no part of language, however small or insignificant, which cannot give pleasure to someone. With good reason Apollodorus—Quintilian quotes his remark taken from Caelius—held that an infinite number of rules would be needed to account for all preferences" (*De ratione dicendi* 42–43). Another reason it is so easy for these rhetoricians to expand the domain of figure is the ampleness and slipperiness of the term. The term *figura* is also a technical reference to forms of syllogisms in logic texts and structures of words and syntax in grammar texts.[67] Lamy also applies the term *scheme* to the idea of the discourse and to its overall shape: "Before we speak, we ought to form a Scheme in our Minds of what we desire to say." He goes on, "We ought therefore in the first place to range our Thoughts, and put such things as we intend to represent by our Words into natural order, disposing them so, that the knowledge of some few of them, may render the rest more easy and intelligible to the Reader" (1.1.5). Even though he does not mean here a "stylistic" figure, others would have so meant. The wide latitude given to this term is also evident when Lamy uses *figure* to mean "the impressions the Objects make upon the sense" and then the brain (4.1.8).

Even another reason these humanists allow the figure category flexibility is that they treat the subject primarily as a matter of pedagogical or practical convenience. These writers are acquainted with a wide variety of classical and contemporary sources and so themselves have a broader exposure to the devices called figures than their own handlists present.[68] These educators select the figures that to them seem either the most common, the most useful, or the most worthy of attention, not wanting to overwhelm the pupil (and perhaps the publisher) with excessive detail. Because their selections differ, the figures listed vary somewhat from manual to manual. Yet nearly all the devices are well-known enough to have multiple citations and belong to a common stock.

This looseness in regard to the figure domain suggests that what is most important to these pedagogues is not fine distinctions among forms but having ready at hand a broad-ranging repertoire of forms for use. This enumeration of textual devices reflects a concern for craftsmanship, for identifying and naming forms and strategies so that they can become tools in the hands of the artist for both interpretation and composition. The impulse to identify and name as many of these strategies as possible comes from the recognition that the more patterns one notices, the more nuanced is one's interpretation of text and the more self-consciously controlled and hence artistic can become one's own composition.

Even though not fully theorized, the looseness with which Renaissance rhetoricians treat figures prevents static and false dichotomies between fiction and nonfiction, unusual and usual expression, or representational and referential forms. Since the same elements receive attention in these discussions of embellishments whether called figures or not; since these forms occur naturally as well as purposefully and can be both authentic and feigned; since they produce all kinds of effects, not merely poetic elevation; since they include both arguments and linguistic patterns; and since the appropriate use of all forms creates artistic discourse, this approach to figures unites without collapsing not only poetics and rhetoric but also content and style, pointing the way to a new definition of figure and providing a single heuristic for both style and invention.

A New Definition of Figure

With figure becoming a plastic notion of form itself, this tradition enables the insight that all forms are figures—that is, all forms derive from tropological processes and have representational functions. This tradition also enables the insight that all figures, however, are also "normal" forms because they result from logical processes and have indicative functions. Perhaps Erasmus glimpses this insight and so refuses to distinguish tropes, figures, and nonfigures. Shaw certainly has it, as we will see at the end of chapter 2. These characteristics of figures will be explained in more detail in chapters 2 and 3. For now it will suffice to say that language, in being a sign system, automatically involves the four basic tropes simultaneously: metonymy—a sign stands for the thing signified; irony—conscious choice denotes purposeful design; synecdoche—forms embody the mental processes that produce them; and metaphor—forms result from placing things in terms of other things. Besides these basic tropes, any number of schemes of both thought and speech also shape any given concept, since these tropes involve logical *topoi* and forms involve arrangements.

While this description of language is not explicit, the overlying of figure upon figure is an insight widely held in this tradition. Quintilian makes one comment alluding to this fact, showing several figures of speech and of thought within one sentence (9.1.16). Renaissance rhetoricians, however, frequently comment on these overlays. Hoskins provides several examples of such overlapping and then asserts, "These examples may make you believe that a sentence may be course[d] through the whole figure-book; and it shall appear in a set treatise that many figures may easily assemble in one clause and any figure may sort with any" (40). Gill provides a similar analysis of a sentence from Edmund Spenser's *The Faerie Queene:* "How great is such an artist? What is the complete sentence? How many figures are there? *Anaphora, Traductio, . . . Isocolon, Schesis, Anadiplosis, Asyndeton, Congeries, Gradatio,* ignoring the finer points. Is there not here comprehended almost the whole rhetoric of *Talaeus* at one view?" (2.170).

This overlap makes all language both poetic (creative) and logical (rational) at its core. The genre of fiction is created not simply through the use of figures but rather through purposeful simulation, so that an additional level of representation is overlaid upon the basic level already present in nonfiction. Literariness is best defined not by specific forms that elevate the style but rather by the degree of artistry in the use of one's forms. Consequently fiction and nonfiction remain separate genres, but both are equally figured and governed by the rules of literariness.

Making these claims does not erase the distinction commonly made in these manuals between figurative and literal meaning. Smith, for example, exhorts the reader, "And herein we must beware that we take not those things literally which are to be understood spiritually, that we go not out to a figurative acceptation of any place of Scripture, where we have not a sufficient reason (grounded upon some word of truth) why the proper sense or signification of the words may not be adhered unto, for we must never leave off the proper sense unless the coherence of the Text, the Analogy of faith, or some other place of Scripture require a figurative Exposition. And it is very dangerous to make figures where the Scripture makes none, or to make the scope and sense bleed with straining it too hard" ("Author to the Reader" A6r–v). There is a formal difference between language that employs tropes to create figurative meaning and ordinary language that merely results from tropological processes. The difference once again is that the first has more levels of representation/indication than has the second.

Style as Invention/Invention as Style

Two additional consequences follow from giving this breadth to the figure domain. The first is that style and invention in Renaissance rhetoric become mirror images of each other. The second is that instruction in style provides a recursive model of composition, which is built into the curriculum and which balances and completes the linear model provided by the typical sequence of rhetoric's departments: invention, arrangement, style, memory, and delivery. Both of these consequences underscore the simultaneously dualistic and monistic relationships inhering between content and expression. Renaissance humanists openly acknowledge these relationships, taking their cue from Cicero and Hermogenes.

Cicero purposely emphasizes the recursiveness among the canons of rhetoric. In the dramatized dialogue in *De Oratore,* Cicero has Antonius, the first speaker, review the precepts of invention, disposition, and memory and then Crassus, the second speaker, take up instruction in style or "the embellishment of oratory." However when Antonius concludes his portion, Crassus points out the impossibility of such a clean, linear division among these offices: "Granted, Antonius, that I allow something to be the case which is in reality quite otherwise, what pray have you to-day left to me, or to anybody, that can possibly be said? . . . Who gave Antonius leave to divide the subject up into shares. . . . And next, if I understood him rightly, listening as I was with great pleasure, he seemed to me to be discussing both the two subjects [matter and style] conjointly" (2.90.365–6). To emphasize the point, Crassus reiterates it when he begins to speak again the next day:

> When in arranging our shares in the debate he took for himself in the subject the proper topics of oratory and left it to me to expound the proper method of embellishing them, he separated from one another things that cannot really stand apart. Every speech consists of matter and words, and the words cannot fall into place if you remove the matter, nor can the matter have clarity if you withdraw the words. . . . Nowadays we are deluged not only with the notions of the vulgar but also with the opinions of the half-educated, who find it easier to deal with matters that they cannot grasp in their entirety if they split them up and take them piecemeal, and who separate words from thoughts as one might sever body from mind—and neither process can take place without disaster. (3.5.19–6.25)

Cicero makes the same point again in the *Orator,* where he deals with each of rhetoric's canons separately and sequentially but also underscores their inevitable inseparability by rehearsing invention, disposition, and delivery as he responds to Brutus's question about the ideal style (1.3).

A similar overlap between invention and style is demonstrated in *On Invention* from the Hermogenic corpus. Books 1–3 of this work cover proofs and arrangement. Book 4 discusses figures of speech and thought. Reciprocally *On Types of Style* incorporates proofs and matters of arrangement within style.

The same awareness of this reciprocity between invention and style appears in Renaissance instruction. Erasmus, for example, emphasizes the recursiveness of the process of composition in his preaching manual, *Ecclesiastes.* He begins his third book, where he discusses disposition, pronunciation, and style, by saying that he is now going to run back through the same things he has just discussed in invention but in a different way (3.7.5–6). His *De copia* is certainly a book that treats both figures and topics as heuristics for both style and invention.[69] Robertellus declares that his figural analyses serve to illustrate the writers' processes of invention as well as to explain obscure parts of a text (37r). Others, such as Veltkirchius (193v) and Smith (A7r), even call the figures "places" of invention.[70] Day explains that schemes and tropes are for the "apt setting forth and delivery of the places therein used" ([1586] 72). The modern literary critic Bernard Weinberg observes that in Italian Renaissance manuals on the art of poetry the topics "are curiously transformed into stylistic procedures" (*History of Literary Criticism* 152). Rhetoric textbooks inevitably cover much of style in invention and arrangement and vice versa. The overlaps are obvious, so much so that Ramus wants to get rid of them. The system, then, does not either bifurcate nor collapse idea and form but suggests that the two are separable but interconnected in essential ways.[71] George Gascoigne (c. 1535–77) can advise the poet to pay attention to both invention and style/figure: "If you do . . . never study for some depth of device in the Invention, and some figures also in the handling thereof, it will appear to the skillful Reader but a tale of a tub" (*Certaine Notes of Instruction* [1575] 48). But Keckermann can teach the student that any given figure contributes to both content and style. He remarks that a *sententia* "to the degree that it explains something, whether it proves or amplifies, pertains to the doctrine of invention, but to the extent that it embellishes speaking, it pertains to the doctrine of elocution" (*Systema* 1475). He explains that *appositio* brings in added information "not only for the sake of the declaration, but also for that of ornament" (1502). Both sets of instructions, both perspectives, are true.[72]

This reciprocity between invention and style has only recently begun to receive some attention from contemporary rhetoricians. Ross Winterowd, for example, has seen that invention can subsume style: "If one views theories of form and theories of style merely as sets of topics—which in most instances they are—then the whole process of composition is unified under the auspices of invention" (48). Reciprocally Paul Butler suggests that if the inventional function of style is seen, style will become important again (*Out of Style* 84). The generative power of stylistic forms, a concept central to the classical and Renaissance rhetorical curricula, underlies Francis Christensen's "A Generative Rhetoric of the Sentence" and Richard Coe's "An Apology for Form; or, Who Took the Form out of the Process?" Forms are heuristics because they are templates that put ideas into relations. Once we perceive the relations evoked by the form, we look for ideas to fit or complete the form. Consequently Lanham acknowledges that even figures without a logical basis still become "a kind of mold for thought, or machinery for generating it" (*Analyzing Prose* 124). Such insights arise naturally from the Renaissance curriculum.

Chapter 2

iscourse, a Web of Schemes

In chapter 1 we learned that nearly all the forms customarily taught in the art of rhetoric appear as stylistic figures in Renaissance handbooks. This practice turns rhetoric into figures. In this chapter we will see that Renaissance rhetoricians apply figures to all genres and styles of expression, as well as to thought and to action, thereby making figures central to discourse, showing discourse to consist of three parallel dimensions—thought, speech, and action—and revealing text, regardless of genre, to be literally what its name declares it to be: a complex web of overlying and interconnected *schemata.* Having to pay attention to all these layers of forms/ideas explains why stylistic mastery is so demanding, yet so important. Seeing discourse as a web of schemes enables further reconciliations between dualisms and monisms within one universal heuristic.

This picture of discourse emerges because, unlike Aristotle and the philosophers who restrict rhetoric to political or literary speech and assign logic to the more academic disciplines of philosophy—a separation that keeps rhetoric, poetics, and philosophy distinct—these humanists unite grammar, logic, and rhetoric into one general theory of human meaning making. Being the umbrella of the arts, rhetoric pulls instruction on thinking and acting into instruction on speaking about all subjects, to all audiences, in all genres and styles, and by means of all media. While their classical forebears provide this general theory of human communication, Renaissance rhetoricians make more evident its extensibility to all expression by applying rhetoric to all human activity, erasing distinctions between enthymematic and syllogistic logic, moving figures into logic instruction, depicting meaning making as schema induction, and elaborating on figures in human behavior. In this view poetics, philosophy, and ethics are both subdisciplines and subgenres of rhetoric. But since rhetoric naturally reflects a philosophy and when well practiced becomes literary, rational, and ethical, these subjects also become identical with rhetoric. Since rhetoric is composed of figures, one's use of figures will reveal one's aesthetic, rational, and moral judgment.

This last statement must wait for attention until chapters 3 and 4, where we will show that although essentially figurative, human thought and expression remain essentially meaningful. For now we will illustrate how Renaissance precepts, despite occasional theoretical naïveté, show the primacy of figures to discourse. We will examine first rhetoric's synonymity with discourse, second the absence of an unfigured style in this curriculum, third indications in both rhetoric and logic manuals of the figurative nature of mind, and fourth indications of the figurative nature of action.

Rhetoric, the Umbrella of the Communication Arts

This unification of the three language arts into one universal art of discourse receives the fullest expression in Cicero but is also evident in the classical and Renaissance texts reflective of the traditional Greco-Roman curriculum, whose roots lie in Isocrates's program. This philosophy of rhetoric differs from that in Aristotle, whose segregation of the arts reduces rhetoric to merely one genre and its subject matter to merely persuasive technique. In all programs the study of grammar is anticipatory to the study of rhetoric and logic, so it is the relationship between logic and rhetoric and the genres of discourse that are of issue.

Classical Precedents

Keeping the arts of logic, dialectic, poetics, and rhetoric distinct—arts he conceives of as instrumental only—Aristotle does not present a unified nor complete theory of human discourse. The first two arts provide tools to guide reason in dialogue between experts focused on building knowledge: logic ascertains certain truths and dialectic probable truths. These two dialogic techniques aid the work of philosophy. The second two are tools for composing continuous speech or monologue directed toward the lay multitude: poetic for fiction and rhetoric for persuasion in the political sphere. Aristotle does not attempt to describe all possible genres of discourse. He restricts persuasion (the moving of an audience) to only one kind of speech act, the rhetorical. He believes that the reasoning one uses for philosophy differs in kind from the reasoning one uses in rhetoric, and he ignores issues of composition for philosophical genres. His analysis of rhetoric also remains limited in scope despite occasional comments that could have wider application. Aristotle designates rhetoric "as the faculty [capacity] of observing in any given case the available means of persuasion" (*Rhetoric* 1.2 1355b26–27) but restricts the "given cases" to three primary, separate genres of political oratory: the deliberative, forensic, and epideictic (1.3 1358b7). These arguments do not require the use of syllogisms or logical demonstration—the tools of logical certainty—but rather enthymemes and examples, both real and apparent, which, because based on audience opinion, are the tools for drawing opposite conclusions impartially in the search for probabilities. He justifies this restriction since "the duty of rhetoric is to deal with such matters as we deliberate upon without arts or systems to guide us, in the hearing of persons who cannot take in at a glance a complicated argument, or follow a long chain of reasoning" (1.2 1357a2–4). This kind of argumentation or reasoning is inferior to both scientific and ethical deliberation: "Moreover, before some audiences not even the possession of the exactest knowledge will make it easy for what we say to produce conviction. For argument based on knowledge implies instruction, and there are people whom one cannot instruct" (1.1 1355a24–26). Aristotle may wish that the orator speak truth and that the function of this art be not simply success in persuading (1.1 1355b10). But he gives his attention to the techniques by which a public speaker does succeed in winning over this "audience of untrained thinkers" (1.1 1354a10; 1.2 1357a11). These techniques can be used equally well for good or ill ends, he claims (1.1 1355b4–6), making rhetoric an amoral art. While Aristotle draws examples for rhetorical argument, structure, and style from not only oratory but also poetry, history, and philosophy, thereby suggesting that many types of discourse may exhibit the same forms (e.g., 1.6–15, 2.19–24, 3.2–18); while he calls rhetoric "an offshoot" of dialectics and ethics (1.2 1356a25–26) since it entails these two (1.4 1359b9); and while he declares that the philosopher trained in reasoning will be a more skilled orator than a speaker who only learns rhetoric (1.2 1356a22–25), his evident disdain for the necessity of rhetoric, belief that this art is inferior to philosophy, restriction of the art's application to political oratory, complaint that rhetoric "has been given a far wider subject-matter than strictly belongs to it" (1.4 1359b7), and failure to acknowledge other types of speech as persuasion indicate that he does not see a unity among the genres nor the principles of judgment applicable to each.[1] Aristotle separates *phronesis,* the practical judgment necessary for rhetoric, from *sapientia,* the wisdom necessary for philosophy and the moral life (*Nicomachean Ethics* 6.3 1139b31–1140b30). In Aristotle mind and speech, truth and opinion, teaching and persuasion, and *phronesis* and *sapientia* are distinctly different things, belonging to different disciplines and genres with different sets of guidelines.

In Cicero and Quintilian, however, the arts of logic and dialectic have been conflated and subordinated to rhetoric, which is the art of human communication in general, applicable to all genres and governed by moral judgment. It is on the question of rhetoric's breadth and identity that Cicero lets his readers know he differs from Aristotle, whom he otherwise admires for having "surveyed these concerns of the art" with "sagacity" and "insight" despite having "disdained" rhetoric (*De Oratore* 2.38.160). In the dialogue dramatized in *De Oratore,* Antonius is the interlocutor whose view aligns quite closely with Aristotle's.[2] He claims that rhetoric is the art for political speech: the orator "is a man who can use language agreeable to the ear, and arguments suited to convince, in law-court disputes and in debates of public business" (1.49.213). He says, "This oratory of ours must be adapted to the ears of the multitude, for charming or urging their minds to approve of proposals, which are weighed in no goldsmith's balance, but in what I may call common scales" (2.38.159). As a consequence he also argues that an orator needs only a general knowledge of law and the techniques of argument (1.55.234–58.246), not familiarity with many subjects or universal culture (1.51.219). Treating rhetoric as an instrumental art, Antonius allows the orator techniques of manipulation, which the moral philosopher would disapprove of (1.53.227–54.233), and claims that "consummate eloquence can exist quite apart from philosophy" (1.54.233). Cicero makes clear that Antonius is an Aristotelian, for he has Antonius claim to have read Aristotle's *Synagoge* and "those other works containing sundry observations of his own on the same art" and acknowledge that his own rhetorical precepts "differ but little" from Aristotle's (2.38.160).[3] Antonius prefers Critolaus, who was a follower of Aristotle (2.38.160).

In contrast Crassus, the spokesman for Cicero's view,[4] laments that philosophers have driven the orator "from the helm of State, shut [him] out from all learning and knowledge of more important things, and thrust [him] down and locked [him] up exclusively in law-courts and petty little assemblies, as if in a pounding mill" (1.11.46). Crassus declares rhetoric's all-encompassing domain and universal reach when he redefines the art: "The art of speaking well, that is to say, of speaking with knowledge, skill and elegance, has no delimited territory, within whose borders it is enclosed and confined" (2.2.5). Whether oratory, philosophy, history, poetry, or epistle, "eloquence is one, into whatever shores or realms of discourse it ranges," and "whether it be delivered to few or to many, among strangers or among friends or by oneself, the flow of language though running in different channels does not spring from different sources, and wherever it goes, the same supply of matter and equipment [*instructu ornatuque*] of style go with it" (3.6.23). Rhetoric is now instruction in how to speak well on any occasion to any audience about any subject. "Speaking well," the aim of the art, is not simply being able to find all the means of persuasion; rather it is achieved in demonstrating total "propriety and discernment" in one's speech act (1.29.132)—in fashioning the aspects of the speech act to be appropriate to its aims, circumstances, audience, speaker, and the public good. Kathy Eden agrees, "Indeed, Cicero defines eloquence as the ability to practice *decorum*" (*Hermeneutics* 26).

In *De officiis,* his treatise on moral philosophy, Cicero describes decorum, linking it to rational and moral judgment. This principle of appropriateness applies to both reason and speech: "For to employ reason and speech rationally, to do with careful consideration whatever one does, and in everything to discern the truth and to uphold it—that is proper" (1.27.94). It also applies to action and is equivalent to moral virtue: "Such is its essential nature, that it is inseparable from moral goodness; for what is proper is morally right, and what is morally right is proper" (1.27.94). The proper speech exhibits decorum in both what is argued for and how the argument is made. In *De Oratore* Crassus emphasizes that rhetoric must include concern for the public good, since human converse, in being social, brings about social consequences. The good speech, or eloquence, must bring about what is good for society:

> For the one point in which we have our very greatest advantage over the brute creation is that we hold converse one with another, and can reproduce our thought in word. Who therefore would not rightly admire this faculty, and deem it his duty to exert himself to the utmost in this field, that by so doing he may surpass men themselves in that particular respect wherein chiefly men are superior to animals? To come, however, at length to the highest achievements of eloquence, what other

> power could have been strong enough either to gather scattered humanity into one place, or to lead out of its brutish existence in the wilderness up to our present condition of civilization as men and as citizens, or, after the establishment of social communities, to give shape to laws, tribunals, and civic rights? And not to pursue any further instances—well nigh countless as they are—I will conclude the whole matter in a few words, for my assertion is this: that the wise control of the complete orator is that which chiefly upholds not only his own dignity, but the safety of countless individuals and of the entire State. (1.8.32–34)

Since speech is action, the manner of speech is also inevitably implicated in moral judgments. What the art teaches primarily, then, is good judgment, or wisdom: "the knowledge of what is appropriate to a particular occasion is a matter of practical sagacity" (3.55.212). Hence he declares, "This method of attaining and of expressing thought, this faculty of speaking, was, I say, designated by the ancient Greeks wisdom" (3.14.56). Consequently as Cicero defines rhetoric in *De Partitione Oratoria,* "Eloquence is nothing else but wisdom delivering copious utterance" (23.79).[5] By wisdom, as Robert W. Cape, Jr. explains, Cicero means both practical and theoretical sagacity, both *phronesis* and *sapientia* (39–41).

Cicero believes these principles of decorum are universals innate to the processes of human reason and speech: "Virtue is reason completely developed; and this is certainly natural; therefore everything honorable is likewise natural" (*De legibus* 1.16.45). Because the principles that determine appropriateness are natural, Cicero has great faith that the opinion of the common people regarding what is appropriate will coincide with that of experts. He says in *De officiis,* "And because that very quality which we term moral goodness and propriety is pleasing to us by and of itself and touches all our hearts both by its inward essence and its outward aspect and shines forth with most lustre through those virtues named above, we are, therefore, compelled by Nature herself to love those in whom we believe those virtues to reside" (2.9.32). He says again in *Brutus,*

> The truth is that the orator who is approved by the multitude must inevitably be approved by the expert. What is right or wrong in a man's speaking I shall be able to judge, provided I have the ability and knowledge to judge; but what sort of an orator a man is can only be recognized from what his oratory effects. Now there are three things in my opinion which the orator should effect: instruct his listener, give him pleasure, stir his emotions. By what virtues in the orator each one of these is effected, or from what faults the orator fails to attain the desired effect, or in trying even slips and falls, a master of the art will be able to judge. But whether or not the orator succeeds in conveying to his listeners the emotions which he wishes to convey, can only be judged by the assent of the multitude and the approbation of the people. For that reason, as to the question whether an orator is good or bad, there has never been disagreement between experts and the common people. (49.184–85)

Speaking well results from both good reasoning and facility with forms of expression. These skills require mastery of the three branches of philosophy—science, logic, and ethics (*De Oratore* 1.15.68)—as well as poetry, history, and oratory. Hence Crassus requires the orator to "take all knowledge for his province" (2.1.5). Cicero admonishes that the orator needs the skills of both logical debate and rhetorical speech-making (*Orator* 32.114–20).

He particularly complains, however, that too often instruction in logic and ethics have been excluded from rhetorical training. Cicero has Crassus criticize Socrates, who "separated the science of wise thinking from that of elegant speaking," the "source from which has sprung the undoubtedly absurd and unprofitable and reprehensible severance between the tongue and the brain, leading to our having one set of professors to teach us to think and another to teach us to speak" (*De Oratore* 3.16.60–61). Cicero remarks that, because of this severance, in his day Aristotle's instruction in logic "is ignored by all except a few of the professed philosophers" (*Topica* 1.3). Cicero's instruction in reason, then, includes Aristotle's logic. However, Cicero mixes Aristotle's logic and dialectic so that distinctions between them disappear, and he allows the orator as needed either to "demonstrate with probability or [to] prove irrefutably" (*De Inventione* 1.29.44).[6] He gives to argumentation two branches, "one concerned with invention of arguments and the other with judgment of their validity." While he considers Aristotle the founder of both (*Topica* 2.6), Cicero's treatment of both the topics of invention and the rules of inference owe more to later developments than to the direct influence of Aristotle.[7] Additionally Cicero insists that the orator must combine the logician's concern for *theses* (general questions) with the rhetorician's concern for *hypotheses* (particular questions), since the general always underlies the particular (21.79–80). One studies the forms of argument not for their own sake but in order to construct "a course of reasoning which firmly establishes a matter about which there is some doubt" (2.8), a matter that will lead to practical decision-making in the affairs of life. For these reasons Cicero declares rhetoric is "broader and logic narrower" (*Orator* 32.114).

Cicero, through Crassus, also insists that the speaker will need to master the division of philosophy "concerned with human life and conduct" (*De Oratore* 1.15.68) in order to speak on questions of justice, honor, and praiseworthiness, as well as in a manner that accords with these virtues. This study of ethics will additionally provide "profound insight into the characters of men, and the whole range of human nature, and those motives whereby souls are spurred on or turned back" (1.12.53). Calling upon precedent and naming Isocrates, Crassus remarks, "For in old days at all events the same system of instruction seems to have imparted education both in right conduct and in good speech; nor were the professors in two separate groups, but the same masters gave instruction in both ethics and in rhetoric" (3.15.57, 59).

Cicero's definition of rhetoric is broader than Aristotle's, then, in three important ways. First the art applies to all speech, which is civic by nature, not merely political orations delivered to the multitude. Second the art must be designed to produce good speech, not merely identify the available means of persuasion. Third the art of speech encompasses the arts of knowledge and applies them to social use.[8] Since all speech is social by nature, Cicero's perspective inverts Aristotle's: it is rhetoric that is fundamentally dialogical, whereas philosophy, inasmuch as it focuses only on the creating of syllogisms, is fundamentally monological.[9] Ernesto Grassi insightfully makes this last point:

> Rational [philosophical] speech is that which strictly, "mathematically" explains or "infers" what is implied in the premises. This speech is "monological" in its deepest structure, for it is not bothered by emotion or place and time determinations in its rational process; . . .
>
> Rhetorical speech on the other hand is a "dialogue," that is, that which breaks out with vehemence in the urgency of the particular human situation and "here" and "now" begins to form a specifically human order in the confrontation with other human beings. (113)

Also inverting Aristotle, Cicero claims that philosophers cannot speak as well as an orator on these subjects because the former lack the added training rhetoric provides for socializing knowledge: "And all this is considered to be the special province of philosophers, . . . but when he [the orator] has granted their knowledge of these things, since they have devoted all their labour to that alone, still he will assert his own claim to the oratorical treatment of them, which without that knowledge of theirs is nothing at all" (*De Oratore* 1.12.53–54). Cicero does not reject Aristotle's analysis of logical and rhetorical techniques, only his inadequate philosophy of discourse, and therefore incorporates Aristotle's technical arts within a broader conception of their relationship, a conception that comes from Isocrates.[10]

The father of the Hellenistic curriculum, Isocrates insists that his *logôn paideia* (discourse education) is concerned with "all the forms of discourse in which the mind expresses itself," both public and private (*Antidosis* §183), and he contrasts the narrower focus of other sophists on *rhetoreia,* political speech-making, to his own broader focus on *logos,* or human communication in general (*Against the Sophists* §21, 32–33; *Panathenaicus* §11).[11] In using the term *logos,* Isocrates emphasizes the union of *ratio* (reason) and *oratio* (speech) in the activity of deliberation/argumentation. He elaborates:

> With this faculty we both contend against others on matters which are open to dispute and seek light for ourselves on things which are unknown: for the same arguments which we use in persuading others when we speak in public, we employ also when we deliberate in our own thoughts; and while we call eloquent those who are able to speak before a crowd, we regard as sage those who most skillfully debate their problems in their own minds. And, if there is need to speak in brief summary of this power, we shall find that none of the things which are done with intelligence take place without the help of speech, but that in all our actions as well as in all our thoughts speech is our guide, and is most employed by those who have the most wisdom. (*Nicocles* §8–9; *Antidosis* §256)

It is the possession of *logos* that distinguishes the human from the animal, and it is the study or mastery of *logos* that will provide the best training for life, because such a study imparts true wisdom, which is that practical, moral judgment used in finding the best course of action and speech in the uncertain and ever-changing contingencies in human affairs (*Against the Sophists* §13; *Antidosis* §184, 271). This problem-solving and decision-making ability is prudence, which "will enable us to govern wisely both our own households and the commonwealth" (*Antidosis* §285). The best speech, resulting from prudence, is a civilizing force devoted to "the welfare of man and our common good" (§276):

> For in the other powers which we possess we are in no respect superior to other living creatures; nay, we are inferior to many in swiftness and in strength and in other resources; but, because there has been implanted in us the power to persuade each other and to make clear to each other whatever we desire, not only have we escaped the life of wild beasts, but we have come together and founded cities and made laws and invented arts; and, generally speaking, there is no institution devised by man which the power of speech has not helped us to establish. For this it is which has laid down laws concerning things just and unjust, and things base and honourable; and if it were not for these ordinances we should not be able to live with one another. It is by this also that we confute the bad and extol the good. (*Nicocles* §5–7; *Antidosis* §253–55)

This description of *logos* suggests that argument is the basic function of all discourse, which is social or political by nature because embedded in human relations. As Takis Poulakos explains, Isocrates does not mean "political" in the sense of self-interested or party maneuvering but rather in the necessary constituting of social bonds and communal well-being (*Speaking for the Polis* 5). In order to speak well, the orator must acquire knowledge on wide-ranging subjects[12] and study human motives and honorable behaviors (*Antidosis* §217, 277). Isocrates concedes that a training in *logos* will not "implant honesty and justice in depraved natures," but he is convinced that such a training will enable people to "become better and worthier," for the desire to speak well and think right will motivate nobility of action (§274–78). Isocrates calls this course of study focused on practical and ethical judgment *philosophia* (§181), thereby uniting in one person the roles of orator, citizen, statesman, moral teacher, and philosopher.[13]

We find in Isocrates's extant writings only a partial anatomy of the discourse art. Cicero and several other ancients have attributed to him a textbook on the subject, but it does not survive.[14] In the years after Isocrates and Aristotle, as Cicero narrates the history, the schools descending from each, "one busy with philosophy, but devoting some attention to the art of rhetoric as well, the other entirely devoted to the study and teaching of oratory, were fused into one group by later teachers who took into their own books from both sources what they thought was correct" (*De Inventione* 2.3.8). For this reason Cicero embraces, by means of the interlocuter Antonius, Aristotle's technical analysis and incorporates it within his own more thorough instruction that derives from "the treatises on the art by [Isocrates's] pupils . . . who carried on his doctrines" (2.3.8). That Antonius in his technical description of the art in book 2 of *De Oratore* presents some precepts not in Aristotle, in fact some clearly in alignment with Crassus's broader view, suggests that Cicero is adding to and correcting Aristotle's precepts to fit his own understanding of the oratorical art.[15] Evidence of this expansion comes when Antonius announces to Crassus that he is no longer concerned with "refuting your arguments" but with enunciating "my own personal views" (2.10.40). As a consequence Antonius speaks for Cicero when he concedes to Crassus that "all reasoning and all teaching really belong to this one art alone" (2.9.37), recognizes that both *thesis* and *hypothesis* apply to oratory (2.10.41–42), reduces the primary genres of speech to the deliberative and judicial, since the epideictic is really not separate from them (2.10.43),[16] and advocates adding instruction in the writing of history (2.15.62–4); the duties of encouraging, comforting, teaching, and warning (2.15.64); the means for developing general questions (*theses*) (2.19.78); and humor or wit (2.57.231). Antonius also speaks for Cicero in his praise for the Peripatetic Carneades, whose oratorical power derived from his skill in argument (2.38.161), which was due to his incorporating into rhetoric Aristotelian logical precepts and the arguing *in utramque partem,* that is, both sides of any issue (Cicero, *De finibus* 5.14).[17] It is this unified theory of discourse that allows Cicero to combine without collapsing not only content and expression but also mind and speech, accomplishing again on the disciplinary level what he accomplishes more locally in his discussion of style.[18]

Quintilian follows Cicero in this broader view of rhetoric, "the science of speaking well" in both public and private discourse: "Those who refused to make the sphere of oratory all-inclusive, have been obliged to make somewhat forced and long-winded distinctions" (2.15.19, 34; 2.21.23). He may even set the precedent for believing Aristotle has the same opinion by remarking that "Aristotle seems to have implied that the sphere of the orator was all-inclusive when he defined rhetoric as the *power to detect every element in any given subject which might conduce to persuasion*" (2.15.16). Specifying that "the aim of rhetoric is *to think and speak rightly*" (2.15.37),[19] Quintilian teaches dialectic as part of the orator's training (2.21.13). Like Cicero, Quintilian dispenses with distinctions between logic and dialectic and requires the speaker to use both certain and probable proofs (5.8.6; 5.10.12), both syllogisms and enthymemes (1.10.37–9; 5.14.27), both *theses* and *hypotheses* (3.5.10). Like Cicero, Quintilian insists that oratory combines philosophy and rhetoric: "These two branches of knowledge were, as Cicero has clearly shown, so closely united, not merely in theory, but in practice, that the same men were regarded as uniting the qualifications of orator and philosopher" (1.Pr.13). He elaborates that the orator studies both moral philosophy and physical science: "Now as a matter of fact we all of us frequently handle those themes which philosophy claims for its own. Who, short of being an utter villain, does not speak of justice, equity and virtue? Who (and even common country-folk are no exception) does not make some inquiry into the causes of natural phenomena?" (1.Pr.16). The orator must acquire broad knowledge through additional study of history, civil law, religion, and poetry (12.2–4). Like Cicero, Quintilian recognizes that the three primary genres of oratory overlap: "All three kinds rely on the mutual assistance of the other. For we deal with justice and expediency in panegyric and with honor in deliberations, while you rarely find a forensic case, in part of which at any rate something of those questions just mentioned is not to be found" (3.4.16). Like Cicero, Quintilian insists that a speech's quality is determined by the degree of congruency within the speech act and between this act and its most complete relevant context but, being more skeptical than his predecessor, does not believe a high level of congruency will automatically also win widespread audience approval. Speaking well cannot be determined by the audience's response, unless it is a discerning audience: "But our orator and his art, as we define it, are independent of results. The speaker aims at victory, it is true, but if he speaks well, he has lived up to the ideals of his art, even if he is defeated. . . . For the art of rhetoric, as I shall show later, is realised in action, not in the result obtained" (2.17.23–26). Judgment is at the center of the art: "I regard it inextricably blent with and involved in every portion of this work" (4.5.1; see also 3.3.6). For this reason Quintilian declares even more explicitly than did Cicero that a rhetorical education can form the good man (12.intr.4) and that "no man can be an orator [worthy of the name] unless he is a good man": "For it is impossible to regard those men as gifted with intelligence who on being offered the choice between the two paths of virtue and of vice choose the latter, nor can we allow them prudence, when by the unforeseen issue of their own actions they render themselves liable not merely to the heaviest penalties of the laws, but to the inevitable torment of an evil conscience" (12.1.3). Because rhetoric is broader and philosophy narrower, it is the rhetorician, not the philosopher, who can speak the best: "But it is surely the orator who will have the greatest mastery of all such departments of knowledge and the greatest power to express it in words" (1.Pr.17), while the speech of dialecticians, "crowded with a mass of *epicheiremes* and *enthymemes,*" is "mechanical" (5.14.27, 32).

The other classical sources influential on Renaissance rhetoric also hold this inclusive, moral perspective on the language arts. The *Ad Herennium* may limit rhetoric to the "theory of Public Speaking" (1.1.1) and may imply that the art of speaking be seen as a subdiscipline of philosophy ("for it is true that copiousness and facility in expression bear abundant fruit, if controlled by proper knowledge and a strict discipline of the mind" [1.1.1]), but this anonymous author, who is less philosophically astute than Cicero, still teaches an art that has assimilated logic instruction within rhetorical invention (2.20–29), illustrates forms of argument with examples from a variety of genres, and extends the art's precepts to "the most ordinary speech of every day" (4.10.14).[20] This manual gives the art more breadth than did Aristotle and reveals the traces of the broad art of discourse that has given shape to the Hellenistic rhetorical curriculum, even though it fell subject to a narrowing over time that Cicero disapproved of.[21] The precepts in this technical manual easily assimilate with those in Cicero's *De Oratore,* even if the definition of rhetoric does not.

Additionally Demetrius, Hermogenes, and Longinus have this broader perspective, for all suppose that the analysis of text they provide applies to any genre, includes cognitive as well as linguistic forms, and develops good judgment and sophistication in readers and speakers. For example Demetrius includes a short discussion of personal letters, showing that the same stylistic elements and principles of decorum apply to them as to conversation, formal oratory, poetry, and philosophy (§223–25). Hermogenes in *On Types of Style* draws examples from all genres.[22] Whereas he remarks in *On Issues* that rhetoric deals with *hypotheses*, not *theses* (28), he nevertheless supposes that *theses* function in rhetorical arguments, for in *On Types of Style* they are one kind of stylistic figure (1.6.245). The author of *On Invention* does not segregate argument forms according to the separate disciplines. Whereas Aristotle distinguishes the *epicheireme,* or the dialectical syllogism, from *apodeixis,* the logical or demonstrative syllogism, this author declares that the *epicheireme* may serve an *apodiectical* function (13.163) and that the syllogism structures the *epicheireme* (14.165–66). Similarly Longinus remarks that when a *phantasia* ("image production") is "combined with factual arguments," whether in oratory, poetry, history, or philosophy, "it not only convinces the audience, it positively masters them" (§15).[23]

Convinced that facility and judgment come through precept, example, and practice, these Greco-Roman educators, following Isocrates, join instruction in the art with the interconnected activities of reading, writing, and speaking. Pupils must find the art's principles at work in both good and poor models, then apply the principles even more decorously in their own written and spoken compositions.[24] Quintilian insists that "every kind of writer must be carefully studied" (1.4.4). Models come from all genres, whether philosophy, history, oratory, epistles, or poetry, to which the same artistic principles apply. Learning to write in all the genres, pupils must "rival and vie" with the originals and seek to surpass their quality (10.5.5). Quintilian explains the need for all three activities: "[Writing, reading, and speaking] are so intimately and inseparably connected, that if one of them be neglected, we shall but waste the labour which we have devoted to the others. For eloquence will never attain to its full development or robust health, unless it acquires strength by frequent practice in writing, while such practice without the models supplied by reading will be like a ship drifting aimlessly without a steersman" (10.1.1–2). Constant practice in both textual analysis and composition, in both written and oral performance, produces not only fluent, effective, and ethical speakers but also discerning readers and listeners. An education in this curriculum, then, centers on critical, moral judgment and creates a sophisticated audience immune to the machinations an unprincipled orator would employ.

Renaissance Rhetoricians

Inspired by this Greco-Roman curriculum, Renaissance humanists also adopt this broad application of the art. Because this breadth has not been much noted, it will be appropriate to cite from many humanists to show its prevalence. In his *Dialecticae disputationes* (1439), the early Italian humanist Valla, whose work significantly influenced northern European humanism, treats rhetoric as "the comprehensive science of human expression" (Monfasani, *George* 305).[25] In his *Oration in Praise of Eloquence,* Trebizond claims that "eloquence contains all of civil life within it" (trans. Rebhorn, *Renaissance Debates* 34) and that "rhetoric alone has undertaken the managing of private as well as public matters. For what could be thought up or said in the conduct of our affairs that does not require the power of oratory?" (32).[26] The Spanish humanist Vives writes his *De ratione dicendi* about speech in general and defines eloquence as "speaking well," "for there is [nothing] more advantageous to human society than well-formed and well-developed language, and nothing more harmful and distressing than language that is not suited to the person, place, or time" (23). He also describes the broad usefulness of rhetoric in his *De causis corruptarum artium* (On the Causes of the Corruption of the Arts), which were published as the first seven books of the *De tradendis disciplinis* (1531): "The faculty of speech, like a kind of universal tool, has been diffused through all things, not unlike grammar and dialectic; nor did Cicero and Quintilian omit to mention that there are more genres of which one might speak—in fact, Quintilian unfolded many of them. However, they thought that what was necessary for the other genres could be derived from the precepts given for those three [judicial, deliberative, and demonstrative oratory]" (159; trans. Rebhorn, *Emperor* 4). Erasmus goes beyond the medieval art of letter writing by expanding the subject matter of epistles to any topic and organizing letters according to the three primary genres of oratory and a fourth type he calls the familiar (*De conscribendis epistoles* 71). Day follows suit in *The English Secretary.* Furthermore Erasmus applies rhetoric to all genres and in *Ecclesiastes* repeats Cicero's definition of rhetoric as "nothing else than the prudence of the one speaking" (1.66.629–31; trans. Boswell). Melanchthon also regards eloquence as "the faculty of speaking wisely and well" (*Elem.* 5r, 78) and declares that these principles have been advanced "to aid all men," not merely lawyers or public speakers (4v, 75). Additionally he gives the three political occasions for speech ubiquitous application: the demonstrative genre includes congratulation, the speech of thanks, laments, eulogies, and panegyrics (7v, 24r); the judicial involves not only legal oratory but also scriptural exegesis and ecclesiastical disputes (10v); and the deliberative consists in persuasion and dissuasion, exhortation and its opposite, requests, petitions, prayers, encouragement, consolations, complaints, consultations, objurgations, and deprecations (7v, 21v, 23v). John Rainolds (1549–1607), an Oxford don, agrees that "rhetoric is diffused throughout all subjects, like some universal tool" (Green, *John Rainolds's Oxford Lectures* [1572–78] 250), and Wilson, who brackets off astronomy, arithmetic, and geometry from much needing this art of utterance (*Art of Rhetoric* 45), nevertheless declares that "rhetoric is an art to set forth by utterance of words matter at large" (45) and that "the use thereof appeareth full oft in all parts of our life" (120). Taking the three genres of oratory as general types of all discourse, Wilson, like Cicero, nevertheless acknowledges that they of necessity overlap:

> Nothing can be handled by this art but the same is contained within one of these three causes. Either the matter consisteth in praise or dispraise of a thing, or else in consulting whether the cause be profitable or unprofitable, or lastly whether the matter be right or wrong. And yet this one thing is to be learned: that in every one of these three causes—these three several ends—may every of them be contained in any one of them. And therefore he that shall have cause to praise any one body shall have just cause to speak of justice, to entreat of profit, and jointly to talk of one thing with another. (54)

Soarez remarks that "eloquence is so great, so distinguished, and such a wonderful thing that it contains almost everything" (260). The Ramist Fenner sees the application of these arts broadly too and encourages that they be used "in understanding and judging the many treatises that are written to hurt or benefit the world. It is necessary and just that skills in judging and speaking be available to all, not merely the expert, since all people participate in communication daily" (146). Puttenham (24, 206, 22) and Scaliger (1.1.4–5) believe the poet to be an orator and poetry to be argument, like other speech genres. Like Wilson, Scaliger even specifies that all genres of discourse, because they function to teach, are fundamentally deliberative oratory, with principles of epideictic and judicial oratory mixed in (1.1.4–5; 3.105.398).[27] Even Lamy still acknowledges rhetoric as the general art of speaking, despite splitting persuasion off as a separate genre: "The Arts of Speaking and Persuading are both comprehended under the name of Rhetoric by several great Masters" (4.88). Lamy also still gives to persuasion an almost unlimited application: "The Art shows itself in the Pulpit, at the Bar, at all manner of business and conversation; for in a word, the whole end of Commerce and Conversation is to persuade those with whom we deal" (4.92–93).

Authors of stylistic handbooks repeat the same broad view. Sherry applies figures to all kinds of great writing ([1550] 13–14) and defines rhetoric as "nothing else but wisdom speaking eloquently" (17). Robertellus insists that the art of eloquence and the figures apply equally to all genres (9r). Peacham declares that these figures are "profitable and necessary, as well for private speech, as for public Orations" ([1593] A.B.i.r). Hoskins designs his treatise for the writing of epistles and for conversation (26), and the Spanish Jesuit Luis de Granada (1504–88) concurs that *elocutio* or style "is open as wide as possible to all disciplines of all kinds" (*Ecclesiastica Rhetorica* 40; trans. Rebhorn, *Emperor* 5).[28] The breadth that these humanists give to rhetoric is evidenced as well in their freely extending its application even beyond classical precedent to personal meditation, prayer, courtiership, manners, painting, music, dancing, archery, and any human art, encompassing not only verbal but also extralinguistic forms of expression.[29]

Humanists also agree that speaking well entails both right thinking and right expressing, and that the speaker who wishes for eloquence must study both philosophy and rhetoric.[30] Although he acknowledges the difficulty of acquiring encyclopedic knowledge and combining it with effective speech, Trebizond still encourages the ideal: "But when both are found together, a common event in antiquity which does not seem possible in these corrupt times, something perfect and truly divine occurs" (*Rhetoricorum* 60r; trans. Boswell).[31] He also teaches that eloquence, the art of good speaking, is divided into dialectic, or "that part of speech by means of which we pry into the secrets of nature," and rhetoric, or "that other part, which is necessary for civic affairs and without which no one ever carried on his business with distinction, especially in the state" ("Oration" 31). The opposite of eloquence is either "muteness" or bad speaking (34). Sturm writes, "Finally, I regard him as eloquent who combines the exercise of speech with the learning of philosophers; who has been aptly and fittingly prepared in both things; who can thus furnish the substance and illustrate it" ("On the Lost Art" 128–29). Rainolds admonishes that "the practice of rhetoric depends upon knowledge of the great arts, and upon practical judgment of public life" ("Introductory Lecture" 99). Hoskins agrees: "Then he that could apprehend the consequence of things, in their truth, and utter his apprehensions as truly were a right orator" (2). Soarez also says that "speaking well" means "to speak the best of thoughts with carefully chosen words" (118) and "with wisdom, experience and polish" (120). Peacham declares that good speaking results when "knowledge may be joined with apt utterance, and [the] copy of speech with matter of importance, that is to say, that their Eloquence may be wise and their Wisdom eloquent" ([1577] A.ii.v). He defines rhetoric, quoting from Cicero, as "wisdom speaking eloquently" ([1577] A.iii.r), with wisdom referring to both knowledge and to good judgment. Sir Thomas Elyot (c. 1490–1546) expresses a similar understanding in *The Boke Named the Governour* (1531): "Wherefore they be much abused that suppose eloquence to be only in words or colours of Rhetoric, for, as Tully saith, what is so furious or mad a thing as a vain sound of words of the best sort and most ornate, containing neither conning nor sentence?" (1.116).

Without exception humanists stress decorum or good judgment as the wisdom the art teaches. Ascham declares, "Decorum, which, as it is the hardest point, in all learning, so is it the fairest and only mark, that scholars, in all their study, must always shoot at" (*Scholemaster* 249). Melanchthon explains that the principles of both rhetoric and dialectic "are necessary in forming judgments" (*Elem.* 5r, 79–80) and "for prudently evaluating and understanding" texts of all kinds (4v, 76). Sherry instructs that eloquence—"to utter the mind aptly, distinctly, and ornately"—arises from good judgment ([1550] 19). Wilson indicates that the good speaker is the one who "can use meet terms and apt order such as all men should have and wise men will use, such as needs must be had when matters should be uttered" (*Art of Rhetoric* 187). Blount also understands that judgment or prudence lies at the heart of eloquence and that eloquence requires both wholesome subject matter and skillful expression: "But Eloquence is chiefly grounded upon Wisdom, & Wisdom arises principally from a due pre-consideration of all our actions; Hence that excellent saying of a modern French Author, . . . 'tis impossible to speak well, without having first well considered what to speak" (A2v–3r). Puttenham indicates that the art rests in "decency" (270), and that it is those "of much observation and greatest experience" that have the best judgment:

> But since the actions of man with their circumstances be infinite, and the world likewise replenished with many judgements, it may be a question who shall have the determination of such controversy as may arise whether this or that action or speech be decent or indecent: and verily it seems to go all by discretion, not perchance of every one, but by a learned and experienced discretion, for otherwise seems the decorum to a weak and ignorant judgement, than it doth to one of better knowledge and experience: which showeth that it resteth in the discerning part of the mind, so as he who can make the best and most differences of things by reasonable and witty distinction is to be the fittest judge or sentencer [*sic*] of decency. (270)

As a consequence of this breadth, logic—or dialectic, as it was called in the Renaissance—belongs to the study of rhetoric or eloquence.[32] Humanists revise medieval Scholastic logic by turning the subject from being an end in itself to being a means to the larger practical and social ends of eloquence. Accordingly they generally argue that this subject should be not the last and ultimate course in the university curriculum but a less specialized study as part of rhetorical training.[33] Whereas Trebizond prepares a simplified logic book as a supplement to his rhetoric but does not equate this introductory course with logic proper,[34] the majority of humanists reject the subtleties and formalisms found in Scholastic logic and argue that a streamlined logic returns the subject to its proper essentials.[35] In real life logic does not stand alone; rather this art provides the skeleton for all argumentation, which must then be fleshed out by rhetoric. Whereas medieval logic focuses primarily on syllogistic judgment,[36] the humanists give to this art both invention and judgment. They insist that dialectic should include both demonstrative and nondemonstrative inference and should function both to find "good" reasons in practical decision-making and to uncover and evaluate the arguments being made in texts.[37] Wilson's *The Rule of Reason* is representative. Wilson begins the textbook with the definitions of logic and its two parts that are traditional in humanist logics:

> Logic is an art to reason probably on both parts, of all matters that be put forth, so far as the nature of every thing can bear.
>
> This Art is divided into two parts. The first part standeth in framing of things aptly together, in knitting words, for the purpose accordingly, and in Latin is called *Judicium.*
>
> The second part consisteth in finding out matter, and searching stuff agreeable to the cause, and in Latin is called *Inventio.* (B.i.r)

The part called "Judgment," also known as "disposition" or "framing," includes rules concerning the categories of words,[38] the forming of propositions and syllogisms, and the method of arranging arguments, so that one can recognize proper order and truth and then order properly. Wilson sets forth the purpose of this instruction: "to declare the nature of every word severally, to set the same words in a perfect sentence, and to knit them up in argument, so that hereby we might with ease espy the right frame in matters, how they agree being lapped up in order" (J.iiii.v). The part known as "Invention" teaches one to find matter, proofs, and propositions by visiting the "store house of places wherein arguments rest" (J.iiii.v). One invents by taking a subject through the places in order to find appropriate predicates, a proposition through in order to find appropriate proofs, or a question through in order to find answers. The logical *topoi* or "places" become fairly standard in these manuals and derive principally from Cicero's list in the *Topica.*[39] Guiding all thinking and the framing of all assertions, dialectic is necessary for prudence, as Agricola in *De inventione dialectica* explains, "since prudence itself seems to consist in knowing the nature of something, and collecting what agrees and disagrees with it, what it causes and what might happen" (1.1.3; trans. Mack, *Renaissance Argument* 139).

Humanist logic even goes beyond classical precedents in explicitly joining probable argumentation and scientific demonstration. Both Ramists and non-Ramists declare that informal and formal reasoning are one and the same process. Fraunce repeats in his *The Lawiers Logike* (1588) what Ramus says in his *Dialectique* (1555)[40] regarding why logic and dialectic are the same:

> Artificial Logic then is the polishing of natural wit, as discovering the validity of every reason, be it necessary, whereof cometh science: or contingent, whence proceedeth opinion. Although I know there is a great controversy and contention among the ancient Philosophers, concerning these two: . . . Aristotle would needs make two Logics, the one for Science, the other for Opinion: wherein (if so it may be said of so great a Philosopher) it seemeth he was but an Opinator [*sic*]. For although among things conceived and known, some be necessary and infallible, some doubtful and contingent, yet the Art of Knowing and Reasoning of the same (I mean Logic) is only one and the same. (5v)

The Non-Ramist Rainolds makes the same argument in his Oxford lectures on rhetoric, although mistakenly giving Aristotle credit for the same insight:

> Furthermore, those ancients assign twofold material to the art of dialectic, "necessary" material for demonstrating and "probable" material for disputing ("captious" material I relegate to the Sophists as repugnant to art). In doing so they seem to act just as if someone should say that tailoring propounds a theory of producing a toga, from either black cloth or red cloth. After all, the art of sewing is precisely the same, no matter what cloth you use to make a garment, and the art of discussing is precisely the same, from whatever matter you construct an argument. Aristotle teaches the same rules of constructing both a probable and a necessary argument. . . . Since the same argument can be both necessary and probable, the distinction is irrelevant to the art of discourse. ("Lecture on Chapter 12" 219)

It is the syllogism, being the fundamental form of thought, that unites the kinds of reasoning by underlying all the forms of argumentation: enthymemes, inductions, deductions, examples, dilemmas, sorites, and so forth. Melanchthon indicates the importance of the syllogism in *Elementorum* when he applies Aristotle's *Analytics* to rhetoric (6v, 86)[41] and analyzes the *status* as a conclusion in the main syllogism underlying the case (11v, 117).[42] Ramus also considers textual analysis a process of "cutting out from the parts of the continuous discourse the many syllogisms which you see in it" and "forming the sum total of the discourse into one syllogism" (*Dialecticae institutiones* [1543] 48r; trans. Rummel, *Humanist-Scholastic Debate* 163). Fraunce insists that each form of argument is at base a syllogism:

> For an Enthymeme is but a contracted and short syllogism: An example, but an argument from the like or equal, . . . and no argumentation of itself without the help of a syllogism: An Induction, which is called the Socratical Argumentation, is but an argument concluded by a syllogism from the enumeration of parts: A Sorites, but an Enthymematical progression by certain degrees. . . . Lastly, a Dilemma is nothing else, but an argument from the contraries or opposites. . . . Nor in that

> called *biaion* . . . is there any new disposition or art of consequence, but only that of syllogism. (*Lawiers Logike* 99r–100r)

These beliefs are common to the northern humanist logic manuals of the period.[43]

When describing the relationship between dialectic and rhetoric, Renaissance humanists either subordinate logic to rhetoric or simply unite the arts under the canopy of "discourse." Either way they all agree that logic and rhetoric (and grammar) are interconnected language arts, naming different dimensions of the same speech act. Valla in *Dialecticae disputationes contra Aristotelicos* (1438) subordinates logic to be a subdivision of rhetoric: "What else is dialectics than a species of confirmation and refutation. These are parts of invention; invention is one of the five parts of rhetoric. Logic is the use of the syllogism. Does not the orator use the same? Certainly he does, and not only that but also the enthymeme and the epichereme, in addition to the induction etc." (*Opera* 693; trans. Monfasani, *George* 304–5).[44] Melanchthon wrote his logic manual *Erotemata dialectices* (1547) as a companion to his rhetoric, believing that Aristotle's *Analytics* and Cicero's *Topica* both belong to rhetoric.[45] In *Elementorum* he explains, "For if Rhetoric is not only concerned with matters that are forensic and persuasive but in general with all matters relating to the subject at hand, no one can in any way divorce it from Dialectics, whose function is to teach with efficiency" (6r; 84). Wilson in his *Art of Rhetoric* is very clear that logic holds a necessary place in rhetoric: "The places of logic, as I said, cannot be spared for the confirmation of any cause. For who is he that in confirming a matter will not know the nature of it, the cause of it, the effect of it, what is agreeing thereunto, what likeness there is betwixt that and other things, what examples may be used, what is contrary, and what can be said against it? Therefore I wish that every man should desire and seek to have his logic perfect before he look to profit in rhetoric, considering the ground and confirmation of causes is for the most part gathered out of logic" (145). Repeating that dialectic treats of matters in a general way (i.e., *theses*) and rhetoric regards both the general and the particular questions (i.e., *theses* and *hypotheses*), Wilson echoes Cicero:

> Things generally spoken, without all circumstances, are more proper unto the logician, who talketh of things universally, without respect of person, time, or place. And yet notwithstanding, Tully doth say that whosoever will talk of a particular matter must remember that within the same also is comprehended a general. As for example, if I shall ask this question, "Whether it be lawful for William Conqueror to invade England and win it by force of armor?," I must also consider this, "Whether it be lawful for any man to usurp power, or it be not lawful?" That if the greater cannot be borne withal, the less cannot be neither. (46)

That the rhetorical topics are added upon the logical and are not a different kind of proof is evident when the schoolmaster at Reading, Leonard Cox (c. 1495–c. 1549), teaches in his *The Arte or Crafte of Rhethoryke* (c. 1530) that the rhetorical places must be reduced to their logical core in order to judge them (48). In the popular textbook *Oratoriae Libri Duo* (1629) that covers all five canons of rhetoric, Charles Butler gives a quite extensive treatment of logic in book 2, drawing from Cicero, Quintilian, and Aristotle.[46] In his grammar text, Gill makes clear the interrelations of the arts when he comments that just as the rhetorician uses logic, so he also uses grammar (*Logonomia Anglica* [1619] 151). All three dimensions work in the creation of ideas and in the framing of them into forms, but they remain separable for pedagogical purposes.

Those who merely unite the arts usually reduce the definition of rhetoric from discourse in general to the embellishment of speech and enlarge dialectic from its focus on the most fundamental of idea relationships to the invention and evaluation of all subject matter. These humanists nevertheless insist that discourse is both dialectical and rhetorical at once. Agricola, for example, in *De inventione dialectica* moves from rhetoric into dialectic the precepts for not only teaching but also moving and pleasing, since all three are necessary for convincing an audience (book 3). He defines the arts of the trivium as follows:

> All language has as its object that someone should make someone else share in his thoughts. Therefore, it is apparent that there should be three things in every speech: the speaker, the hearer and the subject-matter. Consequently, three points should be observed when speaking: that what the speaker intends should be understood; that the person addressed should listen avidly; and what is said should be plausible and should be believed. Grammar, which deals with the method of speaking correctly and clearly, teaches us how to achieve the first goal. The second is taught by rhetoric, which provides us with linguistic embellishment and elegance of language, along with all the baits for capturing ears. Dialectic will lay claim to what remains, that is, to speak convincingly on whatever matter is included in a speech. (192; trans. Mack in "Humanist Rhetoric" 86).[47]

Similar to Agricola, Sturm considers grammar, dialectic, and rhetoric the three divisions of the art of "discourse or oration":

> For the duty of the grammarian is to recommend precepts of pure speech, as if rules. Dialecticians distinguish true from false conclusions and explain the kinds of argumentations, by which necessary things are separated from the merely probable, permanent things from transitory, pure things from corrupted ones. But rhetoricians adorn this truth more splendidly, defend it more bravely, commend it more delightfully . . . so that no discovery or work of man seems to be more admirable than well expressed and eloquent prudence, or prudent and wise eloquence. ("Lauingen School" 212)

In contrast to Agricola, Sturm still gives to rhetoric all five departments while also expanding the concerns of dialectic. In his *Partitiones oratoriae* (1539), rhetoric covers invention, arrangement, style, memory, and delivery, and in his *Partitiones dialecticae* (1539), he acknowledges that rhetoric has five parts and gives to dialectic three parts: invention, judgment, and arrangement.[48] Influenced by both Agricola and Sturm, Ramus draws similar distinctions while keeping the three subjects united in the trivium. The difference with Ramus is that his divisions among grammar, logic, and rhetoric are mutually exclusive in order to eradicate messy overlaps and thereby, so he claims, make instruction more efficient:

> The whole of dialectic concerns the mind and reason, whereas rhetoric and grammar concern language and speech. Therefore dialectic comprises, as proper to it, the arts of invention, arrangement, and memory; . . . To grammar for the purposes of speaking and writing well belong etymology in interpretation, syntax in connection, prosody in the pronunciation of short and long syllables, and orthography in the correct rules for writing. From the development of language and speech only two proper parts will be left for rhetoric, style and delivery; rhetoric will possess nothing proper and of its own beyond these. (*Arguments* 105)

Because Ramus so severely separates dialectic and rhetoric, the ties between the two subjects dissolve later on.[49] But as long as these three arts belong to one unified theory of discourse, the instruction itself prevents this severe division. In fact because of his primary focus on dialectic in his textual analyses, Ramus's commentaries unavoidably point out the argumentative function of figures.[50] With numerous quotations from poetry to exemplify arguments in Ramist logic textbooks, Tuve argues that the Ramist emphasis on the logical basis of all discourse makes more evident the inextricable connections between argument and style (342).

One troublesome aspect of Renaissance theorizing is that the boundaries around these arts are not always defined as precisely as they should be. They are often expressed in overly simplified dualisms and sometimes inconsistent ways even within single texts or authors. These inadequate descriptions reflect theoretical naïveté, however, rather than the true beliefs of the pedagogues, who always undermine the dualisms by insisting upon their unity. Unfortunately it is these oversimplifications, isolated and taken out of context, that scholars have used to produce reductive descriptions of these arts for this period.

One common simplification is the separation of the arts along the lines of content and style. Melanchthon, for example, says at one point in his *Elementorum* that dialectic provides "the bare matter, while rhetoric adds, so to speak, the vesture of words" (5v, 83).[51] In his "Reply to Pico," he adopts a similar position, saying that dialectics "shows the method (*via*) of teaching" and rhetoric "shows by what sort of words things should be explained" (trans. Breen 56). Yet he also explains that eloquence is composed of both dialectic and rhetoric, which are "conjoined by nature" (57).[52] Peacham too divides by content and style, knowledge and speech: "When of late I had considered the needful assistance that the one of these do require of the other, that wisdom do require the light of Eloquence, and Eloquence the fertility of Wisdom, and saw many good books of Philosophy and precepts of wisdom set forth in English, and a very few of Eloquence: I was of a sudden moved to take this little Garden in hand" ("Dedicatory Epistle" [1577] A.ii.v). But he is also careful to warn that when wisdom and eloquence are not united, calamity results:

> Many not perceiving the nigh and necessary conjunction of these two precious Jewels do either affect fineness of speech and neglect the knowledge of things, or

> contrariwise covet understanding and condemn the art of Eloquence: and therefore it cometh to pass that such take great pains and reap small profits: they ever seek and never find the thing they would fainest have, the one sort of these speak much to small purpose, and the other (though they be wise) are not aptly to express their meaning. (A.iii.r)[53]

Another common, but overly simple, division separates dialectic and rhetoric into reason and speech, a division not restricted to Ramists.[54] Soarez, for example, declares, on the one hand, that speech and reason are "so similar that the Greeks, who were foremost not only in thinking but also in speaking, used the same word for both" (110). On the other, he separates them, saying that speech is but "the companion and interpreter of reason" (112). To be eloquent, however, speech must be kept "in close union with reason" (112). Wilson also calls logic the art of reason (*Rule of Reason* B.i.r) and rhetoric the art of speech (*Art of Rhetoric* 45). Yet rhetoric includes logic, and the truly eloquent person is the wise man, who can find "the reasons that best serve to further our cause" (52) and "can plainly, distinctly, plentifully, and aptly utter both words and matter, and in his talk can use such composition that he may appear to keep a uniformity . . . in the uttering of his sentence" (187).[55]

A third distinction separates these two arts according to the functions of oratory that each accomplishes: dialectic's purpose is to teach and rhetoric's to delight and move. Melanchthon also makes this division: "The distinction, to put it perhaps more properly, is that the end or purpose of Dialectics is to teach, but the function of Rhetoric is to move and stimulate the minds and thus to affect a person." Of course since "the rhetorician cannot do without a method of teaching," "dialectics must be used to show what virtue is, and what are its causes, its degrees and its effects. But when we exhort people to be virtuous, the principles of Rhetoric must be followed" (*Elem.* 6r, 85–86). This distinction sounds as though dialectic and rhetoric produce different genres of discourse, but Melanchthon does not hold this belief, for he also declares that every speech/oration has as purposes to give knowledge and prescribe action, and so both arts are always necessary in any genre (8r). Even the philosopher must combine dialectic and rhetoric in order to speak so as to communicate, as Melanchthon explains in his "Reply to Pico":

> As a matter of fact I call a philosopher one who when he has learned and knows things good and useful for mankind, takes a theory (*doctrina*) out of academic obscurity and makes it practically useful in public affairs, and instructs men about natural phenomena, or religions, or about government. Moreover, however much you would relegate the orator to the forum alone, nevertheless those [barbarians] whom you defend have undertaken to explain those parts of philosophy which cannot be illuminated without eloquence. Now first of all, though there is more than one way of saying a thing, yet when we wish to communicate our mind's cogitations to others, it requires the use of a very definite kind of speech to set forth what we are talking about correctly and in order, with words that are known and are rightly put together. This should be a characteristic common to every form of discourse.

> Take those arts which can be considered pretty nearly speechless, Arithmetic and Geometry, yet each must be taught by use of proper words and some kind of method and system if it is to be understood. Without eloquence and without those arts which are comprised in eloquence it is in no wise possible to search out and illustrate the other disciplines, the subject matter of physics, ethics, and theology. (trans. Breen 58)

This relationship Melanchthon further underscores by adding a fourth genre to rhetoric, the didactic (*didaskalikon*), so that the genre of teaching can no longer be relegated to dialectic as a separate discipline (6v).[56] Like Melanchthon, Keckermann distinguishes logic and rhetoric according to their ends: logic teaches and rhetoric more principally moves and delights (*Systema* 1392). Also like Melanchthon, however, he will put all genres of discourse within rhetoric, the universal art of speech (1394), dividing between "dogmatic" and "affective" genres (*Systematis Rhetorici Specialis* 1587).

A fourth division distinguishes the two arts by the kind of style appropriate to each. This distinction, passed along by Quintilian, separates discourse into two basic genres: "there are two kinds of speech, the continuous which is called rhetoric, and the concise which is called dialectic (the relation between which was regarded by Zeno as being so intimate that he compared the latter to the closed fist, the former to the open hand)" (2.20.7). Veltkirchius echos this comment in his commentary on *De copia:* "Dialectic is a direct means of treating and learning something by knowing how to break down something into its parts and investigate them separately and jointly by means of certain questions. Rhetorical invention and dialectical invention are nearly the same. The only difference is in style. Rhetoric requires a more copious treatment of matters than does dialectic and thus employs means of sprucing things up, amplifying them, comparing them, and employing various figures" (186v; trans. Boswell). Wilson echoes this comment in his logic manual:

> Both these Arts are much like saving that Logic is occupied about all matters, and doth plainly and nakedly set forth with apt words the sum of things by the way of Argumentation. Again of the other side Rhetoric useth gay painted Sentences, and setteth forth those matters with fresh colors and goodly ornaments, and that at large.
>
> Insomuch, that Zeno being asked the difference between Logic and Rhetoric, made answer by Demonstration of his hand, declaring that when his hand was closed, it resembled Logic, when it was open & stretched out, it was like Rhetoric. (*Rule of Reason* B.ii.r–v)[57]

This distinction is a misquotation of Cicero, whose more careful precision grants to the eloquent speaker expertise in the genres of both the logician's debate and the rhetorician's oration:

> The man of perfect eloquence should, then, in my opinion possess not only the faculty of fluent and copious speech which is his proper province, but should also acquire that neighboring borderland science of logic; although a speech is one thing

> and a debate another, and disputing is not the same as speaking, and yet both are concerned with discourse—debate and dispute are the function of the logicians; the orator's function is to speak ornately. Zeno, the founder of the Stoic school, used to give an object lesson of the difference between the two arts; clenching his fist he said logic was like that; relaxing and extending his hand, he said eloquence was like the open palm. . . . I therefore expect this perfect orator of ours to be familiar with all the theory of disputation which can be applied to speaking. (*Orator* 32.113–14)

Quintilian later on in his discussion actually declares that dialectic "is really a concise form of oratory" (2.21.13) and considers it identical with conversation (3.4.11). Similarly Renaissance rhetoricians actually opt for Cicero's inclusiveness. Veltkirchius, for example, follows his above distinction between dialectic and rhetoric with the declaration "No orator can truly be eloquent without dialectic. Without it he is merely garrulous and does not know how to treat and manage anything systematically" (186v).

Occasionally in the seventeenth century, we begin to see Aristotle's distinctions between the arts seep into some rhetoric manuals (perhaps because perceived as compatible with the definition of rhetoric in the *Ad Herennium*). But even in these rare cases, Aristotle's distinctions have been merely overlaid upon the Ciceronian curriculum.[58] The three authors from those surveyed who are the most Aristotelian are Keckermann, Vossius, and Lamy.

Keckermann defines logic as reason and assigns to it the role of teaching among experts; rhetoric is "the art of having and arranging speeches with regard to popular knowledge and excitement of souls" (*Systema* 1392–93). Yet like the humanists before him, Keckermann also defines rhetoric more broadly as "language," both "familiar" for private conversation and "serious" for more formal occasions (1394). As we have already seen, he pulls all the types of discourse into rhetoric, placing the dialectical genres, like Melanchthon does, under a category he calls "dogmatic" rhetoric (*Systematis* 1587).

Vossius's *Rhetorices contractae* is, as Thomas Conley notes, "the most 'Aristotelian' of any treatise on rhetoric of the time" (*Rhetoric* 160). Distinguishing logic, dialectic, and rhetoric more exactly along the lines Aristotle does, Vossius says the first and second arts establish and teach among experts absolute and probable knowledge respectively, and the third makes use of popular knowledge in order to move the will and emotions of a lay audience (1.1.5–6). Similar to Aristotle, he also says that rhetoric is "the faculty of seeing in each instance what is likely to lead to persuasion" (1.1.3; trans. Conley, *Rhetoric* 161). But Vossius only follows Aristotle in definitions of the arts and in making memory separate from rhetoric. Otherwise, referring to rhetoric as "the science of good speaking" (1.1.1), Vossius teaches the precepts common in the standard curriculum.[59]

Later on in the century, Lamy had clearly separated reason from speech and explanation from persuasion. Reason belongs to philosophy, whose first part is "call'd Logick" (5.92) and whose concern is knowledge of truth acquired through Descartes's new methods of rationalism, not through syllogistic reasoning or topical invention (which, as he interprets, only rehearses the already known or supposed [5.91, 104–5]). Rhetoric is the art of persuasion directed toward the recalcitrant audience whose sentiments must be changed: "When a truth is eagerly contested, unless we be blinded with Interest, Perverseness, or Passion, good proof is sufficient to convince us; . . . But when the controversy is with people that are not fond of the truth; that are perverse in their inclinations, and prepossess'd by their Passions, Reason is too weak, and we must make use of cunning" (5.90). Hence Lamy separates rhetoric out as a subgenre of the art of speaking, knowing that by doing so he counters the immediate tradition: "Though the Arts of Speaking and Persuading are both comprehended under the name of Rhetoric by several great Masters, yet it is not to be denied but there is great difference betwixt them. Every man who speaks well, has not the secret of working upon the Affections, or working to his side, such as were before of a contrary opinion; and this is call'd to persuade" (5.88–89). Yet the actual content of both arts retains the traditional Ciceronian contours. He still allots to rhetoric its five departments (5.89), emphasizes the importance of "good proof" (5.90), and reviews even if briefly the logical topics, the *thesis* and *hypothesis*, the three primary genres, the *stases,* and the particular topics appropriate to each in order to aid invention (5.91–107).[60] It is true that Lamy assigns the finding and ordering of matter to the "Art of Thinking," but though it "has its [own] bounds," it must still be included in the art of speaking (1.6). It is also true that Lamy devotes only one book to invention and four books to style, but this instruction in style applies to the art of speaking generally and includes subject matter, disposition, and delivery.

A second troublesome aspect of Renaissance theorizing occurs in those who shift between Aristotle's view of rhetoric as a mere tool of persuasion and Cicero's as the art of good speech.[61] This confusion is in Quintilian, who, on the one hand, treats eloquence as a moral ideal: "eloquence has its fountain-head in the most secret springs of wisdom" (12.2.6); and on the other, as skilled dexterity: "to be eloquent is a far less achievement than to be an orator" (12.1.21). The problem continues in some Renaissance texts. Trebizond, for example, sometimes, like Cicero, has the term refer to "aptness of speech," to discourse that "knows how to succor the afflicted, is able to encourage those who are cast down, does not hesitate to offer safety to the despairing, is not ignorant of ways to free people from dangers and preserve men in their city and their very own homes" ("Oration" 33). Sometimes, like Aristotle, Trebizond has the term refer to the instrument of persuasion that can be used by both the good and the wicked: "If the eloquent are indeed wicked, then let them be punished for having abandoned all virtue. We don't think we ought to do anything different in this matter than we do with gladiators and assassins: when they have used their arms wickedly against the state or against some citizen, they themselves, rather than their arms, are removed" (34). Trebizond sometimes identifies "bad speaking" with wickedness, correspondent with "bad doctors," "crafty lawyers," and "vicious steersman" (34), and sometimes equivocally with merely technical ineptness or "inarticulateness" (33).[62] A similar tension, although not as pronounced, is in Soarez, who insists, on the one hand, that rhetoric is the ability to speak well, which "means to speak the best of thoughts with carefully chosen words" (118). On the other Soarez sometimes equates rhetoric with the "power" of speech to persuade (118) and hence worries that "if we were to teach the ability to speak to people who lack [integrity and utter discretion], we would certainly not be training orators but would be providing mad men with weapons" (120). Of course such vicious speakers would not deserve the name of orators and would indeed be "mad," but the issue regarding whether the study of rhetoric produces the good man remains in Soarez unexamined. This ambiguity is surprising given the explicit identification Soarez makes between true eloquence and Christian morality:

> But to draw greater profit from eloquence, we must carefully purify it by Christian teaching. Just as a conscientious farmer makes a vine more fruitful and better to behold by trimming it with his pruning knife when it runs wild and spreads out rather freely in all directions, in the same way eloquence will recover its marvelous beauty, if there is a pruning of the vanity of errors into which it has fallen through the fault of men ignorant of God's laws. Let license in the matter of lying, then, be banished, that license which is sternly forbidden by divine law but which Quintilian and ancient teachers of oratory allow a speaker. Check all boldness and the disgraceful fault of tearing others to pieces by infamous, insulting, and abusive language, which I could wish Demosthenes and Cicero had not indulged too much. Let pride and hankering for vain praise which blunts keenness of mind be pruned away. Let it be understood that it is wicked to envelop an audience in darkness so that they do not perceive the truth; or by speaking, to corrupt their decisions and their way of thinking, which was done time and again by Greek and Roman orators.
>
> After these numerous and serious faults have been eliminated, the divine and heavenly beauty of Christian eloquence will promptly stand forth. It will be all the more brilliant and illustrious in proportion as it will be applied more earnestly to the profit of all men and to proclaiming the praises of Almighty God who gave speech to man for the preservation of society and the union of mankind. (113–14)[63]

The tension is greatest in Ramus, however. On the one hand, he clearly advocates that for a complete education one must study all the humanistic arts, including moral philosophy and Christian theology. On the other he nevertheless insists that grammar, dialectic, and rhetoric are entirely separate from moral philosophy, being instrumental arts only. These three language arts are not moral virtues, but "virtue[s] of the mind and the intelligence," whose "followers can still be men of the utmost moral depravity" (*Arguments* 87). Prudence, the center of these arts, is also "not a moral virtue, but a virtue of the intelligence and mind" (87). He argues vehemently against Quintilian's claim that the orator "cannot be perfect unless he is a good man," because "rhetoric is not an art which explains all the virtuous qualities of character" (84) and because moral philosophy does not fit into any of the proper parts of rhetoric (86–87) or dialectic (88). This refusal to allow overlaps among the arts applies only to their definitions, not to their use, however, for Ramus agrees that all must be used together by the best of speakers (90–91).

Despite insufficient attention among some to reconciling the moral and instrumental conceptions of the art, Renaissance rhetoricians all agree, however, that good speaking equates with moral probity and that the language arts are designed to create the *uomo universale,* the man whose humanity, which is based in reason and speech, has been perfected.[64] Valla proclaims that the true orator must be a good man (Seigel 144). In Erasmus there is no equivocation, for Christ, as the divine *Logos,* which Erasmus argues should be translated not as "Word" (*Verbum*) but as "Speech" (*Sermo*), is both the Father's eloquent discourse and the ideal orator whom all should imitate.[65] As Marjorie O'Rourke Boyle has noticed, to Erasmus "God is the supreme author who has engraved his literature both in his Son and in the human spirit. By focusing on Christ the theologian discovers how to read this text. By imitating Christ the theologian acquires godly eloquence and enhances his own humanity, which was created through that divine discourse. . . . Christ [is] an eloquent persuasion to an audience which comes into its humanity in the imitation of the holy colloquy" (101). Similarly Vives acknowledges the arts as moral training: "The branches of learning are called humanistic, since they make us human. They have their source in God, to make us good men" (*De tradendis disciplinis* 293). Melanchthon declares that "this method of preparing a speech makes manners more civilized" (*Elem.* 32v, 222). Sturm writes that "nothing in the nature of things cultivates morality as does the study of letters" (*De literarum* [1538] 132; trans. Tinsley in "Johann Sturm's Method" 28). Ben Jonson, the poet, also avers "the impossibility of any man's being the good Poet, without first being a good Man" ("Dedicatory Epistle" 12). Late in the seventeenth century, Lamy still asserts that "this Art is no where to be caught so methodically as in the precepts of Morality" (5.110).

Besides these statements all these rhetoricians condemn sophistry as evil and, like Cicero, equate right reason with moral virtue. Erasmus's postulation of this relationship serves as a representative example of a commonplace belief among these educators: "Virtue is a habit of mind in harmony with reason" (*De conscribendis epistolis* 108). Melanchthon's definition of virtue is equally representative: "It is a habit of the will inclining men to be obedient to the judgment of right reason" (*Elem.* 8v, 102).[66]

Like the classical curriculum, so Renaissance schoolroom exercises unite the three language arts. First the reading method applies grammatical, logical, and rhetorical precepts to the interpretation of any text, whether poetry, history, philosophy, epistle, oratory, scripture, prayer, musing, or creative work. Melanchthon explains that the language arts lay down principles not only for directing the preparations of the speaker but also "for prudently evaluating and understanding the writings of others . . . who indeed without this method can in no way be understood" (*Elem.* 4v, 76–77).[67] Second the writing of the composition exercises—the transformations of model texts, the *progymnasnata,* and the *gymnasmata*—all depend upon the successful integration of these three language arts.[68] Third handlists of figures feature dialectical, grammatical, and rhetorical forms, effectually subordinating dialectic and grammar to rhetoric in discussions of style. Commenting on this inclusion of argument forms in the figure domain, Crane observes, "It is confusing to discover in an epitome of tropes and figures much the same material as in a treatise which purports to deal with logic" (6).

The Question of the Plain Style

In addition to uniting all genres of human communication and both reason and speech within one art, Greco-Roman and Renaissance rhetoricians further the insight of the centrality of figures to discourse by teaching that all styles, which range over high, middle, and low registers and the myriad of qualities that make up human expression, are created by means of figures. The distinction between an unfigured plain style and a figured rhetorical style simply does not exist in this rhetorical tradition. Even those who retain a distinction between figured and unfigured language still advocate that all styles and genres partake of figured language. This absence of a plain style without figures in the rhetoricians' teachings further undermines this already problematic distinction between figured and unfigured language, underscores rhetoric's jurisdiction over all genres of discourse, and ensures that decorum remains a suitably flexible standard, stabilized by congruency among all elements and not aligned rigidly with a particular species of form or style.

The notion of a plain style that is nonrhetorical, unfigured, objective, and transparent derives from the precepts of Aristotle and from Scholastic philosophers who demote style to expression and rhetoric to merely "painted" language. By so doing they oppose a dialectical plain style to an ornate rhetorical one. The first is the good style, and the second is the bad. The notion of a nonrhetorical plain style can only come from precepts that reduce the domain of rhetoric to particular genres, restrict figures to poetic alterations of language, and then associate figures with rhetoric, passion, and ambiguity. This fundamental difference between the Renaissance humanists and the philosophers in the definition of a plain style is one of the grounds of the debate between philosophy and rhetoric in the Renaissance. In attributing this basic binary between the oratorical and plain styles to Renaissance rhetoricians' precepts, modern scholars reflect the philosophers' dualistic bias and have failed to understand the rhetoricians' more complex, albeit inadequately explained, view.[69]

The Notions of Philosophers and Scientists

Aristotle, remember, associates poetic ornamentation with an oratorical high style. Debora K. Shuger emphasizes the close kinship in Aristotle's mind between the rhetorical and poetic styles by pointing out that Aristotle uses in the *Poetics* the term *dignity* to describe the language of tragedy (1449a) and again in the *Rhetoric* for the oratorical style that departs from ordinary language (3.2 1404b8). "Similarly," she goes on, "in the *Rhetoric,* Aristotle offers rules for creating loftiness of style (3.6 1407b26), where the Greek word translated as 'loftiness' is actually *ogkos* or 'massiveness'—a term Aristotle associates [in the *Poetics*] with the bulk and richness of epic (1459b)" (17–18).[70] This high style has three variations, each belonging to the three separate genres of epideictic, deliberative, and judicial oratory (3.12 1413b3). The one that most lends itself to written form, the epideictic is "most literary" and aims to display artistic skill (3.12 1414a16).[71] Deliberative requires the more spontaneous, passionate, rougher, less precise style for "actual tussle" (3.12 1413b18). The forensic is finished and precise but with fewer artifices and less passion, since the judge "can take the whole thing in better, and judge of what is to the point and what is not" (3.12 1414a10–14). Aristotle differentiates these oratorical high styles from an ordinary, nonmetaphorical language necessary in logic and philosophy. He specifically rejects metaphor from the language of science, saying,

"Metaphors are poetical and so . . . as to knowledge of nature [they are] unsatisfactory" (*Meteorology* 357a 25–27). He also rejects metaphors in reasoning: "And if one should not argue in metaphors, it is clear too that one should not define either by metaphors or what is said in metaphors" (*Posterior Analytics* 97b 37–38). This fixed segregation of styles according to genres encourages the notion of an unfigured plain style for science and an elevated, figured style for public oratory and poetry.[72]

Scholasticism evinces this influence of Aristotle. Arising in the twelfth century due to the newly available Arab and Jewish scholarship on Aristotle's logical works, medieval Scholasticism elevates dialectic as the most important of the arts. Dialectic provides the method for philosophy, teaching, theological debate, and scriptural hermeneutics. Grammar and rhetoric become mere preliminaries, with grammar, the instrument of eloquence, imparting the virtues of correctness and plainness; and with rhetoric a mere ancillary of grammar instruction, no more than poetic decoration useful for literature, public ceremony, and preaching.[73] John of Salisbury (c. 1115–80) in his *Metalogicon* (1159 A.D.) is representative of this orientation. He assigns to grammar the rules governing a very limited group of tropes and schemes, the only precepts of rhetoric mentioned in the whole book, with the advice that a figure, which is an "excusable departure from the rule" and belongs to poetry (54), be "used only out of necessity or for ornamentation" (56). He treats grammar, which is part of logic (37), as the means for developing eloquence or "the power of verbal expression" (10, 52), cites Augustine and Isidore of Seville as his sources (54–56), and focuses only on correctness and clarity as the virtues of speech (37–38).

This attitude toward rhetoric as "fluff," the fineries of style, is again evident in the charges the Renaissance scholastics bring against the rhetoricians. The scholastics call the rhetoricians, as Erika Rummel documents, nothing but "grammarians, speechifiers, and Greeklings" or philologists and "poets" who "are all imagination and lies" (*Humanist-Scholastic Debate* 11). In the famous 1485 epistolary exchange with Ermolao Barbaro (1454–93), Pico della Mirandola (1463–94) plays the role of the scholastic. He defends philosophers for slighting eloquence, which he defines as flowery words, and criticizes rhetoric as inherently ornamental and hence sophistical and meretricious:

> We should not be blamed for not having yoked eloquence to wisdom, since it is wicked to have joined them at all. For who would not condemn as detestable curly hair and makeup in an upright virgin? Who would not detest it in a Vestal? There is such a great opposition between the functions of the orator and the philosopher that they could not contradict one another more. For what is the office of the rhetor other than to lie, deceive, circumvent, practice sleight-of-hand tricks. It's your business, as you say, to turn black into white and white into black as you will; by means of speech to raise up, cast down, amplify, and diminish whatever you wish; and finally, to transform things themselves, as if by the magical force of eloquence, which you boast about, so that they assume whatever face and dress you wish, not appearing what they are in actuality, but what your will wants them to be—and even though they are not really transformed, they nevertheless appear that

way to your auditors. All this is nothing other than sheer lying, sheer imposture, sheer trickery, since by its nature it enlarges things through amplification or reduces them through diminishment, and by producing the deceptive harmony of words, like so many masks and simulacra, it dupes the minds of your auditors while it flatters them. Can there by affinity between this and the philosopher whose entire activity is consumed in discovering the truth and demonstrating it to others? (trans. Rebhorn, *Renaissance Debates* 59)[74]

The minimal attention in both Aristotle and the scholastics to means for creating linguistic clarity—they focus only on correctness of grammar and word choice—implies its naturalness and relative effortlessness. According to Pico philosophers "seek *what* to write, not *how;* or rather, [they] seek how to do so without the pomp and flowers of speech" (61), and philosophers, whose "chief business" is "to compose [their] minds, not [their] words," believe that auditors should look beyond the harshness and imperfections of their speech to the "gems" and "rare and precious furnishings" in their content (62).

Inasmuch as Scholasticism continued in English universities throughout the Renaissance, this perspective competed with that of the rhetoricians. Its influence can be seen on the poet Samuel Daniels (1562–1619), who in *A Defence of Rhyme* (1603) rejects rhetoric because in his mind it is associated with this artificially painted and empty high style:

> Eloquence and gay words are not of the substance of wit; it is but the garnish of a nice time, the Ornaments that do but deck the house of a State, and *imitatur publicos mores:* Hunger is as well satisfied with meat served in pewter or silver. Discretion is the best measure, the rightest foot in what habit soever it run. Erasmus, Rewcline, and More brought no more wisdom into the world with all their new revived words than we find was before . . . nor are the effects of all this great amass of eloquence so admirable or of that consequence, but that *impexa illa antiquitas* can yet compare with them. (Smith II.372)

Its influence also leads Francis Bacon (1561–1626) to criticize Sturm, Carr, and Ascham unfairly for paying more attention to words than to matter (*Advancement of Learning* I.iv.2) and Descartes to relegate rhetoric to one type of language use (I.6).

This perspective also fuels the efforts of seventeenth-century apologists for the new science, who popularize the idea of a nonrhetorical plain style for the serious work of the Royal Society of London.[75] Restricting eloquence or rhetoric to merely decorated speech, Thomas Sprat (1635–1713), the bishop of Rochester, wishes "that *eloquence* ought to be banish'd out of *civil Societies,* as a thing fatal to Peace and good Manners." Associating the figures with obscurity, Sprat advocates a style free from such devices:

> Who can behold . . . how many mists and uncertainties, these specious *Tropes* and *Figures* have brought on our Knowledge? . . . The only Remedy, that can be found for this *extravagance:* and that has been, a constant Resolution, [is] to reject all the amplifications, digressions, and swellings of style: to return back to the primitive

> purity, and shortness, when men deliver'd so many *things,* almost in an equal number of *words.* They have exacted from all their members, a close, naked, natural way of speaking; positive expressions; clear senses; a native easiness: bringing all things as near the Mathematical plainness, as they can: and preferring the language of Artizans, Countrymen, and Merchants, before that, of Wits, or Scholars. (*History of the Royal Society* [1667] 111–13)

In *Leviathan* (1651) Thomas Hobbes (1588–1679), like Aristotle, abolishes metaphors and other "Rhetorical figures" from proper speech because they tend "to the stirring up of Passion" (307), "openly profess deceit" (137), and lead to fallacious reasoning: "The Light of humane minds is Perspicuous Words, but by exact definitions first snuffed, and purged from ambiguity; *Reason* is the *pace;* Increase of *Science,* the *way;* and the Benefit of man-kind, the *end.* And on the contrary, Metaphors, and senseless and ambiguous words, are like *ignes fatui;* and reasoning upon them, is wandering amongst innumerable absurdities" (116). Robert Plot (1640–96), in the *National History of Staffordshire* (1686), explains his style: "I shall make all *Relations* (as formerly) in a plain familiar Stile, without the Ornaments of *Rhetorick,* least the matter be obscured by too much *illustration;* and with all the imaginable brevity that perspicuity will bear" (1; qtd. in R. F. Jones 83). And Alexander Ross (1590–1654), another member of the Royal Society, reminds his fellow scientists that "Aristotle in his Topics will have us to avoid Metaphors, which cast a mist upon the thing defined; every Metaphor being more obscure than proper words" (*Medicus Medicatus* [1645] 20–21). Equating rhetoric with passionate expression, Ross gives this advice: "If you lay the fault of this upon your Rhetorical expressions, I must answer you, that Rhetoric in such a subject may well be spared: use your Rhetoric when you will work upon the affections, but not when you will inform the understanding; for in this regard you do but cloud, not clear the intellect" (*The Philosophical Touch-stone* [1645] 92; qtd. in Williamson 277).

The Notions of Rhetoricians

In contrast to the philosophers, the rhetoricians, whether classical, humanist, or Ramist, do not strictly conflate the low style with philosophical genres, unfigured language, and the virtue of perspicuity, nor the high style with the oratorical and poetic genres, ornamentation, ambiguity, copia, and verbal display. Rather all genres of discourse exhibit low, middle, and high registers, all registers and styles partake of figures, and all styles to be good must be perspicuous and suited to subject, audience, speaker, occasion, genre, purpose, and civic responsibility. When appropriately used, all levels of style provide adornment and, when faulty, mar the speech with kinds of excess. This more complex and flexible view of style avoids reductive dualisms and stereotypes and enables the rhetoricians better to achieve the aims the philosophers outline by better accounting for the elements of expression that create the good and bad styles. Whereas the philosophers oppose nature (ordinary language) and art (figured language), the rhetoricians treat the two as complements (all language is figured naturally, and all artistic uses of language figure it so as to imitate the natural figures requisite for one's meaning). The rhetoricians' discussion of the "plain style" illustrates their more nuanced approach. The quality of "plainness" has two meanings in humanist manuals: the lowest of registers, whose association with informality approximates conversation and casual deportment; and perspicuity, a fundamental virtue of style necessary in all registers. Both types of style result from art and mirror nature. The rhetoricians oppose the first to either more formal styles or to other faulty low styles. They oppose the second to either obscurity or "artificiality," faults once again possible in any level of utterance.[76]

The Low Style

The Renaissance inherits from classical sources three separate schemes for describing styles. The Romans use two of them, both deriving from earlier Greek traditions. The third comes from Hermogenes.

The first scheme is integral to the rhetorical curriculum and divides styles into what come to be known as the three *genera dicendi:* the plain, the intermediate, and the grand registers. Quintilian briefly introduces these three kinds of style as follows:

> The first would seem best adapted for instructing, the second for moving, and the third (by whichever name we call it) for charming or, as others would have it, conciliating the audience; for instruction the quality most needed is acumen, for conciliation gentleness, and for stirring the emotions force. Consequently it is mainly in the plain style that we shall state our facts and advance our proofs, though it should be borne in mind that this style will often be sufficiently full in itself without any assistance whatever from the other two. The intermediate style will have more frequent recourse to metaphor and will make a more attractive use of figures, while it will introduce alluring digressions, will be neat in rhythm and pleasing in its reflexions; its flow, however, will be gentle, like that of a river whose waters are clear, but overshadowed by the green banks on either side. But he whose eloquence is like to some great torrent that rolls down rocks and "disdains a bridge" and carves out its own banks for itself, will sweep the judge from his feet, struggle as he may, and force him to go whither he bears him. (12.10.59–61)

All three are necessary and correct (12.10.58).

The second scheme serves as a way to indicate the quality of a style and does not become an instructional heuristic in the curriculum. Associated with regional practices and preferences in ancient times, this set of styles comprises the Attic, the Asiatic, and the Rhodian. Quintilian's description of these three styles is as follows:

> The distinction between the Attic and the Asiatic schools takes us back to antiquity. The former were regarded as concise and healthy, the latter as empty and inflated: the former were remarkable for the absence of all superfluity, while the latter were deficient alike in taste and restraint. The reason for this division, according to some authorities, . . . is to be found in the fact that, as Greek gradually extended its range into the neighboring cities of Asia, there arose a class of men who desired to distinguish themselves as orators before they had acquired sufficient command

> of the language, and who consequently began to express by periphrases what could have been expressed directly, until finally this practice became an ingrained habit. My own view, however, is that the difference between the two styles is attributable to the character both of the orators and the audiences whom they addressed: the Athenians, with their polish and refinement, refused to tolerate emptiness and redundance, while the Asiatics, being naturally given to bombast and ostentation, were puffed up with a passion for a more vainglorious style of eloquence. At a later period, the critics, to whom we owe this classification, added a third style, the Rhodian, which they asserted to lie midway between the two and to be a blend of both, since the orators of this school are neither so concise as the Attic nor redundant like the Asiatic school, but appear to derive their style in part from their national characteristics, in part from those of their founder. For it was Aeschines who introduced the culture of Athens at Rhodes, which he had chosen as his place of exile; and just as certain plants degenerate as a result of change of soil and climate, so the fine Attic flavour was marred by the admixture of foreign ingredients. Consequently certain of the orators of this school are regarded as somewhat slow and lacking in energy, though not devoid of a certain weight, and as resembling placid pools rather than the limpid springs of Athens or the turbid torrents of Asia. (12.10.16–19)

To call a style by one of these three titles was to pronounce a judgment upon a speech's quality, with Attic being the best and Asiatic the worst. These styles each included a wide variety of diverse manifestations, with speakers as different as Isocrates, Lysias, Demosthenes, Plato, Aristotle, and Pericles all being examples of the Attic or the good style (12.10.20–26).

At the time of Cicero, a group of Roman orators with a definite program to exalt the lucid, unemotional, unornamented, and severe style of the logician called themselves the "Attici," appropriating the term in order to equate their ideal of style with the "keen and exact judgment" of Attic oratory (Quintilian 12.10.20) and to criticize Cicero for his "Asiatic" exuberance. In the *Orator* Cicero objects to this reduction in the meanings of "Attic" and of the "ideal" style: "There are many kinds of Atticists: but these of our day apprehend the nature of one kind only. They think that the only one who attains the Attic norm is he who speaks in rough and unpolished style, provided only that he is precise and discriminating in thought. Their mistake is in assuming him to be the only one; they are quite right in calling him Attic" (7.28). That is, they are right in recognizing that this one style can be found in ancient Athens, when rhetoric flourished, but wrong in restricting the Attic style from including the wide range of registers extending from grandiloquence and "fiery force" to the "intellectual appeal" of the acute, subtle, and concise style and the "ease," "charm," and "exquisiteness" of the tempered style (5.20–21). Cicero argues that the true ideal showing keenness of judgment is represented by Demosthenes, the master of all good styles (29.104). A similar debate was still going on in Quintilian's day. Acknowledging those critics who preferred a "natural" plain style to a heightened, ornamented one, Quintilian responds by arguing for mastery of a range of styles (12.10.40–44).

The third method for teaching styles comes from Hermogenes, who describes them in a more nuanced way than his predecessors. Identifying twenty different ideas or characters of style, many of which can be combined within one speech, he enumerates the textual features or figures that create each one. The plain style—*saphēneia* or *claritas*—is not a register but one of these characters. Demosthenes is the master of all. This focus on characters derives from Isocrates,[77] and its mixture with the *genera dicendi* must have been a practice in ancient Greece, represented by Demetrius's fourfold set of the plain, the polished, the grand, and the forceful.

In the Renaissance rhetoricians frequently combine in their instruction the three *genera dicendi* with the Hermogenean characters. A few use the terms *Attic, Rhodian,* and *Asiatic* to name a separate assessment of quality. Occasionally these three designations simply become alternate names for the low, middle, and high registers, losing their association with evaluative judgments. To understand the rhetoricians' concept of the low or plain style, then, we must examine the precepts regarding stylistic register and figuration.

Stylistic Register

Because stylistic register depends upon and can be determined from many discourse elements that do not necessarily accompany each other, the low or plain style does not have one predictable identity and will be manifest in many subtypes. The low, middle, and high designations can compare subject matter (whether mundane, delightful, or lofty), emotional level (whether calm, temperate, or passionate), number of words (brief, moderate, or copious), degree of verbal elevation (unadorned, florid, or ornate), degree of polish (rustic, courtly, or majestic), degree of seriousness (trivial, pleasant, or solemn), degree of formality (conversational, academic, or ceremonial), functions of oratory (proving, delighting or moving), and even degree of quality (faulty, careful, or brilliant).[78] The complexity of elements contributing to the level of style permits various combinations, producing various subtypes of each. The low style, for example, can be associated with directness, concision, informality, rusticity, sincerity, simplicity, honesty, pointedness, subtlety, harshness, urbanity, humility, intimacy, artlessness, clarity, and so forth. In other words there can be both a direct and subtle low style, both a calm and forceful low style, both an urbane and a harsh low style, both an artful and artless low style. Many of these same qualities can also appear in a higher style, for urbanity and indirection can combine with elegance to produce a middle style, and harshness and force can combine with grandeur to create a high style. Since a subject matter may be high but its appropriate verbal treatment brief in order to create force, or since passion, copiousness, and ornateness may be combined with a low subject matter to create humor, and each of these two combinations may be expressed in poetry, in oratorical prose, or in conversation, placing particular utterances into mutually exclusive and rigidly distinct stylistic levels does not work.

The three *genera dicendi* are then flexible attributions, whose designations have meaning only in reference to each other and whose identity changes depending upon the kinds of comparisons being made. For example Cicero at one time associates the low style with little decoration, brevity, and clarity: "At the other extreme were the orators who were plain, to the point, explaining everything and making every point clear rather than impressive, using a refined, concise style stripped of ornament" (*Orator* 6.20). At another time he indicates that this low style can result from, on the one hand, a purposeful imitation of rusticity or, on the other, a polished neatness: "Within this class some were adroit but unpolished and intentionally resembled untrained and unskillful speakers; others had the same dryness of style, but were neater, elegant, even brilliant and to a slight degree ornate" (6.20). At still another time, Cicero declares that the plain style is not necessarily "devoid of vigour and force" (*De Oratore* 3.52.199). Quintilian similarly points out the variety of types possible:

> But eloquence cannot be confined even to these three forms of style. For just as the third style is intermediate between the grand and the plain style, so each of these three are separated by interspaces which are occupied by intermediate styles compounded of the two which lie on either side. For there are styles fuller or plainer than the plain, and gentler or more vehement than the vehement, while the gentler style itself may either rise to greater force or sink to milder tones. Thus we may discover almost countless species of styles, each differing from the other by some fine shade of difference. (12.10.66–67)

In the Renaissance Puttenham indicates that these various qualities of style combine in different ways so that the three general registers have varying manifestations: "Howsoever it be, we find that under these three principal complexions (if I may with leave so term them) high, mean and base style, there be contained many other humors or qualities of style, as the plain and obscure, the rough and smooth, the facile and hard, the plentiful and barren, the rude and eloquent, the strong and feeble, the vehement and cold styles, all which in their evil are to be reformed, and the good to be kept and used" (161). Lamy also insists that since the matter regulates the style and "everything subject to our thoughts being matter for Discourse, there are infinite diversity [*sic*] of Styles" (4.23).

This same complexity we find in the Greeks. Demetrius insists that except for the plain and the grand styles, which are polar opposites, "any style may combine with any other" (§37). Since the stylistic characters he describes can be mixed together to create a myriad of combinations, this complexity is most explicit in Hermogenes (1.1.215). Those Renaissance rhetoricians who combine Hermogenes with Cicero merely increase in visibility the variability of qualities that can be combined to create a style. Some in this group do not establish firm correspondences between the Hermogenean *ideas* and the levels of style. In his *Ecclesiastes* Erasmus with his usual resistance to systematization describes various styles by freely mixing together the Latin stylistic virtues with qualities Demetrius and Hermogenes discuss, listing, for example, *perspicuitas* (clarity), *aptum* (appropriateness), *probabilitas* (credibility), *evidentia* (sharpness), *prudentia* (sagacity), *adfectus* (emotions), *copia* (ampleness), *acrimonia* (pungency), *vehementia* (vehemence), *gravitas* (gravity), *jucunditas* (pleasantness), *splendor* (brilliance), *festivitas* (humor), *amplitudo* (richness), *dignitas* (excellence), *venustas* (charm), and *gratia* (grace).[79] These virtues he then later connects in flexible ways to the three *genera dicendi* or *character orationis* (3.162.209–47). Likewise Vives (*De ratione dicendi* 89ff), Sturm (*De universa* 15–30, 544, 569), and Vossius (*Commentariorum* 2:471) freely mix and match qualities and levels. Vives even adds stylistic characters to the list. He describes types of speech as vigorous (110), witty, solid, full, puerile (124), virile and mature (124), mild, grave (125), majestic, sober (126), severe (127), disgusting (128), pleasant (128), urbane (129), and so forth. Actually Vives explains that there are as many qualities of style as there are qualities of mind and character: "Speeches take their names from the state of mind of the speaker or from the quality of the things spoken about. Thus speech is called timid, angry, invidious, accusing, raving, free, furious, burning, excited, relaxed, sedate. . . . Likewise those names which are derived from virtues and vices as pious, just, moderate, temperate, strong, cautious, impious, blaspheming, slothful" (*De ratione dicendi* 123). Others, such as Trebizond (457) and Scaliger (4.1.440), subordinate the various Hermogenean characters to the three levels of style.[80]

The flexibility with which these designations of stylistic register must be taken becomes even more apparent when these rhetoricians, unlike the philosophers, apply these stylistic levels or the Hermogenean *ideas* to all the genres of discourse. Poetry, philosophy, history, epistles, oratory—none aligns universally with any one stylistic level or character. In fact as Cicero tells us, all genres must make use of all three of the *genera dicendi* as appropriate (*De Oratore* 3.55.211). Decorum after all prescribes that "no single kind of oratory suits every cause or audience or speaker or occasion" (3.44.210). As instances he mentions that epideictic oratory requires a lower, more middle style than do the higher deliberative and judicial orations (*Orator* 11.37–42; 19.65); tragedy requires a higher style than comedy, generally speaking (20.67). Hermogenes gives examples of all the *ideas* from Demosthenes's oratory and occasionally from the other genres.

Similarly Renaissance rhetoricians tend not to restrict various genres to particular levels of style.[81] In *De conscribendis epistolis* Erasmus must generalize more than he wishes to in order to describe the epistle as a genre. In this general description, he concedes that the letter "should resemble a conversation between friends" and thus "favours simplicity, frankness, humour, and wit" (20). Consequently he says, "Atticism is best suited to this genre, and a rather low style, closer to comedy than tragedy, or even lower than comic diction, provided that it is a learned simplicity" (21). However he prefaces this generalization with cautions against oversimplification, since the only rule without exception is the necessity to observe decorum. Arguing for appropriate flexibility, Erasmus instructs that "the letter should adapt itself to every kind of subject and circumstance" (19). As a result "those who try to impose a single form and style on this branch of writing are taking on a task that is both fruitless and absurd" (20). Letters, he says, can be dignified, unpretentious, elegant, amusing, powerful, soothing, pithy, modest, vivid, grave, verbose, brief, elaborate, technical, uncomplicated, laconic, artificial and embroidered, archaic, effusive, familiar, harsh, flattering, and so forth:

> A letter's style will not only conform to the topic, but, as befits any good go-between (for a letter performs the function of a messenger), it will take account of times and persons: it will not speak of the same subject on all occasions or to all persons alike; it will present itself in one guise to the old, in another to the young; its aspect will vary according as the person addressed is stern and forbidding, or of a more jovial nature; a courtier or a philosopher; an intimate acquaintance or a total stranger; a man of leisure or one engaged in active pursuits; a faithful companion or a false friend and ill-wisher. At the same time the style will also keep in mind the writer and not merely the recipient or the purpose for which it was sent. Therefore it will play the part of Mercury, as it were, transforming itself into every shape required by the topic at hand, yet in such a way that amid great variety it retains one feature unaltered, namely that of being always refined, learned, and sane. (19)

Likewise Day insists that styles of epistles vary to match subject matter, audience, and speaker ([1599] 1.4–5, 10) and will sometimes express vituperation (1.42), sometimes exhortation (1.50), conciliation (1.83), courtesy (1.99), consolation (1.112), reproach (1.136), accusation (2.4), humble apology (2.37), congratulation (2.67), and so forth.

Just as the epistle will exhibit all three registers and many qualities, so will the other genres. Scaliger applies all three levels and Hermogenean characters to poetry (4.1.440–62), acknowledging the inadequacies of the categories for strict classification of genres (4.1.448). Puttenham puts comedy and love poems in the middle style; tragedies, hymns, and histories in the high style; and pastorals and eclogues in the low style (165). But he emphasizes that the cardinal rule when determining level is decorum, thereby preventing his classification from becoming static: "But by reason of the sundry circumstances, that man's affairs are as it were wrapped in, this [decency] comes to be very much alterable and subject to variety, insomuch as our speech asketh one manner of decency, in respect of the person who speaks: another of his to whom it is spoken: another of whom we speak: another of what we speak, and in what place and time and to what purpose. And as it is of speech, so of all other our behaviors" (270). In *Clavis Scripturae Sacrae,* a book that provides a rhetorical analysis of scripture using the stylistic characters from both Greek and Latin sources, Flacius says the Bible has examples of all three stylistic registers (2:459, Shuger 73). In *Ecclesiastes* Erasmus acknowledges that sermons require all three (3.162.209–12). Sherry even draws examples of low, middle, and high styles from among Cicero's judicial orations ([1550] 22–24).

Stylistic levels vary not merely from work to work but even within single works. Each speech, poem, or tragedy will require, Cicero says, a suitable mixture of the three levels in order to meet the demands of its unique circumstances: "Consequently, at one moment we use a dignified style, at another a plain one, and at another we keep a middle course between the two; thus the style of our oratory follows the line of thought we take, and changes and turns to suit all the requirements of pleasing the ear and influencing the mind of the audience" (*De Oratore* 3.45.177). The delivery of each part must be varied: "The superior orator will therefore vary and modulate his voice; now raising and now lowering it, he will run through the whole scale of tones. He will also use gestures in such a way as to avoid excess" (*Orator* 18.59). What is necessary is a wise adaptability "to suit the business before us" (*De Oratore* 3.45.212). The *Rhetorica ad Herennium* advises similarly, "Thus, by means of the variation, satiety is easily avoided" (4.11.16). Quintilian uses the speeches of Ulysses, Nestor, and Menelaus all from Homer's *Iliad* to exemplify the high, middle, and low styles (12.10.64) and remarks that the orator "will use all styles, as circumstances may demand, and the choice will be determined not only by the case as a whole, but by the demands of the different portions of the case" (12.10.69). Hermogenes makes the same point about flexibility: different *ideas* are appropriate both for different utterances and for various parts of one speech:

> [Demosthenes] had so mastered political oratory that he was always combining styles everywhere. When he gave a deliberative speech, for example, he did not separate it rigorously from a judicial speech or a panegyrical speech, but mixed the characteristics of all three in the same speech, regardless of what kind of oratory he was practicing. . . . He uses each type [*idea*] when and where it should be used. . . . Therefore, as I said before, strictly speaking, it is not possible to find accurately in any of the ancient orators a single style, because it is clearly a mistake to use one and not to vary one's style. (1.1.216–21)

Hermogenes emphasizes that this flexibility is necessary for good speaking: "A so-called practical speech is one that is composed out of all the types of style previously discussed, not used one by one, but in some way blended with one another, as we said earlier. The orator who effects the best blend of these styles will create the best practical speech" (2.10.380).

Besides being necessary for suitable flexibility, stylistic variation also enables the speaker to accomplish successfully the three requisite functions of speech: to teach, to delight, and to move (*De Optimo Genere Oratorum* 1.3; *Brutus* 49.185).[82] Assigning one function to each stylistic level, Cicero therefore declares that every speaker must use all three styles: "For these three functions of the orator there are three styles, the plain style for proof, the middle style for pleasure, the vigorous style for persuasion; . . . Now the man who controls and combines these three varied styles needs rare judgment and great endowment; for he will decide what is needed at any point, and will be able to speak in any way which the case requires" (*Orator* 20.69–70).[83] But even this alignment is not firm in Cicero, for he also asserts that each level of style can exhibit all three of the primary functions of the orator. They all delight: "These three styles should exhibit a certain charm of colouring, not as a surface varnish but as permeating their arterial system" (*De Oratore* 3.52.199). All three "aim on the one hand at neatness of structure and grace in . . . employment of words and on the other hand at impressiveness in expressing . . . thoughts" (3.52.100). They all teach: Cicero says of the ideal, "The style must be in the highest possible degree pleasing and calculated to find its way to the attention of the audience, and . . . it must have the fullest possible supply of facts" (3.24.91). Also they all persuade: one who attains perfection in the plain, in the middle, or in the high style "is a great orator" (*Orator* 28.98–99). Like Cicero, Quintilian summarizes the characteristics of each stylistic level according to function and is also aware that each level of style can function simultaneously to teach, delight, and move. He says, for example, of the maxim and other epigrammatic forms, which are common features of the plain style, that they "strike the mind and often produce a decisive effect by one single blow, while their very brevity makes them cling to the memory, and the pleasure which they produce has the force of persuasion" (12.10.48).[84]

Renaissance rhetoricians repeat these principles. Vives instructs, "What I have said should be understood not only of the entire speech, but also of its parts, and sometimes of each cadence and period" (*De ratione dicendi* 130). He goes on, "The good speaker will employ the style demanded by the circumstances and not only for his major topic, but for each of its parts as well" (131). Erasmus does not associate each of the three *genera dicendi* with either teaching, delighting, or moving because he believes that all discourse must do all three to be effective (*Ecclesiastes* 2.272.536–49; 2.274.595–600).[85] Melanchthon teaches that the three levels of style "are intermingled, just as musicians mix tones" (*Elem.* 63v, 343). In *The Art of Prophecying* (1592), the preaching manual frequently taken to be the quintessential representative of the Puritan plain style, even William Perkins (1558–1602) advises that "in the doctrine he [the preacher] ought to be more moderate, in the exhortation more fervent and vehement" (672). The sermon ought to combine the qualities of soberness, moderation, gravity, truth-speaking, dignity, authority, zeal, graciousness, love, the "affections of the heart," simplicity, and perspicuity in order "to express the Majesty of the Spirit" and the integrity and holiness of the minister, and "to be lively and powerful" in stirring up "godly affections in other men" (671–72). Perkins, it is true, does not mention the *genera dicendi,* nor does he give any specific precepts for how to create these qualities of style. But the flexibility of delivery and the variety of qualities necessary for a good style, along with his emphasis on decorum—he counsels the preacher to "fit" the application of the doctrines "according as place, time, and person do require" (664)—suggest that his "plain style" has less in common with the ideal of the philosophers and more with that of fellow rhetoricians.[86]

The recognition that teaching, delighting, and moving cannot necessarily be separated into different styles or even textual elements also shows up in comments on the functions of arguments and figures. Agricola insists that a fully developed argument moves the passions:

> But if we call argumentation everything by which we consider what is doubtful and uncertain, I would have thought not only that it is necessary for arousing emotions, but that it ought to be very dense and even thickly packed. For strength is necessary for the intellect to be seized and for the mind itself to be carried away from itself and as it were placed outside itself. This technique of argument is so much imitated by creative writers that if they are short of different arguments, they pile on the same point, changing the words, as if they were making several points. (199; qtd. in Mack, *Renaissance Argument* 203–4)

Because reason and emotion are connected, Agricola talks about moving and pleasing in book 3 of his dialectic manual. Figures, too, simultaneously teach, delight, and move. Peacham indicates that metaphors perform these three functions at once: metaphors "give light," "minister a pleasure to his wit," "move affections," and "are forcible to persuade" ([1577] D.iii.r). Butler in *Rhetoricae libri duo* makes the same point about figures of thought: "As these, along with tropes and schemes produce delight and instruction, so they alone also will have greatest efficacy in moving and conquering—the chief matter in oratory" (1.24.113; trans. Shuger 127).

Consequently though the styles of the various genres do differ and they can be compared to each other using the rubric of the three *genera dicendi,* this classification holds only according to the specific texts and qualities being examined. Firm distinctions between them based on stylistic register do not hold generally. It is probably for this reason that when Cicero describes the styles of oratory, poetry, history, and philosophy in the *Orator,* he does not assign each to one of the stylistic levels, except to say that, in his opinion, all are lower than the flexibly modulated, "terse and vigorous language" of the best deliberative and judicial oratory (19.61–20.70). The one genre besides these two types of oratory that he does place into a category is the philosophical writing of the best classical masters. He regards these philosophical texts as a kind of middle, but not low, style (27.95).[87] This middle style, however, is a dynamic mixture of various low, middle, and high elements. Philosophical discourse is like conversation (*sermo*); great philosophers of the past, though, have used highly ornate language; and academic purposes elevate the style above the common but do not ascend to the heights of public oratory:

> Certain philosophers, to be sure, had an ornate style,—for example Theophrastus received his name from his divinely beautiful language, and Aristotle challenged even Isocrates, and the Muses were said to speak with the voice of Xenophon, and Plato was, in dignity and grace, easily the first of all writers or speakers—yet their style lacks the vigour and sting necessary for oratorical efforts in public life. They converse with scholars, whose minds they prefer to soothe rather than arouse; they converse in this way about unexciting and non-controversial subjects, for the purpose of instructing rather than captivating; and some think they exceed due bounds in aiming to give some little pleasure by their style. It is therefore easy to distinguish the eloquence which we are treating in this work from the style of the philosophers. The latter is gentle and academic; it has no equipment of words or phrases that catch the popular fancy; it is not arranged in rhythmical periods, but is loose in structure; there is no anger in it, no hatred, no ferocity, no pathos, no shrewdness; it might be called a chaste, pure and modest virgin. Consequently it is called conversation rather than oratory. (*Orator* 19.62–64)

That "oratory" here is a genre of discourse, not rhetoric itself, Cicero makes clear when he follows this description with the reminder that "while all speaking is oratory, yet it is the speech of the orator alone which is marked by this special name" (19.64). Similarly Hermogenes does not firmly assign disciplines to specific stylistic *characters.*

For example he quotes from several of Plato's philosophical works in his discussions of *semnotēs* (solemnity), *kallos* (beauty), *glykytes* (sweetness), and *epieikeia* (modesty), and he quotes from the philosopher Xenophon for *apheleia* (simplicity), *drimytes* (subtlety), and *aletheia* (sincerity). Philosophical works can exhibit qualities associated with all three of the Roman *genera dicendi,* then. The fact that Hermogenes does not quote from philosophers to illustrate all the stylistic characters does not mean that he could not have done so.

It is because various genres and texts can be compared according to so many different elements that rhetoricians place different genres under different categories at different times. Throughout the period we find philosophers, historians, orators, and literary works classed under all three or multiple genera.[88] This lack of agreement again shows the difficulty of using the three levels of style as a static, prescriptive classification system. Those in the classical or Renaissance periods who use this descriptive mechanism to classify various genres rigidly rather than simply to give illustrative touchstones reify the system contrary to the precepts taught by the rhetoricians.

When we find static categories implied by oversimplified statements in these rhetoricians' instructions, we are witnessing either the results of careless theorizing or of efforts to adjust precepts to young beginners. For example Soarez seems to be simplifying for his audience of youngsters when he aligns the three levels of style more inflexibly with primary functions than does Cicero: "the plain style is occupied with instructing, the middle style with charming, and the grand style with persuading" (413). He also aligns dialectical and expository style with teaching and the low style (416). But even in Soarez such reification of the categories does not separate out a dialectical plain style from the rhetorical styles, for any speaker must use all three of the *genera dicendi* in different parts of the speech and as circumstances require (412–16). Additionally the low style, like the middle and high, requires figures (413–14).

Figuration

That all styles have figures is the second difference distinguishing the stylistic ideal of the rhetoricians from that of the philosophers. Without exception rhetoricians allot figures, whether considered specialized forms or forms in general, to all levels of style. In the *Rhetorica ad Herennium,* we read, "Each type of style, the grand, the middle, and the simple, gains distinction from rhetorical figures" (4.11.16). While some figures do seem more particularly suited to one kind, others are common to all three. *Pathopoeia* (passionate expression) typically makes a style high, but metaphor, according to Cicero, creates any level (*Orator* 23.75–28.99). On this point Cicero differs from Aristotle, who makes metaphor a feature of the high style (even though he acknowledges it is found in conversation) (3.2 1404b36). Cicero also comments on the impossibility of distinguishing stylistic levels according to types of figures. All styles make use of figures of thought, he says (*Orator* 23.76–28.99; 39.136–40.139).[89] He also observes, "It will be open to us to use almost the same ornaments of style on some occasions in a more energetic and on others in a more quiet manner" (*De Oratore* 3.55.212). Cicero's description of the "plain" style, which he gives as "a type and pattern" in the *Orator,* encourages the use of appropriate figures. Paying little attention here to the difference between forms and figures, Cicero contrasts instead the artful low style (eloquence) with the poorly crafted one (ineloquence):

> [This style] is restrained and plain, . . . follows ordinary usage, really differing more than is supposed from those who are not eloquent at all. . . . For that plainness of style seems easy to imitate at first thought, but when attempted nothing is more difficult. For although it is not full-blooded, it should nevertheless have some of the sap of life, so that, though it lack great strength, it may still be, so to speak, in sound health. . . . In this style [rhythms] are to be wholly eschewed. It should be loose but not rambling; so that it may seem to move freely but not to wander without restraint. He should also avoid, so to speak, cementing his words together too smoothly, for the hiatus and clash of vowels have something agreeable about it and show a not unpleasant carelessness on the part of the man who is paying more attention to thought than to words. But his very freedom from periodic structure and cementing his words together will make it necessary for him to look to other requisites. For the short and concise clauses must not be handled carelessly, . . . Also all noticeable ornament, pearls as it were, will be excluded; not even curling irons will be used; all cosmetics, artificial white and red, will be rejected; only elegance and neatness will remain. The language will be pure Latin, plain and clear; propriety will always be the chief aim. . . . He will employ an abundance of apposite maxims. . . . He will not be bold in coining words, and in metaphor will be modest, sparing in the use of archaisms, and somewhat subdued in using the other embellishments of language and of thought. Metaphor he may possibly employ more frequently because it is of the commonest occurrence in the language of townsman and rustic alike. . . . This orator will also use the symmetry that enlivens a group of words with embellishments that the Greeks call *schemata,* figures as it were, of speech. . . . He will, however, be somewhat sparing in using these. . . . There are, as a matter of fact, a good many ornaments suited to the frugality of this very orator I am describing. . . . Other figures of speech he will be able to use freely, provided only he breaks up and divides the periodic structure and uses the commonest words and mildest of metaphors. He may also brighten his style with such figures of thought as will not be exceedingly glaring. . . . For he will be rather subdued in voice as in style. . . . Many of these figures of thought will be appropriate to this plain style, although he will use them somewhat harshly. . . .
>
> A speech of this kind should also be sprinkled with the salt of pleasantry, which plays a rare great part in speaking. There are two kinds, humour and wit. He will use both; the former in a graceful and charming narrative, the latter in hurling the shafts of ridicule. (23.75–26.87)[90]

We have already seen that later Greeks showed figures to create all the types of style. Demetrius mentions figures in his description of the plain style (§190–235). The point is particularly explicit in Hermogenes, who explains that "clarity," as well as "purity" (correctness), "simplicity," "sincerity," "subtlety," and "harshness"—qualities associated with this so-called low style—all result from careful implementation of figures. For example clarity depends upon both purity and distinctness (1.2.226). Purity requires the figures *orthotes* (the simple sentence), simple narrative, and brevity (1.3.227–30). Distinctness requires forewarning (*katastasis*), transition (*symplerosis*), logical ordering (*kosmesis*), definition (*horismus*), dividing the whole into parts (*merismos*), enumeration (*aparithmesis*), asking and answering one's own questions (*hypophora*), repeating the main point after a digression (*epanalepsis*), and majesty (*onkos*) (1.4.236–41). Simplicity adds to purity and distinctness the use of oaths (*orcos*) and comparisons (2.3.326–27). Sincerity depends also upon prayers and appeals (*deesis*), wishes (*euche*), exclamations (*ecphonesis*), amazement (*thaumasmus*), spontaneity (*autoschediasmos*), rapid replies (*lysis*), lack of connectives (*asyndeton*), inversion of word order (*hyperbaton*), abusive language (*convinciari*), addressing an audience not present (*apostrophe*), perplexity (*diaporesis*), and so forth (2.7.354–63). Finally subtlety, which depends upon figures of wit and humor, "expresses cunningly contrived thoughts in a simple style" (2.5.340), and "[harshness] uses almost all the figures" (1.7.259). Since Hermogenes also declares that "the figures that produce Solemnity are the same as those that produce Purity, that is, simple, direct statements and the like" (1.6.250), he shows that the grand style includes a subtype that lacks more obvious ornaments too, prohibiting plainness of dress from being the exclusive marker of a so-called plain style.[91]

Renaissance rhetoricians continue this instruction.[92] Those who draw primarily from Roman and contemporary precedents echo Cicero's description of the low style. Melanchthon, for example, writes that the good low style, which "is highly suitable for teaching," still must resort to figured language and still must be carefully crafted:

> The humble category does not rise above the daily manner of speaking, keeps the peculiarity (characteristics) of the discourse with marvelous care and strives markedly to express the matter with words as highly appropriate as possible. It does not care for crowded figures, uses metaphors freely, not far-fetched ones, but those taken from daily conversation. It enlarges nothing entirely, but the whole aspect of the speech is modest and put together with the idea of dissembling and as if purposely shunning the ornate. It argues the matter with practical discretion and in an orderly manner, almost on purpose does not digress and by the very appearance of simplicity ensnares the listener. It uses very round-about expressions, for it echoes the negligence of daily discourse in the arrangement of words. . . . There are, indeed, faulty spots in this first category, shallow and insipid ones, rough and obscure ones, as in Sallust somewhere in his speeches. (*Elem.* 63v–64r; 344–46)[93]

Those who combine Cicero and Hermogenes make figuration even more ubiquitous. In *Ecclesiastes* Erasmus shows the figures to create all the qualities of style and to "make oratory [discourse] powerful, delightful, and abundant" (3.44.787–88). He also observes that "the entire conversation of man is stuffed full with tropes" (3.176.497). Sturm too describes each of the stylistic characters by enumerating the figures that create them. Even Ramus teaches that all speech and styles have figures: "Indeed tropes and figures exist in every speech, but ornament is increased or diminished in accordance with the nature of the subjects which are treated and the persons who are taught" (*Arguments* 150). Renaissance rhetoricians, then, would be in sympathy with recent work showing figures in science texts.

Such a comment in Ramus brings into question another commonly accepted belief among scholars: that the growing popularity of the philosophical "plain style" in the seventeenth century owes much to Ramus.[94] We must be careful to qualify such a lineage of influence, for Ramus's precepts clearly place him in the rhetoricians' camp. Talon treats of decorum and the three levels of style, which he applies to oratory, history, poetry, and epistles, in the *Rhetorica* ([1548] 99–100). Even though direct instruction in decorum and the three levels of style dropped out of later editions, Ramus continues to treat of them in his editions of *Dialecticae institutione* between 1543 and 1569, only leaving them out afterward because dialectical method naturally produces the varying levels (*Scholae rhetoricae in Scholae in liberales artes,* col. 275ff; in Ong, *Ramus, Method* 212–13). What Ong has called the "Ramist plain style"—a style that is voiceless, transparent, unfigured—cannot be attributed to Ramus directly,[95] nor can it be attributed to English Ramists, who continue to teach that discourse is composed of figures. Fraunce, for example, may distinguish between "simple and natural" speeches and those "finely fashioned and figured artificially" (*Arcadian Rhetoric* B8r). But whether he means by "simple and natural" without self-conscious choice or without particular "excellencies" of style, he certainly does not mean a dialectical plain style. For he includes a large number of figures as examples of arguments in his dialectic textbook, where he also uses the word *plain* to mean a kind of dialectical argument that is not the formal "subtle and strict probation" of the Scholastics but rather the "simple, plain, and easy explication" found in the poets and orators: "Read Homer, read Demosthenes, read Virgil, read Cicero, read Bartas, read Torquato Tasso, read that most worthy ornament of our English tongue, the Countess of Pembroke's *Arcadia,* and therein see the true effects of natural Logic which is the ground of artificial, far different from this rude and barbarous kind of outworn sophistry: which if it had any use at all, yet this was all, to feed the vain humors of some curious heads in obscure schools" (*Lawiers Logike* 3v).

There are those who, in associating "plainness" with directness, simplicity, and nakedness, do sometimes mean by it unfigured language, as we have seen. Quintilian may insist that there is a language with figures (*eschematismen*) and a language without (*aschematiston*) (9.1.13). But in Quintilian this distinction does not align with that between a rhetorical and dialectical, nor a grand and low style, for he applies tropes, when employed to express our meaning, to the low style (12.10.69–70; 8.6.7). Also distinguishing figured speech from "plain language" (35r), Melanchthon still gives figures to the low style and instructs that the high style will not be all figure: "Even as figures that are pleasing and are sparingly used add a very great deal to a topic, a speech is just as greatly defective and inept in which almost nothing is said in a straightforward manner" (*Elem.* 34v, 233). Similarly Scaliger may distinguish figured from "bare" or "nude" speech in poetry (3.93.363), but the fact that both types appear in poetry, as do all the Hermogenean characters (including clarity and purity [4.2–3.459B; 4.1.445]), and that he considers dialectical arguments to be figures (3.71.339–40) means that his distinction does not align with that between the dialectical plain and the rhetorical grand styles. When rhetoricians make reference to dialectical and rhetorical styles differing like Zeno's closed and open hand, they do not mean the unfigured versus the figured, nor the plain versus the grand styles. Rather they mean, to use Fraunce's words, the formal "subtle and strict probation" of the scholastics appropriate for experts versus the "simple, plain, and easy explication" of the poets and orators appropriate for nonexperts. The distinction between philosophy and rhetoric in rhetorical manuals does not correlate with a distinction between the plain and grand styles, then.[96]

There is an additional distinction sometimes made that we cannot confuse as correspondent with a separation between either philosophy and rhetoric or the low and high styles. In the seventeenth century, a few begin to divide figures from nonfigures based on whether the devices produce emotional or unemotional speech. This division, however, does not hold even within the very manuals that assert it.

Keckermann, for example, contrasts a figured and emotional to an unfigured and unemotional kind of speech:

> The word *schemata* is taken from theater into the rhetorical art: just as in the theater men in various scenes represent various characters with the figures of their costumes, so also speech can insert them for various uses of delighting and moving. Figures give various affections, just as costumes, garments, images, colors, or whatever name we call them. Figures, therefore, or, in other words schemes, are habits of speech, by which from the nude and simple custom speech is changed, and it puts on some peculiar appearance for the purpose of delighting and moving the hearer. (*Systema* 1480)

The "dogmatic" genres teach through a "nude" style that is "not expressly meant to move the emotions" (*Systematis* 1587), while the "affective" genres expressly move and delight (1610). These statements may indicate at first glance that Keckermann will make a clean divide between a dialectical plain style and a rhetorical figured style. However he does not do so, for "dogmatic" genres still belong to rhetoric, have emotional effects, involve the use of varied levels of style, and require figures, such as *descriptio, orthotes,* and *enthymema,* to create "vividness" and "clarity" (1590–91). Furthermore he states that all three of the *genera dicendi* are "painted by color" (*Systema* 1480). Encompassing many forms within figures, he also categorizes some under the heading of proofs and others under the heading of emotions, acknowledging that "all figures pertain to emotion either expressing it or moving it . . . ; nevertheless, certain figures more remotely contain emotion . . . and [others] truly take up some emotion" (1490). Such indications suggest that he, like his earlier humanist contemporaries, treats emotional content both topically and holistically: we can identify particular forms at moments in the text that clearly insert emotion, and we can step back and recognize that all the devices in an utterance work together to create the expression of emotion. This general attitude will become more evident in the next chapter when we examine the functions of figures and styles.

Lamy also associates the figures with a passionate style distinguished from an unfigured, natural, and unemotional style: "Our Passions also have their peculiar characters, by which they represent themselves in our Discourse: . . . These ways of Speaking . . . are the famous Figures mentioned by Rhetoricians, and by them defin'd, Manners of Speaking, different and remote from the ways that are ordinary and natural; that is to say, quite other than what we use, when we speak without passion" (2.94–95). Yet self-contradictions abound in Lamy's discussion. He assigns the "plain and naked" low style, the one "cool and in peace" or "calm and sedate" (2.93) or "free from those Ornaments that Passion inspires into an Orator," to discourses of "dogmatical assertion" such as geometry (4.49), as we might expect, but also, as we might not expect, to rhetorical speeches and poetry when the subject is not "extraordinary" or "great" and hence does not merit "commotions and raptures" (4.23, 53). He turns around, however, and says that poets frequently use "metaphors which (as we said before) make everything so plain" (4.54), and he describes a "Poetical Discourse" as "figure all over" (4.53), with verse itself being a figure (2.145). Lamy also acknowledges that we even use tropes "when we are quiet and at ease" (2.123) and figures in "the mildest and most temperate conversation, though no resistance be found in the Mind of the persons with whom we discourse" (2.147), since figures help to "explicate" or "make exact descriptions" or "fix" ideas in the mind (2.147). Furthermore all discourses express attitude, are "colored": "Discourse is the Picture of our Thoughts, the Tongue is the Pencil which draws that Picture; and Words are the Colours" (1.5), which make an action "appear greater, or less, laudable or contemptible, just or unjust" (4.44). Figures are present in all genres, for "thus has Conversation its Figures, as well as Speeches, and Declamations" (2.147–48), and all styles must have the virtues of easiness (perspicuity), strength ("short expressions that signify much" [4.38]), pleasantness (tropes and figures [4.39]), and severity (absence of "whatever is not absolutely necessary" [4.39]). The possibility of nonfigured speech becomes even more questionable since, as we have seen, Lamy treats fundamental sentence components, such as the comma, colon, and period, and arguments as figures. The plain style does not correspond to dialectical genres necessarily, then; nor is there a style that is totally absent of figure, emotion, attitude, or the need for artistic polish.

This association of figures with emotional expression need not accompany an Aristotelian definition of rhetoric. For example Walker associates the figures with "modes of livelier and more passionate expression" (24). Yet Walker's distinction is also blatantly self-contradictory, because he ends up treating all devices as figures and even admits that "all compositions whatever" entail figures (94). Since all these rhetoricians, whether classical or humanist, unanimously teach that all utterance expresses some kind of emotion and attitude, tying figures to emotional content proves accurate but implying that some discourse lacks emotional content is not.

When "plainness" refers to the low style, it is set in opposition not to the faulty high style, as philosophers suppose, but to the more formal middle and high styles and to faulty versions of the low. Each style will fail if indecorous. Rhetoricians name corresponding faulty styles for each of the three levels and for many of the Hermogenean characters. Because each level has various subtypes, each can fail in various ways.

The failed low style, for example, results from numerous errors: unnatural brevity can produce obscurity (*obscuritas*), carelessness a disorderliness (*dissipatio*) and sloppiness (*ameles*), vulgarity crudity (*foedus*), lack of variety aridity (*exilitas*), inadequate expression humiliation (*meiosis* or *tapinosis*), excessive candor offensiveness (*acharis*), and lack of vigor in delivery lifelessness (*atonia*). "Nakedness" can sometimes refer to this failed low style, the one without art. Lamy, for example, remarks that some passages are "dry, flat, barren," leaving the style "half-naked" (4.3). It is this bad low style that Fraunce attributes to the Scholastics (*Lawiers Logike* 3v).

The Clear Style

The second common meaning of *plainness* in these rhetoric manuals is clarity. The understanding of clarity is the third difference distinguishing the stylistic ideal of the rhetoricians from that of the philosophers. To these rhetoricians clarity is a virtue that all styles, not merely the low, must possess in order to achieve eloquence. This perspicuity does not derive solely from correct grammar and precise words used literally—the criteria of the philosophers—but from decorous composition, the construction that best accomplishes all the purposes of the speaker on this occasion to this audience. This composition requires the apt use of the proper figures, whose function is ultimately the perfection of the expressivity of language. When used well figures maximize meaning and perspicuity. It is because figures aid in the creation of clarity by means of vividness, emphasis, order, continuity, coherence, and congruity that these rhetoricians recommend their use.

When "plainness" means "clarity," it is set in opposition not to ornament but to confusion.[97] Because it results from appropriateness, this perspicuity produces true ornateness. Hence Melanchthon defines eloquence as clear speech created through appropriate embellishment, a standard applicable to all styles and requiring consummate art:

> For eloquence is not what those men imagine it to be—adventitious adornment. On the contrary, it is the faculty for proper and clear explication of mental sense and thought; in this it even serves worth and truth, so that they may be aptly and correctly expressed; it makes it possible also for great things to be magnified and for things needing abasement to be humbled. And so, as the object of a painter is to copy bodies truly and properly—how difficult this is to achieve is no secret to the experienced—therefore, not only is art required for it but also a great variety of colors. So the object of the rhetorician, or of eloquence (if you prefer that word), is to paint, as it were, and to represent the mind's thoughts themselves in appropriate and clear language; when he has toiled over it, he will need a great variety of colors as it were, of words, sentences and figures, and finally even a kind of art that at least I think is far greater than the art of a consummate and perfect painter ever can be. ("Reply to Pico" 55–56)

He goes on, asserting that "the proper exposition of things is the chief ornament of eloquence" (62) and that "eloquence is a necessity when it comes to clarifying great subjects" (64). He criticizes the scholastics who condemn rhetoric as "a painted face" by pointing out that their lack of attention to stylistic craftsmanship produces a "hideous" one that is not plain and is inhuman: "Further, if you take from philosophy even the simpler form [the rhetorical low style] you clearly leave her voiceless. How could you explain anything except at least by the use of appropriate and transparent speech? The unlearned imagine that everybody has facility in that sort of discourse; but it really cannot be attained without the very best instruction, without the most intensive study, without long practice" (59). Lamy agrees that sublimity arises from the beauty of appropriate construction (4.60–61). He then asserts that the following example is sublime and forceful because of its clarity: "Longinus in his Book of this Sublimity, has given us an example of a sublime expression taken out of the First Chapter of Genesis, where Moses speaking of the Creation, uses these words; And God said let there be light, and there was light." This statement "gives a strong Idea of the power of God over his Creatures," leading "the mind of the Reader . . . directly to the end of the design" (4.60).

These rhetoricians, then, make a distinction between the obscurity resulting from confusion and the subtlety resulting from a skillful indirection. The first arises from "affection of words, & undigested conceits" (George Chapman, prefatory letter to *Ovids Banquet of Sence* [1595] 49); the second arises from "shadows *per Allegoriam*" (Gascoigne, *Certayne Notes of Instruction* [1575] 48). It is in this second sense of subtlety, not ambiguity, that rhetoricians sometimes say that metaphors and tropes render the speech less plain (Melanchthon, *Elem.* 56r; Puttenham 166).

With the "plain" now meaning the "perspicuous," it becomes one with the appropriate and hence the true high style, opposing the "artificial," inflated, or pretentious style. Cicero, Hermogenes, and Longinus all indicate that the high style can be viewed in two ways: as a heightened, moving, poetic style full of weighty and noble ideas expressed in grand or forceful language; or as a perfectly crafted style, exhibiting the overarching virtues of correctness, clarity, appropriateness, and hence ornateness. This second is Cicero's Attic style (*Orator* 29.100; *De Oratore* 3.25.96). In Hermogenes force has two meanings. He says:

> In my opinion Force in a speech is nothing other than the proper use of all the kinds of style previously discussed. . . . To know what technique must be used and when and how it should be used, and to be able to employ all the kinds of style and their opposites and to know what kinds of proofs and thoughts are suitable in the proemium or in the narration or in the conclusion, in other words, as I said, to be able to use all those elements that create the body of a speech as and when they should be used seems to me to be the essence of true Force. (2.9.369)

Longinus also identifies two kinds of this sublime style: the first expresses grand conceptions with vehement emotion through elevated language (§8); the second is a perfectly crafted style appropriate to the occasion, for style "becomes sublime by being apt to the situation" (§40) and by achieving a mean between extremes (§41–42).[98]

Like Cicero, so Vives uses the term *Attic,* which he conflates with perspicuity, to be the good, natural style. "Naturalness" is now not the opposite of art but the result of true art, of perfect congruency among the elements of the speech act. Vives is describing the truly eloquent style when he describes with the epithets of "beautiful nakedness" and "natural color" the expression whose figures fit the arguments meant to be conveyed. This style has "apt words, clearly set forth," and "figures that are modest, decent, clean, not far-fetched but with the appearance of being fresh and newborn" (*De ratione dicendi* 98). Its opposite, he claims, is "the artificial, the painted, in which the decoration," because unsuitable to the circumstances, "appears as something applied from without" (99). This faulty style arises when speakers believe, as the philosophers do, "that the whole art of speaking can be reduced to verbal expression, e.g., to schemes, tropes, periods, and harmony of diction, things which do not touch upon the body of the discourse or the substance, but pertain to the ornaments and decorations of good speech" (25). Melanchthon uses *Asiatic* to name this faulty high style: "There are faulty places in this category, swollen and puffed up, which try to appear grandiose, which produce nothing effective, but have endless periphrases and monstrous metaphors. These were once called Asiatic, for in Asia where they had a corrupt and improper kind of discourse, they still affected praise of eloquence by a display of immoderate ornament. Rational natures always at first shrank away from this category" (*Elem.* 64v, 347). Puttenham also explains that this "artificial" (inartistic) style results from poorly applied ornamentation:

> Now also be there many other sorts of repetition if a man would use them, but are nothing commendable, and therefore are not observed in good poesie, as a vulgar rimer who doubled one word in the end of every verse, thus: adieu, adieu, my face, my face. And an other that did the like in the beginning of his verse, thus: To love him and love him, as sinners should do. These repetitions be not figurative, but fantastical, for a figure is ever used to a purpose, either of beauty or of efficacy: and these last recited be to no purpose, for neither can ye say that it urges affection, nor that it beautifieth or enforceth the sense, nor hath any other subtlety in it, and therefore is a very foolish impertinency of speech, and not a figure. (211–12)

The style the philosophers condemn as the oratorical, then, the rhetoricians also condemn, but as ineloquence, not eloquence itself. And the plain style, which the philosophers hold up as the ideal, the rhetoricians also embrace, but as perspicuity created by means of figures and artistry, not the absence of them, and as a virtue necessary in all genres, not merely the scientific. Even if the rhetoricians do not fully explain all the reasons why their paradigm is more explanatory of discourse than that of the philosophers, they nevertheless believe that they can better teach how to create and read the varied characters and virtues of style than can the philosophers. Melanchthon asserts, "None more than they [rhetoricians] scorn flattery and empty show; none speak with more chastity than those who by constant practice have accustomed themselves to correct speaking" ("Reply to Pico" 62). The scholastics, on the other hand, have poor style. Valla holds that orators can speak of ethics "much more clearly, weightily, magnificently" than can "the obscure, squalid, and anemic philosophers" ("On the True Good" in *Opera* 906–7; trans. Seigel 142). Keckermann remarks that philosophers explore intricate problems of speculative truth without regard for the audience's capacity, but rhetoricians adjust their speech to reach their listeners (*Systema* 1391).

The Figurative Nature of Mind

An implication to follow from the comprehensive domains of rhetoric, style, and figure in Renaissance language arts instruction is that not only all speech but also all thought is figured. This idea must surely have been around in classical times, as indicated when Alexander Rhetor remarks that there are those who teach that "no unfigured discourse can easily be found . . . since discourse depends on the configuration of the mind" (trans. Russell 176). But this insight becomes more visible in both humanist rhetoric and dialectic textbooks, even when not argued for explicitly. The figuration of mind is implied because in rhetoric manuals all figures tend to be conceived as figures of thought; fundamental thought processes, which are figures themselves, are made general heads of many more particular figures and tropes; and both artificial and natural memory are shown to work on the basis of *schemata.* In turn dialectic manuals reinforce the instruction in rhetoric manuals by treating tropes as arguments and argument forms as figures and by depicting meaning making itself as a function of schema induction and tropological processes.

First Renaissance rhetoricians tend to view all figures as figures of thought. This habit is evident in their consistent use of the principles of scope and analogy to extend the reach of figures. They typically see figures as transferable from one discourse level to another—in other words as capable of being decreased or enlarged in size. This varying of scope is only possible if the form exists in thought. This flexible application of figures is evident everywhere in Renaissance handlists. Cicero had defined a figure of thought in contradistinction to a figure of speech by saying, "The figure suggested by the words disappears if one alters the words, but that of the thoughts remains whatever words one chooses to employ" (*De Oratore* 3.52.200). But in Renaissance discussions even figures of speech are treated as figures of thought. For example in classical texts *anadiplosis* is a figure of speech in which a word ends one phrase or clause and then begins the next. But in Sturm, for example, *anadiplosis* also operates in letters and syllables (2.22.4–7). In classical texts *epistrophe* is the ending of successive phrases or clauses with the same word, but in Keckermann (1505) and Walker (67) this figure includes ending the phrase or clause with the same letter or syllable and in Soarez ending successive clauses with the same idea (309). *Epanalepsis* similarly now applies to repeating not only the same word but also the same syllable, clause, or idea at the beginning and ending of not only a sentence but also a passage or even a whole speech. *Epanados* now has an application on both the level of sentence and of passage. *Climax* (*gradatio*) can appear in a sentence, paragraph, and an extended passage. *Correctio* (correcting a word or idea stated earlier), *diminutio* (diminishing), and *synonymia* (renaming through synonyms) apply to a word, sentence, or passage. We are not surprised, then, to see Sturm come up with a new figure, *chorismos,* which extends syntactical *prolepsis* to the order of ideas in a passage (3.3.498).

We see the same kind of transference from level to level with tropes, which are sometimes called figures of speech and sometimes of thought. Tropes occur in words, sentences, and whole passages. Puttenham even lists *synecdoche* twice, once for the single word (196) and once for the extended passage (205). He does the same thing with *meiosis* (lessening), once as a figure of a word (227) and once as a figure of thought (228).

In the same way, these rhetoricians extend the application of figures of thought from sentence to passage to whole work, pulling full-length genres into the figure domain. *Encomion* (praise), *onedismus* (vituperation), *adhortatio* (exhortation), *dehortatio* (dissuasion), *accusatio* (accusation), and *proecthesis* or *apologia* (defense) name not only small discourse chunks but also the three primary genres of oratory. This extension is self-conscious and explicit in Robertellus and Peacham.[99] Other figures are extended to include other genres. Sherry, for example, gives complaints of the poets as an illustration of *commiseratio* and Cicero's invectives as illustration of *deinosis* ([1550] 68). Peacham includes bills of complaint and supplications to princes as examples of *mempsis* ([1593] 66). Given this principle and the presence of other genres such as *fabula, prosopopoeia,* and *mythos* on figure lists, it seems inconsistent to exclude full-length genres of any kind. This thought seems to motivate Veltkirchius to add *historia,* an extension of the narrative, and *drama,* an extension of *prosopopoeia,* to his list of figures (172r) and to indicate that the commentary is a manifestation of the figure *exegesis* (173v). Given these precedents, how can we keep from seeing other full-length genres as examples of various figures? With flexible scope a principle illustrated over and over again in these handlists, readers would have continued its application and treated all figures as if capable of transference from level to level.[100]

The principle of analogy also operates to fill in the list of forms by creating figures where voids appear but where parallelism dictates figures should be. For example Melanchthon introduces *commiseratio* as a figure. Doing so makes sense with *deinosis* already a figure. *Commiseratio* and *deinosis* are the two emotional appeals commonly suited to the peroration. *Exclamatio* is a general figure capable of manifestation in many other forms. As a consequence *exclamatio* becomes a general type often listed with many species. It is only natural to increase the number of species as Talaeus does by adding *salutatio* (a greeting) or as Butler does by adding *ostentatio* (a boast). Scaliger adds *eidolopoeia,* a species of the *prosopopoeia* commonly introduced in the impersonation exercise of the *progymnasmata.* In similar manner Smith adds *hebraism* to be parallel with *hellenismus*; Blount adds *embleme* as another kind of symbol.

Because of analogy all kinds of style probably become figures. *Ethopoeia* (expression of mild feeling) and *pathopoeia* (expression of passion) are both figures and styles. Quintilian and Robertellus call *apheleia* (simple speech) a figure; *apheleia* is the name of a style in Hermogenes. *Deinotes, celeritas, peribole,* and *brevitas* are figures; they are also styles. Styles belong to sentences, passages, and whole orations. When one can pick up and put down a style as one can pick up and put down a pattern or strategy according to need, or when one can simulate a style as one can simulate a pattern, there seems little value in regarding them as completely different kinds of things. Following Erasmus,

Sturm treats styles in this way. For example Sturm suggests that magnitude (*megethos*) can be used in the high, middle, and low styles (3.6.544), that clarity (*sapheneia*) has a place in both subtle and full styles (3.6.545), and that we must decide where we want to use beauty (*kallos*) (3.6.544). Characters of style and stylistic virtues and vices also overlap. *Claritas* and *puritas* are virtues; they also correspond, as Sturm points out, with Hermogenes's styles of the same names (3.6.544). Scaliger further associates *claritas* with the figure *enargia* (4.1.444). *Copia* is both a style and a virtue. *Obscuritas* and *cacozelia* are vices and are also styles. If these features are figures, consistency would require viewing all virtues, vices, and qualities of style as figures of thought and, in so doing, greatly expanding not only the range of figures but also the number of forms of thought seen as figures.

Second Renaissance rhetoricians frequently elevate some figures to general heads and subordinate others to be species of these. While some general figures vary from manual to manual, those corresponding to the dialectical topics become fairly standard.[101] Melanchthon even comments that "all figures," not just those of amplification, "have origins in dialectical expressions" (*Elem.* 45v, 263–64). Because the topics underlie even figures of speech, Melanchthon advises that the translator must consider these topics in order to translate the scriptures' Hebraic figures accurately (9r, 100). Accordingly *antithesis* has been given the following species: *enantiosis, contentio, contrarium, contraposita, antanaclasis, antimetabole, prosapodosis, anthypophora,* and *diallage. Comparatio* is often the general category for both similitudes and dissimilitudes of all kinds, including not only antithesis and its species but also all metaphor, metonymy, synecdoche, allegory, simile, parable, analogy, fable, and example. These groupings of figures can vary from text to text, so that if a student consults several, he will be encouraged to look for relationships among figures and to see figures of thought as fundamental thought processes.

Like the dialectical topics, so tropes become general heads of other tropes and schemes. Both Cicero and Quintilian acknowledge metaphor as a fountainhead of tropes in general (*De Oratore* 3.149; *Institutio* 8.3.24). A number of Renaissance rhetoricians follow suit. Erasmus, for example, lists as derivatives *similia, collatio, imago, abusio* (*catachresis*), *aenigma, allegoria, proverbium, gnome, effictio,* and *apologus* (fable) (*Eccl.* 3.159.123–168.314). Cicero also speculates that metonymy may be the basic trope (*Brutus* 69), and Vossius follows him (4.3.209). But the Ramists propose something new. Instead of one basic trope, there are four: metaphor, metonymy, synecdoche, and irony. This postulation suggests an awareness of transference, transmutation, substitution, and contrariety as fundamental thought processes by which all other tropes operate. The first to propose these four basic tropes, Talaeus only lists *catachresis, allegory, aenigma, hyperbole,* and *diminutio* as kinds of metaphor and *antonomasia* as a species of synecdoche, but others after him elaborate more. For example Fraunce includes *epitheton* under metonymy and *paralepsis* and *apophasis* under irony (*Arcadian Rhetoric* A4v; A8r–v). Fenner speaks of *meiosis* as a kind of synecdoche when "less is spoken and yet more is understood" (170). Gill adds that *antonomasia, metalepsis, onomatopoeia,* and *barbaralexis* are species of metonymy (154) and that *sarcasmos, antiphrasis, insultatio, paralepsis, asteismos,* and "all those figures in which the discourse departs from the truth of the matter itself" are species of irony (153). The idea that there are four basic tropes is picked up by succeeding non-Ramist rhetoricians and becomes common stylistic doctrine.

Third the depiction of artificial and natural memory creates the impression that thought is figured, for even this art is shown to work by means of *schemata.* Instructions for memory, the process by which one learns one's speech by heart, reveal figuration to be central to cognitive storage and retrieval. Students learn that in order to remember consciously, they must place ideas in patterns—schemes—because the natural memory works on this basis. Two systems for memorizing receive attention. The first has a speaker imagine the rooms of a well-known building and assign one room to each section of the speech, moving in spatial order from room to room as he or she moves from section to section in the speech. Then he or she must take each idea from the speech, associate it with an image, and place each image in order around the appropriate room in strategic relation to the other images. Wilson in *The Art of Rhetoric* and Gulielmus Gratarolus (c. 1516–c. 1568) in *The Castel of Memorie* (1562) also suggest that having the images be dramatic and emotionally moving makes them more memorable (237; H.iii.r). To remember the speech, one then mentally walks back through the rooms in order, translating the images and their relationships back into ideas. In other words one translates symbol, allegory, and narrative back into the dialectical and rhetorical topics. A second procedure involves reducing one's ideas to a general head and then dividing the head into its several parts based upon the dialectical topics. This system, advocated by both Ciceronians and Ramists, creates a well-ordered speech and, as a result, one that is memorable (Brinsley, *Ludus Literarius* 208; Gratarolus F.viii.r–v).[102] Either way memory is shown to work by means of figures and anticipates the theory of twentieth-century cognitive psychologists, who have adopted "schema" or patterning as the explanatory mechanism for the human information processing system or, in other words, for learning, retention, problem solving, reading, writing, and even mathematics.[103]

Fourth further underscoring thought as fundamentally figured is the express awareness of tropes as arguments and arguments as figures. Both humanist rhetoricians and logicians emphasize these correlations. All four primary tropes are defined in terms of the logical topics that produce them, making obvious their status as conflated arguments. As Fraunce writes in his rhetoric manual, "*Metonymia* is a trope which useth the name of one thing for the name of another that agreeth with it, as when the cause is turned to signify the thing caused, the thing caused to signify the cause, the subject to express the adjunct, or the adjunct the subject" (*Arcadian Rhetoric* A3r); "*Ironia* is a Trope, that by naming one contrary intendeth another" (A6v); "A *Metaphor* is when the like is signified by the like: so then a Metaphor is nothing but a similitude contracted into one word" (B1v); and "*Synecdoche* is when the name of the whole is given to the part, or the name of the part to the whole" (B5r). The observation is frequently made that metaphor is a contracted similitude and a similitude is an argument. Wilson, for example, in his rhetoric textbook refers the reader to his logic textbook for more explanation of similitudes: "I have spoken of similitudes heretofore in the book of logic" (*Art of Rhetoric* 215). Reciprocally in his book of logic, he teaches that the argument from similitude is found in metaphors or "things . . . spoken by translation" (*Rule of Reason* O.viii.r). Likewise Fraunce, in *The Lawiers Logike,* gives as examples of arguments from similitude the simile, metaphor, fable, and example (72r–74v), all of them figures. Again Sherry in his rhetoric manual derives metaphor and example from the similitude ([1550) 71–72), and so does Blundeville in his *The Art of Logike* (95, 99). In *Rhetorica libri duo,* Butler obviously relates the figure of irony to the dialectical topic of contraries by discussing how irony is created from the four kinds of opposites, which are always treated in logic: relatives, privatives, contraries, and contradictories (21).[104] Extended or secondary tropes are also clearly seen as arguments. Melanchthon remarks, "For allegory is a kind of comparison in which something similar is indicated yet without the rest of the comparison being expressly stated, or I may put it another way: allegory is a truncated enthymeme" (*Elem.* 36v, 241).

Dialectical arguments are also treated as figures of thought. When they speak of these figures, rhetoricians cross-reference logic texts. The Ramist Fraunce moves these figures to his dialectic manual,[105] as do other non-Ramist logicians. The argument based on definition, which sets out "the very nature of the thing itself," as Wilson describes it in his logic manual (*Rule of Reason* J.viii.r), matches with the figure as Sherry defines it in his rhetoric manual, wherein the "proper pith of any thing is declared briefly and perfectly" ([1555] G.iiii.r). Hoskins clearly connects the argument and the figure when he advises, "But to be most perfectly instructed, read the sixth book of Aristotle's *Topica*" (44). Certain figures are even species of this argument from definition: Fraunce in his logic book lists epithets, "explications, illustrations, amplifications, and extenuations" (*Lawiers Logike* 40r)—or, renamed as figures, *periphrasis, paradigma, amplificatio,* and *diminutio.* Another kind of definition is the description, under which argument Fraunce lists in his logic book *prosopographia, topographia, chorographia, geographia, chronographia, hypotyposis, periphrasis,* and *allusio* (*Lawiers Logike* 62v–63r) and which he illustrates with selections from Spenser's *The Shepheardes Calendar.* Fraunce also is quite explicit in pointing out that the argument from conjugates "cometh from a Rhetorical figure, called *Polyptoton*" (50r). This argument is built on various forms of a word and proceeds as follows: "A just man is to be praised, *ergo* Justice is to be praised" or "He doth all things wisely, *ergo* he is wise" (Blundeville 100). Fraunce in *The Lawiers Logic* again comments that the topic of notation or etymology "seemeth also a Rhetorical agnomination" (50v), sometimes producing "quips, taunts, jests, and conceipts" (51v), all figures. Hoskins in his rhetoric manual associates the figure *partitio* with the logical topic of division: "And so you may divide as many ways as things may differ . . . whereof the proper treaty belongs to logic" (45). Ralph Lever (d. 1584/5) in his *The Art of Reason* (1573) describes the figures *diaresis, enumeratio, eutrepismus, prolepsis,* and *distinctio* as he gives examples of arguments derived from the topic of division, under which he treats of whole/parts and genus/species (212–13). When illustrating the argument from antecedents and consequents, Blundeville depicts the figure *syllogismus,* the implying of consequences by signs or circumstances: "Yesternight was ruddy, and this morning is gray, this day therefore will be fair" or "This woman giveth milk. Ergo she hath had a child" (191). One reasons in both of these arguments on the basis of signs that come before, after, or during an event. Smith's example of the figure is parallel to Blundeville's example of the argument: from "David's sorrowful bewailing of his son Absolom's death" in 2 Samuel 18.33, we may infer "how dearly he loved his son, notwithstanding his evil inclinations" (259). *Enantiotes,* which Quintilian insists is a kind of argument (5.9.3), Sturm treats as a figure, one clearly tied to the topic of contraries: "I call this *Contraria,* which is what it is called in the Topics" (2.23.428).

Not only proofs that derive from the dialectical *topoi* but also logical argument forms are called figures.[106] Veltkirchius, as we have already seen, explicitly brings arguments into the figure domain, naming *syllogismus, enthymema, inductio,* and *consequentia* specifically as figures and commenting that Erasmus views the "arguments and places of invention" as schemes (193v–4v). Wilson in his rhetoric manual remarks that *inductio,* the logical argument, is one species of the figure *imago* (similitude): "By this figure, called in Latin *imago*—that is to say, an image— . . . we might heap many men together and prove by large rehearsal anything that we would, the which of the logicians is called induction" (*Art of Rhetoric* 232). Hoskins identifies the figure *gradatio* as a *sorites:* "If it be turned to an argument, it is a SORITES. . . . Now to make it a sorites, or climbing argument, join the first and the last with an *ergo*" (12). Blundeville says the same in his logic text: "The Rhetoricians use another kind of argument, called *Gradatio,* which is much like to *Sorites,* saving that the subject of the first proposition is not rehearsed in the Conclusion" (154). Puttenham reveals that the figure dilemma is "fit for argumentation, and worketh not unlike the *dilemma* of the Logicians" (230). Peacham comments that the *aetiologia* provides "an authentic seal to an evidence" and that "the speaker in the use of this figure ought to be sure that the reason or cause which he joineth to the proposition be good and sufficient, lest he weaken what he should confirm" ([1593] 185). He describes *apodeixis* as a demonstrative argument based on "known principles, which experience doth prove and no man can deny" ([1593] 86). These ætiologies, Walker says, prove the premises as the orator "lays them down, before he infers his conclusion from them, . . . that he may render the fabric of his speech not only beautiful, but strong" (80–81). Wilson, in his logic text, relates the fallacy of *secundum quid* to the vice of hyperbole, of taking something that is only true in a qualified sense and declaring it true in an absolute sense (*Rule of Reason* R.viii.r). Blundeville adds to the list of argument forms in his logic textbook two figures he borrows from the rhetoricians: the "subjection" (*subjectio*)—"in the which we confute each question with a reason immediately following the same" (157)—and the "violation" (*inversio* or *metastasis*)—"whereby we shew the reason of our adversary, to make for us, and not for him" (158).

The centrality of figure to thought is again implied when *analogia* migrates to figure lists. Analogy is a basic principle of invention, the thought process underlying the similitude or comparison, and the instrument of inductive reasoning. Analogy is also the basic principle guiding judgment in usage and in logical, moral, and artistic decisions. Decorum requires the finding or creating of analogies, consensus, or harmony among the various considerations both inter- and intratextual entailed in any interpretive or communicative act. Erasmus calls this analogy *collatio,* a figure, which he defines as follows: "Just as a metaphor is a brief comparison, so likeness or *collatio* is a metaphor explained and accommodated to the matter" (*Eccl.* 3.218.429–30; trans. Boswell). Hoffmann summarizes the three primary ways Erasmus uses *collatio:* "On a grammatical level, *collatio* establishes the original by comparing a text with its source. When it comes to interpretation, *collatio* serves to compare similar meanings so as to uncover the consensus underlying the various expressions of truth in particular circumstances. In deliberative rhetoric, finally, the rhetorician employs *collatio* to compare both sides of an open question with an eye to that eventual agreement which is suggested by the most probable solution, by the 'equilibrium of truth' at the end of the persuasive process" (179). This awareness of a scheme at the center of the judgment process suggests that Erasmus has a sophisticated understanding of thought structures as figures. Also listing the virtue *analogia* as a scheme, Mosellanus may too (b.iii.r). Not including *analogie* among figures (even though he does include metaphor and similitude), Puttenham still makes reference to it being the fundamental principle of decorum:

> Now because his comeliness resteth in the good conformity of many things and their sundry circumstances, with respect one to another, so as there be found a just correspondency between them by this or that relation, the Greeks call it *Analogie* or a convenient proportion. This lovely conformity, or proportion, or conveniencie between the sense and the sensible hath nature herself most carefully observed in all her own works, then also by kind graft it in the appetites of every creature working by intelligence to covet and desire: and in their actions to imitate and perform: and of man chiefly before any other creature as well in his speeches as in every other part of his behavior. And this in generality and by an usual term is that which the Latins call [*decorum*]. (269)[107]

It is to this standard of judgment, this principle of analogy, that Hoskins must self-consciously refer when he declares, "But let discretion be the greatest and general figure of figures" (15). With principles of judgment figures, these humanists must have assumed that figures structure thought at a fundamental level.

Despite this obvious regarding of thought patterns as figures, there is little explicit rationale given in these manuals for doing so. Scaliger, it seems, comes close to declaring that figures, whether those of thought or diction, are mental patterns that impose structures upon all signs in discourse. He explains thought itself as embellishment. Disagreeing with Trebizond, who had defined *ennoian* or *sententia* (thought) as the matter invented to be polished by words, Scaliger defines it instead as the *ornata* or "furnishings" of an argument, "the fitting out" (*exordandum*), "the explaining" (*explanandum*), or "the interpellation, interruption, or disturbance" (*interpellando*) of the argument (4.1.449). The *sententia* is a subject to be dealt with, "an appendix" of an argument (4.1.449). He explains that since a sentence (*sententia*) is an appearance or image of a mental concept (*imago rei*) and since the words themselves are also an image of the mental image (4.1.449), the thought or matter—the sailing of Aeneas or the destruction of Troy, for example—can only be known by means of the way it has been reflected in the fitting out, by means of the "*temperationes* (combinations or constitutions) in the mind of the poet," which are summoned for the thought (4.1.449; trans. Boswell). In other words we understand the argument and the thought through the "furnishings" or *exornationes.* Scaliger seems to see thinking as a "figuring" process. Robertellus more explicitly endorses the doctrine that all speech is naturally shaped "according to the figuration of the mind" and, disagreeing with Alexander, argues that those natural patterns are as much figures as the artful imitation of them in speech (25v). But these comments are left without further elaboration of their implications. The one exception is Shaw, whose analysis we will examine below.

Fifth the figurative nature of cognition appears in the depiction of meaning making in dialectical invention. The combination of "places" or "categories" produces not only proofs but also predicates and names. This process of thought is treated as a language art, with a focus on both assembling and judging the appropriateness of names and propositions. As Wilson explains, to reason well one must "declare the nature of every word severally, to set the same words in a perfect sentence, and to knit them up in argument, so that hereby we might with ease espy, the right frame in matters, how they agree being lapped up in order" (*Rule of Reason* J.iv.v). In this analysis names themselves are treated as "arguments," and if "arguments," then *schemata.* Fraunce's explanation of this process is most explicit. He explains that "Paris" and "a good shepherd" from the proposition "Paris is no good shepherd" are "singly put down as two arguments, to wit, the subject and the adjunct" (*Lawiers Logike* 6v). To interpret *Paris,* then, we must see that the word refers not merely to a young man but also to the category of substance, and to interpret *shepherd* we must see that the word not only names an occupation but also an adjunct to a substance. The meaning of the word depends upon more than referential semantics; it also depends upon relational semantics—that is, the relationships among the categories evoked by the schemes to which the word is applied.[108] Wilson's explanation of the word *virtue* shows this process at work: "Virtue referred to the mind which containeth it is a word adjoined: compared with vice, it is a contrary; referred to justice, it is a general word [a genus]" (*Rule of Reason* K.vi.r). Being categories that predicate or assert a relation about any given subject, these "places" impose schemes or arguments. *Categoria,* which means "to accuse," sometimes shows up on figure lists. Fraunce explains the term in his logic manual, cognizant it names a *schema:* "These general heads of arguments . . . are called Categoremes, . . . [or] Categories, both which are Greek words of like signification, borrowed from the place of judgment, and applied to philosophical conceipts . . . [which] signify to say, or affirm one thing of an other, . . . where one thing added to an other is affirmed of the same, or else denied" (*Lawiers Logike* 10v–11r).

The principles that guide meaning making are the principles of logic, and these principles are those of decorum, summarized as usual by the metaphor of "agreement." Wilson, for example, states the common rule: "For whereas the places agree (that is to say, all things are referred to the one, that are referred to the other) there the proposition is good, and the latter part of the proposition, is truly spoken of the first. But where the places do not agree (that is to say, some things are referred to the one word, that are not referred to the other) there the things themselves can not agree" (*Rule of Reason* O.ii.v). This picture of meaning making based in "place-theory" has much in common with a new "blended-spaces model" proposed by Gilles Fauconnier and Mark Turner, two linguists working in the field of cognitive or frame semantics, who in *The Way We Think* (2002) suggest that words have meaning by virtue of the categories their use evokes and the blends logically possible among the categories due to context (44). The underlying assumption of frame semantics is that "language does not carry meaning, but guides it" through schema induction (Fauconnier, *Mental Spaces* xxii). In other words ordinary language refers by means of schemes and tropes, not without them. Such a picture of meaning making at the center of Renaissance logic instruction suggests again quite vividly that thought is by nature schematic, figured.

This depiction of meaning making also presents thinking as fundamentally tropological, when *tropological* is taken in the general sense of cognitive transference among frames. It is this general notion of metaphor as transference that I. A. Richards is approaching in *The Philosophy of Rhetoric* when he claims that "thought is metaphoric" (94). He describes metaphor as "two thoughts of different things active together and supported by a single word, or phrase, whose meaning is a resultant of their interaction" (93) and "a borrowing between and intercourse of *thoughts,* a transaction between contexts" (94). In work that has built upon Richard's ideas and spurred contemporary metaphor theory, Max Black calls this approach to metaphor the "interaction view" (38). Kenneth Burke echoes this view in his definition of metaphor in *A Grammar of Motives:* "Metaphor is a device for seeing something *in terms of* something else. . . . If we employ the word 'character' as a general term for whatever can be thought of as distinct (any thing, pattern, situation, structure, nature, person, object, act, role, process, event, etc.), then we could say that metaphor tells us something about one character as considered from the point of view of another character. And to consider A from the point of view of B is, of course, to use B as a perspective upon A" (503). Although Burke uses this definition for the specific figure of metaphor, he applies the notion to thinking generally. He claims such a process is a necessity for all definition: "To tell what a thing is, you place it in terms of something else" (24). Additionally dialectic itself is concerned with the "transformation of terms," and the office of dialectic is "the *dis*position and the *trans*position of terms" in relation to each other (402). Indeed Renaissance "place logic" shows cognition to be such a disposition and transposition of terms, to be a process of rearranging multible overlying "places" in order to create alignments or "common grounds"—to be the tropological acts of transference and of framing that produce conceptual, linguistic, and behavioral invention (that is, transformation).[109]

The Figurative Nature of Human Behavior

Not only do Renaissance humanists populate dialectic with figures, but they also describe human behavior in figural terms. Behavior results from choice and is distinguished from motion, which results from merely physical stimuli. Just as figures can be found in thought and verbal structures, so figures can be found in one's delivery. Some figures require voice and gesture for their full actualization. For example as Peacham explains, the figure *mimesis* (imitating others) occurs when the orator "counterfeits not only what one said, but also his utterance, pronunciation and gesture" ([1593] 138–39). Also *expolitio* (dwelling on a point but varying its presentation) can be effectuated by means of voice and gesture (Peacham [1593] 194). Fraunce tells us that *ironia* (irony) is created sometimes by the contrast between the sense of the words and "the manner of utterance" (*Arcadian Rhetoric* A7r).

Actions themselves can also be recognized as figures. Veltkirchius and Wilson indicate that *gesticulatio* (using gestures) is a figure. Scaliger asserts that silence and gestures alone, like those in the Spanish dances, can express figuratively their *synecdoches* without any words (3.31.305). Smith finds *mycterismus* (privy mocking) in a gesture, "when in shew of disdainful contempt of a person or thing we fling up our nose" (248). *Exuscitatio* (unbridled vociferation) requires the free use of the voice. *Cataphora* (impetus in delivery) and *tasis* (pleasant modulation with fluency, proper accent, and speed) are figures that apply to voice. Some manuals list the phonetic, orthographical, and rhythmic figures as aspects of pronunciation or delivery.

The most explicit treatment of behaviors themselves as figures is found in Samuel Shaw's play *Words Made Visible: or Grammar and Rhetorick Accommodated to the Lives and Manners of Men* (1679),[110] wherein we also find the fundamentality of figures to both human speech and thought. Because this work shows figures to have the center place in all dimensions of human thought and communication, it will serve as a good conclusion to our discussion thus far.

This work contains two plays, which were originally written for Shaw's schoolboys to perform. The first play features as characters the parts of speech, the second the tropes and figures. It is the second that is of relevance here. This second play dramatizes a friendly debate between the brothers Ellogus (elocution) and Eclogus (pronunciation) over which of them has done more in propagating and enlarging their father's dominions. Their father is Prince Eulogus (rhetoric) or "good speech." They each call forth their forces, who describe their conquests. Ellogus calls upon Invention to summon the tropes and figures, and Eclogus calls upon Affection to summon voice and gesture. This depiction shows rhetoric to be all tropes and figures, a doctrine reinforced when Prince Ellogus admits that to his cousins Monsieur Trope and Monsieur La Figure he has "wholly committed the management of [his] affairs" (104) and when Prince Eclogus at the end declares, "But before we part I do here declare that Prince *Elocution* with all his Tropes and Figures signifies nothing without *Pronunciation*" (187).

Shaw proclaims the ubiquity of tropes and figures in human converse. The four primary tropes have subdued the four corners of the earth (111). Metonymy remarks, "and what is most signal, where every thing is signal, it is hard to say" (113). All names result from Metonymy, "the great *Nomenclator* of the World" (114). Irony adds, "Here lies our excellency, that every man of us does all" (115–16). Metaphor declares, "Whatever is not Ironical is Metaphorical at least. . . . There is nothing New in the World: whatever is bears some resemblance, similitude, relation or allusion to what has been formerly; so that the present World is merely *Metaphorical*" (118–19). These basic tropes underlie all others. Synecdoche replies, "But, Sir, if you have a desire, and the fortitude to hear any more of our Conquests, we will send in our four principal Captains *Hyperbole, Catachresis, Metalepsis,* and *Allegory,* to give you a more particular account of the wonderful things, that they, being commissioned by us, have perform'd" (121–22). Figures, too, are fundamental. After Gnome has spoken, Eclogus responds, "I perceive that even plainness itself is *Figurative*" (139).

In the prologue to this play, Shaw places his own philosophy in opposition to that of the philosophers: "Neither the Aristotelian, nor the Cartesian Philosophy (as cunning as it is) have found out all the Tropical points that are in this great Globe. Nay, as this great Mystery has baffl'd Philosophers, so I doubt not to affirm, that it hath escap'd the Divines too" (97). He then announces as a rhetorician that "men live Tropes and Figures as well as speak them: and this is the thing that is principally design'd to be represented to you" (99).

People live tropes and figures, because these forms fundamentally structure their thoughts, speeches, and actions. As the character Prologue announces, "The whole life of man is a *Tropical Figurative* Converse, and a continual Rhetorication. If *Vossius, Ramus, Talaeus, Farnaby, Butler, DuGuard* (I will not say *Walker,* because he is yet alive) and a thousand more of them were hang'd out of the way, there would be no dearth of Rhetorick: for every individual man is a system of it" (98). Prologue also declares, "That the most illiterate people, in their most ordinary communication, do Rhetoricate by *Instinct,* as well as others do by Art, is very obvious, so obvious, that I dare say, take but an ingenious and well practis'd Scold, and with the help of an artificial Interpreter, She shall appear to give Examples of half the Tropes and Figures in Butler in one heat" (98–99). These tropes pattern all three dimensions of discourse—speech, thought, and action—as Trope explains to Prince Eclogus: "I am able in general (Sir) to assure you that all the World is turn'd *Tropical* (save only what's become *Figurative*) and that not only in those babbling things call'd words . . . but in manners and minds, in practices and principles too" (107). For example Hyperbole says of himself,

> I fashion the very minds and manners of men, as I please. By an *Hyperbolical* overweening (which is vulgarly call'd *ambition*) one man attempts to be *Universal Monarch,* and another *Universal Bishop;* and (which is good Rhetoric, though some Critics laugh at it for bad Grammar) one particular Church styles itself *Catholic.* By an *Hyperbolical* ingenuity the *Foot-boy* comes to be a *Butler,* the *Butler* comes to be a *Gentleman,* the *Gentleman* comes to be a *Count.* All that raise Estates, and all that are rais'd to Honours are my Clients. The Common people are all my Subjects too. What is *swearing,* but an *Hyperbolical* way of *affirming*? What is *stealing* and *cheating* but an Hyperbolical way of *getting* an Estate? What is *Superstition,* but an Hyperbolical way of being *Religious*? (127)

Irony points out his manifestations not only verbally but also behaviorally: "It is very usual, Sir, and in some cases al-a-mode to hang up men after they are dead: and that hanging is by my device" (116).

Figures too, whether of thought or speech (129), have equal dominion over all three dimensions. As one figure of thought, Prolepsis, reports, "Men do generally live and act, as well as speak *Proleptically.* All *wise* Men foresee *dangers,* and prevent them; all *good* men foresee *Temptations* to evil and avoid them" (132). Just as "men may act virtuously by the same ingenuity as they commit vice" (134), so "the ingenious *Physician* foresees the too sudden recovery of his Patient, and knowing, that health as well as wit is never ought except it be dear bought, wisely retards the over hasty cure, and keeps him long ill, that when he is once recover'd he may be long well. The Sagacious *Lawyer* foresees the dangerous and disadvantageous agreement that his Client is like to make with his Adversary, and therefore prolongs his suit a Term, or two, or ten, or twenty" (132). Gnome is a figure of thought, who "by a grave and naked propounding of the undoubted Maxims of Divinity, Morality, Policy or Philosophy, . . . tacitly appeal[s] to the Reasons and Judgments of Men, . . . [and achieves] greatest glory . . . in making Men to live Gnomically, as all just and righteous men do, who by keeping their words, make good their Bargains, paying their Debts, and such like things, do most effectually confute and baffle iniquity out of the World" (137–39). Noema works often without words but through "allusive glances and gestures" (140), and by means of Diatyposis "all manner of Tradesmen do put you off with bad wares, or scant measure, or at excessive rates so lively, that you would verily think (but that he swears the contrary) that he cheated you" (146–47). "All *Conquerours* are what they are" by Digression (156), and by Increment "the spiritual *Tyrants* take away first the *Estates* of the Hereticks, then their *liberty,* then their *lives*" (159).

Shaw quite explicitly shows figures of speech to be figures of thought that also structure all three dimensions. Tmesis, a grammatical figure that splits apart a compound word by interposing other words in between, becomes any improper interposition between people: "I have taught . . . all *Trades-men* by the *Interposition* of Covetousness, to part *Honesty* and *Gain;* which of old were great Cronies. But my Masterpiece lies amongst the *Sacrilegious Crew* that meddle with other men's Wives. If men and their Wives be not a close Complex, there is none in Nature, and yet I have suborn'd a Schismatical sort of people to interpose between them, and to make a division without a divorce. What is the most fashionable adultery, but a temporal *Tmesis* in Matrimony?" (181–82). Ellipsis, "commonly call'd *want of the Word,*" applies not only to grammar but also to various kinds of silence. By repressing God's word, "that mighty Prince the *Pope* keeps the people in due obedience to his Laws and Rules, as absolutely as heart can wish. . . . All *Cowards,* that betray the Truth by their unseasonable silence, and all *false Friends,* that have not a word to speak for their Friend in time of danger, are my Disciples" (177). Asyndeton (the lack of conjunctions), causes "the want of Love and Union in all the world and amongst all the members of it. By me States and Kingdoms fight, and kill, and conquer one another. . . . And all the Swarm of Beggars that go together by Apposition, without any Legal Conjunction (and yet prove as fruitful as the best licens'd Couple in the Country)" (178–79).

The inseparable connections among these three dimensions of discourse are further underscored by the representation of thought as the "kinswoman" of style and diction as the "kinswoman" of delivery (129). Additionally from these examples we see that figures do not refer to only those devices of indirectness, dissimulation, or deviation, but also include the straightforward, genuine, and common. As *epanorthosis* or *correctio* includes both the "honest penitents" and the "dissembling *Temporizers*" (165–66), so the other figures have well- and ill-motivated uses.

It is true that Shaw claims originality for this work: these plays offer, in the author's words, "a pleasant new Fancy, clear Wit, brisk Satyre, and good Morality" (preface A1v), and this originality may indeed be his self-conscious recognition of thought and action as figured. But if Shaw sees, it is likely that others also see but simply leave the insight unexplained. Erasmus, Veltkirchius, Sturm, Peacham, Hoskins, Blount, and Smith demonstrate this vision implicitly by showing figures to encompass argument, speech, and behavior without clear distinctions between the figure and nonfigure.

These doctrines anticipate those of twentieth-century theorists who are beginning again to explore tropes and schemes as thought structures. Burke has opined that forms such as comparison, contrast, series, and chiasmus function as "our modes of understanding anything; they are implicit in the processes of abstraction and generalization by which we think" (*Counter-statement* 142). In "The Four Master Tropes," he resurrects the Ramistic set of basic tropes and treats metaphor, metonymy, synecdoche, and irony, like Renaissance rhetoricians do, as lines of thinking or perspectives (*Grammar of Motives* 503–17). George Lakoff and Mark Johnson have argued similarly in *Metaphors We Live By* that metaphors structure and guide thinking; Raymond W. Gibbs in *The Poetics of Mind* shows that tropes play an essential role in our cognitive system and function automatically in our understanding of ordinary language (446). These contemporary studies may be more theoretically astute but are less attuned to the variety and complexity of patterns at work in discourse than are Renaissance depictions.

TREATING SPEECH, THOUGHT, AND BEHAVIOR as constituted by figures pulls all three domains into language but does not lead these humanists to philosophical nihilism, as the same insight does followers of Nietzsche. Dooming humans to the prison house of language and consequently to ultimate epistemological and metaphysical uncertainty, Nietzche in "On Truth and Lies in a Nonmoral Sense" reduces human consciousness to language conventions and trope, defines trope as a mere representation of an object in the world (referential semantics) and language conventions as cultural constructions, denies the existence of universal forms (except trope), and discounts body in favor of mind.[111] In other words, language is a prison house because human consciousness is pure representation, whereas the grounding of truth requires perfect reference, an impossibility since mind is split from body. The monist position that there are only forms without ultimate meaning, ironically, depends upon an underlying dualistic belief that a referential plain style is one thing and a figured, artificial, ambiguous style another. This monism simiply denies the possibility for the first and embraces the second.[112] Another dualism arises when these monists point out, on the one hand, the inadequate referentiality of language, but on the other, language's indicativeness of culture, making culture the perfect referent in a system incapable of perfect reference and their own grounding assumptions as positivist as those of their opponents, the objectivists.

In contrast, Renaissance humanists are neither nihilists nor positivists. They believe that humans are thoroughly immersed in meaning and meaning-making, which is both nonfictional and fictional. Because contextualized in real and shared physical and social worlds, communication involves real knowledge building and character making, but because inescapably perspectival and creative, remains open to further interpretation and transformation. Their middle way results from attributing to consciousness both particular and universal forms and transformational procedures, derived from both individual and common cultural and bodily experience.[113] These forms are both tropes and schemes, which create not only imaginative representations but also rational arguments about the external world—since representations are arguments. Tropes and schemes also guide and reflect their own processes of construction, thereby indicating as well both the internal world of the speaker and the meta-discursive operations of language. What determines truth and reference is not absence of representation in language, but rather the achievement of the universal standards of congruency, relevance, appropriate scope, and suitable balance between adaptability and stability within one's argument and one's performance. In reconciling dualisms and monisms, this philosophy provides a single, consistent hermeneutic/heuristic for the genres within both the humanities and the sciences. We have already seen how place theory shows figures to prompt meaning constructions. The remaining functions of figures will be the subject of the next chapter.

Chapter 3

unctions of Figures and Styles

Tools and Mirrors

Besides conflating rhetoric and figure and then depicting speech, thought, and action as all fundamentally figured, Renaissance rhetoricians also blur the distinction between the figure and the nonfigure by treating all forms as behaviors indicative of points of view and characters. These behaviors function as both persuasive tools and reflective mirrors simultaneously.[1] A speaker employs forms for the purposes of informing and affecting an audience, but those forms reflect the very actions and motives that produced them. A focus on forms/figures and their constitutive role in human thought and communication, then, highlights text as behavior, encourages a hermeneutic that assumes both text and figure are both performance and argument, places ethics at the center of stylistic instruction, and treats the form/figure as the microcosm of human discourse. Renaissance rhetoricians share this view with their classical forebears in the Isocratean tradition but make the paradigm more explicit than do their ancestors through increased attention to the meaning of style and figures.[2] Sherry emphasizes the importance of giving heed to functions when he reprimands the schoolmasters who merely point out figures but fail to examine the purposes for them: "But what profit is herein if they go no further?" he asks ([1550] 12). Even though these pedagogues do not fully explicate the implications of their interpretive practice, all approach textual analysis with the same set of assumptions: their art of rhetoric presents a meaningful utterance as a motivated act of a speaker, who is reading and responding to such acts of others and of self and who is attempting to elicit a response from an audience. (In the Renaissance this audience is multiple, inclusive of others, self, and God.) This hermeneutic is broader and more integrative than the one Aristotle offers; yet it is precisely on this point of meaning that Aristotle's own efforts to separate content and style fail. This failure itself provides evidence that the broader view espoused in the Renaissance is the more realistic view.

Figure/Style/Text as Performance

Ultimately forms/figures are behaviors. Whether verbal or thought patterns such as reversal (*antimetabole*) or contradiction (antithesis); strategies such as enumeration (*enumeratio*) and insinuation (*emphasis*); speech acts such as an insult (*insultatio*), command (*prostaktikon*), and warning (*admonitio*); discourse chunks such as parable (*parabole*) or allusion (*parechesis*); large-scale speech genres such as myth, history, and drama; effects such as correctness (*katharotes*), vividness (*enargia*), and passion (*pathopoeia*); or personal characteristics such as sincerity (*aletheia*) or affectation (*cacozelias*)—all these types of forms are fundamentally behaviors.[3] The latter types differ from the former simply in being more complex behavior sets. In fashioning definitions for each, we can describe each as either a product or a process, for form and behavior are two faces of the same phenomenon. *Conclusio* is both the conclusion to a syllogism and the process of drawing a conclusion; *encomion* is both the genre of praise and the act of praising. *Aletheia* is both the quality of sincerity and the act of speaking truthfully and spontaneously. The behavioral dimension of figures is evident in many of their very names: *metaphora* is a "transference," *anaphora* is a "carrying back," *antimetabole* is a "turning about," *epizeuxis* is "a fastening upon," and *commoratio* is a "lingering." Likewise the names of larger complexes are still behaviors: a *parabola* (parable) is a "placing beside" and a *prosopopoeia* (impersonation) is a "mask making."

While the literal meanings of the terms are obscure to those no longer educated in Latin and Greek, they seem not to be so to the classical and Renaissance rhetoricians. The term *schema* means "posture" and derives from *echein,* meaning "to behave."[4] An awareness of figures as behaviors seems evident when Quintilian refers to figures as "gestures of language" (9.1.13), when Sherry defines a scheme as "a behavior, manner, or fashion either of sentence, oration, or words" ([1550] 25), when Soarez remarks that "since figures are, as it were, the gestures of a speech, it is as ridiculous to pursue them without thought, as it is to seek postures and gestures without a body" (334), and when Vossius says that by "dress[ing] with different schemes . . . speech is brought to life as if with different actions and deeds" (4.11.229). The insight shows up in descriptions of individual figures. Fraunce calls figures of thought "motions of the mind" (*Arcadian Rhetoric* E4v); Smith calls the *enthymema* the "whole action and sentence of the mind" (260); and Peacham, who calls figures "gestures and countenances of speech" ([1593] 1), describes the figure *antonomasia* (renaming) in such expressions as "Your Honor" or "Your worship" as a performance: "for by this form the orator when he speaketh to high dignities, he boweth (as it were) the knee of his speech, and lifteth up the eye of his phrase to the bright beams of earthly glory, thereby declaring his due reverence, and their high dignity" ([1593] 23).

As behaviors figures/forms encode and guide the proper delivery of the text. This insight these humanists make more explicit than do their classical predecessors, who only give general counsel that one's delivery must harmonize with both style and invention. Renaissance rhetoricians, however, specify that figures provide performance clues. Day, for example, declares that figures supply "well ordering and delivery" ([1599] 76). Because "the actor does nothing but what he understands from the manner whereby the text was made, figured, and disposed by the poet," Scaliger instructs that the knowledge of figures "ought not to be foreign" to the poet (7.5.904; trans. Boswell). The Ramists recognize the same connection. Fraunce, echoing Talaeus, counsels that the figures guide the use of both voice and gesture. The voice must enact the figure:

> In the particular applying of the voice to several words, we make tropes that be most excellent plainly appear. For without this change of voice, neither any Irony, nor lively Metaphor can well be discerned. By that kind of voice which belongeth to whole sentences, all kinds of figures and passionate ornaments of speech are made manifest. In figures of words which altogether consist in sweet repetitions and dimensions, is chiefly conversant that pleasant and delicate tuning of the voice, which resembleth the consent and harmony of some well ordered song. In other figures of affections, the voice is more manly, yet diversely, according to the variety of passions that are to be expressed. (*Arcadian Rhetoric* H7r)

Gesture too must follow the figures: "Continued and flowing sentences" may cue the outstretching of the arm (K2r), or doubting (*addubitatio*) and prayers (*deesis*) may require putting both hands together (K3r). John Brinsley (1585–1665) in *Ludus Literarius* (1612), a teaching manual, gives the same advice to the schoolmaster: "Let them [the boys] also be taught carefully, in what word the Emphasis lieth; and therefore which is to be elevated in the pronunciation. As namely those words in which the chief Trope or Figure is" (214). Walker also instructs, "Now those words which the voice is chiefly to stay upon, and give an extraordinary Emphasis to, are such, in which there lies some figure, as all *Antitheta's* and *correspondents,* and words relating to another, and generally the *mediums* (in which lies the greatest burden) of our arguments" (120–21).

Being constituted by figures, style is also fundamentally behavior. This reciprocity between figure and performance justifies delivery's inclusion within style and also explains why in the Ramists and in Farnaby (29–30), the levels and qualities of style appear in the discussion of delivery. The rules of delivery are, after all, the same as those for style. Quintilian instructs, "The rules for delivery are identical with those for the language of oratory itself. For as our language must be correct, clear, ornate and appropriate, so with our delivery" (11.3.30). Talaeus, remember, remarks similarly that delivery is the same thing as style, and both Day and Father Thomas Wright (1561–1624) use the term *delivery* as a synonym for style and speech.[5] Style, then, should not be conceived as one's words or signs but rather one's use and arrangement of them into forms, which activity gives them signification and turns them into signs. Both Donawerth and Waswo have recognized that Renaissance educators emphasize not words but the structured contexts of words as being meaningful (19; 220). These two critics do not equate this structured context with figures. Ernst Cassirer comes closer when he sees that the Renaissance philologists "argued that the scholastics had seen only the outward, grammatical structure of language, while its real kernel, which is to be sought not in grammar but in stylistics, had remained closed to them" (*Philosophy of Symbolic Forms* 1:127). Gerald L. Bruns also recognizes that this tradition views form as a mode of action with meaning: "The most abstruse conceit shows itself, after all, to be an act of predication, even as the most resonant and distracting scheme adumbrates a basic syntactical procedure. Thus it is that the 'veil of words,' however much it may work to conceal thought, is able at the same time to reveal what it conceals. Structure in speech, that is to say, makes signification possible" (251–52). The unspoken but clear implication to follow from Renaissance instruction is that it is the figure or the behavior that is the smallest fundamental unit of meaning.

With discourse a web of schemes, text itself is also fundamentally behavior. The humanists' curriculum encourages this understanding of text because the oration is an oral form, the uniform pedagogical method in the classroom treats texts as performances, and the other departments of the language arts are described in behavioral terms.

Delivery is the culminating manifestation of the oration, the deep-structure paradigm from which all other genres are merely superficial variations. Cicero's advice is commonplace: "But the effect of all of these oratorical devices depends on how they are delivered. Delivery, I assert, is the dominant factor in oratory" (*De Oratore* 3.56.213). This oral dimension requires the text to be seen as drama. Quintilian does so, instructing, "It is at the close of our drama that we must really stir the theatre, when we have reached the place for the phrase with which the old tragedies and comedies used to end, 'Friends, give us your applause'" (6.1.52). The oration's connection to oral performance has not yet been lost in the Renaissance.[6] Wilson repeats the classic reference to Demosthenes's praise of delivery: "Demosthenes therefore, that famous orator, being asked what was the chiefest point in all oratory, gave the chief and only praise to pronunciation, being demanded what was the second and the third, he still made answer, 'Pronunciation,' and would make none other answer till they left asking, declaring hereby that art without utterance can do nothing, utterance without art can do right much" (241).[7] As late as 1679, Shaw, remember, has Prince Eclogus (delivery) proclaim the indivisibility of delivery and style: "But before we part I do here declare that Prince *Elocution* with all his Tropes and Figures signifies nothing without *Pronunciation*" (187).

The regular enactment of text in schoolroom practice helped to keep alive the oral dimension of discourse and its situatedness within a dramatic context. Oral performance is the focus of ideal classroom methodology. The lesson begins with the schoolmaster introducing a text to his schoolboys through an oral reading. The second step, close analysis of text, requires determining the appropriate voice and gesture for such an oral recitation, since reading requires bringing the text back to life. When Quintilian explains reading, he does so with oral performance in mind: "Reading remains for consideration. In this connexion there is much that can only be taught in actual practice, as for instance when the boy should take breath, at what point he should introduce a pause into a line, where the sense ends or begins, when the voice should be raised or lowered, what modulation should be given to each phrase, and when he should increase or slacken speed, or speak with greater or less energy. In this portion of my work I will give but one golden rule: to do all these things, he must understand what he reads" (1.8.1–2). Oral performance is also the goal of William Kempe (c. 1563–1601), who in his instructions to the schoolmaster includes voice and gesture among the textual elements advanced students should observe in such close reading: "all the use of the Arts, as not only the words and phrases, not only the examples of the arguments; but also the axiom, wherein every argument is disposed; the syllogism, whereby it is concluded; the method of the whole treatise, and the passages, whereby the parts are joined together. Again, he shall observe not only every trope, every figure, as well of words as of sentences; but also the Rhetorical pronunciation and gesture fit for every word, sentence and affection" ([1588] 233). The pupils thereby learn that the written text provides performance clues and that a good reading entails bringing the acting of the utterance into harmony with the forms and ideas structuring the utterance. Step three, the memorization of the original passage, requires oral recitation. In step four as the schoolboys imitate the exemplary passages held up for study, they pay attention not only to the materials of the speech but also to the methods the original author used in order to accomplish his designs. This analysis then guides their own efforts to accomplish their own purposes with their own specified audiences and materials. Since the pupils know they must perform their own compositions before a live audience, they approach the task with attention to the impression their speeches will make as "real-life" actions. This focus on performance will guide step five, the revision and memorization of their own compositions. The concluding sixth step requires the schoolboys to deliver their own memorized compositions before an audience of peers and schoolmaster, who provide feedback.[8] This oral exam allows the pupils to practice speaking and acting and serves as the measure of their *facilitas*—the behavioral objective of this extensive language arts training—inclusive of fluency, readiness of invention, oral interpretive skills, and good judgment. Pupils learn that giving the utterance "life" entails portraying a believable human being in full performance. They also learn to see discourse as a conscious, motivated act of a speaker performed before an audience on a given occasion. These lessons are reinforced by the custom of having schoolboys perform plays each year, wherein they must determine, in the words of the Winchester grammar school headmaster Christopher Johnson, "what must be pronounced with what expression [and gesture]" (British Museum MS. Add. 4379 88v; qtd. in Baldwin 1:328) so as to re-create, in the words of the Lothbury schoolmaster Hoole, "the very life" (*New Discovery* 142).

Additionally both classical and Renaissance rhetoricians describe speech and all of its various departments as if composed of behaviors. In *Antidosis* Isocrates provides an explication of several extracts from his previous speeches in order to show evidence "that all [his] writings tend toward virtue and justice" (§67). These explications delineate these speeches as if behaviors. In *To Nicocles* he has, "reproach[ed] monarchs," "enjoin[ed] upon Nicocles not to be easy-going," and "tried to persuade him." Isocrates has not paid "court to his wealth nor to his power, but plead[ed] the cause of his subjects, and strive[n] with all [his] powers to secure for them the mildest government possible" (§70–72). In *De Oratore* Cicero's Crassus describes Antonius's style in terms of behaviors and their effects: "Do you not see what this style of Antonius's is? It is bold, vehement, vigorous in delivery, carefully prepared and safeguarded in respect of every aspect of the case, keen, penetrating, precise, dwelling upon each separate point, making courteous concessions and gallant onsets, intimidating, imploring, employing a vast variety of styles without ever exhausting the appetite of the audience" (3.9.32). Quintilian issues the warning that the speaker should avoid boasting, groveling, flattering, using affected buffoonery, disregarding authority, and immodesty in dealing with obscenity or unseemliness, for these behaviors all show one being "over-anxious either to please or amuse" (11.1.30). Hermogenes teaches that one produces the copious style (*peribolē*) by "discuss[ing] a larger genus to which a species belongs," by "mention[ing] the undefined as well as the defined," by "discuss[ing] the whole to which a part belongs," by "adding a point and then breaking it down into its component parts," or by making "unnecessary statements" (1.11.278–79).

The same focus on behavior prevails in Renaissance descriptions of style. The acute and subtle style, Vives writes, results "whenever one penetrates to the heart of a proposed question and, stripping away all the rind, shows the kernel perfectly clean," "divid[es] and cut[s] up the question into little pieces," and neatly arranges "proper, apt, [and] natural" words (*De ratione dicendi* 116). "Anyone who wishes to give his example the fullest treatment possible," Erasmus instructs, "will set out all the separate points of similarity and dissimilarity and will compare one with another" (*De copia* 619).

The same focus prevails also in the descriptions of the art's other departments. Both invention and disposition, which are shared by logic and rhetoric, are depicted as mental actions. One finds arguments by "drawing" a subject through the "places" one mentally visits, and one frames arguments by "disposing" ideas into proper arrangements. These cognitive behaviors are even called "acts" in logic textbooks. Zachary Coke, a late Renaissance logician, for example, refers to thought as action in his *The Art of Logic* (1654): "The proper end of Logic, is, the ordering and directing of mans cogitations (or the acts of mans understanding) in the knowledge of things" (7). In *The Passions of the Minde in Generall* (1604), Wright reflects this tendency to view action as the essence of human consciousness when he identifies the three basic types of actions that "proceed from mens souls": "Some are internal and immaterial, as the acts of our wits and wills; others be mere external and material, as the acts of our senses, seeing, hearing, moving, &c. Others stand betwixt these two extremes, and border upon them both. . . . Those actions then . . . we call Passions, and Affections, or perturbations of the mind, . . . prosecuting some good thing, or flying some ill thing, causing therewithall some alteration in the body" (7–8). Also described as actions, the processes of memorizing and then remembering are depicted as walking through, populating, and scanning places set in the mind.

Aristotle is the exception, and his approach is similar to language philosophers who define speech as words or linguistic structures. His focus is less on the behavior of the speaker and more on verbal devices and their effects on audiences. While he acknowledges that delivery is a facet of style, he sees delivery as separate from and even less worthy "as an elevated subject of inquiry" than words (*Rhetoric* 3.1 1403b20; 1404a1). This severance between style and delivery leads him to say in the *Poetics* that the poet need not concern himself with "the difference between command and prayer, simple statement and threat, question and answer, and so forth," for "the theory of such matters belongs to acting and the professors of that art. Whether the poet knows these things or not, his art as a poet is never seriously criticized on that account" (1456b8–10). He discounts Protagoras's criticism of Homer for using a command where a prayer was meant, since this detail pertains to delivery (1456b12–15). Scaliger recognizes this effort in Aristotle to sever verbal language, figures, and delivery, and he faults him for it: "Aristotle, however, says that they [figures] are of no importance to the poet, just to the actor. . . . [However,] a command, a vow, a narration, a threat assert some face to a speech. . . . And if it is thus, it ought not to be foreign both to the knowledge and use of the poet." Scaliger instead agrees with Protagoras's evaluation of Homer and then credits the awareness of this unity between style and delivery to the more enlightened Latins (7.5.904).

Figure/Style/Text as Argument: Both Tool of Persuasion and Mirror of Mind

Because they are behaviors situated in temporal, spatial, physical, social, logical, and psychological relations, figures, styles, and texts have meaning. Where there are relations, there is meaning. Because this meaning results from a constructing consciousness both recognizing and imposing forms upon real data, both expression and its interpretation are best understood as someone's argument. Of course with the oration as the master genre, all texts are treated not only as performances but also as arguments. Styles and figures are seen as arguments too. The full meaning or argument of a figure, style, and text derives precisely from all the situated actions that constructed it. These actions always make assertions, express emotions, and both create and reveal characters. These meanings then have two primary effects: they reflect the mind of the speaker, and they move a consenting audience to like-mindedness.

Because of the reflective nature of discourse, Isocrates self-consciously acknowledges his speeches as the "image of my thought and my whole life" (*Antidosis* §189). Renaissance rhetoricians declare the concept even more explicitly.[9] Erasmus calls both speech and behavior "mirrors" (*Cic.* 116), and Agricola remarks that "speech is the sign of what the speaker's mind contains" (1.1; McNally 395). Puttenham expresses the mimetic function clearly: "And because this continual course and manner of writing or speech showeth the matter and disposition of the writer's mind, more than one or few words or sentences can show, therefore there be that have called style, the image of man [*mentis character*] for man is but his mind, and as his mind is tempered and qualified, so are his speeches and language at large, and his inward conceits be the metal of his mind, and his manner of utterance the very warp and woof of his conceits" (160–61). Wright holds the same belief: "Words represent most exactly the very image of the mind and soul: wherefore *Democritus* calleth speech . . . the image of life; for in words, as in a glass may be seen a man's life and inclination. Wherefore *Diogenes* wondered that men would not buy earthen pots before they proved by the sound whether they were whole or broken, yet they would be contented to buy men by sight before they proved their speech" (105). He extends this mimetic function to actions as well: "The internal conceits and affection[s] of our minds are not only expressed with words, but also declared with actions: . . . for indeed words and actions spring from the same root, that is understanding and affections: and as leaves, flowers, and fruit declare the virtues of trees, so words and actions the qualities of minds" (124–25).

Like speech and action, so figures are seen as mirrors of the mind. Peacham declares that figures are those "forms of speech . . . by which the singular parts of man's mind are most aptly expressed, and the sundry affections of his heart most effectually uttered" ([1593] AB.iii.v). A century and a half later, Joseph Priestley (1733–1804) still retained this understanding of figures and makes the point clearly:

> Figurative speech, therefore, is indicative of a person's real feelings and state of mind, not by means of the words it consists of, considered as *signs of separate ideas*, and interpreted according to their common acceptation; but as *circumstances* naturally attending those feelings which compose any state of mind. Those figurative expressions, therefore, are scarcely considered and attended to as *words*, but are viewed in the same light as *attitudes*, *gestures*, and *looks*, which are infinitely more expressive of *sentiments* and *feelings* than words can possibly be. ([1777] 77)

Not only do figures mirror the speaker's mind, but they also then affect the hearer. These rhetoricians attribute to figures a host of effects meant to move the hearers' minds and hearts.[10] As Melanchthon puts it, figures are used "so that they [the hearers] may be either informed or emotionally moved" (*Elem.* 49r, 278).[11] The figures' usefulness as persuasive tools has received some attention by modern critics who espouse a "value-added" theory of figuration.[12] But seldom have critics seen, as humanist rhetoricians do, that this persuasion results because figures are mirrors, making arguments, expressing emotions, and revealing character.

Figures and Styles as Assertions

These rhetoricians read both styles and figures for the assertions they make.[13] Styles make statements. Quintilian observes that "a translucent and iridescent style merely serves to emasculate the subject which it arrays with such a pomp of words" (8.Pr.20–21). Similarly Lamy asserts that the style "denote[s] the quality of the matter that is the subject of the discourse" (4.24). Like styles, so all tropes and schemes are lines of argument. These manual writers indicate that forms of all kinds inevitably make assertions of two types: one is incontrovertible and automatic due to the relations giving the form its identity; the other accrues because of the multiple motives behind the form's use and the multiplex functions the form participates in due to its contexts. (This double nature means, incidentally, that meaning making has both monistic and dualistic properties.) The first kind of meaning results from the relations that give the form its identity. Figures assert about the subject matter the relations they impose on the subject matter. Forms in and of themselves argue regardless of the actual subject matter applied to the form. They assert what they are. For example antithesis argues contrariety, *hypozeuxis* subordination, *isocolon* parallelism, and *orthotes* straightforwardness. This assertion is incontrovertible by definition. The farther away forms are from being fundamental thought patterns, though, the more dependent they are on their contexts for recognition. The *objurgatio* (reproof) relies upon more reinforcing signs than does the antithesis. There are many forms of repetition, all arguing importance of some kind, with the specific reasons for importance dependent upon context.

Both classical and Renaissance rhetoricians point out that figures argue the relations they embody. Demetrius explains that because of the antithetical form in which they are written, clauses that are not really antithetical appear to be so (§24). Cicero remarks that *amplificatio* (augmenting or diminishing) can either increase the importance of a subject or diminish and disparage it (*De Oratore* 3.27.104). Similarly Aquila states that "by this means, the orator elevates petty subjects and extends narrow ones" (22; trans. Leff in "Latin" 275).[14] In the Renaissance Melanchthon points out that a *sententia,* because it identifies a statement as a general truth, can function as the major premise in a syllogism (50r).[15] Hoskins instructs that by means of illustration a speaker argues that something is "evident" (17). Smith indicates that "Auxesis of small things makes great matters, so Meiosis of great matters makes but trifles" (56). He explains that *synoeceiosis* (paradox) "teacheth to conjoin divers things, or contraries, or to reconcile things that differ" (120). Shaw remarks that *incrementum* (growing, increasing) is not appropriate for describing someone's progression toward badness, for with *incrementum* "men only ascend": "Men do not *grow up* in wickedness, but *sink into* it; and this they do by . . . *Decrement*" (159).

When rhetoricians give guidelines for the proper formation of figures, they do so knowing that figures signify given relationships. Wilson, for example, warns about tropes: "Notwithstanding, there ought much wariness to be used in choosing of words translated, that the same be not unlike that thing whereunto it is applied, nor yet that the translation be uncomely, or such as may give occasion of any unclean meaning" (*Art of Rhetoric* 197). Because figures must be formed according to the relations they assert, Peacham says an allegory based on unlikeness is absurd ([1593] 27). He warns that *diaresis,* the form of speech that divides the genus into species, will lead to confusion if it numbers "too few kinds" or reckons "up too many," and "if things of another kind be mingled with it" (124). Similarly he advises that hyperbole not be used "to amplify trifles, or diminish the estimation of good things, [for] by the one it becometh a vice of speech called Bomphiologia, by the other it is turned into Tapinosis" ([1593] 33).

The second kind of meaning accrues from the relations in which these figures participate because of context. These forms make additional arguments when in use, and these assertions change in each new act of construction. For example Hermogenes explains that the figure of division (enumerating parts) can produce "an indirect expression of Abundance" (1.11.291).[16] Puttenham suggests that Caesar expresses the "celerity of his conquest" and thereby his great prowess through his omission of conjunctions (*asyndeton*) in his often-quoted "*Veni, vidi, vici. I came, I saw, I overcame*" (186). The use of *antimetabole* (chiasmus) Peacham says can serve "to praise, dispraise, to distinguish, but most commonly to confute by the inversion of the sentence" ([1593] 164).

Even Ramus shows figures instrumental in argument making. In his commentary on Cicero's first Catilinarian oration, Ramus observes that the digression and exclamation in "O Immortal Gods!" (1.4.9) asserts "the outrageousness of the present situation" (*In Ciceronis orationes* Q1v; trans. Mack in "Ramus Reading" 120). Because figures assert relations, they must be used when the speaker needs to express those relations.

Besides direct explication of textual figures, other evidence suggests that these rhetoricians assume figures to express ideas. For example, remarking that all figures ultimately derive from dialectical topics, Melanchthon implies that all make arguments (*Elem.* 45v, 263). Puttenham connects sound to sense and the auricular figures to argument: "For the ear is properly but an instrument of conveyance for the mind, to apprehend the sense by the sound" (207). Lamy suggests that figures argue when he declares that "as Nature puts the members of the Body into postures proper for defence or insult in a single Duel, so the same Nature prompts us to Figures in our Discourse, and that we give them such touches and circumstances as may justify the controverted truth and refute all that is brought in opposition" (4.46). Also figures are often described by the mental path they direct the hearer along. The author of the *Ad Herennium* describes the cognitive working of *contrarium* (reasoning by contraries): "from a statement which is not open to question it draws a thought which is in question, in such a way that the inference cannot be refuted, or can be refuted only with much the greatest difficulty" (9.18.26).[17] Quintilian explains that *syllogismus* (implying the consequent by signs) leads a hearer to identify an unexpressed conclusion: "One thing is magnified in order to effect a corresponding augmentation elsewhere, and it is by reasoning that our hearers are then led on from the first point to the second which we desire to emphasize" (8.4.15). Similarly Smith views *metalepsis* as a line of thinking that leads to an assertion of relationship: "This Trope is a kind of Metonymy, signifying by the effect a Cause far off by an effect nigh at hand; and it teaches the understanding to dive down to the bottom of the sense, and instructs the eye of the wit to discern a meaning afar off; for which properly it may be aptly compared to an high prospect, which presents to the view of the beholder an object remote, by leading the eye from one mark to another by a lineal direction, till it discerns the object inquired" (52).

This recognition of figures as lines of argument anticipates the recent attention in contemporary scholarship to a figure's argumentative function. Most recent work has focused on metaphor and tropes, but a few studies have begun to explore selected schemes as arguments. Fahnestock shows that certain figures such as antithesis, *gradatio, antimetabole, ploche,* and *polyptoton* have "argumentative content" in that a "premise is conveyed" because they "perfectly epitomize certain patterns of thought or argument" (*Rhetorical Figures* 22, 26). Lanham points out that alliteration, for example, acts like "powerful glue," suggesting "a natural affinity between objects or concepts" through front rhyme (*Analyzing Prose* 125). Chaim Perelman and Lucie Olbrechts-Tyteca have also demonstrated the argumentative function of certain verbal forms. *Antimetabole,* for instance, works to tease apart different senses of the same word, as in "We should not live to eat but eat to live" (*New Rhetoric* 428, 444). Several recent literary scholars are beginning to notice the Renaissance attribution of argumentative content to figures.

In *Renaissance Figures of Speech,* Patricia Parker, for example, cites numerous Renaissance remarks about the figure *hysteron proteron* (inversion of proper order), showing its status as an argument (Adamson, Alexander, and Ettenhuber 136–45). In the same volume, Katrin Ettenhuber shows the Renaissance awareness of hyperbole as argument (210–11). Renaissance precepts suggest, though, that all forms make arguments.

Because figures result from an organizing consciousness that puts elements together in order to convey ideas to and elicit responses from an audience, figures reveal utterances to be a speaker's positions, interpretations, points of view. Not only lines of argument, figures also chart lines of thinking that the speaker followed in constructing the discourse. Figures "color" the subject matter, presenting the speaker's take on things. Lever, the logician, has this general awareness of expression as perspective: "Words are voices framed with heart and tongue, uttering the thoughts of the mind" (1). Twentieth-century theory has emphasized that these constructs have epistemic functions: that is, they reveal an author's ideology and ways of making sense of experience, which, if persuasive, then serve as a model of knowledge making for the audience. Ideologies, which underlie all arguments, have been characterized as grand narratives that give meaning to life's actors and events by placing them in cause/effect relations. Although Renaissance rhetoricians do not explain this ideological connection, they are aware of the same and that a speaker's figures assert relations about not only subject matter, but also audience, self, occasion, and the other circumstances of the utterance. Peacham, for example, reads a speaker's use of a particular figure for the speaker's values and assumptions. He opines that a speaker who uses an *aenigma* (riddle) with an audience who cannot understand it thinks well of himself, ill of his audience, and naught of integrity ([1593] 29). Likewise Shaw proposes that the poor man who can see "the whole World" in his little portion reads God's synecdoche well and reflects an optimism and gratitude born of religious faith, while "the covetous Muck-worm," who misreads the synecdoche and takes the part for the whole, lacks the eternal perspective and "loseth the whole for a little part" (121).

Renaissance precepts accord with Lanham's statement that "to write is to compose a world as well as view one" (*Analyzing Prose* 3), and with Richard Ohmann's belief that stylistic choices indicate a writer's epistemology ("Prolegomena" 187). Renaissance precepts also anticipate some contemporary work in cognitive semantics, tropology, and poetics of mind, wherein tropes are identified as generative cognitive processes "by which people conceptualize their experience and the external world" (Gibbs 1). Tropes are mental constructs that then come to underlie conceptual systems and ideologies, as Hayden White illustrates in his *Metahistory* and *Figural Realism.* Renaissance precepts look forward to the work of Burke, who sees that any form is a line of argument and "a way of experiencing" (*Counter-statement* 143), the guiding premise for the analyses in all his books.

Figures and Styles as Emotional Expressions

Both classical and Renaissance handbooks encourage the speaker to express appropriate emotions during the speech by employing the figures suitable to those emotions. These figures are those that naturally occur in speech when people are moved by each emotion. Such instruction presupposes that the style and the figures then reflect the speaker's emotional state. Of the classical rhetoricians, Longinus explains most clearly this understanding. He says of *hyperbaton,* the arranging of words out of natural sequence:

> [It is] the truest mark of vehement emotion. Just as people who are really angry or frightened or indignant, or are carried away by jealousy or some other feeling—there are countless emotions, no one can say how many—often put forward one point and then spring off to another with various illogical interpolations, and then wheel round again to their original position, while, under the stress of their excitement, like a ship before a veering wind, they lay their words and thoughts first on one track then another, and keep altering the natural order of sequence into innumerable variations—so, too, in the best prose writers the use of *hyperbata* allows imitation to approach the effects of nature. (§22)

After an example of this figure from the speech of Dionysius the Phocaean in Herodotus,[18] Longinus interprets, "He has transposed 'men of Ionia' and started at once with his fears, as though the terror was so immediate that he could not even address the audience first. He has, moreover, inverted the order of ideas. . . . The result is that his words do not seem premeditated but rather wrung from him" (§22). Similarly Quintilian explains that we cannot express anger or sorrow in "neat antitheses, balanced cadences and exact correspondences," because no one in these states talks this way (9.3.102). Demetrius instructs that devices that require conscious attention to verbal pattern, figures such as assonance, *isocolon,* and *homoeoteleuton,* are not appropriate for a forceful style because "anger needs no artifice" and "their studied artifice dissipates the force." Invective instead requires simpleness and spontaneity (§27).[19]

This connection of mental state, speech configuration, and emotion is repeated in Renaissance accounts. Agricola advises the speaker to create emotion in the speech by imitating the language of each emotion:

> In this manner of treating the emotions it is imperative that the language express all the thoughts, vows, regrets, desires, prayers, and disputes in accordance with the nature of each emotion. This is principally achieved by the type of style [employed], so that the language itself recreates tumult and turmoil through mental agitation. Indeed, that force which we sometimes call the "color" of language especially consists of this imitation through the emotions. Thus, even though many say the same thing, whether in exposition or argumentation, still one will exhibit the color of a man advising merely, another of one angry, another of one complaining, another of one grieving. (3.2; McNally 417)

Similarly Lamy advises, "If we would know the Figures of Choler, we need no more than watch what we naturally say, when we are transported with that Passion" (2.124). Consequently writers who wish to depict "a person under commotion" must, as Lamy directs, "represent his Discourse with all its proper Figures, turning and altering them, as Men in passion do generally turn and alter their Discourse. A skillful Painter, to express (as much as in him lies) the thoughts and passions of the person whom he draws, gives his Picture such touches and lines, as he observes to be in the Face after extraordinary provocation, which strokes, are great indications of the temper of the Mind" (2.95). With similar understanding Sherry says that in figures "is the oration and sentence made by them more pleasant, sharp and vehement, after the affection of him that speaketh or writeth" ([1550] 39).

Consequently individual figures are interpreted according to their emotional content. Wilson points out that resting upon a point (*commoratio*) shows "we are earnest in a matter, and feel the weight of our cause" (203). Soarez notes that *aposiopesis* (breaking off an utterance) "displays an emotion of rage" or "shows a state of anxiety and a kind of scrupulousness" (346). Puttenham gives an even more psychologically complex description of this figure's possible meanings: it can show that nothing further needs to be said, or that we are ashamed, or afraid to speak it out, or giving a threat, or showing a moderation of anger, or suddenly startled by an occasion, or suffering from a "fantastical head" and "such that be sudden or lack memory" (178).

While some figures are firmly tied to a particular emotional state—such as *indignatio* (anger), *bdelygma* (hatred), or *pathopoeia* (passion)—others are capable of creating and expressing a range of emotions, whose specific references change depending upon context. Puttenham's analysis of *aposiopesis* above shows this flexibility. Peacham acknowledges that *articulus* or *asyndeton* can express either calm or vehement emotions: "in peaceable and quiet causes it may be compared to a semibreve in Music, but in causes of perturbation and haste it may be likened to thick and violent strokes in fight, or to a thick and thundering peal of ordinance" ([1593] 57). Hoskins says that *polyptoton* likewise "may be used with or without passion" (17). Vickers is right about some of the figures when he observes that "the figures are not fixed, then: they are flexible, and can be effective channels for quite varied states of mind or levels of argument" (*Classical Rhetoric* 121). This flexibility suggests that those rhetoricians in this tradition who associate the figures of speech with the calmer emotions and the figures of thought with the more vehement, as Fraunce (E4v–5r) and Smith do (7), are settling for oversimplification.

This association of figures with emotional states does not presuppose a severance between reason and emotion. Despite the desire in Robertellus to separate forms of argument from forms of emotion, lines of thinking and feeling are not generally opposed in Renaissance rhetoric, as they are in Descartes and the philosophical tradition. As Suzanne K. Langer explains, this Cartesian opposition leads to the belief that formlessness or formal aberration is associated with feeling and form with absence of feeling (*Feeling and Form* 17). Instead figures are both lines of thinking and of feeling; the expression "motions of the mind" refers in Renaissance usage to both acts of reasoning and of emoting.[20] The term *sententia* also refers to both thought and feeling, again suggesting that movements of thoughts are connected to movements of emotions. This relationship is implied by Hoskins's comment "And as no man is sick in thought upon one thing but for some vehemency or distress, so in speech there is no repetition without importance" (12). It is also implied when Lamy observes that logical arguments express the speaker's passions because they derive from an "ardent desire to persuade or dissuade those to whom we speak" (2.134). Similarly Agricola (199–200), Melanchthon (*Elem.* 45v), and Keckermann (*Systematis* 1610) teach that the dialectical places produce not only logical proofs but also emotional proofs.[21] Wright emphasizes that both the manner and matter, the delivery and the reasons, "stir up or suppress the affections of man" (183). Shuger notices that sacred rhetorics in the Renaissance do not differentiate knowing and feeling, love and knowledge, as philosophers do. Flacius, for example, explains, "The Hebrews attribute the whole psychic life of man to the heart and appear to place the rational soul completely in the heart . . . ascribing to the heart the power both of thought and choice, of wishing and doing. . . . On the other hand, the philosophers locate the rational soul . . . in the head or brain; leaving only emotion in the heart" (1:178; Shuger 151). This Christian connection between love and knowledge also appears in Keckermann: "Reason and will should be implicit in emotion, and emotions resolve into knowledge and understanding. . . . Will and emotion derive from reason and knowledge" (*Systematis* 1612; Shuger 151). Shuger concludes that in these manuals emotion "does not subvert reason but animates it, drawing heart and mind toward union with the desired object" (151–52).

Thoughts and feelings are neither opposed in Cicero. Since there is a genuine connection between idea and expression, Antonius asserts, "Now if that player, though acting it daily, could never act that scene without emotion, do you really think that Pacuvius, when he wrote it, was in a calm and careless frame of mind? That could never be" (*De Oratore* 2.46.193). This integrative vision is most obvious in Cicero's explanations of figures' functions. Amplification, for example, works both to argue and to move emotions: it is "requisite in all the lines of argument . . . employed to make a speech convincing, either when we are explaining something or winning sympathy or arousing emotion" (3.27.104–5). Metaphor, too, has both a logical and emotional appeal: it has an "agreeable and entertaining quality" (3.38.155), it leads the hearer's thoughts to "something else and yet without going astray," and its direct appeal to the senses creates vividness (3.39.160). This connection suggests that, as William W. Fortenbaugh aptly explains, "emotional response is intelligent behavior open to reasoned persuasion. When men are angered, they are not victims of some totally irrational force. Rather they are responding in accordance with the thought of unjust insult. Their belief may be erroneous and their anger unreasonable, but their behavior is intelligent and cognitive in the sense that it is grounded upon a belief which may be criticised and even altered by argumentation" (*Aristotle on Emotion* 17). Consequently Trousdale and Vickers, two scholars who have recognized that figures, according to Renaissance doctrines, mirror states of mind but who define emotional states in opposition to reason, are being influenced by Cartesian assumptions that do not influence these rhetoricians. Although Trousdale explains that figures "express a state of mind" or, in other words, "the feeling of the speaker in relation to some particular event," these devices are formal aberrations (*Shakespeare* 90, 82). Vickers sees the doctrines of the figures as "an attempt to classify emotional states and the resulting speech forms, both being regarded as deviations from normal behavior, signalling a loss of balance" (*In Defence* 296).[22]

Because figures express emotion, concealing one's art requires delivering the figure with the appropriate emotional expression and making sure figures and emotions are appropriate to subject matter, occasion, speaker, audience, and purpose. In other words appropriateness of form to content and purpose hides—does not draw the audience's attention to—the form. There is not necessarily disingenuousness in these admonitions, for there is an organic relation between style and substance. As Quintilian says, "It is as ridiculous to hunt for figures without reference to the matter as it is to discuss dress and gesture without reference to the body" (9.3.100). He justifies this advice by arguing, "So too oratory possesses a natural mien, which while it is far from demanding a stolid and immovable rigidity should as far as possible restrict itself to the expression with which it is endowed by nature" (9.3.101). Peacham emphasizes this fitness too: since repetition signifies importance, "heed ought to be taken, that the word which is least worthy or most weak, be not taken to make the repetition, for that were very absurd" ([1593] 42).

When the emotion expressed is consistent with the figures, ideas, circumstances, and multiple relevant contexts, this congruity mirrors nature and persuades an audience of the genuineness of the speaker and appropriateness of the speaker's view.[23] This expression evokes a like-mindedness in the hearers and moves their emotions along similar lines. Smith explains the general figure *pathopoeia* as "a form of speech whereby the Speaker moves the mind of his hearers to some vehemency of affection" because "the speaker himself (being inwardly moved with any of those deep and vehement affections), doth by evident demonstration, passionate pronunciation and suitable gestures make a lively expression thereof" (266). This arousal of emotion does not require that the speaker always express the same emotion he wants the hearer to feel, for, as Agricola explains, sometimes the speech seeks "to arouse and excite another" (3.2; McNally 418). But there is always some kind of emotion expressed and evoked, as Robertellus asserts when he declares that "every utterance that issues forth from us is figured" or "colored" (26r). Figures and emotions, then, are detachable in the sense that we can choose them and the line of thinking they accompany, but not detachable from thought or utterance itself. Hence expressions of emotion are both mirrors and tools. These rhetoricians provide a psychological rationale for the effects of figures, tying effect to cause and justifying their claim that style and figures are crucial tools for eliciting an emotional response.[24]

Both classical and Renaissance rhetoricians stress the figures' power to move the audience's affections. "There is no more effective method of exciting the emotions than an apt use of figures" (9.1.21), Quintilian says. Longinus writes that all schemes "serve to lend emotion and excitement to the style" (§29). Aquila declares that "nothing is their equal for stirring the emotions of hearers or judges" (22; trans. Leff in "Latin" 275). In the Renaissance this doctrine is commonplace throughout the period.[25] Erasmus says that figures all have an affective function on the hearer (*Eccl.* 3.98.903). Peacham prefaces his handlist with the declaration that by means of these figures, what the speaker "commendeth is beloved, what he dispraiseth is abhorred, what he persuadeth is obeyed, & what he dissuadeth is avoided" ([1593] AB.iii.v). The emotional effect of individual figures is also sometimes explained. Wilson says of *epizeuxis* (doublets),

"Thus, the oft repeating of one word doth much stir the hearer and makes the word seem greater, as though a sword were oft digged and thrust twice or thrice in one place of the body" (*Art of Rhetoric* 225).

This ability to evoke emotion is the only function present-day apologists for Renaissance rhetoric generally attribute to figures. Heinrich F. Plett, for example, comments that Renaissance rhetoricians commonly provide "a functional explanation of the stylistic devices in terms of the emotions they are likely to engender" ("Place and Function" 358). Joachim Dyck refutes the widely held belief that figures were meant primarily to adorn and polish by emphasizing their ability to evoke emotion: "But the *ornatus,* the body of rules covering the use of tropes and figures of speech, is also part of the emotional effect to be achieved by words; it is not an adornment to delight the intellect but a means of producing and reducing emotion" (236). James A. Herrick repeats, "This concern for the emotive power of language also revealed itself in the intense interest of Renaissance rhetoricians in *elocutio*" (157). Such a limited view, however, needlessly excludes the rest of the figure's meanings and the explanation for why figures can elicit emotions from an audience.

Figures and Styles as Characters

Because figures mirror the speaker's decisions in this act of communication, all selected with varying degrees of purposefulness and appropriateness, and because utterances are behaviors always situated within social/moral relations, style inevitably reveals not only the speaker's interpretation of both subject matter and social situation but also motives and quality of judgment. Including both conscious and subliminal designs, motives include beliefs, ideologies, habitual lines of thinking, values, attitudes, emotions, and goals.[26] Style reveals how a speaker is treating self, those persons spoken about and to, and those who will ever be affected by the proposal. As a consequence style is the speaker's practice of ethics, and this practice inevitably reflects the speaker's moral philosophy. Quality of judgment, then, points to degree of wisdom and virtue. The resulting composite picture forms an impression of the speaker's character, both the projected persona of this one performance and the more enduring person behind this mask (whose choices both constitute and reveal the quality of mind behind the performance). It is not an exaggeration, then, to equate style and character. This character includes general moral qualities such as sincerity, compassion, and justice that can be shared universally and those personality traits unique to each individual. This character is detachable in the sense that we can choose which qualities/styles we will exhibit in each performance but not detachable from thought, speech, or behavior itself.

This awareness of style and figure as a creation and a reflection of character is again a commonplace in both classical and Renaissance traditions, beginning with Isocrates. Because he believes that discourse both constitutes and embodies one's judgment, Isocrates then reads speech as a reflection of prudence and motives: "For the power to speak well is taken as the surest index of a sound understanding, and discourse which is true and lawful and just is the outward image of a good and faithful soul" (*Antidosis* §255). This mimetic quality of discourse motivates Isocrates to invite his audience to read his speeches for his character (§7). He purposely stages *Antidosis* as a defense of a just man against detractors at a trial in order to call attention to this mimetic dimension of speech (§8).[27] While speech constructs the speaker's identity, Isocrates nevertheless argues that this construction still points in an essential way to the speaker's motives and judgment. He supposes that his own highly crafted style—use of periods, antitheses, *isocola,* and alliterations—underscores the carefulness and conscientiousness he has devoted to arguing on behalf of matters of great civic consequence.[28] He also supposes that all his previous speeches should serve as context for each new speech act. Consequently he quotes from his earlier writings in this particular apologia (defense) to provide evidence of his integrity and nobility of character over time.

Cicero too reads speech as a mirror of complex character, of both a persona and a behind-the-scenes person. On the one hand, a style is a mask that can be picked up and put down as appropriate to occasion. A man is not his style. In *De Oratore* Antonius describes the need to create an appropriate image of self: "Moreover so much is done by good taste and style in speaking, that the speech seems to depict the speaker's character. For by means of particular types of thought and diction, and the employment besides of a delivery that is unruffled and eloquent of good-nature, the speakers are made to appear upright, well-bred and virtuous men" (2.43.184). On the other hand, speech gives clues to the speaker's real state of mind. Antonius suggests that the good orator must "read" the opponent's every action, his style, to discern his "mind": "It is painstaking to listen with close attention to our opponent, and so as to catch not only his periods, but his every word as well, and finally to read all his changes of countenance, which generally gives the clue to his frame of mind" (2.35.148). In this sense a man is his style. Since speech depicts character, Crassus reproves previous rhetoricians who have failed "in understanding what character they are appearing in or what it is that they profess" by means of their styles (*De Oratore* 3.14.54). That their styles have created for them characters of which they are unaware shows that character is a construction, but not always one that results from fully conscious intentions. This gap between intention and effect means that there are always two dimensions to this construction in any speech: the image of self one attempts to create and the image that is actually created. Cicero's definition of eloquence as "nothing else but wisdom delivering copious utterance" (*De Part. Orat.* 23.79) indicates his assumption that speech reflects its author's motives and quality of judgment.

Character entails more than this double image in a speech, for a speaker's reputation also has bearing. Placing a high degree of importance on the personal character of all involved in a courtroom proceeding—the professional advocates, the accuser and accused, the witnesses and the judges—the Romans counted reputation as evidence in a trial.[29] Cicero has Antonius say in *De Oratore:* "A potent factor in success, then, is for the characters, principles, conduct and course of life, both of those who are to plead cases and of their clients, to be approved, and conversely those of their opponents condemned; and for the feelings of the tribunal to be won over, as far as possible, to goodwill towards the advocate and the advocate's client as well. Now feelings are won over by a man's merit, achievements or reputable life, qualifications easier to embellish, if only they are real, than to fabricate where non-existent" (2.43.182). The fact that Cicero also teaches in *De Officiis* that propriety applies both within each speech and among all one's actions shows his interest in reading individual speech acts in the context of a speaker's life: "If there is any such thing as propriety at all, it can be nothing more than uniform consistency in the course of our life as a whole and all its individual actions" (1.31.111). Finally in *De Officiis* Cicero records that there is both a universal and individual nature in man. This dual nature will be manifest in a speaker's character, whether consciously enacted or not:

> We must realize also that we are invested by Nature with two characters, as it were: one of these is universal, arising from the fact of our being all alike endowed with reason and with that superiority which lifts us above the brute. From this all morality and propriety are derived, and upon it depends the rational method of ascertaining our duty. The other character is the one that is assigned to individuals in particular. . . .
>
> For we must so act as not to oppose the universal laws of human nature, but, while safeguarding those, to follow the bent of our own particular nature. (1.30.107–31.110)[30]

This essential particular nature is not as susceptible to artistic control as is universal nature and often imposes restrictions upon one's capacity for artistic achievement.

Like Cicero, Quintilian values stylistic versatility: "But there is no law of heaven which prohibits the possession of all or at any rate the majority of styles by one and the same person" (11.3.181). Also like Isocrates and Cicero, Quintilian is clear that there is a natural connection between the way one speaks and one's mind or character. He says, "For a man's character is generally revealed and the secrets of his heart are laid bare by his manner of speaking, and there is good ground for the Greek aphorism that, 'as a man lives, so will he speak'" (11.1.29–30). This character that emerges is not merely a representation but also a revelation about the real person speaking. This awareness of style's double reflection leads Quintilian to watch for the relationship between the two. While he may be overly optimistic about a dishonest person's inability to hide successfully behind the mask during any one performance, he nevertheless recognizes that a speaker's reliability is determined by the congruency perceived between the mask and the mind behind the mask:

> For however we strive to conceal it, insincerity will always betray itself, and there was never in any man so great eloquence as would not begin to stumble and hesitate so soon as his words ran counter to his inmost thoughts. Now a bad man cannot help speaking things other than he feels. On the other hand, the good will never be at a loss for honourable words or fail to find matter full of virtue for utterance, since among his virtues practical wisdom will be one. And even though his imagination lacks artifice to lend it charm, its own nature will be ornament enough, for if honour dictate the words, we shall find eloquence there as well. (12.1.29–30)

Reputation based on a lifetime's performances is also important to Quintilian, who writes that "if [the orator] is believed to be a good man, this consideration will exercise the strongest influence at every point of the case" (4.1.7). One's integrity arises from congruency between beliefs and actions within and among many performances.

This same awareness of complex character is found in the Hellenistic rhetoricians. Demetrius, Hermogenes, and Longinus all teach the orator to craft stylistic characters. Each, however, acknowledges style's reference to the person behind the mask. Demetrius remarks about authenticity, "In every form of speech it is possible to see the writer's character" (§227). Reading for the speaker's degree of wisdom, he emphasizes that frigidity of style reveals the same kind of poor judgment that produces boastfulness: "In general, there is a sort of analogy between boastfulness and frigidity. The boaster pretends that qualities belong to him even if they do not, while the writer who adds pomp to trifles is himself like the man who boasts about trifles" (§119). Hermogenes is also cognizant of an overall "revelation of Character that necessarily appears throughout the whole speech, like the complexion of a body," a revelation in addition to the particular stylistic qualities the speaker is crafting (2.2.321). Longinus explicitly reads style for the writer's intentions and judgment: "Sublimity is the echo of a noble mind" and "a grand style is the natural product of those whose ideas are weighty" (§9). This connection leads to his conclusion that true sublimity comes from those of noble character motivated by high hopes (§44).

The same complex vision guides the textual explications of Renaissance rhetoricians. They teach an art that reveals character as a construction and a reflection, a manifestation of art and of nature. As Puttenham says, the styles are "complexions," "humors," or "qualities" that result from nature and art: "For if the man be grave, his speech and style is grave; if light-headed, his style and language also light; if the mind be haughty and hot, the speech and style is also vehement and stirring; if it be cold and temperate, the style is also very modest; if it be humble, or base and meek, so is also the language and style. And yet peradventure not altogether so, but that every man's style is for the most part according to the matter and subject of the writer, or so ought to be, and conformable thereunto" (161). Again he explains that a style "is a certain contrived form and quality, many times natural to the writer, many times his peculiar by election and art, and such as either he keepeth by skill, or holdeth on by ignorance, and will not or peradventure cannot easily alter into any other" (160). Style is artificial inasmuch as it results from conscious choice and design; it is natural inasmuch as it results from preference, habit, spontaneous emotion, and unpremeditated choice.[31] In this way style/behavior encompasses both acting and being as two simultaneous but distinct dimensions of reference.

When there is incongruity between these two portrayals, the speaker lacks credibility and appears disingenuous or foolish. Wilson gives his assessment of the applicant who wrote a letter full of inkhorn terms: "What wise man reading this letter will not take him for a very calf that made it in good earnest and thought by his inkpot terms to get a good parsonage" (*Art of Rhetoric* 190). The persona the writer attempted to paint—a well-bred, qualified, and clever man of learning—is not believable, because his misuse of vocabulary reveals instead his deficiency of good judgment. Peacham too reads for both levels: he writes that speakers who "take greater care to paint their speech with fine figures, than to express the truth plainly . . . are prouder of their Eloquence, than diligent to set forth matters with plainness" ([1577] G.iii.v). Recognizing incongruities, Ascham faults Sallust for exhibiting "more labor than Art [good judgment]: and in his labor also, too much toil, as it were, with an uncontented care to write better than he could, a fault common to very many men" (*Scholemaster* 297).[32]

When there is congruity between the two portrayals, the speaker exhibits not only integrity but also true wit or wisdom. Renaissance rhetoricians associate wit with the decorous performance. According to Harvey wit is "an affluent Spirit yielding invention to praise or dispraise, or any ways to discourse with judgment of every subject" (*Triming of Thomas Nashe* [1597] in *Works* III.33). Wilson reveals the same understanding when he asks, "Doth wit rest in strange words, or else standeth it in wholesome matter with apt declaring of a man's mind?" (190). Hoskins reiterates, "Therefore Cicero said much when he said, *dicere recte nemo potest nisi qui prudenter intellegit*" (No one can speak properly unless he understands wisely [2]).

Although the art inculcates stylistic versatility, Renaissance rhetoricians therefore commonly remark on the naturally reflective dimension of style. Melanchthon writes, "You see that even natures and customs are wont to be judged from the kind of speech. For it is a very certain conclusion that from the strange mind comes strange speech" (*Elem.* 34r–v, 230). Discerning the speaker's judgment from the speech, Day asserts: "For this cause seeing before speech had, which is the true note, and testimony either of wisdom or folly, all men in their several callings are holden indifferent, yet do we see that when such men are discerned by their speech, forthwith there falleth a separation, and the reverence that all men for the most part yield to discretion, maketh sufficient appearance, what regard skillful utterance beareth from such hateful folly" ([1586] 16–17). The poet Jonson remarks, repeating Vives, "Language most shows a man: speak that I may see thee. It springs out of the most retired, and inmost parts of us, and is the Image of the Parent of it, the mind. No glass renders a mans form, or likeness, so true as his speech" (*Timber* 625).[33]

Renaissance rhetoricians also emphasize the importance of a speaker's life as context in textual analysis. Erasmus in *Ecclesiastes* stresses that to be persuasive, the preacher's life must be virtuous with demonstrated goodwill toward the hearers: "In a person one examines both past words and past actions because the present and even the future can be judged from the past" (2.372.152–53). Lamy also asserts that the speaker's past life matters: "It is clear our esteem for the probity and prudence of an Orator, makes many times a great part of his Eloquence, and disposes us to surrender even before we know what he will say" (5.111). Even though "ill use may be made of this Art" and "one may pretend love for his Hearers" or "put on the face of an Honest man, only to delude those who have a reverence for the least appearance of truth" (5.124–25), Lamy also suggests that a discerning auditor will consider the life of the speaker as context for the speech, and in this way will avoid being deceived: "A good life is the mark that Christ himself has given to discriminate betwixt Preachers of Truth, and those who are sent by the Spirit of Error to delude and deceive us" (5.113).

With one's life a text for exegesis, one's identity is both constituted and revealed by a lifetime of performances. Hence a person's overall style will be composed of numerous qualities, some apparent at one time and others at another. But despite the variety of qualities, underlying patterns will predominate, revealing the nature of the actor's will or character. Sprat says in his *Account of the Life and Writings of Mr. Abraham Cowley* (1668) that though Cowley "has handled so many different Matters in such various sorts of Style, . . . Yet this is true of them all, that in all the several shapes of his Style there is still very much of the likeness and impression of the same mind: the same unaffected modesty, and natural freedom, and easy vigor, and cheerful passions, and innocent mirth, which appeared in all his Manners" (128).

Because in the Renaissance rhetoric applies to any act of making, any product can be read for the mind that guided its creation. In keeping with this assumption, Sir Walter Raleigh gives expression to the common Renaissance belief that God manifests himself by means of his creations, which function as texts: "But by his own Word, and by this visible World, is God perceived of Men; which is also the understood Language of the Almighty, vouchsafed to all his Creatures, whose Hieroglyphical Characters are the unnumbered Stars, the Sun, and Moon; written on these large Volumes of the Firmament; written also on the Earth and the Seas, by the Letters of all those living Creatures, and Plants, which inhabit and reside therein" (*History of the World* [1677] 2). The excellence of God's creations speaks of his eloquence, as Hoskins asserts: "The order of God's creatures in themselves is not only admirable and glorious, but eloquent" (2).

Not only do these rhetoricians read speech, style, and action for the speaker's character, but they also explicitly read figures the same way. A speaker's use of figures points to motives. The author of the *Ad Herennium* points out that *interrogatio,* when used after a summary of one's refutation, can indicate that the speaker wants to "reinforce the argument that has just been delivered" (4.15.22). Demetrius comments that using an antithesis where subject matter does not warrant it "suggests an intent to deceive," to raise a laugh, or to mock (§24). Quintilian remarks that those who create obscurity through obsolete words "seek to gain a reputation for erudition . . . in order that they may be regarded as the sole depositories of certain forms of knowledge" (8.2.12). Those persons who choose useless words are "allured by false ideals of beauty" or "are unwilling to make a direct and simple statement of the facts" (8.2.17). According to Longinus the orator who combines *asyndeta* and *anaphora* "does just the same as the aggressor[;] he belabours the minds of the jury with blow after blow" (§20).[34]

Renaissance rhetoricians provide even more commentary. Soarez remarks that *gradatio* (a ladder) "shows a rather obvious and studied dexterity" (317). Day interprets the use of hyperbole in an amatory letter as evidence of the writer's being in love: "I have heard the party much discommended, for the application of these immoderate and superlative terms, of those who neither in outward appearance or inward conceit of the Gentlewoman, seemed to perceive any matter at all ministering such great effects, as herein were proposed: but what of that, such was his fancy, and so regarded was his opinion towards her, as he could not but extol, what in others' judgments was but meanly to be commended. Love so wrought, and therefore the less was he to be accuser" ([1586] 237–38). Puttenham says of *asyndeton* that we utter it "when we will seem to make haste, or to be in earnest" (186). Smith notes that through the proper use of *litotes* "the speaker for modesty's sake seems to extenuate that which he expresses" (70).

These rhetoricians also read figures for the speaker's judgment. The author of the *Ad Herennium* comments that a proper use of *litotes* avoids the impression of arrogance and shows prudence (4.38.50). Since *paronomasia* (wordplay), *homoeoptoton* (like case endings) and *homoeoteleuton* (similar ending syllables) serve more for entertainment than serious causes "because their invention seems impossible without labour and pains," the speaker reveals poor judgment by using them in the wrong circumstances: "the speaker's credibility, impressiveness, and seriousness are lessened by crowding these figures together" (4.23.32). Cicero reads the well-used metaphor as "a mark of cleverness" (*De Oratore* 3.40.160). Quintilian warns, "Again, hyperbole will often cause a laugh. If that was what the orator desired, we may give him credit for wit; otherwise we can only call him a fool" (8.6.74).

Renaissance rhetoricians read similarly. Melanchthon asserts that grandiose, pompous beginnings "indicate arrogance and self-conceit" (*Elem.* 13r, 221). Peacham observes that overusing figures of repetition "betrays affectation" ([1593] 44). Harvey notes, "Vain and phantastical Amplifications argue an idle, or mad conceited brain" (*Marginalia* 124). Smith remarks that the good use of oxymoron indicates "wittiness" (122) and that *parrhesia* (frankness) shows "our confidence for the present, our fearfulness for the future, or our ability to confute a false accusation" (226). Lamy declares quite self-consciously that the sentence itself "expresses our Judgment," because every proposition contains two terms and a third (the verb) that relates the two "and signifies that Action of the Mind by which we judge" (1.2.19). Calling the figures "Characters drawn by our Passions in our Discourse" (2.94), Lamy instructs that sophistry (the misuse of figures) indicates either unjust and uncalled-for passions, which reveal a "mad man" and "the Character of an Infant," or designing "Raptures and Enthusiasms, which take away the use of Reason, and make [the audience] see things in a quite contrary manner to what in reality they are," a fault that shows "craft" and "cunning" (2.142–44). In fact so closely do these pedagogues connect figures and character that in Peacham the properly used figures themselves constitute "wisdom speaking eloquently" ([1577] A.iii.r), and in Puttenham the figures are personified as characters: *Histeron proteron* is "the Preposterous" (181), *Tapinosis* "the Abbaser" (195), *Liptote* is "the Moderator" (195) and *Hyperbole* "the Over reacher, otherwise called the loud lyer" (202).

It is because discourse naturally depicts character and one's character functions as a proof in one's argument that instruction in good style matters. Hoskins defends the study of style for this reason:

> Yet cannot his mind be thought in tune whose words do jar, nor his reason in frame whose sentences are preposterous; nor his fancy clear and perfect whose utterance breaks itself into fragments and uncertainties. . . . Careless speech doth not only discredit the personage of the speaker but it doth discredit the opinion of his reason and judgment, it discrediteth the truth, and uniformity of the matter and substance. If it be so, then, in words which fly and escape censure, and where one good phrase begs pardon for many incongruities and faults, how shall he be thought wise whose penning is thin and shallow? How shall you look for wit from him whose leisure and whose head, assisted with the examination of his eyes, could yield you no life and sharpness in his writing? (2)

Blount repeats the admonition: "Now, as 'tis certain, that No harmony can appear in his thoughts, nor soundness in his reason, whose speech is faltering and preposterous: So likewise no clearness nor perfection in that Fancy, which delivers itself by a confus'd abortion. Great is the disparagement which flows from the defilement of the Tongue: it not only dishonours the person of the Speaker, but even sullies the opinion of his reason and judgement with a disrepute, and oft-times renders the very truth suspected" (A3r).

For the same reason, these rhetoricians include instruction regarding both the proper and improper uses of figures. Their skillful use is discerned by how well they accomplish one's multiple intentions and by how appropriate those intentions are to the immediate and distant social contexts. Peacham's cautions are noteworthy. About the use of *antiphrasis* (saying the opposite of what is meant) he warns, "This figure ought not to be used without some urgent cause, neither is it seemly to be used of all persons, in respect of the breach of duty: it were unmeet for the son to say, 'wisely spoken father,' for it were as much, as to call his father fool: and likewise for a servant in his anger to use this figure against his master, it were contrary to good manners: and therefore these two things ought to be observed, that it be not used without great cause, nor of any without some authority, or at the least matched in equality" ([1593] 25). *Medela* (pleasing speech to excuse infirmities) should not be used to defend "things unlawful," deny "matters evident," or extenuate "trangressions that be great," because doing so makes the orator appear "both impudent and wicked" ([1593] 176–77). *Asteismus* (witty jesting) "offendeth against charity, when the mirth toucheth some person to his grief or shame," and it offends against piety "when the occasion of mirth and laughter is taken from the abuse of reverend matters" ([1593] 35). Finally *charientismus* (the mitigating of hard matters with pleasant words) heals wounds and cools tempers, but "two great faults may be committed in this figure, the one is a base and vile submission, the other is open flattery: the one is a shame, the other a sin" ([1593] 37).

Similarly Shaw points out two errors leading to the misuse of figures. The first results from an unawareness of the forms one is using and hence of all the arguments one is making and the freedom one has to reframe or reform the thought. This lack of self-consciousness is folly and turns one's own language into a self-induced prison house. Because of this ignorance, the character Trope boasts, "we have set up . . .

Dominions . . . in the very constitutions of mens minds, and made their conversations voluntary tributaries thereunto" (109). The second error results from deliberately reducing the form to a mere device and hence denying and hiding aspects of its meaning. This obfuscation is evil, "when men have made the most serious *things* dwindle into *mere words;* and *Virtue* and *honesty,* (not to say, *Religion and Conscience* it self) are esteem'd or made use of, but as *Terms of Art* to deceive the ignorant, and serve the *turns* of *interest, faction,* or *ambition*" (Preface).

In contrast to this complex and consistent hermeneutic in the humanist tradition, Aristotle's account of style's meaning remains partial and problematic. Despite perceiving that style's meanings correspond with the three types of proofs belonging to invention, he undermines these correspondences by the strict separations he imposes between them and between style and content and style and mind.

Aristotle sets out to rehabilitate rhetoric from its sophistic abuses by giving the art a theory of proofs, which he separates into *logos* (logical appeals), *pathos* (emotional appeals), and *ethos* (ethical appeals). Interestingly Aristotle gives to style meanings that correspond to these three types of proofs. He advises, "Your language will be appropriate if it expresses emotion and character, and if it corresponds to its subject" (3.7 1408a10). This last criterion implies that forms make assertions: "'Correspondence to subject' means that we must neither speak casually about weighty matters, nor solemnly about trivial ones; nor must we add ornamental epithets to commonplace nouns, or the effect will be comic. . . . To express emotion, you will employ the language of anger in speaking of outrage; the language of disgust and discreet reluctance to utter a word when speaking of impiety or foulness; the language of exultation for a tale of glory, and that of humiliation for a tale of pity" (3.7 1408a11–19). Aristotle even describes several figures as if they mimic logical reasoning and act as tacit persuasion patterns. Antithesis, he says, "has the effect of a logical argument," since "it is by putting two opposing conclusions side by side that you prove one of them false" (3.9 1410a21–22). Metaphor suggests correspondence and so is only appropriate when the things compared do correspond (3.2 1405a11). He says of strings of unconnected words (*asyndeton*) that "they have the further peculiarity of suggesting that a number of separate statements have been made in the time usually occupied by one" and "thus [make] everything more important: e.g. 'I came to him; I talked to him; I entreated him'—what a lot of facts! the hearer thinks" (3.12 1413b29–1414a1).

Yet Aristotle insists upon style's firm separation from and inferior status to content. He insists that logos, pathos, and ethos belong to content. They also remain distinct from each other. For example using examples and enthymemes constitutes logos (1.2 1356b2); depicting the adversaries "as open to such charges and possessed of such qualities as do make people angry" (2.2 1380a2–4) constitutes pathos; and quoting a maxim (2.2 1395b16) or mentioning details that give credit to oneself (3.16 1417a3–4) give a speech a moral character. He insists that logical proofs do not appeal to emotions nor refer to character: "And avoid the enthymeme form when you are trying to rouse feeling; for it will either kill the feeling or will itself fall flat. . . . Nor should you go after the enthymeme form in a passage where you are depicting character—the process of demonstration can express neither character nor choice" (3.17 1418a12–16). None of these above-named devices belong to style or to figures. Additionally, as Bruns argues, Aristotle's attempt to isolate speech from thought reveals itself in his *Categories, De Interpretatione,* and *Poetics,* when he treats words as isolated particles that belong not to logical but merely to grammatical categories (253–55).

Also Aristotle separates style and mind, despite making occasional comments that undermine this separation. On the one hand, style has a reflective function. Style expresses emotion and character, he says. Devices are appropriate when they suit the emotion, when they mirror the way people speak while feeling the emotion: "Compound words, fairly plentiful epithets, and strange words best suit an emotional speech," because "men do speak in this strain when they are deeply stirred" (3.7 1408b11–16). His interest in style derives from its capacity to help give the speech "the right impression" (3.1 1403b17). His remarks about this reflective function connect the thoughts, emotions, and character of the speaker more closely than his account in invention allows. He points out that "two different words will represent a thing in two different lights" (3.2 1405b14), implying that logos (perspective) and pathos (attitude) together result from choice of diction. When he also advises that certain thoughts elicit certain emotions, he suggests another connection between logos and pathos. For example the efficient cause of anger is the belief that one has been unjustly slighted by someone (2.2 1378a31–32). As Fortenbaugh explains, one of Aristotle's significant contributions to rhetoric is that he makes "clear the relationship of emotion to reasoned argumentation. By construing thought or belief as the efficient cause of emotion, Aristotle showed that emotional response is intelligent behaviour open to reasoned persuasion" (*Aristotle on Emotion* 17). When Aristotle remarks that "all style and enthymemes that give us rapid information" give "an impression of smartness" (3.10 1410b3–4), he connects logos with ethos. He also connects pathos and ethos: since expressing the emotions appropriate to the subject gives the impression of being genuine or possessing a credible character, "this aptness of language is one thing that makes people believe in the truth of your story" (3.7 1408a20–26).

On the other hand, Aristotle keeps his focus on style as a tool rather than a mirror and denies the essential connection between style and individual. While some figures prompt lines of thinking, Aristotle refrains from attributing to them the status of either arguments or mirrors. He describes instead their effects on the audience. The metaphor surprises the hearer: "Because the hearer expected something different, his acquisition of the new idea impresses him all the more. His mind seems to say, 'Yes, to be sure; I never thought of that'" (3.11 1412a19–21).[35] Style "charms" and impresses the hearer (3.1 1404a11), for "people like what strikes them, and are struck by what is out of the way" (3.2 1404b1). Style also "stirs" the audience to feel the emotions the speaker expresses, provided that they are appropriate to the subject matter, and "once the audience is in a like state of feeling, approval of course follows" (3.7 1408b18). Aristotle counts as relevant only the appearance of character an orator puts on in the moment of performance: "Bring yourself on the stage from the first in the right character, . . . but do not let them see what you are about," he advises (3.16 1417b7–9). Furthermore this reflected image shows no more than the most general outlines of gender, class, age, and social roles. He does not believe that one's speech reflects one's personal moral character:

> Each class of men, each type of disposition, will have its own appropriate way of letting the truth appear. Under "class" I include differences of age, as boy, man, or old man; of sex, as man or woman; of nationality, as Spartan or Thessalian. By "dispositions" I here mean those dispositions only which determine the character of a man's life, for it is not every disposition that does this. If, then, a speaker uses the very words which are in keeping with a particular disposition, he will reproduce the corresponding character; for a rustic and an educated man will not say the same things nor speak in the same way. (3.7 1408a27–33)

Hyperboles, because "they show vehemence," are "for young men to use" (3.11 1413a29–30). Maxims are only appropriate in the speech of the elderly (2.21 1395a3). The speaker need only craft his ethical appeals in each public speech, for his previous reputation has no bearing: "This kind of persuasion, like the others, should be achieved by what the speaker says, not by what people think of his character before he begins to speak" (1.2 1356a9–10). Aristotle focuses only on the persona and the character type created by each speech act.[36] He does not delineate in much detail how to create this persona, nor does he believe that the orator need worry about self-exposure as long as he plays his expected role.

This separation between style and the individual person Aristotle further underscores when he treats emotion and character as qualities detachable from each other and from discourse. Aristotle does not read all texts as behaviors contextualized within a social drama. Some texts lack character and some lack emotion. For example he conceives of discourses without character: "mathematical treatises depict no character; they have nothing to do with choice, for they represent nobody as pursuing any end" (3.16 1417a19–20). In his *Poetics* he repeats this idea: "Character is that which reveals moral choice—that is, when otherwise unclear, what kinds of thing an agent chooses or rejects (which is why speeches in which there is nothing at all the speaker chooses or rejects contain no character)" (1450b6–10). Aristotle does not think the quality of poetry depends upon the poet's ability to depict character through stylistic mimesis but rather to create realistic plots that represent philosophical truths (1450a13). Distrustful of style's mimetic function—of its depiction of mental states—he makes only an oblique mention of this criterion for poetry and even discounts this reference by excusing Homer for his failing in this regard.[37] Aristotle talks instead about the orator "investing speeches with moral character" (*Rhetoric* 2.18 1391b22), much as he suggests that the orator should add emotional appeals to facts, which themselves do not contain an emotional dimension: "The arousing of prejudice, pity, anger, and similar emotions has nothing to do with the essential facts, but is merely a personal appeal to the man who is judging the case" (1.1 1354a16–17). This detachability accords with Aristotle's desire to see style as merely a "value-added" dimension superimposed on the content and necessary only when an audience cares more for words than matter.

Ethics, the Center of Style

Differing from Aristotle, those in the humanist tradition see that figures supply logical, emotional, and ethical proofs for one's argument. This rhetorical curriculum explicitly moves Aristotle's logos, pathos, and ethos from invention to style. Perceiving this fact but assigning to each figure only one of these functions, Joseph organizes the figures in her collection under the Aristotelian categories. A few years later, J. Donald Ragsdale also argues that in Renaissance stylistic rhetorics, figures are "actually equivalent to inventional devices" and that "it is not inconsistent, therefore, to classify the figures of speech according to their correspondence to one of the three classical divisions of the inventional modes of proof" (164–65).[38] But even more significant, in this tradition these three types of proof are not merely tools but also mirrors, and each figure participates in providing all three types of proof at once, with the logical and emotional subsumed under the ethical, giving the principles of style a moral center. Thought and emotion together in context signify character. When hearers are persuaded by a line of thinking and feeling, they take on the same style and the same character.

Evidence that both classical and Renaissance rhetoricians see this ethical center comes from their explicit equation of aesthetic, rational, and moral propriety. Cicero gives expression to an equation that carries through the Renaissance: Nature = Reason = Truth = Virtue = Wisdom = Art = Beauty = Usefulness.[39] As Cicero observes, the principles of decorum apply equally to reason, speech, and life: "The universal rule, in oratory as in life, is to consider propriety" (*Orator* 21.71).[40] In *De Officiis* he concludes that propriety or prudence follows from "employing reason and speech rationally" to impose order and consistency upon every word and deed (1.27.94; 1.35.126), to do "the right thing at the right time," and to arrange "things in their suitable and appropriate places" (1.40.142–3). Its principles derive from universal nature, produce beauty (1.35.126), and enable one to "discern the truth and to uphold it" (1.27.94).[41] This balance and harmony also accompany usefulness: "nature has contrived with incredible skill that the things possessing most utility also have the greatest amount of dignity, and indeed frequently of beauty also" (*De Oratore* 3.45.178).

The same identification is repeated in the Renaissance. Considering the precepts of the art "natural," Vives declares, "Therefore true and genuine rhetoric is the expression of wisdom, which cannot in any way be separated from righteousness and piety" (*De tradendis disciplinis* 185). Likewise Ascham has merged these ideas: "For this I am sure in learning all other matters, nothing is brought to the most profitable use, which is not handled after the most comely fashion. . . . And virtue it self is nothing else but comeliness [i.e., appropriateness and beauty]" (*Toxophilus* 99–100). Also equating nature with right reason, virtue, wisdom, beauty, and art, Wilson observes, "nature teacheth what is comely and what is not comely for all times" (*Art of Rhetoric* 141, 186, 244; *Rule of*

Reason D.vii.r).[42] Lamy has the same understanding: he remarks that the precepts of rhetoric "are good and just in themselves, and every man that has prudence and charity makes use of them insensibly" (5.125).

Even Ramus declares that the principles of decorum have application in all the arts: "There will never be any separate and distinct precept concerning decorum, however, because decorum itself is that harmonious perfection which the arts by their precepts, and human reason and wisdom by themselves, reveal" (*Arguments* 158). And, even he comes to accept the moral center of rhetoric, for though he rejected the ideal of the orator being the good man in the 1549 *Arguments in Rhetoric Against Quintilian*, in his 1557 *Ciceronianus* he embraces the ideal:

> Let us embrace M. Tullius Cicero not for some fault or toy, but for the whole body, or rather spirit, and for the whole life: let us draw forth the stages of life, prudence of teachers, types of disciplines, labors of studies, and everything of continence, fortitude, wisdom, justice, of the whole life, as if presenting a story, so that it may appear how the good man skilled in speaking well, that is, the orator, is produced, whether in the forum, as a pleader of civil cases, such as the advocates of our country are, or as an interpreter of religion and teacher of the people, such as today our priests and theologians are in the Christian church and assembly: thus may both a good man and one skilled in speaking be perceived. . . . We seek out not a man of a single art, such as a grammarian or geometer, but the good man skilled in speaking, concerning whatever matter and wherever he may speak. For the purpose of effecting him, we assume that the example of Cicero should be considered in all parts. (B2v–3r–E2v–3r; trans. Henderson 46)[43]

Indeed, the principles of decorum translate directly into moral virtues: congruency is integrity, relevance or appropriateness is justice, wholeness in framing wherein the parts all have place is mercy, the golden mean is temperance, a balance between adaptability and stability is prudence, and reconciliation of complementary pairs is a combined humility and confidence.[44]

This identification of decorum and virtue permeates sixteenth-century definitions of *ornament.* Thomas Cooper's *Thesaurus Linguae Romanae and Britannicae* translates *ornatus* with the phrases "advanced to authority and dignity" or "endued with wisdom, virtue, and knowledge" ([1573] Ssss6v). John Florio provides as synonyms for *ornamento* "honor, dignity, promotion, praise, or commendation" (*Worlde of Wordes* [1598] 249). Joseph Barrett in *An Alvearie* [1580] equates "honor" with *ornamentum* (Kkiijv).[45] Day has in mind these multiple connotations when he praises learning as "the ornament of the mind" ([1599] 84). The same polyvalency is expressed when Peacham calls eloquence and wisdom "the only Ornaments whereby man's life is beautified and a praise most precious purchased" ([1577] A.ii.r). The resonance remains even a century later when Sir Henry Sidney reminds his son that "only by virtuous Life and good Action, you may be an Ornament to that illustre Family" (*Letters and Memorials* [1746] I.8–9).[46] The union of aesthetics, reason, and ethics in this rhetorical tradition, then, takes place not merely in the union of artistic style with wise and true content, but also and more fundamentally in the principles of decorum that govern and so unite thought, speech, and action.[47]

Scholars have recognized that Renaissance humanists place great importance on the proper reading of texts and make contributions to hermeneutics. Herrick writes that they "wished to read ancient works for their true meanings, rejecting the limited or false meanings attributed to them during centuries of Christian dominance in Europe" (158). Lauro Martines explains that humanists placed a "supreme emphasis on the importance of getting the texts right." Their methods included, he says, "collating the earliest existing manuscripts and applying the finest philological techniques, with an eye to producing an authentic text" and placing "the text in its historical context, in order to establish the correct value of words and phrases" (*Power and Imagination* 204). In contrast to the medieval scholastic practice of "splintering classical sources into individual statements or *sententiae,*" humanists, as Charles Nauert notices, used the exegetical method proposed by Valla and Erasmus and "insisted on reading each opinion in its context, abandoning the anthologies [of florilegia] and subsequent interpretations and going back to the full original text in search of the author's real meaning." Consequently classical authors "re-emerged as real human beings, living at a particular moment in history and addressing their remarks to specific issues" (*Humanism* 18,193).[48] Eden emphasizes that Erasmus, like Cicero and Quintilian, "recommends investigating those very circumstances of production covered under the rhetorical principle of *decorum:* speaker, audience, time, place, and so on" (*Hermeneutics* 73). Meerhoff notes that Melanchthon in his dedicatory epistle to the *Dispositio* of the Epistle to the Romans (1529) "strongly criticises the scholastics who, by isolating (*decerpere, excerpere*) this or that Biblical verse, resemble people who stand admiringly in front of the torn-off arm or leg of a sculpture and show no appreciation of its essential features, the beauty of the whole and the symmetry of the parts. He argues that to be able to really understand the thinking of the apostle, one must be able to grasp the text as a whole, to see the structural coherence and the way the part links with another, for '*optimum interpretandi genus est* οἰκονομίαν *orationis ostendere*' (The best kind of interpreting is to show the disposition of the speech)" ("Logic" 366).[49]

What we need still to notice, however, is that this reading within textual, social, and historical context, according to the principles of decorum, with an effort to see the writer as a real human being and to understand his or her thinking, gives a moral focus to the humanists' exegetical methods. What we also need to see is that these humanists also read figures in the same way, with the focus on authorial intention and achievement in the social and moral circumstances of the speech act. It is reasonable, of course, to acknowledge that while the precepts of rhetoric do prescribe this ideal reading method, the actual practice of interpretation among the humanists varies in quality. The focus of the interpretation also varies according to the particular humanist's purposes.

Again in contrast to the humanists' moral and unified approach, Aristotle's stylistic instruction lacks both a moral center and a coherent hermeneutic. Separating the intellectual from the moral virtues (*Nicomachean Ethics* 1.13 1103a4–10), Aristotle keeps distinct the practical judgment necessary for rhetoric and the wisdom necessary for the moral life (6.3 1139b31–1140b30). Severing behavior from style and style from content, he removes the essential connections between style and mind and hence between artistic decorum and moral judgment. Designed to explain primarily the technique for the elite speaker who addresses the unsophisticated mob, his *Rhetoric* cannot escape from being branded the art of manipulation, in spite of his desire that the orator accomplish beneficial outcomes for the body politic. Without an equal accounting of style's mirroring capacity and of its inevitable presence in even philosophical genres, Aristotle dismisses from his curriculum the corrective hermeneutic that would fully recuperate rhetoric from its sophistic abuses. These dualisms create in Aristotle's theory unresolvable contradictions.[50]

Conclusion: The Figure as Utterance

Making the figure the center and hence the essence of human thought, speech, and action, the humanist rhetorical tradition depicts the figure itself as utterance. Although the smallest unit of meaning, the figure embodies the whole. The figure is itself a representation of the reconciliation between *verba* and *res,* being on the one hand a behavior / sign and on the other an argument communicating (1) the speaker's interpretation of subject and rhetorical situation and (2) both the speaker's projected image and underlying motives and judgment. As the declamation—the macrocosm—is both a performance and an argument,[51] so the figure—the microcosm—is also the master double frame.

When in a speech we distinguish content and style, we associate content with the argument and style with the performance, and we ascribe to content what is explicitly said and to style what is implicitly said. Finding the fullest meaning requires reading according to both frames, for both what the speaker says and how the speaker says it within the narrative context that surrounds the speech act. Wright emphasizes this dual frame when he specifies that we must read both the matter and the manner of speech (105–6). Agricola also alludes to this dual frame when he divides the speech act into the speech and the speaker, saying, "For he who exploits the stupid credulity of a hearer (and there are many who believe the most incredible and contradictory things because they listen to the speaker, not his speech) no more seems to perform the function of the dialectician than that soldier of the emperor whose victory was the fruit, not of his own valor, but of the enemy's fear" (2.3; McNally 408). When we recognize, however, that choice and development of argument belong to style and that style also serves as proof of the argument, we then apply the dual frame to style itself and read the figure as both performance and argument. Both applications of the dual frame must be brought to the interpretative process for fullest explication.

This dual frame unites in the figure and in utterance the three sets of pairs whose relationships have generated the long-standing debate between the rhetoricians and the philosophers. Poetics and rhetoric are not joined merely by their mutual use of figures nor by their inherent didacticism.[52] They are fundamentally two faces of discourse itself. Philosophy and rhetoric are not joined merely as content and style but rather because both mind and speech operate by means of figures, which themselves entail both logical and tropological processes and hence become both arguments and representations. Ethics and rhetoric are not joined merely when speakers choose to speak truth, advise to an honorable course of action, or create the appearance of a credible persona. Rather aesthetic, rational, and moral judgment are one and the same. Because this critical, moral judgment is the center of a training in the language arts, the humanists can claim that their curriculum shapes the good man.

It is only when we see figures as behaviors that we can unite dualistic pairs without collapsing them, because behavior is their shared common ground. Behavior/style both is and is not the man. The humanist insight of language/figure as behavior, not word or linguistic form, solves the dilemma between dualism and monism by delimiting the territory of language at its broadest boundary. Even though these rhetoricians have not yet adequately theorized their art, their broad and coherent view of style embedded in a philosophy and practice that defines human life itself as both drama and argument distinguishes their understanding of figures from the more limited one of the philosophers, whether of their day or our own.

Seldom in contemporary scholarship or classroom pedagogy is style or text conceived as behavior, although the idea has a few exponents. The compositionists Richard E. Young, Alton L. Becker, and Kenneth L. Pike suggest that this conception is useful for teaching composition: "We propose to view style as a particular way of behaving. Our focus, then, is on characteristics of the process of writing rather than on characteristics of the product" (359). This process of the writer includes "formulating elements of experience and ordering them in coherent and meaningful systems, with formulating his relationship with his readers, and with shaping the notions welling up in his mind into a verbal object that is the best expression of what he has understood and that is at the same time an instrument for inducing activity in other minds. As a creator, then, he must see the art of rhetoric in dynamic terms, as search and choice, as a way of behaving" (360). Others have seen this concept useful for textual interpretation. In the field of communications, Thomas S. Frentz and Thomas B. Farrell in "Language-Action" argue that viewing language as action provides a more complete explanation of a text's meaning (349). The literary theorist Burke sees style as behavior when he characterizes the ideal style as "ingratiation" (*Permanence and Change* 71) and when he proposes as a theoretical grammar to guide textual analysis his concept of "dramatism," which "treats language and thought primarily as modes of action" (*Grammar* xxii). Burke also regards modes of action as arguments, for "wherever there is 'meaning,' there is 'persuasion'" (*Rhetoric of Motives* 172). Researchers in speech act theory have adopted this orientation to enable better theoretical description. John Searle, for example, concludes, "Speaking a language is engaging in a (highly complex) rule-governed form of behavior" (12). Agreeing, Mary Louise Pratt says, "To make an utterance is to perform an act" (80). Researchers in cognitive semantics have come to a similar conclusion. A leading spokesman for the field of frame semantics, Charles J. Fillmore shares this view of text as behavior: "Think of a linguistic text, not as the record of 'small meanings' which give the interpreter the job of assembling these into a 'big meaning' (the meaning of the containing text), but rather as a record of the tools that somebody used in carrying out a particular activity. The job of interpreting a text, then, is analogous to the job of figuring out what activity the people had to be engaged in who used these tools in this order" (112). The linguist Bakhtin has argued for the need to consider text as an utterance or speech act (67).

Even more rarely, however, do contemporary scholars attribute to the language arts or to style a moral center. Burke does, who defines rhetoric as "ways of identification that contribute to social cohesion" (*Rhetoric of Motives* 44), with "communication being a generalized form of love" (37) and the art grounded in "a realism of the act: moral, persuasive" (44). It is Lanham who has perhaps been the most vocal recent advocate for a view of style most like that of the Renaissance humanists. "Every statement about style is, if we know how to interpret it, a statement about behavior," he says (*Analyzing Prose* 9). Prose style provides tacit persuasion patterns (119), makes arguments (29), expresses kinds of feeling and attitude (102), allegorizes mental states (30), and "models human motive" (9). Through style "we socialize ourselves" (132). Because it is behavior, aesthetic judgment is ethical judgment: "Prose style exercises . . . our range of possible behavior. By allowing the luxury of imaginative rehearsal, it confers real ethical choice, and to this extent frees us from necessity. Ethics at this point touches taste, indeed becomes it" (*Style* 133).[53] Extending Lanham's argument, Dion Cautrell concludes that style and ethics overlap because styles result from value judgments: "Because styles are pragmatically inseparable from their rhetorical situations, stylistics bears not only on the underlying language choices that writers and readers make but also—because the choices come in response to a particular situation—on how contexts enable or constrain styles. A given judgment may not rightly apply to this or that style, but this or that style surely entails a value judgment, at times an entire ethical system" (229). These insights were already present in the Renaissance rhetorical curriculum, where they were more fully anatomized and integrated into a broad and coherent view not only of style but also of human discourse.

Chapter 4

tylistic Analysis

The best evidence we have that style was understood to be behavior, to create and reflect character, and to be constituted by figures comes from application of the principles to textual analysis. The hermeneutic model is best embodied in the schoolroom impersonation exercise and in the practice of the best dramatic poets. Using this model and the figures commonly listed in Renaissance handbooks, the following explications of several speeches from literary texts demonstrate not only the primacy of figures to text and their substantive nature but also the comprehensiveness and insightfulness of the reading method.

Inasmuch as one of the *progymnasmata* regularly practiced was the *prosopopoeia* or impersonation, schoolboys would have engaged in textual analysis similar to those that follow. In this exercise students would need to write a speech for a particular character. They could choose a fictional or historical person and must imagine this person speaking to a particular audience on a particular occasion. They would need to craft a speech that imitated the way this person typically spoke. The stipulation for this exercise was that the speech be true to this character, meaning that it must re-create this character. Fraunce describes the figure *prosopopoeia* apropos to the schoolboy exercise: "*Prosopopoia* is a feigning of any person, when in our speech we represent the person of any, and make it speak as though he were there present: an excellent figure, much used of Poets, wherein we must diligently take heed, that the person thus represented have a speech fit and convenient for his estate and nature" (*Arcadian Rhetoric* G2r).

In order to accomplish this task, the pupils would need to study speeches of this person to find the customary behaviors, cognitive, linguistic, and social. The progenitor of modern hermeneutics, Friedrich Schleiermacher, who was also a student of the ancient rhetorical tradition, accurately states the understanding of these rhetoricians when he claims that "every act of understanding is the obverse of an act of discourse, in that one must come to grasp the thought that was at the base of the discourse" (*Hermeneutics* 4.2; trans. Wojcik and Hass 2). This textual analysis would involve a very close reading, noting this person's processes of invention, disposition, and manner of expression. The schoolmaster Brinsley recommends that the scholars note the topics and parts of argument in the left-hand margin of their texts and the stylistic figures in the right (*Ludus* 185). Doing so would surely have made evident to the pupils the crossovers between the two lists. But whether the schoolboys were taught the narrow or broad view of figures, they would have been taught to observe, nevertheless, the same broad range of behaviors in texts.

Once schoolboys had inventoried the speaker's behaviors, they would need to explicate their meanings (assertions, ideologies, feelings, and motives), determine their effects, assess the appropriateness of the speaker's decisions within the physical, logical, psychological, and social contexts of the utterance, and find the predominant patterns. Bringing the text back to life, this approach provides insight into the reasons characters choose their responses to experience and the results of those choices. This approach provides at once a dialectical, psychological, and social/moral reading of text. It involves reading speech patterns as representations of subject matter and indications of cognitive processing. Its focus is ultimately on the judgment of the speaker and the character created by means of this judgment. The density of this analysis draws attention to the variety of qualities that make up any utterance and the complexity of human minds and motives.

This approach to analysis takes into account all perceivable behaviors, all the choices the speaker or writer has made, distinguishing between those used for artistic purposes as representations and those used without the same design.[1] The fact that so many of the observable behaviors do appear as figures in Renaissance handlists suggests that these rhetoricians' concern was with behavioral, as opposed to a narrowly "poetic," analysis. Also if one approaches texts looking for the figures listed in these handlists, one becomes attuned to text as behavior and to the wide variety of behaviors possible. Advanced schoolboys, at least in England, would have commonly known anywhere from one hundred to three hundred figures or more. University students would have known even more, so that their textual analyses could have been dense indeed.[2]

The students would also study how other writers created dramatic monologues for characters. Vives recommends that the schoolmaster point out both the writer's weaknesses and strengths, "which we will mention in order that they may be avoided, . . . or imitated" (*De tradendis disciplinis* 3.7.146). When discussing the works of Terence, Hoole reminds the schoolmaster to show his students how well the playwright has written speeches for his characters: "In reading of this book, it is not amiss for the Master to mind his Scholars of the true decorum of both things and words, and how fitting they are for such persons to do or speak, as are there represented, and upon such occasions as they did, and spake them" (*New Discovery* 139–40).

This schoolroom practice is then extended into the professional work of playwrights, who also recognize that the speeches they write for characters must mirror the characters' states of mind. Richard Edwards (c. 1523–66), in his prologue to *The excellent Comedie of . . . Damon and Pithias* (1571), writes that "the greatest Skill" necessary to the playwright is "rightly to touch/All things to the quick: and eke to frame each person so,/That by his common talk, you may his nature rightly know" (Aiir; qtd. in Donawerth 13).[3] To Renaissance humanists mimesis is the dramatic representation of mental action. Agricola says that delight or pleasure derives from the artist's skill in this imitation when

> words are given to characters according to the nature and condition of each, and a representation (*figura*) of minds and of all emotions is shaped, and this gives rise to the language so that the subject-matter seems not to be expressed but rather enacted and through a sort of insubstantial image, the mind of the listener establishes itself as a medium between the reality and the display of things. . . . One can see in Plato that the disputing characters are so carefully shaped that you seem not to hear the words, but watch the expressions, not of Plato but of his characters. (3.4.396–97; trans. Mack "Rudolph Agricola's Reading" 37–38)[4]

The quality of the playwright depends upon the accuracy of this imitation. The explications that follow show that both Milton and Shakespeare understood mimesis in this way.

Even though the result of the impersonation exercise is a dramatic monologue, a literary creation, the process of writing it is no different from that of writing one's own speech for a given audience on a given occasion. The procedure for analyzing any speech, then, equates with the procedure for analyzing the *prosopopoeia.* As a consequence this exercise makes obvious the fictional dimension of any composition. Inasmuch as the fictional speech also points to the quality of the speaker's judgment, this exercise also makes obvious the nonfictional aspects of fiction. What this perspective provides is an awareness of frames around a text and the need to read each frame for the text's fullest explication. This perspective suggests that the difference between fiction and nonfiction is really only the number of frames one needs to bring to the hermeneutic task, not varying methods of analysis. Nonfiction comes with one dual frame—that of the speaker's argument and performance in the context of his or her dramatic situation. Fiction comes with the dual frame occurring twice—once on the level of characters and their situations and once again on the level of author and his or her situation. When the tale is told by a narrator, the dual frame applies a third time. Because the contexts within which characters act are clearly set forth in fiction, coming to conclusions about character is easier in fiction than in nonfiction, where those contexts must be reconstructed from additional research. Analyzing fictional texts, especially those purposely designed to be psychologically mimetic, then, serves as good practice for reading and responding to the nonfictional texts that constitute our daily living in the workaday world. This reciprocity between fiction and nonfiction motivates these pedagogues to insist that literature be part of this practical rhetorical curriculum.

Since the resulting interpretation of text is fundamentally a *controversia,* an argument about meaning and quality, the interpretation itself is subject to the same criteria as a *controversia* for determining its degree of probability: accuracy, sufficiency, relevancy, and coherence of evidence. This insight would caution the schoolboys against authoritarianism and would promote a responsible attention to well-supported, sound reasoning in these analyses.

Because of the density of meaning in any text, no short explication can unravel all the threads. The following three explications demonstrate only a sampling of the possible foci that can result from a figural/stylistic analysis based on this rhetorical hermenuetic. Nevertheless all three show that when the analysis is carried out to the most general level of meaning—to the speaker's character—stylistic details provide psychological insights that enlarge the reader's understanding of human motivation.

Satan in *Paradise Lost* (1: 249–263)

In the following passage, we see Satan, who is addressing himself, come to terms with the new circumstances in which he finds himself after his expulsion from heaven. Three behavioral patterns predominate, all dramatizing and pointing to Satan's pride: reversal, reduction, and overemphasis.

> Farewell happy Fields
> Where Joy for ever dwells: Hail horrors, hail
> Infernal world, and thou profoundest Hell
> Receive thy new Possessor: One who brings
> A mind not to be chang'd by Place or Time.
> The mind is its own place, and in itself
> Can make a Heav'n of Hell, a Hell of Heav'n.
> What matter where, if I be still the same,
> And what I should be, all but less than hee
> Whom Thunder hath made greater? Here at least
> We shall be free; th' Almighty hath not built
> Here for his envy, will not drive us hence:
> Here we may reign secure, and in my choice
> To reign is worth ambition though in Hell:
> Better to reign in Hell, than serve in Heav'n.[5]

First Satan consistently refuses to interpret his experience according to the perspective of God, who has expelled him. The whole speech functions as a refutation or rejection of the opponent's opinion (*antirrhesis*). Delivered to himself, the speech shows Satan's awareness of God's perspective and Satan's desire and need to reverse it. Upon recognition that he has been cast into Hell, Satan almost immediately transforms Hell into a heaven of his own (*inversio,* turning what was against him for him). We see Satan begin this transformation as he personifies Hell (*conformatio*), announces his arrival, and commands (*prostaktikon*) obeisance: "Hail horrors, hail / Infernal world, and thou profoundest Hell/Receive thy new Possessor." The personification allows Satan to domesticate and then dominate the place. We also see the transformation in the names (*antonomasia*) he assigns to this new abode. At first "horrors" (*metonymy*), Hell quickly becomes the "Infernal world," the pagan home of the dead. This *euphemismus* palliates any fear, guilt, or regret. The third renaming, "profoundest Hell" (*superlatio*), completes a climax (a *decrementum* turned into an *incrementum*), expresses praise (*encomium*) and admiration (*thaumasmus*), and accentuates Hell's greatness and mysteriousness rather than its unfathomable emptiness. As Satan changes the meaning of "Hell" (*antanaclasis*), so he also shifts the meaning of "place" (*ploce*) from physical location to mental construct (*metaphora*): "The mind is its own place." Moving from objective to subjective grounds allows Satan to regain control. Also through the reversal (*antimetabole*) in "Can make a Heav'n of Hell, a Hell of Heav'n," Satan denies the contradiction between contradictories, turning a hierarchy into a parity. The final reversal, phrased as an antithesis, reinstates the hierarchy but turns the tables so that Hell is now the better place: "Better to reign in Hell, than serve in Heav'n." We also see the transformation in his listing (*enumeratio*) of the advantages (*euphemismus*) for being in Hell: freedom, distance from God, secure sovereignty. Here, he argues, he may rule securely forever without competition, interference, or surveillance—good reasons (*aetiologia*) for happiness when what matters most is to reign securely. This attempt to reconstruct the meaning of his situation reflects Satan's rebelliousness: his refusal to feel regret, to acknowledge "natural" consequences for his disobedience, and to admit defeat.

Not only does he recharacterize his new home, but he also refuses to characterize God as God characterizes himself. Rather than accept God as the one supreme, perfect deity of the universe, Satan shows allegiance to a pagan pantheon of gods. We understand this point of view by means of the names (*antonomasia*) once again. Just as Hell is the "Infernal world," so heaven is the "happy Fields" of a pagan Elysium. God's victory was due to the whim of Zeus, or "Thunder" (*metonymy*), the true father of the gods, but one whose will is changeable. This ideology is further evidenced by the *characterismus* Satan gives of God, who, like the other pagan deities, is subject to passions, such as "envy." By choosing this metaphysics, Satan not only justifies his lack of allegiance to the Almighty but also makes room for himself in the pantheon of the gods.

Rather than see himself as the arch traitor consigned to an eternal prison, Satan refashions himself as regal, heroic, self-determining, and free. As "Possessor" and "sovereign" (*characterismus*), he assumes he has not only the right but also the capability to call this place his own. Satan describes himself as steadfast, one with integrity and absolute allegiance to principle, not circumstance: he has "A mind not to be chang'd by Place or Time." He is "what [he] should be." He is no relativist: "What matter where, if I be still the same." With autonomy of mind and self, Satan is no victim but an optimistic and self-directed actor: "The mind is its own place, and in itself / Can make a Heav'n of Hell, a Hell of Heav'n." Satan holds himself in high esteem: he is after all a match for God (*comparatio*), who has won only a temporary victory due to Zeus's whim—his thunderbolt (*metaphora*). So secure is Satan's confidence in his strength that he cannot believe his loss is anything but temporary, this belief expressed in the rhetorical question (*erotema*): "And what I should be, all but less than hee/Whom Thunder hath made greater?" He takes charge: he commands (*prostaktikon*) Hell "to receive" its "new Possessor," and by personifying Hell, place, and time, Satan elevates himself above his circumstances. Having aggrandized Hell (*auxesis*), he has at the same time aggrandized himself as its possessor (*auxesis*).

Milton indicates that Satan's perspective is not as equally possible as that of his opponent. Besides Satan's role as rebel in the Judeo-Christian narrative being retold in *Paradise Lost,* contradictions in this passage point to his inferior argument. A second set of behavioral patterns shows that Satan consistently reduces the picture of reality he views, indicating that he constructs reality as he wishes it to be, not as it is according to the biblical account. Fallacious arguments (*paralogismus*) result. Satan frequently uses *metonymia* as he names things. But these metonymies do not work to represent a thing by means of its quality, adjunct, or cause and thereby to clarify a thing's nature. Rather his metonymies substitute one quality, adjunct, or cause for the thing itself and thereby obscure the thing's essence. In this way Satan reduces the picture he chooses to view.[6] Heaven is only "happy fields" where warrior heroes continually prove their superior strength, not a place for paradisaical social relationships. "Joy," a disembodied emotion, disconnected from angels, God, and even himself, is what dwells in Heaven. Satan is oblivious to other individuals as individuals, seen also in his use of the royal *we* ("Here at least/We shall be free"; "Here we may reign secure"), a *synecdoche* through which he reduces the multitude of his followers into himself. No democrat, Satan thinks of only himself throughout this speech. Also the identification of joy (effect) with war (cause) reveals the joy lost to be Satan's lost ambition for Heaven's throne, not peace, love, justice, nor companionship. The disembodied joy also allows Satan to then disassociate himself from his own feelings, so that he can see himself only as a "mind" (synecdoche), an intellect (metonymy) that can through mental patternings construct feelings. The result of this move is that he then also divorces himself from sensation and sight—from outside evidence. Reality becomes only what the subjective mind creates, becomes completely relative to the viewer. Satan is, then, despite his claim to the contrary, a relativist. When referring to God, Satan uses only a pronoun, "hee," or the metonymy "Almighty," obscuring his opponent again from sight. In using this latter term, Satan is also being ironic (*sarcasmus*), for his taking possession of Hell is predicated on disbelief in God's omniscience, omnipresence, and omnipotence. His irony reveals this metonymy to be for him merely figurative. At the same time, however, by focusing on this one quality, he also discloses how much he wishes that this one quality—power—would become his own essence, would be not merely metonymy for him but impossibly the thing itself. Additionally Satan holds this disbelief in the face of evidence to the contrary: he is in Hell due to the Almighty's command. The reduced view is also evident in Satan's personification of "Hell," "Place," and "Time," by means of which he separates circumstances from himself and makes them entities he believes he can control. Yet Satan is limited by circumstances, and though he identifies himself euphemistically as "Possessor" instead of usurper, or republican instead of dictator, his pattern of aggressive domination belies such self-construction and suggests that he may be hiding from himself his own tyrannical posturings.

Satan's effort to make reality be what he wants it to be is further illuminated by a third set of behavioral patterns—those that show his repeated insistence. We see the insistence in the frequent repetition of words (*conduplicatio*) he wants to emphasize for their transformative tasks: "*Hail,* horrors, *hail* / Infernal world"; "A *mind* not to be chang'd by *Place* or Time. / The *mind* is its own *place*"; "*Here* at least / We shall be free; th' Almighty hath not built / *Here* for his envy, . . . / *Here* we may *reign* secure, and in my choice / To *reign* is worth ambition though in Hell: / Better to *reign* in Hell, than serve in Heav'n." We see this same figure in the repetition of "Hell" and "Heav'n" throughout the passage. The repetition is even intensified through *anaphora* (beginning succeeding lines with the same word): "*Here* for his envy, will not drive us hence:/*Here* we may reign secure." The insistence is also intensified through repetitions of sound, such as alliteration (*paroemion*) in "Farewell . . . Fields" and "Hell" and "Heav'n;" the assonance in "mind" and "time" and "I;" and in the end rhyme (*similiter cadens*) between "we" and "free" or "Almighty" and "envy." Besides repetition Satan's building up step by step (*incrementum*) and elevating through heightened words (*auxesis*) work to create insistence. We also see this insistence as he repeatedly defines himself and Hell through comparisons (*comparatio*) with God and Heaven. If as secure in himself as he assumes, he would not be expending so much energy on making Hell and himself as good as, or better than, Heaven and God. The repetition, insistence, indicates struggle, defiance. Finally this insistence is expressed in his opening *apostrophes* to Heaven and Hell, wherein he mimics (*hypocrisis*) formal ceremony in order to create *hyperbole.* In the dismissal of "happy Fields," the hyperbole expresses a derisive scoff (*sarcasmus*) meant to hide his sense of hopelessness. In the welcoming of the "Infernal world," the hyperbole expresses determination meant to underscore his casting away of hope but finding it in a new way (*apocarteresis*). This insistence suggests not only a stubborn refusal to admit to an inferior argument but also a willingness to deceive himself. This insistence in an argument directed to himself shows his defensiveness and reveals the speech to be also a self-justification (*dicaeologia*) and a consolation (*paramythia*). Milton shows, then, that the motive of fear can underlie the characteristic of pride and that pride manifests itself through rebelliousness, a purposeful reduction of perspective, and excessive insistence.

How self-conscious was Milton of the style he attributes to Satan? On the one hand, it matters not if Milton was consciously using art or relying upon natural ability, habit, or inspiration to produce this character depiction. Either way the important question remains: Is the speech mimetic of Satan's character as depicted in the Judeo-Christian narrative? A figurative analysis shows that it is. On the other hand, because of the difficulty of the task and the quality of the depiction, we can conclude that Milton knows the rules of the art and has exercised good judgment in their use. We can also conclude that he believes this narrative and that his portrayal of Satan works to promote the stated argument of *Paradise Lost:* to "justify the ways of God to men" (I.26).

Shakespeare's Sonnet 129

Th' expense of spirit in a waste of shame
Is lust in action, and till action, lust
Is perjur'd, murd'rous, bloody, full of blame,
Savage, extreme, rude, cruel, not to trust,
Enjoy'd no sooner but despised straight,
Past reason hunted, and no sooner had,
Past reason hated as a swallowed bait
On purpose laid to make the taker mad:
Mad in pursuit and in possession so,
Had, having, and in quest to have, extreme,
A bliss in proof, and prov'd, a very woe,
Before, a joy propos'd, behind, a dream.
    All this the world well knows, yet none knows well
    To shun the heaven that leads men to this hell.[7]

In this *prosopopoeia* Shakespeare dramatizes by means of a vivid portrayal (*enargia*) a courtly lover excusing his promiscuity, despite the torturous enslavement such self-gratification brings. Shakespeare emphasizes through this *exemplum* the selfishness, self-destructiveness, and irrationality of this choice.

The enslavement we see as the speaker's mind circles again and again without escape through the experience of desiring and then gratifying sexual drives. Describing (*descriptio*) lust as a self-perpetuating cycle from desire to fulfillment, to disappointment, and so to desire again, the speaker also rehearses (eight times, in fact) the memory of the experience. This rehearsal is a reliving of the experience and an indication that he is unable to extricate himself, the repetition called *commoratio* (resting on a point). Not only does he repeatedly rehearse the cycle mentally, but he also formulates the movement into shapes that correspond with the cyclical pattern, a pattern that seems to have become habitual in his thinking. This endless circling is represented in the repeated figure *antimetabole* (reversal) in line 2, "Is lust in action, and till action, lust," or in lines 8 and 9 when he describes the bait as being "On purpose laid to make the taker mad: / Mad in pursuit." The *anadiplosis* on "mad" also acts out the speaker being pulled into the cycle again.

This enslavement the speaker is aware of, and he uses it to justify his actions. He chooses the metaphor that likens lust to "swallowed bait." He draws attention to both the cycle and the *antimetaboles* he consistently uses through the reversal in line 10: "Had, having, and in quest to have, extreme." This line forms a self-conscious reversal (*antimetabole*) of the pattern established thus far in the speech. He follows up this *antimetabole* with another in the next line that leads us onward through the cycle to enactment and ironic consequence, as if to underscore the cycle's bitter inevitability: "A bliss in proof, and prov'd, a very woe" (11). That the speaker knowingly chooses to remain entrapped we find in both the content and form of the concluding couplet, wherein he argues hyperbolically that no one knows "to shun" this passion, and he wittily uses *antimetabole* (which has become symbolic to him of the inescapable cycle) to justify the claim as he makes it: "All this the world well knows, yet none knows well" (13). Here we have a pattern functioning as a proof (*pisteis*)—an *antimetabole* arguing that the temptation is irresistible—forming part of an *enthymeme,* whose conclusion, "I cannot change," is implicit. Yet his self-conscious choice to shape his speech and justify his actions belies this determinism.

This choice brings inner turmoil—a constant warring between self-hatred and self-gratification. This turmoil appears in the antitheses between the expectation and the reality—that is, between "enjoyed" and "despised," "a bliss" and "a woe," "a joy" and "a dream," "heaven" and "hell." It also appears in the conflicting attitudes expressed. On the one hand, the speaker feels guilt, admitting to experiencing "a waste of shame" (1). Such shame causes him to feel anger, revulsion, and hatred, expressed in the exacerbation (*deinosis*) of the first ten lines. The definition (*definitio*) of lust as "expensive," "wasteful," and "extreme" and the string of epithets describing lust in lines 3 and 4 are pejorative and upbraiding (*onedismus*). The list of them (*congeries*) is also very lengthy (*amplificatio*), and the rhythmic pattern of the list both stresses each condemning word and imitates staccato speech (*articulus*). The words "despised" and "hated" identify the *execratio* here, so too the pun (*antanaclasis*) on "mad" (8), which emphasizes not only the extremity of the speaker's self-loathing but also the irrationality of the lustful passion. Also emphasis in pronunciation is created through the prevalent devices of word similarity: consonance in "expense," "spirit," "waste," "shame;" *paroemion* (alliteration) in "hunted," "had," "hated," "before" and "behind;" assonance in "hated," "bait," "laid," "make," "taker;" and *polyptoton* in "proof and proved."

But at the same time, the speaker still demonstrates an irrational love for self-gratification. He shifts responsibility (*trajectio in alium*) by separating the lust from himself and personifying it (*conformatio* and *metalepsis*), thereby detaching from himself both the fault and the culpability. His anger gradually abates through the *decensus* we observe in the diction: shame and madness give way to "woe" and then the rather euphemistic "dream" (ll. 12–13). On the one hand, he admits the payoff is insubstantial and disappointing; on the other, though, the consequence is something one can forget. He also returns (*resumptio*) to a contemplation of "bliss" and "joy." He suggests that with time, the sting of conscience wanes. And then he concludes by admitting fault but excusing it with the rationale that everyone else is guilty of the same (*dicaeologia*). The love of self-gratification also appears in now calling the experience "heaven" (*auxesis*) and in the witty jesting (*aestismus*) in the penultimate line, wherein the *antimetabole* of "All this the world well knows, yet none knows well" functions as a self-conscious reversal of his previous feelings. The alliteration (*paroemion*) in "world well" and "none knows" and the surprising paradoxical (*inopinatum*) couplet suggest a sardonic recognition (*ironia*) of the inner turmoil he is choosing to accept but discount. The strength of his love for indulgence is also revealed by the fact that he does not have to offer himself a strong argument in support of his decision, for he is content with fallacious reasoning (*paralogismus*). He excuses himself with the bandwagon (that is, "everyone is doing it") and the slippery slope ("it can't be helped"), both fallacies implied in the hyperbole "the world well knows, yet none knows well." He also neglects to consider ways he could break the cycle, the neglect called *eclipsis* (leaving out necessary matter), and he lets the mere force of the couplet's form as a *sententia* (a wise, pithy sentence) persuade him. Finally the earlier vituperative vehemence we now see as more evidence for the strong addiction he has to self-indulgence, for the stronger the love for the vice, the stronger the anger against it must be to fight the attachment.

Because of both the genre conventions and the unreliability of the speaker, we are aware of two voices here: the speaker's and the author's. If the speaker's argument is ultimately justification for remaining enslaved by passions, Shakespeare's argument warns (*paraenesis*) that such a choice is self-indulgent, self-divisive, and irrational. By showing the psychological consequences of moral compromise, Shakespeare seeks to dissuade (*dehortatio*) his readers against succumbing to the lusts of the flesh. Because he keeps the identity of the speaker generic, he argues that the speaker's experience is universal. Inasmuch as the sonnet is also a parody of the Petrarchan sonnet tradition, Shakespeare reveals the true character of the Petrarchan lover to be lustful, selfish, and self-justifying. He removes the romantic gloss that accompanies this tradition to reveal the darker reality underneath.

We could, if we wished, now evaluate the quality of Shakespeare's writing and what his achievement in this poem communicates about his judgment. The degree to which we think he accurately depicts the cognitive behaviors of this speaker/character—the degree to which this portrayal is realistic—will determine the degree to which we find Shakespeare insightful, reliable, and persuasive.

Titus in Shakespeare's *Titus Andronicus* (III.1.219–33)

A figural analysis of this lament reveals that though Titus believes himself honorable, his inconsistencies in argument and behavior expose him to be blindly egotistical and violent. These characteristics are manifestations and results of his fundamental thought pattern—the improperly used synecdoche. Titus typically takes the part for the whole, a mistake that results because he is unaware of the figure in his thoughts and, as a consequence, the ideology and character his construction of reality argues for.

To Marcus's remonstrance "O brother, speak with possibility, / And do not break into these deep extremes. . . . / But yet let reason govern thy lament" (214–18), Titus responds:

> If there were reason for these miseries,
> Then into limits could I bind my woes:
> When heaven doth weep, doth not the earth o'erflow?
> If the winds rage, doth not the sea wax mad,
> Threat'ning the welkin with his big-swoll'n face?

And wilt thou have a reason for this coil?
I am the sea; hark how her sighs doth blow!
She is the weeping welkin, I the earth:
Then must my sea be moved with her sighs;
Then must my earth with her continual tears
Become a deluge, overflow'd and drown'd:
For why my bowels cannot hide her woes,
But like a drunkard must I vomit them.
Then give me leave, for losers will have leave
To ease their stomachs with their bitter tongues.[8]

Titus argues here, in a *refutatio* to Marcus, that he should be allowed to respond to his miseries without limits because his afflictions have been heaped upon him beyond bounds and without merit or cause. Titus states his *propositio* in "Then give me leave" and gives as evidence his assumption that in nature, for every action there is an inevitable and equal reaction. In an *apodixis* (confirmation based on generally accepted principles), Titus gives two exempla of this inevitable cause/effect sequence: (1) when storms descend, the earth overflows and the sea rages; (2) having imbibed too much, a drunkard will vomit. Then arguing by analogy, he likens these cases to his own. Using metaphor, he says, "I am the sea . . . I the earth." Using simile, he claims that "like a drunkard must I vomit." By comparing himself and the source of his miseries to elements of nature, Titus argues that his unrestrained reaction is therefore natural and unchangeable. The deterministic response in each case he indicates with the word "must," which he repeats (*conduplicatio*) to add emphasis to the point. The causelessness of the original action appears in the one-way relationship he sets up between heaven and earth: the heavens rain down upon the earth and blow upon the sea; the earth and sea have no part in causing that "coil." By implication, then, he has not caused his miseries. The causelessness also appears because his physical organs (bowels, stomach, tongue) respond instinctively to the forces working upon them and cause him to behave as he does, the dividing of himself into parts (*divisio*) emphasizing their independence from his conscious control.

Given the truth of the premise and its applicability to his circumstances, Titus has only to show that his misfortunes are of such an extreme nature that they warrant his extreme outpouring of grief and anger. He suggests the greatness of the forces working upon him through *auxesis:* the sky is the "weeping welkin" with "continual tears," the tempest a "coil." The winds do not merely blow but "rage." He also uses *catachresis,* identifying Lavinia, his mutilated daughter, with the heavens, the cause of his suffering. Without tongue or hands and still bleeding from the fresh wounds, her body becomes for him a *synecdochic* icon of all the injustices that have been heaped upon him: not only is his daughter this bleeding stump, but his two sons have been wrongly condemned to death for the alleged murder of their brother-in-law, another son banished for protecting them, and his own left hand sacrificed to ransom his sons. One injustice stands for all injustices. Through this comparison he also suggests that his daughter is his heaven: she *metonymically* represents ideal "virtue" and "honor." Because she also synecdochically stands for all of Titus's children, she represents the honor of his family, their raison d'être. When she is despoiled, the family is despoiled. As heaven and earth are inextricably bound together, she is bound to him so that her griefs descend upon him. Her sighs and tears, then, naturally move within him the overwhelming tempest, flood, and sickness that cannot be kept within bounds. In these circumstances Titus presents himself as a good man mightily abused, an honorable victim (*characterismus*). He calls himself a "loser" (*tapinosis*), the cause of his suffering beyond his control.

Through these same figures, Titus also vents his grief and anger (*pathopoeia*) in order to reinforce his argument's probity. Using *auxesis,* he reflects and creates vehemence. He calls his sorrows his "miseries" and "woes." The sea does not merely move but "wax[es] mad"; the waters are not merely a flood but a "deluge," drowning the whole earth. The *catachresis* and *tapinosis* also point to extreme passion. Turning his daughter into a storm and himself into the deluged world, Titus makes concrete the causes for his emotions and the emotions themselves (*enargia*). Because he casts himself as both sea and earth, he argues his entire world is overcome by passion. Just as the drunkard has ingested too much, so Titus has felt too much sorrow. By focusing on the parts of himself involved in the acts of ingestion and disgorgement, he moves the deluge and tempest inward, again giving physical motion to these passions.

Not only the tropes but also the schemes reflect and create the vehemence. The *accumulatio* of seven *enthymemes,* the if/then statements, builds emphasis (*palilogia*). Also heightening the passion is repetition wherever it occurs: in the *epanaphora* ("Then must my sea" and "Then must my earth"); in the *conduplicatio* on "must"; in the three rhetorical questions (*eroteses*) that form a *congeries* ("When heaven doth weep, doth not the earth o'erflow? / If the winds rage, doth not the sea wax mad, / Threat'ning the welkin with his big-swoll'n face? / And wilt thou have a reason for this coil?"); in the repetition on "leave" (*antistrophe*); in the restatements of his boundless woes (*exergasia*); and in the alliteration (*paroemion*) throughout the passage. The repeated *z* sounds create a grinding of the teeth, the *r* sounds a clinching of the jaw, the *m* sounds a tightening of the lips, all associated with anger, resentment, pain. The emphasis on *d* in "deluge, overflow'd and drown'd" and "drunkard" hammers out the vehemence, whereas the repetition of *t* in "To . . . stomachs . . . bitter tongues"emphasizes the bitterness. Especially generative of forward, wavelike motion (and emotion) is the alliteration on the *w,* occurring in the first six lines ("were," "woes," "weep," "wax," "welkin," "wilt") and then echoed occasionally in the last nine ("weeping," "welkin," "why," "bowels," "woes"). The enjambment in the lines "Then must my earth with her continual tears / Become a deluge, overflow'd and drown'd" also acts out the overflowing of the passion. In expressing his passion, this speech functions as not only a refutation but also a lament (*threnos*).

Additionally Titus argues not only that moderation and control are impossible, but also that his argument and passion are reasonable. He structures his induction (*epagoge*) into a tight chain of *enthymemes* that, taken together, become an *accumulatio* of reasons that end with the *propositio.* The weight of the list increases the argument's force. He also outlines the analogies step by step (*progressio*) and wittily combines the two disparate but related images of drunkenness and the sea. Personifying the world and heavens, he now uses the similarities between humankind and the elements to reinforce the analogy. The parallel structure (*isocolon*) further underscores the inevitable cause/effect relations in "When heaven doth weep, doth not the earth o'erflow?" and in "I am the sea; . . . she is the weeping welkin," just as the *epanaphora* also underscores the closeness of the analogy between himself and the elements in "Then must my sea" and "Then must my earth." The *chiasmi* in the cognitive movement from wind to sea and then from sea to wind (222–25), and proceeding from heaven, earth, wind, sea (221–23) to sea, wind, earth, heaven (227–28), give the argument a sense of returning to where it started, further reinforcing its logical inevitability. The self-evidence of the argument Titus suggests through the three rhetorical questions (*eroteses*): "When heaven doth weep, doth not the earth o'erflow? / If the winds rage, doth not the sea wax mad, / Threat'ning the welkin with his big-swoll'n face? / And wilt thou have a reason for this coil?"

Finally Titus intends to do more than win allowance for the privilege to vent as he wishes. He also desires this speech to be an emotional utterance that moves the audience, his other family members, to like feelings and thoughts (*exuscitatio*), so that they will join him in his cause. To this end he seeks to involve his listeners in the process of his thoughts. By implying the cause/effect relations through questions, Titus requires his listeners to supply the answers and in doing so to adopt his perspective (*innvitio*). The figures of repetition, amplification, and *enargia* involve the listeners in his passions. The "hark" commands (*prostaktikon*) the audience to notice the compelling reasons for outrage, their attention drawn to mutilated Lavinia and to the grieving father, a tableau vivant or *symbole* of family misery. This acting out of the victimized hero (*mimesis*) moves pity. Such a portrait of his circumstances also makes this speech an appeal for pity (*commiseratio*).

However inconsistencies in his speech reveal Titus to be less noble and justified than he here presents himself, calling into question his conclusions. First there is a contradiction (*paralogismus*) between the helplessness he claims about his response and the control he exhibits in this speech. While he cannot "bind" his passions into "limits," he binds his argument into a neat series of *enthymemes,* proceeding from general law to specific application of the law, from opening proposition to concluding summation. The figures of balance, parallelism, antithesis, and *hypotaxis* also suggest a mind putting ideas into relation; so too does the pun (*antanaclasis*) on "reason" that begins the speech. In reasoning against reason, Titus undermines himself. Furthermore if his response were uncontrollable, he would not need to demand "leave" nor to justify it. This argument functions as a self-justification (*dicaeologia*), indicating that Titus is choosing his response. Making his speech an argument also shows it is constructed. His own behavior, then, demonstrates that his unrestrained reaction is chosen, not inevitable and unchangeable.

Second there are contradictions between Titus's claims and physical and social reality. The comparison of physical to human nature is not commensurate (*paralogismus*); hence the use of philosophical determinism to excuse his actions does not justify them.

Titus further undermines his own plea by personifying the elements, since by doing so he imputes to physical elements human motives, a detail that argues choice. When we also notice that Titus states his initial premise as an unconditional absolute—when it rains, the earth floods—we see that his argument is overgeneralized hyperbole, another *paralogismus.* Also, although Titus disclaims meriting his misfortunes, he has unknowingly brought some of them upon himself. Earlier, to observe the Roman rite of human sacrifice, Titus had sanctioned the martyring of Alarbus, the son of the Goth queen, who becomes the new Roman queen. This act precipitates the revenge now enacted upon him.

Third Titus's imagery implies that he holds inconsistent attitudes toward his daughter, Lavinia. On the one hand, by calling her his heaven, he implies that she is a goddess to be worshiped because of her virtue. On the other, with her "mart'red" body making visible her defilement (*symbole*), she becomes an oppressor forcing him to suffer woes he cannot hide. Titus hints at his anger for this shame by envisioning the sea "threat'ning the welkin with his big-swoll'n face." Further evidence for his contradictory attitudes appears in the image of her tears and sighs becoming his floods and tempests. While suggesting that he feels his daughter's sorrows, this image (icon) also signifies his own resentment, impatience, and shame.

These inconsistencies all result from mistaken synecdochic perspectives. Synecdoche, the part standing for the whole, is misused when the part takes the place of the whole. Titus can only conclude that human emotional reactions are like physical reactions if he takes the laws of material reality as the model for the whole of reality. He can only conclude he is a blameless victim if he fails to see the barbaric qualities of any of his former behavior. He can only conclude that rain always submerges the earth if he ignores other possible and necessary causes and effects. Titus can only turn Lavinia into a symbol by focusing on a part of her—in this case her mutilated body—and in doing so dehumanizing her.

In order to take the part for the whole as consistently as does Titus, he must consistently deny the other parts, an act that, because contrary to reality, requires insistence. This insistence reflects and creates egoism. Titus's insistence appears in the vehemence with which he makes his insufficiently proven argument. Such insistence creates an authoritarianism that belittles the family members he addresses. His *eroteses* function as *epiplexes* (questions used to reproach) and *apodioxes* (indignant rejections of a correction). His *antanaclasis* on "reason" functions as a *sarcasmus.* His "then" declarations become commands (*prostaktikon*). When Titus associates himself with both sea and earth, making himself the world and his woes the world's woes, this synecdoche suggests that he makes himself the whole. He sees only himself wherever he looks. Lavinia and his sons become no more to him than images, synecdoches, of himself.

Because Titus's perspective is limited, his claims, as do his diction and syntax, appear to be exaggerated, excessive, and self-indulgent. The figures all participate in creating hyperbole. Egoism is by nature misapplied hyperbole. His mental movements between extremes point to his penchant for melodrama as well as to his instability and defensiveness. His speech then reveals his argument to be a rationalization, his emotional response a postured self-pity.

By denying parts of reality and insisting upon that denial, Titus is violent. Insisting on the totality of a part is an act of severance, dismemberment of the whole. Titus's attitudes toward his daughter show he has dismembered her and his family, reflected in the violence the sea feels toward the heaven and in the insistence in the tone of voice with which Titus speaks these lines, suggested by the three consecutive spondees in "big-swoll'n face" and the two spondees on "wind rage" and "mad / Threat'ning." Titus's insistence upon his privilege to spew forth his grief sickness so that others also suffer from his woes shows he has also severed the community from himself. The argument of "no limits," of "overflowing" bounds, sets up the possibility for unrestrained retaliation. This insistence represents his counterassertion of power, his defiance, despite his self-characterization as a loser. Inasmuch as the speech itself is Titus's venting, it is an act of violence, of retaliation without limits. Finally Titus divides himself from himself, does violence to himself. Despite the logical control he believes he exhibits, his speech reflects a mind in turmoil. This turmoil is seen in the self-contradictions, the oscillations between extremes, the anatomizing of body parts, the movement between detachment from and identification with his own images, and the characterization of the world and drunkard as self-divided. This dismemberment in his thinking and speaking not only makes this speech act violent but also predicts future acts of violence. This thought pattern also suggests that violence against others follows from self-violence. Indeed this moment in the play is the decisive turning point that forecasts all future action. From this point on, Titus prepares for the sickening mutilations he will perform at the play's close.

Through this depiction Shakespeare provides a psychological analysis not only of a man who would seek revenge by dismembering his foes but also of late Roman culture, which Titus symbolizes. Shakespeare shows here that physical dismemberment follows from mental dismemberment, that the unrecognized misused synecdoche is the destructive thought pattern propelling and structuring physical acts of violence, revenge, and barbarism. These acts, both mental and physical, characterize the Romans at the time of the empire's fall and, as Shakespeare argues, lead to its fall. In this characterization he also shows that he recognizes figures as fundamental thought patterns and warns his auditors to pay attention to and change the poorly fashioned figures in their own thoughts so as to avoid destructive behaviors.

VICKERS HAS ARGUED THAT "the challenge facing students of rhetoric is to integrate the appreciation of stylistic detail into a response to the whole" ("Shakespeare's Use" 92). He has also urged further study of Renaissance rhetorical figures since this subject "of all the aspects of rhetoric . . . remains the least appreciated, the most misunderstood" (*In Defence* 294). What we discover by studying Renaissance doctrines of the tropes and figures is precisely the way to move from stylistic detail to the overriding meanings of the text—to the arguments and characters of speakers and authors. In fact it is only a figural/behavioral analysis that enables the fullest explication of meaning, tying together thought, speech, and action and directing attention to motives and judgment. A figural/behavioral approach to exegesis is, then, useful, insightful, moral, and appropriately ample.

Appendix 1

A Handlist of the Figures

A Note on the Handlist

Since my purpose in collecting this list is to report what textual features Renaissance rhetoricians view as figures, the following handlist provides the definitions and examples these rhetoricians and their classical sources give for the figures. I fashion a definition for each that best encapsulates the descriptions found in all the manuals consulted. When there are multiple definitions, I include all of them. When there is disagreement among these rhetoricians about a figure's name or definition, I place the most agreed upon name and definition in the entry itself and include the aberration in the note at the bottom of the entry. I provide examples for each from the manuals themselves and only supply my own example on rare occasions when a suitable illustration is not offered. Following the pattern begun in these manuals, I segregate the figures by discourse level and arrange them alphabetically within these categories. This rubric is useful in showing that figures structure all the levels that make up language, but sometimes misleading in implying that some forms belong to only one level. Since Renaissance rhetoricians tend to view all figures as figures of thought, we need to keep in mind that even the figures in those levels we associate with linguistic phenomena can have manifestations on cognitive levels. Indeed, Renaissance rhetoricians sometimes apply the same figure to different discourse levels. When they do so, I do too, in order to represent this flexible range of application. I use as the head word the most common name of the figure and list afterward in order of frequency its other most common names. Idiosyncratic names I place in the note, where I also record commentary from these manuals on the figure's nature, function, or derivation. For readability, I standardize spelling and punctuation in all quotations from Renaissance texts.

PHONETIC

antistoechon [G. "change of a letter"] or *antithesis* [G. "opposition"]

Substituting sounds within a word

"Experience hath me tought, for taught; this was a painful wark, for work; so be it that you wull, for, will; a thing so frail and brickle, for, brittle; returning very eft, for oft; slibbery, for slippery, . . ."

(Peacham [1577] E.iii.r)

Note: Alternate spelling is *antistechon*. *Parallaga* under morphological figures below is related.

diaeresis [G. "dismantling, separating"]

Making two syllables of one

"Desier for desire" or "fier for fire."

(Puttenham 174)

Note: Alternate spellings are *dieresis* and *dyaeresis*. Alternate names include *dialysis* and *divisio*.

diastole [G. "distinction, difference"] or *ectasis* [G. "a stretching out, extension"] or *extensio* [L. "a stretching out, extension"]

Making a short syllable long, created by putting the accent on the wrong syllable

"Sovereígn for sóvereign: gracíous for grácious: éndure for endúre: Solómon for Sólomon."

(Puttenham 174)

Note: Additional names include *differentia* and *tasis*.

ecthlipsis [G. "squeeze out"]

In pronunciation, dropping the terminal syllable made of a vowel plus "m," usually when the next word begins with a vowel

"*Monstrum horrendum, informe, ingens*" (Virgil, *Aeneid* 3.658) becomes "*monstr' horrend', informe, ingens.*"

(Hoole 305)

Note: Peacham explains that this figure cannot be applied to English ([1577] E.iii.r).

hiatus ["gaping"]

An effective clash of vowels at the end of one word and the beginning of the next

"*Pulcra oratione ista iacta te.*"

(Boast yourself of that fine speech of yours.)

(Quintilian 9.4.36)

Note: Cicero remarks that *hiatus* well-used produces "something agreeable [. . .] and show[s] a not unpleasant carelessness on the part of the man who is paying more attention to thought than to words" (*Or.* 23.77). *Hiatus* can also be a vice. See *hiatus* under vices below.

homoeoptoton [G. "similar inflection"] or *similiter cadens* [L. "similar closing"]

Words with like case endings or nouns ending with like letters or syllables finish joined phrases or clauses.

"He came into Cilicia, and then spied out Africa: and after that came with his army into Sardinia."

"Art thou in poverty? Seek not principality, but rather how to relieve thy necessity."

(Peacham [1593] 54)

"By earnest affection, men learn discretion."

(Wilson 226)

"It is an abomination to kings to commit wickedness: for the throne is established by righteousness" (Proverbs 16:12).

(Smith 214)

Note: Alternate spellings include *homoioptoton* and *omoioptoton*. Even though the English rhetoricians treat this figure as one occurring at the end of phrases or clauses, Latin rhetoricians acknowledge its appearance anywhere in an utterance, whether with initial, median, or terminal words. For example, Soarez explains, "This arrangement is seen, not only at the end of a sentence, but also initial words match one another, or they may correspond to words placed at the middle or at the end; or the order may be reversed, so that those in the middle correspond to those at the beginning, and those at the end to those at the middle; they can also be made to correspond in any fashion" (324).

homoeoteleuton [G. "ending alike"] or *similiter desinens* [L. "ending alike"]

Words without cases, but with like ending syllables finish joined phrases or clauses.

"He is esteemed eloquent which can invent wittily, remember perfectly, dispose orderly, figure diversely, pronounce aptly, confirm strongly, and conclude directly."

"No marvel though wisdom complaineth that she is either wilfully despised, or carelessly neglected, either openly scorned, or secretly abhorred."

(Peacham [1593] 54–55)

Note: Alternate spellings include *homoioteleuton* and *omoioteleuton*. Puttenham calls this figure "the Like loose" (184). Since English is not an inflected language, the distinction between *homoeoptoton* and *homoeoteleuton* matters little, as long as the first is restricted to the ending of clauses. Consequently, some rhetoricians conflate the two figures. In fact, Puttenham (184) and Gill (163) simply consider this figure to cover all end rhyme. Peacham tries to distinguish between these two by restricting *homoeoteleuton* to clauses finishing with like-ending verbs or adverbs, and *homoeoptoton* to phrases or clauses finishing with like-ending adjectives or nouns. Latin rhetoricians do regard this figure as one occurring at the end of phrases and clauses, as opposed to *homoeoptoton* which can occur anywhere. See note to *homoeoptoton* above.

homoioartron [G. "beginning alike"]

Using close together words with beginning syllables that sound alike

"*ego omni officio caeteris satisfacio omnibus*" (I satisfy every duty with regard to everything else.)

(The figure is in "*omni*" and "*omnibus*" or the repetition of "every").

(Sturm 3.17.668)

hyphen [G. "together"]
When joining two words into a compound word, the last syllable of the first word takes on a strong accent, even though the first syllable of the second word also has a strong accent, putting two strong accents side by side within a word
"*Theos* and *logos* when joined become *theologos* (i.e. *theólógos*)."
(Mancinelli xcvi.)

parechesis [G. "succession of similar sounds, alliteration"] or *paromoia* [G. "assonance"]
Assonance, consonance, and alliteration; repeating one or more sounds or syllables to create euphony
"*Et secum sola sicca spatiatur arena*" [And the lone dry sand spreads itself out].
(Sturm 2.22.407)

"Time tried his truth his travails and his trust,
And time too late tried his integrity."
(Puttenham 185)

"*O fortunatam natam me consule Romam*!" (Cicero, his poem on the consulship).
[O happy Rome, born in my consulship (trans. Butler)]
(Vossius 242)

Note: Puttenham calls this "the Figure of like letter" (185) and an additional name is *assonantia*. Alternate spellings include *parachesis, paromoion, paroemion, paromeon, parimion, parhomoeon,* and *adsonantia*. This figure is often included within the broader figure of *paronomasia*. See *paronomasia* under lexical figures below.

rime or *parisonomata* [G. "comparable words"]
One or several syllables of different words end alike.
"My hart my hand, my hand hath given my hart
The giver given from guilt shall never part."
(Sidney, "Graven Thoughts," from *The Old Arcadia*, book 3, 174)
(Fraunce B8v)

"*in hac calamitosa fama quasi in aliqua perniciosissima flamma*" (Cicero, *Pro Cluentio* 1.4.) ["in this calamitous fame, just as a pernicious flame"]
(Sturm 3.31.784)

synaeresis [G. "yoking together"] or *episynaloepha* [G. "collection"] or *complexio* [L. "a combination, connection"]
Contracting two vowels or syllables in the middle of a word into one
"Virtuous" and "righteous" become instead of three syllables each, only two.
(Peacham [1577] E.iii.r)

"Cannot" becomes "can't."
(example mine)

Note: An alternate spelling is *episynaliphe* and an alternate name is *contractio*. Quintilian treats *synaeresis* and *synaloepha*, the next figure, as if the same (1.5.17; 9.4.36).

synaloepha [G. "stopping of a hiatus, coalescing of two syllables into one"]
Eliding two adjacent vowels at the end of one word and the beginning of the next

"To attain" becomes "t'attain."

(Puttenham 174)

"Th' Arcadian's guise was this."
"Show me no more; I seete" (for "see it").

(Peacham [1577] E.iii.r)

"You are" becomes "you're."

(example mine)

Note: An alternate spelling is *synaliphe* and an alternate name is *delecio*. Quintilian makes this figure synonymous with *synaeresis* (1.5.17). See above.

systole [G. "drawing together, contraction"]
Making a long syllable short, created in English by putting the accent on the wrong syllable
Pronouncing "persevérance" as "perséverance;" or "adhérents" as "adherénts."

(Sherry [1550] 27–28)

Note: Alternate names are *contractio* and *synecphonesis*.

MORPHOLOGICAL/ORTHOGRAPHICAL

aphaeresis [G. "a taking away"] or *ablatio* [L. "a taking away"]
Deleting the beginning syllable of a word
"Twixt for betwixt, gainsay for again say, ill for evil."

(Puttenham 173)

Note: An alternate spelling is *apheresis* and additional name is *detractio*.

apocope [G. "a cutting off"] or *abscissio* [L. "a breaking off"]
Deleting the last syllable or letter of a word
"Morne for morning."

(Puttenham 173)

Note: An alternate spelling is *abcisio* or *absissio*.

epenthesis [G. "insertion"] or *interpositio* [L. "a putting between, insertion"]
Adding a syllable in the middle of a word
"Meeterly, for meetly; goldylocks, for goldlocks."

(Puttenham 173)

Note: *Epectasis and insertio* are additional names.

metaplasmus [G. "a change of form"] or *transformatio* [L. "a change of shape"]
A general category for transformations of words by means of adding, deleting, changing or transposing letters or syllables
The following figures are commonly included under this category: *prothesis*, *aphaeresis*, *epenthesis*, *syncope*, *paragoge*, *apocope*, *systole*, *diastole*, *ecthlipsis*, *synaloepha*, *synaeresis*, *diaresis*, *antistoechon*, and *metathesis*.

(Peacham [1577] E.ii.r)

Note: A barbarism tolerated for the sake of poetic license is *metaplasmus* (Quintilian 1.8.14).

metathesis [G. "transposition"] or *transpositio* [L. "transposition"]
Transposing letters within a word
"Remembre, for remember" or "a Cypers tree, for a Cypress tree."

(Peacham [1577] E.iii.v)

Note: An alternate name is *trajectio.*

paragoge [G. "leading past, derivation"] or *proparalepsis* [G. "taking besides"]
Adding an ending letter or syllable to a word
"'He useth to slacken his matters,' for 'to slack his matters.'"

(Sherry [1550] 27)

"'Hasten your business' for 'Haste your business.'"

(Wilson 202)

Note: An alternate spelling is *prosparalepsis.* Alternate names include *productio, diductio,* and *preassumpcio.*

parallaga [G. "interchange, putting one for the other"]
A possible substitution of a letter in a word or a word in an expression due to dialect

1. In a word
   "*Asuenio* for *aduenio*" (I'm coming.).
2. In an expression
   "*Dete* (about you) instead of *ente* (on you)."

(Mancinelli xxvii.)

Note: Alternate name is *protheseon.*

parelcon [G. "extraneous addition"]
Forming an unusual compound word, by adding either a syllable or a whole word at the end of another in order to intensify
Numnam ("For now"), *etiamnum* ("even now"), *tu Sofia adesdum* ("when you, Sophia, are present").

(Smith 187)

Note: This figure is very rare, if even possible, in English. Peacham provides the only English example, and he treats this construction as a vice ([1577] F.iii.r). See *parelcon* below under vices.

prosthesis [G. "placing before"] or *appositio* [L. "a setting before"]
Adding a beginning syllable to a word
"There am I well beknown."
"Ymade to burn outright."
"Adown to the ground we fall."
"I do beweep my woe."

(Peacham [1577] E.ii.r)

Note: An alternate spelling is *prothesis* and an alternate name is *adjectio.*

syncope [G. "cutting"] or *concisio* [L. "a cutting"]
Deleting letters or syllables from the middle of a word
"You see thus oft it hapth" for "happeneth."

"Peruse well Hercles spear" for "Hercules."
"This is mine enmies' spite" for "enemies."
"With great magnimity" for "magnanimity."
"The prosprous wind it blew" for "prosperous."

(Peacham [1577] E.ii.v)

Note: An alternate spelling is *sincope* or *consicio* and an alternate name is *celeriter*.

GRAMMATICAL

anapodoton [G. "not returned"] or *anantapodoton* [G. "without apodosis"] or *anacoluthon* [G. "inconsequence, anomaly"]

Omitting a clause, usually the *apodosis,* while still retaining the meaning of the missing element

"If you do as I have counseled you, and be ruled by your friends, they will do for you; if not, well, I will say no more."

(Peacham [1577] F.i.v)

Note: See *apodosis* below under syntactical figures.

anthimeria [G. "one part for another"]

Substituting one part of speech for another

"So was all his life," for "Such was all his life."

(Peacham [1577] H.iiii.v)

antiptosis [G. "interchange of cases"] or *anthypallage* [G. "substitution of one case for another"]

Putting one case for another

"Me think it is so," for "I think it is so."

(Sherry [1550] 32)

appositio [L. "a setting before"] or *parathesis* [G. "juxtaposition"]

An appositive

"*Animal equus*, a living creature, a horse."
"Erasmus, a man of a most exact judgement."

(Smith 191)

Note: Alternate names include *epergesis* and *prosodiasaphesis*. Alexander Rhetor spells the name *prosdiasaphesis*. Scaliger explains that many epithets belong here (504). See *epitheton* below under lexical figures.

disjunctio [L. "a separation"] or *diazeugma* [G. "a disjoining"]

Each phrase or clause has its own verb that is similar in meaning and that separates an action into parts.

1. In phrases

"The people of Rome destroyed Numantia, overthrew Carthage, cast down Corinth, and razed Fregels" (*Ad Herennium* 4.27.37).
"Covetousness hurteth the body and corrupteth the mind."

(Sherry [1550] 30)

"But why should I be ashamed, I who have lived in such fashion for so many years that me from them no advantage or leisure of mind has ever separated, no pleasure recalled, or no sleep slowed down?" (Cicero, *Pro Archia* 6.12, trans. Flynn)

(Soarez 321)

2. In clauses

"They occupied Capua; they secured Atella with fortification; they will obtain Cuma with a multitude of their own men; they conquered other cities with strength."

(Aquila §43)

"The Colophonians claim that Homer is their countryman, the Chians insist that he is theirs, the Salaminians claim him, but the Smyrnaeans assert he belongs to them" (Cicero, *Pro Archia* 8.19, trans. Flynn).

(Soarez 321)

Note: An alternate name is *alyton*. Soarez associates this figure with *hypozeugma* (321). See *hypozeugma* below. Quintilian points out that some have equated this figure with *synonymia* (9.3.45). Robertellus indicates that this figure creates *epitrochasmus* (24v). See *epitrochasmus* under Pragmatical–idea figures below.

eclipsis [G. "a deficiency"] or *ellipsis* [G. "an omission"] or *defectus* [L. "a deficiency"]
Leaving out a word or words that are nevertheless understood by the context
"Good morrow" and "good night."

(Sherry [1550] 31)

"But this for that let be, and now to the rest." (The word "sufficient" after "let be" is missing).
"What might be more in the matter?" (for "What might be more done or spoken in the matter.")
"A man of so rare virtue, so deeply to be overseen." (Instead of, "Is it true that a man of so rare virtue should so deeply be overseen?").

(Day 81)

Note: An alternate spelling is *eclypsis* or *elleipsis* or *defectio*. Alternate names include *detractio*, *suppressio*, and *synecdoche*. This association with synecdoche demonstrates the principle of extension at work, since in *eclipsis*, we do infer the missing part from the whole. See *synecdoche* under semantical figures below. Puttenham calls this "the figure of default" (175). *Subticentia* is a term sometimes used to designate the category of figures that work by default. *Ellipsis* has one of three possible applications: it can be a grammatical figure, a pragmatical figure, and a vice. See the other entries under these categories below.

enallage [G. "interchange"] or *alleotheta* [G. "changed construction"]
Substituting one case, gender, number, mood, time, person, or word for another

1. The accusative for the dative: "I give you this gift" for "I give this gift to you."
2. The feminine for the neuter: "The wind is loud, she bloweth cold."
3. The plural verb for the singular: "The greater part of wild beasts do not drink in Summer for want of showers."
4. The subjunctive for the infinitive: "I am sorry that I hear it" for "I am sorry to hear it."
5. The present for the future tense: "If it happen hereafter, that they may bear rule, we are all undone."

6. The third person for the first: "Here he is; what have you to say unto him" for "Here am I; what have you to say unto me."

(Peacham [1577] H.iii.v)

7. The first person for the third: "In that hour/ Be it not mine beneath the open sky/ To court soft sleep nor on the forest ridge/ Amid the grass to lie" (Virgil, *Georgic* III.435, trans. Butler).

(Quintilian 9.3.21)

8. The object pronoun for the subject pronoun: "Me thought it should be you, and so me thinks."
9. Any word substituted for another: "He roused himself full blith, and hastened them until" (Spenser, *The Faerie Queene* I 11.4.9). Here "until" is substituted for "unto."

(Gill 158)

Note: An alternate spelling is *alloiotheta* and a synonym is *alloiosis* or *alloeosis*. Puttenham's name is "the Figure of exchange" (182). Erasmus gives *heterosis* as a synonym here (*DC* 321), but Veltkirchius divides *enallage* into two kinds: *antimeria* (substituting one part of speech for another) and *heterosis* (substituting conjugations) (30r). He also gives *permutatio* as a synonym (30r). Quintilian uses *exallage* as the name of this figure (9.3.12), but *exallage* has another more common meaning. See *exallage* below. Alexander gives *allage* as a synonym (33). Scaliger (505) and Hoole (265) conflate this figure with *anthimeria*. See *anthimeria* above. This figure, along with other grammatical figures, contains solecisms that can be acceptable if appropriate to the circumstances of the speech act. See *solecismus* below under vices.

epizeugma [G. "to join up"] or *injunctio* [L. "to join or fasten into"]

Making a verb or noun inclusive

1. One verb completes a number of phrases or clauses, or *zeugma* (the opposite of *disjunctio*):
   "Lust conquered shame, boldness fear, madness reason" (Cicero, *Pro Cluentio* 6.15, trans. Butler).
2. One noun or pronoun includes both male and female genders:
   "But as many as received him, to them gave he power to become the sons of God, even to them that believe on his name" (John 1:12).
3. A collective noun:
   The committee eat their lunches during their meetings.

(Quintilian 9.3.62; last two examples mine)

Note: Both Quintilian and Aquila (§44) include under the first use *prozeugma*, *hypozeugma*, and *mesozeugma*. See each of these headings below.

evocatio [L. "a calling out, a summoning"]

Using a third person noun with a first or second person verb conjugation

"A great part of us students do seek pleasures."

(Smith 190)

exallage [G. "complete change, alteration"]

Frequent and slight grammatical variations within a sentence's structure

"Having first taken Amphipolis, after this he seized Pydna, likewise Potidaea, then Methone in turn, afterwards he attacked Thessaly" (Demosthenes *Olynthiac I* 12, trans. Wooten).

(Hermogenes 2.1.316)

hebraism [L. "belonging to the Hebrews"]
Imitating Hebrew constructions

1. Instead of an epithet, Hebrews put the substantive in the genitive case: "Men of mercy, for, merciful man."
2. Hebrews sometimes use the imperative mood for the future tense: "Seek the Lord and live, (i.e.) ye shall certainly live" (Amos 5:6).
3. Contrarily, Hebrews sometimes put the future tense for the imperative mood: "'The Priest's lips shall preserve knowledge'; for, 'let the Priest's lips preserve knowledge'" (Malachi 2:7).

(Smith 227–28)

hellenismus [G. "belonging to Greek"] or *graecismus* [L. "Greek 'isms'"]
Imitating Greek constructions

"This Graecism [using the infinitive 'to die' after the preposition 'from'] Edmund Spencer uses also not inelegantly in the English tongue: as,
'For not to have been dipt in Lethe Lake,
Could save the sonne of Thetis [Achilles] from to die;'"
("The Ruines of Time" l. 428–29).

(Smith 193–94)

Note: *Hellenismus* has another meaning, that of correct, idiomatic Greek, a virtue that produces purity of style (Aristotle, *Rhetoric* 3.5.1, 1407a19). See virtues below.

hendiadys [G. "one by means of two"]
Using two nouns connected by 'and' instead of a noun and its qualifier

"'On iron and bit he champed,' for 'on the iron bit he champed.'"
"'By surge and sea we past,' for 'by surging sea we past.'"

(Day 83)

Note: Alternate spellings include *hendiadis*, *endiadis* or *endiadys*. Puttenham calls this "the Figure of Twinnes" (188). Gill explains that turning an adjective into a substantive will produce this figure (158).

hypozeugma [G. "being under a yoke"] or *adjunctio* [L. "a joining, annexing"]
Putting the verb, which applies to all the clauses, in the last

"'You are not the sort of person, Catiline, that shame from crime, or fear from danger, or reason from mad folly has ever recalled'" (Cicero, *In Catilinam* 1.9.22, trans. Knott).

(Erasmus, *De copia* 345)

"Beauty by sickness, by sorrow, or by age decayeth."

(Sherry [1550] 29)

Note: Alternate names are *postjunctio* and *synezeugmenon*. Puttenham's English name is "the Rerewarder" (176). *Adjunctio* has been applied to both *hypozeugma* and *prozeugma*. See *prozeugma* below.

hysterologia [G. "speaking last"]
Joining a preposition to the verb instead of to its object

"I ran after with as much speed as I could, the thief that had undone me."
"He ran against with fury rage, the doors most strong."

(Peacham [1577] F.iiii.r)

Note: Lanham clarifies the definition by saying that a "phrase is interposed between a preposition and its object" (*Handlist* 89).

kainoprepeis [G. "novel"] or *heteroiosis* [G. "unusual alteration"] or *innovatio* [L. "an innovation"]
Altering the normal idiom in a novel and striking way in order to achieve conciseness; an unusual, but effective turn of phrase
"Men in great places are thrice servants: [. . .] Certainly men in great fortunes [. . .] are in the puzzle of business [. . .]; for in evil the best condition is not to will, the second not to can. [. . .] The rising to great place is by a winding stair; and if there be factions, it is good to side a man's self whilst he is in the rising, [. . .]" (Bacon, "Of Great Place," *The Essays*).
"I wasn't caught out" instead of "Nobody discovered me doing it."
(Hermogenes 1.12.306; examples mine)

Note: An alternate spelling is *koinoprepes*. Farnaby conflates this figure with *enallage* (28). Demetrius refers to this behavior as *idioticon de onomatos* (§144).

mesozeugma [G. "a joining in the middle"] or *conjunctio* [L. "a joining together"]
Putting the common verb in the middle of two or more clauses
"Either with disease physical beauty fades, or with age."
(*Ad Herennium* 4.27.38)

"Fair maids beauty, alack, with years it wears away,
And with weather and sickness, and sorrow as they say."
(Puttenham 176)

Note: Puttenham's English name is "the Middle marcher" (176).

prolepsis [G. "preconception, anticipation"]
Stating the whole, then dividing it into its parts, so that the verb or adjective in the first clause is applied in the following phrases to nouns with which the word does not agree.
"We were both in great sorrow, I for the loss of my dear friend, and he for fear of banishment."
"They were both famous, the one for his wisdom in war, the other for his singular eloquence."
(Peacham [1577] F.i.v)

Note: An additional name is *prosynapantesis*. This figure necessarily includes *antiptosis*. See *antiptosis* above.

prozeugma [G. "a yoking at first"] or *protozeugma* [G. "a yoking in front"] or *adjunctio* [L. "a joining, annexing"]
Putting the common verb in the first clause
"A victory was won over modesty by lust, over fear by audacity, over reason by madness" (Cicero, *Pro Cluentio* 6.15, trans. Knott).
(Erasmus, *De copia* 345)

"Her beauty pierced mine eye, her speech mine woeful hart:
Her presence all the powers of my discourse."
(Puttenham 176)

Note: Alternate names are *presozeugma* or *prejunctio*. Puttenham's name is "the Ringleader" (176).

syllepsis [G. "a taking together"] or *conceptio* [L. "a comprehending"]
Comprehending under one verb two natures

1. Attributing a predicate belonging to one subject to another, resulting in one verb conjugation being substituted in place of another
"He runs for pleasure, I for fear."
(Day 82)

"Neither you nor he is able to make me amends."
(Gill 156)

"I and my father are safe."
(Smith 182)

"I never yet failed you in constancy,
Nor never do intend until I die."
(Puttenham 177)

2. Applying one verb to two clauses, but giving it a different meaning in each
"Thus valiantly and with a manly mind,
And by one feat of everlasting fame,
This lusty lad fully requited kind,
His father's death, and eke his mother's shame."
(Here "requite" means "to revenge" in the first clause and "to satisfy" in the second.)
(Puttenham 177)

Note: Alternate spellings are *silepsis* and *sillepsis* and an additional name is *collectio*. Puttenham's name is "the Double supply" (176). Discussing the first meaning of the figure, Gill distinguishes *syllepsis* and *zeugma* as follows: "*Syllepsis* differs from *Zeugma* because in *Zeugma* no change of word is required; in *syllepsis*, however, a word which is associated with one immediately preceding, and related to another clause in the sentence, is changed. Therefore even *syllepsis* has *zeugma*, but not vice-versa." Gill also makes clear that *syllepsis* is not a grammatical deviation when he gives the rule for use: "For a verb, when related to two nominatives of different persons, agrees with its closest antecedent" (156). Discussing the second meaning of the figure, Vossius calls *syllepsis* a trope (223). Lily divides the figure into *conceptio personarum* and *conceptio generum* (G.ii.r-v).

synecdoche [G. "understanding one thing with another"]
Attributing a property of the part to the whole by putting the property into the nominative case, modifying the whole, while the part remains in either the accusative or ablative case.
"*Aethiops albus dentes*." ("An Ethiopian white in respect of his teeth.")
(Lily G.iiii.r)

Note: This figure can only apply to an inflected language, not to English.

synthesis [G. "putting together, composition, combination"]
Joining together in one

1. A collective, singular noun is joined with a plural verb
"The Fowl, which fly in winter season into high countries, in Summer do live in the Fen."
(Peacham [1577] H.iii.v)

2. A hyphenated adjective
   "The tempest-tossed Seas"
   "The earth-encircling Ocean"
   "The Green-mantled Earth."

(Smith 198)

Note: Peacham treats this figure as the *enallage* of number ([1577] H.iii.v).

tmesis [G. "a cutting"] or *diacope* [G. "a gash, cleft"] or *intercisio* [L. "a cutting through"]
Splitting apart a compound word or concept

1. Word
   "Hither should he have come to" for "Hitherto should he have come."

(Day 83)

   "What things soever please me" for "Whatsoever things please me."

(Hoole 264)

2. Concept
   "I have taught . . . all *Trades-men* by the *Interposition* of Covetousness, to part *Honesty* and *Gain*; which of old were great Cronies. But my Masterpiece lies amongst the *Sacrilegious Crew* that meddle with other men's Wives. If men and their Wives be not a close Complex, there is none in Nature, and yet I have suborn'd a Schismatical sort of people to interpose between them, and to make a division without a divorce. What is the most fashionable adultery, but a temporal *Tmesis* in Matrimony?"

(Shaw 181–82)

Note: Additional names include *sectio*, *dissectio*, and *tome*. *Diacope* has another more common meaning, listed below under lexical figures.

zeugma [G. "a yoking"]
Using one verb or predicate for several clauses

"Before I forget Caesar, either the Parthian shall drink of the flood Arar, or Germany of Tigris."

(Sherry [1550] 29)

"John was a Fisher, and Peter."

(Hoole 266)

Note: Quintilian calls this figure *epizeugma*. See above. Additional synonyms include *enezengmenon*, *junctio* and *adjunctio*. Puttenham calls this "the single supply" (175).

RHYTHMICAL

caesura [L. "a cutting"] or *anapausis* [G. "repose, rest"]
An extra-metrical pause within a line, a rest

1. The break between groups of feet in a poetic or prosaic line
   "When raging love, with extreme payne" (Surrey, *Poems of Love and Chivalry*, No. 16, l.1)

(Puttenham 86)

2. The break when one foot ends and another begins in the middle of a word
   "Now, ev'n, that foot/step of lost li/berty
   Is gone, and now, like slave-born Mus/covit',

I call it praise to suf/fer ty/ranny;
And now employ the rem/nant of my wit,
To make myself believe that all is well, [. . .]"
(Sidney, *Astrophel and Stella*, Sonnet 2, l. 9–13)

(Hoole 305; example mine)

3. A break between phrases or clauses within a sentence
"The end then of learning/ is to repair the ruins of our first parents/ by regaining to know God aright,/ and out of that knowledge/ to love him,/ to imitate him,/ to be like him,/ as we may the nearest/ by possessing our souls of true virtue,/ which being united to the heavenly grace of faith/ makes up the highest perfection" (Milton, "Of Education," 4th paragraph).

(Sturm 1.5.11; example mine)

Note: Quintilian talks about "rests" in prose, but does not assign a name nor consider this feature a figure (9.4.51).

dialelymenon [G. "without composition"]
Making meter and rhythm irregular and abrupt in order to create force
"But why waste words? Decimus Brutus is under attack, but it is not a war! Mutina under siege, but that is no war either! Gaul is being laid waste: can any peace be more assured? Who can say it is a war to which we have dispatched a very gallant consul at the head of an army? Ill as he was of a serious, longstanding ailment, he thought there should be no excuse for him summoned to defend the Commonwealth" (Cicero, *Philippic* 8.5, trans. Bailey).

(Demetrius §301; example mine)

metabole [G. "a change of direction"]
The transition from one rhythm to another
"The end then of learning is to repair the ruins of our first parents by regaining to know God aright, and out of that knowledge to love him, to imitate him, to be like him" (Milton, "Of Education," 4th paragraph).

(Quintilian 9.4.50; example mine)

metrum [L. "a measure, poetic meter"]
Meter, the sure number of feet in a poetic line
dimetrum, trimetrum, tetrametrum, pentametrum, hexametrum, etc.

(Butler 92–93)

Note: Sturm, Keckermann, and the Ramists list these features of rhythm as figures. Demetrius, Cicero, Hermogenes, Trapezuntius, and the grammarians treat these concerns as embellishments without clear demarcation between these and figures. Quintilian, Puttenham, Scaliger, Soarez, and Farnaby all treat of prosody, but not as figures. Nevertheless, phonetic features that come to be called figures, such as *synaloepha, eclipsis, synaeresis* and *diaresis,* are commonly treated in these discussions of *prosodia.* Fraunce also identifies a *sapphike, elegum,* and *anacreontica* verse form as figures (C2v-4v). All agree that poets use meter, and that speakers and writers of prose, although avoiding such defined regularity, must also use rhythm.

pes [L. "a foot"]
A foot, made up of between two to five syllables in a patterned unit
spondaeus (two long syllables, as in "learning")
pyrrichius (two short syllables, as in "pretty")
iambus (one short syllable and one long, as in "revenge")
choreus (one long syllable and one short, as in "noble")
molossus (three long syllables, as in "transformings")
trochaeus (three short syllables, as in "prettily")
dactylus (one long and two short syllables, as in "company")
anapoestus (two short syllables and one long, as in "monument")
bacchius (one short and two long syllables, as in "reserving")
palimbacchius (two long syllables and one short, as in "almighty")
creticus (a long, a short and a long syllable, as in "impotent")
amphibrachus (a short, a long, and a short syllable, as in "disorder")

(Fraunce C1v)

tribrachys (three short syllables, as in the first three syllables of "*facilitates* or *temeritates*")

(Quintilian 9.4.97)

paean (a long syllable followed by three short ones, as in "stóp doing it" or three short syllables and then a long, as in "beaten them áll")

(Cicero *De Oratore* 3.183).

epitrite (three long syllables followed by a short, as in "*incantare*")

(Hermogenes 1.6.252; example from Hoole 304)

dichoraeus (two *choraeos* together as in "*arbitrabar*" or "*comprobavit*")
dochymus (five syllables arranged with a short, two long, a short and a long, as in "*amicos tenes*")

(Sturm 3.5.529, 536)

Note: Both Lily (G.vi.r) and Hoole (303) call *palimbacchius* "*antibacchius*" and *creticus* "*amphimacer*." Sturm calls *tribrachys* "*aristocordacis*" (3.5.526). Besides these listed above are various combinations of feet, such as *dispondeus* (two *spondaeis*), *choriambus* (a *trochaeo* and *iambo*), *antispastus* (*iambo* and *trochaeo*), *diambus* (two *iambis*), *proceleusinaticus* (two *pyrrhichiis*), and so forth (see Trapezuntius 543 and Hoole 304, 307–10).

rythmon [G. "regular, recurring, measured motion"] or *numeros* [L. "a numbering"]
The rhythmical patterns in prose, which are less definite than poetic meter, but nevertheless can be described using the designations of poetic feet.

(Sturm 3.5.525)

Note: Alternate spelling is *rithmon* or *rhythmos*. Cicero (*De Or* 3.173) and Quintilian (9.4.45) treat this aspect as a virtue. Cicero explains that it is rhythm that forms words into a "well-knit sentence" (*Or* 51.171). Scaliger calls the virtue of proper numbering in poetry *numerositas* (4.7.462B).

LEXICAL

anaclasis [G. "a bending back, reflection"] or *refractio* [L. "a breaking up, breaking open"]
Turning a word into a contrary signification
"When Proculeius reproached his son with waiting for his death, and the son replied that he was not waiting for it, the former retorted, 'Well then, I ask you to wait for it.'"

(Quintilian 9.3.68)

"I know king Ezechias that all this life is but bitterness, but I pray thee give me such bitterness."

(Sherry [1550] 60)

Note: This figure is a particular kind of *antanaclasis*, or pun. Lausberg gives an apt description of this figure: "a word used by the first interlocutor is received by the second in a changed sense which emphasizes the speaker's point of view" (§663). Quintilian's example comes from Rutilius (I.5). See *antanaclasis* below.

annominatio [L. "the bringing together of two words different in meaning, but similar in sound"]

Repeating a word, but adding a declension to it that turns it into its contrary

"If he had tempered himself from pleasure, he had not been thus distempered out of measure."

(Sherry [1555] D.vii.r)

Note: This term is a variation of *adnominatio* or *agnominatio*, other names for *paronomasia*, and some rhetoricians consider it a synonym of *paronomasia*. Others, however, consider this form a species of *adnominatio* and list it as a separate figure. See *paronomasia* below.

antanaclasis [G. "reflection of light, bending back"]

Punning on various meanings of a word

"Care for those things in your youth which may in old age discharge you of care."

"In thy youth learn some craft, that in old age thou mayest get thy living without craft."

(Smith 107)

Note: An alternate spelling is *atanaclasis* and an alternate name is *reciprocatio*. Puttenham's English name is "the Rebounde" (216). Sometimes this figure is included under *paronomasia* and sometimes the two figures are distinguished. It is included when *paronomasia* is taken as the general category for puns and plays on words of all kinds, and distinguished when *paronomasia* is restricted to the pun based on word resemblance. See *paronomasia* below.

antistasis [G. "counter-faction, opposition, counter-plea"]

Repeating a word in an opposite or different sense

1. In an opposite sense, perhaps created by a declension
   "One safety of the conquered is to not hope for safety."
   (*Una salus victis nullam sperare salutem.*)
2. In a different sense
   "From that time Corydon is Corydon with us."

(Rufinianus, *Lexeos* §24)

Note: Rufinianus seems to include both *annominatio* above and *ploce* below within this figure. In Hermogenes' *On Issues*, *antistasis* is a counter-proposition in which an acknowledged wrong is defended on the grounds of its beneficial consequences (2.72.6).

archaismus [G. "old-world charm; use of obsolete expressions"]

Speaking in an old-fashioned manner

From Spenser's *The Shepheardes Calendar*, "a most singular imitation of ancient speech":

"A Shepeheards boye (no better doe him call)
When Winters wastful° spight was almost spent, °devastating
All in a sunneshine day, as did befall,
Led forth his flock, that had bene long ypent.° °pent up

So faynt they woxe,° and feeble in the folde, °grew
That now unnethes° their feete could them uphold." °scarcely
("Januarye" l. 1–6)

(Peacham [1593] 15)

Note: This figure is more appropriate for poetry than oratory, although Cicero allows an orator an occasional *archaism* if appropriate (*De Or* 3.153). Erasmus warns against the practice of using archaic words, which he considers a vice frequently (*De copia* 312), and Peacham treats the same figure as a kind of *onomatopoeia* ([1593] 14). See *onomatopoeia* below under semantical figures.

conduplicatio [L. "with doubling"]

Repeating a word or phrase in a succeeding clause or passage for vehemence or pity

"You are promoting riots, Gaius Gracchus, yes, civil and internal riots."

(*Ad Herennium* 4.28.38)

"This Phanium to be his cousin, doth Demipho deny? Doth Demipho deny this Phanium to be his cousin?"(Terence, *Phormio* 2.3.353–54).

(Sherry [1555] D.v.r)

"You live—and you live, not to renounce your insolence, but to add to it" (Cicero, *In Catalinam* I 2.4, trans. Flynn).

"The prestige of the leaders was almost equal; not equal, perhaps, was that of their followers" (Cicero, *Pro Ligario* 6.19, trans. Flynn).

(Soarez 310)

Note: Following Hermogenes (*Meth.* §9), Aquila calls the repetition of a word or group of words *epanalepsis* or *repetitio* (§31). Susenbrotus uses *conduplicatio* as a synonym for *epanalepsis* (49). See *epanalepsis* below under syntactical figures. Soarez treats this figure as the general category for repetition of many kinds, including *antistrophe, epanalepsis, epanodos, epimone, anadiplosis* (310–11).

deixin [G. "a pointing out"] or *deiktikon* [G. "able to show, a demonstrative"]

Using the demonstrative adjective or second person pronoun to point out something or someone; the pointing expression

"This wretched eater of iambs" (Demosthenes, *On the Crown* 189, trans. Wooten).

"This is the man who now grieves over the misfortune of the Thebans" (Demosthenes, *On the Crown* 41, trans. Wooten).

(Hermogenes 1.8.263)

"You see that dark man with curly hair who strokes his face so that he should seem shrewd, the one who is holding a tablet and writing, the one who is near? That man is Cauis Claudius" (paraphrase of Cicero, *In C. Verrem* II 2.44.108)

"[W]hat if no engagement for his hearing was ever made between you and Quinctius? by what name ought we to call <u>you</u> then?" (Cicero, *Pro P. Quinctius* 18.56, trans. Freese)

(Sturm 2.14.252)

diacope [G. "a cutting through"] or *interjectio* [L. "insertion"]

Repeating a word or words, with one or few words in between

"I will now frame my song of love, how love hath dealt with me."

"Remember my children, remember that I your father have given you a charge to keep, and a commandment to observe."

"My heart is fixed, O God, my heart is fixed" (Psalm 5:7).

(Peacham [1577] J.iii.v)

Note: Alternate spelling is *diakope* and alternate names include *diastole* and *separatio*. Mosellanus treats this feature as a type of *tmesis* (b.vi.v). Fraunce (C6r), Fenner (171) and Smith (89) include this feature as a type of *epizeuxis*. See *tmesis* above under grammatical figures and *epizeuxis* below.

diallage [G. "interchange"]

Mixing both synonymous and non-synonymous terms in a list

"I ask my enemies whether these plots were investigated, discovered and laid bare, overthrown, crushed and destroyed by me."

(Quintilian 9.3.49)

Note: Robertellus mistakes this figure for *synonymia* (24v). See *synonymia* below.

epitheton [G. "a putting upon"] or *appositio* [L. "a setting before"]

Affixing an adjective to a noun so they become one unit

1. With single modifiers

"Sweet beauty, precious love, friendly fortune" or "unbridled lust, filthy gain, wicked guile, deceitful favor, fond fancy."

(Day 84)

2. With compound modifiers

"The tempest-tossed seas.
The wool-ore-burthened sheep.
The earth-encircling ocean.
An heaven-inspired art.
Soul-subduing graces.
Time-beguiling pleasure."

(Blount 47–48)

Note: Synonyms include *attributio* and *adjectiuum*. Puttenham's name is "the Qualifier" (187) or "the figure of Attribution" (193). Because the adjective often creates a trope, Quintilian lists *epitheton* under tropes (8.6.40). Scaliger broadens the domain of *attributio* to a figure of thought inclusive of any mention of an attribute (318). See *attributio* under Logical–idea figures below. Sturm wants to call the adjective *epithesis* and the noun *epithetos* (2.6.317). See *schesis onomaton* below for a particular species of *epitheton*.

epizeuxis [G. "fastening together"] or *geminatio* [L. "doubling"] or *subjunctio* [L. "to affix or subjoin"]

Repeating a word or group of words with no other words in between

"Awake, awake, put on thy strength, O Zion" (Isaiah 52:1).

"O my son, Absalom, my son, my son Absalom: would God I had died for thee, O Absalom my son, my son" (2 Samuel 18:33).

"The Lord is nigh to all that call upon him, even to all that call upon him in truth" (Psalm 145:18).

(Smith 91–92)

Note: An alternate name is *duplicatio*. Puttenham gives as the English name "the Underlay, or Coocko-spel" (210), and Wilson refers to this figure as "doublets" (224). It has also been called *anadiplosis*. See *anadiplosis* below under syntactical figures. Fraunce gives as an alternate name the more general *palilogia* (C6r) and says the figure remains even with a short parenthesis put in between: "The time is changed, (my lute) the time is changed" (Cleophila in Sidney, *The Old Arcadia*, book 2, 82). See *palilogia* below.

etymologia logon [G. "giving the origin of a word"]

Creating a pun by giving a new interpretation of the word

"As when one hath done a robbery, some will say, 'It is pity, he was a handsome man,' to the which another made answer: 'You say truth, sir, for he hath made these shifts by his hands and got his living with light fingering, and therefore being handsome, as you say he is, I would God he were handsomely hanged.'"

(Wilson 171)

Saying that Numius, a money changer, was named after "*nummis distribuendis*" (money which is about to be handed out).

(Sturm 3.22.712)

Note: See *paronomasia*, the general category of puns, below.

isodynamia [G. "equivalence"] or *aequipollentia* [L. "equivalence"]

Substituting for one phrase a different, but equivalent phrase

1. Through the contrary

"'A remarkably learned man,' for 'a man by no means ignorant.'"

"'He did everything'; for 'there was nothing he did not do.'"

"'One must not employ no deception against the man'; that is, 'one must employ some deception."

(Erasmus, *De copia* 342)

2. Through different words

"She does not want to be the wife of that man" for "She does not want that husband."

(Keckermann 1551)

Note: This figure is a species of *paraphrasis*. See *paraphrasis* below.

ison [G. "equal to; equally distributed"] or *isoteta* [G. "of equal distribution"]

Paralleling a set of items, equal and of like weight, with a corresponding set

1. Paralleling single words of the same number of syllables

"Is it known, tried, proved, evident, open, and assured, that I did such a deed?"

"Such rioting, dicing, carding, picking, stealing, fighting, ruffians, queans, and harlots must needs bring him to naught."

(Wilson 228)

2. Paralleling sets of words

"Unless you will consider, judges, that there is no duty and no right so sacred and integral which his wickedness and perfidy have not threatened and violated, then judge Roscius Capito to be a very great man" (Cicero, *Pro S. Roscio Amerino* 38.109, my translation). The figure is the repeated coupling of "duty and right," "sacred and solemn," "wickedness and perfidy," "tampered with and violated."

(Sturm 2.23.421)

3. Paralleling phrases or clauses with word pairs

"If friendship is cultivated by truth, fellowship by trust, and intimacy by piety, then that man who tried to despoil a friend and ally of his fame and fortune must confess that he is vain and perfidious and wicked" (Cicero, *Pro Quinctio* 6.26, trans. Green).

(Sturm 2.23.414)

onomaton kallon [G. "beautiful words"]

Words that give pleasure to the ear or eye, or have an inherent nobility of thought

1. Aural appeal
   "Silvery sheen"
   "Whistling wind"
2. Visual appeal
   "Rose-colored"
   "Flowery meadow"
3. Intellectual appeal
   "Dignity, peace, justice, magnificence, and so forth."

(Demetrius §164)

Note: Demetrius explains that words can be smooth (those that consist mostly of vowels), rough, or weighty (those with breadth, length, and emphatic pronunciation) (§176–77). The smooth and weighty apply here. Rufinianus includes as a figure the general category of effective word choice (*Lexeos* §41–44).

onomaton koinoteron [G. "common, ordinary words"]

Words that are common, ordinary and prosaic

"He walked down the road with a spring in his step."

(Demetrius §164; example mine)

palilogia [G. "repetition, recapitulation"] or *iteratio* [L. "repetition"] or *repetitio* [L. "repetition"]

Repeating the same word or syllable

This is a general category of repetition, including *diacope, epizeuxis, anaphora, epistrophe, anadiplosis, conduplicatio, complexio, epimone, polyptoton, ploce, traductio.*

Note: Demetrius uses *dilogia* (§103) and *anadiplosis* (§140) as general terms for word repetition. Sturm uses *epanastrophe* (often a synonym for *anadiplosis*) as an alternate term for *iteratio* (2.22.403–9). Soarez treats *conduplicatio* as the general category for duplication of words (310–12). Aquila claims that repetition does not ornament, but makes an utterance more vehement, since such repetition in real life indicates vehemence (§30).

paraphrasis [G. "a paraphrase"]

Rephrasing, saying the same thing in other words or actions

1. In words
   a. Through alteration and transposition
      For "many false oaths" say instead "plentiful perjury"; for "to make a great show of himself" say instead "to make a muster of himself in the island"; for "seeking by courtesy to undo him" say instead "making courtesy the outside of mischief."

      (Hoskins 47)

   b. Through expansion
      The original: "a man not to be condemned"; the paraphrase: "a man against whom contempt might make no just challenge."

      (Hoskins 44)

   c. Through subtraction
      The original: "Two things which have most power in the state—I mean great influence and eloquence—are both working against us to-day" (Cicero, *Pro P. Quinctio*

1.1, trans. Freese). The paraphrase: "Grace and eloquence, which have such influence, both produce against us at this time."

(Keckermann 1536)

2. In actions

"That one thing of *eating*, they *Periphrase* by variety of *dishes* like diversity of *Phrases*; that one thing of *drinking* is *Periphrastically* performed over and over again in several sorts of Liquors: they work and play the same business and sports over and over again, only with some different circumstances; and sleep the same sleep for three or fourscore years together, only with different dreams it may be. What is *old age* but *childhood* acted over again with a little enlargement, and under somewhat a duller and graver form? Playing with *pins* and *points*, and counting *Gold* and *Silver*, are not different things but different ways of acting over the same thing, call'd *childishness*. In a word, the whole World is *Periphrastical*: for these five thousand six hundred and six and twenty years that came last, are nothing but else [*sic*] a periphrase of that first that began the World."

(Shaw 162)

Note: This figure is sometimes included under the term *periphrasis*. See *periphrasis* below under semantical figures. The four methods of paraphrase—subtraction, expansion, transposition, and alteration—correspond to the four methods of transformation schoolboys were to apply to sentences, passages, or full-length genres in their imitation exercises. *Paraphrasis* was one such imitation exercise and involved saying the same thing in either more or fewer words. Hoskins and Keckermann demonstrate the principles of this exercise as they illustrate this figure.

paronomasia [G. "call with a slight change of name; play upon words which sound alike"] or *agnominatio* [L. "the bringing together of two words different in meaning, but similar in sound"] or *prosonomasia* [G. "call by a name"]

Playing on words

1. Using words that sound similar because they differ only in a letter or syllable

"Alas, what can saying make them believe whom seeing cannot persuade?" (Dorus in Sidney, *The Old Arcadia*, book 2, 92).

"You will have but a bare gain of this bargain."

(Hoskins 16)

"This curse to the state could be repressed for a time, but not suppressed for ever" (Cicero, *In Catilinam* I 12.30, trans. Butler).

(Quintilian 9.3.71)

"Wine is the blood of the vine."

"Hardly any treason is guided by reason."

"Such errors will cause terrors."

(Smith 106)

Note: Hermogenes calls this similarity of word *parison* (*Meth.* §16). See *isocolon* below under syntactical figures for a more common use of *parison*.

2. Using homonyms, *homonymia*

"He is going [*mellei*] to besiege the Greeks; he betrays them. For is anyone concerned [*melei*] about the Asiatic Greeks?" (Demosthenes, *On the Chersonese* 27, trans. Wooten)

(Hermogenes 2.5.342)

3. Changing the meaning of a word
   "This very little is more than too much."

   (Hoskins 15)

4. Playing on sounds, or *parechesis*
   "Hector, Hanno, Hannibal dead, Pompey, Pyrrhus spilled;
   Cyrus, Scipio, Caesar slain, and Alexander killed."

   (Hoskins 16)

5. Using a nickname that sounds similar to the proper name
   Claudius Tiberius Nero was a wine bibber; hence, he was called "Caldius Biberius Mero."
   A jesting friar called Erasmus, "Errans mus."

   (Puttenham 212)

Note: *Paranomasia* is an alternate spelling. Alternate names include *adnominatio, annominatio, denominatio, allusio* and *parechia*. Puttenham calls this "the Nicknamer" (212). Some rhetoricians consider this figure as the general category for punning of all kinds and include *anaclasis, antanaclasis, etymologia logon, ploce*, and *pokrisis* as species. See entries for these figures above and below. See also *parechesis* above in phonetic figures. Soarez cautions that "[t]his otherwise trivial figure needs to be weighted with thought" (323).

permutatio [L. "a changing, exchanging, substitution"] or *metallage* [G. "change"]
Changing the language through various substitutions

1. Adding vocabulary from one language into another
   Berowne: "My love to thee is sound, sans crack or flaw."
   Rosaline: "Sans 'sans,' I pray you." (Shakespeare, *Love's Labour's Lost* 5.2.415–16)
2. Trading a noun for a verb or vice versa, or *plotike*
   Instead of saying, "I intended to go," transform the verb into a noun and say, "My intention was to go."
3. Using tropes instead of proper words
   Instead of saying, "He commanded in a loud voice," say, "He trumpeted his commands."

   (Keckermann 1550; examples mine)

4. Changing from third to second or first person pronouns, or vice versa
   "I really fail to see anything in my life, my connections, my public record, or such modest talent as I possess, for Antonius to despise. Perhaps he thought that the Senate was the place where I could most easily be disparaged. [. . .] Before I reply on other matters, let me say a few words about the friendship which he says I violated—a charge which I take extremely seriously. He complained that at some time or other I appeared against his interests in a civil case. Of course I did. [. . .] But I imagine you brought up this incident to recommend yourself to the groundlings, in reminding them all that you were a freedman's son-in-law and that your children were the grandchildren of a freedman, Quintus Fadius." (Cicero, *Philippics* 2.2–3, trans. Bailey).

   (Walker 90)

Note: See *plotike* below. *Permutatio* can also be a synonym for *enallage, antiphrasis*, and most commonly *allegoria*. See *enallage* above under grammatical figures, *antiphrasis* below under semantical figures, and *allegoria* below under semantical figures.

pleonasmus [G. "superfluity, excess"]
Adding a seemingly superfluous word for clarification or emphasis
"*nam neque Parnasi vobis iuga, nam neque Pindi*" (Virgil, *Eclogue* 10.11)
[For neither did the slopes of Parnassus, nor yet the slopes of Pindus make delay for you.]
(Quintilian 9.3.18)

"Do ye thus requite the Lord, O foolish people and unwise?" (Deuteronomy 32:6).
"That which was from the beginning, which we have heard, which we have seen with our eyes, [. . .]" (1 John 1:1).
(Smith 187)

Note: When the superfluous word does not provide needed clarification or emphasis, this strategy becomes a vice. See *pleonasmus* under vices below.

ploce [G. "twining, twisting"] or *copulatio* [L. "a coupling"] or *duplicatio* [L. "a doubling, reflection"]
Repeating a word in close proximity, but with a different meaning or function
1. *Diaphora* [G. "moving hither and thither, variance"] or *traductio* [L. "a leading along"], repeating a common word
"Bread is bread indeed to a hungry stomach."
"Josephus speaking of our Saviour, saith, 'There was a man called Jesus, if it be lawful to call him a man'" (*The Antiquities of the Jews* 18.3.3).
2. Repeating a proper name
"'In that great victory Caesar was Caesar,' (ie.) a serene Conquerer."
(Smith 109)

"Yet for love's sake I rather beseech thee, being such an one as Paul the aged" (Philemon 1:9). "Here [Paul] doth signify by old Paul, his old manners and constancy in the faith of Christ, and his accustomed diligence in preaching the gospel."
(Peacham [1577] J.ii.r-v)

Note: Alternate spelling is *ploke* or *ploche*. Puttenham's English name is "the Doubler" (211). Alexander unites *ploke*, *antimetabole*, and *synchrisis* as types of interchange (37). Peacham includes only the second meaning here; the first he considers a separate figure ([1577] J.ii.v), a distinction not commonly maintained, however.

plotike [G. possibly from "*plotos*" a tablet]
Varying sentence structure by varying the cases of nouns
1. Using the noun style (nominative case), or *onomastikon*
"Nor is only a resolved prostration unto Antiquity a powerful enemy unto knowledge, but any confident adherence unto Authority, or resignation of our judgments upon the testimony of Age or Author whatsoever" (Browne, *Pseudodoxia Epidemica* 7.1).
2. Using the verb style (accusative and dative cases), or *aitiatikon* and *datikos*
We cannot advance our knowledge if we adhere without question to past authorities (a paraphrase of Browne's statement above).
3. Using direct address, or the vocative case
"What things make life more blessed,
my genial friend, are these" (Martial 10.47, trans. Potts).

4. Using the genitive case
   Instead of "Have you returned my books unread?" say, "Have you returned unread these books of mine?"

(Sturm 3.3.485; 1st, 2nd and 4th examples mine)

Note: In Latin, noun cases determine the structure of the sentence and include, besides the four listed above, the ablative. Since English is not an inflected language, this figure entails primarily choosing either a noun or verb style. For a good discussion of these two styles, see Lanham, *Analyzing Prose* (15–32). Hermogenes treats this device under diction (1.6.249) and so I list it under lexical figures, even though it could easily be listed under syntactical as well.

poieticon [G. "poetical vocabulary"]
Using or borrowing poetic vocabulary
Homer describes the island of Crete: "There is a land of Crete, in the midst of the wine-dark sea, beautiful, fertile, wave-surrounded" (*Odyssey* 19.172–73, trans. Innes). From this line, Thucydides borrows "land" and "wave-surrounded" when he has Hermocrates of Syracuse argue that the Sicilians should act in unity, since they all dwell on one single "wave-surrounded land" (*History of the Peloponnesian War* 4.64.3, trans. Innes).

(Demetrius §113)

pokrisis [G. "to the side of a judgment, beside the point"]
Responding to one's word rather than to one's meaning; a type of playing with words
A friend says to Crassus, "Crassus, if I should come to you tomorrow morning before dawn, I will be bothersome to you."
Crassus responds, "You will not be bothersome to me; that is, I want you to bother me."
Says the other, "I don't want to bother you if you are sleeping; therefore, I will command you to wake up."
Crassus replies, "Nevertheless, you promised that you would not be bothersome."

(Sturm 3.22.712)

Note: The figure's full name seems to be *pokrisis pros to onoma* (Sturm 3.22.712).

polyptoton [G. "with or in many cases"] or *paregmenon* [G. "redundancy"] or *traductio* [L. "a leading along, conducting"]
Repeating a word in varying forms

1. Varying the cases
   "Who hath in his life nothing so much pleasing as the very life itself which he enjoyeth, it is impossible that his life with virtue should any ways be adorned."

(Day 86)

Note: This application of the figure applies primarily to inflected languages, not to English. Day's example more properly belongs to *ploce* for this reason.

2. Varying the word stem with its derivations
   "What manhood call you this, so unmanly to deal in those actions, that specially appertaineth to a man?"

(Day 86)

3. Varying the comparative degrees of adjectives
"Much may be said in my defense, much more for love, and most of all for that divine creature which hath joined me and love together" (Pyrocles in Sidney, *The Old Arcadia*, book 1, 21).

(Hoskins 17)

4. Varying the pronominal stem, or *metabole*
Whoever drank the punch fell dead? Who attended the party? To whom did he send invitations? Whose seats in the council remained empty the next day?

(Scaliger 4.36.505; example mine)

Note: An alternate spelling is *poleptoton* and alternate names are *derivatio* and *metabole*. Puttenham's English name is "the Tranlacer" (213). Both the *Ad Herennium* (4.22.31) and Quintilian (9.3.66) include *polyptoton* as one variety of *paronomasia*. Soarez, however, argues that *polyptoton* or *casuum commutatio* should not be considered a type of *paronomasia* (315). Vossius and Smith distinguish between *polyptoton* and *paregmenon*. The first is "a repetition of words of the same lineage that differ only in termination, and it is made by changing (1) the Mood, (2) the Tense, (3) the Person, (4) the Case, (5) the Degree, (6) the Gender, (7) the Number, (8) the part of Speech" (Smith 110). The second is "when words, whereof one is derived of another, are conjoyned," as in "a discreet discretion" or "For they stumbled at that stumbling stone" (Romans 9:32 in Smith 246). Smith takes his definition of *paregmenon* from Peacham ([1593] 55), who, however, does not list *polyptoton*. When used as the basis of an argument, this figure illustrates the locus *conjugatis* or *etymologia*.

schesis onomaton [G. "state or condition of names"]

1. Connecting an adjective to every substantive in a sentence
He is "a man faithful in friendship, prudent in counsels, virtuous in conversation, gentle in communication, learned in all liberal sciences, eloquent in utterance, comely in gesture, pitiful to the poor, an enemy to naughtiness, a lover of all virtue and godliness."
She is "a maid, in conversation chaste, in speech mild, in countenance cheerful, in behavior modest, in beauty singular, in heart humble and meek, in honest mirth merry with measure, in serving of God diligent, to her parents obedient."

(Peacham [1577] G.iiii.v)

2. An adjective made from the name of a country, place, or people
"A Marcian hand" or "a Pelignian cohort."

(Mancinelli xi.)

synonymia [G. "sameness of meaning"] or *interpretatio* [L. "an explanation of one expression by another"] or *isodynamodeta* [G. "equal force or power"]

A heaping together of synonymous words, phrases, or sentences in order to amplify

1. Words
Your seditious actions have caused "tumults, mutinies, uproars, desperate conspiracies, wicked confederacies, furious commotions, traitorous rebellions, associations in villainy, distractions from allegiance, bloody garboils, and intestine massacres of the citizens."
2. Phrases
"He hath a sweet countenance, a most pleasant eye, a most amiable presence, a cheerful aspect; he is a most delectable object."
"Your beauty, sweet lady, hath conquered my reason, subdued my wit, and mastered my judgment."

(Hoskins 24–25)

3. Sentences

"Since this is so, Catiline, proceed on the path which you have entered; depart from the city, it is high time. The gates are open, get you forth" (Cicero, *In Catilinam* I 5.10, trans. Butler).

(Quintilian 9.3.45; Soarez 315)

"Who more worthy of renown, honour and fame, than Caesar? Who more worthily esteemed, beloved, reverenced and honoured than noble Caesar? Who amongst men was his equal in knowledge, understanding, policy and wisdom? What was he that might be compared to him, either in courage of heart, in fortitude of mind, or magnanimity of nature?"

(Peacham [1593] 129)

Note: Butler gives as an alternate name *palilogia* (135). Puttenham's English name is "the Figure of store" (223). This figure is very like the *locus a multiplici appellatione* (Quint. 5.10.85; Cic. *Topica* 12), which is a species of the *locus* of definition and which uses synonyms to color the subject favorably to one's perspective (cf. Melanchthon, *Elem.* 48r). Hoskins warns that this figure "hath his due season after some argument or proof. Otherwise it [. . .] will sooner yield a conjecture of superfluity of words than of sufficiency of matter" (24). Because the figure includes restatements of ideas on the level of the sentence, it clearly functions not only as a figure of speech, but also of thought. See *tautologia* under Pragmatical–idea figures below.

trachea [G. "harsh, rough"] or *skleros* [G. "harsh, rough"]

A harsh, rough word

"Shrieking" instead of "crying out"; "bursting out" instead of "charging."

(Demetrius §49)

traductio [L. "a leading along, conducting"] or *tautoteta* [G. "maintenance of identity"]

Repeating a word throughout a sentence or utterance

1. In a sentence

"Suffer riches to belong to rich men but prefer thou virtue before riches: For if ye wilt compare riches with virtue, thou shalt scarce think them meet to be called riches."

(Sherry [1550] 48)

"In the beginning was the Word, and the Word was with God, and the Word was God" (John 1:1).

"And no man hath ascended up to heaven, but he that came down from heaven, even the Son of man which is in heaven" (John 3:13).

(Peacham [1593] 49)

2. In a passage

"You call him a man, who, had he been a man, would never so cruelly have sought another man's life. But he was his enemy. Did he therefore wish thus to avenge himself upon his enemy, only to prove himself his own enemy?"

(*Ad Herennium* 4.14.20)

Note: Melanchthon gives *tautologia* as the name (*Elem.* 43r). In his first edition, Sherry mistakenly calls this figure *epanodus* ([1550] 48), a mistake he corrects in the second edition. Soarez gives the same example as Sherry above and also includes *ploce* as a species (312–13).

SYNTACTICAL

absolutio [L. "completeness"] or *apheles* [G. "simple"]

A sentence composed of one independent clause; a complete, simple sentence

"I must speak about the unique and lofty virtue of Cneius Pompeius. Such a speech, however, is harder to end than to begin. Thus, abundance must not be sought so much as a limit in speaking" (Cicero, *De Imperio Cn. Pompei* 1.3, trans. Boswell).

(Trapezuntius 505)

Note: In calling a simple sentence *apheles,* Vossius associates it with the simple style known as *apheleia* (281). See *apheleia* below under Discoursal–styles. This figure helps create *orthotes.* See *orthotes* below.

alastasis [G. "placing an exclamation"] or *brevis injectio* [L. "a little injection"]

Interrupting a sentence with a short interjection

"[A]nd I blame, not those who introduced these improvements—far from it!—but you" (Demosthenes, *On Organization* 30, trans. Vince).

(Sturm 2.20.385; example mine)

allophylos [G. "another race, tribe, or class"]

An assertion about another.

"You love me."
"A third party loves either you or me."

(Mancinelli lxxxvi.)

Note: See *idiophasis* below for the opposite figure.

anadiplosis [G. "double, fold"] or *reduplicatio* [L. "redoubled, replicated"] or *epanastrophe* [G. "return"]

Beginning the next word, phrase or clause with the last letter, syllable, word, phrase or clause

1. Letter

"Royal Lear" (Shakespeare, *King Lear* 1.1.139)

(Sturm 2.22.407; example mine)

2. Syllable or root

"*Flens flentem obtestatur*" [The weeper entreats the weeper].
"O *fortunatam natam me consule Romam*" [Oh fortunate Rome, born in my consulship] (Cicero's poem on his consulship, according to Quintilian 9.4.41).

(Sturm 2.22.405)

3. Word or approximate word

"Comfort it is for man to have a wife,
Wife chaste, and wise, and lowly all her life."

(Puttenham 210)

4. Phrase or clause, or *iteratio*

"I will go against him, even if his hands are like fire,
Even if his hands are like fire, and his rage is like flashing steel."
(Homer, *Iliad* 20.371–72, trans. Wooten)

(Hermogenes 1.12.304)

Note: Alternate names include *palilogia* and *reversio*. Puttenham's English name is "the Redouble" (210). Alexander treats *anadiplosis*, *palilogia*, and *epanalepsis* together as types of word repetition (29) and may be the source for conflating *anadiplosis* and *palilogia*. See *palilogia* above under lexical figures. Sturm wants to distinguish between *anadiplosis*, the figure within a clause, and *iteratio*, the figure extending into two phrases or clauses (2.22.404–5). Furthermore, Sturm suggests that the figure is still present even when one or several words come between the repeated word, since he advises that one can hide the figure either by placing one or several words in between the repetition of the word, by changing the form of the word, or by using an approximate word in sound (404–7).

anakampsis [G. "to bend upwards or back"] or *transpositio* [L. "to set over or across"]

Varying word order and syntax in allowable ways without changing the meaning

Instead of saying "[H]e would have written everything," say "[E]verything would he have written."

Instead of saying "[H]e was not present," say "Present he was not."

"He did not praise him, on the one hand; he insulted him, on the other hand." (Here the connectives come at the end instead of at the beginning of each clause.)

(Demetrius §256–57)

Instead of saying "We daily await your vote," say "We, most diligent and zealous, those votes of yours, men, await daily."

(Sturm 3.1.451)

Note: Keckermann calls this transposed construction the "reflective" and the usual the "direct" construction (1543).

anaphora [G. "carrying back"] or *epanaphora* [G. "carrying back"] or *repetitio* [L. "repetition"] or *epibole* [G. "throwing or laying on"]

Beginning successive phrases or clauses with the same word, group of words, or idea

1. Same word

"You pass wakeful nights that you may be able to reply to your clients; he that he and his army may arrive betimes at their destination. You are roused by cockcrow, he by the bugle's reveillé. You draw up your legal pleas, he sets the battle in array. You are on the watch that your clients be not taken at a disadvantage, he that cities or camps be not so taken" (Cicero, *Pro Murena* 9.22, trans. Butler).

(Quintilian 9.3.32)

"Learning bringeth to knowledge, learning maketh wise, learning enableth to virtue, learning is the ornament of the mind, finally, learning is the only substantial prop and guide of man's life, without which nothing in a manner can be pleasant, nothing savory, nothing of value, etc."

(Day 85)

2. Same group of words

"The voice of the Lord is powerful; The voice of the Lord is full of Majesty; The voice of the Lord breaketh the Cedars, etc." (Psalm 29:4–5).

(Smith 97)

3. Same idea

"I grieved, Athenians, when I saw that hidden enemy to be wandering within our walls unpunished; I was angry because I knew the ease of the attack on all through the deceit of one; it disturbed me, because I perceived many showing joy in accepting injury" (Demosthenes, a lost speech).

(Rutilius I.7)

Note: An alternate name is *relatio* and Puttenham's term is "the Figure of Report" (208). Lanham makes a useful distinction between *anaphora* and *epanaphora*, the first term referring to only one word being repeated and the second to several words being repeated at the beginning of successive lines (*Analyzing Prose* 11, 67). This distinction is not observed, however, in either the classical or Renaissance texts consulted for this study.

anastrophe [G. "turning back, inversion"] or *perversio* [L. "a turning about, inversion"]
The backward setting of words

1. Strictly, the transposition of two words:
"'He fell from off the wall,' for 'he fell off from the wall.'"

(Sherry [1550] 31)

2. Loosely, *hyperbaton*:
"Faults, no man liveth without."
"Long when he had confusedly thus lived."

(Day 82)

Note: An alternate name is *reversio.* Sturm treats this form as one kind of *metathesis* ["transposition"] (3.17.678). Quintilian lists this figure as a trope since "its meaning is not complete until the two words have been put together" (8.6.66). It is also a species of *hyperbaton*. See *hyperbaton* below.

anisocolon [G. "unequal clauses"]
A period with unequal or unparallel clauses or members
"I take up this one thing, which gives me your disclosed crime and that manifest."

(Keckermann 1527)

"[P]art of [the island] which is on the one hand cultivated and useful is small; on the other hand the uncultivated part is large, though the island itself is small" (Antiphon, *fragment* 50, in Blass, *Antiphontis Orationes*, trans. Innes).

(Demetrius §53)

Note: This strategy is the opposite of *isocolon.* See *isocolon* below.

antimetabole [G. "transposition"] or *commutatio* [L. "a reciprocal opposition or change"] or *inversio* [L. "an inversion or transposition"] or *chiasmus* [G. "placing crosswise, diagonal arrangement"] or *metathesis* [G. "change of position, transposition"]
Turning a sentence back on itself to form the pattern "abba"

1. Using exact words
"We must eat to live, and not live to eat."
"Not man for the Sabbath, but the Sabbath for man was ordained" (Mark 2:27).
"They are happy whose wisdom is answerable to their fortune, and whose fortune answereth their wit."

(Day 95)

"Withall she laughed, and she blusht withall:
That blushing to her laughter gave more grace,
And laughing to her blushing, as did fall. (Spenser, *The Faerie Queene* II 12.68.1–3)

(Gill 166)

2. Using contrary words, but keeping the same sense
"Parthenia desired above all things to have Argalus; Argalus feared nothing but to miss Parthenia" (Sidney, *Arcadia*, book 1, 33).

"Neither could you have thought so well of me if extremity of love had not made your judgment partial, nor you could have loved me so entirely if you had not been apt to make so great undeserved judgment of me" (Pyrocles in Sidney, *The Old Arcadia*, book 1, 13).

(Hoskins 15)

Note: An alternate spelling is *antemetabole* and an additional name is *antimetathesis*. Puttenham's English name is "the Counterchange" (217). The *Ad Herennium* treats this figure as a species of *contentio* (4.15.21). Trapezuntius remarks that there are twenty-four ways to turn a *commutatio* (512), the insight, according to Monfasani (288), coming from Maximus Planudes (Walz, V.426–28). Tying this figure to argument, Peacham remarks that it serves "most commonly to confute by the inversion of the sentence" ([1593] 164). Melanchthon, who advises that this figure is appropriate for enythymemes built on contraries (*Inst.* 24r), classifies this figure as a species deriving from the dialectical topic of contraries (*Elem.* 52r).

apodosis [G. "giving back, restitution, return"]

The consequent clause of the periodic sentence; that which we return to

"He who praises my friend praises me."

(Sturm 2.24.426)

"If that money can be brought without injury to the farmers, let the Roman people have it" (Cicero, *In C. Verrem* II 3.78.182, trans. Green).

(Keckermann 1527)

Note: Sometimes the *apodosis* precedes the *protasis* for the sake of inversion (Keckermann 1526). See *protasis* below.

articulus [L. "a small member, part, or space"] or *brachiologa* [G. "shortness in speaking"] or *incisio* [L. "a cut, incision"]

Cutting between words in a list; staccato speech

"My friends and faithful soldiers, now is the time to shew yourselves valiant, courageous, hardy, bold, and constant, considering for what value you shall fight, for your religion, for your wives, your children, your goods, your liberty, your lives, and your country, either to die with honor, or live with renown."

(Peacham [1593] 57)

Note: An alternate name is *dialyton*, and alternate spellings include *incisum* and *brachilogia*. Quintilian denies that this device is a figure (9.3.98). Occasionally, *articulus* and *asyndeton* are conflated, but more often they are distinguished. Soarez argues, "They, who think that *dissolutio* and *articulus* are the same, are mistaken" (319), and Puttenham distinguishes by saying that *articulus*, or "the Cutted comma," applies to single words, *asyndeton* to clauses (222). It also seems that *articulus* refers to pronunciation, *asyndeton* to syntax. Hermogenes suggests that *articulus* helps create vehemence (1.8.263). *Incisum* is also the Latin term for the Greek *comma*, referring to a phrase or short clause. See *comma* below. This figure also creates speed or *celeritas* (Day 92). See *epitrochasmus* under Pragmatical–idea figures and *gorgotes* under Discoursal–styles below.

asyndeton [G. "without connection"] or *dissolutio* [L. "a dissolving, breaking up"] or *dialyton* [G. "capable of dissolution"]

Omitting conjunctions; the opposite of *polysyndeton*

"I saw it, I said it, I will swear it."

"*Veni, vidi, vici*" or "I came, I saw, I overcame" (Caesar, reporting his victory over the army of Pharnaces near Zela; qtd. in Plutarch, "Life of Caesar," *The Lives of the Noble Grecians and Romans*).

(Puttenham 185–86)

Note: Alternate spelling is *asyntheton*. Puttenham's term is "the Loose language" (185), and additional names include *brachylogia*, *solutum*,and *inconjunctum*. This figure is sometimes conflated with *articulus*. See the note above for *articulus*. It is also sometimes conflated with *kommata* (see *brevitas* below) or *brachylogia* (see *brevitas* under Pragmatical–idea figures below), probably because *asyndeton* helps create brevity.

brevitas [L. "shortness, brevity"] or *kommata* [G. "short phrases"]

Using very short sentences in succession

"Will we not embark? Will we not set forth? Will we not sail to his land?" (Demosthenes, *Philippic I* 44, trans. Wooten).

"When then, gentlemen of Athens, will we do what must be done? When what happens? When, by Zeus, there is some necessity? But now how should one interpret what is happening?" (Demosthenes, *Philippic I* 10, trans. Wooten).

(Hermogenes 1.7.259)

"He left; he departed; he escaped; he broke out" (Cicero, *In Catalinam* II 1.1, trans. Boswell).

(Trapezuntius 578)

Note: An alternate spelling is *commata*. *Commata* is the plural of *comma*. See *comma* below. See also *brevitas* under Pragmatical–idea figures. I separate these two figures to point out that at times the emphasis is on syntax and at other times on compactness.

circumductio [L. "lengthening" or "prolongation"] or *peribole* [G. "a space enclosed, circuit, circumnavigation"]

A sentence of more than six members that transcends the limits placed upon the *periodus* and produces very full speech

"But if at some time it were to come to pass that someone would plan the destruction of Lucius Flaccus, still I never thought, gentlemen, that Decimus Laelius, the son of a very honourable gentleman, himself possessed of the best of prospects, would undertake for the sake of his own advancement a prosecution which befitted the hatred and madness of debased citizens rather than his own virtue and promise of his youth" (Cicero, *Pro Flacco* 1.2, trans. Boswell).

(Trapezuntius 556)

"And, moreover, we have this additional disadvantage, that Marcus Junius, who has several times pleaded this cause before you, O Aquillius, a man practiced in the conduct of other causes also, and much and frequently concerned in this particular one, is at this moment absent, being engaged on his new commission; and so they have had recourse to me, who, even if I had all other requisite qualifications in ever so high a degree, have certainly scarcely had time enough to be able to understand so important a business, having so many points of dispute involved in it" (Cicero, *Pro P. Quinctio* 1.3, trans. Yonge).

(Sturm 3.3.497)

Note: Scaliger suggests that one can create such a sentence by adding a genus, species, whole, part, person, place, time, mode, instrument, or cause to a nude idea (458). Veltkirchius advises that the periodic sentence is appropriate for oratory, the *peribole* for history (48v). Trapezuntius mentions that a sub-species of *circumductio* is the scheme *conditio cum partitione*, but he gives no example (559). Melanchthon uses *circumductio* as a synonym for the *periodus* (*Elem.* 59v). See *periodus* below for more usual forms of the periodic sentence.

clausula [L. "a close, conclusion, end"]
The final phrase or clause of a sentence

1. The ending of a sentence, which always requires careful crafting of rhythmic, phonetic, syntactic, and logical elements.
"[T]he close of the sentences in my opinion requires even more careful attention than the earlier parts, because it is here that perfection of finish is chiefly tested."
(Cicero, *De Oratore* 3.192)

"As a rule, endings composed of two spondees, a termination which causes comment even in a verse, are to be deprecated, unless the phrase is composed of three separate members, [. . .] Even the dactyl ought not to precede a final spondee, since we condemn verse-endings at the period's close. [Etc.]"
(Quintilian 9.4.101)

2. The final cadence of a period when in the form of an epigram
"I boast nothing, but plainely say, we all labour against our owne cure, <u>for death is the cure of all diseases</u>." (Browne, *Religio Medici* II.9).
(Quintilian 8.5.13, example mine)

Note: Only the second use is technically a figure, and it is usually called an *epiphonema*. See *epiphonema* below under Pragmatical–idea figures. Quintilian categorizes this device not as a figure, but as a reflection (8.5.13).

climax [G. "a staircase, a scaling-ladder"] or *gradatio* [L. "a series of steps"] or *scala* [L. "a staircase, a scaling-ladder"]
Ascending by degrees, combining *anadiplosis, isocolon*, and *incrementum*

1. When the exact words are repeated
"Whom he predestinated, them also he called, and whom he called, them also he justified, and whom he justified, them also he glorified" (Romans 8:30).
(Fenner 172)

"Sweet glove, the sweet despoils of sweetest hand,
Fair hand, the fairest pledge of fairer heart,
True heart, whose truth doth yield to truest band,
Chief band, I say, which ties my chiefest part,
My chiefest part, wherein do chiefly stand
Those secret joys, which heav'n to me impart:"
(Dorus in Sidney, *The Old Arcadia*, book 3, 149)
(Fraunce C8r)

2. When the same idea is repeated through synonyms
"And he not only entrusted himself to the people but also to the senate; not only to the senate but to the public garrisons and troops; and not to these alone but to the power of the man to whom the senate had entrusted the entire republic" (Cicero, *Pro Milone* 23.61, trans. Flynn).
(Soarez 316)

Note: An alternate spelling is *klimax* or *clymax* and an alternate name *ascensus*. Puttenham's English name is "the Marching figure" (217). Melanchthon classifies this figure as a species deriving from the dialectical topic of cause/effect (*Elem.* 52r), and Hoskins calls this figure, when *ergo* joins the first and last clauses, a logical *sorites* or climbing argument (12). Veltkirchius too teaches that this figure is affined to *sorites* (119r, 194v).

comma [G. "that which is cut off"] or *incisum* [L. "severed"]
A phrase or short clause of less than eight to twelve syllables
1. A phrase
"Dionysius in Corinth"
2. A short clause
"Know thyself" or "Follow God" (*Corpus Paroemiographorum Graecorum.* II.19 and 40 [footnote], trans. Innes).

(Demetrius §9)

Note: Alternate spelling is *komma*. According to Quintilian, a *comma* is "the expression of a thought lacking rhythmical completeness; on the other hand, most writers regard it merely as a portion of the colon" (9.4.122). There is some disagreement as to how long a group of words can be and still be considered a *comma*. Sturm (3.1.441) and Keckermann (1524) say eight syllables and Trapezuntius says twelve (498).

conditio [L. "a condition"]
Using a conditional phrase or clause to increase the vividness of the thing
"If now that golden branch from the tree would appear to us!"
"Alas, miserable boy, if only you can overcome this cruel fate, you will be Marcellus."

(Scaliger 3.39.311)

congeries [L. "heap, pile"] or *synathroismos* [G. "collection, union"] or *coacervatio* [L. "a heaping together"] or *accumulatio* [L. "a heaping up"] or *symphoresis* [G. "a bringing together, collecting"]
Heaping up words in a list within a sentence
1. Without conjunctions, i.e., with *asyndeton*
"He was a man wholly malicious, exceedingly proud, utterly arrogant, altogether subtle, by nature cruel, and in speeches contentious."

(Day 92)

2. With conjunctions, i.e., with *polysyndeton*
"His house and home and arms
And Amyclean hound and Cretan quiver." (Virgil, *Georgics* 3.344, trans. Butler)

(Quintilian 9.3.51)

Note: An alternate spelling is *sinathrismus,* and alternate names include *acervatio* and *congestio*. Scaliger calls the list without conjunctions *coagmentatio* and the list with conjunctions *coacervatio* (314). Melanchthon lists this figure as a species deriving from the dialectical topic of division (*Elem.* 50r). This figure helps to create *epitrochasmus*. See *epitrochasmus* under Pragmatical–idea figures below.

dicolon [G. "two clauses"]
A period made up of two clauses
1. When the two *cola* are equal, the sentence is an *isocolon*.
"I went from Athens to Stagira because of the great king, and from Stagira to Athens because of the great storm" (Aristotle, *fragment* 669, in Rose, *Aristotelis qui ferebantur librorum fragmenta*, trans. Innes).

(Demetrius §29)

2. When the two *cola* are unequal, the sentence is an *anisocolon*.
"There is much, gentlemen, that I must inevitably pass over, if I am to deal, sooner or later, to the best of my power, with the matters entrusted to my honorable keeping" (Cicero, *In C. Verrem* II 2.1.1, trans. Greenwood).

(Sturm 3.1.442)

Note: Hoskins refers to this structure as a "double sentence" (40). See *isocolon* below and *anisocolon* above.

dirimens copulatio [L. "a connecting with an interruption"] or *symploke* [G. "intertwining, complication, combination"]

A construction built on "not only, but also"

"Nevertheless, it was not written for him only, that it was reckoned to him for righteousness, but also for us to whom it shall be counted for righteousness" (Romans 4:23–24).

"Wherefore you must needs obey, not only for fear of vengeance, but also for conscience sake" (Romans 13:5).

(Peacham [1577] S.ii.r)

Note: *Symploce*, an alternate spelling, more commonly refers to another figure. See *symploce* below. Sturm gives as an alternate name *complexio negans* (2.16.360). This figure is a kind of *incrementum* when the lesser is placed first and the worthier last, Peacham explains.

epanalepsis [G. "resumption"] or *circulus* [L. "a circle"]

Same syllable, word, clause, or idea begins and ends the sentence, or is taken up again later in the sentence.

1. *Renovatio verbi* [L. "a renewal of a word"] or *replicatio* [L. "a replication"] or *reiteratio* [L. "a reiteration"] or *kyklos* [G. "circle"]
   a. In syllable:
   Fortune brought success and the fame he was longing for.

   (Keckermann 1506; example mine)

   b. In word:
   "In sorrow I was born, and must die in sorrow."
   "Unkindness moved me, and what can so trouble my courses or wrack my thoughts as unkindness?"

   (Hoskins 14)

2. *Resumptio* [L. "a restoration"]
   a. Of a word
   "Are you totally unmoved by our need of a night watch on the Palatine, unmoved by the guards about the city, unmoved by the fears of all the people, unmoved by the assembling of all loyal citizens, unmoved by this impressive building where the Senate has met, unmoved by the faces and the looks of all those here?" (Cicero, *In Catilinam* I 1.1, trans. Knott)

   (Erasmus, *De copia* 345)

   b. Of a phrase or clause:
   "Morning-star give back the day, wherefore delay our joy? Soon comes our Caesar, morning-star give back the day" (Martial 8.21).

   (Keckermann 1507)

c. Of an idea

"By that right hand I ask you, which hand you have extended as a guest to the king Deiotarus, also an August man, this right hand, I say, is the stronger not so much in wars and in battles, as in promises and loyalty" (Cicero, *Pro Rege Deiotaro* 3.8, trans. Boswell).

(Trapezuntius 529)

"This thing confirmed, of which if the Philosophers say true, we cannot doubt, when in death there is no such utter undoing, that not the least suspicion of sense may remain: this then I say well assured, we must discuss this, what it is to lack sorrow."

"But to overcome thy mind, to restrain thine anger, to temper the victory–him that doth those things, I do not compare to the noblest men, but judge most like to God."

(Sherry [1555] C.ii.r-v)

Note: Uncommon synonyms include *prosapodosis, redditio,* and *repetitio*. Puttenham's English term is "the Eccho sound" or "the slow return" (210). Trapezuntius reserves *resumptio* for the brief repetition of either word or idea so that forgetfulness does not overtake the hearer because of the length of the speech or the interposition of a digression (528). Susenbrotus follows Trapezuntius, but also includes as *epanalepsis* the repetition of a word at the beginning and end, calling this species *replicatio, reiteratio,* or *conduplicatio* and explaining that Sulpitius Victor called it *epanadiplosis* (49). Perhaps this is the figure Cicero intends by "*revocatio verbi*" (*De Or.* 3.206). Hermogenes includes under this term repetition of any kind (*Meth.* §9). Alexander does too, associating it with *anadiplosis* and *palilogia* (29) and listing this figure as both a figure of diction and of thought (19, 29). For application on the level of idea, see the term under Pragmatical—idea figures below.

epanodos [G. "return"] or *regressio* [L. "a going back, return"]

Putting the same word at the beginning and middle or the middle and end of a sentence

"So that he as God sitteth in the temple of God, shewing himself that he is God" (2 Thessalonians 2:4).

(Fenner 173)

"Heare then, but then with wonder heare; see but adoring see, . . .
Heare you this soule-invading voice, and count it but a voice?"
(Sidney, *Astrophel and Stella*, Seventh Song l. 13–17)

(Fraunce D4v)

Note: Alternate spelling is *epanados*. Melanchthon includes syntactical *prolepsis* here (*Inst.* 24r). See *prolepsis* below.

epembole [G. "insertion, parenthesis"] or *parembole* [G. "insertion, interpolation"]

A modifying clause or phrase inserted into the middle of a sentence

"As long as the ship is safe, whether it is a large one or a small one, then both the sailor and the pilot and every man without exception must be zealous, but when the sea wins, zeal is useless" (Demosthenes, *Philippic III* 69, trans. Wooten).

"The Olynthians would now have many things to say, which if they had known them before, they would not have been destroyed" (Demosthenes, *Philippic III* 68, trans. Wooten).

"Do not let anyone be acquitted or condemned because this one or that one wants it" (Demosthenes, *De Falsa Legatione* 296, trans. Wooten).

(Hermogenes 1.10.270–71)

epimone [G. "tarrying, delay"]

A refrain

"My true love hath my heart and I have his,
By just exchange one for another given:
I hold his dear, and mine he cannot miss,
There never was a better bargain driven.
My true love hath my heart and I have his.
My heart in me keeps him and me in one,
My heart in him his thoughts and senses guides:
He loves my heart, for once it was his own,
I cherish his because in me it bides.
My true love hath my heart, and I have his."

(Puttenham 233)

"Christ, speaking to *Peter*, '*Simon*, son of *Jonas*, lovest thou me more than these? Feed my sheep,' which saying he repeateth three times" (John 21:15–17).

(Peacham [1593] 70)

Note: Puttenham's English name is "the Love-burden" or "the long repeate" (233). In Hermogenes, *epimone* covers the restatement of the same idea in different words (1.11.286), tying it to *commoratio* or the dwelling upon a point. See *commoratio* under Pragmatical–idea figures below.

epiploke [G. "interweaving"] or *prosaphyn* [G. "a handling"] or *annexio* [L. "connecting"]

Conjoining or connecting clauses; a general category that includes *parenthesis*, *polysyndeton*, *hypostasis*, *plagiasmos*, etc.

"This is not unclear, Athenians, that Leptines, and anyone else who speaks on behalf of this law, will say nothing fair about it, but he will mention some unworthy men who use their exemption to shirk their public responsibilities, and he will use this argument a great deal" (Demosthenes, *Against Leptines* 1, trans. Wooten).

(Hermogenes 1.12.307)

epistrophe [G. "turning about"] or *conversio* [L. "a turning round, revolving"] or *antistrophe* [G. "a turning about"] or *epiphora* [G. "a bringing to or upon"]

Ending successive clauses with the same syllable, word, or idea

1. Syllable

"It is an abomination to kings to commit wickedness: for the throne is established by righteousness" (Proverbs 16:12).

(Keckermann 1506; example mine)

2. Word

"Where affections bear rule, there reason is subdued, honesty is subdued, good will is subdued, and all things else that withstand evil forever are subdued."

(Wilson 225)

3. Idea

"For you have decided; you have passed sentence; you have given judgment."

(Quintilian 9.3.45)

"Do you grieve because three armies of the Roman people have been slaughtered? Antonius slaughtered them. Do you miss our noblest citizens? Antonius snatched them away. Has the authority of this order of ours been torn down? Antonius tore it down" (Cicero, *Philippics* 2.55, trans. Flynn).

(Soarez 309)

Note: Puttenham calls this figure "the Counter turne" (208). When the same syllable ends successive clauses, we also have *homoeoptoton*. See *homoeoptoton* under phonetic figures above. Quintilian explains that *synonymia* and *disjunctio* are also both present in his example above.

episynapsis [G. "an attachment"]

A modifying or parenthetical element attached to the end of a sentence

"If that money can be brought without injury to the farmers, let the Roman people have it, especially when they are in such straits with regard to money" (Cicero, *In C. Verrem* II 3.78.182).

(Keckermann 1527)

Note: An alternate name is *epitasis*. This figure is a type of *epitrechon*. See below.

epitrechon [G. "overrunning"] or *accursio* [L. "a running or coming to"]

Lengthening the sentence by adding *epembole, episynapsis, appositio, transjectio*, or another sentence at the end in a way that makes the sentence keep moving forward and the flow swift

"Since the tribe of Pandionis had not appointed a chorus-master, now two years ago [. . .]" (Demosthenes, *Against Meidias* 13, trans. Wooten).

(Hermogenes 2.1.314)

"Although you, Marcus, my son, already having learned at the feet of Cratippus for a whole year, and this at Athens, it is necessary that you abound in the precepts and teachings of philosophy, on account of the great authority both of your teacher and the city: of which one by instruction, the other by example can increase you" (Cicero, *De Officiis* 1.1).

(Sturm 3.15.655)

Note: Alternate spellings include *epitrekon* and *epitrokon*, and the name for such a sentence is *eukatastrophon*. This figure helps create swiftness, *gorgotes* (see Discoursal–styles below) and the loose style, *oratio soluta* (see Discoursal–styles below). It creates a movement opposite to that of *circuitas*, the periodic sentence that ends with the independent clause, and to *circumscriptio*, the periodic style (see Discoursal–styles below). The second example above illustrates how these added clauses and phrases compromise the tidiness of strict periodic structure. Sturm, however, who treats the *periodus* as the general category of sentences, considers this *eukatastrophon* another species of the period (3.1.443). See *periodus* below. It is also the opposite of *hypostrophe* or *parenthesis*, in that the latter interrupts a thought while *epitrechon* extends the thought. Also see *parenthesis* below.

hirmos [G. "train, series, sequence"]

A sentence containing an unranked series or list; a heaping up of many things of different kinds

"*God in the beginning made heaven, earth, sea, firmament, sun, moon, stars, and all things in them contained*: where you see all these words, *heaven, earth, etc.* have all one continuance until the last end of the sentence."

(Day 84)

"All men exclaim upon these exactions—nobles, gentry, commonalty, poor, rich, merchants, peasants, young, old, high, low—and all cry out upon the hard impositions of these burdens."

"Love's companions be unquietness, longings, fond comforts, faint discomforts, hopes, jealousies, rages, carelessness, carefulness, yieldings, etc."

"Because the daughters of Zion are haughty, and walk with stretched out necks, and with wandering eyes, walking and mincing as they go, and making a tinkling with their feet:" (Isaiah 3:16)

(Smith 163–64).

Note: Alternate spellings are *eirmos, eirmon*, and *syrmos*. For the figure naming a list itself, see *congeries* above.

hypallage [G. "interchange, exchange"] or *immutatio* [L. "interchange, substitution of one thing for another"]

A pardonable exchanging of words; interchanging mutually the relations of things

"Madam, I set your eyes before mine woes" (for "I set my woes before your eyes").

(Puttenham 183)

"'Darkesome wandering by the solitary night,' for 'wandering solitarily by the darkesome night.'"

"'The wicked wound thus given,' for 'having thus wickedly wounded him.'"

(Day 83)

"'Thou hast hid their heart from understanding,' (i.e.) thou has hid understanding from their heart" (Job 17:4).

(Smith 200)

Note: Additional names include *submutatio* and *subalternatio*. Puttenham calls this figure "the Changeling" (182). Cicero claims that grammarians used the term *metonymia* for *hypallage* (Or. 27.93). In the examples above, we can see that metonymy is at work to create this figure. *Hypallage* is sometimes listed as a trope, sometimes as a grammatical figure.

hyperbaton [G. "passing over, transposed"] or *transgressio* [L. "a going across, a going over"]

Transposed word order

1. Putting words in an order that violates normal syntax, most often by moving a word some distance from its original place

   "And you hath he quickened, who were dead in trespasses and sins" (Ephesians 2:1).

   "But fornication, and all uncleanness, or covetousness, let it not be once named amongst you, as becometh Saints" (Ephesians 5:3).

   (Smith 200)

2. *Transjectio* or *trajectio*, separating elements that belong together with a parenthetical insertion

   "Having chosen instead of a life of safety the honor—things that no other king of Macedonia ever achieved—of achieving these things" (Demosthenes, *Olynthiac II* 15, trans. Wooten).

   (Hermogenes 1.12.305)

   "You, O storm ravaging your country,—you whirlwind and tempest dispelling peace and tranquility,—did you hope that the republic would endure what you (in the shipwreck of the state, when darkness was spread over the republic, when the Roman people was overwhelmed, when the senate was overturned and expelled,) pulled down and built up? what you, after having violated every feeling of religion, still polluted under the name of religion? that it would endure the monument of the destruction of the republic which you erected in the house of this citizen who is now speaking, and in the city which he had preserved by his own exertions and dangers, to the disgrace of the knights and the grief of all virtuous men; that it would endure the inscription which you had placed there after having erased the name of Quintus Catulus, one moment longer than the time that it was absent from these walls, from which it had been driven at the same time that I myself was?" (Cicero, *De Domo Sua* 53.137, trans. Yonge).

(Trapezuntius 573)

"O comrades (for we have known evils like this before),
You have suffered worse things: god will give an end even to these" (Virgil, *Aeneid* 1.205–6, trans. Lind).

(Sturm 2.17.365)

Note: Puttenham's English name is "the Trespasser" (180). The *Ad Herennium* talks about two species: *perversio* (*anastrophe*) and *transjectio* (4.32.44). Trapezuntius names the two species *transgressio* and *trajectio* (573). Like Donatus (3.6) and Diomedes (h.i.r), Mancinelli (lix), Despauterius (C6r), Sherry ([1550] 30–31), and Puttenham (180) consider *hyperbaton* a general category containing more specific figures that change normal word order, such as *anastrophe*, *hysteron proteron*, *parenthesis*, *synchisis*, and *tmesis*. Gill simply collapses all distinctions among these figures, saying that *hyperbaton* "seems to be ruled by *Anastrophe* or *Reversio*, *Hysterologia*, *Hysteron Proteron*, in defining which subtly prattling grammarians have differed so trifling, that I am not afraid to group them together" (164). Quintilian explains that this figure, along with *anastrophe*, has been considered a trope when this transposition causes a change in meaning (8.6.67). This figure also works to create suitable rhythm or word emphasis (Quintilian 9.4.27, 29).

hypostasis [G. "standing under, supporting"]

An expression that requires subordination

"I *so* clearly refuted Philip *that* his own allies rose up and agreed" (Demosthenes, *On the Crown* 136, trans. Wooten).

"*Whatever* benevolence I have shown to the city and to you all, *so* much will I receive from you in this trial" (Demosthenes, *On the Crown* 1, trans. Wooten).

(Hermogenes 1.11.290)

Note: This may be the figure Trapezuntius intends by *subcontinuatio*, which results when "a certain particle of speech is placed ahead [so that] a longer series of words is woven together" (560). This figure helps create *plagiasmos* (see below) and corresponds with Lanham's *hypotaxis* (*Analyzing Prose* 29).

hypozeuxis [G. "a subjoining"]

Giving every clause of the sentence its own subject and verb

"Such is man's depraved nature and perverse inclination, that taking away the use of government, every kind of evil shall quickly oppress every part of goodness, ambition shall strive for honor, pride shall disdain obedience, malice proceed to murder, theft deprive true possessors, idleness neglect labor, impiety scorn religion, and raging tumults violate peace, and turn a happy state into a miserable confusion, whereupon it ensueth that open rebellion is raised, good men murdered, virgins deflowered, holy places polluted, houses burned, cities defaced, laws despised, the whole earth confounded, and the omnipotent power of God either little regarded or utterly forgotten."

(Peacham [1593] 60)

"My Lady gave me, my Lady wist not what,
Giving me leave to be her Sovereign:

For by such gift my Lady hath done that,
Which whilest she lives she may not call again."

(Puttenham 177–78)

Note: Puttenham calls this figure "the Substitute" (177).

hysteron proteron [G. "the latter before the former"] or *hysterologia* [G. "speaking last"]
Putting the word or clause that should be second first and the first second

1. The reversed words
"And if I not perform, God let me never thrive."

(Puttenham 262)

2. The reversed clauses
"That which of all others is most sacred and permanent, honored and ever shining virtue, choose unto yourselves."

(Day 83)

Note: Puttenham's name is "the Preposterous" (262). See also the terms under Pragmatical–idea figures and vices below.

idiophasis [G. "an utterance pertaining to oneself"]
An assertion about self; using a self-reflexive pronoun
"I love myself."
"You love yourself."

(Mancinelli lxxxvi.)

Note: See *allophylos* above for the opposite figure.

isocolon [G. "equal clauses"] or *compar* [L. "an equal, a companion"] or *parison* [G. "exactly balanced and even"] or *syzygia* [G. "union of yoke fellows"]
Phrases or clauses in parallel structure that have approximately an equal number of syllables
"If ever I could wish my faith untried and my counsel untrusted [. . .]" (Philanax in Sidney, *Arcadia*, book 3, 467).
"Save his gray hairs from rebuke and his aged mind from despair [. . .]" (Basilius in Sidney, *Arcadia*, book 2, 255).
"Her face with beauty, her head with wisdom, her eyes with majesty, her countenance with gracefulness, her lips with loveliness [. . .]" (Dorus in Sidney, *Arcadia*, book 2, 164).
"My years are not so many but that one death may conclude them, nor my faults so many but that one death may satisfy them" (Philoclea in Sidney, *Arcadia*, book 3, 471).
"Rather seek to obtain that constantly by courtesy which you cannot assuredly enjoy by violence" (Philanax in Sidney, *Arcadia*, book 3, 401).
"Loneliness can neither warrant you from suspicion in others nor defend you from melancholy in yourself" (Basilius in Sidney, *Arcadia*, book 1, 88).

(Hoskins 38)

Note: Alternate spellings are *isokolon* or *conpar*. An additional name is *membrum*. Puttenham calls *parison* "the Figure of even" (222). There is not complete agreement on the exact features required for this figure. The *Ad Herennium*, for example, says *conpar* is comprised of clauses with an approximately equal number of syllables so that they are of equal length, but not necessarily of parallel structure (4.20.27). Puttenham adds that these clauses are "not very long, but yet not so short as the cutted comma" (222). Smith, on the other hand, requires that there be both equality of length and of structure (216). Some rhetoricians consider *isocolon* and *parison* different figures. For example, Hermogenes uses *parison* to refer to paired words that differ only by one syllable (*Meth.* §16) or to parallel phrases (*Id.* 1.12.299) and *isocolon* to parallel clauses (*Id.* 1.12.305). Aquila adds that *parison* allows an unequal number of words, while *isocolon* requires an equal number of words (§24). Quintilian regards *parison* as resemblance between certain words in one phrase or clause with certain words in another; that is, these "words will be of equal length and will have similar terminations." *Isocolon*, on the other hand, refers to a sentence in which clauses are of equal length (9.8.75–80). Keckermann (1506, 1527) and Sturm (2.23.412) follow Quintilian. *Syzygia*, in Cicero's *Topica*, has a different meaning, being associated with *polyptoton* and the argument based on etymology (9.38).

isopleura [G. "being equilateral"]

A sentence that has three members equal in length

They forgot themselves, betrayed their hopes, and destroyed their bliss.

(Sturm 3.1.454; example mine)

isoskelis [G. "having two sides equal"] or *aequicrura* [L. "of equal legs"]

A sentence that has two members equal in length and a third or fourth unequal member

"*Quae res in civitate duae plurimum possunt, eae contra nos ambae faciunt in hoc tempore, summa gratia et eloquentia*;" (Cicero, *Pro Quinctio* 1.1). ["The two things which have the greatest influence in a state,—namely, the greatest interest and eloquence, are both making against us at the present moment," trans. Yonge.]

(Sturm 2.23.418)

Note: The form in the above example is lost somewhat in the English translation. An alternate spelling is *isoscelis*.

macrocolon [G. "a long clause"] or *skhoinotene* [G. "elongated, stretched"]

A very long clause

"To describe unto you the miserable fear Cleophila's lovers lived in while she stood at the discretion of those undiscreet rebels, [. . .] would require as many words as to make you know how full they were now of unspeakable joy that they saw, [. . .] the same wrought (and safely wrought) by her mean in whom they had placed all their delights" (Sidney, *The Old Arcadia*, book 2, 116).

(Sturm 3.1.452; example mine)

Note: Demetrius advises that long clauses produce grandeur (§44) and short clauses produce force (§7).

meiouros [G. "tapering, mouse-tailed"]

A sentence with the final clause the shortest

"So that I am now convinced of the truth of the saying, which when put forward by some of those who are devoted to literature and the study of philosophy seemed to be incredible, that, for a man who has in his soul got a firm grasp of all the virtues, everything that he does turns out well" (Cicero, *Pro Balbo* 1.3, trans. Gardner)

(Sturm 3.1.450, example mine)

membrum [L. "a limb, member"] or *colon* [G. "a limb, clause"]

Joining two, but usually three or four *commata*, forming a compound predicate, subject, or sentence; or, in a more general sense, simply a clause

1. Compound Predicate:
   "'Thou didst both profit thine enemy, and hurt thy friend.' This exornacion may be made of two parts only, but the perfectist [*sic*] is made of three, thus: 'Thou didst profit thine enemy, hurt thy friend, and didst no good to thyself.'"

   (Sherry [1550] 57)

2. Compound Subject:
   "Thou light of our eyes, thou staff of our age, thou comforter of our life, thou hope of our generation, [hear our plea]."

   (Peacham [1593] 58)

3. Compound Sentence:
   "You were helping your enemy, you were hurting your friend, and you were not consulting your own best interests."

   (*Ad Herennium* 4.19.26)

4. A single clause
   a. An independent clause
      "What men plow, sail, build—all these produce fortitude."

      (Melanchthon, *Elem.* 59v, my translation)

   b. A dependent clause
      "Because I grew up in the city, . . ."

      (Quintilian 9.4.123; example mine)

Note: *Membrum* is sometimes a synonym of *compar* or *isocolon*. See *isocolon* above. Quintilian defines the *colon* as "the expression of a thought which is rhythmically complete, but is meaningless if detached from the whole body of the sentence" (9.4.123), and he refuses to regard any form of *membrum* as a figure (9.3.98). Hermogenes says a *colon* must be over seven syllables (*Inv.* 4.4.184), Sturm over eight (3.1.441), and Trapezuntius over twelve (498).

orthotes [G. "straightness"] or *rectitudo* [L. "straightness, directness"]

Directness in speech; a straightforward construction with simple sentences and without subordination; the opposite of obliqueness and *plagiasmos*

1. With simple sentences, *membra directa*
   "For two years the tribe of Pandionis had not appointed a chorus master. The assembly was meeting. The archon was assigning the flute-players. There were arguments and disputes. I came forward and offered my services." (Demosthenes, *Against Meidias* 13, Hermogenes' paraphrase, trans. Wooten)

   (Hermogenes 1.3.231)

2. With a *periodus directa*
   "Caius Hegius is a Mahomertinus, most honored in all things by the city. His house is the best, of Messana certainly the most well known and among our men the most famous."

   (Keckermann 1536)

Note: Sturm also associates grammatical correctness with this figure (2.11.333). Keckermann is the one who divides this figure into the direct *membrum* (1543) and direct *periodus* (1535). This figure requires *absolutio* (see above) and corresponds with Lanham's *parataxis* (*Analyzing Prose* 29). Its opposite is *plagiasmos* below.

parenthesis [G. "putting in beside"] or *interpositio* [L. "a putting between, insertion"] or *interclusio* [L. "a stopping or shutting up"] or *hypostrophe* [G. "turning round or back"]

A parenthetical insertion in the middle of a sentence

"The man (I speak it for no harm) will sometime have his own will."

(Sherry [1550] 31)

"Nevertheless, just as I for my own improvement have always combined Greek and Latin studies—and I have done this not only in the study of philosophy but also in the practice of oratory—so I recommend that you should do the same, so that you may have equal command of both languages" (Cicero, *De Officiis* 1.1, trans. Miller).

(Sturm 3.19.682)

Note: Additional names include *paremptosis* and *injectio*. Susenbrotus (33) and Gill (165) also attribute *dialysis* and *dissolutio* here. Puttenham's English name is "the Insertour" (180). Melanchthon places this figure in the category of those deriving from the dialectical topic of circumstances (*Elem.* 54v). This figure is one type of *epembole*. See *epembole* above.

parisosis [G. "almost equal, just like"]

Parallelisms either lexical or syntactical; a general category for similitudes among words and phrases

1. Lexical, or *isotes*

   "If by truth friendship, by trust fellowship, by piety intimacy is cultivated, it is necessary that that man who tried to despoil a friend and an ally for fame and fortune confess that he is vain and perfidious and wicked."

   (Sturm 2.23.414)

2. Syntactical, or *isocolon*

   "From the expenses of the chorus masters, pleasure is given to the spectators for a small part of the day, but from the abundant funds spent on war equipment, safety is given to the city for all time" (Demosthenes, *Against Leptines* 26, trans. Wooten).

   (Hermogenes 1.11.292)

Note: This category includes *homoioptoton, homoioteleuton, homoioartron, polyptoton, enantiosis, isotetes, isocolon, paronomasia,* and so forth (Sturm 2.23.412).

periodikon [G. "acquired in one's travels"]

A sentence of more than four *cola,* but less than eight, and one that lacks both the *protasis* and the rounding constraints of a *periodus*

"And from the first article to the last, Romans, I find that the only idea of the tribunes, their only scheme, their only aim in what they do is that ten kings of the treasury, the revenues, all the provinces and the entire republic, of friendly kingdoms, of free nations—in fact, ten lords of the whole world, should be set up under the pretended name of an agrarian law" (Cicero, *De Lege Agraria* II 6.15, trans. Freese).

(Sturm 3.1.464)

periodus [G. "going round in a circle"] or *comprehensio* [L. "uniting and grasping as a whole"] or *irmus* [G. "a train, series, sequence"] or *circumscriptio* [L. "a composing"]

A periodic sentence or a complete thought

1. *Circuitus* [L. "a going round, a circling"], a sentence of at least two, but no more than four to six clauses, that contains a *protasis* (proposition) and an *apodosis* (response),

usually, although not always, forming an enthymeme. Such a structure postpones the independent clause, until the end, becoming a dense, rounded, and closed unit.

a. Without an enthymeme

"For it is not to speak nobly that is noble, but after speaking to perform what has been spoken."

(Demetrius §18)

"Next, men of Athens, that it is absolutely contrary to the national character to ratify such a law as this, I will also endeavour to show you briefly by an example of our conduct in the past" (Demosthenes, *Against Leptines* 11, trans. Vince).

(Hermogenes 1.9.267–68)

"[F]inally, had the immortal gods not launched him upon the impulse of attempting, effeminate creature that he was, to slay a very gallant gentleman, your free constitution would be to-day a thing of the past" (Cicero, *Pro Milone* 33.89, trans. Watts).

(Trapezuntius 506)

b. With an enthymeme

"And if fortune may do much against them, which hath put all their accompts upon chance, all are not to be committed to fortune, lest fortune have too great a domination upon them."

(Sherry [1555] E.i.r)

"If waker care, if sudden pale colour,
If many sighs with little speech to plain:
Now joy, now woe, if they my cheer distain,
For hope of small, if much to fear therefore,
To haste, to slack my pace less or more
Be sign of love, then do I love again." (Wyatt, "Sonnet 28" l.1–6)

(Puttenham 187)

2. *Ambitus* [L. "a moving round about"], a sentence with a *protasis* and *apodosis*, but also with multiple interconnected cola, that spreads out rather than rounds back on itself.

"What I entreated of the immortal gods, O judges, according to the manners and institutions of our ancestors, on that day when, after taking the auspices in the *comita centuriata*, I declared Lucius Murena to have been elected consul,—namely, that the fact might turn out gloriously and happily for me and for my office, and for the Roman nation and people,—that same thing do I now pray for from the same immortal gods, that the consulship may be obtained by that same man with safety, and that your inclinations and opinions may agree with the wishes and suffrages of the Roman people, and that that fact may bring to you and to the Roman people peace, tranquillity, ease, and unanimity" (Cicero, *Pro Murena* 1.1, trans. Yonge).

(Trapezuntius 507)

3. *Productio spiritus* [L. "a lengthening, prolonging of the breath"]

a. A sentence with a climactic arrangement of clauses

"But if I had this cause so deserving, so illustrious, and so important; if either the Sicilians had not demanded this of me, or I had not had such an intimate connexion with the Sicilians; and if I were to profess that what I am doing I am doing for the sake of the republic, in order that a man endowed with unprecedented covetousness, audacity and wickedness,—whose thefts and crimes we have known to be most enormous and most infamous, not in Sicily alone, but in Achaia, in Asia, in Cilicia, in Pamphylia, and even at Rome, before the eyes of all men,—should be brought to trial by my instrumentality, still, who would there be who could find fault with my act or my intention?" (Cicero, *In Q. Caecilium* 2.6, trans. Greenwood)

(Trapezuntius 554)

b. *Pneuma* [G. "breath"] or *spiritus* [L. "a breath"], a sentence formed not on the basis of syllables or clauses, but on the breath capacity of the speaker.
"He begs and entreats you, O Chrysogonis, if he has converted no part of his father's most ample possessions to his own use; if he has defrauded you in no particular; if he has given up to you and paid over and weighed out to you all his possessions with the most scrupulous faith; if he has given up to you the very garment with which he was clothed, and the ring off his finger; if he has stripped himself bare of everything, and has excepted nothing,—he entreats you, I say, that he may be allowed to pass his life in innocence and indigence, supported by the assistance of his friends." (Cicero, *Pro S. Roscius* 49.144, trans. Yonge)

(Sturm 3.2.476)

Note: For Hermogenes, the *pneuma* has two kinds: 1. when we stretch out one thought, elaborating it in numerous *cola* and 2. when we divide one subject into its many actions (*Inv.* 4.4).

4. *Continuatio* [L. "following of one thing after another"], a joining together of multiple clauses in a rambling way without force.
"Although I am afraid, gentlemen of the jury, that fear is an unseemly condition in which to begin a speech in defense of the bravest of men; and that it is in the last degree unbecoming, seeing that Titus Annius himself is more anxious for the safety of the state than for his own, that I should be unable to bring to his case a greatness of spirit to equal his; still, the unprecedented aspect of this unprecedented trial alarms my eyes, which, fall where they may, look in vain for the familiar environment of the courts and the traditional procedure of the law." (Cicero, *Pro Milone* 1.1, trans. Watts).

(Trapezuntius 566)

Note: The significant difference between *ambitus* and *continuatio* is hard to see. These two also involve *epitrechon* and, when extended too much, move the highly contained and structured periodic style closer to its opposite, *oratio soluta* (see below under Discoursal—types of styles) or the running style (see Lanham, *Analyzing Prose* 52–56).

5. A *monocolon* [G. "one clause"], a period with one clause in which the thought is suspended until the end or that bends back on itself by completing a pattern.
"Clear expression sheds much light on the listener's thoughts." (The bend is the completion of the antithesis between the speaker's speech and the listener's thoughts.)

(Demetrius §17)

"Let my diligence contest with the avarice of all of them, your integrity with their money, your constancy with the threats and power of the Fathers" (Cicero, *In C. Verrem* II 1.1.3, trans. Green)

(Sturm 3.1.442)

6. A complete thought of any kind, whether formed by *commata* or *cola*.
"Know thyself."

(Scaliger 4.25.495)

Note: An alternate spelling is *periodos*. Puttenham calls this figure "the Long Loose" (186), and Melanchthon gives *circumductio* as a synonym (*Elem.* 59v). See *circumductio* above for the more common use of this name, however. Cicero gives as names for this figure, without distinguishing among them, "*ambitus, circuitus, comprehensio, continuatio*, or *circumscriptio*" (*Orator* 60.204). It is common to find these terms repeated as synonyms in later handbooks. Trapezuntius, however, divides the *comprehensio* into the first four species listed above. Aristotle had said that there were two kinds of period: one that is simple and has only one *colon* and the other that matches the definition of *circuitus* above (*Rhetoric* 3.9.5–6, 1409b). Demetrius acknowledges Aristotle's two kinds (17), but prefers that the period contain two to four clauses (§16) and insists that there are always two essentials: "the length of the clause and the bending back at the end" (§17). Hermogenes also recognizes both the *monocolon* and the varieties of sentence with multiple *cola* all within the period (*Inv.* 4.3), but distinguishes the *pneuma* as a separate figure (*Inv.* 4.4). Cicero, however, restricts the period to a sentence with two *cola* or more, with the full period consisting of four *cola* (*Orator* 66.221). Aquila adds the stipulation that a period must have from two to six *cola* (§18), as does Melanchthon (*Elem.* 59v). Trapezuntius also disallows the *monocolon* as a period and Farnaby follows him (18). Sturm follows Hermogenes, but comes up with *periodikon* for the sentence that has more than four *cola* but less than eight and is free from the constraints of the true period (3.2.473), which must have a proposition (*protasis*) and a response (*apodosis*) (3.1.464). A sentence longer than eight *cola* is *peribole*. See *peribole* (under *circumductio*) and *periodikon* above. Keckermann follows Sturm (1525–32), except that he restricts the perfect period to two *cola* and divides the imperfect period, that without a determined quantity of parts, into *contractio* and *extensio* (1529). *Contractio* has fewer than four *cola*,and they are unequal in length. *Extensio* has four *cola* or more, with one or several of them being unequal (1529). Quintilian says the period must have at least two cola, but that it has two forms: the first "is simple, and consists of one thought expressed in a number of words, duly rounded to a close. The other consists of *commata* and *cola*, comprising a number of different thoughts" (9.4.124). Alexander Rhetor equates the period with the complete sentence (27–29) and Scaliger agrees, but divides it into the simple (made from *commata*) and the composite (made from *cola*) (4.25.493–96). Quintilian argues the *periodus* is not a figure; Melanchthon, Farnaby, Soarez, and Vossius discuss it under *compositio*, not *dignitas*, but do not clearly distinguish it from figures. Melanchthon describes the period as a "*circuitus* or *circumductio* because it joins several ideas with syllogistic, causal, relative, comparative, opposite particles, and even sometimes copulatives" (*Elem.* 59v; La Fontaine 324–25). *Absolutio* (see above) is then sometimes contrasted with and sometimes included in the periodic sentence.

plagiasmos [G. "a sideways, indirect, dependent construction"]

Using subordinate clauses to wind one's way to the point; the opposite of *orthotes*

"When the Phocian war began—not by my fault, for I was still outside politics—you were at first disposed to hope that the Phocians would escape ruin, although you knew that they were in the wrong, and to exult over any misfortune that might befall the Thebans, with whom you were justly and reasonably indignant because of the immoderate use they had made of the advantage they gained at Leuctra." (Demosthenes, *On the Crown* 18, trans. Vince).

(Hermogenes 1.11.288)

"When, as often happens, brother Quintus, I think over and recall the days of old, those men always seem to me to have been singularly happy, who, with the State at her best and while enjoying high distinctions and the fame of their achievements, were able to maintain such a course of life that they could either engage in activity that involved no risk or enjoy a dignified repose" (Cicero, *De Oratore* 1.1, trans. Sutton).

(Keckermann 1536)

Note: Keckermann calls this construction the *periodus indirecta* (1536), in accordance with Demetrius (§104). This figure requires the use of *hypostasis* (see above) and corresponds with Lanham's hypotactic style (*Analyzing Prose* 29).

polysyndeton [G. "many connections"] or *junctio* [L. "a joining, uniting"]
Connecting with many conjunctions; the opposite of *asyndeton*

"And I saw it, and I say it and I
Will swear it to be true."

"For in her mind no thought there is,
But how she may be true iwis:
And tenders thee and all thy heal,
And wisheth both thy health and weal:
And is thine own, and so she says,
And cares for thee ten thousand ways."

(Puttenham 186)

Note: Alternate spellings are *polysyntheton* and *polisyntheton*.

prolepsis [G. "preconception, anticipation"] or *praesumptio* [L. "a taking beforehand, anticipation"] or *anticipatio* [L. "the innate notion of a thing formed before receiving instruction concerning it"]
Giving a general idea and then treating its separate parts within one sentence

"The three worst reproaches are directed against us: that we seem to be envious, ungrateful, and untrustworthy" (Demosthenes, *Against Leptines* 10, trans. Wooten).

(Hermogenes 1.11.279)

"Then dear Lady, I pray you let it be,
That our long love may lead us to agree:
Me since I may not wed you to my wife,
To serve you as a mistress all my life:
Ye that may not me for your husband have,
To claim me for your servant and your slave."

(Puttenham 179)

"Let us take upon us one self charge, I to direct abroad, you to order at home."
"Men diversely do err, some by an ignorant simplicity, others by a most perverse folly."

(Day 82)

Note: Puttenham's English name is "the Propounder" (179). Alternate spellings include *proslepsis* and *presumptio*. An alternate name is *proanaphonesis*. *Prolepsis* is very similar to *epanodos*, but differs in that it does not require, as *epanodos* does, that the terms used in naming the divisions be repeated in the explanation of each part. See *epanodos* among Pragmatical—idea figures below.

protasis [G. "that which is put forward"]
The antecedent, suspense-creating part of the periodic sentence; the initial dependent clause

"If that money can be brought without injury to the farmers, let the Roman people have it" (Cicero, *In C. Verrem* II 3.78.182).

(Keckermann 1527)

Note: See *periodus* and *apodosis* above.

symploce [G. "intertwining, complication, combination"] or *complexio* [L. "a combination"] or *koinotes* [G. "mingling"] or *epanadiplosis* [G. "doubling, folding"]

Combining *anaphora* and *epistrophe* in successive clauses

"Who took Zedekiah prisoner, & put out both his eyes? Nebuchadnezzar. Who put Daniel and his fellows into the burning furnace? Nebuchadnezzer. Who was transformed from a man into a beast, & eat hay with oxen? Nebuchadnezzer." (See 2 Kings 25: 7; Daniel 1–4.)

(Sherry [1550] 47–48)

"Who proposes the law? Rullus. Who deprived a large section of the people of their votes? Rullus. Who presided over the Assembly? Who summoned the tribes he wanted, who drew lots for them, without any custodian being present? Who declared the election of the decemvirs whom he wanted? The same Rullus" (Cicero, *De Lege Agraria* II 9.22, trans. Freese).

(Soarez 309)

Note: Alternate spellings are *symploche* and *conplexio*. Alternate names include *comprehensio*, *conexum*, *complicatio* and *synthesis*. Puttenham's English name is "the figure of replie," and he mistakenly calls this figure *conduplicatio* (209). See both *comprehensio*, a syntactical figure, and *conduplicatio*, a lexical figure, above for the more common attribution of these two terms.

syncrisis [G. "aggregation, comparison"] or *antithesis* [G "opposition"] or *antitheton* [G. "opposed, antithetical"]

Contrasting contrary words, phrases, or clauses within a sentence in parallel structure

1. Counterposing contrary words

   "He that prefers wealthy ignorance before chargeable study, prefers contempt before honor, darkness before light, and death before life."

   (Smith 208)

2. Counterposing contrary phrases or clauses

   "Avarice misses what it has as much as what it does not have" (Publilius Syrus, *Sententiae* §694, Loeb).

   (Keckermann 1483)

   The one thief says to the other, "We indeed are justly here, for we receive the due reward of our deeds, but this man (meaning Christ) hath done nothing amiss" (Luke 23:41).

   "Behold, my servants shall eat, but ye shall suffer hunger; my servants shall drink, but ye shall abide thirst: Behold, my servants shall rejoice, but ye shall be ashamed: Behold, my servants shall sing for joy of heart, but ye shall cry through sorrow of heart, and shall howl through vexation of spirit" (Isaiah 65:13–14).

   "The subtle commit the fault, and the simple bear the blame."

   (Smith 208)

Note: Alternate spellings include *sygchrisis*, *sygkrisis*, *synkrisis*, and *synchrisis*. Quintilian wants to restrict *antithesis,* also called *contrapositum* or *contentio,* to this figure of speech only (9.2.101; 9.3.81). But only Butler and Vossius among Renaissance rhetoricians follow Quintilian in ignoring *antithesis* as a figure of thought. Keckermann, who mistakenly spells the term *synchysis*, considers this figure of speech a particular kind of *antithesis*, one that contrasts the contraries of one thing (1483). Most often, *syncrisis* names a syntactical pattern and *antithesis* names the figure of thought, but this distinction does not hold across the board, for both terms, as well as the other synonyms of each, are commonly used to name both dimensions of the figure. See *antithesis* under Logical–idea figures below. Additionally, the term *syncrisis* is also sometimes used as a synonym of *comparatio*. See also *comparatio* under Logical–idea figures below.

systrophe [G. "a rolling up together, a winding into a ball" or "a coming together, a gathering"] or *convolutio* [L. "a rolling up together"]

A sentence that is so contained in itself that no part can be grasped without the whole; a concise, but packed *period*)

1. A full sentence

   "When we returned from the Euboean expedition and Hierax and Stratocles, the envoys of Amphipolis, mounted this platform and bade you sail and take over their city, if we had shown the same earnestness in our own cause as in defense of the safety of Euboea, Amphipolis would have been yours at once and you would have been relieved of all your subsequent difficulties" (Demosthenes, *Olynthiac I* 8, trans. Vince).

   (Hermogenes 1.11.294)

   "And while it is true that no forgetfulness will ever efface the memory of what you have done for me, I beg you to remember that, whatever enhancements of fortune or honour may accrue to you in the future, you could never have secured them, had you not in the old days of your boyhood hearkened to the advice given you in all sincerity and affection by myself" (Cicero, "Letter to C. Scribonius Curio," *Epistulae ad Familiares* II 1.2, trans. Williams).

   (Trapezuntius 565)

2. A sentence that rotates from proposition to inversion

   "Still, it is a habit of ours to gauge the wisdom of a project by its results, and while imputing foresight to the successful, to charge the unsuccessful with the lack of it" (Cicero, *Pro Rabirio Postumo* 1.1, trans. Green).

   "The two things which have the greatest influence in a state,—namely, the greatest interest and eloquence, are both making against us at the present moment" (Cicero, *Pro P. Quinctio* 1.1, trans. Yonge).

   (Sturm 1.16.362–63)

3. A sentence that heaps up definitions of a thing

   "An history, saith he, is the testimony of times, the light of verity, the maintenance of memory, the schoolmistress of life, and messenger of antiquity" (Cicero, *De Oratore* 2.9.36).

   "Man is the example of imbecility, the image of inconstancy, the spoil of time, the bondman of misery, the vessel of insatiable desire, and the confident castle of sudden ruin."

   (Peacham [1593] 153)

Note: Peacham may confuse his figures here when he conflates *systrophe* and *conglobatio*, or he may simply be using the second meaning of *systrophe*, for his treatment does not fully match that of Hermogenes, Trapezuntius, and Sturm. See *conglobatio* below as a synonym of *congeries* under Pragmatical–idea figures.

taxis [G. "arrangement, order"]

Distributing an adjunct to every subject

"Princes for their dignities, magistrates for their authority, rich men for their wealth, captains for their courage, counselors for their wisdom, & holy men for their profession, are assaulted of the mighty, and envied of the wicked, from whence it commeth that they are often either deprived of their lives, or spoiled of that they possess."

"The divine wisdom hath assigned Kings to reign, Judges to hear causes & give sentence, Advocates to plead, subjects to obey, the wise to give counsel, and the rich to give alms."

(Peacham [1593] 60–61)

Note: Taxis has another more general meaning, that of arrangement or word order. See also *ordo* below under Pragmatical–idea figures.

tetracolon [G. "four clauses"]
A period with four clauses, so that there is one *apodosis* for the first *protasis* and a second *apodosis* for the second *protasis*

"For in providing that no one is to be immune, (the law) took away immunity from those who have it, and in providing further that in the future it will not be permitted for you to give immunity, (it took away from) you the right to give it" (Demosthenes, *Against Leptines* 2, trans. Kennedy).

(Hermogenes, *Invention* 4.3.181)

"If effrontery were as potent before a tribunal of justice as recklessness is effective in the lonely country-side, Aulus Caecina would have as little chance in the conduct of his case today against the effrontery of Sextus Aebutius as once he had in the employment of force against his audacity" (Cicero, *Pro A. Caecina* 1.1, trans. Hodge).

(Sturm 3.1.442)

tricolon [G. "three clauses"]
A period with three clauses

"You were helping your enemy, you were hurting your friend, and you were not consulting your own best interests."

(*Ad Herennium* 4.19.26).

"Passion overcame shame, boldness fear, and madness reason" (Cicero, *Pro Cluentio* 6.15, trans. Flynn).

(Soarez 328)

Note: Hermogenes insists upon a stricter form than later rhetoricians do, for he defines the *tricolon* as a sentence having one *apodosis* that responds to two *protases*, as in the following: "Of the services for which he ought to thank those politicians working in his interest—services for which you ought to require punishment—of these I see it is not now the time to speak" (Demosthenes, *Olynthiac II* 4, trans. Kennedy).

SEMANTICAL

The Four Primary Tropes

ironia [G. "dissimulation, pretense"] or *illusio* [L. "a mocking, jeering; or an illusion, deceit"]
Implying the contrary of what is said or done, or disguising the meaning

1. In words:
   "I am not guilty of those praises."
   "I have hardly escaped good fortune."
   "He threatens me a good turn."

(Blount 6)

2. In ideas:
"Strange, indeed, Gaius Caesar, and hitherto unparalleled is the charge which has been submitted to you by my kinsman Quintus Tubero—that Quintus Ligarius has been in Africa; and this charge, Gaius Pansa, with all his outstanding ability, has made bold to admit; fortified, possibly, by his intimacy with you. For, hoping that you knew nothing of the matter at first hand and that you could have known nothing of it at second hand, I had come prepared to take advantage of your ignorance to save an unfortunate man." (Cicero, *Pro Ligario* 1.1, trans. Watts)

(Soarez 354)

3. In actions:
"A man's whole life may be coloured with *irony*, as was the case with Socrates, who was called an *ironist* because he assumed the role of an ignorant man lost in wonder at the wisdom of others."

(Quintilian 9.2.46)

"[S]aying the opposite of what one wants to be the case in order to accomplish what one wants without seeming to say the opposite of what one wants[.]" In Homer's *Iliad* 2.135, "Agamemnon is making trial of the Greek force and wants them to remain while saying that they should [. . .] flee. [But his argument is so poor that it cannot persuade. Again, in school exercises, you] support the propositions of the opponent and defend them at length and sometimes with witnesses, but you are pretending to speak against them, for in so speaking you will not awaken suspicion and you will get what you want. In such a figure of speech, to win is for the speaker to be defeated, and to be defeated is for the speaker to win."

(Hermogenes, *Method* §22)

4. Inclusive of *dissimulatio* and *simulatio*
"[I]n dissimulation there is a negation of the thing which is. In simulation there is an affirmation of a thing which is not."
   a. *Dissimulatio* = Drances pretends that he is not confident.
   b. *Simulatio* = Socrates pretends that he is ignorant.

(Scaliger 3.85.356)

Note: An alternate spelling is *eironeia*. Puttenham calls this figure "the Drie mock" (199). Peacham lists *irrisio* as an alternate name, but this is a mistake, since *irrisio* is the Latin for *sarcasmus* ([1593] 35). Keckermann points out that irony can also apply to the whole speech (1470). Soarez distinguishes between *ironia*, the trope, and *ironia*, the figure of thought (354), for the same reasons Quintilian does. To Quintilian, the trope is franker in its meaning, without pretense, and with a purely verbal conflict; the figure is a disguise with a conflict between the verbal and the other elements of the communication act (9.2.45). Species of irony include *antiphrasis*, *sarcasmus*, *insultatio*, *paralepsis*, *asteismos*, *charientismus*, *mycterismus*, *chleuasmos*, *diasyrmus*, and all those figures that depart from the truth of the matter. Sometimes irony is listed as a species of allegory. Fraunce says that irony "continued maketh a most sweet allegory" (A6v). See allegory below.

metaphora [G. "transference"] or *translatio* [L. "a carrying from one place to another, a transferring"]

An implied comparison, a similitude contracted into one word, formed by transferring attributes of one thing to another

1. Common "places" from whence we draw metaphors include:
   a. From the sight to the understanding of the mind
   "I see your meaning."

b. From the hearing to the affections of the heart
"He that is scornful will not hear when he is reproved" (Proverbs 13:1). "In this translation refusing to hear signifieth disdain of correction, and hatred of doctrine."

c. From the smelling to the pleasure of the mind or to foresight
"Abominations of sin do stink."
"'A sacrifice of a sweet savor' [Ephesians 5:2], that is, a sacrifice acceptable to God."
"Being wise & provident, by his singular foresight did timely smell out the ungracious practices, and privy conspiracies of the enemies bent against the city and commonwealth."

d. From feeling or touching to provoking affections
"'And they were pricked in their hearts' [Acts 2:37], meaning, pierced with sorrow and repentance."

e. From the tasting to having experience
"There are certain of them which stand here, that shall not taste of death till they see the kingdom of God" (Luke 9:27).

f. From the mind (or passions) to the body
"'Whatsoever mine eyes desired I let them have it' [Ecclesiastes 2:10]. Here *Solomon* attributeth desire to the eyes, which is a word properly belonging to the mind."

g. From living creatures without reason to man
"A tyrant is called a lion, an extortioner a wolf, a man without mercy a tiger, he that is deceitful and subtle a fox, a shameless railer a barking dog."

h. From man to the brute creature
"The mourning dove, the musical nightingale, the proud peacock, the flattering dog."

i. From the living to things without life
"The firmament bewailed his funeral, the sun mourned and would not be seen, and the clouds shed great plenty of sorrowful tears."
("This place for the most part is the fountain of the figure called *Prosopopoeia*.")

j. From things without life to things having life
"A stony heart, a green head, a leaden wit, raw youth."

k. From things senseless to things senseless
"Envy is the canker of fame"; "Idleness is the rust of a common wealth"; "Evil words do corrupt good manners."

l. From the offices and physical actions of men to the spiritual
"They that plow iniquity shall reap the same" (Job 4:8).

m. From certain substantives very much used
"The day dawn and the day star ariseth in your hearts" (2 Peter 1:19).

n. From the four elements
"Kindle not wrath, lest thou beest not able to quench it."
"The raging tempests of sedition, the whirlwinds of trouble."
"The waves of worldly troubles."
"A vale of misery."

o. From men to God
"Hence it is that he is called a King, a Lord, a Lord of hosts, a Judge, a father, an husbandman, a planter of a vineyard, a shepherd, a nurse, a guide."

p. From God to men
"I said ye are Gods" (Psalm 82:6).

(Peacham [1593] 4–13)

2. Examples in speech
   "Being grieved with a matter, we say commonly we cannot digest it."
   "Ah, sirrah, I am glad I have smelled you out."
   "The land crieth for vengeance."
   "Hatred buddeth among malicious men."

(Wilson 198–99)

3. Examples in thought and behavior
   "There is nothing New in the World: whatever is bears some resemblance, similitude, relation or allusion to what has been formerly; so that the present World is merely *Metaphorical.*

   The whole life of man is rather allusive than real. *Kings* and their Governments, *Magistrates* and their Laws are nothing but an allusion to a *superior Monarchy* and *Legislation*: all inferiour *Dominations* are an allusion to them. The Preachers use more allusions than proofs, and the people are even with them, for the best of their practice is rather an *allusion* than a *Conformity* to their Doctrine. [. . .] All *Virtues* are inquir'd by a *Metaphorical* imitation, and all *Diseases* and *Vices* contracted by a *Metaphorical* infection."

(Shaw 119–20)

Note: Puttenham's English name is "the Figure of Transporte" (189). Metaphor did not have special reference to this particular trope until sometime after Aristotle; rather, the translated or transferred word was the common definition for tropes in general (Lausberg §554). We see this notion in Hermogenes (*Inv.* 4.10). We also see this conception carried on, for example, in Cicero (*De Or* 3.149), Quintilian (8.3.24), Erasmus (*Eccl.* 3.159.123), Melanchthon (*Elem.* 35r), Wilson (196), Robertellus (31r-v), Gill (152), Lamy (2.60), and Walker (56), who make clear that allegories, comparisons, proverbs, riddles, fables, personifications, metonymy, and so forth spring from metaphor.

metonymia [G. "change of name"] or *transnominatio* [L. "changing the name"] or *denominatio* [L. "substituting one name for another to which it has some relation"] or *hypallage* [G. "interchange, exchange"]

Substituting adjunct for subject, cause for effect, or vice versa

1. Common places from whence we create metonymies:
   a. When the cause is put for the effect
      1. Efficient cause
         "*Vulcan* for fire. *Neptune* for the sea. *Bacchus* for wine. *Venus* for love. *Mars* for war. *Mercurie* for eloquence."
         "He learned his Arguments of *Aristotle*, and his eloquence of *Tully*."
      2. Material cause
         "'I want silver,' where by silver, money is to be understood."
         "'They eat the finest wheat and drink the sweetest grapes'; by Wheat is understood bread, and by Grapes wine."
      3. Instrumental cause
         The "Crown" for "Kingdom; [. . .] the Tongue for speech; Arms for war."
      4. Formal cause
         "Art is put for an Artificer; pride for a proud man, [. . .] and the soul for man."
   b. When the effect is put for the cause
      "Hereby we say, death is pale, fear sad, anger hasty, wine bold."
      "Two nations art in thy womb" (Genesis 25:23).
      "There is death in the pot" (2 Kings 4:40).
      "He lays honor upon the altar."

c. When the subject is put for the adjunct
   1. The subject for the accident inherent
      "*Curius* victory; *Curius* being the name of a certain victorious Captain."
   2. The container for the thing contained
      "'The cup,' for the wine contained in it."
      "'The purse,' for the money therein."
   3. The place is put for the inhabitants
      "'The City met the General'; for the Citizens."
   4. The place is put for the actions done there
      "'The Hall is done,' (i.e.) the Action of that court of judicature."
   5. The possessor is put for the thing possessed
      "'Some Guardians [. . .] have devoured the Orphans,' intimating the orphans' patrimony."
   6. The seat or place is put for the quality inherent in the same
      "Whoso committeth adultery with a woman wanteth a heart" (Proverbs 6:32)
   7. The Advocate is put for him he represents
      "The Cause will go against the Attorney General."
   8. The time is put for the things done or contrariwise
      "The morning's view corrects the evening's work."
      "Harvest is put for Summer, Cold for Winter, Sleep for the Night."
   9. The name of the thing signified is put for the sign
      "Thus in Gen. 17:10, Circumcision is called the Covenant, when 'twas only a Seal of the Covenant and of the righteousness of faith."
      "The Paschal Lamb is called the Lord's Passover" (Exodus 12:11).

d. When the adjunct is put for the subject
   1. The sign is put for the thing signified
      "'He beareth not the sword in vain,' (i.e.) Authority" (Romans 13:4).
   2. The quality is put for the person
      "'Deserts are preferred'; (i.e.) men deserving are."
   3. Time is put for the persons or things subject thereunto
      "'The days are evil,' (i.e.) the hearts and conversations of the men of these days are evil" (Ephesians 5:16).
   4. Names of the virtues or vices are put for the persons
      "'Justice,' for 'a just man.'"
   5. The thing set in a place for the place itself
      "Books are put for Library or Study. A Play for a play-house."
   6. The thing contained for the container, the abstract for the concrete
      "In 1 Corinthians 1:30, Christ is not called righteous, but righteousness."
   7. The antecedent is put for the consequent
      "To hear is to obey."
   8. The consequent is put for the antecedent
      "In the sweat of thy face shalt thou eat thy bread" (Genesis 3:19).
   9. When several things accompany each other, one is put for the others
      "'Joshua overcame the Canaanites,' (i.e.) he and his Army" (Joshua 11:21).

(Smith 13–32)

2. Examples in thought and behavior
   "I am the great *Nomenclator* of the World: [. . .] I have Metonimiz'd the World indeed. It is by a real Metonymy that men of devout and refin'd minds discern the *Creator*, where others see nothing by the *Creature*; that *Idolatrous*, and covetous, and proud men, put the *Creature* in room of the *Creator*; that all *Hypocrites* present us with the *sign*

instead of the *thing signifi'd*; that all *Lawyers* seek themselves instead of their Client; and indeed in all ill-order'd Common-wealths, that true *Subjects* are respected as *Adjuncts*, and mere *Adjuncts* are embrac'd as the best *Subjects*."

(Shaw 114–15)

Note: Cicero also calls this trope *immutatio* (De Or 3.167), Wilson gives as an alternate name "transmutation" (200), and Puttenham's name is "the Misnamer" (191). Cicero also regards *verborum immutatio* as the definition for a trope (*Brutus* 69); Vossius follows him (209). Gill lists *antonomasia, metalepsis, onomatopoeia,* and *barbaralexis* as species (154).

synecdoche [G. "understanding one thing with another"] or *intellectio* [L. "understanding, comprehension"]

Substituting part for whole, species for genus, or vice versa

1. Common places from whence we derive synecdoches:
   a. The whole is put for the part, or the part for the whole
      "All the world came to hear the wisdom of Solomon" (1 Kings 10:24).
      "I am not worthy that thou shouldest enter under my roof" (Matthew 8:8).
   b. The genus is put for the species, or the species for the genus
      "Preach the gospel to all creatures" (i.e., men).
      "Man shall not live by bread only" (Matthew 4:4).
   c. The plural number for the singular, or the singular for the plural
      "'We deceived the people, and seemed Orators' (Cicero, meaning but himself)." ("Fragment of a letter to Brutus," qtd. in Quintilian 8.6.20)
      "A man borne of a woman hath but a short time to live."
   d. The matter for the thing made
      "They eat the finest wheat, and drink the sweetest grapes."
   e. The consequent for the antecedent, or the antecedent for the consequent
      "Thou shalt eat thy bread in the sweat of thy face" (Genesis 3:19).
      "He put the people to the sword and the city to the fire."

      (Peacham [1593] 17–18)

   f. The sign for the thing signified
      "Lo, now the top of the chimneys in the villages smoke a far off" (Virgil, *Eclogue* I.81–82). Through the smoking chimneys, Virgil signifies "night to be at hand."

      (Sherry [1550] 43–44)

2. Examples in thought and behavior
   "Sir, I am the famous *Synecdoche*, who whensoever I please make a *part* to pass for the *whole*, and at another time make the *whole* to signify no more than the *part*. By me a single *Monarch* makes himself a *multitude*, and the *Parson* as if he had a *Parish* in his belly, cries *We* at every word. By me a whole Kingdom fits in *Parliament* at once; and the whole World is in a *general Council*. I have taught the Ladies to dress themselves, and their Gallants to pay their debts by the same *Trope*. By my means the religious poor man possesseth the whole World, and the covetous Muck-worm loseth the *whole* for a little *part*."

   (Shaw 120–21)

Note: An additional name is *comprehensio*. Puttenham's term is "the Figure of quick conceite" (196). The boundary lines between metonymy and synecdoche are not consistently drawn. For example, Trapezuntius combines the two within *intellectio* (462). Fraunce, Smith, and Shaw consider the figure that substitutes the material for the thing made or the sign for the thing signified to be metonymy, while Erasmus, Peacham, Day, Sherry and Wilson attribute these relations to synecdoche. Lamy treats synecdoche as a kind of metonymy (2.73).

The Secondary Tropes

allegoria [G. "veiled language"] or *inversio* [L. "an inversion"] or *permutatio* [L. "a changing, exchanging, substitution"]

A continued or sustained metaphor

"What strait, what tide-race, think you, is full of so many conflicting motions or vexed by such a variety of eddies, waves and fluctuations, as confuse our popular elections with their wild ebb and flow? The passing of one day, or the interval of a single night, will often throw everything into confusion, and one little breath of rumour will sometimes turn the whole trend of opinion" (Cicero, *Pro Murena* 17.35, trans. Butler).

(Quintilian 8.6.49)

"The clouds of care have covered all my coast,
The storms of strife, do threaten to appear:
The waves of woe, wherein my ship is tossed,
Have broke the banks, where lay my life so dear." (Imitation of Horace, *Ode* 1.14.1)

(Puttenham 198)

Note: *Allusio* is an alternate, but uncommon synonym. Like Diomedes (h.i.r), Mosellanus lists as species *aenigma, paroemia, ironia, sarcasmus, astysmus, mycterismus, antiphrasis* and *charientismus* (b.vi.r). Susenbrotus adds *diasyrmus* and *hyperbole* to the list (13). Melanchthon includes as species *ainigma, eironeia, sarcasmos, mimesis, proverbia, apologus,* and *mythologia* (*Elem.* 41v). Puttenham calls allegory "the Figure of false semblant or dissimulation," and, following Quintilian (8.6.52–59), subordinates all tropes under it including *periphrasis* (196–206). Puttenham's rationale is that allegory is "the ringleader and captain of all other figures, either in the Poetical or oratory science" because "every speech wrested from his own natural signification to another not altogether so natural is a kind of dissimulation, because the words bear contrary countenance to th'intent" (197). Vossius, however, identifies only four kinds of allegory: *apologos* (fable), *mythos, aenigma* and *paroemia* (proverb) (*Commentarium* 198). Gill's description shows his awareness of allegory as argument: "Spenser's whole poem [*The Faerie Queene*] is an allegory which teaches ethics by means of stories. Thus an allegory explores an idea obscurely through a complete metaphor" (153). Melanchthon too has the same awareness: "For allegory is a kind of comparison in which something similar is indicated yet without the rest of the comparison being expressly stated, or I may put it another way: allegory is a truncated enthymeme" (*Elem.* 36v, trans. La Fontaine 241).

anthropopathia [G. "having human feelings"]

Attributing to God human characteristics

"Thus the Lord is said to have a face in Psal. 116:11, 17:15, and eyes, in Psal. 11:4 to signify his omniscience; bowels in Isa. 63:75, and a bosom in Psal. 74:11, to denote unto us his infinite mercy and most ardent love."

(Smith 205)

antiphasis [G. "contradictory proposition"]

Speaking affirmatively in order to heighten the damage done to the adversary

1. Through *confessio*

"You have then, Tubero, the benefit of what is the dearest dream of counsel for the prosecution, a prisoner who pleads guilty, but guilty of having been on the same side as you, Tubero, and as that very estimable gentleman your father" (Cicero, *Pro Ligario* 1.2, trans. Watts).

(Scaliger 3.90.361)

2. Through *concessio*
"Let us assume that the dogma which you teach be true: but, indeed, how can it then be excused that, after the rites of the Church have been changed, you have been the author of such an important schism? There is, however, more evil in a schism than there is good in these dogmas."

(Melanchthon, *Elem.* 53r)

3. Through *consensio*
"The ship's captain ransoms the girls for a price. It is human." (It is surely inhuman and agreeing with the captain's excuse heightens the act's infamy.)

(Scaliger 3.90.361)

Note: This figure is a type of irony and the opposite of *antiphrasis* below. See *concessio*, *confessio* and *consensio* below under Pragmatical–people figures.

antiphrasis [G. "expression by means of negation"]
Using a word contrary to its meaning; contrary speech
Saying to a dwarf, "What a giant have we here."
Saying to him who treats an ordinary matter as if a strange one, "What a wonder telleth he."

(Day 80)

Note: Puttenham's English name is "the Broad floute" (201). Veltkirchius treats this figure as one type of *permutatio* and includes here the vice *paradiastole* (194r). See *paradiastole* below under vices. Scaliger distinguishes between *antiphrasis* (contrary speech) and *antiphasis* (affirmative speech), both kinds being species of irony (3.90.359–61). See *antiphasis* above.

antonomasia [G. "a name instead"] or *pronominatio* [L. "substituting an epithet for a proper name"]
Re-naming in place of proper name
Calling Achilles "the son of Peleus"; the Romans, "the descendants of Romulus"; Aeneas, "the faithless"; Hannibal, "the Phoenician"; the master, "the old man"; Homer, "the poet."

(Erasmus, *De copia* 331)

These alternate names include patronyms (Peliades for Achilles), genus for species ("The City" for Rome), or species for genus (Cato for a wise, stern, austere man).

(Sturm 2.6.311–12)

Note: Puttenham calls this figure "the Surnamer" (192). Gill categorizes this figure under metonymy (154), while Vossius regards it a species of synecdoche (222). Peacham gives *nominatio* and *nominis permutatio* as additional Latin equivalents ([1593] 22). Diomedes subordinates *epitheton* as a species here (g.vi.v).

auxesis [G. "growth, increase"]
Augmenting through a heightened word
"In dispraise, thus a proud man is called Lucifer; a drunkard, a swine; an angry man, mad. In praise, thus a fair virgin is called an Angel; good music, celestial harmony; and flowers in meadows, stars."

(Smith 55)

Note: Most rhetoricians use *auxesis* and *incrementum* as synonyms, but with an awareness that augmentation occurs through both the use of a heightened word and through phrase and sentence sequences. In other words, *auxesis* is both a figure of diction and of thought. Peacham, however, makes a distinction between them, using *auxesis* for augmenting through a word (167) and *incrementum* for mounting by degrees (169). *Auxesis* is also sometimes a synonym for amplification. See *amplificatio* and *incrementum* under Pragmatical–idea figures below. Melanchthon classifies this figure as one that derives from the dialectical topic of definition (*Elem.* 48r). Quintilian categorizes this device as a method of amplification, not a figure (8.4.1).

catachresis [G. "misuse, misapplication"] or *abusio* [L. "abuse, misuse"]
A far-fetched metaphor
"'*I lent my love to loss, and gaged my life in vain.*'
Whereas this word *lent* is properly of money or some such other thing, as men do commonly borrow, for use to be repaid again, and being applied to love is utterly abused, and yet very commendably spoken by virtue of this figure. For he that loveth and is not beloved again, hath no less wrong, than he that lendeth and is never repaid."
(Puttenham 191)

He, who "misliked a picture [of a man] with a crooked nose," declared "the elbow of his nose to be disproportionable."
(Hoskins 12)

Note: An alternate spelling is *katachresis*. Puttenham's name in English is, not surprisingly, "the Figure of abuse" (190).

catatyposis [G. "forming to be correspondent with, after the fashion of"]
A description of one thing in terms of another
"A phantom resembling the god appeared in his dreams,
In all things like Mercury, in voice and complexion and hair
Golden-yellow, with limbs that had the beauty of youth" (Virgil, *Aeneid* 4.558–60, trans. Lind).
(Mancinelli xcviii.)

cateroche [G. "with respect to excellence or eminence"]
Attributing excellence to something through a name
Virgil indicates the excellence of husbandry by attributing the art to a goddess and likening the wild earth to the strong oak of Dadona. Dadona was a town in Epirus famous for the oracular oak tree sacred to Jupiter. Once tamed, the oak becomes a symbol of true strength.
"Ceres of old taught mortal men to delve
The earth with iron share, what evil time
The hallowed groves their acorns and wild fruits
Refused to bear, and from Dadona's tree
No nurture fell" (*Georgics* 1.145–49, trans. Palmer 29).
(Mancinelli xcix.)

chleuasmos [G. "scornful, scoffing jest or mock"] or *epicertomesis* [G. "mock, taunt"]
Mocking derisively through a cunning, implicit comparison that leaves the adversary no reply
"You, Drances, at any rate always have much to say
At a time when war demands action. As elders are summoned,
You are the first to be present. The meeting must not be
Filled with your words that go boastfully flying in safety
As long as the moat and the walls hold the enemy back.

And the ditches not running with blood. Then thunder ahead
With your eloquence after your custom. You, Drances, accuse me
Of fear when your right hand has heaped up as many piles
Of dead Trojans as mine has and dotted the fields here and there
With trophies. (Virgil, *Aeneid* 11.392–401, trans. Lind)

(Rufinianus §2)

"Lie there and measure Hesperian fields,
Trojan, the fields which you sought in war: this prize
They receive who dare to cross swords with me" (Virgil, *Aeneid* 12.364–66, trans. Lind).

(Rufinianus, *Dianoeas* §10)

"And do you think that the consulship is attested by a dog that whines at the heels of a Clodius?" (Cicero, *In L. Calpurnium Piso* 10.23, trans. Watts)

(example mine)

Note: *Insectatio* is an additional name. Keckermann conflates this figure with *subsannatio* (1473). See *mycterismus* below under Discoursal–genres.

hyperbole [G. "excess, overshooting"] or *superlatio* [L. "exaggeration, the highest degree"] or *superjectio* [L. "an exaggeration"]

Exaggeration

1. In speech
   a. Through similitude
      "Words and blows came so thick together as the one seemed lightning to the other's thunder" (Sidney, *Arcadia*, book 3, 456).
   b. Through superiority
      "The world sooner wants occasions than he [Argalus] valor to go through them" (Sidney, *Arcadia*, book 1, 33–34).
      "[H]e besought her to have pity of him, whose love went beyond the bounds of conceit, much more of uttering" (Amphialus in Sidney, *Arcadia*, book 3, 368).
   c. Through impossibility, *adynaton*
      "Though a thousand deaths followed it, and every death were followed with a thousand shames" (Gynecia in Sidney, *The Old Arcadia*, book 2, 81).

(Hoskins 29)

2. In action
   "By an *Hyperbolical* overweening (which is vulgarly call'd *ambition*) one man attempts to be *Universal Monarch*, and another *Universal Bishop*; and (which is good Rhetoric, tho some Critics laugh at it for bad Grammar) one particular Church styles itself *Catholic*. By an *Hyperbolical* ingenuity the *Foot-Boy* comes to be a *Butler*, the *Butler* comes to be a *Gentleman*, the *Gentleman* comes to be a *Count*. All that raise Estates, and all that are rais'd to Honours are my Clients. The Common People are all my Subjects too. What is *swearing*, but an *Hyperbolical* way of *affirming*? What is *stealing* and *cheating* but an Hyperbolical way of *getting* an Estate? What is *Superstition*, but an Hyperbolical way of being *Religious*?"

(Shaw 127)

Note: Puttenham's English name is "the Over reacher, otherwise called the loud lyer" (202). Susenbrotus gives two additional names: *eminentia* and *excessus* (17). *Hyperbole* is also sometimes a vice, as Shaw's examples suggest. See the term below under vices.

hypocrisis [G. "delivery"] or *pronuntiatio* [L. "delivery, action"]

Adding irony through pronunciation in order to undercut the opponent's claims

"You and that one in singing? But when did you ever have a pipe joined with wax?"

(The audience hears: "You cannot sing, but the other one is great in singing.")

"I would not fear you, Daphne, as a judge."

(The audience hears: "Of course, you are unjust to me and you will not judge me rightly.")

(Rufinianus, *Dianoeas* §8)

hypocorismos [G. "talk a child's talk" or "call by endearing names"]

Diminishing through the use of a diminutive

Instead of calling someone "attractive" (*blandus*), you say "little attractive thing" (*blandulus*), or instead of "man" (*homo*), you say "little man" (*homunculus*).

(Sturm 2.27.436)

As a manner of speech with our equals and inferiors, we call a young gentlewoman "Mall" for "Mary, "Nell" for Elner, "Jack" for "John," or "Robin" for "Robert."

(Puttenham 228–29)

Note: This figure is a species of *meiosis*, according to Puttenham, but Sturm lists it separately.

icon [G. "likeness, image, representation"] or *imago* [L. "an image, representation, likeness"]

An image, a contracted simile

"Fierce and untamed war with eyes sparkling as the flaming fire, whose face carried in itself a terror to the lookers on, and his countenance was as it were a present death. His gesture was as the furious assault of a Lion, and his mouth as a devouring pit to swallow the blood of multitudes. Armed he was with fire, with famine, and with sword, crying revengement on the world, and persecuting all nations with a ceaseless dread."

(Day 99–100)

Note: An alternate spelling is *eikon*. Puttenham's name is "Resemblance by Pourtrait or Imagery" (248). Quintilian discusses the *eikon* as a kind of proof , not a figure (5.11.24). Melanchthon specifies that this figure, a species of the similitude, derives from the dialectical topic of comparison (*Elem.* 53v).

koinotes [G. "sharing in common, community"]

Uniting a group by speaking in the plural and sharing alike either deeds worthy of praise or of blame

"And so, if anything is done wrong [or right] by those before whom we are speaking, we will not say, 'You did it!' but 'We did it!'"

(Vossius, *Commentariorum* 179)

Note: Vossius gives as an alternate name *communicatio sermonis* and indicates that this strategy is discussed by Hermogenes, but does not give a source (179).

litotes [G. "plainness, simplicity, smallness"] or *diminutio* [L. "diminution, lessening"]

Understatement

1. By denying the contrary

"I was not the last in the field to fight against the enemies of my country, neither have I been least esteemed or worst accounted of in the love & favor of noble men."

(Peacham [1593] 150–51)

"I know you hate me not, nor wish me any ill."

(Puttenham 195)

2. By denying the rightness of the word

"Those fantastical-minded people which children and musicians call lovers" (Musidorus in Sidney, *The Old Arcadia*, book 1, 16).

"This color of mine, which she in the deceivable style of affection would entitle beautiful" (Pyrocles in Sidney, *Arcadia*, book 2, 279).

(Hoskins 35)

"'That misfortune of letting fall his Dagger,' which the rude Swaggerers of our time call 'being disarmed.'"

"'That opinion of honesty,' which hath lately been so proudly translated by the Soldier into the word 'Honor.'"

(Hoskins 36; Blount 31)

Note: Alternate spellings include *liptote, lyptote* and *leptotes*. An alternate name is *antenantiosis*. Trapezuntius describes this figure with "*per negationem affirmatio*" (569) and Sturm gives as an additional name *antarithmos* (3.17.678). Puttenham translates the term as "the Moderatour" (195). Hermogenes discusses this figure under the name of *apophasis* (*Meth.* §37). See also *enantiosis* below under Logical–idea figures for a related form.

meiosis [G. "a lessening, diminishing"] or *extenuatio* [L. "a lessening, extenuation"]

Lessening, diminishing, or disabling through a word or words

1. Opposite of *auxesis*

"When one had given his fellow a sound blow, being rebuked for the same, said he 'scant touched him.'"

"When two have fought together, to say that the one 'had his leg pricked with a sword,' when perchance he had a great wound."

(Wilson 206)

2. A kind of *hyperbole*

"They scarce cling to their bones."

"He is shorter than a pygmy."

(Erasmus, *De copia* 344)

"Alas, sir, it is not in my power to do it."

"Little, God wot, could man do in such a case."

(Day 84)

Note: Sometimes this figure is also called *tapeinosis* or *diminutio*. Puttenham calls this figure "the Disabler" (195). Like *auxesis* and *incrementum*, so *meiosis* and *diminutio* are sometimes synonyms and sometimes not. When they are not distinguished, this figure includes "lessening" in both words and matter; when distinguished, *meiosis* is the figure of diction, and *diminutio* the figure of thought. Puttenham, however, lists *meiosis* twice, once for the trope (195) and once for the figure of thought (227–29). Melanchthon lists *tapeinosis* as the generic name for the cluster of figures that lessen, in which he includes *meiosis* and *diminutio* (*Inst.* 23r and *Elem.* 48v). Sturm (2.27.435) and Vossius (259) too treat *tapeinosis* as the general category. See *tapinosis* below and *diminutio* under Pragmatical–idea figures. This figure Melanchthon classifies as deriving from the dialectical topic of definition (*Elem.* 48v).

metalepsis [G. "participation, taking one thing instead of another"] or *transumptio* [L. "a taking of one thing for another"]

Substituting a remote cause for a present effect or combining several tropes within one

"*Medea,* cursing her first acquaintance with prince *Jason*, who had very unkindly forsaken her, said:

Woe worth the mountaine that the maste bare
Which was the first causer of all my care.

Where she might as well have said, 'Woe worth our first meeting,' or 'Woe worth the time that *Jason* arrived with his ship at my father's city in *Colchos*, when he took me away with him,' and not so far off as to curse the mountain that bare the pine tree, that made the mast, that bare the sails, that the ship sailed with, which carried her away." (Euripides, *Medea*, I.i.1–2)

(Puttenham 193–94)

Spenser uses "pledges" for "children" in *The Faerie Queene* I. 10.4.8–9:

"But faire Charissa to a lovely fere
Was lincked, and by him had many pledges dere."

(Gill 154)

Note: An alternate spelling is *transsumptio*. Puttenham's name is "the Farrefet, as when we had rather fetch a word a great way off than to use one nearer hand" (193). Erasmus calls this figure a kind of synecdoche (*DC* 339), but Gill (154) and Vossius (221) identify it as a species of metonymy.

onomatopoeia [G. "word coining"] or *nominatio* [L. "naming"] or *nominis confictio* [L. "name inventing"]

The making of words, neologisms

1. *Fictio* [L. "making, fashioning"]
   a. By imitating the sound it signifies
      "Flashing of lightning, clashing of blades, clinking of fetters, chinking of money: and as the poet Virgil said of the sounding a trumpet, ta-ra-tant, taratantara."

      (Puttenham 192)

   b. By imitating the voices of dumb beasts
      "The roaring of Lions, the bellowing of bulls, the bleating of sheep, the grunting of swine, the croaking of frogs, the chattering of Pies, the chirping of sparrows, the howling of dogs, the neighing of horses, and hissing of serpents."
2. *Derivatio* [L. "derivation"] or *paragoge* [G. "derivation"]
   a. By derivation from the original with suffixes or prefixes
      "The city *Troy* was so called by derivation from king *Troe*, and before that it was called *Teucria*, from *Teucrus,* and first of all *Dardania* from *Dardanus*."
   b. By combining two words together and making of them one
      "'Oratorlike, scholarlike': also to call a churl 'thickskin,' a niggard a 'pinchpeny,' a flatterer a 'pickthank,' a glutton a 'bellygod.'"
3. *Trope* [G. "turn, turning"] or *catachresis* [G. "abuse"], adapting the nearest available term when no actual term exists
   a. By imitating antiquity, *archaismus*
      "I will refer the Reader to *Chaucer* & *Gower*, and to the new *Shepheardes Calendar*."
   b. By suggesting that one imitates another's manner
      "To fatherize" or "to Platonize" (that is, to imitate his father or to imitate Plato).
      "I can not court it" (that is, "I can not perform the duty or manners of a courtier").
      "I can not Italian it" (that is, "I can not imitate the fashion of an Italian.")

      (Peacham [1593] 14–15)

Note: Alternate names are *pepoiemenon* and *procreatio.* Puttenham calls this figure "the New namer" (192). This figure becomes the general category for neologisms, which are created in three ways: word coining, word forming, and word translating. It is Quintilian who assigns the term *catachresis* to the third category (8.6.34). Others simply attribute *trope* to the third method when they name it. Both *paragoge* and *catachresis* are names for other figures. See *paragoge* above under morphological figures and *catachresis* above under semantical figures.

periphrasis [G "a circumlocution"] or *circumlocutio* [L. "a circumlocution"] or *circumscriptio* [L. "an encircling"] or *circuitio* [L. "a going round, a circumlocution"]

Replacing one or few words with many either to more fully describe something or to hide unpleasantness

1. Replacing a name with a description of some identifying notable enterprise, native country, sect or opinion

   Calling Aeneas "Goddess born," "Anchises-sprung," or "the Trojan Anchisiade."

   (Scaliger 3.78.346)

   "Calling Scipio 'the destroyer of Carthage and Numantia,' just as Horace called Homer 'the recorder of the Trojan war.'"
2. Using *etymologia*, or replacing the name with the cause or reason for the name

   Instead of philosopher, say "a man pursuing wisdom."

   Instead of parasite, say "a man who is a slave to food and his belly."
3. Using *notatione* or *annotation*, that is, replacing the thing with a description of the signs that accompany it

   Instead of anger, say "a seething of the mind or bile which brings pallor to the face, a glare to the eyes, and a trembling to the limbs."

   Instead of "a salt-fish dealer," say "he wipes his nose on his arm."
4. Using *definitio*, or replacing the word with its definition

   For rhetoric, say "the art of good speaking."

   For peculator, say "one who plundered the public funds."

   For tyrant, say "one who forcibly crushed law and the liberty of citizens."

   (Erasmus, *De copia* 331–32)
5. Replacing a name or phrase with a *metaphor*

   "When they had slept awhile" becomes "When they had a while hearkened to the persuasion of sleep."

   "To put off or lay down this Tabernacle" (1 Peter 1:14), for "to die."

   (Smith 169)

Note: Additional names include *circumitio* and *circuitas.* Puttenham calls this "the Figure of ambage" (203). Gill includes here "all descriptions of places, persons, times, etc. (with which every poem abounds)" (158). This figure works to either make something more clear or more darkened and concealed. For more elaboration on *etymologia, notatio*, and *definitio*, see *definitio* below under Logical–idea figures.

sarcasmus [G. "mockery, sarcasm"] or *irrisio* [L. "a deriding mockery"]

Sarcasm or derision

Upon taking prisoner in battle John Frederick, Duke of Saxony, "a man of monstrous bigness and corpulence," the Emperor Charles V said, "I have gone a hunting many times, yet never took I such a swine before."

(Puttenham 200)

"And they that passed by [our Savior] railed on him, wagging their heads, and saying, 'Ah, thou that destroyest the temple, and buildest it in three days, Save thyself, and come down from the cross.'" (Mark 15:29–30)

(Smith 142)

Note: An alternate spelling is *sarcasmos*. Puttenham's name is "the Bitter taunt" (200). Scaliger makes *irrisio* (derision) a species of *sarcasmus*: it refers to attributing a crime falsely to men of sure dignity and integrity, when without a doubt the attribution is recognized as belonging to the adversary. For example, "With me in command, did the adulterous Dardanius conquer Sparta?" (*Aeneid* 10.97–98); in other words, "It was not I who led the attack against Sparta" (3.86.356). On the other hand, Vossius, probably following Rufinianus (*Dian.* §9), makes *irrisio* into the general category containing the figures *sarcasmos, diasyrmos, charientismus, asteismus, mycterismus,* and *mimesis* (227–28).

symbole [G. "sign, token"]
Symbol
"[I represent] *Whore-Masters*, by the example of *Sardanapalus* or *Heliogabalus*; of all modern *Tyrants*, by the example of *Nero*; of all petty *Hackneys*, by the example of *Helena*; of all modern *Traitors*, by the example of *Cataline* and *Cegetbus*; and of the most ambitious *Usurpers*, by the example of the renown'd *Alexander*."

(Shaw 151)

Note: *Collatio* is an alternate name.

tapinosis [G. "lowering, lessening, humiliation, abasement"] or *exouthenismos* [G. "setting at naught"]
Diminishing by making trivial

1. Through a word
When talking to Iago, Cassio calls his mistress Bianca a "monkey" and a "bauble" (Shakespeare, *Othello* 4.1.127, 135).

(Susenbrotus 35; example mine)

2. Through a statement
"A few, however, who stood nearest to him suspected that he had intended to say something about the agrarian law" (Cicero, *De Lege Agraria* II 5.13, trans. Butler).

(Quintilian 8.4.28)

Note: An alternate spelling is *tapeinosis*. Sometimes this figure is subsumed under *meiosis* or subsumes *meiosis*. See *meiosis* above.

PRAGMATICAL

Treating Ideas

amplificatio [L. "a widening, enlarging, increasing"] or *auxesis* [G. "growth, increase"]
Augmenting; a general category

1. Description
"Amplification . . . consisteth most in augmenting and diminishing of any matter, and that divers ways. All amplification and diminishing either is taken out of the substance in things or else of words."
The means of amplifying include the places of confirmation from both logic and rhetoric, and the following figures, among others:
a. Of words
Palilogia, auxesis, meiosis, hyperbole, prosopopoeia, correctio, progressio, incrementum, dirimens copulatio, congeries, metaphor, exclamatio, paradiastole, etc.

b. Of matter

Comparatio, catacosmesis, exemplum, antithesis, definitio, divisio, color, antisagoge, syllogismus, emphasis, dinumeratio, peristasis, frequentatio, paroemia, sententia, etc.

2. Example

"As for example, where it is said, 'Gentle behavior winneth goodwill and clearly quencheth hatred,' I might in commending a noble gentleman for his lowliness, declare at large how commendable and how profitable a thing gentle behavior is, and of the other side, how hateful and how harmful a proud disdainful man is, and how beastly a nature he hath that being but a man thinketh himself better than any other man is, and also overgood to have a match or fellow in this life. As thus: 'If lowliness and charity maintain life, what a beast is he that through hatred will purchase death? If God warneth us to love one another, and learn of him to be gentle because he was gentle and humble in heart, how cruel are they that dare withstand his commandment? If the subject rebel against his king, we cry with one voice, "Hang him, hang him," and shall we not think him worthy the vilest death of all that being a creature contemneth his creator, being a mortal man neglecteth his heavenly maker, being a vile mould of clay setteth light by so mighty a God and ever-living king? Beasts and birds without reason love one another; they shroud and they flock together: and shall men endued with such gifts hate his even-Christian and eschew company? When sheep do stray, or cattle do strive one against another, there are dogs ready to call them in, yea, they will bite them (as it hath been full often seen) if two fight together, and shall man want reason to bark against his lewd affections, or at the least shall he have none to check him for his faults, and force him to forgive?'"

(Wilson 146–48, 152)

Note: An additional name is *parauxesis.* Denying it to be a figure (9.2.106), Quintilian divides amplification into four types of methods: *incrementum, comparatio, ratiocinatio* (reasoning as in *syllogismus* and *emphasis*), and *congeries* (8.4.3) and distinguishes argument from amplification (8.4.12). Peacham, however, explains, "Now is it to be observed that Amplification is called by the name of a figure, yet as a generall of many specials" and divides it into distribution, description, comparison, and collection ([1593] 120–21). Peacham also regards amplification as argument, for this device affirms with clear, weighty, plentiful, and various proofs thereby moving "the minds of the hearers" ([1593] 120). He follows Cicero, who describes invention of arguments as amplification (*Inv.* 2.48). Cicero divides amplification into intellectual and emotional (*Inv* 2.48), giving *loci communes* for each to aid invention (2.68). Also recognizing the role of amplification in argument, Melanchthon explains that the *thesis* supplies the major premise, while the *auxesis* supplies the minor premise of the syllogism (*Elem.* 48r), and Sturm warns that amplification must have an argumentative quality so that it does not become swaggering and swelling (1.31.123). Hoskins too divides amplification of matter into the categories of comparison, accumulation, intimation and progression, all figures and all arguments (17).

anamnesis [G. "calling to mind, reminiscence"] or *commonitio* [L. "an earnest reminding, admonition"]

Calling to remembrance

1. The speaker recalls something

a. Sincerely

"The Prodigal son, when he came to himself, said, 'How many hired servants of my father's house have bread enough and to spare, and I perish with hunger? I will arise and go to my father, etc.'"(Luke 15:17).

(Smith 249)

b. Ironically, in order to seem more unprepared
"This ring of Piso's reminds me of something which had entirely slipped my memory. How many gold rings do you think Verres has stripped from the fingers of honourable men?" (Cicero, *In C. Verrem* II 4.26.57, trans. Butler)

(Quintilian 9.2.61)

2. The speaker reminds the audience of things that need to be remembered
a. Of what has been said earlier in the speech
Cicero appends this summary at the end of his statement of facts to remind the judge of the central point: "Up to this point, Gaius Caesar, Quintus Ligarius stands clear of all blame. So far from leaving his home at the call of war, he left it when there was not the remotest suspicion of war; he went out as legate in time of peace, and in an utterly peaceable province he so bore himself that peace was its highest interest. His departure at least can give you no just cause of affront. And what of his remaining? Far less this; for while his departure implied an inclination which did him no discredit, his remaining was due to an honorable necessity. These two conjunctures, then, are unimpeachable: the first, when he left Rome as legate; the second, when, in response to the demands of the province, he was given the charge of Africa." (*Pro Ligario* 2.4. trans. Watts).

(Quintilian 4.2.51)

b. Of matters past or present
"And here you must consider, as with the farmers just now, but a good deal more carefully still, what line you mean to take. It will matter a great deal whether you choose to have the Sicilians, individually and collectively, regarded as your friends or as your enemies. If as your enemies, what becomes of you? What refuge will you find, what ground to stand on? You have just quarreled with the farmers, the respectable and wealthy farmers, Sicilian and Roman alike; how will you deal now with the Sicilian cities? Will you declare the Sicilians your friends? And how can you? Never before have they gone so far as to give evidence against anyone officially, in spite of the fact that a number of former governors of the province have been convicted and only two acquitted; yet now here they are, with official letters, official instructions, official evidence. Were they giving you official eulogies, we should think it was more their own practice than your merits that made them do it; and as they are in fact officially denouncing your conduct, are they not showing us that their wrongs are so heavy that they have much preferred abandoning their own practice to being silent about your practices?" (Cicero, *In C. Verrem* II 2.64.155, trans. Greenwood)

(Sturm 1.40.217)

Note: Additional names include *reminiscentia*, *memoratio*, and *recordatio*. Quintilian treats the first (9.2.61), but not the second (9.2.106), application as a figure. Perhaps the figure Soarez describes of "stor[ing] away some points in the hearer's memory and then reclaim[ing] what was deposited there" (361) belongs here.

antenagoge [G. "leading up against, bringing up instead"] or *compensatio* [L. "a weighing, balancing of several things together"]

Balancing a fault by adding a virtue, or a disadvantage by adding an advantage

1. In a positive way:
"I must needs say, that my wife is a shrew,
But such a housewife as I know but a few."

(Puttenham 225)

"It is a thing difficult to attain learning, but yet very commodious."

(Day 89)

2. In a negative way, called *retributio* [L. "retribution"]:
   When we cannot get rid of our crime, we can throw a counter charge at our adversary. For example, if our adversary accuses, "You shattered the moneybox of Daphne," we can respond, "Did I not see you, terrible man, take by treachery the goat of Damo?"

   (Scaliger 3.51.324)

Note: An alternate spelling is *antanagoge* and an alternate name is *anteisagoge*. Puttenham's English name is "the Recompencer" (224). Alexander calls this move a contrastive substitution (25).

apolytos merismos [G. "a loosing from or setting free from a division"]

An unfinished or incomplete division

"That, on the one hand, is my view." Demosthenes does not pick up the second half of the division ["on the other hand"] but immediately proceeds to a conclusion: "Therefore, perhaps, being loud and shameless, they will press hard, . . ." (*De Falsa Legatione* 238, trans. Wooten).

(Hermogenes 2.7.362)

apostasis [G. "causing to revolt, defection, departure from"]

Starting fresh without giving any advance indication or notice to prepare the audience for what one does next

1. In syntax
   "You yourself, Tityrus, the pines,
   the streams, the groves all call you." (Virgil, *Eclogue* 1 l.38–39)
   (This sentence gets stuck and starts over, unlike the continuous flowing sentence: "The pines and the streams call Tityrus.")

   (Sturm 3.12 .617)

2. In argument
   After his speech is interrupted with the reading of the decree, Demosthenes resumes without a transition: "This was the beginning of our dealings with Thebes and the first negotiation, since before this these men had reduced our attitude toward the Thebans to hostility and hatred and distrust. This decree caused the danger surrounding the city to disappear like a cloud" (*On the Crown* 188, trans. Wooten).

   (Hermogenes 1.9.267)

   "Well, I pass by those successes which Philip achieved and maintained before I became a politician and a public speaker, as I do not think that they concern me. I will, however, remind you of enterprises of his which were thwarted after the day on which I entered public life. Of these I will render an account, premising only that Philip started with this enormous advantage. In all the Greek states–not in some but in every one of them–it chanced that there had sprung up the most abundant crop of traitorous, venal, and profligate politicians ever known within the memory of mankind. These persons . . ." (Demosthenes, *On the Crown* 60–61, trans. Vince)

   (Hermogenes 1.10.270)

3. In expressing emotion
   a. Within a sentence
   "When I brought suit against my guardians, when I was a mere boy and neither knew this man nor whether he existed—would that I were not acquainted with him now!—" (Demosthenes, *Against Meidias* 78, trans. Wooten)

   (Hermogenes 2.7.355)

   b. Within a passage
   "At length returning to some use of herself, she began to say to Cleophila that she was sorry she would venture herself to leave her rest, being not altogether healed of her hurt. But as if the opening of her mouth to Cleophila had opened some great flood-gap of sorrow, whereof her heart could not bear the violent issue, she sank to the ground with her hands over her face, crying vehemently: 'Cleophila, help me! O Cleophila, have pity of me!'

   Cleophila ran to her, marvelling what sudden sickness had thus possessed her; and beginning to ask her the cause of her sorrow, and offering her service to be employed by her, Gynecia opening her eyes wildly upon her, pricked with the flames of love and the torments of her own conscience: 'O Cleophila, Cleophila,' said she, 'dost thou offer me physic which art my only poison, or wilt thou do me service which hast already brought me into eternal slavery? [. . .] Alas, [. . .] what shall I say more? Take pity of me, O Cleophila, but not as Cleophila, and disguise not with me in words, as I know thou dost in apparel. [. . .] Alas, Cleophila, [. . .] I perceive you know full little how piercing the eyes are of a true lover. There is no one beam of those thoughts you have planted in me but is able to discern a greater cloud than you do go in. Seek not to conceal yourself further from me, nor force the passion of love into violent extremities!'" (Sidney, *The Old Arcadia*, Book 2, 82–84)

   (Sturm 3.24.725; example mine)

Note: Sturm calls these suddenly proclaimed affections *dikthesin* (3.24.725). Hermogenes advises that this figure creates sincerity (2.7.355). Quintilian describes this strategy as he treats invention, but does not call it a figure (4.5.5). The opposite to this figure is *katastasis*. See *katastasis* below.

aversio [L. "a turning away"] or *apoplanesis* [G. "a leading astray, making to digress"]
Leading away from the point
"Cicero, when he should have answered to an accusation, in which it was objected that Caelius had poisoned Metellus, for as much as it was proved that Caelius had poison prepared in his house: and furthermore that the force of that poison was tried in a servant of his, he digressed by and by to Metellus' death, and maketh a suspicion that he was poisoned by the mischievous deed of Clodius: he sigheth, weepeth and bewaileth that death, whereby he stayeth and appeaseth his adversaries, and causeth them to mourn with him, and to be stricken (as it were) with the same wound, and so by his vehement and forcible persuasion turneth the minds of the Judges from the cogitation of the fact, now and then touching it a little, and slipping from it again" (*Pro Caelio* 24.58–60).

(Peacham [1593] 117)

chorismos [G. "dancing a round in a chorus, any circling motion"]
Dividing a general idea into parts and then dilating upon each part point for point throughout a passage
"The two things which have the greatest influence in a state,—namely, the greatest interest, and eloquence, are both making against us at the present moment; and while I am

awed by the one, O Caius Aquillius, I am in fear of the other:—I am somewhat awed, apprehending that the eloquence of Quintius Hortensius may embarrass me in speaking; but I am in no slight fear lest the interest of Sextus Naevius may injure Publius Quintius. And yet it would not seem so disastrous for us that these things should exist in the highest degree in the other party, if they existed also to a moderate extent in us; but the fact is, that I, who have neither sufficient experience nor much ability, am brought into comparison with a most eloquent advocate; and that Publius Quintius, who has but small influence, no riches, and few friends, is contending with a most influential adversary. And, moreover, we have this additional disadvantage, that Marcus Junius, who has several times pleaded this cause before you, O Aquillius, a man practised in the conduct of other causes also, and much and frequently concerned in this particular one, is at this moment absent, being engaged on his new commission; and so they have recourse to me, who, even if I had all other requisite qualifications in ever so high a degree, have certainly scarcely had time enough to be able to understand so important a business, having so many points of dispute involved in it." (Cicero, *Pro Quinctio* 1.1, trans. Yonge)

(Sturm 3.3.498)

Note: This scheme is syntactical *prolepsis* now applied to ideas throughout a passage. Sturm says this *schema* is especially appropriate for philosophy (1.15.38).

climax [G. "a staircase, a scaling-ladder"] or *gradatio* [L. "a series of steps"]

Climbing the stairs from things smaller to things greater

1. The ascent created not through the repetition of exact words, but through the repetition of ideas connecting one step to the next.

   Keckermann reduces the story of Phoebus and Daphne to a pithy verbal climax to represent the form in the narrative: "*Viderat hanc, visamque cupit potiturque cupita*" ["He saw her, and desired whom he saw, and possessed whom he desired"] (Ovid, *Metamorphoses* I.489).
2. The ascent created by the stacking of cause upon cause

   "Now what remnant of the hope of liberty survives, if those men may do what they please, if they can do what they may, if they dare do what they can, if they do what they dare, and if you approve what they do?" (*Ad Herennium* 4.25.34).

   "In the city luxury arises, from luxury avarice steps forth, from avarice necessarily erupts boldness, whence all crimes and scandals are born." (paraphrase of Cicero, *Pro S. Roscius* 27.75)
3. The ascent created by denying the possibility of exaggerating the thing sufficiently.

   "I cannot find the words with which sufficiently worthily I can express that thing to you, hearers."

(Keckermann 1482, 1488–89)

Note: Keckermann indicates that *climax* can structure an *aetiologia* (1482). Repeating an observation made in Veltkirchius that climax is affined with *sorites* (119r), Hoskins remarks that to make the *gradatio* a *sorites,* or climbing argument, we join the clauses with an *ergo* (12). He illustrates by revising a sentence spoken by Zelmane from Sidney's *Arcadia*, book 2, 317: "Ergo, you cannot enjoy your own goods without government, nor government without a magistrate, nor magistrate without obedience, and no obedience where every man upon his private passion doth interpret the doings of the rulers" (12–13). See *climax* under syntactical figures for the figure of speech. A related figure is *incrementum*, which is sometimes seen as a species of *climax* and sometimes distinguished because it has a looser structure. Keckermann's third application above would more properly fit under *incrementum*. See *incrementum* below.

commoratio [L. "dwelling on a point"] or *epimone* [G. "delay"]
Resting upon a point
1. In a short passage
"Now seeing that all Greece was in such a plight, and still unconscious of a gathering and ever-growing evil, what was the right policy for Athens to adopt, and the right action for her to take? That is the question, men of Athens, which you ought to consider, and that is the issue on which I ought to be called to account; for I was the man who took up a firm position in that department of your public affairs. Was it the duty of our city, Aeschines, to abase her pride, to lower her dignity, to rank herself with Thessalians and Dolopians, to help Philip to establish his supremacy over Greece, to annihilate the glories and the prerogatives of our forefathers? Or, if she rejected that truly shameful policy, was she to stand by and permit aggressions which she must have long foreseen, and knew would succeed if none should intervene?" (Demosthenes, *On the Crown* 62–63, trans. Vince)
(Hermogenes 1.11.286)
2. In a long passage
"*Cicero*, when *Erutius* could show no cause in his accusation why *Roscius* should slay his father, he doth first amplify the wicked fact of Parricide, declaring how great it is, and argueth that without many and great causes, such a wickedness cannot be committed, and contendeth that it cannot fall but upon a mischievous and most lewd man: after this he demandeth of *Erutius* the cause why *Roscius* should slay his father, which place, because it was strongest in *Roscius*' defense, he tarrieth long in it, and very often maketh his return thither; he often demandeth the causes of so great and horrible wickedness, of so shameful a deed; he often amplifieth the greatness of the fact, and that which is great indeed, [. . .]" (*Pro S. Roscio* 13–29).
(Peacham [1593] 152–53)

Note: *Immoratio* is an additional name. Puttenham, who calls this "the figure of Abode," advises the persuader, upon "finding a substantial point in his matter to serve his purpose," to "dwell upon that point longer than upon any other less assured, and use all endeavor to maintain that one, and as it were to make his chief abode thereupon" (240). Robertellus assigns Phalereus as the source for this figure (48v).

congeries [L. "a heap, pile, mass"] or *sinathrismus* [G. "collection, union"] or *accumulatio* [L. "a heaping up"] or *conglobatio* [L. "a heaping, gathering, crowding together"]
Heaping up many things in order to amplify
1. Accumulating details
"They are the Ministers of Christ, I speak as a fool, I am more: in labors more abundant: in stripes above measure: in prison more plenteously: in death oft: of the Jews received I sixty times, every time forty stripes save one: thrice was I beaten with rods: I was once stoned: I suffered thrice Shipwrecks: night and day have I been in the deep Sea: in journeying often: in perils of waters: in perils of robberies: in jeopardies of mine own nation: in jeopardies among the Heathen: in perils in the city: in perils in the wilderness: in perils in the Sea: in perils among false brethren: in labors and travail: in watchings often: in hunger and thirst: in fastings often: in cold and nakedness: beside the things which outwardly happen unto me" (2 Corinthians 11:23–28).
(Peacham [1577] R.i.r)

"Mine eyes, no eyes, but fountains of my tears:
My tears, no tears, but floods to moist my heart:

My heart, no heart, but harbour of my fears:
My fears, no fears, but feeling of my smart.
  My smart, my fears, my heart, my tears, mine eyes
  Are blind, dried, spent, past, wasted with my cries.
And yet mine eyes, though blind, see cause of grief:
And yet my tears though dried, run down amain:
And yet my heart, though spent, attends relief:
And yet my fears, though past, increase my pain:
  And yet I live, and living feel more smart:
  And smarting, cry in vain, Break heavy heart."
(Francis Davidson, *A Poetical Rhapsody*, No. 111, "Breake heavy hart" ll. 8–19)

(Gill 168)

2. Accumulating arguments
"What was that drawn sword of yours, Tuberus, doing in the battle line at Pharsalus? Whose side was that sharp point seeking? What awareness was there of your weapon? What mind? What eyes, hands, fervor of soul? What were you desiring? What did you want?" (Cicero, *Pro Ligario* 3.9, trans. Green)

(Keckermann 1489)

Note: An alternate name is *athroismos*. Puttenham calls this "the heaping figure" (243), and like Sherry ([1555] G.ii.v) includes the heaping of both words and sentences. Quintilian distinguishes between *congeries* and *synathroismos*, with the first a heaping of words or details identical in meaning and the second a heaping of different things, but these are methods, not figures (8.4.27). Peacham uses *dinumeratio* for the heaping of sentences, saying the figure is related to *congeries*, but differs in that "*congeries* heapeth up words, and this sentences" ([1577] R.i.r). See note to *enumeratio* below. Peacham restricts *conglobatio* to the heaping up of definitions ([1577] T.i.r), connecting this figure to *systrophe*, but Sturm treats *conglobatio* as the general term for heaping up "events, consequences, deeds, and actions [. . .] the divisions of a thing" (1.32.129). Sturm tries to distinguish *conglobatio* from *congeries* by indicating that *conglobatio* can include superfluous matters, but *congeries* touches upon things pertinent to the matter at hand (1.33.144). Under *congeries*, Gill includes both the syntactical and pragmatical applications and lists as synonyms *coacervatio* and *synathroesmos* (167). In addition, Gill's comment on the above poem instructs the student to read for overlapping figures: "Here, in addition to *Congeries*, you have continuous *Anaphora, Epanorthosis, Anadiplosis, Asyndeton, Zeugma*, [. . . and] *Regressio*" (168).

decrementum [L. "a decrease"] or *decensus* [L. "a decrease, abatement"]
Descending by degrees

1. In words and ideas:
"Son of man, the house of Israel is unto me as dross: all they are brass and tin, and iron, and lead in the midst of the furnace: they are even the dross of silver" (Ezekiel 22:18).

(Smith 135)

2. In actions:
"By me Kingdoms and Commonwealths, as illustrious in the World, as the Sun and Moon in the Heavens, do set and wain as well as they. By me great Favorites fall gradually, from the *Closet*, then from the *Council*, then from the *Court*, then from the *City*; and never cease tumbling, till they be even with the ground, and under it too. By me the *Apostatizing* part of the World, those *Religious Renegades* fall first from *devotion*, then from *seriousness*, then from *common honesty* and *modesty*, till at last they renounce even *humanity* itself."

(Shaw 160)

Note: This figure is the opposite of *incrementum* and is commonly treated, even if not named, in discussions of *amplificatio*, since attentuation is a necessary counterpart to amplification. See *amplificatio* above and *incrementum* below.

declinatio [L. "a bending aside"]

Digressing briefly

"Then Gaius Varenus, that is, the Varenus who was killed by the slaves of Ancharius:—I beg you, gentlemen, to give careful attention to what I am about to say;" (Cicero, *Pro Vareno*, now lost, trans. Butler).

(Quintilian 9.2.56)

Note: Sturm distinguishes *declinatio* and *digressio*, explaining that *digressio* constitutes a separate part of a speech, whereas *declinatio*, which tends to be short, takes place within a part of a speech. He also suggests that *declinatio* is a kind of *apostasis* (2.20.376). See *apostasis* above.

defectus [L. "a deficiency"] or *detractio* [L. "a taking away, withdrawal"] or *ellipsis* [G. "an omission"]

Leaving out some detail, idea, event, or description that is nevertheless implied

Here Aeneas inserts a quotation without any mention of the speaker, who, we are to understand, was some Trojan, speaking after the departure of the Greeks: "Here the Dolopian host/ Camped, here the fierce Achilles pitched his tent" (Virgil, *Aeneid* 2.30, trans. Butler).

(Quintilian 9.2.37)

Whoever dies in battle, although not mentioned specifically, is nevertheless numbered among those who fought; or contrariwise, those who are named in the enumeration are still believed to have been in the battle even if their actions on the battlefield are not described specifically.

(Scaliger 3.77.344)

Note: Scaliger considers this figure a species of *eclipsis*, which he is transferring from grammar and applying to ideas. He also claims that it can be seen as a species of *aposiopesis*. Quintilian, however, would have disagreed, distinguishing *eclipsis* from *aposiopesis* (9.3.60).

diallage [G. "interchange, change, difference"] or *consummatio* [L. "a reckoning together"]

Concentrating many different arguments to establish one point

"My lords, do not weigh my words and sentences severally, but consider them all altogether. If the accused person here shall receive profit by this other man's death; if his life heretofore hath ever been evil, his nature covetous, his wealth most slender; and that this dead man's goods could turn to no man's avail so much as unto this accused person; and that no man could so easily dispatch him; and that this man could by no better means compass his desire; and that nothing hath been unattempted which might further his naughty purpose, and nothing done that was thought needless; and seeing a meet place was chiefly sought for, and occasion served very well, and the time was most apt for such an attempt, and many reasons heretofore devised to compass this offense, and great hope both to keep it close and also to dispatch it; and besides that, seeing this man was seen alone and little before in the same place where this other man was slain, and that this man's voice which did slay him was heard a little before in the same place where this other man was slain; and seeing it is well known that this man came home late the same night, and the next day after being examined did answer confusedly, fearfully, and as though he were amazed; and seeing all these things are partly showed by witnesses, partly by good reason, partly by his own confession, and partly by the report that commonly goeth of him, which belike is not spoken without some ground—it shall be your parts, worthy judges, weighing all these things together, to give certain judgment of him for this offense, and not to think it a matter of suspicion. For it might have been that three or four of these conjectures being proved might give but only a cause of suspicion, but whereas all these together are plainly proved by him, it cannot be otherwise but that he hath offended."

(Wilson 159)

Note: An additional Latin name is *instantia*, which means "presence or steadiness, constancy, perseverence, force, vehemence, earnestness in speaking." Quintilian lists Gorgias, Rutilius, and Celsus as sources for this figure, but disagrees that it is a figure (9.2.102).

diaskeue [G. "To arm, equip, or prepare oneself"]
Elaborating a topic with rhetorical devices, developing a passage artistically

1. Description
   This is a general category, involving figures such as *diatyposis*, *prosopopoeia*, *aphegesis*, *peristasis*, *paradoxon*, *parepomenon*, and *leptologia*. It does not include *aetiologia*, *ekparasynaptikon*, or *dianoia*, since giving a cause or reason produces *kataskeue*, or the confirmation.

   (Hermogenes, *Invention* 3.15.166–67)

2. Example
   "An awful sight, men of Athens, and piteous. For when recently we were on our way to Delphi, we could not help seeing it all—houses razed to the ground, walls dismantled, the land destitute of men in their prime, only a few weak women and mere boys and miserable old men" (Demosthenes, *De Falsa Legatione* 64, trans. Kennedy).

   (Hermogenes, *Invention* 2.7.124)

Note: Quintilian rejects this device as a figure (9.2.107).

diexodos [G. "for going through, something detailed, an outlet or passage"]
Going through in detail; the opposite of answering with a simple yes or no

"Some have endured this once, while no one has endured it twice, but I have endured it thrice."

(Quintilian 9.3.87)

digestio [L. "an orderly distribution, division"] or *ordinatio* [L. "a setting in order, arranging"] or *eutrepismus* [G. "preparation"]
Numbering, sequencing, and defining the parts beforehand

"'There are three things,' quoth Tully, 'which hinder Sextus Roscius at this time: the accusation of his adversaries, the boldness of them, and the power that they bear. Eruscus, his accuser, hath taken upon him to forge false matter; the Roscians' kinsfolk have boldly adventured and will face out their doings; and Chrysogonus here, that most can do, will press us with his power" (*Pro S. Roscio* 13.35).

(Wilson 223)

"There are three sorts of men which do dispose of all that a man hath, the Lawyer, the Physician, and the Divine. The Lawyer disposeth of his goods, the Physician of his body, and the divine of his soul."

(Peacham [1593] 130)

Note: Alternate names include *endeixis tes taxeos* and *eutaxia*. This figure, when found in the *propositio*, is more specifically referred to as *partitio* or *distributio*. See *partitio* under Discoursal–parts of oration below.

diminutio [L. "diminution, lessening"] or *meiosis* [G. "a lessening, diminishing"] or *extenuatio* [L. "a lessening, extenuation"] or *tapeinosis* [G. "lowering, lessening, humiliation, abasement"]

Extenuating things difficult or diminishing things

1. For encouragement

"As to one that would shun learning, for the tediousness thereof in study, we might show, that besides the great necessity thereof in the life of man, we shall in attaining thereof, take no other nor more labor some course, than others before us have done: that the way thereunto is very plain and easy, the labor (if any be) sweet and pleasant. And whereas in all our ordinary exercises of vanity, there reboundeth for the most part in the end but mere travail, and unprofitable charge: in this the commodity is as great as the delight, the gain as ordinary as the practice, wherein the study is but the least part of a man's life, but the pleasure and commodity infinite."

(Day 94)

2. For modesty

"Not all the skill I have to speak or do,
Which little is God wot (set love apart:)
Liveload not life, and put them both thereto,
Can counterpoise the due of your dessert."

(Puttenham 227–28)

3. For subtle scoffs

To an adversary commended as a very brave soldier, one could reply:

"A jolly man (forsooth) and fit for the war,
Good at hand grips, better to fight afar,
Whom bright weapon in show as it is said,
Yea his own shade, hath often made afraid."

(Puttenham 228)

4. For pleasant familiarity

As a manner of speech with our equals and inferiors, we call a young gentlewoman "Mall" for "Mary, "Nell" for Elner, "Jack" for "John," or "Robin" for "Robert."

(Puttenham 228–29)

Note: Some rhetoricians indicate that this figure applies to both words and matter. Puttenham even lists *meiosis*, or "the Disabler or figure of Extenuation" twice, once for the trope (195) and once for this figure of thought (227–29). Others separate the figures of speech and of thought with separate names. For example, Day (84, 94), Hoskins (35–36, 39), and Blount (31–32, 35) each list *meiosis* and *diminutio* as separate figures, the first for the trope and the second for the figure of thought. Keckermann calls the figure of word *extenuatio* (1468) and that of idea *diminutio* (1489). Also, sometimes *meiosis* and *tapeinosis* are distinguished. See *tapeinosis* above under semantical figures. Veltkirchius suggests that this figure can be created by means of *decrementum, malo comparatio, ratiocinatio, congeries, dissimulatio, irrisio, and insectatio* (139r-140r).

disjunctio [L. "a separation"] or *diastasis* [G. "a standing apart"]

Separating ideas within a sentence, period, or passage; or separating verse and quotations from one's own text

1. Keeping ideas separate, but connected within one sentence
   "Those men ought to be despised; nevertheless, they are endured."
   "On the one hand, . . . ; on the other, . . ."

   (Sturm 2.13.345)

2. Separating ideas that belong together within a passage
   "But if, because we have no faith in day-books, we have adopted the practice of compiling ledgers, ought authority and sanctity to be attributed before the judge to what is considered by all to be feeble and unimportant? [Up to this point the question has been proposed, and then a *diastasin* is interjected.] What is the reason why we write our notes carelessly but make up our ledgers carefully? What is the reason? [After this interval he successively appends the cause.] It is because day-books last for a month, ledgers forever; day-books are immediately destroyed, ledgers are religiously preserved" (Cicero, *Pro Q. Roscio* 2.6–7, trans. Freese).

   (Sturm 2.20.382)

3. Keeping verse and quotations separate from one's own text
   Marcus Scipio said to the auctioneer, regarding L. Manlius, who suffered defeat in seeking the consulate: "Each I judge to be a good and distinguished citizen."

   (Sturm 3.21.708)

Note: The opposite method of quoting is *paraploke*, when we integrate the verse with our own words. See *paraplokas toiematon*, a figure under Logical–evidence below. Hermogenes discusses two ways of incorporating quotations of verse within one's own text, the first "quotation" or *kollesis,* which seems to apply to both this figure and *paraploke* below, and the second "adaptation" or *paroidia* (*Meth.* §30), which corresponds to *parechesis*, also under the Logical–evidence category below. This figure retains similarity with the grammatical figure of the same name. See *disjunctio* above under grammatical figures.

dissipatio [L."a scattering, dispersing"]

Scattering the details loosely throughout: the opposite of *metabole*

"These acres favor corn,
In yonder, vines grow better; elsewhere spring
Fruit-orchards and a wealth of unsown green.
Who knows not how the scented saffron grows
On Timolus, Lydian hill? that ivory
Is India's trade, and frankincense the pride
Of sensual Araby? The Chalybes
Delve naked after iron, Pontus breeds
The Castor drug, and far Epirus sends
Her mettled coursers for Olympian palms." (Virgil, *Georgic* 1.54–63, trans. Williams)

(Quintilian 9.3.39)

distributio[1] [L. "A division, distribution"]

Assigning to each as is due

1. In a sentence
   "He alienated both brothers, one by his uncouth behavior, the other by his meanness."

   (Erasmus, *De copia* 427)

2. In a passage
   "It is the duty of a king to have an especial care over his whole realm. It is the office of his nobles to cause the king's will to be fulfilled, and with all diligence to further

his laws, and to see justice done everywhere. It is the part of a subject faithfully to do his prince's commandment and with a willing heart to serve him at all needs. It is the office of a bishop to set forth God's word and with all diligence to exhort men to all godliness. It is a husband's duty to love his wife and with gentle means to rule her. It is the wife's office humbly to submit herself to her husband's will. Servants should be faithful to their masters, not only for fear of a law but also for conscience' sake. Masters should use their servants accordingly, paying them that which is due unto them. A father should bring up his children in the fear of God. Children should reverence their fathers with all submission."

(Wilson 210–11)

distributio[2] [L. "a division, distribution"] or *merismus* [G. "dividing, division"] or *divisio* [L. "a division"] or *diaeresis* [G. "dismantling, separating"]

Dividing the general into species, the whole into parts, and the subject into accidents for the sake of dilation, or vice versa

1. Adding to the species its genus or to the parts the whole
Demosthenes calls upon precedent by having a public inscription against bribery read during his speech and he amplifies the importance of this precedent by describing the scene (the whole) where this inscription (the part) stands visible: "[A]lthough the whole of our citadel [Acropolis] is a holy place, and although its area is so large, the inscription stands at the right hand beside the great brazen Athena which was dedicated by the state as a memorial of victory in the Persian war, at the expense of the Greeks" (*De Falsa Legatione* 272, trans. Vince).

(Hermogenes 1.11.278–79)

2. Amplifying a general statement by naming and perhaps describing all the particulars
"But ask now the beasts, and they shall teach thee; and the fowls of the air, and they shall tell thee: Or speak to the earth, and it shall teach thee: and the fishes of the sea shall declare unto thee. Who knoweth not in all these that the hand of the Lord hath wrought this? In whose hand is the soul of every living thing, and the breath of all mankind" (Job 12:7–10).

(Peacham ([1593] 123)

"He consumed all his substance in riot," when amplified, becomes, "Whatsoever patrimony he had from his father, what private enrichment by his deceased mother, what large assistance by friends, [. . .] what dowry soever by wife, which no doubt was very great, all this hath he consumed by a most dissolute and wanton living: money, plate, lands, wealth, possessions and all are gone to the devil, his cattle consumed, his household stuff sold, his apparel spent, and the poor miser at this instant hath not left him a farthing."

(Day 97)

3. Dividing a subject into its alternatives
"Had the king shown himself honest, Postumus would have been a monument of sagacity; as the king has deceived him, he is pronounced the greatest of fools" (Cicero, *Pro C. Rabirio Postumo* 1.1, trans. Watts).

(Sturm 3.15.657)

Note: Additional names are *catalogos* and *partitio*, and other spellings include *particio* or *diairesis*. Puttenham's name is "the Distributer" (230). Some rhetoricians, such as Sherry, Day, and Peacham, insist that this figure is used for amplification, not argument; others, such as Hermogenes, Melanchthon, Sturm and Puttenham, acknowledge its use in argument. Peacham's commentary on the example from Job above undermines the distinction between amplification and argument, however, for he explains that the distribution itself argues "their gross ignorance": "by which answer of Job to his friends he declareth that their wisdom was no other than such as the very brute beasts do daily teach, [. . .] whereby he doth pithily and elegantly set forth and amplify their gross ignorance" (123). Sometimes this figure is indistinguishable from those of the same names explicitly connected to the logical treatment of ideas. See the head-term *partitio* below under Logical–idea figures.

electio [L. "a choice, selection"]
Explaining that one is choosing to do something by necessity
"But I resolve thus, gentlemen, that in this case and in the practice of pleading, I must take up the right of piety rather than of defense, the role of complaint rather than of eloquence, and of grief rather than of ability" (Cicero, *Pro Sestio* 2.3, trans. Boswell).
(Trapezuntius 560)

emperibolon [G. "within boundaries"]
Placing divisions within divisions
1. In a sentence
"Therefore, this decree, by giving security to Charidemus, who is directing the affairs of king Cersobleptes, and by instilling fear and dread of being accused in the commanders of the other kings, [. . .] makes those kings weak, and the one who stands alone strong" (Demosthenes, *Against Aristocrates* 10–11, trans. Wooten).
(Hermogenes 1.11.292)

2. In a passage
"This remarkable, extraordinary favour on your part, Romans, I consider a great source of mental enjoyment and delight, but it causes me still more anxiety and solicitude. For my mind is occupied with many serious thoughts, which leave me no share of rest day or night—[thus far, a proposition, made by brief enumeration. Now follows analysis] above all, as regards maintaining the dignity of the consulate, a great and difficult task for anyone, but above all for myself, since no mistake of mine will meet with indulgence; if I am successful, little praise and that forced from unwilling people is in prospect; if I am in doubt, I can see no trustworthy counsel, if I am in difficulties, no loyal support.
But if I alone were brought into danger, I could endure it, Romans, with greater equanimity; but there appear to me to be certain men who, if they think that I have made some slight mistake concerning any matter not only intentionally but even by accident, will be ready to reproach you all for having preferred me to my noble competitors. [Thus far we have seen the first part of the enumeration; after an interval, another follows. . . .] In addition, to this I have a most laborious and difficult task before me in the manner of carrying on my consulship; for I have made up my mind that I ought to follow a different system and principle from those of my predecessors, some of whom have specially avoided the approach to this place and the sight of you, while others have not shown much enthusiasm in presenting themselves" (Cicero, *De Lege Agraria* II 2.5–6, trans. Freese).
(Sturm 3.15.645)

emphasis [G. "suggestion, hint"] or *significatio* [L. "an indication, mark, sign, token"]
Insinuating more than is said
1. Through tropes or circumlocutions
"An example of holy Job 17:14: 'I will say to corruption thou art my father, and to the worm thou art my mother and my sister.' By which saying, Job signifieth that his hope

in father and mother, in sister, and in all worldly matters should cease, & that the worms of the grave should be in their stead."

2. By placing stress on words
"'Darest thou presume to praise him?' That is [. . .] as much as to say: 'Is ignorance fit to commend learning, or folly meet to praise wisdom?'"

(Peacham [1593] 178)

3. By having several words or one sentence impart two ideas at once
"Her bow lay strung, her quiver full, her shield by her head; but they never loosen their belts." (The last clause describes the general custom among Amazons, as well as the particular action of this woman.)

(Demetrius §138)

Note: The English name is "the Renforcer" in Puttenham (194). This figure is a general one and can be created through many other figures. For example, Puttenham explains that the meaning can be added through "a word of more than ordinary efficacie" (194), Smith, through pronunciation (256), and Erasmus, by describing the signs that accompany something, i.e., the figure *annotation* (*De copia* 332). See *periphrasis* under semantical figures above. This figure is sometimes equated with *scematismus*. See *scematismus* below under Pragmatical–people figures. The third example above, that from Demetrius, should perhaps become its own figure.

enosis [G. "a shaking, quake"]

Making two different things into one by listing the different things as if alike; the opposite of *paradiastole*

"I labour to be brief, I turn obscure" (Horace, *Epistle* 2.3 "Art of Poetry" l. 25, trans. Butler).

(Quintilian 9.3.65)

Note: This figure extends through the next several lines of the poem as well. Here is a translation by Charles E. Passage: "I may seek terseness/ Only to wind up obscure; one who tries for a lightness of touch may/ Sacrifice sinew and spirit; the grandiose strays into bombast;" (l. 25–27).

enumeratio [L. "a counting up"] or *dinumeratio* [L. "a counting over, a reckoning up"] or *aparithmesis* [G. "a counting over"]

Numbering parts, species, causes, effects, accidents, antecedents, consequents, circumstances, things annexed, characteristics, etc.

1. With explicit numbering, or *arithmesis*:
"The two things which have the greatest influence in a state,—namely, the greatest interest, and eloquence, are both making against us at the present moment; and while I am awed by the one, O Caius Aquillius, I am in fear of the other" (Cicero, *Pro Quinctio* 1.1, trans. Yonge).

(Sturm 2.12.339)

2. Without numbering, or *aparithesis*:
"What may we think of man, when we consider the heavy burthen of his misery, the weakness of his patience, the imperfection of his understanding, the conflicts of his counsels, the insatiety of his mind, the brevity of his life, and the certainty of his death?"
"Anthony was the cause of civil war, of three slain armies of Roman people, of the death of many noble Citizens, of overthrowing the authority of the Senate, and finally of all evils whatsoever."

(Peacham [1593] 125–26)

Note: Additional names include *athroisis* and *anarithmesis.* Wilson calls this figure "reckoning" (230). Cicero and Quintilian treat *dinumeratio* and *enumeratio* as synonyms. Quintilian acknowledges that Cicero calls *dinumeratio* a figure (9.1.35), but disagrees (9.3.91) since *enumeratio* should occur regularly in the *partitio,* where it is called *distributio,* and in the *peroratio,* where it is called *recapitulatio.* However, Renaissance treatments loosen this stipulation, allowing any appearance of this device to be the figure. In the 1577 edition, Peacham distinguishes *dinumeratio,* numbering up many things in order to amplify (R.i.r) from *enumeratio,* which he lists twice, the first naming "when we gather together those things into a certain number, which straight way we doe briefly declare" (Q.iiii.v), by which he means the *distributio* belonging to the *partitio* (see Discoursal–parts below), and the second, when we list accidents, consequents, causes, circumstances, and effects (R.iii.v–iiii.v). In the second edition, *dinumeratio* has disappeared and *enumeratio* appears only once bearing the second of the definitions (125–26).

epanalepsis [G. "resumption"] or *circulo oratorio* [L. "making speech circular"]

1. Repeating the same idea in the same words
   See *epanalepsis* under syntactical figures above.
2. Repeating the same idea later in the passage or speech using the same words
   "When a speaker uses the same words in the exordium that he uses in the end of the speech."

   (Sturm 2.22.409)

3. Repeating the same idea in different words after a parenthesis, digression, or proofs
   "'Why have I begun by reviving these memories and quoting those old speeches? My first and chief object, men of Athens, is that when you hear me relate some performance that seems to you atrocious and incredible, no one may ask in surprise: 'Then why did you not speak out and give us this information instantly?' Then after interjecting many details and completing his argument on this point, he repeats what he had said earlier so that the argument will be clear: 'That, I say, is my first and main purpose in this narration." (Demosthenes, *De Falsa Legatione* 25–27, trans. Vince and Wooten).

   (Hermogenes 1.4.240)

Note: An alternate name is *renovatio verbi.* For the syntactical application of this figure, see the entry under syntactical figures above.

epanodos [G. "return"] or *regressio* [L. "a going back, return"]

Discussing a general statement part by part, but repeating the words used in the initial statement

1. In a sentence:
   "I never saw a fray more unequally made than that, that was between us today, I with bearing the blows, and he with giving them, till we were both weary" (Terence, *Adelphoe,* 2.2.211–13).

   (Peacham [1593] 129)

2. In a passage:
   "Love, hope and death, do stir in me much strife,
   As never man but I lead such a life:
   For burning love doth wound my heart to death:
   And when death comes at call of inward grief,
   Cold lingering hope doth feed my fainting breath:
   Against my will, and yields my wound relief,
   So that I live, and yet my life is such:
   As never death could grieve me half so much."

   (Puttenham 229)

Note: This figure is like *prolepsis*, but *prolepsis* does not require that the same words be repeated as each part is taken up. Alternate spellings are *epanodis* and *epanados*. Puttenham's English name is "the figure of Retire" (229). Peacham explains that this figure enriches "by partition of the whole and also to garnish the same by the variety of the several differences" ([1593] 129).

epexergasia [G. "continuous treatment"]

An intensified form of *exergasia:* returning often to the strongest and central proofs, clinching our argument through a reassertion of our proofs

Throughout Deuteronomy, Moses attempts to persuade the Hebrews to worship the God of Israel by continually reminding them of God's great goodness to them, but of the penalties that will befall them if they continue in their stubborn disregard for His commandments.

(Veltkirchius 168r)

Note: A synonym is *epexegaroia*. See *expolitio* below. Quintilian would rather regard this device as a method of embellishment, not a figure (8.3.88).

epiphonema [G. "a witty saying added as a finishing touch, or an exclamation"] or *acclamatio* [L. "an exclamation, a shout"]

A pithy, summative *sententia* attached to the close of a sentence, proof, or speech by way of climax and moral instruction

1. At the end of a sentence

   "If reason can persuade, if examples may move, if necessity may help, if pity may provoke, if dangers foreseen may stir us to be wise, I doubt not but you will rather use sharp laws to repress offenders than with dissolute negligence suffer all to perish."

   (Wilson 208)

2. At the end of proofs

   "Such toil it was to found the Roman race!" (Virgil, *Aeneid* I.33, trans. Butler).

   "The virtuous youth preferred to risk his life by slaying him to suffering such dishonor" (Cicero, *Pro Milone* 4.9, trans. Butler).

   (Quintilian 8.5.11)

3. At the end of a speech

   "[A]fter the true relation of Scipio Africanus his course, who, having been chief general of the greatest armies in the world, having all his lifetime kings suitors for his favor and nations kept in awe of his name; yet in fifty-six years never bought or sold goods or lands, never built any house or castle of his own, left not above 40 pounds in gold and 6 pounds in silver behind him at his death; it may be folded up in this acclamation: 'So little need hath he to stoop to private cares that thrives upon public victories, and so small leisure hath he to be desirous of riches, being but the means, who hath been so long possessed of honor, which is the mortal end of mortal actions.'"

   (Hoskins 34–35)

Note: An alternate spelling is *epithonema* or *epiphonesis*. Puttenham's English equivalent is "the Surclose or consenting close" (225). Quintilian categorizes this device as a reflexion, not a figure (8.5.11). In his first edition, Sherry conflates this figure with *exclamatio* (50), but in his second, he lists the two figures separately. Susenbrotus says this figure is particularly appropriate for epigrams (96). Melanchthon places this figure in the category of those deriving from the dialectical topic of genus (*Elem.* 53v).

epitrochasmus [G. "speaking trippingly, fluently; a rapid succession of statements"] or *celeritas* [L. "swiftness, quickness, speed"] or *percursio* [L. "a running through or over"]

A running forward, or rapid movement from one idea to the next

1. In a connected style, using *polysyndeton*

"Two years ago the tribe of Pandionis had failed to appoint a chorus-master, and when the Assembly met at which the law directs the Archons to assign the flute-players by lot to the choruses, there was a heated discussion and mutual recrimination between the Archon and the overseers of the tribe. Thereupon I came forward and volunteered to act as chorus-master, and at the drawing of the lots I was fortunate enough to get the first choice of a flute-player." (Demosthenes, *Against Meidias* 13, trans. Vince)

(Hermogenes 2.1.314)

2. In a disconnected style, using *asyndeton*

"They do not send weapons? And everyone from the city follows? And they are pulling up rafts from other ships? Go, bear flames, pass out spears, push the oars." (Virgil, *Aeneid* 4.596–98, trans. Green)

(Scaliger 3.44.315)

Note: This figure has also been described as a rapid summary without elaboration, being the opposite of *hypotyposis* and *amplificatio* (see Cicero, *De Or* 3.202). Other names include *collectio*, *praecipitatio*, *procursio*, *impressio* and *expeditio*. This figure is the *epitrechon* applied to a passage and helps to create *gorgeteta*, the rapid, running style. In fact, Scaliger equates it with *gorgeteta* (315). See *gorgotes* below under Discoursal–styles. There is a discrepancy between the Loeb text of Cicero's *De Oratore* (3.202) and Quintilian's quotation of the same text in the Loeb edition (9.1.28). In the first, Cicero's word is *praecisio*, the synonym for *aposiopesis*, and in the second, the word is *percursio*. It makes more sense to read *percursio* here, since Cicero has already listed *aposiopesis* as a separate figure.

ergasia [G. "working at, development, treatment"] or *tractatio* [L. "the treatment, handling, discussion of a subject"]

Developing or handling a point or an argument by adding support

1. Description

"Again, we see that the discovery of what to say is wholly insufficient, unless you can handle it when found. But the handling should be diversified, so that your hearer may neither perceive the art of it, nor be worn out by too much monotony. You ought to formulate your proposition, and give the reasons for its being what it is; and from those same commonplaces you should sometimes draw your conclusion, and sometimes abandon them to pass elsewhere; often it is better not to formulate expressly, but to make it plain, by affirming the underlying principle, what the formulation would have been; if you are putting a parallel case to something, you should first show how it is like, and then annex the matter in hand; as a rule you should conceal the intervals between successive proofs, to prevent them from being counted, so that, separate in fact, they may seem blended in statement."

(Cicero, *De Oratore* 2.177)

2. Example

The proposition: "It is permitted to the city to do what it wants with its own." The *ergasia*: "for it is permitted to each master to do what he wants in his own house."

The proposition: "It is a good thing to honor parents." The *ergasia*: "for even wild beasts do this."

(Hermogenes, *Invention* 3.7.150)

Note: Neither Cicero nor Hermogenes identify *ergasia* as a figure, but Sturm and Robertellus do.

erroris inductio [L. "leading into, introducing, admitting error"]
Discovering that we have thought otherwise than the truth is

1. Ironically, with pretended ignorance
"Who would have thought that he ever would have done so? Now of all men upon earth, I would have least suspected him. But such is the world."

(Wilson 213)

"But the sculptor of those pictures—who was he? Now who was he? Oh, yes, thank you; they said it was Polyclitus." (Cicero, *In C. Verrem* II 4.3.5, trans. Flynn)

(Soarez 360)

2. Sincerely
"You think such a man a worthy personage and of much honesty, but I will prove that he is much otherwise; a man would not think it, but if I do not prove it, I will give you my head."

(Wilson 213)

Note: Quintilian only allows the ironical use to be the figure (9.2.61).

eudiasis [G. "fair weather, calmness"] or *attemperatio* [G. "tranquility, temperateness"]
Moderating the speech by using qualifiers, such as "I believe" or "in my opinion"
"The Spartans seem to me to be doing the work of dangerous men" (Demosthenes, *For the People of Megalopolis* 16, trans. Wooten).

(Hermogenes 2.6.350)

Palinurus interjects "I believe" in his recommendation to Aeneas that they dock at Sicily:
"The friendly shore
Of your half-brother Eryx, Sicilian ports,
Lie not far distant, I believe, if only
I still recall the way to steer by stars
I watched before." (Virgil, *Aeneid* 5:25–29, trans. Lind)

(Scaliger 3.36.310)

Note: Hermogenes considers this approach a kind of *endoiasis*, i.e., hesitation (2.6.350). See *aporia* under Pragmatical–people figures below.

evasio [L. "a going out"]
Touching on a point, but not dwelling on it nor explaining it
"Do not dwell on the concession of his murder."

(Scaliger 3.45.315)

Note: An alternate name is *decrectare*. Robertellus attributes this figure to Celsus (45r). Scaliger points out that this figure helps create brevity. This figure may correspond with the second meaning of *metastasis* below.

exaggeratio [L. "a raising up, elevation"]
Heightening by mentioning singular, special, or well-chosen details
"What we require, Aeschines, is not oratory with enfolded hands, but diplomacy with enfolded hands" (Demosthenes, *De Falsa Legatione* 255, trans. Vince).

(Demetrius §277)

Euryalus' mother laments over the death of her son:

"Can this I see be you, the late and last
Resource of my old age? How could you leave me alone,
Euryalus, cruel boy? And I, your wretched mother,
Could not speak to you before you died
Upon a mission of so great a danger.
Ah, in an unknown land you lie, the prey
Of Latin dogs and birds. Your mother could not
Follow your corpse to burial, close your eyes
In death or wash the wounds upon your body,
Cover you with the robe which day and night
I hastily wove for you, consoling the sorrow
Of an old woman with its web and woof.
Where shall I follow you now? What earth shall hold
Your mangled limbs, your corpse? Are these remains
What you have brought me? Is it for this I followed
Over the land and sea? Turn all your spears
On me, if you have pity! Rutulians, kill
Me first, or you, great father of the gods,
Thrust down this head to Tartarus with your bolt,
Since otherwise I cannot end the cruelty
Of life." (Virgil, *Aeneid* 9.488–508, trans. Lind)

(Scaliger 3.46.315)

exclusio [L. "a shutting out, exclusion"]

Excluding points that are useless, dishonest, or incommodious to us, or while harmless to us, beneficial to the adversary

"Let it not be permitted for me to take a nap out in the open."

(Scaliger 3.61.334)

Note: This feature may correspond with *excludere*, a figure Quintilian (9.2.104) and Robertellus (45r) draw from Celsus and both discount.

exegesis [G. "explanation, interpretation"] or *epexegesis* [G. "an extended explanation"]

Adding an interpretation or exposition of a word, statement, or passage

1. Of a word

   "I know that in me, that is to say, in my flesh dwelleth no good thing" (Romans 7:18).

   (Peacham [1593] 191)

2. Of a statement

   "Time at one instant seeming both short and long, short in the pleasingness in calling to mind, long in the stay of his desires" (Sidney, *Arcadia*, book 1, 96).

   (Smith 206)

3. Of a passage

   Interpretation of Romans 2:5–10: "When shall be opened 'the righteous judgement of God, which will reward every man according to his deeds.' That is to say, praise, honor, and immortality to them which continue in well doing, and seek immortality: but unto them that are rebels, and do not obey the truth, but follow unrighteousness, shall come indignation, wrath, tribulation, etc."

   (Peacham [1593] 191)

Note: Additional names include *enarratio*, *ephexegesis*, and *explicatio*. Gill associates this figure with *enargia* (160). When a prolonged explication, this figure comes to include the genre of commentary (Veltkirchius 173v).

expolitio [L. "a polishing, finishing, adorning, embellishing"] or *exergasia* [G. "working out, bringing to completion"]

Dwelling on the same point, but in varied words, figures, and delivery; the development of an argument

1. Dwelling on the same topic, but seeming to say something new
   a. By a change of words
   Psalm 35:1–8: "(1) Plead my cause (O Lord) with them that strive with me: fight against them that fight against me; (2) Take hold of shield and buckler, and stand up for mine help; (3) Draw out also the spear, and stop the way against them that persecute me: say unto my soul, I am thy salvation. (4) Let them be confounded and put to shame that seek after my soul: let them be turned back and brought to confusion that devise my hurt. (5) Let them be as chaff before the wind: and let the angel of the Lord chase them. (6) Let their way be dark and slippery: and let the angel of the Lord persecute them. (7) For without cause have they hid for me their net in a pit, which without cause they have digged for my soul. (8) Let destruction come upon him at unawares; and let his net that he hath hid catch himself: into that very destruction let him fall."

   (Smith 222)

   b. By a change of pronunciation and gesture
   "'Sextus Roscius is convicted that he slew his father.' Now this is said with a plain pronunciation: 'Did Sextus Roscius slay his father?' with an interrogation which is full of marvelling: and likewise that which the Orator hath uttered in hot and vehement speech, he may repeat again with cool and quiet words." (cf. Cicero, *Pro S. Roscio* 13.37)

   (Peacham [1593] 194)

   c. By a change of figures
   "Cicero when he had reckoned up many mischievous deeds of Catiline and many of his wicked doings practiced against the commonwealth, and had accused him most grievously in the Senate, he commanded him to get out of the City. He changed the handling of his sentence and translateth his speech to *Prosopopoeia*: whereby he feigneth the country chiding with Catiline and rehearseth in order all his ungracious, mischievous, and unlucky deeds enterprised against it, accusing him sore and willing him to depart out of it: 'No abominable or wicked deed has been heard or seen these many years but through thee, no naughty facts without thee. Thou only hast slain many citizens and never yet been punished. Thou hast vexed and robbed thy fellows and nothing said unto thee. Thou has not only been able to neglect laws and statutes, but also to overthrow them and break them in pieces. I endured as I could those earlier deeds, although they ought not to have been borne, but now that I should be wholly in fear on account of you alone, that, at the slightest sound, Catiline should be feared, that no plan, it seems, can be undertaken against me uninspired by your villainy, that is not to be borne. Therefore depart and free me from this terror; if it is well founded, that I may not be overwhelmed; if it is false, that now at last I may cease to fear.'" (*In Catilinam* I 7.18)

   (Peacham [1593] 194)

2. Developing a theme or argument through a variety of methods

"[Proposition, with Reasons subjoined] The wise man will, on the republic's behalf, shun no peril, because it may often happen that if a man has been loath to perish for his country it will be necessary for him to perish with her. Further, since it is from our country that we receive all our advantages, no disadvantage incurred on her behalf is to be regarded as severe.

[Restatement] I say, then, that they who flee from the peril to be undergone on behalf of the republic act foolishly, for they cannot avoid the disadvantages, and are found guilty of ingratitude towards the state.

[Argument from the contrary] But on the other hand they who, with peril to themselves, confront the perils of the fatherland, are to be considered wise, since they render to their country the homage due her, and prefer to die for many of their fellow citizens instead of with them. For it is extremely unjust to give back to nature, when she compels, the life you have received from nature, and not to give to your country, when she calls for it, the life you have preserved thanks to your country; and when you can die for fatherland with the greatest manliness and honour, to prefer to live in disgrace and cowardice; and when you are willing to face danger for friends and parents and your other kin, to refuse to run the risk for the republic, which embraces all these and that most holy name of fatherland as well.

[Argument from the comparison] He, who in a voyage prefers his own to his vessel's security, deserves contempt. No less blameworthy is he who in a crisis of the republic consults his own in preference to the common safety. For from the wreck of a ship many of those on board escape unharmed, but from the wreck of the fatherland no one can swim to safety.

[Argument from example] It is this that, in my opinion, Decius well understood, who is said to have devoted himself to death, and, in order to save his legions, to have plunged into the midst of the enemy. He gave up his life, but did not throw it away; for at the cost of a very cheap good he redeemed a sure good, of a small good the greatest good. He gave his life, and received his country in exchange. He lost his life and gained glory, which, transmitted with highest praise, shines more and more every day as time goes on.

[Conclusion] But if reason has shown and illustration confirmed that it is fitting to confront danger in defence of the republic, they are to be esteemed wise who do not shrink from any peril when the security of the fatherland is at stake."

(*Ad Herennium* 4.43.56–44.57)

Note: An alternate spelling is *exargasia*. Puttenham calls this figure "the Gorgious" (254). In the second example above we have the instructions and model for a *chreia*, one of the *progymnasmata*. Erasmus (*De copia* 630), Susenbrotus (90–91), Sherry ([1550] 93–96), and Peacham ([1577] Q.i.r-v; [1593] 194–95) quote this example in full from the *Ad Herennium*, and Sturm provides a similar analysis of Cicero's methods of development in *Pro Lege Manilia* (1.26.89–96). Susenbrotus explains that *expolitio* on the verbal level equals *synonymia*, whereas on the content level it equals the development of a theme. Melanchthon places this figure in the genus of those that derive from the dialectical topic of definition (*Elem.* 48r). To Quintilian, this is a method of embellishment, not a figure (8.3.88).

frequentatio[1] [L. "frequency, a crowding together"] or *sinathrismus* [G. "assemblage, collection"] or *anacephalaeosis* [G. "a summary"]

Gathering together points from the whole into a dense summary, a recapitulation

"If reason can persuade, if examples may move, if necessity may help, if pity may provoke, if dangers foreseen may stir us to be wise, I doubt not but you will rather use sharp laws to repress offenders than with dissolute negligence suffer all to perish."

(Wilson 208)

"Thus when all is done, what vice is he free from, what is the cause Judges why you would deliver him? He is a betrayer of his own chastity; he lieth in wait to do mischief; he is covetous, intemperate, vicious, proud, wicked to his parents, unkind to his friends, troublesome to his kin, stubborn to his betters, disdainful to his equals, cruel to his inferiors, finally intolerable to all men."

(Peacham [1593] 151)

Note: An alternate spelling is *synathroismos*. Sometimes *frequentatio* is distinguished from *congeries* and sometimes not. For example, Sherry refers to both the list within a sentence (*congeries*) and the gathering together of the argument's details (*frequentatio*) as *sinathrismus* ([1550] 50). Puttenham, however, restricts *sinathrismus* to the word list and calls the collecting of one's former points "the collectour" or the "recapitulatour" (243–44), i.e., *frequentatio*. Peacham also distinguishes the word list, *symphoresis*, ([1593] 128) from the summarizing of one's points, *frequentatio* (151). Like Puttenham, Peacham, and Keckermann, Wilson very clearly associates this figure with the epilogue of the argument by calling it "the conclusion, or lapping-up of matter" (208). This recapitulation need not come only in the peroration, of course, but as a conclusion to a digression or to individual parts of the argument. Nevertheless, the lack of strictness in Renaissance texts differs from many earlier texts wherein this device is only a figure when used outside of the peroration (cf. Fortun. 2.31). In fact, *anacephalaeosis* is the standard term for the summary in the epilogue (see Hermogenes, *On Issues* 52.11), along with *enumeratio* (Quintilian 6.1.1) and *recapitulatio* (Fortun 2.31).

frequentatio[2] [L. "frequency, a crowding together"]

Multiple repetitions together of the same idea

The Sausage-seller competes with Paphlagon, the wheedling sycophant, in the following exchange:

Paph: To the Lady who over the city presides, to our mistress Athene, I pray
If beyond all the rest I am stoutest and best, in the service of Demus today,
Except Salabaccho, and Cynna the bold, and Lysicles—then in the Hall
May I dine as of late at the cost of the State for doing just nothing at all.
But O if I hate you, nor stride to the van to protect you from woes and mishaps,
Then slay me, and flay me, and saw me to bits, to be cut into martingale strips.
S.S.: And I, if I love you not, Demus, am game to be slaughtered by chopping and mincing,
And boiled in a sausage-meat pie; and if THAT is, you think, not entirely convincing,
Let me here, if you please, with a morsel of cheese, upon this to a salad be grated,
Or to far Cerameicus be dragged through the streets with my flesh-hook, and there be cremated. (Aristophones, *Knights* 767–72, trans. Rogers)

(Scaliger 3.42.314)

Note: This repetition seems very similar to *commoratio*, but Scaliger keeps this figure distinct. The passage cited above is a clearer example than the one Scaliger cites from *Knights*, and so I have substituted it for his.

gesticulatio [L. "pantomimic motion, gesticulation"]
Using gestures

Gnatho gestures toward the foolish major Thraso, who is standing apart, when he says, "By way of requital to you, Phaedria, and you, Chaerea, I present the main course, a bountiful source of nourishment and laughs. Eat hearty." (Terence, *Eunucho* 5.9.186–87, trans. Parker).

(Veltkirchius 167r)

hypotyposis [G. "sketch, outline"] or *diatyposis* [G. "full and perfect shape; vivid description"] or *demonstratio* [L. "a showing or pointing out"] or *energasia* [G. "a working into"]
Making vivid, bringing the matter before the eyes

1. Through description

"If one were to say that a city had been taken by storm, he would of course imply by such an overall statement all the subsidiary events that such a calamity admits. But, to go on in the exact words of Quintilian: 'If you make explicit everything included in this one phrase, we shall witness the flames spreading through homes and temples, and the crash of falling buildings, and all the cries blending into one overriding sound; some people fleeing, not knowing where they are going, others locked in a last embrace of their loved ones, the wails of babies and women, and old men cruelly preserved by fate to see this day; then we shall see the inevitable plundering of secular and sacred, the running to and fro of men carrying off loot or looking for more, prisoners in chains, each in the charge of his personal robber, mothers resisting the abduction of their children, and, wherever anything of greater value has come to light, the victors fighting among themselves (8.3.67ff).'"

(Erasmus, *De copia* 577–78)

2. By casting the audience in the role of the afflicted

"Go to your bosom,
Knock there, and ask your heart what it doth know
That's like my brother's fault. If it confess
A natural guiltiness such as is his,
Let it not sound a thought upon your tongue
Against my brother's life." (Shakespeare, *Measure for Measure* 2.2.136–40)

(Trapezuntius 548; example mine)

Note: An alternate spelling is *hypotiposis* and an additional name *repraesentatio*. Erasmus and Sherry indicate that the following figures all help to create *hypotyposis*: *effiguratio*, *prosopopoeia*, *characterismus*, *prosopographria*, *ethopoeia*, *pathopoeia*, *sermocinatio*, *mimesis*, *topographia*, *topothesia*, and *chronographia*. Peacham uses this same text from Quintilian as an example of *pragmatographia* ([1577] O.iiii.v; [1593] 139–40). *Hypotyposis* sometimes becomes identified with lively description in general (see *descriptio* under Discoursal-genres). Contrarily, Soarez uses *descriptio* as a synonym here (344). Scaliger wants *tractatio* to refer to various descriptions of people (3.33.307) and *demonstratio* to be descriptions of things (3.34.309). He also indicates that *hypotyposis* acts as a weaker and simpler form of *apodeixis*. See *apodeixis* under Logical—evidence figures below. Melanchthon places this figure in the category of those deriving from the dialectical topic of circumstance (*Elem.* 54v). *Enargeia* is another term that evokes this same figure, but I list it separately under virtues since it most precisely means "vividness," while *hypotyposis* is the means by which this vividness is created.

hysteron proteron [G. "the latter before the former"] or *hysterologia* [G. "speaking last"] or *anastrophe* [G. "turning back, inversion"]

Putting the second idea or event before the first; putting the posterior before the prior

1. In a sentence

"Pluck off my boots and spurs."

(Sherry [1550] 31)

"[the posterior] Thanks to the arrival of Publius Sestius, the new tribunes of the commons, [the prior] who at the time, during the last days of my consulship, were eager to attack what I had accomplished, [back to the posterior] found their assaults and endeavors thwarted, as did the remnants of the conspirators" (Cicero, *Pro Sestio* 5.11, trans. Gardner).

(Sturm 3.14.634)

"'I kissed her cherry lip and took my leave,' for 'I took my leave and kissed her.'"

(Puttenham 181)

2. In a passage

"Am I a consul to fear an assembly of the people, to dread a tribune of the people, to be greatly agitated frequently and without reason, to be afraid of going to live in a prison, if a tribune give orders for me to be taken thither? [Thus far his proposition; next follows that *anastrophe* of proposition and reason.] I, since I am armed with your arms and equipped with the most honourable insignia of my office, with your command and authority, I am not afraid to be able to come forward upon this tribunal and, with you to support me, to resist the wickedness of this man, and I have no fear that the republic, fortified by such strong protectors, can be conquered or crushed by men like these" (Cicero, *De Lege Agraria* II. 37.101, trans. Freese).

(Sturm 3.14.638)

3. In a narrative, or *peribeblemenon* [G. "a throwing around"]

Homer begins the *Iliad* in the middle of things (*in medias res*).

(Sturm 3.14.636)

Note: *Praeposteratio* and *hyperbaton* are other synonyms sometimes. Puttenham calls this figure "the Preposterous" (181). Each of the above terms have either grammatical or syntactical applications as well. See the entries for these terms under grammatical and syntactical figures. Also see *hysteron proteron* under vices.

illustris explanatio [L. "clear, bright, lustrous explanation"]

Clear explanation

"You may perhaps ask, what is the meaning of that terror, that dread, which prevents so many and such eminent men from consenting, in accordance with their constant practice, to plead the cause of one whose civil rights and property are at stake. It is not surprising that you are still in ignorance of this, since the accusers have purposely avoided mentioning the real reason that has brought about this trial. What then is this reason? The property of the father of my client Sextus Roscius is valued at 6,000,000 sesterces, and it is from a most valiant and illustrious citizen, Lucius Sulla (whose name I mention with respect), that a young man, at the present time perhaps the most powerful in the State, claims to have bought the same for 2000 sesterces—I mean Lucius Cornelius Chrysogonus. What he demands from you is this, that because the excuse for his demand was his illegal seizure of this rich and splendid property of another, and because the existence of Sextus Roscius appears to be a hindrance and an obstacle to his enjoyment of it, you should therefore remove all uneasiness from his mind and put an end to his apprehension. As long as Sextus Roscius is alive, Chrysogonus thinks himself unable to retain possession of the large and rich inheritance of an innocent man like my client; but if he is condemned and driven out of his country, he hopes to be able to squander and dissipate in luxury and extravagance what he has obtained by crime. He calls upon you to remove this anxiety from his mind, which torments and stings him night and day, and to avow yourselves his supporters in securing this ill-gotten booty" (Cicero, *Pro S. Roscio* 2.5–6, trans. Freese).

(Cicero, *De Oratore* 3.202; example mine)

Note: Quintilian would rather regard this embellishment as a method than a figure (9.2.2).

incrementum [L. "growth, increase, augmentation"] or *auxesis* [G. "growth, increase"] or *akme* [G. "peak"]

Mounting by degrees to a culmination or climax, whether in language, thought, or delivery

1. In language

The case: "A man killed his son in the presence of his mother in accordance with the law about those not brought to trial. The mother dropped dead, and the father is being tried as responsible for her death." In the trial, the prosecutor says: "And finding him with her, he struck, he wounded, he murdered his son together with his wife, as though they were strangers, as personal enemies, as born from some enemy of the state. Who is not outraged, who is not infuriated, who is not angered at what has been done? Who does not demand condign punishment? Has not the house been filled with pollution, [have there not been] unlawful killings, impious slaughter, a whole family murderously snatched from life, by the very person whom one would least expect?"

(Hermogenes, *Invention* 2.7.125)

"He first set upon him with reproachful words, after assailed him with his weapons, then wounded him, and lastly did most miserably murder him."

"Gold, riches, honor, estate, treasure, kingdoms, life, and all he held of no moment."

(Day 91–92)

2. In ideas

"[F]or when Philip was moving hither and thither, subduing Illyrians and Triballians, and some Greeks as well, when he was gradually getting control of large military resources, and when certain Greek citizens, including Aeschines, were availing themselves of the liberty of the peace to visit Macedonia and take bribes, all these movements were really acts of war upon the states against which Philip was making his preparations. That they failed to perceive it is another story, and does not concern me. My forebodings and expostulations were unceasing; I uttered them in the Assembly and in every city to which I was sent. But all the cities were demoralized. The active politicians were venal and corrupted by the hope of money: the unofficial classes and the people in general were either blind to the future or ensnared by the listlessness and indolence of their daily life; in all the malady had gone so far that they expected the danger to descend anywhere but upon themselves, and even hoped to derive their security at will from the perils of others. In the result, of course, the excessive and inopportune apathy of the common people has been punished by the loss of their independence, while their leaders, who fancied they were selling everything except themselves, discover too late that their own liberty was the first thing they sold. Instead of the name of trusty friend, in which they are dubbed toad-eaters and scoundrels, and other suitable epithets. What did they expect? Men of Athens, it is not because he wants to do a traitor a good turn that a man spends his money; nor, when he has once got what he paid for, has he any further use for the traitor's counsels. Otherwise treason would be the most profitable of all trades. But it is not so. How could it be? Far from it! As soon as the man who grasps at power has achieved his purpose, he is the master of those who sold him his mastery; and then—yes, then!—knowing their baseness, he loathes them, mistrusts them, and reviles them. Look at these instances [. . . .] From these examples it may be clearly discerned that the man who is most vigilant in defence of his country and most vigorous in his opposition to treason—he is the man, Aeshines, who provides you traitors and mercenaries with something that you can betray for a bribe; and, if you are still secure and still drawing your pay, you owe this to the great majority of these citizens, and to those who thwarted your purposes—for your own efforts would long ago have brought you to destruction" (Demosthenes, *De Corona* 44–49, trans. Vince).

(Hermogenes, *Invention* 4.4.189–90)

"If thou hadst done or spoken this in a private audience, among men of the ruder and meaner sort, among such as are less capable of skill than a great many others, thy fault could not have been hid: but to do it before thy betters, in the presence of such as are adjudged both honorable and wise, in the hearing of those of great account, of such as have power to check and authority to compel thee, it was too, too peevish."

(Day 92)

2. In actions

Incrementum speaks, "I am that *Figure*, Sir, whereby men rise from lesser and lower degrees still higher and higher. By me men rise from *Freshmen* to *Sophisters*, from thence to *Curates*, from thence to *Parsons*, from thence to *Dignitaries*. Others from *discontent* to *preaching*, from thence to *plotting*, from thence to *fighting*, from thence to *killing*, and so to *succeeding*. And all men that can hit of the knack of it, from *pence* to *shillings*, from thence to *pounds*, from thence to *hundreds*, from thence to *thousands*, from thence to *tens of thousands*, and so on *in infinitum*. [. . .] The spiritual *Tyrants* take away first the *Estates* of the Hereticks, then their *liberty*, then their *lives*; and of their Proselytes, first the *senses*, then the *reason*, then the *faith*. In a word, by me all men grow rich, wise, honourable, virtuous."

(Shaw 158–59)

Note: Puttenham's English name is "the Avancer" (226). Gill explains that this figure is a *climax* without the *anadiplosis* (161) and Smith retains the understanding of this figure as a species of *climax* (133). See *climax* above. Melanchthon lists this figure as a species deriving from the dialectical topic of division (*Elem.* 50r). Quintilian prefers to categorize this device as a method, not a figure (8.4.3).

innvitio [L. "an invitation, summons, challenge"]

Asserting indirectly and so inviting audience participation in the interpretative act

When Dido defends her suicide, she charges herself with having lived as beasts do, without wedlock and conscience. This self-accusation, however, endorses marriage and shows that she accepts responsibility for her mistake, on account of which she regains honor in her death. But this conclusion remains unspoken:

"I was not permitted to live
Free from a marriage, without reproach, like a beast
Untouched by despair" (Virgil, *Aeneid* 4.552–53, trans. Lind).

(Scaliger 3.80.347)

Note: Scaliger creates this figure and considers it a type of *reticentia* created through circling round a point and thereby requiring the higher and fuller intellect to decipher. Having in mind that this figure is a method of engaging the audience in one's thought process and thereby obtaining identification and winning support, he speculates that the Greek *ennoian* ("thought, reflection, cogitation") could be a synonym (3.80.347). Using this same example to illustrate *emphasis*, Quintilian interprets this quotation from Dido as follows: Even though she "complains of marriage, this passionate outburst shows that she regards life without wedlock as no life for man, but for the beasts of the field" (9.2.64). See *emphasis* under Pragmatical–idea figures above.

interrogatio [L. "a questioning, inquiry, examination"]
Asking for an answer

"Tell us (say they) for whose cause is this evil come upon us? what is thine occupation? and whence comest thou?" (Jonas 1:8)

(Smith 137)

Note: Wilson calls the genuine question *interrogatio* and distinguishes it from *percontatio* or *epiplexis*, the question that chides or sets forth emotion with greater vehemency. Susenbrotus calls the geniune question *pynthanomai*, meaning "to learn through inquiry" (58). Peacham includes both the genuine question and the question that creates vehemency within *interrogatio*, calling only the second figurative ([1593] 105). Smith includes all three kinds of questions within *erotesis* (135–40). Quintilian denies that the genuine question is a figure (9.2.7). Contrarily, Sturm applies the figure *interrogatio* to investigation of any kind (1.25.79–83). See *interrogatio* below under Pragmatical–people figures for the other kinds of questions considered figurative.

inversio [L. "an inversion"] or *metastasis* [G. "a removal"] or *antistrophe* [G. "a turning about"]
Turning what was against us for us

1. By returning the accusation to the accuser and making him the defendant, or *antenklematiko* [G. "counter-accusation"]

Aeschines says that "Philip will be antagonized if you (the Athenian jury) vote to condemn those who arranged the peace," threatening the Athenians with Philip's anger. Demosthenes responds that it is arguments such as this one that have brought about the fall of other cities to Philip (*De Falsa Legatione* 78, 134, trans. Kennedy).

(Hermogenes, *Invention* 3.3.138–39)

"When *Antony* charged *Cicero* that he was the cause of civil war raised between *Pompeius* and *Caesar*, *Cicero* rebounded the same accusation again to *Antony*, saying: 'Thou *Marcus Antony*, thou I say gavest to *Caesar* (willing to turn all upside down) cause to make war against thy country'" (*Philippic* 2.23, 53).

"When *Ahab* likewise charged *Elia* [Elijah], that it was he which troubled all *Israel*, 'Nay,' saith *Elia*, 'It is not I that trouble *Israel*, but thou and thy father's house, in that you have forsaken the commandments of the Lord, and thou hast followed *Baal*'" (1 Kings 18:17–18).

(Peacham [1593] 181–82)

2. By offering a contrasting interpretation of an act

If the opponent remarks, "You have buried him, therefore you have killed him," we may respond, "Indeed, if I had killed him, I should not have buried him. For a man who stops on a public road near a corpse while he buries him, at a place where it is likely that others will come upon him, is not conscious of having done anything bad; that is evident from his assurance of mind."

(Melanchthon, *Elem.* 52v)

"*Romulus* drinking sparingly: at supper one said unto him, 'If all men did so, wine would be cheaper than it is.' To whom *Romulus* answered, 'Yea, but it would be rather dearer, if every one drank as much as he would; for I have drunk as much as I desire.'"

(Smith 126)

Note: In argument, this species of refutation is called *anticategoria* (Quintilian 3.10.4), *biaion* (Hermogenes, *Inv.* 3.3), or *violatio* (Erasmus *DCE* 114), and the contradictory interpretation of evidence is called *antistrephon*, the retort argument (Melanchthon, *Elem.* 15v). Melanchthon lists this figure as one deriving from the dialectical topic of contraries, but also involving causes and circumstances (*Elem.* 52r).

katastasis [G. "a presentation"] or *praemonitio* [L. "foreshadowing"]

Introducing one's forthcoming rebuttal, chain of reasoning, exposition, expression of emotion, or behavior; announcing what one will do

1. In argument

"But before I speak about the accusation itself, I will say a few words about the hopes of the accusers" (Cicero, *Pro Deiotaro* 2.7, trans. Watts).

(Trapezuntius 526)

"Briefly, judges, I will respond to this matter."

(Sturm 3.24.729)

2. In expressing emotion

"Give me the right to call him a lewd fellow" (Aeschines, *On the Embassy* 88, trans. Wooten).

(Hermogenes 2.7.358)

Note: An additional name is *proanaphonesis* [G. "a prediction or warning"]. This advance notice, Hermogenes explains, decreases the impression of sincerity (2.7.355). For the more sincere expression, see *apostasis* above, the figure opposite to this one.

leptologia [G. "discuss in quibbling fashion"]

Elaborating or demonstrating a detail of the whole

For example, if the Gauls are at a luxurious feast, we can elaborate as follows:

"There was noise. There was a loud cry of women. There was music from the orchestra. It seemed to me that I saw some entering and others leaving; one part was reeling from the wine, another was yawning from the drinking bout of yesterday. One Gaul, covered in perfume, was being turned about among them, his head topped with a crown. The ground had been dirtied with wine, with the heads of the languid, and with the bones of fish."

(Aquila §2)

Note: Aquila calls this figure a species of *diatyposis*, but distinguishes because here the details are demonstrated, whereas in *diatyposis* the whole is demonstrated. Veltkirchius considers this figure a vice of overelaboration (9v).

macrologia [G. "speaking at length"] or *perioysia* [G. "that which is over and above, surplus, superiority of numbers or force, speaking at length"]

Using redundancy

1. Adding a redundant phrase or clause for emphasis or weight

"Men of so high and excelling virtue, let them ever live and never die."

(Day 82)

"And vanquished them unable to withstand" (Spenser, *The Faerie Queene* I 10.65.5)
"He followed and pursued fast" (*The Faerie Queene* VI 4.18.9)

(Gill 157)

2. Adding redundancy throughout a passage
Kent berates Oswald, Goneril's servant, in this wise: "A knave, a rascal, an eater of broken meats; a base, proud, shallow, beggerly, three-suited, hundred-pound, filthy worsted-stocking knave; a lily-liver'd, action-taking, whoreson, glass-gazing, superserviceable, finical rogue; one-trunk-inheriting slave; one that wouldst be a bawd in way of good service, and art nothing but the composition of a knave, beggar, coward, pandar, and the son and heir of a mungril bitch; one whom I will beat into [clamorous] whining, if thou deni'st the least syllable of thy addition" (Shakespeare, *King Lear* 2.2.15–24).

(Robertellus 49v; example mine)

Note: Sometimes *perissologia* is taken as a synonym here. Both *macrologia* and *perissologia* are also considered vices when the redundancy is truly unnecessary. See the terms under vices below. Robertellus points out that this strategy is useful for anger to the extent that it reproves (49v).

metabole [G. "exchange, barter; a change of direction"]

1. Changing one's direction in mid-course
"Two hounds were leashed in front of the courtyard. I can tell you the actual names of the hounds. But why should I want to tell you their names?" (Telemachus, unknown).

(Demetrius §148).

2. Amassing a combination of details together; the opposite of *dissipatio*
"I am intentionally omitting many details for fear that even those I have mentioned may seem all too many: you must, however, understand that Oppinanicus was ever himself, at other periods of his life as at this. He it was whom the Town Council of Larinum adjudged by a unanimous finding to have falsified the public records of their censors, with whom no one would have any pecuniary transactions, nor any dealings whatsoever, whom not one of all his kinsmen and connexions ever appointed by will as trustee to his children. No one thought that it was decent to call upon him, to meet him in society, to converse with him, or to ask him to dinner. Everyone shrank from him, everyone loathed him, everyone avoided him as a savage and dangerous brute, a very scourge." (Cicero, *Pro Cluentio* 14.41, trans. Hodge)

(Quintilian 9.3.38)

Note: Robertellus says the second use of this figure creates *epitrochasmos* (24v). See *epitrochasmos* above. See the entries under rhythmical, lexical, and qualitative figures for other uses of the term *metabole*.

metastasis [G. "a removal"] or *translatio* [L. "a carrying or removing from one place to another"] or *transmotio* [L. "a transposition"]

Shifting grounds

1. *Trajectio in alium* [L. "a throwing or putting off upon another"], shifting the blame to someone or something else
   a. A shifting of responsibility
   "Gracchus, when accused of making the treaty with the Numantines [. . .] may plead that he made it as the representative of his commander-in-chief."

"A person who has failed to comply with some testamentary injunction may plead that the laws forbade such compliance."

(Quintilian 7.4.13–14)

b. A shifting of guilt
Cicero says to Tubero, who is guilty of the same offense as Ligarius: "You must needs therefore plead guilty to your own offence, before you proceed to arraign that of Ligarius" (*Pro Ligario* 1.2, trans. Watts).

(Scaliger 3.68.338)

Note: In argumentation, this transference of the blame is called in Greek *metastasis* (Hermogenes, *On Issues* 72.5) or *metalepsis* (Hermogenes, *Invention* 3.12.162). In Latin texts, *remotio criminis* ["removal, elimination"] and *translatio criminis* are the terms used for *traiectio in alium.* Quintilian explains that we can also effectuate this transference by "evad[ing] the charge with the aid of some point of law, making it appear that the action has been brought against us illegally" (3.6.83). Such a move is one of four available to the defendent in any case: we may deny the charge, show the act was never committed, show the act was justifiable, or show that the action is being brought against us illegally—the question of competence (3.6.83). It is thereby a basis for argument, and, consequently, Quintilian denies that this action is a figure (9.2.107).

2. Passing over an issue quickly, changing the subject
When dealing with points that do not support his case, Demosthenes treats them with as few words as possible.

(Hermogenes 1.11.286)

When passing judgment on some authority, the crowd often covers up any good deeds the person might have done, while exaggerating the mistakes.

(Melanchthon, *Elem.* 51v)

Note: Puttenham remarks, "Discretion doth will us sometimes to flit from one matter to another, as a thing meet to be forsaken, and another entered upon. I call him therefore the *flitting* figure, or figure of *remove*" (240).

3. *Color* [L. "coloring"], fictionalizing in an added narrative that involves a transference of time; i.e., by presenting a picture of what is likely to happen or what might have happened or caused an effect, or by using the present tense to narrate a past or future event, and so forth
"Abundance is created in the thought if one not only narrates what was done but also what the consequences would have been if it had not been done, and what had to be done so that such and such would happen, as if we should say: 'Aeschines was nominated for the deputation to Thermopylae; three or four hands were held up, and he was declared elected. He repaired to the Council, invested with all the prestige of Athens, and at once, putting aside and disregarding everything else, addressed himself to the business for which he had taken pay.'" (Demosthenes, *De Corona* 149, trans. Wooten and Vince).

(Hermogenes 1.11.282)

Cicero fictionalizes when he pretends that Clodius had predicted that Milo's death would take place within three days (*Pro Milone* 9.26).

(Melanchton, *Elem.* 51r)

Cicero, in his defense of Milo, shows what Clodius would have done, had he succeeded in securing the praetorship: "And, as a matter of fact, Clodius, by Milo's death, did stand to gain not only that his praetorship would not fall under a consul who would render him powerless for ill, but also that his praetorship would fall under consuls with whose connivance, at least, if not with their aid, he hoped that he might have full scope for the mad schemes which he entertained—men who, so at least he reasoned, would not be anxious to check his efforts if they could, since they would be sensible of the deep debt they owed him, and who, even if they wished, would perhaps scarce be able to crush that audacity in the vilest of scoundrels which time had by now brought to its full vigour" (*Pro Milone* 12.32, trans. Watts).

(Robertellus 44r)

Note: An additional name is *transmutatio.* Prevalent in rhetorical instruction is the use of *color* to mean "external form, outward show, appearance" or "the particular aspect given to a case by the skillful manipulation of the facts—the 'gloss' or 'varnish' put on them by the accused or accuser" (Quintilian 4.2.88, note 1). Quintilian uses the term to imply that we "color" the position so as to "gloss over what is unsightly" (3.8.44). This coloring, although not explicitly treated by Quintilian as a figure, is created by means of other devices: figures of omission, such as *praeteritio* and *brevitas* (4.2.67), of *lexis,* such as *synonymia* (4.2.77), of *pronuntiatio* (4.2.77), and of *dispositio* (4.2.82). "Gloss" Hermogenes treats in detail under *metathesis* [G. "a transposition"] in argument (*On Issues* 49.8). This meaning of the term must be what Scaliger has in mind when he identifies a figure he calls *adnarratio* (see Discoursal–parts of oration below). The meaning of the term "color" has broadened in Lamy, where it now means word choice in general (1.5), which makes an action "appear greater, or less, laudable or contemptible, just or unjust" (4.44).

4. Moving the issue to another ground

"These studies of letters pertain not so much to private utility, but more to the good of the republic."

Cicero exhorts Caesar to take care for his life, not for his own sake, but for the sake of the republic: "And all those wounds of war thus inflicted now require your attention, and there is no one except you who is able to heal them. Therefore, I was concerned when I heard that celebrated and wise saying of yours, 'I have lived long enough to satisfy either nature or glory.' Sufficiently long, if you please, for nature, and I will add, if you like, for glory; but, which is of the greatest consequence of all, certainly not long enough for your country" (*Pro Marcello* 8.24–25, trans. Yonge).

(Melanchthon, *Elem.* 51r)

5. Making the judge a sharer of the same counsel

"What else do we want than what you have wanted, Caesar?" (paraphrase of Cicero's approach in the speech *Pro Ligario*)

(Scaliger 3.68.338)

Note: Melanchthon classifies this figure as one that derives from the dialectical topic of cause/ effect (*Elem.* 50v).

nempe [L. "strengthening an assertion"]

Adding to a statement intensifiers, such as "indeed," "certainly," "without a doubt," "to be sure," "of course," "beyond question," "obviously," "forsooth," and so forth

"He certainly does speak of that."

(Keckermann 1475)

nomimon zetema [G. "inquiry with respect to convention"]

Asking the audience to allow us to use our own order or arrangement and giving the reasons why

"It may, however, be a matter for surprise in some quarters that in an inquiry dealing with statute law, in a public trial held before a specially selected praetor of the Roman people and a jury of high dignity, in the presence of a crowded audience of citizens, my speech should be made in a style out of keeping not merely with the conventions of the bar, but also with forensic language. But I crave your indulgence, an indulgence which will, I trust, cause you no inconvenience, and which is peculiarly applicable to the nature of my client's case; and I would ask you to allow me, speaking as I am on behalf of a distinguished poet and a consummate scholar, before a cultivated audience, an enlightened jury, and the praetor whom we see occupying the tribunal, to enlarge somewhat upon enlightened and cultivated pursuits, and to employ what is perhaps a novel and unconventional line of defense to suit the character of one whose studious seclusion has made him a stranger to the anxious perils of the courts" (Cicero, *Pro Archia* 2.3, trans. Watts).

(Sturm 1.15.41)

ordo [L. "methodical arrangment, order"] or *catacosmesis* [G. "order, arrangement, adornment"] or *kosmesis* [G. "ordering, arrangement, adornment"]

Ordering a list from worthiest to least, or vice versa, or from first to last

1. Worthiest to least

"God and man, men and women, Sun and Moon, Day and Night, the King and his Nobles, Life and Death."

(Peacham [1577] N.ii.r)

2. Least to worthiest, or less vivid to more vivid

Comparing music to a flood, Plato writes, "but when the flood fails to stop and enchants him, at that point he melts and liquefies" (*Republic* 411b, trans. Innes). "Liquifies" is more vivid than "melts."

(Demetrius §51)

"He [Cyrus] gives him gifts too—a horse, a robe, a torque, and the assurance that his country would no longer be plundered" (Xenophon, *Anabasis* 1.2.27, trans. Innes).

(Demetrius §139)

"There was yet never any noble Captain, Prince, King, or Emperor that could deface or vanquish that noble nation."

(Peacham [1577] N.ii.r)

Note: Quintilian rejects *ordo* as a figure (9.3.91), but nevertheless gives the same kinds of examples as these above in his discussion of *ordo*, or artistic structure (9.4.23). The Greek for artistic structure or arrangement is *taxis*, the term Demetrius uses when he discusses the above considerations. Notice that if the order is re-arranged in the sentences above, they lose the effects they have at present. Hermogenes includes here ordering from first to last or vice versa and using the natural order of objection and then refutation or of proposition and then proofs, or vice versa (1.2.238). Robertellus includes within *ordo*, or artistic structure, considerations of *anastophe*, *parenthesis*, and even *synchisis* (30v). See the individual headings for these terms.

paradiastole [G. "putting together of dissimilar things"] or *distinctio* [L. "a distinction"]

Removing ambiguities in words and matter; distinguishing between similar things (often used by granting one thing, but then re-interpreting it); or re-naming vices with near virtues

1. Interpreting words
   "As, being charged that you have brought very light reasons, you may answer: 'If by *light* you mean *clear*, I am glad you do see them; if by *light* you mean of *no weight*, I am sorry you do not feel them.'"
   "A man of hidden learning, hidden as well for the obscure and mean estate of his person as hidden for the unusual and intricate conceit of the matter."
   (Hoskins 42–43)

2. Interpreting propositions
   "*Travel in foreign countries settleth a young man's humors.* If it be taken in this sort: 'It will enforce him to wariness and secrecy and restrain him from pouring forth his counsels,' it is very profitable; for he shall have few friends to put confidence in and few companions to prattle with, upon whom he might bestow his idle time or idle thoughts. But if you intend that by traveling all vanities should be taken away, it seems not so likely and admittable; because he shall walk through many ill examples and great liberty."
   (Hoskins 43)

3. Using words similar in meaning, but in ways that require and highlight their different connotations
   In Latin, the words *vereor* and *metuo* both mean "I fear." However, since Cicero uses both, he forces a slight distinction between them. Because of the contrast, *vereor* feels lighter, like respect, and *metuo* feels heavier, like dread. In the translation below, Yonge translates the first as "I am awed" and the other as "I am in fear." Cicero maintains the distinction as the paragraph goes on:
   "The two things which have the greatest influence in a state,—namely, the greatest interest and eloquence, are both making against us at the present moment; and while I am awed by the one, O Caius Aquillius, I am in fear of the other:—I am somewhat awed, apprehending that the eloquence of Quintius Hortensius may embarrass me in speaking; but I am in no slight fear lest the interest of Sextus Naevius may injure Publius Quintius" (*Pro Quinctio* 1.1).
   (Sturm 2.24.425)

4. Distinguishing matters to clarify them
   "That before was necessary speech, this will be voluntary; that was for the judge, this is for Gaius Piso; that for a defendant, this for Roscius; that for victory, this pointed out for the sake of good judgment" (paraphrase of Cicero, *Pro Q. Roscio* 5.15).
   (Sturm 2.24.424)

   "That was not a punishment, but merely a prevention of crime" (from a lost work of Cicero).
   (Quintilian 9.2.18)

5. Giving faults a more moderate coloration by calling them by neighboring virtues
   "[W]hen we call a subtle person wise; a bold fellow courageous; a prodigal man liberal; a man furious or rash valiant; a parasite a companion; him that is proud, magnanimous; and such like."
   (Day 84)

Note: Other names are *discriminatio*, *diacrisis*, or *substitutio*. Quintilian doubts that this device can be called a figure since it depends upon definition (9.3.65). Keckermann says this figure also arises when we add the opposite *stasis* to the point we explain in order to clarify it further (1483). Farnaby points out that we can use this figure to make false reasoning evident (23), and Melanchthon classifies it as a species deriving from the dialectical topic of contraries (*Elem.* 53r).

paraleipsis [G. "neglect, disregard, omission"] or *praeteritio* [L. "a passing over, omission"]
Omitting arguments and details for the sake of modesty, unimportance, time, effort, or irrelevance

1. Omit something outright
"And there are also many other things which Jesus did, the which, if they should be written every one, I suppose that even the world itself could not contain the books that should be written" (John 21:25).
(Hermogenes 2.6.351; example from Lausberg §308)

2. Mention that we will omit or pass over some points that we leave undefined
"I shall pass over those speeches concerning which there is some dispute whether they were delivered in the city's best interests" (Demosthenes, *On the Crown* 131, trans. Wooten).
(Hermogenes 2.6.351)

"For my part I have no pleasure to lay open other men's errors; it is enough unto me, that by themselves they are made apparent and that the whole world may see them."
"I talk not now of times past."
(Day 95)

3. Narrate the facts while we promise to omit them
"In private life, if any of you are not aware that I have been generous and courteous, and helpful to the distressed, I do not mention it. I will never say a word or tender any evidence about such matters as the captives I have ransomed, or the dowries I have helped to provide, or any such acts of charity. It is a matter of principle with me. My view is that the recipient of a benefit ought to remember it all his life, but that the benefactor ought to put it out of his mind at once, if the one is to behave decently, and the other with magnanimity" (Demosthenes, *On the Crown* 268, trans. Vince).
(Hermogenes 2.6.351)

"His theft, his rapine, his spoil, and all his whole disorderly course of life in those days perpetrated, I now omit and only do come to the times present."
(Day 95)

4. Omit the species and so speak only about the genus
"Now, however, all these things have been sold in open market, and in place of them we have imported vices which have infected Greece with a mortal sickness. And what are those vices? Envy of the man who has secured his gains; contempt for him who confesses; [pardon for those who are convicted;] hatred for him who censures such dealings; and every other vice that goes hand in hand with corruption. For war-galleys, men in abundance, money and material without stint, everything by which one might gauge the strength of our cities, these we as a body possess to-day in number and quantity far beyond the Greeks of former times. But all our resources are rendered useless, powerless, worthless by these traffickers" (Demosthenes, *Philippic* III 39–40, trans. Vince)
(Sturm 3.10.587; example mine)

Note: Alternate spelling is *paralepsis*. I include here primarily the straightforward use of this figure that, according to Hermogenes, creates modesty (2.6.351). For its ironical use, see the entry under Pragmatical–people. By treating types of people, not individuals, we reprehend more gently, as Sturm explains. Quintilian acknowledges the usefulness of this strategy (4.2.49), but denies it is a figure (9.3.99).

partitio conjugata [L. "a mixed partition"]

After dividing, including only a part in the first partition, but the whole in the second

"He was fortunate to find in the occupation of that office two men, one of whom could provide him with a magnificent theme for his pen, and another whose achievements could supply him with a theme and who could also lend him an appreciative hearing" (Cicero, *Pro Archia* 3.5, trans. Watts).

(Trapezuntius 573)

proepipletrein [G. "to make preparations for beforehand"]

Forestalling criticism by commenting on our word choices ourselves

"Cato, a glutton for books, if it is right to use such a word of such a noble subject . . ."

"The master's self, to use a phrase of Plautus' . . ."

". . . , for that is how your favorite moderns speak."

". . . , if I may so express myself, . . ."

"I will say it in Greek, to express my meaning better."

(Erasmus, *De copia* 308–9)

progressio [L. "advancement, progress, growth, increase"]

Mounting through a series of comparisons

1. By increasing in importance at each step

"What a boy art thou in comparison of this fellow here. Thou sleeps, he wakes; thou plays, he studies; thou art ever abroad, he is ever at home; thou never waits, he still doth his attendance; thou carest for nobody, he doth his duty to all men; thou dost what thou canst to hurt all and please none, he doth what he can to hurt none and please all."

(Wilson 226)

"To make table-talk of a mean man's name [were] wrong, to run upon a nobleman's title were a great scandal, to play with a prince's name were a treason; and what shall it be to make a vanity of that name which is most terrible even to tyrants and devils, and most reverend even to monarchs and angels—the name of God?"

(Hoskins 27)

2. By decreasing in importance at each step

"In reprehending the prodigality of monuments [. . .], I begin with the excess of Alphonsus on his father's funeral, thence to Alexander's profusion on his friend's tomb, then to Urbinus towards his servant, thence to Caesar on his horse's burial, after that to the Molossians on their dogs, thence to the Egyptians, that charge themselves with the sumptuous burial of a crocodile."

(Hoskins 26)

prolepsis [G. "preconception, anticipation"] or *procatalepsis* [G. "breaking up, annulling beforehand"] or *praesumptio* [L. "assuming beforehand"] or *ante occupatio* [L. "an anticipation"] or *praeoccupatio* [L. "a seizing beforehand"]

Preventing objections by anticipating and answering them before they are spoken

1. By bringing up the objection and then answering it

"But when he saw many of the Pharisees and Sadducees come to his baptism, he said unto them, O generation of vipers, who hath warned you to flee from the wrath to come? Bring forth therefore fruits meet for repentance: And think not to say within yourselves, We have Abraham to our father: for I say unto you, that God is able of these stones to raise up children of Abraham" (Matthew 3:7–9).

(Smith 130)

2. *Antiphora,* by leaving the objection unstated, but still answering it
   "In the first epistle of Ovid, Penelope willing her husband Ulysses to come home himself, [. . .] when he might have laid for his tarrying the wars, she prively took away the excuse, saying, 'Troy is destroyed'" (*Heroides* I.3).

   (Sherry [1550] 53–54)

   "'Honor the Lord with thy substance, and with the first fruits of all thine increase:' [Objection: So I may begger myself. But this objection is prevented in the words of the next verse;] 'so shall thy barns be filled with plenty.'" (Proverbs 3:9–10).

   (Smith 130)

Note: An alternate spelling is *antypophora.* Sherry indicates that this figure can also be used to "compell our aduersarye to answer" ([1550] 53).

3. By correcting the adversary's understanding of a word
   "Citizens, I say, if I may call them by that name" (Cicero, *Pro Murena* 37.80, trans. Butler).

   (Quintilian 9.2.18)

   "[. . .] though that was not a punishment, but a preventing of crime" (from a lost work of Cicero, qtd. in Quintilian 9.2.18).

   (Soarez 340)

4. By foreseeing and avoiding dangers
   "All *wise* Men foresee *dangers,* and prevent them; all *good* men foresee *Temptations* to evil and avoid them; the ingenious *Physician* foresees the too sudden recovery of his Patient, and knowing that health as well as wit is never ought except it be dear bought, wisely retards the over hasty cure and keeps him long ill, that when he is once recover'd he may be long well. The Sagacious *Lawyer* foresees the dangerous and disadvantageous agreement that his Client is like to make with his Adversary, and therefore prolongs his suit a Term, or two, or ten, or twenty, wisely considering, that of two evils, he ought to choose the least."

   (Shaw 132)

5. By attributing modern knowledge and inventions to former ages when narrating a tale; creating anachronisms
   If the poet should say that a town was sacked by catapults in the time of Aeneas, he would be using this figure, for catapults had not been invented yet.

   (Scaliger 3.49.320)

Note: Other names include *anticipatio,* "prevention," *proanaphonesis,* and *praeceptio.* Puttenham calls it "the presumptuous, otherwise the figure of Presupposall" (239). Quintilian treats this figure as a category inclusive of *praemunitio, confessio, praedictio, emendatio, praeparatio,* and *reprehensio* (9.2.17–18), but he also has reservations about its being a figure (9.3.99). Farnaby makes clear a distinction others also follow. *Prolepsis* has two parts: the first is the raising of the objections the adversary will bring against us, called *praesumptio, objectio, occupatio, anteoccupatio, praeoccupatio,* or *hypophora*; the second is the answering of the objections, called *subjectio* or *anthypophora.* He tells us this figure is suitable for the *proemion* and the *confirmatio* (24). *Hypophora* is applied here with the meaning of indirect or attributed speech, the meaning found in Hermogenes (*Inv.* 4.13.207). Talaeus conflates *prolepsis* and *subjectio* (31). This *subjectio* differs from the *subjectio* listed below under the category of Pragmatical—people, but is like *subjectio*, otherwise *anthypophora*, the answering of objections, under Discoursal–parts below. Sturm treats all forms of answering objections under *occupatio* (1.26.88), with the specific name of *proanaphonesis* for predicting an opponent's argument beforehand (1.28.103). Vossius conflates *prolepsis* and *occupatio*, describing this figure as if equivalent to the *subjectio* listed under the category of Pragmatical–people and giving it two parts: *hypophora* and *anthypophora* (243). See *subjectio* under Pragmatical–people and *occupatio* under Discoursal–parts below. Melanchthon lists this figure as a species of those deriving from the dialectical topic of contraries (*Elem.* 52v).

protimesis [G. "assigning a higher value to"] or *aestimatio* [L. "valuation, appraisement"]
Using superlatives, contrasts, or order to show the dignity of things

1. Using superlatives
"These words are no fables uttered among men, but an assured truth left unto us by writing, and yet not by any common writing, but by such as all the world hath confirmed and agreed upon that it is authentic and canonical; neither are they the words of one that is of the common sort, but they are the words of a doctor in the Church of God; and yet not the words of a divine or doctor of the common sort, but of an Apostle; and yet not of one that is the worst, but of Paul, that is the best of all others and yet not Paul's, but rather the words of the Holy Ghost speaking by the mouth of Paul."
(Wilson 153)

"There is not a better preacher among them all, except Hugh Latimer, the father of all preachers."
(Wilson 154)

2. Using the greatest that can be conceived
"You beat your mother. What more need I say? You beat your mother."
(Quintilian 3.4.7)

3. Using contrasts
"Now Lord, what a man is he; he was not ashamed being a gentleman, yea, a man of good years and much authority, and the head officer in a duke's house, to play at dice in an alehouse with boys, bawds, and varlets. It had been a great fault to play at so vile a game, among such vile persons, being no gentleman, being no officer, being not of such years, but being both a man of fair lands, of an ancient house, of great authority, an officer to a duke, yea, and to such a duke, and a man of such years, that his white hairs should warn him to avoid all such folly, to play at such a game, with such roisters and such varlets, yea, and that in such a house as none come thither but thieves, bawds, and ruffians—now before God I cannot speak shame enough of him."
(Wilson 154)

"Members of the Senate, I recall Quintus Scaevola the augur in the Marsic War. He was very old and broken in health, but every day as soon as it grew light he would give admittance to everyone. Nobody during that war ever saw him in bed. Old and feeble as he was, he was the first to arrive at the Senate-house. I could have wished that those whom it behooved were following his conscientious example; or at least that they were not jealous of someone else's toil" (Cicero, *Philippics* 8.30, trans. Bailey).
(Keckermann 1483)

4. Using order

Homer, in describing the Cyclops, "keeps augmenting his hyperbole and seems to climb higher and higher with it: 'for he was not like men who eat bread but like a wooded summit,' and what is more, the summit of a high mountain, one towering above all the others" (*Odyssey* 9.190–92, trans. Innes).

(Demetrius §52)

"Gentlemen of the jury, it is chiefly because I consider that the State will benefit by the repeal of this law, but partly also out of sympathy with the young son of Chabrias, that I have consented to support the plaintiffs to the best of my ability" (Demosthenes, *Against Leptines* 1, trans. Vince).

(Hermogenes 1.11.287)

Note: Quintilian considers this device a method, not a figure (8.4.6).

remotio [L. "a withdrawing, removing"] or *aphaeresis* [G. "taking away, removal"]

Withdrawing or removing an idea through denial, so that the contrary takes its place whether explicitly or implicitly

1. In a sentence, with *remotio* and *positio*

"To live life tomorrow is too late, live today" (Martial 5.58).

(Sturm 2.21.391)

"Rather reason than stupidity."

(Sturm 2.21.392)

"You will not have enemies, but friends."

(Keckermann 1550)

2. In an argument, with *remotio* and *positio*

"He was chosen, not as one who would make traffic of your interests, not as one who had any confidence in Philip, but as one of the party that was to keep an eye on the rest, [. . .]" (Demosthenes, *De Falsa Legatione* 12, trans. Vince).

(Hermogenes 1.11.293)

Dido to her sister Anna: "But I should prefer that the earth gape open and swallow/ Me first or the Father All-powerful kill me with lightening,/ Drive me to pale shadows of Erebus and deepest night/ Before I should violate honor or break my vows" (*Aeneid* 4:22–25, trans. Lind).

(Scaliger 3.82.348)

3. The removal alone

"When the Phocian war began—not by my fault, for I was still outside politics—you were at first disposed to hope that the Phocians would escape ruin, [. . .]" (Demosthenes, *On the Crown* 18, trans. Vince).

(Hermogenes 1.11.293)

Dido's message to Aeneas: "I never conspired with Greeks at Aulis to ruin/ The Trojan people. I sent no fleet against Troy/ Nor dug up the ashes or spirit of Father Anchises" (*Aeneid* 4:427–29, trans. Lind).

(Scaliger 3.82.348)

Note: Additional names include *ablatio inferens, castigatio, "arsis* and *thesis,"* and *hypexairesis*. Sturm spells the Greek name *aphairhesis* (1.40.224) and uses the term *remotio* to name the removing and *positio* to name the replacing (2.21.392). Hermogenes talks about this figure as negating and then affirming, but explains that these two do not need to follow each other. The negation and the affirmation can each stand alone (1.11.293). When standing alone, the *affirmatio,* like the *negatio,* becomes a figure in its own right (see *affirmatio* and *negatio* under Discoursal–genres below). *Remotio* has another meaning. In discussions of possible means for defense, *remotio* refers to the defendent's acknowledging the deed as wrong, but shifting the blame for it onto someone or something else. Cicero regards such a move a figure, calling it *trajectio in alium.* Such a move is widely known as one kind of *metastasis.* See *metastasis* above.

repetitio [L. "repetition"] or *iteratio* [L. "repetition"]

Repetition of the same idea in different words

"Then overhead a black cloud burst upon me,
Bringing the night and storm and ruffled waves.
The winds beat up the ocean, raised great surges,
And we were scattered on the boiling water.
Clouds wrapped up daylight, and the rainy night
Snatched heaven from us, lightning doubled its flashes
Through clouds torn open. We were driven off
Our course and wandered blindly on the billows.
Our helmsman Palinurus said he could not
Distinguish night from day in heaven, recall
His route in mid-sea. Three days we were derelicts,
Three pitchblack nights without the shining stars." (Virgil, *Aeneid* 3.221–32, trans. Lind)

(Scaliger 3.41.313; example mine)

restrictio [L. "a restriction, limitation"]

Adding an exception to a statement, excluding a part

"We are afflicted on every side, yet are we not in distress: in poverty, yet not overcome of poverty: we are persecuted, but not forsaken: cast down, but we perish not" (2 Corinthians 4:8–9).

"The high thrones of Princes are glorious, yet changeable: dignities are sweet, yet they be dangerous: riches are good things, yet full of trouble: pleasures are the flowers & fruits of life: yet are they full of the causes of misery, and deceitful baits of death and destruction."

(Peacham [1593] 131)

sustentatio [L. "a deferring, delay"] or *suspensio* [L. "suspense"] or *hypomone* [G. "a holding back of the principal thought for a surprise"]

Withholding information until the end, creating suspense

1. Fulfilling expectation

Spenser withholds revealing the author of these deeds until the end of the description:

"Then vp arose a man of matchlesse might,
And wondrous wit to menage high affaires,
Who stird with pitty of the stressed plight
Of this sad Realme, cut into sundry shaires
By such, as claymd themselues *Brutes* rightfull haires,
Gathered the Princes of the people loose,
To taken counsell of their common cares;
Who with his wisedom won, him streight did choose,
Their king, and swore him fealty to win or loose.

Then made he head against his enimies,
And *Ymner* slew, of *Logris* miscreate;
Then *Ruddoc* and proud *Stater*, both allyes,
This of *Albanic* newly nominate,
And that of *Cambry* king confirmed late,
He ouerthrew through his owne valiaunce;
Whose countreis he redus'd to quiet state,
And shortly brought to ciuill gouernaunce,
Now one, which earst were many, made through variaunce.

Then made he sacred lawes, which some men say
Were vnto him reueald in vision,
By which he freed the Traueilers high way,
The Churches part, and Ploughmans portion,
Restraining stealth, and strong extortion;
The gracious Numa of great Britanie:
For till his dayes, the chiefe dominion
By strength was wielded without pollicie;
Therefore he first wore crowne of gold for dignitie.

Donwallo dyde . . ." (*The Faerie Queene* II.10. 37–40)

(Gill 170)

2. *Inopinatum* [L. "something unexpected"] or *paradoxon* [G. "contrary to expectation, incredible"]

Subverting expectations; giving a surprising, paradoxical turn

Cicero, when arguing against Verres, begins a point by saying, "'What next? well, what would you suppose? you will be looking, perhaps, to hear of some piece of theft or robbery.' Then, after keeping the minds of the judges in suspense for a considerable time, he adds something much worse: 'You look to me, gentlemen, still anxious to hear the sequel, knowing as you do that the man never did anything without getting some profit or plunder out of it. But what could be done here? Expect what you will—as rascally a deed as you like to fancy: my tale will surpass your wildest expectations. Those men, after being convicted of the crime of conspiracy, handed over to execution and bound to the stake, were suddenly, before the eyes of thousands of people, unbound and handed over to their owner, the man from Triocala'" (Cicero, *In C. Verrem* II 5.5.10–11, trans. Greenwood)

(Soarez 348–49)

Note: This figure applies the periodic sentence structure to a passage. According to Taleus, the figure additionally creates suspense, promises something big and then does not deliver, or strings someone along (53–54). *Sustentatio* and *hypomene* are sometimes completely equated with *paradoxon*, even though the second has a narrower meaning, and sometimes *paradoxon* has an additional application besides the unexpected turn. See *paradoxon* below under Logical–idea figures.

tautologia [G. "repeating what has been said"]

Following a term with restatements of the same thing in order to explain it

"'The Senate of the Roman people is the greatest council, from which order foreign nations seek privileges.' For here one name, 'The Senate,' receives an honorable notice [. . . and is explained by] the greatest council and that order by which foreign nations seek privileges."

(Aquila §39)

Note: Aquila indicates that this figure is like *synonymia*, but in many words rather than single words. Even though he lists it as a figure of speech, the figure more properly belongs to those of thought since it does not depend upon verbal patterns for its existence. See *synonymia* above under syntactical figures.

Treating People

adulatio [L. "cringing flattery, adulation"] or *hypothyposis* [G. "to win by flattery"]

Using flattery

Goneril flatters her father Lear in this public performance of love:

"Sir, I love you more than words can wield the matter.
Dearer than eyesight, space, and liberty,
Beyond what can be valued, rich or rare,
No less than life, with grace, health, beauty, honor;
As much as child e'er lov'd, or father found;
A love that makes breath poor, and speech unable;
Beyond all manner of so much I love you." (Shakespeare, *King Lear* 1.1.55–61)

(Robertellus 45v, example mine)

Note: Quintilian acknowledges that this feature has been called a figure by Celsus, but is not himself in favor of calling it so (9.2.104).

ad hilaritatem impulsio [L. "an incitement to merriment"]

Using humor

1. Word
   a. A quick altering of some one word or of some one sentence through *irony*
      "According to that merry saying of Nero upon his man that was light-fingered: 'I have one at home,' quod he, 'among all others, to whom there is no coffer locked nor door shut in all my house,' meaning that he was a picklock and a false varlet; and yet these words might have been spoken of a faithful servant."
   b. Playing on words that sound similar by changing a letter or syllable of one to make the other, *paronomasia*
      "'What carry you, master parson,' quod a gentleman to a priest that had his woman on horseback behind him. 'Have you got your mail behind you?' 'No sir,' quod the priest, 'it is my female.'"
   c. Hinting more than is said, *scematismus*
      "'Ah,' quod a certain man, 'do you see yonder fellow, and do you know him?' 'Yea,' quod the other, 'I know him very well.' 'I shall tell you, sir,' said the gentleman, 'there is not a man of greater understanding within this city than he is.' 'Tush, it is not so,' quod he. 'No?,' said the other, 'Mark well the bought of his leg, and you shall see his understanding worthy to be compared with the best and greatest of them all.'"
   d. Interpreting a word, *etymologia logon*
      "As when one hath done a robbery, some will say, 'It is pity, he was a handsome man,' to the which another made answer: 'You say truth, sir, for he hath made these shifts by his hands and got his living with light fingering, and therefore being handsome, as you say he is, I would God he were handsomely hanged.'"
   e. Applying a word to an unexpected context, *antanaclasis*
      "'Such a man hath no fault but one, and if that were amended, all were well.' 'What is that?', quod another. 'In good faith, he is naught.'"

f. Taking a man's word, but not his meaning, *pokrisis*
"As when one had said to another (whose help he must needs have), 'I am sorry, sir, to put you to pains,' the other answered: 'I will ease you, sir, of that sorrow, for I will take no pains for you at all.'"
g. Augmenting or diminishing without all reason; using *hyperbole* or *meiosis*
Diogenes, seeing a tiny town having big gates, said: "Take heed, you men of this town, lest your town run out of your gates."
h. Giving an honest name to an evil deed, or an evil name to a good deed, *antiphrasis* or *paradiastole*
"Some old fellows when they think one to be a heretic, they will say: 'He is a gospeler'" or "a father loving his son tenderly and having no cause to be grieved with him will sometimes say to him, 'Come hither, sir knave.'"

2. Tale
a. Telling fables, tales, histories aptly
b. Applying an old tale to some man living, or *parechesis*
"As if one were called Arthur, some good fellow [. . .] would dub him knight of the Round Table, or else prove him to be one of his kin, or else [. . .] prove him to be Arthur himself."
c. Speaking one thing merrily and thinking another earnestly, or *ironia*
"[O]ur worthy Latimer did set out the devil for his diligence wonderfully and preferred him for that purpose before all the bishops in England."
d. Gathering a meaning the speaker did not intend, or *inopinatum*
"When Livius Salinator, a Roman captain, had kept the castle of Terentum, losing the town to Hannibal his enemy, and that Maximus thereupon had laid siege to the same town and got it again by the sword, then Salinator, which thus kept the castle, desired him to remember that through his means he got the town. 'Why should I not,' quod he, 'think so? For if you had never lost it, I had never got it.'"
e. Dissembling as though we do not understand what one meant, *dissimulatio*
"When Metellus took muster and required Caesar to be there, not abiding that he should be absent though his eyes grieved him, and said: 'What, man, do you see nothing at all?' 'Yes, marry,' quod Caesar, 'as evil as I see, I can see a lordship of yours,' the which was four or five miles from Rome, declaring that his building was oversumptuous and so huge withal–much above his degree–that a blind man might almost see it. Now in those days, overcostly building was generally hated, because men sought by such means to get fame and bear rule in the commonweal."
f. Returning a mock for a mock or accusation, *mycterismus*
"As when one Quintus Opimius, having an evil name for his light behavior, had said to a pleasant man Egilius that seemed to be wanton of living and yet was not so: 'Ah my sweet darling Egilia, when wilt thou come to my house sweet wench, with thy rock and thy spindle?' 'I dare not in good faith,' quod he, 'my mother hath forbid me to come to any suspected house where evil rule is kept.'"
g. Implying more than is said, *emphasis*
"A homely fellow made his woeful lamentation to Diogenes in most pitiful sort because his wife had hanged herself upon a fig tree, hoping to find some comfort at his hand. But Diogenes, hearing this strange deed: 'For the love of God,' quod he, 'give me some slips of that tree, that I might set them in some orchard.'"
h. Giving a churlish answer, *sarcasmus*
"When the father was cast in judgment, the son seeing him weep: 'Why weep you father?', quod he, to whom his father answered: 'What? Shall I sing, I pray thee, seeing by a law I am condemned to die?'"

i. Giving a pleasant, witty reply to a wrong done, *asteismus*
"As when Cato was stricken of one that carried a chest–some say a long pole–when the other said, after he had hit him: 'Take heed, sir, I pray you.' 'Why,' quod Cato, 'dost thou carry anything else?'"

j. Praising in order to dispraise, *antiphasis*
"When an evil man had accused many persons, and none took any harm by him but rather were acquitted from time to time and taken the sooner for honest men: 'Now would to Christ's Passion,' quod a naughty fellow, 'that he were mine accuser, for then should I be taken for an honest man also through his accusation.'"

k. Using irrelevant facts to make the truth seem other than it is, *paralogismos*
"One was charged for robbing a church, and almost evidently proved to be an offender in that behalf; the said man, to save himself harmless, reasoned thus: 'Why,' quod he, 'how should this be? I never robbed house nor yet as ever faulty in any offense besides; how then should I presume to rob a church? I have loved the church more than any other, and will lovers of the church rob the church? I have given to the church; how happeneth that I am charged to take from the church, having so good mind to church dignity?'"

l. Giving advice by means of implication, *significatio*
"When an unlearned lawyer had been hoarse and almost lost the voice with overlong speaking, one Granius gave him counsel to drink sweet wine cold so soon as he came home. 'Why,' quod he, 'I shall lose my voice if I do so.' 'Marry,' quod he, 'and better do so than undo thy client and lose his matter altogether.'"

m. Speaking contrary to expectation, *improvisum quiddam*
"An English physician, riding by the way and seeing a great company of men gathered together, sent his man to know what the matter was, whereupon his man, understanding that one there was appointed to suffer for killing a man, came riding back in all posthaste and cried to his master long before he came at him: 'Get you hence, sir, get you hence for God's love.' 'What means thou?', quod his master. 'Marry,' quod the servant, 'yonder man shall die for killing of one man, and you I dare say have killed a hundred men in your days; get you hence therefore, for God's love, if you love yourself.'"

n. Answering with the unexpected, *improvisum quiddam*
"When Pompilius, a soldier of Julius Caesar, had said often to Caesar, and showed him that he was wounded in the face for his sake, Caesar, being wearied with such his often rehearsal: 'Well,' quod he, 'the next time that thou run'st away, thou wilt not look back.' The soldier therewith was much aghast, as one that looked not for any such answer."

o. Mocking a lie by exaggerating it, *diasyrmus*
"When one being of a low degree and his father of mean wealth had vaunted much of the good house that his father kept, of two beefs spent weekly and half a score tuns of wine drunk in a year, another good fellow hearing him lie so shamefully: 'Indeed,' quod he, 'beef is so plentiful at my master your father's house that an ox in one day is nothing, and as for wine, beggars that come to the door are served by whole gallons. And as I remember, your father hath a spring of wine in the midst of his court: God continue his good housekeeping.'"

p. Competing with another in the dissembling of good manners, *simulatio*
"When two meet together, and the one cannot well abide the other, and yet they both outwardly strive to use pleasant behavior, and to show much courtesy, yea, to contend on both parts which should pass other in using of fair words and making lively countenances, seeking by dissembling the one to deceive the other."

3. Action, *gesticulatio*
   a. Look or gesture
      "One being grieved with another man said in his anger: 'I will set thee out in thy colors, I will show what thou art.' The other being therewith much chafed: 'Show,' quod he, 'what thou canst'; with that he showed him, pointing with his finger, a man with a bottle nose, blob-cheeked, and as red as a butcher's bowl, even as like the other man as anyone in all the world could be."
   b. Laughter
   c. *Mimesis*
      "The matter is told pleasantly, when some man's nature [. . .] is so set forth, his countenance so counterfeited, and all his gesture so resembled, that the hearers might judge the thing to be then lively done, even as though he were there."
   d. Picture
      "Another good fellow, being merrily disposed, called his acquaintance unto him and said: 'Come hither, I say, and I will show thee as very a lout as ever thou sawest in all thy life before.' With that, he offered him at his coming a steel glass to look in."
      (Wilson 167–83)

Note: Wilson calls this figure "mirth-making" (213). Cicero's extended discussion of wit can be found in *De Oratore* 2.235–290 and Quintilian's in 6.3.1–112, but Quintilian does not regard the use of jokes a figure (9.2.104). Scaliger considers the use of jokes a figure only when dressed up by other figures (3.93.363). Demetrius includes another kind of joke, what he calls the release from fear, as in discovering that the strip of leather is really not a snake (§159).

aphorismus [G. "a delimitation, assignment of boundaries"] or *reprehensio* [L. "censure, reprimand"]

Rebuking by questioning the applicability of a term

"Your counselors, if such may be called counselors, as draw unto mischief, are utterly unmeet to such kind of assemblies."

(Day 94)

"Citizens, I say, if I may call them by that name" (Cicero, *Pro Murena* 37, trans. Butler).

(Quintilian 9.2.18)

Note: This figure is a species of *correctio*. See *correctio* below.

apocarteresis [G. "suicide by hunger"]

Casting away hope, but finding it in a new way

"'He hath destroyed me on every side, and I am gone, and he hath removed mine hope like a tree.' Job in these words signifieth that he hath no more hope of worldly prosperity and comfort, and therefore he turneth the eye of his hope to heaven, saying: 'I know that my redeemer liveth, etc.' [Job 19:10, 25–26]. Whereby he comforteth himself the better to endure & suffer so great and heavy a burthen of misery."

"Let the widow weep, and the fatherless children lament. Let kinsfolk sorrow, and friends mourn, yet cannot all this prevail, for he is gone, and cannot be called again; his absence must needs be suffered, when his presence cannot be redeemed, and therefore think on men that live, and let the dead rest."

(Peacham [1593] 83–84)

Note: Peacham gives as the Latin equivalent *tollerantia* ([1593] 83). Robertellus cites Demetrius as his source for this figure (49r).

apodioxis [G. "expulsion"] or *rejectio* [L. "a rejection"]

Rejecting arguments as needless, absurd, false, foolish, or irrelevant

1. Open rejection

"For why should Milo hate Clodius, seeing he is the ground and chief cause of his glory?" (Cicero, *Pro Milone* 13.35)

(Sherry ([1555] E.v.v)

"To the Sadducees captiously inquiring of Christ, concerning the state of marriage in the resurrection, he answered: 'You do err, not knowing the Scriptures, neither the power of God' [Matthew 22:29]: by which answer he rejecteth their captious objection, by noting their ignorance."

(Peacham [1593] 185)

"Thus Christ rejects Peter's argument, touching his endeavor to avert Christ from his suffering: 'Get thee behind me, Satan. Thou art an offence unto me: for thou favourest not the things of God'" (Matthew 16:23).

(Smith 230)

2. Covert dismissal by postponing a point, tabling an issue, or omitting what cannot be said in a timely manner

"What good will it be to talk about this, since it does not contribute anything to the case at hand."

(Melanchthon, *Elem.* 52v).

"I will speak concerning this thing at another more convenient time."

(Keckermann 1489)

Note: An additional name is *reprobatio*. Melanchthon lists this figure as a species of those deriving from the dialectical topic of contraries (*Elem.* 52v).

apophasis [G. "a denial, negation"] or *negatio* [L. "a denial, negation"]

Denying to say or do that which we say or do

"As if Venus, about to persuade Paris to adultery, had said, 'I'm not going to persuade you to be the lord of a most beautiful lady.'"

(Scaliger 3.89.359)

"I say nothing."

"Neither will I mention those things, which if I should, you notwithstanding could neither confute nor speak against them."

(Smith 165)

Note: This figure can be a form of irony and is conflated with *paralepsis* in Aquila (§8), Robertellus (44v), and Soarez (349). See *paralepsis* below.

aporia [G. "being at a loss, perplexity"] or *dubitatio* [L. "uncertainty, doubt"] or *endoiasis* [G. "hesitation"] or *diaporesis* [G. "perplexity"]

Doubting about what to say or do, hesitating, deliberating with ourselves, affecting ignorance, wondering

1. About which of two expressions to use

"Before I begin, I doubt what to name ye. Shall I call you subjects? You deserve it not. My friends ye are not. To call you enemies were overlittle, because your offense is so great. Rebels ye are, and yet that name doth not fully utter your folly. Traitors I may call you, and yet you are worse than traitors, for you seek his death who hath given you life. The offense is so great that no man can comprehend it. Therefore I doubt what to call you, except I should call you by the name of them all."

(Wilson 210)

2. About what action to take
   a. In front of an audience
      "For my part, I confess I know not where to turn. Am I to say that there never was a scandal over the corruption of that court; or that it never was discussed at the street-corners, bandied about in the law courts, commented on in the Senate? Am I to expunge from public opinion such firm impressions, so deeply and so long ingrained? That is beyond my power (Cicero, *Pro Cluentio* 1.4, trans. Hodge).

      (Soarez 341)

   b. In self-deliberations
      "Yet if my desire, how unjust soever it be, might take effect, though a thousand deaths followed it, and every death followed with a thousand shames, yet should not my sepulchre receive me without some contentment. But, alas, sure I am not, that Cleophila is such as can answer my love: and if she be, how can I think she will? since this disguising must needs come for some foretaken conceipt. And either way, wretched Gynecia, where canst thou find any small ground-plot for hope to dwell upon? No, no, it is Philoclea his heart is set upon, if he be a he, it is my daughter which I have born to supplant me. But if it be so, the life I have given thee, unnatural Philoclea, I will sooner with these hands bereave thee of, than my birth shall glory she hath bereaved me of my desires. In shame there is no comfort, but to be beyond all bounds of shame" (Gynecia in Sidney's *The Old Arcadia*, book 2, 81).

      (Fraunce G7v-8r)

3. About what to say
   "What else is there? Have I left anything out?"

   (Quintilian 9.2.60)

4. About some facts
   "Those statues were called the Canephoroe; but the sculptor—who was he? Now who did they say he was? Oh yes, thank you—Polyclitus" (Cicero, *In Verrem* II 4.3.5, trans. Greenwood).

   (Rufinianus §9)

4. Imputing to the audience wonderment or doubt
   When Cicero says that he believes the judges wonder why a man such as himself would undertake a particular case.

   (Sturm 1.16.45)

Note: This figure is also sometimes called *addubitatio* and *deliberatio*. Puttenham's English name is "the Doubtfull" (234). Hermogenes treats *diaporesis* and *endoiasis* as two different behaviors (2.8.367), the first referring to perplexity about which word to use and the second to kinds of hesitations, but this distinction seems to disappear shortly thereafter. Quintilian adds that this device may be employed about the past; that is, "we may equally pretend that we *had* felt hesitation on the subject" (9.2.20). Walker adds that we can use this figure when we do not wish to impose our opinions upon the auditor (91).

aposiopesis [G. "becoming silent"] or *reticentia* [L. "a keeping silent"] or *praecisio* [L. "a breaking off abruptly"] or *interruptio* [L. "an interruption in the thought or expression"]

Breaking off an utterance and leaving things unsaid

1. Breaking off an utterance in mid-sentence, leaving it unfinished
   "Husband come home, or else."
   "Alas, my friends, in this my deep distress, tell me what . . ."

   (Peacham [1577] E.iiii.r)

   "I heard . . . ; I am ashamed to tell it."

   (Peacham [1577] N.i.v)

2. Leaving something unsaid or some details unmentioned so that we end before the natural point for the conclusion
   "I am pressing my point too far; the young man appears to be moved" (Cicero, *Pro Ligario* 3.9, trans. Butler).
   "Why should I say more? You heard the young man tell the story himself" (Cicero, *In C. Verrem* II 5.44.116, trans. Butler).

   (Quintilian 9.2.57)

   "Thou that art a young man of such towardness, having such friends, to play me such a part, well, I will say no more, God amend all that is amiss."

   (Wilson 205)

Note: Puttenham's name is "the Figure of silence" (178). Additional names include *obticentia, ellipsis,* and *abscisio*. Quintilian makes two figures here. The first is *aposiopesis,* which is leaving a sentence unfinished; the second is *praecisio,* which is bringing our words to a close before the natural point for their conclusion (9.2.57). Cicero may have agreed with Quintilian since he lists *reticentia, praecisio,* and even *interruptio* as if separate figures (*De Or* 3.202, 205, 207). Scaliger, too, follows Quintilian here (3.77.344). Quintilian also argues that *ellipsis* should not be conflated with *aposiopesis* (9.3.60).

apostrophe [G. "a turning away"] or *aversio* [L. "a turning away"]
Directly addressing a different audience either present or absent

1. Turning from the judge to the witnesses
   "And herein you witnesses are to consult with your own consciences and to enter into true examination of your memory. Did you mark his looks? Did you note his speeches? Did you truly observe the particular proceedings of the action?"

   (Hoskins 48)

2. Turning from a living audience to some quality or thing personified
   "Hope, tell me, what hast thou to hope for? Love, be ashamed to be called love."

   (Hoskins 48)

3. Turning from the audience to ourselves
   Dido to herself, "There is nothing to do but die, as you well deserve,
   And remove your sorrow with steel" (Virgil, *Aeneid* 4.549–50, trans. Lind).

   (Keckermann 1495)

4. Turning from the immediate audience to God or angels
   "O Jupiter, thou who wast established by Romulus under the same auspices under which this city was established, rightly called by us the Stayer of this city and empire, thou wilt repel him and his allies from thy temples and from the other temples, from the dwellings of this city and its walls, from the lives and fortunes of all the citizens, and these men, enemies of the upright, foes of the state, plunderers of Italy, who are united by a compact of crime in an abominable association, thou will punish living and dead with eternal punishments" (Cicero, *In Catalinam* I 13.33, trans. Lord).

   (Keckermann 1495)

5. Turning from the senators to the defendant
   "In heaven's name, Catiline, how long will you abuse our patience? How long will that madness of yours mock us? To what limit will your unbridled audacity vaunt itself?" (Cicero *In Catilinam* I 1.1, trans. Lord)

(Fraunce G2r)

Note: An additional name is *adversio*. Puttenham's name for this figure is "the turne tale" (244). The *Ad Herennium* treats this figure as an *exclamatio* (4.15.22). Sturm says that poets call this figure *prosphonesis* (1.24.72). Fraunce includes here poet's invocations (F8v).

appellatio conscientia [L. "an accosting of knowledge"]
When consulting with the adversary, we contest his knowledge.
"I call your knowledge itself to the witness stand."

(Keckermann 1495)

Note: Keckermann includes this device as a kind of *communicatio*. See *communicatio* below.

asteismus [G. "wit"] or *urbanitas* [L. "refinement, elegance of manner, affability, wit"]
Witting jesting, often through tropes
"Diogenes was asked on a time what wine he loved best to drink. 'Marry,' quod he, 'another man's wine,' meaning that he loved that drink best that cost him least. The same Diogenes likewise was asked what one should give him to let him have a blow at his head. 'Marry, a helmet,' quod he."

(Wilson 176)

"As Cato said to one that had given him a good knock on the head with a long piece of timber he bare on his shoulder, and then bade him beware: 'What,' quoth Cato, 'wilt thou strike me again?'"

(Puttenham 200)

Note: Alternate spellings include *astismus, asteismos,* and *astysmus*. This figure, called by Puttenham "the Merry scoff" or "the civill jest" (200), is often listed as a trope. Peacham explains that "the merry and pleasant sayings of this figure are called *facetiae*" ([1593] 33).

autoschediasmos [G. "self spontaneity"] or *prospoieisthai schediazein* [G. "to pretend extemporaneousness"]
Sudden and impromptu speech
Demosthenes seems to say something that occurs to him on the spur of the moment rather than something that was thought out in advance: "Indeed this point almost escaped me" (*Against Meidias* 110), or "Indeed I have gone into arguments that it will be more appropriate to use later" (*On the Crown* 42, trans. Wooten).

(Hermogenes 2.7.359)

Note: Sturm calls this kind the opposite of accurate speech (3.35.809).

commemoratio [L. "a calling to mind, commemorating"]
Saying that we know how the audience thinks and feels
1. Implicitly
   "You sit here, then, to avenge the death of one to whom you would refuse to restore life, even did you think you had the power; and a law has been proposed for an inquiry into

his slaying, though, could he by the same law have been brought back to life, that law would never have been proposed" (Cicero, *Pro Milone* 29.79, trans. Watts).

(Melanchthon, *Elem.* 44v)

2. Explicitly
"I know how you feel, judges."

(Keckermann 1495)

Note: Both Melanchthon and Keckermann regard this figure as a kind of *communicatio*. See *communicatio* below.

communicatio [L. "imparting, communicating"] or *anacoenosis* [G. "communication"]
Asking for hearer's opinion; deliberation with audience

"And you, yourself, Labienus–what should you have been doing in such a time of crisis? When the promptings of indolence were driving you to flight and concealment, when the wickedness and madness of Lucius Saturninus were inviting you to the Capitol, when the consuls were calling you to the defence of your country and to freedom, whose authority, whose voice, whose party should you have preferred to follow, whose orders to obey?" (Cicero, *Pro Rabirio* 8.22, trans. Hodge)

(Soarez 341–42)

"Were it your case, what would you answer? Tell me, I appeal unto your secret thoughts. Your friend hath esteemed better of his own stomach than of the eternal love betwixt you vowed, and preferreth the trial of his valor before the regard of both your credits; which must die howsoever either or both of you survive the combat: would you not judge him unworthy ever to be your friend that began not his fidelity with an inviolable covenant never to be your enemy?"

(Hoskins 49)

Note: Alternate spellings include *anakoinosis, anacinosis, anacenosis*, and *koenosis. Idiotismos* is another name. Puttenham's Anglicization is "the Impartener" (235). Sturm probably refers to this figure with the term *epanakenosis* (3.31.779).

comprobatio [L. "approbation, approval"]
Complimenting the judges, jury, or audience

"Nothing is so dear to the people as kindness, and none of your many high qualities arouses such admiration and such pleasure as your compassion. For in nothing do men more nearly approach divinity than in doing good to their fellow-men; your situation has nothing prouder in it than the power, your character nothing in it more noble than the wish, to preserve all whom you can" (Cicero, *Pro Ligario* 12.37–38, trans. Watts).

(Melanchthon, *Elem.* 18r)

"To all that be in Rome, beloved of God, called to be saints: Grace to you and peace from God our Father, and the Lord Jesus Christ. First, I thank my God through Jesus Christ for you all, that your faith is spoken of throughout the whole world" (Romans 1:7–8).

(Melanchthon, *Elem.* 12v)

Note: In pleading it is sometimes necessary for the defendant who has admitted guilt to then call upon the judges' clemency, one of the strategies for defense Cicero is using in the above examples, Melanchthon explains (*Elem.* 18r). Praising one's audience or the judge is also one means useful for securing good will, as Quintilian advises (3.7.24; 4.1.16). Even though neither Quintilian nor Melanchthon treat this strategy as a figure, other Renaissance rhetoricians do.

concessio [L. "a concession"] or *paromologia* [G. "partial admission"] or *synchoresis* [G. "agreement, consent"]

Granting many points, but following with a point that overthrows all to one's favor

1. With pretense

   "But such charges are trifles when it is Verres who is standing his trial. What if he did make this ship's captain, the most notable man in his own community, secure himself by bribery against being flogged? Men do behave thus. What if he took money to acquit some other person? Such a thing has been done before. This nation does not expect us to bring stale charges against Verres. It demands novelties; it yearns for the unprecedented; for this, it feels, is not the trial of a Sicilian governor, but the trial of some foul and evil despot" (Cicero, *In C. Verrem* II. 5.44.117, trans. Greenwood).

   (Soarez 351)

2. Without pretense

   "They are proud, vain, disobedient, I acknowledge it; yet they are our children."

   (Smith 204)

   "Notwithstanding this I say concerning the whole nation of the Greeks, I grant unto them learning, I grant unto them the knowledge of many Arts, I take not from them the comely grace of speech, fine wits, singular eloquence. And furthermore, if they challenge unto themselves any other thing, I will not deny it them, yet religion and faith that nation never favored, what virtue, what authority, what weight there is of all this matter, they know not" (Cicero, *Pro Flacco* 4.9).

   (Peacham [1593] 173–74)

   "[S]uppose you have omitted nothing in your own person of a friend to be performed, that you were no partaker with him of those evil counsels, that you abstained to accompany him in the execution of his mischiefs; yet are you not therefore cleared. For it is not sufficient for a man not to do evil of himself, but that by too much lenity he become not occasion of another's mischief."

   (Day 96)

3. Combined with *sustentatio* and *inopinatum*

   "Solomon rehearseth the parts of his felicity: he mentioneth his riches, possessions, sumptuous buildings and pleasures, but suddenly he concludeth that all this is but vanity and vexation of spirit. This conclusion commeth unlooked for and very unlike to have ensued such premises. The expectation tendeth rather to hear what felicity followed all this wealth and great possession, and not what vanity or vexation of spirit" (Ecclesiastes 2:1–11).

   (Peacham [1593] 174)

Note: Alternate spellings include *paramologia* and *paromologe*. Peacham offers as an even additional name *paralogia* ([1593] 173). Puttenham's Anglicization is "the Figure of Admittance" (235). Keckermann specifies that there are two types of concession: the first brings no damage to the adversary; the second does bring harm (1487). *Concessio* and *confessio* are sometimes conflated into one figure; consequently, *paromologia* and *synchoresis* are sometimes synonyms of *confessio*. See *confessio* below. *Concessio* is also sometimes conflated with *permissio*. See *permissio* below. Quintilian, Soarez, Talaeus, Fenner, and Fraunce allow only the mocking form to count as the figure. Melanchthon shows this figure to derive from the dialectical topic of contraries (*Elem.* 53r).

conciliatio [L. "the gaining over or winning of hearers"]

Putting oneself on terms of intimacy with the audience; ingratiation; wishing the counsel well

1. Simply

   "O Caesar, your dying father entrusted me to you in his will."

2. Elaborately

   "Who should cling more to you in memory than your very strong father? How much by his deeds and sayings? And to be sure what he desired concerning me while he was alive and what he has written in his will in his first commendation—that I be entrusted to you—should be honored now that he is dead. Does this escape your memory completely, you who were accustomed to forget nothing except injuries?"

   (Scaliger 3.93.363)

Note: Scaliger argues that only the elaborate example above should be considered a figure. He says that *conciliatio* then is able to be figured, but is not a figure itself, contrary to Cicero (*De Or* 3.205) and Keckermann (1475), who do regard both the simple and elaborate versions figures.

confessio [L. "a confession"]

Admitting guilt or fault

"You have now, Tubero, the advantage most desired by an accuser: the accused confesses his guilt" (Cicero, *Pro Ligario* 1.2, trans. Butler).

(Quintilian 9.2.51)

"Let not my sins to thy remembrance come,
Nor all those spots which stain'd my youth;
But wash them out, and mindful of thy truth,
Receive the Prodigal returning home,
And let thy Mercy for thy ancient Love make room." (Based on Psalm 25:7)

(Lamy 2.120)

Note: An alternate name is *homologia*. Hoskins (28) and Blount (24) call this figure "admission." Sturm specifies that this confession may be honest, feigned, or ironic (1.21.58). This figure is sometimes conflated with *concessio* and sometimes with *permissio*. See *concessio* above and *permissio* below.

consensio [L. "agreement, common accord"] or *syndrome* [G. "in agreement with"]

Provisional concurrence with an adversary's viewpoint in order to ultimately undermine it

1. By praising the crime of the adversary, so that we press it more gravely

   "The ship's captain ransoms the girls for a price. It is human." (It is surely inhuman and agreeing with the captain's excuse heightens the act's infamy.)

   (Scaliger 3.90.361)

2. By using the adversary's line of reasoning in a new context, so that we show its flaws

   "'Ah,' says he, 'but look at that glorious boast of Cephalus—never once indicted!' Yes, glorious, and also lucky. But why should a man who has been often indicted but never convicted be the more justly open to reproach? However, men of Athens, so far as Aeschines is concerned, I can repeat that glorious boast: for he never indicted me or prosecuted me on indictment; and so, by his own admission, I am no worse a citizen than Cephalus" (Demosthenes, *On the Crown* 251, trans. Vince).

   (Hermogenes 2.1.313)

3. By agreeing to something that will really work to our favor

   "'Come now, do you deny that the court was bribed?' I do not, but maintain that it was not my client who bribed it. 'Who did bribe it, then?' I consider, first, that had there been any uncertainty as to what the issue of the trial would be, the balance of probability would still be in favour of the court having been bribed by the man who was afraid that it would convict himself, and not by the man whose fear was that it would acquit his adversary: second, that, inasmuch as there was no doubt what the verdict must be, it was much more likely to have been he who had no other ground of confidence than he who had every ground: and last, that it was much more likely to have been he who had twice failed before these judges, than he who had twice won his case before them" (Cicero, *Pro Cluentio* 23.63, trans. Hodge).

(Quintilian 9.2.51)

4. By exaggerating the charges brought against us to make them seem incredible

"My client is accused of having killed his father—a criminal and impious act, O immortal gods! of such a nature that all kinds of guilt seem to be included in this single evil deed. In fact, if, as is well said by philosophers, filial duty is often violated by a look, what punishment sufficiently severe can be found for one who has brought death upon his father, for whom all laws human and divine bound him to suffer death himself, if circumstances demanded?

In the case of a crime so grave, so atrocious, so unusual, and one which has been so rarely committed that, whenever it is heard of, it is regarded as a portent and monstrosity, what arguments, I ask you, do you think you ought to employ, Erucius, in your capacity as accuser? Ought you not to show the remarkable audacity of the man who is accused of it, his savage manners and brutal nature, a life given up to every kind of vice and infamy, in short, a character depraved, abandoned, and utterly ruined?" (Cicero, *Pro S. Roscio*, 13.37–38, trans. Freese)

(Quintilian 9.2.53)

Note: Robertellus collapses *concessio*, *confessio*, and *consensio* (44v); Scaliger distinguishes them, but treats them as species of *antiphasis* (3.90.361). See *antiphasis* above under semantical figures.

convinciari [L. "heckling, abuse"] or *vexatio* [L. "vexation"] or *contumelia* [L. "abuse, affront"]

Attacking the adversary through mocks, insults, ridicule, sarcasm, name-calling, and abusive language

"But what if he never forfeited his recognizances at all, if your plea is entirely a tissue of lies, invented by you with the greatest roguery and malice; what if no engagement for his appearing was ever made between you and Quinctius? by what name ought we to call you then? A rascal? But even if he had forfeited his recognizances, in making your application to the praetor and in advertising his goods for sale you still showed yourself to be an utter rascal. Full of malice? You do not deny it. Fraudulent? That is a name which you have already claimed for yourself and glory in it. Audacious, avaricious, perfidious? These terms are commonplace and out-of-date; but the act is unprecedented and unheard of. What term then am I to use? By Hercules! I am afraid of using expressions so harsh that they would outrage nature, or not so strong as the cause demands" (Cicero, *Pro Quinctio* 18.56, trans. Freese).

(Sturm 3.24.730)

Turnus: "You, Drances, at any rate always have much to say
At a time when war demands action. As elders are summoned,
You are the first to be present. The meeting must not be
Filled with your words that go boastfully flying in safety
As long as the moat and the walls hold the enemy back
And the ditches not running with blood. Then thunder ahead

With your eloquence after your custom. You, Drances, accuse me
Of fear when your right hand has heaped up as many piles
Of dead Trojans as mine has and dotted the fields here and there
With trophies. Go test for yourself what a lively courage
Can achieve. I am sure you need not go far to seek
Our enemies; everywhere they stand round the walls.
Are we attacking? Why pause? Or shall Mars exist
Forever upon your windy tongue and flying
Feet? (Virgil, *Aeneid* 11:392–406, trans. Lind)

(Scaliger 3.87.358)

Note: An alternate name is *catachresticos*. The above example from the *Aeneid* also appears as an illustration of *chleuasmos,* a semantical figure that is one species of this larger genus of abusive language. Quintilian prefers to regard this device as a method, not a figure (8.3.89). This figure seems similar to *laesio*, but differs, perhaps, in that *laesio* need not involve abuse. See *laesio* below.

correctio [L. "a correction"] or *epanorthosis* [G. "setting right, correcting"] or *metanoia* [G. "change of mind or heart, repentance"]

Retracting and correcting one's word, idea or action made in error; or correcting another person

1. When the word is corrected before it is spoken

   "We have here brought before you Judges, to have your judgement, not a thief, but a violent robber, not an adulterer, but a breaker of all chastity, not a spoiler of church goods, but a rank enemy to all godly religion, not a quarreling ruffian, but a most cruel murderer" (Cicero, *In C. Verrem* II 1.3.9).

   (Peacham [1593] 172)

   "I have in your service spent not my time only, but my strength and estate."

   (Smith 147)

2. When the word or idea is corrected after it is spoken, or *epidiorthosis*

   "I labored more abundantly than they all, yet not I, but the grace of God in me" (1 Corinthians 15:10).

   (Fenner 174)

   "O peerless you, or else no one alive
   Your pride serves you to freeze them all alone:
   Not pride madame, but praise of the lion.
   To conquer all and be conquered by none."

   (Puttenham 224)

3. When the orator blames himself for mis-speaking

   "Oh, I have made a false step here, gentlemen; he did not rob him of them, he bought them; I am sorry I spoke" (Cicero, *In C. Verrem* II 4.20.43, trans. Greenwood).

   (Quintilian 9.2.60)

   "We are fools that do presume to compare *Drufus Africanus*, *Pompeius*, and our selves with *Clodius*" (Cicero, *Pro Milone* 8.20).

   (Peacham [1593] 173)

4. When the orator asks for pardon

   "I beg you to pardon me, if I have been carried too far."

   (Quintilian 9.2.17)

5. Correcting a word to reprimand someone, or *aphorismus*
   "Ah cruel man, and no man neither, but a beast."

(Day 94)

"O Parthenia! No more Parthenia! What art thou?" (Parthenia in Sidney, *Arcadia*, book 3, 426)

"But if extreme and unresistable violence have oppressed me, who will ever do any of you sacrifice (O you Stars) if you do not succour me. No, no you will not help me. No, no you cannot help me" (Philoclea in Sidney, *Arcadia*, book 2, 174).

(Hoskins 30)

6. When calling the speech back to its purpose after a digression
   See *antanaclasis* under Discoursal–parts below.

(Keckermann 1489)

Note: Alternate spellings are *metanoea* and *metania*. Other names include *emendatio, moderatio, paenitentia,* "repenting," and *epidiorthosis*. Talaeus and Soarez list *correctio* twice, once for the correction of a word (70, 331) and once for the correction of a idea (50, 340). Peacham lists *correctio* and *metania* separately, but considers the second a species of the first and a reprehension ([1593] 172–73), having in mind what Rufinianus describes under *aphorismus* (§14). See *aphorismus* above. Puttenham, however, calling this figure "the Penitent," treats *metanoia* and *correctio* as synonyms, emphasizing the figure's use in praise (223), and Day separates *metonoia* and *aphorismus*, the first a correction of a word in order to praise or blame, and the second, a stronger reprehension (94). Gill treats all these terms as synonyms, including even *paradiastole, disjunctio* and *disterminatio* (164). See *paradiastole* below. This brief introduction suggests the variety of interpretations we find amongst these rhetoricians. Melanchthon classifies this figure as a species deriving from the dialectical topic of contraries (*Elem.* 52v).

deliberatio [L. "a deliberation, consultation"]
Deliberation, a general category

1. *Aporia* (deliberating with self)
2. *Anacoenosis* or *communicatio* (deliberating with audience)

(Butler 121)

Note: Hoskins and Blount restrict *deliberatio* to *aporia*. Fenner, Fraunce and Butler include both figures here. See *aporia* and *communicatio* above.

diakrisis [G. "separating, distinguishing"]
Conceding excessively to the adversary in order to win a concession in return
"In the first place, I request Chrysogonus to be satisfied with our wealth and property, and not to ask for our life-blood" (Cicero, *Pro S. Roscio* 3.7, trans. Freese).

(Sturm 3.23.723)

Note: Sturm points out that in this example, while the request is genuine, the concession contains pretense, inasmuch as it is excessive and the wealth should be restored as well.

diasyrmus [G. "disparagement, ridicule"] or *elevatio* [L. "a lessening, disparaging accomplished through a raising up"]
Disparaging, scoffing at, or debasing the opponent's argument

1. Through "some base similitude" or "some ridiculous example, to which the adversary's objection or argument is compared" (Peacham [1593] 39).

"To say to one's opponent, that he 'fights with leaden Daggers,' meaning weak and slender Arguments."

(Peacham [1577] D.iiii.r)

2. Through criticism
When we claim the arguments "pertain not to the purpose, or that they are unworthy to be answered unto, or that we keep them till another time."

(Sherry [1550] 61)

Note: An alternate spelling is *diasirmus* or *elevacio*. Aquila treats this figure more generally as *irrisio* (36). Scaliger equates this figure with *vexatio* (3.87.358), otherwise called *convinciari*. This figure is often categorized with the tropes and is sometimes conflated with *chleuasmos*. See also the entries for these related terms.

epanorotema [G. "adding questions"]
Interviewing someone by means of the Socratic method with a series of questions until one's point is made
Socrates: "My boy, how much property did your father leave you? Was it a lot and not easily assessed?"
Boy: "It was a lot, Socrates."
Socrates: "Well now, did he also leave you the knowledge of how to use it?"
["Socrates unobtrusively drives the boy into a corner; he reminds him that he does not have knowledge and encourages him to find instruction."]

(Demetrius §297)

Note: Robertellus gives the name to this strategy that he pulls from Demetrius (49r).

eucharistia [G. "thankfulness, gratitude"] or *gratiarum actio* [L. "an act of graciousness"]
Thanking hearers for listening or for a favor
"To thee, O Caesar, we give most hearty thanks, yea great thanks we yield to thee" (Cicero, *Pro Marcello* 11.33).
Jacob prays, "I am not worthy of the least of all thy mercies, and all the truth which thou hast shewed unto thy servant" (Genesis 32:10).
Christ prays, "Father, I thank thee for that thou hast heard me" (John 11:41).

(Peacham [1593] 101–2)

Note: In Melanchthon (*Elem.* 7v) and Vossius (116) *gratiarum actio* names a genre of discourse.

euphemismus [G. "use of an auspicious word in place of an inauspicious one; using words of good omen"]
Palliating something unfavorable in a modest kind of speech

1. By giving something a less offensive name or reference for modesty's sake
"None of you shall approach to any that is near of kin to him, to uncover their nakedness" (Leviticus 18:6). ("Uncover their nakedness" for "incest.")

(Smith 225)

2. By predicting good consequences
To tell "the likely effects of good causes, and to foretell them, as by the good towardness of youth to prognosticate the virtue and felicity of the future age, for a good beginning doth promise a good end, a good cause a good effect, a holy life a happy death, [. . .]"

(Peacham [1593] 90)

Note: Peacham gives *boni ominis captatio* as the Latin equivalent ([1593] 89). He follows Robertellus, who follows Phalereus, in assigning the second meaning, which usually is covered under *ominatio boni*. See *ominatio* under Discoursal–genres below.

excitatio [L. "a rousing up, wakening"]
Arousing the audience from weariness or boredom; getting their attention
"Listen carefully, I beg you."
"The thing I am dealing with possibly seems trivial at first sight, but if you will attend for a little, you will assuredly realize that under this cover lurk the gravest perils to our national security."
"Bear with me for a while, I beg you, I will soon reveal what all this has in view."
"And now you will hear something never heard before."

(Erasmus, *De copia* 649)

Use exclamations or commands, or admonish the audience not to sleep.

(Scaliger 3.61.334)

Note: Quintilian reports the figure *excitare judices* from Celsus, but rejects it (9.2.104). Robertellus requests that it be given a proper name (45r). Scaliger seems to have given this figure such a name.

fastidium [L. "scornful contempt, haughtiness, pride"]
Being haughty, disdainful
Richard III exults to himself after his rapid and successful wooing of Anne, the widow of Edward, Prince of Wales, whom Richard helped to depose and kill. This love conquest he makes following hard upon Edward's funeral:
"Was ever woman in this humor woo'd?
Was ever woman in this humor won?
I'll have her, but I will not keep her long.
What? I, that kill'd her husband and his father,
To take her in her heart's extremest hate,
With curses in her mouth, tears in her eyes,
The bleeding witness of my hatred by,
Having God, her conscience, and these bars against me,
And I no friends to back my suit [at all]
But the plain devil and dissembling looks?
And yet to win her! All the world to nothing!
Hah!" (Shakespeare, *Richard III* 1.2.227–38)

(Robertellus 45v; example mine)

Note: Quintilian attributes this figure to Celsus (9.2.104), but hesitates to accept it as a figure (9.2.107).

fictio [L. "a making, fashioning, feigning, counterfeiting"]
Using invented and simulated speech
A general category inclusive of *prosopopoeia*, *sermocinatio*, *dialogismus*, *paralepsis*, etc.

(Scaliger 3.85.356)

Note: See the entries for these terms individually.

fiducia [L. "trust, reliance, confidence, assurance"] or *eustathia* [G. "steadiness, firmness, tranquility"] or *pepoithesis* [G. "trust, reliance, boldness"]

Promising or protesting constancy, faithfulness, confidence

"I am ready to sail out as a volunteer and suffer any consequences, if this is not true" (Demosthenes, *Philippic I* 29, trans. Wooten).

(Hermogenes 2.7.356)

The apostle Paul avers, "I am persuaded that neither death, nor life, nor angels, nor principalities, nor powers, neither things present, nor things to come, neither height, nor depth, nor any other creature shall be able to separate us from the love of God, which is in Christ Jesus our Lord" (Romans 8:38).

(Peacham [1593] 69)

Expressions such as "I will say confidently," "I will speak faithfully," "See how I do not fear this adversary."

(Keckermann 1498)

Note: Peacham gives *constantia* as another name ([1593] 69).

hypophora [G. "putting forward"] or *sibi ipsi responsio* [L. "a replying to one's own question"]

Answering one's own questions

"Whom hast thou defied and blasphemed? against whom hast thou lifted up thy voice, and exalted thy proud looks? Even against the holy one of Israel" (Isaiah 37:23).

"Shall we continue in sin, that grace may abound? God forbid" (Romans 6:1–2).

(Peacham ([1593] 107–8)

"And is there care in heaven? And is there love
In heavenly spirits to these creatures base,
That may compassion of their evils move?
There is, or else much more wretched [. . .]" (Spenser, *The Faerie Queene* II 8.1.1–4)

(Gill 166)

Note: Hermogenes calls this *erotesis kata diastasin* (1.4.239). This technique is used in *ratiocinatio* and *subjectio*; consequently, examples of either one of these are often cited for *hypophora* and vice versa. Also, for this reason Sturm (1.28.104), Gill (166), and Smith (127) associate *hypophora* with *subjectio*. See *ratiocinatio* and *subjectio* below. *Hypophora* has another meaning, that of indirect or attributed speech. See *prosopopoeia* below under Discoursal–genres.

hyposchesin [G. "undertaking, engagement, promise"]

Speaking modestly about oneself

"[W]hen Demosthenes declares that although he could bring a charge of theft or violence, he is nevertheless content to make an accusation for assault" (*Against Conon* 1, trans. Wooten).

When the orator counts himself "among the common people when [he] is not of that rank," as Demosthenes does in *Against Meidias*: "I myself did what each one of you would have chosen to do if you had been insulted" (1, trans. Wooten).

When the orator says he is going to trial against his will, but that the opponent has compelled him, as Demosthenes does in *Against Aristocrates*: "Although I am not involved in politics nor am I one of those who come into court often, I say that I shall demonstrate that such a crime was perpetrated . . ." (4, trans. Wooten).

When the orator says he is not accustomed to public speaking.

When the orator says that the opponent is prosecuting him, but that he could have brought charges against the opponent although he has not.

(Hermogenes 2.6.345–47)

When the orator removes his own concerns from the matter at hand: "Not, gentlemen, that I have so good a conceit of myself as to presume to fancy that my client's services to myself entitle him to exemption from all prosecution. [. . .] In dealing with them [the theories of the prosecution] I must walk warily, that I may myself be void of offense; and I must not deal with them at all until I have replied to the actual charges, that it may not appear that the case for the defence relies rather upon the recollection of my own crisis than upon my client's innocence" (Cicero, *Pro Plancio* 1.3–2.4, trans. Watts).

(Sturm 3.35.814)

improvisum quiddam [L. "an unforeseen something"] or *para prosdokian* [G. "the unexpected"]
Replying with an unexpected turn of expression

The Cyclops replies, "No-man I will eat last, the rest before him" (Homer, *Odyssey* 9.369–70, trans. Innes).

(Demetrius §152)

"'When is it best to dine?,' quod one to Diogenes. 'Marry,' quod he, 'for a rich man, when he list, for a poor man, when he can.'"

(Wilson 168)

interpellantis coercitio [L. "a restraining or coercing of those who hinder"]
Silencing interrupters; bidding those who have least cause to speak to hold their peace

"Diogenes, being upon the sea among a number of naughty packs in a great storm[, . . .] when divers of these wicked fellows cried out for fear of drowning–some with feigned prayer to Jupiter, some to Neptune, and every one as they best fantasied the gods above–'Whish,' quod Diogenes, 'for by God's Mother, if God himself know you to be here, you were like to be drowned, every mother's son of you.'"

(Wilson 223)

Note: Wilson's name for this figure is "whisht." Quintilian regards this device as a method, not a figure (9.2.2).

interpellatio [L. "a speaking between, interruption, hindrance"]
Interrupting others

Both Hamlet and Polonius interrupt each other in the following interchange:

Pol. Well be with you, gentlemen!

Ham. [Aside to Rosencrantz and Gildenstern] Hark you, Guildenstern, and you too–at each ear a hearer–that great baby you see there is not yet out of his swaddling-clouts.

Ros. Happily he is the second time come to them, for they say an old man is twice a child.

Ham. I will prophesy, he comes to tell me of the players, mark it! [Aloud] You say right, sir, a' Monday morning, 'twas then indeed.

Pol. My lord, I have news to tell you.

Ham. My lord, I have news to tell you. When Roscius was an actor in Rome—

Pol. The actors are come hither, my lord.

Ham. Buzz, buzz!

Pol. Upon my honor—

Ham. "Then came each actor on his ass"—

Pol. The best actors in the world, either for tragedy, comedy, history, pastoral, pastoral-comical, historical-pastoral, [tragical-historical, tragical-comical-historical-pastoral,] scene individable, or poem unlimited; Seneca cannot be too heavy, nor Plautus too light, for the law of writ and the liberty: these are the only men. (Shakespeare, *Hamlet* 2.2.380–402)

(Scaliger 3.91.362; example mine)

interrogatio [L. "a questioning, inquiry, examination"] or *rogatio* [L. "an asking, demanding"]
To make a point and express emotion by asking a question; the rhetorical question to which no answer is expected

1. *Erotesis* or *erotema* [G. "an inquiry, a question"] or *peusis* [G. "inquiry, question"], to affirm, deny, or demand warmly

Love: "How sweet are thy words unto my taste! yea sweeter than honey to my mouth" (Psalm 119:103).

Desire: "How long tarriest thou, Lord?"

Admiration: "What is it that the greedy hunger of gold doth not urge and compel mortal men to attempt?" (Virgil, *Aeneid* 3.63)

Wishing: "Shall I not see him before I die?"

Sorrow: "Why died I not in my birth? Why set they me upon their knees and gave me suck with their breasts?"

(Peacham ([1593] 105–6)

Despair: "Alas, what ground may hold me, what land or shore may possess me, circumvented as I am with so many evils?" (Virgil, *Aeneid* 2.69–70)

Anger: "Shall I yet cover thy villainies, being at thy hands thus hatefully misused?"

(Day 87)

Note: Puttenham's term here is "the Questioner" (220). In his first edition, Sherry distinguishes between *erotesis* and *erotema*, listing *erotema* as a synonym for *ratiocinatio* ([1550] 51–52), but such is an error, which he corrects in his second edition. Alexander restricts *erotema* to a "yes" or "no" question (24). Both Quintilian (9.2.7–11) and Soarez (337) use *erotesis* as a synonym of *interrogatio*, which includes all forms of questions asked not to get information, but to press a point, to create ill will, to excite pity, to express indignation, despair, or surprise, to command, and to assert that which cannot be denied. Peacham lists *interrogatio* and *erotema* separately ([1593] 105–6), treating *interrogatio* as a general category, consisting of two types: the genuine question and the one used to express emotion; and *erotema* as the question used to affirm or deny, within which he includes the question used to upbraid. Similarly, Butler uses *erotesis* for the rhetorical question and *interrogatio* for the question asked as an exclamation. See also *interrogatio* above under Pragmatical–idea figures.

2. *Epiplexis* [G. "blame, rebuke"] or *percontatio* [L. "a question, an inquiry"], to upbraid

"Tully inveighing against Cataline, that Roman rebel, beginneth his oration chidingly, questioning with Catiline of this sort: 'How long, Catiline, wilt thou abuse our sufferance? How long will this rage and madness of thine go about to deceive us?'" (*In Catalinam* I 1.1)

(Wilson 209)

Note: Sherry gives as an alternate name *increpacio* ([1550] 51). Smith (136) and Day (87), like Peacham, include this kind of question within *erotesis*.

3. *Elenktikon* [G. "a refutation"], to refute through cross-examination

"But here was a man annexing Euboea and making it a basis of operations against Attica, attacking Megara, occupying Oreus, demolishing Porthmus, establishing the tyranny of Philistides at Oreus and of Cleitarchus at Eretria, subjugating the Hellespont, besieging Byzantium, destroying some of the Greek cities, reinstating exiled traitors in others: by these acts was he, or was he not, committing injustice, breaking treaty, and violating the terms of peace? Was it, or was it not, right that some man of Grecian race should stand forward to stop those aggressions?" (Demosthenes, *De Corona* 71–72, trans. Vince).

(Demetrius §279)

"In time past there was a greater abundance of such men [whose valour, energy, and good fortune in warfare have been weighed and not found wanting] in our commonwealth than to-day; yet though this was so, not only their safety but also their honour was regarded. And to-day how should you act, now that the profession of arms has fallen out of fashion among our youth; when our best men and our greatest generals have been wasted either by age or civil dissension and public calamity; when wars so numerous are either unavoidably undertaken by us, or sprung upon us with unforeseen suddenness? Do you not think you should retain this man himself against our nation's doubtful hour, while at the same time you kindle his fellow-countrymen to the pursuit of honour and virtue?" (Cicero, *Pro M. Fonteio* 19.42, trans. Watts)

(Sturm 3.10.588)

Note: Sturm, echoing Hermogenes, claims that *elenktikon* "is a powerful and conquering argument" that cannot be refuted (3.11.602). He has in mind that the question is part of an *elenchus*, with the question containing a supposition that cannot be denied (see Hermogenes, *Meth.* §10). See *elenchus* below under Discoursal–parts of oration. Farnaby too says that this type of question is frequently used in enthymemes and inductions (24).

4. To ask questions in order to attract attention to one's point
"You have a resource which you will not find if you look for it now, but if you wait, you will find it. What then is this resource that is not now but will be hereafter? That sounds like a puzzle. I shall explain" (Demosthenes, *On the Navy-Boards* 24, trans. Kennedy).

(Hermogenes, *Method* §10)

Note: Hermogenes explains that asking oneself questions in this manner attracts the attention of the audience and wins their agreement in advance, since the question includes a proof and refutation of suspicion and the listeners know that the orator would not ask a question of himself that he would not be able to answer (*Meth.* §10).

laesio [L. "a hurting, injuring"]
Hard-hitting; making personal attacks

"But since that madman has thought that by pouring abuse upon me in the senate he could win some access to your ears, I shall depart in my speech from a natural arrangement; and shall reply, I will not say to the speech of my infuriated opponent, for a speech is beyond his capacity, but to his scurrility, his practice in which has been reinforced not only by an intolerable impudence, but also by a long-continued impunity.

And first I ask you, Clodius, infatuate lunatic that you are, what Nemesis of your crimes and enormities is it which is so powerfully deluding you to believe that upright men such as these, who bear up the state not merely by their wise deliberations, but by the very impressiveness of their external majesty, are incensed with me, because in a statement of my opinion I identified the welfare of the state with the bestowal of honour upon Gnaeus Pompeius, and that they are likely to hold at this time views on essential matters of religion different from those which they held in my absence?" (Cicero, *De Domo Sua* 1.3, trans. Watts)

(Cicero, *De Oratore* 3.205; example mine)

Note: This figure is similar to *convinciari* above, but differs in that hard-hitting need not entail abuse, even though this particular example does.

medela [L. "a healing, remedy, means of redress"]

Healing offenses when we cannot defend or deny them

"When there was a greater luxurity [*sic*] and riot objected against *Caelius* [than] *Cicero* durst defend, and more evident [than] he could deny: notwithstanding he did extenuate the fault with gentle words, and as much as he could pacified the judges, [. . . by saying] that those things were partly the vices of times rather than of the man, [. . .] that some things ought to be yielded to age, [. . . and that he had] expectation of *Caelius'* modesty and honest behavior for the time to come" (*Pro Caelio* 28–30).

"The Apostle *Paul* giveth a very good example of this figure in his Epistle to *Philemon*, where he useth sundry reasons & diverse means to salve and cure the fault of *Onesimus*, and to appease and pacify the displeasure of *Philemon*": "I beseech thee for my son Onesimus, whom I have begotten in my bonds: Which in time past was to thee unprofitable, but now profitable to thee and me: [. . .] If thou count me therefore a partner, receive him as myself. If he hath wronged thee, or oweth thee ought, put that on mine account" (Philemon 1:10–18).

(Peacham [1593] 176)

Note: Declining to do so, Quintilian reports that Celsus treated *satisfacere* ("satisfaction, reparation, amends, apology") as a figure (9.2.104).

meionektikas [G. "to be at a disadvantage"]

Diminishing ourselves to make the adversary look unjust

"For can anything more iniquitous or more scandalous be spoken of or mentioned, Gaius Aquilius, than the fact that I, who am defending the civil rights, the good name and fortunes of the other party, should have to plead my cause first, above all, when Hortensius, who in this trial fills the part of an accuser, upon whom nature has lavishly bestowed a wealth of language and the greatest eloquence, is going to speak against me?" (Cicero, *Pro Quinctio* 2.8, trans. Freese)

(Sturm 3.23.719)

mimesis [G. "imitation"] or *imitatio* [L. "imitation"]

Imitating others; speaking as if another; using another's words and gestures

"In Psal[m] 2:3, *David* uses the language of rebellious rulers: ' Let us break their bands, and cast away their cords from us.'

So in 1 Cor[inthians] 15:32 *Paul* uses the words of Epicures: 'What advantages it me, if the dead rise not? let us eat and drink, for to morrow we shall die.'"

(Smith 247)

Note: Quintilian gives *ethopoeia* as a synonym (9.2.58). See *ethopoeia* below under Discoursal–genres. Melanchthon indicates that this figure is a species of a more general figure he calls *color* (*Elem.* 51r). See *metastasis* above under Pragmatical–idea figures. Sherry indicates that this figure is the *prosopopoeia* ([1550] 69) and Shaw includes this figure as a kind of *prosopopoeia* (171). When expanded into a full-length drama, this figure becomes a genre in its own right. Keckermann, however, restricts this figure to parody and ridicule, a form of irony (1472).

mystikos hypostamenein [G. "an announcement of a mystery"]
Mystifying the audience; presenting secrets or mysteries
"To discover this is a difficult matter and to reveal it to all once it has been discovered is impossible" (Plato, *Timaeus* 28c, trans. Wooten).

(Hermogenes 1.6.247)

"O the height of the riches, of the wisdom, and of the knowledge of God, how incomprehensible are his judgments and untracktable his paths" (Romans 11:33).

(Sturm 3.9.572)

paralepsis [G. "neglect, disregard, omission"] or *praeteritio* [L. "a passing over, omission"] or *occupatio* [L. "taking possession of"] or *praetermissio* [L. "a leaving out, omission"]
Pretending to bypass what we really do say

1. Without a reason for omitting the information
"I do not say thou receivest bribes of thy fellows. I busy not myself in this thing, that thou spoilest Cities, Kingdoms, and all men's houses: I let pass thy thefts and thy robberies."

(Peacham [1593] 131)

2. With a reason for doing so
"I hold my peace and will not say for shame,
The much untruth of that uncivil dame:
For if I should her colors kindly blaze,
It would so make the chaste ears amaze."

(Puttenham 239–40)

"I do not complain of the decrease of revenues, nor of the crime of this loss and damage; I pass over those things which everyone can lament most truly and most grievously–that we have been unable to preserve the chief part of the public heritage, the fairest possession of the Roman people, the reverse of corn, the war granary, the revenue which the republic kept under seal and bar; lastly, that we have yielded that territory to Publius Rullus, which by itself alone resisted both the absolutism of Sulla and the bribery of the Gracchi. I do not say that this is the only revenue in the State which is left after others have been lost, which does not remain inactive, while others are interrupted; which flourishes in peace, and does lose its value in time of war; which supports the soldiery and is not afraid of the enemy–I say nothing of all this now and reserve what I have to say for a public assembly. I am now speaking of the danger to our safety and freedom." (Cicero, *De Lege Agraria* 1 7.21, trans. Freese)

(Soarez 349–50)

Note: An alternate spelling is *paralipsis* or *paraleipsis* and additional names include *parasiopesis* and *occultatio*. Puttenham calls this figure "the Passager" (239). Quintilian disallows this device as a figure (9.3.99). Both Fraunce (A8v) and Smith (166) acknowledge the figure *apophasis* or *negatio* to be a type of this figure. Keckermann distinguishes by regarding *paralipsis* as an opposite of *apophasis*. In *apophasis* we deny what we greatly affirm; in *paralipsis* we affirm something, but we nevertheless act contrarily (1472). See *apophasis* above.

parrhesia [G. "outspokenness, frankness, freedom of speech"] or *licentia* [L. "freedom, license to do as one pleases"]
Speaking candidly

1. Begging license for the privilege of speaking candidly
   "Pardon if I be tedious, the circumstance of the cause requireth it."
   "If my speech seem vehement, the matter occasioning the same is urgent."
   (Day 90)

   "You may suppose me proud and inconstant, but my sincerity shall out-dare all their calumnies."
   "For do I now persuade men, or God? or do I seek to please men? for if I yet pleased men, I should not be the servant of Christ" (Galatians 1:10).
   (Smith 226–27)

2. Speaking freely without asking for such a privilege
   "Now in the Immortal Gods' name, when I look at you, Dolabella, very dear to me as you are, I cannot keep silent about the mistake which both of you gentlemen are making" (Cicero, *Philippic* 1 29, trans. Bailey).
   (Peacham [1593] 114; example mine)

   Jesus replies to those who accuse the woman caught in adultery, "He that is without sin among you, let him first cast a stone at her." Jesus then says to the woman, "Neither do I condemn thee: go, and sin no more" (John 8:7,11).
   (Keckermann 1498)

3. Censuring our own faults as we censure others' faults
   "When Marcus Cicero maintains in your presence that another was not an adherent of the cause which he admits that he himself embraced, he feels no fear of what unspoken reflections may fill your mind, nor does he shudder at what thoughts about himself may be suggesting themselves to you as you listen to his defense of that other. [. . .] Mark, Tubero, I pray, how I, who flinch not from confessing my own fault, dare not to acknowledge that of Ligarius! And I have spoken thus about myself in order that Tubero might forgive me when I said the same about him;" (Cicero, *Pro Ligario* 2.6–8).
   (Melanchthon, *Elem.* 45r)

Note: Alternate spellings include *parisia* or *parresia.* Puttenham's Anglicization is "the Licentious" (234). Quintilian restricts this figure to occasions when we cloak an ulterior motive by this freedom in speaking (9.2.28). The examples above show that Renaissance rhetoricians are not so restrictive.

permissio [L. "a giving up, yielding"] or *epitrope* [G. "surrender of the power to decide"]
Conceding to and suffering of another's will, sometimes sincerely and sometimes ironically in order to forbid that will in a kind of *concessio*

1. Sincerely
   "Patience is a remedy for every disease."
   "When things cannot be that we would have, we should will that which we can have."
   (Wilson 230)

2. Ironically, showing contempt, bluffing, or pretending ignorance
   "Take your pleasure for a time and do what you list; a time will come when accompt shall be made."
   (Wilson 230)

   "Rejoice, O young man in thy youth, and let thy heart cheer thee in thy young days, & walk in the ways of thine own heart, and in the sight of thine eyes: but know thou, that for all these things God will bring thee into judgment" (Ecclesiastes 11:9).

"*Simo* in *Terence* seemeth by his words very willingly to grant, that his son might marry *Glyceryе*, when in very deed, he endeavoreth with all diligence to withdraw him from her: 'Yes,' quoth he, 'let him take her. God speed him well, let him go dwell and keep house with her'" (*Andria* 5.3.888–89).

(Peacham [1593] 112)

Note: Quintilian (9.2.25), Susenbrotus (64), and Soarez (357) treat *permissio* as *synchoresis*. See *synchoresis* below. Robertellus distinguishes between this more reproaching and debasing kind of *epitrope* and that other more confiding kind, called *synchoresis* (43r). Peacham, Taleus, Fenner and Fraunce allow only the ironic form to be the figure.

phantasia [G. "imagination, a re-presentation"] or *imaginatio* [L. "a mental image, fancy, imagination"]

Imagining vividly the details of a situation so as to evoke within ourselves the emotions we wish to evoke in the hearers

"Shall I not bring before my eyes all the circumstances which it is reasonable to imagine must have occurred in such a connexion? Shall I not see the assassin burst suddenly from his hiding-place, the victim tremble, cry for help, beg for mercy, or turn to run? Shall I not see the fatal blow delivered and the stricken body fall? Will not the blood, the deathly pallor, the groan of agony, the death-rattle, be indelibly impressed upon my mind? [. . .]

Again, when we desire to awaken pity, we must actually believe that the ills of which we complain have befallen our own selves, and must persuade our minds that this is really the case. We must identify ourselves with the persons of whom we complain that they have suffered grievous, unmerited and bitter misfortune, and must plead their case and for a brief space feel their suffering as though it were our own, while our words must be such as we should use if we stood in their shoes. I have often seen actors, both in tragedy and comedy, leave the theatre still drowned in tears after concluding the performance of some moving role."

(Quintilian 6.2.31–35)

Note: Quintilian would rather regard this embellishment as a method, not a figure (8.3.88). This figure inevitably leads to *evidentia* or *enargia* on the one hand and *pathopoeia* on the other. See the entries for these terms.

philophronesis [G. "kind treatment, courtesy"]

Speaking with gentleness and humble submission

"*Jacob*, who fearing the malice and might of his brother *Esau*, used this means to appease his rage and cruelty. He commeth before his family; as soon as he saw *Esau*, he shewed a sign of dutiful submission. He bowed himself seven times most humbly before he came near to him, calling him his Lord, and himself his servant. His family also children came likewise in seemly and suppliant order, and humbled themselves at his presence, yielding obeisance and reverence unto him, by means whereof the fiery and flaming wrath of *Esau* was turned into tears of compassion" (Genesis 33:1–15).

"The Ambassadors of the Israelites do deliver their humble submission to *Olophernes*, in these words saying: 'Behold we are the servants of *Nabucodonozor*, the great King. We lie down before thee; use us as shall be good in thy sight. Behold our houses and all our places, and all our fields of wheat, and our flocks, and our herds, and all our lodges and tabernacles lie before thy face: use them as it pleaseth thee. Behold, even our Cities and the inhabitants thereof are thy servants: come and take them as it seemeth good to thee'" (*Apocrypha*, Judith 3:1–4).

(Peacham [1593] 96–97)

Note: Latin names include *benevolentia* and *exceptio benigna* (Peacham [1593] 96).

pleonektikon [G. "to have an advantage"]

Attributing great power, justice, and the favor and confidence of many to the adversaries

"In the next place, Quinctius has for his opponent nominally Naevius, but in reality the most accomplished men of our time, the bravest and most prosperous of our citizens, who with united efforts and vast resources are defending parties in order that he may be able the more easily to overwhelm anyone he chooses by an iniquitous trial—if that can be called defending" (Cicero, *Pro Quinctio* 2.7, trans. Freese).

(Sturm 3.23.719)

praemunitio [L. "fortifying beforehand"] or *proparasceue* [G. "preparation"]

Defending oneself against an anticipated attack

1. By giving reasons for one's participation in the case before making one's case
   Cicero begins his speech against Caecilius with the following self-defense: "It may be, gentlemen, that some of you, or some of the audience, are surprised that I have departed from the line of action which I have pursued for all these years with regard to criminal proceedings; that having defended many accused persons, and attacked nobody, I have now suddenly changed my policy, and entered the arena as a prosecutor. But anyone whom this surprises has only to understand the motives that govern my action, and he will not only recognize that I am doing right, but will certainly take the view that no one can be held better fitted than myself to conduct the case before us" (*In Q. Caecilium* 1.1, trans. Greenwood).

   (Quintilian 9.2.17)

2. By blaming, censuring, or chiding those guilty before giving reasons to show the innocence of the defendant
   As part of his narration of the event, Cicero includes the fact that Milo's servants, not Milo, killed Clodius in their zeal to revenge their master's supposed murder: "[A]nd those of the servants who had presence of mind to defend themselves, and were faithful to their master, were some of them slain, and the others, when they saw a fierce battle taking place around the chariot, and as they were prevented from getting near their master so as to succour him, when they heard Clodius himself proclaim that Milo was slain, and they thought that it was really true, they, the servants of Milo, (I am not speaking for the purpose of shifting the guilt onto the shoulders of others, but I am saying what really occurred) did, without their master either commanding it, or knowing it, or even being present to see it, what every one would have wished his servants to do in a similar case" (*Pro Milone* 10.29, trans. Yonge).

   (Butler 137)

Note: A synonym is *proyporgasia*. Butler conflates this figure with *praeparatio* (137). See *praeparatio* below.

praeparatio [L. "a making ready"] or *procatasceue* [G. "preface, preliminary exposé"]
Preparing the audience for acceptance of one's ideas

1. By briefly laying out the debate and one's intentions and reasons beforehand in a *digestio*
"I hope, my lords, both to persuade this man by reason and to have your judgment in this matter. For whereas it is a sore thing to be justly accused for breaking friendship, then assuredly if one be wrongfully slandered, a man had need to look about him."
(Wilson 212)

2. By preparing the way for the *probatio,* the section devoted to proofs, through strategic scattering of details in the preceding *exordium* and *narratio*
Dido prepares Anna, her sister, to support her in her desire for marriage with Aeneas in this wise:
"Anna sister, how sleeplessness frightens and worries me now!
What a stranger is this who has come as a guest to our home!
How he carries himself, how brave in heart and with weapons!
He is god-born: at least I believe it; my faith is not empty.
Fear shows a low character. How he is tossed by the Fates!
What wearisome wars he described! If I had not decided
Most firmly to marry no more since my first love deceived me
By dying, if I were not weary of torches and bed
As a bride, I could yield to a sinful love for this man." (Virgil, *Aeneid* 4.9–17, trans. Lind)
(Rufinianus, *Dianoeas* §3)

Demosthenes prepares the Athenian jury to support his complaint against Meidias:
"The brutality and insolence with which Meidias treats everyone alike are, I suppose, as well known to you, gentlemen of the jury, as to all other citizens. For myself, I have simply taken the course which anyone of you would have adopted, had he been the victim of a similar outrage. I lodged a plaint in the Assembly against him as an offender in connexion with the festival, not only for his assault on my person at the Dionysia, but for many other acts of violence during the whole period when I served as chorus-master. But when the whole people, acting honourably and rightly, evinced such anger, such exasperation, such deep concern at the wrongs which they knew I had suffered, that, in spite of the frantic efforts of the defendant and a few supporters, they were deaf to their arguments, shut their eyes to their wealth and their promises, and condemned him by an unanimous show of hands, thereupon, gentlemen of the jury, many citizens, including some of you who are here in court, came to me and demanded and even implored that I should take the further step of bringing Meidias under your jurisdiction; and they did so, I think, for two reasons, men of Athens, because, so help me heaven! they thought that my own wrongs were serious, and they also wished to punish Meidias for conduct which they had witnessed on other occasions, as a scoundrel and a ruffian who could no longer be tolerated. This being so, I have in your interests taken all due precautions, and now that the case is before the court, I am here, as you see, to accuse him, having refused large sums of money, men of Athens, which I might have accepted on condition of dropping the prosecution, and having to steel myself against many appeals and favourable offers—yes, and even menaces. What yet remains to do is in your hands; but my hope is that the more the defendant has pestered you with his solicitations—I observed just now what he was up to in front of the courthouse—the more likely I am to obtain justice. [. . .] But since Meidias bribed the umpires and so robbed

my tribe unfairly of the prize, since I in person was struck by him and insulted as perhaps no chorus-master was ever insulted before, and since I am here to follow up the verdict which the Assembly pronounced in indignation and anger at such conduct, for these reasons I shall not shrink even from an appeal to you. [. . .] For the case stands thus, Athenians. I was the victim and it was my person that was then outraged; but now the question to be fought out and decided is whether Meidias is to be allowed to repeat his performances and insult anyone and everyone of you with impunity. Therefore if perhaps anyone of you hitherto assumed that this action was brought from private motives, when he now reflects that this is a matter of general concern, and that public interest demands that no one shall be allowed to act in this way, let him grant me an attentive hearing, and then let him give what seems to him the fairest verdict.

But first the clerk shall read you the law which provides for the lodging of plaints in the Assembly; [. . .] Now I want to read to you the next law as well, [. . .] You will observe, gentlemen of the jury, that whereas in the first law the public plaint may be lodged against those who violate the laws of the festival, in the latter law you have sanctioned plaints against those who exact money from defaulting debtors or seize any property or use violence to that end. [. . . B]ut Meidias, as I shall prove, chose those very same days [of the festival] to commit offences that call for the severest punishment. I intend to describe in order each outrage of which I have been the victim, before I speak of the blows in which his attacks culminated, for there is not a single one of those attacks for which he will not be shown to have deserved death. (*Against Meidias* 1–12, trans. Vince)

(Hermogenes, *On Issues* 63.7–21)

Note: Rufinianus and Robertellus distinguish between *praemunitio* and *praeparatio*, while Butler (137) and Keckermann (1486) equate the two figures. Quintilian indicates that both *praemunitio* and *praeparatio* are two species of *prolepsis* (9.2.16–17). See *praemunitio* above and *prolepsis* above under Pragmatical–idea figures. This figure corresponds to the preliminary confirmation of one's argument (Hermogenes' *On Issues* 63).

prodiorthosis [G. "setting right by anticipation"]

Prefacing something which will be disagreeable to the hearer or odious to us with some acknowledgment or disclaimer in order to obviate objections

"Although I perceive how much of what I say will give offence, it must be said."

(Aquila §1)

"If you intend, for example, to praise Plato's doctrine that wives should be held in common, you will say that you are well aware that you appear to be proposing something absolutely ridiculous, but you will beg your audience to suspend judgment for a time until they have heard the main points of the argument, as you are quite sure that, once the case has been fully set out, they will be ready to endorse a very different opinion."

(Erasmus, *De copia* 652)

Note: An alternate spelling is *prosdiorthosis*. Robertellus considers this figure a kind of *praeparatio* (47v). Alexander says that when this guarding of one's position occurs both before and after one's statement, the figure is called *amphidiorthosis* (15).

proklesis [G. "calling forth, challenge, invitation"] or *provocatio* [L. "a challenge, provocation"]
Provoking the adversary to the conflict of the controversy

1. By a vehement accusation
   Eliphaz accuses Job: "Is it for fear of thee that I will accuse thee, or go with thee into judgement? Is not thy wickedness great? and thine ungracious deeds abominable? for thou hast taken the pledge from thy brother for nought, and spoiled the clothes of the naked" (Job 22:4–6).
2. Without accusation
   Elihu calls Job to account: "If thou canst give me answer, prepare thyself and stand before me" (Job 33:5).
3. By a confident offer of justification
   Christ says, "Which of you can rebuke me of sin?" (John 8:46).

(Peacham [1593] 83)

Note: An alternate spelling is *proclees.*

promissio [L. "a promise"]
Promising something

1. Promising to be brief
   "We will not dilly-dally longer: the speech is coming to its end."
2. Promising benefit
   "I know it is going to be pleasing to you to hear."

(Keckermann 1489)

3. Promising to speak about something, or to provide proof
   "But as to the nature and size of the force which I think adequate to relieve the situation, the means of defraying the cost, and the best and speediest method of providing for its equipment, I shall now endeavor to state my views, [. . .] Now I believe that I can indicate this, without prejudice to anyone else's proposal. That is a bold promise, but it will soon be put to a practical test, and you shall be my judges" (Demosthenes, *First Philippic* 15, trans. Vince).

(Cicero, *De Oratore* 3.205; example mine)

Note: Sturm even goes so far as to specify a figure he names *hypochesis* for promising great things pertaining to the health of the republic (3.31.784).

pysma [G. "a question requiring an explanatory answer"] or *quaesitum* [L. "a question"]
Inquiry

1. Asking questions that require more than a "yes" or "no" answer
   Cicero asked in behalf of Roscius, "In what place did he speak with them? with whom did he speak? did he hire them? whom did he hire, and by whom? To what end, or how much did he give them?" (*Pro S. Roscius* 27.74)

(Peacham [1593] 107)

2. Asking many questions in one place for vehemence
   "Will the Lord absent himself for ever, and will he be no more entreated? Is his mercy clean gone for ever? and is his promise come utterly to an end for evermore? hath God forgotten to be gracious? and will he shut up his loving kindness in displeasure?" (Psalm 77:7–9)

(Peacham [1593] 107)

Note: Kennedy comments that Diogenes Laertius (7.66) attributes the distinction between *erotesis* and *pysma* to the stoics (*Progymnasmata* 1, footnote 3). See *interrogatio* above.

ratiocinatio [L. "an exercise of the reasoning powers, ratiocination"]
Reasoning with oneself or one's audience by question and answer

1. To come to a conclusion

"Our ancestors if they condemned any woman of one offence, they deemed her by plain judgement to be convicted of many: by what reason? for whom they judged unchaste in life, they esteemed also guilty of poisoning: why so? because it must needs be, that she which addicteth her body to unlawful lust doth fear many: who be they? her husband, her parents, and others to whom she seeth the infamy of her dishonesty doth concern: what then? it must needs be that by any means she may, she will endeavor their destruction, whom she feareth so much: wherefore? because there is no honest means to hold her back whom the greatness of the offence maketh fearful, intemperancy bold, and woman's nature rash."

(*Ad Herennium* 4.16.23)

"How came this good fellow by all that he hath? Did his father leave him any land? Not a foot. Did his friends give him anything? Not a groat. Hath he served in any vocation to heap up so much wealth? None hath lived more idly. Doth he not lean to some nobleman? Yea, but he never received more than four marks' wages. How then cometh he by all that ever he hath, living without labor, having no friends to help him, having so little to take unto by all outward appearance, and spending so liberally, and owing no man a groat in all the world? Assuredly, it cannot be otherwise but that he cometh naughtily by most of that which he hath."

(Wilson 231)

2. To tell ourselves what we will do

"Phaedria, in Terence, being much troubled and out of quiet because he was not received of his woman, but shut out of doors when he was most willing to see her, made as though he would not come to her afterwards, nor yet see her at all, when she did most gently send for him. And therefore, being in anger, thus he said: 'Well, what shall I do? Shall I not go, not even now when she sends for me of her own accord? Or shall I be of such a nature that I cannot abide the despitefulness of harlots? She hath shut me out; she calls me again. Shall I go to her? Nay, I will not, though she entreat me never so fair.'" (*Eunouchus* I.i.45–49)

(Wilson 232)

Note: In his first edition, Sherry mistakenly gives as an alternate name for this figure *erotema* ([1550] 52). *Ratiocinatio* is also the general term for the method of argumentation, which consists of syllogisms, enthymemes and epicheremes. The figure is a specialized use of the term. See also *hypophora* above and *subjectio* below for related figures.

responsio [L. "an answer, reply"]
Replying to a question by giving an answer that was not asked for

"For example, a witness for the prosecution, who was asked whether he had been cudgelled [*sic*] by the defendant, replied, 'And I did no wrong!'"

"The question may be, 'I asked whether you killed the man?' The reply is, 'This man was a robber.'"

(Soarez 338)

revocatio [L. "a calling back"]
Calling oneself back
1. *Correctio*
2. *Aposiopesis*
3. *Antanaclasis* (returning to the matter)

Note: This is a general category used by the Ramists. See each of these figures listed separately.

scematismus [G. "configuration"] or *periploke* [G. "a twining round"]
Speaking circuitously so that we only hint rather than make plain; innuendo
1. For safety's sake
   a. By reproving another person in whom the same evils are
   "If a man should [reprehend] Dionysius the king of Sicilia, he might reprove the cruelty of Phalaris, and by an artificial description and reprehension of that cruelty and tyranny in Phalaris, he may make a most bright and resplendent glass wherein Dionysius must needs behold himself and his deformed tyranny."
   b. By praising another person who shows the contrary virtues
   "An evil man hearing the praises and glorious fame of others [who governed by wisdom, equity, moderation and mercy] is moved in mind and begins to covet commendation and praise, and seeing it cannot be obtained only by desire, he inclineth to the means by which he may deserve it."

(Peacham [1593] 197)

   c. By keeping statements ambiguous
   "I was defending a woman who was alleged to have forged her husband's will, and the heirs were stated to have given a bond to the husband on his deathbed, which latter assertion was true. For since the wife could not legally be appointed his heir, this procedure was adopted to enable the property to be transferred to her by a secret conveyance in trust. [The bond did promise the property to the wife and proved the wife innocent, since it confirmed the will. But the bond was illegal, since the wife could not inherit.] Now it was easy for me to secure the woman's acquittal by openly mentioning the existence of the bond; but this would have involved her loss of the inheritance. I had, therefore, to plead in such a way that the judges should understand that the bond had actually been given, but that informers might be unable to avail themselves of any statement of mine to that effect. And I was successful in both my aims."

(Quintilian 9.2.73–74)

2. For modesty's sake, cloaking obscene or shameful things, *occultatio* [L."insinuation"]
   "Adam knew Eve his wife" (Genesis 4:1).
   "Whose mother is delighted with daily marriages," meaning "her unchaste life."

(Peacham [1593] 197–98)

3. For delight and novelty
   The Earl of Gloucester shows off his wit in this banter with Kent:
   Kent: Is not this your son, my lord?
   Glou: His breeding, sir, hath been at my charge. I have so often blush'd to acknowledge him, that now I am braz'd to't.
   Kent: I cannot conceive you.

Glou: Sir, this young fellow's mother could; whereupon she grew round-womb'd, and had indeed, sir, a son for her cradle ere she had a husband for her bed. Do you smell a fault? (Shakespeare, *King Lear* 1.1.8–16)

(Peacham [1593] 198; example mine)

Note: Scaliger (3.78.346) and Wilson (201) treat this figure as a kind of *periphrasis*. Sometimes this figure is equated with *emphasis*. See *emphasis* under Pragmatical–idea figures. *Occultatio* has some overlap with *euphemismus* above.

sermocinatio [L. "a conversation, discussion"] or *dialogismus* [G. "debate, discussion"]

Imitating a dialogue between people

"As when Doctor Haddon had comforted the Duchess of Suffolk's Grace for her children, and had said they were happily gone because they might have fallen hereafter and lost that worthy name which at their death they had, at last he bringeth in the mother, speaking motherlike in her children's behalf of this sort, and answereth still to her sayings. 'But all these evils whereof you speak,' quod she, 'had not chanced.' Yet such things do chance. 'Yet not always.' Yet full oft. 'Yet not to all.' Yet to a great many. 'Yet they had not chanced to mine.' Yet we know not. 'Yet I might have hoped.' Yet better it had been to have feared."

(Wilson 209)

"Saith the Lord by the Prophet there concerning Ephraim: 'He is a Merchant, the balances of deceit are in his hands; he loveth to oppress.' Then follows the fiction of Ephraim's speech: 'Yet, I am become rich, I have found me out substance: in all my labors they shall find none iniquity in me, that were sin.' Then you have the Lord's answer to this objection: 'And I that am the Lord thy God from the land of Egypt, will yet make thee to dwell in Tabernacles, as in the days of the solemn feast'"(Hosea 12:7–9).

(Smith 255)

Note: Puttenham names this figure "the right reasoner" (242) and Shaw calls it the "ingenious Art of Quotation" (170). Sturm indicates that this dialogue may have three forms: 1. *diegetikos,* when the conversation is narrated; 2. *dialogikos,* when the dialogue is dramatized; 3. a mixture of these two. Sturm also comments that the comic and tragic poets use this figure (1.39.212). *Sermocinatio* also refers sometimes to the dramatized speech of one person (see *prosopopoeia* under Discoursal–genres below). *Dialogismus* is in the Ramists a general category containing the figures *aporia, anacoenosis, hypophora, prolepsis* (with *occupatio* and *subjectio*), *permissio* and *concessio.*

subjectio [L. "an annexing, subjoining"] or *anthypophora* [G. "reply"]

Turning what our adversaries can say into questions, then answering these questions with responses in our own favor

1. By raising our objections to another's argument and answering them in our favor

"Whom hast thou defied and blasphemed? against whom hast thou lifted up thy voice, and exalted thy proud looks? Even against the Holy one of Israel" (Isaiah 37:23).

(Peacham [1593] 107)

"Is this a manner of discipline? [. . .] Had they for this cause the authority of tutors to them given, that in vanities and misliked pleasures, they who are committed unto their charge, should consume their youth under them? Believe me I am of a far other opinion, [. . .]"

(Day 88)

2. By confuting objections others bring against us
   "Now after all these proofs of the happy coming and acknowledgment of our true and only Messias: Let me speak unto you again, ye Jews, enemies, and maligners of our sole and only God and Savior Christ Jesus, with what reasons strengthened do you persist in your madness? Stand ye upon the Oracles of Prophets? We have made plain unto you that they are wholly for us. Look ye after Moses? It was only of our Christ, and none other that he hath written. Wait ye on Types and Figures? They all in one do agree to be in him fulfilled. Prefer you unto us miracles? Who could desire more than by him was shewed. Bring you against us a number of consents? Alas you only bring the smallest number, and lurking as it were in a corner, are the gainsayers of truth itself, sith the whole world round about you doth witness for us."

   (Day 88)

3. By deliberating possible reasons, but refuting them all in order to rebuke
   "What makes you so arrogant? Distinguished parentage? But your family was totally obscure. Wealth? You are poorer than Irus. Education? You have never read a decent book in your life. Looks? You are uglier than Thersites. Ability? You are favoured with the thickest of brains. How can this bragging of yours be anything but sheer madness?"

   (Erasmus, *De copia* 347–48)

4. By refuting through answering our questions with questions, i.e., *antisagoge*
   See *antisagoge* below under Logical–idea figures.

Note: An alternate spelling is *antipophora* and additional names include *hypobole, suggestio*, and *apophasis*. See *apophasis* above, however, for the more common attribution of this term. Puttenham calls this "the Figure of response" (214). Following Rufinianus (8), Soarez associates this figure with *aitiologia* (338). See *aetiologia* below under the Logical–evidence category. In his first edition, Sherry mistakenly equates this figure with *prosapodosis* (53), but corrects his mistake in the second edition. Melanchthon explains that *anthypophora*, the answering of objections, is not equivalent to this figure, but is a part of it (*Elem.* 44r). See *anthypophora* below under Discoursal–parts. Puttenham explains that this "is a figure of argument and also of amplification. Of argument, because proposing such matter as our adversary might object and then to answer it ourselves, we do unfurnish and prevent him of such help as he would otherwise have used for himself: then because such objection and answer spend much language it serves as well to amplify and enlarge our tale" (214).

synchoresis [G. "consent, agreement"] or *epitrope* [G. "surrender of the power to decide"]
Having said enough, leaving the rest to the judges' discretion

"But now Judges I leave the whole, and the most lawful right of my cause, which I have declared, and commit it unto you to judge and determine it, as reason and wisdom shall direct you."

"Whether it be right saith he in the sight of God, to hearken unto you more than unto God, judge ye" (Acts 4:19).

(Peacham [1593] 111)

"Me thinks that I have said, what may well suffice,
Referring all the rest, to your better advise."

(Puttenham 234)

Note: An alternate spelling is *epitropis*. Puttenham's English name is "the Figure of Reference" (234). Quintilian (9.2.25), Susenbrotus (65), and Soarez (356) include this figure in *permissio*. See *permissio* above.

LOGICAL

Basic Idea Relations

antapodosis [G. "a giving back in turn, repayment"] or *redditio* [L. "to give back, return, restore"]

1. Reciprocal representation; comparing two subjects or objects in several aspects side by side in a simile or similitude

"As among Greek musicians (for so they say), only those turn flute-players that cannot play the lyre, so here at Rome we see that those who cannot acquire the art of oratory betake themselves to the study of the law" (Cicero, *Pro Murena* 13.29, trans. Butler).

"For as tempests are generally preceded by some premonitory signs in the heaven, but often, on the other hand, break forth for some obscure reason without any warning whatsoever, so in the tempests which sway the people at our Roman elections we are not seldom in a position to discern their origin, and yet, on the other hand, it is frequently so obscure that the storm seems to have burst without any apparent cause" (Cicero, *Pro Murena* 17.36, trans. Butler).

(Quintilian 8.3.79–80)

Note: This first application of the term seems identical to *analogia*. See *analogia* below under figures of Logical–evidence. An alternate name is *conlatio*. Scaliger gives *comparatio repetita* as an alternate name (3.51.324). Quintilian prefers to regard this embellishment as a method, not a figure.

2. The second part of a division

a. Immediate

"He accuses me [*propositio*], but indicts this man [*redditio*]" (Demosthenes *On the Crown* 15, trans. Wooten).

b. Delayed

"Now I do not choose, Athenians, to enumerate the resources of Philip and by such arguments to call on you to rise to the occasion [the *propositio* or *protasis*]. Do you ask why? Because it seems to me that any dissertation on that topic is a tribute to his enterprise, but a record of our failure. For the higher he has raised himself above his proper level, the more he wins the admiration of the world; but the more you have failed to improve your opportunities, the greater is the discredit that you have incurred. All this then I will waive. [. . .] There are, however, other topics open to me; you will be the better for having heard them, and if you will consent to scrutinize them accurately, men of Athens, you will find in them grave charges against Philip. On these topics I shall endeavor to address you" [the *antapodosis* or *redditio*] (Demosthenes *Olynthiac II* 3–4, trans. Vince).

(Hermogenes 1.11.291)

Note: This second definition of the term corresponds with *protasis* and *apodosis* (see syntactical figures above), but extends the syntactical application to a logical one.

antisagoge [G. "compensatory antithesis"]

Setting up the contraries in order that the preferred choice be more evident

1. Answering our own question with an opposite question

"But if our unrighteousness commend the righteousness of God, what shall we say? Is God unrighteous who taketh vengeance? [. . .] God forbid" (Romans 3:5).

(Susenbrotus 60)

2. Promising reward after virtue and punishment after vice

Moses saith, "If thou shalt obey the voice of the Lord thy God, and observe and do all his commandments, which I command thee this day, then the Lord thy God will set thee on high above all the nations of the earth. And all these blessings shall come upon thee, etc. But if thou wilt not obey the voice of the Lord thy God, to keep and do all his commandments and his ordinances, which I command thee this day, then all these curses shall come upon thee and overtake thee, etc." (Deuteronomy 28:1–2, 15–16).

(Peacham [1593] 93)

3. Opposing a statement with a stronger point
   "The change of the rites is somewhat inconvenient, but false dogmas are even more troublesome."
   "It is a difficult task to practice this mode of speech, but it has many and great uses."

   (Melanchthon, *Elem* 53r)

4. Showing the superiority of one thing through a contrast with another thing
   "As if one should set Lukes velvet against Jean velvet, the Lukes will appear better, and the Jean will seem worser. Or set a fair woman against a foul and she shall seem much the fairer, and the other much the fouler."

   (Wilson 156)

Note: The correct spelling of this figure is *anteisagoge*. Melanchthon lists this figure as a species deriving from the dialectical topic of contraries (*Elem.* 53r).

antithesis [G. "opposition"] or *contentio* [L. "contention, contrast"]
Coupling together contraries; contrasting on the basis of contraries

1. In counterposed words
   "He is gone, [. . .] from painful labour to quiet rest, from unquiet desires to happy contentment, from sorrow to joy, and from transitory time to immortality."
   "So well lighted were the eyes of his mind, that by them he saw life in death, an exaltation in falling, glory in shame, a Kingdom in bondage, and a glorious light in the midst of darkness."

   (Smith 174)

2. In counterposed phrases or sentences
   "Marcellus restored their works of art to the Syracusans though they were our enemies; Verres took them away from them when they were our allies" (Cicero, *In C. Verrem* II 4:115, trans. Knott).

   (Erasmus *De copia* 616)

   "What I have said before was necessary; what I am going to say will be voluntary. Then I was addressing myself to a judge, now I address myself to Gaius Piso; then I was pleading for an accused person, now for Roscius; my former speech was prepared in order to win a cause, the latter to save a good reputation" (Cicero, *Pro Q. Roscio* 5.15, trans. Freese).

   (Sturm 2.24.426)

3. In counterposed ideas within a passage
   "Compare the one's impatience to the other's mildness, the one's impenitency with the other's submission, the one's indignation with the other's humility, and tell me whether he that conquered seemed not rather confounded, [and] he which yielded unto him not anything discouraged. Compare not mind with mind, lest it seem fantastical, and beyond the trial of our senses; but set the one's triumph against the other's captivity, victory against loss, feasts against wounds, a crown against fetters, felicity against misfortune: and the majesty of courage will be found in the overthrow."

   (Hoskins 21)

"You may set the meekness of Christ and the cruelty of the Jews one against another, thus: he wished their salvation, they desired his destruction: he preached peace unto them, they picked quarrels against him: he spake unto them the truth, they devised most wicked lies to condemn him: they laughed him to scorn for his meekness, he was sorry to see their wickedness: they smote him on the face and buffeted him, but he did not so much as lift up his hand against them: he sought to save their life, they most maliciously put him to death."

(Peacham [1577] R.i.v)

4. In debate, a counter proposition to an opponent's argument
In reply to Clodius, Cicero argues that "Clodius cannot rightly describe Cicero as an 'exile,' for he [Cicero] had done nothing to forfeit citizenship, and Clodius' bill was carried by a hired mob of slaves and criminals" (*De Domo Sua* 27.72–34.92, trans. Watts, heading p. 133).

(Sturm 1.20.57)

5. In counterposed ideas in thought
Antithesis says, "I taught the *Lacedemonians* to educate their children soberly, and instruct them in temperance by setting before them the example of a drunken Slave, making a fool and a beast of himself in his drink. I teach all ingenious Youths to give themselves industriously to their studies, by propounding to them the shame and punishment which the Lads meet with. By the *Antithetical* consideration of the disgraces and miseries of Poverty, I encourage the considerate to diligence in their callings, and to frugal living."

(Shaw 154–55)

Note: Additional names include *antitheton, contrapositum, contrarium, syncrisis, sygchrisis, oppositio* and *opposita oratio*. Puttenham gives the English name as "the encounter" or "the Quarreller" (219). *Syncrisis* becomes the commonest name for the figure of speech and *antithesis* for the figure of thought, although sometimes the two terms are simply synonyms. See *syncrisis* under syntactical figures above. Quintilian allows *antithesis* as a figure of speech (9.3.81), but rejects it as a figure of thought (9.2.101). In his 1550 edition, Sherry calls this figure *antitheton* (56) and distinguishes it from *antithesis*, a synonym for *contrarium,* the argument from contraries (172). In his 1555 edition, Sherry makes the same distinction, but this time using the more mainstream names *contentio* (E.vi.v) and *enthymeme* (G.vii.r). Robertellus lists the following figures as species of *antithesis*: *contraposita, antanaclasis, contentio, antimetabole, prosapodosis, anthypophora* and *diallage* (31r). Hoskins treats this figure as a kind of comparison—a comparison of contraries (21). Smith restricts *contentio* to *enantiosis* (118) and gives *oppositio* as an alternate name for *antithesis* (172). Gill groups *enantiosis, contrarium,* and *contentio* with *antithesis*, apparently recognizing all the figures by these names as fundamentally alike (166). Melanchthon lists this figure under the dialectical topic of contraries (*Elem.* 52r).

attributio [L. "an attribute"]

Attributing a quality or associated circumstance to either a person or a thing in order to describe it

"[I]n the year there is sterility, in the air a storm, in the night silence, in a rock roughness."

(Scaliger 3.48.318)

Note: Scaliger indicates that *epithets, similitudes,* detailed narration, *prosopopoeia, sermocinatio,* and *diatyposis* or description of all kinds are species of this figure. This figure corresponds to the dialectical topics of quality, quantity, and circumstance.

comparatio [L. "comparison"] or *collatio* [L. "comparison, similitude, parable"] or *parabole* [G. "comparison, analogy"]

A comparison of both like and unlike things

1. Of like or equal things
"Now as Jannes and Jambres withstood Moses, so do these also resist the truth: men of corrupt minds, reprobate concerning the faith" (2 Timothy 3:8).
2. Of unlike or unequal things
"Behold the fowls of the air, for they sow not, neither doe they reap, nor gather into barn: yet your heavenly Father feedeth them: Are ye not much better than they?" (Matthew 6:26)
3. From the less to the greater
"For if the blood of bulls, and of goats, and the ashes of an heifer sprinkling the unclean, sanctify to the purifying of the flesh: how much more shall the blood of Christ, who through the eternal Spirit offered himself without spot to God, purge your consciences from dead works to serve the living God?" (Hebrews 9:13–14)
4. From the greater to the less
"'If God spared not the Angels that sinned, but cast them down to hell, and delivered them into chains of darkness, to be reserved unto judgement,' etc. much less will he spare the wicked, who 'walk after the flesh in the lusts of uncleanness'" (2 Peter 2:4–10).
(Smith 209–10)

Note: This is a general category covering comparisons of things equal, different and contrary. Occasionally, *syncrisis* is an alternate name. See *syncrisis* above under syntactical figures. Because a feature of argument, Quintilian rejects this strategy as a figure (8.4.3; 9.2.100). This figure corresponds to the dialectical topic of comparison, according to Melanchthon, and includes examples, fables, parables, and icons (*Elem.* 53r). Hoskins explains that comparisons function as examples in argument: "If to protract battle upon advice be cowardice, then Phocion, then Metellus, then Fabius, then all the valiantest captains of all ages were cowards"; or "If to displant the rebellious natives of Ireland, and to root them out of the island be cruelty, then colonies translated into France, into Sicily, into several coasts of Italy and divers other places, by the Romans, testify great cruelty" (20). *Parabole* also has a more specific reference to parable. See *parabola* below under Discoursal–genres.

consecutio [L. "an effect, consequence"] or *parepomenon* [G. "a consequence, necessary or accidental]

Attaching the consequences to an event

"The emptying of the treasury on barbarous troops, the breaking of the youth of the country by hardship, the trampling underfoot of the harvests, the abduction of cattle, the burning of farm and village on every side, the deserted fields, tumbled walls, looted homes, plundered shrines, old men left childless, children fatherless, mothers widowed, girls shamefully raped, the morals of the young ruined by licence, so many deaths, so many sorrows, so many tears, the extinction of the arts, the suppression of law, the obliteration of religion, the total confusion of every divine and human value, the undermining of all civil discipline—all this train of evils, I say, which is born of war, we shall write down to your account alone, if, on your advice, war is declared."
(Erasmus, *De copia* 576–77)

definitio [L. "a boundary, definition"] or *horismus* [G. "a boundary, limit, definition"] or *finitio* [L. "a limit, definition"]

A definition

1. By declaring the nature of a thing pithily and briefly
   "He is free that is subject to no evil."
   "It is a virtue to eschew vice."

   (Wilson 232)

   "Fear is an apprehension of future harm."
   "Thrift is a moderate and lawful increase of wealth by careful government of your own estate."

   (Hoskins 44)

2. By denying one contrary and affirming the other
   "It is no industry as ye call it, but a certain busy brainsickness, for industry is a lively and unwearied search and occupation in honest things, eagerness is an appetite in base and small matters."

   (Puttenham 239)

   "Men cannot be said in virtue to exceed, for in virtue there is ever an excellency, but never an excess, sith the excess is only appropriate unto vices."

   (Day 97)

3. By distinguishing among things of close affinity
   "To pour forth thy curse against thy adversary is malignity, against an innocent cruelty, against thy parent impiety, against God blasphemy."
   "To refuse good counsel is folly, to condemn it is wickedness, to scorn it is madness."

   (Peacham [1593] 128)

4. By enumerating the components of a thing, or *numeri designationem*
   "Here he said two things, this and that."

   (Hermogenes 1.4.238)

5. By enumerating a subject's or situation's attributes, circumstances, or associated details, or *praescriptio*
   "No rescue will come from him,
   The Aetolian, or from his Arpi. Messapus will help,
   And lucky Tolumnius; so will those leaders whom many
   A people sent to the war. No little the glory
   Won by the flower of Latium's troops and Laurentian
   Fields." (Virgil, *Aeneid* 11.448–53, trans. Lind)

   (Scaliger 3.55.331)

6. By giving the definition of a name, or *etymologia*
   A grammarian is "one who teaches grammar."
   "*Pecuniosus* 'a moneyed man' is one 'who possesses an abundance of cattle (*pecus*).'"

   (Erasmus, *De copia* 332)

7. By explaining the nature of anything
   "Let us then define anger as a longing, accompanied by pain, for a real or apparent revenge for a real or apparent slight, affecting a man himself or one of his friends, when such a slight is undeserved" (Aristotle, *Rhetoric* 2.2.1 1378a 30, trans. Freese).

   (Hoskins 43–44)

Note: Alternate spellings include *horysmos* and *orismus*. Wilson calls the brief definition *circumscriptio* (232). See also *etymologia* under *periphrasis*, a semantical figure. Cicero in *Topica* calls *etymologia*, the argument based on the definition of a word, *notatio* (8.35). Quintilian does not regard *etymologia* (1.6.29) or *definitio* (9.3.91) a figure. But, Veltkirchius distinguishes among three kinds of definition, all figures: *etymologia*, the definition of a word; *notatio* or rhetorical definition, the describing of something by means of its accidents and signs; and *finitio*, the dialectical definition that identifies something by means of its essentials, that is, its genus and difference, its causes, its parts, or its effects (33v-34r). By means of this device, Peacham instructs that "every several matter is evidently expressed, plainly distinguished, and brightly adorned with the shining beams of glorious eloquence" ([1593] 129). This figure is equivalent to the dialectical topic of definition, according to Melanchthon (*Elem.* 49v). Hoskins sees this correspondence, for he advises, "Of seven or eight ways of definition, read Valerius's *Logic*. But to be most perfectly instructed, read the sixth book of Aristotle's *Topica*" (44). Puttenham, however, distinguishes between the definition of the logician and that of the rhetorician. The logician, he says, defines "the truth or nature of every thing by his true kind and difference, as to say wisdom is a prudent and witty foresight and consideration of humane or worldly actions with their events." The orator uses the definition derived from contrast amongst similar terms (239).

dianoia [G. "thought, intention, purpose"]

An attribution of intent or motives

"Fury furnishes arms" (Virgil, *Aeneid* 1.159).

"Following the practice of members of the nobility, who, when once they have begun to carry out some plan, whether right or wrong, show such superiority in its execution that is beyond the reach of one in our humble position, Dolabella most manfully persevered in acting wrongfully" (Cicero, *Pro Quinctio* 8.31, trans. Freese).

(Rufinianus §18)

Note: This use of the term here corresponds to Hermogenes' use in discussions of the defendant's intent and the intent of the law (*On Issues* 72.13; 82–83.8).

dissimilitudo [L. "unlikeness, difference, dissimilitude"] or *alloiosis* [G. "difference"]

A contrast on the basis of differences

1. In a sentence

"If we have any disease in our body, we use exercise, and all other means, that we may hence forward be delivered and free from it; but being sick in soul, we dissemble and make delay: we leave the fountain uncured, and count necessary things superfluous" (Chrysostom).

(Smith 212)

2. In a passage

"Sir Francis Drake indeed traveled round about the world in two years, saw divers nations, endured many perils at sea, and returned laden with great treasure. And Vascus Gama first searched the coast of Quiloa, Mozamba, and Calicut, and opened a passage to the East Indias. But it was easy for Drake to proceed further in discoveries, when he had an entrance made by Columbus; so was it most dangerous and difficult for Gama to adventure a course without example and direction. Drake scoured the coast with a sufficient company of ships, made pillage of others, and thereby furnished his own enterprises. Gama went but weak at the first, lost most of his small fleet, and met nothing at sea but tempests and famine. Drake invaded upon opportunities, hazarded but his own fortune, and retired to sea upon all advantage. Gama had in charge an expedition of his sovereign's commandment, was constrained to victual himself amongst barbarous nations, and not only to buy provision in their continent land with the price of his blood, but durst not depart without leaving his king proclaimed and possessed in their territories, divers places of strength established to his use. So that if Gama had been to peruse the example of Drake as Drake had the light of Columbus and Magellus' travels, Vascus Gama's spirit was likely to have conquered the whole world as Drake's fortune was to compass it."

(Hoskins 19–20)

Note: Two alternate names include *diaphora* [G. "difference or distinction"] and *anomoiosis* [G. "difference"]. Although this figure is widely recognized as a sub-species of comparison, it is nevertheless often listed separately. Rejecting it as a figure (9.3.91), Quintilian treats the dissimilitude under arguments and specifies that one can either point out the differences between similar things or the similarity between different things (5.11.30).

ekparasynaptikon [G. "attaching a causal explanation"]

Attaching causes to a statement or event

"Finding that you had got to the end of the regular Assemblies, and that there was no meeting left, and observing that the envoys were still wasting time at Athens instead of starting at once, I proposed a decree as a member of the Council, to which the Assembly had given authority, directing the envoys to sail immediately, and the general Proxenus to convey them to any place in which he should ascertain that Philip was to be found" (Demosthenes, *De Falsa Legatione* 154, trans. Vince).

(Hermogenes 1.11.290)

"After duly performing the religious observances, Romulus summoned his men to an assembly and gave them laws, since there was no way other than by law that they could become a unified community. He thought the rustic population more likely to be bound by these laws if he made himself venerable by adopting symbols of office. Not only did he make himself more impressive in his way of dressing, but he also assumed a retinue of twelve lictors. Some sources think that this number derived from the number of birds that had augured and portended his rule. But I have no problem with the opinion of those who consider that the attendants and their number derive from the neighboring Etruscans, who [. . .] had this number because each of their twelve communities contributed one lictor after they united to elect a king" (Livy, *The History of Rome* 1.8).

(Erasmus, *De copia* 576; example mine)

Note: Veltkirchius identifies the following kinds of causes for consideration: the first or infinite (God), the finite (fate, nature, fortune, will, error, ignorance), the internal and external, the material, the formal, the universal, the essential, the necessary or unnecessary, the immediate, intermediate, and remote, and the final (116r-119r).

enantiosis [G. "opposition"] or *contraria* [L. "opposing"]

Paired contraries in equal, parallel structures; the opposite of *parison*

1. Pairing opposite words

   "Just without partiality, liberal without profusion, wise without curiosity."

   (Smith 119)

2. Pairing opposite ideas

   "Obsequiousness makes friends; truth makes enemies" (Terence, *Andria* 1.1.68, my translation)

   (Keckermann 1483)

   "He is of a strange nature as ever I saw, for to his friend he is churlish, to his foe he is gentle: give him fair words, and you offend him; check him sharply, and you win him.

Let him have his will, and he will fly in thy face; keep him short, and you shall have him at commandment."

(Wilson 223)

"Could not look on, nor would not look off."
"Neither the one hurt her, nor the other help her."
"He is a swaggerer amongst quiet men, but is quiet among swaggerers."

(Smith 119)

3. Pairing opposite arguments or images
"What then is the meaning of this prosecution which finds it easier to climb the Alps than just the few steps which lead to the Treasury, which defends the treasury of the Ruteni more jealously than that of the people of Rome, which prefers unknown witnesses to those whom it knows, foreigners to fellow-citizens, and which thinks that it is establishing a charge more convincingly upon the capricious allegations of barbarians than upon the documentary evidence furnished by our own countrymen?" (Cicero, *Pro M. Fonteio* 3.4, trans. Watts)

(Sturm 2.23.425)

"Did the most innocent vouchsafe it as a part of His glory to pray for His enemies, and shall we, the most sinful, esteem it a blot to our reputation to be unrevenged on our brethren?"

(Hoskins 22)

"Thou therefore which teachest another, teachest thou not thy self? Thou that preachest a man should not steal, dost thou steal?" (Romans 2:21).

(Smith 119)

4. Responding with a contrary word or charge
"As Gallo was objecting to a fellow's drunkenness by saying, 'When will you go out from your dining room in which you dine magnificently?,' the other responded, 'When will you go out from another's bedroom?'"

(Sturm 3.22.713)

Note: Scaliger calls this figure *antenantiosis* (4.37.506), conflating it with *litotes*. See *litotes* above under semantical figures. This figure is sometimes included under *contentio*. Quintilian makes reference to only *enantiotes* or *contrarium*, the pairing of opposite arguments (5.9.3; 5.11.31), and this strategy he denies is a figure because it is argument (9.2.106; 9.3.90). However, Renaissance rhetoricans generally consider this structure a figure and conceive of it in all its forms as argument. Farnaby says this figure "affirms through paired contraries" (23). Smith explains that "we speak that by a contrary which we would have to be understood as it were by affirmation" (118). Sturm clearly ties the figure to the topic of contraries: "I call this *Contraria*, which is what it is called in the Topics. There are three genres of *Contraria*: *privantia*, which contrasts knowns and unknowns; *adversantia*, which contrasts desires with moderations; and *Repugnantia*, which contrasts enemies with loyals" (2.23.428). Hoskins comments that this figure is the opposite of *synoeciosis* (oxymoron), for the latter is a composition of disagreeing terms, but this is an opposition of disagreeing terms (37).

oxymoron [G. "pointedly foolish"] or *synoeciosis* [G. "binding together, bringing into combination"]

A condensed paradox

1. In two words, when one contrary is affirmed to be in the other directly by making one the substantive and one the adjective

   "And with that, she prettily smiled, which, mingled with her tears, a man could not tell whether it were mourning pleasure or delightful sorrow" (Sidney, *Arcadia*, book 3, 490).

   "It was an excellent pastime to those that would delight in the play of virtue, with what a witty ignorance she would not understand" (Sidney, *Arcadia*, book 3, 507).

   (Hoskins 36)

2. In few words, when one contrary is attributed to another indirectly

   "If they are silent, they say enough."

   "But she that liveth in pleasure is dead while she liveth" (1 Timothy 5:6).

   (Smith 122–23)

   "There was so perfect agreement in so mortal disagreement, like a music made of cunning discords" (Sidney, *Arcadia*, book 3, 416).

   (Hoskins 37)

Note: Alternate spellings include *sinoeciosis*, *synaeceosis*, and *syneciosis*.

paradoxon [G. "marvelous, strange, contrary to all expectation"] or *inopinatum* [L. "something unexpected"]

Expressing something as if contrary to expectation and causing wonder

1. In a sentence

   "Not that, lest it should be an injury to you; and not this, lest it should seem that he lacks in his duty."

   (Robertellus 43r)

   "I wonder much to see so many husbands thrive,
   That have but little wit, before they come to wive:
   For one would easily ween who so hath little wit,
   His wife to teach it him, were a thing much unfit."

   (Puttenham 233–34)

   "Could it possibly be thought that learning and place of good education might ever have produced such monstrous effects?"

   (Day 90)

2. In a passage or argument

   Paul used this figure in his defense in front of King Agrippa: "Why should it be thought a thing incredible with you, that God should raise the dead? I verily thought with myself, that I ought to do many things contrary to the name of Jesus of Nazareth. Which thing I also did in Jerusalem: and many of the saints did I shut up in prison, having received authority from the chief priests; and when they were put to death, I gave my voice against them. And I punished them oft in every synagogue, and compelled them to blaspheme; and being exceedingly mad against them, I persecuted them even unto strange cities. Whereupon as I went to Damascus with authority and commission from the chief priests, At midday, O king, I saw in the way a light from heaven, above the brightness of the sun, shining round about me and them which journeyed with me. And when we were all fallen to the earth, I heard a voice speaking unto me, and saying in the Hebrew tongue, Saul, Saul, why persecutest thou me? it is hard for thee to kick against the pricks. And I said, Who art thou, Lord? And he said, I am Jesus whom thou persecutest. But rise, and stand upon thy feet: for I have appeared unto thee for this purpose, to make thee a minister and a witness both of these things which thou hast seen, and of those things in the which I will appear unto thee; Delivering thee from the people, and from the Gentiles, unto whom now I send thee, etc." (Acts 26: 8–23).

(Peacham [1593] 112–13)

Note: Puttenham calls this figure "the Wondrer" (233). *Hypomone* is a rare synonym (43r). Veltkirchius equates *paradoxon* with *admiratio* (50v). See *admiratio* below under Discoursal–genres. Peacham treats *paradoxon* as a form of argument "by which the Orator affirmeth something to be true by saying he would not have believed it, or that it is so strange, so great, or so wonderful that it may appear to be incredible" ([1593] 112). This figure is to be used "when the thing which is to be taught is new, strange, incredible, and repugnant to the opinion of the hearer" (113). Quintilian, however, refuses to allow this kind of paradox to be a figure (9.2.24). See *sustentatio* above under Pragmatical–idea figures for the other use of *paradoxon* as a figure.

partitio [L. "a partition, division"] or *divisio* [L. "a division, separation"] or *distributio* [L. "a division, distribution"]

Division of whole into parts, genus into species, or subject into accidents

1. Of a general word

   In place of animal, we say "man and beast."

   (Keckermann 1550)

2. In a sentence

   "The whole of eloquence consists in subject-matter and expression."

   "Every syllogism requires three components: the major premise, minor premise, and conclusion."

   (Erasmus, *De copia* 426–27)

3. In a passage

   "Every nation hath his team and his plough to get his living, his bed to take his rest, some fruit of his labour for his friend, his bow & his spear for his enemy, [. . .] mourning at burials, mirth at marriages, & religious worship in their Temples. Here the general custom of nations is the whole, which as you see is divided into certain parts."

   (Peacham [1593] 124)

   "He is well seen in all Sciences. He perfectly knoweth all the painful rules of Grammar, the pleasant Flowers of Rhetoric, the subtleties of Logicians, the secrets of natural Philosophy, the difficulty of Wisdom supernatural, the pleasant Fables of Poets, the Mathematical demonstrations, the motions of Stars, the cunning reasons of numbers, the description of the world, the measuring of the earth, the situations, names, distances of Countries, Cities, Mountains, Rivers, Fountains, and Wildernesses, the properties of Soils, the deep mysteries of Divinity, the difference of harmonies, the consent of tunes, histories, old and new, antiquities, novelties, Greek, Latin and Hebrew. Finally, whatsoever good learning hath been found and taught of good Authors, all that hath this man perceived, known and remembered."

   (Peacham [1577] R.iii.v)

Note: Cicero in *Topica* uses *divisio* to refer to the division of a genus into species and *partitio* to refer to the division of the whole into parts (5.17). Celsus apparently follows this distinction and calls both division and partition figures (Quintilian 9.2.105). Quintilian disagrees, however, that either should be a figure (9.2.107). Peacham follows Celsus's distinction, with the figure *divisio* or *diaeresis* (dividing the general into the specials) distinguished from *partitio* (dividing the whole into parts), both species of a general figure he names *distributio*, which also includes *enumeratio* (dividing the subject into accidents, the matter into antecedents, the effect into causes and into things annexed and following after the effect): "*Distributio* is a general word, comprehending diverse special kinds, by which we dilate and spread abroad the general kind, by reckoning up the special kinds, the whole by dividing it into parts, and the subject by rehearsing the accidents" ([1593] 123–24). *Divisio* and *partitio* become folded together in Trapezuntius, Erasmus, Keckermann, Hoskins and Blount, who use the terms generally to cover any kind of division for any purpose. Hoskins (with Blount repeating him) clearly ties this figure to these logical topics: "And so you may divide as many ways as things may differ, as: by their beginnings, endings, properties, marks, effects, times, places, forms, and persons in whom they are, and howsoever; whereof the proper treaty belongs to logic" (45).

peristasis [G. "standing round, surrounding, circumstances, situation"]

Amplifying by adding circumstances

1. In a sentence
   a. Circumstances relating to a person
      1. Parentage: "Thou art of a noble blood, and hast thou made thyself a companion of Rascals?"
      2. Nation: "Is it not a shame for thee, being an Englishman born, to despise the feat of shooting."
      3. Country: "To be born and bred in Middlesex, and to speak ill English is a foul fault."
      4. Kind: "For a Woman to use filthy talk is much uncomely."
      5. Age: "For a child of ten years old to be very wise and sober is a strange hearing, and worthy of wonder."
      6. Education: "To be well brought up in youth, & after to digress and fall from good manners, as Nero did, doth deserve great dispraise and blame."
      7. Discipline: "It is a great fault in a Schoolmaster, that ought to teach good manners to his Scholars, to follow ill manners himself, and for a Preacher to be covetous, envious, unchaste, intemperate, etc., which in his Doctrine teacheth the contrary."
      8. Habit of body: "God hath endowed thee with a beautiful fairness, why dost thou live so filthily?"
      9. Fortune: "For a wealthy man to lose all that he hath in one hour by mischance, and yet to take it patiently, as Job did, doth deserve greater praises than can be given him."
      10. Condition: "Being a servant and to strike his Master, is he not worthy to be punished?"
      11. Nature of the mind: "God hath given you a valiant heart, and shall careful thought overcome you?"
      12. Study: "You practice Law, the maintenance of right. With what face and conscience can you offer this wrong?"
      13. Fore deeds: "He hath been the foremost in the field, to fight for the defense of his country: and by valiant manliness, got always the victory, and now being as lofty as ever he was, he hath no care of his Country, no delight in anything, but only in welfare, sleep, and ease, letting all go which way it will."
      14. Counsel: "You counseled them to do this wickedness; therefore, your fault is the greater, and you most worthy to be punished."
      15. Name: "To be named manly, and to hide yourself so cowardly, was that meet think you?"

b. Circumstances relating to a thing
   1. Cause: "Thou wast the first that kindled the contention, and after caused this murder, therefore thou shalt have the sharpest punishment."
   2. Place: "He defiled the virgin in the Temple, which is abominable to be heard."
   3. Time: "On the Sabbath day, and at the time of prayer, when he should have served God with hearty prayers, he obeyed the Devil with wicked doings, and committed this murder."
   4. Occasion: "When all men were in Godly exercise, he thought it best to go about his wicked practice."
   5. Instrument: "To slay or murder with an Axe, a knife, a Gun, or poison, causeth the murder to be more grievously taken, and judged more cruel and wicked, than if it had been done with weapons of defense, as with a Sword, Dagger, Staff, Bill, or such like."
   6. Manner: "If the murdered body be hanged up spitefully or mangled pitifully, or killed privily, it doth signify a great and wicked cruelty in the murderer."

(Peacham [1577] O.i.r-v)

2. In a passage:
Demosthenes uses this figure in an extended way as he narrates how he became chorus-master: "'I promised to outfit a chorus.' When? 'Two years ago.' Where? 'In the assembly.' Why? 'Because a chorus master had not been established and, therefore, there were arguments and reproaches.' How? 'As a volunteer.' What state was Demosthenes in? 'I was not very rich,' he said, 'and to try to undertake something beyond one's resources may have been an act of madness.' [. . .] What was his intention? 'Because of ambition.'" (*Against Meidias* 13–69)

(Hermogenes 1.11.281)

Note: Quintilian treats *peristasis* as a "place" for the invention of arguments, specifically those deriving from the special circumstances of individual cases (5.10.103–4). Peacham certainly connects this figure with argument, for he remarks, "The use of circumstances is very profitable to Amplify, to extenuate, to express plainly, to prove, and to confirm: for it maketh the Oration to be defenced [*sic*] on every side, with plenty of arguments" ([1577] O.i.v). Hoskins describes this figure as a kind of amplification efficacious for "good invention" (28).

similitudo [L. "likeness, resemblance"] or *homoeosis* [G. "likeness, resesmblance"]
Similarity

1. In a sentence, *simile*
"His whole face was suffused with rage just as iron glows in the fire."

(Erasmus, *De copia* 337)

"Like as they greatly do offend, who going to a public well, whence all a whole city hath their water, do infect the same with a most deadly poison: even so do they most wickedly merit of the common weal, who depraving the mind of a Prince, do lade and frequent the same with most mischievous counsels."

(Day 99)

2. In a passage
"The more precious a thing is, the more diligently should it be kept and better heed taken to it. Therefore, time (considering nothing is more precious) should warily be used, and good care taken that no time be lost without some profit gotten. For if they are to be punished that spend their money and waste their lands, what folly is it not

to think them worthy much more blame that spend their time (which is the chiefest treasure that God giveth) either idly or else ungodly? For what other thing doth man lose when he loseth his time but his life? And what can be more dear to man than his life? If we lose a little money or a ring of gold with a stone in it, we compt that great loss. And I pray you, when we lose a whole day, which is a good portion of a man's life, shall we not compt that a loss, considering though our money be gone we may recover the same again, but time lost can never be called back again? Again, when we lose our money, somebody getteth good by it, but the loss of time turneth to no man's avail."

(Wilson 214)

"Policy is like the sea: it serves for intercourse of profits, for defense against invasion. There are in both ebbings and flowings, calms and tempests, the observation whereof may make a man first wise, then rich. But as the water serves for many outward uses, so can it not please inwardly swallowed. If you sail upon it, it will carry you whither you will desire; but if you drink it, it doth not satisfy but increase a desire."

(Hoskins 18)

Note: Alternate spellings include *homoiosis, homeosis, homeozeuxis, omiosis*, and *omoiosis*. Puttenham's name is "Resemblance" (247). Another name is *eikasia* [G. "likeness, representation"]. This figure includes *icon, parabole*, and *paradeigma* and corresponds to the *locus a simili* for arguments. Hoskins declares that the similitude "is the ground of all emblems, allegories, fables, and fictions" (10). Quintilian discusses similitudes as arguments (5.11.5) or as methods (8.3.72), the difference being that the argument helps our proof and the method makes the picture more vivid. Both are "ornament[s] to oratory," although not figures (8.3.74). Sturm, however, does not distinguish at all between the argument and the figure, but treats the similitude as a form of argumentation used by both philosophers and orators. "The *similitudo* is a figure of oratory," he says, used "in order that the nature of the thing put forth be understood." The similitude has four parts: the proposition, the simile, the *accomodatio*, and the conclusion (1.41.231). He goes on to say that the similitude is not used alone, but joined to other forms of reasoning (233) and that in every *exemplum* there is some similitude (1.42.255). Puttenham has a similar insight: "As well to a good maker and Poet as to an excellent persuader in prose, the figure of *Similitude* is very necessary, by which we not only beautify our tale, but also very much enforce and enlarge it. I say enforce because no one thing more prevaileth with all ordinary judgements than persuasion by *similitude*" (247). Some authors, such as Rufinianus, Erasmus, Sturm, Robertellus, Hoskins, and Blount, list the simile and the longer similitude as separate figures. Rufinianus calls the simile *homoeon* (§25) and the similitude *omoiosis* (§22). Soarez even calls simile a trope (295).

synoeciosis [G. "binding together, bringing into combination"] or *cognatio* [L. "natural connection, affinity"]

Showing that contraries share similar properties; a seeming paradox

"[N]ot only the man who murders another by administering a deadly draught is to be regarded as a poisoner, but also the man who deprives another of his wits by giving him some drug."

(Celsus via Quintilian 9.2.105)

"The covetous and the prodigal are both alike in fault, for neither of them knows to use their wealth aright: they both abuse it, and both get shame by it."

"Gluttonous feasting and starving famine are both as one, for both weaken the body, procure sickness, and cause death."

"The covetous man wants as well what he hath as what he hath not" (Publilius Syrus, *Sententiae* §694, Loeb).

"A dissembler studies to over-reach as well them that trust him, as them that trust him not."

(Smith 120)

Note: Alternate spellings include *synoikeiosis, syneciosis, sinaeciosis,* or *synaeceosis.* Puttenham's English name is "the Crosse-Couple" (216). Melanchthon, perhaps mistakenly, attributes *communicatio* as an additional name (*Elem.* 52v), Scaliger calls this figure *conjunctio* (3.47.317), and Smith gives as an alternate name *conciliatio* (120). Quintilian rejects *cognatio* as a figure of thought as Celsus defines it (9.2.105), but approves of *synoeceiosis* as a figure of speech (9.3.64). Melanchthon treats the figure as a species deriving from the dialectical topic of contraries (52v), and Peacham indicates that this figure makes an argument: by it we "repugn common opinion with reason" ([1593] 170).

Forms of Argument

anastrophe ton pistis [G. "turning upside down in regard of proofs"]

Giving the reasons and proofs before the *protasis* itself

"Observing that the navy was going to pieces, that the wealthy were let off with trifling contributions, while citizens of moderate or small means were losing all they had, and that as a result the government was missing its opportunities [the reasons], I made a statute under which I compelled the wealthy to take their fair share of expense, stopped the oppression of the poor, and, by a measure of great public benefit, caused your naval preparations to be made in good time [the *protasis*]" (Demosthenes, *On the Crown* 102, trans. Vince).

(Hermogenes 1.11.284)

Note: The *protasis* is the proposition to be proved or explained. See *protasis* below under Discoursal–parts.

conclusio [L. "the conclusion of the syllogism"] or *symperasma* [G. "the conclusion of the syllogism"]

Giving the conclusion that follows from what has been said or done before

1. *Consequentia* or *epakolouthesis*, the logical conclusion from the argument or chain of reasoning, also sometimes called a *clausula*

"You must, therefore, first confess your own offence before you accuse Ligarius of anything" (Cicero, *Pro Ligario* 1.2, trans. Butler).

(Quintilian 8.5.13)

"Wherefore you must needs obey, not only for fear of vengeance, but also for conscience sake" (Romans 13:5).

(Peacham ([1577] U.iiii.v)

2. The complete syllogism

"But if the oracle had predicted to the Danaans that Troy could not be taken without the arrows of Philoctetes, and these arrows moreover served only to smite Alexander, then certainly killing Alexander was the same as taking Troy."

(*Ad Herennium* 4.30.41)

"If it be showed by reason, and proved by example, that we ought to venture and jeopardize [ourselves] in peril for the commonwealth, they are to be counted wise men which do shun no danger for the safeguard of their country."

(Peacham [1577] U.iiii.v)

Note: An alternate spelling is *consequens.* Sherry calls this figure *epilogus* [G. "the winding up of the speech"]. Quintilian regards the first use a reflexion (8.5.13; 9.3.98) and the second an argument (9.2.103). See also *syllogismus* below for another figure that includes the complete syllogism.

deuterologian [G. "second word"]
A speech that takes care of many arguments at once
1. When we speak first with many charges to defend
An example of the first is Cicero, when he prosecutes against Gaius Verres, the governor of Sicily, for extortion, misgovernment, and oppression. He speaks first and brings charges sevenfold: Verres has robbed the Treasury, plundered Asia and Pamphylia, and pirated Sicily; illegally abrogated Roman law and custom for personal benefit; unjustly executed, imprisoned and tortured Roman citizens and allies; let pirates and criminals go free; despoiled shrines and sanctuaries; given and taken bribes; and abandoned his public duties for wanton and licentious living.
2. When we speak second and then have both accusations to answer and new points to make
An example of the second is Cicero's defense of Sextus Roscius of Ameria, for Cicero not only defends Roscius from the outrageous charge of parricide, but also prosecutes Roscius' accusers for attempting to frame Roscius with a crime.

(Sturm 3.35.815)

dilemma [G. "double, ambiguous proposition"] or *dialysis* [G. "dissolution, separation"]
An argument from disjunctive propositions that dismisses both
"If he be a good man, why speak you ill of him? If he be naught, why do you keep him company?"
"Why should I sharply reprove him? If he be a good man, a friendly admonition is better; but if he be an evil man, reproof is odious and contemptible with him."

(Smith 262)

Note: Alternate spellings are *dilemmaton* and *dialisis. Divisio* is an alternate name. Puttenham's English name is "the Dismembrer" (230). Quintilian includes the dilemma (which is not a figure) when he discusses the various kinds of arguments which derive from division (5.10.70). Hoskins, on the other hand, lists *dilemma*, *prosapodosis*, and *expeditio* as figures deriving from division (45–46). According to Peacham, this figure "pertaineth properly to confirm or confute, and that after a most mighty and invincible manner of inferring a conclusion" ([1593] 127). Puttenham, too, remarks that the dilemma is "not so figurative as fit for argumentation, and worketh not unlike the *dilemma* of the Logicians" (230). Wilson uses a dilemma to illustrate a kind of *aporia*, or "doubtfulness": "Whether shall I speak, or hold my peace? If I speak, you will not hear; if I hold my peace, my conscience condemneth my silence" (*Art of Rhetoric* 210).

disjunctio [G. "a separation; an opposition of two propositions that are disjunctively connected in a syllogism"]
An argument with only two viable alternatives
"To honor and liberty we were born; let us either retain these or let us die with dignity" (Cicero, *Philippics* 3.36, trans. me).

(Keckermann 1484)

enthematikon [G. "a graft"]

A sentence that has the force of an enthymeme, but is not one

"I am a man; I think nothing human foreign to me" (Terence, *Heautontimorumenos* 1.1.25). (Sturm 1.14.33)

Note: Perhaps a better definition of this figure is that the two clauses are connected by several implicit syllogisms, rather than as premise and conclusion. Sturm credits Aristotle as the source for this form. See *enthymema* below.

enthymema [G. "something in the mind; thought, piece of reasoning, argument"]

An incomplete syllogism

1. *Contrarium* or *antitheton*, an incomplete syllogism that reaches a conclusion by affirming or denying the contrary

   "He that in familiar communication and company of his friends will never say truth, thinkest then that he will abstain from a lie in a common audience?" (Sherry [1550] 57)

   "If it be a great praise to please good men, surely to please evil men it is a great shame." (Sherry [1550] 93)

2. An incomplete syllogism that reaches a conclusion in a positive way

   "If fish bred in the salt water may want salting, then laws may need a law to mend them."

   "If great wealth brings cares, and poverty misery, then the mean between these two extremes is a great blessing." (Smith 261)

Note: Alternate spellings include *enthimema* and *enthymeme*. Rufinianus, Peacham and Sherry restrict the meaning of enthymeme to only *contrarium*; Sturm, Scaliger, Robertellus, Keckermann, and Smith allow it both designations. The notion of an enthymeme as an imperfect syllogism begins in antiquity but is not widely held. It is not in Aristotle. Quintilian acknowledges that "some" have this view (5.14.24). It is most prominent among Byzantine rhetoricians after Hermogenes (see Conley, "The Enthymeme in Perspective"). By the Renaissance, however, the enthymeme is generally defined as the truncated syllogism. Quintilian rejects as a figure the enthymeme proper, since he considers it a "straightforward method of speaking" (9.2.103), but he here acknowledges that Rutilius and Celsus had regarded it a figure and accepts as an adornment the enthymeme from contraries when not the proof and when a finishing off of an epicheireme for a striking effect, as in the following example from Cicero in *Pro Ligario* 4.10: "Caesar, shall the language of those whom it is your glory to have spared goad you to imitate their own cruelty?" (8.5.10). Although an aspect of style, Quintilian wants to regard this enthymeme as not a figure, but a reflexion. (For Quintilian's discussion of both kinds of enthymeme, which he treats as arguments, see 5.10.1 and 5.14.1.) Quintilian's notion seems similar to that of Hermogenes and the author of the *Anonymous Seguerianus*, who says that "an enthymeme is a conclusion of an antecedent epikheireme related to the question at issue in one period" (§146, 157, qtd by Kennedy in Her. *Inv.* 3.8). Isocrates also had regarded the enthymeme as a feature of style (*Against the Sophists* 16). Following Quintilian, Peacham remarks in his first edition that when this form is used for proof, it is not a figure ([1577] U.iii.v); yet, in his second, he has changed positions and erased the distinction, saying that this figure is used "most specially to confirm or confute" ([1593] 163).

epagoge [G. "bringing on, induction"] or *inductio* [L. "a leading into, induction"]

An argument by induction, which, by nature, is based on comparisons

"Tell me, what good did Demosthenes ever get out of his remarkable eloquence? Apart from other misfortunes, an unhappy and pitiable end. What reward did eloquence bring to Tiberius and Gaius Gracchus? A violent death, and that a wretched and shameful one. What to the highly praised Antonius? He too was mercilessly stabbed to death by thugs. Take Cicero, the father of all eloquence, what reward did he get? Death, and a bitter and pitiable one at that. Very well, then, burn the midnight oil and strive to achieve the highest glories of eloquence, when it has always brought destruction on anyone who excelled in it."

"Do you not expect a sailor to talk more knowledgeably about sailing than a doctor? and a doctor more authoritatively about medicine than a painter? and a painter better about the techniques of colour and light and shade and perspective than a cobbler? Will not a charioteer be better at discussing the art of driving a chariot than a sailor? (A number of comparisons like this will make everyone prepared to accept the idea that each person will speak best about the thing he knows best. Then one brings in one's parallel case.) But what will the orator discuss best, when he professes to be able to talk on any topic?"

(Erasmus, *De copia* 623–24)

Note: Quintilian discusses *epagoge* under arguments drawn from similarities (5.10.73).

epenthymeme [G. "added support, additional argument or enthymeme"]

An enthymeme with reasoning added

"As to your sons—if indeed they should really be called yours when you have cruelly put them to death—if you had punished them with beating, or had branded them with exile and disinheritance, I should still regret that so many fine youths should be kept from their illustrious native soil or should be shamefully beaten. But since you have done away with them, not by disinheritance, or exile, or beating, but by death, all three at once, how can I refrain from protest, accusation, and indignation? If I should have cried out in protest if you had put one of them to death, shall I hold my tongue before this threefold slaying?"

"What Coriolanus did must seem to us more than an enemy act; for it is an act of tyranny to attack one's own country. The enemy should not be attacked, for he [Coriolanus] deserved to be pursued with greater hatred than they in that they attack a foreign country, he his own. He is trying to overthrow that to which he is most indebted."

(Erasmus, *De conscribendis epistolis* 122)

Note: Hermogenes treats this feature as belonging both to argument (*Inv.* 3.9.152) and to style (*Meth.* §5).

epicheireme [G. "a laying hands on, a grasping, an undertaking or attempt; dialectical proof"]

A syllogism in which either or both premises are supported by a reason or example

"Things that are done by design are managed better than those which are governed without design. The house that is managed in accordance with a reasoned plan, is in every respect better equipped and furnished than one which is governed in a haphazard way with a total lack of design. The army that is commanded by a wise and shrewd general is guided in all ways more advantageously than one which is governed by someone's folly and rashness. The same line of reasoning is applicable to navigation, for the ship which has the services of the most expert pilot makes the most successful voyage.

Of all things nothing is better governed than the universe. For the risings and settings of the constellations keep a fixed order, and the changes of the seasons not only proceed in the same way by a fixed law but are also adapted to the advantage of all nature, and the alteration of night and day has never through any variation done any harm.

Therefore the universe is administered by design."

(Cicero, *De Inventione* I.34.58–59)

Note: Quintilian indicates that this term frequently refers to the rhetorical syllogism, that is, one built on a major premise that is only probably true, as differentiated from the logical syllogism in which the major premise is certainly true (5.14.14). This is the meaning this term has in Aristotle's *Topics* (8.162a16). However, Quintilian also says that the distinctions the Greeks maintained between the *enthymema*, *epicheireme*, and *apodeixis* have pretty much slipped away so that these terms name the same thing (5.10.1). He also indicates that the *epicheireme*, as a complete proof, "occurs not merely in individual arguments, but in whole *cases*, provided they are of a simple character" (5.14.10)—i.e., a whole, but simple speech could be one *epicheireme*. This application would be true especially if the *epicheireme* followed the five-part structure often prescribed for it during the first century A.D. and after: proposition, supporting reason, proof of the reason, embellishment, and conclusion (*Ad H* 2.18.28). Hermogenes has a simpler notion of the *epicheireme*: it is a reason in support of a premise (*Inv.* 3.5.). Renaissance rhetoricians do not distinguish between the dialectical and the rhetorical syllogism. Quintilian notes that Visellius and Celsus include both the *epicheireme* and the *enthymeme* among the figures, although he rejects the designation (9.2.106). Hermogenes names the *epichereme* as a feature of style (inasmuch as thought is a feature of style), but not as a figure *per se* (2.3.326).

expeditio [L. "a dispatching, removing"] or *enumeratio* [L. "an enumerating"]

Eliminating all arguments in order, one at a time, until only one option remains

Cicero eliminates all other points at once when he asks, "If this is not the point at issue, what is?" (*Pro Caecina* 13.37, trans. Butler)

(Quintilian 5.10.68)

"The goods in question being alleged to be mine, it is requisite you prove, either that you had them by chance, that you have long held or enjoyed them, that you bought them with your money, or otherwise that by some gift you came to them, or lastly, in succession that you have obtained them. That you had them by chance it cannot be, for they were not lost from my keeping. Long have you not held them, for they were always till this in mine own possession. It is plain you never bought them, for you paid me no money for them. By gift you could not have them, for the right was in me to give them. The succession must be void, for myself am yet living. It remaineth, then, if you keep them, that living you do cast me out of mine own possession."

(Day 98)

Note: *Tpophasis* is a rare alternate name. Puttenham's English name is "the speedie dispatcher" (241) and Hoskins's is "inference" (45). Keckermann refers to this figure as *enumeratio per remotionem* (1484), using language similar to Quintilian's when Quintilian describes the argument of elimination (*remotio*) based on division (5.10.66–67). Hoskins points out that "[t]his enumeration and inference thereupon is that which the logicians call induction; as, in reckoning up, it is neither this nor that, therefore it is this; and (as one merrily saith) it is the dog's syllogism in a cross-way, that saith, My master is gone this or that way: but I smell him not this way, nor this; therefore he runs on his conclusion, without smelling" (45).

hypothesis [G. "supposition"]

Arguing from a fictitious or conditional proposition, or a definite proposition

1. A fictitious supposition

   "Upon my word, if my slaves feared me the way all your [fellow citizens] fear you, I should feel that I had better get out of my house" (Cicero, *In Catalinam* I 7.17, trans. Knott).

   (Erasmus, *De copia* 593)

Note: Hermogenes calls this supposition the *plaston* (fictive) *epicheireme* (*Inv.* 3.11.159). Quintilian treats it as another *locus* for the invention of argument, not as a figure (5.10.95).

2. A definite proposition—one restricted to person, time and place—upon which an argument rests

   Cicero should not accept Mark Antony's proposal that he keep his life in return for burning the *Philippics*.

   (Erasmus, *De copia* 597)

Note: The above example comes from Seneca, *Suasoriae* 6 and was a stock theme debated in the ancient schools. Arguments rest on either a definite or indefinite question, although an indefinite proposition always lies behind a definite (Quintilian 3.5.10). The definite question or *hypothesis* is specific to the circumstances, while the indefinite, or *thesis*, is general and not limited to circumstances. Not usually treated as figures in classical rhetoric, these questions pertain to all arguments and to invention. Nevertheless, some Renaissance rhetoricians treat them as figures. See *thesis* below also.

pareuresis [G. "pretext, pretense"] or *exceptio* [L. "the exception of the defendant to the plaintiff's statements"]

An argument with reasons and excuses that are meant to vanquish all objections

Aeneas's answer to Dido, "whereof I have gathered the sum both of the objections of *Dido*, and of the answers & excuses of *Aeneas*":

"First, she objecteth by her suspicion gathered from probable tokens and very likely signs, his unkind and wicked purpose to steal away from her, to whom she declareth her most fervent love, charging him with his promise faithfully plighted to her.

Secondly, she telleth him that for his sake, she is hated of foreign Princes, and despised of her own people, that for his sake her high and exalted fame were utterly lost.

Thirdly, she declareth that for his sake the danger of conquest both of *Carthage* and her kingdom were most like to ensue, if he should wilfully persist & wickedly proceed in this his evil purpose, which did most woefully and grievously appear unto her.

To whose objection *Aeneas* maketh an answer consisting of many parts as followeth: First he confesseth her kindness, goodness, and liberality. Secondly, he utterly denieth that ever his intent was to depart by stealth. Thirdly, he telleth her that wedlock was never his meaning, nor his coming. Fourthly, he saith, that he greatly desireth to restore his ancient city of *Troy*. Fifthly, he allegeth that the Oracle of *Apollo* calleth him from *Carthage* to *Italy*. Sixthly, he argueth from equal comparison that if she might take delight and pleasure to dwell in *Carthage* her native City and country, why might not the Trojans likewise repair to the land which they most longed after? Seventhly, he sheweth her that his father's ghost doth every night warn him away. Eighthly, that he did wrong to his son *Ascanius*, to withhold him so long from Italy, his promised inheritance. Ninthly, he signifieth that by a message from God himself, both appearing to his eyes and sounding in his ears, he is commanded to remove and depart from thence, and therefore wisheth her to content herself, and cease her wailing for his love which might not prevail, and therefore in vain" (*Aeneid* 4.305–62).

(Peacham [1593] 95–96)

Note: Peacham's Latin equivalents include *adinventio* and *excogitata excusatio* ([1593] 95).

propositio [L. "a setting forth, a proposition"]

A premise leading to a conclusion

"As if a man would counsel Tully not to take the condition offered by Antony, that is, that by burning of his books called *philippia* [*Philippics*], he should have his life, he might use commonly these propositions. First that no man ought to buy his life so dear, that thereby he should lose his immortal name. To this general may serve a particular taken out of the circumstances, that it ought not to be done, especially of Cicero, which by so many labors hath gotten unto himself an excellent and everlasting name, and that hath showed most eloquently by putting out so many noble works that death ought to be despised, especially seeing that now he hath not much time to live being an old man. Again, another principal proposition shall be taken of the circumstances. That nothing is worse, than that Cicero being a very good man should owe his life to Antony the worst man of the world. The third proposition shall be conjectural: how that Antony craftily goeth about that the books being burned in the which he perceiveth both his own immortal infamy to be and the immortal glory of Cicero, when he hath afterwards taken away his life, he may utterly extinguish Cicero."

(Sherry [1550] 77)

Note: Sherry here is modeling the logical invention of arguments on a common school exercise (See *Suasoria* 6 in Seneca, *Suasoriae*).

prosapodosis [G. "addition that completes"] or *divisio* [L. "a division, separation"] or *dialysis* [G. "dissolution, separation"]

An argument that separates into the alternatives of a question, resolves each by subjoining explanation or evidence, or uses a number of reasons to support one statement

1. Dividing into alternatives

"The judges are corrupt, partly because of favoritism, partly because of bribes."

(Melanchthon, *Elem.* 50r)

"Time at one instant seeming short and long to them: short in the pleasingness of such presence, long in the stay of their desires" (Sidney, *Arcadia*, book 1, 96)

(Hoskins 46)

2. Supporting each alternative or detail one by one

"If I have evil spoken, bear witness of the evil; but if I have well spoken, why smitest thou me?"

"I demand now whether you will revenge your own injuries or the injuries of the commonwealth? If you do revenge the injury of the commonwealth, what answer will you make concerning your constancy in that behalf? If you revenge your own, beware you err not in thinking that Caesar will be angry and have displeasure with your enemies, when he has forgiven his own" (Cicero, *Pro Ligario* 10.29).

(Peacham ([1577] R.iiii.v)

"Your silence must carry with it a construction of contempt, unkindness, or displeasure. If you take me not for your friend, you offer unkindness. If you deem me unworthy of an answer, it comes of contempt. If your passion defers a reply, it argues your displeasure."

(Hoskins 46)

3. Supporting one statement with more than one reason
   "'Tis oft great gain to set bad lands on fire
   And burn the stubble in sharp crackling flame.
   Haply the earth some secret powers conceives
   And seeds of nourishment; or some disease
   Is burned out and all noisome dews expelled;
   Or heat, more like, the hidden breathing-holes
   And secret channels opens and sets free,
   Whereby the young plants drink the moisture in.
   More often heat gives toughness and contracts
   The soil's large veins, lest soaking showers bring harm,
   Or the swift sun's too fierce extreme of power,
   Or wintry blasts of Boreas' piercing cold."
   (Virgil, *Georgic* I.84–115, trans. Williams)

   (Quintilian 9.3.96)

   "Better it were to rule than to serve, for he that ruleth liveth because he is free. But he that serveth cannot be said to live. For where bondage is, there is no life properly" (Brutus about Gnaeus Pompeius, in Quintilian 9.3.95).

   (Wilson 229)

Note: Alternate spellings are *prosopodosis* or *dialisis*. Sherry lists *prosapodosis* as an alternate name for *subjectio* in his 1550 edition (53), a mistake that he corrects in his second edition. The first application of this figure resembles syntactical *prolepsis*. See *prolepsis* above under syntactical figures. The dilemma is one species of this figure. Consequently, Day conflates *dialysis* with *dilemma* (97). Melanchthon lists this figure as one species that derives from the dialectical topic of division (*Elem.* 50r). When only one reason is added to a statement, we have the figure *aetiologia*. See *aetiologia* below under Logical–evidence.

syllogismus [G. "a collecting, reasoning"] or *ratiocinatio* [L. "an exercise of the reasoning powers"] or *collectio* [L. "a collecting together"]

Implying the consequent by signs or circumstances, or the complete syllogism

1. The conjecture following from the signs or circumstances of a matter. These circumstances are either those that go before, are annexed with, or follow after.
   a. Those that go before
      "'Seven days hence will I cause it to rain upon the earth forty days and forty nights' (Genesis 7:4), whereby the Lord gave to understand what a mighty flood should follow."

      (Peacham [1593] 180)

   b. Those that are annexed with
      1. In tropes
         "He was mistaken for a hat riding on the pommel of a saddle," meaning "a little man on horseback."
         "You had need eat a bushel of salt with him," meaning "you must live many years in his company whom you shall accompt for your friend."

         (Hoskins 25)

2. In appearance
"Cicero, when he is about to reproach Antony with his drunkenness and vomiting, says, 'You with such a throat, such flanks, such burly strength in every limb of your prize-fighter's body,' etc. What have his throat and flanks to do with his drunkenness? The reference is far from pointless: for by looking at them we are enabled to estimate the quantity of the wine which he drank at Hippias' wedding, and was unable to carry or digest in spite of the fact that his bodily strength was worthy of a prize-fighter" (*Philippic* 2.25.63, trans. Butler).

(Quintilian 8.4.16)

3. In actions
By saying that Polyphemus used a pine tree for his staff, Virgil implies that Polyphemus was a giant (*Aeneid* 3.687).

(Sherry [1555] G.i.r)

"Mary Magdalen, who pressed into the feast of the proud Pharisees, and before their faces washed Jesus' feet with her tears and wiped them with the hairs of her head, lamenting her offences: we judge her repentance was great, that cast off all bashfulness and fear, and pressed in so boldly to bewail her wickedness" (cf. Luke 7.37–38).

(Peacham [1577] P.iiii.r)

c. Those that follow after
"Foelix trembled, which did plainly betoken his inward horror, at the hearing of God's judgements" (Acts 24:25).

(Peacham [1593] 180)

2. The complete syllogism, or *syllogicon*, same as *conclusio*
Every just thing is profitable;
Every honest thing is just;
Every honest thing therefore is profitable.

(Smith 260)

Note: This figure has been called in English "intimation." This figure includes the act of implying the greatness of something by describing the greatness of its details. Used in this way, the figure is a type of *emphasis*. Quintilian would rather consider this device a method than a figure (9.2.103). *Ratiocinatio* is also the general term for "reasoning."

thesis [G. "setting down, placing"] or *locus communis* [L. "commonplace"]
An indefinite proposition, unrestricted to a particular person, time or place; a commonplace
When considering whether war should be waged against the Turks, we should also consider whether a Christian should be permitted to go to war.
When Cicero says that Clodius was punished by God for his crimes against religion, he then talks about the reality of the divine power that governs the world: "Assuredly such a power does exist; nor can it be that while in the frail fabric of our bodies there is a Something which energizes and which feels, yet that Something does not exist in the vast and glorious workings of nature; unless perchance they think otherwise just because it does not offer itself to the view or to the sight" (*Pro Milone* 31.84, trans. Watts).

(Melanchthon, *Elem.* 26r)

Note: Melanchthon teaches that the chief method for amplification is converting the *hypothesis*, or particular cause, into the *thesis*, or general principle applicable to the cause (Elem. 46v). From the general principles arise commonplaces, which serve to demonstrate and amplify (26v). Commonplaces contain and serve as major premises in syllogisms (46v); in fact, the central *thesis* of the speech is the commonplace from which the main proof originates (47v). He distinguishes these commonplaces from *sententia* culled like flowers from the poets and orators (27r). Veltkirchius provides a similar discussion, emphasizing that the places of dialectic produce these commonplaces (184v-86r). This *thesis* corresponds to the indefinite question one considers during the process of invention. Quintilian reviews the considerations as follows: "[Q]uestions are either *definite* or *indefinite*. *Indefinite* questions are those which may be maintained or impugned without reference to persons, time or place and the like. The Greeks call them *theses*. [. . .] Cicero distinguishes two kinds, the one concerned with *knowledge*, the other with *action*. Thus 'Is the world governed by providence?' is a question of knowledge, while 'Should we enter politics?' is a question of action. The first involves three questions, whether a thing is, what it is, and of what nature: [. . .] the second involves two, how to obtain the power and how to use it. *Definite* questions involve facts, persons, time and the like. The Greeks call them *hypotheses*, while we call them *causes*. [. . .] But in every special question the general question is implicit, since the *genus* is logically prior to the *species*" (3.5.5–10). See *hypothesis* above. While these basic questions do not produce figures for Quintilian, the indefinite basis does for Hermogenes, who calls the resulting commonplaces *katholikoi logoi* (*Meth.* §5). Erasmus discusses these general or catholic commonplaces under *sententia* (*DC* 627). See also *dignitates* and *sententia* below.

Kinds of Evidence

ainos [G. from *parainesis* or "advice"]

Using a moral from a fable or tale

"[T]he tale of Icarus falling into the sea warns that no one should rise higher than his lot in life allows, and the story of Phaëthon that no one should undertake to perform a task that is beyond his powers."

(Erasmus, *De copia* 611)

Note: An alternate spelling is *aenos*. Theon gives the origin of this name ("The Exercises of Aelius Theon," in Kennedy, *Progymnasmata* 24).

aetiologia [G. "giving a cause"] or *subjecta ratio* [L. "placing a reason under"] or *causa* [L. "a cause, reason"]

Confirming a word or statement by giving a reason or reasons

1. Confirming the use of a word by reference to its definition
   a. In vituperation
      "Are you not a citizen who is an enemy of the nation? Should this man be considered strong who deserted his weapons?"
   b. In praise
      "I am truly a citizen, who fought back the weapons of enraged men."
   c. In combination
      "Had the king shown himself honest, Postumus would have been a monument of sagacity; as the king has deceived him, he is pronounced the greatest of fools" (Cicero, *Pro Rabirio Postumo* 1.1, trans. Watts).

(Sturm 2.27.434)

2. Confirming a statement
   "He brought me forth into a place of liberty, he brought me forth even because he had a favor unto me. The Lord rewarded me according to my righteousness; according to the cleanness of my hands hath he recompensed me" (Psalm 18:19–20).

   (Peacham [1593] 184)

   "Thus saith the Lord; For three transgressions of Edom, and for four, I will not spare him: because he did pursue his brother with the sword, and did cast off all pity, and his anger did tear perpetually, and kept his wrath for ever" (Amos 1:11).

   (Smith 125)

Note: Alternate spellings include *etiologia, aitiologia*, or *caussa*. Puttenham's Anglicization is "the Reason rend or the Tell Cause" (236). Quintilian rejects this form as a figure (9.3.93). But, Melanchthon classifies this figure as a species deriving from the dialectical topic of cause (*Elem.* 50v). Peacham's description of the use of this figure demonstrates its function as argument: "This figure is usual in all good Authors and is of great strength in speech, for that the sentence said hath always the reason joined unto it as an authentic seal to an evidence: and it serveth to confirmation and confutation. The speaker in the use of this figure ought to be sure that the reason or cause which he joineth to the proposition be good and sufficient, lest he weaken that which he should confirm and disgrace that which he should beautify" (185). Puttenham concurs, "In many cases we are driven for better persuasion to tell the cause that moves us to say thus or thus: or else when we would fortify our allegations by rendering reasons to every one" (236).

analogia [G. "correspondence, resemblance"]

Using an analogy or parallel, a comparison in which all the parts of the parallel correspond

"[A] ship raising or lowering sail to suit the force of the wind, and tacking from one side to the other, would be a parallel, showing that the sensible man should yield to circumstances and accommodate himself to his situation."

"Those just sailing into harbour after a long sea-voyage eagerly give information to those setting out about the likelihood of storms and the pirate situation and what the different places are like, because it is natural to feel kindly towards those who are about to face the dangers which we have just escaped. What then should be my feelings, who am just coming into sight of land after a terrible tossing, towards this man who, as I can see, must go out to face dreadful storms?" (Cicero, *Pro Murena* 2.4, trans. Knott)

(Erasmus, *De copia* 621)

Note: This figure seems to correspond with *antapodosis*, a figure listed above under the Logical–idea category. I list *analogia* here because Erasmus (*DC* 607) and Veltkirchius (159v) treat it as one kind of illustrative example. Quintilian deems *analogia* as a kind of similarity that functions as argument, not figure (5.11.34). *Analogia* is commonly identified as the principle upon which metaphors are built (see Erasmus [*Eccl.* 3.159.123], Robertellus [37r], and Sturm [2.2.275]).

apodeixis [G. "showing forth, making known, exhibiting; proof"]

Confirming a statement with both argument and examples; demonstration

"An example of *Paul* the Apostle: 'Be not deceived, God is not mocked, for whatsoever a man soweth that shall he also reap'" (Galatians 6:7).

"Another of *Solomon*: 'Can a man take fire in his bosom, and his clothes not be burnt: or can a man go upon coals, and his feet not be burnt?' (Proverbs 6:27–28). Here in these two examples taken from the experience of Nature, are the reasons of their conclusions grounded."

(Peacham [1593] 86)

Note: An alternate spelling is *apodixis*. Peacham gives as the Latin equivalent *experientia* and *evidens probatio* and describes this figure as occurring when the orator "inferreth his reason and confirmation from known principles, which experience doth prove and no man can deny" ([1593] 86). The term *apodeixis* in Aristotle refers to scientific demonstration and belongs to philosophy, not rhetoric. Quintilian includes *apodeixis* in his discussion of rhetorical argument, but not style (5.10.1–8). Demetrius treats this feature as a stylistic option, but not specifically as a figure (§233). That *apodeixis* has become a figure of rhetoric in Renaissance texts indicates a significant departure from classical precedents. Peacham and Smith (231) both include here proverbs and common sayings.

apomnemonsysis [G. "memorial, record, commemoration, recounting"] or *kollesis* [G. "gluing"]
Quoting a statement of another
Matthew 15:7–8 quotes Isaiah 29:13: "O hypocrites *Esay* prophesied well of you, saying: 'This people draweth near unto me with their mouth and honoureth me with their lips, but their heart is far from me.'"

(Peacham [1593] 87)

Note: Peacham gives the Latin equivalent as *dicti commemoratio* ([1593] 87). Robertellus gives Demetrius as the source for this figure (48v), but it seems more likely that the source is Hermogenes's discussion of the *chreia* in his *Progymnasmata* (see Kennedy, *Progymnasmata* 76). Hermogenes identifies two kinds of borrowing: the first is direct quotation or *kollesis*; the second is adaptation or *paroidia* (*Meth.* §30). See *parechesis* below.

asphalia [G. "assurance, certainty, security, pledge, bond"]
Offering self as surety for one's word
"*Judah* persuading his father *Jacob* to let *Benjamin* his youngest son go into *Egypt* with the rest of his brothers, who used this form of speech, saying: 'I will be surety for him, of my hand shalt thou require him, if I bring him not to thee, and set him before thee, then let me bear the blame for ever'" (Genesis 43:9).

(Peacham [1593] 68)

Note: *Securitas* and *certitudo* are Latin equivalents.

bebaiosis [G. "confirmation, strengthening"]
Confirming by reference to tradition or long-held opinion
"That opinion is old which is established from the most ancient literature of the Greeks, that the island of Sicily was consecrated to Ceres and Liber."

(Sturm 3.35.816)

Note: The term comes from *Rhet. ad Alex.*, ch. 36 (1442b 34), where it means confirmation in general.

chreia [G. "use, advantage, service; a pregnant maxim, frequently illustrated by an anecdote"]
Using a short exposition of a saying or deed of a known authority
1. Of a saying
"In that [Isocrates] sayeth, 'The root of learning is bitter and the fruits pleasant': he signifieth [that] no excellent quality or gift, virtue, art or science can be attained, except pain, labour, diligence do plant and set the same: but when that noble gift, either learning, or any excellent quality, is lodged and reposed in us, then we gather by painful labours, great profit, comfort, delectable pleasures, wealth, glory, riches, which be the fruits of it" (Hermogenes, *Progymnasmata* §3).

2. Of a deed
   "As Diogenes being asked of Alexander the Great, if he lacked anything, that he was able to give him, thinking his demand under his power, for Diogenes was at the same time warming himself in the beams of the Sun: Diogenes answered, 'Ye take away that, that ye are not able to give,' meaning that Alexander by his body, shadowed him, and took away that, which was not in his power to give. Alexander turned himself to his men and said, 'If I were not Alexander, I would be Diogenes.'" [An exposition of the meaning or significance of this event would follow.]
3. Of both
   "Diogenes, seeing a boy wanton & dissolute, did strike his teacher with a staff, uttering these words: 'Why dost thou teach thy scholar so dissolutely.'" [An exposition of the meaning or significance of this example would follow.] (Hermogenes, *Progymnasmata* §3)

(Rainolde D.iiii.v-E.i.r)

Note: Sherry lists this figure as a kind of *indicacio*, an appeal to authorities. See *kriseis* below. Melanchthon and Erasmus treat it as a kind of *sententia*. Inasmuch as the exposition of the saying can stand alone, *chreia* is also a name for a genre of essay, being one of the *progymnasmata*. Aphthonius explains that the essay has its name because it is useful ["*khreiodes*"] (*Progymnasmata* §3, in Kennedy, *Progymnasmata* 97). See Quintilian also for a description of this moral essay (1.9.3–6).

dignitates [L. "authoritative principles"]

Confirming by using the common, general axioms and first principles of each science

For example, we can calculate from its known kinetic energy how much gravitational potential energy an object will gain, if the first kind of energy is completely converted to the second kind, or vice versa, because in an isolated system, energy will be transformed but not lost when a force operates upon an object and because potential energy decreases as kinetic energy increases and vice versa.

(Veltkirchius 164r, example mine)

Note: Both Sherry and Veltkirchius would allow a scientific principle as an example here. Veltkirchius treats this figure as a species of *kriseis*, specifically the catholic or universal maxim. See *kriseis* below and *thesis* above.

firmamentum [L. "a strengthening, support, prop"]

The good reasons supporting one's position; or the strongest argument of one's defense

"[A]nyone urging Cicero not to accept Mark Antony's proposal that he should keep his life in return for burning the *Philippics* could use the following propositions [reasons]: 'No man of eminence ought to buy his life at the cost of his immortal fame.' This general proposition could be reinforced by one dependent on the specific circumstances of this case: 'Especially Cicero, who by his labours won for himself a name and a glory that will live for ever and eloquently demonstrated in so many wonderful books that death is of no account, particularly as, being already an old man, he probably has not many years still to live.' A second major proposition can be derived from the circumstances of the case: 'Nothing could be more distressing than to have a fine man like Cicero indebted for his life to a villain like Antony.' The third proposition will be conjectural: 'Antony is acting treacherously; when the *Philippics*, which he knows enshrine his own eternal infamy and Cicero's deathless glory, have been burned, he will then take Cicero's life and so blot out the man entirely'" (Seneca, *Suasoria* 6).

(Erasmus, *De copia* 597–98)

Note: The Latin name *firmamentum* is in Cicero's *De Inventione* I.13.18–19, *Part. Orat.* 29.103, and Quintilian 3.11.19. The *Ad Herennium* uses the term instead to mean "the central point of the accusation," and Caplan's footnote provides *synechon* as the Greek term (1.16.26). *Synechon* means "connection, holding together like a sinew, pressing in and around so as to leave little room for movement."

invocatio [L. "an invocation"]
Confirming one's statement with an invocation to the gods
"In heaven's name, Catiline, how long will you abuse your patience?" (Cicero, *In Catilinam* I 1.1, trans. Lord)

(Robertellus 45v)

Note: Quintilian, who reports that this figure comes from Celsus, rejects it (9.2.104).

kriseis [G. "judgments"] or *indicatio* [L. "a valuation"] or *auctoritas* [L. "a judgment"]
Confirming through an appeal to authorities or testimony

1. In general
"According to Epicurus, happiness lies in pleasure."
"Pyrrho denies the possibility of knowledge."
"He cites a number of authorities holding this opinion."

(Erasmus, *De copia* 438)

2. *Procrisis*, putting this proof before one's own argument
"And so, while from many other things we can understand that our ancestors have surpassed other nations not only in arms, but also in wisdom and prudence, this is especially shown by the fact that they devised a remarkable punishment for the undutiful. In this matter, consider how in sagacity they excelled those who are reputed to have been the wisest men of all other nations" (Cicero, *Pro S. Roscio* 25.69, trans. Freese).

(Sturm 3.9.578)

3. *Epencrisis*, putting this proof in the middle of one's own argument
"According to tradition, Athens, while she possessed the hegemony of Greece, was the most sagacious of all the states; moreover, the wisest of her citizens is said to have been Solon, the man who drew up the laws which are still in force among them at the present day. When he was asked why he had killed his father, he answered that he thought no one would be guilty of such a crime. He is said to have acted wisely in not appointing any penalty for a crime which until then had never been committed, for fear he might appear to suggest rather than prevent it. How much greater the wisdom of our ancestors! Aware that nothing was so sacred that it might not some day be violated by an act of audacity, they thought out a remarkable punishment for parricides, with the object of deterring from crime, by the greatness of the punishment, those whom nature alone had been unable to keep loyal to duty: they ordered that they should be sewn alive into a sack, and then thrown into a river" (Cicero, *Pro S. Roscio* 25.70, trans. Freese).

(Sturm 3.9. 578)

Note: Additional names include *judicatio* and *judicia*. Alternate spellings include *indicacio, autoritas,* and *authoritee*. The names Quintilian applies to the argument from testimony are the Latin *auctoritas* and the Greek *kriseis* (not figures). These forms of proof include opinions (*judicationes*), proverbs, common sayings, popular beliefs, and quotations from the poets (5.11.36–39). Melanchthon includes here laws, proverbs and the sayings of famous men, but subordinates all these under the figure *sententia* (*Elem.* 53v), as Susenbrotus also does (96). Sherry indicates that the species of this figure include *sententia, dignities, proverb, chreia, enthymeme, epiphonema, noema, aenos*, and *oraculum* ([1550] 92–93; [1555] G.vi.v-vii.v).

martyria [L. "a testimony"]
Confirming a statement with one's own experience
"The Physician maketh report of his own proof in diseases and cures, and sometime doth record them to the great benefice and good of the posterity."
"The Captain which hath been in many battles, at many sieges, assaults, defenses, and encounters, and hath had experience in many stratagems, doth teach younger soldiers, and confirmeth that which he counseleth by his own testimony founded upon often proof."
"That which was from the beginning, which we have heard, which we have seen with our eyes, which we have looked upon, and our hands have handled, of the Word of life; (For the life was manifested, and we have seen it, and bear witness, and shew unto you that eternal life, which was with the Father, and was manifested unto us;) That which we have seen and heard declare we unto you" (1 John 1:1–3).

(Peacham [1593] 85)

Note: Peacham gives *testatio* as a Latin equivalent ([1593] 85).

mythologia [G. "storytelling"]
Confirming by using fables or myths combined with explanation
"Do not think, as often happens in fables, that those who commit wickedness and impiety are agitated and terrified by the fiery torches of their violent passions."

(Sturm 1.42.253)

oraculum [L. "a divine announcement"] or *chrismos* [G. "oracular response"]
Confirming a statement with God's word or commandments
"All things that are spoken and commanded in the Bible."

(Sherry [1555] G.vii.v)

Note: Quintilian treats proof based on oracles under the category of *kriseis* (5.11.42).

paradeigma [G. "pattern, model, precedent, example"] or *exemplum* [L. "an example"]
Confirming by giving an example

1. Fictional, or *parabole*

   "But now because this offense is an evil most odious, and the principal occasion of all other mischief, I will set forth three notable examples, the one of a dragon, the second of a dog, and the third of a lion, which all three in thankfulness, if that be true which is reported of them, wonderfully exceeded; and the rather I seek to set them out, that the wicked hereby may well know what they themselves are when brute beasts shall set them all to school."

   (Wilson 217)

2. Historical, or *paradeigia*

   "And consulting upon the affairs of the low countries at this day, peradventure her Majesty might be thus advised: The Flemings are a people very unthankful and mutable, and rebellious against their Princes, for they did rise against *Maximilian* Archduke of Austria, who had married the daughter and heir of the house of Burgundy, and took him prisoner, till by the Emperor *Frederike* the third his father, he was set at liberty. They rebelled against *Charles* the fifth Emperor, their natural Prince. They have falsified their faith to his son *Philip,* king of Spain, their sovereign Lord: and since to Archduke *Matthias*, whom they elected for their governor, after to their adopted Lord Monsieur of France, Duke of Anjou: I pray you what likelihood is there they should be more assured to the Queen of England, than they have been to all these princes and governors, longer than their distress continueth, and is to be relieved by her goodness and puissance."

(Puttenham 252–53)

Note: An alternate spelling is *paradigma*. Puttenham's name is "Resemblance by example" (248). Quintilian treats both *parabole* and the historical parallel as kinds of inductive proofs, not figures (5.11.125). Rufinianus seems to be the only rhetorician to use the term *paradeigia* (§22); nevertheless, many make reference to the historical parallel as a kind of example. Explaining that these two modes of example are helpful in confirming arguments (*Inst.* 18v), Melanchthon points out that this figure derives from the dialectical topic of comparison (*Elem.* 53r), and Susenbrotus has the student use the dialectical topic of circumstances to create this figure (103). This figure is often listed as a species of the similitude.

paraplokas toiematon [G. "interweaving poetical quotations in prose"] or *versibus uti* [L. "the use of verse"]

1. The incorporating of verse quotations and poetic reminiscences in one's text generally
2. Quoting poetry, but integrating the quotations with paraphrase in prose, logical connection, explicit attribution, and commentary into one's own text

Plato, for example, integrates a quotation from Homer in this manner: "But also in Homer we see that it is just to honor such young men as are noble. Indeed Homer says that Ajax, who was distinguished in the war, 'was honored with whole chines,' since this was a suitable reward for a young and courageous man, from which he would derive honor and increase his strength" (*Republic* 5.468c-d; *Iliad* 7.321).

(Hermogenes 2.4.336–37)

Note: The other way to use quotations is by keeping them entirely separate from our own words. See *disjunctio*, a Pragmatical–idea figure above. Quintilian (9.2.104) and Robertellus (45r) say the quoting of verse, or *versibus uti*, is a figure of thought in Celsus. Quintilian disapproves of including this strategy as a figure (9.2.107); Robortellus prefers to view the device not as a figure of thought, but as a figure of words (45r).

parechesis [G. "supplying as one's own"] or *allusione* [L. "allusion"] or *paroidia* [G. "adaptation"]

Using another's words with a new purpose, sometimes without attribution; an allusion

"I shall be speaking with the propriety of the Tragic Muse, when I say to the jury: 'Who on an embassy delights in the company' of Philocrates, 'I never inquired, knowing' that he took money, as Philocrates admits he did" (Demosthenes, *De Falsa Legatione* 245, quoting Euripides's *Phoenix*, trans. Kennedy).

(Hermogenes, *Method* §30)

"I may say of an ill conscience, as *Socrates* of a wandering traveler, 'It is no wonder if it be out of temper, when it hath it's self for it's companion.'"

(Smith 244)

Note: For direct quotation see *apomnemonsysis* and *paraplokas toiematon* above.

paroemia [G. "a proverb, adage"] or *proverbium* [L. "an old saying, proverb"] or *adagium* [L. "applicable to life, an adage"] or *apophthegma* [G. "a terse, pointed saying"]

Using a proverb or common saying as proof

"Who so toucheth pitch shall be defiled therewith."
"It early pricketh that will be a thorn."
"Many hands make light work."

(Day 80)

Note: Alternate spellings include *parimia, paromia, paremia* and *paronomia.* Although Celsus listed this device as a figure, Quintilian disapproves (9.2.104) unless it involves allegory or irony (8.6.57). Vives distinguishes among these terms as follows: popular and trite expressions are adages; sayings and deeds of great men are apothegms; and apothegms that are repeated frequently are proverbs (*De ratione dicendi* 118–19). Keckermann also distinguishes them: an apothegm is a sharp, brief and polished response; proverbs or adages are *sententia* frequently repeated by the common man (1478–79). Sherry distinguishes between common moral sentences and proverbs ([1550] 92–93). This figure is sometimes listed as a kind of allegory, a trope. Susenbrotus indicates that this figure serves to confirm (19).

sententia [L. "thought, opinion, judgment, sentiment"] or *gnome* [G. "thought, judgment, opinion"]

Using a pithy, terse, weighty aphorism or maxim about general truth invented by ourselves

1. In words
   a. Without a reason
      "Envy brings its own punishment."
      "A prince who will know everything has many things to learn."
      "Complaisance wins friends; truth begets ill will" (Terence, *Andria* 1.1.68).
      (Erasmus, *De copia* 627)

      "Lecherous and intemperate youth maketh a feeble body in old age."
      (Peacham ([1577] U.iii.r)

   b. With a reason
      "They who think that the sins of youth deserve indulgence are deceived, because that time of life does not constitute a hindrance to sound studious activities. But they act wisely who chastise the young with especial severity in order to inculcate at the age most opportune for it the desire to attain those virtues by which they can order their whole lives."
      (*Ad Herennium* 4.17.25)

2. In deeds
   "But my greatest glory lies in making Men to live *Gnomically*, as all just and righteous men do, who by keeping their words, make good their bargains, paying their Debts, and such like things, do most effectually confute and baffle iniquity out of the World. Let the principle be what it will, it matters not; let men live thus *Gnomically*, and I will undertake one *Quaker* shall both have more credit, and make more Converts than an hundred *Metonimical* Devices, or *Metaphorical* Philosophers."
   (Shaw 138–39)

Note: Puttenham's name for this figure is "the Director" or "the Sage sayer" (243). Quintilian prefers to consider *sententia* and its related forms (*gnome, enthymema, epiphonema, noema*, and *clausula*) as reflexions, not figures (8.5.1–14). Scaliger qualifies by saying that the *sententia* is not necessarily a figure, but admits of figures (3.94.363). The rest make no such distinctions. Erasmus (*DC* 627–30) includes as kinds of maxims *theses* (catholic or universal statements) and *hypotheses*, those with and without reasons, those that are single and those that are double (either based on a similarity or a contrary), the *epiphonema*, the *noema*, and the explicit or the concealed. Examples of the latter two are these: Ovid gives the explicit maxim: "More fiercely burns the fire that is concealed" (*Metamorphoses* 4.64) and Virgil alludes to this maxim obliquely in his line "She is consumed with hidden fire" (*Aeneid* 4.2). Keckermann considers *gnome* a special kind of *sententia*, one that is complex, having conjoined themes; that is, it does not so much explain a thing as persuade that something must be done or not done (1476–77). Day includes quotations from other authors here (99). Hoskins explains that a *sententia* can be created by "putting the general name for the special; as they say, drawing it a *thesi* ad *hypothesin*" (40). Peacham, too, declares that the *thesis*, "a sentence universal," can serve as a *gnome* ([1577] U.iii.r). Saying that this figure derives from the dialectical topic of genus, Melanchthon teaches that the major premise of a syllogism is in most cases a commonplace saying and he includes here laws, proverbs, and sayings of famous men, or in other words, *kriseis* or judgments (*Elem.* 53v). See *kriseis* above and *thesis* under Logical–argument forms above.

DISCOURSAL

Parts of an Oration

adnarratio [L. "a narrative near by"] or *schesis* [G. "state or condition which is alterable"] or *adfictio* [L. "a fashioning near by"]

Adding a narrative to our oration that colors our case positively and/or the adversary's case negatively, in response to the adversary's contrary narration and in order to prevent attacks and to obscure the adversary's case

Venus downplays her own influence in the war between the Trojans and the Italians by attributing to Juno its causes:

"Now Juno even
Stirs up the spirits of death—this lot of creation
Had remained yet unthrown—and Allecto is suddenly loosed
On the earth and has rioted through the Italian cities."

In response, Juno not only points out Venus's role as supporter of the Trojan attack, but also begins her defense of the Italians by laying down the premise Venus herself has already argued and then uses it to reach a contrary conclusion:

"For the people of Italy it is unworthy
To burn nascent Troy and for Turnus to take a stand
On the soil of his own fatherland, he whose grandfather was
Pilumnus, his mother the goddess Venilia. Why
Do the Trojans attack the Latins with torches that make
A black ruin, and press down their yoke on fields not their own,
Or drive off their booty?" (Virgil, *Aeneid* 10.39–82, trans. Lind)

(Scaliger 3.73.342)

Note: Rufinianus gives the same example (*Dian.* §5). An alternate name is *parantegnosis* (342). Quintilian mentions the need for this strategy, but does not call it a figure (4.2.80–82). This figure seems to differ from *color*, a kind of *metastasis* (see Pragmatical–idea figures), by not relying solely upon suppositional additions to the narrative. This figure can be applied in the statement of facts or as a narrative digression within a speech.

anasceue [G. "carry away, remove, demolish"] or *destructio* [L. "a pulling down, destruction"] or *evacuatio* [L. "a weakening"] or *confutatio* [L. "confutation"]

The refutation, wherein we contradict the greatest point of the adversary's case

In his defense of Sextus Roscius of Ameria, Cicero demolishes the prosecutor's charge of parricide by showing that Roscius had neither motive, disposition, nor opportunity to kill his father, whereas Capito and Magnus, on whom the blame should be fixed, had all three. He disproves the prosecution's accusation that the son was afraid of being disinherited by showing such a charge to be mere gossip. Furthermore, Roscius is of good character without a smirch upon his reputation. Additionally, Roscius could not have killed his father since he was not in Rome, knew few people in Rome inasmuch as he seldom left Ameria, and did not send his servants to do the deed.

(Rufinianus, *Dianoias* §6; example mine)

Note: In logic, this move is the opposite of *kataskeue*, the confirming of one's proofs. Quintilian mentions both of these terms in his discussion of the narrative exercise in the *progymnasmata* (2.4.18). *Anaskeue* is the name in Greek for the refutation exercise of the *progymnasmata* and *kataskeue* is name for the confirmation (Hermogenes, *Progymnasmata* §5).

antanaclasis [G. "reciprocation or bearing back"] or *reditus ad rem* [L. "returning to the subject"]
Returning to the matter after a digression

1. After a long parenthesis
"Assure thyself (most wicked woman! that hast so plaguily a corrupted mind as that thou canst not keep thy sickness to thyself, but must most wickedly infect others) assure thyself, I say, etc." (Pamela in Sidney, *Arcadia*, book 3, 410)

(Hoskins 44)

2. After a digression
"I knew a preacher that was a whole hour out of his matter, and at length remembering himself said, 'Well, now to the purpose.'"

(Wilson 207)

Note: Keckermann (1489) and Vossius (272) regard this figure as a kind of *revocatio*. See *revocatio* above under Pragmatical–people figures. Shaw includes this figure within *epanados* (157). See *epanados* above under syntactical and Pragmatical–idea figures.

anthypophora [G. "reply"] or *subjectio* [L. "an annexing, subjoining"] or *objectio* [L. "a throwing or putting before"] or *lysis* [G. "a loosening, rupture"]
Answering objections the adversary brings against us

1. By granting the objection, but then following with a contrary point that overcomes the initial concern
"I grant there is in it great labors and many perils, yet by painful travail and valiant adventures therein shall ensue immortal glory."
"Indeed it is good to hope for the best, yet it is better to fear the worst."
"It is good to be merry, but yet with measure."
"I grant to learn tongues is a painful thing, yet is it necessary, and being once attained, a thing that bringeth both pleasure and profit."

(Peacham [1577] S.i.v)

2. By refuting the objection with the contrary argument
"Yea, but you say he hath done these things so that all men knew it not. I think there be no man which hath heard of his name, but can also rehearse his mischievous acts" (Cicero, *In C. Verrem* I 5.15).

(Sherry [1555] E.vii.v)

"You will say to me that in a factious country it is the only policy to stand neutral. I say, no, unless many circumstances help you; *videlicet*, these: if none of those friends by whom your love is scanned be entered into a quarrel; if you be assured that your wealth and discretion is equal to the best; if there be likelihood of scattering the reliance of both sides and making a new pack. Then is it wisdom to stand aloof off a while, that if you please, you may add the victory to which side you will."

(Hoskins 49)

"The chief priests and the elders of the people came unto Christ, as he was teaching, and said, 'By what authority doest thou these things? and who gave thee this authority?' And Jesus answered and said unto them, 'I also will ask you one thing, which if ye tell me, I in likewise will tell you by what authority I do these things. The baptism of John, whence was it? from heaven, or of men?' And they reasoned with themselves, saying, 'If we shall say, "From heaven," he will say unto us, "Why did ye not then believe him?" But if we shall say, "Of men;" we fear the people; for all hold John as a prophet.' And they answered Jesus, and said, 'We cannot tell.' And he said unto them, 'Neither tell I you by what authority I do these things.'" (Matthew 21:23–27)

(Smith 128)

Note: Alternate spellings include *antipophra* and *anthipophora.* Quintilian rejects this device as a figure (9.2.106). Melanchthon treats it as a species deriving from the dialectical topic of contraries (*Elem.* 53r). The answering of the objection may be short or long. Consequently, Sturm includes under *lysis* (3.20.697) what Hermogenes has called *choris katastaseos*—rapid replies, often without formal introduction of either the objections or the replies (2.7.356).

antiprotasis [G. "a counter-proposition"]

The counter-statement to a proposition, or *protasis*, of the adversary

If the adversary objects that it is impossible to dig a trench through the Isthmus, we would reply that doing so is not impossible (paraphrase from Hermogenes, *Inv.* 3.4.134).

(Sturm 1.28.104)

Note: Although he talks about this counter-proposition in his treatment of argument, Hermogenes calls it "an ornament of speech" (*Inv.* 3.4.134). For an example of the whole argument one makes, see the note to *protasis* below.

antirrhesis [G. "gainsaying, refutation"]

Rejecting the authority or opinion of some person through refutation

"Job, to his wife saying to him, 'Blaspheme God and die,' made this answer, saying: 'Thou speakest like a foolish woman'" (Job 2:10).

"This same form of speech Christ useth against Satan [. . . ,] where he rejecteth the subtle attempts and false allegations of Satan by the mighty power and truth of his answers" (see Matthew 4:3–10).

(Peacham [1593] 89)

Note: An alternate spelling is *antirrhysis.* Quintilian rejects refutation as a figure (9.2.106). Robertellus says that this refutation can occur without emotion or be mixed with other figures that do introduce emotion (45v). *Antirrhesis* may be a synonym of *anasceue.* According to Michel Patillon and Giancarlo Bolognesi, who provide a French translation of an Armenian manuscript of Theon's *progymnasmata*, *antirrhesis* ("contradiction") is "a discourse that attacks the credibility of another discourse," by showing it to be "obscure, impossible, incredible, deceitful, or inadequate in thought or expression; or conversely, redundant or lacking vigor, or confused; or [. . . self-] contradictory" (§17 in Kennedy, *Progymnasmata* 72). See *anasceue* above.

apantesis [G. "a meeting, encountering"]

A brief statement of the adversary's proposition that will now be refuted; a brief *occupatio*

Demosthenes repeats the question of his opponents: "'Where indeed shall we land?' someone has asked.'" Then he gives his refutation without a formal introduction: "The war itself, Athenians, will find his [Philip's] weak spots" (*Philippic* I 44, trans. Wooten).

"Are the Byzantines wretches? Of course. But nevertheless they must be saved. For that is beneficial to Athens" (Demosthenes, *On the Chersonese* 16, trans. Wooten).

(Hermogenes 2.7.356)

Note: This figure is the counterpart to the rapid reply. See note to *anthypophora* above.

aphegesis [G. "leading the way, narration"]

A brief, simple, straightforward narrative; one part of the *diegesis* or statement of the case

"He says that he had had a sale by auction in Gaul; that he had sold what he thought fit; that he had taken care that the partnership should owe him nothing; that he would have no more to do with summoning any one, or with giving security; if Quintius had any business to transact with him, he had no objection. He, as he was desirous to revisit his farm in Gaul, does not summon the man at present; so he departs without giving security. After that, Quintius remains at Rome about thirty days. He gets any securities which he had given other people respited, so as to be able to go without hindrance into Gaul. He goes; he leaves Rome on the twenty-ninth of January, in the Consulship of Scipio and Norbanus;—I beg of you to remember the day. Lucius Albius the son of Sextus of the Quirine tribe, a good man and of the highest reputation for honour, set out with him. When they had come to the place called the fords of Volaterra, they see a great friend of Naevius, who was bringing him some slaves from Gaul to be sold, Lucius Publicius by name, who when he arrived in Rome told Naevius in what place he had seen Quintius; and unless this had been told Naevius by Publicius, the matter would not so soon have come to trial. Then Naevius sends his slaves round to his friends; he summons himself all his associates from the halls of Licinius and from the jaws of the shambles, and entreats them to come to the booth of Sextus by the second hour of the next day. They come in crowds; he makes oath that Publius Quintius has not appeared to his bail, and that he has appeared to his. A long protest to this effect is sealed with the seals of noble men. They depart: Naevius demands of Burrienus the praetor, that by his edict he may take possession of Quintius' goods." (Cicero, *Pro Quinctio* 6.23–25, trans. Yonge)

(Sturm 1.15.37)

argumentatio [L. "argumentation, proof"] or *pistis* [G. "proof"]

Confirmation by means of proofs

1. Inartificial proofs
   a. Previous legal judgments, hearsay, evidence extracted under torture, written documents, oaths, witnesses, and oracles
   b. Signs, which are referred to time
      (1) the past: threatenings
      (2) the present: a cry heard at a specific place
      (3) the future: he turns pale when asked about the murder
2. Artificial proofs (from the "places")
   a. The circumstances of persons include kindred, nation, country, kind, age, education, physical condition of body and mind, material circumstances, state, disposition, studies or occupation, character, previous statements, previous deeds, emotional state, and name.
   b. The circumstances of things include cause (material, formal, efficient and final), place, time, opportunity, means, instrument, and manner.
   c. The commonplaces of deliberative discourse include the honest, profitable, pleasant, easy, necessary, possible, and precedent; of judicial discourse include affirmation or denial of witnesses, motive, opportunity, character, definition of the act, and intent of the law; and of demonstrative discourse include those listed in a. above.
   d. *Sententia*
   e. The logical topics (whole/ part; genus/ species, etc.)

(Sherry [1550] 78–88)

Note: An alternate name is *agonas*. The *argumentatio* section of the speech contains both the *confirmatio* (Cicero *Inv.* 1.34) or *probatio* (Quintilian 5.pr 5) and the *refutatio* (Quintilian 3.9.1). *Pistis* is Aristotle's term for the *argumentatio* (3.13.4, 1414b). *Kataskeue* is the term in Hermogenes (*Inv.* 3.4.133). Precedent for regarding the argument itself as a figure comes from Cicero's inclusion of argumentation in his discussion of ornamentation, the third virtue of style (*De Or* 3.91–95, 104–124). Sherry may not intend for the entire *confirmatio* to be regarded as a figure, but only for the proofs (*pisteis*) themselves, as long as they function to amplify a speech. But others take the more inclusive view.

conclusio [L. "a shutting up, closing"] or *epilogus* [G. "the winding up of the speech"] or *peroratio* [L. "the finishing part, peroration"]

The peroration or conclusion to either a speech or the various sections of the speech

"Consider therefore whether you should have any hesitation in plunging whole-heartedly into a war which will defend the glorious name of the Roman people, the security of your allies, vast revenues, the investments of many of your fellow citizens, and the state itself" (Cicero, *Pro Lege Manilia* 7.19, trans. Knott).

(Erasmus, *De copia* 653)

digressio [L. "a going aside, deviation"] or *parecbasis* [G. "a going aside from, deviation"] or *egressio* [L. "a going out, digression"]

A long digression which can appear anywhere in a speech

"We swerve sometimes from the matter upon just considerations, making the same to serve for our purpose as well as if we had kept the matter still. As in making an invective against rebels and largely setting out the filth of their offense, I might declare by the way of a digression what a noble country England is, how great commodities it hath, what traffic here is used, and how much more need other realms have of us than we have need of them. Or when I shall give evidence, or rather declaim against a heinous murderer, I may digress from the offense done and enter in praise of the dead man, declaring his virtues in most ample wise, that the offense done may be thought so much the greater, the more honest he was that hath thus been slain."

(Wilson 206–7)

Note: Puttenham, who gives as an English name "the Straggler" (240), spells this figure *parecnasis* (240) and Day *pareonasis* (100). Additional names include *excursio, ecbasis, diexodon* and *ecbolen.* Quintilian says others call this figure *aphodos* ["departure"] (9.3.87), but rejects both the digression and return to the point as figures (9.2.4). Against those who believe otherwise, Soarez defends *digressio* as a figure based on Cicero's authority (354). Erasmus teaches that material for the digression comes from the topics and includes the use of commonplaces (589); Vossius reiterates that a kind of digression includes the bringing in of the *thesis* as support for the *hypothesis* (257).

elenchus [G. "an argument of disproof, a refutation"]

The refutation based on the results of scrutiny, cross-examination

"Was it the duty of our city, Aeschines, to abase her pride, to lower her dignity, to rank herself with Thessalians and Dolopians, to help Philip to establish his supremacy over Greece, to annihilate the glories and the prerogatives of our forefathers? Or, if she rejected that truly shameful policy, was she to stand by and permit aggressions which she must have long foreseen, and knew would succeed if none should intervene? I would now like to ask the man who censures our past conduct most severely, what party he would have wished our city to join. That party that shares the guilt of all the disasters and dishonours that have befallen Greece,—the party, as one may say, of the Thessalians and their associates? Or that which permitted those disasters in the hope of selfish gain, the party in which we may include the Arcadians, the Messenians, and the Argives?" (Demosthenes, *De Corona* 63–65, trans. Vince)

"What we require, Aeschines, is not oratory with enfolded hands, but diplomacy with enfolded hands" (Demosthenes, *De Falsa Legatione* 255, trans. Vince).

(Hermogenes 1.10.271)

Note: The first example above also illustrates *elenktikon*, since it develops by means of questions. See *elenktikon* above under Pragmatical–people figures. The second example can be paraphrased as follows: Aeschines should use hand gestures in oratory, but should not accept bribes in diplomacy.

enstasis [G. "opposition"]

A direct contradiction to an opponent's claim

The opponent claims, "There is a need to innovate." We respond, "It is nothing new." To the claim "To do this is disagreeable," we respond, "It is not disagreeable."

(Hermogenes, *Invention* 3.6.137)

Note: There is also an indirect objection called *antiparastasis*. For example, the opponent says, "I am not liable for what I said." The *enstasis* is "But you are not without liability." The *antiparastasis* is "Even if you are not liable, it is not so you can insult the city" (Hermogenes, *Inv.* 3.6.137). Hermogenes suggests that the *enstasis* makes a "fine figure" (4.4.187). He does not say the same for the *antiparastasis*, but if the one, why not the other? See example #4 of *antithesis* under Logical–idea figures above.

entechna [G. "introduce an elaborate argument; within the range or province of art"]

An argument when the refutation is put first and the adversarial position being refuted is put second

This technique Demosthenes uses in his speech *Against Aristocrates*. He begins the *proemium* with the declaration that "the purpose of all my exertions in this case is that you may hold the Chersonese securely, and may not for the second time be cheated out of the possession of that country. If, then, it is your desire to learn the truth about this business, and to give a righteous and legitimate verdict on the indictment, you must not confine your attention to the mere phrasing of the decree, but also take into consideration its probable consequences. [. . .] It is essential that at the outset I should explain to you the circumstances to which you owe the secure possession of the Chersonese, for in light of that knowledge you will get a clear perception of the wrong that has been committed."

After this review, he indicts both Charidemus, who wishes with seditious purposes to be the general of the Athenian forces, and Aristocrates, who has made a decree to make him so, for plotting to enable Cersobleptes to become monarch over all of Thrace and threaten Athenian democracy. In this indictment, he then reviews the proposals and reasons this duo are presenting to the Athenian people, ones he has already established to be shams (1–18).

(Hermogenes 1.4.235–36)

epidiegesis [G. "after or repeated narration"]

Repeating the brief opening statement of facts or narration at greater length and with more elaboration; a supplementary narration

Cicero, in *Pro S. Roscio*, briefly makes the charges that Sextus Roscius was both robbed of his wealth and property and then framed for the murder of his father at 2.6, but then

Cicero returns to the subject later, providing the detailed story of how these events came about from 6.15 to 10. 29.

(Erasmus, *De copia* 650; example mine)

Note: Aristotle talks of the *prodiegesis*, *diegesis*, and *epidiegesis*, attributing this division to the school of Theodorus of Byzantium (*Rhetoric* 3.13.5, 1414b). Quintilian treats this feature (not figure) in his discussion of the statement of facts (4.2.128).

exordium [L. "beginning, commencement"]

The opening or introduction of a speech

"As nature hath ever abhorred murder, and God in all ages most terribly hath plagued bloodshedding, so I trust your wisdoms, most worthy judges, will speedily seek the execution of this most hateful sin. And whereas God revealeth to the sight of men the knowledge of such offenses by divers likelihoods and probable conjectures, I doubt not but you being called of God to hear such causes will do herein as reason shall require and as this detestable offense shall move you upon rehearsal of the matter."

(Wilson 126)

Note: Another name is *prooimion* (*Ad H* 1.3.6). The above example illustrates a direct beginning. For an indirect approach, see *insinuatio* below.

insinuatio [L. "insinuation"]

The subtle beginning

"So then whenever the subject obliges us to win over the good will of the person to whom we are writing if his loyalty is uncertain, or to regain it if he has been offended, or strengthen it if our message is somewhat unpleasant, or revive it because of a rather long interval in our acquaintance, we shall attempt to capture his favour [. . .] as follows. We may say that there was the deepest affection and the closest intimacy between our ancestors and his, and that very many services were rendered on both sides; that this good will has been handed on to us in a hereditary succession and has never been neglected; that true affection, which we imbibed with our nurse's milk, as it were, has increased with the years, and that what was ordained more by fate than by human wisdom has now been so firmly established through close association and numerous favours that absolutely no mischance can eradicate it."

(Erasmus, *De conscribendis epistolis* 76)

Note: Another name is *ephodos* (*Ad H* 1.3.6; Era 75).

narratio [L. "a narrative"] or *diegesis* [G. "setting out in detail, a leading through, a narrative"]

The exposition; the statement of facts

"Publius Quinctius, my client, had a brother named Gaius, undoubtedly a careful and industrious manager of an estate in every respect except one. He showed rather less caution than usual in entering into partnership with Naevius, a worthy man I dare say, but one who had not been brought up in such a manner as to give him the opportunity of becoming acquainted with the rights of a partnership and the duties of a trustworthy manager; [. . .] However, Quinctius, being acquainted with and familiar with the man, was induced to admit him, as I have said, into a partnership in his business in Gaul, where he had a considerable grazing farm, well cultivated and very productive. [. . .]

After the partnership had lasted for several years, Naevius had more than once been suspected by Gaius Quinctius, since he was unable to render a satisfactory account of certain transactions which he had carried on [. . . .] In the meantime Gaius Quinctius dies in Gaul, while Naevius was there; his death was sudden. [. . .] Soon after his brother's death Quinctius set out for Gaul, where he lived on the most friendly terms with this fellow Naevius. They were together for nearly a year, during which time they had several discussions both about the partnership and everything connected with the management of the farm and the property in Gaul. In the meantime, Naevius never put in a word to the effect that either the partnership owed him anything or that Quinctius was personally indebted to him. Since a certain number of debts had been left unpaid which had to be settled at Rome, my client had a notice put up in Gaul that he would sell some private property of his at Narbo. Then it was that this excellent man Naevius endeavored, at great length, to dissuade him from making the sale. He told him [. . .] that he himself had plenty of money at Rome, which my client, if he had any sense, ought to look upon as belonging to both, considering his intimacy with his late brother and his relationship to himself, Naevius having married a cousin of Quinctius by whom he had children. [. . .] Since Gaius was indebted to Publius Scapula, his brother Publius [. . .] settled how much he had to pay to Scapula's children. [. . .]

All this took place at the suggestion and on the urgent advice of Naevius. Nor was it surprising that Quinctius took the advice of a man of whose assistance he felt assured; for Naevius had promised him not only in Gaul, but every day in Rome, that he would pay down the money as soon as Quinctius had given him a hint. [. . . Then when Naevius] thought that Quinctius was reduced to the greatest straits, so that he could tie him down at the critical moment on his own terms, [h]e refused to advance Quinctius a penny until a settlement had been arranged in regard to all the affairs and accounts of the partnership, [. . .] And so from that time the matter had to be settled in the courts. [. . .]

Naevius next declared that he had sold by auction in Gaul whatever he thought fit; [. . . When Naevius learned that Quinctius was in Gaul, Naevius] got together all his acquaintances from the Licinian halls and the entrance to the market by his own efforts, and invited them to meet him at the counting-house of Sextius at the second hour of the following day. They attended in great numbers. Naevius called them to witness that 'Publius Quinctius had not answered to his bail, and that he had answered'[. . . .] Naevius then applied to the praetor Burrienus for permission to take possession of the defaulter's estate in accordance with the edict. [. . .]

Quinctius returns to Rome, and appears to his bail. This Naevius, a most violent fellow, who had taken possession of the property, had driven Quinctius out and robbed him of it, for eighteen months made no claim, kept quiet, amused Quinctius as long as he could with proposals for coming to terms, and finally applied to the praetor Gnaeus Dolabella that Quinctius should give him security for payment of the judgement according to the formula: IN THAT HE IS CLAIMING FROM ONE WHOSE GOODS HAVE BEEN POSSESSED FOR THIRTY DAYS ACCORDING TO THE PRAETOR'S EDICT. [. . .] Quinctius's supporters demurred; [. . .] Quinctius himself emphatically declared that his reason for being unwilling to give security was to avoid the appearance of himself thereby giving a verdict that his goods had been possessed in accordance with the edict; [. . . Dolabella] ordered that either security must be given or an engagement entered into, [. . .] Quinctius preferred to enter into the 'engagement.' [. . . H]e proposed you as judge, Aquilius; and then sued Naevius on the 'engagement.' This is the essential point of the trial, this is the gist of the whole cause." (Cicero, *Pro Quinctio* 3.11–19.32, trans. Freese)

(Sturm 1.15.37)

Note: The example for *aphegesis* above is one part of this longer statement of the facts. Hermogenes uses *katastasis* as an alternate name for this part (*Inv.* 2.1). This *katastasis* has a different meaning from the same term above under Pragmatical–idea figures.

occupatio [L. "a seizing, occupying; anticipation"] or *praeoccupatio* [L. "a seizing beforehand"]

Anticipating and laying out the objections the adversary could or does bring against us, the first half of the figure *prolepsis*

"An unused thing it is, and I think not heretofore seen, *Arcadians*, that a woman should give public counsel to men, a stranger to the country people, and that lastly in such a presence a private person, as I am, should possess the regal throne." Beginning the refutation with these objections, Cleophila now answers them. (Sidney, *The Old Arcadia*, book 2, 113).

(Fraunce H3v)

Note: Sturm says there are two kinds of *occupatio*: one that lays out all the objections the adversary could bring and the other that is brief, using only an *apantesis* and some kind of *antithesis*, i.e., a denial, condemnation, or expression of anger in response to the objection (1.26.99). The first kind appears in the *refutatio* section of the speech; the brief kind can appear anywhere in the speech. Sturm also cites three ways to respond to an adversary's case: with *episteme*, when we say we know the adversary's case; with *doxa*, when we say we believe we know the adversary's case; and with *akoe*, when we say we have heard about the adversary's case (1.27.100). Sturm says that Quintilian called this figure *praesumptio*. Keckermann, however, treats the *occupatio* as the full *refutatio*, with two parts: *prolepsis* (the laying out of the objections) and *subjectio* (the answering of the objections) (1485).

paradiegesis [G. "an incidental narrative"]

A subtle beginning using a narration to introduce and teach a principle

"Then *Paul* stood in the midst of *Mars* street, & said: 'Ye men of *Athens*, I perceive that in all things ye are too superstitious, for as I passed by, I found an altar wherein is written unto the unknown GOD, whom ye then ignorantly worship, him shew I unto you, God that made the world, and all things that are therein, seeing he is Lord of heaven & earth, dwelleth not in temples made with hands, neither is worshiped with men's hands, as though he needed any thing, seeing he giveth to all life and breath and all things.' And so consequently, he proceedeth to the full declaration of his purpose" (Acts 17:22–25).

(Peacham [1593] 94)

Note: Although others have listed it, Quintilian rejects this form as a figure (9.2.107).

partitio [L. "a partition, division"] or *enumeratio* [L. "a counting up"] or *distributio* [L. "a division, distribution"]

The partition of the proposition into the argument's sub-topics

"It is also called a distribution when we divide the whole into several parts, and say we have four points, whereof we purpose to speak, comprehending our whole talk within compass of the same." For example, Cicero speaking to the Senate, lays out his argument: "Why, then, am I against peace? Because it is dishonorable, because it is dangerous, because it is impossible. While I explain these three points, Members of the Senate, may I request you to listen to my words with your customary benevolence?" (*Philippic* 7.9, trans. Bailey)

(Wilson 211; example mine)

Note: Quintilian does not accept *partitio* as a figure, even though Celsus does (9.2.105), but he does treat it as an adornment that "greatly add[s] to the lucidity and grace of our speech" (4.5.22). Even when not listed separately, *partitio* receives attention in discussions of the *propositio*. Peacham, for example, gives three guidelines for the *propositio*, which he calls a figure: "First that it absolutely containeth whatsoever pertaineth to the cause. Secondly that it be well divided. Lastly, that it be disposed in an order most meet for the same cause" ([1593] 193). See *propositio* below.

prodiegesis [G. "preliminary narration"]

The preliminary narration, giving the necessary background information at the beginning of the *diegesis*

"It is necessary, men of Athens, and not improper, to remind you of the position of affairs in those days, so that you may consider each transaction with due regard to its occasion.

When the Phocian war began—not by my fault, for I was still outside politics—you were at first disposed to hope that the Phocians would escape ruin, etc. [. . .]" (Demosthenes, *De Corona* 17–18).

(Hermogenes 1.4.236)

Note: Hermogenes also calls this preliminary narration *prokatastasis* (*Inv.* 2.1). See notes to *narratio* and *epideigesis* above.

propositio [L. "a principal subject, theme; a proposition"] or *prothesis* [G. "statement of the case, thesis, proposition"]

The proposition that summarizes the matter whereof we will speak

1. A main idea without partition into subtopics

"I will tell you [. . .] there is none hath a worse name than this fellow; none hath been so often in trouble; he may be faultless, but I can hardly believe it; there are enow that will testify of his naughtiness and avouch his evil demeanor to be such that the like hath not been heard heretofore."

(Wilson 207)

"I have now to speak of the excellent and singular virtues of Pompeius" (Cicero, *Pro Lege Manilia* I.3).

(Peacham [1593] 192)

2. A main idea with partition into sub-topics

"I understand, gentlemen, that the accusation falls into three parts, the first aspersing my client's character, the second dealing with his candidature for the magistracy, and the third with charges of bribery" (Cicero, *Pro Murena* 5.11, trans. Butler).

(Quintilian 4.5.12)

Note: Quintilian acknowledges that Celsus calls this device a figure, but disagrees (9.2.105). Sturm treats the *propositio* as a kind of *katastasis* (3.7.559). See *katastasis* above under Pragmatical–idea figures. Erasmus explains that propositions come from the *stases* and *topoi* (*De copia* 605).

protasis [G. "standing before"]

Each proposition with which we begin a section of our *confirmatio* or *refutatio*; a topic sentence

We declare that a trench should be dug through the Isthmus.

(Sturm 1.28.104)

Note: Such a proposition could be followed with the anticipated response of the opponent, "Digging such a trench is impossible" (*hypophora*); then an *antiprotasis*, or our counterstatement, "It is not impossible"; then the *lysis*, or the evidence to support our *antiprotasis* and refute the objection: "for the excavation is an easy thing since the ground is level" (Sturm 1.28.104). This example comes from Hermogenes (*Invention* 3.4.134), where he calls the *protasis* "an ornament of speech."

reditus ad propositum [L. "returning to the central point"]

Repeating the central proposition in the peroration and then drawing our formal conclusions

The central proposition: "We deny, Sextus Naevius, that you have taken possession of the goods of Publius Quinctius in accordance with the praetor's edict."

The return: "From this and all Naevius's other words, deeds, and intentions, anyone can understand that he had, and has, no other object than to enable himself to secure the whole estate (which belongs in common to both), as his own personal property by violence, injustice, and unfair legal procedure.

Now that I have finished my pleading, the nature of the case and the greatness of the danger seem to make it necessary for my client to implore and beseech you, Aquilius, and you, his assessors, in the name of old age and forlorn condition, simply to follow the dictates of your natural goodness of heart, so that, since he has the truth with him, his distress may have greater power to incline you to pity than the resources of Naevius to incline you to cruelty" (Cicero, *Pro Quinctio* 10.36; 29.90–30.91).

(Cicero *De Oratore* 3.203; example mine)

Note: Quintilian (9.3.87) treats this device as if equivalent with *reditus ad rem*, returning to the point after a digression (see *antanaclasis* above), but Cicero clearly has in mind these two returns as two distinct figures, since he mentions them separately in the same list. From Cicero's description, this figure seems to belong to the peroration. Vossius identifies this figure as a kind of *epanodos* (258). See *epanodos* above under Pragmatical–idea figures.

transitio [L. "a going across or over"] or *metabasis* [G. "passing over"] or *metastasis* [G. "removal, shifting, migration"]

A transition; reviewing briefly what has been said and previewing what will next be said

1. From one point to the next

"I have told you the cause of all this evil; now I will tell you a remedy for the same."

"You have heard of justification by faith only; now you shall hear of the dignity of works and how necessary they are for every Christian body."

(Wilson 207)

"These things you will say are pleasant, but the rest yet untold are far more delightful."

"But why stay we so long in trifles? I will go to the head of the matter."

(Day 96)

2. From addressing one person to addressing another

Cicero turns from addressing the judges to addressing the prosecutor: "Now, Erucius, I come to you" (*Pro S. Roscio* 29.79, trans. Freese).

(Melanchthon, *Institutiones* 25r; example mine).

Note: An additional name is *symplerosis* (3.7.559). Melanchthon places this figure within the category of those deriving from the dialectical topic of circumstances (*Elem.* 54v).

Genres

accusatio [L. "accusation, indictment"] or *categoria* [G. "a speaking against, accusation"]

An accusation

Paul accusing Elymas, the sorcerer: "O full of all subtlety and all mischief, thou child of the devil, and enemy of all righteousness, wilt thou not cease to pervert the strait ways of the Lord?" (Acts 13:10)

(Peacham [1593] 81)

Note: Peacham gives *criminis reprehensio* as an additional name ([1593] 80).

adhortatio [L. "an exhortation, encouragement"] or *protrope* [G. "exhortation, encouragement"] or *parainetikon* [G. "advice, exhortation"]

An exhortation with or without reasons attached

"If ever God have had respect to a just cause, or ever gave victory where it was due, or ever lent his hand to equity against tyranny, or ever preferred his people and confounded his enemies, he will this day fight with us, and for us, and give us a glorious victory, be our enemies never so many, and we never so few; and therefore shew yourselves this day valiant, courageous and constant; fight this day for your honour and for your country; cast off this day all fear that may make you weak, & arm yourselves with hope that may make you strong; and be ye assured of an honourable and glorious conquest, after which shall ensue incomparable joy, great wealth, and immortal fame."

(Peacham [1593] 77)

Note: Another name is *apophonema*. Quintilian rejects straightforward exhortation as a figure (9.2.103). Although he does not call it a figure, Scaliger places *adhortatio* under the general heading of *deliberatio* or the deliberative argument and includes herein several other features that have been otherwise identified as figures: *admonitio*, *consolatio*, and *dehortatio*, its opposite (3.123.399).

adianoeta [G. "unintelligible"]

An expression with an obvious meaning on the surface, yet a secret one underneath

1. Secret passwords
2. Deliberate ambiguity, so that the audience will read a statement one way, but the privileged insiders will read it another way and, since the statement could have such a meaning, are protected from perjury.

(Quintilian 8.2.20)

adjuratio [L. "a swearing"] or *orcos* [G. "an oath"]

An oath

"Now therefore up, come out, and speak comfortable unto thy servants, for I swear by the Lord, except thou come out, there will not tarry with thee one man this night, and that will be worse unto thee, than all the evil, that fell on thee from thy youth hitherto" (2 Samuel 19:7).

(Peacham [1593] 75)

Note: An alternate name is *jusiurandum*. Peacham's example above also illustrates *obtestatio*, a swearing by the gods. See *obtestatio* below.

admiratio [L. "wonder, surprise, astonishment"] or *thaumasmus* [G. "marvelling"]

An expression of marvel, wonder, surprise

"Although he is well aware of how he has lived his life, this filthy scoundrel will dare to look you in the eye and with his sonorous voice will discourse upon how he has lived, which makes me choke with rage. Don't these men know you?" (Demosthenes, *De Falsa Legatione* 199, trans. Wooten)

"Are you deliberating, Athenians, although the Thebans are on the island, about what you should do?" (Demosthenes, *On the Chersonese* 74)

(Hermogenes 2.7.355)

"O Lord, how excellent is thy Name!" (Psalm 8:1)

(Fenner 173)

admonitio [L. "an admonition"] or *paraenesis* [G. "advice, exhortation"]

An admonition, warning

"By this warning *Cicero* dissuadeth the Senate from making league with *Antony*: 'For God's sake take heed, Judges, lest through hope of present peace you bring not in continual war'" (*Philippic* 7.25).

"Beware of false Prophets which come unto you in sheep's clothing, but inwardly they are ravening wolves; you shall know them by their fruits" (Matthew 7:15–16).

(Peacham [1593] 78–79)

Note: Quintilian rejects this behavior as a figure, even though Celsus lists it (9.2.104).

adynaton [G. "without power; impossible"]

An impossibility

"I cannot put down in words how much your letter delighted me."

"Not if I had a hundred tongues, a hundred mouths and a cast-iron larynx [could I] include all the forms of crime, etc."

(Melanchthon, *Elem.* 44v)

"To recline is to labor."

(Sturm 3.22.715)

aenigma [G. "a dark saying, a riddle"]

A riddle

"'I consume my mother that bare me, I eat up my nurse that fed me, then I die, leaving them all blind that saw me.' This is meant of the flame of a Candle, which when it hath consumed both wax and wick, goes out, leaving them in the dark that saw by it."

(Smith 86)

"The dreams and visions there of Pharaoh's chief Butler and chief Baker, as likewise Pharaoh's own dreams, were Aenigmatical" (Gen. 40–41).

(Smith 88)

Note: Alternate spellings include *ainigma* and *enigma*. Puttenham's name is "the Riddle" (198). Demetrius also gives as a synonym *griphos* and explains that this figure can result from incoherence as well, therein becoming a vice (§153). See *enigma* below under vices. This figure is sometimes listed as a trope, a kind of allegory. See *allegoria* under semantical figures above. Smith argues, however, that it is not properly a trope (4) and gives as one kind of example a word problem in mathematics (87).

affirmatio [L. "an affirmation, averment of a fact"] or *thesis* [G. "a position, affirmation"]

An affirmative assertion

"However, that rustic life, which you call 'hick,' is the teacher of frugality, diligence, and justice."

(Sturm 3.16.660)

"To retire and dissemble excellencies is only good policy in him whom his course must at length necessarily draw into light and proof, and then all that he shows will be admirable, because expectation forestalled nothing of his worth."

(Hoskins 32)

"The credit of behavior is to cover imperfection and set forth your good parts better."

(Blount 27)

anairesis [G. "taking away, destruction"] or *remotio* [L. "a withdrawing"] or *negatio* [L. "a negation"]

A direct denial or negation

"I did not fortify Athens with masonry and brickwork; they are not the works on which I chiefly pride myself" (Demosthenes, *On the Crown* 299, trans. Vince).

(Hermogenes 1.9.267)

"At first you were so disposed, not because of me, for I was not then in politics" (Demosthenes, *On the Crown* 18, trans. Wooten).

(Hermogenes 1.11.293)

Note: Sturm spells the name variously (*anairhesis* [2.15.353], *anairesis* [3.12.616], and *aneresis* [3.12.616]) and distinguishes between the *remotio* associated here and the *remotio* associated with *aphairhesis,* the withdrawing or denying of each particular alternative (1.40.224). See *remotio* under Pragmatical–idea figures above.

apagoresis [G. "a prohibition, interdict"] or *detrectatio* [L. "a declining, refusing"] or *prohibitio* [L. "a hindering, forbidding"]

A prohibition

"Thou shalt not kill. Thou shalt not commit adultery. Thou shalt not steal. Thou shalt not bear false witness against thy neighbour. Thou shalt not covet thy neighbor's house, thou shalt not covet thy neighbor's wife, nor his manservant, nor his maidservant, nor his ox, nor his ass, nor any thing that is thy neighbor's." (Exodus 20:13–17)

(Scaliger 3.83.349; example mine)

Note: Quintilian rejects this form as a figure (9.2.104, 107).

apodeiktikon [G. "affording proof, demonstrative"]

A sentence that serves as part of an argument, of which there are three kinds: a proposition, a reason, and a conclusion

1. A proposition or declaration
   "Two things which have most power in the state—I mean great influence and eloquence—are both working against us to-day; the one, Gaius Aquilius, fills me with apprehension, the other with dread" (Cicero, *Pro Quinctio* 1.1, trans. Freese).
2. A reason
   "Did you resort with such eager haste to these extreme and most unfriendly legal measures, in order that there might be nothing more grievous or more cruel which you kept back for future employment? [. . .] But the man whose property has been sold, who has not only seen his rich possessions but even the necessities of food and clothing ignominiously put up for sale under the hand of an auctioneer, that man is not only banished from the company of the living, but is relegated to a position lower than the dead, if that be possible" (Cicero, *Pro Quinctio* 15.48–49, trans. Freese).
3. A conclusion
   "Therefore, by Hercules! if a man's goods are possessed by virtue of an edict, his character and reputation are taken possession of together with his goods" (Cicero, *Pro Quinctio* 15.50, trans. Freese).

(Sturm 3.3.487)

Note: Sturm also uses the term *apodeiktikon* to refer to argumentation in general (1.38.201). See note to *apodeixis* above under Logical–evidence. Used along side of *ethikon* and *pathetikon,* both of which Sturm treats as kinds of styles, *apodeiktikon,* by inference, would also become a kind of style

(1.38. 201). Hermogenes (*Inv.* 3.13.167) and Cicero (*De Or* 3.182, 185, 212 and *Or.* 37.128) also use these terms to refer to both styles and topics. Hermogenes additionally distinguishes the apodeictic from the panegyric (*Inv.* 3.13.168).

apologia [G. "a speech in defense"]
A confession fortified with a defense against incrimination
In the *Iliad* book 3, when Helen is brought forward to watch the duel between her two husbands, Paris and Menelaus, her tears confess both her guilt and sorrow for this conflict.
(Sturm 1.29.109)

asseveratio [L. "a vehement assertion, asseveration"] or *apophansis* [G. "a declaration, decision"]
A strongly confident assertion
"Nevertheless, because of the more stubborn critics I do not shrink from affirming what I said with reasons and the clear testimonies of scripture."
"Who is so blind that he does not see this? Who is so stubborn that he will deny it? Scratch your forehead and dare to deny it!"
(Erasmus, *Ecclesiastes* 2.465.418–24)

Note: Quintilian gives as an additional name *adfirmatio* (6.3.70), but denies this device is a figure if straightforward (9.2.104). Scaliger indicates this figure can be created through the use of *obtestatio* or by the addition of either a cause or an explanation to a *sententia* (3.38.311; 3.60.334).

astrothesiam [G. *ia* "constellation" with Latin ending "*m*"]
A description of stars
"The old man had scarcely spoken when suddenly thunder
Crashed on the left, a star fell out of the sky
And fled with its dazzling torch through the darkness of night.
We saw it slip over the top of our house and light up
The roads as it vanished, still shining, in woods on Mount Ida.
It dragged a long furrow of brilliance and scattered the smell
Of smoking sulphur widely about" (Virgil, *Aeneid* 2.733–39, trans. Lind).
(Sherry [1550] 69; example mine)

Note: The correct spelling should be *astrothesia*.

cataphronesis [G. "a low opinion of others"]
An expression of contempt
Goneril to her husband Albany:
"Milk-liver'd man,
That bear'st a cheek for blows, a head for wrongs,
Who hast not in thy brows an eye discerning
Thine honor from thy suffering, [that not know'st
Fools do those villains pity who are punish'd
Ere they have done their mischief, where's thy drum?
France spreads his banners in our noiseless land,
With plumed helm thy state begins [to threat],
Whilst thou, a moral fool, sits still and cries,
'Alack, why does he so?']" (Shakespeare, *King Lear* 4.2.50–59)
(Sturm 3.13.623; example mine)

cataplexis [G. "amazement, consternation"] or *comminatio* [L. "a threatening, menacing"]
A threat of punishment, misfortune, or disaster

"Yet forty days, and Nineveh shall be destroyed" (Jonah 3:4).

(Peacham [1593] 80)

Note: Additional names include *apeile* and *perculsio*. Quintilian denies that a straightforward threat is a figure (9.2.103).

characterismus [G. "characterization"] or *notatio* [L. "describing, depicting, characterizing"]
A description of body or mind; character delineation

"There is no such pinch penny alive as this good fellow is. He will not lose the paring of his nails. His hair is never rounded for sparing of money. One pair of shoes serveth him twelve months: he is shod with nails like a horse. He hath been known by his coat this thirty winter. He spent once a groat at good ale, being forced through company and taken short at his word, whereupon he hath taken such conceit since that time that it hath almost cost him his life."

(Wilson 212)

Note: Keckermann treats *characterismus* as the general category for all descriptions of things and people (1482). Gill does too, remarking that "all these Characterisms clarify, explain, and embellish" (158). Quintilian denies this form as a figure (9.3.99). Sometimes this figure is seen as one type of *ethopoeia*. See *ethopoeia* below.

charientismus [G. "wit"] or *scomma* [G. "jest, gibe"]
Mild, appeasing, benevolent, light, charming, witty speech

"He that heard one call him all to nought and say, 'Thou art sure to be hanged ere thou die,' [replied] very soberly, 'Sir, I know your mastership speaks but in jest.'"

(Puttenham 201)

"A certain man being apprehended, and brought before *Alexander* the Great, King of Macedonia, for railing against him, and being demanded by *Alexander* why he and his company had so done, he made this answer: 'Had not the wine failed, we had spoken much worse'; whereby he signified that those words proceeded rather from wine than malice: by which free and pleasant confession, he assuaged *Alexander's* great displeasure and obtained remission."

(Smith 77)

Note: Puttenham's English name is "the Privy nippe" (201). This figure is sometimes listed as a trope and as a form of irony. According to Demetrius, this feature is the chief characteristic of the elegant style (§128). See *glaphyria* below under Discoursal–styles.

chronographia [G. "chronological record, annals"]
A description of time

The spring is "that season which bringeth comfort to every living creature, when the Sun visiteth the face of the earth with his warm shine, the air became temperate, fountains and streams were clear, pastures green, when the flowers of every field, and the blossoms of every tree do present their beauty to the eyes of the beholder, and the new and tender breed of beasts and birds are brought forth and presented to man by the liberal hand of nature, at which time the birds sing, lambs play, music is heard, youth rejoice, and the hearts of men become more glad: this is that time which bringeth calmness to the sea, temperature to the air, beauty to the earth, clearness to the firmament, and a comfort to every creature."

(Peacham [1593] 142–43)

Note: An alternate spelling is *cronographia.* Puttenham calls this figure "the Counterfait time" (246). This genre results from the *locus* of time. Quintilian points out that time can be treated generally, as in the historical period, or specifically, as in particular circumstances or *kairos* (5.10.42; 3.6.25), but does not regard this description as a figure.

commendatio [L. "a commendation, recommending"] or *encomion* [G. "eulogy"]

Praise or commendation of a person or thing

1. Briefly

"[A]n example from Plutarch could be introduced by saying that this writer was of all authors particularly worthy of respect in that he combined a thorough knowledge of philosophy with the eloquent style of a historian, so that one would rightly expect to find in him not only a trustworthy account of events, but also the authority and judgment of a revered and learned philosopher."

(Erasmus, *De copia* 608)

2. At length

Cicero praising Pompey: "Such a man he was of whom being a young man and a Roman knight, the Senate might oftentimes have required aid and defense, whose noble acts with a most renowned victory both by land and sea had spread over all nations whose three honorable triumphs are witnesses, that all the world was in our government and dominion, whom the people of Rome had commended with singular honors, now if you should say that he hath done something against the league of peace, who will believe you? truly no man, for when death had quenched envy, his noble acts should have flourished in glory of an eternal renown: whose virtues being bruted, should have given no place to doubts: and shall the friendly, approved, and perfect virtue of this man be hurt by the false report of backbiters?" (*Pro Balbo* 6.16).

(Peacham [1593] 155)

Note: Other names are *metaepaina* and *laudatio.* When writing the *progymnasmata,* especially the *chreia* and proverb exercises, schoolboys are directed to praise either the authority or the proverb they quote. It is clear from the example above that Erasmus considers such a move a kind of *commendatio.* Another schoolboy exercise is the *encomium,* in which this praise fills the entire essay. Hermogenes distinguishes between short praise *epainos* and the genre of praise *enkomion* (*Progymnasmata* §7).

commiseratio [L. "exciting compassion"] or *conquestio* [L. "bewailing"] or *oictros* [G. "pitiable, lamentable"] or *eleos* [G. "pity, mercy, compassion"]

The awakening of sympathy in the audience

1. In a short passage

"O poor me! Where will I turn?! Where will I flee?! What advocate will I seek?!"

(Keckermann 1499)

"O Jerusalem, Jerusalem, which killest the Prophets, etc. How often would I have gathered thy children together, as a hen doth gather her brood under her wings, and ye would not!" (Luke 13:34)

(Smith 142)

2. In a whole work

Complaints of the poets. For example, Colin Cloute complains of his unfortunate love in this wise:

"Ye Gods of love, that pitie lovers payne,
(If any gods the paine of lovers pitie:)
Looke from above, where you in joyes remaine,

And bowe your eares unto my dolefull dittie.
And Pan thou shepheards God, that once didst love,
Pitie the paines, that thou thy selfe didst prove.

"Thou barrein ground, whome winters wrath hath wasted,
Art made a myrrhour, to behold my plight:
Whilome thy fresh spring flowrd, and after hasted
Thy sommer prowde with Daffadillies dight.
And now is come thy wynters stormy state,
Thy mantle mard, wherein thou maskedst late.

"Such rage as winters, reigneth in my heart,
My life bloud friesing with unkindly cold:
Such stormy stoures do breede my balefull smart,
As if my yeare were wast, and woxen old.
And yet alas, but now my spring begonne,
And yet alas, yt is already donne. Etc."
(Spenser, *The Shepheardes Calendar*, "Januarye" l. 13–30)

(Sherry [1550] 68; example mine)

Note: *Miseratio* is an additional name. Cicero treats the *conquestio* as a "place" of invention, especially appropriate for the peroration, and observes that we use the places of argument to invent the concrete detail that will move this sympathy (*De Inventione* 1.106–9; *Or* 37.130). The *Ad Herennium* applies the name *commiseratio* to this appeal to pity (2.31.50). Martianus Capella regards the appeal to pity as a kind of argument from inartificial proof (§504), appropriate wherever necessary in the speech (§565). Trapezuntius lists *conquestio* as a genre when he illustrates the range of vocal flexibility (*mollitudo*) differing genres require of the oartor (410). Melanchthon refers to this figure as "*lachrymos*" [tears], a kind of *exclamatio* (*Elem.* 44r). Veltkirchius seems to be the earliest Renaissance rhetorician to list this device as a figure on its own. Keckermann lists *commiseratio* and *conquestio* as separate figures (1499).

comprecatio [L. "a common or public imploring of a deity"]
A public prayer
Aeneas speaks:

"We follow you, holy one
Of the gods, whoever you are, we obey your order
And greet you once more. Be present and help us, we pray;
O graciously bring us the stars that we need in the sky." (Virgil, *Aeneid* 4.579–82, trans. Lind)

(Veltkirchius 167r; example mine)

Note: See *deprecatio* below for a similar figure. *Obsecratio* could be a synonym. See *obsecratio* below.

dehortatio [L. "a dissuading"] or *apotropon* [G. "dissuasion"]
Dissuasion; opposite of *adhortatio*
"Also, for God's sake take heed, you Judges, that through hope of present peace, you bring not in continual war and contention" (Cicero, *Philippic* 7.25). "Here Cicero dissuadeth the Senate, from making league with Anthony."

(Peacham [1577] L.i.v)

deinosis [G. "exacerbation when in dire straits"]

A vehement, forceful expression of fear, anger, madness, hatred, envy, despair

Cicero's invectives. For example, here is the opening of the first speech against Lucius Sergius Catiline:

"In heaven's name, Catiline, how long will you abuse our patience? How long will that madness of yours mock us? To what limit will your unbridled audacity vaunt itself? Is it nothing to you that the Palatine has its garrison by night, nothing to you that the city is full of patrols, nothing that the populace is in a panic, nothing that all honest men have joined forces, nothing that the senate is convened in this stronghold, is it nothing to see the looks on all these faces?" (1.1, trans. Lord)

(Sherry [1550] 68; example mine)

Note: An alternate spelling is *donysis*. Wilson calls this figure "stomach grief" (224). To Quintilian, *deinosis* is a method of embellishment, not a figure (8.3.88). See *deinotes* under Discoursal–styles below.

deprecatio [L. "a warding off or averting by prayer"] or *deesis* [G. "entreaty"]

A petition, entreaty, or supplication to gods or men, sometimes as an oath and sometimes as a prayer

1. As an oath

"I now invoke all the gods and goddesses whose domain is the land of Attica. I invoke also Pythian Apollo [. . .] and I solemnly beseech them all that, if I shall speak the truth now, [. . .] they may grant to me prosperity and salvation" (Demosthenes, *On the Crown* 141, trans. Vince).

"Unless it was only out of a desire to rescue those men, may I utterly perish from the face of the earth if any amount of money would have persuaded me to go on an embassy with these men" (Demosthenes, *De Falsa Legatione* 172, trans. Wooten).

(Hermogenes 2.7.354)

2. As a prayer

"May the gods, if ever their power respects the loyal,
If ever their hearts are just and their minds know right,
Give you worthy reward" (Virgil, *Aeneid* 1.620–22, trans. Lind).

(Butler 114)

3. As a supplication to a ruler

"By your honour, consistency, and clemency, therefore, [Caius] Caesar, free us from this fear first, that we may have no misgivings that any particle of resentment lingers in your heart. I ask it by the right hand of hospitality which you have extended to King Deiotarus, as you have grasped his in return, a right hand, no less steadfast in promises and pledges than in wars and encounters" (Cicero, *Pro Rege Deiotaro* 3.8, trans. Watts).

(Soarez 357)

4. As a plea for pardon

"But now that his dark secret has been disclosed by an indefatigable opponent, there is nothing for it, I suppose, but to plead guilty to the charge, especially as, thanks to my friend Pansa, it is no longer a debatable question. So I must needs eschew controversy and convert my whole speech into an appeal for your compassion, to which so many have owed their safety, winning from you not indeed absolution from guilt but pardon for their errors" (Cicero, *Pro Ligario* 1.1, trans. Watts).

(Melanchthon, *Elem.* 18r)

Note: Sturm calls a plea to the judges *axiosis* and the plea to God *euche* (3.31.784). See *euche* below. Because this supplication is sometimes in the form of an oath, occasionally *obsecratio* and *obtestatio* are collapsed into this figure. See *obsecratio* and *obtestatio* below. Melanchthon suggests this figure derives from the dialectical topic of circumstances (*Elem.* 54v). As a plea for pardon, *deprecatio* joins *purgatio* and *translatio criminis* as options for defense when one admits guilt (see Quintilian 5.13.1 ff). This figure corresponds to the counter-proposition in argumentation that acknowledges the wrong doing, but excuses it due to factors outside the defendant's control (see Hermogenes' *On Issues* 65.10–71.17). Quintilian acknowledges Celsus as a source for this figure, which he himself does not accept (9.2.104).

descriptio [L. "delineation, description"] or *hypotyposis* [G. "sketch, outline"] or *diatyposis* [G. "full and perfect shape; vivid description"] or *ekphrasis* [G. "description"]

Description in general

1. Setting forth the particulars of persons, events, places, circumstances, etc.

   "What personages and affections are set forth in *Arcadia*. For men: pleasant idle retiredness in King Basilius, and the dangerous end of it; unfortunate valor in Plangus; courteous valor in Amphialus; proud valor in Anaxius; hospitality in Kalander; the mirror of true courage and friendship in Pirocles and Musidorus; miserableness and ingratitude in Chremes; fear and rudeness, with ill-affected civility in Dametas. [. . .]

   And for actions of persons, there are many, rarely described: as a mutiny and fire in a ship; causes of an uproar; the garboil; an armed skirmish; policy and preparation; [. . .] managing a horse is described; tilting shows. Many other notable and lively portraits are, [. . .]"

   (Hoskins 41–42)

2. After speaking of thing in general, we descend into particulars

   "If you desire that I make you a picture or lively description of the nature of Desire, I will tell you: 'It is a strange country, whereunto the Prodigal child failed when he forsook his father's house to undertake a banishment: a country where corn is still in grass; vines in the bud; trees perpetually in blossom, and birds always in the shell; you neither see corn, fruit, nor any thing fully shaped, all is there only in expectation: A country where the Inhabitants are never without fevers, one is no sooner gone, but another comes into its place: here time looks on you afar off, and never comes near you, but shews you an enchanted looking-glass, wherein you see a thousand false colours, which amuse you. Here at best you have nothing to dinner but smoke and expectation.'"

   (Smith 251–52)

3. Laying out vividly the consequences of an act

   "But, men of the jury, if by your votes you free this defendant, immediately, like a lion released from his cage, or some foul beast loosed from his chains, he will slink and prowl about in the forum, sharpening his teeth to attack every one's property, assaulting every man, friend and enemy, known to him or unknown, now despoiling a good name, now attacking a life, now bringing ruin upon a house and its entire household, shaking the republic from its foundations. Therefore, men of the jury, cast him out from the state, free every one from fear, and finally, think of yourselves. For if you release this creature without punishment, believe me, gentlemen, it is against yourselves that you will have let loose a wild and savage beast."

   (*Ad Herennium* 4.39.51)

Note: Additional names include *deformatio* and *hypographia*. Puttenham calls this figure "the counterfeit representation" (245). Peacham, Day, Puttenham, and Farnaby use *hypotyposis* for the general category of description. In fact, as species of *hypotyposis* Farnaby lists *pragmatographia, topographia, topothesia, prosopographia, pathopoeia, chronographia, diatyposis, enargia*, and *characterismus* (23) and Puttenham also includes *prosopopoeia* (246). Smith, however, uses the term *diatyposis* for description in general (251–52), distinguishing it from *hypotyposis* or *enargia* (112–14). Scaliger distinguishes between *diatyposis* and *hypotyposis*, the first the longer sketch and the second the shorter, weaker, and simpler—i.e., description in a sentence or two. Also, he uses *tractatio* to refer to descriptions of people and *demonstratio* to refer to descriptions of things (3.34.309). Melanchthon, Hoskins, and Blount use *descriptio* as the general category for all the other species. Melanchthon places description under the dialectical topic of circumstance (*Elem.* 54r).

desperatio [L. "hopelessness, despair"]

An expression of desperation or despair

1. Sincere

Gynecia laments, "But wretch that I am, my torment is beyond all succour, and my evil deserving doth exceed my evil fortune. For nothing else did my husband take this strange resolution to live solitary: for nothing else have the winds delivered this strange guest to my country: for nothing else have the destinies reserved my life to this time, but that only I, most wretched I, should become a plague to my self, and a shame to womankind" (Sidney, *The Old Arcadia*, Book 2, 80).

(Fraunce E5r)

2. Simulated

"Oh in vain my undertaken labors! Oh my false hopes! Oh my inane cogitations!" (Cicero, *Pro Milone* 34.94, my translation)

(Keckermann 1499)

diatyposis [G. "regulation, apportionment"]

Rules, precepts

"Jethro giv[es] rules to Moses for the election of Judges, saying: 'Moreover provide thou among all the people, men of courage, fearing God, men dealing truly, hating covetousness, and appoint such over them to be rulers over thousands, rulers over hundreds, rulers over fifties, and rulers over ten, and then let them judge the people at all seasons, etc.'" (Exodus 18:21–22).

(Peacham [1593] 92)

Note: Peacham's Latin equivalents are *informatio* and *testamentum* ([1593] 92). Demetrius suggests that we can sometimes use the form of a precept to present ideas, just as we can use questions, direct statements, or accusations (§296).

dicaeologia [G. "plea in justification"] or *anangeon* [G. "force, constraint, necessity"] or *necessitas* [L. "unavoidableness, necessity, compulsion"] or *purgatio* [L. "a cleansing, purging"]

A self-justification by admitting, but then reasonably excusing the fault

1. With excuses or *excusatio*

"I did it by mistake."
"I did it while I was angry."
"I did it with no thought of harming."

(Melanchthon, *Elem.* 17v)

"I confess that this I did. But the woman that thou gavest me, did deceive me" (Genesis 3:12).

(Sherry [1550] 60)

2. With allowable reasons that show necessity

   "I forsook my friend, but the laws compelled me: I kept friendship most faithfully, as long as the laws permitted me, and now I am not cast off by will, but by force of law."

   (Peacham [1593] 115)

   "When you blamed me because I used sharp correction of your child, you did not well, for is it not better that correction be used, than life abused, and the child weep rather than the father should wail?"

   (Peacham [1577] M.iiii.v)

   "It is permitted to those who have a place to go to be timid and lazy, but it is necessary for you to be brave men, since no refuge is available to you" (Hannibal, *The Second Punic War*, book 1, trans. La Fontaine).

   (Melanchthon, *Elem.* 50v)

Note: Alternate spellings include *dichaologia*, *dichologia*, *anankeon*, and *necessum*. Puttenham calls this "the Figure of Excuse" (237) and Scaliger gives *rationabilitas* as an additional name (3.67.337). Rutilius, Quintilian, Melanchthon, Sherry and Scaliger distinguish between *dicaeologia/ purgatio* and *anangeon/ necessitas*, saying that the first is self-justification in general and the second is one type of the first—the declaration of the action's necessary causes. This distinction comes from the discussion regarding the argument known as the qualitative assumptive (when the deed itself is unjustified, but favorably viewed nevertheless). *Purgatio*, the admittance that the deed was bad but the intent was good, is one option in such an argument. One's choices here include arguing *error* (ignorance)—corresponding to the first example above—, *casus* (blaming fortune), *necessitas* (compulsion)—corresponding to the second example above—, and *oblivio* (forgetfulness). Other options include *comparatione causa* (the act was the lesser of two evils), *translatio criminis* (transference of criminal responsibility) and *deprecatio* (plea for pardon), the last two of which have also become figures. See *trajectio in alium*, a kind of *metastasis,* above under Pragmatical–idea figures and *deprecatio* above. In his first edition, Peacham includes all forms of defense within this figure (M.iiii.v), but in his second, he restricts this figure to the defense against an admitted act (115) and uses *proecthesis* for the other types of defense (102). There is even a third kind of defense, the *apologia*. See these other figures under Discoursal-genres above and below. Treating this figure as one deriving from the dialectical topic of cause, Melanchthon broadens this defense to include justifications based on honor, possibility and necessity (50v). Although he mentions that Rutilius lists these defenses as figures, Quintilian disallows them (9.2.106–7; 9.3.99). Scaliger, too, claims that only in its dressed up forms is this defense a figure (3.93.363).

drama argumentum [G. "an argument made by means of action represented on the stage"]
Dramatic portrayal

The "Murder of Gonzago" play in Shakespeare's *Hamlet*.

(Veltkirchius 172r; example mine)

effictio [L. "a representing of corporeal peculiarities"]
A description of a person's physical appearance

"I mean him, men of the jury, the ruddy, short, bent man, with white and rather curly hair, blue-grey eyes, and a huge scar on his chin, if perhaps you can recall him to memory."

(*Ad Herennium* 4.49.63)

Note: Susenbrotus considers *effictio* a synonym for *prosopographia* (86), while Melanchthon uses *effictio* for a lively description (*Elem.* 54v). Soarez spells the term *effectio* and associates it with *notatio* and *ethopoeia* (346–47). See related figures above and below.

effiguratio [L. "a representation"]
A description of a thing

"Neptune himself struck the earth with his trident; it trembled, and by its movement threw open channels for the waters. Across the wide plains the rivers raced, overflowing their banks, sweeping away in one torrential flood crops and orchards, cattle and men, houses and temples, sacred images and all. Any building which did manage to survive this terrible disaster unshaken and remain standing, was in the end submerged when some wave yet higher than the rest covered its roof, and its gables lay drowned beneath the waters. Now sea and earth could no longer be distinguished: all was sea, and a sea that had no shores.

Some tried to escape by climbing to the hilltops, others, sitting in their curved boats, plied the oars where lately they had been ploughing; some sailed over cornlands, over the submerged roofs of their homes, while some found fish in the topmost branches of the elms. [. . .] The Nereids wondered to see groves and towns and houses under the water; dolphins took possession of the woods, and dashed against high branches, shaking the oak trees as they knocked against them. Wolves swam among the flocks, and the waves supported tawny lions, and tigers too. The lightning stroke of his strong tusk was of no use, then, to the wild boar, nor his swift legs to the stag—both alike were swept away. Wandering birds searched long for some land where they might rest, till their wings grew weary and they fell into the sea" (Ovid, *Metamorphoses*, Book 1, "The Flood" 278–309, trans. Innes).

(Sherry [1555] F.v.r)

Note: Rufinianus also lists this term, but applies it to *prosopopoeia* (*Dian.* §14).

eidolopoeia [G. "formation of an image by putting words in the mouth of one dead"]
A dramatization of a dead person

"Hector slain, speaketh to Aeneas [:] 'O Aeneas, thou god's son, fly and save thyself, from this ruin and fire: the enemies hath taken the walls, and lofty Troy is prostrate to the ground. I would have thought, I had died valiantly enough to my country, and my father Priamus, if with this my right hand, Troy had been defended'" (Virgil, *Aeneid* 2.300–4).

Cicero about Lucius Brutus: "If it so were, that Lucius Brutus, that noble and famous man were alive, and before your presence: would he not use this oration: 'I Brutus, sometime did banish and cast out for cruelty, the state and office of kings, by the horrible fact of Tarquinius, against Lucretia, and all that name banished, but you have brought in tyrants. I, Brutus, did reduce the Roman Empire, to a freedom and liberty: but you foolishly can not uphold and maintain, the same given to you. I, Brutus, with the danger of my life, have saved my country of Rome, but you without all danger, lose it.'" (*Ad Herennium* 4.53.66)

(Rainolde N.i.v-ii.r)

Note: The source for this figure seems to be Aphthonius's *Progymnasmata* §11 and Hermogenes's *Progymnasmata* §9. This feature is commonly treated in most texts under *prosopopoeia.*

elogium [L. "an inscription"]
Elegy

1. In blame

Turnus speaks after defeating Pallas:

"Remember, Arcadians, carry my words to Evander:

I send him back Pallas just as he deserved to receive him.
I give him largess of whatever the tomb may bestow
Of honor, whatever solace of burying him.
No little price shall he pay as a host to Aeneas." (*Aeneid* 10.511–15, trans. Lind)

2. In praise
   Virgil says of Euryalus and Nisus:
   "Fortunate both, if my poems shall have any power;
   No day shall ever remove your memory from Time
   So long as the house of Aeneas, immovable stone
   Of the Capitol, shall be dwelt in, a Roman father
   Continue to wield there a general's command over men." (*Aeneid* 9.451–55, trans. Lind)

(Scaliger 3.40.312)

embleme [from L. *emblema* "raised ornaments on vessels"]
A visual symbol with a motto or explication
"Paint a castle, compassed with Rivers, and let the *Motto* be[:] 'Neither by siege nor undermining.'"

(Blount 4)

Note: Emblems were a popular visual and poetic genre during the Renaissance.

epicrisis [G. "judgment"] or *adjudicatio* [L. "a judicial adjudging of a matter"]
A judgment or evaluation; speaking dogmatically
"An example of our Savior Christ, saying: 'Ye have heard that it was said to them of old time, Thou shalt not commit adultery, but I say unto you, That whosoever looketh on a woman to lust after her, hath committed adultery with her already in his heart'" (Matthew 5:17–18).

(Peacham [1593] 99)

"Alas, the minds of priests are ignorant."

(Scaliger 3.40.311)

Note: Alternate spelling is *epikrisis* and an alternate name is *judicatio*.

epitimesis [G. "censure, criticism"] or *obiurgatio* [L. "a chiding, reproof, rebuke"] or *inter se pugnantia* [L. "contending between themselves"]
A chastisement, reproof, or rebuke

1. Generally, a reproof
   a. Gentle
      "Out of one mouth proceedeth blessing and cursing, my brethren these things ought not so to be: doth a fountain send forth at one place sweet water and bitter?" (James 3:10–11)

      (Peacham [1593] 163)

   b. Biting and derogatory
      "If you have a brain in your head!"

      (Sturm 3.10.584)

      "Ye stiffnecked and uncircumcised in heart and ears, ye do always resist the Holy Ghost: as your fathers did, so do ye. Which of the prophets have not your fathers persecuted? and they have slain them which showed before of the coming of the Just

One; of whom you have been now the betrayers and murderers: Who have received the law by the disposition of angels, and have not kept it." (Acts 7:51–53)

(Smith 142)

2. Specifically, objecting to a charge by throwing the same charge back at the adversary
   Speaking to Jupiter, Venus charges Juno, "If there is no region your pitiless wife will allow/ To the Trojans [. . . ,]" blaming her for the war with the Italians. Juno answers by blaming Venus for the war: "Which man or god ever drove Aeneas to warfare/ Or to face King Latinus in enmity?" (Virgil, *Aeneid* 10.45–68, trans. Lind)

   (Rufinianus, *Dianoeas* §7)

Note: Attributing the figure to Celsus (9.2.105), Quintilian hesitates to accept it as a figure (107). The second use of this figures appears to be a more vehement kind of *inversio*. See *inversio* above under Pragmatical–idea figures. Inasmuch as this charge is often delivered by means of a question, both Rufinianus (§21) and Robertellus (43v) conflate *epitimesis* and *epiplexis*. *Objurgatio* is frequently associated with invective. See also *barytes* below under Discoursal–styles.

ethopoeia [G. "to make or produce character"] or *ethikon* [G. "arising from habit"] or *ethologia* [G. "description of character"]

A portrayal of manners, character, and mild affections

1. A portrayal of manners and character
   a. Through dramatic presentation
      1. Of others
         "So Terence setteth out boasting Thraso, Plautus, a cracking soldier. And this fashion properly belongeth to Comedies, and Dialogues."

         (Sherry [1555] F.v.v)

      2. Of self
         "Everyone writes a letter in the virtual image of his own soul."

         (Demetrius §227)

   b. Through description, or *characterismus*
      "Finally, the tribunes enter upon their office. The speech of Publius Rullus is at last expected because he was the chief promoter of the agrarian law and conducted himself more harshly than his colleagues. Once he was elected, he put on a different expression, another tone of voice, and a different gait; his clothes were worn out, his person neglected and rugged in appearance, while his hair and beard were longer than our style approve, so that his eyes and manner seemed to denounce the tribunal power and to threaten the republic" (Cicero, *De Lege Agraria* II 5.13, trans. Flynn).

      (Soarez 347)

Note: An alternate spelling is *aetopeia.* In this sense, the term refers to a character sketch. *Moralis confictio* is an alternate name. Soarez gives *mimesis, effictio,* and *notatio* as synonyms here (346). See the separate entry for *characterismus* above.

2. An expression of mild emotions, such as love, hope and mirth, or character traits, such as fairness, truthfulness, temperance, humility, modesty, and wit
   "As of the father's love toward the children, the husband and wife, of friends, [. . .] In expressing of these among the Latins, Livius is very cunning. For an history chiefly setteth out the desire of minds, purposes, and deeds, without any great outcries and rages."

   (Sherry [1555] F.v.v)

"[Mamercus] prepared to weaken the censorship, [. . .] Summoning an assembly, he said that the immortal gods had undertaken to manage the foreign policy of the state and keep everything safe; he himself would do what needed to be done inside the city to defend the liberty of the Roman people. Currently its greatest safeguard was that great power should not be long-lasting and that a term limit should be imposed on men to whom the law could not be applied. Other magistracies lasted one year, whereas the censorship was for five. It was a serious matter to live under such an obligation to the same men for a great part of one's life. So, he was going to propose a law whereby the censorship should last no more than a year and a half. With great agreement on the part of the people, Mamercus passed the law on the following day with the words, 'Fellow citizens, so that you may know how displeasing prolonged power is to me, I hereby resign from the dictatorship.' And so, having laid down his own magistracy and imposed a term limit on the other, he was escorted to his home with great rejoicing and popular support" (Livy, *The History of Rome* 4.24, trans. Warrior).

(example mine)

Note: Sherry explains that expressing these gentle emotions aids the orator in winning men's favor. This is the method for creating *delectare* (delight and amusement), one of the three necessary means for persuasion. These gentle passions are called *ethoi* and are also associated with a kind of style that exhibits a civilized kind of speaking (see *epieikeia* under Discoursal–styles below). Sturm points out that when a style transcends these limits, it becomes *pathetikon* (3.23.719). This depiction of the gentler emotions may be accomplished through either the use of dramatic soliloquy or narrative description. Quintilian only allows the *ethopoeia* created through *mimesis* to be a figure (9.3.99).

euche [G. "prayer, vow, wish or aspiration"] or *votum* [L. "a solemn promise, a vow"]

A covenant; a wish for something affixed to a solemn vow; or a wish generally

1. A vow in exchange for obtaining an aspiration, a covenant

   Jacob vows, "If God will be with me, and will keep me in this journey which I go, and will give me bread to eat, and cloth to put on, so that I come again unto my father in safety. Then shall the Lord be my God, and this stone which I have set up as a pillar, shall be God's house, and of all that thou shalt give me, will I give the tenth unto thee" (Genesis 28:21).

   (Peacham [1593] 67)

2. A wish of any kind

   "Would that we were at this stage of alarm!" (Aristides, *On Sending Reinforcements to Sicily* 40, trans. Wooten)

   (Hermogenes 2.7.354)

   "Oh would God that the adulterer had been drowned in the raging sea, when with his navy of ships he sailed to Lacedemonia."

   (Sherry [1550] 51)

Note: Sometimes *euche* and *optatio* are conflated and sometimes distinguished. See *optatio* below. This figure, according to Melanchthon, belongs to the category of those deriving from the dialectical topic of circumstances (*Elem.* 54v).

eulogia [G. "a speaking well, or a blessing"] or *benedictio* [L. "a blessing"] or *makarismos* [G. "a pronouncing or esteeming happy, a blessing"]

A blessing or an expression of joy

"And *David* sent messengers unto the men of *Jabesh Gilead*, and said unto them: Blessed are ye of the Lord, that ye have shewed such kindness unto your Lord *Saul*, that you have buried him" (2 Samuel 2:5).

(Peacham [1593] 65)

"In the wide-branching beech-trees' shade reclined
Thou, Tityrus, playst on thy slender reed
A shepherd song. I from my fatherland,
My fatherland and pastures ever dear,
To exile fly, while Tityrus at ease
In cooling shadows bids the woodland sing
Of lovely Amaryllis.
'Twas a god,
O Meliboeus, gave these idle hours,
One of my gods forever. A young lamb,
From my full folds a thankful offering,
Shall oft his altar stain. For it was he
Gave yonder herds their leave to roam so far,
And me to play whatever song I will
On sylvan pipes the happy, livelong day." (Virgil, *Eclogue* 1.1–14, trans. Williams)

(Sturm 3.24.729)

Note: Peacham takes the term *benedictio* ([1593] 65) from Henri Estienne, who in his *Thesaurus graecae linguae* gives the term theologians used for this figure (Crane, "Introduction" to Peacham's 1593 edition, 22).

exclamatio [L. "a crying out, an exclamation"] or *ecphonesis* [G. "a crying out, an exclamation"]
A crying out; an interjection
"O death, where is thy sting? oh grave, where is thy victory?" (1 Corinthians 15:55)

(Smith 143)

Note: Puttenham gives the English name as "the Outcry" (221). This figure is generally treated as a genus, with species deriving from varied emotions, such as *admiratio, irrisio, optatio, deprecatio, imprecatio, execratio, indignatio, desperatio, ostentatio, threnos, commiseratio, paenismus, interrogatio, epiphonema*, and so forth. Quintilian accepts only the feigned emotions and the feigned outcry as figures (9.2.27). Renaissance rhetoricians, however, regard the genuine exclamations to be figures as well. Melanchthon suggests that this figure derives from the dialectical topic of circumstances (*Elem.* 54v).

execratio [L. "a curse, an expression of hatred"] or *bdelygmia* [G. "abomination"] or *abominatio* [L. "an abominating"]
An expression of hate; an abhorrent rejection
"O wretched man that I am! who shall deliver me from the body of this death" (Romans 7:24).
"O do not this abominable thing that I hate, etc." (Jeremiah 4:4).

(Smith 141–42)

Note: *Detestatio* is an additional name (338). This figure is sometimes conflated with *ara* or *imprecatio*. See *imprecatio* below. Sturm also says that *execratio* is frequently joined with *optatio* (1.24.70). See *optatio* below.

exuscitatio [L. "awakening, arousing"]
A moving speech; free use of the voice; unbridled vociferation

1. In praise
"What one is he of so slender or contemptible a spirit amongst us, or who of all our Nation would be counted so envious, as upon so great and large a desert had by a man so worthy, would not willingly render unto him all honour and due commendation?"
(Day 99)

2. In dispraise
"Who is of so careless a mind that seeing these things can hold their peace and let them pass? You put my father to death before he was condemned, and being put to death, you registered him among the number of condemned men. You thrust me out of mine own house by violence. You possessed my patrimony. What will you more? Came you not to the seats as you do now that you may put to death or condemn Sextus Roscius?" (Cicero, *Pro S. Roscio* 11.32)
(Peacham [1577] U.i.r)

Note: An alternate spelling is *exsuscitatio.*

fable or *fabula* [L. "a fictitious narrative, a fable"] or *apologus* [G. "a story, tale, fable"] or *fabella* [L. "a brief narrative, a fable"] or *mythos* [G. "fiction"]
A short tale about beasts who represent human affections and behaviors; or fictional narratives in general

1. A short tale featuring beasts as characters
"Themistocles persuaded the Athenians not to change their officers by rehearsing the fable of a scabbed fox. 'For,' quod he, 'when many flies stood feeding upon his raw flesh and had well fed themselves, he was contented at another's persuasion to have them flapped away, whereupon there ensued such hungry flies afterwards, that the sorry fox being all alone was eaten up almost to the hard bone, and therefore cursed the time that ever he agreed to any such evil counsel.'"
(Wilson 222)

2. Any fictional narrative
"And it is therefore, gentlemen of the jury, that men of the greatest learning have recorded in their fictitious narratives that one who had killed his mother to avenge his father [Orestes] was acquitted, when the opinion of men was divided as to his guilt, not merely by the decision of a deity, but by the vote of the wisest of goddesses" (Cicero, *Pro Milone* 3.8, trans. Butler).
(Quintilian 5.11.18)

Note: Some rhetoricians collapse the beast fable and the fictional narrative into one figure; others separate them. See *mythos* below. Quintilian distinguishes between the *fabula* (fictional narrative) and *fabella* (the cruder beast fable that appeals to the lower class), but treats these genres as kinds of *exemplum* that function as proofs, not as figures (5.11.17–19). This figure derives from the dialectical topic of comparison (Melanchthon, *Elem.* 53r).

historia [L. "a narrative of past events, a history"]
A history
The History of Rome by Titus Livius (Livy).
(Veltkirchius 172r)

Note: See also *paradeigia*, the historical example, treated under *paradeigma*, a figure of Logical—evidence.

ignocentia [L. "forgiveness"] or *syngnome* [G. "forbearance, allowance"]

A pardon

Christ on the cross, praying for his enemies: "Father forgive them, for they know not what they do" (Luke 23:34).

As he was being stoned, Stephen cried, "Lord, lay not this sin to their charge" (Acts 7:60).

(Peacham [1593] 98)

Note: Quintilian acknowledges that Celsus regarded this behavior a figure, but disallows it (9.2.104).

imprecatio [L. "an invoking of evil"] or *ara* [G. "a prayer, vow, curse"]

A curse

Pyrocles to Philoclea: "There is none here &c. but only the almighty powers, whom I invoke to be the triers [*sic*] of my innocency. And if ever my thoughts did receive so much as a faint in their true affection: if they have not continually with more and more ardour, from time to time pursued the possession of your sweetest favour: if ever in that possession they received either spot or fellowship, then let there most horrible plagues fall upon me: let mine eyes be deprived of the light, which did abuse the heavenly beams that stroke them: let my falsified tongue serve to no use, but to bemoan mine own wretchedness. Let my heart impoisoned [*sic*] with detestable treason, be the seat of infernal sorrow: let my soul with the endless anguish of his conscience, become his own tormentor" (Sidney, *The Old Arcadia*, book 3, 205).

(Fraunce F3r)

"Perdition seize you, Master Runaway! not content with being a worthless scoundrel, you must also be a driveling idiot!" (Cicero, *Pro Rege Deiotaro* 7.21, trans. Watts)

(Soarez 358)

Note: Alternate spellings are *areia* and *aria*. This figure is a particular kind of *execratio* and is sometimes conflated with *execratio*. See *execratio* above.

indignatio [L. "an exciting of indignation"] or *iracundia* [L. "irascibility"] or *ira* [L. "anger, wrath, rage"] or *aganactesis* [G. "irritation, vexation"]

An expression of anger

"O incredible boldness, or rather impudency of a shameless creature: not fit to be suffered."

"What kind of people are you to rage in so vile a madness? Was ever seen a multitude so fierce, a company so careless, an assembly so desperate? What inconsiderate dealing do you use? I shame to see you, & grieve to behold you."

(Day 89)

Note: Cicero treats this emotion as a "place" of invention, especially appropriate for the peroration, which has three parts: the summing up (*enumeratio*), the *indignatio*, and the *conquestio* (*De Inventione* 1.98). Trapezuntius applies to this genre the name *cohortatio*, which is the magnifying of some crime to incite the hearer to anger (410). See *deinosis* under *pathopoeia* below.

insultatio [L. "a scoffing, reviling, insulting"]

An insult

"And they that passed by (our Savior) railed on him, wagging their heads, and saying, 'Ah thou that destroyest the Temple and buildest it in three days!'" (Mark 15:29)

(Smith 142)

Note: Puttenham's English name is "the Disdainefull" or "the Reprochfull or scorner" (218).

modus imperativus [L. "the imperative mode"] or *prostaktikon* [G. "a command, the imperative mood"]

A direct command

"Give license to the bold, give prizes to the wicked, throw out the good!"

(Sturm 3.10.591)

modus optativus [L. "the optative mode, expressing a wish"] or *eikteron* [G. "supplication"]

The indirect command formed by the hortatory subjunctive

"Accordingly, let us imitate men like our Bruti, Camilli, Ahalae, Decii, Curii, Fabricii, Maximi, Scipiones, Lentuli, Aemilii, and countless others, who firmly established this State, whom, indeed, I reckon among the company and number of the Immortal Gods. Let us love our country; let us obey the Senate, let us serve the interests of loyal citizens; let us disregard present advantages, let us work for glory in years to come; let us regard that as best which is most truly good; let us hope for our wishes, but let us bear what comes" (Cicero, *Pro Sestio* 69.143, trans. Gardner).

(Sturm 2.14.349)

mycterismus [G. "sneering, mockery"] or *subsannatio* [L. "mockery by gestures, derision in pantomime"]

A privy, scornful mock or scoff

1. In word

"A glorious gentleman that had two servants, and belike would be known not only to have them but also to have more, said in the presence of a worshipful man: 'I marvel much where all my servants are?' 'Marry, sir,' quod one that thought to hit him home, 'they were here, all two, even now.'"

(Wilson 210)

Saying to one whose words we do not believe, "No doubt, Sir, of that."

(Puttenham 201)

2. In gesture

"A scorning by some gesture of the face, as by writhing the nose, putting out the tongue, petting, or such like."

(Sherry [1550] 46)

"And sometime is a figure, when in shew of disdainful contempt of a person or thing, we fling up our nose."

(Smith 248)

Note: Puttenham's name is "the Fleering frumpe" (201). Keckermann associates this figure with *chleuasmos* (1473), listed above under semantical figures and sometimes considered a form of irony.

mythos [G. "fiction, legend, myth"] or *poet's tale*

A myth or any fictional narrative

1. A myth

"The story is that once, before the birth of the Muses, cicadas were human beings. When the Muses were born and song came into the world, some of the men of that age were so ravished by its sweetness that in their devotion to singing they took no thought to eat and drink, and actually died before they knew what was happening to them. From them sprang thereafter the race of cicadas, to whom the Muses granted the privilege that they should need no food, but should sing from the moment of birth till death without eating and drinking, and after that go to the Muses and tell how each of them is honoured on earth and by whom. So the cicadas make report to Terpsichore of those who have honoured her in the dance, and thus win her favour for them; to Erato of those who have occupied themselves in matters erotic, and similarly to the other Muses, according to the nature of the activity over which each Muse presides. But to Callipe the eldest of the Muses and her next sister Urania they make report of those who spend their lives in philosophy and honour the pursuit which owes its inspiration to these goddesses; among the Muses it is these that concern themselves with the heavens and the whole story of existence, divine and human, and their theme is the finest of them all. So you see that there are many reasons why we should proceed with our discussion instead of indulging in a mid-day sleep" (Plato, *Phaedrus* 259b, trans. Hamilton).

(Hermogenes 2.4.330)

2. Any fictional story

"If a man would speak against covetous caitiffs, can he better show what they are than by setting forth the strange plague of Tantalus, who is reported to be in hell, having water coming still to his chin and yet never able to drink, and an apple hanging before his mouth and yet never able to eat?

Icarus would needs have wings and fly contrary to nature, whereupon when he had them set together with wax and joined to his side, he mounted up into the air. But so soon as the sun had somewhat heated him, and his wax began to melt, he fell down into a great river and was drowned out of hand, the which water was ever after called by his name. Now what other thing doth this tale show us but that every man should not meddle with things above his compass?

Midas desired that whatsoever he touched, the same might be gold, whereupon Jupiter had granted him his boon, his meat, drink, and all other things turned into gold, and he choked with his own desire, as all covetous men lightly shall be that can never be content when they have enough."

(Wilson 220)

Note: Alternate names include *mythikon, narratio poetica*, and *ficcion*. Sometimes myth and fictional narratives are seen as the same figure, and sometimes they are separate genres and separate figures. Sometimes fiction and *fabula* or *apologus* are also conflated. See fable above.

narratio [L. "a narrative"] or *diegema* [G. "a narrative"]

A narrative that can appear anywhere in the speech

"I remember a case which occurred when I was in Asia: how a certain woman of Miletus, who had accepted a bribe from the alternative heirs and procured her own abortion by drugs, was condemned to death: and rightly, for she had cheated the father of his hopes, his name of continuity, his family of its support, his house of an heir, and the Republic of a citizen-to-be. How much more severely did the same crime deserve to be punished in Oppianicus; for she in doing violence to her body brought pain upon herself, but he produced the same result as she by painful death of another" (Cicero, *Pro Cluentio* 11.32, trans. Hodge).

(Sturm 1.30.112)

Note: Hermogenes distinguishes between *diegema* and *diegesis*, the first a story about one thing and the second a collection of stories. For example, the history of Herodotus or Thucydides is a *diegesis*, but the story of Arion in Herodotus (1.23) or of Alcmeon in Thucydides (2.102) is a *diegema* (*Progymnasmata* §2). However, Hermogenes calls the statement of facts or narrative of a speech a *diegesis*, and an illustrative story a *diegesis* in his *On Types of Style*. The distinction between these two terms, then, may not matter much. See *narratio* above under Discoursal–parts. Hermogenes specifies four species of narrative: the mythical, the fictional or dramatic, the historical, and the legal. He also specifies five schemata or methods of narrative: the direct declarative, the indirect declarative, the interrogative, the asyndetical, and the comparative (*Progymnasmata* §2). Sturm calls a little narrative *narratiuncula*, of which the above is an example (1.30.112).

noema [G. "that which is perceived"] or *methodeuthesis* [G. "a crafty assertion"]

An insinuating, subtle remark; speaking indirectly

"*Pawlet* Lord Treasurer of England, and first Marques of Winchester, with the like subtle speech gave a quip to Sir *William Gyfford*, who had married the Marques' sister, and all her lifetime could never love her nor like her company, but when she was dead made the greatest moan for her in the world. [. . .] 'O good brother,' quoth the Marques, 'I am right sorry to see you now love my sister so well,' meaning that he shewed his love too late, and should have done it while she was alive."

"A great counselor somewhat forgetting his modesty, used these words: 'Gods lady, I reckon myself as good a man as he you talk of, and yet I am not able to do so.' 'Yea sir,' quoth the party, 'Your Lordship is too good to be a man. I would ye were a Saint,' meaning he would he were dead, for none are shrined for Saints before they be dead."

(Puttenham 238)

Instead of saying, "The judges are corrupt," we say, "The people require other judges."

(Sturm 3.10.584)

Note: Puttenham's English name is "the Figure of close conceit" (238) and an additional name is *cogitatum*. Quintilian categorizes this device as a reflexion, not a figure (8.5.12). Melanchthon places this figure in the category of those deriving from the dialectical topic of genus (*Elem.* 54r).

obsecratio [L. "a beseeching, a supplication"]

A request made with the words "for the sake of"

"O Chremes, I beseech thee for God's sake and for our old friendship's sake, which hath continued ever since we were children, which time hath also increased, and for thy only daughter's sake, and my son's, whom I have committed wholly to thy government, help me in this matter" (Terence, *Andria* 3.3.537–42).

"O Caesar, for thy promise, thy constancy, and thy mercy's sake, discharge us from this fear, especially that we may not so much as suspect that any part of anger remaineth in thee, for thy right hand's sake I beseech which thou gavest to Deiotarus in promise" (Cicero, *Pro Rege Deiotaro* 3.8).

(Peacham [1593] 71)

Note: This figure is a species of *deprecatio*. See *deprecatio* above. Because *obsecratio* can also mean a public prayer, it is sometimes conflated with *deesis*. Because it has a third meaning, that of an asseveration or protestation coupled with an invocation, it is sometimes conflated with *obtestatio.* See *deesis* above and *obtestatio* below.

obtestatio [L. "an adjuring by calling God to witness"]
An oath that calls as a witness either God, others, or oneself
"Being himself, I think, a marvelous soldier, by Zeus" (Demosthenes, *De Falsa Legatione* 113, trans. Wooten).
"But Androtion is the one who repairs the vessels that you use in solemn processions: Androtion—O Earth and Gods!" (Demosthenes, *Against Androtion* 78, trans. Wooten)

(Hermogenes 2.7.352–53)

Note: This figure is a species of *adjuratio* or *orcos.* See *adjuratio* above. It has on occasion been considered the same as *deesis.* See *deprecatio* above.

ominatio [L. "a foreboding, prognostic"] or *praedictio* [L. "a foretelling, prediction"]
A prediction

1. A warning of evil to come, or *ominatio mali* or *diabole* [G. "false accusation, slander"]
"But, as I see it, Lucius will rule the roost. He is patron of thirty-five tribes, whose votes he took away by the law in which he shared out the magistracies with Gaius Caesar. He is patron of the centuries of Roman knights, whom he likewise chose to disenfranchise, patron of the ex-military tribunes, patron of the Exchange. Who will be able to stand up to his power, especially when he has settled those same on lands? Who ever had all the tribes, the Roman knights, the military tribunes, the Exchange for clients? Do you imagine the Gracchi had greater power than this gladiator will have?" (Cicero, *Philippic* 7.16–17, trans. Bailey)

(example mine)

"How long wilt thou sleep, O sluggard, when wilt thou arise out of thy sleep? Therefore thy poverty cometh upon thee as one that traveleth by the way & thy necessity like an armed man" (Proverbs 6:10–11).

(Peacham [1593] 90)

2. A prediction of good fortune or things hoped for, or *ominatio boni*
"There will come a time when we will see the republic in a flowering state."

(Keckermann 1499)

3. An attempt to forestall a consequence
"For I will say without any intention of aggravating the charge [. . .]"

(Quintilian 9.2.17)

Note: Peacham in his second edition remarks that *ominatio* most often refers to the warning of evil consequences and, consequently, assigns to *euphemismus* the prediction of good (89–90), since this Greek term also means "the use of words of good omen." See *euphemismus* above under Pragmatical–people figures. Melanchthon suggests that this figure derives from the dialectical topic of circumstances (*Elem.* 54v).

onedismus [G. "a reproach"]
A vituperation; upbraiding of ingratitude or impiety
Dido to Aeneas:
"No Goddess never was thy Dam, nor thou of Dardan's kind.
Thou traitor wretch but under rocks, and mountains rough unkind.

Thou wert begot, some brood thou art of Beast or Monster wild.
Some Tigers thee did nurse and gave to thee their milk unmild.
[. . .]
No steadfast truth there is, this naked miser up I took,
Whom seas had cast to shore, and of my Realm a part I gave,
His fleet I did relieve, and from their death his people save."

(Virgil, *Aeneid* 4: 366–77, trans. Thomas Phaer)

"The Prophet *Esay*, by this [. . .] vineyard fruitfully planted and carefully fenced, doth set before the people's eyes, God's goodness and mercy towards them. And by the wild and evil fruit, which that vineyard brought forth, he accuseth them of most sinful ingratitude" (Isaiah 5).

(Peacham [1593] 74)

Note: Sturm calls *oneidismos* the inimical and hostile reproach, while *epitimesis* is the friendly reproach (1.23.70). Sturm also gives another name for reproach, *elegchein* (3.10.591).

optatio [L. "the expression of a wish"]

A wish to God or men, expressing the speaker's desire

"I only wish, gentlemen, that you had so large a supply of brave and upright men as to make it difficult for you now to decide whom to put in charge of these great issues and of this great war!" (Cicero, *Pro Lege Manilia* 10.27, trans. Hodge)

(Soarez 358)

"O that thou wouldst rent the heavens!" (Isaiah 64:1)

"O that I might have my request! and that God would grant me the thing I long for!" (Job 6:8)

"O that I had the wings of a Dove, that I might fly and be at rest!" (Psalm 55:6)

(Smith 142)

Note: This figure is sometimes conflated with *euche*. See *euche* above.

ostentatio [L. "a vain display, ostentation"]

A boast, vaunt

Prince Hal: "What, fought you with them all?"

Falstaff: "All? I know not what you call all, but if I fought not with fifty of them, I am a bunch of radish. If there were not two or three and fifty upon poor old Jack, then am I no two-legged creature. [. . .] I have pepper'd two of them. Two I am sure I have paid, two rogues in buckroom suits. [. . .] These four came all afront, and mainly thrust at me. I made me no more ado but took all their seven points in my target, thus. [. . .] These nine in buckroom that I told thee of [. . .] their points being broken—[. . .] began to give me ground; but I follow'd me close, came in, foot and hand, and with a thought seven of the eleven I paid" (Shakespeare, *1 Henry IV* 2.4.184–218).

(Butler 114; example mine)

paeanismus [G. "singing a hymn of triumph or praise"]

An expression of joy

"O death, where is thy sting? oh grave, where is thy victory?" (1 Corinthians 15:55)

(Peacham [1593] 82)

"O how amiable are thy Tabernacles, thou Lord of Hosts!" (Psalm 84:1)

(Smith 142)

parabola [G. "a parable, parallel, comparison; a placing beside"]

A parable

"A great Eagle with great wings, long winged, full of feathers, which had divers colours, came unto Lebanon, and took the highest branch of the Cedar; he cropped off the top of his young twigs, and carried into a land of traffic; [he set it in a city of merchants]" (Ezekiel 17:3–4).

The explication is as follows: "The great Eagle signifies the King of Babylon; by Lebanon is signified Jerusalem; and by the highest branch of the Cedar and the top of his young twigs, the King and Princes of Jerusalem; by a land of traffic and a City of Merchants is signified Babylon."

(Smith 221)

Note: An alternate spelling is *parabole*. Occasionally, *collatio* is an alternate name. Puttenham calls this figure "Resemblance morall or misticall" (248). Melanchthon specifies that this figure, a species of the similitude, derives from the dialectical topic of comparison (*Elem.* 53r).

paramythia [G. "speaking soothingly, giving comfort, consolation, encouragement"]

A remedy or "medicine" to an opponent's charges or to our audience's sorrow and heaviness

1. *Consolatio,* an expression of consolation or comfort

   "*Eliphas*, the Themanite, [. . .] ministreth his medicine of spiritual comfort, in these words saying: 'Blessed is the man whom God correcteth, therefore refuse not thou the chastening of the almighty, for he maketh the wound and bindeth it up, he smiteth and his hand maketh whole.' After this he addeth many branches of God's mercy, loving kindness, and fatherly protection towards his children, and thereupon concludeth that *Job* ought to apply all these considerations to himself, as most precious medicines able to minister consolation and strength to his fainting spirit" (Job 5:17–18).

   (Peacham [1593] 100)

   "Be of good cheer my sweet heart. Hurt not thyself with sorrow. I warrant thee, I will find out thy Pamphilus, wheresoever he be and will bring him with me." (Terence, *Andria* 4.2.1–3)

   (Peacham [1577] L.i.v)

2. Any method of remedy, including forms of *confessio* and *excusatio*

   See *confessio* under Pragmatical–people figures and *dicaeologia* under Discoursal–genres above.

   (Sturm 1.29.107–110)

pathopoeia [G. "excitement of the passions"]

A passionate, moving speech

1. When the orator, being himself moved with any affection, seeks to move his hearers to the same, called "Imagination" or *Phantasia*

   "Can a woman forget her sucking child? yea they may forget, yet will I not forget thee: Behold, I have graven thee upon the palms of my hands, etc." (Isaiah 49:15–16).

   (Smith 266)

   For "moving mirth and laughter," comedies contain examples.

   (Peacham [1593] 144)

2. When the orator moves the hearers to pity, compassion, or mercy by telling a "lamentable" tale or "woeful sufferings and pitiful miseries," called *Commiseratio*
   "[T]he cruel murdering of the Infants in Bethlehem and the Coasts there about by Herod."
   "[H]earing of the bitter passion of Christ."
   "Histories do serve and likewise poets complaints may give good examples to move men to pity, and to pardon offences the perorations of Cicero shall teach you."
   (Peacham [1577] P.iii.r-v)

3. When the orator moves the hearers to anger, consternation, bitterness and the more violent emotions, called *Deinosis*
   "What will you do when I invade your special province, that is, when I show that, as far as abuse is concerned, you are a mere ignoramus?" (Cassius Severus is here upbraiding his opponent for being abusive.)
   (Quintilian 8.3.88–89)

   "Examples hereof be common in Tragedies."
   (Peacham [1577] P.iii.r)

Note: Gill's term *pathographia* (158) probably corresponds here. Additional names include *empatheia* and *pathetikon*. *Pathoi* are the violent passions differentiated from *ethoi*, the mild affections. *Pathetikon* can also be seen as a kind of style. See below under Discoursal–styles for a full-length example. The *deinosis* type is known in discussions of argument as *cohortatio* (Trapezuntius 410). Melanchthon categorizes this figure among those that derive from the dialectical topic of circumstances (*Elem.* 54v). It is this figure, along with *enumeratio* [or *frequentatio*] and sometimes *amplificatio*, that characterize the peroration (Quintilian 6.1.1, 9, and 52). Quintilian advises that actions as well as words can be employed to move the emotions: "Hence the custom of bringing accused persons into court wearing squalid and unkempt attire, and of introducing their children and parents, and it is with this in view that we see blood-stained swords, fragments of bone taken from the wound, and garments spotted with blood, displayed by the accusers, wounds stripped of their dressings, and scourged bodies bared to view" (6.1.30). Despite an extensive discussion, Quintilian does not categorize *pathetikon* as a figure, however (6.2.8–36). This figure is a means for creating *energeia* (Sherry [1550] 66–68). See *energeia* below under virtues. Hermogenes prescribes this figure for creating *aletheia*, the sincere style (2.7.352–56), whose two primary emotions correspond to the two emotions of pity and anger included here. See *aletheia* below under Discoursal–Styles. See also the individual entries for *phantasia*, *commiseratio*, *indignatio*, and *deinosis*.

phobos [G. "panic, fear, dread"]
An expression of fear

"I am entrapped in many ways, by sickness, exile, poverty:
Also alarm my fainting heart of every shred of wisdom robs:
My mother menaces my life with direful torture and with death,
And none could be so firm of spirit, none so confident of heart
But that hereat his blood would ebb with terror and his face turn pale" (Ennius, *Alcmeo* [Remains, i. p. 230], trans. Rackham).

(Sturm 3.32.785; example in Cicero, *De Oratore* 3.218)

pragmatographia [G. "description of an action or affair"]
A description of an action or event, such as wars, tempests, shipwrecks, conquests, murders, triumphs, assaults, and so forth

1. In poetry
   "When Cupid scaled first the fort,
   Wherein my heart lay wounded sore
   The battery was of such a sort,
   That I must yield or die therefore.
   There saw I love upon the wall,
   How he his banner did display,
   Alarm, alarm he gan to call,
   And bad his soldiers keep array.
   The arms the which that Cupid bare,
   Were pierced hearts with tears besprent:
   In silver and fable to declare
   The steadfast love he always meant.
   There might you see his band all dressed
   In colours like to white and black,
   With powder and with pellets pressed,
   To bring them forth to spoil and sack,
   Good will the master of the shot,
   Stood in the Rampire brave and proud,
   For expense of powder he spared not,
   Assault assault to cry aloud.
   There might you hear the Canons roar,
   Each piece discharging a lover's look, etc."

   (Puttenham 247)

2. In prose
   To describe a city overcome with an assault, say "there shall appear many fires and scattered flames upon houses and temples, the noise of houses falling down, a confused sound of many things and woeful cries, some flying with great peril, others embracing their friends and bidding them farewell forever, infants shrieking, women most bitterly weeping, old men reserved by most unhappy destiny to see that day, the spoiling of temporal and profaning of hallowed things, the running forth of them that carry away the spoils, and the submission of them that entreat for their own goods, every captive led chained before his taker, the mother wrestling to retain her sucking babe, and wheresoever where great wealth is, there is also great fighting and contention among the spoilers themselves."

   (Peacham [1593] 140)

Note: Puttenham's name for this figure is "the Counterfait action" (246).

proecthesis [G. "prefatory account"]

A defense answering accusations, containing reasons that prove one ought not to be blamed

Christ defends eating with publicans and sinners by saying, "They that are whole need not the Physician, but they that are sick: [. . .] I am not come to call the righteous, but sinners to repentance" (Matthew 9:12–13).

"In like manner he defendeth his Disciples being accused for pulling the ears of corn on the Sabbath day, by alleging the example of David eating the shew bread in his great hunger. Secondly by showing his authority being Lord of the Sabbath. And thirdly by citing a sentence of [Hosea 6:6], which he thus applieth: 'If you knew (saith he) what this meaneth, I will have mercy and not sacrifice, you would not have condemned the Innocents'" (Luke 6:1–5).

(Peacham [1593] 103)

Note: Quintilian defines this device somewhat differently, as "pointing out what ought to have been done, and then what actually has been done," a strategy that he rejects as a figure (9.2.106). Scaliger defines the figure as Quintilian does, gives *praeexpositio* as the Latin name, but accepts it as a figure (3.72.341). Peacham appears to have lost the sense of this figure having to be part of the preface or introduction.

prosopographia [G. "description of a person"]

A description of a person in either mind and/ or body

An old man can be described "with crooked limbs, and trembling joints, his head white, his eyes hollow, his sight dim, his hearing thick, his hands shaking, his legs bowing, his colour pale, his skin wrinkled, weak of memory, childish yet covetous, suspicious, testy, greedy of news, credulous, misliking of the present world, and praising the former times."

(Peacham [1593] 135)

Note: An alternate spelling is *prosographia*. Puttenham's name is "the Counterfait countenance" (246). Both Hermogenes in *Progymnasmata* §7 and Priscian in *Praeexercitamina* §7 point out the close connection between this genre as literary portrait or biography and the *loci* of persons associated with *epideictic* discourse.

prosopopoeia [G. "making faces; the making or representing of a person"]

Impersonation; a dramatization of a person, thing or idea through imaginary sayings or writings

1. Indirect speech, *hypophora* [G. "putting forward"]

   "At length, staying, he came a little nearer her again, but still without the compass of blows, holding one leg as it were ready to run away; & then fell to scolding and railing, swearing, it was but a little bashfulness in him, that had made him go back, and that if she stayed any longer, he would make her see, his blood came out of the eldest shepherds house in that Country" (about Dametas in Sidney, *The Old Arcadia*, book 1, 29–30).

   (Fraunce G2r-v)

2. Direct speech

   a. *Personae confictio* [L. "a fabricating of people"] or *sermocinatio* or *prosopopoeia* or *antiprosopopoeia*, having a specific person speak

   Cicero has Appius Claudius, who was dead at the time, address Clodia in *Pro Caelio*: "Woman, what hast thou to do with Caelius, with a stripling, with a stranger? Why hast thou been either so intimate with him as to lend him gold, or such an enemy as to fear poison? Hadst thou not seen that thy father, hadst thou not heard that thy uncle, thy grandfather, thy great grandfather, thy great-great grandfather, and his father were consuls? Lastly, didst thou not know that lately thou hadst in marriage Quintus Metellus, a most illustrious and most courageous man, most devoted to his country, who had only to step outside his own door to surpass nearly all his fellow-citizens in courage, in glory and in prestige?" (14.34, trans. Gardner)

   (Talaeus 34)

"She might perceive afar off one coming towards her in the apparel of a shepherd, with his arms hanging down, going a kind of languishing pace, with his eyes sometimes cast up to heaven, as though his fancy strave to mount up higher; sometimes thrown down to the ground, as if the earth could not bear the burden of his pains: at length she heard him with a lamentable tune sing these few verses:

Come shepherds weeds, become your master's mind,
Yield outward shew, what inward change he tries,
Nor be abashed, since such a guest you find,
Whose strongest hope in your weak comfort lies.
Come shepherd's weeds, attend my woeful cries,
Disuse your selves from sweet Menalcaus voice,
For other be those tunes which sorrow ties,
From those clear notes which freely may rejoice.
Then pour out plaints, and in one word say this,
Helpless his plaint who spoils himself of bliss.

And having ended, she might see him strike himself upon the breast, uttering these words: 'O miserable wretch, whither do thy destinies guide thee?'" (Pamela and Musidorus in Sidney, *The Old Arcadia*, book 1, 36)

(Fraunce G3v-4r)

b. Having an indefinite person speak
"At this point some one will interpose, '. . .'" or "Some one will say, ' . . .'"

(Quintilian 9.2.36)

c. *Dialogismus,* having people speak in dialogue
See under pragmatical–people figures above.

d. *Conformatio* [L. "shaping, forming"] or *empsychosis* [G. "animating"] or *animatio* [L. "animating, a living being"], personification
Our country accuses us of negligence: "Unkind people and Citizens whom I have engendered in my bowels, nourished with my paps, fostered with my delights, why do you thus ungratefully not only abstain to tender me, but give me an open proy [*sic*] to my foes to suppress me: yea, which is most loathsome of all others, become proper murtherers and parricides of your own parentage and family, cruel destroyers of your own patrimony, and wretched renders and tearers of your mothers' bowels, without all regard or pity."

(Day 91)

e. *Commutatio personarum* [L. "a changing of person"], introducing an *empsychosis* with a proposition or narration
"Could [the public] meet and hold discourse with you now, it would say, 'I have not preferred Plancius to you, Laterensis, but, since there was no choice between you as good patriots, I chose to bestow my favours upon the man who importuned me for them, rather than upon the man who would not demean himself to the homage of a supple knee'" (Cicero, *Pro Plancio* 5.12, trans. Watts).

(Sturm 1.37.188).

3. *Mimesis* [G. "imitation"] or *imitatio* [L. "imitation"]
"I am that *Figure* [. . .] whereby men act some other person living or dead. [. . .] I raise the dead as familiarly as any *Conjurer*: I make the vilest *Usurper* upon earth to pass for a *Reformer*, the falsest *Traitors* to be esteem'd as faithful *Counselors*, a mere *Ass* to pass for a *Lion*, and a Carrion *Crow* for a *Peacock*; and all this without any change of

natures at all: I make a *Fencer* to pass for a serious *Dueler*, the miserable *Churl* for a good *Housekeeper*, the rich *Friar* for a very *Mendicant*, and a very *Bankrupt* for a *Gentleman* of good fortune. [. . .] For in one word, all men act over again the lives of other men, and whatever is done in the World is done by *Prosopope*."

(Shaw 171)

4. General category for descriptions of people
comprehending *characterismus*, *prosopographia*, *ethopoeia*, *pathopoeia*, *conformatio*, *sermocinatio*, and *mimesis*.

(Sherry [1555] F.v.r-vii.r)

Note: An alternate spelling is *prosopopoiia*. Puttenham calls this figure "the Counterfait inpersonation" (246). *Hypomnematon* is an additional name for personification. This figure includes the reading out of imaginary documents as well. Melanchthon specifies that this figure derives from the dialectical topic of comparison (*Elem.* 53v).

querela [L. "a complaint"] or *mempsis* [G. "a blaming, censure, complaint"] or *querimonia* [L. "a complaint"]

A complaining request for help

1. In a sentence or passage
"For thy sake also are we killed all the day long, and are counted as sheep appointed to be slain. Awake, why sleepest thou, O Lord? arise, cast us not off for ever" (Psalm 44:22–23).

(Peacham [1593] 66)

Charinus to himself:

"Oh, it's past words, it's past belief to find
A human being with such a twisted mind,
A nature that gets pleasure out of pain
And mischief, making other's loss his gain.
Can it be true? It is. What's more, the worst
Are those who can't for shame say no at first,
But when their promises should be redeemed
They're forced to show they're not the men they seemed.
They face it out, though, bold as bold can be,
'Well, who are you? Or what are you to me?
Hell, charity begins at home. She's mine.
Give her to you? Why should I?' That's their line.
They gave their word, you say. Well, what about it?
Where shame would be appropriate, they're without it.
They're timid at the wrong time. Well, what now?
Shall I accost him, challenge him, have a row?
That's not much use you say. Ah, but it is.
It helps to ease my feelings and hurt his." (Terence, *Andria* 4.l. 625–42, trans. Clayton)

(Veltkirchius 167r)

2. In a whole work
"By this form bills of complaint are exhibited to the Courts of judgement, and supplications to Princes."

(Peacham [1593] 66)

salutatio [L. "a greeting, salutation"]
A greeting or salutation

"Hail, the country
The Fates have destined for me! Hail, gods of the household,
Faithful to Troy!" (Virgil, *Aeneid* 7.130–32, trans. Lind)

(Talaeus 24)

schetliasmos [G. "indignant or passionate complaint"]
An *indignatio* with a complaint and with irony

"Ah, how loud would be the lamentation of those great men who laid down their lives for glory and for liberty, and left behind them the monuments of many noble achievements, if they could see how to-day the progress of our city has ended in the form and rank of a dependant, and that the question of the hour is—whether Charidemus is entitled to personal protection! Charidemus! Heaven help us!" (Demosthenes, *Against Aristocrates* 210, trans. Vince)

(Hermogenes 2.7.353)

semeiologia [L. "the interpretation of signs"] or *semeosis* [G. "divination"]
A prophecy or portent; divination

1. The reading of portents
"The first omen I saw
Were four horses who browsed in a pasture, as white as the snow.
And Father Anchises spoke: 'O strange land, you bring war.
These horses are armed for war, this herd threatens war.
Yet often such creatures are trained to draw chariots too
And to travel in harness without any baulking; there is
Hope for peace,' he said." (Virgil, *Aeneid* 3.568–74, trans. Lind)
2. A prophecy
The harpy Celaeno prophesies to Aeneas: "Hear what I say
And fix my words within your souls, predictions
Apollo heard from the Almighty Father
And told to me, the greatest of the Furies.
You sail to Italy with winds called to your aid.
You shall reach Italy, be allowed to enter its ports.
But you cannot circle with walls the city Fate gives you,
Until, requiting your assaults upon us,
A frightful hunger forces you to gnaw
And to devour the very tables you use!" (*Aeneid* 3.284–93, trans. Lind)
3. A dream and its interpretation
"And the chief butler told his dream to Joseph, and said to him, In my dream, behold, a vine was before me; And in the vine were three branches: and it was as though it budded, and her blossoms shot forth; and the clusters thereof brought forth ripe grapes: And Pharaoh's cup was in my hand: and I took the grapes, and pressed them into Pharaoh's cup, and I gave the cup into Pharaoh's hand. And Joseph said unto him, This is the interpretation of it: The three branches are three days: Yet within three days shall Pharaoh lift up thine head, and restore thee unto thy place: and thou shalt deliver Pharaoh's cup into his hand, after the former manner when thou wast his butler" (*Genesis* 40: 9–13).

4. The interpretation of a divine parable

   Jesus tells and interprets the parable of the sower: "A sower went out to sow his seed: and as he sowed, some fell by the way side; and it was trodden down, and the fowls of the air devoured it. And some fell upon a rock; and as soon as it was sprung up, it withered away, because it lacked moisture. And some fell among thorns; and the thorns sprang up with it, and choked it. And other fell on good ground, and sprang up, and bare fruit an hundredfold. And when he had said these things, he cried, He that hath ears to hear, let him hear. And his disciples asked him, saying, what might this parable be? And he said, Unto you it is given to know the mysteries of the kingdom of God: but to others in parables; that seeing they might not see, and hearing they might not understand. Now the parable is this: The seed is the word of God. Those by the way side are they that hear; then cometh the devil, and taketh away the word out of their hearts, lest they should believe and be saved. They on the rock are they, which, when they hear, receive the word with joy; and these have no root, which for a while believe, and in time of temptation fall away. And that which fell among thorns are they, which, when they have heard, go forth, and are choked with cares and riches and pleasures of this life, and bring no fruit to perfection. But that on the good ground are they, which in an honest and good heart, having heard the word, keep it, and bring forth fruit with patience" (Luke 8: 5–15).

   (Veltkirchius 173r)

threnos [G. "a dirge, a lament"] or *lamentatio* [L. "a lamentation"]

A lament

1. In a sentence or passage

   "O that my head were full of water, and mine eyes a fountain of tears, that I might weep day and night, for the slain of the daughter of my people" (Jeremiah 9: 1).

   (Peacham [1593] 66)

   "O cruel and lamentable times wherein we live, subject as we are to so manifold miseries!"

   (Day 89)

2. In a whole work

   "The greatest part of Jeremiah's lamentations is framed by this form of speech."

   (Peacham [1593] 66–67)

topographia [G. "a description of a country or region"]

A description of a real place

Examples are "Virgil's description of Carthage and its harbour, Pliny's accounts in his Letters of his Laurentine villa, and Statius' account of Pollio's villa at Sorrento and Manilius' villa at Tivoli, [. . .] the eruption of Vesuvius in the Younger Pliny, and the fires of Etna in Claudian."

(Erasmus *De copia* 587)

Note: Puttenham's name for this figure is "the Counterfait place" (246). *Cosmographia* [G. "a description of the world"] is a species here.

topothesia [G. "a description of a place"]
A description of a feigned place
Examples include "Ovid's evocation of the Abode of Sleep, the House of Fame, the Palace of the Sun, Virgil's of the Underworld and the lair of Cacus, the description of Taenarum in Statius, a hall in Lucian, and Psyche's fairy palace in Apuleius."
(Erasmus, *De copia* 587)

Note: Both of the figures above result from the *locus* of place.

*Types of Styles (*Figurae dicendi *or* orationis*)*

acharis [G. "without grace or charm, unpleasant, disagreeable"]
The repulsive style, a vice; the opposite of forcefulness or *deinotes*

1. Description
The subjects treated are obscene, crude, or disgusting; the composition is either disjointed, with clauses that are not linked to each other, but seem like broken fragments, or with long, continuous periods that cause the speaker to run out of breath; and the diction presents either the charming or the disgusting as great and terrible.
(Demetrius §302–4)

2. Example
"The man who accused Timandra of being a prostitute [. . . ,] spewed out over the court her basin, her fees, her mat, and many similar ugly details."
Clitarchus describes the wasp: "It lays waste the hillsides, and rushes into the hollow oaks" (FGrHist 137 Clitarchus F 14 [cf. T 10], trans. Innes).
(Demetrius §302, 304)

Note: Scaliger gives *foedus* [L. "foul, filthy, unseemly, loathsome"] as an alternate name (4.16.473). Demetrius explains that repulsiveness and frigidity are separate, but related qualities that "lie next to each other" (§304). See *psychrotes* or frigidity below.

akme [G. "point, edge"] or *vehementia* [L. "vehemence"] or *acris* [L. "sharp, pointed, piercing"]
The florescent, vigorous style

1. Description
To be vigorous, speak about important subjects directly with *epitimesis, epicrisis, onedismus, apeilai, cataphronesis, metaphora, onomatopoeia (pepoiemenon), cacemphaton, apostasis, epembole, hypostasis, apostrophe, elenchus, ironia, elenktikon, anairesis, thesis, amplificatio, apostrophe, deixin, erotesis, symploke, articulus,* and *asyndeton* between *macrocola*. Vigor shares characteristics with asperity, vehemence, and brilliance.
(Hermogenes 1.10.269–77; Sturm 3.13.619–29)

2. Examples
"But as for you, Caecilius, [. . .] estimate again and again your capacity, and gather yourself together, and consider who you are and what you are fit for" (Cicero, *In Q. Caecilium* 12.37).
(Sturm 3.13.619)

"While the vessel is safe, whether it be a large or a small one, then is the time for sailor and helmsman and everyone in his turn to show his zeal and to take care that it is not capsized by anyone's malice or inadvertence; but when the sea has overwhelmed it, zeal is useless" (Demosthenes, *Philippic III* 69, trans. Vince).
(Hermogenes 1.10.270)

Note: Scaliger also describes this style with the adjective *acre* (4.15.467) and, like Trapezuntius (552), associates *vehementia* here (4.18.483). According to Hermogenes, this style is a species of the grand style. See *grandis* below. *Vehementia* is also associated with *sphodrotes*. See *sphodrotes* below.

aletheia [G. "truthfulness, sincerity"] or *veritas* [L. "truthfulness"]

Speech that is sincere, true, unaffected, spontaneous, animated with the cogitations of the soul, straight from the heart

1. Description

   To create this sincerity, use the simple and modest styles, adding when necessary *dikthesin*, such as *schetliasmos*, *orcos* and its various kinds (*obtestatio*, *obsecratio*, *euche*, *deesis*), *threnos*, *convinciari*, and various kinds of *ecphonesis* (showing the various kinds of emotions) to create *pathetikon*. For approaches use *apantesis*, *apostasis*, *hyperbaton*, *anastrophe*, and *autoschediasmos*. For diction use vehement and coined words for anger (*skleros*); use pure, simple and sweet words for pity. For figures, use *apostrophe*, *interrogatio*, *deiktikon*, *diaporesis*, *aposiopesis*, *epikrisis*, *epidiorthosis*, *apolytos merismos*, *expolitio*, *oneidismos*, *metanoia*, and *solecismus*. For vehement emotions use the clauses, word order, cadence and rhythms of asperity; for pity and the milder emotions use the techniques of simplicity.

   (Hermogenes 2.7.352–63; Sturm 1.23.66–70; 3.20.697–98; 3.24.725–34)

2. Example

   King Richard III, alone, awakes from his dream, in which the ghosts of his victims have all condemned him:

   "Give me another horse! Bind up my wounds!
   Have mercy, Jesu! Soft, I did but dream.
   O coward conscience, how dost thou afflict me!
   The lights burn blue. It is now dead midnight.
   Cold fearful drops stand on my trembling flesh.
   What do I fear? Myself? There's none else by.
   Richard loves Richard, that is, I [am] I.
   Is there a murtherer here? No. Yes, I am.
   Then fly. What, from myself? Great reason why—
   Lest I revenge. What, myself upon myself?
   Alack, I love myself. Wherefore? For any good
   That I myself have done unto myself?
   O no! Alas, I rather hate myself
   For hateful deeds committed by myself.
   I am a villain; yet I lie, I am not.
   Fool, of thyself speak well; fool, do not flatter:" (Shakespeare, *Richard III* 5.3.177–92)

   (example mine)

Note: Patterson describes this style as that of "one plain-dealing man addressing another in whose judgment he has perfect confidence" (186) and points out the correspondence between this style, *pathopoeia*, and *energeia* (127–31). See *pathopoeia* under Discoursal–genres above and *energeia* under Qualitative–virtues below.

ameles [G. "careless, negligent"]

The careless and neglected style, a vice; the opposite of *epimeleia*

1. Description

   Full of *barbarismus*, *solecismus*, *arithmon*, and the various vices of style.

   (Sturm 3.17.667)

2. Example

"When I was in Cambridge, and a student in the King's College, there came a man out of the town with a pint of wine in a pottle pot to welcome the provost of that house that lately came from the court. And because he would bestow his present like a clerk dwelling among the scholars, he made humbly three curtsies and said in this manner: 'Cha good even my good lord, and well might your lordship vare. Understanding that your lordship was come, and knowing that you are a worshipful Pilate and keeps a bominable house, I thought it my duty to come incantivantee and bring you a pottle of wine, the which I beseech your lordship take in good worth.'"

"Another good fellow of the country, being an officer and mayor of a town and desirous to speak like a fine learned man, having just occasion to rebuke a runagate fellow, said after this wise in a great heat: 'Thou ingram and vacation knave, if I take thee anymore within the circumcision of my damnation, I will so corrupt thee that all vacation knaves shall take ilsample by thee.'"

(Wilson 190)

Note: Scaliger calls this failed middle style *negligentia* (4.24.491).

apheleia [G. "artlessness, simplicity"] or *tenuitas* [L. "thinness, fineness, smallness"]

The unaffected and simple style; the opposite of *drimytes* and *oxytes*

1. Description

To create this style, use thoughts that are common to all men and occur to everyone, that are not deep or complex, that are trivial, and that even children and country people speak about. Proofs (*epicheirema*) are constructed out of comparisons with animals and plants. Approaches include, along with those that create the pure style, those that have an appearance of superficiality: *aphegesis*, *proslepsis*, *merismos*, proving one's point with an oath instead of facts, *deesis*, brief *apantesis* and *lysis*. Diction shares features with the pure style and sometimes includes striking words. Figures and clauses are those of purity, except word order is more artless and loose. The rhythmical close must be stately, solemn.

(Hermogenes 2.3.322–29; Sturm 3.20.697–98)

2. Examples

"How handsome Granddaddy seems to me, Mother" (Xenophon, *Cyropaedia* 1.3.2, trans. Wooten).

"[A]s Cyrus says of the Assyrians, 'They are bad men themselves, and they ride bad horses'" (Xenophon, *Cyropaedia* 1.4.19, trans. Wooten).

"I am serenading Amaryllis, and my goats are grazing on the mountain" (Theocritus, *Idylls* 3.1, trans. Wooten).

"except for harvesters and diggers and binders and shepherds and herdsmen."

(Hermogenes 2.3.322–23)

Note: *Simplicitas* is another name Scaliger gives (4.19.484). Both Trapezuntius and Scaliger associate this style with the low style. See *subtilitas* below. Sturm also includes here "loose oratory" or *logadis* (3.4.512), a feature commonly associated with the low or plain style. See *logadis* below. Robertellus calls *apheleia* a virtue, not a style (30r).

apocope [G. "a cutting off, abruptness"]

An abrupt form of speaking

1. Description

Inclusive of extended *asyndeton*, *eclipsis*, *scematismus*, *dialelymenon*, and like figures.

2. Example
   Sir Plume in Pope's *The Rape of the Lock*:
   "My Lord, why, what the devil!
   Z____ds! damn the lock! 'fore Gad, you must be civil!
   Plague on 't! 'tis past a jest—nay prithee, pox!
   Give her the hair" (l. 127–30).

(Demetrius §238, 301; example mine)

asapheia [G. "uncertainty, obscurity"] or *obscuritas* [L. "darkness, obscurity"]
The obscure style, a vice; the opposite of *sapheneia*

1. Description
   Obscurity results from obsolete or provincial words, technical jargon, homonyms, or useless words. Also from sentences that are too long, delay the conclusion by means of excessive hyperbaton, have confused word order or too many parentheses, or that strive for too much brevity and omit words or ideas necessary for the sense. Additionally, from the misuse of words and figures, from *adianoeta*, and from numerous other solecisms.

(Quintilian 8.2.12–21)

2. Example
   The writings of Heraclitus.

(Sturm 3.6.545)

"Pleasures deliver ecstasy for fulfillment, for perfection, for desperation. Their chief concern for fulfillment is in the expectation and desires; for perfection, in the completion of one's soul; and for desperation, in the constant fixing in mind and spirit the pleasing of the body and consistently striving to quench all misery and woe. To spend too little time or too much effort in pleasure is in the will of the one, for how fulfilled is possible, for how whole is sufficient, and for how desperate is in our striving to attain the plethora of joy. There is little importance in which way to turn until one honestly analyzes the levels of fulfillment, the levels of perfection, and the levels of desperation necessary to sacrifice to be right as rain in the kind of path chosen" (name withheld).

(Example mine)

Note: *Obscuritas* is talked about in Quintilian as a vice, not a style *per se*; yet, Renaissance rhetoricians treat *obscuritas* as a style. Scaliger discusses this style, but does not call it a figure (4.1.445). Sturm distinguishes between *asapheia* and *kryptikon*, the first the opposite of *sapheneia* and the second the opposite of *kekrimmenon*, a kind of *deinotes*. See *deinotes* below. *Kryptikon* [G. "concealed, hidden"] would seem to result from *exilitas*, the failed low style below.

barytes [G. "importunity, arrogance, gravity"] or *objurgatio* [L. "reproof"]
The angry, indignant, grave style

1. Description
   To create this style, use thoughts and approaches that include *epitimesis*, *aganactesis*, *syncrisis*, *meionektikas*, and *ironia* mixed with *diaporesis*, *endoiasis*, *eudiasis*, *epikrisis*, *epitrope* (*permissio*), and *anangeon*. Also use elements appropriate to simplicity and modesty.

(Hermogenes 2.8.364–68)

2. Example
   "You know that, since I bought you as a child,
   You've found me a fair master, tolerant, mild.
   From slave I made you freedman, since as slave

You did free-hearted service. So I gave
The best reward I had."
[This speech is said in a reproachful manner.] (Terence, *Andria* 1.1.35–39, trans. Clayton)

(Sturm 3.25.735)

Note: An alternate name is *baryteta*. Hermogenes and followers consider this style a species of *veritas* or *aletheia*. See *aletheia* above.

brevitas [L. "brevity, conciseness"] or *brachylogia* [G. "brevity in speech"] or *brachiepia* [G. "laconic style"]

Using the very minimum of necessary words; being brief, terse, concise; the opposite of *peribole*

1. By means of symbols or images
   "The cicadas will sing to you from the ground" carries more meaning and impact than "your trees will be cut down" (Stesichorus, according to Aristotle, *Rhetoric* 2.11.9, 1395a).
   (Demetrius §243)

   "Sallust's description of Mithridates as 'huge of stature, and armed to match.'"
   (Quintilian 8.3.82)

2. By means of very short sentences
   "The man is sore wounded: I fear me he will die. The physicians mistrust him."
   "The party is fled: none pursueth. God send us good luck."
   (Wilson 206)

3. By means of leaving out details
   "Just recently consul, next he [Marius] was first man of the state; then he sets out for Asia; next he is declared a public enemy and exiled; after that he is made general-in-chief and finally consul for the seventh time."
   (*Ad Herennium* 4.54.68)

   "As he passed by, he took Lemnum; then he left a garrison at Tharsus: after he took a city in Bythinia; driven from thence, forthwith he won Abydus."
   (Sherry ([1555] G.viii.v)

   "The corps (saith Simo) goeth before, we follow after" (Terence, *Andria* I.i.116–17).
   "We come to the grave, it is put into the fire, a lamentation is made" (*Andria* I.i.126–28).
   (Peacham [1593] 182)

Note: Scaliger calls this style *abcissio* (3.77.344). The term *brachylogia* also refers, when well-used, to comprehending many things in a few words (a virtue), or when ill-used, to speaking too briefly (a vice). See this term under both virtues and vices below. In addition, it is another name for *asyndeton*. See *asyndeton* above under syntactical figures. The examples from Sherry and the *Ad Herennium* also appear as examples of *epitrochasmus*, suggesting that *brevitas* can also be seen as a pragmatical figure that creates speed. See *epitrochasmus* under Pragmatical–idea figures and *gorgotes* below. Soarez instructs that figures of speech formed by omission create *brevitas* (317). Peacham remarks that this figure is to be used "either when matters need no long speech, or when time requireth speed," and he warns that too much brevity produces obscurity ([1593] 182). For the opposite style, see *peribole* below.

cacozelias [G. "affectation"]

The affected, sentimental style; the opposite of *glaphyria*.

1. Description

   This subject matter and diction are too cute, ingenious, and emotional, with anapestic or undignified meter.

2. Examples

   "[O]ne writer spoke of 'a centaur riding himself.'"

   "[O]n the theme of Alexander deliberating whether to compete in the Olympic games, another said, 'Alexander, run in your mother's name.'"

   "[T]he sweet-coloured rose laughed."

   "[T]he pine was whistling to the accompaniment of the gentle breezes."

   "[B]randishing the ash spear Pelian to the right over his shoulder" (Sotades 17) instead of the more noble rhythm in "brandishing the Pelian ash spear over his right shoulder (Homer, *Iliad* 22.133, trans. Innes)."

   (Demetrius §186–89)

Note: To Demetrius and Hermogenes, *caozelia* is a style, but to Quintilian, the grammarians, and the Renaissance rhetoricians, it is one of the vices of speech. See *cacozelia* below under vices.

circumscriptio [L. "a composing"] or *eiromenin lexin* [G. "words in continuation"]

The periodic, continuous, connected style

1. Description

   In this style, the speaker uses periodic sentences, wherein "the language runs on as if enclosed in a circle until it comes to an end with each phrase complete and perfect." Additionally, this style requires a concern for rhythm, making clauses no longer than one's breath capacity, balance, *isocolon*, *anisocolon*, *clausulae*, *antithesis*, *hyperbaton*, *anakampsis*, and at times *homoeoteleuton*. The words too must be smoothly connected to avoid *hiatus* and a harsh clash of consonants (*cacemphaton*). "This style should not be maintained for a long time," for "[i]f you use it constantly, it not only wearies the audience, but even the layman recognizes the nature of the trick," and it "takes the feeling out of the delivery, it robs the audience of their natural sympathy, and utterly destroys the impression of sincerity. [. . .] It is to be used, then, in an ornate laudatory passage [. . .] in telling a story which calls for dignity rather than pathos [. . .] often in amplification[. . . .] It is effective when the audience have been won and held by the speaker; they no longer are intent on watching or catching him, but are now on his side, and wish him success; overcome with admiration for the vigour of his oratory, they do not seek points to criticize." It is also appropriate in history and epideictic genres. Two good models of this style are Isocrates and Theopompus.

   (Cicero, *Orator* 61.207–62.226; *De Oratore* 3.43.171–46.181)

   The connections need not come only from periods of the circuitous type, but also from other forms of the period and from repetitions of significant words, such as *resumptio*, *epimone*, *anadiplosis*, and so forth. This style, which is found in Isocrates, is suitable for history and description, but must not ever be used for extended passages, for it wearies those listening as well as talking.

   (Aquila §18–19)

2. Example

   "Wherefore, Publius Africanus, when he had destroyed Carthage, adorned the cities of the Sicilians with most beautiful statues and monuments, in order to place the greatest number of monuments of his victory among those whom he thought were especially delighted at the victory of the Roman people. Afterwards that illustrious man, Marcus Marcellus himself, whose valour in Sicily was felt by his enemies, his mercy by the conquered, and his good faith by all the Sicilians, not only provided in that war for the advantage of his allies, but spared even his conquered enemies. When by valour and skill he had taken Syracuse, that most beautiful city, which was not only strongly fortified by art, but was protected also by its natural advantages—by the character of the ground about it, and by the sea—he not only allowed it to remain without any diminution of its strength, but he left it so highly adorned, as to be at the same time a monument of his victory, of his clemency, and of his moderation; when men saw both what he had subdued, and whom he had spared, and what he had left behind him. He thought that Sicily was entitled to have so much honour paid to her, that he did not think that he ought to destroy even an enemy's city in an island of such allies. And therefore we have always so esteemed the island of Sicily for every purpose, as to think that whatever she could produce was not so much raised among the Sicilians as stored up in our own homes. When did she not deliver the corn which she was bound to deliver, by the proper day? When did she fail to promise us, of her own accord, whatever she thought we stood in need of? When did she ever refuse anything which was exacted of her? Therefore that illustrious Marcus Cato the wise called Sicily a storehouse of provisions for our republic—the nurse of the Roman people. But we experienced, in that long and difficult Italian war which we encountered, that Sicily was not only a storehouse of provisions to us, but was also an old well filled treasury left us by our ancestors; for, supplying us with hides, with tunies, and with corn, it clothed, armed, and fed our most numerous armies, without any expense at all to us." (Cicero, *Against Verres* II, 2.2, trans. Yonge)

(Cicero, *Orator* 62.210)

Note: Cicero gives *comprehensio*, *continuatio* and *ambitus* as other names for this style (*Orator* 61.207), equating it with the *periodus*. See *periodus* under syntactical figures above. Other figures that help create this periodic style include *antimetabole*, *climax*, *enthymema*, *syllogismus*, *antithesis*, *hypostasis*, *dirimens copulatio*, and *epembole*. This style is often set as an opposite to the loose style. See *oratio soluta* below.

deinotes [G. "force" or "cleverness"] or *gravitas* [L. "weightiness"]

Forceful, weighty speech; or decorous speech

1. Description

   "Force in a speech is nothing other than the proper use of all the kinds of style." To cover the subject, one needs instruction in the entire art of rhetoric. The following are the two different types of forceful speech:

   a. One that is forceful and appears to be so

      Thoughts are paradoxical, profound, compelling or cleverly contrived, with approaches and diction typical of grandeur, solemnity and vehemence. Figures, word order and all the other elements are those appropriate to solemnity, fluorescence, brilliance and abundance. Especially effective is *systrophe*.

   b. One that is forceful but does not seem to be so, or *kekrimmenon* [G. "in a mixed manner"]

      This type is not produced by the thought, but exclusively by the approach: one seems to speak simply and in an artless manner, thereby understating the significance of what is said.

(Hermogenes 2.9.369–80)

2. Examples
   a. One that is forceful and appears to be so

   "It is a question of parricide, which no one attempts to commit without many motives; it is pleaded before men of the greatest shrewdness, who know that no one commits even the most trifling misdemeanour without a motive.

   Very well; you cannot bring forward any motive. Although it ought to be considered at once that I have won my case, I will not insist upon my right, and will make a concession to you in this case, which I would not make in any other, so convinced am I of my client's innocence. I do not ask you to say why Sextus Roscius killed his father, I ask you how he killed him. Yes, I ask you how, O Gaius Erucius, and I will so deal with you that, although it is my time for speaking, I will give you full permission to answer, to interrupt, or, even if you desire it, to ask me questions. How did he kill him? Did he strike the blow himself, or entrust the task to others? If you maintain that he did it himself, I answer that he was not in Rome; if you say that he did it by the hands of others, I ask you, who were they? Slaves or free men? If free men, who are they? from the same place Ameria, or some of these assassins from Rome? If from Ameria, who are they? why are their names not given? if from Rome, how did Roscius, who for several years did not come to Rome and never stayed there more than three days, make their acquaintance? Where did he meet them? how did he get an interview with them? how did he persuade them? He gave them a bribe. To whom, and through whom, did he give it? where did the money come from, and how much was it? Is it not by following up all such traces that the starting-point of the crime is usually reached? (Cicero, *Pro S. Roscio* 26.73–27.74, trans. Freese)

   (Sturm 3.26.745–49)

   b. One that is forceful, but does not appear so

   In the reconciliation with her father, Cordelia's replies are simple and short, yet powerful expressions of her love:

   Lear: Do not laugh at me,
   For (as I am a man) I think this lady
   To be my child Cordelia.
   Cordelia: And so I am; I am.
   Lear: Be your tears wet? Yes, faith. I pray weep not.
   If you have poison for me, I will drink it.
   I know you do not love me, for your sisters
   Have (as I do remember) done me wrong:
   You have some cause, they have not.
   Cordelia: No cause, no cause. (Shakespeare, *King Lear* 4.7.67–75)

   (example mine)

Note: In his commentary on Hermogenes, Sturm gives as synonyms for this style *eloquentia* or *decorum* (see Patterson 67, 179). The correct spelling for the second kind is *kekramenon*. When Demetrius identifies a kind of forceful style that he calls *deinos*, he means by the term a passionate intensity that evokes fear or terror. He opposes this forceful style to the elegant style, *glaphyria* (§258). See *deinosis* under Discoursal–genres above for this sense of the term and its opposite *glaphyria* below. Because the term *deinotes* also means "cleverness," Hermogenes expands his notion of this style to mean the masterful and appropriate combination of all qualities and styles into an effective whole. In doing so, he makes the "terrible" into a subspecies of "the appropriate." Taking Odysseus as the model of the truly forceful speaker, who changes styles as circumstances demand, Hermogenes says, "Was the same man forceful at times, but not at others? I would argue that the same man is speaking in all these passages and is using the same Force and the same craft, since he knows that it is necessary to use different kinds of style and is able to do so" (2.9.372). Trapezuntius, then, identifies two kinds of *deinotes*: *gravitatis verbo solum* or grand themes spoken in grand language and *gravitatis vere et re* or appropriateness (603). Like Hermogenes, both Trapezuntius and Sturm keep forcefulness separate from the grand style. Contrarily, Scaliger associates this style, which he calls *gravitas*, with the grand style, while defining it as "that prudence which organizes all the parts of an oration into a composite whole" (4.18.483, trans. Patterson 179). See *oratio grandis* below. There are two faulty opposites to *deinotes*: *spumosus*, that opposing A, and *kryptikon*, that opposing B (Sturm 3.26.749). See *spumosus* below and the note to *asapheia* (*kryptikon*) above. A speech that has force or power also corresponds to the virtues *energeia* and discretion. See these two entries under virtues below. This style matches one definition Cicero gives to "eloquence"—the mastery of the art (*Orator* 29.100).

dissolutum [L. "lax, disconnected, careless"]
The slack style; the failed middle style

1. Description

"[I]t is without sinews and joints; accordingly I may call it the Drifting, since it drifts to and fro, and cannot get under way with resolution and virility. [. . .] Speech of this kind cannot hold the hearer's attention, for it is altogether loose, and does not lay hold of a thought and encompass it in a well-rounded period."

(Ad Herennium 4.11.16)

"[I]t waveth hither and thither, as it were without sinews and joints, standing surely in no point. And such an Oration cannot cause the hearer to take any heed, when it goeth in and out, and comprehendeth not anything with perfect words."

(Sherry [1555] H.v.r)

2. Example

"Our allies, when they wished to wage war with us, certainly would have deliberated again and again on what they could do, if they were really acting of their own accord and did not have many confederates from here, evil men and bold. For they are used to reflecting long, all who wish to enter upon great enterprises."

(Ad Herennium 4.11.16)

Note: Alternate names are *aneimeson* [G. "careless, without restraint, without accent"] and *trepidatio* [L. "agitation, confusion"]. This style seems to include both *ameles* and *hyptiotes*, from the Hermogenean forms. See each of these listed above and below.

drimytes [G. "subtlety"] and *oxytes* [G. "sharpness"] or *acuitas* [L. "sharpness"]
Superficial profundity

1. Two kinds:
    a. To express something pointedly, using striking words and turns of phrase.
    b. To combine the serious and comic for the sake of a laugh.
2. Description

Whereas pure or solemn diction remains pure or solemn despite the thought, "the diction of [Subtlety] has no element of Subtlety if it is separated from the thought that it expresses or from the preceding context of the thought." The diction expresses some thought in an unusual, witty or ironic way through tropes or forms of *paronomasia*. Also useful are *apophthegmata*, *paroemia*, various kinds of quotations from other writers, *allegoria*, *archaismus*, various kinds of jokes and witticisms (*ad hilaritatem impulsio*), *antiphrasis*, and *enantiosis*.

(Hermogenes 2.5.339–45; Sturm 3.22.708–15)

3. Example

   "Hence those people whose indignation went so far as to make them humorists: some of these made the remark you have often heard repeated, that *ius verrinum* was of course poor stuff: others were still sillier, only that their irritation passed them off as good jesters, when they cursed Sacerdos for leaving such a miserable hog behind him. I should not recall these jokes, which are not particularly witty, nor, moreover in keeping with the serious dignity of this Court, were it not that I would have you remember how Verres' offences against morality and justice became at the time the subject of common talk and popular catchwords" (Cicero, *In C. Verrem* II 1.46.121, trans. Greenwood).

   (Trapezuntius 589)

Note: Scaliger's name is *acumen* [L. "a point to prick or sting with"] (4.14.466). In the above example, *ius verrinum* has two possible meanings: "Verres' administration of the law" and "pork gravy." *Sacerdos*, or "Mr. Priest," was also the name of Verres' predecessor, who erred in giving up his position to Verres (i.e., failing to sacrifice this animal).

epieikeia [G. "reasonableness, fairness"] or *modestia* [L. "modesty"]

Mildness, moderation, modesty; the opposite of vehemence

1. Description

   This style is produced primarily by the thought, exemplified in statements that show the speaker is aiming at less than he could otherwise attain (*hyposchesin*).

   Approaches include first giving up some of one's advantages by means of *meionektikas*, *pleonektikon*, *syncrisis* (contrasting our justice with the injustice of the adversary), *paramythia* and *diakrisis* and second toning down or softening arguments in presentation and delivery, using *meiosis*, *euphemismus*, *eudiasis*, *paraleipsis* (omitting some facts or comments), and *apheleia* (the simple style). The diction, figures, clauses, word order and cadences should be those of the simple style.

   (Hermogenes 2.6.345–52; Sturm 3.23.716–24)

2. Examples

   "Why, then, if not some, but all, were unworthy in most respects, did he consider you and them worthy of the same treatment?" (Demosthenes, *Against Leptines* 2, trans. Wooten). The more vehement version would have been, "Why, if not some, but all, were unworthy in most respects, did he condemn you and them to the same dishonor?"

   (Hermogenes 2.6.349)

   "[H]ow often would I have gathered thy children together, even as a hen gathereth her chickens under her wings, and ye would not!" (Matthew 23:37)

   (Sturm 3.11.595)

Note: Sturm associates this style with *ethikon*, the depiction of the mild emotions and just character (3.17.679). See *ethopoeia* above under Discoursal–genres.

epimeleia [G. "care, attention, diligence"] and *kallos* [G. "beauty"] or *pulchritudo* [L. "beauty"]

The carefully wrought, beautiful style; the opposite of *ameles*

1. Description

   The speech must have symmetry, harmony, proportion, and unity. It will have the diction appropriate to purity. This style will have "adornments applied from without for the sake of embellishment," such as *parisosis*, *homoioteleuton*, *homoioptoton*, *homoioartron*, *epanaphora*, *antistrophe*, *epanastrophe*, *climax*, *isocolon*, *hyperbaton*, *kainoprepeis*, *liptote*, *polyptoton*, *epitheton*, *metathesis*, *enallage*, *geminatio*, *diaeresis*, *tmesis*, *anastrophe*, *anthimeria*, *antiptosis*, *ethikon*, and *antarithmos*. Clauses will be moderately long and conjoined (*mediestekota*), without *hiatus* but with *euphonia;* or short clauses will be closely connected and interwoven (*epiploken*) in the manner of insertions (*epembole* and *hypostrophe*). Word order must have configurations similar to meter and *clausulae* should end in monosyllables. The meter must be appropriate to the passage, but not too obviously metrical. A beautiful passage can be added to a speech for the sake of ornament.

2. Example
"There are people who frown upon eloquence and censure men who study philosophy, asserting that those who engage in such occupations do so, not for the sake of virtue, but for their own advantage. Now, I should be glad if those who take this position would tell me why they blame men who are ambitious to speak well, but applaud men who desire to act rightly; for if it is the pursuit of one's own advantage which gives them offence, we shall find that more and greater advantages are gained from actions than from speech. Moreover, it is passing strange if the fact has escaped them that we reverence the gods and practise justice, and cultivate the other virtues, not that we may be worse than our fellows, but that we may pass our days in the enjoyment of as many good things as possible. They should not, therefore, condemn these means by which one may gain advantage without sacrifice of virtue, but rather those men who do wrong in their actions or who deceive by their speech and put their eloquence to unjust uses" (Isocrates, *Nicocles* 1–2, trans. Norlin).

(Hermogenes 1.12.296–311; Sturm 3.17–18)

Note: V*enustas* [L. "charm"] is an additional name. This style is one species of the middle style. See *mediocris* below. Scaliger associates this decorated, florid style with poetry (4.9.463).

ethos [G. "custom, habit"] or *affectio* [L. "a state of mind or feeling"]
A style that reveals character

1. Description
Hermogenes explains,"[B]y 'character' I do not mean simply the revelation of Character that necessarily appears throughout the whole speech, like the complexion of a body, but also that which is naturally combined with the other styles [. . . .] The first kind of revelation of Character that I mentioned, that which naturally appears throughout the whole speech, involves attributing suitable and characteristic words and arguments to [. . .] persons. [. . .] But the kind of revelation of Character that we are now discussing, in all its various manifestations, can be employed anywhere in the speech like the other styles" and includes *apheleia* (simplicity), *glykytes* (sweetness), *drimytes* (subtlety), *epieikeia* (modesty), *aletheia* (sincerity), and *baryteta* (indignation).

(Hermogenes 2.2.321)

2. Example of modesty
"By both these statutes, then, the defendant Conon is amenable for what he has done; for he committed both assault and highway robbery. If I on my part have not chosen to proceed against him under these statutes, that should fairly prove that I am a peaceful and inoffensive person, not that he is any less a villain" (Demosthenes, *Against Conon* 24, trans. Murray).

(Hermogenes 2.6.345)

Note: Both Trapezuntius (579) and Sturm (3.6.543) apply to this style the adjective *moratus* [L. "adapted to the manners or character of a person or to the subject"]. See the entries for these individual styles above and below and *ethopoeia* above under Discoursal–genres.

eukrinea [G. "clear-sightedness"] or *claritas* [L. "clearness, brightness, splendor"]
The clear style
See *sapheneia* below.

Note: *Dilucidas* is an additional name.

exilitas [L. "thinness, meagerness, weakness"] or *tò xeron* [G. "aridity"]
The meager, dry style; the failed low style

1. Description

This style results when great events are trivialized through inadequate expression, an unconnected series of phrases goes on too long, and there is too much abruptness of detail or too much disguising of a subject's unpleasantness—features of *apocope*.

(Demetrius §236–39)

"Those who cannot skillfully employ that elegant simplicity of diction [. . .] arrive at a dry and bloodless kind of style which may aptly be called the Meager. [. . .] This language, to be sure, is mean and trifling, having missed the goal of the Simple type, which is speech composed of correct and well-chosen words."

(*Ad Herennium* 4.11.16)

2. Example

Saying about the cruel tyrant Phalaris, "Phalaris was a bit of a nuisance to the people of Acragas."

"Life is short, art long, opportunity fleeting, experience deceptive" (Hippocrates, *Aphorisms* 1.1, trans. Innes).

"But Demeter came uninvited and fought on our side in the sea battle, but Aristides not."

"Someone says of a man who lay with his wife's corpse: 'he does not lie with *her* again.'"

(Demetrius §237–39)

"Now this fellow came up to this lad in the baths. After that he says: 'Your slave boy here has beat me.' Afterwards this fellow called the lad names and shouted louder and louder, while a lot of people were there."

(*Ad Herennium* 4.11.16)

Note: Scaliger's name is *sicca* [L. "dry"] (4.23.489). Quintilian also applies the term *meiosis* to this meager and inadequate expression (8.3.51). See *meiosis* below under vices.

glaphyria [G. "elegance"]
The elegant, charming, graceful, polished style; the opposite of *cacozelias*

1. Description

Use as subjects gardens of the nymphs, marriage songs, loves, beauty, and spring. In content, use *charientismus*, proverbs (*paroimia*), *mythos*, *hyperbole*. In diction and composition, use beautiful, smooth, and noble words with *euphonia*, subtle rhythms, brevity (*syntomia*), *progressio* in word order, *metaphora*, personification (*prosopopoeia*), compound words, *heteroiosis* (*idiotikon*), neologisms (*pepoiemenon*), comparison (*parabole*), *metabole*, parody (*parodia*), allegory, adding the unexpected (*improvisam quiddam*), and figures such as *epizeuxis*, *anaphora*, *epanalepsis* (forms of *anadiplosis*).

(Demetrius §128)

2. Example

"And thus it was: Gynecia, with her two daughters, Cleophila, the shepherds Dorus and Dametas, being parted from the duke whom they left solitary at the lodge, came into the fair meadow appointed for their shepherdish pastimes. It was, indeed, a place of great delight, for through the midst of it there ran a sweet brook which did both hold the eye open with her beautiful streams and close the eye with the sweet purling noise it made upon the pebble-stones it ran over; the meadow itself yielding so liberally all sorts of flowers that it seemed to nourish a contention betwixt the colour and the smell whether in his kind were the more delightful. Round about the meadow, as if it had been to enclose a theatre, grew all such sorts of trees as either excellency of fruit, stateliness of growth, continual greenness, or poetical fancies have made at any time famous. In most part of which trees there had been framed by art such pleasant arbours that it became a gallery aloft, from one tree to the other, almost round about, which below yielded a perfect shadow, in those hot countries counted a great pleasure.

In this place, under one of the trees, the ladies sat down, inquiring many questions of young Dorus (now newly perceived of them), whilst the other shepherds made them ready to the pastimes. Dorus, keeping his eye still upon the princess Pamela, answered with such a trembling voice and abashed countenance, and oftentimes so far from the matter, that it was some sport to the ladies, thinking it had been want of education which made him so discountenanced with unwonted presence. But Cleophila (that saw in him the glass of her own misery), taking the fair hand of Philoclea, and with more than womanish ardency kissing it, began to say these words: 'O love, since thou art so changeable in men's estates, how art thou so constant in their torments?'" (Sidney, *The Old Arcadia*, book 1, 41–42).

(example mine)

Note: Demetrius points out that this style is opposite to the forceful style or *deinotes* (§258). It also seems it could be a species of *glykytes* below.

glykytes [G. "sweetness, pleasantness"] or *suavitas* [L. "sweetness, pleasantness"] or *jucunditas* [L. "agreeableness, delight"]

The style of sweetness, gracefulness, prettiness, and pleasure

1. Description

This style results from thoughts that deal with *mythos, fabula, ekphrasis* (especially which appeals to all the senses), *chronographia, notatio, epainos* of ourselves or topics that we value, *empsychosis* or *animatio*. Approaches are the same as purity and simplicity, with poetic references or reminiscences (*parechesis*) that are woven into one's own text (*paraplokas toiematon*) and proverbs (*paroemia*). For diction, use *epitheton* and striking words and turns of phrase (per the subtle style). Figures are those of simplicity and purity. Word order is like that in beauty (*kallos*)—almost metrical—and cadences should be solemn and stately. This style creates the beauty of simplicity.

(Hermogenes 2.4.330–339; Sturm 3.21.698–708)

2. Example

"First, then, in ancient times, as we are told by tradition, in this court alone [the Court of Areopagus] the gods condescended both to render and to demand satisfaction for homicide, and to sit in judgement upon contending litigants,—Poseidon, according to legend, deigning to demand justice from Ares on behalf of his son Halirrothius, and the twelve gods to adjudicate between the Eumenides and Orestes" (Demosthenes, *Against Aristocrates* 66, trans. Vince).

"It is indeed a lovely spot for a rest. This plane is very tall and spreading, and the agnus-castus splendidly high and shady, in full bloom too, filling the neighbourhood with the finest possible fragrance. And the spring which runs under the plane;

how beautifully cool its water is to the feet. The figures and other offerings show that the place is sacred to Achelous and some of the nymphs. See too how wonderfully delicate and sweet the air is, throbbing in response to the shrill chorus of the cicadas—the very voice of summer. But the most exquisite thing of all is the way the grass slopes gently upward to provide perfect comfort for the head as one lies at length." (Plato, *Phaedrus* 230b, trans. Hamilton)

(Hermogenes 2.4.330, 332)

Note: This style is a species of the middle style. See *mediocris* below. Patterson points out that this style, along with beauty, depends for its effects upon schemes more than tropes, and upon "figures which are either purely 'auricular' or figures of 'copious amplification, or enlargement of language [which] do also contain a certain sweet and melodious manner of speech'" (Puttenham 206). In other words, these are figures that appeal more to the ear than to the mind (125–26).

gorgotes [G. "rapidity"] or *celeritas* [L. "swiftness"] or *velocitas* [L. "rapidity"]

The speedy and concise style; the opposite of *hyptiotes*

1. Description

   To create this style, use *kommata, apostrophe, hypostrophe, epiploken, epitrechon, asyndeton, exallage, anaphora, antistrophe, symploke, plagiasmos, systrophe,* immediate *antapodosis,* short *epembole,* and trochaic meter.

   (Hermogenes 2.1.312–20)

2. Example

   "What therefore should I do? Should I not go? Not even now when I am summoned to the other side? She excluded me, she recalled me, should I return? Not if she begs me." (adapted from Terence, *Eunuchus* 1.1.45–48)

   (Sturm 3.19.682)

Note: Trapezuntius adds *subcontinuatio, interpretatio, incisio, interrogatio, adversio* and *excusitatio* as schemes that create *celeritas* (577–78). *Celeritas* is also a synonym for *epitrochasmus*. See *epitrochasmus* above under Pragmatical–idea figures.

hyptiotes [G. "supine, careless, negligent"]

The languid style, a vice; the opposite of *gorgotes*

1. Description

   Lacking vigor, bite, and wit. Languishing and slow.

2. Example

   "There dwelleth not far hence, one Allinus, that mortally hateth my father, and all that belong unto him, whose son Ornatus was, whom if I should commend, you might think me too cruel to refuse his love so unkindly, only thus much I will say of him, he was every way worthy to be beloved, though my fancy could never be drawn to like of him: who upon what occasion I know not, but as Adellena told me, made his love known to her, which she likewise told me of: but I refusing to hear her, answered her plainly, that I was greatly offended with her, for making any such motion: and forbade her forever to speak of him again. But now this day you have heard what she hath told me, which I can hardly believe to be true, or that Ornatus would be so rash without wisdom to enter into such extremes. But if it be so (as I would it were not) it grieveth me for him, and I wish that I had not refused to hear his suit, though I am not willing to yield thereto. For I would not have it said of me, nor my name so much blazed, that my cruelty procured him to that extremity, though his wisdom might have foreseen such mischief, and he more moderately have tempered his love.

Ornatus taking occasion said, I neither know this gentleman, nor how constant his love was, but thus much my mind persuadeth me, that had not his love been great, he would not have grieved so much at your unkindness: but love is of this force, that it turneth the mind into extremes, or utterly breaketh the heart: which force belike it had in him, else would he not have done himself so much harm. But it may be (as you say) Ornatus hath not done himself outrage, but only abandoning company, liveth in despair and so meaneth to die: which if it be so, then in my fancy, you might do well to let him by some means understand that you did pity him. Stay there, quoth Artesia, you must first know, whether I can do it or no: for if I should say I pity with my lips, and he not find it so, it would drive him to more despair, and therefore I will leave off to do that, until I can find whether I can do so or no" (Emanuel Ford, *Ornatus and Artesia*, chapter 5, D2v).

(Sturm 3.19.682; example mine)

Note: This slack style Scaliger refers to as *paresis* [G. "a slackening of strength, paralysis, neglect"], a vice opposite to the virtue *energeia* (3.27.294). See *energeia* below under virtues.

katharotes [G. "purity, cleanness, correctness"] or *puritas* [L. "cleanness, purity"]

Purity and leanness; the opposite of *peribole*

1. Description

   See *sapheneia* below.

2. Example

   "I shall relate the facts to you from the beginning as well as I can. My father, men of the jury, is Sopaeus; all who sail to the Pontus know that his relations with Satyrus are so intimate that he is ruler of an extensive territory and has charge of that ruler's entire forces. Having heard reports both of this state and of the other lands where Greeks live, I desired to travel abroad. And so my father loaded two ships with grain, gave me money, and sent me off on a trading expedition and at the same time to see the world. Pythodorus, the Phoenician, introduced Pasion to me and I opened an account at his bank" (Isocrates, *Trapeziticus* 3–4, trans. Van Hook).

(Hermogenes 1.3.229)

Note: *Hellenismos* and *latinitas*, in their original designations as correct Greek or correct Latin, are synonyms here, as Sturm points out (3.6.545). See virtues below.

krypsis [G. "concealed, hidden"]

A style moderately wrought, half way between *epimeleia* and *ameles*

"The causes and motives of seditions are: innovation in religion, taxes, alteration of laws and customs, breaking of privileges, general oppression, advancement of unworthy persons, strangers, dearths, disbanded soldiers, factions grown desperate, and whatsoever in offending people joineth and knitteth them in a common cause.

The first remedy or prevention is to remove by all means possible that material cause of sedition whereof we spake, which is want and poverty in the estate. To which purpose serveth the opening and well-balancing of trade; the cherishing of manufactures; the banishing of idleness; the repressing of waste and excess by sumptuary laws; the improvement and husbanding of the soil; the regulating of prices of things vendible; the moderating of taxes and tributes; and the like. Generally, it is to be foreseen that the population of a kingdom (especially if it be not mown down by wars) do not exceed the stock of the kingdom which should maintain them. Neither is the population to be reckoned only by number: for a small number, that spend more and earn less, do wear out an estate sooner than a greater number that live lower and gather more. Therefore the multiplying of nobility and other degrees of quality, in an over-proportion to the common people, doth speedily bring a state to necessity; and so doth likewise an overgrown clergy, for they bring nothing to the stock; and in like manner when more are bred scholars than preferments can take off" (Bacon, "Of Seditions and Troubles," *The Essays* §15).

(Sturm 3.17.668; example mine)

Note: *Krypsios* is the proper spelling. Sturm's name for this style probably results from its character as neither too obviously fashioned nor too obviously unfashioned and hence as "natural" or unseen, an ideal achieved when one uses art to hide art. It is one kind of middle style.

lamprotes [G. "brilliancy, splendor, distinctness"] or *splendor* [L. "brilliance, lustre, brightness"]
The brilliant or a splendid style

1. Description
We achieve brilliance when we have confidence in what we are saying, we describe remarkable events and glorious deeds, we introduce the thought directly, deliver an unbroken narration, speak nobly (i.e., swear an oath [*orcos*]), use *anairesis* and *thesis*, *comparatio*, *apostasis*, *asyndeton*, *plagiasmos*, *auxesis* (amplification), *ekphrasis*, *merismos*, *macrocola*, and cadences typical of solemnity.

(Hermogenes 1.9.264–69; Sturm 3.12.604–18)

2. Example
"When an army of traitorous citizens, herded together for secret crime, had prepared for the country a most cruel and terrible end, and when, for the overthrow and destruction of the state, Catiline had been made commander in the camp and Lentulus commander in these very temples and dwellings, I the consul, by my precaution and my toil, at the risk of my life, without a riot, without a levy, without arms, without an army, by the arrest and confession of five men only, freed the city from conflagration, the citizens from murder, Italy from devastation, the state from ruin. I saved the lives of all the citizens, the peace of the world, this city, the home of us all, the citadel of foreign kings and nations, the light of mankind, the home of empire, by the punishment of five mad, abandoned men" (Cicero, *Pro Sulla* 11.33, trans. Lord).

(Sturm 3.12.604)

Note: Trapezuntius also calls this style *illustris oratio* (531, 549) and Scaliger gives as an alternate name *nitor* (4.1.444). This style is one kind of *megethos*, or the grand style. Erasmus even conflates this style with the grand style (*Eccl.* 3.98.905). See *oratio grandis* below.

oratio grandis [L. "great, abundant, full speech"] or *gravis* [L. "heavy, weighty, ponderous"] or *megaloprepes* [G. "magnificent"]; also called *megethos* [G. "greatness, magnitude"], *axioma* [G. "dignity"], *onkos* [G. "majesty"], *sublimitas* [L. "loftiness, height"], *magnitudo* [L. "greatness"], or *amplitudo* [L. "amplitude, fullness"]
The grand, sublime, noble, mighty and full style; amplitude, grandeur; the high style

1. Description
The characteristics of style that produce grandeur include *semnotes* (solemnity), *trachytes* (asperity), *sphodrotes* (vehemence), *lamprotes* (brilliance), *akme* (florescence) and *peribole* (abundance) or *mestotes* (fullness).

(Hermogenes 1.5.242)

"The orator of the [grand] style is magnificent, opulent, stately and ornate; he undoubtedly has the greatest power." He is brilliant, fluent, copious, impetuous and fiery, whose "eloquence rushes along with the roar of a mighty stream" and "has power to sway men's minds and move them in every possible way." He discusses "lofty matters impressively," either "storm[ing] the feelings" or "creep[ing] in," either "implant[ing] new ideas" or "uproot[ing] the old." This orator shows "splendid power of thought and majesty of diction." He is "forceful, versatile, copious and grave," sometimes through "a rough, severe, harsh style, without regular construction or rounded periods" and sometimes through "a smooth, ordered sentence-structure with a periodic cadence."

(Cicero, *Orator* 28.97–99; 5.20)

"A discourse will be composed in the Grand style if to each idea are applied the most ornate words that can be found for it, whether literal or figurative; if impressive thoughts are chosen, such as are used in Amplification and Appeal to Pity; and if we employ figures [*exornationes*] of thought and figures of diction which have grandeur."

(*Ad Herennium* 4.8.11–12)

"The great, the noble, the mighty, and the full kind of inditing, with an incredible and a certain divine power of oration, is used in weighty causes: for it hath with an ample majesty very garnished words: proper, translated, and grave sentences, which are handled in *amplificatio* and *commiseratio*: and it hath exornations both of words and sentences: whereunto in orations they ascribe very great strength and gravity. And they that use this kind be vehement, various, copious, grave, well and thoroughly appointed to move and turn men to their purpose. This kind did Cicero use in the oration for Aulus Cluencius, for Sylla, for Titus Annius Milo, for Caius Rabirius, against Catiline, against Verres, [and] against Piso."

(Sherry [1555] H.iii.v–iiii.r)

2. Example

"'Who of you, pray, men of the jury, could devise a punishment drastic enough for him who has plotted to betray the fatherland to our enemies? What offence can compare with this crime, what punishment can be found commensurate with this offence? Upon those who had done violence to a freeborn youth, outraged the mother of a family, wounded, or—basest crime of all—slain a man, our ancestors exhausted the catalogue of extreme punishments; while for this most savage and impious villainy they bequeathed no specific penalty. In other wrongs, indeed, injury arising from another's crime extends to one individual, or only to a few; but the participants in this crime are plotting, with one stroke, the most horrible catastrophes for the whole body of citizens. O such men of savage hearts! O such cruel designs! O such human beings bereft of human feeling! What have they dared to do, what can they now be planning? They are planning how our enemies, after uprooting our fathers' graves, and throwing down our walls, shall with triumphant cry rush into the city; how when they have despoiled the temples of the gods, slaughtered the Conservatives and dragged all others off into slavery, and when they have subjected matrons and freeborn youths to a foeman's lust, the city, put to the torch, shall collapse in the most violent of conflagrations! They do not think, these scoundrels, that they have fulfilled their desires to the utmost, unless they have gazed upon the piteous ashes of our most holy fatherland. Men of the jury, I cannot in words do justice to the shamefulness of their act; yet that disquiets me but little, for you have no need of me. Indeed your own hearts, overflowing with patriotism, readily tell you to drive this man, who would have betrayed the fortunes of all, headlong from this commonwealth, which he would have buried under the impious domination of the foulest of enemies.'"

(*Ad Herennium* 4.8.11–12)

Note: Cicero also describes this style as *grandiloqui* (*Or.* 5.20) or *vehemens* and claims persuasion as its primary function (*Or.* 21.69). He seems to have combined the two styles *megaloprepes* and *deinos* that Demetrius wishes to keep separate (§36). To Hermogenes, *megethos* becomes a subtype of *deinotes*. See *deinotes* above. Demetrius considers *megaloprepes* the opposite of *ischnos*, the plain style (§36). Quintilian gives the Greek *adron* as a synonym (12.10.58), associates the grand style with *pathopopeia* (8.10.59–61), and cites Ulysses as the character in the *Iliad* who orates in the high style (12.10.64). Trapezuntius associates Hermogenes's *megethos* with the Roman high or grand style (531). Scaliger says that *dignitas*, *gravitas* and *vehementia* are characteristics of this grand style (4.18.483). See the other entries for these terms above and below.

oratio mediocris [L. "moderate speech"] or *floridus* [L. "flowery"]

The temperate, middle style

1. Description

Between the high and the plain is the "tempered style, which uses neither the intellectual appeal of the latter class nor the fiery force of the former; [. . .] bringing nothing except ease and uniformity, or at most adding a few posies as in a garland, and diversifying the whole speech with simple ornaments of thought and diction." In this style for pleasure (*delectando*), "there is perhaps a minimum of vigour, and a maximum of charm. For it is richer than the unadorned style, but plainer than the ornate and opulent style. All the ornaments are appropriate to this type of oration, and it possesses charm to a high degree." The speaker can use metaphor, hypallage or metonymy, catachresis, and allegory. "This speaker will likewise develop his arguments with breadth and erudition, and use commonplaces without undue emphasis. [. . .] It is commonly the philosophic schools which produce such orators: [. . .] It is, as a matter of fact, a brilliant and florid, highly coloured and polished style in which all the charms of language and thought are intertwined. The sophists are the source from which all this has flowed into the forum[.]"

(Cicero, *Orator* 6.21; 21.69; 26.91–27.97)

"The intermediate style will have more frequent recourse to metaphor and will make a more attractive use of figures, while it will introduce alluring digressions, will be neat in rhythm and pleasing in its reflexions [*sententia*]; its flow, however, will be gentle, like that of a river whose waters are clear, but overshadowed by the green banks on either side."

(Quintilian 12.10.60)

"The mean and temperate kind of inditing standeth of the lower, and yet not of the lowest, and most common words and sentences. And it is rightly called the temperate kind of speaking, because it is very nigh unto the small and to the great kind[s], following a moderation and temper betwixt them both. And it followeth (as you would say) in one tenor distinguishing all the oration with small ornaments both of words and sentences. Cicero useth this for the law of Manilius, for Aulus Cecinna, for Marcus Marcellus, and most of all in his books of Offices."

(Sherry [1555] H.v.r)

2. Example

"First of all, Nature has endowed every species of living creature with the instinct of self-preservation, of avoiding what seems likely to cause injury to life or limb, and of procuring and providing everything needful for life—food, shelter, and the like. A common property of all creatures is also the reproductive instinct (the purpose of which is the propagation of the species) and also a certain amount of concern for their offspring.

But the most marked difference between man and beast is this: the beast, just as far as it is moved by the senses and with very little perception of past or future, adapts itself to that alone which is present at the moment; while man—because he is endowed with reason, by which he comprehends the chain of consequences, perceives the causes of things, understands the relation of cause to effect and of effect to cause, draws analogies, and connects and associates the present and the future—easily surveys the course of his whole life and makes the necessary preparations for its conduct" (Cicero, *De Officiis* 1.4.11, trans. Miller).

(example mine)

Note: *Enmeson* is an alternate name. Cicero also calls this style *temperatus* (*Or.* 6.21) or *modicum* (*Or.* 21.69); Quintilian adds *medium* and *antheron* (12.10.58) and associates it with *delectare* and *ethopoeia* (8.10.59–60). This style seems to correspond with *epimeleia* of the Hermogenean forms. See *epimeleia* above. Quintilian says that Homer assigns to Nestor this middle style of "speech sweeter than honey" (12.10.64). Scaliger says this *oratio aequabile* has both *rotunditas* [L. "roundness, smoothness"] and *volubilitas* [L. "fluency"] (4.22.485). The middle style is most often defined as a register midway between the high and the low. See *oratio grandis* above and *subtilitas* below. The high, middle and low styles form the *genera dicendi* (kinds of speaking) in the Latin tradition.

oratio soluta [L. "loose speech"] or *logadis* [G. "having to do with words"]

The loose, disconnected, discontinuous style

1. Description

To present ideas without seeming order or rhythm, but in such a way that "those who use it could be considered, not stupid, but on the whole wise."

(Cicero, *Orator* 71.236)

This "looser texture, such as is found in dialogues and letters, except when they deal with some subject above their natural level, such as philosophy, politics or the like [. . .] has its own peculiar rhythms," does not demand *hiatus*, compactness, or tight structural cohesion, but still has cohesion.

(Quintilian 9.4.19–21)

The loose style is not bound by well-arranged rhythms, fixed periodic structure, or continuous and connected thoughts and sentences. It is appropriate for conversation, epistles, and judicial oratory when we wish to copy conversation.

(Aquila §18)

2. Example

"For some time now I would have responded to your letter, except that a certain shame of denying to you something held me back in the very threshold of friendship. And moreover that which you were asking was of a sort that even they who were dealing with me on your behalf understood could not be offered by me conveniently. For I was never a good poet, nor did I think it reasonable enough to be involved in an argument of the sort that was proposed by you to me, nor to be held bound by an agreement, embraced many years ago, due to my old age and life. And so, since I neither wanted to say no to you nor to give in to you, my utterance stuck, impeded by a certain roughness. Now, knowing that you have accepted my excuse and that you moreover so desire something of literary quality from me, I will not fail in my duty in this regard. And since there is no other argument for writing something now, I would ask of you that you pardon me because I could not gratify you who were desiring so much, and, in other matters when it will be advantageous to you, that you test my good will toward you. Believe me, with one little word from you, you will get in the future whatever I can provide." (M. Antonius Muretus to Scipio Montius, a distinguished man, on April 1, 1584; trans. Boswell)

(Muret 437, 450)

Note: This style is one opposite of the periodic style or *circumscriptio* (see above). It corresponds to Lanham's "running" style (*Analyzing Prose* 52–56) and is characterized by *epitrechon, episynapsis, epembole, appositio*, and *epiploke*. See these entries above under syntactical figures.

pathetikon [G. "impassioned, pathetic"]

An emotional style

"It is pitiable to be ejected from all one's possessions, still more pitiable to be ejected unjustly; galling to be deceived by a kinsman; it is a calamity to be driven out of one's property, a still greater calamity to be driven out in disgrace; it is disastrous to be slain by a brave and honourable man, still more disastrous to be slain by one whose voice has been prostituted in the trade of a public crier; it is mortifying to be conquered by one's equal or superior, still more mortifying to be conquered by one's inferior or by one who is beneath us; it is grievous to be handed over with one's property to another, still more grievous to be handed over to an enemy; it is awful to have to plead for one's life, still more awful to plead before having heard the charge. Quinctius has turned his eyes everywhere, he has tried all the chances of safety; not only has he been unable to find a praetor from whom he could obtain the kind of trial he wanted; he has not even been able to get any assistance from the friends of Naevius, at whose feet he often and for a long time prostrated himself, begging them by the immortal gods either to contend with him according to law or at any rate to inflict injustice upon him unaccompanied by disgrace. Finally, he faced the haughty looks of his enemy Sextus Naevius himself; he seized his hand with tears—that hand experienced in proscribing the estates of his kinsmen; he implored him by the ashes of his dead brother, in the name of the relationship which united them and of his own wife and children, whose nearest relative is Publius Quinctius, to show at length some compassion, to have some consideration, if not for their relationship, at least for his age; if not for the man himself, at least for humanity; and to come to some arrangement with him on any terms, provided only they were endurable and his reputation were left unimpaired. Repulsed by Naevius himself, having received no assistance from his enemy's friends, harassed and browbeaten by all the magistrates, he has no one to appeal to but yourself, Aquilius; to you he commits himself, to you he entrusts all his fortunes and everything he possesses; in your hands he places his reputation and all the hopes of the life that still remains to him. Worried by numerous affronts, tormented by many wrongs, he takes refuge with you, not disgraced but in misery; driven out from a rich estate, assailed by every kind of indignity, seeing this man lording it over his paternal heritage, unable to provide a dowry for his marriageable daughter, he has, in spite of this, done nothing to belie his past life." (Cicero, *Pro Quinctio* 31.95–98, trans. Freese)

(Sturm 3.23.719)

Note: This passage is Cicero's peroration, where *pathopoeia* is expected. This style corresponds with *pathopoeia* (see Discoursal–genres), but I list it here because Sturm uses the term to refer to a style.

peribole [G. "an enclosure, circuit"] or *mestotes* [G. "fullness"] or *circumductio* [L. "a leading or conducting around"] or *plenitudo* [L. "fullness"]

The abundant, full, copious style; an opposite of *katharotes* and of *brevitas*

1. Description

To create this style, bring in arguments from every source, such as comparisons, opposites, the genus, the whole and the species or parts, the causes, the consequences, and so forth. *Paradeigma* and *enthymema* are created by these means. Hermogenes admits, "[A] discussion of this would entail a section on proofs." Even add points that are unnecessary, such as discussing the genus to which a species belongs when talking about the species (*thesis*). Also bring in a counter-example, *ekphrasis, merismos, proslepsis*, or *peristasis*. Use *anastrophe* of events, *epembole, auxesis* (amplification), qualification (*attributio* or *descriptio*), and *anastrophe ton pistis*. In reference to diction, use *isodynamodeta* and *synonymia*. Other figures include *aparithmesis, epimone, epanalepsis* of idea, *protimesis, hypothesis, plagiasmos, hypostasis, merismos, emphasis, ekparasynaptikon*, delayed *antapodosis, emperibolon, episynapsis, arsis* and *thesis, dirimens copulatio*, and *systrophe*.

(Hermogenes 1.11.278–95; Sturm 3.14.630–16.664)

2. Example

"Now seeing that all Greece was in such a plight, and still unconscious of a gathering and ever-growing evil, what was the right policy for Athens to adopt, and the right action for her to take? That is the question, men of Athens, which you ought to consider, and that is the issue on which I ought to be called to account; for I was the man who took up a firm position in that department of your public affairs. Was it the duty of our city, Aeschines, to abase her pride, to lower her dignity, to rank herself with Thessalians and Dolopians, to help Philip to establish his supremacy over Greece, to annihilate the glories and the prerogatives of our forefathers? Or, if she rejected that truly shameful policy, was she to stand by and permit aggressions which she must have long foreseen, and knew would succeed if none should intervene? I would now like to ask the man who censures our past conduct most severely, what party he would have wished our city to join. The party that shares the guilt of all the disasters and dishonors that have befallen Greece,—the party, as one may say, of the Thessalians and their associates? Or that which permitted those disasters in the hope of selfish gain, the party in which we may include the Arcadians, the Messenians, and the Argives? Why, the fate of many, indeed of all, of those nations is worse than ours. For if, after his victory, Philip had at once taken himself off, and relapsed into inactivity, harassing neither his own allies nor any other Greeks, there might have been some reason for finding fault with the opponents of his enterprises; but seeing that, wherever he could, he destroyed the prestige, the authority, the independence, and even the constitution of every city alike, who can deny that you chose the most honourable of all policies when you followed my advice?

To resume my argument: I ask you, Aeschines, what was the duty of Athens when she perceived that Philip's purpose was to establish a despotic empire over all Greece? What language, what counsels, were incumbent upon an advisor of the people at Athens, of all places in the world, when I was conscious that, from the dawn of her history to the day when I first ascended the tribune, our country had ever striven for primacy, and honour, and renown, and that to serve an honourable ambition and the common welfare of Greece she had expended her treasure and the lives of her sons far more generously than any other Hellenic state fighting only for itself; and knowing as I did that our antagonist Philip himself, contending for empire and supremacy, had endured the loss of his eye, the fracture of his collar-bone, the mutilation of his hand and his leg, and was ready to sacrifice to the fortune of war any and every part of his body, if only the life of the shattered remnant should be a life of honour and renown? [. . .] Tell me; what ought I to have done? I put the question to you, Aeschines, dismissing for the moment everything else [. . . .] Was it, or was it not, right that some man of

Grecian race should stand forward to stop these aggressions? (Demosthenes, *On the Crown* 63–71, trans. Vince)

(Hermogenes 1.11.286)

Note: Hermogenes identifies this quality as one type of grandeur or *megethos*. See *oratio grandis* above. For its stylistic opposites, see *katharotes* and *brevitas* above.

psychrotes [G. "coldness, flatness, lifelessness, insipidity, vanity"] or *frigidum* [L. "the cold"] or *sufflata* [L. "puffed up, inflated"] or *spumosus* [L. "foamy, bombastic"] or *euteleia* [G. "cheapness"]

The swollen, undignified, bombastic style; frigidity, bad taste; the failed grand style and the opposite of *deinotes*

1. Description

"Frigidity is defined by Theophrastus as 'that which exceeds its appropriate form of expression'" and may occur in thought, diction, or composition.

(Demetrius §114)

This style appears to be forceful, but is not really so. Thoughts are shallow and commonplace, but the diction is rough, vehement, and solemn; the figures and other aspects of style are typical of beauty, fluorescence, and solemnity; and the approaches include unjustified *epitimesis*, *convinciari*, and other vehement attacks. In addition, approaches from the other styles are employed at the wrong time and place.

(Hermogenes 2.9.377–78)

"[To t]hose who are inexperienced, turgid and inflated language often seems majestic—when a thought is expressed either in new or in archaic words, or in clumsy metaphors, or in diction more impressive than the theme demands."

(Ad Herennium 4.10.15)

"[An oration] which swelleth and is puffed up, which useth strange words hardly translated, or too old, and that be now long since left off from use of daily talk, or more grave than the thing requireth."

(Sherry [1550] 23)

2. Examples

a. In thought

One writer grotesquely elaborates on Homer, *Odyssey* 9.481, by describing the rock Cyclops throws at Odysseus' ship with "as the rock was rushing along, goats were browsing on it."

(Demetrius §115)

"*torva mimalloneis inplerunt cornua bombis*" (Persius, *Satire* 1.99).
("the savage horns filled with Bacchic buzzings")

(Sturm 3.26.749)

b. In diction

Instead of "a cup without a base is not put on the table," say "an unbased cup is not tabled" (Sophocles, *Triptolemus*, fragment 611, trans. Innes).

(Demetrius §114)

"'For he who by high treason betrays his native land will not have paid a condign penalty albeit hurtl'd into gulfs Neptunian. So punish ye this man, who hath builded mounts of war, destroyed the plains of peace.'"

(Ad Herennium 4.10.15)

c. In composition

"A line of verse in prose is out of place, and as frigid as too many syllables to the line in verse or as meter which is too regular."

(Demetrius §118)

The style of the sophists, i.e., of Gorgias, Polus, and Meno.

(Hermogenes 2.9.377)

Note: Scaliger's name is *pingue* ["fat, grease"] (4.24.490). This style corresponds with *bomphiologia* listed under vices below. Melanchthon associates this bad style with the Asiatic style (*Elem.* 64v).

sapheneia [G. "clearness, distinctness"] or *perspicuitas* [L. "transparency, clearness"]

The pure, clear, open style; the opposite of obscurity

1. Description

This perspicuous style is created by the virtues of *katharotes* (purity) and *eukrineia* (clarity), which can also be considered as separate styles. To achieve *katharotes*, use simple *diegema* (without *amplificatio* or *peristasis*), *orthotes*, *hellenismos* or *latinitas*, and begin sentences with iambic or trochaic meter (which are most similar to conversation), but mix meters so the style does not become strictly metrical. To achieve *eukrineia*, use common *sententia*, *katastasis*, *propositio*, *digestio*, *symplerosis*, *horismus*, *aparithmesis*, *merismos*, *erotesis kata diastasin*, and *epanalepsis* of idea, and follow the natural order of events or arguments, placing the *antithesis* (counter-proposition) before the *lysis*.

(Hermogenes 1.3.227–4.240; Sturm 3.6.545–64)

2. Example

"There is, for instance, Sannio, the trainer of the tragic choruses, who was convicted of shirking military service and so found himself in trouble. After that misfortune he was hired by a chorus-master—Theozotides, if I am not mistaken—who was keen to win a victory in the tragedies. Well, at first the rival masters were indignant and threatened to debar him, but when they saw that the theatre was full and the crowd assembled for the contest, they hesitated, they gave way, and no one laid a finger on him. One can see that the forbearance which piety inspires in every one of you is such that Sannio has been training choruses ever since, not hindered even by his private enemies, much less by any of the chorus-masters" (Demosthenes, *Against Meidias* 58–59, trans. Vince).

(Hermogenes 1.11.289)

Note: Sturm notes that *sapheneia* is called a virtue by Aristotle, a figure by the teacher of Herennianus, and a form or idea by Hermogenes (3.6.545). Hermogenes also calls this style a virtue in his *Progymnasmata* §10 (See Kennedy, *Progymnasmata* 86). This style corresponds to *perspicuitas* (see below under virtues) and is a quality that belongs to all good styles, Hermogenes says (1.1.226).

semnotes [G. "solemnity, dignity"] or *dignitas* [L. "dignity"]

Solemnity; the opposite of simplicity

1. Description

Solemn thoughts are those about religion, metaphysics, science, philosophy, ethics and high accomplishment. Solemn approaches include direct statements made without hesitation, the use of *allegoria*, *ekphrasis*, and *mystikos hypostamenein.* Solemn diction requires broad sounds, long syllables, long vowels, *metaphora*, and the noun style (*onomastikon*). The figures that create solemnity are the same as those for purity (*katharotes*), along with *apophansis* and *epicrisis*. Like purity, solemnity requires short *kola* that sound like aphorisms (*paroemia*), *clausulae* that end with a complete foot and preferably a noun with three syllables, and rhythms that are dactylic, anapestic, paeonic, and epitritic.

(Hermogenes 1.6.243–54)

2. Example

"You say that I was afraid of death. But the truth is, that I could not look upon even immortality as desirable, if it was to be achieved at my country's cost; far less could I choose to die, and carry my country with me to perdition. For I have always thought—call me a fool if you will—that those who have sacrificed their lives for the state have not died so much as achieved immortality" (Cicero, *Pro Plancio* 37.90, trans. Watts).

(Trapezuntius 536)

Note: *Semnotes* is one kind of *megethos*, the grand style. See *oratio grandis* above.

sphodrotes [G. "vehemence, violence"] or *vehementia* [L. "vehemence"] or *acrimonia* [L. "acrimony, sharpness, austerity"]

Vehemence, acrimony; the opposite of modesty or *epikeikeia*

1. Description

This style is directed against persons less important than ourselves or those the audience delights to hear criticized. The thoughts involve criticism and refutation. The approach is open and straightforward. Hence, this style is created by means of *epitimesis, epicrisis, antirrhesis* and *orthotes,* The diction requires *skleros* or *trachea*, *epitheton,* and *onomatopoeia.* Figures include *apostrophe, interrogatio, elenktikon, deiktikon, metaphor, synecdoche, hyperbole, aganactisis, ekphonesis,* and *parrhesia*. Clauses are *kommata* with pauses after single words, or *articulus.* Cadence and rhythm are identical to those of asperity.

(Hermogenes 1.8.261–64; Sturm 1.17.45; 3.11.598–603)

2. Examples

"Therefore, will this man gain his release, this man who is the scapegoat, the public pest, whom anyone when he saw him would shun as a bad omen rather than address him?" (Demosthenes, *Against Aristogeiton* 80, trans. Wooten)

"Why, then, wretch, do you spread slanders? Why do you compose speeches? Why do you not take a dose of hellebore?" (Demosthenes, *On the Crown* 121, trans. Wooten)

(Hermogenes 1.8.261–64)

Note: Quintilian treats *acrimonia* as a method of embellishment (8.3.89). Trapezuntius and Scaliger associate *vehementia* with *akme.* See *akme* above. *Vehementia* is also a quality of grandeur. See *oratio grandis* above.

subtilitas [L. "fineness, thinness, keenness, acuteness, exactness, subtlety"] or *ischnos* [G. "spare, plain, unadorned"]

The low, pressed, filed, precise, urbane, plain, and common style

1. Description

In the plain style, which is appropriate for proof, the orator follows "ordinary usage," ignores the "bonds of rhythm," is "loose but not rambling," carefully uses *hiatus* and short and concise clauses, excludes "all noticeable ornament," and seeks for purity, clarity, and propriety. "He will employ an abundance of apposite maxims" and "will be modest" in his use of metaphor, neologism, archaism, and schemes of symmetry. But "[t]here are, as a matter of fact, a good many ornaments suited to the frugality of this very orator," mostly figures of thought, which are less obvious and which he will use "somewhat harshly," even though "he will be rather subdued in voice" and "will employ only slight movements of the body." He will "reveal in a well-bred manner the feeling with which each thought is uttered." This orator will use both humor and wit with propriety, "the former in a graceful and charming narrative, the latter in hurling the shafts of ridicule." He will be "to the point, explaining everything and making every point clear rather than impressive, using a refined, concise style [. . . .] Within this class some were adroit but unpolished and intentionally resembled untrained and unskillful speakers; others had the same dryness of style, but were neater, elegant, even brilliant and to a slight degree ornate."

(Cicero, *Orator* 21.69–26.90; 5.20)

"[I]t is mainly in the plain style that we shall state our facts and advance our proofs, though it should be borne in mind that this style will often be sufficiently full in itself without any assistance whatever from the other two [ie., middle and high]."

(Quintilian 12.10.59)

"[I]t is a kind of oration that is let down even to the most used custom of pure and clear speaking. It hath fine sentences, subtle, [and] sharp, teaching all things and making them more plain, not more ample. And in this same kind (as Cicero saith in his Orator) some be crafty, but unpolished, and of purpose like the rude and unskillful. Other [features include being] trim, that is, merry conceited, flourishing also, and a little garnished. Cicero used this kind in his philosophical disputations, in the oration for Quintius, [and] for Roscius the comedy player; and Terence and Plautus in their Comedies."

(Sherry [1555] H.iiii.r-v)

2. Examples

"Now our friend happened to enter the baths, and, after washing, was beginning to be rubbed down. Then, just as he decided to go down into the pool, suddenly this fellow turned up. 'Say, young chap,' said he, ' your slave boys have just beat me; you must make it good.' The young man grew red, for at his age he was not used to being hailed by a stranger. This creature started to shout the same words, and more, in a louder voice. With difficulty the youth replied: 'Well, but let me look into the matter.' Right then the fellow cries out in that tone of his that might well force blushes from any one; this is how aggressive and harsh it is—a tone certainly not practised in the neighbourhood of the Sundial, I would say, but backstage, and in places of that kind. The young man was embarrassed. And no wonder, for his ears still rang with the scolding of his tutor, and he was not used to abusive language of this kind. For where would he have seen a buffoon, with not a blush left, who thought of himself as having no good name to lose, so that he could do anything he liked without damage to his reputation."

(*Ad Herennium* 4.10.14)

"But let us examine the point at issue. Certain persons thought that the name of war ought not to be in the motion. They preferred to call it 'tumult,' showing their ignorance not only of the facts but of words. For while a war can exist without a tumult, a tumult cannot exist without a war. For what else is a tumult but a commotion so serious that fear beyond the ordinary arises from it—that being the origin of the word 'tumult.'[. . .] And that a tumult is something more serious than a war can be inferred from the fact that exemptions are valid in a war but not a tumult. [. . .] After all, there is no halfway house between war and peace. If 'tumult' does not come under the heading of war, it must come under the heading of peace—than which nothing more incongruous can well be said or thought.

But I have dwelt too long upon a word. Let us rather look at substance, Members of the Senate—which indeed I have noticed is sometimes apt to be made worse by a word. We do not want this to be seen as a war. [. . .]

Decimus Brutus is under attack, but it is not a war! Mutina under siege, but that is no war either! Gaul is being laid waste: can any peace be more assured?" (Cicero, *Philippic* 8.2–5, trans. Bailey)

(example mine)

Note: Adjectives that describe this style include *attenuata, humile, infima, subtile, tenue* and *bare.* Quintilian associates the low style with *docere* or teaching (8.10.59), uses *gracile* as an additional adjective describing this style (12.10.66), and says that Menelaus is the character in the *Iliad* who speaks in this refined and precise style (12.10.64). Scaliger attributes the characteristics of *tenuitas, simplicitas* and *securitas* (a consistent adherence to a common mode of presentation) to this style (4.20.484). See *apheleia* above. Melanchthon mentions that writers often call this style Attic, despite Cicero's contention that true Atticism uses all three of the *genera dicendi* appropriately (64r).

trachytes [G. "harshness"] or *asperitas* [L. "roughness, harshness"] or *aphodrotes* [G. "asperity"]
The style of harshness or asperity; the opposite of *glykytes*

1. Description

This style, which is bitter and critical, is directed against persons who must be scolded and corrected. The thoughts involve reproaches and the approach is to make the criticism openly and boldly without extenuation (*epitimesis*). The diction is tropical (*metaphora*). The following figures are among those that create harshness or asperity: *prostaktikon, epiplexis, elencticon, parrhesia, epicrisis, antirrhesis, methodeuthesis,* and *aposiopesis.* Clauses are *kommata* (*brachiepia*); word order should create *cacemphaton* and *arithmon.*

(Hermogenes 1.7.255–60; Sturm 3.10.580–92)

2. Examples

"[. . .] if indeed you carry your brains in your heads and not trampled down in your heels" (Demosthenes, *On Halonnesus* 45, trans. Wooten).

"And you, hamstrung and robbed of your money and your allies, have taken the role of servants and hangers-on, content if they hand over to you the Theoric or the Boidic [*sic*] Fund for your festivals" (Demosthenes, *Olynthiac III* 31, trans. Wooten).

"For indeed, men of Athens, you seem to me to have become altogether slack, idly waiting for the advent of disaster. You see the distresses of others, but take no precaution for yourselves; you have no thought for the steady and alarming deterioration of your commonwealth" (Demosthenes, *De Falsa Legatione* 224, trans. Vince).

(Hermogenes 1.7.256)

Note: Sturm divides this style into two: *trachytes* for the use of harshness with friends and *aphodrotes* for the use of harshness with enemies (3.10.583). Hermogenes lists this quality as a type of grandeur. See *oratio grandis* above.

QUALITATIVE

Vices

acyron [G. "without authority"] or *acyrologia* [G. "incorrect phraseology"] or *improprietas* [L. "improper use"]
An improper use of a word or phrase

1. Word
   "'You shall have six stripes which you long for': when they long for them not one whit."
   (Sherry [1555] A.vi.v)

   "'Her hair surmounts Apollo's pride,
   In it such beauty reigns.'
   Whereas this word *reign* is ill applied to the beauty of a woman's hair, and might better have been spoken of her whole person, in which beauty, favour and good grace, may perhaps in some sort be said to reign[.]"
   (Puttenham 263)

2. Phrase
   Sentence fragments
   (Sturm 3.1.442)

Note: An alternate spelling is *akyron*. Puttenham calls this vice "the Uncouthe" (262). Hermogenes specifies two kinds of improper words: using the wrong word and corrupting a word or *paraphthora* (*Meth.* §3).

amphibologia [G. "ambiguity"] or *amphibolia* [G. "uncertainty of mind"] or *ambiguitas* [L. "ambiguity"]

Ambiguity due to composition errors

1. Lexical homonymy
   "A merry fellow on a time was sent to hire his mistress a maid, and in hiring the maid, he did much commend his mistress' liberality towards her maids, and told her that he would warrant her that his mistress would give her a mark besides her wages before the year went out. Now whether he meant a mark in money or a mark about head or shoulders I know not, but the maid after learned."
   (Peacham [1577] G.i.v)

2. Several possible meanings for a word
   "'Buy you any mutton today, neighbor?' quoth one neighbor to another. 'No, by my troth,' quoth the other, 'for I mean to have a leg or a shoulder of my father.' Another man riding by understood the meaning of this saying, according to the order of his words. 'Surely,' quoth he, 'he is an hungry child that can find in his heart to eat his father.' With that they all fell a laughing."
   (Peacham [1577] G.i.v)

3. Misleading order
   a. Misplaced modifiers
      "'I sat by my lady soundly sleeping,
      My mistress lay by me bitterly weeping.'
      No man can tell by this, whether the mistress or the man slept or wept."
      (Puttenham 267)

   b. Structural ambiguity
      "His father loveth him better than his mother."
      (Sherry [1550] 33)

   c. Ambiguous pronoun reference
      "'I suppose you said Myrrina told you that Bacchis hath her ring' (Terence, *Hecyra* 5.4.845). Here through fault of composition we know not to whom the ring doth belong."
      (Peacham [1577] G.i.v)

Note: Puttenham's name is "the Ambiguous" (267). Quintilian speaks about most of these causes of linguistic ambiguity at length, but not as if they are figures (7.9.2–10; 8.2.16; 9.4.32).

anacoluthon [G. "inconsequence, anomaly"] or *anantapodoton* [G. "without *apodosis*"]
When members of a sentence or speech do not cohere grammatically or logically

1. Grammatical incoherence
   "He blundered—he slipped—he never thought—if ever again." (Cicero, *Pro Ligario* 10.30, trans. Watts)
   (Keckermann 1501)

2. Logical incoherence
   "Because money is hardly worth anything anymore, we might as well spend it."
   (Melanchthon, *Elem.* 20r; example mine)

Note: Even though Melanchthon does not treat this feature as a figure, his use of this term to describe an illogical argument shows the breadth of the term's application.

arithmon [G. "without rhythm"]
Without sweet and round composition; arrhythmical

1. Too much regularity
   a. "Again it is a blemish to have too many monosyllables in succession, since the inevitable result is that, owing to the frequency of the pauses, the rhythm degenerates into a series of jerks. [. . . T]he converse also is true as regards long syllables, since their accumulation makes our rhythm drag."
   (Quintilian 9.4.42)

   b. "It is a fault of the same class to end a number of successive sentences with similar cadences, terminations and inflexions."
   (Quintilian 9.4.42)

   Example: "Bewailing, imploring, weeping, protesting."
   (*Ad Herennium* 4.12.18)

   c. "It is likewise inartistic to accumulate long series of verbs, nouns or other parts of speech, since even merits produce tedium unless they have the saving grace of variety."
   (Quintilian 9.4.42)

   d. "The appearance of a complete verse in prose has a most uncouth effect, but even a portion of a verse is ugly, especially if the last half of a verse occurs in the cadence of a period or the first half at the beginning."
   (Quintilian 9.4.72)

2. Too much irregularity
   a. Avoid ending periods with a word of many syllables
   (Quintilian 9.4.66)

   b. "[I]n parts which are absolutely continuous without a breathing space, there must [still] be almost imperceptible pauses."
   "I note, gentlemen, that the speech for the prosecution falls sharply into two divisions" (Cicero, *Pro Cluentio* 1.1, trans. Butler).

"[T]he groups formed by the first [three] words, the next three, and then again by the next [three and two and then three] have each their own special rhythms and cause a slight check in our breathing."

(Quintilian 9.4.67–68)

c. Use the arrangement of accents with an awareness of their effects: strength or weakness, rising and falling, speed or slowness, emphasis and de-emphasis, gentleness or harshness, smoothness or jerkiness.

(Quintilian 9.4.91–111)

Note: Alternate spellings include *arrythmon* and *arithmus*. Veltkirchius (11v) references Quintilian 9.4 for the full treatment of *compositio* or artistic structure, within which is included "the structural art which welds thoughts together in the body of the period or rounds them off at the close" (9.4.13). Composition consists of order, connection, and rhythm, which three are interdependent (9.4.22). Hence, I pull the explanation of arrhythmical errors from Quintilian, even though he does not treat these as figures. Quintilian asserts that when prose lacks rhythm, the deficiency "would stamp the author as a man of no taste or refinement" (9.4.56). Wilson points out that those who "end their sentences all alike, mak[e] their talk rather to appear rimed meter than to seem plain speech" (193).

aschematiston [G. "without form or schemes"]

Absence of or unskillful use of figures

For example, too much repetition of one word shows unskillfulness:

"If a man knew what a man's life were, no man for any man's sake would kill any man, but one man would rather help another man, considering man is born for man to help man and not to hate man."

(Wilson 193)

Note: Veltkirchius explains that this vice covers whatever is "unadorned, inelegant, artless, rude" and includes both the overabundant, pretentious use of figures characteristic of sophistic discourse and the uncrafted, inept use, characteristic of the unskilled (11r). In his second edition, Sherry equates this figure with *homoiologia*: "[W]hen in the oration there is no variety, nor pleasantness, but it is all alike, and by no variety taketh away tediousness" ([1555] B.ii.r). See *homoiologia* below.

asiatismus [G. "Asianism"]

Full of figures and words, but lacking matter; the Asiatic style

1. Description

"Of the Asiatic style there are two types, the one sententious and studied, less characterized by weight of thought than by the charm of balance and symmetry. Such was Timaeus the historian; in oratory Hierocles of Alabanda in my boyhood, and even more so his brother Menecles, both of whose speeches are masterpieces in this Asiatic style. The other type is not so notable for wealth of sententious phrase, as for swiftness and impetuosity—a general trait of Asia at the present time—combining with this rapid flow of speech a choice of words refined and ornate. This is the manner of which Aeschylus of Cnidus and my contemporary Aeschines of Miletus were representatives. Their oratory had a rush and movement which provoked admiration, but it lacked elaborate symmetry of phrase and sentence. Both of these styles, as I have said, are better suited to youth; in older men they lack weight and dignity."

(Cicero, *Brutus* 325)

2. Example
   See those for *sufflata* above under Discoursal–styles.

Note: This vice could be listed under Discoursal–styles, but since in the Renaissance it appears amongst the vices, I list it here. The opposing Attic style corresponds to the virtue *syntomia*. See the entry below under virtues.

atonia [G. "slackness, enervation, laziness"]
Lack of vigor in delivery; without accentuation

(Scaliger 3.27.294)

Note: Scaliger calls this vice one opposite to *energeia*. See *energeia* below under virtues.

barbaralexis [G. "using foreign words"]
Improperly mixing into one's speech foreign, regional, or archaic words; applying the rules of one language to another; inkhornisms

A Letter Devised by a Lincolnshire Man for a Paid Benefice to a Gentleman That Then Waited upon the Lord Chancellor for the Time Being

"Pondering, expending, and revoluting with myself your ingent affability and ingenious capacity for mundane affairs, I cannot but celebrate and extol your magnifical dexterity above all others. For how could you have adepted such illustrate prerogative and dominical superiority, if the fecundity of your ingeny had not been so fertile and wonderful pregnant. Now, therefore, being accersited to such splendent renown and dignity splendidious, I doubt not but you will adjuvate such poor adnichilate orphans as whilom were condisciples with you, and of antique familiarity in Lincolnshire. Among whom I, being a sholastical panion, obtestate Your Sublimity to extol mine infirmity. There is a sacerdotal dignity in my native country contiguate to me where I now contemplate, which your worshipful benignity could soon impetrate for me, if it would like you to extend you [*sic*] schedules and collaud me in them to the right honorable lord chancellor, or rather archigrammatian of England. You know my literature, you know the pastoral promotion: I obtestate your clemency to invigilate thus much for me, according to my confidence, and as you know my condign merits for such a compendious living. But now I relinquish to fatigate your intelligence with any more frivolous verbosity, and therefore he that rules the climates be evermore your beautreux, your fortress, and your bulwark. Amen.

Dated at my dome, or rather mansion place, in Lincolnshire, the penult of the month sextile. *Anno millimo, quillimo, trillimo. Per me Johannes Octo.*"

(Wilson 189)

Note: Like Quintilian (1.5.8), some consider this vice a kind of barbarism, while others, like Donatus (3.1), use *barbarolexis* as a synonym for *barbarismus*. See *barbarismus* below.

barbarismus [G. "speaking like a barbarian; using one's own language amiss"]
Improper pronunciation or spelling of words, or general category of improper word usage

1. Improper pronunciation or spelling
   "A dousand for a thousand, isterday, for yesterday."

(Puttenham 257)

2. Incorrect use of words
   a. Unidiomatic word
      "The form *piissimus* [as the superlative of *pius*], which according to Cicero was never heard by Latin ears."

b. Misapplication of a word
"*Compilare* 'gather up'" cannot be used as a synonym for "*colligere* 'to collect,'" because although "*compilare* is a good Latin word, [. . .] it has acquired a different sense, 'remove by stealth.'"

c. Improper combination of words
"You can say *facere aes alienum* for 'contract debts,' and also *facere vorsuram* for 'raise a second loan,' but you cannot use *facere* like this in the phrases *facere invidiam* or *facere simultatem* to mean 'generate ill will or animosity against oneself.'"

d. Inappropriate word
"'What is this fellow after?' is appropriate, but [. . .] 'what is this mortal after?' is foolish."

(Erasmus *De copia* 304–6)

Note: Puttenham calls this vice "Forrein speech" (256). Bonner explains that "Under Stoic influence, it became accepted that a barbarism was a fault in the use of a single word, and a solecism was one arising in words in conjunction, that is, an error of syntax" (*Education* 198). When used appropriately in poetry, barbarisms become not faults, but *metaplasmus.* See *metaplasmus* above under grammatical figures.

battologia [G. "stammering speech; saying the same thing over and over again"]
Gibberish

"Some public speakers of otherwise distinguished reputation, especially among the Italians, actually set out to waste time with strings of synonyms [. . . ,] as if that were some splendid achievement. It is just like someone expounding the verse from the psalm, 'Create in me a clean heart, O God' by saying 'Create in me a clean heart, a pure heart, an unsullied heart, a spotless heart, a heart free from stain, a heart untainted by sin, a purified heart, a heart that is washed, a heart white as snow,' and so on, right through the psalm. 'Richness' of this sort is practically *battologia.*"

(Erasmus *De copia* 321)

bomphiologia [L. "booming words"] or *tumiditas* [L. "swollenness, pomposity"] or *ogkologia* [G. "speaking in a hollow voice"]
Bombast; making trifling matters great

"[. . .] in making trifles, treasures; cottages, castles; thistles, mighty Oaks; and pebble stones, precious pearls."

A beggar speaks fair to the constable, lifting him up "to a high dignity," when being taken to the stocks: "I beseech your worship forgive me, if ever your honor take me here again, then let me be punished according to your honor's discretion."

(Peacham [1577] G.ii.v)

Note: Puttenham calls this "Pompious speech" (266) and, like Peacham, points out that this vice is the opposite of the vice *tapinosis* ([1577] G.ii.v). See below. See *sufflata* above under Discoursal–styles for the corresponding style.

brachylogia [G. "brevity in speech"]
Speaking too briefly

"Some again will be so short, and in such wise curtail their sentences, that they had need to make a commentary immediately of their meaning, or else the most that hear them shall be forced to keep counsel."

(Wilson 192)

Note: *Brachylogia* is also sometimes an alternate name for *asyndeton*, for both syntactical and pragmatical *brevitas*, and for the virtue *syntomia*. See these entries above and below.

cacemphaton[1] [G. "ill-sounding"] or *cacophonia* [G. "ill-sound"]
Disagreeable and inharmonious sounds

1. *Hiatus* [G. "gaping"], a clash or collision of vowels
"Some will so set their words that they must be fain to gape after every word spoken, ending one word with a vowel and beginning the next with another, which undoubtedly maketh the talk to some most unpleasant. As thus: 'Equity assuredly every injury avoideth.'"

(Wilson 193)

2. Harsh clash of consonants
The hissing sound produced by the collision of "s" as in "*ars studiorum*."

(Quintilian 9.4.38)

"*Quadrupedate putre sonitu quatit ungula capu.*"
("A hoof shakes the foul field with a galloping sound.")

(Veltkirchius 11r)

3. Too much alliteration
"Your strength is not to strive, or strike against the stream so strong."
"A planted place of pleasure plain, where pleasure shall me please."
"In my drowsy, dreadful dream, I thought I drank of Dragon's deadly drink."

(Peacham [1577] G.iii.r-v)

4. Immediate repetition of the same syllable
"*res mihi invisae visae sunt, Brute*" (Cicero, *Letter to Brutus*, now lost).
["The situation seemed hateful to me, Brutus" (trans. Butler).]
"*O fortunatam natam me consule Romam*" (Cicero, the poem on his consulship).
["O happy Rome, born in my consulship" (trans. Butler).]

(Quintilian 9.4.41)

Note: An alternate spelling is *casemphaton* or *cacephaton*. Alternate names include *dysphonia, absurditas, absonum* and *cacophaton*. *Cacophonia* or *dysphonia* is sometimes a virtue, especially in forceful or acrimonious styles. To this category of vice also belongs *chalinos* [G. "a bridle"] in Quintilian (1.1.37) or *dysprophoron* [G. "impeding forward movement"] in Martianus Capella, a cluster of sounds difficult to pronounce, a tongue twister, exemplified in "*persuasitrices praestigiatrices atque inductrices striges*" (Capella §514). The Latin grammarians also list *mytacismus* or *metacismus* (the overuse of "m"), *labdacismus* (the overuse of "l"), and *iotacismus* (the overuse of "j") as additional species of vices here. See also *lambdacismus* and *tautologia* below.

cacemphaton[2] [G. "ill-sounding"] or *aeschrologia* [G. "foul language, obscenity"]
Lewd or vulgar language

1. Through inappropriate application
"For example, 'dung' and the verb 'to dung' are not vulgar if you are talking about farming to farmers, but they are if you are making a speech on affairs of state in the presence of the ruler."

(Erasmus, *De copia* 309)

2. Through foul double entendre
"[. . .] as [a man] that in the presence of Ladies would use this common Proverb,
'Jape with me, but hurt me not,

Bourde with me but shame me not.'

For it may be taken in another perverser [*sic*] sense by that sort of persons that hear it, in whose ears no such matter ought almost to be called in memory."

(Puttenham 261)

Note: Puttenham's English name is "the figure of foule speech" (260). For a correspondent style, see *acharis* under Discoursal–styles above.

cacosyntheton [G. "ill-composed"]

Words ill-applied or ill-placed

1. Words ill-applied

"But lest you too indignantly turn up your nose at all this smoke of fumigation, I will bind you a garland of goat's beard."

(Gill 168)

"There is (quoth one) small adversity between your Mare and mine" ('adversity' for 'diversity').

(Peacham [1577] G.iiii.r)

2. Words ill-placed

"A foolish fellow, when I saw before the King, stand laughing."

(Peacham [1577] G.iiii.r)

Note: An alternate spelling is *cacosintheton*. Puttenham calls this vice "the Misplacer" (260).

cacozelia [G. "affectation"] or *affectatio* [L. "affectation, conceit"]

Affectation; misusing styles or words; using new-fangled words to appear educated

A man selling his colt told a prospective buyer, a gentleman, that "his Gelding was of as stout an opinion as any Gelding in England, and all the faults he had were, that he was very scrupulous of the Spur." The gentleman replied, laughing, "If thy Gelding be of so stout an opinion, it may be, that he and I shall never agree, for I would have such a one, as I might persuade with reason."

"A man coming through a Gentleman's pastures, and seeing there a great number of Sheep, [. . .] speaking with the Gentleman, 'Sir,' said he, 'Your worship have goodly audience of sheep': whereby the Gentleman perceived that he was more fit to talk among sheep, then speak among men."

(Peacham [1577] G.ii.v-iii.r)

Note: An alternate spelling is *cacozelon*. Puttenham's English name is "Fonde affectation" (258) and an additional name is *mala affectatio*. Hermogenes says this fault also arises from the misuse of content (*Inv.* 4.12.202). For the corresponding style, see *cacozelias* above under Discoursal–styles.

calumnia [L. "a misrepresentation, false statement"]

Purposely misinterpreting an adversary's statement or deed

Because Christ allowed a multitude to come to him for the sake of teaching them, the Pharisees accused him of bringing about a kingdom.

Because Christ lived by common custom, the Pharisees accused him of intemperance.

(Melanchthon, *Elem.* 51v)

Note: Melanchthon treats this vice as an inappropriate kind of *metastasis*. In making this behavior a vice, Melanchthon rejects the suggestion of Hermogenes that telling a lie is an acceptable figure (see *Meth.* §19).

catachresis [G. "misuse, misapplication"] or *abusio* [L. "abuse, misuse"]
An overly strained metaphor or a sentence fragment

1. The overly strained metaphor
"A voice beautiful to his ears."
"The elbow of his nose is disproportionable."

(Smith 49)

2. A sentence fragment

(Sturm 3.1.442)

Note: An alternate spelling is *katakreson*. See *catachresis* above under semantical figures for its legitimate use. Sturm refers to sentence fragments as both *acyron* and *catachresis*. See *acyron* above.

eclipsis [G. "a deficiency"] or *ellipsis* [G. "an omission"] or *defectus* [L. "a failure, deficiency"]
Leaving out necessary words or matter

1. Words
"Many of these are in Cicero's Epistles written to Atticus." [For example, Cicero writes, "I have already given you a description of Pompey's first public speech—of no comfort to the poor or interest to the rascals; on the other hand the rich were not pleased and the honest men were not impressed. So—a frost" (I.14, trans. Bailey).]

(Sherry [1555] A.vi.v; example mine)

2. Matter
a. Leaving out a necessary reason
In *Doctor Faustus*, Faustus reads from Romans 6.23 and 1 John 1.8–9 as he considers choosing divinity as his field of study. But in his deliberations, he omits not only the second half of each scripture, which teaches repentance and forgiveness, but he neglects to acknowledge salvation as the central message of Christianity, and hence concludes without proof that religion offers him nothing substantial:
"When all is done, divinity is best:
Jerome's Bible, Faustus, view it well:
Stipendium peccati mors est: ha! *Stipendium, etc.*
The reward of sin is death? That's hard.
Si pecasse negamus, fallimur, et nulla est in nobis veritas.
If we say that we have no sin,
We deceive ourselves, and there's no truth in us.
Why then belike we must sin,
And so consequently die.
Ay, we must die an everlasting death.
What doctrine call you this? Che sará, sará:
What will be, shall be! Divinity, adieu! (Marlowe, Text A 1.37–48)

(Day 81; example mine)

b. Leaving undone or unspoken what should be done or spoken
Ellipsis speaks, "By me (commonly call'd *want of the Word*) the mighty Prince the *Pope* keeps the people in due obedience to his Laws, [. . .] All *Cowards*, that betray the Truth by their unseasonable silence, and all *false Friends*, that have not a word to speak for their Friend in time of danger, are my Disciples."

(Shaw 177)

Note: An alternate spelling is *eclypsis*. For its proper use, see *eclipsis* above under grammatical figures or *defectus* above under Pragmatical–idea figures.

enigma [G. "a dark saying, a riddle"] or *skotison* [G. "darken it"]
Obscuring the meaning

"Some use so many interpositions both in their talk and in their writing, that they make their sayings as dark as hell."

(Wilson 194)

"The [fallacy] in Method is when to deceive withall, the end is set in the beginning, the special before the general, good order begone, confounded: And finally, when darkness, length, and hardness is laboured after."

(Fenner 180)

Note: Alternate spelling is *aenigma*. The *enigma* becomes a vice when the meaning is overly obscure. For its proper use, see *aenigma* under Discoursal–genres above. Fenner ends his discussion of logic and sophistry with the above description of purposeful obfuscation. He does not give this deliberate obfuscation a name, but we recognize the behavior as this vice. Inasmuch as Fenner names *amphibolia, archaismus, onomatopoeia, homonymia*, and *tautologia* as causes of fallacious arguments (177–80), he could very well have had *skotison* in mind here.

homoiologia [G. "uniformity of style"] or *homoeideia* [G. "sameness of form"]
No variety to prevent tediousness

"He came thither to the bath, yet he said afterwards, 'Here one servant bet me.' Afterwards he said unto him: 'I will consider.' Afterwards he chid with him, and cried more and more when many were present."

(Sherry [1550] 33)

Note: Alternate spellings include *homiologia* and *homoeologia*.

hypallage [G. "interchange, exchange"]
Words inappropriately exchange places

"He took his ear from his fist."
"Open the day, and see if it be the window."
"I would make no more ado, but take a door and break open the Axe."

(Peacham [1577] G.i.r)

"A certain sorry man of law, that gave his Client but bad council, and yet found fault with his fee, [. . .] said: 'My fee, good friend, hath deserved better counsel.' 'Good master,' quoth the Client, 'if your self had not said so, I would never have believed it: but now I think as you do.'"

(Puttenham 183)

Note: For the proper use of this figure, see *hypallage* under both syntactical and semantical figures above.

hyperbaton [G. "passing over, transposed"] or *perplexitas* [L. "perplexity, obscurity"]
Awkward transposition of words

"In the midmost sea/ Rocks are there by Italians altars called" (Virgil, *Aeneid* I.109, trans. Butler).

(Quintilian 8.2.14)

"As I rose in the morning, I met a cart full of stones empty."

(Wilson 194)

Note: For this figure's proper use, see *hyperbaton* above under syntactical figures.

hyperbole [G. "excess, overshooting"]
Deceptive or unmeasured exaggeration
1. In speech
"Those that hate me are more in number than the hairs of my head."
(Fenner 168)

2. In action/ thought
"By an *Hyperbolical* overweening (which is vulgarly call'd *ambition*) one man attempts to be *Universal Monarch*, and another *Universal Bishop*; and (which is good Rhetoric, tho some Critics laugh at it for bad Grammar) one particular Church stiles it self *Catholic*. [. . .] What is *swearing*, but an *Hyperbolical* way of *affirming*? What is *stealing* and *cheating* but an Hyperbolical way of *getting* an Estate? What is *Superstition*, but an Hyperbolical way of being *Religious*?"
(Shaw 127)

Note: See also *hyperbole* under semantical figures above.

hyrmos [G. "train, series, sequence"] or *circumductio* [L. "lengthening" or "prolongation"]
An unfashioned sentence is too long continued; an excessive circumlocution
"Harken all you that love justice, and would have reason bear rule, in all controversies and debates, knowing how all men ought to the uttermost of their power, not having regard to men, maintain the same from time to time, against all such, as would by their good wills and hearts' desire, bring in all manner of disorders among good men, that do daily wish to live in such peace, as might both please God, which commandeth concord and justice to be among us men, here upon the earth, wherein debates do daily grow, and increase to a huge heap, that cannot well by man's wisdom be abated."
(Peacham [1577] H.i.r)

Note: This vice is related to both the syntactical figure *hirmos* and the periodic sentence called *irmus*, but the different spellings of the word do strictly correspond to its three different applications.

hysteron proteron [G. "the latter before the former"]
Putting "the cart before the horse"
1. A misplaced word or phrase
"A corral lip of hew"
(Puttenham 262)

2. A misplaced idea
"Vesper shewed his face, and Phoebus fled from sight." [The evening star does not appear before the sun has gone down.]
(Peacham [1577] F.iiii.r)

"After he had given sail to the wind and taken the Seas."
(Day 83)

Note: Puttenham calls this vice "the Preposterous" (262). See *hysteron proteron* above under both syntactical and Pragmatical–idea figures for its proper uses.

lambdacismus [G. "a defect in pronunciation"]
Cacophany created by the undue repetition of one letter or syllable
"*O fortunantam natam me consule Romam*" (Cicero's poem on his consulship).
["Oh fortunate Rome, born in my consulship."]
(Sturm 2.22.408)

Note: In the Latin tradition, this vice names the undue repetition of the letter "l." In Sturm, the figure has become generalized. The example above contains several repeating sounds and syllables. This vice is a sub-species of the first *cacemphaton* above and *tautologia* below.

macrologia [G. "speaking at length"] or *garrulitas* [L. "a chattering, prating, talkativeness"]
Too long-winded in either a sentence or a whole oration

1. A superfluous restatement within a sentence
"He is alive yet, God be praised, and is not dead."
"He hath drunk up all, and left none."
"He was not then awake, but was fast asleep."
"He was never out of England, but always in England."
(Peacham [1577] F.ii.v)

2. A wearisome passage
Polonius: "My liege, and madam, to expostulate
What majesty should be, what duty is,
Why day is day, night night, and time is time,
Were nothing but to waste night, day, and time;
Therefore, since brevity is the soul of wit,
And tediousness the limbs and outward flourishes,
I will be brief. Your noble son is mad:
Mad call I it, for to define true madness,
What is't but to be nothing else but mad?
But let that go.
Queen: More matter with less art.
Polonius: Madam, I swear I use no art at all.
That he's mad, 'tis true, 'tis true 'tis pity,
And pity 'tis 'tis true—a foolish figure,
But farewell it, for I will use no art.
Mad let us grant him then, and now remains
That we find out the cause of this effect,
Or rather say, the cause of this defect,
For this effect defective comes by cause:
Thus it remains, and the remainder thus:
Perpend.
I have a daughter—have while she is mine—
Who in her duty and obedience, mark,
Hath given me this." (Shakespeare, *Hamlet* 2.2.86–108)
(example mine)

Note: Puttenham, who calls this vice "Long language," conflates this vice with *perissologia* (264), as do others. See *perissologia* below.

meiosis [G. "a lessening, diminishing"] or *diminutio* [L. "diminution, lessening"]
Meagerness or inadequacy of expression for the subject matter
"There is a rocky wart upon the mountain's brow."
(Quintilian 8.3.48–50)

Note: Quintilian says this meagerness contributes to an obscure style. This meagerness also corresponds to *exilitas*, the arid style. See *exilitas* above under Discoursal–styles.

paradiastole [G. "putting together of dissimilar things"]
Excusing vices by calling them virtues

"When we call him that is crafty, wise: a covetous man, a good husband: murder a manly deed: deep dissimulation, singular wisdom: pride, cleanliness: covetousness, a worldly or necessary carefulness: whoredom, youthful delight & dalliance: Idolatry, pure religion: gluttony and drunkenness, good fellowship: cruelty, severity."

(Peacham [1577] N.iiii.v)

Note: Peacham makes clear that this vice is only well-used when put in the mouth of "a shameless person," who uses it as an "excuse serving to self-love, partial favor, blind affection," and "the better maintenance of wickedness" ([1593] 169). Puttenham, however, allows a freer use of this figure, which he calls "the Curry favell," and which can moderate and abate "the force of a matter by craft, and for a pleasing purpose" (195). Quintilian mentions this strategy (not figure), but advises that this "a good man will never do, unless perhaps he is led to do so by consideration for the public interest" (3.7.25). For its other meaning, see *paradiastole* above under Pragmatical–idea figures.

paralogismus [G. "fallacious, fraudulent reasoning"] or *eudialyta* [G. "easy to destroy"]
Fallacious reasoning

"All sin is evil.
Every Christian doth sin:
Therefore, every Christian is evil."

"No Pope is a Devil.
No man is a Devil:
Therefore, no man is a Pope."

(Smith 265)

parelcon [G. "extraneous addition"]
A superfluous word

"For why I could not otherwise do, when that I call" or "Why what is the matter?" The figure is in the combination of "for why," "when that," and "why what."

(Peacham [1577] F.iii.r)

Note: *Parelcon* is not always a vice. See the entry above under morphological figures.

periergia [G. "over-elaboration; wasting one's labor's on a thing"] or *curiositas* [L "bestowing care or pains"]
Over-elaboration; excessive carefulness

"'The tenth of March when Aries received
Dan Phoebus rays into his horned head,
And I myself by learned lore perceived
That Ver approached and frosty winter fled
I crossed the Thames to take the cheerful air,
In open fields, the weather was so fair.'

First, the whole matter is not worth all this solemn circumstance to describe the tenth day of March, [. . . I]t is not only more than needs, but also very ridiculous, for he makes wise, as if he had not been a man learned in some of the mathematics (by learned lore) that he could not have told that the x. of March had fallen in the spring of the year: which every carter, and also every child knoweth without any learning. Then also, when he saith [Ver approached, and frosty winter fled . . .] it were a surplusage (because one season must needs give place to the other)[.]"

(Puttenham 265)

"'I came to the stairs, I took a pair of oars. They launched out, rowed apace, I landed at the Court-gate, I paid my fare, went up to the presence, asked for my lord. I was admitted.' All this is but: 'I went to the Court and spake with my lord.'"

(Hoskins 6)

Note: Puttenham's English name is "the Over labour, otherwise called the curious" (265) and an additional name is *microlochia*. Veltkirchius places *leptologia* here as well (9v). See *leptologia* above under Pragmatical–idea figures.

perissologia [G. "over-talking, wordiness"]

Superfluous words of no weight

"*Quintilian* taketh this example out of *Livy*: 'The Ambassadors, peace not being obtained, returned home again from whence they came'" (*Fragment* 62, Hertz, in Q. 8.3.53).

(Peacham [1577] F.ii.v)

"He followed and pursued fast" (Spenser, *The Faerie Queene* VI 4.18.9).

(Gill 157)

Note: Donatus deems this device useful when the redundancy adds meaning (3.3). Soarez explains that *"perisologia"* results when *periphrasis* falls into excess (299). Sometimes *macrologia* is a synonym. See *macrologia* above and under Pragmatical–idea figures.

pleonasmus [G. "superfluity, excess"] or *superfluitas* [L. "superfluity"]

Redundancy

1. Needless repetition in phrases
   "I heard it with mine ears."
   "She spake it with her mouth."
   "*Antiocus* was sorry in his mind."

(Peacham [1577] F.ii.r)

2. Any unnecessary words
   "I am that *Figure*, whereby any word unnecessarily abounds in discourse. I cannot deny, neither am I asham'd of my acquaintance with the female Sex, so long as no worse comes of it than this, that by me they prove big with Words, but these, Sir, (although they are a pretty sight when they are together) are but a small part of my Conquest. The *Trades-men* (who are the staple Party of every Kingdom) are all mine; and so are all their *Customers*. The greatest part of *Scholars* are mine, especially the *Grammarians*."

(Shaw 177–78)

3. Any unnecessary possession
   "In Morals I have prevail'd yet more. All *ambitious Princes* are my Vassals, and so are all *covetous rich men*, who trouble themselves for a great deal more than they need. There is but a third sort of men, the *Sensualists*, and amongst these I have a considerable interest too; especially among the *Veneral Pluralists*, who keep *many* women; when it is well known any man may have his belly full of *one*."

(Shaw 178)

Note: Puttenham's name is "Too ful speech" (264). For the proper use of this figure, see the entry under lexical figures above.

poicilogia [G. "elaborately colored"]

Excessive ornamentation

"This young gallant, of more wit than wealth, and yet of more wealth than wisdom, seeing himself inferior to none in pleasant conceits, thought himself so apt to all things that he gave himself almost to nothing but practising of those things commonly which are incident to these sharp wits—fine phrases, smooth quips, merry taunts—jesting without mean and abusing mirth without measure. As therefore the sweetest rose hath his prickle, the finest velvet his brack, the fairest flour his bran, so the sharpest wit hath his wanton will and the holiest head his wicked way. And true it is that some men write, and most men believe, that in all perfect shapes a blemish bringeth rather a liking every way to the eyes than a loathing any way to the mind. Venus had her mole in her cheek which made her more amiable; Helen her scar in her chin which Paris called *cos amoris*, the whetstone of love; Aristippus his wart, Lycurgus his wen. So likewise in the disposition of the mind, either virtue is over-shadowed with some vice or vice overcast with some virtue: Alexander valiant in war, yet given to wine; Tully eloquent in his glozes, yet vainglorious; Solomon wise, yet too too wanton; David holy, but yet an homicide; none more witty than Euphues, yet at the first none more wicked" (Lyly, *Euphues: The Anatomy of Wit*, chapter 1, 1st paragraph, 32–33).

(Veltkirchius 11v; example mine)

solecismus [G. "incorrectness in the use of language"]

Ungrammatical constructions

"As when we speak false English, that is by misusing the *Grammatical* rules to be observed in cases, genders, tenses and such like, every poor scholar knows the fault, and calls it the breaking of *Priscian's* head, for he was among the Latins a principal Grammarian."

(Puttenham 258)

Note: Alternate spelling is *soloecismus*. Puttenham's English term is "Incongruitie" (258). The grammatical schemes that are species of *enallage* are also species of *solecismus*, formed by means of adding, deleting, changing or transposing words in a sentence. They become appropriate transformations and not the vice *solecismus* if congruent with the speaker's purposes.

soraismus [G. "heaping up of something"] or *sardismus* [G. "mixture of dialects"] or *koinismos* [G. "mixture of dialects"]

Mingling diverse languages, dialects, or styles inappropriately

"And of ingenious invention, infanted with pleasant travail" (the French word "enfante" means "borne as a child").

"I will freddon in thine honour" (the French word "freddon" means "to shake or quiver the fingers").

(Puttenham 260)

Note: An alternate spelling is *soroesmus*. Puttenham calls this vice "the mingle mangle" (259). Quintilian also includes within this fault "the indiscriminate mixture of grand words with mean, old with new, and poetic with colloquial, the result being a monstrous medley" (8.3.60).

synchisis [G. "commingling, confusion"] or *anoiconometon* [G. "not set in order, unarranged"] or *confusio* [L. "confusion, disorder"] or *dissipatio* [L. "a scattering, dispersing"]

All without order, confused arrangement; the opposite of elegance, clarity, and *digestio*

1. In a sentence

"'The wines good which afterward had in pipes laid aboard *Acestes* one *Cicilian* shore, and given to the *Trojans* departing, the noble man did distribute' (Virgil, *Aeneid* 1.202–4). This saying, by confusion of order is so darkened, that it is almost impossible to be understood, for the plain order placeth it thus: 'The noble man *Aeneas* did afterward distribute the wines, which good *Acestes,* King of *Cicilia*, had laid aboard and given to the *Trojans* departing one *Cicilian* shore.'"

(Peacham [1577] G.i.r)

2. In extended discourse

Panthus in his wild flight from Troy gives the following confused speech:
"That last of days, that hour we cannot dodge,
Has come to Troy. Trojans we were, and Troy
Has been, and Troy's great glory. Jupiter
Fiercely transfers the gods to Argos now.
The Greeks are masters in a ruined city.
Their horse stands high amid our walls and pours
Out armored men, and jeering Sinon stirs
The flames; he triumphs. Others, massed in thousands,
Stand at the open gates, as many men
As ever came to Troy from great Mycenae.
Some block the narrow streets with spear-points levelled;
Their naked sword-blades glitter along the columns,
Ready to kill; the sentries at the gateway
Try to fight back; theirs is a blind resistance." (Virgil, *Aeneid* 2.340–53, trans. Lind)

(Trapezuntius 530)

Note: Alternate spellings include *synchesis, synchysis* and *sygchysis* and an additional name sometimes is *anastrophe*. Trapezuntius counsels that *confusio* "must be avoided unless we want to show the effects of a deranged mind. Nature itself teaches us that there are some impulses of the mind that cannot be spoken elegantly, so that, when we imitate them, confusion necessarily follows" (530). Melanchthon comments that if a speech "lacks order in the presentation of the matter, [it] is just sounds without meaning" (*Elem.* 31v). Also, Wilson warns, "Some will rove so much, and babble so far without order, that a man would think they had a great love to hear themselves speak" (192). Sometimes this vice is a species of *hyperbaton*. See *hyperbaton* above under syntactical figures.

tapinosis [G. "lowering, lessening, humiliation, abasement"] or *humilitas* [L. "littleness of mind, meanness, baseness"]

Meanness and humiliation

1. Too much condescension

"As if we should say to a great prince or a king: 'If it please your mastership.'"

(Sherry [1550] 34)

2. Too much dilution of the truth

"How then shall I, Apprentice of the skill,
That whylome in divinest wits did raine,
Presume so high to stretch mine humble quill?"
(Spenser belittles his own ability too much in *The Faerie Queene* III Proem 3.)

(Gill 152)

Note: Alternate spelling is *tapeinosis.* Puttenham calls this figure "the Abbaser" (266). For the accepted use of this figure, see its entry under semantical figures above.

tautologia [G. "repeating what has been said"] or *nugatio* [L. "a babbling, bragging, swaggering"]
Excessive repetition of the same sounds, words, or ideas

1. Sounds
"The deadly drops of dark disdain,
Do daily drench my due deserts."
(Puttenham 261)

2. Words
"If you have a friend, I would wish you to keep a friend, for an old friend is to be preferred before a new friend; if I were your friend, I would never take you again for my friend, if you should once forsake me your old friend and take a new friend."
(Peacham [1577] F.iii.r-v)

3. Ideas
"Some will tell one thing twenty times, now in, now out, and when a man would think they had almost ended, they are ready to begin again as fresh as ever they were."
(Wilson 194)

Note: Puttenham calls this "the figure of selfe saying" (261). Martianus Capella uses the term *homoeoprophoron* for the irritating repetition of the same consonant and specifies the following additional species: *mytacism* for the constant use of "m," *labdacism* for the overuse of "l," *iotacism* for the overuse of "j," and *polysigma* for the overuse of "s" (514). The first three of these species Donatus lists (3.1). See *lambdacismus* above also.

Virtues

analogia [G. "correspondence, resemblance"] or *collatio* [L. "comparison, similitude"]
Well-proportioned

1. Usage remains in accordance with the known practice of native speakers
Quintilian explains, "The essence of analogy is the testing of all subjects of doubt by the application of some standard of comparison about which there is no question, the proof that is to say of the uncertain by reference to the certain. This can be done in two different ways: by comparing similar words, paying special attention to their final syllables [i.e., declensions . . .] and by the study of diminutives (1.6.4). [. . .] For analogy was not sent down from heaven at the creation of mankind to frame the rules of language, but was discovered after they began to speak and to note the terminations of words used in speech. It is therefore based not on reason but on example, nor is it a law of language, but rather a practice which is observed, being in fact the offspring of usage" (1.6.16).
(Sherry [1550] 37)

Note: This reference of the term would correlate to the virtues *ciriologia* and *latinitas* below.

2. The decorous speech in all regards
"Now because his comeliness resteth in the good conformity of many things and their sundry circumstances, with respect one to another, so as there be found a just correspondence between them by this or that relation, the Greeks call it *Analogie*, or a convenient proportion. This lovely conformity, or proportion, or convenience between the sense and the sensible hath nature herself first most carefully observed in all her own works, then also by kind graft it in the appetites of every creature working by intelligence to covet and desire: and in their actions to imitate and perform: and of man chiefly

before any other creature as well in his speeches as in every other part of his behavior. And this in generality and by an usual term is that which the Latins call *decorum.* [. . .] But by reason of the sundry circumstances, that man's affairs are as it were wrapped in, this *decency* comes to be very much alterable and subject to variety, insomuch as our speech asketh one manner of *decency* in respect of the person who speaks: another of his to whom it is spoken: another of whom we speak: another of what we speak, and in what place and time and to what purpose. And as it is of speech, so of all other our behaviors."

(Puttenham 269–70)

Note: This second reference correlates to "discretion" below. For Quintilian's treatment of this principle of judgment, see 1.6.3.

cataphora [G. "attack, tirade"] or *incitatio* [L. "an inciting, rousing"]

Impetus in delivery

"They do not send weapons? And everyone from the city follows? And they are pulling up rafts from other ships? Go, bear flames, pass out spears, push the oars" (adaptation of Virgil, *Aeneid* 4.596–98).

(Scaliger 4.11.465)

Note: Vossius suggests that this virtue produces *celeritas* and is appropriate for accusation. He opposes it to *tasis* (284). See *celeritas* above under Pragmatical–idea figures and *tasis* below.

ciriologia [G. "authoritative speech"]

Proper and natural speech; normal usage

"But let us examine the point at issue. Certain persons thought that the name of war ought not to be in the motion. They preferred to call it 'tumult,' showing their ignorance not only of the facts but of words. For while a war can exist without a tumult, a tumult cannot exist without a war. For what else is a tumult but a commotion so serious that fear beyond the ordinary arises from it—that being the origin of the word 'tumult.'[. . .] And that a tumult is something more serious than a war can be inferred from the fact that exemptions are valid in a war but not a tumult. [. . .] After all, there is no halfway house between war and peace. If 'tumult' does not come under the heading of war, it must come under the heading of peace—than which nothing more incongruous can well be said or thought" (Cicero, *Philippic* 8.2–5, trans. Bailey).

(Puttenham 168; example mine)

Note: An alternate spelling is *cyriologia* or *kyriologia.* This virtue would encompass *hellenismos* and *latinitas* (see *latinitas* below), as well as *proprietas* (see *proprietas* below).

concinnitas [L. "an elegant and skillful joining of things"] or *commensuratio* [L. "symmetry, uniformity"]

Beauty of style produced by a skillful connection of words and clauses; symmetry, elegance

"For this law, gentlemen of the jury, is not written, but born; we did not learn, receive and read it, but we seized, plucked and wrested it from Nature herself; for this we were not taught, but made; we know it not by training, but by instinct" (Cicero, *Pro Milone* 4.10, trans. Hubbell).

(Cicero, *Orator* 49.165)

Note: This particular virtue is an element of *compositio*, along with euphony and rhythm (Cicero, *Or* 60.201). See *synthesis* below.

copia [L. "abundance"] or *perittotes* [G. "abundance"]
The abundant style; the opposite of the compressed style or *syntomia*

1. Description
   Enriching and expanding a subject so that nothing can be added; elaborating using a variety of thoughts and means of expression.
2. Example
   "Come is the final day, fate's inevitable doom
   Upon Dardanus' city; we Trojans are no more;
   Gone is Ilium, gone the mighty fame of Teucer's sons.
   Jove is become our foe and has bestowed
   All that was ours on Argos.
   Greeks now triumph in all the blazing city. [. . .]
   O my country, O Ilium the dwelling place of gods!
   O ramparts of Dardanus' race with all your fame in war! [. . .]
   Who can unfold in words that murderous night?
   Can any weep the tears those toils deserve?" (Virgil, *Aeneid* 2.340–46, 249–50, 383–84, trans. Knott)

   "Lives he still and breathes the air of heaven?
   Rests he not yet among the cruel shades?" (Virgil, *Aeneid* 3.348–49, trans. Knott)
   (Erasmus, *De copia* 298)

Note: Like *syntomia* below, this virtue is also a kind of style, in fact, one species of *peribole,* and could be listed under Discoursal–styles above. Erasmus in *De copia* treats *copia* as a virtue and in *Ecclesiastes* treats it as a style (3.154.25). Quintilian treats *copia* as a method of embellishment (8.3.87). It is, however, most often considered a virtue. The vice that arises from overabundant and extravagant expression is "mere glibness, which is both silly and offensive" (Erasmus, *DC* 295). Its counterpart style would be *psychrotes* or *sufflata.* See these entries above under Discoursal–styles.

discretion [E. "prudence; being careful about what one says and does"]
Good judgment; following decorum

"Last is respect, to discern what fits yourself, him to whom you write, and that which you handle; which is a quality fit to conclude the rest because it doth include the rest, and that must proceed from ripeness of judgment, [. . .] But let discretion be the greatest and general figure of figures."

(Hoskins 7,15)

Note: Theophrastus had listed four virtues of style: purity (correctness), clarity, propriety and ornamentation. Hoskins calls *proprietas* "discretion" or "respect," but he broadens the category so it involves not only matching words to subject matter, but also tailoring all one's discursive choices to the requisites of the particular speech act. This virtue corresponds to the second reference of *analogia* above and to Hermogenes' notion of force. See *deinotes* above under Discoursal–styles. His category also corresponds to Cicero's fourth virtue of style—aptness, wherein Cicero teaches that "the knowledge of what is appropriate to a particular occasion is a matter of practical sagacity [*prudentia*]" (*De Or* 3.212). Cicero has expanded "aptness" from a mere focus on using proper words (see *proprietas* below) to good judgment in general. Scaliger also cites as one of the four stylistic virtues *prudentia,* which is good judgment in the selection of words and figures and which is also called *venustas,* because it produces charm and beauty in all styles (4.6.461B).

enargeia [G. "clearness, distinctness, vividness"] or *evidentia* [L. "clearness, distinctness"] or *illustratio* [L. "vivid representation"] or *energeia* [G. "activity"]

Vividness; bringing before the eyes

"Is there anybody so incapable of forming a mental picture of a scene that, when he reads the following passage from the Verrines, he does not seem not merely to see the actors in the scene, the place itself and their very dress, but even to imagine to himself other details that the orator does not describe? 'There on the shore stood the praetor, the representative of the Roman people, with slippered feet, robed in a purple cloak, a tunic streaming to his heels, and leaning on the arm of this worthless woman'" (Cicero, *In C. Verrem* II 5.33.86, trans. Butler).

(Quintilian 8.3.64)

Note: Alternate spellings are *enargia* or *energia*. *Suffiguratio* is a snynonym. Sturm makes a useful distinction: *amplificatio* provides magnitude, whereas *evidentia* provides "splendor and light" (1.36.159). This vividness is created by means of many figures: narrations, descriptions, dramatizations, *ethopoeia*, personifications, *sermocinatio*, and so forth. Vividness is so closely associated with *hypotyposis* that the two often become synonyms of each other. See *hypotyposis* above under Pragmatical–idea figures. Sturm suggests that the logical topics help one to invent the detail necessary for *illustratio* (1.36.167). Quintilian points out that this method of embellishment increases the clarity and probability of the narrative or argument (4.2.63–64; 8.3.61–62). See *energeia* below.

energeia [G. "vigor of style; activity; energy"] or *tropus* [G. "way, manner, fashion, guise"]

Vigor; lively and stirring speech

Crassus's remark has vigor: "Shall I regard you as a consul, when you refuse to regard me as a senator?"

(Quintilian 8.3.89)

Note: An alternate spelling is *tropos*. *Energeia* and *enargia* differ slightly in meaning, and several rhetoricians use the terms according to the distinction. *Energeia* refers to whatever creates vigor in the speech, *enargeia* to whatever creates vividness. Vividness, along with other devices such as *asseveratio*, *obtestatio*, *orthotes*, *adhortatio*, and so forth, can create vigor. But vigor does not necessarily create vividness. Vigor is the larger category. Hoskins refers to this virtue as "life" and treats it as one of the four virtues of style in the place of "exornation," as if to suggest that attention to ornamentation creates a life-like representation and vigor (7). See *eschematismon* below. Mosellanus lists the tropes as species (b.iii.v). Sherry emphasizes the roles of *pathopoeia* and *ethopoeia* in creating *energeia* ([1550] 66–67) and thereby connects vigor to involving the audience in the passions of the speaker. Antonio Minturno then connects *energeia* to the Hermogenic style of sincerity, *aletheia* (see Patterson 127). See *aletheia* above under Discoursal–styles. Puttenham distinguishes *enargeia* and *energeia* somewhat differently, the first created by figures of speech that have an aural appeal and the second by figures of thought or "such words and speeches inwardly working a stir to the mind" (155).

eschematismon [G. "possessing form, esp. a form created through artifice"] or *exornation* [from L. "an adorning, decorating, embellishing"] or *ornatus* [L. "a furnishing, providing, preparing"]

Figured, garnished, polished speech

There are two kinds of ornamentation, both necessary:

1. The first that through discretion creates comeliness by holding true to the appropriate level of style (the high, middle or low) one establishes in the speech and using the appropriate tropes and figures so as to fashion clarity and pleasing variety in diction and sentence structure.

2. The second that sprinkles figures here and there "as stars stand in the firmament."

(Wilson 195)

Note: Fraunce calls this virtue "bravery of speech" (A2v) and Hoskins calls it "life, which is the very strength and sinews, as it were, of your penning" (7). This virtue is one of the four Theophrastus designates as the primary virtues of style. Mosellanus places *synthesis*, *cyriologia*, and *tropus* as species (b.iii.v). See entries for these terms above and below. Wilson has taken these two kinds of ornamentation from Cicero's instruction (*De Or* 3.25.96).

euphonia [G. "goodness of voice"] or *suavitas* [L. "sweetness, pleasantness, agreeableness"]

Elegant, pleasing, smooth, harmonious sounds

1. Description

Avoid ugly or inappropriate words, choose fullness and agreeableness of sound, and make elegant connections between words (avoiding hiatus and cacophony).

(Keckermann 1511)

2. Example

"Come live with me and be my love,
And we will all the pleasures prove
That valleys, groves, hills, and fields
Woods, or steepy mountain yields.

And we will sit upon the rocks,
Seeing the shepherds feed their flocks,
By shallow rivers to whose falls
Melodious birds sing madrigals. Etc. (Marlowe, "The Passionate Shepherd to His Love" l. 1–8).

(example mine)

Note: *Molle* [L. "to be soft"] is a synonym. Quintilian regards *euphonia* a virtue, but not a figure, and gives *vocalitas* as the Latin equivalent (1.5.4). Keckermann treats the phonetic figures as species of *euphonia* (1515).

hellenismus [G. "belonging to Greek"]

Grammatically correct, idiomatic Greek

See *katharotes* above under Discoursal–styles.

(Sturm 3.6.545)

Note: For its other meaning, see the entry under grammatical figures above.

latinitas [L. "pure Latin style, Latinity"]

Imitating proper Latin constructions, purity in language use

See *katharotes* above under Discoursal–styles.

(Sturm 3.6.545)

Note: Like *hellenismus*, *latinitas* means correct, idiomatic Latin, a virtue producing purity of style. Its opposites are the vices *barbarismus*, for single words, and *solecismus*, for conjoined words. This virtue, applied to English, would entail using English according to grammatical rules and acceptable diction, based on the custom and practice of educated speakers. In this last sense, this virtue becomes synonymous with the virtues *ciriologia* and *analogia* (the first meaning). See *analogia* and *ciriologia* above. Sturm treats both *latinitas* and *hellenismus* as synonyms of *katharotes*.

perspicuitas [L. "transparency, clearness"]
Clarity, plainness

1. Description
   This virtue arises from propriety in diction and in word order, periods that do not long postpone the conclusion, with nothing lacking and nothing superfluous.
   (Quintilian 8.2.22)

2. Example
   See *sapheneia* above under Discoursal–styles.

Note: This virtue joins *puritas* (*latinitas*), *proprietas*, and *ornatus* to complete the four primary virtues of style as identified by Theophrastus and repeated frequently after Cicero (*De Or* 3.37). Scaliger remarks that *perspicuitas* or transparency is nothing else than *evidentia* or *enargeia*, what Hermogenes calls *sapheneia* and Trebizond *claritas* (4.1.444). See these entries above under virtues and styles.

pithanotetos [G. "persuasiveness"]
Persuasiveness

1. Description
   This virtue is achieved when the style is clear and familiar, the diction is not elaborate nor inflated, the composition moves steadily along without a formal rhythm and leaves some points for the listener to infer and work out for himself, since "when he infers what you have omitted, he is not just listening to you but he becomes your witness and reacts more favourably to you. For he is made aware of his own intelligence through you, who have given him the opportunity to be intelligent. To tell your listener every detail as though he were a fool seems to judge him one."
   (Demetrius §221–22)

2. Example
   Iago: "I am glad of this, for now I shall have reason
   To show the love and duty that I bear you
   With franker spirit; therefore (as I am bound)
   Receive it from me. I speak not yet of proof.
   Look to your wife, observe her well with Cassio,
   Wear your eyes thus, not jealious nor secure,
   I would not have your free and noble nature,
   Out of self-bounty, be abus'd; look to't.
   I know our country disposition well:
   In Venice they do let [God] see the pranks
   They dare not show their husbands; their best conscience
   Is not to leave't undone, but keep't unknown.
   Othello: Dost thou say so?
   Iago: She did deceive her father, marrying you
   And when she seem'd to shake and fear your looks,
   She lov'd them most.
   Othello: And so she did.
   Iago: Why, go to then.
   She that so young could give out such a seeming
   To seel her father's eyes up, close as oak,
   He thought 'twas witchcraft—but I am much to blame;
   I humbly do beseech you of your pardon
   For too much loving you" (Shakespeare, *Othello* 3.3.193–213).
   (example mine)

Note: Demetrius focuses on the verbal features of persuasiveness and treats this virtue as a kind of style, as does also Hermogenes (1.11.280). It perhaps corresponds to *apodeiktikon*, when the latter is used to name a style, although the latter, in connoting argument, shifts the focus from verbal to logical features. See *apodeiktikon* above under Discoursal–genres. In the commentary on the *Progymnasmata* of Aphthonius attributed to John of Sardis, a text dating from the 9th century, we find *apithanon* (without persuasiveness) listed as a vice (2.20 in Kennedy, *Progymnasmata* 185).

poikilia [G. "an embroidering in many colors"]

Variety, either by repeating one thing in divers ways or by altering sentence structures

1. With words

   "He escaped; he broke out; he fled."

   "Let me not do it; let me not yield; let me not allow it."

   (Sturm 3.34.799)

2. With sentence structure, or *metaschematismos* [G. "changed scheme"]

   a. Description

      1. By means of *plotike* and *metaplasmos*
      2. By means of lengthening, shortening, inverting, turning back, interrupting
      3. By means of *apodeiktikon*, considering the sentence's function in argument

   b. Example

      "Two things which have the most power in the state—I mean great influence and eloquence—are both working against us to-day; the one, Gaius Aquilius, fills me with apprehension, the other with dread. That the eloquence of Quintius Hortensius may embarrass me in my pleading is a thought that causes me some disquietude; that the influence of Sextus Naevius may injure the cause of Publius Quinctius—of that I am gravely afraid. Yet I should not consider the possession of these advantages in so high a degree by my opponents to be so greatly deplored, if we possessed at least a moderate share of either; but the position is such that I, who have little natural ability and insufficient experience, am pitted against a most accomplished advocate, while my client Quinctius, whose resources are small, who has no opportunities and only a few friends, has to contend with a most influential adversary. An additional disadvantage for us is that Marcus Junius, who has several times pleaded this cause before you, Aquilius, who has had great experience at the bar, and has given great and frequent attention to this cause in particular, is prevented by a new commission from being present to-day. So then I was applied to—I who, even if I possessed all other qualifications in the highest degree, have scarcely had time enough to make myself acquainted with a matter of such importance and one involving so many disputed points. Thus what has generally been a help to me in other causes also fails me in this." (Cicero, *Pro Quinctio* 1.1–4, trans. Freese)

      (Sturm 3.1.452)

Note: An additional name for *poikilia* is "exposition" and for *metaschematismos* is *metabole*. *Metaschematismos* was also an oratorical exercise in which boys were to dissolve, add, transpose, invert, and vary periods, by changing cases, verb forms, lengths, orders, structures, continuity, and so forth (Sturm 3.1.463).

probabilitas [L. "probability, credibility"]

Probability, credibility

Shakespeare's depiction of Iago as the embodiment of evil

(Erasmus, *Ecclesiastes* 3.98.904; example mine)

Note: Erasmus regards this quality as both a virtue and a style.

proprietas [L. "proper signification"]

Without faults in diction; the opposite of *acyron*

1. Calling things by their right names

   "[A man], standing in much need of money and desirous to have some help at a gentleman's hand, made his complaint in this wise: 'I pray you, sir, be so good unto me as forbear this half year's rent. For so help me God and halidom, we are so taken on with contrary bishops, with revives, and with Southsides to the king, that all our money is clean gone.'" The words he should have used were "contributions," "reliefs," and "subsidies."

   (Quintilian 8.2.1; example from Wilson 190)

2. When a word has a number of meanings, using it for its original or proper meaning

   "[T]he word *vertex* means a whirl of water, or of anything else that is whirled in a like manner: then, owing to the fashion of coiling the hair, it comes to mean the top of the head, while finally, from this sense it derives the meaning of the highest point of a mountain. All these things may correctly be called *vertices*, but the proper use of the term is the first."

   (Quintilian 8.2.7)

3. Using the special names that apply to particular contexts

   "Thus we use *urbs* in the special sense of Rome, *venales* in the special sense of newly-purchased slaves, and *Corinthia* in the special sense of bronzes, although there are other cities besides Rome, and many other things which may be styled *venales* besides slaves, and gold and silver are found at Corinth as well as bronze."

   (Quintilian 8.2.8)

4. Using words with the maximum of significance

   "Caesar was thoroughly sober when he undertook the task of overthrowing the constitution" (Cato, *Suet. Caes.* 53, trans. Butler).

   Virgil spoke of a "thin-drawn strain" (Eclogue 6.5) and Horace of the "shrill pipe" (Ode 1.12.1) and "dread Hannibal" (Ode 3.4.36).

   (Quintilian 8.2.9)

5. Using words that become proper names because they sum up someone's salient characteristics

   "Fabius was called 'Cunctator,' the Delayer, on account of the most remarkable of his many military virtues."

   (Quintilian 8.2.11)

6. Using words that are congruent with importance of subject matter, level of style, and purpose

   "wherewith arrives
   Many a pest to plague thee: such as he
   Of subterranean house and granary,
   The small mouse; or, though prisoned by his eyes,
   The mole digs deep his bed; or lurking toad
   Peers from his hole; and many a prodigy
   The earth unnumbered breeds: the weevil tribes
   Whose legions ravage the high heap of corn,
   And ants, whose fear is age and poverty." (Virgil, *Georgic* 1.181, trans. Williams)

   (Quintilian 8.3.20)

Note: Quintilian does not consider this virtue a figure *per se*, but because his discussion is the most thorough on *proprietas*, I summarize him. He does say, however, that "without propriety ornament is impossible" (8.3.16). Wilson calls this virtue "aptness" and stresses that decorum is at the center: "Such are thought apt words that properly agree unto that thing which they signify, and plainly express the nature of the same. Therefore they that have regard of their estimation do warely speak and with choice utter words most apt for their purpose. In weighty causes grave words are thought most needful, that the greatness of the matter may the rather appear in the vehemency of their talk. So likewise of others" (191). This virtue is one of the four primary virtues of style identified by Theophrastus. Cicero takes a broader view of this virtue, treating not only proper words, but also appropriateness in all facets of the speech act. See discretion above. Mosellanus, who also takes the broader view, includes the virtues of *analogia*, *tasis*, and *syntomia* as species here (b.iii.r). See entries for these terms above and below.

synthesis [G. "putting together, composing"] or *compositio* [L. "a putting together, arranging"] or *oeconomia* [G. "direction, management, arrangement"]

Apt composition, with good order and pleasant variety

"Composition is an apt joining together of words in such order that neither the ear shall espy any jar, nor yet any man shall be dulled with overlong drawing out of a sentence, nor yet much confounded with mingling of clauses, such as are needless, being heaped together without reason and used without number. For by such means the hearers will be forced to forget full oft what was said first, before the sentence be half ended, or else be blinded with confounding of many things together." In order to achieve this virtue, one must be neither too brief, nor too prolix; neither too poetical, nor too vulgar; neither too repetitive, nor wholly without repetition. Avoid *eclipsis*, *amphibologia*, *synchisis*, *hiatus*, *tautologia*, *hysteron proteron*, *hypallage*, *hyperbaton*, *homoiologia*, *arithmon*, *periergia*, *macrologia*, and the overuse of interpositions. Observe *ordo* and *poikilia*.

(Wilson 192–94)

Note: Composition is a virtue of style the *Ad Herennium* adds to those of Theophrastus, and as such becomes a widely discussed central division of instruction regarding style. Cicero treats euphony, symmetry and rhythm as the three divisions of composition or word arrangement (*Or.* 60.201). The term *oeconomia* also applies to the principles of good disposition, the second canon of rhetoric (see Melanchthon, *Elem* 29r).

syntomia [G. "conciseness"] or *brevitas* [L. "brevity, conciseness"] or *brachylogia* [G. "brevity in speech"]

The concise, compressed, but compendious style

1. The opposite of *copia*

   "What could be more concisely expressed than [this] line: 'the plains where Troy once stood'? [*Aeneid* 3.13–14]. Macrobius says, in a very few words [Virgil] has here consumed and swallowed up the city without even allowing the ruins to remain" (see *Saturnalia* 5.1.8, trans. Knott).

   (Erasmus, *De copia* 298)

2. The style that is only as long as it needs to be

   "[The speech is] not tediously long, but brief and compendious, as the matter might bear."

   (Puttenham 168)

Note: Veltkirchius also calls this kind of speech *Atticos*, associating it with the Attic style (169r). Just as there are two ways to apply *syntomia*, so the Attic style has been defined in the same two ways (see

Cicero, *Brutus* 82.284–91 or *Orator* 25.83). Like *asiatismus* under vices and *copia* above, this discussion could have been listed under Discoursal–styles. Hoskins substitutes brevity for composition as one of his four virtues of style (4). Quintilian's discussion of this virtue is found in 4.2.42.

tasis [G. "stretching, tension, intensity"]

Pleasant pronunciation and modulation, with fluency, proper accent, and proper speed

"[A]nd if that day brought great glory to you and great joy to the people of Rome, have no hesitation, I beg you, Gaius Caesar, in earning on every possible occasion the title to a like glory. Nothing is so dear to the people as kindness, and none of your many high qualities arouses such admiration and such pleasure as your compassion. For in nothing do men more nearly approach divinity than in doing good to their fellow-men; your situation has nothing prouder in it than the power, your character nothing in it more noble than the wish, to preserve all whom you can. The case might be held to call for a longer speech, your character to demand a briefer. Deeming it therefore more profitable that you yourself should speak rather than that I or anyone else address you, I will now close, merely reminding you that in granting life to the absent Ligarius you will grant it to all these here present" (Cicero, *Pro Ligario* 12.38, trans. Watts).

(Sherry [1550] 37; example mine)

Note: This feature has also been alternately called *enargia* and *extensio*. Vossius suggests that *tasis* produces a calming effect and is appropriate for the defense. Its opposite is *cataphora* (284). See *cataphora* above. Wilson, in his discussion of delivery, makes reference to this virtue, along with a good number of vices of pronunciation (241–42).

Appendix 2

Chronology and Abbreviations of Authors Cited in Appendix 3

c. 2nd to early 1st century B.C.	Demetrius, *On Style*	Dem
c. 85 B.C.	Anonymous, *Ad Herennium*	AdH
55, 46 B.C.	Cicero, *De Oratore*	Cic (De Or)
	Orator	Cic (Or)
	Brutus	Cic (B)
	De Inventione	Cic (*Inv.*)
c. 15 A.D.	Rutilius, *De figuris sententiarum et elocutionis libri II*	Rut
c. 90 A.D.	Quintilian, *Institutio Oratoria* I do not cite Quintilian for figures he mentions but rejects, unless he cites the source of the figure or is the source.	Qui
c. 1st century A.D.	Longinus, *On the Sublime*	Lon
c. 2nd century A.D.	Alexander Rhetor, *On Figures of Thought and Speech* Spengel Ed.	Ale
180 A.D.	Hermogenes, *On Types of Style*	Her
	On Invention	Her (*Inv*)
	On the Method of Forcefulness	Her (*Meth*)
	Progymnasmata	Her (*Pro*)
c. 200 A.D.	Aquila, *De figuris sententiarum et elocutionis*	Aqu
c. 300 A.D.	Rufinianus, *De figuris sententiarum et elocutionis*	Ruf
c. 350 A.D.	Donatus, *Ars grammatica*	Don
c. 370 A.D.	Diomedes, *De schematibus and Tropis.* In *Diomedes doctissimi ac diligentissimi linguae latinae perscrutatoris de arte grammatica opus utilissimum* 1511 ed.	Dio
1470	Trebizond (Trapezuntius), *Rhetoricorum libri quinque* 1538 ed. The Olms edition.	Tra
1489	Mancinelli, *Carmen de figuris*, 1514 ed.	Man
1512	Despauterius, *De figuris*, 1631 ed.	Des

1512	Erasmus, *De duplici copia rerum et verborum*	Era (DC)
	De conscribendis epistolis, 1521	Era (DCE)
	Ecclesiastae sive de ratione concionandi libri quatuor, 1535 The Amsterdam edition, with book, page, line #'s	Era (E.)
1516	Mosellanus, *Tabulae de schematibus et tropis*	Mos
1521	Melanchthon, *Institutiones rhetoricae,* 1528 ed.	Mel (I.)
	Elementorum rhetoricae libri duo, 1531 ed.	Mel (E.)
	Tabulae de schematibus et tropis	Mel (T.)
1534	Veltkirchius, M. (Joannes Velcurio), *In duplicem Erasmi copiam, commentarii; accessit nova in utraque copiam epitome;* 1573 ed. called *D. Erasmi Roterodami De Duplici Copia Verborum ac Rerum Commentarii Duo* All of the figures in *De copia* appear in Veltkirchius's commentary. I do not list Veltkirchius for these, but only for those figures that he adds to the book or provides a name for when Erasmus only describes and does not name the figure.	Vel
c. 1535	Susenbrotus, *Epitome Troporum ac Schematum, Grammaticorum et Rhetoricorum*, 1562 ed.	Sus
1540	Lily, *A Short Introduction of Grammar,* 1567 ed.	Lil
1545	Talaeus, *Rhetorica*, 1548 ed.	Tal
1550	Sherry, *A Treatise of Schemes and Tropes*	She ([1550])
	A Treatise of the Figures of Grammer and Rhetorike, 1555	She ([1555])
1553	Wilson, *The Arte of Rhetorique*, 1560 ed.	Wil
1557	Soarez, *De arte rhetorica*, 1568 ed.	Soa
1561	Scaliger, *Poetices libri septem*, 2nd ed., 1581	Sca
1563	Rainolde, *A Booke Called the Foundacion of Rhetorike*	Rai
1567	Robertellus, *De artificio dicendi*	Rob
1575	Sturm, *De universa ratione elocutionis rhetoricae, libri IIII*, 1576 ed.	Stu
1577	Peacham, *The Garden of Eloquence*	Pea ([1577])
	and the second edition, 1593	Pea ([1593])
1584	Fenner, *The Artes of Logike and Rethorike, plainelie set foorth in the Englishe tounge.*	Fen
1588	Fraunce, *The Arcadian Rhetoric*	Fra
1589	Puttenham, *The Arte of English Poesie*	Put
1592	Day, *The English Secretary*, 1599 ed.	Day

1598	Butler, *Rhetorica libri duo*, 1649 ed.	But
1599	Hoskins, *Directions for Speech and Style*	Hos
1606	Keckermann, *Systema Rhetoricae*	Kec
1619	Gill, *Logonomia Anglica*	Gil
1621	Vossius, *Rhetorices contractae, sive partitionum oratoriarum libri quinque*, Editio ultimo 1711.	Vos
1625	Farnaby, *Index Rhetoricus*	Far
1651	Hoole, *The Latine Grammar*	Hoo
1653	Blount, *The Academie of Eloquence, Containing a Compleat English Rhetorique, Exemplified*, 1654 ed.	Blo
1657	Smith, *The Mystery of Rhetoric Unveiled*	Smi
1659	Walker, *Some Instructions Concerning the Art of Oratory*	Wal
1672	Lamy, *The Art of Speaking*, translated into English 1676. 1688 ed., rpt. 1708	Lam
1679	Shaw, *Words Made Visible: or Grammar and Rhetorick Accommodated to the Lives and Manners of Men*	Sha

Appendix 3

An Alphabetical Listing of the Figures

Figure Name	*Discourse Level*	*Head Word*	*Sources*
Ablatio	Morphological	aphaeresis	She ([1550] 26), Sus (20)
Ablatio inferens	Pragmatical—Idea	remotio	Tra (564)
Abominatio	Discoursal—Genres	execratio	Era (DC 347), Pea ([1593] 82)
Abscisio	Pragmatical—People	aposiopesis	Ad H (4.54.67)
Abscissio	Morphological	apocope	She ([1550] 27), Hoo (263), Smi (171), Sus (21)
Absolutio	Syntactical		Tra (505)
Absonum	Vice	cacemphaton[1]	Vel (10v)
Absurditas	Vice	cacemphaton[1]	Vel (10v)
Abusio	Semantical	catachresis	Ad H (4.33.45), Blo (5), Era (DC 336), Hos (11), Mel (I. 16r), Pea ([1593] 16), Qui (8.6.34), She ([1550] 41), Stu (2.5.304), Sus (10), Tal (13), Tra (465), Vos (225), Wil (200)
Abusio	Vice	catachresis	Gil (151), Smi (48)
Acclamatio	Pragmatical—idea	epiphonema	Blo (29), Era (DC 629), Gil (165), Hos (34), Put (225), Sca (3.40.311), Smi (143), Sus (96)
Accumulatio	Syntactical	congeries	Blo (19, 27), Hos (24, 31)
Accumulatio	Pragmatical—Idea	congeries	Sca (3.46.315)
Accursio	Logical—Idea	epitrechon	Stu (3.15.655)

Figure Name	*Discourse Level*	*Head Word*	*Sources*
Accusatio	Discoursal—Genres		Era (DC 447), Pea ([1593] 80), Sca (3.66.336), Vos (298), Wil (224)
Acervatio	Syntactical	congeries	Qui (9.3.53), Sca (3.43.314)
Acharis	Discoursal—Styles		Dem (§302)
Acrimonia	Discoursal—Styles	sphodrotes	Era (E.3.98.912), Tra (546)
Acris	Discoursal—Styles	akme	Era (E.3.162.211)
Acuitas	Discoursal—Styles	drimytes	Tra (589)
Acyrologia	Vice	acyron	Des (C2r), Dio (g.iv.r), Don (3.3), Man (v.), Pea ([1577] D.i.r.), She ([1550] 32), Sus (11)
Acyron	Vice		Des (C2r), Era (DC 305), Her (*Meth.* §3), Mos (a.viii.v), Put (262), Qui (8.2.4), [Rob (29v)], Stu (3.1.442), Sus (11)
Ad hilaritatem impulsio	Pragmatical—People		Cic (De Or 3.205), Sca (3.93.363), Stu (3.22.708–15), Wil (167–83, 213)
Adagium	Logical—Evidence	paroemia	Mel (I. 17v), Sca (3.84.353), She ([1550] 45), Sus (14), Vel (164r)
Addubitatio	Pragmatical—People	aporia	Aqu (§10), Blo (44), But (121), Far (25), Fen (175), Fra (G7r), Hos (48), Ruf (§9), Smi (150), Tal (26),
Adfictio	Discoursal—Parts of Oration	adnarratio	Ruf (*Dian.* §5)
Adfirmatio	Discoursal—Genres	asseveratio	Qui (6.3.70)
Adhortatio	Discoursal—Genres		Era (DC 498, 510), Kec (1475), Mel (I. 22r), Pea ([1577] L.i.r;[1593] 77), Ruf (§35)
Adianoeta	Discoursal—Genres		Qui (8.2.20)
Adjectio	Morphological	prosthesis	Hoo (263)
Adjectiuum	Lexical	epitheton	Pea ([1593] 146)
Adjudicatio	Discoursal—Genres	epicrisis	Pea ([1593] 99), Stu (2.21.385), Tra (538)
Adjunctio	Grammatical	hypozeugma, prozeugma	Ad H (4.27.38), Cic (De Or 3.206), Soa (320)

Figure Name	*Discourse Level*	*Head Word*	*Sources*
Adjunctio	Grammatical	zeugma	Gil (156), Man (xxx.)
Adjunctio	Lexical	epizeuxis	Smi (89)
Adjuratio	Discoursal—Genres		Era (DC 347, 550), Mel (E. 54v), Qui (9.2.98)
Admiratio	Discoursal—Genres		But (113), Cic (Or 39.135), Era (DC 347), Fen (173), Fra (E5r), Kec (1500), Mel (E. 44r), Pea ([1593] 72), Sca (4.42.513), Sha (183), Smi (141), Stu (1.24.77), Sus (58), Tal (51), Vos (270), Wal (92)
Admonitio	Discoursal—Genres		Pea ([1593] 78), [Qui (9.2.104)], Rob (45v), Sca (3.61.334)
Adnarratio	Discoursal—Parts of Oration		Sca (3.73.342)
Adnominatio	Lexical	paronomasia	Ad H (4.21.29), Era (E. 3.134.571), Qui (9.3.66), Ruf (*Lex.* §15)
Adsonantia	Lexical	paronomasia	Gil (163)
Adulatio	Pragmatical—Idea		Lam (2.133), [Qui (9.2.104)], Rob (45v)
Adversio	Pragmatical—People	apostrophe	Man (xc.), Tra (577)
Adynaton	Discoursal—Genres		Dem (§125), Mel (E. 44v), Rob (39r), Stu (3.22.715)
Aenigma	Discoursal—Genres		Cic (De Or 3.167), Day (80), Dem (§99), Des (C2v), Dio (h.i.v), Don (3.6), Era (DC 336), Far (22), Gil (152–3), Kec (1474), Lam (2.77), Man (lxviii.), Mel (E. 41r; I. 17v), Mos (b.v.v), Pea ([1577] D.ii.r; [1593] 27), Put (198), Qui (8.6.52), Sca (3.84.351), She ([1550] 45; [1555] D.ii.r), Smi (83), Soa (297), Stu (2.3.296), Sus (13), Tal (15), Tra (466), Vos (224)
Aenos	Logical—Evidence		Mel (I. 22r), She ([1550] 93; [1555] G.vii.v), Sca (3.84.351), Vel (164v)

Figure Name	*Discourse Level*	*Head Word*	*Sources*
Aequicrura	Syntactical	isoskelis	Kec (1528)
Aequipollentia	Lexical	isodynamia	Era (DC 342), Kec (1551)
Aeschrologia	Vice	cacemphaton[2]	Des (C2v), Dio (g.iv.v), Mos (b.i.v), She ([1555] B.ii.r), Vel (10v)
Aestimatio	Lexical	protimesis	Stu (2.15.355)
Aetiologia	Logical—Evidence		Ale (17), Day (95), Era (DC 414–16), Far (24), Kec (1482), Mel (E. 50v; I. 26r), Mos (b.vii.v), Pea ([1577] S.iiii.r; [1593] 184), Put (236), Rob (19v), Ruf (§8), Rut (II.19), Sha (142–5), She ([1555] E.viii.r), Smi (123), Soa (338), Sus (84), Vos (249), Wal (80), Wil (229)
Aetopeia	Discoursal—Genres	ethopoeia	She ([1550] 67–8)
Affectio	Discoursal—Styles	ethos	Tra (497)
Affectatio	Vice	cacozelia	Qui (8.3.56), Vel (11r)
Affirmatio	Discoursal—Genres		Blo (24,27), Hos (32), Stu (1.18.48)
Aganactesis	Discoursal—Genres	indignatio	Her (2.7.356), Kec (1499), Rob (37v), Ruf (§11), Stu (1.23.66)
Agnominatio	Lexical	paronomasia	Fra (D5r), Gil (163), Hos (16), Mel (E. 43v; I. 21r), Mos (z.vi.r), Sca (3.56.332), Smi (105), Sus (55), Tra (588), Vel (45v), Vos (240)
Agnominatio	Semantical	antanaclasis	Tra (588)
Agonas	Discoursal—Parts	argumentatio	Stu (3.34.796)
Akme	Pragmatical—idea	incrementum	Her (*Inv.* 4.4.189)
Akme	Discoursal—Styles		Her (1.10.269), Stu (3.8.570; 3.13 [8], 618)
Alastasis	Syntactical		Stu (2.20.385)
Aletheia	Discoursal—Styles		Her (2.7.352), Stu (3.24.725)

Figure Name	*Discourse Level*	*Head Word*	*Sources*
Allegoria	Semantical		Blo (2), But (3), Cic (Or 27.94), Day (79), Dem (§99), Des (C6r), Dio (h.i.r), Don (3.6), Era (DC 336), Far (21), Fen (168), Fra (B4r–v), Gil (152), Her (1.6.246), Hos (9), Kec (1473), Lam (2.76), Man (lxv.), Mel (E. 36v; I. 16v), Mos (b.v.v), Pea ([1577] D.i.r; [1593] 25), Put (197), Qui (8.6.44), Rob (31v), Sca (3.53.330), She ([1550] 45; [1555] D.i.v), Smi (59), Soa (294), Stu (2.3.292), Sus (11), Tal (14), Tra (466),Vos (223), Wal (58), Wil (201)
Alleotheta	Grammatical	enallage	Des (C8r), Far (28), Gil (158), Man (xciiii.), Pea ([1577] H.iii.r), Sus (42)
Alloiosis	Grammatical	enallage	Ale (33), Gil (158), Man (xciiii.), Sca (4.36.505), Sus (42)
Alloiosis	Logical—Idea	dissimilitudo	Qui (9.3.92), Rob (19v), Rut (II.2), Sca (4.36.505), Stu (2.24.424)
Allophylos	Syntactical		Man (lxxxvi.)
Allusio	Lexical	paronomasia	Sca (4.33.503)
Allusio	Semantical	allegoria	Sca (3.84.349), Vel (172v)
Allusione	Logical—Evidence	parechesis	Era (DC 630), Lam (5.145)
Alyton	Grammatical	disjunctio	Soa (321)
Ambiguitas	Vice	amphibologia	Ad H (4.53.67), Qui (8.2.16), She ([1550] 33; [1555] A.vi.v), Vel (9r)
Ambitus	Syntactical	periodus	Aqu (§18), Cic (Or 60.204), Kec (1525), Stu (3.1.437), Tra (507), Vos (279)
Ameles	Discoursal—Styles		Her (1.12.296), Stu (3.17.667)
Amphibolia	Vice	amphibologia	Dem (§196), Don (3.3), Fen (177), Her (*Meth.* §35), [Qui (9.4.32)], Vos (206)

Figure Name	*Discourse Level*	*Head Word*	*Sources*
Amphibologia	Vice		Des (C2r), Dio (g.iv.v), Man (x.), Mos (b.i.r), Pea ([1577] G.i.r), Put (267), [Rob (29v)], She ([1550] 33), Wil (192, 194)
Amphidiorthosis	Pragmatical—People	prodiorthosis	Ale (15)
Amplificatio	Pragmatical—Idea		Blo (11), Cic (Or 36.126), Era (DC 592), Hos (17), Kec (1475), Mel (E. 33r), Pea ([1577] N.ii.r–iii.v; [1593] 120–2), [Qui (8.4.1; 9.2.106)], Sca (3.46.315), She ([1550] 70; [1555] F.viii.r), Stu (1.30.111), Wal (66), Wil (147–160)
Amplitudo	Discoursal—Styles	oratio grandis/ megethos	Era (E.3.64.252), Stu (3.6.543)
Anacephalaeosis	Pragmatical—Idea	frequentatio[1]	Era (E. 2.468.486), Her (*Meth.* §12), Stu (1.40.229)
Anaclasis	Lexical		Qui (9.3.68, 97), Rob (24r), Rut (I.5), She ([1550] 60)
Anacoenosis	Pragmatical—People	communicatio	But (121), Far (25), Gil (166), Mel (I. 22v), Pea ([1577] M.ii.r; [1593] 110), Put (235), Rob (43v), Ruf (§10), Sha (134–6), She ([1550] 55), Smi (152), Soa (341), Stu (3.31.779), Sus (64), Tal (27), Vos (245)
Anacoluthon	Grammatical	anapodoton	Kec (1501)
Anacoluthon	Vice		Dem (§153), Kec (1501)
Anadiplosis	Lexical	epizeuxis	Dem (§267), Ruf (*Lex.* §8), Stu (2.22.399)

Figure Name	*Discourse Level*	*Head Word*	*Sources*
Anadiplosis	Syntactical		Ale (29), Aqu (§32), Blo (6), But (104), Cic (De Or 3.206), Day (85), Dem (§66), Des (C4v), Dio (g.iii.v), Don (3.5), Far (22), Fen (172), Fra (C6v), Gil (160), Hos (12), Kec (1505), Lam (3.160), Man (xxxv.), Mos (a.vi.r), Pea ([1577] J.iii.r; [1593] 46), Put (210), Qui (9.3.44), Rob (24v), Sca (4.29.498), She ([1550] 48; [1555] D.v.r), Smi (92), Soa (310), Sus (50), Tal (66), Vos (236), Wal (33)
Anairesis	Discoursal—Genres		Her (1.9.267), Stu (2.15.353)
Anakampsis	Syntactical		Dem (§256), Era (DC 345), Her (4.3.181), Kec (1543), Stu (3.1.451)
Analogia	Logical—Evidence		Era (DC 607), Stu (2.2.275), Vel (159v)
Analogia	Virtue		Mos (b.iii.r), Put (168), Rob (18r, 31v), She ([1550] 37), Stu (2.2.275)
Anamnesis	Pragmatical—Idea		Pea ([1593] 76), Qui (9.2.61, 106), Rob (45v), Sca (3.91.362), Smi (249), Soa (361), Stu (1.37.192)
Anangeon	Discoursal—Genres	dicaeologia	Her (2.8.368), Mel (E. 50v; I. 26r), Rob (19v), Rut (I. 20), Sca (3.66.336), She ([1550] 60; [1555] E.viii.v), Stu (3.35.807), Sus (85)
Anapausis	Rhythmical	caesura	Her (1.1.218), Stu (1.5.11)
Anantapodoton	Grammatical	anapodoton	Kec (1501), Mel (E. 43v; I. 21r)
Anantapodoton	Vice	anacoluthon	Era (E. 3.7.12), Kec (1501), Mel (E. 57r)

Figure Name	*Discourse Level*	*Head Word*	*Sources*
Anaphora	Syntactical		Blo (7), But (106), Cic (De Or 3.206), Day (84), Dem (§141), Des (C4v), Dio (g.iii.v), Don (3.5), Far (22), Fen (172), Fra (C8v), Gil (159), Her (2.1.316), Hos (13), Kec (1505), Lam (3.158), Lon (§20), Man (xxx-viii.), Mos (a.vi.r), Pea ([1593] 41), Put (208), Qui (9.3.30), Sca (4.30.500), She ([1555] D.iiii.r), Smi (96), Soa (368), Stu (3.35.816), Sus (49), Tal (59), Vos (235), Wal (44)
Anapodoton	Grammatical		Pea ([1577] F.i.v), Sus (24)
Anarithmesis	Pragmatical—Idea	enumeratio	Rob (49r)
Anasceue	Discoursal—Parts of Oration	antirrhesis	Her (*Meth.* §26), Ruf (*Dian.* §6)
Anastrophe	Syntactical		Day (82), Des (C6r), Dio (h.i.r), Don (3.6), Far (28), Gil (164), Hoo (268), Kec (1502), Man (lx.), Mos (b.vi.v), Pea ([1577] F.iii.v), Qui (8.6.65), Rob (30v), She ([1550] 31; [1555] C.ii.v), Smi (198), Stu (1.19.51), Sus (31)
Anastrophe	Pragmatical—Idea	hysteron proteron	Her (1.11.282), Stu (3.13.633)
Anastrophe	Vice	synchisis	Qui (1.5.40), Vos (208)
Anastrophe ton pistis	Logical—Argument Forms		Her (1.11.283), Stu (3.14.643)
Aneimeson	Discoursal—Styles	dissolutum	Stu (3.19.682)
Animatio	Discoursal—Genres	conformatio	Stu (1.37.185)
Anisocolon	Syntactical		Dem (§53), Kec (1529), Stu (2.23.417)
Annexio	Syntactical	epiploke	Stu (3.18.680)
Annominatio	Lexical		Aqu (§27), Qui (9.3.71), Rob (22r), She ([1555] D.vii.r)
Annominatio	Lexical	paronomasia	Soa (322), Tal (68)
Annotation	Semantical	periphrasis	Era (DC 332), Pea ([1577] H.i.v; [1593] 148)

Figure Name	*Discourse Level*	*Head Word*	*Sources*
Anoiconometon	Vice	synchisis	Qui (8.3.59), [Rob (29v)], She ([1555] B.ii.v), Vel (12r)
Anomoiosis	Logical—Idea	dissimilitudo	Vos (254)
Antanaclasis	Semantical		Day (87), Far (23), Gil (162), Kec (1508), Man (xxxix.), Mel (E. 43v; I. 21r), Pea ([1577] K.ii.v; [1593] 56), Put (216), Qui (9.2.99; 9.3.68), Rob (31r), Sha (182–3), Smi (107), Sus (56), Vel (45v), Vos (232), Wil (170)
Antanaclasis	Discoursal—Parts of Oration		Blo (40), Hos (44), Smi (107)
Antapodosis	Logical—Idea		Her (1.11.291), [Qui (8.3.78)], Rob (30r), Sca (3.51.324)
Antarithmos	Semantical	liptote	Stu (3.17.678)
Anteisagoge	Pragmatical—Idea	antenagoge	Ale (25), Aqu (§14)
Antenagoge	Pragmatical—Idea		Aqu (§14), Day (89), Put (224), Sca (3.51.324), Wil (161)
Antenantiosis	Semantical	litotes	Ale (37)
Antenklematiko	Pragmatical—Idea	inversio	Her (2.6.347), Stu (3.35.814)
Ante occupatio	Pragmatical—Idea	prolepsis	Cic (De Or 3.205), Far (24), Soa (339)
Anthimeria	Grammatical		Era (DC 322), Hoo (265), Pea ([1577] H.iiii.v), Qui (9.3.10), Sca (4.36.505), Stu (3.17.678)
Anthropopathia	Semantical		Pea ([1593] 13), Smi (204)
Anthypallage	Grammatical	antiptosis	Dem (§59), Vos (291)
Anthypophora	Pragmatical—People	subjectio	Day (87), Put (214)
Anthypophora	Discoursal—Parts of Oration		But (121), Des (C7r), Far (24), Lam (2.127), Man (lxxxiiii.), Mel (E. 53r; I. 24v), Pea ([1577] S.i.v; [1593] 170), Ruf (*Dian.* §4), Rob (31r), She ([1555] E.vii.r), Smi (128), Stu (1.28.104), Sus (61), Vos (243)
Anticipatio	Syntactical	prolepsis	Ruf (Lex §1)

Figure Name	*Discourse Level*	*Head Word*	*Sources*
Anticipatio	Pragmatical—Idea	prolepsis	Ruf (*Dian.* §2), Sca (3.49.320), Smi (127), Wil (213)
Antimetabole	Syntactical		Ale (37), Blo (9), Day (95), Far (23), Gil (166), Hos (14), Lam (3.161), Mel (E. 52r; I. 24r), Mos (a.vii.v), Pea ([1577] R.ii.r; [1593] 164), Put (217), Qui (9.3.85), Rob (31r), Rut (I.6), Sca (4.37.506), Smi (116), Soa (330), Stu (2.26.431), Sus (81), Vos (256), Wil (229)
Antimetathesis	Syntactical	antimetabole	Ale (37), Sca (4.37.506), Sha (183), Vos (237)
Antiphasis	Semantical		Sca (3.90.361), Wal (93)
Antiphora	Pragmatical—Idea	prolepsis	Blo (46), Fen (175), Hos (50), Mos (a.vii.r), She ([1550] 53), Smi (129)
Antiphrasis	Semantical		Day (80), Des (C6v), Dio (h.i.v), Don (3.6), Far (21), Gil (153), Kec (1467), Man (lxvii.), Mel (I. 18r), Mos (b.vi.r), Pea ([1577] C.iiii.v; [1593] 24), Put (201), Qui (8.6.57; 9.2.47), Ruf (*Dian.* §12), Sca (3.90.359), She ([1550] 46), Smi (45, 74), Stu (3.22.713), Sus (11, 16), Tra (465), Vel (37r), Vos (229), Wil (171)
Antiprosopopoeia	Discoursal—Genres	prosopopoeia	Stu (3.10.587)
Antiprotasis	Discoursal—Parts of Oration		Her (*Inv.* 3.4.134), Stu (1.28.104)
Antiptosis	Grammatical		But (131), Era (DC 326), Far (27), Gil (158), Hoo (266), Kec (1502), Lil (G.iiii.r), Man (lxxix.), Mel (I. 19v), Pea ([1577] H.iii.r), She ([1550] 31), Smi (192), Stu (3.17.678), Sus (34), Vos (291)
Antirrhesis	Discoursal—Parts of Oration		Her (1.8.262), Pea ([1593] 88), Rob (45v), Stu (3.11.602)
Antisagoge	Logical—Idea		Mel (E. 53r; I. 24v), Pea ([1593] 93), Rob (48r), Sus (61), Wil (156)

Figure Name	*Discourse Level*	*Head Word*	*Sources*
Antistasis	Lexical		Rob (23v), Ruf (*Lex.* §24)
Antistoechon	Phonetic		But (52), Far (26), Gil (180), Hoo (264), Man (xxv.), Mos (a.iiii.v), Pea ([1577] E.iii.r), Put (174), She ([1550] 28; [1555] B.iii.v), Smi (172), Sus (22)
Antistrophe	Syntactical	epistrophe	Ale (29), Aqu (§35), Day (85), Gil (160), Her (1.12.303), Put (208), Rob (24r), She ([1550] 47), Soa (309), Stu (2.22.400), Sus (51), Tra (571)
Antistrophe	Pragmatical—Idea	inversio	Smi (125), Stu (2.23.429)
Antithesis	Phonetic	antistoechon	But (52), Des (C3v), Don (3.4), Far (26), Gil (180), Hoo (264), Man (xxv.), Mos (a.iiii.r), Rob (29r), Smi (172), Sus (22)
Antithesis	Syntactical	syncrisis	Ale (36), But (130), Far (18), Kec (1534), Qui (9.2.101), Rob (22r), Ruf (*Lex.* §13), Stu (1.31.115)
Antithesis	Logical—Idea		Cic (Or 39.135), Day (92), Dem (§22), Era (DC 616), Gil (166), Her (1.11.282), Kec (1475), Lam (2.110), Mel (E. 52r; I. 23v), Pea ([1577] R.i.r; [1593] 160), Rob (31r), Ruf (§37), Sca (4.37.506), Sha (152–5), Smi (172), Soa (328), Stu (1.20.57; 1.26.88), Sus (71), Wil (229)
Antitheton	Syntactical	syncrisis	Aqu (§22), Des (C7v), Her (*Inv.* 4.2.173), Man (lxxxv.), Qui (9.3.81), Rob (19v), Vos (255)
Antitheton	Logical—Idea	antithesis	Era (E. 3.124.385), Her (*Meth.*§15), Put (219), Rob (31r), Rut (II.16), Sca (3.59.334), She ([1550] 56), Soa (328), Sus (71), Vos (255), Wal (121)
Antitheton	Logical—Argument Forms	enthymema	She ([1550] 56), Stu (2.23.428)

Figure Name	*Discourse Level*	*Head Word*	*Sources*
Antonomasia	Semantical		But (31), Day (79), Des (C5v), Dio (g.vi.v), Don (3.6), Era (DC 331), Far (21), Gil (154), Kec (1459), Lam (2.74), Man (liii.), Mel (E. 36r; I. 16r), Mos (b.v.r), Pea ([1577] C.iii.v; [1593] 22), Put (192), Qui (8.6.29), Rob (28v), She ([1550] 44; [1555] C.viii.v), Smi (66), Soa (288), Stu (2.6.311), Sus (8), Tal (21), Tra (465), Vos (222), Wil (201)
Apagoresis	Discoursal—Genres		[Qui (9.2.107)], Rob (46r), Sca (3.83.349)
Apantesis	Discoursal—Parts of Oration		Her (2.7.356), Rob (49r), Stu (1.20.57; 1.26.88)
Aparithmesis	Pragmatical—Idea	enumeratio	Her (1.4.239), Stu (3.7.563), Vos (244)
Apeile	Discoursal—Genres	cataplexis	Stu (3.13.623)
Aphaeresis	Morphological		But (45), Des (C3r), Dio (g.v.r), Don (3.4), Era (DC 329), Far (26), Gil (179), Hoo (262), Kec (1515), Lil (G.i.r), Man (xviii.), Mel (T. c.iiii.v), Mos (a.iiii.r), Pea ([1577] E.ii.r), Put (173), Rob (28v), She ([1550] 26; 1555] B.iii.v), Smi (170), Sus (20), Wil (202)
Aphaeresis	Pragmatical—Idea	remotio	Kec (1483), Stu (1.40.224), Vos (244)
Aphegesis	Discoursal—Parts of Oration		Stu (1.15.37; 1.26.90)
Apheleia	Discoursal—Styles		Her (2.3.322), Qui (8.3.87), Rob (30r), Stu (3.20.691)
Apheles	Syntactical	absolutio	Vos (281)
Aphodos	Discoursal—Parts of Oration	digressio	[Qui (9.3.87)]
Aphodrotes	Discoursal—Styles	trachytes	Stu (3.10.583)

Figure Name	*Discourse Level*	*Head Word*	*Sources*
Aphorismus	Pragmatical—People		Day (94), Gil (165), Mel (I. 25v), Rob (42v), Ruf (§14), Stu (1.28.104), Sus (75)
Apocarteresis	Pragmatical—People		Pea ([1593] 83), Rob (49r)
Apocope	Morphological		But (45), Cic (Or 45.153), Des (C3r), Dio (g.v.r), Don (3.4), Era (DC 329), Far (26), Gil (179), Hoo (262), Kec (1515), Lil (G.i.v), Man (xx.), Mel (T. c.iiii.v), Mos (a.iiii.r), Pea ([1577] E.ii.v), Put (173), Rob (28v), She ([1550] 27; [1555] B.iii.v), Smi (171), Sus (21), Wil (202)
Apocope	Discoursal—Styles		Dem (§238)
Apodeiktikon	Discoursal—Genres		Her (*Inv.* 3.13.162), Stu (1.38.201; 3.3.487)
Apodioxis	Pragmatical—People		But (138), Mel (E. 52v; I. 25v), Pea ([1577] S.iiii.r; [1593] 185), Rob (43v), Ruf (§12), Sha (183), Smi (229), Vos (271)
Apodeixis	Logical—Evidence		Dem (§233), Era (DC 580), Kec (1535), Pea ([1593] 86), Smi (230), Stu (3.3.487)
Apodosis	Syntactical		Far (18), Her (*Inv.* 4.3.179), Kec (1526), Stu (2.24.426), Vos (281)
Apologia	Discoursal--Genres		Her (*Meth.* §32), Sca (3.84.350), Stu (1.29.109)
Apologus	Discoursal—Genres	fable	Era (DC 607), Mel (E. 41v), Pea ([1593] 188), Sca (3.84.350), Stu (3.21.707)
Apolytos merismos	Pragmatical—Idea		Her (2.7.362)
Apomnemonsysis	Logical—Evidence		Pea ([1593] 87), Rob (48v), Stu (3.22.712)
Apophansis	Discoursal—Genres	asseveratio	Dem (§296), Her (1.6.246), Stu (3.9.571)

Figure Name	*Discourse Level*	*Head Word*	*Sources*
Apophasis	Semantical	litotes	Her (*Meth.* §37)
Apophasis	Pragmatical—People		But (20), Far (25), Fra (A8v), Kec (1472), Rob (44v), Sca (3.89.359), Sha (183), Smi (164), Soa (349)
Apophasis	Pragmatical—People	subjectio	Rob (43v), Ruf (§8)
Apophonema	Discoursal—Genres	adhortatio	Rob (43r), Ruf (§19)
Apophthegma	Logical—Evidence	paroemia	Era (DC 646), Kec (1478) Mel (T. c.v.v), Stu (3.22.708), Sus (96), Vos (278)
Apoplanesis	Pragmatical—Idea	aversio	Pea ([1577] N.i.r; [1593] 117), Rob (43v), Ruf (§13)
Aporia	Pragmatical—People		But (121), Day (89), Far (25), Mel (E. 44r; I. 22r), Pea ([1577] M.i.v; [1593] 109), Put (234), Rob (43v), Ruf (§9), Rut (II.10), Sha (164–5), She ([1550] 54), Smi (150), Sus (63), Tal (26), Vos (262), Wil (210, 230)
Aposiopesis	Pragmatical—People		Ad H (4.30.41), Ale (22), Aqu (§5), But (116), Day (81), Dem (§103), Des (C2r), Era (E. 3.110.146), Far (25), Fen (174), Fra (F6v), Gil (156), Her (2.7.361), Kec (1490), Lam (2.105), Man (xii.), Mel (I. 21v), Mos (a.vii.r), Pea ([1577] E.iiii.r. & N.i.v; [1593] 118), Put (178), Qui (9.2.54), Rob (30r), Sca (3.77.344), Sha (168–9), She ([1555] B.viii.v), Smi (148), Soa (345), Stu (2.19.374), Sus (25), Tal (50), Vos (263), Wil (205)
Apostasis	Pragmatical—Idea		Her (1.9.267; 2.7.355), Stu (3.12.617; 3.24.729)

Figure Name	*Discourse Level*	*Head Word*	*Sources*
Apostrophe	Pragmatical—People		Ad H (4.15.22), Ale (23), Aqu (§9), Blo (44), But (116), Day (90), Des (C8r), Era (DC 325), Far (25), Fen (174), Fra (F7v), Her (2.1.313), Hos (48), Kec (1494), Lam (2.118), Man (xc.), Mel (E. 44v; I. 22v), Mos (b.vii.v), Pea ([1577] M.iiii.v; [1593] 116), Put (244), Qui (9.2.38), Rob (44r), Ruf (*Lex.* §26), Sca (4.1.456), Sha (183), She ([1550] 60), Smi (157), Soa (343), Stu (1.22.63), Sus (67), Tal (47), Vos (269), Wal (94)
Apotropon	Discoursal—Genres	dehortatio	Rob (37v)
Appellatio conscientia	Pragmatical—People		Kec (1495)
Appositio	Morphological	prosthesis	She ([1550] 26), Smi (170), Sus (20)
Appositio	Grammatical		Des (C7r), Era (DC 591), Far (27), Hoo (264), Kec (1502), Lil (G.i.v), Man (cii.), Mos (a.viii.r), She ([1555] B.vi.v; [1550] 30), Wal (53)
Appositio	Lexical	epitheton	Pea ([1593] 146), Qui (8.6.40), Soa (288), Sus (39), Tra (465)
Ara	Discoursal—Genres	imprecatio	Fen (174), Pea ([1593] 64), Rob (43r), Stu (1.24.70), Vos (270)
Archaismus	Lexical		Cic (De Or 3.153), Era (DC 312), Hoo (264), Pea ([1593] 15), Qui (9.3.14), Stu (3.22.712)
Areia	Discoursal—Genres	imprecatio	Mel (I. 22r), Ruf (§15), She ([1550] 51), Soa (358), Sus (62)
Argumentatio	Discoursal—Parts of Oration		Kec (1475), Sca (3.71.339), Stu (2.27.434)
Arithmon	Vice		Ad H (4.12.18), Dem (§117), Her (1.7.259), Put (83), [Qui (9.4.56)], She ([1555] B.ii.v), Vel (11v), Wil (193)

Figure Name	*Discourse Level*	*Head Word*	*Sources*
Arsis and Thesis	Pragmatical—Idea	remotio	Her (1.11.293), Stu (3.16.660)
Articulus	Syntactical		Ad H (4.19.26), Era (E. 3.102.976), Her (1.8.263), Mel (E. 43r; I. 20v), Pea ([1577] J.iiii.v; [1593] 57), She ([1550] 57; [1555] D.vii.v), Soa (319), Sus (53), Tra (549), Vel (46r), Wal (76)
Articulus	Syntactical	asyndeton	Far (27), Gil (156), Mel (E. 43r), Smi (183)
Asapheia	Discoursal—Styles		Stu (3.6.545)
Ascensus	Syntactical	climax	Aqu (§40)
Aschematiston	Vice		Mos (b.i.v), Qui (8.3.59; 9.1.4), [Rob (29v)], She ([1550] 35; [1555] B.ii.r), Vel (11r), Wil (193)
Aeschrologia	Vice	cacemphaton[2]	She ([1550] 34; [1555] B.ii.r)
Asiatismus	Vice		Cic (B. 325), She ([1555] B.ii.r), Vel (10v), Wil (194)
Asperitas	Discoursal—Styles	trachytes	[Sca (4.1.456)], Tra (544)
Asphalia	Logical—Evidence		Pea ([1593] 68), Rob (46v)
Asseveratio	Discoursal—Genres		Era (DC 653), Qui (9.2.104), Rob (45r), Sca (3.38.311; 3.60.334), Stu (1.16.42), Tra (536)
Assonantia	Phonetic	parechesis	Era (E. 3.132.568), Gil (163), Sus (56)
Asteismus	Pragmatical—People		Day (80), Des (C6v), Dio (h.i.v), Don (3.6), Far (22), Gil (153), Kec (1472), Man (lxxii.), Mel (I. 18r), Mos (b.vi.r), Pea ([1577] D.iiii.r; [1593] 33), Put (200), Qui (8.6.57), Rob (43r), Ruf (§4), Sha (183), She ([1550] 46; [1555] D.ii.r), Smi (77), Sus (15), Vos (228), Wil (206)
Astrothesiam	Discoursal—Genres		She ([1550] 69), Vel (129r)

Figure Name	*Discourse Level*	*Head Word*	*Sources*
Asyndeton	Syntactical		Ale (32), Aqu (§41), Blo (33), But (128), Day (83), Dem (§268), Des (C4r), Dio (g.iii.v), Era (DC 345), Far (27), Gil (156), Her (1.9.267), Hoo (266), Hos (38), Kec (1502), Lon (§20), Man (xxxiii.), Mel (E. 43v; I. 20v), Mos (a.vii.r), Pea ([1577] G.iiii.r/J.iiii.r; [1593] 52), Put (185), Qui (9.3.50), Rob (23v), Ruf (*Lex.* §20), Sca (4.28.497), Sha (178–9), She ([1550] 59; [1555] D.vii.v), Smi (182), Soa (318), Stu (2.25.428), Sus (37), Vos (230), Wal (35), Wil (229)
Athroisis	Pragmatical—Idea	enumeratio	Stu (2.12.338)
Athroismos	Pragmatical—Idea	congeries	Lon (§23)
Atonia	Vice		Her (2.11.399), Sca (3.27.294)
Attemperatio	Pragmatical—Idea	eudiasis	Sca (3.36.310)
Attenuata	Discoursal—Styles	subtilitas	[Ad H (4.8.11)], She ([1555] H.iiii.r), Tra (457)
Attractio	Morphological	parelcon	Lil (G.v.r)
Attributio	Lexical	epitheton	Sus (39)
Attributio	Logical—Idea		Era (DC 458), Sca (3.48.318)
Auctoritas	Logical—Evidence	kriseis	Kec (1475), She ([1550] 92; [1555] G.vi.v), Vel (151r), Wal (70)
Autoschediasmos	Pragmatical—People		Stu (3.35.809)
Auxesis	Semantical		But (4), Era (DC 343), Far (21), Mel (E. 48r; I. 23r), Pea ([1577] N.iii.r; [1593] 167), Qui (8.4.1), Sha (183), She ([1550] 70; [1555] F.viii.v), Smi (55), Sus (70), Vos (259), Wil (152)
Auxesis	Pragmatical—Idea	amplificatio	Cic (Or. 36.125), Her (1.11.283), Mel (E. 47v), Stu (2.27.435)
Auxesis	Pragmatical—Idea	incrementum	Day (91), Kec (1487), Put (226), Sus (70)

Figure Name	*Discourse Level*	*Head Word*	*Sources*
Aversio	Pragmatical—Idea		Cic (De Or 3.205), Qui (9.2.39), Sca (3.82.348), Stu (3.35.810)
Aversio	Pragmatical—People	apostrophe	Aqu (§9), Day (90), Kec (1494), Mel (E. 44v; I. 22v), Qui (9.2.38), She ([1550] 60), Smi (157), Soa (343), Sus (67), Tal (47), Vel (30v)
Axioma	Discoursal—Styles	oratio grandis/megethos	Her (1.5.242), Stu (3.8.567)
Barbaralexis	Vice		Des (C1v), Dio (g.iv.v), Don (3.1), Era (DC 304, 312), Gil (154), Mos (b.ii.v), Rob (28v), She ([1555] A.v.r), Wil (188)
Barbarismus	Vice		Ad H (4.12.17), Des (C1v), Dio (g.iv.v), Don (3.1.), Era (DC 304, 314), Man (ii.), Mos (b.i.v), Put (257), Qui (1.5.6), Rob (28v), Sca (3.31.306), She ([1550] 36; [1555] A.v.r)
Bare	Discoursal—Styles	subtilitas	Stu (3.29.766)
Barytes	Discoursal—Styles		Her (2.8.364), Stu (3.25.734), Tra (601)
Battologia	Vice		But (136), Era (DC 318)
Bdelygmia	Discoursal—Genres	execratio	Fen (174), Pea ([1593] 82), Smi (141)
Bebaiosis	Logical—Evidence		Her (*Meth.* §28), Stu (3.35.816)
Benedictio	Discoursal—Genres	eulogia	Pea ([1593] 65)
Benevolentia	Pragmatical—People	philophronesis	Pea ([1593] 96)
Bomphiologia	Vice		Pea ([1577] G.ii.r; [1593] 168), Put (266), She ([1550] 61; [1555] B.ii.r)
Brachiepia	Discoursal—Styles	brevitas	Pea ([1577] T.iiii.v; [1593] 182), Rob (20r), Stu (3.18.680), Wil (205–6)
Brachiologa	Syntactical	articulus	Day (92), Dio (g.iv.r), Put (222)
Brachylogia	Syntactical	asyndeton	Qui (9.3.50), Sus (53)

Figure Name	*Discourse Level*	*Head Word*	*Sources*
Brachylogia	Discoursal—Styles	brevitas	Dem (§242), Her (*Meth.* §33), Qui (8.3.82), Rob (30r), Rut (II.8)
Brachylogia	Vice		She ([1555] A.vii.r), Vel (10r), Vos (207), Wil (192)
Brachylogia	Virtue	syntomia	She ([1555] A.vii.r)
Brevis injectio	Syntactical	alastasis	Tra (577)
Brevitas	Syntactical		Rob (50r), Stu (2.22.400), Vos (297), Wil (205–6)
Brevitas	Discoursal—Styles		Ad H (4.54.68), Cic (De Or 3.202), Era (DC 300), She ([1555] G.viii.v),
Brevitas	Virtue	syntomia	Cic (Or 40.139), Vel (169r)
Cacemphaton[1]	Vice		Dio (g.iv.v), Gil (168), Lam (3.210), Man (xv.), Pea ([1577] G.iii.r), Put (261), Qui (8.3.44), She ([1555] B.ii.r), Sus (36), Vel (10v), Vos (275), Wil (192)
Cacemphaton[2]	Vice	(aeschrologia)	Don (3.3), Era (DC 309, 315), Mos (b.i.v), Put (260), Qui (8.3.44)
Cacophaton	Vice	cacemphaton[1]	Des (C2v), Gil (168)
Cacophonia	Vice	cacemphaton[1]	Cic (De Or 3.171), Dem (§105), Her (1.7.259), Stu (2.22.408), Vel (10v)
Cacosyntheton	Vice		Des (C2v), Dio (g.iv.v), Don (3.3), Gil (168), Man (xvi.), Mos (b.i.v), Pea ([1577] G.iiii.r), Put (260), Qui (8.3.59), [Rob (29v)], She ([1550] 35; [1555] B.ii.v), Sus (36), Vel (12r), Wil (190, 192)
Cacozelia	Vice		Des (C2v), Dio (g.iv.v), Era (E. 3.26.405), Gil (168), Her (*Inv.* 4.12.202), Mos (b.i.v), Pea ([1577] G.ii.v), Put (258), Qui (8.3.56), [Rob (29v)], She ([1550] 34; [1555] B.ii.r), Vel (11r), Vos (298), Wil (190)
Cacozelias	Discoursal—Styles		Dem (§186), Her (*Inv.* 4.10.199)

Figure Name	*Discourse Level*	*Head Word*	*Sources*
Caesura	Rhythmical		Hoo (305), Lil (G.vi.v), Put (86)
Calumnia	Vice		Mel (E. 51v)
Castigatio	Pragmatical—Idea	remotio	Sca (3.82.348)
Catachresis	Semantical		Blo (5), But (3), Cic (Or 27.94), Day (79), Des (C5r), Dio (g.iv.v), Don (3.6), Era (DC 336), Far (21), Hos (11), Kec (1469), Lam (2.80), Man (xlix.), Mel (E. 36v; I. 16r), Mos (b.iiii.v), Pea ([1577] C.iiii.r; [1593] 16), Put (190), Qui (8.6.34), Rob (31v), She ([1550] 41; [1555] C.vii.v), Smi (48), Soa (291), Stu (2.5.304), Sus (10), Tal (13), Vos (225), Wil (200)
Catachresis	Vice		Era (DC 313), Fen (168), Far (21), Gil (151), Kec (1469), Smi (49), Stu (3.1.442)
Catachresticos	Pragmatical—People	convinciari	Man (l.)
Catacosmesis	Pragmatical—Idea	ordo	Pea ([1593] 118)
Catalogos	Pragmatical—Idea	distributio[2]	Mos (b.vii.v)
Cataphora	Virtue		Her (*Inv.* 4.5.192), Vos (284)
Cataphronesis	Discoursal—Genres		Stu (3.13.623)
Cataplexis	Discoursal—Genres		Lam (2.97), Mel (E. 54v), Pea ([1593] 79), Qui (9.2.103), Rob (45r), Sca (3.62.335), Stu (3.31.784)
Catatyposis	Semantical		Man (xcviii.)
Categoria	Discoursal—Genres	accusatio	Dem (§296), Her (1.10.277), Pea ([1593] 80)
Cateroche	Semantical		Man (xcix.)
Causa	Logical—Evidence	aetiologia	Mel (I. 26r), Sus (84)
Celeritas	Pragmatical—Idea	epitrochasmus	Sca (3.44.315), Stu (1.20.55)
Celeritas	Discoursal—Styles	gorgotes	Tra (576)
Celeriter	Morphological	syncope	Sca (4.44.519)

Figure Name	*Discourse Level*	*Head Word*	*Sources*
Certitudo	Logical—Evidence	asphalia	Pea ([1593] 68)
Chalinos	Vice	cacemphaton[1]	Qui (1.1.37)
Characterismus	Discoursal—Genres		Far (23), Gil (158), Kec (1482), Rut (II.7), She ([1550] 66; [1555] F.v.r), Vel (127v), Wil (212)
Charientismus	Discoursal—Genres		Day (80), Dem (§128), Des (C6v), Dio (h.i.v), Don (3.6), Far (22), Kec (1472), Man (lxix.), Mel (I. 18r), Mos (b.vi.r), Pea ([1577] D.iiii.v; [1593] 36), Put (201), Rob (42v), Ruf (§3), Sha (183), She ([1550] 46; [1555] D.ii.v), Smi (76), Sus (16), Vel (37r), Vos (227)
Chiasmus	Syntactical	antimetabole	Her (*Inv.* 4.4.182), Sca (4.38.508), Stu (3.3.503), Tra (513)
Chleuasmos	Semantical		Fen (173), Fra (E8v), Kec (1473), Rob (42v), Ruf (§2),
Chorismos	Pragmatical—Idea		Stu (1.15.38)
Chreia	Logical—Evidence		Era (DC 626), Kec (1476), Mel (E. 53v), Rob (43v), Ruf (§18), She ([1550] 93; [1555] G.vii.r–v)
Chrismos	Logical—Evidence	oraculum	Vel (164v)
Chronographia	Discoursal—Genres		Des (C7r), Era (DC 588), Far (23), Gil (158), Man (lxxxii.), Mel (E. 54v), Mos (b.vii.v), Pea ([1577] P.i.v–ii.v; [1593] 142), Put (246), She ([1550] 69; [1555] F.vii.r), Smi (223), Stu (3.21.700), Sus (89)
Circuitio	Semantical	periphrasis	Era (DC 331), Gil (158), Soa (299), Stu (2.6.312), Sus (39), Tra (573)
Circuitas	Syntactical	peribole	Vel (46r)
Circuitas	Syntactical	periodus	Cic (Or 60.204), Lam (3.150), Man (lvii.), Mel (E. 59v), Stu (3.1.437), Tra (506), Vos (279)
Circuitas	Semantical	periphrasis	Gil (158), Sus (39)
Circulo Oratorio	Pragmatical—Idea	epanalepsis	Stu (2.22.408)

Figure Name	*Discourse Level*	*Head Word*	*Sources*
Circulus	Syntactical	epanalepsis	Tra (588)
Circumductio	Syntactical		Kec (1529), Sca (4.1.458), Stu (1.9.19), Tra (556)
Circumductio	Discoursal—Styles	peribole	Tra (556)
Circumductio	Vice		Sca (4.1.458)
Circumitio	Semantical	periphrasis	Ad H (4.32.43)
Circumlocutio	Semantical	periphrasis	Des (C5v), Don (3.6), Gil (158), Mos (b.vi.v), Qui (8.6.61), Sca (3.78.346), Smi (167), Sus (39), Vel (33r), Wal (34), Wil (201)
Circumscriptio	Syntactical	periodus	Aqu (§18), Cic (Or 60.204), Sca (3.36.310), Stu (3.1.437), Vos (279)
Circumscriptio	Semantical	periphrasis	Cic (De Or 3.208)
Circumscriptio	Logical—Idea	definitio	Wil (232)
Circumscriptio	Discoursal—Styles		Aqu (§18), Cic (Or 61.207)
Ciriologia	Virtue		Mos (b.iii.v), Put (168)
Claritas	Discoursal—Styles	eukrinea	Stu (3.6.545), Tra (496)
Clausula	Syntactical		Cic (De Or 3.192), Dem (§244), Her (1.6.253), Kec (1526), Mel (T. c.v.v), Qui (9.4.70; 9.4.101)
Clausula	Logical—Argument Forms	conclusio	[Qui (8.5.13)]
Climax	Syntactical		Ale (31), Aqu (§40), Blo (7), But (105), Day (94), Dem (§270), Des (C5r), Dio (g.iv.r), Far (22), Fen (172), Fra (C7v), Gil (161), Her (1.12.304), Hos (12), Kec (1488), Lon (§23), Man (xlvi.), Mel (E. 52r; I. 23v), Mos (a.vii.r), Pea ([1577] Q.iii.r; [1593] 133), Put (217), Qui (9.3.54), Rob (23v), Ruf (*Lex.* §19), Sca (4.31.502), She ([1550] 58), Smi (94), Soa (316), Stu (3.17.676), Sus (80), Tal (66), Tra (572), Vel (119r), Vos (238)

Figure Name	*Discourse Level*	*Head Word*	*Sources*
Climax	Pragmatical—Idea		Hos (12), Kec (1488)
Coacervatio	Syntactical	congeries	Aqu (§6), Gil (167), Mel (I. 23v), Rob (23r), Sca (3.43.314), Sus (71), Vel (26v)
Coagmentatio	Syntactical	congeries	Sca (3.43.314)
Cogitatum	Discoursal—Genres	noema	Vos (248)
Cognatio	Logical—Idea	synoeciosis	[Qui (9.2.105)], Rob (45v)
Collatio	Semantical	symbole	Sca (3.50.322), Vos (253)
Collatio	Logical—Idea	comparatio	Cic (*Inv.* 1.30.49), Era (DC 337), Mel (E. 36v), Qui (8.3.77)
Collatio	Logical—Idea	dissimilitudo	Blo (14), Hos (20), Stu (3.22.713)
Collatio	Discoursal—Genres	parabola	Era (DC 607), Sus (102)
Collatio	Virtue	analogia	Era (E. 3.184.642)
Collectio	Grammatical	syllepsis	Gil (156)
Collectio	Pragmatical—Idea	epitrochasmus	Sus (71)
Collectio	Logical—Argument Forms	syllogismus	Qui (9.2.103), Rob (45r)
Colon	Syntactical	membrum	Ale (27), Aqu (§18), Cic (Or 61.206), Dem (§1), Era (DCE 93), Far (18), Her (*Inv.* 4.4.184), Kec (1524), Lam (3.149), Mel (E. 59v), Sca (4.25.493), Sha (144), She ([1550] 57), Stu (3.1.442), Vel (45v)
Color	Pragmatical—Idea	metastasis	Cic (Or 61.206), Her (1.11.282), Kec (1482), Lam (4.44), Mel (E. 51r), Qui (4.2.88), Vel (194r), Vos (250)
Comma	Syntactical		Ale (27), Aqu (§18), Cic (Or 61.206), Dem (§9), Far (18), Her (1.7.259), Kec (1524), Lam (3.148), Mel (E. 59v), Sca (4.25.493), Stu (3.1.441), Vel (45v)
Commemoratio	Pragmatical—People		Kec (1495), Mel (E. 44v), Stu (3.34.800)

Figure Name	*Discourse Level*	*Head Word*	*Sources*
Commendatio	Discoursal—Genres		Ad H (4.37.49), Cic (De Or 3.205), Era (DC 608), Mel (E. 7v), Pea ([1577] T.ii.v), Stu (3.28.759)
Commensuratio	Virtue	concinnitas	[Rob (31r)]
Comminatio	Discoursal—Genres	cataplexis	Cic (Or 40.138), Kec (1499), Pea ([1593] 79), Sca (3.62.335)
Commiseratio	Discoursal—Genres		But (114), Fen (173), Fra (F2r), Kec (1499), Lam (2.132), Mel (E. 44r), Rob (38r), Smi (142), Sus (63), Tal (52), Wil (163)
Commonitio	Pragmatical—Idea	anamnesis	Qui (4.2.51), Stu (1.40.217)
Commoratio	Pragmatical—Idea		Ad H (4.45.58), Cic (De Or 3.202), Day (98), Era (DC 320), Gil (150), Pea ([1577] T.iiii.r; [1593] 152), Put (240), Rob (49v), Sca (3.46.315), Smi (233), Stu (1.33.143), Sus (99), Wil (203)
Communicatio	Pragmatical—People		Blo (44–45), Cic (De Or 3.204), Era (E. 3.110.132), Fen (175), Fra (H1v), Hos (49), Kec (1495), Lam (2.119), Mel (E. 44v; I. 22v), Qui (9.2.20), Rob (44r), Ruf (§10), Sca (3.68.338), She ([1555] E.iiii.r), Smi (152), Soa (341), Sus (64), Tal (27), Vel (50v), Vos (245), Wil (212)
Commutatio	Syntactical	antimetabole	Ad H (4.28.39), Blo (9), Day (95), Era (E. 3.142.762), Gil (166), Hos (14), Kec (1483), Mel (E. 52r; I. 24r), She ([1555] E.vi.r), Smi (116), Soa (330), Sus (81), Tra (512), Vel (194r), Vos (256), Wal (64)
Compar	Syntactical	isocolon	Ad H (4.20.27), Blo (32), Cic (De Or 3.207), Era (E. 3.104.996), Hos (37), Pea ([1577] K.i.r; [1593] 58), She ([1550] 57), Smi (216), Soa (327), Sus (54), Tra (587), Vos (282)

Figure Name	*Discourse Level*	*Head Word*	*Sources*
Comparatio	Logical—Idea		Ad H (4.45.59), Blo (11–16), Day (93), Era (DC 593), Gil (152–53), Hos (17), Kec (1534), Lam (2.111), Mel (E. 53r), Pea ([1577] Q.iii.v; [1593] 156), [Qui (9.2.100)], [Rob (45r)], Rut (II.16), Sca (3.50.321), She ([1550] 71–76; [1555] F.viii.v), Smi (208–10), Stu (1.31.115), Sus (72), Vos (252), Wal (121), Wil (214, 231)
Compensatio	Pragmatical—Idea	antenagoge	Aqu (§14)
Complexio	Phonetic	synaeresis	Hoo (263), Qui (1.5.17)
Complexio	Syntactical	symploce	Ad H (4.14.20), Blo (8), Era (E. 3.100.913), Fra (D2v), Gil (161), Hos (13), Mel (I. 20r), Put (209), She ([1555] D.iiii.v), Smi (100), Soa (309), Stu (2.22.401), Sus (51), Vos (235)
Complicatio	Syntactical	symploce	Tal (63)
Compositio	Virtue	synthesis	Stu (2.27.435)
Comprecatio	Discoursal—Genres		Vel (167r)
Comprehensio	Grammatical	syllepsis	Smi (181)
Comprehensio	Syntactical	periodus	Cic (Or 60.204), Sca (4.25.493), Soa (377), Stu (3.1.437), Tra (505), Vel (46r), Vos (279)
Comprehensio	Syntactical	symploce	Fra (D2v), Wil (226)
Comprehensio	Semantical	synecdoche	Smi (32), Vel (41r), Vos (218)
Comprobatio	Pragmatical—People		Pea ([1577] L.ii.v), Wil (224)
Conceptio	Grammatical	syllepsis	Des (C4r), Gil (156), Man (ciii.), Ruf (*Lex.* §2), Sca (3.77.345), She ([1550] 30), Sus (27)
Concessio	Pragmatical—People		Blo (46), Fen (175), Fra (H5v), Hos (50), Kec (1486), Lam (2.127), Mel (E. 53r), Qui (9.2.51), Rob (37v), Sca (3.57.333), Smi (203), Soa (351), Stu (2.27.436), Tal (29), Vos (246), Wal (93)

Figure Name	*Discourse Level*	*Head Word*	*Sources*
Conciliatio	Pragmatical—People		Cic (De Or 3.205), Kec (1475), Sca (3.93.363), Stu (3.28.759)
Conciliatio	Logical—Idea	synoeceiosis	Smi (120)
Concinnitas	Virtue		Pea ([1577] B.i.r), Stu (3.4.519)
Concisio	Morphological	syncope	Hoo (263), Lil (G.v.v), She ([1550] 27), Smi (171)
Conclusio	Logical—Argument Forms		Ad H (4.30.41), Cic (De Or 3.203), Kec (1475), Pea ([1577] U.iiii.v), Sca (3.71.341), She ([1550] 55), Vos (244)
Conclusio	Discoursal—Parts of Oration		Era (DC 653), Kec (1475), Wil (208)
Conditio	Syntactical		Sca (3.39.311)
Conduplicatio	Lexical		Ad H (4.28.38), Cic (Or 39.135), Era (E. 3.108.74), Lam (3.161), She ([1555] D.v.r), Soa (310), Sus (49), Tra (599)
Conexum	Syntactical	symploce	Aqu (§36)
Confessio	Pragmatical—People		Blo (24), Hos (28), Lam (2.120), Mel (I. 26r), Qui (9.2.17, 51), Rob (44v), Sca (3.58.333), She ([1555] E.vii.v), Stu (1.21.58), Sus (85), Vel (194r), Vos (246)
Confirmatio	Discoursal—Parts of Oration	argumentatio	Era (DC 648)
Conformatio	Discoursal—Genres	prosopopoeia	Ad H (4.53.66), Cic (Or 25.85), Era (DC 553), Fra (G5r), Pea ([1577] O.iii.r; [1593] 136), Qui (9.2.32), Rob (50r), She ([1555] F.vi.v), Smi (153), Soa (342), Sus (67), Tra (580)
Confusio	Vice	synchysis	Des (C6r), Mos (b.vii.r), Sus (33), Tra (530)
Confutatio	Discoursal—Parts of Oration	antirrhesis	Era (DC 648)

Figure Name	*Discourse Level*	*Head Word*	*Sources*
Congeries	Syntactical		Dem (§238), Era (DC 320), Gil (150), Kec (1548), Mel (E. 50r; I. 23v), Pea ([1577] Q.ii.r; [1593] 128), Qui (9.3.48), Rob (5v), She ([1555] D.viii.r), Stu (1.33.144), Sus (71), Vos (298), Wil (158)
Congeries	Pragmatical—Idea		Era (DC 594), Gil (167), Kec (1489), Lam (2.129), She ([1555] G.ii.v), Stu (1.33.143)
Congestio	Syntactical	congeries	Rob (31r)
Conglobatio	Pragmatical—Idea	congeries	Pea ([1577] T.i.r), Stu (1.32.126)
Conjunctio	Grammatical	mesozeugma	Ad H (4.27.38), Soa (321)
Conjunctio	Syntactical	polysyndeton	Vel (45v)
Conjunctio	Logical—Idea	synoeciosis	Sca (3.47.317)
Conlatio	Logical—Idea	antapodosis	Ad H (4.45.59)
Conquestio	Discoursal—Genres	commiseratio	Kec (1499)
Consecutio	Logical—Idea		Era (DC 576), Tra (560)
Consensio	Pragmatical—People		Qui (9.2.51), Rob 44v), Sca (3.90.361)
Consequentia	Logical—Argument Forms	conclusio	Ad H (4.54.67), [Qui (9.2.103)], Vel (194v)
Consolatio	Discoursal—Genres	paramythia	Mel (E. 23v), Pea ([1577] L.i.v; [1593] 100), Sca (3.123.399)
Consummatio	Pragmatical—Idea	diallage	[Qui (9.2.103)], Rob (45r), Vel (194v)
Contentio	Syntactical	syncrisis	Man (lxxxv.), Qui (9.3.81)
Contentio	Logical—Idea	antithesis	Ad H (4.15.21; 4.45.58), Blo (16, 32), Cic (De Or 3.205), Day (92), Era (DC 616), Gil (166), Hos (21, 37), Mel (E. 52r; I. 23v), Rob (49v), Sca (4.37.506), She ([1550] 56; [1555] E.vi.v), Soa (328), Sus (71)
Contentio	Logical—Idea	enantiosis	Hos (37), Smi (118)
Continuatio	Syntactical	periodus	Ad H (4.19.27), Cic (Or 60.204), Era (E. 3.140.694), She ([1555] E.i.r), Stu (3.1.437), Sus (98), Tra (566), Vos (279)

Figure Name	*Discourse Level*	*Head Word*	*Sources*
Contractio	Phonetic	synaeresis	Smi (177)
Contractio	Phonetic	systole	She ([1550] 27)
Contrapositum	Syntactical	syncrisis	Qui (9.3.81)
Contrapositum	Logical—Idea	antithesis	Rob (31r), Sca (3.59.334)
Contraria	Logical—Idea	enantiosis	Era (E. 3.166.272), Rob (31r), Stu (2.23.425), Vel (42v)
Contrarium	Logical—Idea	antithesis	Gil (166), Ruf (*Lex.* §13), Sus (71)
Contrarium	Logical—Argument Forms	enthymema	Ad H (4.18.25), Cic (De Or 3.207), Era (E. 3.140.688), She ([1550] 56), Stu (2.27.434), Vel (167v)
Contumelia	Pragmatical—People	convinciari	[Qui (8.3.89)]
Conversio	Syntactical	epistrophe	Ad H (4.13.19), Aqu (§35), Cic (De Or 3.207), Era (E. 3.100.913), Gil (160), Put (209), She ([1555] D.iiii.r), Smi (98), Soa (309), Stu (2.22.400), Sus (51), Tra (571), Vos (235), Wal (67), Wil (225)
Convinciari	Pragmatical—People		Her (2.7.358), Stu (3.24.730)
Convolutio	Syntactical	systrophe	Pea ([1593] 153), Tra (565)
Copia	Virtue		Era (DC 5), Kec (1546), [Qui (8.3.87)]
Copulatio	Lexical	ploce	Aqu (§28), Gil (162), Mel (E. 43r; I. 20v), She ([1555] D.vi.r), Sus (52), Vel (45r)
Correctio	Pragmatical—People		Ad H (4.26.36), Blo (25), Cic (De Or 3.203, 207), Era (DC 436, 529, 594), Gil (165), Hos (29), Kec (1490), Lam (2.82), Mel (E. 52v; I. 25v), Pea ([1577] R.ii.v; [1593] 172), Qui (9.2.17), Ruf (*Lex.* §17), Sca (3.37.310), She ([1550] 70; [1555] G.iii.v), Smi (146), Soa (331, 340), Stu (2.21.388), Sus (75), Tal (50, 70), Tra (600), Vos (237), Wal (69), Wil (211)

Figure Name	*Discourse Level*	*Head Word*	*Sources*
Cosmographia	Discoursal—Genres	topographia	Man (lxxxiii.)
Curiositas	Vice	periergia	Vel (9v)
Decensus	Pragmatical—Idea	decrementum	Qui (8.4.28), Smi (135)
Declinatio	Pragmatical—Idea		Cic (De Or 3.207), Qui (9.2.56), Stu (2.20.376), Vel (194r)
Decrectare	Pramatical—Idea	evasio	Rob (45r)
Decrementum	Pragmatical—Idea		Sha (159–60), Sus (78), Vel (139r)
Deesis	Discoursal—Genres	deprecatio	Era (DC 424), Her (2.3.327), Mel (I. 22r), Rob (43r), Ruf (§16), She ([1550] 51), Soa (357), Stu (62), Vos (270)
Defectus	Grammatical	eclipsis	Mel (I. 21r), Sca (4.27.497), She ([1550] 31), Smi (178)
Defectus	Pragmatical—Idea		Lam (2.105), Sca (3.77.344)
Defectus	Vice	eclipsis	Vel (10r)
Definitio	Logical—Idea		Ad H (4.25.35), Blo (39), Day (97) Era (DC 332), Hos (43), Kec (1475), Mel (E. 49v), Pea ([1577] H.i.v; [1593] 148), [Qui (9.3.91)], Rob (20r), Sca (3.55.331), She ([1550] 58; [1555] G.iiii.r), Smi (235), Sus (85)
Deformatio	Discoursal—Genres	descriptio	Aqu (§13), Sca (3.33.307), Sus (86)
Dehortatio	Discoursal—Genres		Pea ([1577] L.i.v; [1593] 78)
Deiktikon	Lexical	deixin	Dem (§289), Her (1.8.263), Stu (2.14.252)
Deinosis	Discoursal—Genres		Era (DC 320), [Qui (8.3.88; 9.2.104)], Rob (30r), Sca (3.66.336), Stu (1.29.109), Wil (224)
Deinotes	Discoursal—Styles		Dem (§240), Era (E. 3.98.911), Her (2.9.369), Stu (3.26.739), Tra (603)
Deixin	Lexical		Her (1.8.263)
Delecio	Phonetic	synaloepha	She ([1550] 28)

Figure Name	*Discourse Level*	*Head Word*	*Sources*
Deliberatio	Pragmatical—People		Blo (44), But (121), Fen (175), Fra (G7r), Hos (48), Wal (92)
Demonstratio	Pragmatical—Idea	hypotyposis	Ad H (4.55.68), Era (E. 3.126.458), Rob (50r), Sca (3.34.309), She ([1555] F.iv.v), Soa (344), Sus (86), Tra (548)
Denominatio	Lexical	paronomasia	Des (C4v), Man (xxxix.), Sus (56)
Denominatio	Semantical	metonymia	Ad H (4.32.43), Soa (285), Stu (2.4.297)
Deprecatio	Discoursal—Genres		But (114), Cic (De Or 3.205), Era (E. 2.466.437), Lam (2.133), Mel (E. 54v), Rob (45v), Sca (3.83.349), Soa (357), Stu (1.24.71), Tal (24), Vel (194r)
Derivatio	Lexical	polyptoton	Ruf (*Lex.* §16), Vos (239)
Derivatio	Semantical	onomatopoeia	Qui (8.6.32), Tra (460)
Descriptio	Pramatical—Idea	hypotyposis	Soa (344)
Descriptio	Discoursal—Genres		Ad H (4.39.51), Aqu (§13), Blo (35–37), Cic (De Or 3.205), Des (C7r), Era (DC 577), Hos (41–42), Kec (1475), Lam (2.135), Mel (E. 54r), Pea ([1593] 134), Rob (49v), Sca (3.34.309), She ([1555] F.iii.r), Smi (251), Soa (344), Stu (2.27.434), Sus (86), Wal (73)
Desperatio	Discoursal—Genres		But (114), Fen (173), Fra (E5v), Kec (1499), Sca (4.42.513)
Destructio	Pragmatical—Idea	anasceue	Ruf (*Dian.*§6)
Detestatio	Discoursal—Genres	execratio	Sca (3.69.338)
Detractio	Morphological	aphaeresis	Hoo (263)
Detractio	Grammatical	eclipsis	Aqu (§46), Qui (9.3.18)
Detractio	Pragmatical—Idea	defectus	Qui (9.2.37)
Detrectatio	Discoursal—Genres	apagoresis	Qui (9.2.104), Rob (46r), Sca (3.61.334)
Deuterologian	Logical—Forms		Her (*Meth.* §27), Stu (3.35.815)
Diabole	Discoursal—Genres	ominatio	Rob (43r), Ruf (§17)

Figure Name	*Discourse Level*	*Head Word*	*Sources*
Diacope	Grammatical	tmesis	Day (83), Dio (h.i.r), Gil (180), Man (lxi.), Mos (b.vi.v), Sus (33)
Diacope	Lexical		Fen (171), Fra (C6r), Pea ([1577] J.iii.v; [1593] 48), Rob (23v), Ruf (*Lex.* §11), Smi (89), Stu (1.18.49)
Diacrisis	Pragmatical—Idea	distinctio	Stu (2.24.424)
Diaeresis	Phonetic		But (48), Des (C3v), Don (3.4), Far (26), Gil (180), Hoo (262, 306), Lil (G.vi.v), Man (xxiiii.), Mos (a.iiii.r), Pea ([1577] E.iii.r), Put (174), Qui (1.5.17), Rob (28v), She ([1555] B.iii.v), Smi (177), Stu (3.17.677), Sus (22)
Diaeresis	Pragmatical—Idea	distributio/ merismus	Kec (1483), Pea ([1593] 123), Rob (25r), Ruf (*Lex.* §23), Stu (1.32.126)
Diakrisis	Pragmatical—People		Stu (3.23.723)
Dialelymenon	Rhythmical		Dem (§301)
Diallage	Lexical		Qui (9.3.49), Rob (24v)
Diallage	Pragmatical—Idea		[Qui (9.2.103)], Rob (31r), Sca (3.64.335), Wil (158)
Dialogismus	Pragmatical—People	sermocinatio	But (121), Day (97), Era (DC 586), Far (25), Mel (E. 53v), Put (242), Rob (43r), Ruf (§20), She ([1550] 69), Smi (254), Stu (1.39.208), Sus (93), Tal (37), Vos (267), Wil (209)
Dialysis	Phonetic	diaeresis	Gil (180)
Dialysis	Syntactical	asyndeton	Ale (32), Dem (§61), Kec (1538), Rob (19v), Rut (I.15), Vos (291)
Dialysis	Syntactical	parenthesis	Dio (h.i.r), Gil (165), Man (lxii.), Mos (b.vi.v), Sus (33)
Dialysis	Logical—Argument Forms	prosapodosis	Day (97), Mel (E. 50r; I. 26v), Put (230), She ([1550] 55), Sus (93)
Dialyton	Syntactical	articulus	Dio (g.iv.r), She ([1550] 57)

Figure Name	*Discourse Level*	*Head Word*	*Sources*
Dialyton	Syntactical	asyndeton	Don (3.5), Far (27), Man (xxxiii.), Mel (E. 43v), Ruf (*Lex.* §20), Smi (182), Soa (318), Sus (37)
Dianoia	Logical—Idea		Era (DC 413), Mel (T. c.v.r), Rob (43v), Ruf (§18), Sus (85)
Diaphora	Lexical	ploce	Pea ([1577] J.ii.v; [1593] 45), Rob (24r), Rut (I.12), She ([1555] D.vi.v), Stu (3.1.453)
Diaphora	Logical—Idea	dissimilitudo	Vos (254)
Diaporesis	Pragmatical—People	aporia	Ale (24), Aqu (§10), Her (2.7.361), Rob (44r), Ruf (§9), Soa (340), Stu (2.19.373), Sus (63), Tal (26)
Diaskeue	Pragmatical—Idea		Her (*Inv.* 4.12.202), [Qui (9.2.107)]
Diastasis	Pragmatical—Idea	disjunctio	Her (2.4.338), Stu (2.20.381)
Diastole	Phonetic		But (52), Des (C3r), Far (26), Gil (179), Hoo (306), Man (xxi.), Pea ([1577] E.iii.r), Put (174), Qui (1.5.18), She ([1555] B.iii.v), Smi (177), Sus (21)
Diastole	Lexical	diacope	Rob (23v), Ruf (*Lex.* §11)
Diasyrmus	Pragmatical—People		Ale (26), Aqu (§15), Cic (De Or 3.203), Pea ([1577] D.iiii.r; [1593] 39), Rob (42v), Ruf (§5), Sca (3.87.358), Sha (183), She ([1550] 61), Sus (16), Vos (227), Wil (181)
Diatyposis	Pragmatical—Idea	hypotyposis	Ale (25), Far (23), Her (*Inv.* 4.9.197), Lon (§20), Sca (3.33.308), Sha (145–7), Vos (250)
Diatyposis	Discoursal—Genres		Dem (§296), Pea ([1593] 92)
Diatyposis	Discoursal—Genres	descriptio	Aqu (§13), Rob (48r), Smi (251), Sus (86)
Diazeugma	Grammatical	disjunctio	Aqu (§43), She ([1550] 30; [1555] C.i.v)

Figure Name	*Discourse Level*	*Head Word*	*Sources*
Dicaeologia	Discoursal—Genres		Day (96), Mel (E. 50v; I. 26r), Pea ([1577] M.iiii.v; [1593] 115), Put (237), Rut (II.3), Sca (3.67.337), She ([1555] E.viii.r), Sus (85), Vel (194r)
Dicolon	Syntactical		Ale (28), Blo (35), Dem (§251), Her (*Inv.* 4.3.179), Hos (40), Kec (1526), Stu (3.1.442), Vel (47r), Vos (281)
Diductio	Morphological	paragoge	Sus (21)
Diegema	Discoursal—Genres	narratio	Her (*Pro.*§2)
Diegesis	Discoursal—Parts of Oration	narratio	Her (*Meth.* §28), Stu (1.15.37)
Diexodon	Discoursal—Parts of Oration	digressio	Vos (257)
Diexodos	Pragmatical—Idea		Qui (9.3.87)
Differentia	Phonetic	diastole	Lil (Gvr)
Digestio	Pragmatical—Idea		Cic (De Or 3.205), Sca (3.70.339), Stu (1.15.39; 1.35.155), Wil (223)
Dignitas	Discoursal—Styles	semnotes	Era (E. 3.154.24), [Sca (4.16.467)], Tra (532)
Dignitates	Logical—Evidence		She ([1550] 92), Vel (164r), Wal (70)
Digressio	Discoursal—Parts of Oration		Cic (De Or 3.203), Day (100), Era (DC (589), Lam (4.57), Pea ([1577] U.iiii.r; [1593] 154), Rob (44v), Sca (3.75.343), Sha (155–8), Smi (241), Soa (354), Stu (2.20.378), Sus (104), Tal (42), Vos (257), Wal (96), Wil (206)
Dikthesin	Pragmatical—Idea	apostasis	Her (2.7.355), Stu (3.24.725)
Dilemma	Logical—Argument Forms		Blo (41), Day (97), Era (E. 3.122.374), Her (*Inv.* 4.6.192), Hos (46), Kec (1484), Lam (2.134), Pea ([1577] T.ii.r; [1593] 127), Sha (136), Smi (262), Stu (1.40.213), Tra (548), Wil (210)
Dilogia	Lexical	palilogia	Dem (§103)

Figure Name	*Discourse Level*	*Head Word*	*Sources*
Dilucidas	Discoursal—Styles	eukrinea	Stu (3.6.545)
Diminutio	Semantical	litotes	Ad H (4.38.50), Blo (31), Hos (35), Lam (78), Rob (49v), She ([1555] E.v.r)
Diminutio	Semantical	meiosis	Era (DC 344)
Diminutio	Pragmatical—Idea		Blo (31), Day (94), Era (E. 3.122.367), Fen (170), Hos (35), Kec (1489), Mel (E. 48v), She ([1550] 61), Sus (77), Tra (593)
Diminutio	Vice	meiosis	Vel (10r)
Dinumeratio	Pragmatical—Idea	enumeratio	Cic (De Or 3.207), Pea ([1577] R.i.r)
Dirimens Copulatio	Syntactical		Her (1.11.294), Hos (27), Pea ([1577] S.ii.r; [1593] 171), Tra (564)
Discretion	Virtue		Blo (10), Hos (15)
Discriminatio	Pragmatical—Idea	paradiastole	Kec (1483), Ruf (*Lex.* §22)
Disjunctio	Grammatical		Ad H (4.27.37), Aqu (§43), Era (DC 345), Qui (9.3.45), Rob (24v), She ([1550] 30), Soa (321), Tra (572)
Disjunctio	Pragmatical—Idea		Cic (De Or 3.207), Soa (321), Stu (2.13.342), Wal (63)
Disjunctio	Logical—Argument Forms		Kec (1484)
Dissectio	Grammatical	tmesis	She ([1550] 31)
Dissimilitudo	Logical—Idea		Blo (13), Era (DC 619), Hos (19), Pea ([1593] 160), Put (248), Smi (212), Stu (1.41.241), Vos (254), Wal (63)
Dissimulatio	Semantical	ironia	Cic (De Or 3.203), Kec (1466), Pea ([1593] 35), Qui (6.3.85), Rob (44r), Ruf (*Dian.* §9), Sca (3.76.343), She ([1550] 45), Smi (45), Soa (298), Stu (3.22.713), Sus (14), Tal (8), Vel (140r), Vos (220), Wil (176)
Dissipatio	Pragmatical—Idea		Cic (De Or 3.207), Qui (9.3.39)

Figure Name	*Discourse Level*	*Head Word*	*Sources*
Dissipatio	Vice	synchisis	Sca (3.70.339)
Dissolutio	Syntactical	asyndeton	Ad H (4.30.41), Cic (De Or 3.207), Mel (E. 43v), Qui (9.3.50), Rob (31r), Ruf (*Lex.* §20), She ([1550] 59), Soa (318), Stu (2.25.428), Sus (37), Tra (578), Vel (45v), Vos (291)
Dissolutio	Syntactical	parenthesis	Gil (165), Man (lxii.), Sus (33)
Dissolutum	Discoursal—Styles		[Ad H (4.11.16)], She ([1550] 24; [1555] H.v.r)
Distinctio	Pragmatical—Idea	paradiastole	Blo (37–8), Hos (42–3), Kec (1475), Qui (9.3.65), Smi (114), Stu (2.1.270; 2.24.424)
Distributio[1]	Pragmatical—Idea		Ad H (4.35.47), Cic (Or 40.138), Era (DC 427), Kec (1483), Pea ([1577] R.iiii.r; [1593] 126), Rob (49v), She ([1555] F.ii.r), Soa (356), Stu (2.27.435), Wil (210)
Distributio[2]	Pragmatical—Idea	merismus	Cic (De Or 3.203), Day (97), Era (DC 572), Lam (2.109), Mel (E. 50r; I. 26v), Pea ([1577] R.iii.r), Ruf (*Lex.* §23), Sca (3.70.339), Soa (355), Sus (91), Vos (248)
Distributio	Logical—Idea	partitio	Pea ([1593] 123
Distributio	Discoursal—Parts of Oration	partitio	Wil (211)
Divisio	Phonetic	diaeresis	Hoo (263), Man (xxiiii.), Smi (177)
Divisio	Pragmatical—Idea	distributio/ merismus	Blo (17), Hos (22), Pea ([1593] 123)
Divisio	Logical—Idea	partitio	Blo (40), Cic (Or 40.137), Hos (45), Mel (I. 26v)
Divisio	Logical—Argument Forms	dilemma	Era (E. 3.122.374)
Divisio	Logical—Argument Forms	prosapodosis	Ad H (4.40.52), Pea ([1577] R.iiii.v), Rob (49v), She ([1550] 55; [1555] G.iii.v), Sus (93)
Donysis	Discoursal—Genres	deinosis	She ([1550] 68), Vel (128v)

Figure Name	*Discourse Level*	*Head Word*	*Sources*
Drama Argumentum	Discoursal—Genres		Vel (172r)
Drimytes	Discoursal—Styles		Her (2.5.339), Stu (3.22.708)
Dubitatio	Pragmatical—People	aporia	Ad H (4.29.40), Cic (De Or 3.203, 207), Day (89), Era (DC 347), Kec (1491), Lam (2.102), Mel (E. 44r; I. 22r), Qui (9.2.19), Rob (44r), She ([1550] 54; [1555] E.iii.v), Soa (332, 340), Stu (1.16.45), Sus (63), Tra (593), Vos (262), Wal (91)
Duplicatio	Lexical	epizeuxis	Ruf (*Lex.* §8)
Duplicatio	Lexical	ploce	Gil (162), Sus (52)
Duplicatio	Syntactical	anadiplosis	Man (xxxv.), Sca (4.29.498)
Dysphonia	Vice	cacemphaton[1]	Dem (§48)
Ecbasis	Discoursal—Parts of Oration	digressio	Sca (3.75.343)
Ecbolen	Discoursal—Parts of Oration	digressio	Vos (257)
Eclipsis	Grammatical		But (128), Day (81), Des (C3v), Far (26), Lil (G.vi.r), Mel (E. 43v; I. 21r), Pea ([1577] E.iii.v), Put (175), She ([1550] 31; [1555] B.viii.r), Soa (317), Sus (24), Vel (45v)
Eclipsis	Vice		Day (81), Des (C2r), Dio (g.iv.v), Don (3.3), Man (xi.), Mos (b.i.r), She ([1555] A.vi.v), Vel (10r)
Ecphonesis	Discoursal—Genres	exclamatio	But (113), Day (89), Far (24), Gil (165), Pea ([1577] K.iiii.r; [1593] 62), Put (221), Sha (163–4), Smi (140), Stu (3.11.602), Sus (61), Vos (262)
Ectasis	Phonetic	diastole	Des (C3r), Don (3.4), Far (26), Gil (179), Man (xxi.), Mel (T. c.iiii.v), Mos (a.iiii.r), She ([1550] 27), Sus (22)

Figure Name	*Discourse Level*	*Head Word*	*Sources*
Ecthlipsis	Phonetic		But (42), Dio (g.v.r), Don (3.4), Far (26), Fra (C1v), Gil (179), Hoo (305), Man (xxii.), Mos (A.iiii.v), Pea ([1577] E.iii.r), Qui (9.4.40), Rob (29r), Smi (176), Sus (22)
Effictio	Discoursal—Genres		Ad H (4.49.63), Era (E. 3.160.165), Mel (E. 54v; I. 26v), Rob (49v), Sca (3.34.309), Soa (347), Sus (86)
Effiguratio	Discoursal—Genres		Ruf (*Dian.* §14), She ([1550] 66; [1555] F.v.r), Vel (127r)
Egressio	Discoursal—Parts of Oration	digressio	Era (DC 589), Sca (3.75.343), Sus (104)
Eidolopoeia	Discoursal—Genres		Rai (N.i.r–v), Sca (3.33.307)
Eikasia	Logical—Idea	similitudo	Dem (§80)
Eikteron	Discoursal—Genres	modus optativus	Stu (3.10.591)
Eiromenin lexin	Discoursal—Styles	circumscriptio	Aqu (§18)
Ekparasynaptikon	Logical—Idea		Era (DC 576), Her (1.11.290), Qui (4.2.83), Stu (3.15.655)
Ekphrasis	Discoursal—genres	descriptio	Her (1.6.244)
Electio	Pragmatical—Idea		Tra (560)
Elenchus	Discoursal—Parts of Oration		Her (1.10.271), Stu (3.13 [8].625)
Elenktikon	Pragmatical—People	interrogatio	Dem (§279), Her (1.8.262), Stu (3.10.588)
Eleos	Discoursal—Genres	commiseratio	Her (2.7.356), Stu (1.24.77)
Elevatio	Pragmatical—People	diasyrmus	Aqu (§15), She ([1550] 61), Sus (16), Vel (139r)
Ellipsis	Grammatical	eclipsis	Ale (33), Aqu (§46), But (128), Des (C3v), Gil (155), Hoo (266), Kec (1500), Lam (1.37), Rob (24v), Sca (4.27.497), Sha (176), Smi (178), Vos (230)
Ellipsis	Pragmatical—Idea	defectus	Lam (2.104)

Figure Name	*Discourse Level*	*Head Word*	*Sources*
Ellipsis	Pragmatical—People	aposiopesis	Kec (1501)
Ellipsis	Vice	eclipsis	Qui (8.6.22), [Rob (29v)], Smi (176–7)
Elogium	Discoursal—Genres		Sca (3.40.312)
Embleme	Discoursal—Genres		Blo (3), Hos (9)
Emendatio	Pragmatical—People	correctio	Qui (9.2.17), Rob (44r), Smi (146), Stu (2.21.389)
Eminentia	Semantical	hyperbole	Sus (17)
Empatheia	Discoursal—Genres	pathopoeia	Stu (3.32.785)
Emperibolon	Pragmatical—Idea		Her (1.11.292), Stu (3.15.645), Tra (560)
Emphasis	Pragmatical—Idea		Dem (§155), Des (C8r), Era (DC 657), Her (1.4.241), Kec (1467), Man (xcv.), Mos (b.vii.r), Pea ([1577] H.ii.r; [1593] 178), Put (194), Qui (9.2.64), Rob (30r), Sca (3.79.346), Smi (256), Soa (347), Sus (44), Vel (194v), Vos (226), Wil (158)
Empsychosis	Discoursal—Genres	conformatio	Dem (§81), Her (2.4.333), Stu (1.37.185)
Enallage	Grammatical		Era (DC 321), Far (28), Gil (158), Her (*Inv.* 4.4.188), Hoo (264), Kec (1503), Lon (§23), Pea ([1577] H.iii.v–iiii.r), Put (182), Qui (9.3.6–11), Sca (4.36.505), Smi (195), Stu (2.23.417), Sus (35)
Enantiosis	Logical—Idea		Blo (16,32), Far (23), Gil (166), Her (*Meth.* §34), Hos (22, 37), Kec (1483), [Rob (46r)], Sca (4.37.506), Smi (118), Stu (2.23.425), Wil (223)
Enargeia	Virtue		Cic (Or 40.139), Dem (§209), Era (DC 577), Far (23), Gil (158), Her (2.5.343), [Qui (8.3.61)], Ruf (*Dian.* §15), She ([1550] 66), Sus (86)

Figure Name	*Discourse Level*	*Head Word*	*Sources*
Enargia	Virtue	tasis	Put (155)
Enarratio	Pragmatical—Idea	exegesis	Vel (173v)
Encomion	Discoursal—Genres	commendatio	Pea ([1593] 155)
Endeixis tes taxeos	Pragmatical—Idea	digestio	Her (1.4.236), Stu (1.15.39)
Endoiasis	Pragmatical—People	aporia	Her (2.8.367), Rob (31r), Stu (3.9.571)
Energasia	Pragmatical—Idea	hypotyposis	Stu (1.36.159)
Energeia	Virtue		Hos (7), Put (155), Qui (8.3.89), Rob (30r), Sca (3.25.293)
Energeia	Virtue	enargeia	Dem (§81), Era (DC 577), She ([1550] 66), Stu (1.36.159)
Enezengmenon	Grammatical	zeugma	Man (xxx.)
Enigma	Vice		Dem (§153), Des (C2v), Dio (g.iv.v), Man (xiii.)
Enmeson	Discoursal—Styles	oratio mediocris	Stu (3.29.766)
Enosis	Pragmatical—Idea		Qui (9.3.65), Stu (2.24.425)
Enstasis	Discoursal—Parts of Oration		Her (*Inv.* 4.4.187), Wal (90)
Entechna	Discoursal—Parts of Oration		Her (1.4.235), Stu (3.7.565)
Enthematikon	Logical—Argument Forms		Stu (1.14.33)
Enthymema	Logical—Argument Forms		Era (E. 3.150.932), Kec (1476), Lam (2.134), Pea ([1577] U.iii.v; [1593] 162), [Qui (8.5.9)], [Rob (43r)], Ruf (§30), Sca (3.71.339), She ([1550] 93; [1555] G.vi.v), Smi (260), Stu (1.28.105), Vel (144v; 164v), Wal (80)
Enumeratio	Pragmatical—Idea		Blo (41), Era (DC 574), Lam (2.135), Pea ([1577] R.iii.v/Q. iiii.v; [1593] 125), She ([1550] 63–5; [1555] F.i.v), Stu (2.12.338), Tra (559), Vos (244), Wal (73), Wil (230)

Figure Name	*Discourse Level*	*Head Word*	*Sources*
Enumeratio	Logical—Argument Forms	expeditio	Day (98), Hos (45), Kec (1484), Sus (98)
Enumeratio	Discoursal—Parts of Oration	partitio	Pea ([1577] Q.iiii.v)
Epagoge	Logical—Argument Forms		Era (DC 623), Rob (42v), Ruf (§26), Wil (215, 232)
Epainos	Discoursal—Genres	commendatio	Her (*Pro.*§7)
Epakolouthesis	Logical—Argument Forms	conclusio	[Qui (9.2.103)], Rob (45r)
Epanadiplosis	Syntactical	symploce	Rob (23v), Ruf (*Lex.* §9)
Epanalepsis	Lexical	conduplicatio	Aqu (§31)
Epanalepsis	Syntactical		Ale (19, 29), Blo (8), But (108), Cic (De Or 3.206), Day (85), Dem (§196), Des (C4v), Dio (g.iii.v), Don (3.5), Era (DC 345), Far (23), Fen (172), Fra (D3r), Gil (160), Her (*Meth.* §9), Hos (14), Kec (1506), Man (xxxvi.), Mos (a.vi.r), Pea ([1577] F.ii.r; [1577] J.ii.v; [1593] 46), Put (210), Qui (9.3.31), Rob (22r), Ruf (*Lex.* §5), Rut (I.11), Sca (4.29.498), She ([1555] C.ii.r, D.v.v), Smi (101), Stu (2.22.397), Sus (30; 49), Tal (65), Vos (236)
Epanalepsis	Pragmatical—Idea		Her (1.4.239), Ruf (§31)
Epanaphora	Syntactical	anaphora	Ale (20, 29), Aqu (§34), Dem (§59), Era (DCE 93), Gil (159), Her (1.10.276), Pea ([1577] H.iiii.v; [1593] 41), Rob (23v), Ruf (*Lex.* §6), Sca (498), She ([1550] 47), Stu (2.22.393), Sus (49), Tra (569)
Epanastrophe	Syntactical	anadiplosis	Her (1.12.304), Sca (4.30.500), Stu (2.22.393), Tra (571)

Figure Name	*Discourse Level*	*Head Word*	*Sources*
Epanodos	Syntactical		Ale (30), Blo (8), But (108), Far (23), Fen (172), Fra (D4r), Hos (14), Kec (1507), Lam (3.158), Man (xcvii.), Mos (b.vii.v), Qui (9.3.35), Rob (31r), Sca (4.30.500), Sha (157), Smi (103), Tal (64), Vos (237)
Epanodos	Pragmatical—Idea		Cic (De Or 3.207), Day (92), Gil (167), Mel (I. 24r), Pea ([1577] S.i.r; [1593] 129), Put (229), Qui (9.3.34), Rob (23v), Ruf (*Lex.* §21), Smi (103), Sus (82)
Epanorotema	Pragmatical—People		Dem (§297), Rob (49r)
Epanorthosis	Pragmatical—People	correctio	But (115), Far (25), Fen (174), Fra (F6r), Gil (165), Kec (1490), Lam (2.103), Mel (E. 52v; I. 25v), Rob (25r), Ruf (*Lex.* §17), Sha (165–7), Gil (165), Smi (146), Stu (3.24.733), Sus (75), Tal (50), Vos (237)
Epectasis	Morphological	epenthesis	Man (xix.)
Epembole	Syntactical		Her (1.10.271), Kec (1537), Sca (4.1.458), Stu (2.17.363), Tra (562)
Epencrisis	Logical—Evidence	kriseis	Stu (3.9.578)
Epenthesis	Morphological		But (45), Des (C3r), Don (3.4), Era (DC 329), Far (26), Gil (179), Hoo (262), Lil (G.i.r), Man (xix.), Mel (T. c.iiii.v), Mos (a.iiii.v), Pea ([1577] E.ii.r), Put (173), Rob (29r), She ([1550] 27; [1555] B.iii.r), Smi (171), Sus (20), Wil (202)
Epenthymeme	Logical—Argument Forms		Era (DCE 122), Her (*Meth.* §5)
Epergesis	Grammatical	appositio	She ([1550] 30)
Epexegaroia	Pragmatical—Idea	epexergasia	Vel (168r)

Figure Name	*Discourse Level*	*Head Word*	*Sources*
Epexegesis	Pragmatical—Idea	exegesis	Des (C8r), Man (lxxxix.), Gil (160), Pea ([1577] T.i.r; [1593] 191), Sus (69)
Epexergasia	Pragmatical—Idea		[Qui (8.3.88)], Rob (30r), Stu (3.34.800)
Ephexegesis	Pragmatical—Idea	exegesis	Man (lxxxix.)
Epibole	Syntactical	anaphora	Rob (22r), Rut (I.7), Soa (308), Sus (49)
Epicertomesis	Semantical	chleuasmos	Rob (42v), Ruf (§2)
Epicheireme	Logical—Argument Forms		Kec (1535), [Qui (9.2.106)], Sca (3.71.339), Smi (258), Stu (1.28.105), Wal (80)
Epicrisis	Discoursal—Genres		Her (1.6.250), Pea ([1593] 99), Rob (48r), Stu (2.21.385), Tra (538)
Epidiegesis	Discoursal—Parts of Oration		Era (DC 650)
Epidiorthosis	Pragmatical—People	correctio	Ale (15), Her (2.7.362), Stu (3.24.733)
Epieikeia	Discoursal—Styles		Her (2.6.345), Stu (3.11.595; 3.23.715)
Epilogus	Logical—Argument Forms	conclusio	She ([1550] 55)
Epilogus	Discoursal—Parts of Oration	conclusio	Era (DC 653)
Epimeleia	Discoursal—Styles		Her (1.12.296), Stu (3.17.665)
Epimone	Syntactical		Dem (§280), Des (C7r), Gil (169), Her (1.11.286), Kec (1504), Man (lxxvii.), Pea ([1593] 70), Put (233) Smi (233), Sus (42)
Epimone	Pragmatical—Idea	commoratio	Ale (17), Her (1.11.286), Rob (48v), Smi (233), Stu (3.2.481)

Figure Name	*Discourse Level*	*Head Word*	*Sources*
Epiphonema	Pragmatical—Idea		But (115), Day (98), Dem (§106), Era (DC 609, 629), Far (25), Fen (174), Fra (F3v), Gil (165), Her (*Inv.* 4.9.196), Kec (1478), Lam (2.116), Mel (E. 53v), Pea ([1577] L.ii.v; [1593] 104), Put (225), [Qui (8.5.11)], Rob (43r), Ruf (§29), Sca (3.51.325), She ([1550] 50; [1555] G.vii.r), Smi (143), Soa (359), Sus (96), Tal (52), Vos (258), Wal (83), Wil (208)
Epiphora	Syntactical	epistrophe	Pea ([1577] J.i.v; [1593] 42), Rob (22r), Rut (I.8), Soa (309), Vos (235)
Epiplexis	Pragmatical—People	interrogatio	Her (1.7.259), Kec (1499), Rob (43v), Ruf (§21), She ([1550] 51)
Epiploke	Syntactical		Her (2.1.314), Stu (3.18.680)
Epiploke	Syntactical	gradatio	Rob (24r), Rut (I.13)
Epistrophe	Syntactical		Blo (8), But (107), Cic (Or 39.135), Far (23), Fen (172), Fra (D1v), Gil (160), Hos (13), Kec (1505), Lam (3.158), Qui (9.3.30), Rob (23v), Ruf (*Lex.* §18), Smi (98), Sus (51), Tal (62), Vos (235)
Episynaloepha	Phonetic	synaeresis	Don (3.4), Man (xxiii.), Rob (28v), Sus (22)
Episynapsis	Syntactical		Her (1.11.293), Kec (1527), Stu 2.17.363)
Epitasis	Syntactical	episynapsis	Her (*Inv.* 4.1.172)
Epitheton	Lexical		Blo (47), But (16), Day (84), Des (C5v), Dio (g.vi.v), Dem (§85), Don (3.6), Era (DC 590), Fra (A4v), Gil (157), Her (2.4.338), Kec (1549), Mel (I. 16v), Mos (b.v.r), Pea ([1577] H.i.r; [1593] 146), Put (187), Qui (8.6.40), Rob (31v), Sca (3.48.318), Smi (68), Soa (290), Stu (2.6.316), Sus (39), Tra (465), Vos (228), Wal (51)

Figure Name	*Discourse Level*	*Head Word*	*Sources*
Epitimesis	Discoursal—Genres		Ale (40), Her (1.7.256), Kec (1499), Lam (2.133), Rob (43v), Ruf (*Dian.* §7), Sca (4.1.460), Smi (142), Stu (1.23.70;3.8.569; 3.10.583)
Epitrechon	Syntactical		Her (2.1.314), Stu (3.19.682; 3.15.655)
Epitrochasmus	Pragmatical—Idea		Ale (22), Aqu (§6), Gil (167), Her (2.1.314), Mel (I. 23v), Rob (24v), Sus (71)
Epitrope	Pragmatical—People	permissio	But (125), Far (24), Her (2.8.367), Lam (2.120), Pea ([1577] M.iiii.r; [1593] 112), Rob (19v), Ruf (§27) Sca (333), Sha (183), She ([1550] 55), Smi (130), Stu (3.31.779)
Epitrope	Pragmatical—People	synchoresis	Day (90), Put (234), Rob (43r), Rut (II.17), Sus (66), Vos (246)
Epizeuxis	Lexical		Blo (6), But (103), Cic (Or 39.135), Day (85), Des (C4v), Dio (g.iii.v), Don (3.5), Far (22), Fen (171), Fra (C5v), Gil (159), Hos (12), Kec (1504), Lam (3.159), Man (xxxvii.), Mos (a.vi.r), Pea ([1577] J.iii.r; [1593] 47), Put (210), Qui (9.3.28), Rob (31r), She ([1555] D.vi.r), Smi (89), Stu (1.16.43), Sus (50), Tal (58), Vos (237), Wil (224)
Epizeugma	Grammatical		Aqu (§44), Qui (9.3.62), Rob (24r)
Ergasia	Pragmatical—Idea		Lam (2.129), Rob (39r), Stu (1.28.105)
Erotema	Pragmatical—People	interrogatio	Ale (24), Aqu (§11), Day (87), Dem (§279), Des (C8r), Man (lxxxviii.), Mel (I. 21v), Pea ([1577] L.iii.v; [1593] 106), Put (220), Rob (48r), Sus (57)
Erotesis	Pragmatical—People	interrogatio	But (133), Dem (§297), Far (24), Her (1.8.262), Lon (§18), Sha (183), She ([1550] 51), Smi (135), Soa (336), Stu (1.25.81)

Figure Name	*Discourse Level*	*Head Word*	*Sources*
Erotesis kata diastasin	Pragmatical—People	hypophora	Her (1.4.239), Stu (3.7.564)
Erroris Inductio	Pragmatical—Idea		Cic (De Or 3.205), Qui (9.2.61), Sca (3.92.363), Soa (360), Wil (213)
Eschematisman	Virtue		Qui (9.1.14), Rob (25v), Sus (47)
Ethos	Discoursal—Styles		Her (2.2.321), Stu (3.20.690), Tra (579)
Ethikon	Discoursal—Genres	ethopoeia	Cic (Or 37.128), Dem (§227), Her (*Meth.* §36), Stu (1.38.201; 3.17.679)
Ethologia	Discoursal—Genres	ethopoeia	Qui (1.9.3), Vel (172v)
Ethopoeia	Discoursal—Genres		Ale (21), Aqu (§4), Cic (Or 40.139), Era (DC 654), Qui (9.2.58; 9.3.99), Rai (N.i.r), Rob (47r), Ruf (*Dian.* §13), Rut (I.21), Sca (3.33.307), She ([1555] F.v.v), Soa (346), Stu (1.38.200), Tal (38), Vel (127v), Wal (74)
Etymologia	Logical—Idea	definitio	Era (DC 332), Kec (1550), Pea ([1577] H.i.v; [1593] 148), [Qui (1.6.29)], Sca (3.55.331), Stu (3.22.712), Sus (41)
Etymologia logon	Lexical		Stu (3.22.712), Wil (171)
Eucharistia	Pragmatical—People		Era (DC 461), Pea ([1593] 101)
Euche	Discoursal—Genres		Era (DC 494), Her (2.7.354), Pea ([1593] 67), Rob (43v), Ruf (§28), She ([1550] 51), Stu (3.31.784), Vos (270)
Eudialyta	Vice	paralogismus	Stu (3.35.813)
Eudiasis	Pragmatical—Idea		Era (DC 474), Her (2.6.350), Stu (3.32.786)
Eukatastrophon	Syntactical	epitrechon	Stu (3.1.443)
Eukrineia	Discoursal—Styles		Her (1.4.235), Stu (3.6.545; 3.7.558)
Eulogia	Discoursal—Genres		Pea ([1593] 65), Sca (3.40.311), Smi (142)

Figure Name	*Discourse Level*	*Head Word*	*Sources*
Euphemismus	Pragmatical—People		Dem (§281), Her (2.3.325), Pea ([1593] 89), Qui (9.2.92), Rob (48v), Smi (224), Vos (223)
Euphonia	Virtue		Cic (Or 49.163), Dem (§69), Des (C8r), Her (1.12.307), Kec (1511), Man (xciii.), Stu (3.4.518), Vel (12r), Vos (274)
Eustathia	Pragmatical—People	fiducia	Pea ([1593] 69)
Eutaxia	Pragmatical—Idea	digestio	Stu (1.15.40)
Euteleia	Discoursal—Styles	psychrotes	Her (2.10.383), Stu (3.8.567)
Eutrepismus	Pragmatical—Idea	digestio	Pea ([1593] 129)
Evacuatio	Pragmatical—Idea	anasceue	Ruf (*Dian.* §6)
Evasio	Pragmatical—Idea		Her (1.11.286), Rob (45r), Sca (3.45.315)
Evidentia	Pragmatical—Idea	enargeia	Era (DC 577), Qui (6.2.32), She ([1550] 66), Sus (86), Wil (203)
Evocatio	Grammatical		Des (C7r), Far (27), Lil (G.i.v), Man (ci.), Mos (a.viii.r), Smi (190), Vel (49v)
Exaggeratio	Pragmatical—Idea		Dem (§277), Kec (1475), Sca (3.46.315), Stu (1.32.126)
Exallage	Grammatical		Her (2.1.316), Qui (9.3.64), Stu (3.19.687)
Exallage	Grammatical	enallage	Qui (9.3.12), Sca (3.31.306)
Exceptio	Logical—Argument Forms	pareuresis	Rob (48v)
Excessus	Semantical	hyperbole	Sus (17)
Excitatio	Pragmatical—People		Era (DC 649), Kec (1475), [Qui (9.2.104)], Rob (45r), Sca (3.61.334)

Figure Name	*Discourse Level*	*Head Word*	*Sources*
Exclamatio	Discoursal—Genres		Blo (29), But (115), Cic (De Or 3.207), Day (89), Era (DC 347), Far (24), Fen (173), Fra (E5r), Gil (165), Hos (33), Kec (1490), Lam (2.101), Mel (E. 44r; I. 22r), Pea ([1593] 62), Qui (9.2.27), Rob (44r), Sca (3.40.311), She ([1555] E.iii.r), Smi (140), Soa (359), Stu (2.21.386), Sus (61), Tal (51), Vos (262), Wal (92), Wil (229)
Exclusio	Pragmatical—Idea		[Qui (9.2.104)], [Rob (45r)], Sca (3.61.334)
Excursio	Discoursal—Parts of Oration	digressio	Era (DC 589), Sca (3.75.343), Sus (104)
Excusatio	Discoursal—Genres	dicaeologia	Sca (3.66.336), Sus (85), Vel (167r)
Execratio	Discoursal—Genres		Cic (De Or 3.205), Fen (174), Kec (1499), Ruf (§15), Sca (3.69.338), Sha (183), She ([1550] 51; [1555] E.iii.v), Smi (141), Soa (358), Stu (1.24.70), Tal (52), Vos (270)
Exegesis	Pragmatical—Idea		Des (C8r), Era (DC 332), Gil (160), Smi (206), Wal (79)
Exemplum	Logical—Evidence	paradeigma	Ad H (4.49.62), Blo (12–3), Cic (De Or 3.205), Des (C7r), Era (DC 607), Hos (18), Mel (E. 53r), Pea ([1593] 186), Rob (49v), Sca (3.71.339), She ([1550] 72–5/88–9; [1555] G.iiii.v), Stu (1.42.242), Sus (103), Vos (252), Wal (80), Wil (215)
Exergasia	Pragmatical—Idea	expolitio	Cic (De Or 3.205), Put (254), Qui (8.3.88), Rob (30r), She ([1550] 93), Smi (221), Stu (1.26.89), Sus (90), Vel (166r), Vos (232)
Exilitas	Discoursal—Styles		[Ad H (4.11.16)], Cic (De Or 3.97), Mel (E. 64r), She ([1555] H.ii.v), Stu (3.8.569)

Figure Name	*Discourse Level*	*Head Word*	*Sources*
Exordium	Discoursal—Parts of Oration		Era (DC 648), Kec (1475)
Exornation	Virtue	eschematis-man	She ([1550] 39), Wil (194)
Exouthenismos	Semantical	tapinosis	Rob (43r), Ruf (§6)
Expeditio	Pragmatical—Idea	epitrochasmus	Sca (3.44.315)
Expeditio	Logical—Argument Forms		Ad H (4.29.40), Blo (40), Day (98), Hos (45), Kec (1484), Pea ([1577] Tiiii.r; [1593] 186), Put (241), She ([1550] 54), Smi (250), Stu (1.40.219), Sus (98), Wal (78)
Explicatio	Pragmatical—Idea	exegesis	Smi (206)
Expolitio	Pragmatical—Idea		Ad H (4.42.54), Era (DC 630), Kec (1551), Mel (E. 48v; I. 26v), Pea ([1577] P.iiii.v; [1593] 193), Put (254), Rob (49v), She ([1555] G.viii.r), Smi (221), Stu (3.24.729), Sus (90), Vos (232), Wal (70)
Exposition	Virtue	poikilia	Pea ([1577] F.iii.v)
Extensio	Phonetic	diastole	Gil (179), She ([1550] 27), Smi (177), Sus (21)
Extensio	Virtue	tasis	She ([1550] 37)
Extenuatio	Semantical	meiosis	Cic (De Or 3.202), Kec (1468), Mel (E. 36v), Sca (3.81.347), She ([1550] 61)
Extenuatio	Pragmatical—Idea	diminutio	Cic (Or 40.137), Kec (1475), Sca (3.81.347), Stu (2.27.434), Sus (80), Vel (139r)
Exuscitatio	Discoursal—Genres		Ad H (4.43.55), Cic (De Or 3.205), Day (99), Pea ([1577] U.i.r; [1593] 177), Sus (99), Tra (578)
Fabella	Discoursal—Genres	fable	Vel (171v)
Fable	Discoursal—Genres		Blo (3), Hos (9), Pea ([1593] 188), Wil (221)
Fabula	Discoursal—Genres	fable	Era (DC 631), Sca (3.84.351), Stu (1.42.253), Vel (173r)

Figure Name	*Discourse Level*	*Head Word*	*Sources*
Fastidium	Pragmatical—People		[Qui (9.2.104)], Rob (45v)
Fictio	Semantical	onomatopoeia	Qui (8.6.31), Smi (72), Stu (2.10.328), Tra (459)
Fictio	Pragmatical—People		Sca (3.85.356), Tal (33)
Ficcion	Discoursal—Genres	mythos	She ([1550] 72)
Fiducia	Pragmatical—People		Kec (1499), Stu (1.24.77)
Finitio	Logical—Idea	definitio	Ad H (4.8.11), Day (97), Era (DC 332), Mel (I. 26v), Sca (3.55.331), Sus (41)
Firmamentum	Logical—Evidence		Era (DC 595), Wal (121)
Floridus	Discoursal—Styles	oratio medi-ocris	Cic (De Or 3.98), [Qui (12.10.58)], [Sca (4.9.463)]
Frequentatio[1]	Pragmatical—Idea		Ad H (4.40.52), Blo (27), Cic (De Or 3.202), Cic (Or 40.137), Era (DC 651), Hos (32), Kec (1484) Pea ([1577] T.iii.v; [1593] 151), Put (244), Rob (49v), She ([1555] G.ii.r), Stu (1.40.229), Sus (98), Wil (208)
Frequentatio[2]	Pragmatical—Idea		Sca (3.42.314)
Frigidum	Discoursal—Styles	psychrotes	[Qui (5.10.31)]
Garrulitas	Vice	macrologia	Vel (9v)
Geminatio	Lexical	epizeuxis	Cic (De Or 3.206), Des (C4v), Man (xxxvii.), Qui (9.3.28), Sca (3.41.313), Stu (1.16.43), Sus (50)
Gesticulatio	Pragmatical—Idea		Vel (167r), Wil (174)
Glaphyria	Discoursal—Styles		Dem (§128)
Glykytes	Discoursal—Styles		Her (2.4.330), Stu (3.21.699)
Gnome	Logical—Evidence	sententia	Era (E. 3.148.883), Her (*Inv.* 4.3.180), Kec (1476), Mel (E. 53v), Pea ([1577] U.iii.r; [1593] 189), Put (243), [Qui (8.5.3)], Rob (46r), Sha (137), She (136–9), Smi (244), Stu (1.14.32), Sus (94), Vel (164r), Vos (247)

Figure Name	*Discourse Level*	*Head Word*	*Sources*
Gorgotes	Discoursal—Styles		Era (E. 3.98.910), Her (2.1.312), [Sca (3.44.315)], Stu (3.19.682)
Gradatio	Syntactical	climax	Ad H (4.25.34), Blo (7), But (105), Cic (De Or 3.207), Day (94), Des (C5r), Dio (g.iv.r), Era (E. 3.140.720), Far (22), Gil (161), Hos (12), Man (xlvi.), Mel (E. 52r; I. 23v), Mos (a.vii.r), Qui (9.3.54), Rob (31r), Ruf (*Lex.* §19), Sca (4.31.502), She ([1550] 58; [1555] E.vi.r), Smi (94), Soa (316), Stu (2.24.422), Sus (80), Tal (66), Tra (572), Vel (119r), Vos (238), Wal (33), Wil (228)
Graecismus	Grammatical	hellenismus	But (131), Far (28), Kec (1503), Qui (9.3.17), Ruf (*Lex.* §32), Smi (193)
Gratiarum Actio	Pragmatical—People	eucharista	Mel (E. 7v), Pea ([1577] L.ii.r; [1593] 101)
Gravis	Discoursal—Styles	oratio grandis	[Ad H (4.8.11)], [Sca (4.17.482)], Tra (457)
Gravitas	Discoursal—Styles	deinotes	Era (E. 3.132.549), [Sca (4.18.483)], Stu (3.6.543), Tra (603)
Griphos	Discoursal—Genres	aenigma	Dem (§153)
Hebraism	Grammatical		Smi (227)
Hellenismus	Grammatical		But (131), Far (28), Hoo (268), Kec (1503), Smi (193), Stu (3.6.545)
Hellenismus	Virtue		Stu (3.6.545)
Hendiadys	Grammatical		Day (83), Des (C7v), Far (28), Gil (158), Kec (1502), Man (lxxx.), Mos (a.vi.v), Pea ([1577] H.iiii.r), Put (188), Smi (194), Sus (35)
Heteroiosis	Grammatical	kainoprepeis	Far (28), Qui (9.3.12)
Heterosis	Grammatical	enallage	Era (DC 321)
Hiatus	Phonetic		Cic (Or 23.77), Dem (§68), Her (1.3.232), Kec (1516), Qui (9.4.36), Stu (3.4.521)

Figure Name	*Discourse Level*	*Head Word*	*Sources*
Hiatus	Vice	cacemphaton[1]	Ad H (4.12.18), Cic (Or 44.151), Dio (g.v.r), Don (3.1), Her (1.12.308), Kec (1511), Stu (3.4.519), Tra (579), Wil (193)
Hirmos	Syntactical		Day (83), Don (3.5), Far (25), Gil (163), Rob (31r), Sha (184), She ([1555] F.viiii.v), Smi (163), Sus (38)
Historia	Discoursal—Genres		Vel (172r), Wal (74)
Homeozeuxis	Logical—Idea	similitudo	Dio (h.i.v)
Homoeideia	Vice	homoiologia	Qui (8.3.52)
Homoeoptoton	Phonetic		Ale (36), Aqu (§25), Des (C5r), Dio (g.iii.v), Don (3.5), Era (E. 3.134.589), Far (18), Her (1.12.302), Kec (1504), Man (xliii.), Mel (E. 43v; I. 20v), Mos (a.vi.v), Pea ([1577] K.i.v; [1593] 53), Qui (9.3.78), Rob (19v), Rut (II.13), Sca (4.41.512), She ([1550] 58), Smi (213), Soa (324), Stu (2.23.412), Sus (54), Tal (81), Vos (241), Wal (35), Wil (226)
Homoeosis	Logical—Idea	similitudo	Des (C6v), Dio (h.i.v), Don (3.6), Man (lxxiii.), Mos (b.vii.r), Rob (42v), Ruf (§25), Sca (3.50.321), Stu (3.22.713), Sus (99)
Homoeoteleuton	Phonetic		Ale (35), Aqu (§26), But (107), Day (86), Dem (§26), Des (C4v), Dio (g.iii.v), Don (3.5), Era (E. 3.134.590), Far (18), Gil (163), Her (1.12.302), Kec (1506), Lam (3.158), Man (xlii.), Mel (E. 43v; I. 21r), Mos (a.vi.v), Pea ([1577] K.i.v); [1593] 54), Put (184), Qui (9.3.77), Rob (19v), Rut (II.14), Sca (4.41.512), She ([1550] 58), Smi (214), Soa (326), Stu (2.23.412), Sus (55), Tal (81), Vos (241), Wil (226)
Homoioartron	Phonetic		Her (1.12.302), Stu (3.17.668)

Figure Name	*Discourse Level*	*Head Word*	*Sources*
Homoiologia	Vice		Era (DC 302), Mos (a.vii.v), [Rob (29v)], She ([1550] 33), Wil (194)
Homoiosis	Logical—Idea	similitudo	Era (E. 2.414.165), Stu (1.41.231)
Homologia	Pragmatical—People	confessio	Her (*Meth.* §32)
Homonymia	Lexical	paronomasia	Her (2.5.342)
Homonymia	Vice	amphibologia	Qui (7.9.2), Vel (18r), Vos (206)
Horismus	Logical—Idea	definitio	Day (97), Her (1.4.238), Mel (I. 26v), Pea ([1577] S.iiii.v; [1593] 128), Put (239), Rob (20r), Rut (II.5), Sca (3.55.331), She ([1550] 58), Smi (235), Stu (3.7.563), Sus (85)
Humile	Discoursal—Styles	subtilitas	Era (E. 3.162.212), Mel (I. 13r)
Humilitas	Vice	tapinosis	Vel (10r)
Hypallage	Syntactical		Ale (40), But (131), Cic (Or 27.93), Day (83), Des (C7v), Era (E. 3.176.500), Far (28), Gil (164), Hoo (268), Kec (1469), Man (lxxviii.), Mel (E. 43v; I. 21r), Mos (a.vi.v), Put (182), Smi (200), Stu (3.35.814), Sus (34), Vel (45v), Vos (229)
Hypallage	Semantical	metonymia	Cic (Or 27.93), Qui (9.3.92), Soa (288), Stu (2.4.297), Sus (7), Tal (3)
Hypallage	Vice		Era (DC 305), Pea ([1577] G.i.r), Put (183), Wil (194)
Hyperbaton	Syntactical		Ale (38), But (129), Des (C5v), Dio (h.i.r), Don (3.6), Far (28), Gil (164), Her (1.12.305), Kec (1537), Lam (1.41), Lon (§22), Man (lix.), Mel (E. 42v; I. 19v), Mos (b.vi.v), Pea ([1577] F.iii.v), Put (180), Qui (8.6.65), Rob (24v), Sca (4.38.508), She ([1550] 30), Smi (199), Soa (300), Stu (2.17.365), Sus (31), Tal (71), Tra (573), Vel (45v)

Figure Name	*Discourse Level*	*Head Word*	*Sources*
Hyperbaton	Pragmatical—Idea	hysteron proteron	Stu (3.14.637)
Hyperbaton	Vice		Ad H (4.12.18), Put (180), Qui (8.2.14), She ([1555] A.vi.v), Vel (9r), Wil (194)
Hyperbole	Semantical		Blo (24), But (3), Cic (De Or 3.203), Day (80), Dem (§161), Des (c6r), Dio (h.i.r), Don (3.6), Era (DC 344), Far (21), Fra (B3r), Hos (29), Kec (1468), Lam (2.79), Man (lviii.), Mel (E. 36v; I. 18r), Mos (b.vii.r), Pea ([1577] D.iiii.v; [1593] 31), Put (202), Qui (8.6.67), Rob (43r), Ruf (§38), Sca (3.74.342), Sha (123–7), She ([1550] 71), Smi (54), Soa (301), Stu (2.8.322), Sus (17), Tal (15), Vos (223), Wil (208)
Hyperbole	Vice		Dem (§124), Fen (168), Fra (A2v), Gil (151), Qui (8.3.49), Sha (123–7), Smi (54), Stu (2.8.324)
Hypexairesis	Pragmatical—Idea	remotio	Ale (16)
Hyphen	Phonetic		Man (xcvi.)
Hypobole	Pragmatical—People	subjectio	Lam (2.118), Sca (4.36.505), Sha (183), Vos (244)
Hypochesis	Pragmatical—People	promissio	Stu (3.31.784)
Hypocorismos	Semantical		Era (DC 348), Put (228), Stu (2.27.436), Sus (77)
Hypocrisis	Semantical		Ruf (*Dian.* §8)
Hypographia	Discoursal—Genres	descriptio	Vel (127r)
Hypomene	Pragmatical—Idea	sustentatio	Dem (§216), Rob (44r), Ruf (§34), Soa (348)
Hypomnematon	Discoursal—Genres	prosopopoeia	Soa (343)
Hypomone	Logical—Idea	paradoxon	Rob (43r)

Figure Name	*Discourse Level*	*Head Word*	*Sources*
Hypophora	Pragmatical—People		But (120), Cic (Or 40.137), Des (C7r), Man (lxxxiiii.), Pea ([1577] L.iiii.v; [1593] 107), Qui (9.2.14), Rob (44r), Smi (127), Stu (1.28.104), Wil (232)
Hypophora	Pragmatical—People	prolepsis	Vos (243)
Hypophora	Discoursal—Genres	prosopopoeia	Her (*Inv.* 4.13.207)
Hyposchesin	Pragmatical—People		Her (2.6.348), Stu (3.35.814)
Hypostasis	Syntactical		Her (1.11.290), Rob (49r), Stu (3.8.626)
Hypostrophe	Syntactical	parenthesis	Her (1.6.251), Stu (3.19.682)
Hypothesis	Logical—Argument Forms		Era (DC 593, 597), Her (1.11.288), Smi (263), Stu (2.16.357), Vel (146r)
Hypothyposis	Pragmatical—People	adulatio	Rob (44r)
Hypotyposis	Pragmatical—Idea		But (136), Cic (De Or 3.202), Era (DC 577), Lam (2.108), Mel (E. 54v), Qui (9.2.40), Rob (27r), Sca (3.33.308), She ([1555] F.v.r), Smi (112), Soa (344), Wil (161)
Hypotyposis	Discoursal—Genres	descriptio	Day (97), Far (23), Gil (158), Mel (I. 26v), Pea ([1577] O.ii.r), Put (245), Sus (86), Vos (251)
Hypozeugma	Grammatical		But (130), Dio (g.iii.r), Era (DC 345), Man (xxx.), Mos (a.v.v), Pea ([1577] K.iii.r; [1593] 51), Put (176), She ([1550] 29; [1555] C.i.r), Smi (180), Soa (320), Sus (26)
Hypozeuxis	Syntactical		Des (c4r), Dio (g.iii.r), Don (3.5), Man (xxxi.), Mos (a.v.v), Pea ([1577] K.iii.r; [1593] 59), Put (177), Rob (24v), Ruf (*Lex.* §4)
Hyptiotes	Discoursal—Styles		Her (2.1.314), Stu (3.19.682)

Figure Name	*Discourse Level*	*Head Word*	*Sources*
Hyrmos	Vice		Ad H (4.12.18), Dem (§303), Des (C5r), Dio (g.iv.r), Man (xlv.), Pea ([1577] H.i.r), She ([1555] A.vi.v), Smi (163), Wil (192)
Hysterologia	Grammatical		Kec (1502), Pea ([1577] F.iiii.r), She ([1555] C.ii.v), Sus (32)
Hysterologia	Syntactical	hysteron proteron	But (131), Des (C6r), Dio (h.i.r), Don (3.6), Gil (164), Man (lxiiii.), Mos (b.vii.r)
Hysterologia	Pragmatical—Idea	hysteron proteron	Far (28), She ([1550] 31), Smi (201)
Hysteron Proteron	Syntactical		But (130), Day (83), Des (C6r), Dio (h.i.r), Don (3.6), Gil (164), Man (lxiiii.), Mos (b.vii.r), Put (262)
Hysteron Proteron	Pragmatical—Idea		Day (83), Far (28), Put (181), She ([1555] C.iii.r), Sus (32)
Hysteron Proteron	Vice		Day (83), Pea ([1577] F.iiii.r), Put (262), Wil (193)
Icon	Semantical		Day (99), Des (C6v), Dio (h.i.v), Don (3.6), Era (DC 623), Man (lxxiiii.), Mel (E. 53v; I. 18v), Mos (b.vii.r), Pea ([1577] U.ii.r; [1593] 145), Put (250), Rob (31v), Ruf (§24), Sha (184), She ([1550] 91), Stu (2.27.436), Sus (101), Vos (228)
Idiophasis	Syntactical		Man (lxxxvi.)
Idiotismos	Pragmatical—People	communicatio	Rob (43v)
Ignocentia	Discoursal—Genres		Era (DC 477), Pea ([1593] 98), [Qui (9.2.104)], Rob (45v)
Illusio	Semantical	ironia	Cic (De Or 3.202), Kec (1466), Mel (I. 17v), Pea ([1593] 35), Qui (8.6.54), Sca (3.85.356), Soa (298), Sus (14), Tra (465), Vos (220)
Illustratio	Virtue	enargeia	Stu (1.36.159), Sus (86)
Illustris explanatio	Pragmatical—Idea		Cic (De Or 3.202)

Figure Name	*Discourse Level*	*Head Word*	*Sources*
Imaginatio	Pragmatical—People	phantasia	Smi (266), Pea ([1577] P.iii.r; [1593] 144)
Imago	Semantical	icon	Ad H (4.49.62), Cic (De Or 3.207), Era (DC 623), Sca (3.50.321), She ([1550] 91; [1555] G.v.v), Stu (2.27.434), Sus (101), Vos (251), Wil (232)
Imitatio	Pragmatical—People	mimesis	Cic (De Or 3.204), Era (E. 3.22.332), Smi (247), Vos (228)
Imminutio	Semantical	meiosis	Cic (De Or 3.207), Stu (2.27.434)
Immoratio	Pragmatical—Idea	commoratio	Sus (99), Tra (578)
Immutatio	Syntactical	hypallage	Cic (De Or 3.207), Smi (200), Stu (2.23.415)
Immutatio	Semantical	metonymia	Cic (De Or 3.167)
Imprecatio	Discoursal—Genres		But (114), Era (DC 494), Fen (174), Fra (F2v), Kec (1499), Mel (E. 44r; I. 22r), Pea ([1577] K.iiii.r; [1593] 64), Put (221), Stu (3.32.785), Sus (62), Tal (24), Wil (224)
Impressio	Pragmatical—Idea	epitrochasmus	Sca (3.44.315)
Improprietas	Vice	acyron	Mos (a.viii.v), She ([1550] 32; [1555] A.vi.v), Vel (9r)
Improvisum quiddam	Pragmatical—People		Cic (De Or 3.207), Wil (167)
Incisio	Syntactical	articulus	Tra (577)
Incisum	Syntactical	articulus	Ad Her (4.19.26), Soa (319), Vel (46r)
Incisum	Syntactical	comma	Cic (Or 62.211), Kec (1540), Stu (3.1.442), Vel (46r)
Incitatio	Virtue	cataphora	Sca (4.11.465)
Inconjunctum	Syntactical	asyndeton	Sus (37)

Figure Name	*Discourse Level*	*Head Word*	*Sources*
Incrementum	Pragmatical—Idea		Cic (De Or 3.207), Day (91), Era (DC 592), Far (24), Gil (161), Kec (1487), Mel (E. 50r; I. 23v), Pea ([1577] Q.ii.v; [1593] 169), Rob (5v), Sha (158–9), She ([1550] 71; [1555] F.viii.v), Smi (132), Sus (70), Vos (260), Wal (72), Wil (153)
Indicatio	Logical—Evidence	kriseis	Era (DC 438), She ([1550] 92)
Indignatio	Discoursal—Genres		But (114), Day (89), Fra (E7v), Kec (1499), Ruf (§11), Sca (4.42.513), Smi (141), Stu (1.23.66)
Inductio	Logical—Argument Forms	epagoge	Sca (3.71.339), Vel (144v), Wal (80)
Inference	Logical—Argument Forms	expeditio	Blo (41), Hos (45)
Infima	Discoursal—Styles	subtilitas	[Sca (4.21.484)], Tra (457)
Injectio	Syntactical	parenthesis	Tra (565)
Injunctio	Grammatical	epizeugma	Aqu (§44)
Innovatio	Grammatical	kainoprepes	Tra (573)
Innvitio	Pragmatical—Idea		Sca (3.80.347)
Inopinatum	Pragmatical—Idea	sustentatio	But (122), Qui (6.3.84; 9.2.24), Ruf (§34), Vos (297)
Inopinatum	Logical—Idea	paradoxon	But (122), Mel (E. 44r; I. 22r), Sus (64)
Insectatio	Semantical	chleuasmos	Ruf (*Dian.* §10), Vel (140r)
Insertio	Morphological	epenthesis	Hoo (263)
Insinuatio	Discoursal—Parts of Oration		Era (DCE 75)
Instantia	Pragmatical—Idea	diallage	Era (E. 3.102.964), Sca (3.64.335)
Insultatio	Discoursal—Genres		Day (89), Gil (153), Put (218), Sus (63), Vos (299)

Figure Name	*Discourse Level*	*Head Word*	*Sources*
Intellectio	Semantical	synecdoche	Ad H (4.33.44), Era (DC 341), Gil (151), Mel (I. 15v), Pea ([1593] 17), Put (196), She ([1550] 42), Soa (282), Sus (7), Tal (19), Tra (462), Wil (199)
Inter se pugnantia	Discoursal—Genres	epitimesis	Pea ([1577] R.i.v; [1593] 163)
Intercisio	Grammatical	tmesis	Gil (180), Sus (20)
Interclusio	Syntactical	parenthesis	Qui (9.3.23), Soa (353), Sus (33)
Interjectio	Lexical	diacope	Stu (1.18.49)
Interpellantis coercitio	Pragmatical—People		Cic (Or 40.138), Wil (223)
Interpellatio	Pragmatical—People		Cic (De Or 3.205), Sca (3.91.362)
Interpositio	Morphological	epenthesis	She ([1550] 27), Sus (20)
Interpositio	Syntactical	parenthesis	Des (C6r), Gil (165), Mel (E. 54v; I. 25v), Qui (9.3.23), Sca (4.38.508), She ([1550] 31; [1555] C.iii.r), Smi (188), Stu (2.17.363), Sus (33), Vel (30v), Wal (43)
Interpretatio	Lexical	synonymia	Ad H (4.28.38), Era (DC 320), Mel (E. 48v; I. 23v), Sca (3.56.332), She ([1555] D.v.v), Sus (69), Tra (578), Vos (232)
Interrogatio	Pragmatical—Idea		Pea ([1577] L.iii.r; [1593] 105), She ([1555] E.ii.r), Smi (137), Stu (1.25.79), Sus (58), Wil (209)
Interrogatio	Pragmatical—People		Ad H (4.15.22), Aqu (§11), Blo (27), But (114), Day (87), Des (C8r), Era (DC 347), Hos (32), Kec (1494), Lam (2.117), Mel (E. 44r; I. 21v), Pea ([1577] L.iii.r; [1593] 105), Qui (9.2.7–11), Rob (43v), Sca (4.42.513), She ([1555] E.ii.r), Smi (135), Soa (336), Sus (57), Tra (578), Vos (268), Wal (82)
Interruptio	Pragmatical—People	aposiopesis	Cic (De Or 3.207), Qui (9.2.54), Rob (44v), Soa (346), Sus (25)

Figure Name	*Discourse Level*	*Head Word*	*Sources*
Intimation	Logical—Argument Forms	syllogismus	Blo (20), Hos (25)
Inversio	Syntactical	antimetabole	Gil (166), Sca (4.33.503), Smi (116), Stu (2.26.431)
Inversio	Pragmatical—Idea		Era (DC 647), Far (24), Kec (1485), Mel (E. 52v), Smi (125)
Invocatio	Logical—Evidence		[Qui (9.2.104)], Rob (45v)
Iotacismus	Vice	cacemphaton[1]	Dio (g.v.r), Don (3.1), Mos (b.ii.v)
Ira	Discoursal—Genres	indignatio	Stu (1.24.77)
Iracundia	Discoursal—Genres	indignatio	Cic (De Or 3.205), Day (89), Fra (E7v), Smi (141)
Irmus	Syntactical	periodus	Kec (1526), Mos (a.vi.v), Put (186), Vel (48r)
Ironia	Semantical		Ale (22), Aqu (§7), Blo (6), But (18), Day (80), Dem (§291), Des (C6v), Dio (h.i.r), Don (3.6), Era (DC 347), Far (21), Fen (170), Fra (A6v), Gil (153), Her (1.10.272), Hos (28, 30), Kec (1466), Lam (2.80), Man (lxvi.), Mel (E. 41r; I. 17v), Mos (b.vi.r), Pea ([1577] D.iii.r; [1593] 35), Put (199), Qui (8.6.54; 9.2.44), Rob (31v), Ruf (§1), Sca (3.85.354), Sha (115–8), She ([1550] 45; [1555] D.ii.r), Smi (45), Soa (298, 354), Stu (2.9.324), Sus (14), Tal (8), Tra (465), Vos (220), Wal (93), Wil (209)
Irrisio	Semantical	sarcasmus	Aqu (§15), But (113), Kec (1500), Ruf (*Dian.* §9), Sca (3.86.356), Smi (79), Sus (15), Vel (140r), Vos (227)
Ischnos	Discoursal—Styles	subtilitas	Dem (§36, §190), [Qui (12.10.58)]

Figure Name	*Discourse Level*	*Head Word*	*Sources*
Isocolon	Syntactical		Aqu (§23), Dem (§25), Far (18), Gil (170), Her (1.12.305), Kec (1527), Pea ([1577] k.i.r; [1593] 58), Qui (9.3.80), Rob (19v), Rut (II.15), She (1550] 57), Soa (327), Stu (2.23.417), Tal (81), Tra (572), Vos (282), Wal (38), Wil (227–8)
Isodynamia	Lexical		Era (DC 342), Kec (1551), Qui (10.1.12), Ruf (*Lex.* §37), Stu (2.7.318)
Isodynamodeta	Lexical	synonymia	But (136), Era (DC 307), Her (1.11.285), Stu (3.14.641)
Ison	Lexical		Aqu (§42), Cic (De Or 3.206), Stu (2.23.421), Wil (228)
Isopleura	Syntactical		Stu (3.1.454)
Isoskelis	Syntactical		Her (1.12.301), Kec (1528), Stu (2.23.418)
Isoteta	Lexical	ison	Stu (2.23.421)
Iteratio	Lexical	palilogia	Aqu (§29), Cic (Or. 25.85), Rob (31r), Stu (2.22.403)
Iteratio	Syntactical	anadiplosis	Stu (2.22.403)
Iteratio	Syntactical	anaphora	Ruf (*Lex.* §5)
Jucunditas	Discoursal—Styles	glykytes	Era (E. 3.98.904), Tra (584)
Judicatio	Logical—Evidence	kriseis	Vel (151r)
Judicatio	Discoursal—Genres	epicrisis	Sca (3.40.311)
Judicia	Logical—Evidence	kriseis	Era (DC 607)
Junctio	Grammatical	zeugma	She ([1550] 29), Stu (3.17.668)
Junctio	Syntactical	polysyndeton	Stu (2.25.428)
Jusiurandum	Discoursal—Genres	adjuratio	Era (E. 2.466.437), Pea ([1593] 75), Rob (44v), Stu (1.18.50)
Kainoprepeis	Grammatical		Dem (§144), Her (1.12.306), Stu (3.17.677), Tra (573)
Kallos	Discoursal—Styles	epimeleia	Her (1.12.296), Stu (3.17.665), Tra (568)
Katastasis	Pragmatical—Idea		Her (1.4.239), Stu (3.24.729)

Figure Name	*Discourse Level*	*Head Word*	*Sources*
Katharotes	Discoursal—Styles		Her (1.3.227), Stu (3.6.545)
Kekrimmenon	Discoursal—Styles	deinotes	Stu (3.27.753)
Koinismos	Vice	soraismus	[Rob (29v)]
Koinotes	Syntactical	symploce	Rob (22r), Rut (I.9), Stu (3.35.807)
Koinotes	Semantical		Vos (223)
Kollesis	Logical—Evidence	apomnemonsysis	Her (*Meth.* §30)
Kommata	Syntactical	brevitas	Dem (§241), Era (DCE 93), Her (1.7.259), Stu (2.22.400), Tra (578)
Kosmesis	Pragmatical—Idea	ordo	Her (1.2.238), Stu (1.28.104)
Kriseis	Logical—Evidence		Era (DC 626), Mel (E. 53v), Sus (96)
Krypsis	Discoursal—Styles		Stu (3.17.668)
Kryptikon	Discoursal—Styles	asapheia	Stu (3.26.749)
Kyklos	Syntactical	epanalepsis	Her (*Inv.* 4.8.195)
Laesio	Pragmatical—People		Cic (De Or 3.205)
Lambdacismus	Vice		Dio (g.v.r), Don (3.1), Mos (b.ii.v), Qui (1.5.32), Stu (2.22.408)
Lamentatio	Discoursal—Genres	threnos	Pea ([1593] 66)
Lamprotes	Discoursal—Styles		Her (1.9.264), Stu (3.8.570), Tra (549)
Latinitas	Virtue		Ad H (4.12.17), Stu (3.6.545), Vel (9r)
Laudatio	Discoursal—Genres	commendatio	Ad H (4.37.49)
Leptologia	Pragmatical—Idea		Ale (18), Aqu (§2), Rob (47v), Vel (9v)
Licentia	Pragmatical—People	parrhesia	Ad H (4.36.48), Cic (Or 40.138), Era (E. 3.122.348), Fen (174), Fra (F4v), Mel (E. 45r; I. 22v), Qui (9.2.27), Rob (49v), Sca (4.24.491), She ([1555] E.iiii.v), Smi (225), Soa (350), Sus (66), Tal (55), Vel (50v)

Figure Name	*Discourse Level*	*Head Word*	*Sources*
Liptote	Semantical	litotes	Day (84), Des (C7v), Man (lxxxi.), Pea ([1577] H.ii.v; [1593] 150), Put (195), Qui (10.1.12), She ([1550] 61), Sus (41)
Litotes	Semantical		Far (21), Her (1.12.306), Lam (2.78), Qui (10.1.12), Sha (184), Smi (69), Tra (569), Vos (222)
Locus communis	Logical—Argument Forms	thesis	Cic (Or. 36.126), Era (DC 605, 637), Mel (E. 46r)
Logadis	Discoursal—Styles	oratio soluta	Stu (3.4.512)
Lysis	Discoursal—Parts of Oration	anthypophora	Her (2.7.356), Stu (1.28.104; 3.7.564)
Macrocolon	Syntactical		Dem (§44), Stu (3.1.452), Vos (282)
Macrologia	Pragmatical—Idea		Day (82), Gil (157)
Macrologia	Vice		Des (C2r), Dio (g.iv.r), Don (3.3), Man (viii.), Mos (b.i.r), Pea ([1577] F.ii.v), Put (264), Qui (8.3.53), She ([1550] 34; [1555] B.i.v), Sus (30), Vel (9v), Vos (207)
Macrologia	Vice	perissologia	Gil (157), Put (264), Qui (8.3.53), [Rob (29v)]
Magnitudo	Discoursal—Styles	oratio grandis	[Sca (4.18.483)], Tra (531)
Makarismos	Discoursal—Genres	eulogia	Stu (3.24.729)
Mala affectatio	Vice	cacozelia	Qui (8.3.56), She ([1550] 34)
Martyria	Logical—Evidence		Pea ([1593] 85), Rob (45v), Smi (232)
Medela	Pragmatical—People		Pea ([1577] T.ii.v; [1593] 176)
Megaloprepes	Discoursal—Styles	oratio grandis	Dem (§36, §38), [Qui (4.2.61)], Stu (3.34.800)
Megethos	Discoursal—Styles	oratio grandis	Her (1.5.242), Stu (3.8.567)
Meionektikas	Pragmatical—People		Her (2.6.347), Stu (3.23.719)

Figure Name	*Discourse Level*	*Head Word*	*Sources*
Meiosis	Semantical		Blo (35), But (4), Day (84), Era (DC 344), Far (21), Fen (170), Hos (39), Mel (E. 48v; I. 23r), Pea ([1577] N.iiii.v; [1593] 168), Put (195), She ([1550] 61), Smi (55), Sus (75–6), Vos (259), Wil (206)
Meiosis	Pragmatical—Idea	diminutio	But (4), Cic (Or 40.137), Far (21), Put (227), Qui (8.3.50), Smi (55), Sus (77)
Meiosis	Vice		Gil (151), Qui (8.3.50), [Rob (29v)], Vel (10r)
Meiouros	Syntactical		Stu (3.1.450)
Membrum	Syntactical		Ad H (4.19.26), Aqu (§18), Cic (Or 62.211), Era (E. 3.102.976), Kec (1524), Lam (3.149), Pea ([1577] J.iiii.v; [1593] 58), She ([1550] 57; [1555] D.viii.r), Stu (3.1.437), Sus (53), Tra (572), Vel (46r)
Membrum	Syntactical	isocolon	Day (86), Sus (54)
Memoratio	Pragmatical—Idea	anamnesis	Sca (3.91.362)
Mempsis	Discoursal—Genres	querela	Pea ([1593] 65)
Merismus	Pragmatical—Idea	distributio	Day (97), Her (1.4.238), Kec (1483), Mel (E. 50r; I. 26v), Put (230), Rob (19v), Rut (I.18), Sha (183), Soa (355), Stu (3.15.646), Sus (91), Vos (248)
Mesozeugma	Grammatical		But (130), Dio (g.iii.r), Era (DC 345), Man (xxx.), Mos (a.v.v), Pea ([1577] K.iii.r; [1593] 51), Put (176), She ([1550] 29; [1555] C.i.r), Smi (180), Sus (26)
Metabasis	Discoursal—Parts of Oration		Mel (I. 25r), Pea ([1577] T.i.v; [1593] 175), Qui (9.3.25), Ruf (*Lex.* §25), Rut (II.1), Sca (3.76.343), Sha (183), She ([1550] 59), Smi (237), Wil (207)
Metabole	Rhythmical		Qui (9.4.50)

Figure Name	*Discourse Level*	*Head Word*	*Sources*
Metabole	Lexical	polyptoton	Lon (§23), Sca (4.36.505)
Metabole	Pragmatical—Idea		Dem (§148), Qui (9.3.38), Rob (24v)
Metabole	Virtue	poikilia	Ale (35)
Metacismus	Vice	cacemphaton[1]	Dio (g.v.r), Don (3.1), Mos (b.ii.v)
Metaepaina	Discoursal—Genres	commendatio	Rob (37v)
Metalepsis	Semantical		But (3), Day (79), Des (C5v), Dio (g.vi.v), Don (3.6), Era (DC 339), Fen (168), Far (21), Gil (154), Kec (1459), Man (li.), Mel (E. 35v; I. 16r), Mos (b.iiii.v), Pea ([1577] C.iiii.v; [1593] 23), Put (193), Qui (8.6.37), Rob (31v), She ([1550] 41; [1555] C.viii.r), Smi (51), Soa (293), Stu (2.6.314), Sus (10), Vos (221)
Metalepsis	Pragmatical—Idea	metastasis	Qui (9.2.106)
Metallage	Lexical	permutatio	Sca (4.36.506)
Metanoia	Pragmatical—People	correctio	Day (94), Gil (165), Mel (I. 25v), Pea ([1577] R.iii.r; [1593] 173), Put (223), Rob (19v), Rut (I.16), Sca (3.37.310), Stu (3.24.730), Sus (75)
Metaphora	Semantical		Blo (1), But (22), Day (77), Dem (§78), Des (C5r), Dio (g.vi.v), Don (3.6), Era (DC 333), Far (20), Fen (170), Fra (B1v), Gil (151), Her (1.6.249), Hos (8), Kec (1464), Lam (2.75), Lon (§32), Man (xlviii.), Mel (E. 35r; I. 15v), Mos (b.iiii.r), Pea ([1577] B.ii.r; [1593] 3), Put (189), Qui (8.6.4), Rob (31v), Sha (118–9), She ([1550] 40; [1555] C.vii.r), Smi (9), Soa (276), Stu (2.2.274), Sus (6), Tal (9), Vos (211), Wal (54), Wil (198)

Figure Name	*Discourse Level*	*Head Word*	*Sources*
Metaplasmus	Morphological		But (42), Cic (De Or 3.206), Des (C3r), Dio (g.iv.v), Don (3.4), Era (DC 329), Gil (178), Hoo (264), Man (xvi.), Mos (a.iiii.v), Pea ([1577] E.i.v), Qui (9.1.33), She ([1555] B.iii.r), Smi (170), Stu (3.3.491), Sus (19), Wil (225)
Metaschematismos	Virtue	poikilia	Kec (1535–9), Stu (3.1.452; 3.3.483–507)
Metastasis	Pragmatical—Idea		Ale (26), Aqu (§16), Cic (De Or 3.207), Her (1.11.286), Mel (E. 50v), Put (240), [Qui (7.4.14; 9.2.41)], Rob (44r), Sca (3.65.336)
Metastasis	Pragmatical—Idea	inversio	Her (2.6.347), Pea ([1577] T.iii.r; [1593] 181), Smi (126)
Metastasis	Discoursal—Parts of Oration	metabasis	Day (96), Rob (25r), Ruf (*Lex.* §25), Sus (83)
Metathesis	Morphological		But (52), Cic (De Or 3.207), Des (C3v), Don (3.4), Far (26), Gil (180), Hoo (264), Man (xxvi.), Mos (a.iiii.v), Pea ([1557] E.iii.v), She ([1555] B.iii.v), Smi (176), Soa (323), Stu (3.17.672), Sus (23)
Metathesis	Syntactical	antimetabole	Mel (E. 52r; I. 24r), Rob (23v), Ruf (*Lex.* §10), Soa (330), Sus (81)
Methodeuthesis	Discoursal—Genres	noema	Stu (3.10.584)
Metonymia	Semantical		Blo (4), But (4), Cic (Or 27.9), Day (78), Des (C5v), Dio (g.vi.v), Don (3.6), Era (DC 339), Far (20), Fen (169), Fra (A3r–6v), Gil (151), Hos (10), Kec (1458), Lam (2.72), Man (lii.), Mel (E. 6r; I. 15v), Mos (b.v.r), Pea ([1577] C.ii.r; [1593] 19), Put (191), Qui (8.6.23), Rob (31v), Sca (4.35.505), Sha (113), She ([1550] 42; [1555] C.vii.v), Smi (12), Soa (285), Stu (2.4.297), Sus (7), Tal (3), Vos (213), Wal (34), Wil (200)

Figure Name	*Discourse Level*	*Head Word*	*Sources*
Metra and pedes	Rhythmical		But (90–8), Dem (§38–44), Far (19), Fen (171), Fra (B8v–C4v), Kec (1518), Lam (2.145), Stu (3.5.525–36), Tal (72–82), Tra (539–43), Wal (121)
Microlochia	Vice	periergia	Stu (3.4.520)
Mimesis	Pragmatical—People		Kec (1472), Mel (E. 41v), Pea ([1577] O.iiii.r; [1593] 138), Qui (9.2.58), Rob (44v), Sha (183), She ([1555] F.vi.v), Smi (247), Soa (347), Tal (38), Vel (129r), Vos (228), Wil (167)
Mimesis	Discoursal—Genres	prosopopoeia	Far (25), Sha (171), She ([1550] 69)
Miseratio	Discoursal—Genres	commiseratio	Era (E. 3.102.964)
Moderatio	Pragmatical—People	correctio	Sca (3.37.310)
Modestia	Discoursal—Styles	epieikeia	Tra (592)
Modus imperativus	Discoursal—Genres		Era (DC 439), Qui (9.2.48), Stu (2.14.349), Tra (544)
Modus optativus	Discoursal—Genres		Stu (2.14.349), Tra (544)
Molle	Virtue	euphonia	Sca (4.10.464)
Monocolon	Syntactical	periodus	Aqu (§18), Dem (§17), Her (*Inv.* 4.3.179), Kec (1524), Stu (3.1.442), Vel (47r)
Moralis confictio	Discoursal—Genres	ethopoeia	Aqu (§4)
Mycterismus	Discoursal—Genres		Mel (I. 18r), Mos (b.vi.r), Pea ([1577] D.iii.v; [1593] 38), Put (201), Qui (8.6.58), She ([1550] 46; [1555] D.ii.v), Smi (248), Sus (15), Vos (228), Wil (209)
Mystikos hypostamenein	Pragmatical—Idea		Her (1.6.247), Stu (3.9.572)
Mythikon	Discoursal—Genres	mythos	Her (2.4.330), Stu (3.21.699)
Mythologia	Logical—Evidence		Mel (E. 41v), Stu (1.42.253), Vel (156r)
Mythos	Discoursal—Genres		Dem (§157), Era (DC 610), Sca (3.84.351), Vel (171v)

Figure Name	*Discourse Level*	*Head Word*	*Sources*
Mythos	Discoursal—Genres	fable	Her (*Pro* §1)
Narratio	Discoursal—Parts of Oration		Era (DC 648), Kec (1475), Stu (1.30.112; 1.36.167), Vel (172r)
Narratio	Discoursal—Genres		Stu (1.30.112)
Narratio poetica	Discoursal—Genres	mythos	Vel (171v)
Necessitas	Discoursal—Genres	dicaeologia	Mel (E. 50v), Sca (3.66.336), She ([1550] 60), Vel (194r)
Negatio	Pragmatical—People	apophasis	But (20), Fra (A8v), Qui (9.2.47), Rob (44v), Smi (164)
Negatio	Discoursal—Genres	anairesis	Ad H (4.46.59), Tra (536)
Nempe	Pragmatical—Idea		Kec (1475)
Noema	Discoursal—Genres		Dem (§291), Era (DC 629), Kec (1478), Mel (E. 54r), Pea ([1577] U.iiii.r; [1593] 180), Put (238), [Qui (8.5.12)], Sha (139–41), She ([1555] G.vii.r), Sus (97), Vos (248)
Nominatio	Semantical	onomatopoeia	Ad H (4.31.42), Pea ([1593] 14), Soa (290)
Nominis confictio	Semantical	onomatopoeia	Era (DC 337), Pea ([1593] 14), Sus (9)
Nomimon zetema	Pragmatical—Idea		Stu (1.15.41)
Notatio	Logical—Idea	definitio	Mel (T. c.v.r), Vel (33v)
Notatio	Discoursal—Genres	characterismus	Ad H (4.50.63), Cic (Or 40.138), Era (E. 3.144.804), Rob (50r), Sca (3.33.308), Soa (347), Stu (1.38.197), Tra (580)
Notatione	Semantical	periphrasis	Era (DC 332), Sus (41)
Nugatio	Vice	tautologia	Vel (9v)
Numeri designationem	Logical—Idea	definitio	Her (1.4.238), Stu (3.7.563)
Numeros	rhythmical	rythmon	Lam (3.202), Stu (1.4.11)
Objectio	Discoursal—Parts of Oration	anthypophora	Ruf (*Dian.* §4), Vel (194r)

Figure Name	*Discourse Level*	*Head Word*	*Sources*
Objurgatio	Discoursal—Genres	epitimesis	Cic (De Or 3.205), Kec (1499), Ruf (*Dian.* §7), Sca (4.1.460), Stu (1.24.71), Tra (601), Vel (167r), Vos (268)
Objurgatio	Discoursal—Styles	barytes	Tra (601)
Obscuritas	Discoursal—Styles	asapheia	Qui (8.2.12), [Sca (4.1.445)], Vel (10r)
Obsecratio	Discoursal—Genres		Cic (De Or 3.205), Era (E. 2.466.443), Kec (1500), Ruf (§16), Sca (4.83.349), Sha (183), Soa (357), Vos (270)
Obtestatio	Discoursal—Genres		But (114), Era (E. 2.466.437), Fra (F1r), Kec (1500), Lam (2.129), Mel (E. 44r; I. 22r), Pea ([1577] K.iiii.v; [1593] 71), Put (221), Ruf (§16), Sca (3.38.311), Soa (357), Stu (3.35.802), Sus (62), Tal (52), Vel (51r), Wil (224)
Obticentia	Pragmatical—People	aposiopesis	Qui (9.2.54), Rob (44v), Sus (25)
Occultatio	Pragmatical—People	paralepsis	Ad H (4.27.37)
Occultatio	Pragmatical—People	scematismus	Her (*Inv.* 4.11.200), Qui (9.3.98), Stu (1.26.97)
Occupatio	Pragmatical—Idea	prolepsis	Blo (45), Hos (49), Mel (E. 52v), Smi (127), Tra (593), Vel (194r), Vos (243)
Occupatio	Pragmatical—People	paralepsis	Day (95), Era (DC 347), Pea ([1593] 130), She ([1550] 59), Soa (349), Sus (72), Wil (213)
Occupatio	Discoursal—Parts of Oration		But (121), Fen (175), Kec (1485), She ([1555] E.vii.r), Stu (1.26.88)
Oeconomia	Virtue	synthesis	Vel (12r)
Ogkologia	Vice	bomphiologia	Vel (10v)
Oictros	Discoursal—Genres	commiseratio	She ([1550] 68), Vel (128v)
Ominatio	Discoursal—Genres		Era (DC 454), Kec (1499), Mel (E. 44r; I. 22r), Pea ([1577] L.i.r; [1593] 90), Sus (62)
Omoiosis	Logical—Idea	similitudo	Day (99), Era (DC 615), Put (247), Ruf (§22)

Figure Name	*Discourse Level*	*Head Word*	*Sources*
Onedismus	Discoursal—Genres		Pea ([1593] 73), Rob (49r), Sca (4.1.460), Stu (1.23.68)
Onkos	Discoursal—Styles	oratio grandis/ megethos	Her (1.4.241), Stu (3.8.567)
Onomastikon	Lexical	plotike	Her (1.6.240), Stu (3.3.485)
Onomaton kallon	Lexical		Dem (§164), Ruf (*Lex.* §41–44), Stu (3.21.706)
Onomaton koinoteron	Lexical		Dem (§164), Stu (3.21.706)
Onomatopoeia	Semantical		Cic (De Or 3.154), Day (79), Des (C5v), Dio (g.vi.v), Don (3.6), Era (DC 337) Far (21), Gil (154), Kec (1469), Man (lvi.), Mel (E. 36v; I. 16r), Mos (b.v.v), Pea ([1577] C.iiii.r; [1593] 14), Put (192), Rob (28v), Qui (8.6.31), Smi (72), Soa (290), Stu (2.10.328), Sus (9), Vos (229), Wil (199)
Opposita oratio	Logical—Idea	antithesis	Tra (562)
Oppositio	Logical—Idea	antithesis	Ruf (*Lex.* §13), Smi (172)
Optatio	Discoursal—Genres		But (113), Cic (De Or 3.205), Era (DC 424), Fen (173), Fra (E7r), Kec (1498), Pea ([1577] K.iiii.v; [1593] 72), Sca (3.81.348), Smi (142), Soa (358), Stu (1.24.70), Tal (23), Wil (224)
Oraculum	Logical—Evidence		Kec (1478), She ([1550] 93; [1555] G.vii.v), Wal (70)
Oratio grandis	Discoursal—Styles		Cic (Or 5.20), Era (E. 3.162.211), Mel (E. 63v), She ([1550] 21; [1555] H.i.v)
Oratio mediocris	Discoursal—Styles		[Ad H (4.8.11)], Cic (De Or 3.199), Era (E. 3.162.211), Mel (E. 63v), [Qui (12.10.58)], She ([1550] 21; [1555] H.i.v), Tra (457)
Oratio soluta	Discoursal—Styles		Aqu (§18), Cic (Or 71.236)
Orcos	Discoursal—Genres	adjuratio	Her (1.9.267), Lon (§16), Pea ([1593] 75), Stu (1.18.50)
Ordinatio	Pragmatical—Idea	digestio	Pea ([1577] S.iii.r; [1593] 129), Tra (527)

Figure Name	*Discourse Level*	*Head Word*	*Sources*
Ordo	Pragmatical—Idea		Cic (De Or 3.207), Man (cii.), Pea ([1577] N.ii.r; [1593] 118), Tra (566), Wil (232)
Ornatus	Virtue	eschematis-mon	Mos (b.iii.v), She ([1550] 38)
Orthotes	Syntactical		Her (1.3.231), Kec (1535), Sca (4.1.455), Stu (2.11.333)
Ostentatio	Discoursal—Genres		But (114)
Oxymoron	Logical—Idea		Far (24), Sha (184), Smi (121), Vos (256)
Oxytes	Discoursal—Styles		Her (2.5.339), Stu (3.22.708)
Paeanismus	Discoursal—Genres		Pea ([1593] 81), Fen (174), Rob (49v), Sha (183), Smi (143), Sus (63), Vos (270)
Paenitentia	Pragmatical—People	correctio	Qui (9.2.59)
Palilogia	Lexical		Ale (29), Aqu (§29), Fra (C6r), Lam (2.107), Smi (160), Sca (4.29.498), Wal (66)
Palilogia	Syntactical	anadiplosis	Rob (24v), Ruf (*Lex.* §7), Sus (50)
Para prosdokian	Pragmatical—People	improvisum quiddam	Dem (§152), Her (*Meth.* §34)
Parabola	Discoursal—Genres		Dem (§89), Des (C7r), Dio (h.i.v), Don (3.6), Era (DC 616), Lam (2.136), Man (lxxv.), Mel (E. 53v; I. 18v), Mos (b.vii.v), Pea ([1577] U.ii.r), Put (251), Ruf (§22), Sca (3.53.330), Sha (183), She ([1550] 90), Smi (218), Stu (2.9.325), Sus (102), Vos (252)
Parabole	Logical—Idea	comparatio	Dem (§146), Her (*Inv.* 4.179), Qui (8.3.77), Vos (252)
Paradeigia	Logical—Evidence	paradeigma	Era (DC 616), Mel (I. 18v), Put (252), Ruf (§22), Sus (103)

Figure Name	*Discourse Level*	*Head Word*	*Sources*
Paradeigma	Logical—Evidence		Day (100), Des (C7r), Dio (h.i.v), Don (3.6), Era (DC 606), Her (1.11.282), Man (lxxvi.), Mel (I. 18v), Mos (b.vii.v), Pea ([1577] U.ii.v; [1593] 186), Put (252), Rob (42v), Ruf (§23), Sca (3.50.321), Sha (147–9), Stu (3.31.779), Sus (103), Vos (252)
Paradiastole	Pragmatical—Idea		Day (84), Des (C7v), Far (23), Gil (165), Kec (1483), Man (c.), Mel (E. 53r), [Qui (9.3.65)], Rob (23v), Ruf (*Lex.* §22), Rut (I.4), Sca (3.52.329), Sha (183), She ([1555] E.viii.r), Smi (114), Sus (46), Vos (255)
Paradiastole	Vice		Pea ([1577] n.iiii.v; [1593] 168), Put (195), Smi (115–6), Sus (45–6), Wil (152)
Paradiegesis	Discoursal—Parts of Oration		Pea ([1593] 94), [Qui (9.2.107)], Rob (46r)
Paradoxon	Pragmatical—Idea	sustentatio	Qui (9.2.24), Ruf (§34), Soa (348)
Paradoxon	Logical—Idea		But (122), Day (90), Her (2.9.374), Man (xx.), Mel (E. 44r; I. 22r), Pea ([1577] M.ii.v; [1593] 112), Put (233), Rob (43r), Sha (184), Sus (64), Vel (50v)
Paraenesis	Discoursal—Genres	admonitio	Pea ([1593] 78), Qui (9.2.104), Rob (45r), Sca (3.61.334)
Paragoge	Morphological		But (45), Des (C3r), Don (3.4), Era (DC 329), Far (26), Gil (179), Hoo (262), Lil (G.i.v), Mel (T. c.iiii.v), Pea ([1577] E.ii.v), Put (173), She ([1555] B.iii.v), Smi (172), Sus (21), Wil (202)
Paragoge	Semantical	onomatopoeia	Era (DC 308)
Parainetikon	Discoursal—Genres	adhortatio	Qui (9.2.103)

Figure Name	*Discourse Level*	*Head Word*	*Sources*
Paraleipsis	Pragmatical—Idea		Cic (Or 40.137), Day (95), Her (1.11.290; 2.6.351), Stu (3.10.587), Vos (260)
Paralepsis	Pragmatical—People		Ale (23), Aqu (§8), Blo (26), But (20), Cic (Or. 39.135), Day (95), Dem (§263), Era (DC 650), Far (25), Fra (A8r), Hos (30), Gil (153), Kec (1472), Lam (2.105), Mel (E. 44v; I. 24v), Pea ([1593] 130), Put (239), Rob (44v), Sha (183), She ([1550] 59), Smi (165), Soa (349), Stu (3.23.723), Sus (82), Tal (39), Wil (213)
Parallaga	Morphological		Des (C3v), Dio (g.v.r), Man (xxvii.), Mos (a.iiii.v)
Paralogismus	Vice		Far (23), Smi (264), Vel (145v), Wil (180)
Paramythia	Discoursal—Genres		Her. (*Meth.* §31), Lam (2.133), Pea ([1593] 100), Sca (3.123.399), Stu (1.29.107)
Paranomasia	Lexical	paronomasia	Blo (10), Dio (g.iii.v), Kec (1509), Man (xxxix.), Pea ([1577] K.iir; [1593] 56], Soa (322), Stu (3.22.712)
Parantegnosis	Discoursal—Parts of Oration	adnarratio	Sca (3.73.342)
Paraphrasis	Lexical		Blo (43), Era (DC 303), Her (*Meth.* §24), Hos (47), Kec (1537), Wal (96), Wil (201)
Paraplokas toiematon	Logical—Evidence		Her (2.4.336), Stu (3.21.705)
Parasiopesis	Pragmatical—People	paralepsis	Rut (II.11)
Parathesis	Grammatical	appositio	But (135), Smi (190)
Parauxesis	Pragmatical—Idea	amplificatio	Qui (9.2.106)
Parecbasis	Discoursal—Parts of Oration	digressio	Era (DC 589), Put (240), Smi (241), Stu (2.27.436), Sus (104), Tal (42), Vos (257)

Figure Name	*Discourse Level*	*Head Word*	*Sources*
Parechesis	Phonetic		Era (E. 3.132. 568), Far (17), Gil (163), Her (*Inv.* 4.7.194), Lam (3.158), Stu (2.22.407), Sus (56), Vos (242)
Parechesis	Logical—Evidence		Rob (46r), Smi (243), Stu (3.31.779), Wil (173)
Parechia	Lexical	paronomasia	Gil (163)
Paregmenon	Lexical	polyptoton	Pea ([1577] K.ii.r; [1593] 55), Rob (25r), Ruf (*Lex.* §16), Smi (246), Vos (239)
Parelcon	Morphological		Cic (De Or 3.206), Des (C8r), Far (27), Lil (G.v.r), Smi (187), Sus (30)
Parelcon	Vice		Pea ([1577] F.iii.r)
Parembole	Syntactical	epembole	Ale (39), Sca (4.38.508), Vos (238)
Paremptosis	Syntactical	parenthesis	Qui (9.3.23)
Parenthesis	Syntactical		Blo (39), But (133), Day (83), Des (C6r), Dio (h.i.r), Don (3.6), Era (DC 325), Far (27), Gil (165), Hos (44), Kec (1537), Man (lxii.), Mel (E. 54v; I. 25v), Mos (b.vi.v), Pea ([1577] F.iiii.v; [1593] 198), Put (180), Qui (9.3.23), Rob (19v), Ruf (*Lex.* §12), Rut (I.17), Sca (3.36.310), She ([1550] 31), Smi (188), Soa (353), Sus (33), Tal (46), Vos (238), Wal (79)
Pareonasis	Discoursal—Parts of Oration	digressio	Day (100)
Parepomenon	Logical—Idea	consecutio	Dem (§217), Rob (40r)
Paresis	Discoursal—Styles	hyptiotes	Sca (3.27.294)
Pareuresis	Logical—Argument Forms		Pea ([1593] 95), Rob (48v)
Parison	Lexical	paronomasia	Her (*Meth.* §16)

Figure Name	*Discourse Level*	*Head Word*	*Sources*
Parison	Syntactical	isocolon	Ale (40), Aqu (§24), Era (E. 3.104.996), Kec (1506), Pea ([1577] K.i.r; [1593] 58), Put (222), Qui (9.3.76), Rob (24r), Sca (4.39.511), Sus (54)
Parisonomata	Phonetic		Cic (De Or 3.207), Stu (3.31.784)
Parisosis	Syntactical		Her (1.11.292), Rob (31r), Stu (2.23.412), Sus (49)
Parodia	Discoursal—Genres		Dem (§150), Her (*Meth.* §34), Kec (1472), Qui (9.2.35), Rob (45r), Stu (3.35.816)
Paroemia	Logical—Evidence		Day (80), Dem (§156), Des (C6v), Dio (h.i.v), Don (3.6), Era (DC 336), Far (22), Her (1.6.251), Kec (1474), Man (lxx.), Mel (I. 17v), Mos (b.vi.r), Pea ([1577] D.ii.v; [1593] 29), Put (199), [Qui (8.6.57)], Rob (31v), Sca (3.84.352), She ([1550] 45; [1555] d.ii.r), Smi (81), Soa (360), Stu (3.22.712), Sus (13)
Paroemion	Phonetic	parechesis	Des (C4v), Dio (g.iii.v), Man (xli.), Mos (a.vi.v), Pea ([1577] G.iii.v; [1593] 49), Put (185), Sus (36)
Paroidia	Logical—Evidence	parechesis	Her (*Meth.* §30)
Paromoion	Phonetic	parechesis	Dem (§25), Don (3.5), Her (1.12.302), Rob (19v), Rut (II.12)
Paromologia	Pragmatical—People	concessio	Day (96), Mel (E. 53r; I. 26r), Pea ([1577] S.i.v; [1593] 173), Put (235), Rob (19v), Rut (I.19), Sca (3.57.333), Sha (183), Smi (115), Sus (85), Vos (246)
Paronomasia	Phonetic	paroemion	Blo (10), Fra (E4v), Hos (15), Mel (E. 43v)

Figure Name	*Discourse Level*	*Head Word*	*Sources*
Paronomasia	Lexical		Ale (36), Aqu (§27), But (109), Cic (Or 25.84), Dem (§97), Des (C4v), Don (3.5), Far (23), Fen (173), Fra (D5r), Gil (163), Her (2.5.342), Hos (16), Mel (I. 21r), Mos (a.vi.r), Qui (9.3.66), Rob (22r), Ruf (*Lex.* §15), Rut (I.3), Sca (3.56.332), Smi (105), Sus (56), Tal (68), Vos (240), Wil (225)
Parrhesia	Pragmatical—People		But (132), Day (90), Era (E. 3.122.348), Fen (174), Kec (1497), Mel (E. 45r; I. 22v), Pea ([1577] M.ii.v; [1593] 113), Put (234), Qui (9.2.27), Rob (20r), Ruf (§33), Rut (II.18), Sca (3.67.337), Smi (225), Soa (350), Stu (1.17.45), Sus (66), Tal (55), Wil (223)
Partitio	Pragmatical—Idea	distributio/ merismus	She ([1550] 62; [1555] F.i.r)
Partitio	Logical—Idea		Era (DC 426, 574), Kec (1550), Pea ([1577] R.iii.v; [1593] 124), Tra (527, 560)
Partitio	Discoursal—Parts of Oration		Era (DC 648), Rob (45v), Stu (3.28.759)
Partitio conjugata	Pragmatical—Idea		Tra (573)
Pathetikon	Discoursal—Styles		Cic (Or 37.128), Stu (1.38.201; 3.23.719)
Pathographia	Discoursal—Genres	pathopoeia	Gil (158)
Pathopoeia	Discoursal—Genres		Era (DC 654), Far (23), Mel (E. 54v; I. 22r), Pea ([1577] P.iii.r; [1593] 143), Rob (42v), Ruf (§36), She ([1550] 68; [1555] f.vi.r), Smi (266), Stu (3.32.785), Sus (62), Vel (128v), Wil (160)
Pepoiemenon	Semantical	onomatopoeia	Dem (§144), Her (1.8.262), Stu (3.11.599)
Pepoithesis	Pragmatical—People	fiducia	Her (1.9.265), Stu (1.24.77)

Figure Name	*Discourse Level*	*Head Word*	*Sources*
Percontatio	Pragmatical—People	interrogatio	Cic (De Or 3.203), Era (E. 3.102.956), Qui (5.7.27), Sca (4.42.513), Wil (209)
Perculsio	Discoursal—Genres	cataplexis	Sca (3.62.335)
Percursio	Pragmatical—Idea	epitrochasmus	Aqu (§6), Cic (De Or 3.202), Qui (9.1.28), Sus (71)
Peribeblemenon	Pragmatical—Idea	hysteron proteron	Stu (3.14.636)
Peribole	Syntactical	circumductio	Sca (4.1.458), Stu (3.3.498), Vel (45v), Vos (281)
Peribole	Discoursal—Styles		Her (1.11.277), Stu (3.14.630)
Periergia	Vice		Hos (6), Mos (b.i.r), Pea ([1577] G.iii.v), Put (265), Qui (8.3.55), [Rob (29v)], She ([1550] 33; [1555] B.i.v), Vel (9v), Vos (234), Wil (192)
Periodikon	Syntactical		Stu (3.1.464), Vos (283)
Periodus	Syntactical		Ale (27), Aqu (§18), Cic (Or 60.204), Dem (§10), Far (18), Her (*Inv.* 4.3.176), Kec (1525), Lam (3.150), Mel (E. 59v), Sca (4.25.493), Stu (3.1.437), Vel (45v), Wal (37)
Perioysia	Pragmatical—Idea	macrologia	Rob (49v)
Periphrasis	Lexical	paraphrasis	Sha (162), Wil (201)
Periphrasis	Semantical		Ale (32), Blo (42), But (135), Day (84), Dem (§92), Des (C5v), Dio (g.vi.v), Don (3.6), Era (DC 331), Far (25), Gil (158), Hos (46), Kec (1550), Lam (2.122), Lon (§28), Man (lvii.), Mel (T. c.iiii.r), Mos (b.vi.v), Pea ([1577] H.i.v; [1577] R.iii.r; [1593] 148), Put (203), Qui (8.6.59), Rob (37v), Sca (3.78.346), She ([1550] 44; [1555] D.i.r), Smi (167), Soa (299), Stu (2.6.312), Sus (39), Vos (228)
Periploke	Pragmatical—People	scematismus	Her (*Meth.* §8), Stu (3.35.803)

Figure Name	*Discourse Level*	*Head Word*	*Sources*
Perissologia	Pragmatical—Idea	macrologia	Gil (157)
Perissologia	Vice		Des (C2r), Dio (g.iv.r), Don (3.3), Era (DC 318), Man (vii.), Mos (a.viii.v), Pea ([1577] F.ii.v), Put (264), Qui (8.6.61), She ([1550] 32; [1555] B.i.r), Soa (299), Sus (30)
Peristasis	Logical—Idea		Blo (23), Era (DC 591), Her (1.11.281), Hos (28), Pea ([1577] N.iiii.v; [1593] 164), She ([1555] G.i.r), Wal (73), Wil (153)
Perittotes	Virtue	copia	Her (*Meth.* §5), Stu (3.34.799)
Permissio	Pragmatical—People		Ad H (4.29.39), Cic (De Or 3.207), Era (E. 3.108.96), Fen (175), Fra (H4v), Kec (1496), Mel (E. 44v; I. 22v), Qui (9.2.25), Rob (44r), Sca (3.51.324), She ([1550] 55; [1555] E.iiii.r), Smi (130), Soa (356), Stu (2.27.434), Sus (65), Tal (29), Tra (593), Wil (230)
Permutatio	Grammatical	enallage	Vel (30r)
Permutatio	Lexical		Kec (1550), Wal (90)
Permutatio	Semantical	allegoria	Ad H (4.34.46), Smi (59), Sus (11), Tal (14), Tra (466)
Permutatio	Semantical	antiphrasis	Era (E. 3.118.302), Vel (194r)
Peroratio	Discoursal—Parts of Oration	conclusio	Era (DC 648), Kec (1475)
Perplexitas	Vice	hyperbaton	Vel (9r)
Personae fictio	Discoursal—Genres	prosopopoeia	Aqu (§3), Cic (De Or 3.205), Des (C7v), Mel (I. 23r), Qui (9.2.30), Rob (47v), Sca (3.48.318), Smi (153), Sus (67), Tal (33)
Perspicuitas	Discoursal—Styles	sapheneia	Era (E. 3.98.904), [Sca (4.1.444)], Stu (3.6.543)
Perspicuitas	Virtue		Sca (4.1.444), Vel (10r)
Perversio	Syntactical	anastrophe	Ad H (4.32.44), Tra (587)

Figure Name	*Discourse Level*	*Head Word*	*Sources*
Peusis	Pragmatical—People	interrogatio	Her (*Meth.* §10), Lon (§18), Stu (3.35.804)
Phantasia	Pragmatical—People		[Qui (6.2.29; 8.3.88)], Rob (30r), Wil (163)
Philophronesis	Pragmatical—People		Pea ([1593] 96), Rob (49r)
Phobos	Discoursal—Genres		Her (2.7.356), Smi (143), Stu (3.32.785)
Pisteis	Discoursal—Parts of Oration	argumentatio	Era (DC 605), She ([1550] 78–93)
Pithanotetos	Virtue		Dem (§221), Her (1.11.280)
Plagiasmos	Syntactical		Dem (§104), Her (1.11.288), Kec (1536), Sca (4.1.455), Stu (2.11.336; 3.15.653), Vos (291)
Plenitudo	Discoursal—Styles	peribole	Sca (4.8.462B)
Pleonasmus	Lexical		Ale (32), Aqu (§45), But (128), Day (82), Far (27), Gil (157), Hoo (266), Kec (1502), Lam (2.108), Pea ([1577] F.ii.r), Qui (9.3.18, 46), Rob (24v), Ruf (*Lex.* §40), Sca (4.34.504), She ([1555] C.ii.r), Smi (186), Sus (29), Vos (231), Wal (50)
Pleonasmus	Vice		Des (C2r), Dio (g.iv.r), Don (3.3), Kec (1551), Man (v.), Mos (a.viiii.v), Pea ([1577] F.ii.r), Put (264), Qui (8.3.53), [Rob (29v)], Sha (177–8), She ([1550] 32; [1555] B.i.r), Stu (2.18.369), Vel (9v)
Pleonektikos	Pragmatical—People		Stu (3.23.719)
Ploce	Lexical		Ale (37), Aqu (§28), Cic (De Or 3.206), Day (86), Far (23), Lam (3.159), Mel (E. 43r), Pea ([1577] J.ii.r; [1593] 44), Put (211), Qui (9.3.41), Rob (22r), Ruf (*Lex.* §14), Sca (4.37.506), Smi (109), Sus (52), Vos (232)

Figure Name	*Discourse Level*	*Head Word*	*Sources*
Plotike	Lexical		Dem (§65), Her (1.6.249), Kec (1550), Ruf (*Lex.* §28–33), Stu (3.3.485)
Pneuma	Syntactical	periodus	Her (*Inv.* 4.4.183), Kec (1532), Stu (3.2.473), Tra (555), Vos (283)
Poet's tale	Discoursal—Genres	mythos	Blo (4), Hos (9), Pea ([1593] 188), Wil (219)
Poicilogia	Vice		She ([1555] B.ii.r), Vel (11v)
Poieticon	Lexical		Dem (§112)
Poikilia	Virtue		Her (*Meth.* §4), Sca (4.32.503), Stu (3.34.799)
Pokrisis	Lexical		Stu (3.22.712), Wil (171)
Polyptoton	Lexical		Ad H (4.22.31), Ale (34), Aqu (§37), Blo (11), But (109), Cic (De Or 3.207), Day (86), Des (C5r), Dio (g.iv.r), Don (3.5), Era (E. 3.134.586), Far (23), Fen (173), Fra (D6v), Gil (163), Her (1.12.306), Hos (17), Kec (1509), Lon (§23), Man (xliiii.), Mos (a.vi.v), Qui (9.3.37,66), Rob (24r), Rut (I.10), Sha (179–80), Smi (110), Soa (313), Stu (2.23.412), Sus (53), Tal (67), Tra (588), Vos (239), Wal (34)
Polysyndeton	Syntactical		But (128), Day (83), Dem (§54, §63), Des (C4v), Dio (g.iv.r), Don (3.5), Era (DC 345), Far (27), Gil (158), Her (*Meth.* §11), Hoo (266), Kec (1502), Lon (§21), Man (xxxiiii.), Mel (E. 43v; I. 20v), Mos (a.vii.I), Pea ([1577] G.iiii.v/J.iiii.r; [1593] 53), Put (186), Qui (9.3.51), Rob (19v), Rut (I.14), Sca (3.43.314), Sha (179), Smi (184), Soa (316), Stu (2.25.428), Sus (37), Vos (231)
Postjunctio	Grammatical	hypozeugma	She ([1550] 29)
Praeceptio	Pragmatical—Idea	prolepsis	Ruf (*Dian.* §2)

Figure Name	*Discourse Level*	*Head Word*	*Sources*
Praecipitatio	Pragmatical—Idea	epitrochasmus	Sca (3.44.315)
Praecisio	Pragmatical—People	aposiopesis	Ad H (4.30.41), Cic (De Or 3.202), Era (E. 3.110.146), Sca (3.77.344), Soa (345), Stu (2.19.375), Sus (25), Tra (600)
Praedictio	Discoursal—Genres	ominatio	Era (DC 454), Qui (9.2.17)
Praeexpositio	Discoursal—Genres	proecthesis	Sca (3.72.341)
Praemonitio	Pragmatical—Idea	katastasis	Tra (526)
Praemunitio	Pragmatical—People		But (137), Cic (De Or 3.204), Kec (1486), Qui (9.2.17), Rob (43v), Ruf (§32), Stu (1.27.101)
Praeoccupatio	Pragmatical—Idea	prolepsis	Day (95), Fra (H3r), Sus (83), Wal (92)
Praeparatio	Pragmatical—People		But (137, Era (DC 652), Qui (9.2.17), Rob (47v), Ruf (*Dian.* §3), Wil (212)
Praeposteratio	Pragmatical—Idea	hysteron proteron	Sus (32)
Praescriptio	Logical—Idea	definitio	Sca (3.55.331)
Praesumptio	Syntactical	prolepsis	Des (C4r), Don (3.5), Man (xxix.), Mos (a.v.r), Ruf (*Lex* §1), She ([1550] 28), Sus (28)
Praesumptio	Pragmatical—Idea	prolepsis	Far (24), Mel (I. 24v), Qui (9.2.16), Sca (3.49.320), Soa (339), Stu (1.26.88), Sus (83)
Praeteritio	Pragmatical—Idea	paraleipsis	Ad H (1.9.14)
Praeteritio	Pragmatical—People	paralepsis	Aqu (§8), But (20), Fra (A8r), Mel (E. 44v; I. 24v), Pea ([1577] S.ii.v; [1593] 130), Smi (165), Soa (349), Sus (82), Vel (51r), Vos (260)
Praetermissio	Pragmatical—People	paralepsis	Soa (349), Tal (39), Tra (593)
Pragmatographia	Discoursal—Genres		Far (23), Gil (158), Pea ([1577] O.iiii.v; [1593] 139), Put (246), Sus (87), Wil (204)
Preassumpcio	Morphological	paragoge	She ([1550] 27)

Figure Name	*Discourse Level*	*Head Word*	*Sources*
Prejunctio	Grammatical	prozeugma	She ([1550] 29)
Presozeugma	Grammatical	prozeugma	She ([1550] 29)
Prevention	Pragmatical—Idea	prolepsis	Blo (45), Hos (49), Sca (3.49.320), Wil (213)
Proanaphonesis	Syntactical	prolepsis	Far (28)
Proanaphonesis	Pragmatical—Idea	prolepsis	Stu (1.28.103)
Proanaphonesis	Pragmatical—Idea	katastasis	Her (2.7.355), Stu (3.24.728)
Probabilitas	Virtue		Era (E. 3.98.904)
Procatalepsis	Pragmatical—Idea	prolepsis	Ale (16), Day (95), Far (24), Mel (E. 52v; I. 24v), Pea ([1577] S.iii.v; [1593] 183), Put (239), Ruf (*Dian.*§2), Sus (83)
Procatasceue	Pragmatical—People	praeparatio	Her (*Inv.* 3.2.126), Rob (47v), Ruf (*Dian.* §3)
Proclees	Pragmatical—People	proklesis	Pea ([1593] 83)
Procreatio	Semantical	onomatopoeia	Pea ([1593] 14)
Procrisis	Logical—Evidence	kriseis	Stu (3.9.578)
Procursio	Pragmatical—Idea	epitrochasmus	Sca (3.44.315)
Prodiorthosis	Pragmatical—People		Ale (14), Aqu (§1), Era (DC 652), Rob (47v), Stu (3.32.786)
Prodiegesis	Discoursal—Parts of Oration		Her (1.4.236)
Productio	Morphological	paragoge	Hoo (263), Smi (171)
Productio spiritus	Syntactical	periodus	Tra (554)
Proecthesis	Discoursal—Genres		Her (*Meth.* §12), Pea ([1593] 102), Rob (46r), Sca (3.72.341), Smi (253), Stu (3.34.796)
Proepipletrein	Pragmatical—Idea		Era (DC 308), Her (*Meth.* §6)
Progressio	Pragmatical—Idea		Blo (21), Cic (De Or 3.206), Hos (26), Wil (226)
Prohibitio	Discoursal—Genres	apagoresis	Sca (3.83.349)
Proklesis	Pragmatical—People		Rob (49v)

Figure Name	*Discourse Level*	*Head Word*	*Sources*
Prolepsis	Grammatical		Des (C4r), Dio (g.iii.r), Far (27), Hoo (266), Kec (1501), Lil (G.ii.v), Man (xxix.), Mel (I. 19v), Mos (a.vii.v), Pea ([1577] F.i.v), Sca (3.49.320), She ([1555] C.i.v), Smi (130), Vel (49v)
Prolepsis	Syntactical		Cic (Or 40.138), Day (82), Des (C4r), Dio (g.iii.r), Don (3.5), Man (xxix.), Mos (a.v.r), Put (179), Ruf (*Lex* §1), She ([1550] 28), Sus (28)
Prolepsis	Pragmatical—Idea		But (123), Dio (g.iii.r), Far (24), Her (*Meth.* §23), Kec (1485), Lam (2.118), Man (xxix.), [Qui (9.2.16)], Rob (44r), Rut (II.4), Sca (3.49.320), Sha (130–3), Smi (127), Soa (339), Stu (1.26.88), Sus (83), Tal (31), Vos (243)
Promissio	Pragmatical—People		Cic (De Or 3.205), Era (DC 494), Kec (1489), Sca (3.63.335)
Pronominatio	Semantical	antonomasia	Ad H (4.31.42), Era (E. 3.112.159), She ([1550] 44), Soa (288), Sus (8), Tra (461), Vel (32v), Vos (222)
Pronuntiatio	Semantical	hypocrisis	Ruf (*Dian.* §8)
Proparalepsis	Morphological	paragoge	Man (xx.), Mos (a.iiii.r), Rob (28v), She ([1550] 27), Sus (21)
Proparasceue	Pragmatical—People	praemunitio	Rob (47v), Ruf (§32)
Propositio	Logical—Argument Forms		Era (DC 600), She ([1550] 77), Stu (3.1.442), Vel (145r)
Propositio	Discoursal—Parts of Oration		Cic (De Or 3.203), Era (DC 650), Kec (1475), Pea ([1577] S.ii.v; [1593] 192), She ([1550] 77), Stu (1.40.226), Vos (251), Wil (207)
Proprietas	Virtue		Mos (b.iii.r), She ([1550] 37)
Prosaphyn	Syntactical	epiploke	Stu (3.18.680)
Prosapodosis	Syntactical	epanalepsis	Aqu (§33)

Figure Name	*Discourse Level*	*Head Word*	*Sources*
Prosapodosis	Logical—Argument Forms		Blo (41), But (123), Cic (De Or 3.207), Hos (46), Rob (31r), Rut (I.1), Stu (2.24.426), Wal (78), Wil (229)
Proslepsis	Syntactical	prolepsis	Her (1.11.279), Stu (3.20.697)
Prosodiasaphesis	Grammatical	appositio	Ale (31), Sca (4.34.504)
Prosographia	Discoursal—Genres	prosopographia	Pea ([1577] O.ii.r–v; [1593] 135)
Prosonomasia	Lexical	paronomasia	Day (86), Era (E. 3.134.571), Put (212), Rob (24v), Sus (55)
Prosopographia	Discoursal—Genres		Era (DC 582), Far (23), Gil (158), Mel (E. 54v), Put (245), She ([1550] 66; [1555] F.v.r), Stu (1.38.197), Sus (86), Wil (204)
Prosopopoeia	Discoursal—Genres		Ale (19), Aqu (§3), But (117), Blo (43), Cic (Or 25.85), Day (90), Dem (§265), Des (C7v), Era (DC 582), Far (25), Fen (174), Fra (G2r), Her (*Inv.* 3.15.169), Hos (48), Kec (1492), Lam (2.114), Lon (§27), Man (xcii.), Mel (E. 53v; I. 23r), Mos (a.vii.r), Pea ([1577] O.iii.r; [1593] 136), Put (246), Qui (9.2.30), Rai (N.i.r), Rob (44r), Ruf (*Dian.* §14), Rut (II.6), Sca (3.48.318), Sha (171), She ([1550] 66; [1555] F.v.r), Smi (153), Soa (342), Stu (1.37.183), Sus (67; 87), Tal (33), Vos (267), Wal (91), Wil (204)
Prosparalepsis	Morphological	paragoge	Era (DC 329)
Prospoieisthai schediazein	Pragmatical—People	autoschediasmos	Her (2.7.359; *Meth.* §17)
Prostaktikon	Discoursal—Genres	modus imperativus	Her (1.7.258), Stu (3.10.591), Vel (147r)
Prosthesis	Morphological		But (45), Des (C3r), Don (3.4), Era (DC 329), Far (26), Gil (179), Hoo (262), Kec (1515), Lil (G.i.r), Man (xviii.), Mel (T. c.iiii.v), Mos (a.iii.v), Pea ([1577] E.ii.r), Put (173), Rob (28v), She ([1550] 26); [1555] B.iii.r), Smi (170), Sus (20), Wil (202)

Figure Name	*Discourse Level*	*Head Word*	*Sources*
Prosynapantesis	Grammatical	prolepsis	Ale (40)
Protasis	Syntactical		Far (18), Her (*Inv.* 4.3.178), Kec (1526), Sca (3.51.324), Stu (3.1.442), Vos (281)
Protasis	Discoursal—Parts of Oration		Her (*Inv.* 3.4.134), Stu (1.28.104)
Protheseon	Morphological	parallaga	Des (C3v), Man (xxvii.)
Prothesis	Discoursal—Parts of Oration	propositio	Rob (45v), Stu (3.1.454)
Protimesis	Pragmatical—Idea		Dem (§52), Her (1.11.287), Kec (1483), Stu (2.15.355), Wil (153)
Protozeugma	Grammatical	prozeugma	But (130), Man (xxx.), Smi (180), Soa (320)
Protrope	Discoursal—Genres	adhortatio	Pea ([1593] 77), Rob (43r), Ruf (§35)
Proverbium	Logical—Evidence	paroemia	Era (DC 645), Gil (152–3), Kec (1479), Man (lxx.), Mel (E. 41v), Pea ([1593] 29), She ([1550] 93), Sus (14), Wal (70), Wil (151)
Provocatio	Pragmatical—People	proklesis	Pea ([1593] 83)
Proyporgasia	Pragmatical—People	praemunitio	Rob (43v), Ruf (§32)
Prozeugma	Grammatical		Era (DC 345), Mos (a.v.v), Pea ([1577] K.ii.v; [1593] 51), Put (176), She ([1555] C.i.r), Sus (26)
Psychrotes	Discoursal—Styles		Dem (§114), Her (2.5.341)
Pulchritudo	Discoursal—Styles	epimeleia	[Sca (4.1.446)], Tra (568)
Purgatio	Discoursal—Genres	dicaeologia	Cic (De Or 3.205), Sca (3.94.363)
Puritas	Discoursal—Styles	katharotes	[Sca (4.13.466)], Tra (500)
Pynthanomai	Pragmatical—People	interrogatio	Stu (1.25.81), Sus (58)
Pysma	Pragmatical—People		Ale (25), Aqu (§12), Blo (28), Hos (33), Mel (I. 22r), Pea ([1577] L.iiii.r; [1593] 106), Rob (43r), Sus (58)

Figure Name	*Discourse Level*	*Head Word*	*Sources*
Quaesitum	Pragmatical—People	pysma	Aqu (§12)
Querela	Discoursal—Genres	mempsis	Mel (E. 42v), Vel (167r)
Querimonia	Discoursal—Genres	querela	Pea ([1593] 65)
Questio	Discoursal—Genres	querela	Cic (Or 39.135)
Ratiocinatio	Pragmatical—People		Ad H (4.16.23), Era (E. 3.136.629), She ([1550] 52), Sus (76), Tra (529), Wil (231–2)
Ratiocinatio	Logical—Argument Forms	syllogismus	Era (DC 499), Qui (9.3.98), Smi (258), Stu (1.34.147)
Rationabilitas	Discoursal—Genres	dicaeologia	Sca (3.67.337)
Reciprocatio	Lexical	antanaclasis	Smi (107)
Recordatio	Pragmatical—Idea	anamnesis	Pea ([1593] 76)
Rectitudo	Syntactical	orthotes	Stu (2.11.333), Tra (503)
Redditio	Syntactical	epanalepsis	Aqu (§33)
Redditio	Logical—Idea	antapodosis	Qui (8.3.79), Tra (560), Vos (251)
Reditus ad propositum	Discoursal—Parts of Oration		Cic (De Or 3.203), Stu (1.32.141), Vos (258)
Reditus ad rem	Discoursal—Parts of Oration	antanaclasis	Cic (De Or 3.203), Wil (207)
Reduplicatio	Syntactical	anadiplosis	Aqu (§32), Gil (160), Mos (a.vi.r), Sca (4.1.457), She ([1550] 48), Smi (92), Tra (529), Sus (50)
Refractio	Lexical	anaclasis	She ([1550] 60; [1555] D.vi.r)
Refutatio	Discoursal—Parts of Oration	antirrhesis	Kec (1475)
Regressio	Syntactical	anadiplosis	Ruf (*Lex.* §7)
Regressio	Syntactical	epanodos	Man (xcvii.)
Regressio	Pragmatical—Idea	epanodos	Gil (167), Kec (1507), Mel (I. 24r), Qui (9.3.35), Ruf (*Lex.* §21), Smi (103), Sus (82), Tal (64), Wil (228)
Reiteratio	Syntactical	epanalepsis	Sus (49)

Figure Name	*Discourse Level*	*Head Word*	*Sources*
Rejectio	Pragmatical—People	apodioxis	But (138), Kec (1489), Mel (E. 52v; I. 25v), Ruf (§12), Sca (3.68.338), She ([1555] E.v.v), Smi (229), Vel (194r), Vos (271), Wil (211–2)
Relatio	Syntactical	anaphora	Aqu (§34), Cic (De Or 3.207), Kec (1505), Man (xxxviii.), Mos (a.vi.r), Sca (4.30.500), Smi (96), Sus (49)
Reminiscentia	Pragmatical—Idea	anamnesis	Sca (3.91.362)
Remotio	Pragmatical—Idea		Kec (1483, 1550), Stu (1.40.221; 2.21.392), Vos (244)
Remotio	Discoursal—Genres	anairesis	Stu (2.15.353)
Renovatio	Pragmatical—Idea	epanalepsis	Stu (2.18.371)
Renovatio verbi	Syntactical	epanalepsis	Kec (1506)
Repetitio	Lexical	conduplicatio	Aqu (§31)
Repetitio	Lexical	palilogia	Lam (2.106), Mel (E. 43r; I. 20r), Sca (3.41.313)
Repetitio	Syntactical	anaphora	Ad H (4.13.19), Era (E. 3.100.912), Gil (159), Man (xxxviii.), Mel (E. 43r; I. 19v), Rob (22r), Sca (4.1.457), She ([1550] 47; [1555] D.iiii.r), Soa (308), Stu (2.22.392), Sus (48), Tal (57), Tra (569), Vel (45r), Wil (225)
Repetitio	Syntactical	epanalepsis	Ruf (*Lex.* §5)
Repetitio	Pragmatical—Idea		Lam (2.106), Sca (3.41.313), Wil (207)
Replicatio	Syntactical	epanalepsis	Des (C4v), Sus (49)
Repraesentatio	Pragmatical—Idea	hypotyposis	Smi (112)
Reprehensio	Pragmatical—People	aphorismus	Cic (De Or 3.207), Qui (9.2.18), Ruf (§14), Sus (75)
Reprobatio	Pragmatical—People	apodioxis	Ruf (§12)
Responsio	Pragmatical—People		Qui (9.2.12), Soa (338), Vel (194r)
Restrictio	Pragmatical—Idea		Era (DC 533), Pea ([1577] R.ii.r; [1593] 131)

Figure Name	*Discourse Level*	*Head Word*	*Sources*
Resumptio	Syntactical	epanalepsis	Kec (1507), Ruf (*Lex.* §5), Sca (4.29.498), Smi (101), Stu (3.7.564), Sus (30), Tra (527)
Reticentia	Pragmatical—People	aposiopesis	Aqu (§5), Cic (De Or 3.205), Des (C2r), Era (E. 3.110.146), Fra (F6v), Gil (156), Kec (1490), Man (xii.), Mel (E. 44r; I. 21v), Qui (9.2.54), Rob (44v), Sca (3.77.344), Soa (345), Smi (148), Stu (2.19.374), Sus (25), Tal (50), Vel (45v)
Retributio	Pragmatical—Idea	antenagoge	Sca (3.51.324)
Reversio	Syntactical	anadiplosis	Tra (571)
Reversio	Syntactical	anastrophe	Gil (164), She ([1550] 31), Sus (31)
Revocatio	Pragmatical—People		But (113), Fen (173), Fra (E5r), Kec (1489), Stu (3.7.564), Tal (50), Vos (263)
Revocatio verbi	Syntactical	epanalepsis	Cic (De Or 3.206)
Rime	Phonetic		Fen (171), Fra (B8v)
Rogatio	Pragmatical—People	interrogatio	Cic (De Or 3.203), Qui (4.1.33)
Rythmon	rhythmical		Kec (1518), Stu (3.5.525), Tra (550)
Salutatio	Discoursal—Genres		Tal (24)
Sapheneia	Discoursal—Styles		Dem (§197), Her (1.2.226), Stu (3.6.545)
Sarcasmus	Semantical		Cic (Or 40.137), Day (80), Des (C6v), Dio (h.i.v), Don (3.6), Era (DC 653), Far (22), Gil (153), Kec (1472), Man (lxxi.), Mel (E. 41r; I. 18r), Mos (b.vi.r), Pea ([1577] D.iii.v; [1593] 37), Put (200), Qui (8.6.57), Rob (42v), Ruf (§7), Sca (3.86.356), Sha (172–5), She ([1550] 46; [1555] D.ii.r), Smi (79), Sus (15), Vos (227)
Sardismus	Vice	soraismus	Qui (8.3.59)

Figure Name	*Discourse Level*	*Head Word*	*Sources*
Satisfacere	Pragmatical—People	medela	[Qui (9.2.104)]
Scala	Syntactical	climax	Kec (1487), Sca (4.31.502)
Scematismus	Pragmatical—People		Dem (§287), Her (*Inv.* 4.11.200), Pea ([1593] 196), Qui (9.2.65–6), Rob (46v), Ruf (*Dian.* §1), Wil (168)
Schesis	Discoursal—Parts of Oration	adnarratio	Ruf (*Dian.* §5)
Schesis Onomaton	Lexical		Des (C4v), Dio (g.iii.v), Don (3.5), Gil (157), Man (xl.), Mos (a.vi.r), Pea ([1577] G.iiii.v), Rob (31r), Sus (38)
Schetliasmos	Discoursal—Genres		Her (2.7.352), Stu (1.23.66)
Scomma	Discoursal—Genres	charientismos	Dem (§128), Ruf (§3), Sus (15)
Sectio	Grammatical	tmesis	Sus (33)
Securitas	Logical—Evidence	asphalia	Pea ([1593] 68)
Semeiologia	Discoursal—Genres		Vel (173r)
Semeosis	Discoursal—Genres	semeiologia	Stu (3.32.786)
Semnotes	Discoursal—Styles		Her (1.6.242), Stu (3.8.567)
Sententia	Logical—Evidence		Ad H (4.17.24), Blo (34), Cic (Or 23.79), Day (99), Era (DC 627), Far (22), Hos (38), Kec (1475), Lam (2.115), Mel (E. 53v), Pea ([1593] 189), Put (243), [Qui (8.5.1)], Sca (3.84.353), She ([1550] 92; [1555] G.vi.v), Smi (244), Stu (3.12.611), Sus (94), Vos (247), Wal (82), Wil (149)
Separatio	Lexical	diacope	Ruf (*Lex.* §11)
Sermocinatio	Pragmatical—People		Ad H (4.43.55; 4.52.65), Day (97), Era (DC 649), Kec (1493), Pea ([1577] O.iii.v; [1593] 137), Qui (9.2.32), Rob (50r), Sca (3.35.309), Sha (170), She ([1555] F.vi.v), Smi (254), Soa (342), Stu (1.39.208), Sus (93), Tra (580), Vos (265), Wil (209)

Figure Name	*Discourse Level*	*Head Word*	*Sources*
Sermocinatio	Discoursal—Genres	prosopopoeia	Mel (E. 53v)
Sibi ipsi responsio	Pragmatical—People	hypophora	Cic (De Or 3.207), Stu (2.27.434)
Significatio	Pragmatical—Idea	emphasis	Ad H (4.53.67), Cic (De Or 3.202), Era (E. 3.148.859), Rob (50r), Soa (347), Sus (44)
Simile	Logical—Idea	similitudo	Blo (4), Era (DC 337), Kec (1464), Qui (5.11.27), Sca (3.84.353), Soa (295), Vos (295)
Similiter Cadens	Phonetic	homoeoptoton	Ad H (4.20.28), Blo (33), Cic (De Or 3.206), Day (86), Era (E. 3.134.589), Hos (37), Mel (E. 43v; I. 20v), Pea ([1593] 53), She ([1555] E.i.v), Smi (213), Soa (324), Stu (2.23.412), Sus (54), Tal (81), Tra (587), Vel (45v), Vos (241)
Similiter Desinens	Phonetic	homoioteleuton	Ad H (4.20.28), But (107), Cic (De Or 3.206), Era (E. 3.134.589), Mel (E. 43v; I. 21r), Pea ([1593] 54), She ([1555] E.i.v), Smi (214), Soa (326), Stu (2.23.412), Sus (55), Tra (587), Vel (45v), Vos (241)
Similitudo	Logical—Idea		Ad H (4.45.59), Blo (12), But (22), Cic (De Or 3.205), Era (DC 480–1), Hos (9; 18), Lam (2.111), Mel (E. 41v), Pea ([1577] U.i.r; [1593] 158), [Qui (8.3.72)], Rob (30r), Sca (3.84.354), She ([1550] 74; [1555] G.v.r), Smi (211), Stu (1.41.231), Sus (99), Tal (16), Wal (61), Wil (213)
Simulatio	Semantical	ironia	Aqu (§7), But (18), Qui (6.3.85; 9.2.26), Sca (3.85.356), Smi (45), Sus (14), Tal (8), Vel (194v), Wil (182)
Sinathrismus	Syntactical	congeries	Day (92), Put (243)
Sinathrismus	Pragmatical—Idea	frequentatio[1]	Put (243), She ([1550] 50)
Skhoinotene	Syntactical	macrocolon	Her (*Inv.* 4.4.184), Stu (3.1.446)

Figure Name	*Discourse Level*	*Head Word*	*Sources*
Skleros	Lexical	trachea	Stu (3.24.732)
Skotison	Vice	enigma	Qui (8.2.18), Vos (208), Wil (194)
Solecismus	Vice		Ad H (4.12.17), Des (C1v), Dio (g.v.r), Don (3.2), Era (DC 305), Man (iii.), Mos (b.ii.v), Put (258), Qui (1.5.34), Sca (3.31.306), She ([1550] 36; [1555] A.v.r)
Solutum	Syntactical	asyndeton	Aqu (§41)
Soraismus	Vice		Mos (b.i.v), Pea ([1577] G.iiii.r), Put (259), She ([1550] 35; [1555] B.ii.v), Vel (11v)
Sphodrotes	Discoursal—Styles		Her (1.8.260), Stu (3.8.570)
Spiritus	Syntactical	periodus/ pneuma	Kec (1532), Stu (3.2.472), Vos (283)
Splendor	Discoursal—Styles	lamprotes	Era (E. 3.98.905), [Sca (4.1.444)], Tra (531)
Spumosus	Discoursal—Styles	psychrotes	Stu (3.26.749)
Suavitas	Discoursal—Styles	glykytes	[Sca (4.11.465)], Stu (3.21.699)
Suavitas	Virtue	euphonia	Kec (1511)
Subalternatio	Syntactical	hypallage	Gil (164), Man (lxxviii.), Sus (34)
Subcontinuatio	Syntactical	hypostasis	Tra (560)
Subjecta ratio	Logical—Evidence	aetiologia	Cic (De Or 3.207), Stu (2.27.434)
Subjectio	Pragmatical—Idea	prolepsis	Tal (31)
Subjectio	Pragmatical—People		Ad H (4.23.33), Cic (De Or 3.207), Day (87), Era (DC 347), Gil (166), Mel (E. 44r; I. 22r), Rob (44r), She ([1550] 53; [1555] E.ii.v), Soa (338), Sus (58), Vos (244), Wil (208)
Subjectio	Discoursal—Parts of Oration	anthypophora	Blo (46), But (124), Far (24), Fen (175), Fra (H3v), Hos (50), Kec (1485), Tal (31)
Subjunctio	Lexical	epizeuxis	Gil (159), Put (210), Sus (50)

Figure Name	*Discourse Level*	*Head Word*	*Sources*
Sublimitas	Discoursal—Styles	oratio grandis	Era (E. 3.98.905), Mel (I. 13r), Tra (457)
Submutatio	Syntactical	hypallage	Gil (164), Sus (34)
Subsannatio	Discoursal—Genres	mycterismus	Kec (1473), She ([1550] 46), Smi (248), Vos (228)
Substitutio	Pragmatical—Idea	paradiastole	Sca (3.52.329)
Subticentia	Grammatical/ Pragmatical—Idea	defectus	Sca (3.77.344), Vos (230)
Subtilitas	Discoursal—Styles		Cic (Or 21.69), [Qui (12.10.58)], Stu (3.8.569)
Suffiguratio	Virtue	enargeia	Sus (86)
Sufflata	Discoursal—Styles	psychrotes	[Ad H (4.10.15)], Mel (E. 64v), She ([1550] 23; [1555] H.iiii.r)
Suggestio	Pragmatical—People	subjectio	Qui (9.2.15; 9.3.98)
Superfluitas	Vice	pleonasmus	Vel (9v)
Superjectio	Semantical	hyperbole	Qui (8.6.67), Sus (17), Vos (226)
Superlatio	Semantical	hyperbole	Ad H (4.33.44), Cic (Or 40.139), Era (DC 344), Pea ([1593] 31), Qui (12.10.62), Sca (3.74.342), Smi (54), Soa (301), Stu (2.8.322), Sus (17), Tra (467)
Suppressio	Grammatical	eclipsis	Sca (3.77.344)
Suspensio	Pragmatical—Idea	sustentatio	Kec (1496), Lam (2.113), Sca (3.77.344), Tal (53)
Sustentatio	Pragmatical—Idea		But (122), Gil (170), Kec (1496), Qui (9.2.23), Rob (44r), Ruf (§34), Soa (348), Tal (53)
Sygchrisis	Logical—Idea	antithesis	Ruf (§37)
Syllepsis	Grammatical		Day (82), Des (C4r), Dio (g.iii.v), Don (3.5), Era (DC 324), Far (27), Gil (156), Hoo (266), Kec (1501), Lil (G.ii.r), Man (xxxii.; ciii.)Mel (I. 19v), Mos (a.viii.r), Pea ([1577] F.i.r), Put (176), Qui (9.3.8), Rob (25r), Ruf (*Lex.* §2), Sca (3.77.345), She ([1550] 30), Smi (181), Sus (27), Vos (223)

Figure Name	*Discourse Level*	*Head Word*	*Sources*
Syllogismus	Logical—Argument Forms		Era (DC 593), Lam (2.134), Mos (b.vii.v), Pea ([1577] P.iii.v; [1593] 179), [Qui (8.4.15; 9.2.103)], Rob (45r), Sca (3.71.339), She ([1550] 76; [1555] G.i.r), Smi (258), Stu (1.34.147; 3.31.781), Vel (144v), Wal (80), Wil (205)
Symbole	Semantical		Dem (§243), Sca (3.50.322), Sha (150–2), Vos (253)
Symperasma	Logical—Forms	conclusio	Vos (244)
Symphoresis	Syntactical	congeries	Pea ([1593] 132)
Symplerosis	Discoursal—Parts of Oration	transitio	Her (1.4.237), Stu (3.7.559)
Symploce	Syntactical		Ale (30), Aqu (§36), Blo (8), But (107), Cic (De Or 3.206), Day (85), Far (23), Fen (172), Fra (D2v), Gil (161), Her (*Inv.* 4.3.177), Hos (13), Lam (3.159), Pea ([1577] J.i.v; [1593] 43), Put (209), Qui (9.3.31), Rob (24r), She ([1550] 47), Smi (100), Soa (309), Sus (51), Tal (63), Vos (235), Wal (45), Wil (226)
Symploke	Syntactical	dirimens copulatio	Her (1.10.277), Stu (2.16.360)
Synaeresis	Phonetic		But (48), Cic (Or 46.155), Des (C3v), Far (26), Gil (179), Hoo (262, 306), Kec (1515), Lil (G.vi.v), Man (xxiii.), Pea ([1577] E.iii.r), Qui (1.5.17), She ([1555] B.iii.v), Smi (177), Sus (22)
Synaloepha	Phonetic		But (42), Cic (Or 45.153), Dem (§70), Des (C3v), Don (3.4), Far (26), Gil (179), Hoo (305), Kec (1512), Lil (G.vi.r), Man (xxii.), Mel (T. Ciiii.v), Mos (a.iiii.v), Pea ([1577] E.iii.r), Put (174), Qui (9.4.36), Rob (29r), She ([1550] 28), Smi (176), Sus (22), Wal (125)

Figure Name	*Discourse Level*	*Head Word*	*Sources*
Synathroismos	Syntactical	congeries	Ale (17), Era (DC 320), Gil (167), Mel (E. 50r; I. 23v), [Qui (8.4.27)], Rob (24r), Rut (I.2), Sca (3.43.314), She ([1550] 50), Sus (71), Vos (298), Wal (74)
Synathroismos	Pragmatical—Idea	frequentatio	Sus (98)
Synchisis	Vice		Des (C6r), Dio (h.i.r), Don (3.6), Gil (164), Her (1.4.240), Hoo (268), Kec (1538), Man (lxiii.), Mos (b.vii.r), Pea ([1577] G.i.r), Rob (30v), Stu (2.18.369), Sus (33), Vos (208)
Synchoresis	Pragmatical—People		But (126), Pea ([1577] M.iii.v; [1593] 111), Qui (9.2.21, 25), Sha (183), Sus (66)
Synchoresis	Pragmatical—People	concessio	Her (2.1.313), Smi (203), Stu (1.20.56)
Syncope	Morphological		But (45), Des (C3r), Dio (g.v.r), Don (3.4), Era (DC 329), Far (26), Gil (179), Hoo (262), Kec (1515), Lil (G.i.v), Man (xix.), Mel (E. 42v), Mos (a.iiii.r), Pea ([1577] E.ii.v), Put (173), Qui (9.3.22), Rob (28v), She ([1550] 27; [1555] B.iii.v), Smi (171), Sus (20), Wil (202)
Syncrisis	Syntactical		Ale (37), Blo (15–16), Hos (21), Kec (1483), Pea ([1593] 162), Sca (3.50.321), Smi (207)
Syncrisis	Logical—Idea	comparatio	Her (1.11.282), Kec (1489), Sca (3.50.322), Smi (207), Stu (1.42.255)
Syndrome	Pragmatical—People	consensio	Her (2.1.313)
Synecdoche	Grammatical		Des (C7r), Far (27), Hoo (266), Lil (G.iiii.r), Mel (I. 19v), Mos (a.viii.r), Smi (44)
Synecdoche	Grammatical	eclipsis	Qui (9.3.58), Rob (24v), Soa (317)

Figure Name	*Discourse Level*	*Head Word*	*Sources*
Synecdoche	Semantical		Blo (5), But (27), Day (78), Des (C5v), Dio (g.vi.v), Don (3.6), Era (DC 341), Far (21), Fen (170), Fra (B5r–7v), Gil (151), Hos (11), Kec (1461), Lam (2.73), Man (lv.), Mel (E. 35v; I. 15v), Mos (b.v.r), Pea ([1577] C.iii.r; [1593] 17), Put (196, 205), Qui (8.6.19), Rob (31v), Sca (3.31.305), Sha (120–1), She ([1550] 42; [1555] C.viii.r), Smi (32), Soa (282), Stu (2.6.309), Sus (7), Tal (19), Vos (218), Wal (34), Wil (199)
Synecphonesis	Phonetic	Systole	Smi (177)
Synezeugmenon	Grammatical	hypozeugma	Rob (24v)
Syngnome	Discoursal—Genres	ignocentia	Pea ([1593] 98), Rob (45v)
Synoeciosis	Logical—Idea	oxymoron	Blo (31), Hos (36)
Synoeciosis	Logical—Idea		Day (95), Far (23), Mel (E. 52v), Pea ([1593] 170), Put (216), Sha (183), Smi (120), Sus (82), Wal (64)
Synoikeiosis	Logical—Idea	synoeciosis	Mel (I. 24r), [Qui (9.3.64)], Rob (20r), Rut (II.9), Sca (3.47.317), Soa (321)
Synonymia	Lexical		Ale (30), Aqu (§38), Blo (19), But (135), Day (91), Era (DC 307), Far (25), Gil (157), Hos (24), Kec (1548), Lam (2.108), Mel (E. 48v; I. 23v), Pea ([1577] P.iiii.r; [1593] 149), Put (223), Qui (9.3.45), Rob (24v), Sca (4.32.502), She ([1550] 49), Smi (159), Soa (315), Sus (69), Vos (232), Wal (34)
Synthesis	Grammatical		Des (C7r), Far (28), Gil (158), Hoo (266), Kec (1503), Lil (G.iii.v), Man (xci.), Mel (I. 19v), Pea ([1577] H.iii.v), Rob (28v), Sca (4.40.511), Smi (197), Vel (49v)

Figure Name	*Discourse Level*	*Head Word*	*Sources*
Synthesis	Virtue		Mos (b.iii.v), Put (168), She ([1550] 38), Stu (3.4.507)
Syntomia	Virtue		Dem (§103), Her (*Meth.* §33), Mos (b.iii.r), Put (168), Vel (169r)
Syrmos	Syntactical	hirmos	Gil (163)
Systole	Phonetic		But (52), Des (C3v), Don (3.4), Far (26), Gil (179), Hoo (306), Man (xxi.), Mel (T. c.iiii.v), Mos (a.iiii.r), Pea ([1577] E.ii.v), Put (174), Qui (1.5.18), Rob (29r), She ([1550] 27; [1555] B.iii.v), Smi (176), Sus (21)
Systrophe	Syntactical		Her (1.11.294), Pea ([1593] 153), Stu (2.16.361; 3.16.662)
Syzygia	Syntactical	isocolon	Her (1.11.291), Stu (3.17.677)
Tapeinosis	Semantical	meiosis	Mel (E. 48v; I. 23r), Stu (2.27.435), Vos (259)
Tapeinosis	Pragmatical—Idea	diminutio	But (4), Mel (E. 48v; I. 23r), Stu (2.27.435)
Tapinosis	Semantical		Sha (183), Sus (35)
Tapinosis	Vice		Des (C2v), Dio (g.iv.v), Don (3.3), Era (DC 309), Gil (151), Man (xiiii.), Mos (b.i.v), Pea ([1577] G.ii.r; [1593] 168), Put (266), Qui (8.3.48), [Rob (29v)], She ([1550] 34; [1555] B.ii.r), Smi (57)
Tasis	Phonetic	diastole	Gil (179)
Tasis	Virtue		Her (*Inv.* 4.5.191), Mos (b.iii.r), Put (168), She ([1550] 37), Vos (284)
Tautologia	Pragmatical—Idea		Aqu (§39), Rob (24v), Sca (4.32.503)
Tautologia	Vice		Ad H (4.12.18), But (136), Des (C2r), Dio (g.iv.v), Don (3.3), Era (DC 302), Fen (178), Man (x.), Mos (a.viii.v), Pea ([1577] F.iii.r; [1593] 193), Put (261), Qui (8.3.50), [Rob (29v)], She ([1550] 33; [1555] B.i.r), Stu (2.18.369), Wil (194)

Figure Name	*Discourse Level*	*Head Word*	*Sources*
Tautoteta	Lexical	traductio	Her (*Meth.*§4), Mel (E. 43r), Sca (4.29.498), Stu (3.34.799)
Taxis	Syntactical		Pea ([1577] K.iii.v; [1593] 60), Rob (20r), Rut (II.20)
Taxis	Pragmatical—Idea	ordo	Dem (§139)
Tenue	Discoursal—Styles	subtilitas	Cic (Or 5.20), She ([1550] 21; [1555] H.i.v)
Tenuitas	Discoursal—Styles	apheleia	[Sca (4.21.484)], Tra (580)
Tetracolon	Syntactical		Ale (28), Her (*Inv.* 4.3.179), Kec (1529), Stu (3.1.442), Vel (47r), Vos (281)
Thaumasmus	Discoursal—Genres	admiratio	Her (2.7.355), Pea ([1593] 72), Rob (48v), Stu (3.31.779)
Thesis	Discoursal—Genres	affirmatio	Her (1.11.293), Stu (1.40.226; 3.16.660)
Thesis	Logical— Argument Forms		Blo (35), Cic (Or 36.125), Era (DC 59), Her (1.6.245), Hos (40), Kec (1552), Mel (E. 46r), Smi (263), Vel (146r), Wal (81)
Threnos	Discoursal—Genres		But (114), Day (89), Fen (173), Fra (F1v), Mel (E. 44r), Pea ([1593] 66), Smi (142), Tal (51)
Tmesis	Grammatical		But (52), Day (83), Des (C6r), Dio (h.i.r), Don (3.6), Far (28), Gil (180), Hoo (264), Kec (1537), Man (lxi.), Mos (b.vi.v), Pea ([1577] F.iiii.v), Rob (28v), Sca (4.40.511), Sha (180–1), She ([1550] 31; [1555] C.iii.r), Smi (194), Stu (3.1.451), Sus (33)
Tò xeron	Discoursal—Styles	exilitas	Dem (§236)
Tome	Grammatical	tmesis	Stu (3.1.451)
Topographia	Discoursal—Genres		Des (C7r), Era (DC 587), Far (23), Gil (158), Man (lxxxiii.), Mel (E. 54r), Mos (b.vii.v), Pea ([1577] P.i.r; [1593] 141), Put (246), Qui (9.2.44), Rob (44r), She ([1555] F.vii.r), Sus (88)

Figure Name	*Discourse Level*	*Head Word*	*Sources*
Topothesia	Discoursal—Genres		Era (DC 587), Far (23), Gil (158), Man (lxxxiii.), Mos (b.vii.v), Pea ([1577] P.i.v; [1593] 141), She ([1550] 69; [1555] F.vii.r), Sus (88)
Tpophasis	Logical—Argument Forms	expeditio	She ([1550] 54)
Trachea	Lexical		Dem (§49), Her (2.7.359), Stu (3.24.732)
Trachytes	Discoursal—Styles		Her (1.7.255), Stu (3.8.569)
Tractatio	Pragmatical—Idea	ergasia	Kec (1475), Stu (3.34.799)
Tractatio	Pragmatical—Idea	hypotyposis	Sca (3.33.307)
Traductio	Lexical		Ad H (4.14.20), Mel (E. 43r; I. 20v), Pea ([1577] J.iii.v; [1593] 49), She ([1550] 48), Soa (312), Tra (572), Vel (45r), Wil (229)
Traductio	Lexical	ploce, diaphora	Ad H (4.14.21), Era (E. 3.132.554), Qui (9.3.71), Soa (313)
Traductio	Lexical	polyptoton	Blo (11), Day (86), Gil (163), Hos (17), Put (213), She ([1555] D.vi.v), Stu (2.23.412), Sus (52)
Trajectio	Morphological	metathesis	Hoo (265)
Trajectio	Syntactical	hyperbaton	Tra (573)
Trajectio in alium	Pragmatical—Idea	metastasis	Cic (De Or 3.204)
Transformatio	Morphological	metaplasmus	Hoo (265), Sus (19)
Transgressio	Syntactical	hyperbaton	Ad H (4.32.44), Cic (De Or 3.207), Gil (164), Qui (9.3.91), Sha (157), She ([1550] 30), Smi (199), Sus (31), Tra (573), Vel (46r)
Transitio	Discoursal—Parts of Oration	metabasis	Ad H (4.26.35), But (137), Cic (De Or 3.203), Day (96), Era (DC 410), Kec (1489), Mel (E. 54v; I. 25r), Qui (9.3.98), Sca (3.76.343), She ([1550] 59; [1555] G.iiii.r), Smi (237), Stu (3.7.559), Sus (83), Vos (271), Wal (89)
Transjectio	Syntactical	hyperbaton	Ad H (4.32.44), Stu (2.17.365)

Figure Name	*Discourse Level*	*Head Word*	*Sources*
Translatio	Semantical	metaphora	Ad H (4.34.45), Blo (1), But (22), Cic (De Or 3.157), Cic (Or 23.80), Era (DC 333), Gil (151), Hos (8), Mel (E. 50v; I. 15v), Qui (8.6.4), Sca (3.50.321), She ([1550] 40), Smi (9), Soa (276), Stu (2.2.275), Sus (6), Tra (462), Vos (211)
Translatio	Pragmatical—Idea	metastasis	Mel (E. 50v), Sca (3.65.336), Vel (194r)
Transmotio	Pragmatical—Idea	metastasis	Aqu (§16), Sca (3.65.336)
Transmutatio	Pragmatical—Idea	metastasis	Sca (3.65.336)
Transnominatio	Semantical	metonymia	But (4), Day (78), Gil (151), Mel (I. 15v), Pea ([1593] 19), Smi (12), Sus (7), Vos (213)
Transpositio	Morphological	metathesis	Far (26), Lil (G.v.r), She ([1550] 28), Smi (176)
Transpositio	Syntactical	anakampsis	Kec (1536), Wal (41)
Transumptio	Semantical	metalepsis	Day (79), Des (C5v), Era (DC 339), Mel (I. 16r), Mos (b.iiii.v), Pea ([1593] 23), Qui (8.6.37), She ([1550] 41), Smi (51), Soa (293), Stu (2.6.314), Sus (10), Vos (221), Wil (200)
Trepidatio	Discoursal—Styles	dissolutum	[Sca (4.24.489)]
Tricolon	Syntactical		Ale (28), Dem (§17), Her (*Inv.* 4.3.179), Kec (1528), Qui (9.3.77), Soa (328), Stu (3.1.442), Vel (47r), Vos (281)
Tropus	Virtue	energeia	Mos (b.iii.v), Put (168)
Tumiditas	Vice	bomphiologia	Vel (10v)
Urbanitas	Pragmatical—People	asteismus	Mos (b.vi.r), Pea ([1593] 33), She ([1550] 46), Smi (77), Sus (15)
Vehementia	Discoursal—Styles	akme	[Sca (4.18.483)], Tra (552)
Vehementia	Discoursal—Styles	sphodrotes	Era (E. 3.98.905), Stu (3.8.570)
Velocitas	Discoursal—Styles	gorgotes	[Sca (4.1.447)], Stu (3.6.543), Tra (576)

Figure Name	*Discourse Level*	*Head Word*	*Sources*
Venustas	Discoursal—Styles	epimeleia	Era (E. 3.154.24), Stu (3.6.543), Tra (496)
Veritas	Discoursal—Styles	aletheia	Stu (3.6.543), Tra (594)
Versibus uti	Logical—Evidence	paraplokas toiematon	[Qui (9.2.104)], Rob (45r)
Vexatio	Pragmatical—People	convinciari	Sca (3.87.358)
Votum	Discoursal—Genres	euche	Kec (1499), Mel (E. 54v), Pea ([1593] 67), Sca (3.83.349), Sha (184), She ([1550] 51), Vos (270)
Zeugma	Grammatical		Ale (35), Blo (34), But (130), Day (82), Des (C4r), Dio (g.iii.r), Don (3.5), Era (DC 345), Far (26), Gil (156), Hoo (266), Hos (39), Kec (1501), Lil (G.iii.r), Man (xxx.), Mel (I. 19v), Mos (a.v.v), Pea ([1577] E.iiii.v; [1577] K.ii.v; [1593] 51), Put (175), Rob (30r), Ruf (*Lex.* §3), Sca (4.38.508), She ([1550] 29); [1555] C.i.r), Smi (179), Sus (26), Wal (36)

Appendix 4

The Figures and the Elements of the Trivium

The trivium includes grammar, logic and rhetoric, which describe three dimensions of one art of discourse. The following chart shows that nearly all the forms commonly taught in each of these three subjects appear also as figures of style. Throughout I do not name all the figures that could correspond to each feature, but only one or several that are representative.

I. Grammar

Inasmuch as schoolboys begin the course of study by learning Latin along with their native tongue, they begin with grammar. After the alphabet and vowels, consonants, syllables and diphthongs, schoolboys learn the parts of speech and their forms, such as the declensions of nouns, adjectives, and pronouns; the moods, tenses, and conjugations of verbs; and the comparisons of nouns, adjectives and adverbs. Then they learn syntax, or the rules governing the declensions and uses of words when parts of speech are combined with one another. Normal features of syntax have correspondent figures.

FEATURES OF SYNTAX	FIGURES
phrase	*comma*
clause	*colon, membrum*
simple sentence	*absolutio, orthotes, periodus*
compound sentence	*dicolon, periodus*
complex sentence	*periodus* and its types, *hypostasis, circumductio*
an appositive	*appositio*
adding modifying phrases or clauses	*epitrechon, epembole, episynapsis*
parenthesis	*parenthesis*
adding adjectives	*epitheton*

Syntax also includes acceptable grammatical anomalies and some options for syntactical variation. These last two categories are actually presented as figures in most grammar textbooks.

ANOMALIES	FIGURES
antiptosis	*antiptosis*
enallage	*enallage*
evocatio	*evocatio*
ellipsis	*ellipsis*

ANOMALIES	FIGURES
synecdoche	*synecdoche*
tmesis	*tmesis*
hyperbaton	*hyperbaton*
synthesis	*synthesis*
syllepsis	*syllepsis*
prolepsis	*prolepsis*

OPTIONS	FIGURES
anakampsis	*anakampsis*
hyperbaton	*hyperbaton*
isodynamia	*isodynamia*
permutatio	*permutatio*
plotike	*plotike*
zeugma	*zeugma* and its various types
metaschematismus	*metaschematismus*

Because schoolboys learn language from poetry, it being an excellent model of usage, grammatical instruction includes the principles of prosody. These forms are also sometimes considered figures.

PROSODY	FIGURES
rythmon, numeros	*rythmon, numeros*
caesura	*caesura, anapausis*
the phonetic figures	the phonetic figures
the morphological figures	the morphological figures

Finally, the pupils learn the virtues and vices of grammar. These also appear frequently as figures.

VIRTUES AND VICES	
Correctness	*katharotes, puritas*
hellenismus, for Greek	
latinitas, for Latin	*latinitas*
compositio	*synthesis*
Incorrectness	
obscuritas	*acyrologia, eclipsis, tautologia,* etc.
inordinatae	*cacemphaton, cacosyntheton,* etc.
barbarae	
barbarismus	*barbarismus*
	metaplasmus
	lambdacismus, etc.
solecismus	*solecismus*

II. Dialectic

Renaissance humanists collapse Aristotle's logic and dialectic into one art of reasoning they call dialectic, which they divide into two departments: *inventio* and *dispositio* (or "judgement" or "framing").

INVENTION

Invention teaches the student to find predicates or propositions for the subject of debate by visiting the "store house of places wherein arguments rest" (Wilson, *Rule of Reason* J.iiii.v). The list of these topics or "places" has become standard, deriving from Cicero's list in his *Topica*, so that whether traditional or Ramistic, Renaissance logic textbooks predictably itemize the following as the dialectical places. Since the Ramists discard rhetorical invention, they add description and its various subtypes as places in logic.

These topics have direct corollaries among the tropes and figures.

TOPIC	TROPE	FIGURE OF THOUGHT
definition		*definitio*
description	epithet, *antonomasia*	*descriptio*
chronographia, etc.	*meiosis, hyperbole*	*chronographia, pragmatographia, topographia, prosopographia, characterismus*, etc.
whole/part	*synecdoche*	*divisio, distributio, partitio*
		thesis/ hypothesis
notation/ conjugates		*etymologia, polyptoton*
genus/ species	*synecdoche*	*divisio, distributio, partitio,*
		thesis/ hypothesis
similarity	*metaphora*	*similitudo*
examples		*exemplum*
analogy		*analogia, antapodosis*
fiction		*fabula, ficcion, mythos*
simile		*icon, imago, simile*
difference		*dissimilitudo*
comparison	*metaphora*	*comparatio*
adjuncts:		
property	*metonymia*	*attributio*
antecedents/consequents	*metonymia*	*peristasis*
cause/ effect	*metonymia*	*dianoia, ekparasynaptikon, consecutio, aetiologia*
contraries/ contradictions	*ironia*	*enantiosis, synoeciosis, antithesis*
testimony		*kriseis*
divine		*oraculum*
human		*chreia, paroemia, kollesis*

DISPOSITION

The second part of dialectic, *dispositio*, teaches the proper arrangement of propositions into sound arguments. Herein the student learns to recognize the types of propositions, argument forms, and fallacies. Once again, there is agreement as to the standard forms, and all but one of these types reappear as figures.

KINDS OF PROPOSITION	FIGURES
premise	*propositio*
conclusion	*consequentia*
the disjunctive	*disjunctio*

The Dialectical "Places"

Cicero	*Wilson*	*Lever*	*Macllmaine*	*Fraunce*	*Fenner*	*Blundeville*
definition	definition/subject	substance division	definition description distribution	definition description distribution	definition description distribution	definition description division
whole/parts	whole/parts	whole/parts	whole/parts	whole/parts	whole/parts	whole/parts
notation/conjugates	notation/conjugates	offspring	notation/ etimologie	notation/ conjugates		notation/conjugates/ cases
genus/species	genus/species	general/special	genus/species	general/special	genus/species	genus/species principal or not
similarity examples fiction	similitudes simile, analogy, metaphor	similitude	similitudes quality	like/unlike quality fiction	like/unlike quality simile	like/unlike
difference	differences	differing terms	differences	differences	differences	difference
comparison quantity quality	comparisons quantity	aslike quantity	comparisons quantity	comparisons quantity	comparisons quantity	comparisons quantity example

Cicero	*Wilson*	*Lever*	*MacIlmaine*	*Fraunce*	*Fenner*	*Blundeville*
adjuncts	adjuncts	withcommers	adjuncts	adjuncts	adjuncts	adjuncts
		preparation				
	manner of doing	doing				actions
	suffering	suffering				
	property					
	quality	quality				use/abuse
	quantity	quantity				property
antecedents/	things chancing	forecommers/				circumstances
consequences		aftercommers				
	place	place	place	place	place	place
	time	time	time	time	time	time
	things annexed	things annexed	things annexed	things annexed	things annexed	common accidents
causes	causes	cause	causes	causes	causes	causes
	efficient	efficient	efficient	efficient	efficient	efficient
	material	material	material	material	material	material
	formal	formal	formal	formal	formal	formal
	final	final	final	final	final	final
effects	effects	effect	effects	effects	effects	effects
	effecta					
	destinata					

The Dialectical “Places” (*continued*)

Cicero	*Wilson*	*Lever*	*MacIlmaine*	*Fraunce*	*Fenner*	*Blundeville*
contraries	discordants	gainsets	oppositions	opposites	oppositions	oppositions
	contraries	contraries	contraries	contraries	contraries	contraries
	relatives	relatives	relatives	relatives	relatives	relatives
	privatives	privatives	privatives	privatives	privatives	privatives
contradictions	contradictories	contradictories	contradictories	contradictories	contradictories	contradictories
		order				
		likelier/				
		unlikelier				
		proportion				proportion
						persons
						figurative speech
						apposition
testimony	testimony	witnesses	testimony	testimony	testimony	testimony
	divine	divine/infernal	divine	divine	divine	divine
	human	human	human	human	human	human
						written
						spoken
						custom

KINDS OF PROPOSITION	FIGURES
the categorical	
affirmation	*affirmatio*
negation	*remotio*
universal	*thesis*
particular	*hypothesis*
the hypothetical	*hypothesis*

ARGUMENT FORMS	
syllogism	*syllogismus, conclusio*
demonstrative (certain)	*apodeixis*
dialectical (probable)	*epicheireme*
enthymeme	*enthymema, aetiologia, contrarium*
sorites (a chain of abridged syllogisms)	*gradatio*
induction	*epagoge* or *inductio*
example	*exemplum*
comparison, analogy	*comparatio, imago, similitudo, analogia*
dilemma	*dilemma*
enumeratio	*expeditio, prosapodosis, dialysis*
antistrephon (opponent's arguments can also be used against him; the contradictory interpretation of evidence)	*inversio*
anticategoria or *biaion* (making the accuser the defendant)	*inversio, antenklematiko*

FALLACIES	
fallacy in general	*paralogismus*
amphibologia	*amphibologia*
secundum quid	*hyperbole*
tautologia	*tautologia*
bomphiologia	*bomphiologia*
heterogenium (arguing beside the point)	

III. Rhetoric

Rhetoric consists of five departments: invention, arrangement, style, delivery and memory.

INVENTION OR *INVENTIO*

Rhetorical invention includes two sets of *topoi* or "places": the logical and the rhetorical. Even though the Ramists split logic and rhetoric, they still insist that the the dialectical topics are primary in the invention of any argument and that invention does not differ whether one is composing an argument for specialists or one for the populace in either non-fiction or fiction. The great disservice of the Ramists arises from their reduction of invention to merely the places and forms of logic, slighting the rhetorical places which are standard in the fuller Ciceronian rhetorics.

These rhetorical *topoi* are always treated within a discussion of the three primary oratorical genres: the epideictic or demonstrative (praise and blame), the deliberative (exhortation or dehortation), and the judicial (accusation or defense). The following chart lists these topics and shows the correlative figures. Even the genres themselves appear as figures.

RHETORICAL TOPICS BY GENRE	FIGURES
Demonstrative	
Encomium	*Encomion*
Vituperation	*Onedismus*/ *Objurgatio*
1. Places of person	
Qualities of the mind, the body, and fortune from before, during, and after a person's life.	*Characterismus* *Prosopographia*, *Ethopoeia*
2. Places of deeds	*Pragmatographia*
Qualities of honorability, difficulty, expediency, usefulness, necessity, possibility, and the seven circumstances.	*Peristasis*
3. Places of ideas and things	*Descriptio*, *Chronographia*,
Qualities of honorability, profitability, difficulty, usefulness, necessity, possibility, and the seven circumstances.	*Topothesia*, *Effiguratio*, etc. *Peristasis*, *Diatyposis* (commend rules and precepts)
Deliberative	
Entreat, exhort	*Adhortatio*, *Admonitio*
Dehort, Dissuade	*Dehortatio*
1. Places of exhortation/ dehortation	
Praise or criticism	*Commendatio*/ *Epitimesis*
Expectations (motives) of men	*Dianoia*
Greatness/ smallness of reward	*Ominatio*, *Antisagoge*
Hope of victory	
Hope of renown	
Fear of shame, etc.	*Cataplexis*
Examples, precedents	*Exemplum*, Fable, *Parabole*
2. Places of moving pity	*Commiseratio*
Set before the eyes the lamentable wrongs	*Hypotyposis*
Put the audience in the place of the wronged	*Similitude*
3. Places of comforting	*Paramythia*
Slight reason to be sad	
Share fellowship of sorrow	
4. Places of moving laughter	*Ad Hilaritatem Impulsio*
5. Places of argument	*Argumentatio*
Qualities of honorability, profitability, difficulty, usefulness, necessity, possibility, the seven circumstances, and precedent.	*Pragmatographia*, *Ethopoeia* *Peristasis* *Exemplum*, *Kriseis*
Judicial	
Accusation	*Accusatio*
Heap all faults together	*Congeries*, *Epitimesis*
Extenuate any virtues	*Diminutio*

RHETORICAL TOPICS BY GENRE	FIGURES
Defense	*Proecthesis*, *Apologia*, *Dicaeologia*
Heap all virtues together	*Congeries*, *Commendatio*
Extenuate any faults	*Paradiastole*, *Antenagoge*, *Diminutio*, *Dicaeologia*
The four *stases* (issues of controversy). The issue is also called the *status*, *constitutio*, *kephalaion*, *quaestio*, or *hypothesis*.	*Hypothesis*
1. Conjectural (whether the person committed the act)	
Inartificial proofs	*Pisteis*
Artificial proofs	
Will to do evil (intention)	
Motives: impulse or premeditation	*Dianoia*
Quality of man	*Characterismus*
Power to do evil (possibility)	
Circumstances	*Peristasis*
Quality of man	*Characterismus*
Witnesses	*Auctoritas*
Confession	*Confessio*
2. Definitional (what kind of an act it is)	*Definitio*
Contrary laws or *antinomia*	*Comparatio*, *Antithesis*
Superior/ inferior	
General/ special	
God's law/ man's law	
New/ old	
Intention of the lawmaker	*Dianoia*, *Exegesis*
Ambiguous laws	*Epicrisis*
Analogy or parallel cases	*Analogia*, *Inductio*
Meaning of a word	*Definitio*, *Etymologia*
Counter-definition (*anthorismos*)	
3. Qualitative/ juridicial or *dikaiologikon* (whether the act is justified)	
State absolute (question of right/ wrong)	
Counterplea (*antilepsis*)	
Comparison of law with justice	*Comparatio*
Comparison of act and reward or punishmentwith law and justice	*Comparatio*
Grounds of the "right":	
Nature	*Dignitates*
Law, whether God's or man's	*Dignitates*, *Oraculum*
Custom	*Bebaiosis*
Equity	*Bebaiosis*
Previous judgments	*Kriseis*
Agreement	*Paroemia*, *Sententia*
State assumptive (byways used to purchase favor)	

RHETORICAL TOPICS BY GENRE	FIGURES
Concessio	*Confessio*
Purgatio (deed acknowledged, but intent denied)	*Purgatio*
Deprecatio (deed and intent acknowledged, and forgiveness requested)	*Deprecatio*
Appealing to judge's clemency	*Comprobatio*
Remotio criminis (shifting responsibility)	*Trajectio in alium,*
Blaming one who commanded us	*Metastasis, Metalepsis*
Blaming evil company	
Blaming the law or circumstances	
Blaming the victim	*Antenklematiko*
Relatio criminis or *translatio criminis* or *antithesis* (counter-position; deed was lawful because done in self-defense)	*Necessitas*
Comparatio or *antistasis* (counter-statement; (deed was done to make possible a greater good)	*Necessitas*
4. Translative (*translatio/ metastasis/ exceptio*)	*Metastasis, Metalepsis*
Arguing for a change in court procedure, as in who ought to bring the action against whom, in what manner, before what court, under what law, or at what time.	

Rhetorical invention also includes the point being decided upon, the *krinomenon* or *judicatio*. *Judicatio* is a figure, broader than the precise point being decided upon, but inclusive of such a point. *Firmamentum* or *synechon* is the proof of the *krinomenon* and the strongest argument of the defense. *Firmamentum* has been called a figure. The case or *apodiektikon* (also a figure) is either simple or complex. If complex, it deals with several questions or a comparison. These two complex kinds of cases have correlative figures: *deuterologicon* and *comparatio*. We must also determine whether the case turns on general reasoning or written documents. The devices we use in general reasoning (*syllogicon, inductio, enthymema,* etc.) and in interpretation of written documents (*exegesis*) are figures.

ARRANGEMENT OR DISPOSITIO

Rhetorical arrangement has two parts: the first, explanation of how the various parts of an oration function, and the second, advice regarding how to arrange the order of the parts and the strategies within each part. Even though arrangement is differentiated from invention by name, these instructions, especially those relating to the first division, regularly come in discussions of invention. The oration's parts sometimes appear on figure lists (probably due to Erasmus's *De copia*) and the strategies associated with each part do too. Because they collapse rhetorical arrangement into dialectical arrangement, the Ramists slight instruction in these strategies, mentioning only a few.

PARTS OF THE ORATION	FIGURES
Exordium (to make the audience receptive, well-disposed, and attentive, we use the topics of good-will)	*Exordium*
Prooimion, the direct approach (when the audience holds us in favor)	
1. Topics from our own person	
Refer to our service record without arrogance	*Hyposchesin*, *Fiducia*
Weaken the effect of the charges	*Diminutio*, *Euphemismus*, *Paradiastole*, *Antenagoge*, etc.
Dilate on our misfortunes or difficulties	*Commiseratio*
Use prayers, entreaties	*Deesis*, *Deprecatio*
2. Topics from the person of the opponent	
Bring adversary into contempt	*Accusatio*, *Insultatio*, *Objurgatio*
Depreciate opponent's case with snide allusions	*Diasyrmus*, *Chleuasmos*
3. Topics from the person of the auditors	
Praise their virtuous acts, judgments, reputations	*Comprobatio*
Conciliate the audience	*Conciliatio*
4. Topics from the case itself	
Praise our own cause	*Encomion*
Promise to speak of weighty, wholesome matter	*Promissio*
Ephodos or *insinuatio*, the indirect approach	*Insinuatio*
1. Topics when the case is believed scandalous	
Substitute for the offensive person one who is favored	*Metastasis*
Agree with the hostile audience on some point	*Concessio*, *Consensio*
Refer to a similar case that is held in approval	*Analogia*
Approach defense little by little	*Circumlocutio*
Conceal the unpopular point until later in the speech	*Dissimulatio*
2. Topics when the second speaker	
Begin with the strongest point of the adversary's case	*Anasceue*
Express doubt about what to say first	*Dubitatio*
Then speak confidently	*Fiducia*
Use an oath	*Obtestatio*
Use a reproof, if you possess authority	*Objurgatio*
Use an admonition	*Admonitio*
Use an apology	*Deprecatio*

PARTS OF THE ORATION	FIGURES
3. Topics when the hearers are weary	*Excitatio*
Promise to speak briefly or to provide the better argument	*Promissio*
Use a jest or humor	*Ad Hilaritatem Impulsio*
Tell about a terrible wonder	*Admiratio*
Use a fable or narrative	Fable, *Paradiegesis*
Begin with a new topic	*Apostasis*
Use a rapid style	*Celeritas*
Narratio	
1. The statement of facts, or *diegesis*	*Diegesis*
a. *aphegesis*	*Aphegesis*
b. *epidiegesis*	*Epidiegesis*
c. *paradiegesis*	*Paradiegesis*
2. A narrative digression inserted anywhere	*Narratio, diegema*
a. one that colors the case positively or negatively	*Adnarratio*
b. one that is preliminary (*prodiegesis*)	*Prodiegesis*
3. A *fabula* (could not have occurred), *historia* (did occur), or *argumentum* (could have occurred)	*Fabula, historia, mythikon*
Propositio and *Partitio*	
1. Shows in what we agree with the opponent and what is left in dispute	*Propositio*
2. Sets out the matters we intend to discuss briefly in a methodical way	*Partitio*
3. Preliminary confirmation (*procatasceue*)	*Procatasceue*
Confirmatio or *katasceue*[1]	*Argumentatio*
1. Topics suitable for each genre	(see invention above)
2. Degree of certainty	
a. Irrefutable: *Apodeixis, Dilemma, Enumeratio, Conclusio*	*Apodeixis, Dilemma, Expeditio, Conclusio*
b. Probable:	
What usually happens	
Ordinary beliefs of mankind	*Bebaiosis, Paroemia*
Analogies to these ordinary beliefs	*Analogia*
Signs	*Pisteis*
A prior judgment	*Kriseis, Gnome*
An appeal to precedence	*Paradeigma*
An appeal to a parallel example	*Comparatio*
An appeal to experience	*Martyria, Bebaiosis*
3. Manner of reasoning	
a. *Inductio*	*Inductio*
b. *Ratiocinatio* (deduction)	*Syllogismus*
Epicheireme	*Epicheireme*
Enthymeme	*Enthymeme*
Epenthymeme	*Epenthymeme*

PARTS OF THE ORATION	FIGURES
Refutatio or *anasceue*	*Anasceue, Antirrhesis*
1. Anticipating and laying out the objections the opponent brings against us	*Prolepsis, Occupatio, Apantesis*
2. Answering these objections	*Antiprotasis, Anthypophora*
3. Raising objections to the opponent	*Enstasis* or *Antithesis*
4. Conceding when necessary	*Concessio*
5. Providing an argument of disproof	*Elenchus*
a. Rejecting the opponent's assumption	*Remotio*
b. Showing the fallacies, denying the consequent	*Paralogismus*
c. Showing a stronger argument to the contrary	*Antithesis*
d. Show that opponent's evidence works in our behalf	*Inversio*
e. Interpret opponent's evidence differently (*absolutio*)	*Metastasis* (*color*)
f. Making finer distinctions	*Distinctio*
g. Destroying the strongest point of the adversary	*Anasceue*
h. Showing that opponent's premises do not lead to opponent's conclusions (*antiparastasis*)	
Digressio	*Digressio*
And a return to the subject	*Antanaclasis, Reditus ad rem*
Peroratio	*Peroratio, Frequentatio*
1. Repeating the *propositio*	*Reditus ad propositum*
2. *Enumeratio*, *recapitulatio*, or *anacephalaeosis*	*Frequentatio, Anacephalaeosis*
3. *Indignatio* or *cohortatio*	*Indignatio* or *Deinosis*
a. Appeal to divine law and oracles	*Oraculum, Semeiology*
b. Use arguments based on authority	*Kriseis*
c. Show that evil will result	*Ominatio, Cataplexis*
d. Say this act will become a precedent	*Praedictio, Admonitio*
e. Heighten the degree of the crime	*Exaggeratio, Protimesis*
f. Review all the circumstances	*Peristasis*
g. Use reproaches and denunciations	*Objurgatio*
h. Ask audience to consider injuries as their own	*Hypotyposis*
i. Use comparison/ contrast	*Comparatio*
j. Express anger	*Indignatio*
4. *Conquestio*	*Commiseratio*
a. Use commonplaces	*Loci communes*
b. Show the fall from prosperity to misfortune	*Hypotyposis*
c. Show the long-term future troubles	*Ominatio*
d. Deplore the separate misfortunes	*Execratio, Onedismus*
e. Put audience in the place of the distressed	*Hypotyposis*
f. Use apostrophe	*Apostrophe*
g. Use complaints	*Mempsis*

PARTS OF THE ORATION	FIGURES
h. Implore the audience for mercy	*Deprecatio*
i. Show our unselfishness, mercy and patience	*Ethopoeia*
j. Give audience the duty for the help of the distressed	*Admonitio*

The second part of arrangement, also called *ordo* or *oeconomia*, has to do with strategies for ordering ideas and approaches within a speech. Typically, we have two options: either we order according to nature and proceed through the speech via the outline above, or we vary the order as circumstances require and good judgment dictates. The natural order stipulates that we begin with an exordium, put the confirmation first and confutation second, or state the proposition or *protasis* first and the proof second. Natural order also stipulates that we place the weakest arguments in the middle, or at least progress from weaker to stronger, and that we present the adversary's case before refuting it. Discretionary order calls for exceptions to these rules.

The natural sequence does not appear as a figure, but some of the possible variations do. When the refutation comes before the presentation of the adversary's argument, we have *entechna*. When the proof comes first and the *protasis* second, we have *anastrophe ton pistis*. Melanchthon explains that the confutation can sometimes come before the confirmation (*Elem.* 29r, La Fontaine 206), but this reversal is not given a name. *Ordo* names a figure that sets ideas in either a descending or ascending order within a sentence or passage, but does not carry into its figurative connotation the more general rhetorical notion of arrangement. Instead, the virtue *synthesis* does. Explicitly asking the audience's permission for one's use of discretion in arrangement is a figure—*nomimon zetema*. Also, other figures such as *protimesis*, *climax*, *decrementum*, *incrementum*, *hysteron proteron*, *anastrophe*, *progressio*, and *sustentatio* are types of order.

The Ramists, in their logic texts, also acknowledge these two options for ordering a text. Natural order to them, however, results from recognizing the proper logical division of ideas and placing the arguments from most general to most specific, the method of the syllogism. The second or "the concealed or hidden method" has broad application. Fraunce explains that "the method of wit and discretion, for that it is rather seen in the provident conceit of him that writeth or speaketh, than perceived by any general rule of art" belongs to

> Historiographers, Poets, Orators, and such other speakers or writers, [who] are not bound so strictly to observe the perfection of the first method: but may, according to their matter, meaning, purpose, time, place, persons, wisely observe the best for the intent, altering, hiding, adding, detracting, when and how they list. (*The Lawiers Logike* 114)

Treating the subject more than any other Ramist, Fraunce lists the following strategies in this discussion (114). Only one lacks a corresponding figure.

STRATEGIES	FIGURES
beginning a narrative *in medias res*	*Peribeblemonon*
omitting orderly distributions	*Synchisis*
purposely obscuring things	*Skotison*
amplifying	*Amplificatio*
digressing	*Digressio*
flattering	*Adulatio*
insinuating	*Emphasis*
placing the best arguments first and last	
using plain exordiums when the cause is good	*Exordium*
using *insinuatio* when the audience suspects the cause is bad	*Insinuatio*

Progymnasmata

The *progymnasmata* are the preliminary exercises that prepare students for the more advanced declamations or *gymnasmata*. Each of these preliminary exercises are both a whole composition and a discourse-chunk that can function as a piece of a longer text. Consequently, these exercises become features of invention and arrangement. All but two of them appear on figure lists. The two that do not appear, the commonplace and the legislation, however, are genres that combine several others and so are obviously made up of figures nevertheless. Their appearance on figure lists is probably due to the influence of Erasmus's *De copia*.

mythos (fable)	Fable, *Mythos*
diegema (narrative)	*Diegema*, *Narratio*
chreia (anecdote)	*Chreia*
gnome (maxim, proverb)	*Gnome*, Proverb
katasceue (confirmation)	*Argumentatio*
anasceue or *antirrhesis* (refutation)	*Anasceue*, *Antirrhesis*
koinos topos (commonplace)	
encomion (praise)	*Encomion*
psogos (invective)	*Objurgatio*
synchrisis (comparison)	*Syncrisis*, *Comparatio*
prosopopoeia or *ethopoeia* (speech-in-character)	*Prosopopoeia* or *Ethopoeia*
ecphrasis (description)	*Ecphrasis*, *Descriptio*
thesis (defense of a general question)	*Thesis*
nomos or legislation (defense or criticism of a law)	

Gymnasmata

These advanced exercises produce full-length declamations and include the *suasoria*, an advisory speech given by a particular person to a particular audience on a particular occasion, and the *controversia,* a judicial speech determining the guilt or innocence (or quality) of a person, law, idea, or thing. This judgment includes sometimes a pronouncement of a consequence. These speeches correspond to the genres of deliberative and judicial oratory, which, as we have seen, are also figures.

STYLE OR *ELOCUTIO*

Style is the third department of rhetoric. The common topics covered in style include the precepts, virtues, and vices applying to words considered singly, words in combination, and the various characters or levels of style. Frequently, style is divided into three parts, following the *Ad Herennium*: *elegantia* (purity and perspicuity), *compositio* (euphony and synthesis), and *dignitates* (ornament). While traditional textbooks retain these categories and often fill them all with figures, in handlists of figures, these categories disappear and are often all covered through figures. Note the overlaps among these various parts of style.

WORD CHOICE OR *ELEGANTIA*	FIGURE
proper	
coined or new	*Onomatopoeia*
old	*Archaismus*
tropes	Tropes (semantic figures)
virtues	
purity	*Ciriologia*, *Latinitas*, *Proprietas*, *Analogia*
clarity	*Perspicuitas*
vices	*Acyron*, *Barbaralexis*, *Cacosyntheton*, *Cacozelia*, *Catachresis*

WORDS IN COMBINATION OR *COMPOSITIO*

phrases and clauses	*Comma, Colon, Periodus*
rhythm	*Rythmon*, meter, feet, orthographical figures
cadences	*Clausula*
sound	*Euphonia, Cacophonia, Hiatus, Homoeoptoton, Homoeoteleuton*
word order	*Ordo, Synthesis, Hyperbaton, Chiasmus, Epembole, Isocolon*, etc.
periodic or loose styles[2]	*Polysyndeton, Asyndeton, Periodus, Hypostasis, Epiploke*, etc.
virtues	
artistic composition,	*Synthesis*
symmetry	*Concinnitas*
pleasant sounding	*Euphonia*
vices	*Arithmon, Cacemphaton, Hypallage, Hyperbaton, Hyrmos, Hysteron proteron, Synchisis*

EMBELLISHMENT OR *DIGNITATES*

figures of speech	These vary from list to list
of prosody	
of grammar	
of syntax	
figures of thought	
of words	
of sentences	
of oration	
virtues	
appropriateness	*Analogia, Proprietas*
ornateness	*Eschematismon*
variety	*Poikilia*
"life"	*Energeia*
copiousness	*Copia*
conciseness	*Syntomia*
vividness	*Enargia*
persuasiveness	*Pithanotetos*
vices	*Aschematiston, Brachylogia, Eclipsis, Homoiologia, Hyperbole, Macrologia, Meiosis, Paradiastole, Parelcon, Periergia, Perissologia, Pleonasmus, Poicilogia, Skotison, Soraismus, Tapinosis, Tautologia*, etc.

CHARACTERS OF STYLE

good styles	
clarity	*Sapheneia*
purity	*Katharotes, puritas*
distinctness	*Eukrinea, claritas*
grandeur	*Megethos, magnitudo, sublimitas*
solemnity	*Semnotes, dignitas*
asperity	*Trachytes, asperitas*
vehemence	*Sphodrotes, vehementia*

CHARACTERS OF STYLE

brilliance	*Lamprotes*
florescence	*Akme, energeia*
abundance	*Copia, peribole*
beauty	*Epimeleia, kallos*
elegance	*Glaphyria*
rapidity	*Gorgotes, celeritas*
character	*Ethos, affectio*
simplicity	*Apheleia, tenuitas*
sweetness	*Glykytes, suavitas, jucunditas*
subtlety	*Drimytes, acuitas*
modesty	*Epieikeia, modestia*
sincerity	*Aletheia, veritas*
indignation	*Barytes, objurgatio*
forcefulness	*Deinotes, gravitas*
bad styles	
meagerness, dryness	*Exilitas*
repulsiveness	*Acharis*
carelessness	*Ameles*
abruptness	*Apocope*
obscurity	*Asapheia, obscuritas*
affectation	*Cacozelias*
slackness	*Dissolutum, hyptiotes*
bombast	*Psychrotes, sufflata, asiatismus*

LEVELS OF STYLE:	GOOD	BAD
the high	*Grandis, gravis, megaloprepis*	*Frigidum, sufflata*
the middle	*Mediocris, floridus, temperatus*	*Dissolutum, trepidatio*
the low	*Subtilitas, ischnos, tenuitas*	*Exilitas*

DELIVERY OR *PRONUNTIATIO*

Because rhetoric was first devised to teach oral public speech, instruction in delivery was necessary. Delivery remains a part of the curriculum even after the educational objective is no longer merely public speech because the oral performance is the mark of the art's mastery and text of any kind is still viewed ultimately as oral performance. Delivery includes instruction in voice and gesture.

ASPECTS OF VOICE	VICES DUE TO IMPROPER DELIVERY	VIRTUES DUE TO PROPER DELIVERY
strength	*atonia*	*energeia*
pitch and register	*cacemphaton*	*deinotes*
resonance		*euphonia*
breath-control		*synthesis*
volume	*bomphiologia*	
speed		*cataphora* or *tasis*
pacing	*homoiologia*	*poikilia*
rhythm	*arithmon*	*rythmon*
enunciation	*barbarismus*	*puritas*
intonation	*cacozelia*	*perspicuitas*

Aspects of gesture—facial expressions, movements of the hands and body, gaits, stances, and dress—all manifest figures and contribute to the making of figures.

MEMORY OR *MEMORIA*

Memorization depends upon the use of tropes and schemes, whether concepts are turned into images or positioned within an overriding logical pattern. Figures, such as *symbole*, *allegoria*, *icon*, *narratio*, and logical *topoi* all apply here.

Notes

Introduction

1. Style and substance, "fluff and stuff," are Richard A. Lanham's designations in *Economics of Attention* (157).

2. Sharon Crowley and Debra Hawhee in *Ancient Rhetorics for Contemporary Students* attribute this view to classical rhetoric as a whole: "Ancient rhetoricians devoted an entire canon of their art to the study of unusual uses or arrangements of words. They called this canon 'style' (*lexis,* or 'words,' in Greek; *elocutio,* or 'speaking out,' in Latin). Defined as persuasive or extraordinary uses of language, style can be distinguished from grammar, which is the study of ordinary uses of language" (278).

3. Benedetto Croce and Monroe C. Beardsley are strong proponents of this view. Beardsley, for example, defines style as "the recurrent features of its texture of meaning" (222) or as "detail of meaning or small-scale meaning" (223).

4. Louis T. Milic coined the term *individual* or *psychological monism* in his article "Theories of Style and Their Implications for the Teaching of Composition." This article provides the taxonomy of views scholars of style still use to chart the field. I have elaborated on the three Milic identifies and added a fourth, what I am calling "cultural monism." Heinrich F. Plett offers a different taxonomy in "Concepts of Style: A Classificatory and a Critical Approach," which creates classifications based on the feature of the communication act analysts focus on: (1) style's expressivity of a speaker's personality; (2) style's effects upon an audience; (3) style's relationship to subject matter; (4) style as a set of linguistic choices (269). However Plett admits that all these classifications "lack terminological precision and critical rigour" (270). Other taxonomies are offered in Richard Ohmann's "Generative Grammars and the Concept of Literary Style" and "Speech, Action, and Style."

5. For a translation of this speech, see Lane Cooper, *Theories of Style* 169–79. This view of style became the mantra for nineteenth-century Romanticism. However once the history of style is revised, Buffon's remark will be seen less as an expression of emerging Romanticism and more as a carryover from a common Renaissance belief, as M. H. Abrams has already recognized (229). For a more detailed analysis of the Romantic view toward style, see Abrams and Wolfgang G. Müller's "Style."

6. For examples of reading for the writer's personal idiolect, see Nils Erik Enkvist, "On Defining Style," and Roderick P. Hart and Suzanne Daughton, *Modern Rhetorical Criticism.* Hart, for instance, defines style as "the rhetor's characteristic or distinctive manner of communication (as compared to other rhetors)" (160). For an example of reading for the writer's cognitive orientation, see Ohmann, *Shaw: The Style and the Man.* Ohmann concludes his book with the assertion that Shaw's "quest for likenesses," his embracing of "discontinuities," his "affection for the everlasting 'nay,'" and his "cerebral control" all point to his "confirmed

epistemic stance"—"an affirmation of human mind and order, as against the destructive forces of mechanism and chance" (153; see also xiii).

7. A well-known example of this approach occurs in *Linguistics and Literary History* when Leo Spitzer identifies "the particular Diderotian essence" from Diderot's style and concludes among other things that this author's "self-accentuating rhythm" was "conditioned by a certain nervous temperament" (135). A second example is given by Edmund Wilson in *Axel's Castle:* "The real elements, of course, of any work of fiction, are the elements of the author's personality: his imagination embodies in the images of characters, situations, and scenes the fundamental conflicts of his nature or the cycle of phases through which it habitually passes. His personages are personifications of the author's various impulses and emotions: and the relations between them in his stories are really the relations between these" (176).

8. See Nietzche's "On Truth and Lies in a Nonmoral Sense." Also see Samuel Ijsseling's summary of Nietzche's philosophy in *Rhetoric and Philosophy in Conflict* 103–14.

9. Benjamin Lee Whorf's work in *Language, Thought and Reality* provides the base for this theory. Whorf's focus on the linguistic is evident from comments such as the following: "When we attempt to apply the configurative principle to the understanding of human life, we immediately strike the cultural and the linguistic (part of the cultural), especially the latter, as the great field par excellence of the configurative on the human level" (41); "Meaning will be found to be intimately connected with the linguistic: its principle is symbolism, but language is the great symbolism from which other symbolisms take their cue" (42); "The problem of thought and thinking in the native community is not purely and simply a psychological problem. It is quite largely cultural. It is moreover largely a matter of one especially cohesive aggregate of cultural phenomena that we call a language. It is approachable through linguistics" (65–66); "What has been called 'the deep well of unconscious cerebration' is constituted by linguistic patterning operations, and all entitled to be called thinking" (68).

10. For example, Kathryn Flannery in *The Emperor's New Clothes* asserts, "What counts as style, what counts as valued written form, is part of and derives its meaning from a matrix of elements that comprise a given culture. The material arrangement of words on the page has no essential or intrinsic meaning apart from a given culture, apart from the conventions for reading and writing. Style is thus not a natural exhalation of either the individual or the nation. It is, as Quintilian put it, necessarily schooled. And schools, Henry Giroux reminds us, 'are not merely instructional sites but also sites where the culture of the dominant society is learned and where students experience the difference between those status and class distinctions that exist in the larger society'" (3–4). Her quotation from Giroux is found in *Teachers as Intellecutals: Toward a Critical Pedagogy of Learning* (Granby, Mass.: Bergin and Garvey, 1988, 5–6).

11. Peter Elbow and Ken Macrorie are two recent exponents of this pedagogy, which reflects this advice from Frederic Harrison: "There is nothing more to be said. Be natural, be simple, be yourself: shun artifices, tricks, fashions. Gain the tone of ease, plainness, self-respect. To thine own self be true. Speak out frankly that which you have thought out in your own brain and have felt within your own soul. This, and this alone, creates a perfect style" (154).

12. This view belongs to "current-traditional rhetoric," which stems from the work of later nineteenth-century rhetoricians such as Adams Sherman Hill and held sway throughout much of the twentieth century. William Strunk and E. B. White's *Elements of Style* enshrines this plain style.

13. Lanham's discussion of this preference for the transparent style in *Analyzing Prose* 1–12 is useful. See also Paul Butler, *Out of Style* 53–54 and Kenneth Cmiel 260–61.

14. See Laura R. Micciche 250; Robert J. Connors, " Erasure" 102, and Butler, "Style and the Public Intellectual" 394–99, all in Butler, *Style in Rhetoric and Composition.*

15. I have taken this notion of "at/through" reading from Lanham's *Analyzing Prose* xii–xiii and *Economics of Attention* 143.

16. Today a theoretical inconsistency permits that in expressive genres we assume a genuine image of the author to emerge from his or her works, while in nonfictional persuasion we assume any such image to be a mask. We assume no presence of the author at all in exposition and may or may not believe that literature reveals the author's psyche.

17. Walker Gibson's *Tough, Sweet, and Stuffy,* for example, characterizes the types of personae most common in current persuasive writing. In *Rhetoric of Fiction* and *Company We Keep,* Wayne Booth argues that literature is a rhetorical genre and therefore an "implied author" or persona emerges from the work.

18. See, for example, Milic, "Rhetorical Choice and Stylistic Option."

19. See the collection of essays under "Style and Culture" in Butler's *Style in Rhetoric and Composition* 279–336.

20. Insightful treatments of grammar as part of style can be found in Richard Weaver, Micciche, Virginia Tufte, and Martha Kolln. For including larger discoursal forms in style, see Donald C. Bryant, Wendy Bishop, Winston Weathers, Frank J. D'Angelo, and Hans Ostrom. For including sound see T. R. Johnson.

21. Milic, "Metaphysical Criticism" 164; Connors, *Composition-Rhetoric* 260.

22. Others who comment on this neglect include Edward P. J. Corbett ("Approaches" 95), Neil R. Leroux ("Perceiving Rhetorical Style" 29), Plett ("Concepts" 270), Tom Pace ("What Happened" 1), and Butler (*Out of Style* 13–14).

23. James J. Murphy has observed that this period in rhetoric's history still includes "one thousand neglected authors" ("One Thousand" 20). Since a comprehensive history of Renaissance rhetoric has yet to be written, I am basing my conclusions on the textbooks stipulated in British grammar school and university statutes, on key texts that reflect important achievements in the field, and on English manuals that popularize the arts.

24. Clark, *Rhetoric and Poetry in the Renaissance* 58; Lewis 281; Bolgar, "Humanism" 211; Kristeller, *Renaissance Thought* 251; Baldwin 2:182; and Croll 61, 293–94.

25. John Porter Houston treats rhetoric as style in *The Rhetoric of Poetry in the Renaissance and Seventeenth Century.* John Monfasani claims that northern European rhetoricians tended to reduce rhetoric to style ("Humanism and Rhetoric" 208). Richard Halpern credits the sixteenth-century addiction to style with producing both a textual and a cultural imbalance (20). Neil Rhodes believes that Renaissance rhetoric provided the art to harness the magical power of the word (8).

26. See Murphy, *Rhetoric in the Middle Ages* 88, 359–62; Brian Vickers, *In Defence* 254; Don Paul Abbott 145–46; Thomas O. Sloane, *On the Contrary* 59–62; and Peter Mack, *Elizabethan Rhetoric* 11–47.

27. W. S. Howell, *Logic and Rhetoric* 65; Warren Taylor 30; Russell H. Wagner 1–2; William P. Sanford, *English Theories* 40, 49.

28. While Kennedy makes this remark about classical rhetoric, his description also summarizes the common assessment of Renaissance rhetoric, inasmuch as historians generally see Renaissance views as repetitions of classical ones. Kennedy believes this himself (*Classical Rhetoric* 228, 249), and Murphy shares the same view of classical rhetoric ("Habit" 43), as does D. A. Russell (129–30). The linguists Geoffrey N. Leech and Michael H. Short reflect this opinion when they describe as "one of the earliest and most persistent concepts of style," especially characteristic of the Renaissance, the notion that style is the "adornment" or "dress of thought" (15). A more recent historian of Elizabethan rhetoric, Mack still concurs that Renaissance stylistics involves "clothing the ideas of the speech in the most effective words" (*Elizabethan Rhetoric* 9). This commonplace belief is repeated by John Tinker (87) and by Butler (*Out of Style* 45–46).

29. Connors also believes that all stylistic instruction before the nineteenth century was founded in stylistic dualism (*Composition-Rhetoric* 276). Similarly Vickers calls rhetoric "critical dualism" (*In Defence* 209).

30. Other important literary critics characterize Renaissance figures as mere decorations. Hardin Craig in *The Enchanted Glass* claims, "The elaborate system of technical devices was discussed only with reference to the form and structure of each device, never with reference to its emotional or aesthetic effects" (162–63). In *Endeavors of Art,* Madeleine Doran writes, "Suggestions of a concept of style which recognizes it as organically functional appear occasionally in critical theory, but the decorative function is far more common" (43). M. M. Mahood in *Shakespeare's Wordplay* asserts, "While the books of rhetoric can show us how the average Elizabethan was taught to embellish his Latin and English verses, they tell us nothing of the poetic and dramatic function of these ornaments" (19).

31. Trousdale cites the edition of Puttenham's *Arte of English Poesie* edited by Gladys Doidge Willcock and Alice Walker (Cambridge: Cambridge University Press, 1970), 247.

32. Others who emphasize Renaissance rhetoric as sophistry, a vehicle for manipulation motivated by a desire for power, include O. B. Hardison, Jr. (34), Frank Whigham (1–2), and Wayne A. Rebhorn (*Emperor* 15).

33. See Jones's articles in *The Seventeenth Century: From Bacon to Pope;* Jackson I. Cope and Harold Whitmore Jones's introduction to *Thomas Sprat's History of the Royal Society;* Croll's essays in *Style, Rhetoric, and Rhythm;* George Williamson's *The Senecan Amble;* Robert Adolph's *The Rise of Modern Prose Style;* Wesley Trimpi's *Ben Jonson's Poems;* Perry Miller's *The New England Mind;* W. Fraser Mitchell's *English Pulpit Oratory;* Debora K. Shuger's *Sacred Rhetoric;* and G. L. Hendrickson in "The Origin and Meaning of the Ancient Characters of Style," who expresses the belief that this same distinction is fundamental in classical rhetoric.

34. Considering these precepts only in terms of literature, Abrams does not attempt to reconcile them (229). Müller argues that "the concept of style as an index of the soul," while on the whole rare in this age of imitation, begins in the Renaissance but is "dissociated from rhetorical *elocutio.*" He concludes, "There is thus an opposition in the Renaissance between the traditional elocutionary concept of style as dress of thought (*exornatio*), which is associated with rhetorical decorum, and the modern individualistic concept of style as the incarnation of thought and mind. These two positions may occur side by side in one and the same theoretician and it may be difficult to disentangle them, as is the case in George Puttenham's courtly poetic" ("Style" 750–51).

35. Lorenzo Valla makes a similar comment: "The dialectician uses so to speak a nude syllogism, the orator uses one which is clothed and armed and decorated with gold and purple and precious gems" (*Disputationes dialecticae,* cited by Seigel 162).

36. Hanna H. Gray also notes the humanist emphasis on fusing form and content according to "fitness between them" (513). Thomas M. Greene sees this fusion to be more fundamental, claiming that Roger Ascham, "far from separating words and matter, . . . approached an almost Crocean intuition of their unity" ("Roger Ascham" 615).

37. Ernst Robert Curtius notes that the metaphor "life is a stage" seems to be endemic to societies influenced by classical rhetoric (138–44).

38. Although Agricola distinguishes between "exposition, which merely explains the mind of the speaker without employing anything by means of which belief results in the hearer," and argumentation, "in which one attempts to produce belief in the matter about which he speaks" (1.1; McNally 395), both forms create belief and both result from dialectical invention: the "places" provide "everything which can be said or thought about any subject" (1. *epilogus;* McNally 402). Both J. R. McNally and Mack interpret Agricola's perspective similarly (McNally 393–94; Mack, *Renaissance Argument* 190–92).

39. Marijke Spies calls Scaliger's work "the most elaborate poetical treatise" of the sixteenth century (21).

40. Quintilian reflects an awareness of this textual double frame when he, on the one hand, treats the oration as a drama—"It is at the close of our drama that we must really stir the theatre" (6.1.52)—and, on the other, treats Ovid's *Metamorphoses* as an oration (4.1.77).

41. Quintilian insists that "there is absolutely no difference between writing and speaking well, and that a written speech is merely a record of one that has actually been delivered" (12.10.51).

42. Rosemund Tuve in *Elizabethan and Metaphysical Imagery* sees most tenets of this same philosophy of style in the approach to poetics at the time.

43. This passage is quoted in full by Hoyt H. Hudson in his editorial notes to Hoskins, *Directions for Speech and Style* 55.

44. Cf. Adolph 135.

45. Cf. A. C. Howell 141.

46. Cf. Grassi 35–37.

47. For more discussion of this emphasis on probabilistic reasoning, see Lisa Jardine, "Humanist Logic" 192.

48. This skepticism has been recognized, for instance, by Rita Guerlac, *Juan Luis Vives* 30; Victoria Kahn, *Rhetoric, Prudence* 20; and Sloane, *On the Contrary* 53, although the nature of this skepticism has not always been adequately explained.

49. For the definitions and issues cultural monists identify in the foundationalist/antifoundationalist debate, see Fish, *Doing What Comes Naturally* 316–55, 482.

50. Waswo has noticed the same: "The absorption of logic by rhetoric is the more fundamental acknowledgment that language is the shaping medium of the whole human world" (219). Waswo's insight remains somewhat compromised, though, by his assumption that language is only verbal, linguistic expression (18–20), despite his acknowledgment that language is "a performing art" (14).

51. Sloane does suggest, though, that humanist rhetoric brings contraries into reconciliation (see *Donne, Milton* 65–84 in particular).

52. Johann Sturm, whom Ascham freely acknowledges as his mentor, makes a comment very similar to Ascham's: "Unless the zeal for speaking purely should be revived, in a few years we will sink back into barbarism. Corruption of the doctrine of the Church follows barbarism, corruption in turn of pagan rite. For just as the fear of God has been recovered through the study of literature, so also shall we come to this very barbarism if it is despised and neglected" (*De Imitatione Oratoria Libri Tres* [1574] K1r–v; trans. Vos, "Good Matter" 12).

53. Others who see prudence at the center of rhetoric include Kahn, *Rhetoric, Prudence* 9; Kathy Eden, *Hermeneutics* 26–27; and Edward Armstrong 32. This particular relationship between wisdom and eloquence has not received enough attention.

54. Baldwin 2:677; W. S. Howell, *Logic and Rhetoric* 10, 64; Izora Scott 124; Sister Joan Marie Lechner 236; Grafton and Jardine xiv, 24; Arthur F. Kinney, *Humanist Poetics* 11; Eugene R. Kintgen 31.

55. Scholars who have attempted to correct this misunderstanding of Renaissance imitation include Harold Ogden White, Nancy Struever 145–51; Trousdale, "Recurrence"; John M. Steadman 149–50; Greene, *Light in Troy* 81–103; and G. W. Pigman III.

56. Comments such as these reveal that there were two kinds of Ciceronians at this time: those who were preoccupied narrowly and servilely with Cicero's verbal behaviors and those who more broadly adopted his way of thinking, both his critical judgment and his understanding of the arts. Alvin Vos discusses both in "'Good Matter and Good Utterance': The Character of English Ciceronianism."

57. Halpern, a cultural monist, notes the democratic appearance of this methodology of imitation but believes it functions ultimately as a "monarchical model of political subordination," since he assumes the principles and practices the "subject" internalizes are those of the dominant culture. He says, "This mimetic or imaginary or imitative or 'interpellating' mode of ideological domination is distinctive in that the subject comes to assimilate or internalize a set of practices and thus enacts his subjection 'automatically,' as if he himself had chosen it" (29–30).

He does not believe, as Renaissance humanists do, that the principles of decorum include not only particular but also universal, metadiscursive requisites to which all humans are subject by virtue of sharing the faculties of reason and speech.

58. David M. Knauf begins to unravel the complex relationships between nature and art in Puttenham's theory in "George Puttenham's Theory of Natural and Artificial Discourse."

59. Baldwin 2:617; Kenneth Charlton 239.

60. This tendency to view the classical rhetorical tradition as essentially Aristotelian has been much remarked upon recently for both good and ill. For a positive assessment, see Kennedy, *On Rhetoric* ix; Crowley and Hawhee 12; and James L. Kastely 8. For a negative assessment, see Sloane, *On the Contrary* 36; Jeffrey Walker viii; and Ekaterina V. Haskins, *Logos and Power* 4.

61. I believe that there are four primary rhetorical philosophies in these two periods: sophistic, Platonic, Aristotelian, and Isocratean. While we can find sophists and Platonists in the Renaissance, they are few and do not appear among the schoolroom rhetoricians who openly denounce both.

62. It is Isocrates who is the "father" of the Hellenistic *paideia* (curriculum), not Aristotle nor even his teacher Plato. Isocrates ran a school in Greece in competition with Plato's Academy, where Aristotle was first a student and then a teacher. Subsequently Aristotle set up his own school, also in competition with Isocrates. H. I. Marrou contrasts the competing curricula of Plato and Isocrates in *A History of Education in Antiquity* (61–91) and writes, "This fact must be emphasized from the start. On the level of history Plato had been defeated: posterity had not accepted his educational ideals. The victor, generally speaking, was Isocrates, and Isocrates became the educator first of Greece and then of the whole ancient world" (194). The Hellenistic curriculum was organized officially and instantiated in Greek schools in the generation after Aristotle and Alexander the Great (95). Takis Poulakos and David Depew rightly claim that "of all the ancient Greek writers," Isocrates "is closest to the textualist, aestheticist, and ethical impulses of the humanist tradition" (5).

63. Grube, *Greek and Roman Critics* 144.

64. Shortly after completing *De Oratore,* Cicero declares in a letter to a friend that his new book "disagree[s] entirely with the commonly accepted rules, and embrace[s] all the theories of rhetoric held by the ancients, including those of Aristotle and Isocrates" (*Epistulae Ad Familiares* 1.9.23).

65. Murphy, *Rhetoric in the Middle Ages* 88, 359; Vickers, *In Defence* 254; F. H. Colson lxiv–lxxxix; Sloane, *On the Contrary* 36–37. In contrast Struever argues that it was not so much the discovery of these texts and the broadening of knowledge about antiquity but rather the "fresh reading of them" that mattered (47). Monfasani argues that "the difference between medieval and Renaissance rhetoric had nothing essential to do with the amount of classical rhetoric available. Rather, the difference lay in the view each period took of the use and value of rhetoric" ("Humanism and Rhetoric" 173). The latter two scholars, however, seem to me mistaken.

66. Scholars widely acknowledge rhetoric to be at the center of the humanist program. See Kristeller, *Renaissance Thought* 9–11; Hanna H. Gray; Jerrold E. Seigel vii; William J. Bouwsma, *Culture* 9; Vickers, "On the Practicalities" 133; Monfasani, "Humanism and Rhetoric" 171; Abbott 145–47; Thomas M. Conley, *Rhetoric* 143; and Geoffrey Elton 272.

67. See also Marrou 142–216, 265–91; Clark, *Rhetoric in Greco-Roman Education* 59–66; Stanley F. Bonner, *Education in Ancient Rome* 165–327.

68. Kennedy, *Classical Rhetoric* 232.

69. Whether this Hermogenes is the Hermogenes of Tarsus has recently come into question, but late Greek, Roman, and Renaissance scholars accepted this identification. Besides *On Types of Style,* the four other texts in this corpus attributed to Hermogenes were *On Invention, On Stases, On Method of Forcefulness,* and *Progymnasmata.* Modern scholars, however, believe that

only *On Stases* and *On Types of Style* are truly Hermogenes's work. See Kennedy's introduction to Hermogenes's *Invention and Method* xiii.

70. Monfasani notes that it was not until the second half of the sixteenth century that Longinus was studied and even then received little attention ("Byzantine" 184–85). Still Robertellus, Sturm, Farnaby, Keckermann, Vossius, and Lamy make reference to Longinus, whose influence, Shuger argues, is widely seen in sacred rhetorics (110), so that Longinus is an ancient to be reckoned with. Judging by the number of editions, translations, and commentaries, Monfasani opines that Demetrius, who was a minor authority in Byzantium, became more popular in the Latin West than did Hermogenes ("Humanism and Rhetoric" 183). However, if we judge by the stylistic precepts included within rhetoric manuals, the influence of Hermogenes is more widespread. Shuger notes that Hermogenes, Demetrius, and Longinus are significant influences on the development of the Christian grand style in preaching (110, 157). For the copies of Longinus available before 1600, see Weinberg, "Translations and Commentaries of Longinus."

71. Carl Halm documents that these texts were first printed in 1519 and 1521 (*Rhetores Latini Minores* v–vii). Monfasani summarizes the humanists' recovery efforts of classical culture ("Humanism and Rhetoric" 178–79). Scholars who do not see the liberal arts united in rhetoric prefer to define humanism by its avid classicism. Nicholas Mann, for example, finds this interest in classical antiquity the defining characteristic of humanism: "It involves above all the rediscovery and study of Greek and Roman texts, the restoration and interpretation of them, and the assimilation of the ideas and values they contain" (2).

72. Recently philosophers such as Ijsseling (28–36), classicists such as Walker (38–40), and early modernists such as Sloane (*On the Contrary* 36–37) and Armstrong (32, 94–100) have begun to distinguish differences between Aristotle's and Cicero's rhetorical philosophies, but none sees differences in their beliefs about style. Similarly recent classicists have begun to examine the contrasting philosophies of Isocrates and Aristotle. (See T. Poulakos, Depew, Haskins, *Logos and Power,* and Eugene Garver's "Philosophy, Rhetoric, and Civic Education.") Scholars commonly trace Aristotle's and later Peripatetics's influence on the three later Greeks: Demetrius (Kennedy, *New History* 88; Innes, introduction to Demetrius, *On Style* 315–18; W. Rhys Roberts 57; Walker 56–57), Hermogenes (Cecil W. Wooten, introduction to *On Types of Style* xvii), and Longinus (Kennedy, *New History* 227). Much more needs to be done in tracing the influence of Isocrates and the Hellenistic curriculum on these three later Greeks, as does Dirk M. Schenkeveld for Demetrius in "The Intended Public of Demetrius' *On Style*" and Conley for Longinus and Hermogenes in *Rhetoric* (44–45, 54–59). Russell notes differences between Aristotle and these later Greeks (137–47) and Grube between Aristotle and Demetrius (*Greek and Roman Critics* 111).

73. The few recent scholars, such as Whigham, Cave, Armstrong, and Rebhorn in *Emperor of Men's Minds*, who treat Renaissance rhetoric as sophistic overgeneralize as much as do those who call it Aristotelian. Although Isocrates calls himself a sophist (meaning a philosopher), he also distinguishes his philosophy and curriculum from those of the other sophists (see *Antidosis* and *Against the Sophists*) and so cannot be simply lumped together with them.

74. Murphy, *Rhetoric in the Middle Ages* 90–101, 360. Monfasani explains that in the Middle Ages "Aristotle's *Rhetoric* had almost ceased to function as a textbook in rhetorical education, and his *Poetics* was barely known." The *Rhetoric* was primarily studied in ethics or psychology. Even for the Byzantines, these works were only rhetoric texts of "a minor sort." George of Trebizond's translation of the *Rhetoric* in the mid-1440s was the first Renaissance translation, and Trebizond "treated the work as primarily a text in psychology" and "his own *Rhetoric* owed relatively little to Aristotle's *Rhetoric*" ("Humanism and Rhetoric" 182).

75. Weinberg makes a similar observation about the Cinquecento Italian humanists' tendency to read Aristotle's *Poetics* as if in agreement with Horace's *Ars poetica.* Whereas Aristotle

keeps poetry and rhetoric separate, Horace brings a thoroughly rhetorical view of poetry in harmony with Cicero's and Quintilian's view. Weinberg, however, disapproves and calls this practice "dangerous in the sense that it must inevitably result in hopeless deformation of the texts involved. The mere fact that it should have been practiced so widely is symptomatic of the philosophical naivete of its users" (*History of Literary Criticism* 56).

76. Bakhtin 67.

77. Good descriptions of the curriculum can be found in Baldwin; Sister Miriam Joseph 8–13; Clark, *John Milton;* Abbott; Mack, *Elizabethan Rhetoric* 11–75; and Howard Jones 153–90.

78. Sloane agrees: "Why read or write theory, humanists seemed to ask, when textual analysis of successful rhetorical practice teaches all we need to know about how language works while preserving something of the flavor of circumstance?" (*On the Contrary* 53).

79. Waswo also quotes Steadman and makes the same warning (78). Both also note the Renaissance focus on practice.

80. For a description of Ramus's reforms and influence, see Walter J.Ong, *Ramus* 196–318; Miller 329–30; W. S. Howell, *Logic and Rhetoric* 146–281; Francis A. Yates 231–42; Chaim Perelman and L. Olbrechts-Tyteca 2–3; and Peter Sharratt.

81. Louis B. Wright 67.

82. A full history of stylistic beliefs in the eighteenth and nineteenth centuries has not yet been written. Important work on this subject includes Abrams; P. W. K. Stone; Connors, *Composition-Rhetoric;* Vickers, *In Defence* 196–213; and Bizzell and Herzberg 791–812, 983–98.

Chapter 1: The Comprehensiveness of Figures

1. Crane's study perspicuously notes many of the important overlaps between the dualistic pairs of reason and speech, invention and style, and rhetoric and poetic in Renaissance thought but does not proceed beyond these observations to consider their theoretical importance. In his 1937 collection of Tudor figures (published in 1972), Taylor also notices in passing that "the listings included figures which deal with argument and proof, the arrangement of the elements of sentences, and the development of discourse" (43). He makes this observation even though he believes figures are and were conceived as external ornaments.

2. Previously in "Rhetoric as Character-Fashioning," I wrote mistakenly that no Renaissance rhetorician taught that all language was figured (326).

3. Haskins agrees that in Aristotle "style is conceived as the outer layer of a properly conceptualized techne" (*Logos* 34, 27). Conley remarks that an Aristotelian separates arguments and figures ("Enthymeme" 177). Richard Leo Enos acknowledges that to Aristotle style is a necessary evil (88). Lanham even more explicitly declares that Aristotle is "radically biased against words"; Aristotle's description of style "is not the way things are" and consequently "is riddled with self-contradictions" (*Analyzing Prose* 190). Because Lanham does not see Cicero's differences from Aristotle, he dismisses Cicero too.

4. Aristotle's bias against style is evident in the *Poetics* as well, where he separates again substance, the plot, from style, the external elements, and therefore claims that the power of the tragedy does not depend on the dramatic performance (1450b17) and that infelicity of style does not merit censure (1456b10–12). Haskins again provides an insightful discussion (*Logos* 52–55).

5. Surprisingly Cicero's comprehensive view of style has received little scholarly attention. A. D. Leeman, a classicist, does point out that Cicero, in contrast to the *Ad Herennium,* refuses to detach content and expression, philosophy and rhetoric (122–23), in order to prevent "mere verbalism and complete insincerity" (134), but he also claims that Cicero's ideal "is a no man's land" (123). Butler, the recent compositionist, notices that Cicero sees "a natural connection . . . among style, invention, and arrangement" (*Out of Style* 41). Finally rhetoricians S. Michael Halloran and Merrill D. Whitburn, with more understanding, recognize that Cicero "does not assert a clear and sharp dualism" between content and style (62).

6. See Ong's discussion in *Ramus* 277–79 and Vickers's *In Defence* 284, 314. Because neither sees the expansiveness of style or figures, though, neither sees the full implications of figures being embellishments.

7. Raymond DiLorenzo 255; Grassi 91; Harry Caplan in Cicero, *Ad Herennium* 274, note b.

8. These virtues, which are briefly mentioned in Aristotle, are systematized in Theophrastus (c. 370–c. 285 B.C.), Aristotle's student, and come to be known as one of Theophrastus's contributions to style theory. Despite these four becoming standard, in *De Partitione Oratoria,* Cicero identifies five stylistic virtues or embellishments: lucidity, brevity, acceptability, brilliance, and charm (6.19).

9. Leeman notes that Cicero regards stylistic *ornatus* as "the adequate form of expression of a rich mind, nourished by philosophy" (121, 124). DiLorenzo sees with more completeness that in *De Oratore* "*ornatus* is a concept whose meaning includes much more than the techniques of ornamentation," that Cicero sets out "a comprehensive theory of *ornatus*" (251), which includes "the formal perfection of a speech as a work" (257) and "partakes of the nature of wisdom" (258).

10. In the *Orator* Cicero also indicates that subject matter belongs to style. He remarks that philosophers provide ideas or "the raw material" that imparts a "richness" to style (3.12). Besides ideas, style also includes voice and gesture, for "there can be no eloquence without [proper delivery]," which is "a sort of language of the body" that the speaker will use "according as he wishes to seem himself to be moved and to sway the minds of his audience" (17.55).

11. The Aldine edition, which Monfasani claims to be the best, attributes the stylistic characters to "Isocrates' school" (67v). The Wecheli edition of 1538 says "Socrates' school" (494), which is obviously a misprint since Socrates did not have a school.

12. In his *Latin Grammar* (1559), Ramus mentions *ellipsis* (a defect of any kind [96]), *polysyndeton* (a superfluous conjunction), and *asyndeton* (the removal of a conjunction [107]) under grammatical "anomalies"; under grammatical options he describes but does not name *evocatio* (101), *synthesis* (97), synecdoche (110), *eclipsis* (97, 137, 139), *enallage* (122, 139), *tmesis* (133), and *hysterologia* (136).

13. Hildebrandt in "Amplification in a Rhetoric on Style" rightly points out that in the Renaissance the figure *amplificatio* (to increase or decrease) involves not only issues of intensity and elevation but also length, impressiveness, and development of an idea.

14. Kennedy, *Art of Persuasion* 289.

15. Kennedy, *Art of Persuasion* 277–78 and *New History* 86.

16. Kennedy, *Art of Persuasion* 297–99 and *New History* 91–92; Russell 145–46; Caplan, introduction to Cicero, *Ad Herennium* xiii; Lausberg §501, 600, 858.

17. Spengel, in Alexander of Numenius, *Rhetores Graeci* 3.11.18–3.13.20. We must also note that the concept of *mimesis* or "imitation" here is different from that in Aristotle's *Poetics.* To Aristotle *mimesis* takes place when the poet's tale imitates plots that embody general truths of human experience. Imitation refers here to depiction of the mind. When Alexander uses an example from literature to illustrate a "natural" expression revealing character, he demonstrates the inadequacy of *mimesis* alone as the distinguishing marker of literature.

18. Conley also argues that in Demetrius and Hermogenes we find a focus on the broad view of schema ("Byzantine Teaching" 339 note 12).

19. For other later Greek manuals, see Conley, "Byzantine Teaching."

20. Most of these devices are not named in Aristotle.

21. Quintilian cites Aristotle as one of his sources (2.17.14–15).

22. Conley provides a list of Alexander's figures in "Byzantine Teaching" 368–69. Philip Rollinson and Richard Geckle also provide a list in their summary of "On Figures of Thought and Speech" in *A Guide to Classical Rhetoric* 3-5. The definition of figure and trope comes from Rollinson (3).

23. Such a statement, however, should not have been made in general terms, for the advice is true if similar figures are used closely together but not if a great variety are. Both Aristotle (3.3 1406a3) and Demetrius (§78) give the same advice but apply it to the use of one figure. This sloppiness is an indication of the *Ad Herennium*'s theoretical naïveté.

24. When Renaissance rhetoricians reference Aristotle on style, they do so usually in regard to his discussion of periodicity or metaphor.

25. Unfortunately Vickers assigns this same view indiscriminately to Aristotle, Quintilian, Longinus, Puttenham, and Fraunce (111). He also inconsistently holds to the view that figures remain "deviations" and "abnormalities" (*Classical Rhetoric* 85 and *In Defence* 296).

26. Reviewing its publication history with twenty-four fifteenth-century Italian manuscripts, thirteen editions divided among Italy and France, a reprint in Spain, and appearance on the statutes of Salamanca, Mack concludes, "This pattern suggests a good availability in the first half of the sixteenth century but not a great success" (*History* 45).

27. Hoffmann 186.

28. While Hoffmann notices Erasmus's laxness in making distinctions among these various features of style (172), he does not notice Erasmus's equal laxness toward distinguishing figures from nonfigures (184–85). Hoffmann does insightfully point out that in Erasmus "*ornatus* equips oratory with the means to carry out its proper business and achieve its appropriate goal," that "literary art for art's sake distorts the nature of language by making speech artificial instead of affective," and that "ornamental devices, just as the means of *aptum,* are subservient to both the duties of speaking and the virtues of speech" (185).

29. Mack records that *De copia* "went through 150 editions in the sixteenth century" ("Humanist Rhetoric" 88). Green and Murphy list 93 printings of *De conscribendis epistolis* before 1700 and 10 of *Ecclesiastes* (*Renaissance Rhetoric* 183–88, 190). For texts on school statutes, see Mack, *Elizabethan Rhetoric* 24, 31, 52, 54.

30. Unless otherwise specified, a text's number of printings comes from Green and Murphy's *Renaissance Rhetoric.*

31. "On the Corruption of Rhetoric" in *De disciplinis libri xx* from *Obras Completas,* trans. Lorenzo Riber (Madrid, 1948), 2:453–75, as cited by James Francis Cooney, introduction to *De Ratione Dicendi* 3.

32. He also cites from Aristotle, Quintilian, Seneca, Dionysius of Halicarnassus, Rutilius, Capella, Macrobius, Agricola, and Valla, combining all within the Ciceronian/Hermogenean perspective.

33. Baldwin 1:82, 2:34; Porter 50; Mack, *Elizabethan Rhetoric* 52.

34. Cf. William P. Weaver 379.

35. Mack, *Elizabethan Rhetoric* 46.

36. Green also observes that in the Renaissance the "Hermogenean *ideas* were understood to have a rhetorical impact akin to that of various figures of speech" ("Aristotelian *Lexis*" 154).

37. Mack identifies the classical grammarian Diomedes and the early Renaissance grammarian Despauterius as the sources for this division of vices and their inclusion as figures (*History* 213, 215).

38. Ibid. 214.

39. Baldwin 1:82.

40. Susenbrotus lists as his sources Cicero, the *Ad Herennium,* Quintilian, Rutilius, Celsus, Rufinianus, Trapezuntius, Erasmus, Melanchthon, Mosellanus, and Veltkirchius and the grammarians Donatus, Diomedes, Mancinellus, and Linacre (A.i.v and throughout). He also names Fortunatianus, Sulpitius Victor, and Martianus Capella, but these last have only minor importance for his project. Mack shows Susenbrotus's borrowing of definitions and examples from the *Ad Herennium* and Erasmus's *De copia* and *Ecclesiastes* (*Elizabethan Rhetoric* 86).

41. Baldwin 1:161. Green has argued that there may not have been enough copies of Susenbrotus to be a school textbook as widely used as Baldwin claims and so suggests that grammar school students probably learned figures from standard grammar texts and from supplementation provided by the individual schoolmasters ("*Grammatica movet*" 77–79, 105).

42. Sherry was the schoolmaster of Magdalen College until 1540, when he retired to pursue writing (W. S. Howell, *Logic and Rhetoric* 125).

43. The *Ad Herennium* refers to the three levels of style as *figuras,* not including them among the *exornatione* (4.8.11), and Sherry may simply be retaining the name without conscious intent to equate them with schemes. Nevertheless by calling them figures, he in effect equates them with the other devices he also calls figures.

44. Peacham was ordained at the age of twenty-eight, holding the living of North Mimms in Hertfordshire until 1578, when he became rector at Leverton in Lincolnshire.

45. Crane cites as additional sources "the Latin-English dictionary of Sir Thomas Elyot and Thomas Cooper, Robert Estienne's *Thesaurus linguae latinae,* 1531, and Henri Estienne's *Thesaurus graecae linguae,* 1572–73" (introduction to *Garden of Eloquence* 9) and provides a quite extensive comparison between Peacham and his sources, especially Susenbrotus (11–23).

46. Despite admitting that a few terms he includes are not figures (A8r), he leaves these terms unidentified, and their inclusion works to categorize them among the figures.

47. Receiving his MA from Oxford in 1592, Hoskins taught school in Somerset and then became a lawyer and eventually "Serjeant Hoskins" in 1623. He served as a member of the House of Commons three times and was also a poet (Hudson, introduction to *Directions* ix–xi).

48. Green and Murphy identify five known copies of Hoskins's manuscript (242).

49. For a detailed comparison between Hoskins's work and that of Jonson, Blount, and Smith, see Louise B. Osborn in the "Literary Supplement" of *The Times* (London), May 1, 1930, and Hudson's introduction to *Directions* xxvii–xxxviii.

50. R. C. Alston, introductory note to the 1969 facsimile reprint of Smith's *Mystery.*

51. Hudson, introduction to *Directions* xxxvii.

52. Revised and republished by a colleague, Peter John Perpinian, in 1565, this book was reprinted 134 times in 45 different European cities during the next 173 years, remaining in use among Jesuits until 1836. This text was not adopted by English schools, but three English rhetoric manuals cite Soarez as a source: Thomas Vicar's *Manuductio ad Artem Rhetoricam* (1621), Thomas Farnaby's *Index Rhetoricus* (1646), and John Holmes's *Art of Rhetoric Made Easy; or the Elements of Oratory in Two Books* (1739) (Flynn, introduction to *De Artes Rhetorica* 1, 37, 53).

53. Conley notes that this work was used in "dissenting English schools until the end of the seventeenth century" and that Bacon was familiar with this text (*Rhetoric* 157). The textbook had four printings and then was published an additional time in Keckermann's complete works.

54. Keckermann also acknowledges as his sources Plato, Aristotle, Aphthonius, Agricola, Scribonius, Mancinelli, Philippus, Ligatio, Reisnerus, Talaeus, Treutlerus, Rivius, Junius, Melchioris, Erythraeus, and Horatius.

55. Vossius identifies this genre with *ethikon* (2.15.6).

56. Cf. C. S. M. Rademaker 177–78; Mack, *History* 192–93; and Conley, *Rhetoric* 160.

57. See also *Arguments* 132, 147.

58. Cf. Mack, *History* 144.

59. See examples of these commentaries in Mack, "Ramus Reading."

60. Crane observes that Ramus "insisted in turning over to dialectic nearly all of the figures and devices which most other rhetoricians of the sixteenth century considered under the heading of style" (introduction to Peacham, *Garden of Eloquence* 8). In Ramus's logic, though, these devices lose their identity as figures. (See MacIlmaine, *Logike of the Moste Excellent Philosopher.*) In Fraunce, however, these devices remain figures, even though they appear in his logic manual.

61. Under quantity Scaliger treats of *parison, tmesis,* and *synthesis* (4.39.511). Under quality he includes, for example, *homoeoteleuton, homoioptoton,* and forms of *interrogatio* expressing different emotions (4.42.512).

62. In his introduction to the 1994 reprinting of the *Poetices libri septem,* Luc Deitz shows Scaliger's use of Aquila, Rufinianus, the *Ad Herennium,* Quintilian, and Trapezuntius in book 3 (30–59). Francis Cairns has shown Scaliger's indebtedness to Alexander in book 4 ("*Poetices libri septem*"). See Mack, *History* 223.

63. Baldwin documents all these grammars on English grammar school records (1:108, 124–25, 156, 186, and 191). Mack cites the number of printings of Mancinelli as forty before 1590 and of Despauterius as fourteen before 1620 (*History* 212–13). Green and Murphy, however, document forty-one of Mancinelli by 1547 (287–88) and thirty of Despauterius before 1582 (409–10).

64. John Milton was one of his pupils (Fletcher 114).

65. John Brinsley, a fellow schoolmaster, recommends this book "for strangers, who understand the Latin tongue, at least in some sort, and would learn our tongue themselves, or would teach it unto others" (*Consolation* 77).

66. Common distinctions between nonfigures and figures include the acceptable and unacceptable, typical and atypical, not noticed and noticed, informal and formal, ordinary (referential) and poetic (representational), frequent and infrequent, simple and complex, straightforward and indirect, and real and simulated.

67. Green observes the same ("*Grammatica Movet*" 79–80).

68. Cf. Mack, *Elizabethan Rhetoric* 84–102.

69. Modern scholars have tended to interpret *De copia* one-dimensionally. Mack calls it a book on style (*Renaissance Argument* 311), Baldwin regards the first half to be on style and the second half to be on invention (2:25), and Sloane treats it as a book on invention (*On the Contrary* 64). Vos, however, recognizes that the schemes and tropes appear as heuristic devices ("*De Copia*" 288).

70. Cf. Lechner 126.

71. From a brief look at seventeenth-century stylistic rhetorics, J. Donald Ragsdale noticed the same: "When the figurist rhetorics of the late Renaissance are termed 'stylistic,' one may easily infer that a treatment of invention is missing. From an examination of these stylistic rhetorics, however, one must conclude that there are many figures of speech which very closely correspond to the logical, emotional, and ethical modes of proof in the classical theory of invention" (167). Edward M. Shafter Jr. in his dissertation, "A Study of Rhetorical Invention in Selected English Rhetorics, 1550–1600," also remarks: "The Tudor interpretation of 'figures' is surprisingly complex, flexible, and inclusive. The techniques or processes of rhetorical invention are there, but under the guise of figures of speech. It is the label that is misleading; the substance of sound rhetorical theory is plainly apparent despite the fact that it is presented with stylistic flourish. . . . As a group, the figures of argument are the greatest in number and seemingly the most important as well, since they are strong evidence that reasoned amplification of a theme was a factor of utmost importance in Tudor rhetorical composition" (207–9).

72. Murphy has expressed the need for scholars to explore the question of "the relation between *Topos* (Topic) and *Figura* (Figure)" in the rhetorical traditions extending from ancient Greece through Renaissance Europe in order to address the issues surrounding the relations between thought and speech, invention and style ("*Topos* and *Figura*" 240, 247).

Chapter 2: Discourse, a Web of Schemes

1. In his *Poetics* Aristotle declares that poetry will draw upon rhetoric as characters attempt to persuade each other (1456a35), and he suggests that from tragedy philosophical spectators

derive illumination regarding the causes and effects of human action (Haskins, *Logos* 53–54), but he does not treat poetry itself as a poet's argument. Walker notes these same ambiguities but still argues that Aristotle reconstructs "a philosophically respectable and ethically responsible version of *rhêtorikê*" because he focuses the art on proofs and because his ideal is not the speech of the popular assembly but of the senate (38). Walker also claims that Aristotle adopts the Isocratean position that a genuine art of rhetoric "cannot exist apart from, or must be embedded in, a broadly 'philosophic,' *wisdom-loving* discourse art and education," even though his definition of philosophy differs from Isocrates's (40). But Aristotle's failure to apply the declamation as model for all genres, his preference for philosophy and the contemplative life over rhetoric and the active life, and his focus on rhetoric as technique rather than as wisdom create dualisms not found in Isocrates. The fact that Aristotle's treatment of rhetoric "cannot be detached from a more general art of *logos,*" as Walker argues (40), shows that Aristotle's attempt to distinguish it is unrealistic. Others who also point out Aristotle's dualisms, begrudging attention to rhetoric, his concern with technique, or his self-contradictions include Ijsseling (16); Carol Poster (222); Barbara Warnick (310); Alan G. Gross (35); Depew (159): and Haskins, *Logos* (3–9).

2. Seigel agrees that Antonius expresses Aristotle's views toward rhetoric in book 1 of *De Oratore* (14–15). Others who see Antonius in book 2 of *De Oratore* as a representation of Aristotle's views include Friedrich Solmsen ("Aristotle and Cicero" 397), Kennedy (*New History* 144), and Walker (79–80). These last three, however, do not distinguish Aristotle's and Cicero's views. Walker believes that Antonius in book 1 does not represent Aristotle's view but that of "pragmatic Romans, typically impatient with Greek philosophizing and mainly interested in practical advantage," who were "drawn to the narrower versions of Greek rhetoric" (77).

3. In the *Synagoge Technon,* Aristotle compiles rhetorical works that antedate his own. The "other works" probably include the *Gryllus,* an antirhetorical tract, and the *Rhetoric,* since Cicero was in contact in 46 B.C. with the grammarian Tyrannio, who in 40 B.C. along with Andronicus of Rhodes published for the first time Aristotle's *Rhetoric.* Up until this time, Aristotle's rhetorical teachings are known only in *florilegia* or summaries (Kennedy, *New History* 62–63; Poster 228–29). But whether Cicero became acquainted with Aristotle's teachings directly through the *Rhetoric* or through later renderings we cannot be sure. Antonius does not present Aristotle's precepts as they were discussed in his *Rhetoric,* but there are similarities. For the similarities see Solmsen, "Aristotle and Cicero." For the differences see Kennedy, *New History* 144 and Michael Leff, "Genre and Paradigm." For arguments doubting the likelihood of Cicero's direct acquaintance with Aristotle's *Rhetoric,* see Leeman 114 and William W. Fortenbaugh, "Cicero's Knowledge."

4. Scholars generally recognize Crassus as Cicero's spokesman. Leeman defends this identification (112–13).

5. In *De Inventione* Cicero restricts eloquence to political oratory, makes it a branch of politics, and declares that its function is to persuade an audience (1.5.6–7). He also restricts *theses* to philosophy and *hypotheses* to oratory (1.6.8). In *De Oratore* he has corrected what he calls his youthful mistakes (1.2.5).

6. Hendrickson argues that Aristotle's division of logic into the apodeictic and the dialectical was melded back together by the Stoics, and this melding "became thenceforth the prevailing and universal conception" (263). Quirinus Breen also recognizes that Cicero equates logic and dialectic (102).

7. Kneale and Kneale 178–79.

8. Others who recognize differences between Aristotle's and Cicero's philosophies of rhetoric include Seigel, who points out their disagreement about the fields of knowledge an orator can treat (13–14), and Armstrong, who contrasts Aristotle's divorcing of reason and speech,

narrowing of rhetoric to public persuasion, and focus on technical norms to Cicero's broader conception of the union of reason and speech, rhetoric's concern with both public and private language, and focus on decorum (7–9, 32, 94–96).

9. Independent of the ancient rhetorical tradition, the twentieth-century linguist Mikhail Bakhtin has argued that discourse itself is dialogical (72).

10. What remains a matter of debate are the particular aspects of Aristotle and Isocrates Cicero adopts. R. C. Jebb observes Cicero's imitation of Isocrates's style and personal character (2:32, 68). Harry Mortimor Hubbell emphasizes Cicero's adoption of Isocrates's conception of the ideal orator but believes rhetoric is verbal skill (16–40). Believing Aristotle more advanced than Isocrates, Solmsen argues that Cicero adopts from Aristotle the idea that ethos and pathos are necessary elements for the whole speech rather than merely the exordium and peroration, the division of the art into its offices rather than into the parts of the oration, the focus on the *enthymeme* for rhetoric, the inventing of proofs rather than a retrieving of ready-made arguments, the division into the three genres of political oratory, and the virtues of style ("Aristotelian Tradition" 46–50). S. E. Smethurst says that Cicero adopts Isocrates's concern for general culture and practical, moral judgment in preparing the statesman and Aristotle's concern for dialectic and the three *officia oratoris* (274–80). Grube claims Cicero is "combining the Isocratean ideal of education with the Aristotelian requirements for competence in oratory" ("Educational" 240). Leff argues that Cicero adopts Isocrates's emphasis on rhetoric as a practice unbounded by genre that puts the teaching of judgment foremost and Aristotle's emphasis on rhetoric as technique bounded by genre that puts the teaching of rule foremost, so that Cicero can reunite fixity and flexibility ("Genre and Paradigm"). Walker sees in Cicero the combination of the broad Isocratean *logôn technê* and the Aristotelian "discourse art embodied in the genres of practical civic discourse" (79).

11. Kennedy admits that Isocrates does not refer to his art with the term *rhetorike,* which usually means that form of *logos* found in civic or political discourse, but concludes nevertheless that this more restricted species is really what Isocrates teaches (*New History* 43). Walker more accurately points out that Isocrates is the first to use the term *rhetoreia* (oratory) to refer to the restricted political speech-making of the sophists, whom he condemns, contrasting to this narrow view his own broader focus on discourse (*logos*) in general (32–33). See also Edward Schiappa, who argues against viewing Isocrates as representative of sophistic rhetoric (163–73), and Terry Papillion, who argues that Isocrates's refusal to associate his curriculum with rhetoric reveals his objection to the segregating and reifying program of Plato and Aristotle (153).

12. Isocrates models this breadth as he covers in his writings subjects as diverse as duties of a citizen, values of different forms of government, foreign relations, principles of warfare, municipal problems, the management of private affairs, the virtues an educated man possesses, parent/child relations, literary criticism, current national issues, astronomy, and geometry.

13. Hubbell points out all of these similarities between Isocrates's and Cicero's views, except the broad-ranging focus on discourse in general (16–40). Erika Rummel comments insightfully on Isocrates's equation of rhetorical excellence and moral goodness ("Isocrates' Ideal" 32–35). John Poulakos agrees that to Isocrates the study of rhetoric is the study of moral philosophy (128–31), and Schiappa notes that Isocrates refuses to separate thought from expression, so that learning to speak and think well equals moral training (173). Takis Poulakos rehearses many of the same components of Isocrates's curriculum (93–104).

14. Cf. *De Inventione* 2.3.8 and Papillion's discussion (154–59).

15. Cicero may also be drawing from later sources that have modified Aristotle.

16. Leff correctly argues that Antonius's treatment of the oratorical genres "becomes a vehicle for subverting a generically motivated definition of the scope of the art" and allows Cicero to resolve the tension between a purely technical approach and one focused on imparting the

flexible judgment necessary ("Genre and Paradigm" 312–13, 317). It was Aristotle who divides speeches into the three fixed oratorical genres, not Isocrates, who instead combines the three in order to promote "virtue and justice" (*Antidosis* §67). Papillion argues that scholars who pigeonhole Isocrates into the epideictic tradition have missed both his rejection of "mere showpieces" (as he does in *Helen* §1–13) and his specified purpose to use praise and blame, comparisons, and examples in order to encourage proper behavior and wise policies for the future (157–58). Rummel similarly points out that Isocrates condemns pure *epideixis* in *Panegyricus* ("Isocrates' Ideal" 31). Schiappa too argues that Isocrates does not associate the epideictic with pure aesthetics but with artistry in the service of good counsel on important matters (198–200).

17. Kennedy explains that Carneades "brought a new vigor to the languishing Peripatetic school and a return to some of the serious concerns of Aristotle" (*Art of Persuasion* 322). Conley specifies that Carneades argued both sides of any issue because in the absence of certain knowledge, this method tested the probability of claims and enabled the negotiation of different points of view (*Rhetoric* 37).

18. Scholars generally interpret Cicero's ideal of "general culture" to be a union of philosophy and rhetoric or a harmonious relationship between matter and style. Vos, for example, points out that Cicero "opposes this educational compartmentalism and cultural fragmentation. Neither his mastery of words nor his knowledge of his matter may predominate: Cicero's model orator will integrate the two" ("Good Matter" 5). This association of philosophy with content and rhetoric with expression, however, imposes an oversimplified dualism on Cicero's more complex view. What has received less attention is Cicero's union of mind and speech. While both Ijsseling (35, 40) and Armstrong (9, 32, 94–100) note it, both interpret speech as words instead of behavior, putting "talk" at the center of Cicero's conception of mind instead of "form/argument" and so privileging word over meaning.

19. Grassi points out several recurrent discussions in Quintilian regarding the union of *res* and *verba* (46–52).

20. Hence Kennedy's observation that the *Ad Herennium* "confines oratorical style to three specific kinds" (*Art of Persuasion* 267) is only partially correct.

21. Walker believes that "the predominant version of Greek rhetorical instruction that took hold at Rome during the second and early first centuries B.C. . . . was the kind we see embodied in the *Ad Herennium* and *De Inventione*" (77), one with broad application but without full philosophical self-awareness.

22. Cf. Walker 116–17.

23. Walker agrees that these authors see their works as part of a broad discourse education (56–57, 114–19). Walker, however, retains a distinction between eloquence and conversation.

24. Papillion provides evidence that Isocrates's method of teaching is the same and that his lost textbook contained either whole or large pieces of speeches with analytical commentary (156–58).

25. See also Salvatore I. Camporeale 79–81. The first title of Valla's *Dialectic* was *Repastinatio dialecticae et philosophiae.* Kristeller points out that Valla's work, because of its influence and authority, forms "a bridge, as it were, between Italian and Northern humanism" (*Eight Philosophers* 35).

26. Monfasani argues that Trebizond shifts inconsistently between a cultural and political conception of the art in his writings (*George* 266–68; 294–99). Monfasani sees a political conception in Trebizond's *Oration in Praise of Eloquence,* though, whereas I see a cultural conception.

27. A common belief among scholars has been that rhetoric and poetics are linked through style, that is, figures (see, for example, Bizzell and Herzberg 573). In the classical and Renaissance periods, however, they are linked because poetry is oration. Monfasani misses this link when he remarks that to both Erasmus and Vives "rhetoric was really literary rather than oratorical

training" ("Humanism and Rhetoric" 200). Another common belief has been that literature was viewed in this tradition as epideictic oratory (Vickers, "Rhetoric and Poetics" 744). Instead literature partakes of all three oratorical genres in combination.

28. Several modern scholars, including Vickers (*In Defence* 285), Bouwsma ("Anxiety" 234), Rebhorn (*Emperor* 4–6), and Mack (*Elizabethan Rhetoric* 2–3), have noticed that rhetoric in the Renaissance has become a "universal tool." Those few who notice that it has become the general art for human communication include Ong, *Rhetoric* 53; Abbott 156; Barbara S. Tinsley 26; and Grant M. Boswell 110.

29. For meditation and prayer, see Thomas Wright, *Passions of the Minde in Generall* (1604) and Richard Baxter, *Saint's Everlasting Rest* (1650); for manners Baldesar Castiglione, *Book of the Courtier* (1528) and Stephano Guazzo, *Civile Conversation* (1574); for painting Michael Baxandall, *Giotto and the Orators;* for the visual and musical arts, Kennedy, *Classical Rhetoric* 240 and Vickers, *In Defence* 340–74. Scaliger finds figures, such as synecdoche, in Spanish dances (3.31.305), and Ascham extends the art to archery and any creative act in *Toxophilus* (1545). Gerald P. Mohrmann notes that Guazzo has extended rhetoric "to encompass the entire range of human communication" ("*The Civile Conversation*" 201).

30. Hanna H. Gray has also argued that these humanists viewed the arts as "an interconnected whole" (502) and that the ideal orator would strive for "a harmonious union between wisdom and style" (498) in order to persuade people to right thinking and action (505).

31. Trebizond, however, divides philosophy and rhetoric according to the kinds of questions each considers, relegating speculative theses to philosophy but moral and political theses to the orator (Monfasani, *George* 295).

32. A full history of Renaissance dialectic has not yet been written, but scholars generally note this subordination of logic to rhetoric in humanist texts. See Kristeller, *Eight Philosophers* 34; Ong, *Ramus* 100; Monfasani, "Humanism and Rhetoric" 191; Jardine, "Humanist Logic" 176–77; and Mack, *Renaissance Argument* 14–15. W. S. Howell does not distinguish carefully enough between Scholastic and humanist logic (*Logic and Rhetoric* 32–63).

33. Even though Ramus reserves dialectic as the last of the three language arts to introduce to schoolboys, this dialectic functions to teach critical thinking in textual analysis and argument formation in discourse.

34. Monfasani summarizes Trebizond's *Isagoge dialectica* in *George* 300–317.

35. Mack, *Renaissance Argument* 10–12; Charles G. Nauert, "Humanist Infiltration" 807.

36. Gabriel Nuchelmans 143–44.

37. The three earliest humanist logics, Trebizond's *Isagoge dialectica* (1433), Valla's *Dialecticae disputationes* (1439), and Agricola's *De inventione dialectica* (finished 1479, published 1515), are less complete than those that follow but still indicative of the same content to be found in humanist logics later on. Since Agricola's book treats primarily invention and Trebizond's primarily judgment, Monfasani believes that these two manuals were joined together for logic instruction in the first half of the sixteenth century (*George* 333).

38. These categories include the Predicables, Predicaments, Forepredicaments, and Postpredicaments or Transcendentals. A synthesis of Porphyry's *Isagoge* and Aristotle's *Categories, Prior Analytics, Posterior Analytics, De interpretatione, Topica,* and *De sophisticis elenchis* continued to form the foundation for humanist logic, as it did for medieval, but the humanists generally claim that they teach a purer Aristotelian logic than do the Scholastics and than did Aristotle himself. See particularly Sir Thomas More's "Letter to Martin Dorp" (1515), in Guerlac 167–95; Vives, *Adversus pseudodialecticos* (1519), in Guerlac 47–109; and Guerlac's summary of Vives's *De Aristotelis operibus censura* (1538), in Guerlac 37–42.

39. See the chart "The Dialectical Places" in appendix 4.

40. Ramus writes, "But because of these two species, Aristotle wished to make two Logics, one for science, and the other for opinion; in which (saving the honor of so great a master) he

has very greatly erred. For . . . the art of knowing, that is to say, Dialectic or Logic, is one and the same doctrine in respect to perceiving all things" (3; trans. Zappen 74). Cf. W. S. Howell, *Logic and Rhetoric* 154.

41. Aristotle teaches the syllogism in his *Prior Analytics.*

42. Meerhoff says of Melanchthon, "As early as the 1519 *Rhetoric* he contended that the logical 'deep structure' of a text is reducible to an underlying syllogism, the conclusion of which coincides with the rhetorical *status causae*" ("Significance" 55–56).

43. Brief surveys of some of these logic manuals can be found in W. S. Howell, *Logic and Rhetoric* 12–32, 173–317, and Mack, *Elizabethan Rhetoric* 55–57, 67–80, 83–84.

44. For Monfasani's discussion of both Trebizond's and Valla's views, see *George* 300–317 and "Humanism and Rhetoric" 191. Others who point out Valla's subordination of logic to rhetoric include Kristeller, *Eight Philosophers* 34 and Seigel 161. A similar quotation can be found in Valla's *Repastinatio dialecticae et philosophiae* in Mack, *Renaissance Argument* 110.

45. Breen relates that Melanchthon made this remark about Aristotle's *Analytics* to Stadianus, according to a story in Melanchthon's 1518 oration on education (*Corpus Reformatorum* 12:20), and cites Karl Hartfelder, *Philipp Melanchthon als Praeceptor Germaniae.* 1889. Rpt. Nieuwkoop: B. De Graaf, 1964, 39 as his source (102).

46. Sanford, "English Rhetoric" 518–21.

47. Ong, *Ramus* 100; Mack, *Renaissance Argument* 244, 251; Guerlac 32; and Conley, *Rhetoric* 127 all point out Agricola's "rhetoricizing of logic" and oppose Monfasani's conclusion that in Agricola's work "logic, which had the specific task of teaching, retained primacy over rhetoric" ("Humanism and Rhetoric" 196). James A. Herrick is another who passes along the oversimplified attribution that Agricola splits wisdom and eloquence, with dialectic "the clear winner, walking away with all of the substance, the wisdom, of the speech" (166). We would do well to note the views of fellow Renaissance humanists. Alard of Amsterdam's opinion was that Agricola had succeeded better than any other in uniting dialectic and eloquence; Bartholomew Latomus found Agricola comparable to Cicero and Quintilian; and Melanchthon, who himself united the arts, adopted Agricola's methods of reading (Meerhoff, "Logic and Eloquence" 361–62).

48. Monfasani, "Humanism and Rhetoric" 204.

49. Lanham notes that because Ramus "separated thought from language," speech becomes merely "cosmetic" and "reason breaks free of speech" (*Electronic Word* 157–58). We cannot blame only Ramus for this split, however.

50. Mack notes that in his commentaries, Ramus "shows how rhetoric and dialectic work together" ("Ramus Reading" 131).

51. This comment divides between content and style, not between a "naked" and ornamented style, as Ong claims (*Ramus* 277). Unfortunately Monfasani takes this division as fully representative of Melanchthon's view ("Humanism and Rhetoric" 201).

52. It is possible that this "reply" was actually written by one of Melanchthon's pupils, Franz Burchard, according to Rummel (*Humanist-Scholastic Debate* 9, 147).

53. Gabriel Harvey is another who makes this division: "Unite dialectic and knowledge with rhetoric, thought with language. Learn from Erasmus to conjoin an abundance of matter with an abundance of words" (*Ciceronianus* [1577] 83). Shuger has also noted that despite the fact that the early humanists divide philosophy and rhetoric according to content and style (143), rhetoric and philosophy are not antagonistic in general rhetorics of the Renaissance and "the very complexity of Renaissance rhetoric discouraged any clear-cut bifurcations" (152).

54. This division is the most common one in the scholarship on the period. Vickers assumes that this division between the arts characterizes the Renaissance view. He writes that the humanists' emphasis on rhetoric is driven by the beliefs that "reason cannot do man any good unless bodied forth in speech" ("Rhetoric and Poetics" 729); that men had to be persuaded to virtue

in order to establish civilization; and that eloquence and reason had to be kept together, for eloquence alone "could be a very dangerous art indeed!" ("'Power of Persuasion'" 422).

55. Monfasani sees only the division between the arts in Wilson ("Humanism and Rhetoric" 205). Medine, Wilson's modern editor, however, notices that Wilson's theory may lack total consistency but reduces the inconsistencies found in some former accounts: "While the *Art of Rhetoric* does not present a perfectly integrated theory of rhetoric, it orders the five great procedures in a sequence that for all practical purposes obviates much of the inherent tension among them" (introduction to *Art of Rhetoric* 15).

56. Meerhoff points out that to Melanchthon "the reading of classical orations serves as a model for reading" Paul's letter to the Romans, and interpretation involves the "uncovering of logical invention as a chain of arguments supporting one basic contention," looking for "textual coherence" ("Significance" 51, 55).

57. Wagner accounts for these incompatible definitions of the arts by arguing that between 1551, when he published his logic manual, and 1553, when he published his rhetoric manual, Wilson changed his view of rhetoric from ornate phrasing or style to "the whole art of the orator" (12). This account is possible.

58. Another oversimplification in modern scholarship results from distinguishing the sixteenth and seventeenth centuries according to particular brands of rhetoric. Sanford declares that the view toward rhetoric changed from the sixteenth-century focus on ornate style to the seventeenth-century return to Aristotelianism ("English Rhetoric" 503). Sloane sees the beginning of the seventeenth century as the decisive end of humanist rhetoric, the end of the practice of *controversia* that fosters awareness of dialogue, voice, and relativistic truths, and the triumph of Ramism and science, which foster algorithms, voicelessness, and philosophical certainty (*Donne, Milton* 133–44). Actually of those examined for this study, all the textbooks in both the sixteenth and seventeenth centuries retain the Ciceronian perspective.

59. The author of the definitive study to date of Vossius's life and work, Rademaker similarly recognizes that his work derives from primarily humanist sources: "Since it covered the entire tremendous terrain of humanistic learning, its great value lies first and foremost in this, that it contained everything that the past and his own time had discovered and developed, summarized in an extremely systematical fashion" (353). Cf. Conley, *Rhetoric* 160–61. J. Zappen emphasizes Vossius's debts to Aristotle (75–77).

60. Lamy has been widely regarded as embodying Port Royalist attitudes because he rejects rhetorical invention and favors instead Descartes's rationalistic methods. The Port Royalists, or the Jansenists, who were a Roman Catholic sect in Port-Royal, France, advocated curricular reform, emphasizing modern studies in the spirit of Descartes and teaching the vernacular before turning to the classics (Bizzell and Herzberg 576). Yet Lamy cannot be so easily categorized. Technically he belonged to the Congregation of the Oratory, and his version of rhetoric mixes the Ciceronian view with the Port Royalist opposition to the "places." Cf. W. S. Howell, *Logic and Rhetoric* 379.

61. Because of these tensions, Sloane has called the Renaissance "a nexus of contraries" (*Donne, Milton* 97–99). Kahn has also noticed that "tension exists within the humanist tradition between rhetoric conceived as an activity of ethical deliberation, which is a good in itself, and rhetoric conceived as a neutral technique of argument." By ethical deliberation she means, however, only the means of argument used "in the service of the good" (*Machiavellian Rhetoric* 5). For an analysis of this tension in Italian humanists, see Monfasani, "Episodes of Anti-Quintilianism."

62. Monfasani notes that in the writings of Trebizond this shift "is especially jarring and significant because he gave full expression to both the cultural and pragmatic conceptions of rhetoric and then was never able to resolve the tension between them" (*George* 242).

63. Classical rhetoricians from Aristotle to Quintilian held to a code of ethics that allows the ends to justify the means. Quintilian permits the orator to lie if by doing so he can bring about justice and the greater good (2.17.19–21, 27).

64. Hanna H. Gray corroborates this observation but without as clear a connection to moral perfection: "The humanists' *uomo universale,* if such there was, is to be found in their picture of the ideal orator, master of many arts and governor of his fellowmen, through the force of his eloquence forging a link beween the intellectual and practical spheres of human experience" (504). Donald R. Kelley does see the connection to moral perfection: "in many ways indeed the master of rhetoric fulfilled the idea of the *uomo universale* in moral and political as well as in literary and philosophical terms. The Orator, in other words, was the very prototype and paradigm of the Renaissance man" (18). However Kelley does not explore what kind of ethical roots underlie rhetoric's controversial "civic humanism" (93). Jane Donawerth explains the connection as linear: one studies words in order to get to knowledge, which enables moral action (128–29). Vos sees the indissolubility of virtue and good letters in Ascham and Sturm but not in their classical ancestors ("Good Matter" 18).

65. *Annotationum in Evangelium Joannis* 1:2. In this note Erasmus writes, "First, *sermo* more perfectly explains why the evangelist wrote *logos,* because among Latin speakers *verbum* does not express speech as a whole, but one particular saying." Then, he explains, "But Christ is for this reason called *logos,* because whatsoever the Father speaks, he speaks through the Son" (trans. Boyle 9). By using *sermo* Erasmus reveals he sees rhetoric broadly as discourse. In *Enchiridion militis Christiani,* Erasmus identifies God as the author of the scriptures (3.49).

66. To Vives God, being "the Creator of our reason," is "the Canon and Rule of our reason," so that "reason shows the way by which we may come to God, which is the end for which man is created" (*De tradendis disciplinis* 251–52). Wilson defines virtue as "a constant habit of mind, making them praiseworthy in whom it is" (*Rule of Reason* D.vii.r). Hoskins says similarly, "Virtue is a quality settled in reason" (44).

67. Others who have noticed the Renaissance application of rhetoric and the language arts to textual analysis include Meerhoff, "Significance"; Kahn, *Rhetoric, Prudence* 10; and Eden, *Hermeneutics* 64–100.

68. See appendix 4 for a description of these exercises.

69. In spite of agreement regarding the two-part division, notions of what constitutes this high and this plain style vary considerably, reflecting the lack of knowledge these scholars actually have of rhetorical precepts. Echoing Hendrickson, who first makes this bipartite division (266), Croll declares that "the history of Greek and Roman style is chiefly the story of the relations of the genus grande and the genus humile," the first whose origin is in the rhetoricians Gorgias and Isocrates and whose purpose is display, the second whose origin is in the philosophers Plato and Aristotle and whose purpose is to express reality (59–61). The grand, oratorical style, which he also calls Asiatic, is characterized by the use of figures of speech for their own sake. In contrast the philosophical Attic style uses the figures of thought to convey ideas with clearness, brevity, naturalness, and persuasiveness (89). He then categorizes Renaissance prose styles as either the decorated, Ciceronian high style of the rhetoricians, the fashion most popular in the sixteenth century, or the plain, brief, and rationalistic Anti-Ciceronian, Senecan, or Attic style of the philosophers, the fashion most popular in the seventeenth century (84–85). Retaining this formulation, Williamson then divides the rhetorical high style into three Renaissance manifestations, what he calls the Ciceronian, Isocratean, and Euphuist (31), and the plain style into two, what he calls the Attic (brief and plain) and the Senecan (brief and pointed) (52). R. F. Jones retains the distinction between these two basic styles in the Renaissance but identifies them instead as the rhetorical, characterized by figured, passionate, exuberant language, and the dialectical, characterized by unfigured, natural, naked, and plain language (in *Seventeenth*

Century 76–79, 106–7). He disengages Croll's sententious Anti-Ciceronian style from philosophy, making it and the exuberant Ciceronian style two different rhetorical (grand) types (78–79, 105–7), and identifies a new, unfigured plain style as the preferred mode for science and philosophy (107–9). Shuger concludes that Jones's assessment is the accurate one, identifying Croll's two styles as antithetic types of the grand style: that is, Croll's Asiatic style is really the faulty high style, the rhetoric of display that arises from figures of speech, a type described in Roman rhetoric under the auspices of the middle style and exemplified by Gorgias and Isocrates; and his Attic style is the truly grand style exemplified by Demosthenes and produced by figures of thought (127–29). She then categorizes Renaissance preaching styles as belonging to either the figured or unfigured species of the rhetorical or grand style, suggesting that the plain type is a new hybrid that can be called "the passionate plain style" (164–65, 169).

70. Cf. Hendrickson 252–55.

71. Schiappa argues that Aristotle provides "the first theoretical explication of a genre called epideictic," a genre he identifies with the art of display (198).

72. Vickers notes the same ("Royal Society" 11). G. E. R. Lloyd provides an extended analysis of Aristotle's rejection of both image and analogy from philosophy, science, and reasoning (403–14.). Further evidence to suggest that this distinction between oratorical and philosophical styles derives from Aristotle is found in Theophrastus, who makes this division (Hendrickson 255–56). Croll agrees that Aristotle is the inspiration for the seventeenth-century plain style, but he supposes this inspiration must come from the first two books of Aristotle's *Rhetoric,* wherein Aristotle connects style to reason, Croll says. He opines that "Anti-Ciceronian" plain stylists ignore book 3 of the *Rhetoric,* wherein Aristotle describes the oratorical or high style (58).

73. Scholars agree on this assessment. See Bolgar, *Classical Heritage* 200–211; Murphy, *Rhetoric in the Middle Ages* 89–130; Rummel, *Humanist-Scholastic Debate* 154; Bizzell and Herzberg 440–41.

74. At the end of the letter, Pico reveals that he has merely argued as a scholastic would: "This is what those philosophers might assert, my dearest Ermolao, in defense of their barbarity—or perhaps they would even say much better things if they employed their skill at subtle argument. I do not completely agree with their opinion, nor do I think that a noble and liberal person will do so" (66). This admission reveals the letter as a mock attack on rhetoric, parodying the position of the scholastic logician. Cf. Vickers, "Rhetoric and Poetics" 744.

75. R. F. Jones correlates this stylistic reform with the development of referential semantics (106). W. S. Howell attributes the beginning of this preference for a style without figures to Bacon (*Logic and Rhetoric* 386). Halloran and Whitburn also note that Sprat and the Royal Society through these arguments promote "a serious split between form and content" (65).

76. Adolph is right to distinguish two plain styles, one taught by the rhetoricians and one by the scientists. But his distinction between them is not completely accurate. The difference between the two styles, he says, has to do with whether words approximate the ideas of the speaker or name material objects in the outside world (132–33). Both styles derive from philosophy and belong to the low, Attic style, being clear, brief, conversational, emotionally restrained, unfigured, polite conveyors of truth (135). There are two opposites to this bipartite plain style: either the lofty, ornate, oratorical style that gives attention to words alone (135–38) or the sloppy, overly brief or prolix, raw, and undigested style (145), both of which are obscure (148). But Adolph correctly argues that neither the terms *Ciceronian, Anti-Ciceronian,* nor *Senecan* can be affixed to any of these styles (137–40).

77. See chapter 1, note 11.

78. Because the levels of style can be realigned to measure degree of appropriateness, all faulty styles can be considered low and all supremely crafted styles can be considered sublime. It is in this sense of faulty that Hoskins uses the term *plain style,* associating it with "rusticity" or

lack of art. He admonishes that "a style [of a good letter or good conversation] should be both familiar and unfamiliar, unambiguous, yet not too ordinary and plain, for 'It is as it is in many dishes at our tables: our eyes and taste give them commendation, nor for the substance but for the dressing and service'" (46). This advice is meant to encourage letter writers to strive for not the full and mighty style but the carefully crafted, good style.

79. See *Ecclesiastes* 3.44.787–88; 3.64.248–52; 3.98.903; 3.132.549–55; and 3.154.23–27.

80. Despite her treatment of these levels as fairly stable categories, Shuger has nevertheless noticed that "this syncretism entailed that each of the genera dicendi acquired considerable latitude" and are "multiplex" (162). See also Annabel M. Patterson 27, 34.

81. Tuve also has argued that in Renaissance instruction the levels of style cannot be rigidly assigned to kinds of diction, figures, or subjects (194–215, 237).

82. Cicero changes the terms to *probare* (to prove), *conciliare* (to win favor), and *movere* (to stir) in *De Oratore* 2.27.115, 121, and to *decere* (to speak appropriately), *movere* (to stir), and *delectare* (to delight) in *De Oratore* 1.28.130.

83. A. E. Douglas argues that the association of the three functions of the orator with the three levels of style is Cicero's contribution to rhetorical theory ("Ciceronian Contribution" 18).

84. Shuger errs when she claims that Roman rhetoricians do not combine *docere* and *movere* (147).

85. Cf. Hoffmann 190–91.

86. For Perkins as a representative spokesman for the Puritan plain style—a low style without figures—see Miller 335, 338–40, Mitchell 99–101, and Shuger 71.

87. Halloran and Whitburn also notice that Aristotle prescriptively assigns styles to genres, while Cicero, who focuses instead on description, does not (62). Typically scholars have treated these categories as fairly stable identities. No doubt sometimes literary fashions do make these categories stable, but we must not confuse fashions with the general principles taught in rhetoric.

88. Cf. Patterson 30; Shuger 144, 161, 163.

89. Croll's assertion that the high style has primarily schemes of words and the low or plain style primarily figures of thought (54) has no grounding in either classical or Renaissance rhetoric.

90. Halloran and Whitburn have noticed similarly that in Cicero "the plain style is simply more subtle in its use of the figures of speech" (62). Himself distinguishing figured from plain speech, Vickers mistakes when he claims that Cicero does not want figures in the plain style (*In Defence* 299, 332).

91. Shuger misses the fact that the simple direct statement is a figure and so concludes that Hermogenes and Longinus "allowed for an austerely simple and unornamented form of the grand style" (163).

92. By the 1631 edition of Vossius's *Rhetorices Contractae,* no mention is made of figures being in the low style (5.5.539). Perhaps this omission contributes to the eventual dominance of the philosophers' notion of the plain style.

93. See also Sherry [1550] 23–24 and Soarez 413–14.

94. Cf. Miller 342, 362; Bizzell and Herzberg 569.

95. Ong supposes more than he should when he remarks that Ramist dialectic is "radically visualist," not performative, and that out of this submersion of style into dialectic "emerges the Ramist plain style. . . . It is the phoenix which rises from the holocaust of all three styles, the verbal counterpart of the coming visualist universe of 'objects,' voiceless and by that very fact depersonalized, which would soon recommend to the Royal Society, as Thomas Sprat records in his history, 'a close, naked, natural way of speaking,' as near the 'mathematical' as possible" (*Ramus* 213). He even admits that "there is little evidence from Ramus' contemporaries that

anything very new and distinctive resulted immediately from Ramus' or Talon's prescriptions regarding actual style" (283). This caution does not mean, however, that later on misreadings of Ramistic precepts do not play a part in encouraging the growth of this notion of a plain style.

96. Shuger has also noticed the same (143), but she mistakenly believes that rhetoric manuals apply the three levels of style to only figured, rhetorical language and assume that an unfigured, nonrhetorical language is suitable for dialectic (164–65).

97. Cf. Tuve 30–31.

98. Grube also argues that Longinus is discussing not a particular style at all but only great writing (*Greek and Roman Critics* 342).

99. Scaliger and Vossius do not, like these two, list *adhortatio* as a figure, but they do regard it as the deliberative genre (3.105.399; [1631] 2.21.245).

100. My students do not need to be told to see all figures as figures of thought but do so automatically and look for the patterns on all levels of discourse.

101. Lechner observes, "It is evident that most of these figures of thought correspond exactly to the dialectical places!" (128).

102. Cf. Yates 231–42; Ong, *Rhetoric* 104–12.

103. For an introduction to this approach in cognitive psychology, see Gagné and Perkins.

104. Wilson gives the following examples of these relations in his logic text: white and black are contraries; master and servant are relatives; sight and blindness are privatives; and "Christ is in the Sacrament really" and "Christ is not in the Sacrament really" are contradictions (*Rule of Reason* N.ii.r–N.v.r).

105. Ramus, however, objects that classical rhetoricians do not distinguish logical topics and methods of style (*Arguments* 114).

106. Conley points out that citations of the enthymeme in rhetoric texts from fourth century B.C. to the end of the Byzantine Empire (about two thousand years) have "an ambiguity—perhaps a confusion—about the line which divides argumentation from style" ("Enthymeme" 176). Solmsen notes that the enthymeme in Isocrates and other rhetoricians "had been merely a particular way of formulating a thought (in other words, a concept of stylistic rather than logical complexion)" but in Aristotle becomes the rhetorical syllogism, a feature of argument ("Aristotelian Tradition" 39 note 15).

107. Cf. Sherry [1550] 37; Robertellus 18r, 31r–v, 37r.

108. This approach to meaning making via "place-theory" is an original contribution of Renaissance humanists. The scholastics had supposed that logic's role was to provide a philosophy of language accounting for the meaning and reference of terms. Humanists objected to the arid and algorithmic approach of the scholastics, whose supposition theory with speculations on the properties of terms concentrated on explaining the meaning of individual words removed from context and according to set grammatical categories. Instead of supposition theory, the humanists offer place-theory. For an explanation of supposition theory, see Kneale and Kneale 246–74.

109. Metaphor theory needs a more careful discrimination between the genus of tropes and the individual species of tropes, a more precise accounting of the senses in which language and thought are metaphorical or tropological, and a more thorough explication of the ontological and epistemological implications of this phenomenon. Confusion abounds on these issues.

110. This book was reprinted twice more in 1679 and then reissued under the title of *Minerva's Triumph* in 1680 and again in 1683.

111. "We have to cease to think if we refuse to do it in the prison-house of language; for we cannot reach further than the doubt which asks whether the limit we see is really a limit" (qtd. in Jameson i). The original source is Friedrich Nietzsche, "Nachglassene Schriften 1870–1873," *Werke,* vol. 3, ed. Karl Schlecta (Munich: Hanser, 1954–65), 862.

112. Fish characterizes the long-standing debate between philosophy and rhetoric by attributing to the philosophers the dualistic belief in these two types of language, with a preference for only the first, and to the rhetoricians the monistic belief in the reality of only the figured, artificial, ambiguous language. Fish sides with the rhetoricians (*Doing* 474–78, 480–81, 493–94).

113. Lakoff and Johnson demonstrate that many of our foundational metaphors derive from our physical interactions with the world (194). I submit that the logical *topoi* are universal abstractions that derive from common physical experience in space, time, and materiality and that the rhetorical *topoi* are universal abstractions that derive from common social experience in narrative, drama, and argument.

Chapter 3: Functions of Figures and Styles

1. While there is value in explaining the different processes required to interpret literal and figurative expressions (to use the customary terms), when it comes to explaining their broader meanings in the discourse—that is, the assertions they make, the emotions they express, and the intentions and quality of judgment they reflect—this difference is of secondary importance. It is not my purpose here to explain this difference, which is never adequately explored in either the important classical or Renaissance handbooks.

2. Vickers also claims that Renaissance rhetoricians gave more attention to the functional possibilities of figures than did their classical sources (*Classical Rhetoric* 106).

3. According to speech act theory, there are three kinds of speech acts: locutionary (producing a recognizable grammatical utterance in a given language), illocutionary (representing, directing, promising, expressing, or declaring), and perlocutionary (achieving certain effects in the hearers, such as frightening, convincing, and so forth). Notice that Renaissance figure lists provide a broader sweep of behaviors.

4. Lausberg §499.

5. Talaeus 83–86; Day [1599] 1–4; Wright 104–44. In his introduction to Wright's *Passions,* Sloane writes, "Wright uses 'delivery' to mean all the external operations of the understanding in transmitting concepts to other men or in creating discourse—what today we signify by 'communication'" (xxxiii).

6. Typically scholars have assumed that Renaissance rhetoricians ignored delivery and the oral dimension of speech. See Clark, *Rhetoric and Poetry* 30 and *John Milton* 12; Crane 57; Joseph 21; Ong, *Rhetoric* 58; Vickers, "Some Reflections" 84. Noting this trend, Mohrmann has called for a reexamination of the Renaissance attitude toward delivery in "Oratorical Delivery" 65.

7. See also Wright 571.

8. For a summary of the methodology Quintilian and Renaissance educators prescribe to inculcate rhetorical facility, see Murphy, *Short History* 35–78; Abbott 158–62; and my article "Double Master Frame" 72–80. For original Renaissance sources, see Sturm, *Nobilitatas literata* (in Spitz 133–73 or T.B.'s translation, *A Ritch Storehouse or Treasurie for Nobilitye and Gentlemen*) and Ascham, *Scholemaster* 242–88.

9. Cassirer in *Das Erkenntnisproblem in der Philosophie und Wissenschaft der neuern Zeit* Vol. 1. (Berlin, 1906) observes that these humanists saw language as a reflection of the thinking that produced it (122–23; cited in Breen 44).

10. Taylor observes that comments about figures in these manuals show this focus on persuasive effect (43). Hudson recognizes that Hoskins reduces the emphasis on "figures as ends in themselves, or as ornaments," and redirects it instead onto the functions and purposes of them (xx). Medine notices the same in Wilson (introduction to *Art of Rhetoric* 21–22), and Crane in Peacham (introduction to *Garden of Eloquence* 23).

11. Cf. Farnaby 20.

12. Inasmuch as these effects can be used as tools, they can, in a sense, be disconnected from the artist. This detachability leads Fahnestock to assert that "all of these functional explanations of the figures as sources of emotion, charm, vividness, force, vivacity, or elegance can be grouped together as value-added theories of figuration. According to a 'value-added' view, one begins with a plain message and then adds secondary features that make it more memorable or convincing than it would be without them" (*Rhetorical Figures* 20).

13. Tuve argues that the Renaissance conception of style as the garment of thought means "its [thought's] bodying-forth or manifestation" (61). She explicates the arguments of poetic images in Renaissance poetry, noting that Renaissance writers understood images to be arguments (146–79, 251–381).

14. Leff notices that Aquila is similar to Renaissance rhetoricians in not considering figures as ends in themselves and subject matter as independent of style ("Latin" 276).

15. Medine notices that figures serve for both argumentation and style in both Melanchthon and Wilson (introduction to *Art of Rhetoric* 13, 17–22).

16. Wooten praises Hermogenes because he "discusses both what a particular figure of speech is called and also what function or effect it has in the speech or in the particular passage in which it appears—in other words, how form reflects content" (Hermogenes, *On Types of Style* 133). Fahnestock also sees Hermogenes's recognition of figures as constitutive, not "after-the-fact embellishment" (*Rhetorical Figures* 28).

17. Because the *Ad Herennium* does not make obvious that some figures are "epitomes" of certain patterns of thought, Fahnestock believes this book assumes figures to be "value-added" devices merely (*Rhetorical Figures* 20). This conclusion seems premature, however, for this manual still retains a clear awareness that figures direct cognitive movement. Vickers argues that this author "is perceptive in charting the figures' appeal to the reason, their union of logic, insinuation and probability" (*Classical Rhetoric* 98).

18. *The Histories* 6.11.

19. As James S. Baumlim has noticed, "That style should reflect a speaker's emotional state is a commonplace from classical rhetoric" (444).

20. Cf. Fraunce, *Arcadian Rhetoric* E4v; Wright 7–8; Day 47; and Bulwer 151.

21. Agricola may say that "discourse can teach without moving or delighting, but that it cannot move or delight without teaching" (1.1; McNally 395). Yet he does not identify "moving" with all emotions, only the forceful ones, for to move means "disturbing the peaceful and tranquil mind" or overcoming "the unbeliever" by "drawing him against his will" (2.4, 1.1; McNally 409, 395).

22. Vickers in *Classical Rhetoric* also points out the "intellectual expression" found in figures, but he focuses on emotional expression and does not integrate the two (96, 100).

23. Cf. Longinus §17, 32; Quintilian 9.3.102; Wilson 195.

24. Vickers concurs in *In Defence* 305–39. Fahnestock expresses the more common belief that figures' being associated with emotions necessarily reinforces "their detachability" (*Rhetorical Figures* 19). She sees that "figures are an effective delivery system for both the speaker's point and the degree of intensity or conviction behind it." But because she takes figures as a small, specialized set and because emotions can therefore be expressed without figures, she considers the association of emotion with figures to be "value-added" (20–21). Although not addressing the subject of figures, several contemporary scholars are rediscovering that stylistic forms provide a symbolism of emotional configurations. See Langer, *Philosophy* 70–71, 79; Ohmann, "Prolegomena" 188; Tufte 7–9; and Butler, *Out of Style* 144. Langer and Ohmann even recognize these forms as rational and the dichotomy between thought and emotion as artificial (Langer, *Philosophy* 79–80; Ohmann, "Prolegomena" 190).

25. Conley argues that beginning with Soarez and then becoming characteristic of seventeenth-century rhetorics is the increased focus on affect (*Rhetoric* 152, 154, 159). Nadeau believes that Farnaby, who says that "the emotional drive must pervade the entire speech" (11–12), is unusual in emphasizing pathos ("Thomas Farnaby" 344). Shuger believes that in Renaissance sacred rhetorics passion replaces persuasion as the aim of rhetorical speech (120). She also sees the same trend in Trebizond and Hermogenes (59). All three scholars' conclusions seem inaccurate given the constant focus on the affective dimension of speech in this rhetorical tradition, a dimension that always connects expressivity with persuasiveness.

26. Lamy reads the passions themselves as motives: "His Passion renders him dexterous and cunning, it furnishes him with Arms, and he makes use of everything he can reach for his defence" (2.128), for "we pursue what we love, we avoid what we hate" (2.139).

27. Since Isocrates believes that ethos preexists a person's texts, Baumlin and Baumlin emphasize the essentialism here (*Ethos* xvi). Yun Lee Too assumes Isocrates's textual voices are constructed personae only (6). In contrast Haskins sees both layers to the constructed identity Isocrates creates by means of his speeches and life (*Logos* 21–22).

28. Cf. Conley, *Rhetoric* 18.

29. Cf. Kennedy, "Classical Rhetoric," in Sloane, *Encyclopedia of Rhetoric* 112; May 6–10. May focuses primarily on the essentialism of identity, however: "The Romans believed that character remains essentially constant in man and therefore demands or determines his actions. Since character does not evolve or develop, but rather is bestowed or inherited by nature, an individual cannot suddenly, or at will, change or disguise for any lengthy period his ethos or way of life. . . . The Romans further believed that in most cases character remains constant from generation to generation of the same family" (6). Given that Cicero and Quintilian advocate stylistic flexibility, performative mimesis, and conscious artistry, however, May's formulation is too stark. Herrick expresses a similar notion of simple essentialism when he notices that "in keeping with Roman thinking on the subject, character was a natural trait of an individual that gradually revealed itself through the course of a life" (102).

30. Russell has recognized that the ancients generally see this double reflection of the author in the text. One image reflects the unique traits of the individual and the other the general moral qualities people evince: "'Style' in modern usage is very much an individual matter. We think of it as a kind of finger-print, unique to every individual, and interestingly unique to every interesting individual. Something like this is of course found in antiquity. The style of a great exemplar, Lysias or Demosthenes, is naturally called the 'Lysian' or 'Demosthenic' *charaktēr.* The fact that sensitive critics sometimes felt sure enough to identify authors by their style points the same way. Yet the maxim, *talis oratio qualis vita,* a way of saying that 'speech reflects life,' seems to be of a different application altogether. It asserts that speech is an indication of the moral characteristics of the speaker, marking not his individuality, but his type" (131).

31. The few scholars who have taken account of this focus on character in Renaissance rhetoric miss the complexity of the concept and the widespread acceptance of the doctrine. The predominant assumption is that this reference to character means a persona (Vickers, *Classical Rhetoric* 103; Webber 1; Agnew 97). In contrast Greene notes the "humanist faith in the symptomatic importance of style, with all its ethical, psychological, and even sociological implications," but considers such faith problematic ("Roger Ascham" 615). Similarly, observing that to Ascham and Sturm "the orator's style of speaking becomes a window into the deepest reaches of his psyche," Vos concludes that these two see only the symptomatic link between style and speaker, differing from Cicero, Erasmus, and other humanists in doing so ("Good Matter" 7, 18). Aware of a more complex view, Struever sees that in early Italian humanists personal identity is both separable and inseparable from one's speech (144–63, 162). Lanham identifies as two opposing identities operating in speech the rhetorical and serious selves (*Motives of Eloquence* 5).

32. Because he misunderstands rhetorical decorum, Crane believes that wit in both classical and Renaissance periods was associated with copiousness and ornateness or, in other words, with the high style (*Wit* 4, 7–8, 20, 86). Kahn comes closer to Renaissance understanding when she aligns rhetorical decorum with practical judgment and prudence, but she stops short of explicating the rhetoricians' ideal because she restricts rhetoric to the faculty of arguing both sides of a question (*Rhetoric* 35–36).

33. Vives originally makes this remark in *De ratione dicendi* 2.270.

34. Russell praises Longinus for making "a serious effort to explain how the identification of these abnormalities can contribute to our understanding of the writer's intentions and qualities" (146).

35. Comments such as these that reveal stylistic devices as lines of argument lead Fahnestock to attribute to Aristotle a nonornamental view of figures, for to him, she says, figures "express perfectly, efficiently, and unobtrusively the precise idea the speaker is trying to convey" (*Rhetorical Figures* 27). Similarly his emphasis on the appropriateness of style to subject leads some scholars to find in Aristotle an "organic" or monistic notion of form (Kinneavy 358; Lerner 814–17). Aristotle's focus on the disconnection between style and idea, however, leads other scholars, such as Milic and Kennedy, to see him as spokesman for a dualistic notion of style. Both views are in Aristotle but appear as unresolved contradictions rather than complements.

36. Herrick points out that to Aristotle all that matters is the persona created by the speech; to the Romans the orator brings with him the character created throughout his life (102). Baumlin and Baumlin note the same contrast: "If Isocratean tradition asserts the speaker's need to be good, Aristotelian tradition asserts the sufficiency of seeming good" (*Ethos* xv).

37. See *Poetics* 1454a12f; 1455a20f; 1456a33–34. Scholars who believe that Aristotle does embrace performative mimesis as a criterion for poetry include Gerald F. Else 492–93; Richard McKeon 164–65; and Mack, "Rudolph Agricola's Reading" 37–38. Vickers believes Aristotle embraces it for rhetoric too (*In Defence* 296–97). Haskins, however, points out more persuasively that Aristotle skirts the issue. This denial of style as performative mimesis enables Aristotle to extend Plato's efforts to "curtail the influence of performance culture upon civic education" ("*Mimesis*" 31).

38. Cf. Shafter 11, although Schafter regards only figures of thought.

39. Cf. Quintilian 8.3.11; 9.4.3–7; 12.10.13. DiLorenzo argues that this equation of wisdom and *ornatus* underscores Cicero's critique of Socrates in *De Oratore.* Because Socrates reduces wisdom to knowledge, he disrupts *kosmos* or *ornatus,* the unity among all things. Cicero argues instead that wisdom, being *ornatus,* must include the effective communication of knowledge: "Wisdom is knowledge embodied in speech which, by attracting others at the level of their senses, enters into them at the level of their convictions and becomes the impetus of their actions. . . . The critique does not explicate the content of wisdom. It points rather to its essential bondedness to speech" (258).

40. Smethurst recognizes that Cicero, "true to his *humanitas,* considers decorum to be an aesthetic and literary principle as well as a moral ideal." Even though based on the "Golden Mean" and on uniform consistency, Smethurst discounts the universality of this criteria by attributing them to "the standards of conduct prevailing among the aristocracy, and especially the minority who appreciate Ciceronian *humanitas*" and concludes that such guidelines lead inevitably to rigidity and formalism (311–12).

41. Scholars have typically regarded Cicero's three duties of the orator—teaching, delighting (winning the good will of the audience), and moving—to parallel Aristotle's three types of proof: logos, ethos, and pathos. Ciceronian ethos they identify as the presentation of the gentler emotions or *ethopoeia,* which does not overlap at all with either argumentation or the presentation of passions. (See Solmsen, "Aristotle and Cicero" 397; Kennedy, *Art of Rhetoric* 222–23; Elaine Fantham 271; May 5; Jakob Wisse 249; and Fortenbaugh, "*Trials of Character*"

506). Richard Leo Enos and Karen Rossi Schnakenberg describe instead Cicero's ideal of virtue: *ingenium* (a natural capacity for eloquence), *prudentia* (an ability to adapt one's discourse to the circumstances and advocate for a proper course of action), and *diligentia* (a "passion of commitment" that demonstrates "an individual willing to act on ethical principles for the sake of justice"). They say that *prudentia* entails appealing "not to the expediency of the moment" but "to communal standards." They also emphasize only the persona created in the speech but do acknowledge that this persona can exercise benefits beyond the speech, contributing to the speaker's reputation and ethos in succeeding speeches (199–205).

42. Wagner contends that Wilson focuses only on emotional proofs to the exclusion of logical and ethical proofs (14, 19). In agreement are Sanford (*English Theories* 34) and Sloane (*Donne, Milton* 136). This criticism results from failing to see the moral center Wilson assumes the art to have. Agnew more accurately concludes, "Wilson assumes that style serves as the foundation for ethical proof because it both embodies and develops the rhetor's character," but she sees this proof as merely an external image (93).

43. Green also recognizes that generally style "is an ethical enterprise for the Renaissance mind" ("Aristotelian *Lexis*" 159). Vickers is unfair to the Ramists, whom he claims have little awareness of the figures' mirroring functions (*Classical Rhetoric* 108–9).

44. Eden's central argument is precisely this "correspondence between formal and ethical categories" in classical and Renaissance rhetoric (*Hermeneutics* 31). She provides a nice enumeration of these correspondences in this tradition's hermeneutics: reading for the spirit as well as the letter (intention and achievement), reading with equity (accommodation), and reading both historical and textual contexts (considering the whole and the part in relationship).

45. These three writers are all referenced in Mary E. Hazard 18.

46. Ibid. 15.

47. Critics who reject the moralistic claims of these rhetoricians are staunch dualists. Vickers debunks what he calls the Renaissance "optimism about the innate goodness of speech and rhetoric," because one can, by controlling one's speech, as Iago does, "suggest 'privie thoughtes and secret conceites,' while reserving his real feelings to some deeper level of language and dissimulation" ("'Power of Persuasion'" 422). Kinney also responds to Renaissance panegyrics about rhetoric's goodness with disbelief: "Eloquence for many Tudor writers was not—could not have been, in any realistic sense—the golden language of the good and wise man as Quintilian has seemed to premise, but the manipulation of words in a country where eristics was respected and daily practiced." Orators would have been "actors" merely ("Rhetoric and Fiction" 387). Grafton and Jardine's rejection of the humanists' program as mere propaganda demonstrates their fundamental misunderstanding of the kind of ethical center present in Ciceronian rhetorical theory, that is, critical thinking that derives from combined training in logic, language, and social awareness. They regard the humanists' rhetorical version of dialectic as an inferior form of reasoning to philosophers' logic, the ideal end product of rhetoric to be a public, political speaker, and the methods of rhetorical instruction as merely literary and without a precise "discipline" or clear order (78–82, 124, 136–37, 143). Mohrmann, however, recognizes the moral center Guazzo sees in a rhetorical education, pointed out explicitly when Guazzo writes, "Gentry and renown is not got by our birth, but by our life" and is inculcated through the study of rhetoric: "a right Gentleman is not born as the Poet, but made as the Orator" (*Civile Conversation* 1.182; qtd. in Mohrmann 200). Vos also recognizes this moral center in Ascham and Sturm ("Good Matter" 6–7).

48. But both Nauert (*Humanism* 13) and Martines (191) believe humanists provided a primarily literary education to prepare an aristocratic elite for practical decision making in political affairs.

49. *Oeconomion* has connotations of economy, accommodation, suitable arrangement, and judgment.

50. This double vision provokes Renaissance rhetoricians to argue over how style and ethics relate in Aristotle. See Green, "Aristotelian *Lexis*" 154–58. In *Aristotle's Rhetoric* Garver's reconciliation of the contradictions in Aristotle to prove that rhetoric is fundamentally ethical fits better with rhetoricians in the Isocratean/Ciceronian vein than with Aristotle.

51. Other master genres have been proposed as overarching schemes to guide the interpretation of texts. Andrea Lunsford and John J. Ruszkiewicz in *Everything's an Argument* have suggested that all texts are arguments, Mark Turner in *The Literary Mind* and Walter Fisher in *Human Communication as Narration* that all are narratives. Fisher has also argued that reason itself is fundamentally narrative and that narratives are fundamentally moral (68). Walker takes oral poetry, particularly the lyric, as the model underlying the classical rhetorical paradigm (17, 21). None are complete enough by themselves, however.

52. Vickers associates rhetoric and poetics in these two ways ("Rhetoric and Poetics" 715–16).

53. Others who have similar views of style are noteworthy. Carl H. Klaus has argued in the introduction to his book *Style in English Prose* (1968), "Style is the man; style is not the man. Both statements are true. . . . If we are indifferent to style, we sacrifice our freedom to think and 'think more clearly.' If we care about style, we can most truly be ourselves" (1, 14). Robert J. Graham agrees, urging in "Composing Ourselves in Style" that "we must begin to move notions of style away from the periphery of our teaching and place them firmly in the center," because "by means of language individuals can make and remake themselves within society" (52–54). "Our identities are entirely implicated in, and constituted by, our uniquely characteristic style of being-in-the-world, a style students can discover and refine through their guided experiments with language" (55).

Chapter 4: Stylistic Analysis

1. Most critics believe that only those deviations purposely used are representational. See, for example, Müller, "Iconicity" 306, 308–9, 311 and Fahnestock, *Rhetorical Figures* 23. In contrast Lanham sees form itself as figure and figures as allegorical whether purposeful or subliminal (*Analyzing Prose* 30, 41). In *Captive Victors* Heather Dubrow, a Renaissance literary critic, reads the figures allegorically but does not consider whether Renaissance rhetorical handbooks do. Although they do not analyze figures per se, M. A. K. Halliday in "Linguistic Function and Literary Style" and Ohmann in *Shaw* also read forms as mimetic of mental states.

2. Baldwin has noted that in England in the early part of the sixteenth century, the handlists of both Mosellanus (with 98 figures) and Melanchthon's *Elementorum* (with 97 figures) appear on grammar school statutes (1:82). In the second half of the century, the two manuals stipulated were Erasmus's *De copia* (with about 182 figures) and Susenbrotus's *Epitome* (with 168 figures). If the edition of Erasmus included Veltkirchius's commentary, then the number of figures in *De copia* increased to 230. Additionally figures appear in the grammar manuals. If pupils consulted Quintilian, whose *Institutio Oratoria* was also on both English grammar school and university reading lists, their exposure to figures would have exceeded 300. (For the school statutes, see Baldwin 1:103–4, 106, 299–300; Mack, *Elizabethan Rhetoric* 51). In the early seventeenth century, Butler's *Rhetoric* (with 102 figures) was widely used. Since none of these figure lists are identical, the total number of figures pupils could have been taught was large indeed. Vickers estimates that the commonly known figures total about 100 (*In Defence* 258), but this number seems truer for students who dropped out of grammar school than for those who matriculated or who attended university, where the *Ad Herrenium,* Quintilian, Cicero's *De Oratore,* and Hermogenes were common textbooks, as well (Mack, *Elizabethan Rhetoric* 52).

3. Donawerth recognizes that "when Elizabethan playwrights held the mirror up to nature, their mirror, like that in old fairy tales, was a speaking one" (14).

4. Mack calls this an aesthetic approach to discourse (37). It is a moral approach as well.

5. *John Milton: Complete Poems and Major Prose* 217–18.

6. Like Renaissance rhetoricians, Burke also examines how misused tropes signify reductive perspectives (*Grammar* 510–11).

7. *The Riverside Shakespeare* 1773.

8. *The Riverside Shakespeare* 1037.

Appendix 4

1. *Kataskeue* is the Greek term for "ornamentation" (Kennedy, *A New History* 86).

2. Lanham uses the terms *hypotaxis* and *parataxis* for these two kinds of sentence structure (*Analyzing Prose* 33). These terms are also found in Havelock, *A Preface to Plato* (183-4) and *The New Princeton Encyclopedia of Poetry and Poetics* (879-80), but not in the classical or Renaissance texts consulted for this study.

Bibliography

Primary Sources

Alexander of Numenius. "On Figures of Thought and Speech." In *A Guide to Classical Rhetoric,* edited by Philip Rollinson and Richard Geckle, 3–5. Signal Mountain, Tenn.: Summertown, 1998.

———. "*Περι Των Τησ Διανοιασ Και Τησ Λεξεωσ Σχηματων.*" In *Rhetores Graeci,* edited by Leonard Spengel, 3:9–40. Leipzig: Teubner, 1966.

Aphthonius. *The Progymnasmata of Aphthonius.* Trans. Ray Nadeau. In *Speech Monographs* 19 (1952): 264–85.

Aquila Romanus. *De figuris sententiarum et elocutionis.* In *Rhetores Latini Minores,* edited by Carl Halm, 22–37. Leipzig: Teubner, 1863.

Aristophanes. *Aristophanes.* Trans. Benjamin Bickley Rogers. Loeb Classical Library. Cambridge, Mass.: Harvard University Press, 1924.

Aristotle. *The Complete Works of Aristotle.* Vols. 1–2. Ed. Jonathan Barnes. Princeton, N.J.: Princeton University Press, 1984.

Ascham, Roger. *The Scholemaster.* 1570. In *English Works of Roger Ascham,* edited by William Aldis Wright, 171–302. Cambridge: Cambridge University Press, 1904 (rpt. 1970).

———. *Toxophilus.* 1545. In *English Works of Roger Ascham,* edited by William Aldis Wright, 1–119. Cambridge: Cambridge University Press, 1904 (rpt. 1970).

Bacon, Francis. *The Advancement of Learning.* Ed. William Aldis Wright. 5th ed. Oxford: Clarendon, 1926.

———. *The Essays.* Ed. John Pitcher. London: Penguin Books, 1985.

Baxter, Richard. *The Saint's Everlasting Rest.* 1650. Liverpool: Forshaw, 1798.

Blount, Thomas. *The Academy of Eloquence.* 1654. Ed. R. C. Alston. English Linguistics 1500–1800, no. 296. Menston, Yorkshire: Scolar, 1971.

Blundeville, Thomas. *The Art of Logike.* 1599. Ed. R. C. Alston. English Linguistics 1500–1800, no. 23. Menston, Yorkshire: Scolar, 1967.

Brinsley, John. *A Consolation for Our Grammar Schooles.* 1622. The English Experience, no. 203. Amsterdam: Theatrum Orbis Terrarum, 1969.

———. *Ludus Literarius.* 1612. Ed. R. C. Alston. English Linguistics 1500–1800, no. 62. Menston, Yorkshire: Scolar, 1968.

Browne, Sir Thomas. *The Major Works.* Ed. C. A. Patrides. London: Penguin Books, 1977.

Butler, Charles. *Oratoriae Libri Duo.* Oxford: Turner, 1629.

———. *Rhetoricae libri duo quorum prior de tropis & figuris, posterior de voce & gestu praecipit.* Early English Books, 1641–1700. London: Ex officina Guilielmi Bentley, pro Johanne Williams, 1649.

Bulwer, John. *Chirologia and Chironomia.* 1644. Ed. James W. Cleary. Carbondale: Southern Illinois University Press, 1974.

Capella, Martianus. *The Marriage of Philosophy and Mercury.* Trans. William Harris Stahl and Richard Johnson, with E. L. Burge. In *Martianus Capella and the Seven Liberal Arts.* Vol. 2. New York: Columbia University Press, 1977.

Carmen de Figuris vel Schematibus. In *Rhetores Latini Minores,* edited by Carl Halm, 63–70. Leipzig: Teubner, 1863.

Castiglione, Baldesar. *The Book of the Courtier.* 1528. Trans. Charles S. Singleton. Garden City, N.Y.: Doubleday, 1959.

Caxton, William. *Caxton's Mirrour of the World.* 1481. Ed. Oliver H. Prior. Early English Text Society. Extra Series no. 110. Oxford: Oxford University Press, 1913.

———. *The Myrrour: & dyscrypcyon of the worlde.* Microfilm series, no. 24764, reel 12.

Chapman, George. *Ovids Banquet of Sence.* London: James Roberts, 1595.

———. *The Poems of George Chapman.* Ed. Phyllis Brooks Bartlett. New York: Russell & Russell, 1962.

Cicero, Marcus Tullius. *Brutus. Orator.* Trans. G. L. Hendrickson and H. M. Hubbell. Loeb Classical Library. Cambridge, Mass.: Harvard University Press, 1939.

———. *Cicero Philippics.* Trans. D. R. Shackleton Bailey. Chapel Hill: University of North Carolina Press, 1986.

———. *Cicero's Orations.* Vols. 1–4. Trans. C. D. Yonge. London: Bell, 1893.

———. *De Inventione. De Optimo Genere Oratorum. Topica.* Trans. H. M. Hubbell. Loeb Classical Library. Cambridge, Mass.: Harvard University Press, 1949.

———. *De Officiis.* Trans. Walter Miller. Loeb Classical Library. Cambridge, Mass.: Harvard University Press, 1990.

———. *De Oratore.* Books 1–2. Trans. E. W. Sutton and H. Rackham. Loeb Classical Library. Cambridge, Mass.: Harvard University Press, 1942.

———. *De Oratore.* Book 3. *De Partitione Oratoria.* Trans. H. Rackham. Loeb Classical Library. Cambridge, Mass.: Harvard University Press, 1942.

———. *De Republica. De Legibus.* Trans. Clinton Walker Keyes. Loeb Classical Library. Cambridge, Mass.: Harvard University Press, 1990.

———. *Letters to Atticus.* Vol. 1. Trans. D. R. Shackleton Bailey. Loeb Classical Library. Cambridge, Mass.: Harvard University Press, 1999.

———. *Letters to Atticus.* Books 1–6. Trans. E. O. Winstedt. Loeb Classical Library. Cambridge, Mass.: Harvard University Press, 1912.

———. *Letters to Friends.* Vols. 1–3. Trans. W. Glynn Williams and D. R. Shackleton Bailey. Loeb Classical Library. Cambridge, Mass.: Harvard University Press, 1927 (rpt. 2001).

———. *M. Tullius Cicero: The Fragmentary Speeches.* Ed. Jane W. Crawford. American Classical Studies no. 37. Atlanta: Scholars, 1994.

———. *Orations.* Vols. 6–15. Trans. H. G. Hodge, Louis E. Lord, N. H. Watts, R. Gardner, J. H. Freese, L. H. G. Greenwood. Loeb Classical Library. Cambridge, Mass.: Harvard University Press, 1923–79.

———. *Orations of Marcus Tullius Cicero.* Trans. C. D. Yonge. New York: Colonial, 1900.

———. *Rhetorica Ad Herennium.* Trans. Harry Caplan. Loeb Classical Library. Cambridge, Mass.: Harvard University Press, 1954.

———. *Tusculan Disputations.* Trans. J. E. King. Loeb Classical Library. Cambridge, Mass.: Harvard University Press, 1945.

Coke, Zachary. *The Art of Logic.* 1654. Ed. R. C. Alston. English Linguistics 1500–1800 no. 192. Menston, Yorkshire: Scolar, 1969.

Cox, Leonard. *The Arte or Crafte of Rhethoryke.* Ca. 1530. Ed. Frederic Ives Carpenter. Chicago: University of Chicago Press, 1899.

Day, Angel. *The English Secretorie.* 1586. Ed. R. C. Alston. A Scolar Press Facsimile. Menston, Yorkshire: Scolar, 1967.

———. *The English Secretary.* 1599. Gainesville, Fla.: Scholars' Facsimiles & Reprints, 1967.

Demosthenes. Vols. 1–3, 6. Trans. J. H. Vince and A. T. Murray. Loeb Classical Library. Cambridge, Mass.: Harvard University Press, 1926.

Demetrius, *On Style.* Trans. Doreen C. Innes. In *Aristotle XXIII,* 311–525. Loeb Classical Library. Cambridge, Mass.: Harvard University Press, 1999.

Descartes, Rene. *A Discourse on Method.* Trans. John Veitch. Everyman's Library. London: Dent, 1912.

Despauterius, Johannes [Johannes de Spauter]. *Artis versificatoriae compendium . . . Item de Figuris liber.* C1v–C8r. Edinburgh: Andreas Hart, 1631.

Diomedes Grammaticus. *Diomedes doctissimi ac diligentissimi linguae latinae perscrutatoris de arte grammatica opus utilissimum.* In *Diomedis vetustissimi ac diligentissimi grammatici.* Venice: Joannes Rivius Recensuit, 1511.

Donatus, Aelius. *Ars grammatica (maior).* In *Grammatici latini,* ed. Heinrich Keil, 4:355–402. Leipzig: Teubner, 1864.

Elyot, Sir Thomas. *The Boke Named the Governour.* Ed. S. E. Lehmberg. London: Aldine, 1962.

Erasmus, Desiderius. *Ciceronianus.* Trans. Izora Scott. New York: Teacher's College, Columbia University, 1908.

———. *De conscribendis epistolis.* Trans. J. K. Sowards, 10–254. *Collected Works of Erasmus.* Vol. 25. Toronto: University of Toronto Press, 1985.

———. *De copia.* Trans. Craig R. Thompson, 284–659. *Collected Works of Erasmus.* Vol. 24. Toronto: University of Toronto Press, 1978.

———. *De ratione studii.* Trans. Brian McGregor, 666–91. *Collected Works of Erasmus.* Vol. 24. Toronto: University of Toronto Press, 1978.

———. *Ecclesiastae sive de ratione concionandi libri IIII.* In *Opera Omnia Desiderii Erasmi Roterodami.* Vols. 4–5. Ed. Jacques Chomarat. Amsterdam: Elsevier, 1991.

———. *Ecclesiastae sive de ratione concionandi libri IIII.* In *Opera Omnia.* Vol. 5. Hildesheim, Germany: Olms, 1962.

———. *Enchiridion Militis Christiani.* Trans. Raymond Himelick. Gloucester, Mass.: Smith, 1970.

———. *Methodus.* Ed. G. B. Winkler. In Erasmus, *Ausgewählte Schriften,* edited by W. Welzig III, 38–77. Darmstadt: Wissenschaftliche Buchgesellschaft, 1967.

———. *Parabolae.* Ed. Craig R. Thompson, 123–277. *Collected Works of Erasmus.* Vol. 23. Toronto: University of Toronto Press, 1978.

Ernesti, Johann Christian Gottlieb. *Lexicon Technologiae Graecorum Rhetoricae.* 1795. Hildesheim, Germany: Olms, 1983.

———. *Lexicon Technologiae Latinorum Rhetoricae.* 1797. Hildesheim, Germany: Olms, 1983.

Farnaby, Thomas. *Index Rhetoricus.* 1625. Ed. R. C. Alston. English Linguistics 1500–1800, no. 240. Menston, Yorkshire: Scolar, 1970.

Fenner, Dudley. *The Artes of Logike and Rethorike.* 1584. In *Four Tudor Books on Education,* edited by Robert D. Pepper, 143–80. Gainesville, Fla.: Scholars' Facsimiles & Reprints, 1966.

Ford, Emanuel. *The Most Pleasant Historie of Ornatus and Artesia.* London: Printed by Thomas Creede, 1599(?).

Fortunatus, C. Chirii. *Artis Rhetoricae Libri III.* In *Rhetores Latini Minores,* edited by Carl Halm, 81–134. Leipzig: Teubner, 1863.

Fraunce, Abraham. *The Arcadian Rhetoric.* 1588. Ed. R. C. Alston. English Linguistics 1500–1800, no. 176. Menston, Yorkshire: Scolar, 1969.

———. *The Lawiers Logike.* 1588. Ed. R. C. Alston. English Linguistics 1500–1800, no. 174. Menston, Yorkshire: Scolar, 1969.

Gascoigne, George. *Certayne Notes of Instruction.* 1575. In *Elizabethan Critical Essays,* vol. 1, edited by G. Gregory Smith, 46–57. London: Oxford University Press, 1937.

Gill, Alexander. *Logonomia Anglica.* 1619. Vol. 2. Trans. Bror Danielsson and Arvid Gabrielson. Stockholm Studies in English no. 27. Stockholm: Almqvist & Wiksell, 1972.

Grataroluś, Gulielmus. *The Castel of Memorie.* Englished by Willyam Fulwod. 1562. The English Experience no. 382. New York: Da Capo, 1971.

Guazzo, Stephano. *The Civile Conversation.* 1574. Trans. George Pettie and Bartholomew Young. 1581 and 1586. Rpt. 2 Vols. London: Constable and Co., 1925.

Harvey, Gabriel. *Gabriel Harvey's Ciceronianus.* Trans. Clarence A. Forbes. Studies in the Humanities no. 4. Lincoln: University of Nebraska Studies, 1945.

———. *Marginalia.* Ed. G. C. Moore Smith. Stratford-upon-Avon: Shakespeare Head, 1913.

———. *Rhetor, vel duorum dierum Oratio, De Natura, Arte, & Exercitatione Rhetorica.* London, 1577.

———. *The Works of Gabriel Harvey.* Vols. 1–3. Ed. Alexander B. Grosart. New York: AMS, 1966.

Hawes, Stephen. *The Pastime of Pleasure.* Ed. William Edward Mead. Early English Text Society. Original Series no. 173. London: Oxford University Press, 1928.

Hermogenes. *Invention and Method.* Trans. George A. Kennedy. Atlanta: Society of Biblical Literature, 2005.

———. *On Issues.* Trans. Malcolm Heath. Oxford: Clarendon, 1995.

———. *On Types of Style.* Trans. Cecil W. Wooten. Chapel Hill: University of North Carolina Press, 1987.

———. *Progymnasmata.* In *Progymnasmata: Greek Textbooks of Prose Composition and Rhetoric,* translated by George A. Kennedy, 73–88. Atlanta: Society of Biblical Literature, 2003.

Hobbes, Thomas. *Leviathan.* Ed. C. B. Macpherson. New York: Penguin Books, 1968.

Homer. *The Iliad.* Trans. Richmond Lattimore. Chicago: University of Chicago Press, 1951.

———. *The Odyssey of Homer.* Trans. Richmond Lattimore. New York: Harper & Row, 1967.

Hoole, Charles. *A New Discovery of the Old Art of Teaching Schoole.* 1660. Ed. R. C. Alston. English Linguistics 1500–1800, no. 133. Menston, Yorkshire: Scholar, 1969.

———. *The Latine Grammar.* 1651. Ed. R. C. Alston. English Linguistics 1500–1800, no. 131. Menston, Yorkshire: Scholar, 1969.

Hoskins, John. *Directions for Speech and Style.* 1599. Ed. Hoyt H. Hudson. Princeton Studies in English, no. 19. Princeton, N.J.: Princeton University Press, 1935.

Isocrates. *Isocrates.* Vols. 1–3. Trans. George Norlin and La Rue Van Hook. Loeb Classical Library. Cambridge, Mass.: Harvard University Press, 1929.

John of Salisbury. *The Metalogicon of John of Salisbury.* Trans. Daniel D. McGarry. Berkeley: University of California Press, 1955.

Jonson, Ben. "Dedicatory Epistle of *Volpone.*" 1607. In *Critical Essays of the Seventeenth-Century,* vol. 1, edited by J. E. Spingarn, 11–16. Oxford: Clarendon, 1908.

———. *Timber* or *Discoveries.* In *Ben Jonson,* vol. 8, edited by C. H. Herford Percy and Evelyn Simpson, 561–649. Oxford: Clarendon, 1974.

Keckermann, Bartholomeus. *Systema rhetoricae.* 1607. In *Operum onmium quae extant,* 1391–1581. Geneva: Apud Petrum Aubertum, 1614.

———. *Systematis Rhetorici Specialis.* 1607. In *Operum onmium quae extant,* 1581–1736. Geneva: Apud Petrum Aubertum, 1614.

Kempe, William. *The Education of Children in Learning.* 1588. In *Four Tudor Books on Education.* Ed. Robert D. Pepper, 181–240. Gainesville, Fla.: Scholars' Facsimiles & Reprints, 1966.

Lamy, Bernard. *The Art of Speaking.* 1675. 2nd ed. London: Printed for W. Taylor and H. Clements, 1708.

Lever, Ralph. *The Art of Reason, Rightly Termed Witcraft.* 1573. English Linguistics 1500–1800, no. 323. Menston, Yorkshire: Scolar, 1972.

Lily, William. *A Shorte Introduction of Grammar.* 1567. New York: Scholars' Facsimiles & Reprints, 1945.

Livy. *The History of Rome.* Books 1–5. Trans. Valerie M. Warrior. Indianapolis, Ind.: Hackett, 2006.

Longinus. *On the Sublime.* Trans. W. H. Fyfe. Revised by Donald Russell. In *Aristotle XXIII,* 145–307. Loeb Classical Library. Cambridge, Mass.: Harvard University Press, 1995.

Lyly, John. *Euphues: The Anatomy of Wit* and *Euphues and His England.* Ed. Leah Scragg. Manchester: Manchester University Press, 2003.

Mancinelli, Antonio. *Carmen de figuris.* 1489. In Joannes Sulpitius Verulanus, *Quinta recognitio atque additio ad grammaticen Sulpitianam,* images 129–42, 157–61. London: Wynandum de Worde, 1514.

MacIlmaine, Roland. *The Logike of the Moste Excellent Philosopher P. Ramus Martyr.* 1574. Ed. Catherine M. Dunn. The Renaissance Editions, no. 3. Northridge, Cal.: San Fernando Valley State College, 1969.

Melanchthon, Philip. *Elementorum rhetorices libri duo.* Paris: Apud Simone Colinaeum, 1532.

———. *Elementorum rhetorices libri duo.* Trans. Sister Mary Joan La Fontaine. In *A Critical Translation of Philip Melanchthon's "Elementorum Rhetorices Libri Duo."* PhD diss. University of Michigan, 1968.

———. *Institutiones Rhetoricae.* Paris: Apud Simonem Colinaeum, 1531.

———. "Reply to Pico." Trans. Quirinus Breen. *Christianity and Humanism: Studies in the History of Ideas,* 52–68. Grand Rapids, Mich.: Eerdmans, 1968.

———. *Tabulae de schematibus et tropis.* In Petri Mosellanus, *Tabulae de schematibus et tropis,* c.iiii.r–c.v.v. Paris: Ex officina Roberti Stephani, 1536.

———. "The Praise of Eloquence." In *Renaissance Debates on Rhetoric,* translated by Wayne A. Rebhorn, 97–110. Ithaca, N.Y.: Cornell University Press, 2000.

Milton, John. *Paradise Lost.* In *John Milton: Complete Poems and Major Prose,* edited by Merritt Y. Hughes, 207–469. Indianapolis, Ind.: Bobbs-Merrill, 1957.

Mirandola, Giovanni Pico della. "Letter to Ermolao Barbaro." In *Renaissance Debates on Rhetoric,* translated by Wayne A. Rebhorn, 57–67. Ithaca, N.Y.: Cornell University Press, 2000.

More, Sir Thomas. "Letter to Martin Dorp." 1515. In *Juan Luis Vives against the Pseudodialecticians,* translated by Rita Guerlac, 166–95. Dordrecht, Holland: Reidel, 1979.

Mosellanus, Petri. *Tabulae de schematibus et tropis Petri Mosellani.* Ed. Georgius Maior. Paris: Ex officina Roberti Stephani, 1536.

Muret, Marc Antoine. *Opuscula Varia.* In *Opera Omnia.* Vol. 1. Ed. Carolus Henricus Frotscher, 437–50. Leipzig: Serigiana Libraria, 1834 (rpt. Geneva: Slatkine, 1971).

Nashe, Thomas. "The Preface to Sidney's *Astrophel and Stella.*" 1591. In *Elizabethan Critical Essays,* vol. 2, edited by G. Gregory Smith, 223–28. London: Oxford University Press, 1937.

Ovid. *Heroides.* Trans. Harold Isbell. London: Penguin Books, 1990.

———. *Metamorphoses.* Trans. Mary M. Innes. London: Penguin Books, 1955.

Peacham, Henry. *The Garden of Eloquence.* 1577. Ed. R. C. Alston. English Linguistics 1500–1800, no. 267. Menston, Yorkshire: Scolar, 1971.

———. *The Garden of Eloquence.* 1593. Ed. William G. Crane. Gainesville, Fla.: Scholars' Facsimiles & Reprints, 1954.

Perkins, Williams. *The Art of Prophecying.* Trans. Thomas Tyre. London: Legatt, 1631.

Priestley, Joseph. *A Course of Lectures on Oratory and Criticism.* 1777. Ed. R. C. Alston. *English Linguistics 1500-1800,* no. 126. Menston, Yorkshire: Scolar, 1968.

Priscian. *De figuris numerorum quos antiquissimi habent codices.* In *Grammatici Latini,* vol. 3, edited by Heinrich Keil, 406–40. Hildesheim: Olms, 1961.

Puttenham, George. *The Arte of English Poesie.* 1589. Kent English Reprints. Kent, Ohio: Kent State University Press, 1970.

Quintilian, Marcus Fabius. *Institutio Oratoria.* Vols. 1–4. Trans. H. E. Butler. Loeb Classical Library. Cambridge, Mass.: Harvard University Press, 1920.

Rainolde, Richard. *The Foundacion of Rhetorike.* 1593. Ed. Francis R. Johnson. The English Experience, no. 91. Amsterdam: Theatrum Orbis Terrarum, 1969.

Raleigh, Sir Walter. *The History of the World.* 2nd Ed. London: Stansby, 1617.

Ramus, Peter. *Arguments in Rhetoric against Quintilian.* 1549. Trans. Carole Newlands. Dekalb: Northern Illinois University Press, 1986.

———. *Latin Grammar.* 1585. Ed. R. C. Alston. English Linguistics 1500–1800, no. 305. Menston, Yorkshire: Scolar, 1971.

———. *Peter Ramus's Attack on Cicero: Text and Translation of Ramus's "Brutinae Quaestiones."* Trans. Carole Newlands. Ed. James J. Murphy. Davis, Cal.: Hermagoras, 1992.

Robertellus, Franciscus. *De artificio dicendi.* Bonn: 1567.

Rufinianus, Julius. *De figuris sententiarum et elocutionis libri I.* In *Rhetores Latini Minores,* edited by Carl Halm, 38–62. Leipzig: Teubner, 1863.

Rutilius Lupus, Publius. *De figuris sententiarum et elocutionis.* Ed. Edward Brooks Jr. Mnemosyne Bibliotheca Classica Batava. Leiden: Brill, 1970.

Scaliger, Julius Caesar. *Poetices libri septem.* 2nd ed. [Geneva?]: Apud Petrum Santandreanum, 1581.

Shaw, Samuel. *Words Made Visible: Or Grammar and Rhetorick Accommodated to the Lives and Manners of Men.* 1679. Ed. R. C. Alston. English Linguistics 1500–1800, no. 317. Menston, Yorkshire: Scolar, 1972.

Shakespeare, William. *Sonnets* and *Titus Andronicus.* In *The Riverside Shakespeare.* 2nd ed. Boston: Houghton, Mifflin, 1997. 1019–54 and 1745–80.

Sherry, Richard. A *Treatise of Schemes and Tropes.* 1550. Ed. Herbert W. Hildebrandt. Gainesville, Fla.: Scholars' Facsimiles & Reprints, 1961.

———. A *Treatise of the Figures of Grammer and Rhetorike.* London: Tottel, 1555.

Sidney, Sir Philip. *The Countesse of Pembrokes Arcadia.* In *The Complete Works of Sir Philip Sidney.* Vols. 1–2. Ed. Albert Feuillerat. Cambridge: Cambridge University Press, 1939.

———. *The Old Arcadia.* Ed. Katherine Duncan-Jones. Oxford: Oxford University Press, 1985.

Smith, John. *Mystery of Rhetoric Unveiled.* 1657. Ed. R. C. Alston. English Linguistics 1500–1800, no. 205. Menston, Yorkshire: Scolar, 1969.

Soarez, Cyprian, SJ. *De Artes Rhetorica.* 1568. In "The *De Artes Rhetorica* (1568) by Cyprian Soarez, S.J.: A Translation with Introduction and Notes." Trans. Lawrence J. Flynn. PhD diss. University of Florida, 1955.

Sprat, Thomas. *Account of the Life and Writings of Abraham Cowley.* 1668. In *Critical Essays of the Seventeenth Century,* vol. 2, edited by J. E. Spingarn, 119–46. Oxford: Clarendon, 1908.

———. *History of the Royal Society.* Eds. Jackson I. Cope and Harold Whitmore Jones. St. Louis: Washington University Studies, 1958.

Sturmius, Joannes. *De universa ratione elocutionis rhetoricae libri tres.* Strasbourg: Jobin, 1576.

———. "The Lauingen School." 1565. In *Johann Sturm on Education: The Reformation and Humanist Learning,* translated by Lewis W. Spitz and Barbara Sher Tinsley, 201–54. St. Louis: Concordia, 1995.

———. *Nobilitatas literata.* 1549. Or *Liberally Educated Nobility.* In *Johann Sturm on Education: The Reformation and Humanist Learning,* translated by Lewis W. Spitz and Barbara Sher Tinsley, 133–73. St. Louis: Concordia, 1995.

———. *Nobilitatas literata.* 1549. Or *A Ritch Storehouse or Treasurie for Nobilitye and Gentlemen.* Trans. T.B. (Thomas Browne?). London: Denham, 1570.

———. "On the Lost Art of Speaking." 1538. In *Johann Sturm on Education: The Reformation and Humanist Learning,* translated by Lewis W. Spitz and Barbara Sher Tinsley, 121–32. St. Louis: Concordia, 1995.

Susenbrotus, Joannes. *Epitome troporum ac schematum et Grammaticorum & Rhetorum, ad Authores tum profanos tum sacros intelligendos non minus utilis quam necessaria.* London: Dewes, 1562.

Swift, Jonathan. *Gulliver's Travels.* Ed. Louis A. Landa. Riverside Editions. Boston: Houghton Mifflin, 1960.

Talaeus, Audomarus. *Rhetorica.* Paris: 1548.

Terence. *The Comedies of Terence.* Trans. Frederick W. Clayton. Exeter: University of Exeter Press, 2006.

———. *The Complete Comedies of Terence.* Trans. Palmer Bovie, Constance Carrier, and Douglass Parker. New Brunswick, N.J.: Rutgers University Press, 1974.

Theocritus. *The Poems of Theocritus.* Trans. Anna Rist. Chapel Hill: University of North Carolina Press, 1978.

Trapezuntius, Georgius. "An Oration in Praise of Eloquence." In *Renaissance Debates on Rhetoric,* translated by Wayne A. Rebhorn, 31–34. Ithaca, N.Y.: Cornell University Press, 2000.

———. *Rhetoricorum libri quinque.* In *Continentur Hoc Volumine.* Venice: Aldine Press Quarto, 1523.

———. *Rhetoricorum libri quinque.* Ed. Luc Deitz. Hildesheim: Olms, 2006.

Veltkirchius, M. (Joannes Velcurio or John Doelsch). *D. Erasmi Roterodami De Duplici Copia Verborum ac Rerum Commentarii Duo.* London: Apud Henricum Middeltonum, 1573.

Victoris, Sulpitii. *Institutiones Oratoriae.* In *Rhetores Latini Minores,* edited by Carl Halm, 313–52. Leipzig: Teubner, 1863.

———. *Oratoriarum Institutionu praecepta.* In *Veterum aliquot de arte rhetorica traditiones, de tropis in primis & schematis uerborum & sententiaru[m]* . . . Basilea: Joannis Frobenii, 1521.

Virgil. *Vergil's Aeneid.* Trans. L. R. Lind. Bloomington: Indiana University Press, 1962.

———. *The Georgics and Eclogues of Virgil.* Trans. Theodore Chickering Williams. Cambridge, Mass.: Harvard University Press, 1915.

Vives, Juan Luis. *Adversus pseudodialecticos* and "On Dialectic" from *The Causes of the Corruptions of the Arts.* In *Juan Luis Vives against the Pseudodialecticians,* translated by Rita Guerlac, 46–153. Dordrecht: Reidel, 1979.

——— *Rhetoricae, sive de ratione dicendi.* 1533. In "*De Ratione Dicendi:*" *A Treatise on Rhetoric.* Trans. James Francis Cooney. PhD diss. Ohio State University, 1966.

———. *De tradendis disciplinis.* In *On Education.* 1531. Trans. Foster Watson. Cambridge: Cambridge University Press, 1913.

Vossius, Gerhard Johannes. *Commentariorum rhetoricorum, sive oratorium institutionum libri sex.* London: Ioannis Maire, 1630 (rpt. Kronberg Ts.: Scriptor, 1974).

———. *Rhetorices contractae, sive partitionum oratoriarum libri v.* Oxford: Pro Guilel. Turner, & Th. Higgins, 1631.

———. *Rhetorices contractae, sive partitionum oratoriarum libri v.* Amsterdam: Hollandia & Westfrisiae DD. Ordinum, 1711.

Walker, Obadiah. *Some Instructions Concerning the Art of Oratory.* London: Royston, 1659.

Wilson, Thomas. *The Art of Rhetoric.* 1560. Ed. Peter E. Medine. University Park: Pennsylvania State University Press, 1994.

———. *The Rule of Reason.* 1551. Amsterdam: Theatrum Orbis Terrarum, 1970.

Wright, Thomas. *The Passions of the Minde in Generall.* 1604. Ed. Thomas O. Sloane. Urbana: University of Illinois Press, 1971.

Xenophon. *Xenophon's Works.* Trans. Ashley Cooper et al. Philadelphia: Wardle, 1845.

Secondary Sources

Abbott, Don Paul. "Rhetoric and Writing in the Renaissance." In *A Short History of Writing Instruction from Ancient Greece to Modern America,* 2nd ed., edited by James J. Murphy, 145–72. Davis, Cal.: Hermagoras, 2001.

Abrams, M. H. *The Mirror and the Lamp.* London: Oxford University Press, 1953.

Adamson, Sylvia, Gavin Alexander, and Katrin Ettenhuber, eds. *Renaissance Figures of Speech.* Cambridge: Cambridge University Press, 2007.

Adolph, Robert. *The Rise of Modern Prose Style.* Cambridge, Mass.: MIT Press, 1968.

Agnew, Lois. "Rhetorical Style and the Formation of Character: Ciceronian Ethos in Thomas Wilson's *Arte of Rhetorique.*" *Rhetoric Review* 17.1 (1998): 93–106.

Armstrong, Edward. *A Ciceronian Sunburn: A Tudor Dialogue on Humanistic Rhetoric and Civic Poetics.* Columbia: University of South Carolina Press, 2006.

Auerbach, Erich. "Figura." In *Scenes from the Drama of European Literature,* 11–76. Gloucester, Mass.: Smith, 1973.

Bakhtin, M. M. "The Problem of Speech Genres." In *Speech Genres and Other Late Essays.* Trans. Vern W. McGee. Ed. Caryl Emerson and Michael Holquist, 60–102. Austin: University of Texas Press, 1986.

Baldwin, T. W. *William Shakspere's Small Latine and Lesse Greeke.* Vols. 1 and 2. Urbana: University of Illinois Press, 1944.

Barthes, Roland. "Style and Its Image." In *Literary Style: A Symposium,* edited by Seymour Chatman, 3–10. Oxford: Oxford University Press, 1971.

Barnett, Mary Jane. "Erasmus and the Hermeneutics of Linguistic Praxis." *Renaissance Quarterly* 49.3 (1996): 542–72.

Baumlin, James S. "Generic Contexts of Elizabethan Satire: Rhetoric, Poetic Theory, and Imitation." In *Renaissance Genres,* edited by Barbara Kiefer Lewalski, 444–67. Harvard English Studies no. 14. Cambridge, Mass.: Harvard University Press, 1986.

Baumlin, James S., and Tita French Baumlin, eds. *Ethos: New Essays in Rhetorical and Critical Theory.* Dallas: Southern Methodist University Press, 1994.

Baxandall, Michael. *Giotto and the Orators.* Oxford: Clarendon, 1971.

Beardsley, Monroe C. *Aesthetics: Problems in the Philosophy of Criticism.* New York: Harcourt, Brace, 1958.

Bennett, James Richard. "Style." In *The New Princeton Encyclopedia of Poetry and Poetics,* edited by Alex Preminger and T. V. F. Brogan, 1225–27. Princeton, N.J.: Princeton University Press, 1993.

Benoit, William. "Isocrates and Aristotle on Rhetoric." *Rhetoric Society Quarterly* 20.3 (1990): 251–59.

Bishop, Wendy, ed. *Elements of Alternate Style: Essays on Writing and Revision.* Portsmouth, N.H.: Boynton/Cook, 1997.

Bizzell, Patricia, and Bruce Herzberg, eds. *The Rhetorical Tradition: Readings from Classical Times to the Present.* 2nd ed. Boston: Bedford/St. Martins, 2001.

Black, Max. *Models and Metaphors.* Ithaca, N.Y.: Cornell University Press, 1962.

Bolgar, R. R. *The Classical Heritage and Its Beneficiaries: From the Carolingian Age to the End of the Renaissance.* 1954. New York: Harper & Row, 1964.

———. "Humanism as a Value System, with Reference to Budé and Vivès." In *Humanism in France at the End of the Middle Ages and in the Early Renaissance,* edited by Anthony H. T. Levi, 199–215. Manchester: Manchester University Press, 1970.

Bonner, Stanley F. *Education in Ancient Rome.* Berkeley: University of California Press, 1977.

———. *Roman Declamation.* Liverpool: Liverpool University Press, 1969.

Booth, Wayne. *The Company We Keep: An Ethics of Fiction.* Berkeley: University of California Press, 1988.

———. *The Rhetoric of Fiction.* Chicago: University of Chicago Press, 1961.

Boswell, Grant M. "The Rhetoric of Pedagogy: Changing Assumptions in Seventeenth-Century English Rhetorical Education." *Rhetoric Society Quarterly* 16.3 (1986): 109–23.

Bouwsma, William J. "Anxiety and the Formation of Early Modern Culture." In *After the Reformation: Essays in Honor of J. H. Hexter,* edited by Barbara C. Malament, 215–46. Philadelphia: University of Pennsylvania Press, 1980.

———. *The Culture of Renaissance Humanism.* Washington, D.C.: American Historical Association, 1973.

Boyle, Marjorie O'Rourke. *Erasmus on Language and Method in Theology.* Toronto: University of Toronto Press, 1977.

Breen, Quirinus. *Christianity and Humanism: Studies in the History of Ideas.* Grand Rapids, Mich.: Eerdmans, 1968.

Brummett, Barry. *A Rhetoric of Style.* Carbondale: Southern Illinois University Press, 2008.

Bruns, Gerald L. "Rhetoric, Grammar, and the Conception of Language as a Substantial Medium." *College English* 31.3 (1969): 241–62.

Bryant, Donald C. "Of Style: Buffon and Rhetorical Criticism." In *Essays on Rhetorical Criticism,* edited by Thomas Nilsen, 50–63. New York: Random House, 1968.

Bullinger, E. W. *Figures of Speech Used in the Bible.* 1898. Grand Rapids, Mich.: Baker Book House, 1968.

Burke, Kenneth. *Counter-Statement.* Berkeley: University of California Press, 1931.

———. *A Grammar of Motives.* 1945. Berkeley: University of California Press, 1969.

———. *Language as Symbolic Action.* Berkeley: University of California Press, 1966.

———. *Permanence and Change: An Anatomy of Purpose.* 3rd ed. Berkeley: University of California Press, 1984.

———. *The Philosophy of Literary Form: Studies in Symbolic Action.* 2nd ed. Baton Rouge: Louisiana State University Press, 1967.

———. *A Rhetoric of Motives.* Berkeley: University of California Press, 1950.

Butler, Paul. *Out of Style.* Logan: Utah State University Press, 2008.

———. "Style and the Public Intellectual: Rethinking Composition in the Public Sphere." In *Style in Rhetoric and Composition: A Critical Sourcebook,* edited by Paul Butler, 389–409. Boston: Bedford/St. Martin's, 2010.

Butler, Paul, ed. *Style in Rhetoric and Composition: A Critical Sourcebook.* Boston: Bedford/St. Martin's, 2010.

Cairns, Francis. "The *Poetices libri septem:* An Unexplored Source." *Res Publica Litterarum.* 9 (1986): 49–57.

Camporeale, Salvatore I. *Lorenzo Valla: Umanesimo e Teologia.* Florence: Istituto Nazionale Di Studi Sul Rinascimento, 1972.

Cape, Robert W., Jr. "Cicero and the Development of Prudential Practice at Rome." In *Prudence: Classical Virtue, Postmodern Practice,* edited by Robert Hariman, 35–65. University Park: Pennsylvania State University Press, 2003.

Carroll, William C. *The Great Feast of Language in "Love's Labour's Lost."* Princeton, N.J.: Princeton University Press, 1976.

Cassirer, Ernst. *The Philosophy of Symbolic Forms.* Vol. 1. Trans. Ralph Manheim. New Haven, Conn.: Yale University Press, 1953.

Cautrell, Dion. "Rhetor-Fitting: Defining Ethics through Style." In *Refiguring Prose Style: Possibilities for Writing Pedagogy,* edited by T. R. Johnson and Tom Pace, 228–40. Logan: Utah State University Press, 2005.

Cave, Terence. *The Cornucopian Text: Problems of Writing in the French Renaissance.* Oxford: Clarendon, 1979.

Charlton, Kenneth. *Education in Renaissance England.* London: Routledge & Kegan Paul, 1965.

Chatman, Seymour, ed. *Literary Style: A Symposium.* Oxford: Oxford University Press, 1971.

Christiansen, Nancy L. "The Double Master Frame and Other Lessons from Classical Education." In *Intertexts: Reading Pedagogy in College Writing Classrooms,* edited by Marguerite Helmers, 71–100. Mahwah, N.J.: Erlbaum, 2003.

———. "Rhetoric as Character-Fashioning: The Implications of Delivery's 'Places' in the British Renaissance *Paideia.*" *Rhetorica* 15.3 (1997): 297–334.

———. "Synecdoche, Tropic Violence, and Shakespeare's *Imitatio* in *Titus Andronicus.*" *Style* 34.3 (2000): 350–79.

Christensen, Francis. "A Generative Rhetoric of the Sentence." *College Composition and Communication* 14 (1963): 155–67.

Christensen, Francis, and Bonniejean Christensen. *Notes toward a New Rhetoric: Nine Essays for Teachers.* 2nd ed. New York: Harper & Row, 1978.

Clark, Donald Lemen. *John Milton at St. Paul's School.* New York: Columbia University Press, 1948.

———. *Rhetoric in Greco-Roman Education.* New York: Columbia University Press, 1957.

———. *Rhetoric and Poetry in the Renaissance.* 1922. New York: Russell & Russell, 1963.

Cmiel, Kenneth. *Democratic Eloquence: The Fight over Popular Speech in Nineteenth-Century America.* New York: Morrow, 1990.

Coe, Richard. "An Apology for Form; or, Who Took the Form out of the Process?" *College English* 49.1 (1987): 13–28.

Colson, F. H. "Knowledge and Use of Quintilian after 1416." In *M. Fabii Quintiliani institutionis oratoriae, liber 1,* lxiv–lxxxix. Cambridge: Cambridge University Press, 1924.

Conley, Thomas M. "Byzantine Teaching on Figures and Tropes." *Rhetorica* 4.4 (1986): 335–74.

———. "The Enthymeme in Perspective." *Quarterly Journal of Speech* 70 (1984): 168–87.

———. *Rhetoric in the European Tradition.* New York: Longman, 1990.

Connors, Robert J. *Composition–Rhetoric: Backgrounds, Theory and Pedagogy.* Pittsburgh: University of Pittsburgh Press, 1997.

———. "The Erasure of the Sentence." In *Style in Rhetoric and Composition,* edited by Paul Butler, 82–107. Boston: Bedford/St. Martin's, 2010.

Cooper, Lane, ed. *Theories of Style.* New York: Macmillan, 1912.

Corbett, Edward P. J. "Approaches to the Study of Style." In *Teaching Composition: Ten Bibliographic Essays,* edited by Gary Tate, 73–109. Fort Worth: Texas Christian University Press, 1976.

———. *Classical Rhetoric for the Modern Student.* 3rd ed. Oxford: Oxford University Press, 1990.

———. "Teaching Style." In *Style in Rhetoric and Composition: A Critical Sourcebook,* edited by Paul Butler, 209–18. Boston: Bedford/St. Martin's, 2010.

Craig, Hardin. *The Enchanted Glass: The Elizabethan Mind in Literature.* New York: Oxford University Press, 1936.

Crane, William G. *Wit and Rhetoric in the Renaissance.* New York: Columbia University Press, 1937.

Croce, Benedetto. *Benedetto Croce: Essays on Literature and Literary Criticism.* Trans. M. E. Moss. Albany: State University of New York Press, 1990.

Croll, Morris W. *Style, Rhetoric, and Rhythm.* Ed. J. Max Patrick et al. Princeton, N.J.: Princeton University Press, 1966.

Crowley, Sharon, and Debra Hawhee. *Ancient Rhetorics for Contemporary Students.* 3rd ed. New York: Pearson, 2004.

Curtius, Ernst Robert. *European Literature and the Latin Middle Ages.* Trans. Willard R. Trask. Princeton, N.J.: Princeton University Press, 1953.

D'Angelo, Frank J. "Style as Structure." *Style* 8 (1974): 322–64.

Davidson, Donald. *Twenty Lessons in Reading and Writing Prose.* New York: Scribner, 1955.

Deitz, Luc. ed. Iulius Caesar Scaliger. *Poetices libri septem: Sieben Bücher über die Dichtkunst.* Vol. 2. Stuttgart: Fromman-Holzboog, 1994.

Depew, David. "The Inscription of Isocrates into Aristotle's Practical Philosophy." In *Isocrates and Civic Education,* edited by Takis Poulakos and David Depew, 157–85. Austin: University of Texas Press, 2004.

DiLorenzo, Raymond. "The Critique of Socrates in Cicero's *De Oratore: Ornatus* and the Nature of Wisdom." *Philosophy and Rhetoric* 11.4 (1978): 247–61.

Donawerth, Jane. *Shakespeare and the Sixteenth-Century Study of Language.* Urbana: University of Illinois Press, 1984.

Doran, Madeleine. *Endeavors of Art: A Study of Form in Elizabethan Drama.* Madison: University of Wisconsin Press, 1954.

Douglas, A. E. "A Ciceronian Contribution to Rhetorical Theory." *Eranos* 55 (1957): 18–26.

———. "The Intellectual Background of Cicero's *Rhetorica*: A Study in Method." In *Aufstieg und Niedergang der romischen Welt: Geschichte und Kultur Roms im Spiegel der neueren Forschung* 3.1 (1973): 95–138.

Dubrow, Heather. *Captive Victors: Shakespeare's Narrative Poems and Sonnets.* Ithaca, N.Y.: Cornell University Press, 1987.

Dyck, Joachim. "The First German Treatise on Homiletics: Erasmus Sarcer's Pastorale and Classical Rhetoric." In *Renaissance Eloquence: Studies in the Theory and Practice of Renaissance Rhetoric,* edited by James J. Murphy, 221–37. Berkeley: University of California Press, 1983.

Eden, Kathy. "Hermeneutics and the Ancient Rhetorical Tradition." *Rhetorica* 5.1 (1987): 59–86.

———. *Hermeneutics and the Rhetorical Tradition.* New Haven, Conn.: Yale University Press, 1997.

Elbow, Peter. *Writing with Power: Techniques for Mastering the Writing Process.* New York: Oxford University Press, 1981.

Else, Gerald F. *Aristotle's Poetics: The Argument.* Cambridge, Mass.: Harvard University Press, 1957.

Elton, Geoffrey. "Humanism in England." In *The Impact of Humanism on Western Europe,* edited by Anthony Goodman and Angus MacKay, 259–78. London: Longman, 1990.

Enkvist, Nils Erik. "On Defining Style." In *Contemporary Essays on Style,* edited by Glen A. Love and Michael Payne, 120–32. Glenview, Ill.: Scott, Foresman, 1969.

———. "On the Place of Style in Some Liniguistic Theories." In *Literary Style: A Symposium,* edited by Seymour Chatman, 47–61. Oxford: Oxford University Press, 1971.

Enos, Richard Leo. *Greek Rhetoric before Aristotle.* Prospect Heights, Ill.: Waveland, 1993.

Enos, Richard Leo, and Karen Rossi Schnakenberg. "Cicero Latinizes Hellenic *Ethos.*" In *Ethos: New Essays in Rhetorical and Critical Theory,* edited by James S. Baumlin and Tita French Baumlin, 191–209. Dallas: Southern Methodist University Press, 1994.

Enos, Theresa. *Encyclopedia of Rhetoric and Composition.* New York: Garland, 1996.

Espy, Willard R. *The Garden of Eloquence: A Rhetorical Bestiary.* New York: Dutton, 1983.

Ettenhuber, Katrin. "Hyperbole: exceeding similitude." In *Renaissance Figures of Speech.* Eds. Sylvia Adamson, Gavin Alexander, and Katrin Ettenhuber, 197–213. Cambridge: Cambridge University Press, 2007.

Fahnestock, Jeanne. "Aristotle and Theories of Figuration." In *Rereading Aristotle's Rhetoric,* edited by Alan G. Gross and Arthur E. Walzer, 166–84. Carbondale: Southern Illinois University Press, 2000.

———. *Rhetorical Figures in Science.* New York: Oxford University Press, 1999.

Fantham, Elaine. "Ciceronian *Conciliare* and Aristotelian *Ethos*." *Phoenix* 27 (1973): 262–75.

Fauconnier, Gilles. *Mental Spaces: Aspects of Meaning Constructing in Natural Language*. Cambridge: Cambridge University Press, 1994.

Fauconnier, Gilles, and Mark Turner. *The Way We Think*. New York: Basic Books, 2002.

Fillmore, Charles J. "Frame Semantics." In *Linguistics in the Morning Calm*, 111–37. Seoul: Hanshin, 1982.

Fish, Stanley. *Doing What Comes Naturally*. Durham: Duke University Press, 1989.

———. *Is There a Text in This Class?* Cambridge, Mass.: Harvard University Press, 1980.

Fisher, Walter R. *Human Communication as Narration*. Columbia: University of South Carolina Press, 1989.

Flannery, Kathryn T. *The Emperor's New Clothes: Literature, Literacy, and the Ideology of Style*. Pittsburgh: University of Pittsburgh Press, 1995.

Fletcher, Harris F. *The Intellectual Development of John Milton*. Urbana: University of Illinois Press, 1956.

Fontanier, Pierre. *Les Figures du Discours*. Paris: Flammarion, 1977.

Fortenbaugh, William W. *Aristotle on Emotion*. New York: Harper & Row, 1975.

———. "Cicero's Knowledge of the Rhetorical Treatises of Aristotle and Theophrastus." In *Cicero's Knowledge of the Peripatos*, edited by William W. Fortenbaugh and Peter Steinmetz, 39–60. New Brunswick, N.J.: Transaction, 1989.

———. "[Review of] *Trials of Character: The Eloquence of Ciceronian Ethos*, James M. May." *Quarterly Journal of Speech* 95 (1989): 505–7.

Freedman, Joseph S. "Cicero in Sixteenth- and Seventeenth-Century Rhetoric Instruction." *Rhetorica* 4.3 (1986): 227–54.

Freeman, Donald C. "'Catch[ing] the Nearest Way': Macbeth and Cognitive Metaphor." *Journal of Pragmatics* 24 (1995): 689–708.

Freeman, Donald C., ed. *Linguistics and Literary Style*. New York: Holt, Rinehart & Winston, 1970.

Frentz, Thomas S., and Thomas B. Farrell. "Language-Action: A Paradigm for Communication." *Quarterly Journal of Speech* 62.4 (1976): 333–49.

Fulkerson, Richard P. "The Public Letter as a Rhetorical Form: Structure, Logic, and Style in King's 'Letter from Birmingham Jail.'" *Quarterly Journal of Speech* 65 (1979): 121–36.

Gage, John T. "Philosophies of Style and Their Implications for Composition." *College English* 41.6 (1980): 615–22.

Gagné, Ellen D. *The Cognitive Psychology of School Learning*. Boston: Little, Brown, 1985.

Gaines, Robert N. "Isocrates, Ep. 6.8." *Hermes* 118.2 (1990): 165–70.

Galyon, Linda. "Puttenham's *Enargeia* and *Energeia:* New Twists for Old Terms." *Philological Quarterly* 60 (1981): 29–40.

Garver, Eugene. *Aristotle's Rhetoric: An Art of Character*. Chicago: University of Chicago Press, 1994.

———. "Philosophy, Rhetoric, and Civic Education in Aristotle and Isocrates." In *Isocrates and Civic Education*, edited by Takis Poulakos and David Depew, 186–213. Austin: University of Texas Press, 2004.

Gibbs, Raymond W., Jr. *The Poetics of Mind*. Cambridge: Cambridge University Press, 1994.

Gibson, Walker. *Persona: A Style Study for Readers and Writers*. New York: Random House, 1969.

———. *Tough, Sweet, and Stuffy*. Bloomington: Indiana University Press, 1966.

Grafton, Anthony, and Lisa Jardine. *From Humanism to the Humanities: Education and the Liberal Arts in Fifteenth-and Sixteenth-Century Europe*. Cambridge, Mass.: Harvard University Press, 1986.

Graham, Robert J. "Composing Ourselves in Style: The Aesthetics of Literacy in 'The Courtier.'" *Journal of Aesthetic Education* 24.3 (1990): 45–56.

Grassi, Ernesto. *Rhetoric as Philosophy: The Humanist Tradition.* University Park: Pennsylvania State University Press, 1980.

Gray, Bennison. *Style: The Problem and Its Solution.* The Hague: Mouton, 1969.

Gray, Hanna H. "Renaissance Humanism: The Pursuit of Eloquence." *Journal of the History of Ideas* 24 (1963): 497–514.

Green, Lawrence D. "Aristotelian *Lexis* and Renaissance *Elocutio.*" In *Rereading Aristotle's Rhetoric,* edited by Alan G. Gross and Arthur E. Walzer, 149–65. Carbondale: Southern Illinois University Press, 2000.

———. "*Grammatica Movet:* Renaissance Grammar Books and *Elocutio.*" In *Rhetorica Movet: Studies in Historical and Modern Rhetoric in Honour of Heinrich F. Plett,* edited by Peter L. Oesterreich and Thomas O. Sloane, 73–115. Leiden: Brill, 1999.

Green, Lawrence, D., trans. *John Rainolds's Oxford Lectures on Aristotle's "Rhetoric."* Newark: University of Delaware Press, 1986.

Green, Lawrence, D., and James J. Murphy. *Renaissance Rhetoric: Short Title-Catalogue 1460–1700.* 2nd ed. Aldershot, England: Ashgate, 2006.

Greenblatt, Stephen. *Renaissance Self-Fashioning: From More to Shakespeare.* Chicago: University of Chicago Press, 1980.

Greenblatt, Stephen, ed. *The Norton Anthology of English Literature.* 8th ed. New York: Norton, 2006.

Greene, Thomas M. *The Light in Troy: Imitation and Discovery in Renaissance Poetry.* New Haven, Conn.: Yale University Press, 1982.

———. "Roger Ascham: The Perfect End of Shooting." *ELH* 36.4 (1969): 609–25.

Gross, Alan G. "What Aristotle Meant by Rhetoric." In *Rereading Aristotle's Rhetoric,* edited by Alan G. Gross and Arthur E. Walzer, 24–37. Carbondale: Southern Illinois University Press, 2000.

Gross, Alan G., and Arthur E. Walzer. *Rereading Aristotle's Rhetoric.* Carbondale: Southern Illinois University Press, 2000.

Grube, G. M. A. "Educational, Rhetorical, and Literary Theory in Cicero." *Phoenix* 16.4 (1962): 234–57.

———. *The Greek and Roman Critics.* London: Methuen, 1965.

Guerlac, Rita. *Juan Luis Vives against the Pseudodialecticians.* Dordrecht, Holland: Reidel, 1979.

Halliday, M. A. K. "Linguistic Function and Literary Style: An Inquiry into the Language of William Golding's *The Inheritors.*" In *Literary Style: A Symposium,* edited by Seymour Chatman, 330–65. Oxford: Oxford University Press, 1971.

Halloran, S. Michael, and Merrill D. Whitburn. "Ciceronian Rhetoric and the Rise of Science: The Plain Style Reconsidered." In *The Rhetorical Tradition and Modern Writing,* edited by James J. Murphy, 58–72. New York: Modern Language Association of America, 1982.

Halm, Carl, ed. *Rhetores Latini Minores.* Leipzig: Teubner, 1863.

Halpern, Richard. *The Poetics of Primitive Accumulation: English Renaissance Culture and the Genealogy of Capital.* Ithaca, N.Y.: Cornell University Press, 1991.

Hardison, O. B., Jr. "The orator and the poet: the dilemma of humanist literature." *Journal of Medieval and Renaissance Studies* 1 (1971): 33–44.

Hariman, Robert, ed. *Prudence: Classical Virtue, Postmodern Practice.* University Park: Pennsylvania State University Press, 2003.

Harmon, William, and Hugh Holman. *A Handbook to Literature.* 10th ed. Upper Saddle River, N.J.: Pearson/Prentice Hall, 2006.

Harrison, Frederic. *Tennyson, Ruskin, Mill and Other Literary Estimates.* New York: Macmillan, 1900.

Hart, Roderick P., and Suzanne Daughton. *Modern Rhetorical Criticism.* 3rd ed. Boston: Pearson, 2005.

Haskins, Ekaterina V. *Logos and Power in Isocrates and Aristotle.* Columbia: University of South Carolina Press, 2004.

———. "*Mimesis* between Poetics and Rhetoric: Performance Culture and Civic Education in Plato, Isocrates, and Aristotle." *Rhetoric Society Quarterly* 30.3 (2000): 7–33.

Havelock, Eric A. *Preface to Plato.* Cambridge, Mass.: Belknap Press of Harvard University Press, 1963.

Hawkes, Terence. *Metaphor.* The Critical Idiom, no. 25. London: Methuen, 1972.

Hazard, Mary E. "An Essay to Amplify 'Ornament': Some Renaissance Theory and Practice." *Studies in English Literature* 16 (1976): 15–32.

Henderson, Judith Rice. "Must a Good Orator Be a Good Man? Ramus in the Ciceronian Controversy." In *Rhetorica Movet: Studies in Historical and Modern Rhetoric in Honour of Heinrich F. Plett,* edited by Peter L. Oesterreich and Thomas O. Sloane, 43–56. Leiden: Brill, 1999.

Hendrickson, G. L. "The Origin and Meaning of the Ancient Characters of Style." *American Journal of Philology* 26 (1905): 249–90.

Herrick, James. A. *The History and Theory of Rhetoric.* 3rd ed. Boston: Allyn & Bacon, 2005.

Hildebrandt, Herbert W. "Amplification in a Rhetoric on Style." *Southern Speech Communication Journal* 30 (1965): 294–307.

Hoffmann, Manfred. *Rhetoric and Theology: The Hermeneutic of Erasmus.* Toronto: University of Toronto Press, 1994.

Houston, John Porter. *The Rhetoric of Poetry in the Renaissance and Seventeenth Century.* Baton Rouge: Louisiana State University Press, 1983.

Howell, A. C. "Res et Verba: Words and Things." *ELH* 13.2 (1946): 131–42.

Howell, Wilbur Samuel. *Logic and Rhetoric in England, 1500–1700.* New York: Russell & Russell, 1956.

———. *Poetics, Rhetoric, and Logic: Studies in the Basic Disciplines of Criticism.* Ithaca, N.Y.: Cornell University Press, 1975.

Hubbell, Harry Mortimor. *The Influence of Isocrates on Cicero, Dionysius and Aristides.* New Haven, Conn.: Yale University Press, 1914.

Ijsseling, Samuel. *Rhetoric and Philosophy in Conflict.* The Hague: Nijhoff, 1976.

Jameson, Fredric. *The Prison-House of Language.* Princeton, N.J.: Princeton University Press, 1972.

Jardine, Lisa. "Humanist Logic." In *The Cambridge History of Renaissance Philosophy,* edited by Charles B. Schmitt and Quentin Skinner, 173–98. Cambridge: Cambridge University Press, 1988.

Jebb, R. C. *The Attic Orators.* Vols. 1–2. New York: Russell & Russell, 1962.

Jensen, Kristian. *Rhetorical Philosophy and Philosophical Grammar: Julius Caesar Scaliger's Theory of Language.* Munich: Fink, 1990.

Johnson, Mark, ed. *Philosophical Perspectives on Metaphor.* Minneapolis: University of Minnesota Press, 1981.

Johnson, T. R. *A Rhetoric of Pleasure: Prose Style and Today's Composition Classroom.* Portsmouth, N.H.: Boynton/Cook, 2003.

Johnson, T. R., and Tom Pace, eds. *Refiguring Prose Style: Possibilities for Writing Pedagogy.* Logan: Utah State University Press, 2005.

Jones, Howard. *Master Tully: Cicero in Tudor England.* Nieuwkoop, the Netherlands: De Graaf, 1998.

Jones, Richard Foster. *The Seventeenth Century: From Bacon to Pope.* Stanford, Cal.: Stanford University Press, 1951.

Joseph, Sister Miriam. *Shakespeare's Use of the Arts of Language.* New York: Columbia University Press, 1947.

Kahn, Victoria. *Machiavellian Rhetoric: From the Counter-Reformation to Milton.* Princeton, N.J.: Princeton University Press, 1994.

———. *Rhetoric, Prudence, and Skepticism in the Renaissance.* Ithaca, N.Y.: Cornell University Press, 1985.

Kallendorf, Craig, and Carol Kallendorf. "Careful Negligence: Cicero's Low Style and Business Writing." *Rocky Mountain Review of Language and Literature* 41 (1987): 33–49.

Kastely, James L. *Rethinking the Rhetorical Tradition: From Plato to Postmodernism.* New Haven, Conn.: Yale University Press, 1997.

Kelley, Donald R. *Renaissance Humanism.* Boston: Twayne, 1991.

Kennedy, George. *The Art of Persuasion in Greece.* London: Routledge & Kegan Paul, 1963.

———. *The Art of Rhetoric in the Roman World, 300 b.c.–a.d. 300.* Princeton, N.J.: Princeton University Press, 1972.

———. "Classical Rhetoric." In *Encyclopedia of Rhetoric.* Ed. Thomas O. Sloan. Oxford: Oxford University Press, 2001. 92–114.

———. *Classical Rhetoric and Its Christian and Secular Tradition.* 2nd ed. Chapel Hill: University of North Carolina Press, 1999.

———. *Greek Rhetoric under Christian Emperors.* Princeton, N.J.: Princeton University Press, 1983.

———. *A New History of Classical Rhetoric.* Princeton, N. J.: Princeton University Press, 1994.

———. *On Rhetoric: A Theory of Civic Discourse.* New York: Oxford University Press, 1991.

Kennedy, George, trans. *Progymnasmata: Greek Textbooks of Prose Composition and Rhetoric.* Atlanta: Society of Biblical Literature, 2003.

Kimball, Bruce A. *Orators and Philosophers: A History of the Idea of Liberal Education.* New York: Teachers College Press at Columbia University, 1986.

Kinneavy, James L. *A Theory of Discourse.* Englewood Cliffs, N.J.: Prentice-Hall, 1971.

Kinney, Arthur F. *Humanist Poetics.* Amherst: University of Massachusetts Press, 1986.

———. "Rhetoric and Fiction in Elizabethan England." In *Renaissance Eloquence: Studies in the Theory and Practice of Renaissance Rhetoric* edited by James J. Murphy, 385–93. Berkeley: University of California Press, 1983.

Kintgen, Eugene R. *Reading in Tudor England.* Pittsburgh: University of Pittsburgh Press, 1996.

Klaus, Carl H. *Style in English Prose.* New York: Macmillan, 1968.

Knauf, David M. "George Puttenham's Theory of Natural and Artificial Discourse." *Speech Monographs* 34 (1967): 35–42.

Kneale, William, and Martha Kneale. *The Development of Logic.* Oxford: Clarendon, 1962.

Kolln, Martha. *Rhetorical Grammar.* 5th ed. New York: Pearson, 2007.

Kraye, Jill. *The Cambridge Companion to Renaissance Humanism.* Cambridge: Cambridge University Press, 1996.

Kretzoi, Charlotte M. "Changes in the Meaning and Function of Plain Style." In *Classical Models of Literature,* edited by Zoran Konstantinovic, Warren Anderson, and Walter Dietze, 249–53. Innsbruck: Inst. fur Sprachwissenschaft der Univ. Innsbruck, 1981.

Kristeller, Paul Oskar. *Eight Philosophers of the Italian Renaissance.* Stanford, Cal.: Stanford University Press, 1964.

———. "Humanism." In *The Cambridge History of Renaissance Philosophy,* edited by Charles B. Schmitt and Quentin Skinner, 113–37. Cambridge: Cambridge University Press, 1988.

———. *Renaissance Thought: The Classic, Scholastic, and Humanist Strains.* 1955. New York: Harper & Row, 1961.

———. *Renaissance Thought and Its Sources.* Ed. Michael Mooney. New York: Columbia University Press, 1979.

Lakoff, George. *Women, Fire, and Dangerous Things.* Chicago: University of Chicago Press, 1987.

Lakoff, George, and Mark Johnson. *Metaphors We Live By.* Chicago: University of Chicago Press, 1980.

———. *More Than Cool Reason: A Field Guide to Poetic Metaphor.* Chicago: University of Chicago Press, 1989.

Lang, Berel. "Style as Instrument, Style as Person." *Critical Inquiry* 4.4 (1978): 715–39.

Langer, Suzanne K. *Feeling and Form: A Theory of Art.* New York: Scribner, 1953.

———. *Philosophy in a New Key.* New York: New American Library, 1949.

Lanham, Richard A. *Analyzing Prose.* 2nd ed. New York: Continuum, 2003.

———. *The Economics of Attention: Style and Substance in the Age of Information.* Chicago: University of Chicago Press, 2006.

———. *The Electronic Word: Democracy, Technology, and the Arts.* Chicago: University of Chicago Press, 1993.

———. *A Handlist of Rhetorical Terms.* 2nd ed. Berkeley: University of California Press, 1991.

———. *Literacy and the Survival of Humanism.* New Haven, Conn.: Yale University Press, 1983.

———. *The Motives of Eloquence.* New Haven, Conn.: Yale University Press, 1976.

———. *Style: An Anti-Textbook.* New Haven, Conn.: Yale University Press, 1974.

Lausberg, Heinrich. *Handbook of Literary Rhetoric.* 1960. Eds. David E. Orton and R. Dean Anderson. Leiden: Brill, 1998.

Lechner, Sister Joan Marie. *Renaissance Concepts of the Commonplaces.* New York: Pageant, 1962.

Leddy, J. F. "Tradition and Change in Quintilian." *Phoenix* 7.2 (1953): 47–56.

Leech, Geoffrey N. *A Linguistic Guide to English Poetry.* London: Longman, 1969.

———. "Linguistics and the Figures of Rhetoric." In *Essays on Style and Language,* edited by Roger Fowler, 135–56. London: Routledge & Kegan Paul, 1966.

Leech, Geoffrey N., and Michael H. Short. *Style in Fiction.* New York: Longman, 1981.

Leeman, A. D. *Orationis Ratio: The Stylistic Theories and Practice of the Roman Orators, Historians, and Philosophers.* Amsterdam: Hakkert, 1986.

Leff, Michael. "Genre and Paradigm in the Second Book of *De Oratore.*" *Southern Speech Communication Journal* 51.4 (1986): 308–25.

———. "The Latin Stylistic Rhetorics of Antiquity." *Speech Monographs* 40 (1973): 273–79.

Lerner, Lawrence D. "Style." In *Encyclopedia of Poetry and Poetics,* edited by Alex Preminger, 814–17. Princeton, N.J.: Princeton University Press, 1965.

Leroux, Neil R. *Luther's Rhetoric.* St. Louis: Concordia, 2002.

———. "Perceiving Rhetorical Style: Toward a Framework for Criticism." *Rhetoric Society Quarterly* 22 (1992): 29–44.

Lewis, C. S. *English Literature in the Sixteenth Century Excluding Drama.* Vol. 3, *Oxford History of Literature.* Eds. F. P. Wilson and Bonamy Dobree. Oxford: Clarendon, 1954.

Liddell, Henry George, and Robert Scott. *A Greek-English Lexicon.* Vols. 1–2. Oxford: Clarendon, 1940.

Lloyd, G. E. R. *Polarity and Analogy: Two Types of Argumentation in Early Greek Thought.* Cambridge: Cambridge University Press, 1966.

Love, Glen A., and Michael Payne, eds. *Contemporary Essays on Style.* Glenview, Ill.: Scott, Foresman, 1969.

Lunsford, Andrea A., and John J. Ruszkiewicz. *Everything's an Argument.* Boston: Bedford/St. Martin's, 1999.

Mack, Peter. *Elizabethan Rhetoric: Theory and Practice.* Cambridge: Cambridge University Press, 2002.

———. *A History of Renaissance Rhetoric 1380–1620.* Oxford: Oxford University Press, 2011.

———. "Humanist rhetoric and dialectic." In *The Cambridge Companion to Renaissance Humanism,* edited by Jill Kraye, 82–99. Cambridge: Cambridge University Press, 1996.

———. "Ramus Reading: The Commentaries on Cicero's *Consular Orations* and Vergil's *Eclogues* and *Georgics." Journal of the Warburg and Courtauld Institutes.* 61 (1998): 111–41.

———. *Renaissance Argument: Valla and Agricola in the Traditions of Rhetoric and Dialectic.* Leiden: Brill, 1993.

———. "Rudolph Agricola's Reading of Literature." *Journal of the Warburg and Courtland Institutes* 48 (1985): 23–41.

Mack, Peter, ed. *Renaissance Rhetoric.* New York: St. Martin's, 1994.

Macrorie, Ken. *Uptaught.* New York: Hayden, 1970.

Mahood, M. M. *Shakespeare's Wordplay.* London: Methuen, 1968.

Mann, Nicholas. "The origins of humanism." In *The Cambridge Companion to Renaissance Humanism,* edited by Jill Kraye, 1–19. Cambridge: Cambridge University Press, 1996.

Marrou, H. I. *A History of Education in Antiquity.* Trans. George Lamb. Madison: University of Wisconsin Press, 1956.

Martines, Lauro. *Power and Imagination: City-States in Renaissance Italy.* New York: Knopf, 1979.

May, James M. *Trials of Character: The Eloquence of Ciceronian Ethos.* Chapel Hill: University of North Carolina Press, 1988.

Mazzeo, Joseph A. "Seventeenth-Century English Prose Style: The Quest for a Natural Style." *Mosaic: A Journal for the Interdisciplinary Study of Literature* 6.3 (1973): 107–44.

McAlindon, T. *Shakespeare and Decorum.* London: Macmillan, 1973.

McDonald, Russ. *Shakespeare and the Arts of Language.* Oxford: Oxford University Press, 2001.

McKeon, Richard. "Literary Criticism and the Concept of Imitation in Antiquity." In *Critics and Criticism Ancient and Modern,* edited by R. S. Crane. 147–75. Chicago: University of Chicago Press, 1952.

McNally, J. R. "Rudolph Agricola's *De Inventione Dialectica Libri Tres:* A Translation of Selected Chapters." *Speech Monographs* 34.4 (1967): 393–422.

Meerhoff, Kees. "Logic and Eloquence: A Ramusian Revolution?" *Argumentation* 5 (1991): 357–74.

———. "The Significance of Philip Melanchthon's Rhetoric in the Renaissance." In *Renaissance Rhetoric,* edited by Peter Mack, 46–62. New York: St. Martin's, 1994.

Mesnard, Pierre. "The Pedagogy of Johann Sturm (1507–1589) in Its Evangelical Inspiration." *Studies in the Renaissance* 13 (1966): 200–219.

Micciche, Laura R. "Making a Case for Rhetorical Grammar." In *Style in Rhetoric and Composition,* edited by Paul Butler, 250–66. Boston: Bedford/St. Martin's, 2010.

Milic, Louis T. "Metaphysical Criticism of Style." In *New Rhetorics,* edited by Martin Steinmann, Jr., 161–75. New York: Scribner, 1967.

———."Rhetorical Choice and Stylistic Option: The Conscious and Unconscious Poles." In *Literary Style: A Symposium,* edited by Seymour Chatman, 77–94. London: Oxford University Press, 1971.

———. "Theories of Style and Their Implications for the Teaching of Composition." *College Composition and Communication.* 16.2 (1965): 66–69, 126.

Miller, Perry. *The New England Mind: The Seventeenth Century.* Cambridge, Mass.: Belknap Press of Harvard University Press, 1939.

Mitchell, W. Fraser. *English Pulpit Oratory from Andrewes to Tillotson: A Study of Its Literary Aspects.* New York: Russell & Russell, 1962.

Mohrmann, Gerald P. "*The Civile Conversation:* Communication in the Renaissance." *Speech Monographs* 39.3 (1972): 193–204.

———. "Oratorical Delivery and Other Problems in Current Scholarship on English Renaissance Rhetoric." In *Renaissance Eloquence: Studies in the Theory and Practice of Renaissance Rhetoric,* edited by James J. Murphy, 56–83. Berkeley: University of California Press, 1983.

Monfasani, John. "The Byzantine Rhetorical Tradition and the Renaissance." In *Renaissance Eloquence: Studies in the Theory and Practice of Renaissance Rhetoric,* edited by James J. Murphy, 174–87. Berkeley: University of California Press, 1983.

———. "Episodes of Anti-Quintilianism in the Italian Renaissance: Quarrels on the Orator as a *Vir Bonus* and Rhetoric as the *Scientia Bene Dicendi.*" *Rhetorica* 10.2 (1992): 119–38.

———. *George of Trebizond: A Biography and a Study of His Rhetoric and Logic.* Leiden: Brill, 1976.

———. "Humanism and Rhetoric." In *Renaissance Humanism: Foundations, Forms, and Legacy,* vol. 3, edited by Albert Rabil, Jr., 171–235. Philadelphia: University of Pennsylvania Press, 1988.

Müller, Wolfgang G. "Iconicity and rhetoric: A note on the iconic force of rhetorical figures in Shakespeare." In *The Motivated Sign: Iconicity in Language and Literature 2,* edited by Olga Fisher and Max Nänny, 305–22. Amsterdam: Benjamins, 2001.

———. "Style." In *Encyclopedia of Rhetoric,* edited by Thomas O. Sloane, 745–57. Oxford: Oxford University Press, 2001.

Murphy, James J. "Habit in Roman Writing Instruction." In *A Short History of Writing Instruction: From Ancient Greece to Modern America,* 2nd ed., edited by James J. Murphy, 35–78, Mahwah, N.J.: Erlbaum, 2001.

———. "One Thousand Neglected Authors: The Scope and Importance of Renaissance Rhetoric." In *Renaissance Eloquence: Studies in the Theory and Practice of Renaissance Rhetoric,* edited by James J. Murphy, 20–36. Berkeley: University of California Press, 1983.

———. *Rhetoric in the Middle Ages: A History of Rhetorical Theory from St. Augustine to the Renaissance.* Berkeley: University of California Press, 1974.

———. "*Topos* and *Figura:* Historical Cause and Effect?" In *De Ortu Grammatica: Studies in Medieval Grammar and Linguistic Theory in Memory of Jan Pinborg,* edited by G. L. Bursill-Hall et al., 239–53. Amsterdam: Benjamins, 1990.

Murphy, James J., ed. *Renaissance Eloquence: Studies in the Theory and Practice of Renaissance Rhetoric.* Berkeley: University of California Press, 1983.

———. *A Short History of Writing Instruction: From Ancient Greece to Modern America.* 2nd ed. Mahwah, N.J.: Erlbaum, 2001.

———. *A Synoptic History of Classical Rhetoric.* New York: Random House, 1972.

Nadeau, Ray. "A Renaissance Schoolmaster on Practice." *Speech Monographs* 16 (1950): 171–79.

———. "Thomas Farnaby: Schoolmaster and Rhetorician of the English Renaissance." *Quarterly Journal of Speech* 36 (1950): 340–44.

Nash, Walter. *Rhetoric: The Wit of Persuasion.* Oxford: Blackwell, 1989.

Nauert, Charles G. *Humanism and the Culture of Renaissance Europe.* 2nd ed. Cambridge: Cambridge University Press, 2006.

———. "Humanist Infiltration into the Academic World: Some Studies of Northern Universities." *Renaissance Quarterly* 43.4 (1990): 799–812.

Nietzsche, Friedrich. "On Truth and Lies in a Nonmoral Sense." In *The Rhetorical Tradition: Readings from Classical Times to the Present,* 2nd ed., edited by Patricia Bizzell and Bruce Herzberg, 1171–79. Boston: Bedford/St. Martin's, 2001.

Nuchelmans, Gabriel. *Late-Scholastic and Humanist Theories of the Proposition.* Amsterdam: North Holland, 1980.

Ohmann, Richard. "Generative Grammars and the Concept of Literary Style." In *Linguistics and Literary Style,* edited by Donald C. Freeman, 258–78. New York: Holt, Rinehart & Winston, 1970.

———. "Prolegomena to the Analysis of Prose Style." In *Contemporary Essays on Style,* edited by Glen A. Love and Michael Payne, 177–90. Glenview, Ill.: Scott, Foresman, 1969.

———. *Shaw: The Style and the Man.* Middletown, Conn.: Wesleyan University Press, 1962.

———. "Speech, Action, and Style." In *Literary Style: A Symposium,* edited by Seymour Chatman, 241–54. Oxford: Oxford University Press, 1971.

———. "Speech Acts and the Definition of Literature." *Philosophy and Rhetoric* 4 (1971): 1–19.

Ong, Walter J. *Ramus, Method, and the Decay of Dialogue.* Cambridge, Mass.: Harvard University Press, 1958.

———. *Rhetoric, Romance and Technology.* Ithaca, N.Y.: Cornell University Press, 1971.

Ostrom, Hans. "Grammar J, As in Jazzing Around: The Roles 'Play' Plays in Style." In *Elements of Alternate Style,* edited by Wendy Bishop, 75–81. Portsmouth, N.H.: Boynton/Cook, 1997.

Ortony, Andrew. *Metaphor and Thought.* 2nd ed. Cambridge: Cambridge University Press, 1993.

Pace, Tom. "What Happened: The Rise and Fall of Stylistics in Composition." In *Refiguring Prose Style: Possibilities for Writing Pedagogy,* edited by T. R. Johnson and Tom Pace, 1–2. Logan: Utah State University Press, 2005.

Panther, Klaus-Uwe, and Günter Radden, eds. *Metonymy in Language and Thought.* Philadelphia: Benjamins, 1999.

Papillion, Terry. "Isocrates' *techne* and Rhetorical Pedagogy." *Rhetoric Society Quarterly* 25 (1995): 149–63.

Parker, Patricia. "Hysteron proteron: or the preposterous." In *Renaissance Figures of Speech.* Eds. Sylvia Adamson, Gavin Alexander, and Katrin Ettenhuber, 133–45. Cambridge: Cambridge University Press, 2007.

Patterson, Annabel M. *Hermogenes and the Renaissance.* Princeton, N.J.: Princeton University Press, 1970.

Perelman, Chaim, and L. Olbrechts-Tyteca. *The New Rhetoric: A Treatise on Argumentation.* Trans. John Wilkinson and Purcell Weaver. Notre Dame, Ind.: University of Notre Dame Press, 1969.

Perkins, D. N. "Thinking Frames." *Educational Leadership* 43.8 (1986): 4–10.

Pigman, G. W., III. "Versions of Imitation in the Renaissance." *Renaissance Quarterly* 33 (1980): 1–32.

Plett, Heinrich F. "Concepts of Style: A Classificatory and a Critical Approach." *Language and Style* 12 (1979): 268–81.

———. "The Place and Function of Style in Renaissance Poetics." In *Renaissance Eloquence: Studies in the Theory and Practice of Renaissance Rhetoric,* edited by James J. Murphy, 356–75. Berkeley: University of California Press, 1983.

———. "Die Rhetorik der Figuren: Zur Systematik, Pragmatik und Asthetik der 'Eleocutio.'" In *Rhetorik: Kritische Positionen zum Stand der Forschung,* edited by Heinrich F. Plett, 125–65. Munich: Fink, 1977.

Plett, Heinrich F., ed. *Renaissance-Rhetorik: Renaissance Rhetoric.* Berlin: de Gruyter, 1993.

Porter, H. C. *Reformation in Tudor Cambridge.* Cambridge: Cambridge University Press, 1958.

Poster, Carol. "Aristotle's Rhetoric against Rhetoric: Unitarian Reading and Esoteric Hermeneutics." *American Journal of Philology* 18.2 (1997): 219–49.

Poulakos, John. *Sophistical Rhetoric in Classical Greece.* Columbia: University of South Carolina Press, 1995.

Poulakos, Takis. *Speaking for the Polis: Isocrates' Rhetorical Education.* Columbia: University of South Carolina Press, 1997.

Poulakos, Takis, and David Depew, eds. *Isocrates and Civic Education.* Austin: University of Texas Press, 2004.

Pratt, Mary Louise. *Toward a Speech Act Theory of Literary Discourse.* Bloomington: Indiana University Press, 1977.

Preminger, Alex, and T. V. F. Brogan, eds. *The New Princeton Encyclopedia of Poetry and Poetics.* Princeton, N.J.: Princeton University Press, 1993.

Quinn, Arthur. *Figures of Speech: 60 Ways to Turn a Phrase.* Davis, Cal.: Hermagoras, 1993.

Rademaker, C. S. M. *Life and Work of Gerardus Joannes Vossius.* Assen, the Netherlands: Van Gorcum, 1981.

Ragsdale, J. Donald. "Invention in English 'Stylistic' Rhetorics: 1600–1800." *Quarterly Journal of Speech* 51 (1965): 164–67.

Rankin, Elizabeth D. "Revitalizing Style: Toward a New Theory and Pedagogy." *Freshman English News* 14 (1985): 8–13.

Rebhorn, Wayne A. *The Emperor of Men's Minds: Literature and the Renaissance Discovery of Rhetoric.* Ithaca, N.Y.: Cornell University Press, 1995.

Rebhorn, Wayne A., ed. *Renaissance Debates on Rhetoric.* Ithaca, N.Y.: Cornell University Press, 2000.

Rhodes, Neil. *The Power of Eloquence and English Renaissance Literature.* New York: St. Martin's, 1992.

Rice, Eugene F., Jr. *The Renaissance Idea of Wisdom.* Cambridge, Mass.: Harvard University Press, 1958.

Richards, I. A. *The Philosophy of Rhetoric.* 1936. Oxford: Oxford University Press, 1965.

———. "The Places and the Figures." *Kenyon Review* 11.1 (1949): 17–30.

Ricoueur, Paul. *Hermeneutics and the Human Sciences.* Trans. John B. Thompson. Cambridge: Cambridge University Press, 1981.

Roberts, W. Rhys. *Greek Rhetoric and Literary Criticism.* New York: Cooper Square, 1963.

Robins, R. H. *A Short History of Linguistics.* 3rd ed. London: Longman, 1990.

Robbins, Vernon K. *Exploring the Texture of Texts.* Valley Forge, Pa.: Trinity Press International, 1996.

Rubel, Vere L. *Poetic Diction in the English Renaissance: From Skelton through Spenser.* New York: Modern Language Association of America, 1941.

Rudd, Niall. "The Style and the Man." *Phoenix* 18.3 (1964): 216–31.

Rummel, Erika. *The Humanist-Scholastic Debate in the Renaissance and Reformation.* Cambridge, Mass.: Harvard University Press, 1995.

———. "Isocrates' Ideal of Rhetoric: Criteria of Evaluation." *Classical Journal* 75.1 (1979): 25–35.

Russell, D. A. *Criticism in Antiquity.* London: Duckworth, 1981.

Sanford, William Phillips. "English Rhetoric Reverts to Classicism, 1600–1650." *Quarterly Journal of Speech* 25 (1929): 503–25.

———. *English Theories of Public Address, 1530–1828.* Columbus, Ohio: Hendrick, 1938.

Schenkeveld, Dirk M. "The Intended Public of Demetrius' *On Style:* The Place of the Treatise in the Hellenistic Educational System." *Rhetorica* 18.1 (2000): 29–48.

Schiappa, Edward. *The Beginnings of Rhetorical Theory in Classical Greece.* New Haven, Conn.: Yale University Press, 1999.

Schmitt, Charles B., and Quentin Skinner, eds. *The Cambridge History of Renaissance Philosophy.* Cambridge: Cambridge University Press, 1988.

Schroeder, Christopher, Helen Fox, and Patricia Bizzell, eds. *Alternative Discourses and the Academy.* Portsmouth, N.H.: Boynton/Cook, 2002.

Scott, Izora. *Controversies over the Imitation of Cicero as a Model for Style.* New York: Teachers College, Columbia University, 1910.

Searle, John. *Speech Acts: An Essay in the Philosophy of Language.* London: Cambridge University Press, 1969.

Seigel, Jerrold E. *Rhetoric and Philosophy in Renaissance Humanism: The Union of Eloquence and Wisdom, Petrarch to Valla.* Princeton, N.J.: Princeton University Press, 1968.

Shafter, Edward M., Jr. "A Study of Rhetorical Invention in Selected English Rhetorics, 1550–1600." PhD diss. University of Michigan, 1956.

Sharratt, Peter. "Recent Work on Peter Ramus (1970–1986)." *Rhetorica* 5 (1987): 163–94.

Short, Mick. *Exploring the Language of Poems, Plays and Prose.* London: Longman, 1996.

Shuger, Debora K. *Sacred Rhetoric: The Christian Grand Style in the English Renaissance.* Princeton, N.J.: Princeton University Press, 1988.

Skinner, Quentin. "Moral Ambiguity and the Renaissance Art of Eloquence." *Essays in Criticism* 44.4 (1994): 267–92.

———. "Thomas Hobbes: Rhetoric and the Construction of Morality." *Proceedings of the British Academy* 76 (1991): 1–61.

Sloane, Thomas O. *Donne, Milton, and the End of Humanist Rhetoric.* Berkeley: University of California Press, 1985.

———. *On the Contrary: The Protocol of Traditional Rhetoric.* Washington, D.C.: Catholic University of America Press, 1997.

———. "A Renaissance Controversialist on Rhetoric: Thomas Wright's *Passions of the Minde in Generall.*" *Speech Monographs* 36 (1969): 38–54.

Sloane, Thomas O., ed. *Encyclopedia of Rhetoric.* Oxford: Oxford University Press, 2001.

Sloane, Thomas O., and Raymond B. Waddington. *The Rhetoric of Renaissance Poetry from Wyatt to Milton.* Berkeley: University of California Press, 1974.

Smethurst, S. E. "Cicero and Isocrates." *Transactions and Proceedings of the American Philological Association* 84 (1953): 262–320.

Smith, Gregory G., ed. *Elizabethan Critical Essays.* Vols. 1–2. Oxford: Clarendon, 1904.

Solmsen, Friedrich. "The Aristotelian Tradition in Ancient Rhetoric." *American Journal of Philology* 62.1 (1941): 35–50.

———. "Aristotle and Cicero on the Orator's Playing upon the Feelings." *Classical Philology* 33.4 (1938): 390–404.

Sonnino, Lee A. *A Handbook to Sixteenth-Century Rhetoric.* London: Routledge & Kegan Paul, 1968.

Sontag, Susan. "On Style." *Partisan Review* 32 (1965): 543–60.

Spencer, John, ed. *Linguistics and Style.* London: Oxford University Press, 1964.

Spies, Marijke. *Rhetoric, Rhetoricians and Poets: Studies in Renaissance Poetry and Poetics.* Amsterdam: Amsterdam University Press, 1999.

Spingarn, J. E, ed. *Critical Essays of the Seventeenth Century.* Vols. 1–3. Oxford: Clarendon, 1908.

Spitzer, Leo. *Linguistics and Literary History.* Princeton, N.J.: Princeton University Press, 1948.

Staton, Walter F. "The Characters of Style in Elizabethan Prose." *Journal of English and German Philology* 62 (1958): 197–207.

Steadman, John M. *The Lamb and the Elephant: Ideal Imitation and the Context of Renaissance Allegory.* San Marino, Cal.: Huntington Library, 1974.

Stone, P. W. K. *The Art of Poetry 1750–1820.* London: Routledge & Kegan Paul, 1967.

Struever, Nancy S. *The Language of History in the Renaissance.* Princeton, N.J.: Princeton University Press, 1970.

Strunk, William, Jr., and E. B. White. *The Elements of Style.* 3rd ed. New York: Macmillan, 1979.

Taylor, Warren. *Tudor Figures of Rhetoric.* Whitewater, Wis.: Language Press, 1972.

Tinker, John. "Vagrant Sympathies: From Stylistic Analysis to a Pedagogy of Style." *Style* 37.1 (2003): 86–100.

Tinsley, Barbara Sher. "Johann Sturm's Method for Humanistic Pedagogy." *Sixteenth Century Journal* 20.1 (1989): 23–40.

Too, Yun Lee. *The Rhetoric of Identity in Isocrates.* Cambridge: Cambridge University Press, 1995.

Trimpi, Wesley. *Ben Jonson's Poems: A Study of the Plain Style.* Stanford, Cal.: Stanford University Press, 1962.

Trousdale, Marion. "Recurrence and Renaissance: Rhetorical Imitation in Ascham and Sturm." *English Literary Renaissance* 6 (1976): 156–79.

———. *Shakespeare and the Rhetoricians.* Chapel Hill: University of North Carolina Press, 1982.

Tufte, Virginia. *Grammar as Style.* New York: Holt, Rinehart & Winston, 1971.

Turner, Mark. *The Literary Mind.* New York: Oxford University Press, 1996.

Turner, Mark, and Gilles Fauconnier. "Metaphor, metonymy, and binding." In *Metaphor and Metonymy at the Crossroads,* edited by Antonio Barcelona, 133–45. New York: de Gruyter, 2000.

Tuve, Rosemund. *Elizabethan and Metaphysical Imagery.* Chicago: University of Chicago Press, 1947.

Ullmann, Stephen. *Meaning and Style.* Oxford: Blackwell, 1973.

Valiavitcharska, Vessela. "Figure, Argument, and Performance in the Byzantine Classroom." *Rhetoric Society Quarterly* 41.1 (2011): 19–40.

Varga, A. Kibedi. "Rhetoric, a Story or a System? A Challenge to Historians of Renaissance Rhetoric." In *Renaissance Eloquence: Studies in the Theory and Practice of Renaissance Rhetoric,* edited by James J. Murphy, 84–91. Berkeley: University of California Press, 1983.

Vickers, Brian. *Classical Rhetoric in English Poetry.* Carbondale: Southern Illinois University Press, 1970.

———. *English Renaissance Literary Criticism.* Oxford: Oxford University Press, 1999.

———. *In Defence of Rhetoric.* Oxford: Clarendon, 1988.

———. "On the Practicalities of Renaissance Rhetoric." In *Rhetoric Revalued,* edited by Brian Vickers, 133–41. Binghamton, N.Y.: Medieval & Renaissance Texts & Studies, 1982.

———. "'The Power of Persuasion': Images of the Orator, Elyot to Shakespeare." In *Renaissance Eloquence: Studies in the Theory and Practice of Renaissance Rhetoric,* edited by James J. Murphy, 411–35. Berkeley: University of California Press, 1983.

———. "Rhetoric and Poetics." In *The Cambridge History of Renaissance Philosophy,* edited by Charles B. Schmitt and Quentin Skinner, 715–45. Cambridge: Cambridge University Press, 1988.

———. "Rhetorical and anti-rhetorical tropes: On writing the history of *elocutio.*" *Comparative Criticism* 3 (1981): 105–32.

———. "The Royal Society and English Prose Style: A Reassessment." *In Rhetoric and the Pursuit of Truth: Language Change in the Seventeenth and Eighteenth Centuries,* 2–76. Los Angeles: University of California Press, 1985.

———. "Shakespeare's Use of Rhetoric." In *A New Companion to Shakespeare Studies,* edited by Kenneth Muir and Samuel Schoenbaum, 83–98. Cambridge: Cambridge University Press, 1971.

———. "Some Reflections on the Rhetoric Textbook." In *Renaissance Rhetoric*. Ed. Peter Mack. New York: St. Martin's 1994. 81–102.

Vos, Alvin. "*De Copia* and Classical Rhetoric." *Classical and Modern Literature* 7.4 (1987): 285–94.

———. "'Good Matter and Good Utterance': The Character of English Ciceronianism." *Studies in English Literature, 1500–1900* 19.1 (1979): 3–18.

Wagner, Russell H. "Thomas Wilson's *Arte of Rhetorique.*" *Speech Monographs* 27 (1960): 1–32.

Walker, Jeffrey. *Rhetoric and Poetics in Antiquity.* Oxford: Oxford University Press, 2000.

Wallace, Karl. *Francis Bacon on Communication and Rhetoric.* Chapel Hill: University of North Carolina Press, 1943.

Warnick, Barbara. "Judgment, Probability, and Aristotle's *Rhetoric.*" *Quarterly Journal of Speech* 9 (1989): 299–311.

Waswo, Richard. *Language and Meaning in the Renaissance.* Princeton, N.J.: Princeton University Press, 1987.

Weathers, Winston. *An Alternate Style: Options in Composition.* Rochelle Park, N.J.: Hayden, 1980.

Weaver, Richard M. *The Ethics of Rhetoric.* Davis, Cal.: Hermagoras, 1985.

Weaver, William P. "*Triplex est Copia:* Philip Melanchthon's Invention of the Rhetorical Figures." *Rhetorica* 29.4 (2011): 367–402.

Webber, Joan. *The Eloquent "I": Style and Self in Seventeenth-Century Prose.* Madison: University of Wisconsin Press, 1968.

Weinberg, Bernard. *A History of Literary Criticism in the Italian Renaissance.* Vol. 1. Chicago: University of Chicago Press, 1961.

———. "Translations and Commentaries of Demetrius, *On Style* to 1660: A Bibliography." *Philological Quarterly* 30.3 (1951): 353–80.

———. "Translations and Commentaries of Longinus, *On the Sublime,* to 1600: A Bibliography." *Modern Philology* 47.3 (1950): 145–51.

Whigham, Frank. *Ambition and Privilege: The Social Tropes of Elizabethan Courtesy Theory.* Berkeley: University of California Press, 1984.

Whissen, Thomas. *A Way with Words.* Oxford: Oxford University Press, 1982.

White, Harold Ogden. *Plagiarism and Imitation during the English Renaissance.* Cambridge, Mass.: Harvard University Press, 1935.

White, Hayden. *Figural Realism: Studies in the Mimesis Effect.* Baltimore: Johns Hopkins University Press, 1999.

———. *Metahistory.* Baltimore: Johns Hopkins University Press, 1973.

Whorf, Benjamin Lee. *Language, Thought and Reality: Selected Writings of Benjamin Lee Whorf.* Ed. John B. Carroll. Cambridge: MIT Press, 1956.

Wildermuth, Mark E. "The Rhetoric of Wilson's *Arte:* Reclaiming the Classical Heritage for English Protestants." *Philosophy and Rhetoric* 22.1 (1989): 43–58.

Williamson, George. *The Senecan Amble: A Study in Prose Form from Bacon to Collier.* London: Faber & Faber, 1951 (rpt. Chicago: University of Chicago Press, 1966).

Wilson, Edmund. *Axel's Castle: A Study in the Imaginative Literature.* New York: Scribner, 1936.

Winterbottom, Michael. "Quintilian and the *Vir Bonus.*" *Journal of Roman Studies* 54 (1964): 90–97.

Winterowd, Ross. *Contemporary Rhetoric: A Conceptual Background with Readings.* New York: Harcourt Brace Jovanovich, 1975.

Wisse, Jakob. *Ethos and Pathos: From Aristotle to Cicero.* Amsterdam: Hakkert, 1989.

Woodman, Leonora. "A Rhetorical Model of Prose Style: Notes toward a Synthesis of Rhetoric and Poetics." *Journal of Advanced Composition* 2 (1981): 69–78.

Wright, Louis B. *Middle-Class Culture in Elizabethan England.* Chapel Hill: University of North Carolina Press, 1935.

Wojcik, Jan, and Roland Hass, trans. "*The Hermeneutics:* Outline of the 1819 Lectures [of Friedrich Schleiermacher]." *New Literary History* 10 (1978): 1–16.

Yates, Frances A. *The Art of Memory.* Chicago: University of Chicago Press, 1966.

Young, Richard. "Arts, Crafts, Gifts and Knacks: Some Disharmonies in the New Rhetoric." In *Reinventing the Rhetorical Tradition,* edited by Aviva Freedman and Ian Pringle, 53–60. Conway, Alas.: Canadian Council of Teachers of English, 1980.

Young, Richard E., Alton L. Becker, and Kenneth L. Pike. *Rhetoric: Discovery and Change.* New York: Harcourt, Brace & World, 1970.

Zappen, J. "Aristotelian and Ramist Rhetoric in Thomas Hobbes' *Leviathan:* Pathos versus Ethos and Logos." *Rhetorica* 1 (1983): 65–91.

Index

www.ingramcontent.com/pod-product-compliance
Lightning Source LLC
LaVergne TN
LVHW082003060826
844660LV00006B/276

* 9 7 8 1 6 1 1 1 7 2 4 0 9 *